essentials of

ABNORMAL PSYCHOLOGY

in a changing world **third canadian edition**

JEFFREY S. NEVID
St. John's University

BEVERLY GREENE
St. John's University

PAUL A. JOHNSON
Confederation College

STEVEN TAYLOR
University of British Columbia

MELANIE MACNAB
Seneca College

PEARSON

Toronto

Vice-President, Editorial Director: Gary Bennett
Editor-in-Chief: Michelle Sartor
Acquisitions Editor: Matthew Christian
Marketing Manager: Lisa Gillis
Supervising Developmental Editor: Suzanne Schaan
Developmental Editor: Suzanne Simpson Millar
Project Manager: Ioana Gagea
Manufacturing Manager: Susan Johnson
Production Editor: Tara Tovell
Copy Editor: Stephanie Fysh
Proofreaders: Linda Jenkins, Karen Alliston
Compositor: Aptara®, Inc.
Photo Researcher: Diane Hartmann
Permissions Researcher: Dominic Farrell
Art Director: Julia Hall
Cover Designer: Miriam Blier
Interior Designer: Opus House Inc/Sonya Thursby
Cover Image: Patrick Mac Sean/ès/Corbis

Credits and acknowledgments for the material borrowed from other sources and reproduced, with permission, in this textbook appear on the appropriate page within the text or on page 492.

Original edition published by Pearson Education, Inc., Upper Saddle River, New Jersey, USA. Copyright © 2001 Pearson Education, Inc. This edition is authorized for sale only in Canada.

If you purchased this book outside the United States or Canada, you should be aware that it has been imported without the approval of the publisher or the author.

10 9 8 7 6 5   [CKV]

Library and Archives Canada Cataloguing in Publication

Essentials of abnormal psychology in a changing world / Jeffrey S. Nevid ... [et al.]. — 3rd Canadian ed.
ISBN 978-0-13-276745-3

1. Psychology, Pathological—Textbooks. I. Nevid, Jeffrey S

RC454.E88 2012   616.89   C2011-907983-6

PEARSON

ISBN 978-0-13-276745-3

In fond memory of Merritt, Mary, and Gloria
—PJ

To Anna, Alex, and Amy
—ST

To Michael, who is full of curiosity each day, and to Alvin and Ruth
—MM

BRIEF CONTENTS

1   What Is Abnormal Psychology?   1

2   Assessment, Classification, and Treatment of Abnormal Behaviour   40

3   Anxiety Disorders   98

4   Mood Disorders and Suicide   140

5   Dissociative and Somatoform Disorders   185

6   Personality Disorders   213

7   Substance Abuse and Dependence   249

8   Eating Disorders and Sleep Disorders   293

9   Gender Identity Disorder, Paraphilias, and Sexual Dysfunctions   320

10   Schizophrenia   357

11   Abnormal Behaviour Across the Lifespan   393

Appendix: Research Methods in Abnormal Psychology   433

CONTENTS

Preface xi

Acknowledgments xviii

About the Authors xix

1

What Is Abnormal Psychology? 1

How Do We Define Abnormal Behaviour? 3
Criteria for Determining Abnormality 3
Risk Factors 7
Prevention and Resilience 8
Personal and Social Costs of Poor Mental Health 8
REVIEW IT How Do We Define Abnormal
Behaviour? 8

**Historical Perspectives on Abnormal
Behaviour 9**
The Demonological Model 9
Origins of the Medical Model: An "Ill Humour" 9
Medieval Times 10
Witchcraft 10
Asylums in Europe and the New World 11
The Reform Movement and Moral Therapy in Europe and
North America 11
Drugs and Deinstitutionalization: The Exodus from
Provincial Psychiatric Hospitals 12
Pathways to the Present: From Demonology to
Science 13
REVIEW IT Historical Perspectives on Abnormal
Behaviour 17

**Current Perspectives on Abnormal
Behaviour 18**
Biological Perspectives on Abnormal
Behaviour 18
REVIEW IT Biological Perspectives 22
Psychological Perspectives on Abnormal
Behaviour 22
REVIEW IT Psychological Perspectives 32
Sociocultural Perspectives on Abnormal
Behaviour 34
REVIEW IT Sociocultural Perspectives 34
Interactionist Perspectives 35
REVIEW IT Interactionist Perspectives 36

CONCEPT MAP 38

2

Assessment, Classification, and Treatment of Abnormal Behaviour 40

Systems of Classification 41

Methods of Assessment 41
The Clinical Interview 41
Psychological Tests of Intelligence and
Personality 43
Neuropsychological Assessment 51
Behavioural Assessment 52
Cognitive Assessment 54
Physiological Measurement 56
Probing the Workings of the Brain 56
REVIEW IT Methods of Assessment 58

**Classification of Abnormal Behaviour:
The DSM System 59**
Features of the DSM 60
Evaluation of the DSM System 63
Advantages and Disadvantages of the
DSM System 63
REVIEW IT Classification of Abnormal
Behaviour 66

Methods of Treatment 66
Types of Mental Health Professionals
in Canada 67
Biological Therapies 68
Deep Brain Stimulation 72
Psychodynamic Therapies 72
Behaviour Therapy 75
Humanistic-Existential Therapies 76
Cognitive-Behaviour Therapies 78
Eclectic Therapy 81
Group, Family, and Marital Therapy 81
Computer-Assisted Therapy 82
Does Psychotherapy Work? 83
REVIEW IT Methods of Treatment 87

Abnormal Psychology and Society 87
Psychiatric Commitment and Patients' Rights 87
Mental Illness and Criminal Responsibility 91
REVIEW IT Mental Illness and Criminal
Responsibility 94

CONCEPT MAP 96

3

Anxiety Disorders   98

Types of Anxiety Disorders   101
Panic Disorder   101
Agoraphobia   103
Generalized Anxiety Disorder   105
Phobic Disorders   107
Adjustment Disorders   112
Acute and Posttraumatic Stress Disorders   113
REVIEW IT Types of Anxiety Disorders   117

Theoretical Perspectives   118
Psychodynamic Perspectives   118
Behavioural Perspectives   118
Cognitive Perspectives   120
Biological Perspectives   123
REVIEW IT Theoretical Perspectives   127

Treatment of Anxiety Disorders   128
Psychodynamic Approaches   128
Humanistic Approaches   128
Biological Approaches   128
Behaviour-Based Approaches   129
REVIEW IT Treatment of Anxiety Disorders   136

CONCEPT MAP   138

4

Mood Disorders and Suicide   140

Types of Mood Disorders   141
Major Depressive Disorder   142
Dysthymic Disorder   149
Bipolar Disorder   150
Cyclothymic Disorder   152
REVIEW IT Mood Disorders   153

Theoretical Perspectives   153
Stress and Mood Disorders   154
Psychodynamic Perspectives   154
Learning Perspectives   156
Cognitive Perspectives   157
Biological Perspectives   162
Tying It Together   164
REVIEW IT Theoretical Perspectives on Mood Disorders   165

Treatment   165
Psychodynamic Approaches   165
Behavioural Approaches   167
Cognitive Approaches   168
Biological Approaches   169
REVIEW IT Treatment of Depression   175

Suicide   175
Who Commits Suicide   176
Why Do People Commit Suicide?   176
Theoretical Perspectives on Suicide   178

Predicting Suicide   179
REVIEW IT Suicide   181
CONCEPT MAP   183

5

Dissociative and Somatoform Disorders   185

Dissociative Disorders   187
Dissociative Identity Disorder   187
Dissociative Amnesia   191
Dissociative Fugue   192
Depersonalization Disorder   193
Theoretical Perspectives   194
Tying It Together   196
Treatment of Dissociative Disorders   197
REVIEW IT Dissociative Disorders   199

Somatoform Disorders   199
Conversion Disorder   201
Hypochondriasis   202
Somatization Disorder   204
Other Somatoform Disorders   204
Theoretical Perspectives   205
Treatment of Somatoform Disorders   208
REVIEW IT Somatoform Disorders   209

CONCEPT MAP   211

6

Personality Disorders   213

Types of Personality Disorders   214
Personality Disorders Characterized by Odd or Eccentric Behaviour   214
Personality Disorders Characterized by Dramatic, Emotional, or Erratic Behaviour   218
Personality Disorders Characterized by Anxious or Fearful Behaviour   228
Problems with the Classification of Personality Disorders   232
REVIEW IT Types of Personality Disorders   234

Theoretical Perspectives   235
Psychodynamic Perspectives   235
Learning Perspectives   236
Family Perspectives   238
Cognitive-Behavioural Perspectives   239
Biological Perspectives   239
Sociocultural Views   241
REVIEW IT Theoretical Perspectives   242

Treatment   242
Psychodynamic Approaches   243
Behavioural Approaches   243
Biological Approaches   244
Canadian Treatment Services   245
REVIEW IT Treatment of Personality Disorders   245

CONCEPT MAP   247

7

Substance Abuse and Dependence   249

Classification of Substance-Related Disorders   252
Substance Abuse and Dependence   253
Addiction, Physiological Dependence, and Psychological Dependence   255
Pathways to Drug Dependence   256
REVIEW IT Classification of Substance-Related Disorders   259

Drugs of Abuse   257
Depressants   257
Stimulants   266
Hallucinogens   270
Inhalants   272
REVIEW IT Drugs of Abuse   272

Theoretical Perspectives   273
Biological Perspectives   273
Learning Perspectives   275
Cognitive Perspectives   277
Psychodynamic Perspectives   278
Sociocultural Perspectives   279
Tying It Together   280
REVIEW IT Theoretical Perspectives   281

Treatment   281
Biological Approaches   281
Nonprofessional Support Groups   284
Residential Approaches   284
Psychodynamic Approaches   285
Behavioural Approaches   285
Relapse-Prevention Training   287
REVIEW IT Treatment   289

CONCEPT MAP   291

8

Eating Disorders and Sleep Disorders   293

Eating Disorders   294
Anorexia Nervosa   295
Bulimia Nervosa   297
Causes of Anorexia and Bulimia   299
Treatment of Anorexia Nervosa and Bulimia Nervosa   303
Binge-Eating Disorder   305
REVIEW IT Eating Disorders   307

Sleep Disorders   308
Dyssomnias   308
Parasomnias   311
Treatment of Sleep Disorders   313
REVIEW IT Sleep Disorders   316

CONCEPT MAP   318

9

Gender Identity Disorder, Paraphilias, and Sexual Dysfunctions   320

Gender Identity Disorder   322
Theoretical Perspectives   324
REVIEW IT Gender Identity Disorder   326

Paraphilias   326
Types of Paraphilias   327
Fetishism   328
Theoretical Perspectives   333
Treatment of Paraphilias   334
Sexual Assault   336
REVIEW IT Paraphilias   340

Sexual Dysfunctions   340
Types of Sexual Dysfunctions   341
Theoretical Perspectives   343
Sex Therapy   348
Biological Treatments of Male Sexual Dysfunctions   352
REVIEW IT Sexual Dysfunctions   353

CONCEPT MAP   355

10

Schizophrenia   357

Clinical Features of Schizophrenia   359
Historical Contributions to Concepts of Schizophrenia   359
Prevalence and Costs of Schizophrenia   360
Phases of Schizophrenia   361
Major Features of Schizophrenia   362
Subtypes of Schizophrenia   368
Categorical Model   370
REVIEW IT Clinical Features of Schizophrenia   371

Theoretical Perspectives   371
Psychodynamic Perspectives   371
Learning Perspectives   372
Biological Perspectives   373
The Diathesis-Stress Model   377
Family Theories   380
REVIEW IT Theoretical Perspectives   383

Treatment   383
Biological Approaches   383
Psychoanalytic Approaches   385
Learning-Based Approaches   385
Psychosocial Rehabilitation   387
Family-Intervention Programs   387
Early-Intervention Programs   389
REVIEW IT Treatment Approaches   389

CONCEPT MAP   391

11

Abnormal Behaviour Across the Lifespan   393

Pervasive Developmental Disorders   395
Autism   395
REVIEW IT Pervasive Developmental Disorders   399

Mental Retardation   400
Causes of Mental Retardation   401
Intervention   404
REVIEW IT Mental Retardation   407

Learning Disorders   407
Types of Learning Disorders   407
Intervention   409
REVIEW IT Learning Disorders   410

Attention-Deficit and Disruptive Behaviour Disorders   410
Attention-Deficit/Hyperactivity Disorder   410
Conduct Disorder   414
Oppositional Defiant Disorder   415
REVIEW IT Attention-Deficit and Disruptive Behaviour Disorders   418

Anxiety and Depression in Childhood and Adolescence   418

Separation Anxiety Disorder   418
Perspectives on Anxiety Disorders in Childhood   420
Depression in Childhood and Adolescence   420
REVIEW IT Anxiety and Depression   423

Delirium   423
Clinical Picture   423
Diagnosis   424
Treatment and Outcomes   424
REVIEW IT Delirium   425

Dementia   426
Clinical Picture   426
Neuropathy   426
Causes and Diagnosis   427
Treatment and Outcomes   428
REVIEW IT Dementia   429
CONCEPT MAP   431

Appendix: Research Methods in Abnormal Psychology   433
Glossary   448
References   458
Credits   492
Name Index   493
Subject Index   500

Abnormal psychology is among the most popular areas of study in psychology for good reason. The problems it addresses are of immense personal and social importance—problems that touch the lives of us all in one way or another. They include problems that are all too pervasive, such as depression, sexual dysfunctions, obesity, and alcohol and substance abuse. They include problems that are less common but have a profound impact on all of us, such as schizophrenia.

The problems addressed in this book are thus not those of the few. The majority of us will experience one or more of them at some time or another, or a friend or loved one will. Even those who are not personally affected by these problems will be touched by society's response—or lack of response—to them. We hope that this text will serve both as an educational tool and as a vehicle to raise awareness among students and general readers alike.

Essentials of Abnormal Psychology in a Changing World, Third Canadian Edition, uses case examples and self-scoring questionnaires; a clear and engaging writing style that is accessible but does not compromise rigour; research-based and comprehensive coverage; superior pedagogy; and integration of sociocultural material throughout, including coverage of issues relating to Canadian cultural diversity, gender, and lifestyle.

Essentials of Abnormal Psychology provides students with the basic concepts in the field in a convenient 11-chapter format. These chapters cover historical and theoretical perspectives, approaches to psychological assessment and treatment, and the major types of psychological disorders—including adjustment disorders, anxiety disorders, mood disorders, substance-related disorders, personality disorders, gender identity and sexual disorders, schizophrenia, and disorders of childhood, adolescence, and aging. Throughout the text, we highlight important Canadian research, case examples, and societal and legal perspectives on abnormal psychology. We also present the best international research from a Canadian perspective.

NEW TO THE THIRD EDITION

One major change in this third edition of *Essentials of Abnormal Psychology in a Changing World* is a reduction of the length of what were the first three chapters of the text by more than 40 pages. This was achieved primarily by combining the first three chapters into two and eliminating nonessential material. The first "disorder" chapter is now Chapter 3, "Anxiety Disorders." While the integrity of the introductory material remains, we have cut material extraneous to an "essentials" text, allowing instructors to move to the first disorder chapter earlier in their schedules. For those teaching this subject to psychology majors, the text now contains less material typically covered in introductory psychology. For those delivering this subject to non-majors, the crucial historical and current perspectives are introduced but they do not overwhelm the reader.

Chapter 1, "What Is Abnormal Psychology?" now consists of carefully condensed material defining abnormal psychology and covering historical and current perspectives.

Chapter 2 now includes **Assessment, Classification, and Treatment of Abnormal Behaviour** plus a slightly reduced section on abnormal behaviour in society. Many instructors prefer to introduce the concepts of patient rights and issues of mental illness and society early in their course, rather than at the end, as was done using the second edition. Since both the perspectives section in Chapter 1 and the treatment sections in Chapter 2 are repeated structurally in each subsequent chapter, those sections in these first chapters focus on the essentials.

We have moved **"Research Methods in Abnormal Psychology"** to an Appendix. In the previous edition, this was covered in Chapter 2. Since this text is used by a wide variety of students with varied backgrounds in research methods, we thought it made sense to shift this material to the Appendix, giving the choice of whether to cover it, and when. The content has remained intact.

At the suggestion of several reviewers we have removed the chapter titled "Stress, Psychological Factors, and Health." We have retrieved from this chapter the clinical disorders, adjustment disorders, and posttraumatic stress disorders, and placed them in **Chapter 3, "Anxiety Disorders."**

Also new to the third edition is a section on cognitive disorders of aging, in **Chapter 11, "Abnormal Behaviour Across the Lifespan."**

A new feature called **Normal/Abnormal Behaviour** has been developed for the third edition. These boxes take a topic relevant to students and present two scenarios: one showing an example of "normal" behaviour and one showing an example of when that behaviour has become "abnormal." This will reach students in their everyday lives who are asking if, for example, their interest in food or body image is normal, or their friend's drinking is abnormal.

New research has been added to each chapter, increasing currency and relevancy. A clinical contributor, Karen Rowa, from McMaster University, was involved in this edition from the beginning, scouring databases and periodicals for the best, most recent, and most applicable research. The visuals and cases have been updated to better reflect the diversity of our students.

Upcoming proposed changes to the DSM are introduced in two "Closer Look" boxes: "DSM-5: The Future of Psychiatric Diagnosis" (Chapter 2) and "Personality Change in the New DSM-5?" (Chapter 6).

This new third Canadian edition updates and integrates sociocultural material relating to ethnicity, gender, culture, and lifestyle throughout the text and in highlighted boxed features ("Focus on Diversity"). Attention to issues of diversity is clearly consistent with the importance given to cultural factors in the DSM-IV-TR and with the need to bring these important issues to the attention of the beginning student in abnormal psychology.

GENERAL APPROACH

We approached the writing of this text with the belief that a textbook should do more than offer a portrait of a field of knowledge. It should be a teaching device—a means of presenting information in ways that arouse interest and encourage understanding and critical thinking. To these ends, we speak to the reader in a clear expository style. We attempt to render complex material accessible. We put a human face on the subjects we address by including many case examples drawn from our own clinical files, those of other mental health professionals, and those from DSM casebooks. We stimulate and involve students through carefully chosen pedagogical features, questionnaires, highlights, and applications. We also include built-in study tools designed to help students master difficult material. And yes, we keep abreast of our ever-changing subject by bringing to our readers a wealth of new scientific information drawn from leading scientific journals and organizations. To summarize the material covered in each chapter in an easy-to-remember visual format, we also include Concept Maps at the end of each chapter.

Essentials of Abnormal Psychology exposes students to the multiple perspectives that inform our present understandings of abnormal behaviour—the psychological, sociocultural, and biological domains. We adopt an interactionist approach, which recognizes that abnormal behaviour typically involves a complex interplay of multiple factors representing different domains. Because the concept of integrating diverse perspectives is often difficult for beginning students to grasp, the unique "Tying It Together" features interspersed through the text help students explore how multiple factors interact in the development of psychological disorders.

FEATURES OF THE TEXT

Textbooks walk balance beams, as it were, and they can fall off in three directions, not just two. That is, they must do justice to their subject matter while also meeting the needs of both instructors and students.

In subject matter, *Essentials of Abnormal Psychology* is comprehensive, providing depth and breadth as well as showcasing the most important new research discoveries. It covers the history of societal response to abnormal behaviours, historical and contemporary models of abnormal behaviours, methods of assessment, psychological and biological models of treatment, contemporary issues, the comprehensive range of problem behaviours set forth in the DSM, and a number of other behavioural problems that entail psychological factors—most notably in the interfaces between psychology and health.

Canadian Content

The third Canadian edition of *Essentials of Abnormal Psychology in a Changing World* showcases a wealth of Canadian content. We chose to do this for several reasons. First and foremost, there is a great deal of important, internationally acclaimed Canadian work being done on the research and treatment of abnormal behaviour. In other words, we have tried to present the best research on abnormal psychology while at the same time alerting our readers to the fact that much of this work comes from Canada. Why would we do this? The answer is to help our readers understand that there is important, relevant research being conducted right where they live, and quite likely on their own campus. Our Canadian focus helps readers understand that key research does not originate just in other countries—it's happening in students' own backyards, perhaps being done by the professor who is teaching their course.

The second reason for highlighting Canadian content is to refute the myth that mental disorders are things that happen to people who live someplace else, such as in other regions or countries. Mental disorder touches all of us; there are people in our country and communities and on our campuses who are afflicted with psychological problems. By citing Canadian examples of people who have battled psychological problems, we hope to bring home the fact that mental illness can reach any of us. Fortunately, effective treatments are available for many of these disorders.

Our third reason for a Canadian focus is pragmatic. The prevalence of mental disorders differs from country to country, as do the treatments of and laws regarding mental disorders and patient rights. Some disorders, such as dependence on crack cocaine, are much more common in the U.S. than in Canada. Substance-use disorders in Canada more commonly involve other substances. The health-care system in Canada is also different from systems in other countries. Accordingly, it is important to have a Canadian focus so that readers can understand how people with mental health problems are treated in Canada.

Finally, the issues regarding mental disorders and the law are different in Canada than in many other countries. For example, in the U.S., a person might be deemed to be "not guilty by reason of insanity." In Canada, such a judgment would be "not criminally responsible on account of a mental disorder." In other words, the Canadian courts often recognize that an accused is guilty of a given crime but not responsible because he or she is under the influence of a mental disorder.

This text illustrates the important fact that abnormal psychology does not occur in a cultural vacuum; the expression and treatment of psychological problems are strongly influenced by cultural factors. Our task of updating and Canadianizing this text was made much easier by the fact that so much of the key research on abnormal behaviour has been conducted in Canada.

"Did You Know That" Chapter Openers

Each chapter begins with a set of "Did You Know That" questions designed to whet students' appetites for specific information contained in the chapter and to encourage them to read further. These chapter-opening questions (e.g., "Did You Know That . . . you can become psychologically dependent on a drug without becoming physically addicted?" or "... as many as 17% of people will suffer from an anxiety disorder at some point in their lives?") also encourage students to think critically and evaluate common conceptions in light of scientific evidence.

"Normal/Abnormal" Features (*New to the Third Edition)

Instructors often hear the question "So what is the difference between normal behaviour and a psychological disorder?" In an effort to bring the material back to real life and to separate normal emotional distress from a psychological disorder, we've introduced case comparisons called "Normal/Abnormal Behaviour"—for example, "Alcohol Use: No Disorder" and "Alcohol Abuse: Disorder," "Normal Perfectionism: No Disorder" and "OCPD: Disorder." These have been written to inspire discussion and engagement with students in class. Students will encounter a variety of symptom severities and can discuss the differences between the cases. These cases are not meant to encourage labelling but are designed to show real-life examples written in non-clinical language. The cases are entirely new and have been written for this edition by Dr. Karen Rowa, Assistant Professor, McMaster University and Associate Director at St. Joseph's Healthcare Clinical Psychology Residency Program.

"Focus on Diversity" Features

The third Canadian edition of *Essentials of Abnormal Psychology* helps broaden students' perspectives so that they understand the importance of issues relating to gender, culture, ethnicity, and lifestyle in the diagnosis and treatment of psychological disorders. Students will see how behaviour deemed normal in one culture could be labelled abnormal in another, how states of psychological distress might be experienced differently in other cultures, how some abnormal behaviour patterns are culture-bound, and how therapists can cultivate a sensitivity to cultural factors in their approach to treating people from diverse backgrounds. Multicultural material is incorporated throughout the text and is highlighted in boxed "Focus on Diversity" features that cover specific topics such as the following:

- Healing the Whole Person: The Canadian Aboriginal Perspective (Chapter 1)
- Culture-Bound Syndromes (Chapter 2)
- Koro and Dhat Syndromes: Asian Somatoform Disorders? (Chapter 5)
- Ethnicity and Alcohol Abuse (Chapter 7)

"A Closer Look" Features

The Closer Look features highlight cutting-edge developments in the field (e.g., virtual reality therapy) and in practice (e.g., suicide prevention) that enable students to apply information from the text to their own lives. Here is a quick preview of features:

- A New Vision of Stigma Reduction and Mental Health Support for Young Adults (Chapter 1)
- DSM-5: The Future of Psychiatric Diagnosis (Chapter 2)
- Virtual Therapy (Chapter 3)
- Concussions, Depression, and Suicide Among NHLers (Chapter 4)
- The Controlled Social Drinking Controversy (Chapter 7)
- A New View of Women's Sexual Dysfunctions? (Chapter 9)
- Psychosis Sucks! Early Psychosis Intervention Programs (Chapter 10)

Self-Scoring Questionnaires

Self-scoring questionnaires (for example, the "Fear of Fat Scale" in Chapter 8 and the "Dissociative Experience Scale" in Chapter 5) involve students in the discussion at hand

and permit them to evaluate their own behaviour. In some cases, students may become more aware of troubling concerns, such as states of depression or problems with drug or alcohol use, which they may wish to bring to the attention of a professional. We have screened the questionnaires to ensure that they will provide students with useful information to reflect on and to serve as a springboard for class discussion.

Review It: In-Chapter Study Breaks

Essentials of Abnormal Psychology contains a built-in study break for students. These in-chapter study breaks conclude each major section in the chapters. This feature provides students with the opportunity to review the material they have just read, and gives them a review break before reading on to a new section.

Define It: End-of-Chapter Glossary Terms

Key terms introduced throughout the text are listed here, with page references for easy retrieval and to help students as they study.

Think About It: End-of-Chapter Discussion Material

End-of-chapter questions ask students to think critically about the issues that were raised in the preceding passages of the text, and invite students to relate the material to their own experiences. Additional multiple-choice questions are available on MySearchLab for students to practise.

Concept Maps

Concept Maps are diagram spreads at the end of each chapter that summarize key concepts and findings in bubble form. Concept Maps provide readers with a "big picture" and are a useful way of understanding and remembering the material covered in each chapter.

SUPPLEMENTS

No matter how comprehensive a textbook is, today's instructors and students require a complete educational package to advance teaching and comprehension. *Essentials of Abnormal Psychology* is accompanied by the following supplements.

Supplements for Students

MYSEARCHLAB (www.mysearchlab.com) MySearchLab offers extensive help to students with their writing and research projects and provides round-the-clock access to credible and reliable source material.

- *Research*. Content on MySearchLab includes immediate access to thousands of full-text articles from leading Canadian and international academic journals, and daily news feeds from the Associated Press. Articles contain the full downloadable text—including abstract and citation information—and can be cut, pasted, emailed, or saved for later use.

- *Writing*. MySearchLab also includes a step-by-step tutorial on writing a research paper. Included are sections on planning a research assignment, finding a topic, creating effective notes, and finding source material. Our exclusive online handbook provides grammar and usage support. Pearson SourceCheck™ offers an easy way to detect accidental plagiarism issues, and our exclusive tutorials teach how to avoid them in the future. MySearchLab also contains AutoCite, which helps students cite sources correctly using MLA, APA, CMS, and CBE documentation styles for both endnotes and bibliographies.

- *Text-specific content.* In addition to the eText, MySearchLab provides students with an opportunity to check their understanding of key chapter concepts with Review It, Define It, Recall It, and Think About It sections associated with each chapter.
- *Pearson eText.* Pearson eText gives students access to the text whenever and wherever they have access to the Internet. eText pages look exactly like the printed text, offering powerful new functionality for students and instructors. Users can create notes, highlight text in different colours, create bookmarks, zoom, click hyperlinked words and phrases to view definitions, and view in single-page or two-page view. Pearson eText allows for quick navigation to key parts of the eText using a table of contents and provides full-text search.

COURSESMART FOR STUDENTS   CourseSmart goes beyond traditional expectations—providing instant, online access to the textbooks and course materials you need at an average savings of 60%. With instant access from any computer and the ability to search your text, you'll find the content you need quickly, no matter where you are. And with online tools like highlighting and note-taking, you can save time and study efficiently. See all the benefits at www.coursesmart.com/students.

Supplements for Instructors

Instructors can download these supplements from our online catalogue. Simply visit www.pearsoncanada.ca/highered and look up this textbook using the catalogue's search function.

INSTRUCTOR'S RESOURCE MANUAL   The Instructor's Resource Manual is a true "course organizer," integrating a variety of resources for teaching abnormal psychology. It includes a summary discussion of the chapter content, a full chapter outline, lecture and discussion questions, a list of learning goals for students, demonstrations, and activities.

MYTEST   (www.pearsonmytest.com) MyTest from Pearson Education Canada is a powerful assessment generation program that helps instructors easily create and print quizzes, tests, exams, and homework or practice handouts. Questions and tests can all be authored online, allowing instructors ultimate flexibility and the ability to efficiently manage assessments at any time, from anywhere. MyTest for *Essentials of Abnormal Psychology*, Third Canadian Edition, includes more than 3000 questions in multiple-choice, true/false, and short-answer/essay format.

TEST ITEM FILE   All the questions from the MyTest are also available in Microsoft Word format.

POWERPOINT® PRESENTATIONS   Students often learn visually, and in a world where multimedia is almost an expectation, a full set of presentations will help you present course material to students.

IMAGE LIBRARY   Electronic versions of key figures and tables in the text are available for your use.

MYSEARCHLAB   The moment you know.
Educators know it. Students know it. It's that inspired moment when something that was difficult to understand suddenly makes perfect sense. Our MyLab products have been designed and refined with a single purpose in mind—to help educators create that moment of understanding with their students.
MySearchLab delivers proven results in helping individual students succeed. It provides engaging experiences that personalize, stimulate, and measure learning for each student. And, it comes from a trusted partner with educational expertise and an eye on the future.

MySearchLab can be used by itself or linked to any learning management system. To learn more about how MySearchLab combines proven learning applications with powerful assessment, visit www.mysearchlab.com.

MySearchLab—the moment you know.

COURSESMART FOR INSTRUCTORS   CourseSmart goes beyond traditional expectations—providing instant, online access to the textbooks and course materials you need at a lower cost for students. And even as students save money, you can save time and hassle with a digital eTextbook that allows you to search for the most relevant content at the very moment you need it. Whether it's evaluating textbooks or creating lecture notes to help students with difficult concepts, CourseSmart can make life a little easier. See how when you visit www.coursesmart.com/instructors.

TECHNOLOGY SPECIALISTS   Pearson's Technology Specialists work with faculty and campus course designers to ensure that Pearson technology products, assessment tools, and online course materials are tailored to meet your specific needs. This highly qualified team is dedicated to helping schools take full advantage of a wide range of educational resources, by assisting in the integration of a variety of instructional materials and media formats. Your local Pearson Education sales representative can provide you with more details on this service program.

PEARSON CUSTOM LIBRARY   For enrollments of at least 25 students, you can create your own textbook by choosing the chapters that best suit your own course needs. To begin building your custom text, visit www.pearsoncustomlibrary.com. You may also work with a dedicated Pearson Custom editor to create your ideal text—publishing your own original content or mixing and matching Pearson content. Contact your local Pearson Representative to get started.

PEERSCHOLAR   Firmly grounded in published research, peerScholar is a powerful online pedagogical tool that helps develop your students' critical and creative thinking skills. peerScholar facilitates this through the process of creation, evaluation, and reflection. Working in stages, students begin by submitting a written assignment. peerScholar then circulates their work for others to review, a process that can be anonymous or not depending on your preference. Students receive peer feedback and evaluations immediately, reinforcing their learning and driving the development of higher-order thinking skills. Students can then re-submit revised work, again depending on your preference. Contact your Pearson Representative to learn more about peerScholar and the research behind it.

ACKNOWLEDGMENTS

The field of abnormal psychology is a moving target, because the literature base that informs our understanding is continually expanding. We are deeply indebted to a number of talented individuals who helped us hold our camera steady in taking a portrait of the field, focus in on the salient features of our subject matter, and develop our snapshots through prose.

First, our professional colleagues, who reviewed chapters from the first and second Canadian editions: Carolyn Szostak, University of British Columbia-Okanagan; Kathy Foxall, Wilfrid Laurier University; Thomas Keenan, Niagara College; Linda Knight, John Abbott College; Joanna Sargent, Georgian College; Rajesh Malik, Dawson College; Kristen Buscaglia, Niagara College; Jillian Esmonde Moore, Georgian College; Beverley Bouffard, York University; and Jocelyn Lymburner, Kwantlen University College.

Second, we are thankful to those who provided feedback to develop this new third Canadian edition: Mark Benner, Fanshawe College; Stephane Gaskin, Dawson College; Stuart Keenan, Sir Sandford Fleming College; Linda Knight, John Abbot College; Ronald Laye, University of the Fraser Valley; Karen Moreau, Niagara College; Ravi Ramkissoonsingh, Niagara College; Sandy Schlieman, Algonquin College; Dana Shapero, University of Windsor; and Abe Worenklein, Dawson College.

And finally, to the publishing professionals at or collaborating with Pearson Education Canada who helped guide the development, editing, proofreading, and marketing of this edition, especially Matthew Christian, acquisitions editor; Suzanne Simpson Millar, developmental editor; Lisa Gillis, marketing manager; Tara Tovell, production editor; Stephanie Fysh, copy editor; Linda Jenkins, proofreader; Dominic Farrell, literary permissions researcher; and Diane Hartmann, photo researcher.

JEFFREY S. NEVID is Professor of Psychology at St. John's University in New York, where he directs the Doctoral Program in Clinical Psychology, teaches at the undergraduate and graduate levels, and supervises doctoral students in clinical practicum work. He received his Ph.D. in Clinical Psychology from the State University of New York at Albany and was a staff psychologist at Samaritan Hospital in Troy, New York. He later completed a National Institute of Mental Health Post-Doctoral Fellowship in Mental Health Evaluation Research at Northwestern University. He holds a Diplomate in Clinical Psychology from the American Board of Professional Psychology, is a Fellow of the American Psychological Association and the Academy of Clinical Psychology, and has served on the editorial boards of several journals and as Associate Editor of the *Journal of Consulting and Clinical Psychology*. His publications have appeared in journals such as *Journal of Consulting and Clinical Psychology, Health Psychology, Journal of Occupational Medicine, Behavior Therapy, American Journal of Community Psychology, Professional Psychology: Research and Practice, Journal of Clinical Psychology, Journal of Nervous and Mental Disease, Teaching of Psychology, American Journal of Health Promotion,* and *Psychology and Psychotherapy*. Dr. Nevid is also author of the book *Choices: Sex in the Age of STDs* and the introductory psychology text *Psychology: Concepts and Applications*, as well as several other college texts in the fields of psychology and health coauthored with Dr. Spencer Rathus. Dr. Nevid is also actively involved in a program of pedagogical research focusing on helping students become more effective learners.

BEVERLY A. GREENE is Professor of Psychology at St. John's University, a fellow of seven divisions of the American Psychological Association, and a fellow of the American Orthopsychiatric Association and the Academy of Clinical Psychology. She holds a Diplomate in Clinical Psychology and serves on the editorial boards of numerous scholarly journals. She received her PhD in Clinical Psychology from Adelphi University and worked in public mental health for over a decade. She was founding coeditor of the APA Society for the Study of Lesbian, Gay, and Bisexual Issues series, *Psychological Perspectives on Lesbian, Gay and Bisexual Issues*. She is also coauthor of the recent book *What Therapists Don't Talk About and Why: Understanding Taboos That Hurt Ourselves and Our Clients*, and has more than 80 professional publications that are the subject of nine national awards. Dr. Greene was recipient of the APA 2003 Committee on Women in Psychology Distinguished Leadership Award; 1996 Outstanding Achievement Award from the APA Committee on Lesbian, Gay, and Bisexual Concerns; the 2004 Distinguished Career Contributions to Ethnic Minority Research Award from the APA Society for the Study of Ethnic Minority Issues; the 2000 Heritage Award from the APA Society for the Psychology of Women; the 2004 Award for Distinguished Senior Career Contributions to Ethnic Minority Research (APA Division 45); and the 2005 Stanley Sue Award for Distinguished Professional Contributions to Diversity in Clinical Psychology (APA Division 12). Her coedited book *Psychotherapy with African American Women: Innovations in Psychodynamic Perspectives and Practice* was also honoured with the Association for Women in Psychology's 2001 Distinguished Publication Award. In 2006, she was the recipient of the Janet Helms Award for

Scholarship and Mentoring from the Teacher's College, Columbia University Cross Cultural Roundtable, and of the 2006 Florence Halpern Award for Distinguished Professional Contributions to Clinical Psychology (APA Division 12). In 2009, she was honoured as recipient of the APA Award for Distinguished Senior Career Contribution to Psychology in the Public Interest. She is an elected representative to the APA Council and member at large of the Women's and Public Interest Caucuses of the Council.

PAUL JOHNSON has 25 years' experience in post-secondary education as a professor, program co-ordinator, and curriculum and program validation adviser at Confederation College. Paul recently served on the Ontario Ministry of Training, Colleges and Universities (MTCU) committee that developed the new provincial college curriculum standards for general education and essential employability skills. He has received international recognition for academic leadership from the Chair Academy and the National Institute for Staff and Organizational Development (NISOD). Paul has also practised psychology in the Psychotherapy and Psychiatric departments of St. Joseph's Hospital in Thunder Bay. As well, he has been a health-promotion consultant in his community for many years. Along with Helen Bee and Denise Boyd, Paul co-authored *Lifespan Development* (Pearson Education Canada), now in its fourth Canadian edition.

STEVEN TAYLOR, PHD, ABPP, is a professor and clinical psychologist in the Department of Psychiatry at the University of British Columbia and is editor-in-chief of the *Journal of Cognitive Psychotherapy*. He serves on the editorial board of several journals, including the *Journal of Consulting and Clinical Psychology*. He has published over 200 journal articles and book chapters, and over a dozen books on anxiety disorders and related topics. Dr. Taylor has received career awards from the Canadian Psychological Association, the British Columbia Psychological Association, the Association for Advancement of Behaviour Therapy, and the Anxiety Disorders Association of America. He is a fellow of several scholarly organizations, including the Canadian Psychological Association, the American Psychological Association, the Association for Psychological Science, and the Academy of Cognitive Therapy. His clinical and research interests include cognitive-behavioural treatments and mechanisms of anxiety disorders and related conditions, as well as the behavioural genetics of these disorders.

MELANIE MACNAB has over 10 years' experience teaching psychology at Seneca College in Toronto. She has held positions as professor, program co-ordinator, and associate chair. During her time as associate chair in the School of Communication Arts, Melanie helped implement new and successful programs and was a leader to teams of faculty members. Known for being in the forefront of innovative teaching practices and the development of various delivery modes (fully online and hybrid delivery), she serves as a mentor to many in curriculum development. She currently serves on Seneca's Faculty Advisory Committee and thinks that profound intellectual and interpersonal growth can happen in the classroom.

1

What Is Abnormal Psychology?

CHAPTER OUTLINE

How Do We Define Abnormal Behaviour?
Criteria for Determining Abnormality
Risk Factors
Prevention and Resilience
Personal and Social Costs of Poor Mental Health

Historical Perspectives on Abnormal Behaviour
The Demonological Model
Origins of the Medical Model: An "Ill Humour"
Medieval Times
Witchcraft

Asylums in Europe and the New World
The Reform Movement and Moral Therapy in
   Europe and North America
Drugs and Deinstitutionalization: The Exodus from
   Provincial Psychiatric Hospitals
Pathways to the Present: From Demonology to Science

Current Perspectives on Abnormal Behaviour
Biological Perspectives on Abnormal Behaviour
Psychological Perspectives on Abnormal Behaviour
Sociocultural Perspectives on Abnormal Behaviour
Interactionist Perspectives

Did You Know That...

- About one in five adults in Canada will be diagnosed with a psychological disorder at some point in their lives?

- Behaviour we consider abnormal may be perceived as perfectly normal in another culture?

- The modern medical model of abnormal behaviour can be traced to the work of a Greek physician some 2500 years ago?

- A night on the town in London, Ontario, in the 19th century may have included peering at the residents of a local asylum?

- At one time, there were more patients occupying psychiatric hospital beds than there were patients in hospital beds due to all other causes?

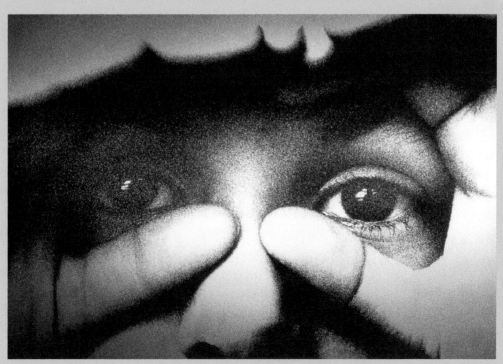

Abnormal behaviour might appear to be the concern of only a few. After all, only a minority of the population will ever be admitted to a psychiatric hospital. Most people never seek the help of a **clinical psychologist** or **psychiatrist**. Only a few people plead not criminally responsible on account of a mental disorder. Many of us have what we call an "eccentric" relative, but few of us have relatives we would consider truly bizarre.

The truth of the matter is that abnormal behaviour affects virtually everyone in one way or another. Abnormal behaviour patterns that involve a disturbance of psychological functioning or behaviour are classified as **psychological disorders** (also called *mental disorders*). Health Canada's (2002b) *Report on Mental Illness in Canada* suggests that about 20% of Canadians will experience a psychological disorder at some time in their lives. Table 1.1 shows the percentage of people who have one of several major classes of psychological disorders during any one-year period. The report also found that psychological disorders requiring hospitalization were most common among people in the 25- to 44-year age range and declined with increasing age. Women, essentially at all ages, had higher rates and more days of hospitalization for the seven most common psychological disorders leading to hospital admission (Health Canada, 2002b). If we also include the mental health problems of our family members, friends, and co-workers, then perhaps none of us remain unaffected.

Abnormal psychology is the branch of the science of psychology that addresses the description, causes, and treatment of abnormal behaviour patterns. Let us pause for a moment to consider our use of terms. We prefer to use the term *psychological disorder* when referring to abnormal behaviour patterns associated with disturbances of psychological functioning, rather than *mental disorder*. There are a number of reasons why we have adopted this approach. First, *psychological disorder* puts the study of abnormal behaviour squarely within the purview of the field of psychology. Second, the term *mental disorder* is generally associated with the **medical model** perspective, which considers abnormal behaviour patterns to be symptoms of underlying mental illnesses or disorders. Although the medical model remains a prominent perspective for understanding abnormal behaviour patterns, we shall see that other perspectives, including psychological and sociocultural perspectives, also inform our understanding of abnormal behaviour. Third, *mental disorder* as a phrase reinforces the traditional distinction between mental and physical phenomena. As we'll see, there is increasing awareness of the interrelationships between the body and the mind that calls into question this distinction.

TABLE 1.1

Prevalence of DSM-IV Disorders in Adults

	1-year (%)	Lifetime (%)
Any Anxiety Disorder	18.1	28.8
Any Mood Disorder	9.5	20.8
Any Substance-Abuse Disorder	3.8	14.6
Any Disorder	26.2	46.4

Source: Adapted from Kessler, Berglund et al., 2005; Kessler, Chiu et al., 2005.

In this chapter, we first address the task of defining abnormal behaviour. We see that throughout history, and even in prehistory, abnormal behaviour has been viewed from different perspectives or according to different models. We chronicle the development of concepts of abnormal behaviour and its treatment. We see that, historically speaking, *treatment* usually referred to what was done *to*, rather than *for*, people with abnormal behaviour. Finally, we'll introduce you to current perspectives on abnormal behaviour.

HOW DO WE DEFINE ABNORMAL BEHAVIOUR?

Most of us become anxious or depressed from time to time, but our behaviour is not deemed abnormal. It is normal to become anxious in anticipation of an important job interview or a final examination. It is appropriate to feel depressed when you have lost someone close to you or when you have failed at a test or on the job. But when do we cross the line between normal and abnormal behaviour?

One answer is that emotional states like anxiety and depression may be considered abnormal when they are not appropriate to the situation. It is normal to feel down because of failure on a test, but not when one's grades are good or excellent. It is normal to feel anxious during a job interview, but not whenever entering a department store or boarding a crowded elevator.

Abnormal behaviour may also be suggested by the magnitude of the problem. Although some anxiety is normal enough before a job interview, feeling your heart hammering away so relentlessly that it might leap from your chest—and consequently cancelling the interview—is not. Nor is it normal to feel so anxious in this situation that your clothing becomes soaked with perspiration.

Criteria for Determining Abnormality

Abnormal behaviour thus has multiple definitions. Depending on the case, some criteria may be weighted more heavily than others. But in most cases, a combination of these criteria is used to define abnormality. Precisely how mental health professionals assess and classify abnormal behaviour is described in Chapter 2, "Assessment, Classification, and Treatment of Abnormal Behaviour."

Psychologists generally apply some combination of the following criteria in making a determination that behaviour is abnormal:

1. *Behaviour is unusual.* Behaviour that is unusual is often considered abnormal. Only a few of us report seeing or hearing things that are not really there; "seeing things" and "hearing things" are almost always considered abnormal in our culture, except, perhaps, in cases of religious experience. Yet **hallucinations** are not deemed unusual in some non-Western cultures. Being overcome with feelings of panic when entering a department store or when standing in a crowded elevator is also uncommon and considered abnormal. But uncommon behaviour is not in itself abnormal. Only one person can hold the record for swimming or running the fastest 100 metres. The record-holding athlete differs from the rest of us but, again, is not considered abnormal.

2. *Behaviour is socially unacceptable or violates social norms.* All societies have norms (standards) that define the kinds of behaviours acceptable in given contexts. Behaviour deemed normal in one culture may be viewed as abnormal in another. In our society, standing on the street corner and repeatedly shouting "Kill 'em!" to passersby would be labelled abnormal; shouting "Kill 'em!" in the arena at a professional wrestling match is usually within normal bounds.

hallucinations Perceptions that occur in the absence of an external stimulus that are confused with reality.

When is anxiety abnormal? Negative emotions such as anxiety are considered abnormal when they are judged to be excessive or inappropriate to the situation. Anxiety is generally regarded as normal when it is experienced during a job interview, so long as it is not so severe that it prevents the interviewee from performing adequately. Anxiety is deemed to be abnormal if it is experienced whenever one boards an elevator.

Although the use of norms remains one of the important standards for defining abnormal behaviour, we should be aware of some limitations of this definition.

One implication of basing the definition of abnormal behaviour on social norms is that norms reflect relative, cultural standards, not universal truths. What is normal in one culture may be abnormal in another. For example, Canadians who assume strangers are devious and try to take advantage are usually regarded as distrustful, perhaps even **paranoid**. But such suspicions were justified among the Mundugumor, a tribe of cannibals in Papua New Guinea studied by anthropologist Margaret Mead (1935). Within that culture, male strangers, even the male members of one's own family, *were* typically spiteful toward others.

Clinicians such as psychologists and psychiatrists need to weigh cultural differences in determining what is normal and abnormal. In the case of the Mundugumor, this need is more or less obvious. Sometimes, however, differences are subtler. For example, what is seen as normal, outspoken behaviour by most Canadian women might be interpreted as brazen behaviour when viewed in the context of another, more traditional culture. Moreover, what strikes one generation as abnormal may be considered by others to fall within the normal spectrum. For example, until the mid-1970s, homosexuality was classified as a mental disorder by the psychiatric profession (see Chapter 9, "Gender Identity Disorder, Paraphilias, and Sexual Dysfunctions"). Today, however, the psychiatric profession no longer considers homosexuality a mental disorder. Indeed, roughly two thirds of Canadians now express approval of same-sex relationships (Bibby, 2006).

Another implication of basing normality on compliance with social norms is the tendency to brand nonconformists as mentally disturbed.

3. *Perception or interpretation of reality is faulty.* Normally speaking, our sensory systems and cognitive processes permit us to form fairly accurate mental representations of the environment. But seeing things and hearing voices that are not present are considered hallucinations, which in our culture are often

paranoid Having irrational suspicions.

taken as signs of an underlying disorder. Similarly, holding unfounded ideas or **delusions**, such as **ideas of persecution** that the Mounties or the Mafia are out to get you, may be regarded as signs of mental disturbance—unless, of course, they *are*.

It is normal in Canada to say that one "talks" to God through prayer. If, however, a person claims to have literally seen God or heard the voice of God—as opposed to, say, being divinely inspired—we may come to regard her or him as mentally disturbed.

4. *The person is in significant personal distress.* States of personal distress caused by troublesome emotions, such as anxiety, fear, or depression, may be considered abnormal. As noted earlier, however, anxiety and depression are sometimes appropriate responses

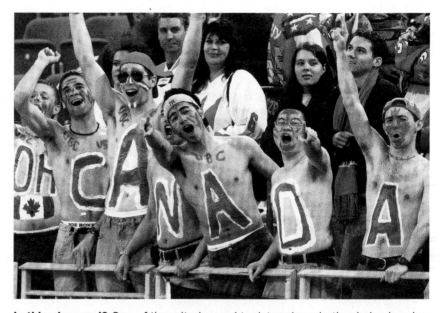

Is this abnormal? One of the criteria used to determine whether behaviour is abnormal is whether it deviates from acceptable standards of conduct or social norms. The behaviour and attire of these spectators might be considered abnormal in the context of a classroom or workplace, but perhaps not at a sporting event.

to a situation. Real threats and losses occur from time to time, and the *lack* of an emotional response to them would be regarded as abnormal. Appropriate feelings of distress are considered normal unless they become prolonged or persist long after the source of anguish has been removed (after most people would have adjusted) or if they are so intense that they impair the individual's ability to function.

5. *Behaviour is maladaptive or self-defeating.* Behaviour that leads to unhappiness rather than self-fulfillment can be regarded as abnormal. Behaviour that limits our ability to function in expected roles or to adapt to our environments may also be considered abnormal. According to these criteria, then, heavy alcohol consumption that impairs health or social and occupational functioning may be viewed as abnormal. **Agoraphobia,** behaviour characterized by an intense fear of venturing into public places, may be considered abnormal in that it is uncommon and also maladaptive because it impairs the individual's ability to fulfill work and family responsibilities.

6. *Behaviour is dangerous.* Behaviour that is dangerous to oneself or other people may be considered abnormal. Here, too, social context is crucial. In wartime, people who sacrifice themselves or charge the enemy with little apparent concern for their own safety may be characterized as courageous, heroic, and patriotic. But people who threaten or attempt suicide because of the pressures of civilian life are usually considered abnormal.

Football and hockey players (and even adolescents) who occasionally get into altercations may be normal enough. Given the cultural demands of these sports, nonaggressive football and hockey players would not last long in varsity or professional ranks. But individuals involved in frequent unsanctioned fights may be regarded as abnormal.

Cultural differences in how abnormal behaviour patterns are expressed lead us to realize that we must determine that our concepts of abnormal behaviour are recognizable and valid before we apply them to other cultures (Bebbington, 1993; Kleinman, 1987). The reverse is equally true. The concept of "soul loss" may characterize psychological distress in some non-Western societies but has little or no relevance to middle-class North Americans. Evidence from multinational studies conducted by the World Health

delusions Firmly held but inaccurate beliefs that persist despite evidence that they have no basis in reality.

ideas of persecution A form of delusional thinking characterized by false beliefs that one is being persecuted or victimized by others.

agoraphobia Excessive, irrational fear of open places.

Canadian census data show that our Aboriginal population continues to be the fastest-growing segment of the population. The highest concentrations of Canada's more than 1.3 million Aboriginal peoples are in the North and West, and just over one half are now living in urban centres throughout Canada (Statistics Canada, 2003). Along with rapid population growth, there is evidence of the resurgence of Canadian Aboriginal cultures, especially in the arts, media, education, commerce, and health (Aboriginal Planet, 2002; Arthur & Stewart, 2001; Fraser, 1994; Letendre, 2002).

Despite this optimistic outlook, Aboriginal peoples in Canada are still dealing with the effects of generations of physical, mental, emotional, and spiritual distress caused by the decimation of their communities, lands, and cultural identities. Consequently, both on- and off-reserve Aboriginal peoples have to contend with extensive mental health, addiction, and medical issues in their communities as compared to the rest of Canadians. In particular, Canadian Aboriginals suffer from disproportionately higher rates of major depression, anxiety, posttraumatic stress disorder, alcoholism and substance abuse, sexual abuse, family violence, chronic disease such as heart disease and diabetes, lower life expectancy, and suicide (Statistics Canada, 2002).

Centuries of extreme social, cultural, and geographic disruption have contributed to the distress suffered by Aboriginal people. The arrival of European settlers resulted in an estimated 90% decline in Aboriginal populations (Trigger & Swagerty, 1996). The remaining Aboriginals were exposed to widespread, inescapable social and cultural disruption caused by government-sanctioned separation of children from their parents and communities plus systematic efforts to force Aboriginal people to take on non-Aboriginal cultural values at the cost of becoming disconnected from their own. This process of cultural assimilation was enforced by the relocation and social regrouping of Aboriginal peoples onto remote reserves, by placing Aboriginal children into residential boarding schools, and by unwittingly creating a forced dependence on government support. Poverty and powerlessness further marginalized Aboriginal peoples and their cultural traditions from mainstream society (Poonwassie & Charter, 2001). Aboriginal peoples' survival of and recovery from this long-standing personal and social devastation are a testament to their strength and long-suffering determination. Moreover, it gives credence to the significance and legitimacy of their perception of life, and, despite great odds, a distinctive Aboriginal perspective has survived to challenge the established Canadian ideas of treatments and cures.

MAINSTREAM TREATMENT OF ABORIGINAL ILLNESSES HAS PROVED LACKING

Mainstream health-care approaches have not been readily accessible or reasonably successful at treating and preventing Aboriginal peoples' physical and mental health problems (McCormick, 2000; Wieman, 2001). There were well-intentioned attempts to change the way that "experts" dealt with Aboriginal health problems during the last decades of the 20th century, but, at best, medical and

Organization (WHO) in the 1960s and 1970s shows that the behaviour pattern we characterize as schizophrenia exists in countries as wide-ranging as Colombia, India, China, Denmark, Nigeria, and the former Soviet Union (Jablensky et al., 1992). Rates of schizophrenia and its general features were actually quite similar among all countries studied. Societal views or perspectives on abnormal behaviour also vary across cultures. In our society, models based on medical disease and psychological factors have achieved prominence in explaining abnormal behaviour. But in traditional cultures, concepts of abnormal behaviour often invoke supernatural causes, such as possession by demons or the devil (Lefley, 1990).

It is one thing to recognize and label behaviour as abnormal; it is another to understand and explain it. Philosophers, physicians, natural scientists, and psychologists have used various approaches, or *models*, in the effort to explain abnormal behaviour. Some approaches have been based on superstition; others have invoked religious explanations. Some current views are predominantly biological; others are psychological. We consider various historical and contemporary approaches to understanding abnormal behaviour. First, let us look further at the importance of cultural beliefs and expectations in determining which behaviour patterns are deemed abnormal.

counselling professionals adopted as truth a range of over-generalized, simplified, and under-researched beliefs about Aboriginal cultural values and behaviours. Overreliance on Aboriginal cultural stereotypes led to a cookie-cutter, one-size-fits-all, condescending approach to treatment and counselling that has netted few overall gains in health and well-being for Aboriginal peoples. This lack of success creates a formidable challenge and opportunity, especially for the non-Aboriginal health-care practitioner to become an effective partner in a meaningful healing process (Waldram, 2001, 2004).

ABORIGINAL HEALING

Aboriginal healing and wellness promotion place a high value on the balance between the interconnected physical, mental, emotional, and spiritual aspects of life. As such, healing and wellness promotion are multi-levelled, targeting the individual as well as the family and the community, while respecting both individual and group languages, customs, history, and environment (D. B. Smith & Morrissette, 2001). This may ultimately evolve into a healing paradigm in which not only will Canadian health practitioners change the way they approach Aboriginal peoples but the Aboriginal healing perspective will influence how practitioners approach members of any and all cultural minority groups. Ultimately, a holistic healing perspective may come to permeate and transform mainstream health, mental health, social services, and care practices in Canada (Poonwassie & Charter, 2001).

A Canadian Aboriginal smudging ceremony. Sacred medicinal plants such as sweetgrass, tobacco, sage, and cedar are ignited in a bowl or seashell and allowed to smoulder. Following ancient, traditional rituals, the smoke is used to purify, cleanse, and heal the mind, body, soul, and spirit. Although there is no one thing that on its own leads to healing, a smudging ceremony is an important aspect of the larger Aboriginal healing perspective. It serves to strengthen cultural identity, which builds self-respect. As the Aboriginal people become aware of who they are, then a sense of connectedness with nature and the Creator, healthier ways of living, and improved physical and mental well-being will follow (A. Magiskan, personal communication, February 10, 2004).

Source: Ann Magiskan is of Ojibwa heritage and is responsible for the Native Heritage programs at Fort William Historical Park.

Risk Factors

In a major Canadian study of psychological health, Stephens, Dulberg, and Joubert (1999) determined that key risk factors include age, education, childhood traumas, current stress, life events, social supports, gender, and physical health. To confuse matters, exposure to multiple risk factors can have an exponential effect that dramatically increases the likelihood of adverse outcomes (Masten, 2001). Exposure to just two risk factors can engender a fourfold increase in adverse outcomes, and four or more risk factors can increase adversity tenfold (Luthar & Cicchetti, 2000; Rutter, 1999). In addition to acting synergistically, risk factors can generate a negative chain reaction whereby exposure to new risks perpetuates and intensifies existing problems.

This can set into motion a self-reinforcing negative spiral (Baylis, 2002). Individually, risk factors do not present a high probability of psychopathology, but they have a strong effect in combination. Multiple risk factors greatly increase the likelihood of adverse outcomes (Masten, 2001).

Prevention and Resilience

Prevention efforts focus on risk factors with the expectation that when these are reduced or eliminated, the incidence of mental health problems will drop. Strategies that promote resilience and enhance an individual's psychological resources can also contribute to problem reduction and even prevention (Stephens et al., 1999). In light of this, viable mental health promotion strategies are needed to establish conditions that foster resilience and support. For instance, the more protective factors there are available to a child, the more likely the child is to experience resilience in the face of adversity and to cope effectively with challenges to both mental and physical functioning (Baylis, 2002).

Resilience is the display of positive adaptation in the face of adversity (Baylis, 2002). It's the capacity to bounce back from our lows and learn from them in a positive way. It's the vital sense of flexibility and the capacity to re-establish one's own balance. It's the essential feeling of being in control with regard to oneself and the outside world (Mental Health Promotion [MHP], 2003). Resilience does not come solely from within an individual but is engendered by family and community. We need to foster resilience within families and communities rather than merely try to make an individual resilient. Neither children nor adults should be viewed in isolation as the sole focus of change, treatment, or enhancement (Baylis, 2002).

Personal and Social Costs of Poor Mental Health

While most Canadians would agree that mental health care is a priority, the true extent and cost of poor mental health have been underestimated (Canadian Alliance on Mental Illness and Mental Health [CAMIMH], 2000; Prevention-Dividend Project, 2003; Stephens & Joubert, 2001). Measures of nonmedical services and of short-term disability are excluded because large numbers of Canadians seek treatment outside of the medical system. Specifically, direct costs related to visits to nonmedical mental health professionals are not fully accounted for. Indirect costs, including lost days of work, lowered productivity, and the drain on other resources (such as family and co-workers), are even harder to track. When morbidity and mortality issues are factored into the equation, poor mental health is one of the costliest health conditions in Canada (CAMIMH, 2000), with the conservative estimated cost of treatment to be over $14 billion annually (Stephens & Joubert, 2001). We'll come back to current views later in the chapter, but for now we'll take a step back in time to explore the historical roots of abnormal behaviour.

REVIEW IT

How Do We Define Abnormal Behaviour?

- **What are the criteria used by mental health professionals to define abnormal behaviour?** Psychologists generally consider behaviour abnormal when it meets some combination of the following criteria: (1) unusual or statistically infrequent; (2) socially unacceptable or in violation of social norms; (3) fraught with misperceptions or misinterpretations of reality; (4) associated with states of severe personal distress; (5) maladaptive or self-defeating; and (6) dangerous.

- **What are psychological disorders?** Psychological disorders (also called *mental disorders*) involve abnormal behaviour patterns associated with disturbances in mental health or psychological functioning.

- **How are cultural beliefs and norms related to the classification and understandings of abnormal behaviour?** Behaviours deemed normal in one culture may be considered abnormal in another. Concepts of health and illness may have different meanings in different cultures. Abnormal behaviour patterns may also take different forms in different cultures, and societal views or models explaining abnormal behaviour vary across cultures as well.

HISTORICAL PERSPECTIVES ON ABNORMAL BEHAVIOUR

Throughout the history of Western culture, concepts of abnormal behaviour have been shaped, to some degree, by the prevailing **world view** of the time. Throughout much of history, beliefs in supernatural forces, demons, and evil spirits held sway. Abnormal behaviour was often taken as a sign of **possession**. In more modern times, the predominant—but by no means universal—world view has shifted toward beliefs in science and reason. Abnormal behaviour has come to be viewed in our culture as the product of physical and psychosocial factors, not demonic possession.

The Demonological Model

Let us begin our journey with an example from prehistory. Archaeologists have unearthed human skeletons from the Stone Age with egg-sized cavities in the skulls. One interpretation of these holes is that our prehistoric ancestors believed abnormal behaviour reflected the invasion of evil spirits. Perhaps they used this harsh method—called **trephining**—to create a pathway through the skull to provide an outlet for those irascible spirits. Fresh bone growth indicates that some people managed to survive the ordeal.

Threat of trephining may have persuaded people to comply with group or tribal norms to the best of their abilities. Because no written records or accounts of the purposes of trephination exist, other explanations are possible. Perhaps trephination was used as a primitive form of surgery to remove shattered pieces of bone or blood clots that resulted from head injuries (Maher & Maher, 1985).

Explanation of abnormal behaviour as a result of supernatural or divine causes is termed the **demonological model**. Ancient peoples explained natural forces in terms of divine will and spirits. The ancient Babylonians believed that the movements of the stars and planets were fashioned by the adventures and conflicts of the gods. The ancient Greeks believed that their gods toyed with humans; when aroused to wrath, the gods could unleash forces of nature to wreak havoc on disrespectful or arrogant humans, even clouding their minds with madness.

Origins of the Medical Model: An "Ill Humour"

Not all ancient Greeks believed in the demonological model. The seeds of naturalistic explanations of abnormal behaviour were sown by Hippocrates and developed by other physicians in the ancient world, especially Galen.

Hippocrates (ca. 460–377 BC), the celebrated physician of the Golden Age of Greece, challenged the prevailing beliefs of his time by arguing that illnesses of the body and mind were the result of natural causes, not of possession by supernatural spirits. He believed that the health of the body and mind depended on the balance of **humours** or vital fluids: phlegm, black bile, blood, and yellow bile. An imbalance of humours, he thought, accounted for abnormal behaviour. A lethargic or sluggish person was believed to have an excess of phlegm, from which we derive the word **phlegmatic**. An overabundance of black bile was believed to cause depression, or **melancholia**. An excess of blood created a **sanguine** disposition: cheerful, confident, and optimistic. An excess of yellow bile made people "bilious" and **choleric**—quick-tempered, that is.

Hippocrates's theory of bodily humours is of historical importance because of its break from demonology. It also foreshadowed the development of the modern medical model, the view that abnormal behaviour results from underlying biological processes. Medical schools continue to pay homage to Hippocrates by having new physicians swear the Hippocratic oath in his honour.

world view Prevailing view of the times. (English translation of the German *Weltanschauung*.)

possession In demonology, a type of superstitious belief in which abnormal behaviour is taken as a sign that the individual has become possessed by demons or the devil, usually as a form of retribution or the result of making a pact with the devil.

trephining Harsh prehistoric practice of cutting a hole in a person's skull, possibly as an ancient form of surgery for brain trauma, or possibly as a means of releasing the demons that prehistoric people may have believed caused abnormal behaviour in the afflicted persons.

demonological model The model that explains abnormal behaviour in terms of supernatural forces.

humours Four fluids in the body: phlegm, black bile, blood, and yellow bile. Hippocrates believed that the health of the body and mind depended on their balance.

phlegmatic Slow and stolid.

melancholia State of severe depression.

sanguine Cheerful.

choleric Having or showing bad temper.

Medieval Times

The Middle Ages, or medieval times, cover the millennium of European history from about AD 476 through AD 1450. Belief in supernatural causes, especially the doctrine of possession, increased in influence and eventually dominated medieval thought. The doctrine of possession held that abnormal behaviours were a sign of possession by evil spirits or the devil. This belief was embodied within the teachings of the Roman Catholic Church, which became the unifying force in Western Europe following the decline of the Roman Empire. Although belief in possession dates from before the Church and is found in ancient Egyptian and Greek writings, the Church revitalized it. The treatment of choice for abnormal behaviour was **exorcism**. Exorcists were employed to persuade evil spirits that the bodies of their intended victims were basically uninhabitable. Their methods included prayer, waving a cross at the victim, beating and flogging, and even starving the victim. If the victim still displayed unseemly behaviour, there were yet more powerful remedies, such as the rack, a device of torture. It seems clear that recipients of these "remedies" would be motivated to behave acceptably as much as possible.

exorcism Ritual intended to expel demons or evil spirits from a person believed to be possessed.

Witchcraft

The late 15th through the late 17th centuries were especially dangerous times to be unpopular with your neighbours. These were times of massive persecutions of people, particularly women, who were accused of witchcraft. Officials of the Roman Catholic Church believed that witches made pacts with the devil, practised satanic rituals, and committed heinous acts such as eating babies and poisoning crops. In 1484, Pope Innocent VIII decreed that witches must be executed. Two Dominican priests compiled a manual for witch-hunting, called the *Malleus Maleficarum* ("The Witches' Hammer"), to help inquisitors identify suspected witches. Over 100 000 accused witches were killed in the next two centuries.

Modern scholars once believed the so-called witches of the Middle Ages and the Renaissance were actually people who were mentally disturbed. They were believed to have been persecuted because their abnormal behaviour was taken as evidence that they were in league with the devil. It is true that many suspected witches confessed to impossible behaviours; however, most of these confessions can be discounted because they were extracted under torture by inquisitors who were bent on finding evidence to support accusations of witchcraft (Spanos, 1978). Accusations of witchcraft appeared to be a convenient means of disposing of social nuisances and political rivals, of seizing property, and of suppressing heresy (Spanos, 1978). In English villages, many of the accused were poor, unmarried elderly women, who were forced to beg their neighbours for food. If misfortune befell people who declined to help, the beggar might be accused of causing misery by having cast a curse on the uncharitable family (Spanos, 1978). If the woman was generally unpopular, accusations of witchcraft were more likely to be followed up.

Historical trends do not follow straight lines. Although the demonological model held sway during the Middle Ages and much of the Renaissance, it did not universally replace belief in naturalistic causes (Schoeneman, 1984). In medieval England, for example, demonic possession was only rarely invoked as the cause of abnormal behaviour in cases in which a person was held to be insane by legal authorities (Neugebauer,

Exorcism. This medieval woodcut illustrates the practice of exorcism, which was used to expel evil spirits who were believed to have possessed people.

1979). Most explanations of unusual behaviour involved natural causes, such as illness or trauma to the brain. In England, in fact, some disturbed people were kept in hospitals until they were restored to sanity (Allderidge, 1979). The Renaissance Belgian physician Johann Weyer (1515–1588) also took up the cause of Hippocrates and Galen by arguing that abnormal behaviour and thought patterns were caused by physical problems.

Asylums in Europe and the New World

By the late 15th and early 16th centuries, asylums, or *madhouses*, began to crop up throughout Europe. Many were former leprosariums that were no longer needed as a result of the decline in leprosy that occurred in the late Middle Ages. Asylums often gave refuge to beggars as well as the disturbed, and conditions were generally appalling. Residents were often chained to their beds and left to lie in their own waste or wander about unassisted. Some asylums became public spectacles. In the 19th century, it was standard operating procedure at many Ontario asylums (found in Toronto, Hamilton, and London) to open to public viewing from noon until 3 p.m. every day (Miron, 2006).

Madhouse, spectacle, or hospital? Standard operating procedures in many Ontario asylums was to allow the public to view the patients, making the hospitals a public spectacle.

The first asylum in what is now North America was the Hôtel Dieu in Quebec City. It was founded in 1639 by the Duchesse d'Aiguillon to care for people with psychological disorders and intellectual disabilities, as well as the poor, the destitute, and the physically disabled. The Catholic community took responsibility for the treatment of patients and oversaw the development of other asylums throughout Quebec (Hurd et al., 1916). Outside Quebec, however, people with psychological disorders received little treatment and were commonly shut away in jails, poorhouses, charity shelters, or another convenient stronghold. No means of addressing their needs came until well into the 19th century, when mental hospitals began to appear in other parts of Canada (Sussman, 1998).

The Reform Movement and Moral Therapy in Europe and North America

The modern era of treatment can be traced to the efforts of individuals such as the Frenchmen Jean-Baptiste Pussin and Philippe Pinel in the late 18th and early 19th centuries. They argued that people who behave abnormally suffer from diseases and should be treated humanely. This view was not popular at the time. Deranged people were generally regarded by the public as threats to society, not as sick people in need of treatment.

From 1784 to 1802, Pussin (1746–1811), a layman, was placed in charge of a ward for people considered "incurably insane" at La Bicêtre, a large mental hospital in Paris. Although Pinel is often credited with freeing the inmates of La Bicêtre from their chains, Pussin was actually the first official to unchain a group of the "incurably insane." These unfortunates had been considered too dangerous and unpredictable to be left unchained. But Pussin believed that if they were treated with kindness, there would be no need for chains. As he predicted, most of the shut-ins became manageable and calm when their chains were removed. They could walk the hospital grounds and take in fresh air. Pussin also forbade the staff from treating the residents harshly, and he discharged employees who ignored his directives.

Pinel (1745–1826) became medical director for the incurables' ward at La Bicêtre in 1793 and continued the humane treatment Pussin had begun. Pinel also spent hours

The unchaining of inmates at La Bicêtre by 18th-century French reformer Philippe Pinel. Continuing the work of Jean-Baptiste Pussin, Pinel stopped harsh practices such as bleeding and purging and moved inmates from darkened dungeons to sunny, airy rooms. Pinel also took the time to converse with inmates in the belief that understanding and concern would help restore them to normal functioning.

moral therapy A 19th-century treatment philosophy that emphasized that hospitalized mental patients should be treated with care and understanding in a pleasant environment, not shackled in chains.

talking to inmates, in the belief that showing understanding and concern would help restore them to normal functioning.

The philosophy of treatment that emerged from these efforts was labelled **moral therapy** (a mistranslation of the words for "well-being" or "morale") (Dix, 1999). It was based on the belief that providing humane treatment in a relaxed, decent, and encouraging environment could restore functioning. Similar reforms were instituted at about this time in England by William Tuke and later in the United States and Canada by Dorothea Dix.

Dix (1802–1887), a Boston schoolteacher, travelled throughout the United States, Europe, and Canada decrying the deplorable conditions in jails and charitable housing, where deranged people were often placed. As a direct result of her social activism, mental hospitals were established in Canada outside of Quebec, initially in the Maritimes during the 1840s, and later in the century in the other provinces.

Drugs and Deinstitutionalization: The Exodus from Provincial Psychiatric Hospitals

phenothiazines Group of antipsychotic drugs or "major tranquillizers" used in the treatment of schizophrenia.

An important factor that spurred the exodus from psychiatric hospitals was the advent of a new class of drugs—**phenothiazines**. The phenothiazines, a group of antipsychotic drugs that helped suppress the most flagrant behaviour patterns associated with schizophrenia, were introduced in Canada in the early 1950s. Two psychiatrists, unbeknownst to each other, had begun experimenting with chlorpromazine, a drug that was being used in conjunction with anaesthetics for surgery. They were curious about its soothing qualities and potential worth as a treatment for psychotic symptoms, and it wasn't long before their pioneering research produced far-reaching outcomes. In 1954, Dr. Ruth Kajander was the first in North America to publicly report on the drug's therapeutic value (Sussman, 1999). A month later, McGill University psychiatrist Heinz Lehmann published the first research paper for the North American audience describing his success in using chlorpromazine to treat schizophrenia (Griffin, 1993; Sussman, 1999). As a result of Kajander's and Lehmann's research, the widespread use of chlorpromazine as an antipsychotic drug in Canada and the United States quickly followed. Chlorpromazine reduced the need for indefinite hospital stays and permitted many people with schizophrenia to be discharged to less restrictive living arrangements in their community, such as halfway houses, group homes, and independent living arrangements. This was a crucial moment in the mental health-care system in Canada.

In response to the growing call for reform in the mental health system, the Canadian Mental Health Association (CMHA) published a report, *More for the Mind: A Study of Psychiatric Services in Canada* (Tyhurst et al., 1963), that recommended that mental illness be treated as a medical condition in a medical facility. This report paved the way for long-term custodial care patients, the so-called back-ward patients in bleak institutions, to be integrated into community general hospitals. This policy of **deinstitutionalization** was based on the belief—the hope, perhaps—that psychiatric patients would benefit from the opportunity to lead more independent and fulfilling lives in the community while relying on general hospitals for short-term care during episodes of illness. Indeed, the psychiatric hospital population across Canada plummeted from more than 50 000 in 1960 to 15 000 by 1975 (Wasylenki, 2001).

In the initial stages, during the 1960s and 1970s, there was a shift from long stays in provincial psychiatric hospitals to shorter but more frequent stays in general hospital psychiatric units. However, although the number of general hospital beds used for this purpose rose, it failed to match the shrinking number of psychiatric hospital beds. At the same time, the availability of more community mental health supports and services lagged far behind the rapid exodus of mental health patients from psychiatric hospitals (Sealy & Whitehead, 2004). The general hospital psychiatric units treated patients with less severe forms of mental disorders, while patients with severe and persistent mental disorders had to rely on the much-scaled-down provincial psychiatric hospital system. In effect, this created a two-tier mental health-care system, whereby middle- and upper-class patients had easier access to psychiatrists and general hospital psychiatric care than less fortunate Canadians, who were relegated to shrinking psychiatric hospital services or, worse, were left to lead a barely sufficient existence in the community (Kirby & Keon, 2004).

Services continued to be narrow in focus and were not well co-ordinated, thus making it difficult for patients to receive adequate and consistent care. The community programs and services that were supposed to replace institutional care have thus far been inadequate (Kirby & Keon, 2004; Wasylenki, 2001). Deinstitutionalization in Canada has left mental patients to rely on dramatically fewer hospital beds and a fragmented system of community services and supports. In "A Closer Look: The Homeless in Canada" on page 16, we consider the plight of the homeless Canadians with mental health issues who got lost in the shuffle between the movement toward the closure of psychiatric institutions and the promised, but thus far inadequate, community mental health-care system.

Until recently, Canada lacked a comprehensive mental health-care policy. In 2006, senators Michael Kirby and Wilbert Keon conducted the most comprehensive study of its kind in Canada on mental health, mental illness, and addiction. Their report, *Out of the Shadows at Last: Transforming Mental Health, Mental Illness and Addiction Services in Canada*, focused squarely on mental health promotion, prevention of mental illness, and the creation of a continuum of care for those who suffer from mental illness and addiction. The report recommended that a Canadian Mental Health Commission be established to implement a national mental health-care strategy. In March 2007, the federal government announced funding for the Commission, to be led by Senator Kirby.

deinstitutionalization Practice of discharging large numbers of hospitalized mental patients to the community and of reducing the need for new admissions through the development of alternative treatment approaches such as halfway houses and crisis intervention services.

Pathways to the Present: From Demonology to Science

Beliefs in possession or demonology persisted until the rise of the natural sciences in the late 17th and early 18th centuries. Society at large began to turn toward reason and science as ways of explaining natural phenomena and human behaviour. The emerging sciences of biology, chemistry, physics, and astronomy offered promise that knowledge could be derived from scientific methods of observation and experimentation. The 18th and 19th centuries witnessed rapid developments in medical science. Scientific discoveries uncovered the microbial causes of some kinds of diseases and gave rise to preventive measures. Emerging models of abnormal behaviour also began to surface, including the medical model, psychological models, and sociocultural models.

A FAMILY INSPIRES COMPASSION AND CARE AFTER LOSING THEIR SON TO SUICIDE

Jack Windeler was a first-year student at Queen's University who died by suicide in March of 2010. Jack's note asked that no fuss be made of his passing, but to "help others." Jack's parents began the Jack Windeler Memorial Fund in partnership with Kids Help Phone, Canada's leading counselling service for youth aged 5–20.

As an initiative of Kids Help Phone, and in partnership with the Mental Health Commission of Canada, the project seeks to promote mental health awareness and support for youth aged 15–20+ who are transitioning from high school to college, university, or independent living.

THE JACK PROJECT AT KIDS HELP PHONE

The mission of the project is to inspire a national culture of informed compassion and care for youth impacted by mental health challenges.

TWOFOLD SUPPORT SYSTEM

School Outreach: The Jack Project has aligned with Canadian mental health organizations to develop a pilot program (2011–12 school year) at 36 schools across Ontario. Through this work, the team plans to develop a model of care and a best practices toolbox that will be available to be implemented over time in institutions across Canada. These resources will be comprehensive, effective, and inclusive for assisting not only young people in transition, but also their peers, community members, and caregivers.

Technology Investment: The Jack Windeler Memorial Fund will make specific investments to Kids Help Phone's

Jack Windeler died by suicide during his first year of studies at Queen's University. He asked that others be helped.

existing technologies. Key to this will be the launch of new support technology at Kids Help Phone, including:

(a) the launch of online chat and mobile applications that will link youth to the trained professionals at Kids Help Phone, and

(b) the automation of key aspects of Kids Help Phone's leading database of 37 000 referral youth-serving agencies across Canada.

Through these integrated online efforts, Kids Help Phone will educate and support youth where they spend increasing amounts of time (online), and will assist more youth to "self-navigate" to be better able to find assistance in their community.

MEDICAL MODEL Against the backdrop of advances in medical science, German physician Wilhelm Griesinger (1817–1868) argued that abnormal behaviour was rooted in diseases of the brain. Griesinger's views influenced another German physician, Emil Kraepelin (1856–1926), who in 1883 wrote an influential textbook on psychiatry in which he likened mental disorders to physical diseases. Griesinger and Kraepelin paved the way for the development of the modern medical model, which attempts to explain abnormal behaviour on the basis of underlying biological defects or abnormalities, not evil spirits. According to the medical model, people behaving abnormally suffer from mental illnesses or disorders that can be classified, like physical illnesses, according to their distinctive causes and symptoms and whose features can be conceptualized as symptoms of underlying disorders, whatever their cause.

Kraepelin specified two main groups of mental disorders or diseases: **dementia praecox** (from roots meaning "precocious [premature] insanity"), which we now call *schizophrenia*, and *manic-depressive psychosis*, which is now labelled *bipolar disorder*. Kraepelin believed that dementia praecox was caused by a biochemical imbalance and manic-depressive psychosis by an abnormality in body metabolism. But his major contribution was the development of a classification system that forms the cornerstone of current diagnostic systems.

dementia praecox Term given by Emil Kraepelin to the disorder we now call *schizophrenia*.

The medical model was supported by evidence that a form of derangement called **general paresis** represented an advanced stage of syphilis in which the syphilis bacterium directly invades brain tissue. Scientists grew optimistic that other biological causes, as well as treatments, would soon be discovered for other so-called mental disorders. This early optimism has remained largely unfulfilled because the causes of most patterns of abnormal behaviour remain obscure.

Much of the terminology in current use reflects the influence of the medical model. Because of the medical model, many professionals and laypeople speak of people whose behaviour is deemed abnormal as being mentally *ill*. It is because of the medical model that so many speak of the *symptoms* of abnormal behaviour rather than its *features* or *characteristics*. Other terms spawned by the medical model include *mental health, syndrome, diagnosis, patient, mental patient, mental hospital, prognosis, treatment, therapy, cure, relapse*, and *remission*.[1]

The medical model is a major advance over demonology. It inspired the idea that abnormal behaviour should be treated by learned professionals and not be punished. Compassion replaced hatred, fear, and persecution.

PSYCHOLOGICAL MODELS Although the medical model was gaining influence in the 19th century, there were those who believed that organic factors alone could not explain the many forms of abnormal behaviour. In Paris, a highly respected neurologist, Jean-Martin Charcot (1825–1893), experimented with the use of **hypnosis** in treating **hysteria** (which is now called *conversion disorder*), a condition in which people present with physical symptoms such as paralysis or numbness that cannot be explained by any underlying physical cause. The thinking at the time was that they must have an affliction of the nervous system that caused their symptoms. Yet Charcot and his associates demonstrated that these symptoms could be removed in hysterical patients or actually induced in normal patients by means of hypnotic suggestion.

Among those who attended Charcot's demonstrations was a young Austrian physician named Sigmund Freud (1856–1939). Freud reasoned that if hysterical symptoms could be made to disappear or appear through hypnosis—the mere "suggestion of ideas"—they must be psychological in origin (E. Jones, 1953). He concluded that whatever psychological factors give rise to hysteria, they must lie outside the range of conscious awareness. This was the kernel of the idea that underlies his model of abnormal behaviour, the **psychodynamic model**, which holds that the causes of abnormal behaviours lie in the interplay of forces within the unconscious mind. "I received the proudest impression," Freud wrote of his experience with Charcot, "of the possibility that there could be powerful mental processes which nevertheless remained hidden from the consciousness of men" (cited in Sulloway, 1983, p. 32).

Freud's theoretical model was the first major psychological model of abnormal behaviour. As we'll see later in this chapter, other psychological perspectives on abnormal behaviour soon followed, based on behavioural, humanistic, and cognitive approaches. We'll also see that each of these psychological perspectives, as well as the physiological perspective, spawned particular forms of therapy to treat psychological disorders.

SOCIOCULTURAL MODELS Sociocultural theorists believe that to better understand the roots of abnormal behaviour, we must consider the broader social contexts in which behaviour occurs. They believe that the causes of abnormal behaviour may be found in the failures of society rather than of the person. Psychological problems may be rooted in the social ills of society, such as poverty, lack of economic opportunity, rapidly changing social values and morals, and racial and gender discrimination. This view of abnormal behaviour will be addressed further later in this chapter.

[1]Because the medical model is not the only way of viewing abnormal behaviour patterns, we adopt a more neutral language in this text in describing abnormal behaviour patterns. For example, we often refer to "features" or "characteristics" of abnormal behaviour patterns or psychological disorders rather than "symptoms." But our adoption of nonmedical jargon is not an absolute rule. In some cases, there may be no handy substitutes for terms that derive from the medical model, such as the term *remission* or the reference to patients in mental hospitals as "mental patients." In other cases we may use terms such as *disorder, therapy*, and *treatment* because they are commonly used by psychologists who "treat" "mental disorders" with psychological "therapies."

general paresis Degenerative brain disorder that occurs during the final stage of syphilis.

hypnosis Trancelike state, induced by suggestion, in which one is generally passive and responsive to the commands of the hypnotist.

hysteria Former term for *conversion disorder*.

psychodynamic model Theoretical model of Freud and his followers in which behaviour is viewed as the product of clashing forces within the personality.

The Homeless in Canada: Still Waiting for True Community Mental Health Care

The number of homeless people across Canada has more than doubled in the last decade. Projections state that nightly, tens of thousands of Canadians are homeless (Hwang, 2001). Although difficult to measure, it is estimated that between 20% and 35% of homeless people need treatment for their mental health problems (R. N. Golden et al., 1999; Milstone, 1995). A year-long study of Toronto homeless shelter users found that about one third (31%) of homeless people were experiencing both psychological and substance-use disorders, while roughly equal numbers were experiencing either a psychological disorder (19%) or a substance-use disorder (21%) (Tolomiczenko & Goering, 1998). In 5% of the cases, a prevalence of severe psychological disorder, primarily schizophrenia, was found.

FACING THE CHALLENGE OF MENTAL HEALTH PROMOTION FOR HOMELESS PEOPLE

While it's true that many provincial psychiatric hospitals closed their doors and general hospitals reduced the number of psychiatric beds beginning in the 1990s, problems arose when provinces failed to adequately fund or integrate community support services intended to replace the need for long-term hospitalization (Muckle & Turnbull, 2006). Far too often, homeless people with a range of psychological problems fell through the cracks of the mental health and social service systems and were left largely to fend for themselves. In particular, there has been an ongoing lack of available housing, transitional care facilities, and effective case management for homeless Canadians who have psychological disorders and addictions (Kirby & Keon, 2006). To compound the problem, not only is there limited access to adequate housing and community support services, magnifying the length and severity of a homeless person's mental health problems (R. N. Golden et al., 1999; Social Services Ottawa, 1999; H. L. Stuart & Arboleda-Florez, 2000), but also large numbers of those who suffer from medical ailments are typically forced to endure increased hospital stays and treatment costs (Podymow, Turnbull, Tadic, & Muckle, 2006).

DEINSTITUTIONALIZATION: THE FINAL PHASE

At long last, we may be on the verge of a new era in Canadian mental health care. In their comprehensive report, *Out of the Shadows at Last*, senators Kirby and Keon (2006) described how a continuum of mental health care could be made available to every Canadian,

Homeless with mental health issues. A multifaceted effort is needed to meet the needs of the psychiatric homeless population, including access to affordable housing and to medical, drug and alcohol, and mental health treatment, as well as other social services. Far too often, homeless people with a range of psychological problems fall through the cracks of the mental health and social service systems, and are left largely to fend for themselves.

including some of our most vulnerable members of society—homeless Canadians with psychological disorders. Based on the recommendations of Kirby and Keon's report, the Canadian Mental Health Care Commission will develop a national strategy to oversee the delivery of mental health services, such as integrated, seamless access to personalized and culturally sensitive care through community mental health-care services and supports (Kirby & Keon, 2006). Such a system may include, but would not be limited to, the following: access to non-health services including safe and adequate housing, employment assistance, and adequate income; opportunities to rely on peer support and develop meaningful social relationships; opportunities to foster self-respect and a sense of being an accepted member of society (Kirby & Keon, 2006; L. B. Russell, Hubley, & Palepu, 2005); and harm reduction programs that target alcohol and drug abuse (Everett, 2002; Turnbull, Muckle, & Tadic, 2004; Wasylenki, 2001).

According to the more radical sociocultural theorists, such as the psychiatrist Thomas Szasz, mental illness is no more than a myth—a label used to stigmatize and subjugate people whose behaviour is socially deviant (Szasz, 1961). Szasz argues that so-called mental illnesses are really "problems in living," not diseases in the sense that influenza, hypertension, and cancer are. Nearly half a century later, Canadian psychiatrist Gordon Warme (2006) has rekindled these sentiments by claiming that biological explanations of abnormal behaviour are still unconvincing and that "most, if not all, of the effects of psychiatry are magical" (p. 2).

Sociocultural theorists maintain that once the label of "mental illness" is applied, it is very difficult to remove. The label also affects other people's responses to the "patient." Mental patients are stigmatized and socially degraded. Job opportunities may be denied, friendships may dissolve, and the "patient" may become increasingly alienated from society. Szasz argues that treating people as mentally ill strips them of their dignity because it denies them responsibility for their own behaviour and choices. He claims that troubled people should be encouraged to take more responsibility for managing their lives and solving their problems (Szasz, 1961).

Although not all sociocultural theorists subscribe to Szasz's more radical views, they alert us to consider the importance of taking sociocultural factors relating to gender, race, ethnicity, lifestyle, and social ills such as poverty and discrimination into account in understanding people whose behaviour leads them to be perceived as mentally ill or abnormal. It should come as no surprise that the effects of stigma and discrimination remain a daily experience for many Canadians diagnosed with psychological or addictive disorders—a topic we'll come back to in Chapter 2, "Assessment, Classification, and Treatment of Abnormal Behaviour."

REVIEW IT

Historical Perspectives on Abnormal Behaviour

- **How have views about abnormal behaviour changed over time?** Ancient societies attributed abnormal behaviour to divine or supernatural forces. There were some authorities in ancient times, such as the Greek physicians Hippocrates and Galen, who believed that abnormal behaviour reflected natural causes. In medieval times, belief in possession held sway, and exorcists were used to rid people who behaved abnormally of the evil spirits that were believed to possess them. The 19th-century German physician Wilhelm Griesinger argued that abnormal behaviour was caused by diseases of the brain. He and another German physician who followed him, Emil Kraepelin, were influential in the development of the modern medical model, which likens abnormal behaviour patterns to physical illnesses.

- **How has the treatment of people with psychological disorders changed over time?** Asylums, or madhouses, began to crop up throughout Europe in the late 15th and early 16th centuries. Conditions in these asylums were dreadful, and in some, such as Bethlehem Hospital in England and 19th-century hospitals in Ontario, a circus atmosphere prevailed. With the rise of moral therapy in the 19th century, largely spearheaded by the Frenchmen Jean-Baptiste Pussin and Philippe Pinel, conditions in mental hospitals improved. Proponents of moral therapy believed that mental patients could be restored to functioning if they were treated with dignity and understanding. The decline of moral therapy in the latter part of the 19th century led to a period of apathy and to the belief that the "insane" could not be successfully treated. Conditions in mental hospitals deteriorated, and they offered little more than custodial care.

  Not until the middle of the 20th century did public outrage and concern about the plight of mental patients mobilize a change in government policy. As a consequence, psychiatric services were commonly relocated to general hospital psychiatric units as an alternative to long-term hospitalization. This movement toward deinstitutionalization was spurred by the introduction of psychoactive drugs, called *phenothiazines*, that curbed the more flagrant features of schizophrenia.

- **What are the roles of psychiatric hospitals and general hospital psychiatric units today?** The hospitals provide a structured treatment environment for people in acute crisis and for those who are unable to adapt to community living. Mental health care in a hospital today aims to restore patients to community functioning. Community mental health-care services are meant to provide continuing care outside of the hospital to people with psychological disorders.

- **What is deinstitutionalization and how successful has it been?** Deinstitutionalization is the policy of reducing the need for long-term hospitalization of mental patients by shifting care to community-based settings. Although deinstitutionalization has greatly reduced the population of provincial psychiatric hospitals, it has not yet fulfilled its promise of restoring people with psychological disorders to a reasonable quality of life in the community. One example of the challenges yet to be met is the number of homeless people with psychological and substance-abuse problems who are not receiving adequate care in the community.

CURRENT PERSPECTIVES ON ABNORMAL BEHAVIOUR

Biological Perspectives on Abnormal Behaviour

The medical model, inspired by physicians from Hippocrates through Kraepelin, remains a powerful force in contemporary understanding of abnormal behaviour, representing a biological perspective. We prefer to use the term *biological perspectives* rather than *medical model* to refer to approaches that emphasize the role of biological factors in explaining abnormal behaviour and the use of biologically based components in treating psychological disorders.

Knowledge of the biological underpinnings of abnormal behaviour has grown rapidly in recent years, and exciting advances are being made in genetics, epigenetics, and stem cell research that are taking us to an entirely new level of understanding of abnormal behaviour. We know that other biological factors, especially the functioning of the nervous system, are also involved in many forms of abnormal behaviour. To better understand the role of biological systems in abnormal behaviour patterns, we first need to learn the basics of how molecular structures alter and regulate cellular function, how the nervous system is organized, and how nerve cells communicate with each other.

GENETICS   Heredity plays an important role in human behaviour. From a biological perspective, heredity is described in terms of genetics—the study of how traits are passed down from one generation to the next and how these traits affect the way we look, function, and behave. We'll begin this section by looking at the latest groundbreaking research on the role genetics plays in the origin of abnormalities.

The Human Genome   A genome comprises all the genetic material encoded in the **DNA** (deoxyribonucleic acid) located in the nucleus of cells in living organisms (see Figure 1.1). DNA—the long, complex molecular structures that make up the genome—is characterized by essential organic compounds that determine our unique genetic code.

In each of our cells, there are an estimated 2.8 billion of the base-pair compounds that form the familiar DNA double-helix structures of the human genome.

Most of our genes contain the cellular instructions for combining 20 standard amino acids to build a wide array of **proteins** (35 000 or so). Each protein is a unique combination of amino acids, and every cell in our body is constructed and maintained by proteins. For example, different proteins are used to build everything from bones, muscles, and organs to brain cells. In addition, all biological processes—metabolism, immune function, muscle contraction, and neurotransmission—rely on proteins.

Genetic errors occur when the number or order of the DNA base pairs is wrong. When the DNA sequence is interrupted, the result can be an alteration or breakdown of a cell's normal protein production, maintenance, and repair processes. If these errors are serious enough, bodily structures and functions can become abnormal or fail.

Epigenetics   Recent genetics research has revealed that DNA errors tell only one part of the story when it comes to explaining the causes of human diseases and disorders. Each of your body's cells contains an identical DNA code. But if each cell carries the same genetic code (your genotype), how is it that they come to differentiate into specialized cell types (your phenotype), such as muscle, skin, or brain cells? The answer seems to be found in a molecular structure that overlays the genome, called the **epigenome** (Callinan & Feinberg, 2006).

Epigenetics research, particularly in recent years (Weinhold, 2006), has shown that the epigenome plays a vital role in gene regulation through two key means: **gene expression** and **gene silencing**. Under normal circumstances, some genes are expressed (turned

---

DNA Deoxyribonucleic acid is a double-strand complex molecule of helical structure that contains the genetic instructions for building and maintaining living organisms.

proteins Organic compounds consisting of amino acids that perform most life functions and make up the majority of cellular structures.

epigenome The sum total of inherited and acquired molecular variations to the genome that lead to changes in gene regulation without changing the DNA sequence of the genome itself.

epigenetics The study of the heritable and acquired changes in gene regulation (phenotype) that occur without affecting DNA sequence (genotype).

gene expression The process by which a gene sequence becomes activated ("turned on") and is translated into the proteins that determine the structure and functions of body cells.

gene silencing The process of preventing or suppressing ("switching off") a gene sequence from being translated into proteins.

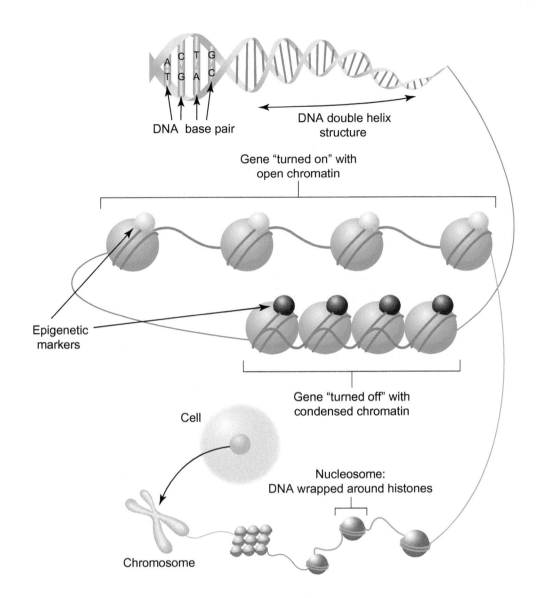

DNA base pair

DNA double helix structure

Gene "turned on" with open chromatin

Epigenetic markers

Gene "turned off" with condensed chromatin

Cell

Nucleosome: DNA wrapped around histones

Chromosome

FIGURE 1.1 **The genome and the epigenome.** The genome is all the hereditary information or all the information necessary to build and maintain life. Each cell contains the same genetic code. The genome is actually made up of chromosomes, found in each nucleus of each cell, that are further segmented into genes which are then wrapped around histones. Gene-coiled histones are called nucleosomes, and groups of these look like beads on a necklace. Along the nucleosomes are epigenetic markers which actually regulate the gene—in gene expressions or gene silencing. It is in this process that epigenetic errors happen and interfere with normal gene regulation.

on) while others are silenced (turned off). So, for example, although a person's muscle cells and brain cells both have the same genome (DNA sequence), it is each cell's unique epigenome that dictates which pattern of genes within that cell will be activated. Simply put, we could say that it is the epigenome that causes "brain" genes to be active in brain cells but silenced in muscle cells and vice versa. The epigenome also regulates hundreds of other critically precise tasks in our cells.

In the area of mental health, Canadian researchers are at the forefront of investigating the role epigenetics plays in the origin and course of psychological disorders such as schizophrenia, bipolar disorders, and Alzheimer's disease (Schumacher & Petronis, 2006). Epigenetics has suddenly provided scientists with a significant reinterpretation of the interplay between genes and the environment. We are just now beginning to understand what may well be the next revolution in the theory and treatment of human disease and disorders.

Stem Cells Stem cell research has recently opened up new avenues for studying the development and treatment of various conditions such as schizophrenia, autism, and bipolar disorder. Stem cells, found in all multicellular organisms, are biological cells that can divide (through mitosis) and differentiate into diverse specialized cell types and can self-renew to produce more stem cells. Stem cells can now be artificially grown and transformed through cell culture into specialized cell types with characteristics consistent with cells of various tissues, such as muscles or nerves.

The inability to actually watch living human brain cells in action has hampered scientists in their efforts to understand psychiatric disorders. However, researchers have identified a promising new approach that may revolutionize the study and treatment of conditions. A team led by researchers at the Salk Institute for Biological Studies in La Jolla, California, took skin cells from a patient with schizophrenia, turned them into adult stem cells, and then grew those stem cells into neurons (Brennand et al., 2011). The resulting tangle of brain cells gave neuroscientists their first real-time glimpse of human schizophrenia at the cellular level.

Scientists have used the disease-in-a-dish strategy to gain insight into sickle-cell anemia and heart arrhythmias. But the Salk team, led by neuroscientist Fred H. Gage, was the first to apply the approach to a genetically complex neuropsychiatric disorder. The group found that neurons derived from patients with schizophrenia formed fewer connections with one another than those derived from healthy patients; they also linked the deficit to the altered expression of nearly 600 genes, four times as many as had been previously implicated. The approach may eventually improve therapy, allowing psychiatrists to screen a variety of drugs to find the one that would be most effective for each patient.

THE NERVOUS SYSTEM Perhaps you would not be nervous if you did not have a nervous system, but even calm people have nervous systems. The nervous system is made up of nerve cells called **neurons**. Neurons communicate with one another, or transmit "messages." These messages somehow account for events as diverse as sensing an itch from a bug bite; co-ordinating a figure skater's vision and muscles; composing a symphony; solving an architectural equation; and, in the case of hallucinations, hearing or seeing things that are not really there.

Every neuron has a cell body, or **soma**, dendrites, and an axon (see Figure 1.2). The cell body contains the nucleus of the cell and metabolizes oxygen to carry out its work. Short fibres called **dendrites** project from the cell body to receive messages from adjoining neurons. Each neuron has a single **axon** that projects trunk-like from

neurons Nerve cells.

soma Cell body.

dendrites Root-like structures at the end of a neuron that receive nerve impulses from other neurons.

axon Long, thin part of a neuron along which nervous impulses travel.

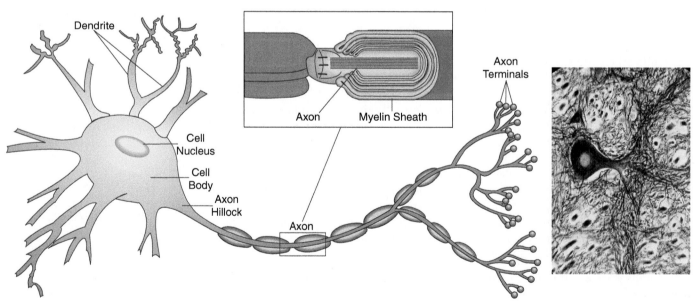

FIGURE 1.2 Anatomy of a neuron.
Neurons typically consist of cell bodies (or somas), dendrites, and one or more axons. The axon of this neuron is wrapped in a myelin sheath, which insulates it from the bodily fluids surrounding the neuron and facilitates transmission of neural impulses (messages that travel within the neuron).

the cell body. Axons can extend over a metre if they are conveying messages between the toes and the spinal cord. They may branch and project in various directions. Axons terminate in small branching structures that are aptly termed **terminals**. Swellings called **knobs** occupy the tips of axon terminals. Neurons convey messages in one direction, from the dendrites or cell body along the axon to the axon terminals. The messages are then conveyed from terminal knobs to other neurons, muscles, or glands.

Neurons transmit messages to other neurons by means of chemical substances called **neurotransmitters**. Neurotransmitters induce chemical changes in receiving neurons. These changes cause axons to conduct the messages in electrical form.

The junction between a transmitting neuron and a receiving neuron is termed a **synapse**. A transmitting neuron is termed *presynaptic*. A receiving neuron is said to be *postsynaptic*. A synapse consists of an axon terminal from a transmitting neuron, a dendrite of a receiving neuron, and a small fluid-filled gap between the two called the *synaptic cleft*. The message does not jump the synaptic cleft like a spark. Instead, axon terminals release neurotransmitters into the cleft like myriad ships casting off into the seas (see Figure 1.3).

Each kind of neurotransmitter has a distinctive chemical structure. It will fit only into one kind of harbour or **receptor site** on the receiving neuron. Consider the analogy of a lock and key. Only the right key (neurotransmitter) operates the lock, causing the postsynaptic neuron to forward the message.

Once released, some molecules of a neurotransmitter reach port at receptor sites of other neurons. "Loose" neurotransmitters may be broken down in the synaptic clefts by enzymes or be reabsorbed by the axon terminal (a process termed *reuptake*) so as to prevent the receiving cell from continuing to fire.

Malfunctions in neurotransmitter systems in the brain are linked to various kinds of mental health problems. For example, excesses and deficiencies of the neurotransmitter **norepinephrine** have been connected with mood disorders (see Chapter 4, "Mood Disorders and Suicide") and eating disorders (see Chapter 8, "Eating Disorders and Sleep Disorders"). **Alzheimer's disease**, which involves the progressive loss of memory and cognitive functioning, is associated with reductions in the levels in the brain of the

terminals In neuropsychology, the small branching structures found at the tips of axons.

knobs Swollen endings of axon terminals.

neurotransmitters Chemical substances that serve as a type of messenger by transmitting neural impulses from one neuron to another.

synapse Junction between the terminal knob of one neuron and the dendrite or soma of another, through which nerve impulses pass.

receptor site Part of a dendrite on the receiving neuron that is structured to receive a neurotransmitter.

norepinephrine Type of neurotransmitter of the catecholamine class.

Alzheimer's disease Progressive brain disease characterized by gradual loss of memory and intellectual functioning, personality changes, and eventual loss of ability to care for oneself.

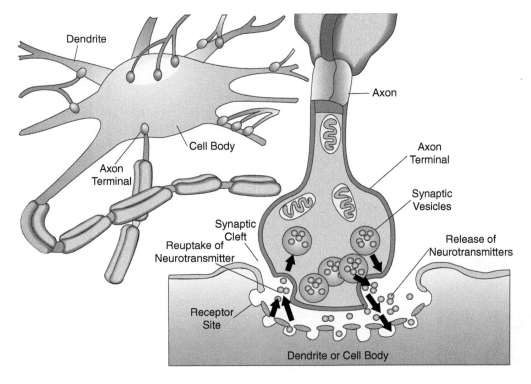

FIGURE 1.3 Transmission of neural impulses across the synapse.
Neurons transmit messages or neural impulses across synapses, which consist of the axon terminal of the transmitting neuron; the gap, or synaptic cleft, between the neurons; and the dendrite of the receiving neuron. The "message" consists of neurotransmitters that are released by synaptic vesicles (sacs) into the synaptic cleft and taken up by receptor sites on the receiving neuron. Finally, neurotransmitters are broken down and reabsorbed by the axon terminal (reuptake) to be recycled.

acetylcholine Type of neurotransmitter involved in the control of muscle contractions. Abbreviated *ACh*.

dopamine Neurotransmitter of the catecholamine class that is believed to play a role in schizophrenia.

neurotransmitter **acetylcholine**. Irregularities involving excessive availability of the neurotransmitter **dopamine** appear to be involved in schizophrenia (see Chapter 10, "Schizophrenia"). **Serotonin**, another neurotransmitter, is linked to various psychological disorders, including anxiety disorders (see Chapter 3, "Anxiety Disorders"), mood disorders (see Chapter 4), sleep disorders (see Chapter 8), and eating disorders (see Chapter 8). Although neurotransmitters are believed to play a role in various psychological disorders, precise causal relationships have not yet been determined.

REVIEW IT

Biological Perspectives

- **What is the distinguishing feature of the biological perspectives on abnormal behaviour?** Biological perspectives focus on the biological underpinnings of abnormal behaviour, including the roles of genetics, neurotransmitter functioning, and brain abnormalities and defects.

---

serotonin Type of neurotransmitter, imbalances of which have been linked to mood disorders and anxiety.

psychoanalytic theory Theoretical model of personality developed by Freud. Also called *psychoanalysis*.

Psychological Perspectives on Abnormal Behaviour

Researchers are investigating whether the combination of psychological and drug treatments for such problems as depression, anxiety disorders, and substance-abuse disorders may increase the therapeutic benefits of either of the two approaches alone. Although Canadian psychiatry has become increasingly medicalized in recent years, some within the psychiatric community have warned their colleagues not to overlook the role of psychological factors in explaining and treating mental health problems (Leszcz, MacKenzie, el-Guebaly, Atkinson, & Wiesenthal, 2002).

At about the time biological models of abnormal behaviour were beginning to achieve prominence with the contributions of Kraepelin, Griesinger, and others, another approach to understanding the bases of abnormal behaviour began to emerge. This approach emphasized the psychological roots of abnormal behaviour and was most closely identified with the work of Freud. Over time other psychological models would emerge from the behaviourist, humanistic-existential, and cognitivist traditions. Let's begin our study of psychological perspectives with Freud's contribution and the development of psychodynamic models.

PSYCHODYNAMIC MODELS Psychodynamic theory is based on the contributions of Sigmund Freud and his followers. The psychodynamic model espoused by Freud, called **psychoanalytic theory**, is based on the belief that psychological problems are derived from unconscious psychological conflicts, which can be traced to childhood. Freud held that much of our behaviour is driven by unconscious motives and conflicts of which we are unaware. These underlying conflicts revolve around primitive sexual and aggressive instincts or drives and the need to keep these primitive impulses out of direct awareness. Why? Because awareness of these primitive impulses, including murderous urges and incestuous impulses, would flood the conscious self with crippling anxiety.

The Structure of the Mind Freud's clinical experiences led him to conclude that the mind is like an iceberg (see Figure 1.4). Only the tip of an iceberg is visible above the surface of the water. The great mass of the iceberg lies below the surface, darkening the deep. Freud came to believe that people, similarly, perceive but a few of the ideas, wishes, and impulses that dwell within them and determine their behaviour. Freud held that the larger part of the mind, which includes our deepest wishes, fears, and instinctual urges, remains below the surface of consciousness.

Sigmund Freud at about the age of 30.

Freud labelled the region that corresponds to our present awareness the **conscious** part of the mind. The regions that lie beneath the surface of awareness were labelled the **preconscious** and the **unconscious**.

In the **preconscious** mind, memories of experience can be found that are not in awareness but can be brought into awareness with focus. Your telephone number, for example, remains in the preconscious until you focus on it. The **unconscious** mind, the largest part of the mind, remains shrouded in mystery. Its contents can be brought to awareness only with great difficulty, if at all. Freud believed the unconscious is the repository of biological drives or instincts such as sex and aggression.

The Structure of Personality   According to Freud's **structural hypothesis**, the personality is divided into three mental entities or **psychic** structures: the id, ego, and superego. Psychic structures cannot be seen or measured directly, but their presence is suggested by observable behaviour and expressed in thoughts and emotions.

The **id** is the only psychic structure present at birth. It is the repository of our baser drives and instinctual impulses, including hunger, thirst, sex, and aggression. The id, which operates completely in the unconscious, was described by Freud as "a chaos, a cauldron of seething excitations" (1933/1964, p. 73). The id follows the **pleasure principle**. It demands instant gratification of instincts without consideration of social rules or customs or the needs of others. It operates by **primary process thinking**, which is a mode of relating to the world through imagination and fantasy. This enables the id to achieve gratification by conjuring up a mental image of the object of desire.

During the first year of life, the child discovers that its every demand is not instantly gratified. It must learn to cope with delay of gratification. The **ego** develops during this first year to organize reasonable ways of coping with frustration. Standing for "reason and good sense" (Freud, 1933/1964, p. 76), the ego seeks to curb the demands of the id and to direct behaviour in keeping with social customs and expectations. Gratification can thus be achieved, but not at the expense of social disapproval. The id floods your consciousness with hunger pangs. Were it to have its way, the id might also prompt you to wolf down any food at hand or even to swipe someone else's plate. But the ego creates the ideas of walking to the refrigerator, making yourself a sandwich, and pouring a glass of milk.

The ego is governed by the **reality principle**. It considers what is practical and possible, as well as the urgings of the id. The ego engages in **secondary process thinking**—the remembering, planning, and weighing of circumstances that permit a compromise between the fantasies of the id and the realities of the world outside. The ego lays the groundwork for the development of the conscious sense of the **self**.

During middle childhood, the **superego** develops. The moral standards and values of parents and other key people become internalized through a process of **identification**. The superego operates according to the **moral principle**; it demands strict adherence to moral standards. The superego represents the moral values of an ideal self, called the **ego ideal**. It also serves as a conscience or internal moral guardian that monitors the ego and passes judgment on right and wrong. It metes out punishment in the form of guilt and shame when it finds that the ego has failed to adhere to the superego's moral standards. Ego stands between the id and the superego. It endeavours to satisfy the cravings of the id without offending the moral standards of the superego.

Freud believed that there is a thin line between normal and abnormal. Both normal and abnormal behaviour are motivated or driven by irrational drives of the id. The difference may be largely a matter of degree. Normality is a matter of the balance of energy among the psychic structures of id, ego, and superego. In normal people, the ego has the

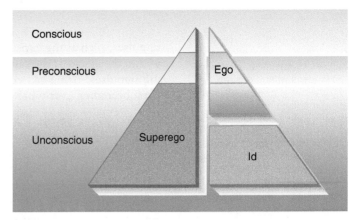

FIGURE 1.4   The parts of the mind, according to Sigmund Freud.
According to psychodynamic theory, the mind is akin to an iceberg in that only a small part of it rises to conscious awareness at any moment in time. Although material in the preconscious mind may be brought into consciousness by focusing our attention on it, the impulses and ideas in the unconscious tend to remain veiled in mystery.

conscious Aware.

preconscious In psychodynamic theory, descriptive of material that lies outside of present awareness but that can be brought into awareness by focusing attention. See also *unconscious*.

unconscious (1) In psychodynamic theory, pertaining to impulses or ideas that are not readily available to awareness, in many instances because they are kept from awareness by means of *repression*. (2) Also in psychodynamic theory, the part of the mind that contains repressed material and primitive urges of the id. (3) More generally, a state of unawareness or loss of consciousness.

structural hypothesis In Freud's theory, the belief that the clashing forces within the personality could be divided into three psychic structures: the id, the ego, and the superego.

psychic (1) Relating to mental phenomena. (2) A person who claims to be sensitive to supernatural forces.

id In psychodynamic theory, the unconscious psychic structure that is present at birth. The id contains instinctual drives and is governed by the pleasure principle.

pleasure principle In psychodynamic theory, the governing principle of the id, involving the demands for immediate gratification of instinctual needs.

primary process thinking In psychodynamic theory, the mental process in infancy by which the id seeks gratification of primitive impulses by means of imagining it possesses what it desires. Thinking that is illogical and magical, and fails to discriminate between reality and fantasy.

ego In psychodynamic theory, the psychic structure corresponding to the concept of the self. The ego is governed by the reality principle and is responsible for finding socially acceptable outlets for the urgings of the id. The ego is characterized by the capacity to tolerate frustration and delay gratification.

reality principle In psychodynamic theory, the governing principle of the ego that involves consideration of what is socially acceptable and practical in gratifying needs.

secondary process thinking In psychodynamic theory, the reality-based thinking processes and problem-solving activities of the ego.

self Centre of consciousness that organizes sensory impressions and governs one's perceptions of the world. The sum total of a person's thoughts, sensory impressions, and feelings.

superego In psychodynamic theory, the psychic structure that represents the incorporation of the moral values of the parents and important others and floods the ego with guilt and shame when it falls short of meeting those standards. The superego is governed by the moral principle and consists of two parts: the conscience and the ego ideal.

identification (1) In psychodynamic theory, the process of incorporating the personality or behaviour of others. (2) In social learning theory, a process of imitation by which children acquire behaviours similar to those of role models.

moral principle In psychodynamic theory, the principle that governs the superego to set moral standards and enforce adherence to them.

ego ideal In Freud's view, the configuration of higher social values and moral ideals embodied in the superego.

strength to control the instincts of the id and to withstand the condemnation of the superego. The presence of acceptable outlets for the expression of some primitive impulses, such as the expression of mature sexuality in marriage, decreases the pressures within the id and at the same time lessens the burdens of the ego in repressing the remaining impulses. Being reared by reasonably tolerant parents might prevent the superego from becoming overly harsh and condemnatory.

Defence Mechanisms   Although part of the ego rises to consciousness, some of its activity is carried out unconsciously. In the unconscious, the ego serves as a kind of gatekeeper or censor that screens impulses from the id. It uses **defence mechanisms** (psychological defences) to prevent socially unacceptable impulses from rising into consciousness. If it were not for these defence mechanisms, the darkest sins of our childhoods, the primitive demands of our ids, and the censures of our superegos might disable us psychologically. **Repression,** or motivated forgetting (banishment of unacceptable ideas or motives to the unconscious), is considered the most basic of the defence mechanisms. A number of these defence mechanisms are described in Table 1.2.

The use of defence mechanisms to cope with feelings like anxiety, guilt, and shame is considered normal. These mechanisms enable us to constrain impulses from the id as we go about our daily business. Freud noted that slips of the tongue and ordinary forgetfulness could represent hidden motives that are kept out of consciousness by repression. If a friend means to say "I hear what you're saying" but it comes out "I hate what you're saying," perhaps the friend is expressing a repressed emotion. If a lover storms out in anger but forgets his umbrella, perhaps he is unconsciously creating an excuse for returning. Defence mechanisms

TABLE 1.2

Major Defence Mechanisms in Psychodynamic Theory

Type of Defence Mechanism	Description	Example
Repression	Expulsion from awareness of unacceptable ideas or motives.	A person remains unaware of harbouring hateful or destructive impulses toward others.
Regression	The return of behaviour that is typical of earlier stages of development.	Under stress, a university student starts biting his nails or becomes totally dependent on others.
Displacement	The transfer of unacceptable impulses away from threatening persons toward safer or less threatening objects.	A worker slams a door after his boss chews him out.
Denial	Refusal to recognize a threatening impulse or desire.	A person harshly rebukes his or her spouse but denies feeling angry.
Reaction formation	Behaving in a way that is the opposite of one's true wishes or desires in order to keep these repressed.	A sexually frustrated person goes on a personal crusade to stamp out indecency.
Rationalization	The use of self-justifications to explain unacceptable behaviour.	A woman says, when asked why she continues to smoke, "Cancer doesn't run in my family."
Projection	Imposing one's own impulses or wishes onto another person.	A sexually inhibited person misinterprets other people's friendly approaches as sexual advances.
Sublimation	The channelling of unacceptable impulses into socially constructive pursuits.	A person channels aggressive impulses into competitive sports.

may also give rise to abnormal behaviour, however. The person who regresses to an infantile state under pressures of enormous stress is clearly not acting adaptively to the situation.

Perpetual vigilance and defence take their toll. The ego can weaken and, in extreme cases, lose the ability to keep a lid on the id. **Psychosis** results when the urges of the id spill forth into consciousness, untempered by an ego that either has been weakened or is under-developed. The fortress of the ego is overrun, and the person loses the ability to distinguish between fantasy and reality. Behaviour becomes detached from reality. Psychoses are characterized, in general, by more severe disturbances of functioning than neuroses, by the appearance of bizarre behaviour and thoughts, and by faulty perceptions of reality, such as hallucinations ("hearing voices" or seeing things that are not present). Speech may become incoherent and there may be bizarre posturing and gestures.

Freud equated psychological health with the abilities to love and to work. The normal person can care deeply for other people, find sexual gratification in an intimate relationship, and engage in productive work. Other impulses must be channelled (sublimated) into socially productive pursuits, such as work, enjoyment of art or music, or creative expression. When some impulses are expressed directly and others are sublimated, the ego has a relatively easy time of it repressing those that remain in the boiling cauldron.

Other Psychodynamic Theorists Freud left a rich intellectual legacy that has stimulated the thinking of many theorists. Psychodynamic theory has been shaped over the years by the contributions of other theorists who are sometimes referred to collectively as **neo-Freudians** (Carl Jung, Alfred Adler, Karen Horney, and Harry Stack Sullivan). They shared certain central tenets in common with Freud, such as the belief that behaviour reflects unconscious motivation, inner conflict, and the operation of defensive responses to anxiety. They tended to de-emphasize the roles of basic instincts such as sex and aggression, however, and placed greater emphasis on roles for conscious choice, self-direction, and creativity.

Evaluating Psychodynamic Perspectives Psychodynamic theory has had a pervasive influence not only on concepts of abnormal behaviour but more broadly on art, literature, philosophy, and the general culture. It has focused attention on our inner lives—our dreams, fantasies, and hidden motives. People unschooled in Freud habitually look for the symbolic meanings of each other's slips of the tongue and assume that abnormalities can be traced to early childhood. Terms like *ego* and *repression* have become commonplace, although their everyday meanings do not fully overlap with those intended by Freud.

One of the major contributions of the psychodynamic model was the increased awareness that people may be motivated by hidden drives and impulses of a sexual or aggressive nature. Freud's beliefs about childhood sexuality were both illuminating and controversial. Before Freud, children were perceived as pure innocents, free of sexual desire. Freud recognized, however, that young children, even infants, seek pleasure through stimulation of the oral and anal cavities and the phallic region.

Yet for all the criticism and skepticism directed at psychoanalytic theory, new research shows support for some of Freud's specific predictions and claims. For example, modern cognitive psychology has confirmed that through repetition, our behaviour can become automatic and as a consequence we perform many everyday tasks with minimal conscious awareness (Power, 2000). Neuropsychological studies are also helping us to better understand conscious and unconscious mental processes and how early life experiences can influence one's susceptibility to abnormal behaviour (D. J. Stein, Solms, & van Honk, 2006).

BEHAVIOURAL PERSPECTIVES The psychodynamic models of Freud and his followers were the first major psychological theories of abnormal behaviour, but other relevant psychologies were also taking shape early in the 20th century. Among the most important was the behavioural perspective, or **behaviourism**, which is identified with contributions by the Russian physiologist Ivan Pavlov (1849–1936), the discoverer of the conditioned reflex, and the American psychologists John B. Watson (1878–1958) and B. F. Skinner (1904–1990). The behavioural perspective focuses on the role of learning in explaining both normal and abnormal behaviour. From a learning perspective, abnormal

defence mechanisms In psycho-dynamic theory, the reality-distorting strategies used by the ego to shield itself from conscious awareness of anxiety-evoking or troubling material.

repression In psychodynamic theory, a type of defence mechanism involving the ejection from awareness of anxiety-provoking ideas, images, or impulses, without the conscious awareness that one has done so.

psychosis Type of major psychological disorder in which people show impaired ability to interpret reality and difficulties in meeting the demands of daily life. Schizophrenia is a prominent example of a psychotic disorder. Plural: *psychoses.*

neo-Freudians Term used to describe the "second generation" of theorists who followed in the Freudian tradition. On the whole, neo-Freudians (such as Jung, Adler, Horney, and Sullivan) placed greater emphasis on the importance of cultural and social influences on behaviour and lesser importance on sexual impulses and the functioning of the id.

behaviourism School of psychology that defines psychology as the study of observable or overt behaviour and focuses on investigating the relationships between stimuli and responses.

FIGURE 1.5 **The apparatus used in Ivan Pavlov's experiments on conditioning.**
Pavlov used an apparatus such as this to demonstrate the process of conditioning. To the left is a two-way mirror, behind which a researcher rings a bell. After the bell is rung, meat is placed on the dog's tongue. Following several pairings of the bell and the meat, the dog learns to salivate in response to the bell. The animal's saliva passes through the tube to a vial, where its quantity may be taken as a measure of the strength of the conditioned response.

behaviour represents the acquisition or learning of inappropriate, maladaptive behaviours. Abnormal behaviour can also be described in terms of not learning or underlearning appropriate, adaptive behaviours.

From the medical and psychodynamic perspectives, abnormal behaviour is symptomatic, respectively, of underlying biological or psychological problems. From the behavioural perspective, however, abnormal behaviour need not be symptomatic of anything. The abnormal behaviour itself is the problem. Abnormal behaviour is regarded as learned in much the same way as normal behaviour. Why, then, do some people behave abnormally? One reason is found in situational factors. For example, harsh punishment for early exploratory behaviour, such as childhood sexual exploration in the form of masturbation, might give rise to adult anxieties over autonomy or sexuality. Poor child-rearing practices, such as a lack of praise or rewards for good behaviour and harsh and unpredictable punishment of misconduct, might give rise to antisocial behaviour. Then, too, children with abusive or neglectful parents might learn to pay more attention to inner fantasies than to the world outside, giving rise, at worst, to difficulty in separating reality from fantasy.

Watson, Skinner, and other behaviourists believed that human behaviour is basically the product of genetic endowment and environmental or situational influences. Like Freud, Watson and Skinner discarded concepts of personal freedom, choice, and self-direction. But whereas Freud saw us as driven by irrational unconscious forces, behaviourists see us as products of environmental influences that shape and manipulate our behaviour. To Watson and Skinner, even the belief that we have free will is determined by the environment, just as surely as is raising our hands in class before speaking. Behaviourists focus on the roles of two major forms of learning in shaping normal and abnormal behaviour: classical conditioning and operant conditioning.

Role of Classical Conditioning Pavlov discovered the conditioned reflex (now called a *conditioned response*) quite by accident. In his laboratory, he harnessed dogs to an apparatus like that in Figure 1.5 to study their salivary response to food. Yet he observed that the animals would start salivating and secreting gastric juices even before they started eating. These responses appeared to be elicited by the sounds made by his laboratory assistants when they wheeled in the food cart. So Pavlov undertook a clever experimental program that showed that animals could learn to salivate to other stimuli, such as the sound of a bell, if these stimuli were associated with feeding.

Because dogs don't normally salivate to the sound of bells, Pavlov reasoned that they had acquired this response, called a **conditioned response** (CR) or conditioned reflex, because it had been paired with a stimulus, called an **unconditioned stimulus** (US)—in this case, food—which naturally elicits salivation (see Figure 1.6). The salivation to food, an unlearned response, is called the **unconditioned response** (UR), and the bell, a previously neutral stimulus, is called the **conditioned stimulus** (CS). Can you recognize classical conditioning in your everyday life? Do you flinch in the waiting room at the sound of the dentist's drill? The drill sounds may be conditioned stimuli for conditioned responses of fear and muscle tension.

A now-famous study was conducted in a laboratory by John B. Watson and his assistant, Rosalie Rayner (Watson & Rayner, 1920). The participant in this study, known as "Little Albert," was a healthy and emotionally stable infant. When tested initially, he showed no fear except of the loud noise Watson made by striking a hammer against a steel bar. Rosalie then presented Little Albert with a white rat, in the hope of conditioning him to associate the rat with a loud noise. This pairing was repeated until Albert

conditioned response (1) In classical conditioning, a learned or acquired response to a previously neutral stimulus. (2) A response to a conditioned stimulus. Abbreviated *CR*.

unconditioned stimulus Stimulus that elicits an instinctive or unlearned response from an organism. Abbreviated *US* or *UCS*.

unconditioned response Unlearned response or a response to an unconditioned stimulus. Abbreviated *UR* or *UCR*.

conditioned stimulus Previously neutral stimulus that comes to evoke a conditioned response following repeated pairings with a stimulus (unconditioned stimulus) that had already evoked that response. Abbreviated *CS*.

FIGURE 1.6 Schematic diagram of the process of classical conditioning.

Before conditioning, food (an unconditioned stimulus, or US) that is placed on a dog's tongue will naturally elicit salivation (an unconditioned response, or UR). The bell, however, is a neutral stimulus that may elicit an orienting response but not salivation. During conditioning, the bell (the conditioned stimulus, CS) is rung while food (the US) is placed on the dog's tongue. After several conditioning trials have occurred, the bell (the CS) will elicit salivation (the conditioned response, or CR) when it is rung, even though it is not accompanied by food (the US). The dog is said to have been conditioned or to have learned to display the conditioned response (CR) in response to the conditioned stimulus (CS). Learning theorists have suggested that irrational excessive fears of harmless stimuli may be acquired through principles of classical conditioning.

jumped violently, fell forward, and began to whimper. A week later, the rat was paired with the loud noise five more times. At the sight of the white rat alone, Albert began to cry. This is a great example of how phobias or excessive fears may be acquired by classical conditioning.

For instance, a person may develop a phobia for riding on elevators following a traumatic experience while riding on an elevator. In this example, a previously neutral stimulus (elevator) becomes paired or associated with an aversive stimulus (trauma), which leads to the conditioned response (phobia). From the learning perspective, normal behaviour involves responding adaptively to stimuli—including conditioned stimuli.

Role of Operant Conditioning Operant conditioning involves the acquisition of behaviours, called *operant behaviours*, that are emitted by an organism and that operate upon or manipulate the environment to produce certain effects. Skinner (1938) showed that food-deprived pigeons would learn to peck buttons when food pellets drop into their cages as a result. It takes a while for the birds to happen on the first peck, but after a few repetitions of the association betweeen button pecking and food, pecking behaviour, an operant response, becomes fast and furious until the pigeons have had their fill.

In operant conditioning, organisms acquire responses or skills that lead to **reinforcement**. Reinforcers are changes in the environment (stimuli) that increase the frequency of the preceding behaviour.

Positive reinforcers boost the frequency of behaviour when they are presented. Food, money, social approval, and the opportunity to mate are examples of positive reinforcers. **Negative reinforcers** increase the frequency of behaviour when they are removed. Fear, pain, discomfort, and social disapproval are examples of negative reinforcers. We learn responses that lead to their removal (like learning to turn on the air conditioner to remove unpleasant heat and humidity from a room).

Adaptive, normal behaviour involves learning responses or skills that permit us to obtain positive reinforcers and escape or avoid negative reinforcers. But if our early learning environments do not provide opportunities for learning new skills, we might be hampered in our efforts to develop the skills needed to obtain reinforcers. A lack of social skills, for example, may reduce opportunities for social reinforcement (approval or praise from others), especially when a person withdraws from social situations. This may lead to depression and social isolation. In Chapter 4, "Mood Disorders and Suicide," we examine links between changes in reinforcement levels and the development of depression.

reinforcement Stimulus that increases the frequency of the response it follows. See *positive* and *negative* and *primary* and *secondary* reinforcers.

positive reinforcers Types of reinforcers that increase the frequency of a behaviour when they are presented. Food and social approval are generally, but not always, positive reinforcers. Contrast with *negative reinforcer*.

negative reinforcers Reinforcers whose removal increases the frequency of an operant behaviour. Anxiety, pain, and social disapproval often function as negative reinforcers; that is, their removal tends to increase the rate of the immediately preceding behaviour. Contrast with *positive reinforcer*.

B. F. Skinner. American psychologist, author, and pioneer of operant conditioning.

primary reinforcers Natural reinforcers or stimuli that have reinforcement value without learning. Water, food, warmth, and relief from pain are examples of primary reinforcers. Contrast with *secondary reinforcers*.

secondary reinforcers Stimuli that gain reinforcement value through their association with established reinforcers. Money and social approval are typically secondary reinforcers. Contrast with *primary reinforcers*.

punishments Unpleasant stimuli that suppress the frequency of the behaviours they follow.

behaviour therapy A learning-based model of therapy.

We can also differentiate primary and secondary, or conditioned, reinforcers. **Primary reinforcers** influence behaviour because they satisfy basic physical needs. We do not learn to respond to these basic reinforcers; we are born with that capacity. Food, water, sexual stimulation, and escape from pain are examples of primary reinforcers. **Secondary reinforcers** influence behaviour through their association with established reinforcers. Thus, we learn to respond to secondary reinforcers. People learn to seek money—a secondary reinforcer—because it can be exchanged for primary reinforcers like food and heat (or air conditioning).

Punishments are aversive stimuli that decrease or suppress the frequency of the preceding behaviour when they are applied. Negative reinforcers, by contrast, increase the frequency of the preceding behaviour when they are removed. A loud noise, for example, can be either a punishment (if by its introduction the probability of the preceding behaviour decreases) or a negative reinforcer (if by its removal the probability of the preceding behaviour increases).

Reinforcing desirable behaviour is generally preferable to punishing misbehaviour. But reinforcing appropriate behaviour requires paying attention to it, and not just to misbehaviour. Some children who develop conduct problems can gain the attention of other people only by misbehaving. They learn that by acting out, others will pay attention to them. For them, getting scolded may actually serve as a positive reinforcer, increasing the rate of response of the behaviour it follows. Learning theorists point out that it is not sufficient to expect good conduct from children. Instead, adults need to teach children proper behaviour and regularly reinforce them for performing it.

Evaluating Behavioural Perspectives   One of the principal values of behavioural models, in contrast to psychodynamic approaches, is their emphasis on observable behaviour and environmental factors, such as reinforcers and punishments, that can be systematically manipulated to observe their effects on behaviour. Learning perspectives have spawned a major model of therapy called **behaviour therapy** (also called *behaviour modification*), which involves the systematic application of learning principles to help people make adaptive behavioural changes. Behaviour therapy techniques have been applied to helping people overcome a wide range of psychological problems, including phobias and other anxiety disorders, sexual dysfunctions, and depression. Moreover, reinforcement-based programs are now widely used in helping parents learn better parenting skills and helping children learn in the classroom.

Critics contend that behaviourism cannot explain the richness of human behaviour and that human experience cannot be reduced to observable responses. Many learning theorists too, especially social-cognitive theorists, have been dissatisfied with the strict behaviouristic view that environmental influences—reinforcements and punishments—mechanically control our behaviour. Humans experience thoughts and dreams and formulate goals and aspirations; behaviourism seems not to address much of what it means to be human.

A Neo-humanistic Perspective   Psychologist Leslie Greenberg of York University has been at the forefront of advancing the humanistic approach, which has been influenced by contemporary developments in the areas of neuroscience and cognitive theory. A key feature of his neo-humanistic approach is that it attempts to reconcile the theoretical differences between the major psychological theories we have discussed so far in this chapter. For example, Greenberg (2002a, 2002b) views humans as comprising multiple facets—emotions, motivations, cognitions, and actions—each of value for survival. In comparison, the different psychological theories have traditionally emphasized that one domain of human functioning is superior to the others (L. S. Greenberg, 2002a, 2002b). This theoretical competition has created major theoretical dilemmas by pitting emotions against reason, conscious against unconscious processes, conformity against self-determination, and mind against both behaviour and biology, to name a few. Accordingly, each theory has given rise to divergent therapeutic approaches. However, despite their serious differences, they all have a common therapeutic goal: to regulate and minimize undesirable emotions (L. S. Greenberg, 2002a, 2002b). Greenberg's theory, instead of emphasizing the mere reduction of unpleasant emotions, embraces the notion that emotions—both pleasant and unpleasant—serve essential adaptive purposes and should therefore be heeded. For example, emotions have survival value when they warn us of potentially dangerous situations, aid us in interpersonal communications (especially nonverbal), and enhance learning by arousing attention and motivation. To suppress or radically modify our emotions is to deny ourselves this important survival function.

The cornerstone of this approach is our **emotional intelligence**. Emotional intelligence dictates how well we experience and express our emotions in a purposeful way to cope with life. Strengthening our emotional intelligence leads to well-being, and this is the premise for a neo-humanistic therapy referred to as *emotion-focused therapy* (EFT).

The strengths of humanistic-existential perspectives in understanding abnormal behaviour lie largely in their focus on conscious experience and their innovation of therapy methods that assist people along pathways of self-discovery, self-acceptance, and self-determination. The humanistic-existential movement put concepts of purpose, free choice, inherent goodness, responsibility, and authenticity back on centre stage and brought them into modern psychology. Ironically, the primary strength of the humanistic-existential approach—its focus on conscious experience—may also be its primary weakness. Conscious experience is private and subjective. Therefore, the validity of formulating theories in terms of consciousness has been questioned. How can psychologists be certain they accurately perceive the world through the eyes of their clients?

There is now a Canadian initiative to study these types of issues. Founded in Langley, British Columbia, in 1998, the International Network on Personal Meaning (INPM; see www.meaning.ca) is an organization of 300 members, in 30 countries, dedicated to the scientific research and advancement of the role of meaning in our daily lives (Wong, 2002). This multidisciplinary society addresses, through scholarly and educational activities, our needs for health, spirituality, and community. The INPM has also spawned a professional branch of its organization to advance the role of existential psychology and therapy within psychology, the International Society for Existential Psychology and Psychotherapy (ISEPP), and it launched a peer-reviewed journal in 2004, *The International Journal of Existential Psychology and Psychotherapy*.

Critics suggest that neo-humanistic intervention is best suited for personal growth and development, and, indeed, Greenberg (2002a) agrees that it is inappropriate for acute conditions such as panic disorder or disorders of impulse control. Nonetheless, it has been shown to be effective in the treatment of moderate depression, of disorders related to childhood maltreatment and trauma, and of interpersonal problems, and in couples therapy.

COGNITIVE-BEHAVIOURAL PERSPECTIVES In their attempt to turn psychology into a scientific discipline, the early behaviourists focused on outward measurable behaviour and denied the legitimacy of internal mental processes in human behaviour. But the pioneering Canadian psychologist Donald Hebb (1904–1985) thought differently. He believed that "psychology without thought was unthinkable," notes fellow McGill University psychologist Peter Milner (2006, p. 36). In *The Organization of Behavior*, Hebb (1949/2002) outlined his pivotal theory describing how mental process could be explained

Dr. Leslie Greenberg is a psychology professor at York University and the director of the Emotion-Focused Therapy Clinic, which is affiliated with the York University Psychology Clinic (YUPC). Dr. Greenberg is one of the originators of emotion-focused therapy for individuals and couples.

emotional intelligence "The ability to perceive emotions, to access and generate emotions so as to assist thought, to understand emotions and emotional knowledge, and to reflectively regulate emotions so as to promote emotional and intellectual growth" (Mayer & Salovey, 1997).

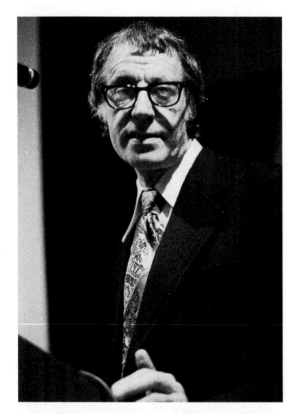

Albert Ellis. Psychologist who developed rational-emotive behaviour therapy (REBT), in which therapists help people adjust their thinking and behaviour to treat emotional and behavioural problems. Ellis is considered one of the originators of cognitive-behavioural therapy.

catastrophize To exaggerate or magnify the negative consequences of events; to "blow things out of proportion."

by neural functioning, and this opened the way for cognition to become a worthy scientific field of study (Milner, 2006).

The word *cognitive* derives from the Latin *cognitio*, meaning "knowledge." Cognitive-behaviour theorists study the cognitions—the thoughts, beliefs, expectations, and attitudes—that accompany and may underlie abnormal behaviour. They focus on how reality is coloured by our expectations, attitudes, and so forth, and how inaccurate or biased processing of information about the world—and our place within it—can give rise to emotional difficulties and dysfunctional behaviours. Cognitive-behaviour theorists believe that our interpretations of the events in our lives, and not the events themselves, determine our emotional states and actions.

Albert Ellis Psychologist Albert Ellis (1913–2007) (1977, 1993, 2003) was a prominent cognitive-behaviour theorist who believed that troubling events in themselves do not lead to anxiety, depression, or disturbed behaviour. Rather, it is the irrational beliefs about unfortunate experiences that foster negative emotions and maladaptive behaviour. Consider someone who loses a job, becomes anxious and despondent about it, and spends the day just moping around the house. It may seem that being fired is the direct cause of the person's misery, but the misery actually stems from the person's beliefs about the loss and not directly from the loss itself.

Ellis used an "ABC approach" to explain the causes of the misery. Being fired is an activating event (A). The ultimate outcome or consequence (C) is a dysfunctional emotional, physiological, and behavioural response (Ellis, 2003; Harris, Davies, & Dryden, 2006). But the activating event (A) and the consequences (C) are mediated by various beliefs (B). Some of these beliefs might include "That job was the major thing in my life," "What a useless washout I am," "My family will go hungry," "I'll never be able to find another job as good," or "I can't do a thing about it." These exaggerated and irrational beliefs compound depression, nurture helplessness, and distract us from evaluating what to do. For instance, the beliefs "I can't do a thing about it" and "What a useless washout I am" promote helplessness.

The situation can be diagrammed like this:

Activating events ⟶ Beliefs ⟶ Consequences

Ellis emphasized that apprehension about the future and feelings of disappointment are perfectly normal when people face losses. However, the adoption of irrational beliefs leads people to **catastrophize** the magnitude of losses, leading in turn to profound distress and states of depression. By intensifying emotional responses and nurturing feelings of helplessness, such beliefs impair coping ability.

Ellis asserted that there are three core irrational beliefs held by many people worldwide:

1. "I must be thoroughly competent, adequate, achieving, and lovable at all times, or else I am an incompetent worthless person. . . ."
2. "Other significant people in my life must treat me kindly and fairly at all times, or else I can't stand it, and they are bad, rotten, and evil persons who should be severely blamed, damned, and vindictively punished for their horrible treatment of me. . . ."
3. "Things and conditions absolutely must be the way I want them to be and must never be too difficult or frustrating. Otherwise life is awful, terrible, horrible, catastrophic, and unbearable. . . ." (Ellis, 2003, pp. 236–237)

Ellis noted that the desire for others' approval is understandable but that it is irrational to assume you cannot survive without it. It would be marvellous to excel in everything we do, but it's absurd to demand it of ourselves. Sure, in tennis it would be great to serve and volley like a pro, but most people haven't the leisure time or aptitude to perfect the game. Insisting on perfection deters people from playing simply for fun.

Ellis developed a model of therapy called *rational-emotive behaviour therapy* (REBT) to help people dispute these conditioned habitual irrational beliefs and substitute more rational ones. Ellis admitted that childhood experiences are involved in the origins of irrational beliefs but stated that cognitive appraisal—the here and now—causes people misery. For most people who are anxious and depressed, the ticket to greater happiness lies not in discovering and liberating deep-seated conflicts but in recognizing and modifying irrational self-demands.

Aaron Beck Another prominent cognitive theorist, psychiatrist Aaron Beck, proposes that depression may result from "cognitive errors" such as judging oneself entirely on the basis of one's flaws or failures and interpreting events in a negative light (as though wearing blue-coloured glasses) (A. T. Beck, Rush, Shaw, & Emery, 1979). Beck stresses the pervasive roles of four basic types of cognitive errors that contribute to emotional distress, which are explained in Table 1.3 (on page 32).

Like Ellis, Beck has developed a major model of therapy, called *cognitive therapy* (now commonly referred to as *cognitive behavioural therapy*), that focuses on helping individuals with psychological disorders identify and correct faulty ways of thinking.

Social-cognitive theorists, who share much in common with the cognitive-behaviour theorists, focus on the ways in which social information is encoded. Let's now consider social-cognitive theory, which broadens the focus of both traditional behaviourist and cognitive theories by considering the role of social factors in learning and behaviour.

Albert Bandura **Social-cognitive theory** represents the contributions of theorists such as Alberta-born Albert Bandura (Zimmerman & Schunk, 2002). Social-cognitive theorists emphasize the roles of thinking or cognition and of learning by observation or modelling in human behaviour. For example, social-cognitive theorists suggest that phobias may be learned vicariously, by observing the fearful reactions of others in real life or as shown on television or in movies.

Social-cognitive theorists also view people as affecting their environment, just as the environment affects them. They see people as self-aware and purposeful learners who seek information about their environment, who do not just respond automatically to the stimuli that impinge on them. Bandura (1986, 1989, 2001) uses the term **reciprocal determinism** to describe how a person's behaviour both acts upon and is influenced by one's personal and environmental factors. For example, if you were lost and approached someone for help, you might elicit a different reaction from a stranger depending on whether you came across as friendly or as fearful or threatening. In turn, the stranger's reaction to your request for help might, in part, be influenced by his or her interpretation of your intentions based on your behaviour. As well, the circumstances play a role—the intentions of a smiling stranger may be viewed quite differently on a dimly lit street corner than in a shopping mall.

Social-cognitive theorists concur with traditional behaviourists that theories of human nature should be tied to observable behaviour. They assert, however, that factors within a person should also be considered in explaining human behaviour. For example, behaviour cannot be predicted from situational factors alone (Rotter, 1972). Whether or not people behave in certain ways also depends on certain cognitive factors, such as the person's **expectancies** about the outcomes of behaviour. For example, we see in Chapter 7 that people who hold more positive expectancies about the outcomes of using drugs are more likely to use them and to use them in larger quantities.

Aaron Beck. One of the leading cognitive theorists. His theories are used in the treatment of clinical depression. Beck deveoped the widely used self-report inventories called the Beck Depression Inventory (BDI) and the Beck Anxiety Inventory (BAI).

Albert Bandura. A Canadian/American psychologist whose greatest contribution to the field was his social learning theory, which later became social-cognitive theory. He played a crucial role in the transition between behaviourism and cognitive psychology.

TABLE 1.3

Beck's Four Cognitive Errors

Cognitive Error	Description
Selective Abstraction	People may selectively abstract (focus exclusively on) the parts of their experiences that reflect on their flaws and ignore evidence of their competencies.
Overgeneralization	People may overgeneralize from a few isolated experiences. For example, they may see their futures as hopeless because they were laid off or believe they will never marry because they were rejected by a dating partner.
Magnification	People may blow out of proportion or magnify the importance of unfortunate events. Students may catastrophize a bad test grade by jumping to the conclusion that they will flunk out of university and their lives will be ruined.
Absolutist Thinking	People see the world in black and white terms rather than in shades of grey. Absolutist thinkers may assume any grade less than a perfect "A" or a work evaluation less than a rave is a total failure.

social-cognitive theory A broader view of learning theory that emphasizes both situational determinants of behaviour (reinforcements and punishments) and cognitive factors (expectancies, values, attitudes, beliefs, etc.).

reciprocal determinism The ongoing process of two-way interactions among personal factors (cognitive abilities—expectancies, values, attitudes, and beliefs— as well as affective and biological characteristics), behaviours (skills, talents, habits, and interpersonal relations), and environmental factors (physical surroundings and other people).

expectancies In social-cognitive theory, a personal variable describing people's predictions of future outcomes.

Donald Meichenbaum University of Waterloo professor emeritus Donald Meichenbaum is a co-founder of cognitive-behavioural modification (CBM). Like the other cognitive behaviourists, Meichenbaum's perspective (1976, 1977) considers the interdependence of thoughts, emotions, and actions (interpersonal in particular). Aggressive boys and adolescents, for example, are likely to incorrectly encode other people's behaviour as threatening (see Chapter 11, "Abnormal Behaviour Across the Lifespan"). They assume other people intend them ill when they do not. Aggressive children and adults may behave in ways that elicit coercive or hostile behaviour from others, which serves to confirm their aggressive expectations (Meichenbaum, 1993). Information may also be distorted by what cognitive-behaviour therapists call *cognitive distortions*, or errors in thinking. For example, people who are depressed tend to develop an unduly negative view of their personal situation by exaggerating the importance of unfortunate events they experience (Meichenbaum, 1993). From Meichenbaum's perspective, behavioural interventions can be used to initiate change anywhere along the chain of cognitive, affective, and behavioural events.

Evaluating Cognitive-Behavioural Perspectives As we'll see in later chapters, cognitive-behavioural theorists have had an enormous impact on our understanding of abnormal behaviour patterns and the development of therapeutic approaches. The overlap between the behavioural-based and cognitive approaches is best represented by the emergence of cognitive-behavioural therapy (CBT), a form of therapy that focuses on modifying self-defeating beliefs in addition to overt behaviours. A major issue concerning cognitive-behavioural perspectives is their range of applicability. Cognitive-behavioural therapists have largely focused on emotional disorders relating to anxiety and depression but have had less impact on the development of treatment approaches or conceptual models of more severe forms of disturbed behaviour, such as schizophrenia. Moreover, in the case of depression, it remains unclear, as we see in Chapter 4, to what extent distorted thinking patterns are causes of depression or effects of depression.

REVIEW IT

Psychological Perspectives

- **What are the major psychological perspectives on abnormal behaviour?** Psychodynamic perspectives reflect the views of Freud and his followers, who believed that abnormal behaviour stems from psychological causes involving underlying psychic forces within the personality. Learning theorists posit that the principles of learning can be used to explain both abnormal and normal behaviour. Humanistic-existential theorists believe that it is important to understand the obstacles that people encounter as they strive toward self-actualization and authenticity. Cognitive-behavioural theorists focus on the role of distorted and self-defeating thinking in explaining abnormal behaviour.

PROMOTING MENTAL HEALTH

Mental health promotion is a proactive, holistic, multi-levelled, synergistic process that fosters resilience as one progresses toward an optimal sense of well-being (see Figure 1.7 in this box) (P. A. Johnson, 1989). It is proactive to the extent that it builds up knowledge, resources, and strengths for overall wellness and enhances the capacity of individuals to take control of their lives (MHP, 2003). Through education, community efforts, and government policy, mental health promotion champions optimal mental health, reduces the stigma of mental illness, and engenders a mental wellness style of life (Baylis, 2002). Mental health promotion also moves beyond the commonly held notion that mental health is the mere absence of mental illness (Kahan & Goodstadt, 2002). Moreover, it applies equally to all people, sick or well, disabled or not, problematic or not (MHP, 2003). Mental health promotion is also holistic in nature and places high importance on mental, emotional, social, physical, and spiritual functioning (WHO, n.d.). It considers the reciprocal interactions of these personal domains on multiple levels, including the physical environment, family, community, and population culture, politics, and economics (MHP, 2003; Kahan & Goodstadt, 2002). As is true with risk factors, there is a synergistic effect among health-promoting factors. Exposure to a combination of mental health promotion factors can be greater than the sum total effect of the individual factors (J. Dryden, Johnson, Howard, & McGuire, 1998).

MENTAL HEALTH PROMOTION INITIATIVES

There is a demonstrated need for a different kind of investment in the mental health of Canadians of all ages (Stephens & Joubert, 2001). Canada is sitting on the cusp of change when it comes to mental health promotion and prevention (CAMIMH, 2000), and psychology's role will likely expand across all health-related areas (J. L. Arnett, 2006). Below are just some of the initiatives that cover the full spectrum of mental health promotion services and supports:

- Health Canada (2001b) sponsors four Centres of Excellence for Children's Well-Being across Canada that focus on child welfare, communities, early childhood development, special needs, and youth engagement.
- The federal government introduced the Public Health Agency of Canada (2004) to focus on illness prevention and health promotion.
- In their report *Out of the Shadows at Last: Transforming Mental Health, Mental Illness and Addiction Services in Canada*, Canadian senators Kirby and Keon (2006) recommended that a Canadian Mental Health Commission be established for mental health promotion and prevention of mental illness. The commission was established in 2007.

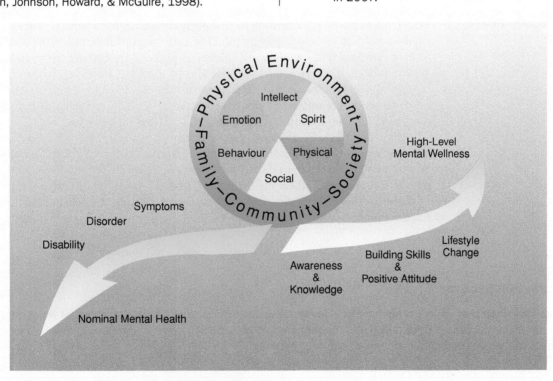

FIGURE 1.7 **The mental wellness continuum.**
Original figure created by author from concepts taken from various sources.

Sociocultural Perspectives on Abnormal Behaviour

To what extent does abnormal behaviour arise from forces within a person, as the psychodynamic theorists propose, or from the learning of maladaptive behaviours, as the learning theorists suggest? The sociocultural perspective informs us that a fuller accounting of abnormal behaviour requires that we also consider the impact of social and cultural factors, including factors relating to ethnicity, gender and social roles, and poverty. Sociocultural theorists seek causes of abnormal behaviour that may reside in the failures of society rather than in the person.

Acadia University community psychologist Patrick O'Neill (2004) says that when dealing with social problems, it is important to keep the focus on dysfunctional social systems rather than on an individual's dysfunction. O'Neill cautions that it is easy for social researchers to inadvertently divert their attention toward an individual's "problem" rather than focus on the social causes of that problem, and that doing so contributes to a "blame the victim" mentality. For example, if we were to consider the problem of drug abuse from a sociocultural perspective, we should focus on the social structures that underlie substance-abuse problems instead of on the personal characteristics or "failings" of the drug addict. The former requires sweeping social changes that, for example, would reduce poverty and improve living conditions. The latter perpetuates interventions that deal with the problem of drug dependence one drug user or one drug dealer at a time.

EVALUATING SOCIOCULTURAL PERSPECTIVES   As you recall from the discussion of homelessness, low-income Canadians experience higher rates of mental health problems than the rest of society. The reasons why are not easy to determine. One line of thinking suggests that poverty gives rise to mental illness. Psychosocial stress resulting from chronic unemployment, financial difficulties, or inadequate housing can create a sense of futility or emotional upset that may lead to the development of mental illness (Health Canada, 2002b). Additionally, low-income Canadians have less access to mental health counselling opportunities than higher-income individuals, and this creates a further barrier to getting well (Health Canada, 1999b).

An alternative view is the **downward drift hypothesis**, which suggests that mental illness leads to poverty. According to this perspective, having a mental illness makes it difficult to hold down a well-paying job. The lack of gainful employment may lead people to drift downward in social status, thereby explaining the linkage between low socioeconomic status and severe behaviour problems (Canadian Health Network, 1999).

Yet another view posits that the connections are not so simple. There may be one or more other variables that influence both poverty and mental illness, such as discrimination, dysfunctional family relationships, interpersonal conflict, or a lack of social-support networks.

All in all, the sociocultural theorists have focused much-needed attention on the social stressors that may lead to abnormal behaviour. Throughout the text we consider how sociocultural factors relating to gender, race, ethnicity, and lifestyle better inform our understanding of abnormal behaviour and our response to people deemed mentally ill. Later in this chapter we consider how issues relating to race, culture, and ethnicity impact the therapeutic process.

downward drift hypothesis The belief that people with psychological problems may drift downward in socioeconomic status.

REVIEW IT

Sociocultural Perspectives

- **What is the basic idea that underlies sociocultural perspectives?** Sociocultural theorists believe that we need to broaden our outlook on abnormal behaviour by taking into account the role of social ills in society, including poverty, racism, and lack of opportunity, in the development of abnormal behaviour patterns.

Interactionist Perspectives

We have seen several models or perspectives for understanding and treating psychological disorders. The fact that there are different ways of looking at the same phenomenon does not mean one model must be right and the others wrong.

No one theoretical perspective can account for the complex forms of abnormal behaviour we encounter in this text. Each of the perspectives we have discussed—the biological, psychological, and sociocultural frameworks—contributes something to our understanding, but none offers a complete view. We are only beginning to uncover the subtle and often complex interactions involving the multitude of factors that give rise to abnormal behaviour patterns.

Many theorists today adopt an interactionist perspective. They believe we need to take into account the interaction of multiple factors representing biological, psychological, sociocultural, and environmental domains in order to explain abnormal behaviour. We'll describe two prominent interactionist models—the diathesis-stress and the biopsychosocial models.

THE DIATHESIS-STRESS MODEL   The leading interactionist model is the **diathesis-stress model**, which holds that psychological disorders result from the combination or interaction of a diathesis (vulnerability or predisposition) with stress (see Figure 1.8). The model proposes that some people possess a vulnerability or **diathesis**, possibly genetic in nature, that increases their risk of developing a particular disorder. Yet whether they develop the disorder depends on the kinds and level of stress they experience. Stress may take the form of biological events such as prenatal trauma, birth complications, or physical illness; psychosocial factors such as childhood sexual or physical abuse or family conflict; and negative life events such as prolonged unemployment or loss of loved ones. This model is crucial to an understanding of the development of mental health issues.

In some cases, people with a diathesis for a particular disorder may remain free of the disorder or develop a milder form of the disorder if the level of stress in their lives remains low or they develop effective coping responses for handling the stress they encounter. However, the stronger the diathesis, the less stress is generally needed to produce the disorder. In some cases the diathesis may be so strong that the disorder develops even under the most benign life circumstances.

The diathesis-stress hypothesis was originally developed as an explanatory framework for understanding the development of schizophrenia (see Chapter 10). It has since been applied to other psychological disorders, such as depression. Although the term *diathesis* generally refers to an inherited predisposition, a diathesis may involve psychological factors such as dysfunctional thinking patterns or personality traits. For example, a dysfunctional pattern of thinking may put individuals at greater risk of developing depression in the face of upsetting or stressful life events such as prolonged unemployment or divorce (see Chapter 4).

THE BIOPSYCHOSOCIAL (SYSTEMS) MODEL   The diathesis-stress model is not the only interactionist account of how abnormal behaviour patterns develop. Another prominent interdisciplinary approach is the **biopsychosocial model**, which, compared to the diathesis-stress model, expands and more clearly delineates the number of factors and dynamic interactions between a person and his or her environment. The biopsychosocial

diathesis-stress model Model of abnormal behaviour that posits that abnormal behaviour patterns, such as schizophrenia, involve the interaction of genetic and environmental influences. In this model, a genetic or acquired predisposition, or *diathesis*, increases an individual's vulnerability to developing the disorder in response to stressful life circumstances. If, however, the level of stress is kept under the person's particular threshold, the disorder may never develop, even among people with the predisposition.

diathesis A predisposition or vulnerability.

biopsychosocial model A conceptual model that emphasizes that human behaviour is linked to complex interactions among biological, psychological, and sociocultural factors.

FIGURE 1.8   The diathesis-stress model.

model encompasses the dynamic interplay of three major systems or domains. Two systems can be thought of as being internal: the biological, which includes genetic, epigenetic, and neurophysiologic factors; and the psychological, which includes psychoanalytic, behavioural, humanistic-existential, and cognitive-behavioural factors. The third system consists of what is considered to be external or outside of us: the sociocultural and environmental factors. Together, these biopsychosocial systems determine the range of known variables involved in the development of abnormal behaviour (Schumacher & Petronis, 2006; Szyf, 2006).

EVALUATING INTERACTIONIST PERSPECTIVES Research shows how biopsychosocial factors play a major role in the aging process, diseases, and abnormal behaviour. Indeed, the discovery of epigenetic factors and the pivotal role they play in our overall well-being may prove to be the proverbial "missing link" that helps us explain how psychological, sociocultural, and environmental factors interact with our genetic code. Throughout the rest of the book, you will also find that many forms of abnormal behaviour involve a complex interplay of multiple influences that include psychological, biological, and/or sociocultural factors.

REVIEW IT

Interactionist Perspectives

- **What is the distinguishing feature of the interactionist perspectives?** The diathesis-stress model posits that some people have predispositions (diatheses) for particular disorders but that whether these disorders actually develop depends on the type and severity of the stressors these people experience. The biopsychosocial approach examines the interplay of biological, psychological, and sociocultural factors in abnormal behaviour. External and internal factors can alter epigenetic patterns, which can affect gene expression. This can lead to an increased risk of both physical and psychological disorders.

Define It

abnormal psychology, 2
acetylcholine, 22
agoraphobia, 5
Alzheimer's disease, 21
axon, 20
behaviour therapy, 28
behaviourism, 25
biopsychosocial model, 35
catastrophize, 30
choleric, 9
clinical psychologist, 2
conditioned response, 26
conditioned stimulus, 26
conscious, 23
defence mechanisms, 25
deinstitutionalization, 13
delusions, 5
dementia praecox, 14
demonological model, 9
dendrites, 20
diathesis, 35
diathesis-stress model, 35
DNA, 18
dopamine, 22

downward drift hypothesis, 34
ego ideal, 24
ego, 24
emotional intelligence, 29
epigenetics, 18
epigenome, 18
exorcism, 10
expectancies, 32
gene expression, 18
gene silencing, 18
general paresis, 15
hallucinations, 3
humours, 9
hypnosis, 15
hysteria, 15
id, 23
ideas of persecution, 5
identification, 24
knobs, 21
medical model, 2
melancholia, 9
moral principle, 24
moral therapy, 12
negative reinforcers, 27

neo-Freudians, 25
neurons, 20
neurotransmitters, 21
norepinephrine, 21
paranoid, 4
phenothiazines, 12
phlegmatic, 9
pleasure principle, 23
positive reinforcers, 27
possession, 9
preconscious, 23
primary process thinking, 24
primary reinforcers, 28
proteins, 18
psychiatrist, 2
psychic, 23
psychoanalytic theory, 22
psychodynamic model, 15
psychological disorders, 2
psychosis, 25
punishments, 28
reality principle, 24
receptor site, 21
reciprocal determinism, 32

reinforcement, 27
repression, 25
sanguine, 9
secondary process thinking, 24
secondary reinforcers, 28
self, 24

serotonin, 22
social-cognitive theory, 32
soma, 20
superego, 24
synapse, 21
terminals, 21

trephining, 9
unconditioned response, 26
unconditioned stimulus, 26
unconscious, 23
world view, 9

Think About It

- What criteria would you use to distinguish abnormal behaviour from normal behaviour?

- What behaviours in your own cultural group might be considered abnormal by members of other groups?

- Do you believe abnormal behaviour is a function more of nature (biology) or of nurture (environment)? Explain.

- Do you believe biology is destiny? Why or why not?

- What role did hypnotism play in the development of psychological models of abnormal behaviour?

- What do you believe should be done about the problem of homelessness for people with psychological disorders?

Weblinks

Canadian Psychological Association (CPA)
www.cpa.ca
This is the homepage for Canada's national psychological association. It is the central source for information about the profession of psychology in Canada.

Canadian Psychiatric Association (CPA)
www.cpa-apc.org
This is the homepage for Canada's national professional association for psychiatrists. It contains psychiatric e-journals and information on a variety of professional matters.

Canadian Mental Health Association (CMHA)
www.cmha.ca
The CMHA is a voluntary organization that is dedicated to the promotion of mental health for all Canadians. Its website contains a diverse selection of mental health resources.

Mental Health Commission of Canada
www.mentalhealthcommission.ca

The MHCC promotes mental health in Canada, and works with stakeholders to change the attitudes of Canadians toward mental health problems and to improve services and support. Its website contains reports and videos.

Mental Health Page at Health Canada
www.hc-sc.gc.ca/hl-vs/mental/index_e.html
This website provides convenient access to a range of online materials related to the promotion of mental health, mental health programs and services in Canada, and the mental health issues, problems, and disorders encountered by Canadians.

Centre for Addiction and Mental Health (CAMH)
www.camh.net
CAMH is Canada's largest teaching and research centre for mental health and addiction problems. The site contains resources on a wide range of mental health and addiction concerns.

 MySearchLab offers you extensive help with your writing and research projects and provides round-the-clock access to credible and reliable source material. Chapter quizzes and a full electronic version of the text are also provided. Take a tour at www.mysearchlab.com.

What Is Abnormal Psychology?

How Do We Define Abnormal Behaviour?

Criteria for Determining Abnormality
Psychologists generally apply some combination of the following criteria in determining that a behaviour is abnormal:

- Unusualness
- Social deviance
- Faulty perceptions or interpretations of reality

- Significant personal distress
- Maladaptive or self-defeating behaviours
- Dangerousness

Historical Perspectives on Abnormal Behaviour

Views About Abnormal Behaviour and Treatment Change Over Time
Prevailing world views shape concepts of abnormal behaviour and treatment.

The Demonological Model
- Ancient societies attributed abnormal behaviour to divine or supernatural forces.

Origins of Naturalistic Explanations
- Hippocrates (460–377 BC) believed that an imbalance of vital bodily fluids caused abnormal behaviour.

Medieval Times (AD 4761–1450)
- Belief in demonic possession held sway and exorcists were used to rid people who behaved abnormally of the evil spirits that were believed to possess them.

Witchcraft (1400s–1600s)
- During the Renaissance, ideas about demonic possession coexisted with naturalistic explanations of abnormal behaviour.

Asylums in Europe and the New World
- As a refuge for both beggars and the disturbed, asylums in Europe were generally dreadful or circus-like. In North America, treatment-based asylums first appeared in Quebec (1639).

The Reform Movement and Moral Therapy (1700s–1800s)
- Proponents believed that mental patients could be restored to functioning if they were treated with dignity and understanding.

Transition in the Modern Era
Institutionalization dominated from the late 1800s until the 1950s as new treatments and community supports became available.

Decline of Moral Therapy
- The belief that the "insane" could not be successfully treated led to deteriorating conditions in mental hospitals until the 1950s.

Deinstitutionalization
- Shifting care to community-based settings began in the 1960s.

Community Mental Health
- A work still in progress today in Canada, where mental patients rely on dramatically fewer hospital beds and a fragmented system of community services and supports.

Scientific Models of Abnormal Behaviour
Core explanations of abnormal behaviour are based on the medical, psychological, and sociocultural models.

Medical Model
- Abnormal behaviour is based on underlying biological defects or abnormalities. Disorders can be classified, like physical illnesses, according to their distinctive causes and symptoms.

Psychological Models
- The first psychological explanation of abnormal behaviour originated with Freud. His psychodynamic model holds that the causes of abnormal behaviours lie in the interplay of forces within the unconscious mind. A diversity of psychological models soon followed.

Sociocultural Models
- Psychological problems may be rooted in the failures of society, such as poverty, social decay, discrimination, and lack of economic opportunity. The stigma of "mental Illness" can also strip people of their dignity and give rise to discrimination.

Biological Perspectives

Genetics

Genome
- All the genetic material encoded in the DNA located in the nucleus of cells in living organisms.

DNA
- Long, complex molecular structure that determines our unique genetic code.

Genetic and Chromosomal Disorders
- Genetic errors occur when the number or order of the DNA base pairs is wrong. Chromosomal diseases result from too many, too few, or incomplete chromosomes.

Epigenetics

Epigenome
- Inherited and acquired molecular variations to the genome.

Epigenetic Mechanisms
- Regulates gene expression (turned on) and gene silencing (turned off).

Epigenetic Errors
- Failure to properly regulate or signal genes to turn on or off.

Stem Cells

- Undifferentiated cells that are capable of indefinite self-replication and differentiation into specialized cells.

The Nervous System

Neurons
- Cells of the nervous system that use neurotransmission to communicate with each other and with the body.

Neurotransmitters
- Chemical substances that foster neural impulses.

Parts of the Nervous System
- Central Nervous System (CNS): the brain and spinal cord send and receive messages in the body.
- Peripheral Nervous System (PNS): the somatic and autonomic nervous systems carry messages between the CNS and the body.

Psychological Perspectives

Psychodynamic Models
Theories based on the belief that psychological problems are derived from unconscious psychological conflicts that can be traced to childhood.

Sigmund Freud—Psychoanalysis
- Levels of consciousness, personality structures (id, ego, super ego), stages of psychosexual development.

Humanistic-Existential Models
Theories that focus on self-actualization and living authentically.

- Carl Rogers
- Neo-Humanism

Learning Models
The view that abnormal behaviour can be described in terms of learning or unlearning behaviours.

Ivan Pavlov—Classical Conditioning
- The conditioned response, unconditioned stimulus, unconditioned response, and conditioned stimulus.

B. F. Skinner—Operant Conditioning
- The effect of reinforcers and punishments on behaviour.

Cognitive-Behavioural Models
Focus on the cognitions—the thoughts, beliefs, expectations, and attitudes—that accompany and may underlie abnormal behaviour.

- Albert Ellis—Rational-Emotive Behaviour Therapy
- Aaron Beck
- Albert Bandura
- Donald Meichenbaum—Cognitive-Behaviour Modification

Assessment, Classification, and Treatment of Abnormal Behaviour

CHAPTER OUTLINE

Methods of Assessment
The Clinical Interview
Psychological Tests of Intelligence and Personality
Neuropsychological Assessment
Behavioural Assessment
Cognitive Assessment
Physiological Measurement
Probing the Workings of the Brain

Classification of Abnormal Behaviour: The DSM System
Features of the DSM
Evaluation of the DSM System
Advantages and Disadvantages of the DSM System

Methods of Treatment
Types of Mental Health Professionals in Canada
Biological Therapies
Deep Brain Stimulation
Psychodynamic Therapies
Behaviour Therapy
Humanistic-Existential Therapies
Cognitive-Behaviour Therapies
Eclectic Therapy
Group, Family, and Marital Therapy
Computer-Assisted Therapy
Does Psychotherapy Work?

Abnormal Psychology and Society
Psychiatric Commitment and Patients' Rights
Mental Illness and Criminal Responsibility

Did You Know That...

- Researchers find that people report more personal problems when they are interviewed by computers than by humans?

- The most widely used personality inventory includes a number of questions that bear no obvious relationship to the traits the instrument purports to measure?

- Some clinicians form diagnostic impressions on the basis of how people interpret inkblots?

- Researchers today can probe the workings of the brain without surgery?

- One form of treatment for depression involves electrical impulses transmitted through the electrodes deep within the brain?

- People can't be committed to a psychiatric hospital just because they're eccentric?

- Despite beliefs to the contrary, the insanity defence is used in very few trials and is successful in fewer still?

- Psychologists and other mental health professionals are not very accurate when it comes to predicting dangerousness?

SYSTEMS OF CLASSIFICATION

There are really two aspects to consider when thinking about a person's symptoms and problems: the psychological assessment and the clinical diagnosis. In the psychological assessment, the clinician is trying to develop a summary of the symptoms and problems using psychological tests, observations, and interviews. In the clinical diagnosis, the clinician arrives at a summary classification by following a defined system, such as the DSM-IV-TR or the ICD-10.

While systems of classification of abnormal behaviour date to ancient times, as we saw in Chapter 1, the current systems are called the *Diagnostic and Statistical Manual of Mental Disorders* (DSM) and the *International Classification of Diseases* (ICD). These two systems classify abnormal behaviour patterns as mental disorders on the basis of specified diagnostic criteria.

Why is it important to classify abnormal behaviour? For one thing, classification is the core of science. Without labelling and organizing patterns of abnormal behaviour, researchers could not communicate with one another, and progress toward understanding these disorders would come to a halt. Moreover, important decisions are made on the basis of classification. Certain psychological disorders respond better to one therapy or drug than others. Classification also helps clinicians predict behaviour. Some patterns of abnormal behaviour, such as schizophrenia, follow more or less predictable courses of development. Classification also helps researchers identify populations with similar patterns of abnormal behaviour. By classifying groups of people as depressed, for example, researchers might be able to identify common factors that help explain the origins of depression.

This chapter reviews the classification and assessment of abnormal behaviour, beginning with the major systems clinicians use in Canada to classify and report abnormal behaviour patterns: the *Diagnostic and Statistical Manual of Mental Disorders* (DSM) and the *International Classification of Diseases* (ICD). We then introduce you to treatment methods that you will see later in the text alongside the specific disorders.

METHODS OF ASSESSMENT

Here we explore methods of assessment that clinicians use to arrive at diagnostic impressions, including interviews, psychological testing, self-report questionnaires, behavioural measures, and physiological measures. The role of assessment, however, goes further than classification. A careful assessment provides a wealth of information about clients' personalities and cognitive functioning. This information helps clinicians acquire a broader understanding of their clients' problems and recommend appropriate forms of treatment.

The Clinical Interview

The clinical interview is the most widely used means of assessment. The interview is usually a client's first face-to-face contact with a clinician. Clinicians often begin by asking clients to describe the presenting complaint in their own words. They may say something like, "Can you describe to me the problems you've been having lately?" The clinician will then usually probe aspects of the presenting complaint, such as behavioural abnormalities and feelings of discomfort, the circumstances regarding the onset of the problem, the history of past episodes, and how the problem affects the client's daily functioning. The clinician may explore possible precipitating events, such as changes in life circumstances, social relationships, employment, or schooling. The interviewer encourages the client to describe the problem in her or his own words in order to understand it from the client's point of view.

Although the format of an intake process may vary from clinician to clinician, most interviews cover topics such as

1. *Identifying data.* Sociodemographic characteristics: marital status, age, gender, racial/ethnic characteristics, religion, employment, family composition, and so on.
2. *Description of the presenting problem(s).* How does the client perceive the problem? What troubling behaviours, thoughts, or feelings are reported? How do they affect the client's functioning? When did they begin?
3. *Psychosocial history.* Information describing the client's developmental history: educational, social, and occupational history; early family relationships.
4. *Medical/psychiatric history.* History of medical and psychiatric treatment and hospitalizations. Is the present problem a recurrent episode of a previous problem? How was the problem handled in the past? Was treatment successful? Why or why not?
5. *Medical problems/medication.* Description of present medical problems and present treatment, including medication.

INTERVIEW FORMATS Of course, every interviewer brings his or her own theoretical orientation to the assessment; however, interviewing skills and techniques have a few features in common. Psychologists and other professionals are trained to establish rapport with and feelings of trust on the part of a client. These feelings help put the client at ease and encourage candid communication. Effective interviewers do not pressure clients to disclose sensitive information. Clients are generally more willing to disclose their personal feelings and experiences to someone who shows concern and understanding, someone they feel they can trust.

There are three general types of clinical interviews: unstructured interviews, semi-structured interviews, and structured interviews. In an **unstructured interview,** the clinician adopts his or her own style of questioning rather than following any standard format. In a **semi-structured interview,** the clinician follows a general outline of questions designed to gather essential information but is free to ask the questions in any order and to branch off in other directions to follow up on clinically important information. In a **structured interview,** the interview follows a preset series of questions in a particular order.

The major advantage of the unstructured interview is its spontaneity and conversational style. There is an active give-and-take between the interviewer and the client because the interviewer is not bound to follow any specific set of questions. The major disadvantage is the lack of standardization. Different interviewers may ask questions in different ways. For example, one interviewer might ask, "How have your moods been lately?" and another might pose the question "Have you had any periods of crying or tearfulness during the past week or two?" Client response may depend to a certain extent on how the questions were asked. Another drawback is that the conversational flow of the interview may fail to touch on important clinical information needed to form a diagnostic impression.

Structured interviews (also called standardized interviews) provide the highest level of reliability and consistency in reaching diagnostic judgments, which is why they are used frequently in research settings (J. B. Williams et al., 1992). Yet many clinicians prefer using a semi-structured approach because of its greater flexibility. A leading example of structured interview protocol is the Structured Clinical Interview for the DSM (SCID). The SCID

unstructured interviews Type of clinical interview in which interviewers determine which questions to ask rather than following a standard interview format.

semi-structured interviews Type of clinical interview in which interviewers are guided by a general outline but are free to modify the order in which questions are asked and to branch off in other directions.

structured interviews Means by which an interviewer obtains clinical information from a client by asking a fairly standard series of questions concerning such issues as the client's presenting complaints or problems, mental state, life circumstances, and psychosocial or developmental history.

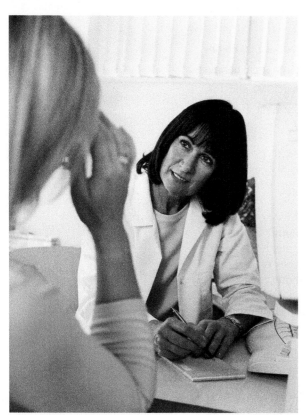

The clinical interview. During the clinical interview, the format might vary, but it typically includes gathering information about present complaints, possible precipitating events, and how the problem affects the person's daily functioning.

includes closed-ended questions to determine the presence of behaviour patterns that suggest specific diagnostic categories and open-ended questions that allow clients to elaborate their problems and feelings.

In the course of an interview, a clinician may also conduct a more formal assessment of the client's cognitive functioning by administering a **mental status examination**. This involves a formal assessment of the client's appearance (appropriateness of attire and grooming), mood, attention, perceptual and thinking processes, memory, orientation (knowing who they are, where they are, and the present date), level of awareness or insight into their problems, and judgment in making life decisions. The interviewer compiles all the information available from the interview and review of the client's background and presenting problems to arrive at a diagnostic impression.

mental status examination Structured clinical evaluation to determine various aspects of a client's mental functioning.

Psychological Tests of Intelligence and Personality

Psychological tests are structured methods of assessment used to evaluate reasonably stable traits such as intelligence and personality. Tests are usually standardized on large numbers of subjects and provide norms that compare clients' scores with an average. By comparing test results from samples of people who are free of psychological disorders with those of people who have diagnosable psychological disorders, we may gain some insight into the types of response patterns that are indicative of abnormal behaviour.

INTELLIGENCE TESTS The assessment of abnormal behaviour often includes an evaluation of intelligence. Formal tests of intelligence are used to help diagnose mental retardation. They evaluate the intellectual impairment that may be the result of other disorders, such as organic mental disorders caused by damage to the brain. They also provide a profile of a client's intellectual strengths and weaknesses, which helps in the development of a treatment plan suited to the client's competencies.

Intelligence is a controversial concept in psychology, however. Even attempts at definition stir debate. David Wechsler, the originator of a widely used series of intelligence tests, defined intelligence as "capacity . . . to understand the world . . . and . . . resourcefulness to cope with its challenges" (1975). From his perspective, intelligence has to do with the ways in which we (1) mentally represent the world and (2) adapt to its demands.

intelligence (1) Global capacity to understand the world and cope with its challenges. (2) Trait or traits associated with successful performance on intelligence tests.

The Stanford-Binet Intelligence Scale (SBIS) was originated by Frenchmen Alfred Binet and Theodore Simon in 1905 in response to the French public school system's quest for a test that could identify children who might profit from special education. The initial Binet-Simon scale yielded a score called a **mental age** (MA) that represented a child's overall level of intellectual functioning. A child who received an MA of 8 was said to be functioning as a typical eight-year-old. Children received "months" of credit for correct answers, and their MAs were determined by adding them up.

mental age Age equivalent that corresponds to the person's level of intelligence, as measured by performance on the Stanford-Binet Intelligence Scale. Abbreviated *MA*.

Louis Terman of Stanford University adapted the Binet-Simon test for American children in 1916, and it became known by its full current name: the Stanford-Binet Intelligence Scale (SBIS). The SBIS also yielded an **intelligence quotient** (IQ), which reflected the relationship between a child's MA and chronological age (CA), according to this formula:

intelligence quotient Measure of intelligence derived on the basis of scores on an intelligence test. Called a *quotient* because it was originally derived by dividing a respondent's mental age by her or his actual age. Abbreviated *IQ*.

$$IQ = MA/CA \times 100$$

Examination of this formula shows that children who received identical mental age scores might differ markedly in IQ, with a younger child attaining a higher IQ.

Today, the SBIS is used for children and adults, and test takers' IQ scores are based on their deviation from the norms of their age group. A score of 100 is defined as the mean. People who answer more items correctly than the average obtain IQ scores above 100; those who answer fewer items correctly obtain scores of less than 100.

This method of deriving an IQ score, called the **deviation IQ**, was used by psychologist David Wechsler in developing various intelligence tests for children and adults,

deviation IQ Intelligence quotient derived by determining the deviation between the individual's score and the norm (mean).

A CLOSER LOOK

Would You Tell Your Problems to a Computer? Or Online Therapist?

Picture yourself seated before a computer screen. A message on the screen asks you to type in your name and press Enter. Not wanting to offend, you comply. This message then appears: "Hello, my name is Sigmund. I'm programmed to ask you a set of questions to learn more about you. May I begin?" You nod your head yes, momentarily forgetting the computer can only "perceive" keystrokes. You type "yes" and the interview begins.

Computerized clinical interviews have been used for more than 25 years. Consider a computerized interview system named CASPER. Interview questions and response options, such as the following, are presented on the screen:

About how many days in the past month did you have difficulty falling asleep, staying asleep, or waking too early (include sleep disturbed by bad dreams)?

During the past month, how have you been getting along with your spouse/partner? (1) Very satisfactory; (2) Mostly satisfactory; (3) Sometimes satisfactory, sometimes unsatisfactory; (4) Mostly unsatisfactory; (5) Very unsatisfactory.

A. D. Farrell, Camplair, & McCullough, 1987, p. 692

The client presses a numeric key to respond to each item.

CASPER is a branching program that follows up on problems suggested by the client's responses. For example, if the client indicates difficulty in falling or remaining asleep, CASPER asks whether sleep has become a major problem—"something causing you great personal distress or interfering with your daily functioning" (A. D. Farrell Camplair & McCullough, 1987, p. 693). If the client indicates yes, the computer will return to the problem after other items have been presented and ask the client to rate the duration and intensity of the problem. Clients may also add or drop complaints—change their minds, that is.

A study found that a brief diagnostic interview conducted over the phone by a computer equipped with voice-response technology achieved similar results to a human interviewer using a more intensive interview protocol, the SCID (Kobak, Greist, Jefferson, & Katzelnick, 1997). Moreover, people generally reveal more personal problems to CASPER than they do when interviewed by a human. Perhaps people are less concerned about being "judged" by computers. Perhaps the computer interview is especially helpful in identifying problems the client is embarrassed or unwilling to

Computer therapy? Would you be more or less open about your problems if you were using a computer-based therapy system? Would you prefer a video-chat with a real therapist?

report to a human. Perhaps the computer seems more willing to take the time to note all complaints.

Reviews of research suggest that computer programs are as capable as skilled clinicians of obtaining information from clients and reaching an accurate diagnosis, and are less expensive and more time-efficient (B. L. Bloom, 1992; Kobak et al., 1996). It seems that most of the resistance to using computer interviews for this purpose comes from clinicians rather than clients.

Computer-assisted treatments for mental health problems are also available. The most basic form of e-therapy is through email correspondence and generally addresses less serious problems—it more often entails giving advice or is psycho-educational in nature (Rochlen, Zack, & Speyer, 2004). Text messaging and chat rooms have also been gaining in popularity because of their "real-time" quality, which allows for immediacy and clarification (Castelnuovo, Gaggioli, Mantovani, & Riva, 2003). Self-help groups, such as Alcoholics Anonymous, have been using a chat-room format as a form of group therapy since the 1990s (Griffiths, 2005). Today, computer video-conferencing between therapists and clients offers a promising alternative mode of mental health treatment (Bouchard et al., 2004; Ruskin et al., 2004). It may prove to be especially useful in circumstances in which face-to-face therapy is impractical, such as in many remote and northern regions of Canada.

known as the *Wechsler scales*. The Wechsler scales group questions into subtests like those shown in Table 2.1, each of which measures a different intellectual task. The Wechsler scales are thus designed to offer insight into a person's relative strengths and weaknesses, and not simply to yield an overall score.

TABLE 2.1

Examples of Subtests from the Wechsler Adult Intelligence Scale

Verbal Subtests	Performance Subtests
Information	**Digit Symbol**
Who wrote the *Iliad*?	Fill in as many boxes as you can with symbols corresponding to particular numbers within the time allowed.
Comprehension	**Picture Completion**
Why do people need to obey traffic laws? What does the saying "The early bird catches the worm" mean?	Determine the missing parts of a picture.
Arithmetic	**Block Design**
John wanted to buy a shirt that cost $31.50, but only had $17.00. How much more money would he need to buy the shirt?	Use blocks like those in Figure 3.1 to match particular designs.
	Picture Arrangement
Similiarities	Arrange story-book pictures in the correct order to tell a coherent story.
How are a stapler and a paper clip alike?	
Digit Span	**Symbol Search**
(Forward order) Listen to this series of numbers and repeat them back to me in the same order: 4 7 5 6	Determine whether either of two target shapes matches those presented in a row of shapes.
(Backward order) Listen to this series of numbers and then repeat them backward: 3 9 7 1	**Object Assembly**
	Arrange the pieces of a puzzle so that they form a meaningful object.
Vocabulary	
What does *capricious* mean?	
Letter-Number Sequencing	
Listen to this series of numbers and letters and repeat them back, first saying the numbers from least to most, and then saying the numbers in alphabetical order.	

Sample items similar to those found in the *Wechsler Adult Intelligence Scale*, Third Edition (WAIS-III). Copyright © 1997 NCS Pearson, Inc. Reproduced with permission. All rights reserved. "Wechsler Adult Intelligence Scale" and "WAIS" are trademarks, in the US and/or other countries, of Pearson Education, Inc. or its affiliate(s).

Wechsler's scales include both verbal and performance subtests. Verbal subtests generally require knowledge of verbal concepts; performance subtests rely more on spatial-relations skills. (Figure 2.1 on page 46 shows items similar to those on performance subtests of the Wechsler scales.) Wechsler's scales allow for computation of verbal and performance IQs.

Students from various backgrounds yield different profiles. Post-secondary students, generally speaking, perform better on verbal subtests than on performance subtests. Australian Aboriginal children outperform white Australian children on performance-type tasks that involve visual-spatial skills (Kearins, 1981). Such skills are likely to foster survival in the harsh Australian outback. Intellectual attainments, like psychological adjustment, are connected with the demands of particular sociocultural and physical environmental settings.

Wechsler IQ scores are based on how respondents' answers deviate from those attained by age-mates. The mean whole test score at any age is defined as 100. Wechsler distributed IQ scores so that 50% of the scores of a population would lie within a "broad average" range of 90 to 110.

Most IQ scores cluster around the mean (see Figure 2.2 on page 46). Just 5% are above 130 or below 70. Wechsler labelled people who attained scores of 130 or above as "very superior," those with scores below 70 as "intellectually deficient." IQ scores below 70 are one of the criteria used in diagnosing mental retardation.

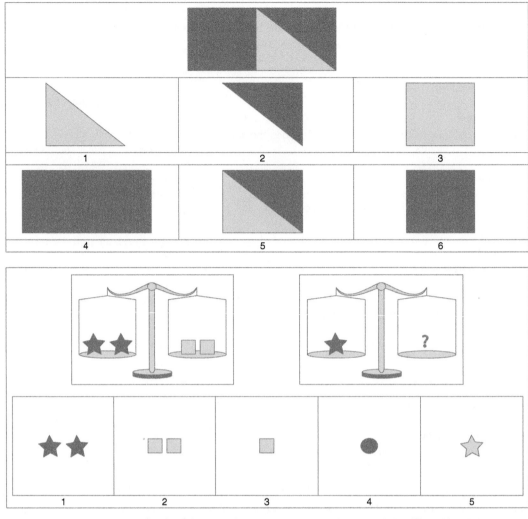

FIGURE 2.1 **Items similar to those on the performance subtests of the Weschler Adult Intelligence Scale IV.**

Source: Dozois & Firestone, 2010, p. 69. Reprinted with permission by Pearson Canada Inc.

FIGURE 2.2 An idealized distribution of IQ scores. The distribution of IQ scores is based on a bell-shaped curve, which is referred to by psychologists as a *normal curve*. Wechsler defined the deviation IQ in such a way that 50% of the scores fall within the broad average range of 90 to 110.

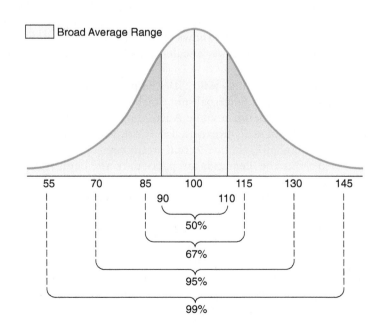

PERSONALITY TESTS Clinicians use various formal tests to assess personality. We consider two types of personality tests: self-report tests and projective tests. Some self-report tests are intended to measure a particular trait or construct, such as anxiety or depression. Here, our focus is on multidimensional self-report personality tests or inventories, as represented by the most widely used of these instruments, the Minnesota Multiphasic Personality Inventory (MMPI).

Do you like automobile magazines? Are you easily startled by noises in the night? Are you bothered by periods of anxiety or shakiness? Self-report inventories use structured items similar to these to measure personality traits such as anxiety, depression, emotionality, hypomania, masculinity–femininity, and introversion. Comparison of clients' responses on scales measuring these traits to those of a normative sample reveals their relative standing.

Self-report personality inventories are also called **objective tests**. They are objective in that the range of possible responses to items is limited. Empirical objective standards—rather than psychological theory—are also used to derive test items. Tests might ask respondents to check adjectives that apply to them, to mark statements as true or false, to select preferred activities from lists, or to indicate whether items apply to them "always," "sometimes," or "never." Tests with **forced-choice formats** require respondents to mark which of a group of statements is truest for them or to select their most preferred activity from a list. They cannot answer "none of the above." Forced-choice formats are commonly used in interest inventories, as in this item:

> I would rather
> a. be a forester.
> b. work in an office setting.
> c. play in a band.

With objective personality tests, items are selected according to some empirical standard. The MMPI-2 contains more than 500 true–false statements that assess interest patterns, habits, family relationships, somatic complaints, attitudes, beliefs, and behaviours characteristic of psychological disorders. It is widely used as a test of personality as well as assisting in the diagnosis of abnormal behaviour patterns. The MMPI-2 consists of a number of individual scales comprising items that tended to be answered differently by members of carefully selected diagnostic groups, such as patients diagnosed with schizophrenia or depression, than by members of normal comparison groups.

Many items that distinguish normal people from clinical groups are transparent in meaning, such as "I feel down much of the time." Some items are subtler in meaning or bear no obvious relationship to the measured trait.

The clinical scales are described in Table 2.2 on page 49. The MMPI-2 also has **validity scales** that assess tendencies to distort test responses in a favourable ("faking good") or unfavourable ("faking bad") direction.

MMPI profiles may suggest possible diagnoses that can be considered in light of other evidence. Moreover, instead of making a full diagnosis, many clinicians use the MMPI to gain general information about respondents' personality traits and attributes that may underlie their psychological problems.

The validity of the original and revised MMPI is supported by a large body of research demonstrating its ability to discriminate between control and psychiatric samples and between groups composed of people with different types of psychological disorders, such as anxiety versus depressive disorders (Keiller & Graham, 1993).

The Personality Assessment Inventory (PAI) is a commonly used objective personality test that is closely tied to the DSM Axis I and II categories (Piotrowski, 2000). The PAI has several subscales, including ones that have treatment implications (e.g., they measure potential for harm to self or others, level of stress, and motivation for treatment). The validity of the PAI is about equal to that of the MMPI (Braxton, Calhoun, Williams, & Boggs, 2007; Kurtz & Blais, 2007), but the PAI can be completed in almost half the time—an important feature for clients who may have difficulty staying on a task for extended periods of time, such as those who are cognitively impaired, impulsive, or depressed.

objective tests Tests that allow a limited, specified range of response options or answers so that they can be scored objectively.

forced-choice formats Method of structuring test questions that requires respondents to select among a set number of possible answers.

validity scales Groups of test items that serve to detect whether the results of a particular test are valid or whether a person responded in a random manner or in a way intended to create a favourable or unfavourable impression.

MMPI-2™
Minnesota Multiphasic Personality Inventory-2™

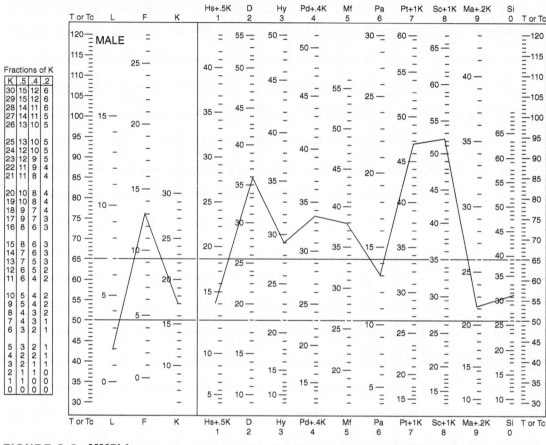

FIGURE 2.3 MMPI form.

Source: Form for use with the MMPI-2™ test as published and copyrighted by the Regents of the University of Minnesota. All rights reserved. "MMPI-2" and "Minnesota Multiphasic Personality-2" are trademarks owned by the Regents of the University of Minnesota.

The above is a profile of a patient referred to [a] clinic by a physician. The physician was concerned about possible schizophrenic ideations, level of depression, and possible suicidal tendencies. It was interpreted by a senior psychologist who specializes in the MMPI, and who knew only the patient's sex, age, level of education, and marital status. This is called a *blind interpretation.*

REPORT

This is the blind analysis of an MMPI profile completed by Mr. Smith. This profile is valid. The MMPI profile completed by Mr. Smith suggests that he is currently experiencing a considerable amount of psychological distress in the form of tension, worry, and anxiety. He is a pas-

sive, dependent man who is having considerable difficulty coming to grips with his underlying dependency needs. It would not be unusual for such an individual to form very strong passive relationships. He is an angry man, whose anger is modified somewhat by his own self-image as a soft, esthetically inclined individual who has rejected the traditionally masculine role. However, he pays for this role rejection with a high level of anxiety and tension, and also experiences a moderate level of depression.

Although the level of anxiety may produce some interference in his thinking, it is unclear from the profile whether a thought disorder exists. It would be necessary to definitively ascertain this from other data sources.

>

However, he is a ruminative and obsessive man, who tends to externalize sources of anger. He is subtly suspicious of the motives of others but feels uncomfortable in stating this directly. Again, this is reflective of his own difficulty in dealing with anger in a direct, but still very controlled, way.

Individuals with profiles such as this often do engage in self-destructive behaviour. However, I would suspect Mr. Smith would give some warning about any such acts.

It should be noted that he is highly vulnerable to loss and does have the potential to become seriously disorganized around such issues. Should he sustain the loss of a significant other person, or significant function, he may become actually suicidal.

Source: Dozois & Firestone, 2010, p. 73. Reprinted with permission by Pearson Canada Inc.

Self-report tests have the benefits of relative ease and economy of administration. Once the examiner has read the instructions to clients and ascertained that they can read and comprehend the items, clients can complete the tests on their own. Such tests often uncover information that might not be revealed during a clinical interview or by observing a person's behaviour.

A disadvantage of self-rating tests is that they rely on clients themselves as the source of data. Test responses may therefore reflect underlying response biases, such as tendencies to answer items in a socially desirable direction, rather than accurate self-perceptions. For this reason, self-report inventories like the MMPI contain validity scales to help uncover response biases. Yet even validity scales may not detect all sources of bias (Bagby, Nicholson, & Buis, 1998). Examiners may also look for additional supporting information, such as by interviewing others who are familiar with a client's behaviour.

Psychodynamically oriented critics suggest that self-report instruments tell us little about possible unconscious processes. The use of such tests may also be limited to relatively high-functioning individuals who can read well, respond to verbal material, and focus on a potentially tedious task. Clients who are disorganized, unstable, or confused may not be able to complete tests.

TABLE 2.2

Sample Clinical Scales of the MMPI-2

Scale Number	Scale Label	Items Similar to Those Found on MMPI Scale	Sample Traits of High Scorers
1.	Depression	Nothing seems to interest me anymore. My sleep is often disturbed by worrisome thoughts.	Depressed mood; pessimistic, worrisome, despondent, lethargic
2.	Hysteria	I sometimes become flushed for no apparent reason. I tend to take people at their word when they're trying to be nice to me.	Naïve, egocentric, little insight into problems, immature; develops physical complaints in response to stress
3.	Psychopathic Deviate	My parents often disliked my friends. My behaviour sometimes got me into trouble at school.	Difficulties incorporating values of society, rebellious, impulsive, antisocial tendencies; strained family relationships; poor work and school history
4.	Paranoia	I would have been more successful in life but people didn't give me a fair break. It's not safe to trust anyone these days.	Suspicious, guarded, blames others, resentful, aloof, may have paranoid delusions
5.	Social Introversion	I don't like loud parties. I was not very active in school activities.	Shy, inhibited, withdrawn, introverted, lacks self-confidence, reserved, anxious in social situations

PROJECTIVE PERSONALITY TESTS   Projective tests, unlike objective tests, offer no clear, specified answers. Clients are presented with ambiguous stimuli, such as vague drawings or inkblots, and are usually asked to describe what the stimuli look like or to relate stories about them. The tests are called *projective* because they were derived from the psychodynamic projective hypothesis, the belief that people impose or "project" their psychological needs, drives, and motives, much of which may lie in the unconscious, onto their interpretations of unstructured or ambiguous stimuli.

The psychodynamic model holds that potentially disturbing impulses and wishes, often of a sexual or aggressive nature, are frequently hidden from consciousness by defence mechanisms. Defence mechanisms may thwart direct probing of threatening material. Indirect methods of assessment, however, such as projective tests, may offer clues to unconscious processes. More behaviourally oriented critics contend that the results of projective tests are based more on clinicians' subjective interpretations of test responses than on empirical evidence.

The two most prominent projective techniques are the Rorschach inkblot test and the Thematic Apperception Test (TAT). The Rorschach test, in which a person's responses to inkblots are used to reveal aspects of his or her personality, was developed by Swiss psychiatrist Hermann Rorschach (1884–1922). As a child, Rorschach was intrigued by the game of dripping ink on paper and folding the paper to make symmetrical figures. He noted that people saw different things in the same blot, and he believed that their percepts reflected their personalities as well as the stimulus cues provided by the blot. Five of the inkblots are black and white and the other five have colour (see Figure 2.4). Each inkblot is printed on a separate card, which is handed to subjects in sequence. Subjects are asked to tell the examiner what the blot might be or what it reminds them of. A follow-up inquiry explores what features of the blot (its colour, form, or texture) the person used in forming an impression of what it resembled.

Clinicians who use the Rorschach tend to interpret responses in the following ways. Clients who use the entire blot in their responses show ability to perceive part–whole relationships and integrate events in meaningful ways. People whose responses are based solely on minor details of the blots may have obsessive-compulsive tendencies that, in psychodynamic theory, protect them from having to cope with the larger issues in their lives. Clients who respond to the negative (white) spaces tend to see things in their own way, suggestive of negativism or stubbornness.

The validity of the Rorschach has been the subject of extensive debate. While the Rorschach is widely used, its use is very controversial and the empirical basis of its use is regularly questioned. For example, recent research refutes the idea that the Rorschach test is sensitive in discriminating psychopaths from nonpsychopaths (Wood et al., 2010).

One problem is the lack of a standard scoring procedure. Interpretation of a person's responses is not objective; it depends to some degree on the subjective judgment of the examiner. Two examiners may interpret the same Rorschach response differently. Recent attempts to develop a comprehensive scoring approach, such as the Exner system (Exner, 1991, 1993), have advanced the effort to standardize scoring of responses. But the debate over the reliability of the Rorschach, including the Exner system, also known as the Rorschach Comprehensive System (RCS), continues (Wood, Nezworski, & Stejskal, 1996, 1997). Yet even if a Rorschach response can be scored reliably, the interpretation of the response—what it means—remains an open question.

The Thematic Apperception Test (TAT) was developed by psychologist Henry Murray (1943) at Harvard University in the 1930s. *Apperception* is a French word that can be translated as "interpreting (new ideas or impressions) on the basis of existing

FIGURE 2.4   An inkblot similar to those found on the Rorschach Inkblot Test.
What does the blot look like to you? What could it be? Rorschach assumed that people project their personalities into their responses to ambiguous inkblots as well as responding to the stimulus characteristics of the blot.

ideas (cognitive structures) and past experience." The TAT consists of a series of cards, like that shown in Figure 2.5, each of which depicts an ambiguous scene. Respondents are asked to construct stories about the cards. It is assumed that their tales reflect their experiences and outlooks on life—and, perhaps, also shed light on deep-seated needs and conflicts.

Respondents are asked to describe what is happening in each scene, what led up to it, what the characters are thinking and feeling, and what will happen next.

Psychodynamically oriented clinicians assume that respondents identify with the protagonists in their stories and project their psychological needs and conflicts into the events they apperceive. On a more superficial level, the stories suggest too how respondents might interpret or behave in similar situations in their own lives. TAT results are also suggestive of clients' attitudes toward others, particularly family members and lovers.

One criticism of the TAT is that the stimulus properties of some of the cards, such as cues depicting sadness or anger, may exert too strong a "stimulus pull" on the subject. The pictures themselves may pull for certain types of stories. If so, clients' responses may represent reactions to the stimulus cues rather than projections of their personalities (Murstein & Mathes, 1996). The TAT, like the Rorschach, is open to criticism that the scoring and interpretation of responses largely depends on clinicians' subjective impressions. The validity of the TAT in eliciting deep-seated material or tapping underlying psychopathology also remains to be demonstrated.

Proponents of projective testing argue that in skilled hands, tests like the TAT and the Rorschach can yield meaningful material that might not be revealed in interviews or by self-rating inventories (Stricker & Gold, 1999). Moreover, allowing subjects freedom of expression through projective testing reduces the tendency of individuals to offer socially desirable responses. Despite the lack of direct evidence for the projective hypothesis, the appeal of projective tests among clinicians remains high (Camara, Nathan, & Puente, 2000).

FIGURE 2.5 **The Thematic Apperception Test (TAT).** Psychologists ask test takers to provide their impressions of what is happening in the scene depicted in the drawing. They ask test takers what led up to the scene and how it will turn out. How might your responses reveal aspects of your own personality?

Neuropsychological Assessment

Neuropsychological assessment is used to evaluate whether or not psychological problems reflect underlying neurological damage or brain defects. Neuropsychological inventories may be used in conjunction with brain-imaging techniques, such as MRI and CT scans, not only to suggest whether clients are suffering from brain damage but also to determine which parts of the brain might be involved (Fiez, 2001). When neurological impairment is suspected, a neurological evaluation may be requested from a neurologist—a medical doctor who specializes in disorders of the nervous system. A clinical neuropsychologist may also be consulted to administer neuropsychological assessment techniques, such as behavioural observation and psychological testing, to reveal signs of possible brain damage.

The Luria-Nebraska Test Battery is based on the work of the Russian neuropsychologist A. R. Luria (1902–1977) and was developed by psychologists at the University of Nebraska (C. J. Golden, Hammeke, & Purisch, 1980). The Luria-Nebraska reveals patterns of skill deficits that are suggestive of particular sites of brain damage.

A wide range of skills is assessed. Tests measure tactile, kinesthetic, and spatial skills; complex motor skills; auditory skills; receptive and expressive speech skills; reading, writing, and arithmetic skills; and general intelligence and memory functioning. Although the Luria-Nebraska is promising, and there is research to support its internal consistency (Teichner, Golden, Bradley, & Crum, 1999), more research is needed to substantiate its overall reliability and validity.

neuropsychological assessment Methods of psychological assessment used to detect signs of underlying neurological damage or brain defects.

Neuropsychological tests attempt to reveal brain dysfunctions without surgical procedures. We will later consider other contemporary techniques that allow us to probe the workings of the brain without surgery.

Behavioural Assessment

The traditional model of assessment, or **psychometric approach,** holds that psychological tests reveal signs of reasonably stable traits or dispositions that largely determine behaviour. The psychometric approach aims to classify people in terms of personality types according to traits such as anxiety, introversion–extraversion, obsessiveness, hostility, impulsivity, and aggressiveness. This model inspired development of trait-based tests such as the Rorschach, TAT, and MMPI.

The alternative model of **behavioural assessment** treats test results as samples of behaviour that occur in specific situations rather than signs of underlying personality types or traits. According to the behavioural approach, behaviour is primarily determined by environmental or situational factors, such as stimulus cues and reinforcements.

The examiner may conduct a **behavioural interview** by posing questions to learn more about the history and situational aspects of problem behaviour. If a client seeks help because of panic attacks, the behavioural interviewer might ask how the client experiences these attacks—when, where, how often, and under what circumstances. The interviewer looks for precipitating cues, such as thought patterns (e.g., thoughts of dying or losing control) or situational factors (e.g., entering a department store) that may provoke an attack. The interviewer also seeks information about reinforcers that may maintain the panic. Does the client flee the situation when an attack occurs? Is escape reinforced by relief from anxiety? Has the client learned to lessen anticipatory anxiety by avoiding exposure to situations in which attacks have occurred?

The examiner may also use observational methods to connect the problem behaviour to the stimuli and reinforcements that help maintain it. Consider the case of Kerry:

> A seven-year-old boy, Kerry, is brought by his parents for evaluation. His mother describes him as a "royal terror." His father complains he won't listen to anyone. Kerry throws temper tantrums in the supermarket, screaming and stomping his feet if his parents refuse to buy him what he wants. At home, he breaks his toys by throwing them against the wall and demands new ones. Sometimes, though, he appears sullen and won't talk to anyone for hours. At school, he appears inhibited and has difficulty concentrating. His progress at school is slow and he has difficulty reading. His teachers complain he has a limited attention span and doesn't seem motivated.
>
> The Authors' Files

The psychologist may use direct home observation to assess the interactions between Kerry and his parents. Alternatively, the psychologist may observe Kerry and his parents through a one-way mirror in the clinic. Such observations may suggest interactions that explain the child's noncompliance. For example, Kerry's noncompliance may follow parental requests that are vague (e.g., a parent says, "Play nicely now," and Kerry responds by throwing toys) or inconsistent (e.g., a parent says, "Go play with your toys but don't make a mess," to which Kerry responds by scattering the toys). Observation may suggest ways in which Kerry's parents can improve communication and cue and reinforce desirable behaviours.

There are advantages and disadvantages to direct observation. One advantage is that direct observation does not rely on a client's self-reports, which may be distorted by efforts to make a favourable or unfavourable impression. In addition to providing accurate measurements of problem behaviour, behavioural observation can suggest strategies for intervention. A mother might report that her son is so hyperactive he cannot sit still long enough to complete homework assignments. By using a one-way mirror, the clinician may discover that the boy becomes restless only when he encounters a problem he cannot solve right away. The child may thus be helped by being taught ways of coping with frustration and of solving certain kinds of academic problems.

Direct observation also has its drawbacks. One issue is the possible lack of consensus in defining problems in behavioural terms. In coding a child's behaviour for hyperactivity, clinicians must agree on which aspects of the behaviour represent hyperactivity. Another potential problem is a lack of reliability or inconsistency of measurement across time or between observers. Reliability is reduced when an observer is inconsistent in the coding of specific behaviours or when two or more observers code behaviour inconsistently.

Observers may also show response biases. An observer who has been sensitized to expect that a child is hyperactive may perceive normal variations in behaviour as subtle cues of hyperactivity and erroneously record them as instances of hyperactive behaviour. Such expectations are less likely to affect behavioural ratings when the target behaviours are defined concretely (Foster & Cone, 1986).

Behavioural clinicians may supplement behavioural observations with traditional forms of assessment, such as the MMPI, or perhaps even with projective tests, such as the Rorschach or TAT. However, they are likely to interpret test data as samples of clients' behaviour at a particular point in time, and not as signs of stable traits. Trait-oriented clinicians may similarly employ behavioural assessment to learn how personality "traits" are "revealed" in different settings and to see how particular traits affect clients' daily functioning.

In addition to behavioural interviews and direct observation, behavioural assessment may involve the use of other techniques, such as self-monitoring, contrived or analogue measures, and behavioural rating scales.

SELF-MONITORING Training clients to record or monitor the problem behaviour in their daily lives is another method of relating problem behaviour to the settings in which it occurs. In **self-monitoring**, clients assume the primary responsibility for assessing the problem behaviour.

self-monitoring In behavioural assessment, the process of recording or observing one's own behaviour, thoughts, or emotions.

Self-monitoring permits direct measurement of the problem behaviour when and where it occurs. Behaviours that can be easily counted, such as food intake, cigarette smoking, nail-biting, hair pulling, study periods, and social activities, are well suited for self-monitoring. Clients are usually best aware of the frequency of these behaviours and their situational contexts. Self-monitoring can also produce highly accurate measurement because the behaviour is recorded as it occurs, not reconstructed from memory.

Behavioural diaries can also help clients increase desirable but low-frequency behaviours, such as assertive behaviour and dating behaviour. Unassertive clients might track occasions that seem to warrant an assertive response and jot down their actual responses to each occasion. Clients and clinicians then review the log to highlight problematic situations and rehearse assertive responses. A client who is anxious about dating might record social contacts with the opposite gender. To measure the effects of treatment, clinicians may encourage clients to engage in a **baseline** period of self-monitoring before treatment is begun.

baseline Period of time preceding the implementation of a treatment. Used to gather data regarding the rate of occurrence of the target behaviour before treatment is introduced.

Self-monitoring, though, is not without its disadvantages. Some clients are unreliable and do not keep accurate records. They become forgetful or sloppy, or they under-report undesirable behaviours, such as overeating or smoking, because of embarrassment or fear of criticism. To offset these biases, clinicians may, with clients' consent, corroborate the accuracy of self-monitoring by gathering information from other parties, such as clients' spouses. Private behaviours such as eating or smoking alone cannot be corroborated in this way, however. Sometimes, other means of corroboration, such as physiological measures, are available. For example, biochemical analysis of the carbon monoxide in clients' breath samples or of nicotine metabolites in their saliva or blood can be used to corroborate reports of abstinence from smoking.

Self-monitoring may actually be an important, perhaps even necessary, feature of some behaviour change programs, such as weight management programs. A study showed that the more consistently participants monitored what they ate, the more weight they lost (Baker & Kirschenbaum, 1993). This is not to imply that self-monitoring alone is sufficient to produce a desired behaviour change. Motivation to change and skills needed to make behaviour changes are also important.

ANALOGUE OR CONTRIVED MEASURES Analogue or contrived measures are intended to simulate the setting in which a behaviour naturally takes place but are carried out in laboratory or controlled settings. Role-playing exercises are common analogue measures. Clinicians cannot follow clients who have difficulty expressing dissatisfaction to authority figures throughout the day. Instead, they may rely on role-playing exercises, such as having the clients enact challenging an unfair grade. A scene might be described to the client as follows: "You've worked very hard on a term paper and received a very poor grade, say a D or an F. You approach the professor, who asks, 'Is there some problem?' What do you do now?" The client's enactment of the scene may reveal deficits in self-expression that can be addressed in therapy or assertiveness training.

The behavioural approach task, or BAT (Lang & Lazovik, 1963), is a popular analogue measure of a phobic person's approach to a feared object such as a snake. Approach behaviour is broken down into levels of response, such as looking in the direction of a snake from about six metres, touching a box holding a snake, and touching a snake. The BAT provides direct measurement of a response to a stimulus in a controlled situation. The subject's approach behaviour can be quantified by assigning a score to each level of approach. These types of measures tend to be part assessment and part treatment.

BEHAVIOURAL RATING SCALES A behavioural rating scale is a checklist that provides information about the frequency, intensity, and range of problem behaviours. Behavioural rating scales differ from self-report personality inventories in that items assess specific behaviours rather than personality characteristics, interests, or attitudes.

Behavioural rating scales are often used by parents to assess children's problem behaviours. The Child Behaviour Checklist (CBCL) (Achenbach, 2001), for example, asks parents to rate their children on more than 100 specific problem behaviours, including the following:

> refuses to eat
>
> is disobedient
>
> hits
>
> is unco-operative
>
> destroys own things

The scale yields an overall problem behaviour score and subscale scores on dimensions such as delinquency, aggressiveness, and physical problems. A clinician can compare a child's score on these dimensions with norms based on samples of age-mates.

Cognitive Assessment

Cognitive assessment involves the measurement of cognitions—thoughts, beliefs, and attitudes. Cognitive therapists believe that people who hold self-defeating or dysfunctional cognitions are at greater risk of developing emotional problems, such as depression, in the face of stressful or disappointing life experiences. They help clients replace dysfunctional thinking patterns with self-enhancing, rational thought patterns.

THOUGHT RECORDS Several methods of cognitive assessment have been developed. One of the most straightforward is the thought record or diary. Depressed clients may carry such diaries to record dysfunctional thoughts as they arise. Aaron Beck (A. T. Beck et al., 1979) designed a thought diary or Daily Record of Dysfunctional Thoughts to help clients identify thought patterns connected with troubling emotional states.

behavioural rating scale Method of behavioural assessment that involves the use of a scale to record the frequency of occurrence of target behaviours.

Each time a client experiences a negative emotion such as anger or sadness, entries are made to identify

1. the situation in which the emotional state occurred
2. the automatic or disruptive thoughts that passed through the client's mind
3. the type or category of disordered thinking that the automatic thought(s) represented (e.g., selective abstraction, overgeneralization, magnification, or absolutist thinking)
4. a rational response to the troublesome thought
5. the emotional outcome or final emotional response

A thought diary can become part of a treatment program in which a client learns to replace dysfunctional thoughts with rational alternative thoughts.

Cognitive assessment of a man's travel phobia might, for example, involve asking him to describe the thoughts that pass through his mind when he imagines himself approaching the fearful situation. He might also be asked to keep a diary of the thoughts he experiences while preparing for a drive or while driving toward a phobic stimulus, such as a bridge or an overpass. By examining thoughts, a therapist can help him identify styles of thinking that are linked to phobic episodes, such as catastrophizing ("I'm going to lose control of the car") and self-deprecation ("I'm just a jerk. I can't handle anything"). Several more formal methods of assessing cognitions have been developed, including those described next.

AUTOMATIC THOUGHTS QUESTIONNAIRE The Automatic Thoughts Questionnaire (ATQ-30) (Hollon & Kendall, 1980) has clients rate the weekly frequency of and degree of conviction associated with 30 automatic negative thoughts. (Automatic thoughts are thoughts that seem to just pop into our minds.) Sample items include the following:

I don't think I can go on.

I hate myself.

I've let people down.

A total score is obtained by summing the frequencies of occurrence of each item. Higher scores are considered typical of depressive thought patterns. The scale discriminates between subjects who attain high or low scores, with higher scores being more indicative of depressive symptoms (Blankstein & Segal, 2001). The 30-item ATQ has been statistically sorted into four categories or factors of related thoughts (see Table 2.3).

TABLE 2.3

Items Defining Factors on the Automatic Thoughts Questionnaire

Factor 1: Personal Maladjustment and Desire for Change	Something has to change. What's the matter with me? I wish I were a better person. What's wrong with me? I'm so disappointed in myself.
Factor 2: Negative Self-Concept and Negative Expectations	My future is bleak. I'm a failure. I'll never make it. My life's not going the way I wanted it to. I'm a loser. Why can't I ever succeed? I'm no good.
Factor 3: Low Self-Esteem	I'm worthless. I hate myself.
Factor 4: Giving Up/Helplessness	I can't finish anything. It's just not worth it.

Source: Adapted from Hollon & Kendall, 1980, pp. 383–395. Copyright Springer. Reprinted with the kind permission of Springer Science+Business Media B.V.

EVALUATING METHODS OF COGNITIVE ASSESSMENT Cognitive assessment has opened a new domain to the psychologist in understanding how disruptive thoughts are related to abnormal behaviour. Over the past three decades or so, cognitive and cognitive-behavioural therapists have been exploring what B. F. Skinner labelled the "black box"—people's internal states—to learn how thoughts and attitudes influence emotional states and behaviour.

The behavioural objection to cognitive techniques is that clinicians have no direct means of verifying clients' subjective experiences—their thoughts and beliefs. These are private experiences that can be reported but not observed and measured directly. Even though thoughts remain private experiences, reports of cognitions in the form of rating scales or checklists can be quantified and validated by reference to external criteria.

Physiological Measurement

We can also learn about abnormal behaviour by studying people's physiological responses. Anxiety, for example, is associated with arousal of the sympathetic division of the autonomic nervous system (see Chapter 3). Anxious people, therefore, show elevated heart rates and blood pressure, which can be measured directly by means of the pulse and a blood pressure cuff. People also sweat more heavily when they are anxious. When we sweat, our skin becomes wet, increasing its ability to conduct electricity. Sweating can be measured by means of the **electrodermal response** or **galvanic skin response** (GSR). (*Electrodermal* contains the Greek word *derma*, meaning "skin." The galvanic skin response is named after the Italian physicist and physician Luigi Galvani, who was a pioneer in research in electricity.) Measures of the GSR assess the amount of electricity that passes through two points on the skin, usually on the hand. We assume that the person's anxiety level correlates with the amount of electricity conducted across the skin.

The GSR is just one example of a physiological response measured through probes or sensors connected to the body. Another example is the **electroencephalograph** (EEG), which measures brainwaves by attaching electrodes to the scalp.

Changes in muscle tension are also often associated with states of anxiety or tension. They can be detected through the **electromyograph** (EMG), which monitors muscle tension through sensors attached to targeted muscle groups. (*Myo-* derives from the Greek *mys*, meaning "mouse" or "muscle." The Greeks observed that muscles moved mouselike beneath the skin.) Placement of EMG probes on the forehead can indicate muscle tension associated with tension headaches. Other probes are used to assess sexual arousal (see Chapter 9, "Gender Identity Disorder, Paraphilias, and Sexual Dysfunctions").

Ambulatory blood pressure devices allow clinicians to monitor clients' blood pressure at intervals throughout the day. Clients may log their concurrent activities or feeling states to reveal how changes in blood pressure are connected with stress.

P. J. Lang (1968) suggested that fear or anxiety consists of three different response systems: behavioural, physiological, and verbal. The behavioural response is avoidance of fear-inducing objects or situations. The physiological response can be measured in terms of changes in heart rate, GSR, or other bodily responses. The verbal system involves measurement of the subjective experience of anxiety. These response systems may act independently, however, so changes in one may not generalize to another. For example, people may report that they feel progressively less anxious when they confront a fearful situation, but their hearts may continue to pound. Or people may be able to approach a phobic situation although they report lingering feelings of anxiety or fear. Because response systems can be independent, most researchers recommend that investigations include multiple measures of anxiety or fear across response domains, such as self-reports of subjective feelings, behavioural approach measures, and physiological measurement.

Probing the Workings of the Brain

Advances in medical technology have made it possible to study the workings of the brain without the need for surgery (see Table 2.4).

electrodermal response Changes in the electrical conductivity of the skin following exposure to a stimulus.

galvanic skin response Measure of the change in electrical activity of the skin caused by increased activity of the sweat glands that accompanies states of sympathetic nervous system arousal, such as when a person is anxious. Abbreviated *GSR*.

electroencephalograph Instrument for measuring the electrical activity of the brain (brainwaves). Abbreviated *EEG*.

electromyograph Instrument often used in biofeedback training for measuring muscle tension. Abbreviated *EMG*.

ambulatory Able to walk about on one's own.

TABLE 2.4

Brain Activity and Imaging Techniques

Technique	How It Works
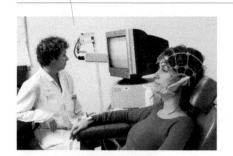	The **electroencephalograph** (EEG) is a record of the electrical activity of the brain. The EEG detects minute amounts of electrical activity in the brain, or brainwaves, that are conducted between electrodes. Certain brainwave patterns are associated with mental states such as relaxation and with the different stages of sleep. The EEG is used to examine brainwave patterns associated with psychological disorders, such as schizophrenia, and with brain damage. It is also used to study various abnormal behaviour patterns. The EEG is also used by medical personnel to reveal brain abnormalities such as tumours.
	Computerized tomography (CT scan) consists of a narrow X-ray beam aimed at the head. The radiation that passes through is measured from multiple angles. The CT scan reveals abnormalities in shape and structure that may be suggestive of lesions, blood clots, or tumours. A computer enables scientists to integrate the measurements into a three-dimensional picture of the brain. Evidence of brain damage that was once detectable only by surgery may now be displayed on a monitor.
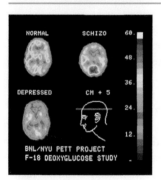	**Positron emission tomography** (the PET scan) is used to study the functioning of various parts of the brain. A small amount of a radioactive compound or tracer is mixed with glucose and injected into the bloodstream. When it reaches the brain, patterns of neural activity are revealed by measurement of the positrons—positively charged particles—emitted by the tracer. The glucose metabolized by parts of the brain generates a computer image of neural activity. Areas of greater activity metabolize more glucose. The PET scan has been used to learn which parts of the brain are most active (metabolize more glucose) when we are listening to music, solving a math problem, or using language. It can also be used to reveal differences in brain activity in people with schizophrenia.
	In **magnetic resonance imaging (MRI)**, a person is placed in a doughnut-shaped tunnel that generates a strong magnetic field. Radio waves of certain frequencies are directed at the head. As a result, parts of the brain emit signals that can be measured from several angles. As with the CT scan, the signals are integrated into a computer-generated image of the brain, which can be used to investigate brain abnormalities associated with schizophrenia (see Chapter 10) and other disorders such as obsessive-compulsive disorder (OCD).
	Functional magnetic resonance imaging (fMRI) is a form of resonance imaging that yields far more information than a basic MRI and produces static pictures of brain structure. In fMRI, computer-generated images show which regions of the brain are active during a specific mental activity, whether it is solving verbal riddles or visual puzzles, experiencing feelings, or initiating actions. The fMRI procedure has recently brought forth many intriguing discoveries in the neurobiology of stress.

(Continued)

TABLE 2.4 *(Continued)*

Technique	How It Works
(a) **(b)**	**Brain electrical activity mapping** (BEAM) is a type of EEG in which electrodes are attached to the scalp (photo a) to measure electrical activity in various regions of the brain. The left column of photo b shows the average level of electrical activity in the brains of 10 normal people (controls) at four time intervals. The right-hand column shows the average level of activity of subjects with schizophrenia during the same intervals. Higher activity levels are represented in increasing order by yellows, reds, and whites. The computer-generated image in the bottom centre summarizes differences in activity levels between the brains of normal subjects and those with schizophrenia. Areas of the brain depicted in blue show small differences between the groups. White areas represent larger differences
	Magnetoencephalography (MEG) measures brain activity in real time. In some cases, MEG can pinpoint the source of an epileptic seizure much more accurately than the traditional method of electroencephalography. Using a combination of MEG and MRI, neurosurgeons have a detailed brain map that allows them to remove just the damaged tissue while preserving healthy cells.

In conclusion, people's psychological problems, which are no less complex than people themselves, are assessed in many ways. In hospital settings, for instance, clients are commonly reviewed by a multidisciplinary team that may include psychologists, psychiatrists, social workers, neuropsychologists, neuroimaging specialists, and other mental health experts as needed. Clients are generally asked to explain their problems as best they can, and sometimes a computer does the asking. Psychologists can also draw on batteries of tests that assess anything from intelligence and personality to neuropsychological integrity. Many psychologists prefer to observe people's behaviour directly when possible, and sometimes devices that measure and record physiological markers of emotional states (e.g., changes in blood pressure, muscle tension, perspiration) are also used. Modern technology has provided several means of studying the structure and function of the brain. The methods of assessment selected by clinicians reflect the problems of their clients, the clinicians' theoretical orientations, and the clinicians' mastery of specialized technologies.

REVIEW IT

Methods of Assessment

- **What is a clinical interview?** A clinical interview involves the use of a set of questions designed to elicit relevant information from people seeking treatment. Interview formats include structured, semi-structured, and unstructured approaches.
- **What are psychological tests?** Psychological tests are structured methods of assessment used to evaluate reasonably stable traits such as intelligence and personality.
- **What are the major types of psychological tests used by clinicians?** Tests of intelligence, such as the Stanford-Binet Intelligence Scale and the Wechsler scale, are used for various purposes in clinical assessment, including determining evidence of mental retardation or cognitive impairment and assessing strengths and weaknesses. Self-report personal-

ity inventories, such as the MMPI, use structured items to measure various personality traits, such as anxiety, depression, and masculinity–femininity. These tests are considered objective in the sense that they offer a limited range of possible responses to items and use an empirical or objective method of test construction. Projective personality tests, such as the Rorschach and TAT, ask subjects to interpret ambiguous stimuli in the belief that their answers may shed light on their unconscious processes. Concerns persist about the validity of these tests, however.

- **What is neuropsychological assessment?** Neuropsychological assessment involves the use of psychological tests to indicate possible neurological impairment or brain defects. The Luria-Nebraska Test Battery measures perceptual skills, cognitive skills, and motor skills and performance that relate to specific areas of brain function.

- **What are some of the methods used in behavioural assessment?** In behavioural assessment, test responses are taken as samples of behaviour rather than as signs of underlying traits or dispositions. The behavioural examiner may conduct an assessment, which relates a problem behaviour to its antecedents and consequents. Methods of behavioural assessment include behavioural interviewing, self-monitoring, analogue or contrived measures, direct observation, and behavioural rating scales.

- **What is cognitive assessment?** Cognitive assessment focuses on the measurement of thoughts, beliefs, and attitudes in order to help identify distorted thinking patterns. Specific methods of assessment include the use of a thought record or diary and the use of rating scales such as the Automatic Thoughts Questionnaire (ATQ-30).

- **How do clinicians and researchers study physiological functioning?** Measures of physiological functioning include heart rate, blood pressure, galvanic skin response (GSR), muscle tension, and brainwave activity. Brain-imaging techniques such as EEG, CT scans, PET scans, MRI, fMRI, and BEAM probe the inner workings and structures of the brain.

CLASSIFICATION OF ABNORMAL BEHAVIOUR: THE DSM SYSTEM

First introduced in 1952, the DSM is now in its fourth edition, called the DSM-IV. Recently, a text revision—the *Diagnostic and Statistical Manual of Mental Disorders, 4th Edition, Text Revision*, better known as the DSM-IV-TR—was published, in which the descriptive and background information on each disorder was updated (American Psychiatric Association [APA], 2000a). The definitions, diagnostic categories, and diagnostic criteria in DSM-IV-TR remain the same as those in DSM-IV. The next revision comes in 2013 (see the Closer Look box "DSM-5: The Future of Psychiatric Diagnosis").

The WHO first published an international mortality and morbidity diagnostic classification standards manual in 1893 (WHO, 2001). The series, the *International Statistical Classification of Diseases and Related Health Problems*, is now in its 10th edition and, for brevity, is known as ICD-10. The Canadian Institute for Health Information (CIHI, 2001) petitioned the WHO for permission to make Canadian enhancements to the ICD-10, and the result was the ICD-10-CA, the Canadian modification.

We focus on the DSM as a method of classification because of its widespread adoption by mental health professionals. However, many psychologists and other professionals criticize the DSM on several grounds, such as relying too strongly on the medical model. Our focus on the DSM reflects recognition of its widespread use and should not be interpreted as a wholesale endorsement.

In the DSM, abnormal behaviour patterns are classified as *mental disorders*. Mental disorders involve emotional distress (typically depression or anxiety) and/or significant impairment in psychological functioning. Impaired functioning involves difficulties in meeting responsibilities at work, within the family, or within society at large. It also includes behaviour that places people at risk for personal suffering, pain, or death.

We should recognize that the DSM is used to classify disorders, not people. Rather than classify someone as a schizophrenic or a depressive, we refer to the person as an individual with schizophrenia or a person with major depression. This difference in terminology is not simply a matter of semantics. To label someone a schizophrenic carries an unfortunate and stigmatizing implication that a person's identity is defined in terms of the disorder that he or she may have or exhibit.

Diagnosis of mental disorders in the DSM system requires that the behaviour pattern not represent an expected or culturally appropriate response to a stressful event, such as the loss of a loved one. People who show signs of bereavement or grief following the death of loved ones are not considered disordered, even if their behaviour is significantly impaired. If their behaviour remains significantly impaired over an extended period of time, however, a diagnosis of a mental disorder might become appropriate.

The DSM system, like the medical model, treats abnormal behaviours as signs or symptoms of underlying pathologies. However, the DSM does not assume that abnormal behaviours necessarily reflect biological causes or defects. It recognizes that the causes of

Science as quackery? Scientologists like actor Tom Cruise view psychiatry as a barbaric and corrupt profession and encourage alternative care based on spiritual healing. The Church of Scientology says psychiatry has had a long history of improper and abusive care. The group's views have been strongly disputed, criticized, and condemned by experts in the medical and scientific community and have been a source of public controversy.

most mental disorders remain uncertain: some disorders may have purely biological causes, and some psychological; still others are likely to reflect a multifactorial model that comprises the interaction of biological, psychological, social (socioeconomic, sociocultural, and ethnic), and physical environmental factors.

J. C. Wakefield (1992a, 1992b, 1997, 2001) proposed that the term *disorder* be conceptualized as "harmful dysfunction." A harmful dysfunction represents a failure of a mental or physical system to perform its natural function, resulting in negative consequences or harm to an individual. By this definition, dysfunction alone is not enough to constitute a disorder. For example, a dysfunction involving a breakdown in the brain's ability to store or retrieve information would constitute a disorder if it leads to harmful consequences such as memory deficits that make it difficult for the person to function effectively. We find Wakefield's conceptualization of disorders as harmful dysfunctions to be instructive in our approach to this text, although we recognize that not all psychologists share his point of view (see Lilienfeld & Marino, 1995).

Features of the DSM

The DSM is descriptive, not explanatory. It describes the diagnostic features—or, in medical terms, symptoms—of abnormal behaviours, and does not attempt to explain their origins. An example of diagnostic criteria for pathological gambling, an impulse-control disorder, is shown in Table 2.5. As in other disorders, only a subset of the symptoms of disorders is required to consider a person as having the given disorder.

Abnormal behaviour patterns are categorized according to the clinical features they share. For example, abnormal behaviour patterns chiefly characterized by anxiety are classified as anxiety disorders (see Chapter 3, "Anxiety Disorders"). Behaviours chiefly characterized by disruptions in mood are categorized as mood disorders (see Chapter 4, "Mood Disorders and Suicide"). The DSM

TABLE 2.5

Sample Diagnostic Criteria for Pathological Gambling

A. Persistent and recurrent maladaptive gambling behavior as indicated by five (or more) of the following:

   (1) is preoccupied with gambling (e.g., preoccupied with reliving past gambling experiences, handicapping or planning the next venture, or thinking of ways to get money with which to gamble)

   (2) needs to gamble with increasing amounts of money in order to achieve the desired excitement

   (3) has repeated unsuccessful efforts to control, cut back, or stop gambling

   (4) is restless or irritable when attempting to cut down or stop gambling

   (5) gambles as a way of escaping from problems or of relieving a dysphoric mood (e.g., feelings of helplessness, guilt, anxiety, depression)

   (6) after losing money gambling, often returns another day to get even ("chasing" one's losses)

   (7) lies to family members, therapist, or others to conceal the extent of involvement with gambling

   (8) has committed illegal acts such as forgery, fraud, theft, or embezzlement to finance gambling

   (9) has jeopardized or lost a significant relationship, job, or educational or career opportunity because of gambling

   (10) relies on others to provide money to relieve a desperate financial situation caused by gambling

B. The gambling behavior is not better accounted for by a Manic Episode.

Source: Reprinted with permission from the *Diagnostic and Statistical Manual of Mental Disorders*, Fourth Edition, Text Revision, (Copyright ©2000). American Psychiatric Association. p. 674.

TABLE 2.6

The Multiaxial Classification System of the DSM-IV-TR

Axis I	Clinical Disorders Other Conditions That May Be a Focus of Clinical Attention
Axis II	Personality Disorders Mental Retardation
Axis III	General Medical Conditions
Axis IV	Psychosocial and Environmental Problems
Axis V	Global Assessment of Functioning

Source: Reprinted with permission from the *Diagnostic and Statistical Manual of Mental Disorders,* Fourth Edition, Text Revision, (Copyright ©2000). American Psychiatric Association. p. 27.

employs a multiaxial or multidimensional system of assessment that provides a broad range of information about an individual's functioning, not just a diagnosis. The system contains the following axes (see Table 2.6 for a summary):

1. *Axis I: Clinical Syndromes and Other Conditions That May Be a Focus of Clinical Attention.* Axis I incorporates a wide range of diagnostic classes such as anxiety disorders, mood disorders, schizophrenia and other psychotic disorders, adjustment disorders, and disorders usually first diagnosed during infancy, childhood, or adolescence (except for mental retardation, which is coded on Axis II). This axis also includes relationship problems, academic or occupational problems, and bereavement, which do not in themselves constitute definable psychological disorders. Psychological factors that affect medical conditions, such as anxiety that exacerbates an asthmatic condition or depressive symptoms that delay recovery from surgery, are also coded on Axis I.

2. *Axis II: Personality Disorders and Mental Retardation.* Personality disorders are enduring and rigid patterns of maladaptive behaviour that generally impair interpersonal relationships and social adaptation.

   People may be given either Axis I or Axis II diagnoses or a combination of the two when both apply. For example, a person may receive a diagnosis of an anxiety disorder (Axis I) and a second diagnosis of a personality disorder (Axis II).

3. *Axis III: General Medical Conditions.* All medical conditions and diseases that may be important to the understanding or treatment of an individual's mental disorder are coded under Axis III. Such would be the case if, for example, hypothyroidism is a direct cause of an individual's mood disorder (such as major depression). Medical conditions that affect the understanding or treatment of a mental disorder but are not direct causes of the disorder are also listed on Axis III. For instance, the presence of a heart condition may determine whether a particular course of pharmacotherapy should be prescribed to a depressed person.

4. *Axis IV: Psychosocial and Environmental Problems.* Axis IV identifies any psychosocial and environmental problems believed to affect a diagnosis, treatment, or outcome of a mental disorder. Psychosocial and environmental problems include negative life events (such as a job termination or a marital separation or divorce), homelessness or inadequate housing, lack of social support, the death or loss of a friend, and exposure to war or disasters. Some positive life events may also be listed, such as a job promotion, but only when they create problems for an individual, such as difficulties adapting to a new job.

5. *Axis V: Global Assessment of Functioning (GAF).* The clinician uses a scale similar to that shown in Table 2.7 (on page 62) to judge a client's current level of overall psychological, social, and occupational functioning.

An example of a diagnosis in the DSM-IV-TR multiaxial system is shown in Table 2.8.

syndromes Clusters of symptoms that are characteristic of particular disorders.

TABLE 2.7

Global Assessment of Functioning (GAF) Scale

Code

100 | 91	Superior functioning in a wide range of activities, life's problems never seem to get out of hand, is sought out by others because of his or her many positive qualities. No symptoms.
90 | 81	Absent or minimal symptoms (e.g., mild anxiety before an exam), **good functioning in all areas, interested and involved in a wide range of activities, socially effec-tive, generally satisfied with life, no more than everyday problems or concerns** (e.g., an occasional argument with family members).
80 | 71	If symptoms are present, they are transient and expectable reactions to psycho-social stressors (e.g., difficulty concentrating after family argument); **no more than slight impairment in social, occupational, or school functioning** (e.g., temporarily falling behind in schoolwork).
70 | 61	**Some mild symptoms** (e.g., depressed mood and mild insomnia) **OR some difficulty in social, occupational, or school functioning** (e.g., occasional truancy, or theft within the household), **but generally functioning pretty well, has some meaningful interper-sonal relationships.**
60 | 51	**Moderate symptoms** (e.g., flat affect and circumstantial speech, occasional panic attacks) **OR moderate difficulty in social, occupational, or school functioning** (e.g., few friends, conflicts with peers or co-workers).
50 | 41	**Serious symptoms** (e.g., suicidal ideation, severe obsessional rituals, frequent shoplifting) **OR any serious impairment in social, occupational, or school functioning** (e.g., no friends, unable to keep a job).
40 | 31	**Some impairment in reality testing or communication** (e.g., speech is at times illogi-cal, obscure, or irrelevant) **OR major impairment in several areas, such as work or school, family relations, judgment, thinking, or mood** (e.g., depressed man avoids friends, neglects family, and is unable to work; child frequently beats up younger children, is defiant at home, and is failing at school).
30 | 21	**Behavior is considerably influenced by delusions or hallucinations OR serious impairment in communication or judgment** (e.g., sometimes incoherent, acts grossly inappropriately, suicidal preoccupation) **OR inability to function in almost all areas** (e.g., stays in bed all day; no job, home, or friends).
20 | 11	**Some danger of hurting self or others** (e.g., suicide attempts without clear expectation of death; frequently violent; manic excitement) **OR occasionally fails to maintain min-imal personal hygiene** (e.g., smears feces) **OR gross impairment in communication** (e.g., largely incoherent or mute).
10 | 1	**Persistent danger of severely hurting self or others** (e.g., recurrent violence) **OR per-sistent inability to maintain minimal personal hygiene OR serious suicidal act** with clear expectation of death.
0	Inadequate information.

Source: Reprinted with permission from the *Diagnostic and Statistical Manual of Mental Disorders*, Fourth Edition, Text Revision, (Copyright ©2000). American Psychiatric Association. p. 34.

TABLE 2.8

Example of a Diagnosis in the Multiaxial DSM-IV-TR System

Axis I	Generalized Anxiety Disorder
Axis II	Dependent Personality Disorder
Axis III	Hypertension
Axis IV	Problem With Primary Support Group (marital separation); Occupational Problem (unemployment)
Axis V	GAF = 62

Evaluation of the DSM System

The two basic criteria used in assessing the value of a diagnostic system such as the DSM are reliability and validity. A diagnostic system may be considered **reliable** or consistent if various diagnosticians using the system arrive at the same diagnoses when they evaluate the same cases.

The most appropriate test of the **validity** of the DSM is its correspondence with observed behaviour. Certain DSM classes, such as anxiety disorders, appear to have generally good validity in terms of grouping people who display similar behaviours (T. A. Brown, Di Nardo, Lehman, & Campbell, 2001; Turner, Beidel, Dancu, & Keys, 1986). Both the validity and reliability of some other diagnostic classes, such as personality disorders, remain areas of active study and debate (Kendell & Jablensky, 2003).

Another measure of validity, called *predictive validity*, is based on the ability of the diagnostic system to predict the course the disorder is likely to follow or its response to treatment. Evidence is accumulating that individuals classified in certain categories respond better to certain types of medication. Individuals with bipolar disorder, for example, respond reasonably well to lithium (see Chapter 4). Specific forms of psychological treatment may also be more effective with certain diagnostic groupings. For example, individuals who have specific phobias (such as fear of heights) are generally highly responsive to behavioural techniques for reducing fears (see Chapter 3).

McGill University transcultural psychiatrists (e.g., Engelsmann, 2000; Kirmayer, 2001; Kirmayer & Minas, 2000; Prince, 2000) have argued that psychiatry in general and the DSM in particular should become more sensitive to diversity in culture and ethnicity. The behaviours included as diagnostic criteria in the DSM are determined by a consensus of mostly U.S.- and Canadian-trained psychiatrists, psychologists, and social workers. Had the American Psychiatric Association asked Asian-trained or Latin American–trained professionals to develop the diagnostic manual, for example, there might have been some different or revised diagnostic categories.

The Chinese Society of Psychiatry (CSP) has published its own system of classification of mental disorders, called *The Chinese Classification of Mental Disorders* (CCMD). Many Chinese psychiatrists believed the CCMD has special advantages over other manuals, such as simplicity, stability, the inclusion of culture-distinctive categories, and the exclusion of certain Western diagnostic categories. The Chinese translation of the ICD-10 was seen as linguistically complicated, containing very long sentences and awkward terms and syntax, and Chinese psychiatrists therefore developed their own classification (S. Lee, 2001).

Advantages and Disadvantages of the DSM System

Many consider the major advantage of the DSM to be its designation of specific diagnostic criteria. The DSM permits a clinician to readily match a client's complaints and associated features with specific standards to see which diagnosis best fits a case. The multiaxial system paints a comprehensive picture of clients by integrating information concerning abnormal behaviours, medical conditions that affect abnormal behaviours, psychosocial and environmental problems that may be stressful to an individual, and level of functioning. The possibility of multiple diagnoses prompts clinicians to consider presenting problems (Axis I) along with the relatively long-standing personality problems (Axis II) that may contribute to them.

Criticisms have also been levelled against the DSM system. As noted, questions remain about the system's reliability and validity. Some critics challenge specific diagnostic criteria, such as the requirement that major depression be present for two weeks before diagnosis (Kendler & Gardner, 1998). Others challenge its reliance on the medical model—a categorical approach to diagnosis in which a disorder is either present or absent. In the DSM system, problem behaviours are viewed as symptoms of underlying mental disorders in much the same way that physical symptoms are signs of underlying physical disorders. The very use of the term *diagnosis* presumes that the medical model is an appropriate basis for classifying abnormal behaviours. An alternative approach, the

reliable In psychological assessment, the consistency of a measuring instrument, such as a psychological test or rating scale. There are various ways of measuring reliability, such as test-retest reliability, internal consistency, and interrater reliability. Also see *validity*.

validity (1) With respect to tests, the degree to which a test measures the traits or constructs that it purports to measure. (2) With respect to experiments, the degree to which an experiment yields scientifically accurate and defensible results.

In May 2013, the fifth edition of the *Diagnostic and Statistical Manual of Mental Disorders* will be published. There are proposed revisions in almost every area of the field, all based on current research, peer review, and a lengthy investigation process.

WHY CHANGE TO DSM-5?

In the past 20 years there has been a great deal of new research and understanding in areas such as neurology, genetics, and behaviour that has significantly improved our understanding of mental health issues.

WHAT ARE THE MAJOR CHANGES?

Dimensional Rather Than Categorical

There will be a deliberate attempt to portray disorders as dimensional rather than categorical, showing the disorders as they truly are experienced rather than with a "one-size-fits-all" label. One good example is a significant reformulation in how personality disorders are identified and assessed. The change integrates disorder types with pathological personality traits and, most important, levels of impairment in what is known as personality functioning. In other words, an attempt will be made to incorporate an assessment of all clients' personality traits rather than simply those of clients who might have a personality disorder.

This would allow clinicians to systematically evaluate patients on the full range of symptoms they may be experiencing. For instance, information about depressed mood, anxiety level, sleep quality, and substance use would be important for clinicians to know regardless of the patient's diagnosis. Dimensional assessments would allow clinicians to rate both the presence and the severity of the symptoms as "very severe," "severe," "moderate," or "mild."

With its multidimensional framework, this hybrid model is very different from the way personality disorders are presented in the DSM-IV-TR, as rigid behavioural categories. The goal for the new criteria is to maximize their utility to clinicians and their benefit to patients.

One of the challenges in accurately diagnosing mental disorders is to evaluate the range of symptoms and other factors that appear in a single patient.

While specific criteria for disorders were a vast improvement over previous diagnostic guidelines for patients with mental disorders, there are real-world problems with this system of diagnosis. The categorical syndromes do not always fit with the reality of the range of symptoms that individuals experience. For example, individuals with schizophrenia often have other symptoms that do not match the criteria for diagnosing schizophrenia—insomnia, for example, or symptoms of depression and anxiety. Also, because the criteria for diagnosis are "yes/no" (i.e., does the individual have this disorder or not?), in most cases there is no method in DSM-IV to account for the severity of the disorder, and thus no specified way to determine if the patient is improving with treatment.

Reorganizing in a Developmental Lifespan Fashion

In the DSM-5, all the chapters will be organized according to a developmental lifespan, starting with neurodevelopmental disorders, which are often diagnosed in infancy and early childhood, and progressing through diagnostic areas more commonly diagnosed in adulthood, such as sleep-wake disorders. Within each category, the individual disorders are arranged so that those typically diagnosed in childhood are listed first. There is also emphasis on placing diagnostic areas that are similar closer to one another.

Criterion Changes and Replacement of DSM-IV Disorders With More Relevant Disorders

Criterion changes reflecting current research will be seen in almost every disorder. Several new disorders are to be included in the DSM-5, including, for example, under mood disorders, premenstrual dysphoric disorder, mixed features specifier, and mixed anxiety depression. The elimination of the following DSM-IV disorders has been proposed, also under mood disorders: mixed episode (to be replaced by mixed features specifier), bipolar I disorder–single manic episode, and mood disorder not otherwise specified. It is the hope that these updates better reflect the range and experience of mood disorders.

Example of a New Disorder: Hoarding Disorder

Proposed criteria for Hoarding Disorder (at the time of printing these were still under discussion):

A. Persistent difficulty discarding or parting with possessions, regardless of the value others may attribute to these possessions.

B. This difficulty is due to strong urges to save items and/or distress associated with discarding.

C. The symptoms result in the accumulation of a large number of possessions that fill up and clutter active living areas of the home or workplace to the extent that their intended use is no longer possible. If all living areas are uncluttered, it is only because of the interventions of third parties (e.g., family members, cleaners, authorities).

D. The symptoms cause clinically significant distress or impairment in social, occupational, or other important areas of functioning (including maintaining a safe environment for self and others).   >

E. The hoarding symptoms are not due to a general medical condition (e.g., brain injury, cerebrovascular disease).

F. The hoarding symptoms are not restricted to the symptoms of another mental disorder (e.g., hoarding due to obsessions in Obsessive-Compulsive Disorder, decreased energy in Major Depressive Disorder, delusions in Schizophrenia or another Psychotic Disorder, cognitive deficits in Dementia, restricted interests in Autism Spectrum Disorder, food storing in Prader-Willi Syndrome). (APA, 2010b)

dimensional model, quantifies multiple aspects of behaviour on the basis of degree of severity—a person may rate low on depression but high on psychosis. The dimensional model is under consideration for the upcoming revision of the DSM (DSM-V) (Trull, Tragesser, Solhan, & Schwartz-Mette, 2007). (See the Closer Look box for further details on the upcoming dimensional model.)

An additional problem is that the medical model focuses on categorizing psychological (or mental) disorders rather than describing people's behavioural strengths and weaknesses. Nor does the DSM attempt to place behaviour within a contextual framework that examines the settings, situations, and cultural contexts in which behaviour occurs.

Another concern about the DSM system is the potential for stigmatization of people labelled with psychiatric diagnoses. Our society is strongly biased against people who are labelled as mentally ill (Everett, 2006). They are often shunned by others and treated unfairly when it comes to many aspects of daily living, such as finding safe and adequate housing, landing employment, or obtaining insurance benefits. This, in turn, impedes their prospects for social integration and can contribute to a cycle of social disadvantages, including unemployment, family discord, divorce, and substance abuse (Kirby &

culture-bound disorders Patterns of behaviour that are found within only one or a few cultural contexts.

taijin-kyofu-sho Psychiatric syndrome found in Japan that involves excessive fear of offending or causing embarrassment to others. Abbreviated *TKS*.

FOCUS ON DIVERSITY
Culture-Bound Syndromes

Some patterns of psychological distress are limited to just one or a few cultures (Osborne, 2001). These **culture-bound disorders** are believed to be a manifestation, however exaggerated, of common folklore and belief patterns within the particular culture. For example, the psychiatric syndrome **taijin-kyofu-sho** (TKS) is common in Japan but rare elsewhere. TKS is characterized by excessive fear that one may behave in ways that will embarrass or offend other people (McNally, Cassiday, & Calamari, 1990). People with TKS may dread blushing in front of others for fear of causing them embarrassment, not for fear of embarrassing themselves. In Western culture, an excessive fear of social embarrassment is called a *social phobia* (see Chapter 3). Unlike people with TKS, however, people with social phobias have excessive concerns that they will be rejected by or embarrassed in front of others, not that they will embarrass other people. TKS primarily affects young Japanese men and is believed to be related to an emphasis in Japanese culture on not embarrassing others as well as deep concerns about issues of shame (McNally et al., 1990; Spitzer, Gibbon, Skodol, Williams, & First, 1994). S. C. Chang (1984) reports that TKS is diagnosed in 7% to 36% of the people treated by psychiatrists in Japan.

Culture-bound syndromes are portrayed in the same way as other psychological disorders in the DSM. However, in the case of some culture-bound disorders, there is scant evidence that they exist today (Trimble, Manson, Dinges, & Medicine, 1984). Such may be the case with two exotic conditions attributed to Aboriginal peoples on this continent: *pibloktoq*, a dissociative episode of excitement, seizures, and short-term coma allegedly found in Inuit communities; and ghost sickness, a psychotic-like preoccupation with death. These conditions are either extremely rare or may have never existed at all—at least not in the same way that depression, schizophrenia, or alcoholism exist in Aboriginal cultures (Waldram, 2004).

We generally think of culture-bound syndromes as abnormal behaviour patterns associated with folk cultures in non-Western societies. Yet some disorders, such as anorexia nervosa (discussed in Chapter 8, "Eating Disorders and Sleep Disorders") and dissociative identity disorder (formerly called *multiple personality disorder*; discussed in Chapter 5, "Dissociative and Somatoform Disorders"), are recognized as culture-bound syndromes specific to industrialized or technological societies such as Canada (T. M. Hall, 2011). They occur rarely, if at all, in other societies.

Keon, 2006; H. L. Stuart, 2005). Stigma also affects individuals directly when they internalize negative stereotypes, which can contribute to feelings of guilt, shame, and inferiority and to the wish to conceal their condition (Everett, 2006; H. L. Stuart, 2005). Indeed, the burden of stigmatization has been portrayed as causing greater and longer-lasting suffering than the mental disorder itself (Schulze & Angermeyer, 2003). Even family members, by association, may adopt attitudes of self-loathing and self-blame when they share in the negative stereotyping of people identified as mentally ill.

Some critics argue that recent editions of the DSM have been overzealous in removing theoretical concepts that explain the causes of abnormal behaviours. Description alone, such critics claim, is too superficial, and many clinicians are recommending a return to a more etiologically based diagnostic system for the next edition of the DSM. For instance, given the advances being made in the areas of genetics and brain-imaging research, some say an effort should be made to include neurobiological explanations of abnormal behaviour in the DSM-5 (Charney et al., 2002).

Many critics also claim that the DSM focuses too much on current behaviours and not enough on a person's history or childhood experiences. To address this, there are plans to incorporate developmental factors into the next edition. For example, the interactions between an individual and his or her social and physical environments play an important role in that person's development over the life course. By including in the DSM the salient risks and vulnerabilities at each stage of life for each mental disorder, clinicians will be in a better position to intervene or even prevent the onset of abnormal behaviours at earlier stages of development (Pine et al., 2002).

The DSM system, despite its critics, has become part and parcel of the everyday practice of most Canadian mental health professionals. It may be the one reference manual found on the bookshelves of nearly all such professionals, dog-eared from repeated use. Perhaps the DSM is best considered a work in progress, not a final product.

Now let us consider various ways of treating abnormal behaviour.

REVIEW IT

Classification of Abnormal Behaviour

- **What is the DSM and what are its major features?** The *Diagnostic and Statistical Manual of Mental Disorders* (DSM) is the most widely accepted system for classifying mental disorders. The DSM uses both specific diagnostic criteria to group patterns of abnormal behaviours that share common clinical features and a multiaxial system of evaluation.
- **Why is the DSM considered a multiaxial system?** The DSM system consists of five axes of classification: Axis I (Clinical Syndromes), Axis II (Personality Disorders), Axis III (General Medical Conditions), Axis IV (Psychosocial

and Environmental Problems), and Axis V (Global Assessment of Functioning, or GAF).
- **What are the major strengths and weaknesses of the DSM?** Strengths of the DSM include its use of specified diagnostic criteria and a multiaxial system to provide a comprehensive picture of an individual's functioning. Weaknesses may include the reliability and validity of certain diagnostic categories and, for some, the adoption of a medical model framework for classifying abnormal behaviour patterns.

METHODS OF TREATMENT

Carla, a 19-year-old undergraduate student, had been crying more or less continuously for several days. She felt that her life was falling apart, that her academic aspirations were in shambles, and that she was a disappointment to her parents. The thought of suicide had crossed her mind. She could not seem to drag herself out of bed in the morning and had withdrawn from her friends. Her misery seemed to descend on her from nowhere, although she could pinpoint some pressures in her life: a couple of poor grades at school, a recent breakup with a boyfriend, and some adjustment problems with roommates.

The psychologist who examined her arrived at a diagnosis of major depressive disorder. Had she broken her leg, her treatment from a qualified professional would have followed a fairly standard course. Yet the treatment that Carla or someone else with a psychological disorder receives is likely to vary not only with the type of disorder involved but also with the therapeutic orientation and professional background of the helping professional. A psychiatrist might recommend a course of antidepressant medication, perhaps in combination with some form of psychotherapy. A cognitively oriented psychologist might suggest a program of cognitive therapy to help Carla identify dysfunctional thoughts that may underlie her depression, whereas a psychodynamic therapist might recommend she begin psychodynamically oriented therapy to uncover inner conflicts originating in childhood that may lie at its root.

In these next sections, we focus on ways of treating psychological disorders. In later chapters, we see how these treatment approaches are applied to particular disorders. Here we focus on introducing the treatments themselves. We will see that the biological and psychological perspectives have spawned corresponding approaches to treatment. First, however, we consider the major types of mental health professionals who treat psychological or mental disorders and the different roles they play.

Types of Mental Health Professionals in Canada

Clinical psychologists, psychiatrists, and social workers constitute the majority of licensed mental health professionals in Canada. These three groups are regulated under provincial and territorial jurisdictions. But for the fourth broad cluster, psychotherapists and counsellors, there remains a lack of common pan-Canadian titles and clearly defined scopes of practice. To date, only Quebec, Alberta, British Columbia, and Ontario have passed or are in the process of passing legislation that regulates the practices of psychotherapy and/ or counselling. Distinguishing among the various helping professionals can be confusing to the public (Farberman, 1997), and thus people seeking treatment are advised to inquire about the training and licensure of helping professionals. In Ontario, there is a movement toward a College of Registered Psychotherapists and Registered Mental Health Therapists to regulate these professionals, who come from a wide variety of backgrounds.

Another reason for confusion is that all the different types of mental health providers, such as clinical psychologists, psychiatrists, clinical social workers, and a wide range of other mental health professionals, practise **psychotherapy** or "talk therapy"—a psychologically based method of treatment involving a series of verbal interchanges between clients and therapists taking place over a period of time, usually on a one-session-per-week basis. The particular approach used by individual psychotherapists reflects their theoretical orientation, such as psychodynamic, behavioural, humanistic, and cognitive. Some therapists adopt an **eclectic orientation**, which means they draw on the theories and techniques espoused by two or more theoretical orientations. We'll return to look at these different approaches to psychotherapy. But first, let's consider the different roles that the major types of mental health professionals play.

psychotherapy Method of helping involving a systematic interaction between a therapist and a client that brings psychological principles to bear on influencing the client's thoughts, feelings, or behaviours in order to help that client overcome abnormal behaviour or adjust to problems in living.

eclectic orientation Adoption of principles or techniques from various systems or theories.

CLINICAL PSYCHOLOGISTS A clinical psychologist is a psychologist trained in the assessment, diagnosis, and treatment of psychological problems. All psychologists, including clinical psychologists, must have at least a master's degree. In most provinces, they must have a doctoral degree (PhD or PsyD) to be licensed to practise psychology independently (H. P. Edwards, 2000). Psychologists use various techniques to diagnose psychological problems, including clinical interviews, psychological tests, and behavioural observations (Canadian Psychological Association [CPA], 2002). They also use psychotherapy as a means of treating these problems. Psychologists often receive extensive training in research, which helps them conduct studies in clinical settings and critically evaluate the clinical literature.

PSYCHIATRISTS Psychiatrists are licensed physicians who have earned medical degrees such as the Doctor of Medicine (MD). They have also completed a post-doctoral residency program in psychiatry that provides specialized training in diagnosing and treating psychological problems. Like psychologists, psychiatrists conduct psychotherapy and diagnostic interviews. Unlike psychologists, they can prescribe drugs and administer other biological treatments, such as electroconvulsive therapy (ECT). Psychiatrists often rely on psychologists for psychological testing to help determine a diagnosis or course of treatment.

SOCIAL WORKERS   Social workers earn a graduate degree in social work at the master's level (Master of Social Work, MSW) or doctoral level (Doctor of Social Work, DSW). They receive supervised training in helping people adjust and utilize social-support services and community agencies. Many social workers conduct psychotherapy or specialize in marital or family therapy.

Biological Therapies

There is a growing emphasis in Canadian psychiatry on the biologically based treatment of abnormal behaviour, especially drug therapies (Gauthier, 1999). Biologically based approaches are generally administered by medical doctors, many of whom have specialized training in psychiatry or **psychopharmacology**. Many family physicians or general practitioners also prescribe psychotherapeutic or psychotropic drugs for their patients, however.

Although the biological or medical approaches have had dramatic success in treating some forms of abnormal behaviour, they also have their limitations. For one, biological therapies may have unwelcome or dangerous side effects. There is also the potential for abuse. One of the most commonly prescribed minor tranquillizers, Valium, has become a major drug of abuse among people who become psychologically and physiologically dependent on it. Psychosurgery has been all but eliminated as a form of treatment because of serious harmful effects of earlier procedures. There are, however, some new experimental biologically based techniques that show promise, such as transcranial magnetic stimulation (TMS), gene splicing, epigenetic therapy, and stem cell interventions.

Different classes of psychotropic drugs are used in the treatment of various types of mental health problems.

ANTI-ANXIETY DRUGS   Anti-anxiety drugs (also called *anxiolytics*, from the Greek *anxietas*, meaning "anxiety," and *lysis*, meaning "bringing to an end") are drugs that combat anxiety and reduce states of muscle tension. They include mild tranquillizers, such as diazepam (Valium); barbiturates, such as meprobamate (Miltown); and sedative-hypnotics, such as triazolam (Halcion) and flurazepam (Dalmane). Clonazepam and lorazepam are widely used in practice, and fall into the category of mild tranquillizers like Valium.

Anti-anxiety drugs depress the level of activity in certain parts of the central nervous system (CNS). In turn, the CNS decreases the level of sympathetic nervous system activity, reducing the respiration rate and heart rate and lessening states of anxiety and tension. Minor tranquillizers such as Valium grew in popularity when physicians became concerned about the use of more potent sedatives, such as barbiturates, which are highly addictive and extremely dangerous when taken in overdoses or mixed with alcohol. Unfortunately, it has become clear that the minor tranquillizers also can, and often do, lead to physiological dependence (addiction). People who are dependent on Valium may go into convulsions when they abruptly stop taking it. Deaths have been reported among people who mix mild tranquillizers with alcohol or who are unusually sensitive to them. There are other less severe side effects, such as fatigue, drowsiness, and impaired motor co-ordination, which might reduce one's ability to function or to operate an automobile. Regular usage of benzodiazepines can also produce **tolerance**, a physiological sign of dependence: the need over time for increasing dosages of a drug to achieve the same effect. Quite commonly, patients become involved in tugs of war with their physicians as they demand increased dosages despite their physicians' concerns about the potential for abuse and dependence.

When used on a short-term basis, anti-anxiety drugs can be safe and effective in treating anxiety and insomnia. Yet drugs by themselves do not teach people more adaptive ways of solving their problems and may encourage them to rely on a chemical agent to cope with stress rather than develop active means of coping. Drug therapy is thus often combined with psychotherapy to help people with anxiety complaints deal with the

psychopharmacology Field of study that examines the effects of drugs on behaviour and psychological functioning and explores the use of psychoactive drugs in the treatment of emotional disorders.

tolerance Physical habituation to a drug so that with frequent usage, higher doses are needed to attain similar effects.

psychological and situational bases of their problems (Talbot & McMurray, 2004). However, combining drug therapy and psychotherapy may present special problems and challenges. For one, drug-induced relief from anxiety may reduce clients' motivation to try to solve their problems. For another, medicated clients who develop skills for coping with stress in psychotherapy may fail to retain what they have learned once the tranquillizers are discontinued, or find themselves too tense to employ their newly acquired skills.

Rebound anxiety is another problem associated with regular use of minor tranquillizers. Many people who regularly use anti-anxiety drugs report that anxiety or insomnia returns in a more severe form once they discontinue them. For some, this may represent a fear of not having the drugs to depend on. For others, rebound anxiety might reflect changes in biochemical processes that are not well understood at present.

ANTIPSYCHOTIC DRUGS Antipsychotic drugs, also called **neuroleptics**, are commonly used to treat the more flagrant features of schizophrenia or other psychotic disorders, such as hallucinations, delusions, and states of confusion. Many of these drugs, including chlorpromazine (Thorazine), belong to the phenothiazine class of chemicals. Phenothiazines appear to control psychotic features by blocking the action of the neurotransmitter dopamine at receptor sites in the brain. Risperidone (Risperdal) and quetiapine (Seroquel) are also antipsychotics. Although the underlying causes of schizophrenia remain unknown, researchers suspect a dysregulation of the dopamine system in the brain may be involved (see Chapter 10). Clozapine (Clozaril), a neuroleptic of a different chemical class than the phenothiazines, has been shown to be effective in treating many people with schizophrenia whose symptoms were unresponsive to other neuroleptics (see Chapter 10). The use of clozapine must be carefully monitored, however, because of potentially dangerous side effects.

The use of neuroleptics has greatly reduced the need for more restrictive forms of treatment for severely disturbed patients, such as physical restraints and confinement in padded cells, and has lessened the need for long-term hospitalization. The introduction of major tranquillizers in the mid-1950s was one of the major factors that led to a massive exodus of chronic mental patients from institutions. Many ex-hospitalized patients have been able to resume family life and hold jobs while continuing to take their medications.

Neuroleptics are not without their problems, including potential side effects such as muscular rigidity and tremors. Although these side effects are generally controllable by the use of other drugs, long-term use of antipsychotic drugs (except possibly clozapine) can produce a potentially irreversible and disabling motor disorder called tardive dyskinesia (see Chapter 10), characterized by uncontrollable eye blinking, facial grimaces, lip smacking, and other involuntary movements of the mouth, eyes, and limbs. Researchers are experimenting with lowered dosages, intermittent drug regimens, and the use of new medications to reduce the risk of such complications.

ANTIDEPRESSANTS Three major classes of **antidepressants** are used in treating depression: **tricyclics**, **monoamine oxidase (MAO) inhibitors**, and **selective serotonin-reuptake inhibitors (SSRIs)**. The first two kinds of antidepressants, tricyclics and MAO inhibitors, increase the availability of the neurotransmitters norepinephrine and serotonin in the brain. Some of the more common tricyclics are imipramine (Tofranil) and amitriptyline (Elavil). The MAO inhibitors include such drugs as phenelzine (Nardil) and tranylcypromine (Parnate). Tricyclic antidepressants (TCAs) are commonly favoured over MAO inhibitors because of potentially serious side effects associated with MAO inhibitors.

The third class of antidepressants, SSRIs, has more specific effects on serotonin function in the brain. Drugs in this class, which include fluoxetine (Prozac), are now the most widely prescribed antidepressants on the market. They increase the availability of serotonin in the brain by interfering with its reuptake by the transmitting neuron.

Many of the newer antidepressants are not pure SSRIs. These include Effexor, Cymbalta, and Pristiq, which are serotonin-norepinephrine reuptake inhibitors (SNRIs), and Remeron, a noradrenergic and specific serotonergic antidepressant (NaSSA).

Slightly more than half of the people with clinically significant depression who are treated with antidepressants of the tricyclic class will respond favourably (Depression Guideline Panel, 1993). A favourable response to treatment does not mean depression is

rebound anxiety Occurrence of strong anxiety following withdrawal from a tranquillizer.

neuroleptics Group of antipsychotic drugs used in the treatment of schizophrenia, such as the phenothiazines (e.g., Thorazine).

antidepressants Types of drugs that act to relieve depression. Tricyclics, MAO inhibitors, and selective serotonin-reuptake inhibitors are the major classes of antidepressants.

tricyclics Group of antidepressant drugs that increase the activity of norepinephrine and serotonin in the brain by interfering with the reuptake of these neurotransmitters by transmitting neurons. Also called *TCAs* (tricyclic antidepressants).

monoamine oxidase (MAO) inhibitors Antidepressants that act to increase the availability of neurotransmitters in the brain by inhibiting the actions of an enzyme, monoamine oxidase, that normally breaks down or degrades neurotransmitters (norepinephrine and serotonin) in the synaptic cleft.

selective serotonin-reuptake inhibitors (SSRIs) Type of antidepressant medication that prevents serotonin from being taken back up by the transmitting neuron, thus increasing its action.

Putting a public face on mental illness. Oscar-winning actress Catherine Zeta-Jones suffers from bipolar disorder, and has previously checked herself into a mental health facility for treatment. Bipolar disorder can usually be controlled with a combination of medication and therapy. Lithium is one of the most common treatments.

eliminated, however. Overall, the effects of tricyclic antidepressants (TCAs) appear to be modest (R. P. Greenberg, Bornstein, Greenberg, & Fisher, 1992). Nor does a particular antidepressant appear to be clearly more effective than any other (Kennedy, Lam, Cohen, Ravindran, & CANMAT Depression Working Group, 2001). Even Prozac, which was hailed by some as a "wonder drug," appears, on the basis of present evidence, to be no more effective than the TCAs (R. P. Greenberg, Bornstein, Zborowski, Fisher, & Greenberg, 1994). The preferred antidepressant depends on individual patient characteristics, including the subtype and severity of depression, tolerance of side effects and safety, and interaction with other approaches such as psychotherapy (Kennedy et al., 2001). Overall, the magnitude of the effect of antidepressant medication compared with a placebo increases with the severity of depression; for patients with very severe depression, the benefit of medications over a placebo is substantial (Elkin, 2010).

We shall see that antidepressants also have beneficial effects in treating a wide range of psychological disorders, including an array of anxiety disorders (see Chapter 3) and eating disorders (see Chapter 8). As research into the underlying causes of these disorders continues, we may find that dysregulation of neurotransmitters plays a key role in their development.

LITHIUM Lithium carbonate, a salt of the metal lithium in tablet form, has demonstrated remarkable effectiveness in stabilizing the dramatic mood swings associated with bipolar disorder (formerly called manic depression) (see Chapter 4). Because of its potential toxicity, the blood levels of patients maintained on lithium must be carefully monitored (Yatham et al., 2005). Like people with diabetes who must take insulin throughout their lifetimes to control their disease, people with bipolar disorder may have to continue using lithium indefinitely to control the disorder.

electroconvulsive therapy Induction of a convulsive seizure by means of passing an electric current through the head; used primarily in the treatment of severe depression. Abbreviated *ECT*.

ELECTROCONVULSIVE THERAPY In 1939, the Italian psychiatrist Ugo Cerletti (1877–1963) introduced the technique of **electroconvulsive therapy** (ECT) in psychiatric treatment. Cerletti had observed in some slaughterhouses the practice of using electric shock to render animals unconscious. He saw that the shocks also produced convulsions. Cerletti incorrectly believed, as did other researchers in Europe at the time, that convulsions of the type found in epilepsy were incompatible with schizophrenia and that a method of inducing convulsions might be used to cure the disorder.

After the introduction of the phenothiazines in the 1950s, the use of ECT became generally limited to the treatment of severe depression. The introduction of antidepressants has further limited the use of ECT. Even though rates of ECT use are down from the 1960s, one Ontario study found that rates (roughly 12.5 per 100 000) have remained constant since the 1990s and are three times higher for elderly than for younger patients (Rapoport, Mamdani, & Herrmann, 2006).

Electroconvulsive therapy remains a source of controversy. For instance, many people, including many professionals, are uncomfortable about the idea of passing an electric shock through a person's head, even if the level of shock is closely regulated and the convulsions are controlled by drugs. Then there are the potential side effects. ECT often produces dramatic relief from severe depression, but concerns remain about its potential for inducing cognitive deficits, such as memory loss. A review of the evidence, however, finds memory losses following ECT to be temporary, except perhaps for some persistent loss of memory for events transpiring immediately around the time of the procedure itself (Devanand, Dwork, Hutchinson, Bolwig, & Sackeim, 1994).

A recent Canadian review found that up to 15% of depressive patients experience treatment-resistant depression (TRD) (Berlim & Turecki, 2007). Although controversies concerning the use of ECT persist, the facts support its effectiveness in helping people overcome severe depression that fails to respond to psychotherapy or antidepressant medication (Rabheru, 2001; Rapoport et al., 2006). Moreover, ECT may help reduce the risk of suicide among severely depressed people (Martin, Cloninger, Guze, & Clayton, 1985). However, ECT is usually considered a treatment of last resort, after less intrusive methods of treating TRD have been tried and have failed.

An alternative form of brain stimulation treatment for depression—**repetitive transcranial magnetic stimulation** (rTMS)—is now used in Canada. In rTMS, a strong magnetic field is directed through a coil held against the head for several daily hour-long sessions. Some early indications have shown rTMS to be an effective, painless, noninvasive procedure with zero to low side effects (Fitzgerald, Benitez, et al., 2006; Fitzgerald, Huntsman, Gunewardene, Kulkami, & Daskalakis, 2006). In some cases, it can be a practical alternative to ECT, as it is a less costly treatment and is not associated with anaesthetic and other ECT risks (Rosa et al., 2006; Schulze-Rauschenbach et al., 2005). Find out more about the use of rTMS in the treatment of depression in Chapter 4.

PSYCHOSURGERY Psychosurgery is even more controversial than ECT and rarely practised today. The most widely used form of psychosurgery was the **prefrontal lobotomy**, no longer performed, in which the nerve pathways linking the thalamus to the prefrontal lobes of the brain are surgically severed. It was believed that by severing the connections between the thalamus and the higher brain centres in the frontal lobe of the cerebral cortex, the patient's violent or aggressive tendencies could be controlled. The prefrontal lobotomy was developed by the Portuguese neurologist António Egas Moniz, who in 1949 won a Nobel Prize for the procedure. By the 1960s, more than 10 000 mental patients in Canada had undergone the operation (Simmons, 1987). Although the operation did reduce violent and agitated behaviour in many cases, it was not always successful. In a cruel, ironic twist, one of Moniz's treatment failures later shot him, leaving him paralyzed from a bullet that lodged in his spine.

Electroconvulsive therapy (ECT). ECT is helpful in many cases of severe or prolonged depression that do not respond to other forms of treatment. Still, its use remains controversial.

Many distressing side effects are associated with the prefrontal lobotomy, including hyperactivity, impaired learning ability and reduced creativity, distractibility, apathy, overeating, withdrawal, epileptic-type seizures, and even death. One famous case was that of Rosemary Kennedy, the sister of John F. Kennedy, who was reportedly subject to violent mood swings and a stormy personality; however, some observers have since attributed this behaviour to her difficulties in keeping up with her active siblings. In 1941, when Rosemary was 23, her father, Joseph Kennedy, was told by her doctors that a new procedure would help calm her mood swings, which the family found difficult to handle at home. Her father gave permission for the prefrontal lobotomy to be performed by Walter Freeman and James Watts. During the surgery Rosemary had a mild tranquillizer but was awake. Dr. Freeman asked her to recite the Lord's Prayer or sing "God Bless America" or count backwards. An estimate of how far to cut was based on how she responded. When she became incoherent, they stopped. After the surgery, Rosemary was reduced to an infantile mentality that left her incontinent and staring blankly at walls for hours. Her verbal skills were reduced to unintelligible babble. In 1949, Rosemary moved to an institution and was visited on regular occasions by her sister Eunice Kennedy Shriver, who became the founder of the Special Olympics.

The occurrence of these side effects, combined with the introduction of the phenothiazines, led to the elimination of the operation. Several more sophisticated psychosurgery techniques have been introduced in more recent years for various purposes. Generally speaking, they are limited to smaller parts of the brain and produce less damage than the prefrontal lobotomy. These operations have been performed to treat such problems as

Stimulating the brain to improve mood? In deep brain stimulation (DBS), electrodes are inserted into the brain, transmitting impulses to brain cells. The method is already approved by the FDA as a treatment for obsessive-compulsive disorder and is showing promise for other mental illnesses.

intractable aggression, depression, and psychotic behaviour; chronic pain; some forms of epilepsy; and persistent obsessive-compulsive disorder (Baer et al., 1995; Irle, Exner, Thielen, Weniger, & Rüther, 1998; Sachdev & Hay, 1996). Follow-up studies of such procedures have shown marked improvement in about one quarter to one half of cases. Concerns about possible complications of these procedures, including decrements in intellectual functioning (Irle et al., 1998), have greatly limited their use.

Deep Brain Stimulation

Deep brain stimulation involves implanting electrodes within the part of the brain that affects mood. During deep brain stimulation, electrical impulses transmitted through the electrodes deep within the brain affect brain cells and chemicals to relieve depression. The amount of stimulation delivered by the electrodes is controlled by a pacemaker-like device placed under the skin in the upper chest. A wire that travels under the skin connects the device, called a *pulse generator*, to the electrodes in the brain.

Although it's approved for other conditions, deep brain stimulation for depression hasn't been approved by the U.S. Food and Drug Administration (FDA). It's still being studied as an experimental treatment. Most candidates for deep brain stimulation are participants in clinical trials.

Deep brain stimulation is an established treatment for essential tremor and Parkinson's disease. Some people with Parkinson's who underwent deep brain stimulation reported an improved mood. Because of those results, deep brain stimulation is being studied as a possible depression treatment to be used when standard treatments don't work. Standard treatments include antidepressants, psychological counselling (psychotherapy), and electroconvulsive therapy (ECT).

Sending electrical impulses to areas of the brain linked with mood affects brain cells and brain chemistry. While this can help ease depression symptoms, researchers are still investigating exactly how deep brain stimulation improves mood.

Deep brain stimulation also shows some promise for some other mental illnesses. It has been approved by the FDA as a treatment for severe and debilitating obsessive-compulsive disorder (OCD). It's also being investigated to see whether it may help with Tourette syndrome, chronic pain, and other disorders.

Although initial results are promising, more research is needed to determine whether deep brain stimulation can be considered a safe and effective treatment for depression. Researchers are still trying to identify the best locations for the electrode implants to help reduce symptoms while causing the fewest and least severe side effects.

In a systematic review of clinical trials of deep brain stimulation for OCD and treatment-resistant depression, Lakhan and Callaway (2010) found that about half of patients did show dramatic improvement. They caution that procedures differed from study to study, and the numbers of patients were usually too small to produce meaningful statistics or make valid inferences as to who will respond to treatment; however, deep brain stimulation is a promising technique for both OCD and treatment-resistant depression.

We now consider the major types of psychotherapy and their relationships to the theoretical models from which they derive.

Psychodynamic Therapies

Psychoanalysis is the form of psychodynamic therapy originated by Sigmund Freud. Practitioners of psychoanalysis, called *psychoanalysts*, view psychological problems as rooted in early childhood experiences and unconscious conflicts. Freud used psychoanalysis to help clients gain insight into and resolve unconscious conflicts. Working through these conflicts, the ego would be freed of the need to maintain defensive behaviours—such as phobias, obsessive-compulsive behaviours, and hysterical complaints—that shield it from recognition of inner turmoil.

Freud summed up the goal of psychoanalysis by saying, "Where id was, there shall ego be." This meant, in part, that psychoanalysis could help shed the light of awareness, represented by the conscious ego, on the inner workings of the id. But Freud did not expect or intend that clients should seek to become conscious of all repressed material—of all their impulses, wishes, fears, and memories. The aim, rather, was to replace defensive behaviour with more adaptive behaviour. By so doing, clients could find gratification without incurring social or self-condemnation.

Through this process a man with a phobia of knives might become aware he had been repressing impulses to vent a murderous rage against his father. His phobia keeps him from having contact with knives, thereby serving a hidden purpose of keeping his homicidal impulses in check. A woman with a loss of sensation in her hand that could not be explained medically might come to see that she harboured guilt over urges to masturbate. The loss of sensation may have prevented her from acting on these urges. Through confronting hidden impulses and the conflicts they produce, clients learn to sort out their feelings and find more constructive and socially acceptable ways of handling their impulses and wishes. The ego is then freed to focus on more constructive interests.

The major methods that Freud used to accomplish these goals were free association, dream analysis, and analysis of the transference relationship.

FREE ASSOCIATION You are asked to lie down on a couch and to say anything that enters your mind. The psychoanalyst (or *analyst*, for short) sits in a chair behind you, out of direct view. For the next 45 or 50 minutes, you let your mind wander, saying whatever pops in, or saying nothing at all. The analyst remains silent most of the time, prompting you occasionally to utter whatever crosses your mind, no matter how seemingly trivial, no matter how personal. This process continues, typically for three or four sessions a week, for a period of several years. At certain points in the process, the analyst offers an interpretation, drawing your attention to connections between your disclosures and unconscious conflicts.

TRANSFERENCE Freud found that clients responded to him not only as an individual but also in ways that reflected their feelings and attitudes toward other important people in their lives. A young female client might respond to him as a father figure, transferring, in an act of **displacement**, onto Freud her feelings toward her own father. A man might also view him as a father figure, responding to him as a rival in a manner Freud believed might reflect the man's unresolved Oedipal complex.

The process of analyzing and working through the **transference relationship** is considered an essential component of psychoanalysis. Freud believed that the transference relationship provides a vehicle for the re-enactment of childhood conflicts with parents. Clients may react to the analyst with the same feelings of anger, love, or jealousy they felt toward their own parents. Freud termed the enactment of these childhood conflicts the *transference neurosis*. This "neurosis" had to be successfully analyzed and worked through for clients to succeed in psychoanalysis.

Childhood conflicts usually involve unresolved feelings of anger or rejection or needs for love. For example, a client may interpret any slight criticism by the therapist as a devastating blow, transferring feelings of self-loathing that the client repressed from childhood experiences of parental rejection. Transferences may also distort or colour the client's relationships with others, such as a spouse or employer. Clients might relate to their spouse as they had to their parents, perhaps demanding too much from them or unjustly accusing them of being insensitive or uncaring. Or they might not give new friends or lovers the benefit of a fair chance if they had been mistreated by others who played similar roles in their past. The analyst helps the client recognize transference relationships, especially the therapy transference, and to work through the residues of childhood feelings and conflicts that lead to self-defeating behaviour in the present.

According to Freud, transference is a two-way street. Freud felt he transferred his underlying feelings onto his clients, perhaps viewing a young man as a competitor or a

displacement In psychodynamic theory, a type of defence mechanism that involves the transferring of impulses toward threatening or unacceptable objects onto more acceptable or safer objects.

transference relationship In psychoanalysis, a client's transfer or generalization to the analyst of feelings and attitudes the client holds toward important figures in his or her life.

woman as a rejecting love interest. Freud referred to the feelings that he projected onto clients as **countertransference**. Psychoanalysts in training are expected to undergo psychoanalysis themselves to help them uncover motives that might lead to countertransferences in their therapeutic relationships. In their therapeutic training, psychoanalysts learn to monitor their own reactions in therapy so as to become better aware of when and how countertransferences intrude on the therapy process.

Although the analysis of the therapy transference is a crucial element of psychoanalytic therapy, it generally takes months or years for a transference relationship to develop and be resolved. This is one reason why psychoanalysis is typically a lengthy and expensive process.

MODERN PSYCHODYNAMIC APPROACHES   Although some psychoanalysts continue to practise traditional psychoanalysis in much the same manner as Freud, briefer and less intensive forms of psychodynamic treatment have emerged (Strupp, 1992). These newer approaches are often referred to as *brief psychodynamic therapies*. They are able to reach clients who are seeking more focused and less costly forms of treatment, perhaps once or twice a week.

Like Freudian psychoanalysis, the newer psychodynamic approaches aim to uncover unconscious motives and break down resistances and psychological defences, yet they focus more on the client's present relationships and encourage the client to make adaptive behaviour changes. As a result of the briefer format, therapy may entail a more open and direct exploration of the client's defences and transference relationships than was traditionally the case. Unlike the traditional approach, the client and therapist generally sit facing each other. Rather than offer an occasional interpretation, the therapist engages in more frequent verbal give-and-take with the client, as in the following vignette. Note how the therapist uses interpretation to help the client, Mr. Arianes, achieve insight into how his relationship with his wife involves a transference of his childhood relationship with his mother:

Mr. Arianes:	I think you've got it there, Doc. We weren't communicating. I wouldn't tell her [his wife] what was wrong or what I wanted from her. Maybe I expected her to understand me without saying anything.
Therapist:	Like the expectations a child has of its mother.
Mr. Arianes:	Not my mother!
Therapist:	Oh?
Mr. Arianes:	No, I always thought she had too many troubles of her own to pay attention to mine. I remember once I got hurt on my bike and came to her all bloodied up. When she saw me she got mad and yelled at me for making more trouble for her when she already had her hands full with my father.
Therapist:	Do you remember how you felt then?
Mr. Arianes:	I can't remember, but I know that after that I never brought my troubles to her again.
Therapist:	How old were you?
Mr. Arianes:	Nine. I know that because I got that bike for my ninth birthday. It was a little too big for me still, that's why I got hurt on it.
Therapist:	Perhaps you carried this attitude into your marriage.
Mr. Arianes:	What attitude?
Therapist:	The feeling that your wife, like your mother, would be unsympathetic to your difficulties. That there was no point in telling her about your experiences because she was too preoccupied or too busy to care.
Mr. Arianes:	But she's so different from my mother. I come first with her.
Therapist:	On one level you know that. On another, deeper level there may well be the fear that people—or maybe only women, or maybe only

	women you're close to—are all the same, and you can't take a chance at being rejected again in your need.
Mr. Arianes:	Maybe you're right, Doc, but all that was so long ago, and I should be over that by now.
Therapist:	That's not the way the mind works. If a shock or a disappointment is strong enough it can permanently freeze our picture of ourselves and our expectations of the world. The rest of us grows up—that is, we let ourselves learn about life from experience and from what we see, hear, or read of the experiences of others, but that one area where we really got hurt stays unchanged. So what I mean when I say you might be carrying that attitude into your relationship with your wife is that when it comes to your hopes of being understood and catered to when you feel hurt or abused by life, you still feel very much like that nine-year-old boy who was rebuffed in his need and gave up hope that anyone would or could respond to him.

Source: Basch, 1980, pp. 29–30. Copyright Basic Books. Reprinted with permission.

Behaviour Therapy

Behaviour therapists apply the principles of learning to help clients make adaptive changes in their behaviour. Because the focus is on changing behaviour—not on personality change or deep probing into the past—behaviour therapy is relatively brief, lasting typically from a few weeks to a few months. Behaviour therapists, like other therapists, seek to develop warm therapeutic relationships with clients, but they believe the special efficacy of behaviour therapy derives from learning-based techniques rather than from the nature of the therapeutic relationship.

Behaviour therapy first gained widespread attention as a means of helping people overcome fears and phobias, problems that had proved resistant to insight-oriented therapies. Among these methods are systematic desensitization, gradual exposure, and modelling. **Systematic desensitization** involves a therapeutic program of exposure (in imagination or by means of pictures or slides) to progressively more fearful stimuli while one remains deeply relaxed.

In **gradual exposure**, also called *in vivo* ("in life") *exposure*, people troubled by phobias purposely expose themselves to the stimuli that evoke their fear. Like systematic desensitization, the person progresses at his or her own pace through a hierarchy of progressively more anxiety-evoking stimuli. A person with a fear of snakes, for example, might first look at a harmless, caged snake from across the room and then gradually approach and interact with the snake in a step-by-step process, progressing to each new step only when feeling completely calm at the prior step. Gradual exposure is often combined with cognitive techniques that focus on replacing anxiety-arousing irrational thoughts with calming rational thoughts.

In modelling, clients first observe and then imitate others who approach or interact with fear-evoking situations or objects. After observing the model, the client may be assisted or guided by the therapist or the model in performing the target behaviour. The client receives ample reinforcement from the therapist for each attempt. Modelling approaches were pioneered by Albert Bandura and his colleagues, who had remarkable success using modelling techniques to treat various phobias, especially fears of animals, such as snakes and dogs (Bandura, Blanchard, & Ritter, 1969; Bandura, Jeffery, & Wright, 1974).

systematic desensitization Behaviour therapy technique for overcoming phobias by means of exposure (in imagination or by means of slides) to progressively more fearful stimuli while one remains deeply relaxed.

gradual exposure In behaviour therapy, a method of overcoming fears through a stepwise process of direct exposure to increasingly fearful stimuli.

Modelling. Modelling techniques are often used to help people overcome phobic behaviours. Here, a child observes an adult handling a spider. As in phobia treatment, the client observes the harmless engagement with the phobic object and is then, with reinforcement from the therapist, more likely to imitate that behaviour.

token economies Behavioural treatment programs, in institutional settings, in which a controlled environment is constructed such that people are reinforced for desired behaviours by receiving tokens (such as poker chips) that may be exchanged for desired rewards or privileges.

Behaviour therapists also use techniques based on operant conditioning, or systematic use of rewards and punishments, to shape desired behaviour. For example, parents and teachers may be trained to reinforce children systematically for appropriate behaviour by showing appreciation and to extinguish inappropriate behaviour by ignoring it. In institutional settings, **token economies** seek to increase adaptive behaviour by allowing patients to earn tokens for performing appropriate behaviours, such as self-grooming and making their beds. The tokens can eventually be exchanged for desired rewards. Token systems have also been used to treat children with conduct-disorder problems.

Other techniques of behaviour therapy discussed in later chapters include aversive conditioning (used in the treatment of substance-abuse problems such as smoking and alcoholism), social-skills training (used in the treatment of social anxieties and skills deficits associated with schizophrenia), and self-control techniques (used in helping people reduce excess weight and quit smoking).

Humanistic-Existential Therapies

Psychodynamic therapists tend to focus on unconscious processes such as internal conflicts. By contrast, humanistic therapists focus on clients' subjective, conscious experiences. Like behaviour therapists, humanistic-existential therapists focus more on what clients are experiencing in the present—the here and now—than on the past. But there are also similarities between the psychodynamic and humanistic-existential therapies. Both assume that the past affects present behaviour and feelings and both seek to expand clients' self-insight. The major form of humanistic therapy is **person-centred therapy** (formerly called **client-centred therapy**), which was developed by the psychologist Carl Rogers.

person-centred therapy Carl Rogers's method of psychotherapy, emphasizing the establishment of a warm, accepting therapeutic relationship that frees clients to engage in a process of self-exploration and self-acceptance.

client-centred therapy Another name for Carl Rogers's *person-centred therapy*.

PERSON-CENTRED THERAPY Rogers (1951) believed that people have natural motivational tendencies toward growth, fulfillment, and health. In Rogers's view, psychological disorders develop largely from the roadblocks that others place in the journey toward self-actualization. When others are selective in their approval of our childhood feelings and behaviour, we may come to disown the criticized parts of ourselves. To earn social approval, we may don social masks or facades. We learn "to be seen and not heard" and may become deaf even to our own inner voices. Over time, we may develop distorted self-concepts that are consistent with others' views of us but are not of our own making and design. As a result, we may become poorly adjusted, unhappy, and confused as to who and what we are.

Person-centred therapy creates conditions of warmth and acceptance in the therapeutic relationship—conditions that help clients become more aware and accepting of their true selves. Rogers was a major shaper of contemporary psychotherapy and was rated the single most influential psychotherapist in a survey of therapists (D. Smith, 1982). Rogers did not believe therapists should impose their own goals or values on their clients. His focus of therapy, as the name implies, is centred on the person.

Person-centred therapy is nondirective. The client, not the therapist, takes the lead and directs the course of therapy. The therapist uses reflection—the restating or paraphrasing of the client's expressed feelings without interpreting them or passing judgment on them. This encourages the client to further explore his or her feelings and get in touch with deeper feelings and parts of the self that have become disowned because of social condemnation.

unconditional positive regard In Carl Rogers's view, the expression of unconditional acceptance of another person's basic worth as a person, regardless of whether one approves of all of the behaviour of the other person. The ability to express unconditional positive regard is considered a quality of an effective person-centred therapist.

Rogers stressed the importance of creating a warm therapeutic relationship that would encourage the client to engage in self-exploration and self-expression. The effective person-centred therapist should possess four basic qualities or attributes: **unconditional positive regard**, empathy, genuineness, and congruence between their thoughts, feelings, and behaviour. The therapist must be able to express unconditional positive regard for clients, in contrast to the conditional approval the client may have received from parents and others in the past. This provides clients with a sense of security that encourages them to explore their feelings without fear of disapproval.

Therapists serve as models of psychological integrity to their clients. Here, Rogers (C.R.) uses reflection to help a client, Jill, focus more deeply on her inner feelings:

Jill: I'm having a lot of problems dealing with my daughter. She's 20 years old; she's in college; I'm having a lot of trouble letting her go. . . . And I have a lot of guilt feelings about her; I have a real need to hang on to her.

C. R.: A need to hang on so you can kind of make up for the things you feel guilty about. Is that part of it?

Jill: There's a lot of that. . . . Also, she's been a real friend to me, and filled my life. . . . And it's very hard . . . a lot of empty places now that she's not with me.

C. R.: The old vacuum, sort of, when she's not there.

Jill: Yes. Yes. I also would like to be the kind of mother that could be strong and say, you know, "Go and have a good life," and this is really hard for me, to do that.

C. R.: It's very hard to give up something that's been so precious in your life, but also something that I guess has caused you pain when you mentioned guilt.

Jill: Yeah. And I'm aware that I have some anger toward her that I don't always get what I want. I have needs that are not met. And, uh, I don't feel I have a right to those needs. You know . . . she's a daughter; she's not my mother. Though sometimes I feel as if I'd like her to mother me . . . it's very difficult for me to ask for that and have a right to it.

C. R.: So, it may be unreasonable, but still, when she doesn't meet your needs, it makes you mad.

Jill: Yeah I get very angry, very angry with her.

C. R.: (Pause) You're also feeling a little tension at this point, I guess.

Jill: Yeah. Yeah. A lot of conflict . . . (C. R.: M-hm.). A lot of pain.

C. R.: A lot of pain. Can you say anything more about what that's about?

Source: Farber, Brink, & Raskin, 1996, pp. 74–75. Copyright Guilford Press. Reprinted with permission.

EMOTION-FOCUSED THERAPY Emotion-focused therapy (EFT) is based on the premise that "emotion, motivation, cognition, and action occur as an integrated response package" (L. S. Greenberg, 2002a, p. 26). From this perspective, there are multiple factors that contribute to maladaptive emotions, including our genetic makeup and temperament. Early in our development, reciprocal interpersonal relationships are formed with "significant others" and gradually we develop well-ingrained patterns of emotional responses. If our early emotional responses were intense, we may fall prey to "reliving" past hurts, fears, and rages in current situations. For example, "inattentiveness from a spouse can activate intense feelings of neglect from a loveless childhood. These feelings then become maladaptive responses to the present situation" (L. S. Greenberg, 2002a, p. 32).

An essential tenet of EFT is not to eliminate intense or uncomfortable feelings but to view them as a signal to take action—"emotion moves us and reason guides us" (L. S. Greenberg, 2002a, p. x). The challenge is to know "when to change emotion and when to be changed by it" (L. S. Greenberg, 2002a, p. xi). During a counselling session, for instance, an emotion-focused therapist acts as a coach who begins by helping people become more aware and accepting of their emotions. This is followed by helping them transform their negative emotions into more adaptive ones—for example, turning unproductive anger into adaptive sadness and then acceptance through the use of emotion-shifting techniques such as role play or guided imagery. This strategy is based on the premise that even though "thinking usually changes thoughts[;] only feeling can change emotions" (L. Greenberg, 2006, p. 91). Lastly, the emotional experiences are reflected upon and assimilated to allow a new meaning of self to emerge (L. Greenberg, 2006). This type of therapeutic collaboration between therapist and client promotes the development of the client's emotional intelligence (Elliot, Watson, Goldman, & Greenberg, 2004).

Cognitive-Behaviour Therapies

There is nothing either good or bad, but thinking makes it so.

—SHAKESPEARE, *HAMLET*

In these words, Shakespeare did not mean to imply that misfortunes or ailments are painless or easy to manage. His point, rather, is that the ways in which we evaluate upsetting events can heighten our discomfort and impair our ability to cope. Several hundred years later, cognitive therapists adopted this simple but elegant expression as a kind of motto for their approach to therapy.

Cognitive-behaviour therapists focus on helping clients identify and correct maladaptive beliefs, automatic types of thinking, and self-defeating attitudes that create or compound emotional problems and dysfunctional ways of behaving. They believe that negative emotions such as anxiety and depression are caused by the interpretations we place on troubling events, not by the events themselves. Canadian psychologists Keith Dobson (University of Calgary) and David Dozois (University of Western Ontario) suggest that all cognitive-behavioural therapies share three fundamental propositions:

1. cognitive activity affects behaviour
2. cognitive activity may be monitored and altered
3. desired behaviour change may be effected through cognitive change (K. S. Dobson & Dozois, 2001, p. 4)

Here, we focus on the contributions of three prominent types of cognitive-behavioural therapy: Albert Ellis's rational-emotive behaviour therapy, Aaron Beck's cognitive therapy, and the cognitive-behavioural therapy of Donald Meichenbaum.

RATIONAL-EMOTIVE BEHAVIOUR THERAPY Albert Ellis (1977, 1993, 2003) believed that the adoption of irrational, self-defeating beliefs gives rise to psychological problems and negative feelings. Consider the irrational belief that one must have the approval almost all the time of the people who are important to you. Ellis found it understandable to want other people's approval and love, but he argued that it is irrational to believe we cannot survive without it. Emotional difficulties such as anxiety and depression are directly caused not by negative events but rather by how we distort their meaning by viewing them through the dark-coloured glasses of irrational beliefs. Thinking irrationally transforms challenging events, such as forthcoming examinations, into looming disasters ("It would be so awful if I did poorly—I wouldn't be able to stand it"). Ellis's rational-emotive behaviour therapy (REBT) seeks to free people from such irrational beliefs and their consequences. In REBT, therapists actively dispute irrational beliefs and their premises and help clients develop more rational, adaptive beliefs.

Ellis and Dryden (1987) described the case of a 27-year-old woman, Jane, who was socially inhibited and shy, particularly with attractive men. Through REBT, Jane identified some of her underlying irrational beliefs, such as "I must speak well to people I find attractive" and "When I don't speak well and impress people as I should, I'm a stupid, inadequate person!" (p. 68). REBT helped her discriminate between these irrational beliefs and rational alternatives, such as "If people do reject me for showing them how anxious I am, that will be most unfortunate, but I can stand it" (p. 68). REBT encouraged her to debate or dispute irrational beliefs by posing challenging questions to herself: "Why must I speak well to people I find attractive?" and "When I don't speak well and impress people, how does that make me a stupid and inadequate person?" (p. 69). Jane learned to form rational responses to her self-questioning; for example, "There is no reason I must speak well to people I find attractive, but it would be desirable if I do so, so I shall make an effort—but not kill myself—to do so" and "When I speak poorly and fail to impress people, that only makes me a person who spoke unimpressively this time—not a totally stupid or inadequate person" (p. 69).

Ellis recognized that irrational beliefs may be formed on the basis of early childhood experiences. Changing those beliefs requires finding rational alternatives in the here and now, however. Rational-emotive behaviour therapists also help clients substitute more effective interpersonal behaviour for self-defeating or maladaptive behaviour.

BECK'S COGNITIVE THERAPY   As formulated by psychiatrist Aaron Beck and his colleagues (A. T. Beck, 1976; A. T. Beck et al., 1979, 2004), cognitive therapy, like REBT, focuses on clients' maladaptive cognitions. Cognitive therapists encourage clients to recognize and change errors in their thinking, called *cognitive distortions*, that affect their moods and impair their behaviour, such as tendencies to magnify negative events and minimize personal accomplishments.

Cognitive therapists have clients record the thoughts that are prompted by upsetting events they experience and note the connections between their thoughts and their emotional responses. They then help them dispute distorted thoughts and replace them with rational alternatives. Therapists also use behavioural homework assignments, such as encouraging depressed clients to fill their free time with structured activities like gardening or completing work around the house. Carrying out such tasks serves to counteract the apathy and loss of motivation that tend to characterize depression and may also provide concrete evidence of competence, which helps combat self-perceptions of helplessness and inadequacy.

Another type of homework assignment involves reality testing. Clients are asked to test out their negative beliefs in the light of reality. For example, a depressed client who feels unwanted by everyone might be asked to call two or three friends on the phone to gather data about the friends' reactions to the calls. The therapist might then ask the client to report on the assignment: "Did they immediately hang up the phone? Or did they seem pleased you called? Did they express any interest at all in talking to you again or getting together sometime? Does the evidence support the conclusion that no one has any interest in you?" Such exercises help clients replace distorted beliefs with rational alternatives.

Consider this case, in which a depressed man was encouraged to test his belief that he was about to be fired from his job. The case also illustrates several cognitive distortions or errors in thinking, such as selectively perceiving only one's flaws (in this case, self-perceptions of laziness) and expecting the worst (expectations of being fired):

A 35-year-old man, a frozen-foods distributor, had suffered from chronic depression since his divorce six years earlier. During the past year, the depression had worsened and he found it increasingly difficult to call upon customers or go to the office. Each day that he avoided working made it more difficult for him to go to the office and face his boss. He was convinced that he was in imminent danger of being fired because he had not made any sales calls for more than a month. Since he had not earned any commissions in a while, he felt he was not adequately supporting his two daughters and was concerned that he wouldn't have the money to send them to college. He was convinced that his basic problem was laziness, not depression. His therapist pointed out the illogic in his thinking. First of all, there was no real evidence that his boss was about to fire him. His boss had actually encouraged him to get help and was paying for part of the treatment. His therapist also pointed out that judging himself as lazy was unfair because it overlooked the fact that he had been an industrious, successful salesman before he became depressed. While not fully persuaded, the client agreed to a homework assignment in which he was to call his boss and also make a sales call to one of his former customers. His boss expressed support and reassured him that his job was secure. The customer ribbed him about "being on vacation" during the preceding six weeks but placed a small order. The client discovered that the small unpleasantness he experienced in facing the customer and being teased paled in comparison to the intense depression he felt at home while he was avoiding work. Within the next several weeks he gradually worked himself back to a normal routine, calling upon customers and making future plans. This process of viewing himself and the world from a fresh perspective led to a general improvement in his mood and behaviour.

Adapted from Burns & Beck, 1978, pp. 124–126. Copyright Springer.
Reprinted with the kind permission of Springer Science+Business Media B.V.

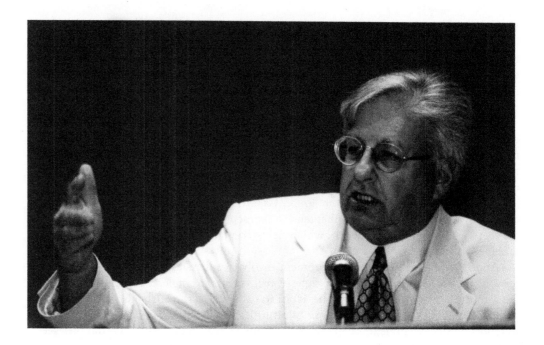

Donald Meichenbaum, co-founder of cognitive-behavioural therapy. Voted one of the 10 most influential therapists of the 20th century, Meichenbaum was a professor at University of Waterloo for 33 years. He is currently research director for the Melissa Institute, an organization that utilizes psychological research to educate government and the public about violence and trauma.

Rational-emotive behaviour therapy and Beck's cognitive therapy have much in common, especially the focus on helping clients replace self-defeating thoughts and beliefs with more rational ones. Perhaps the major difference between the two approaches is one of therapeutic style. REBT therapists tend to be more confrontational and forceful in their approach to disputing clients' irrational beliefs (W. Dryden, 1984; Ellis, Young, & Lockwood, 1987). Cognitive therapists tend to adopt a more gentle, collaborative approach in helping clients discover and correct the distortions in their thinking.

MEICHENBAUM'S COGNITIVE-BEHAVIOURAL THERAPY Today many, if not most, behaviour therapists identify with the broader cognitive-behavioural therapy (CBT). Donald Meichenbaum's cognitive-behavioural therapy developed from the attempt to integrate therapeutic techniques that focus not only on making overt behavioural changes but also on changing dysfunctional thoughts and cognitions (Meichenbaum, 1977). Cognitive-behavioural therapy draws on the assumptions that cognitions and information processing play important roles in the genesis and maintenance of maladaptive behaviour and that the impact of external events is filtered through thinking processes (Beidel & Turner, 1986).

Cognitive-behavioural therapists use an assortment of behavioural and cognitive techniques in therapy. The following case illustration shows how behavioural techniques (exposure to fearful situations) and cognitive techniques (changing maladaptive thoughts) were used in the treatment of agoraphobia, a type of anxiety disorder characterized by excessive fears of venturing out in public:

Ms. X was a 41-year-old woman with a 12-year history of agoraphobia. She feared venturing into public places alone and required her husband or children to accompany her from place to place. In vivo (actual) exposure sessions were arranged in a series of progressively more fearful encounters—a fear-stimulus hierarchy. The first step in the hierarchy, for example, involved taking a shopping trip while accompanied by the therapist. After accomplishing this task, she gradually moved upward in the hierarchy. By the third week of treatment, she was able to complete the last step in her hierarchy—shopping by herself in a crowded supermarket. Cognitive restructuring was conducted along with the exposure training. Ms. X was asked to imagine herself in various fearful situations and to report the self-statements (self-talk) she experienced. The therapist helped her identify disruptive self-statements, such as "I am going to make a fool of myself." This particular self-statement was challenged by questioning whether it was realistic to believe that she would actually lose control and by disputing the belief that the consequences of losing control, were it to happen, would truly be disastrous. She progressed rapidly with treatment and became capable of functioning more independently. But she still harboured concerns about relapsing in the future. The therapist focused at this point on deeper cognitive structures involving her fears of abandonment by the people she loved if she were to relapse and be unable to attend to their needs. In challenging these beliefs, the therapist helped her realize that she was not as helpless as she perceived herself to be and that she was loved for other reasons than her ability to serve others. She also explored the question "Who am I improving for?" She realized that she needed to find reasons to overcome her phobia that were related to meeting her own personal needs, not simply the needs of her loved ones. At a follow-up interview nine months after treatment, she was functioning independently, which allowed her to pursue her own interests, such as taking night courses and seeking a job.

Adapted from Biran, 1988, pp. 165–178. Copyright Springer. Reprinted with the kind permission of Springer Science+Business Media B.V.

It could be argued that any behavioural method involving imagination or mental imagery, such as systematic desensitization, bridges behavioural and cognitive domains. Cognitive therapies such as Ellis's rational-emotive behaviour therapy and Beck's cognitive therapy might also be regarded as forms of cognitive-behavioural therapy because they incorporate cognitive and behavioural treatment methods. The dividing lines between the psychotherapies may not be as clearly drawn as authors of textbooks—who are given the task of classifying them—might desire. Not only are traditional boundaries between the cognitive and behavioural therapies blurred, but many therapists endorse an eclectic orientation in which they incorporate principles and techniques derived from different schools of therapy.

Eclectic Therapy

Each of the major psychological models of abnormal behaviour—the psychodynamic, learning theory, humanistic-existentialist, and cognitive-behavioural approaches—has spawned its own approaches to psychotherapy. Although many therapists identify with one or another of these schools of therapy, an increasing number of therapists identify with an eclectic approach that draws on techniques and teachings of different therapeutic approaches. Eclectic therapists look beyond the theoretical barriers that divide one school of psychotherapy from another in an effort to define what is common among the schools of therapy and what is useful in each of them.

Surveys of therapists have consistently shown that the largest single group of psychologists and other psychotherapists (ranging from around one third to more than half of those sampled) identified with an eclectic therapeutic orientation (Garfield, 1994). Researchers find that therapists who adopt an eclectic approach tend to be older and more experienced (Beitman, Goldfried, & Norcross, 1989). Perhaps they have learned through experience the value of drawing on diverse contributions to the practice of therapy.

Group, Family, and Marital Therapy

In group therapy, a group of clients meet together with a therapist or pair of therapists. Group therapy has several advantages over individual treatment. For one, group therapy is less costly because several clients are treated at the same time. Many clinicians also believe that group therapy may be more effective in treating groups of clients who have similar problems, such as complaints relating to anxiety, depression, lack of social skills, or adjustment to divorce or other life stresses. The group format provides clients with the opportunity to learn how people with similar problems cope with them and provides the social support of the group as well as the therapist. Group therapy also provides members with opportunities to work through their problems in relating to others. For example, the therapist or other members may point out to a particular member when he or she acts in a bossy manner or tends to withdraw when criticized, patterns of behaviour that may mirror the behaviour the client shows in relationships with others outside the group. Group members may also rehearse social skills with one another in a supportive atmosphere.

In family therapy, the family, not the individual, is the unit of treatment. Family therapy aims to help troubled families resolve their conflicts and problems so that they function better as a unit and individual members are subjected to less stress from family conflicts.

Faulty patterns of communications within the family often contribute to family problems. In family therapy, members of the family unit learn to communicate more effectively and to air their disagreements constructively. Family conflicts often emerge at transitional points in the life cycle when patterns are altered by changes in one or more members. Conflicts between parents and children, for example, often emerge when adolescent children seek greater independence or autonomy. Family members with low self-esteem may be unable to tolerate different attitudes or behaviours from other members of the family and may resist their efforts to change or become more independent.

One widely adopted approach to family therapy, called *conjoint family therapy*, was developed by Virginia Satir (1967). Satir conceptualized the family in terms of a pattern or system of communications and interactions that needs to be studied and changed to enhance family functioning as well as the growth of individual family members.

Another prominent approach to family therapy is structural family therapy (Minuchin, 1974). This approach also adopts a family system model of abnormal behaviour. It conceptualizes problem behaviours of individual members of the family as arising from dysfunctional relationship patterns within the family system, rather than as involving only the individuals themselves. Family members may develop psychological or physical problems in response to stressful role relationships in the family. The structural family therapist would help the family understand the hidden messages in a child's behaviour and assist the family to make changes in their relationships to meet the child's needs more adequately. In so doing, the therapist shows the family how the member with the identified problem is responding to wider problems in the family.

Marital therapy may be considered a subtype of family therapy in which the family unit is the marital couple. Like other forms of family therapy, marital therapy focuses on improving communication and analyzing role relationships in order to improve the marital relationship. For example, one partner may play a dominant role and resist any request to share power with the other. The marital therapist would help bring these role relationships into the open, so that alternative ways of relating to each other could be explored that would lead to a more satisfying relationship.

Computer-Assisted Therapy

Computer-based interventions and therapy come in all forms, from online cognitive-behavioural therapy with a live therapist using a video-chat service to self-guided behaviour therapy for children with anxiety, in which they monitor their own progress. Support for this type of therapy, often to increase access to help for individuals, has been growing over the years. Evidence of its efficacy has been shown. One study (Wright et al., 2005) compared the efficacy of computer-assisted cognitive therapy against standard

Computer-based interventions. Evidence for the efficacy of computer-assisted therapy, especially cognitive therapy, has been repeatedly found, and this treatment is a viable option for some.

cognitive therapy and a control group without treatment for outpatients with nonpsychotic major depressive disorder. They found that computer-assisted cognitive therapy had more robust effects than standard cognitive therapy in reducing measures of cognitive distortion and in improving knowledge about cognitive therapy. Also, in a systematic review of computer-based interventions for drug-abuse disorders, researchers from the Yale University School of Medicine found that, compared to treatment as usual, computer-based interventions led to less substance use and higher motivation to change, better retention, and greater knowledge of presented information (Moore, Fazzino, Garnet, Cutter, & Barry, 2011). Computer-based interventions for various disorders have the potential to dramatically expand and alter the landscape of treatment.

Does Psychotherapy Work?

What, then, of the effectiveness of psychotherapy? Does psychotherapy work? Are some forms of therapy more effective than others? Are some forms of therapy more effective for some types of clients or for some types of problems than for others? The effectiveness of psychotherapy receives strong support from the research literature. Reviews of the scientific literature often utilize a statistical technique called **meta-analysis**, which averages the results of a large number of studies in order to determine an overall level of effectiveness.

In the most frequently cited meta-analysis of psychotherapy research, M. L. Smith and G. V. Glass (1977) analyzed the results of some 375 controlled studies comparing various types of therapies (psychodynamic, behavioural, humanistic, etc.) against control groups. The results of their analyses showed that the average psychotherapy client in these studies was better off than 75% of the clients who remained untreated. In 1980, Smith and Glass and their colleague T. I. Miller reported the results of a larger analysis, based on 475 controlled outcome studies, that showed that the average person who received therapy was better off at the end of treatment than 80% of people who did not (M. L. Smith, Glass, & Miller, 1980). A fairly recent meta-analyis of long-term psychoanalytic psychotherapy showed significantly higher outcomes in overall effectiveness, target problems, and personality functioning than shorter forms of psychotherapy (Leichsenring & Rabung, 2008).

Meta-analyses show only negligible differences overall in outcomes between the various therapies when the therapies are compared to control groups (Wampold, Mondin, Moody, & Ahn, 1997; Wampold, Mondin, Moody, Stick, et al., 1997). Such minor differences suggest that the effectiveness of psychotherapy may have more to do with the features that different modes of therapy share than with the specific techniques that set them apart (Lambert & Bergin, 1994).

These common features are called **nonspecific treatment factors**. Nonspecific or common factors in psychotherapy stem largely from the therapist–client relationship. These factors include empathy, support, and attention shown by the therapist; therapeutic alliance, or the attachment the client develops to the therapist and the therapy process; and the working alliance, or the development of an effective working relationship in which the therapist and client work together to identify and confront the important issues and problems the client faces (Binder & Strupp, 1997).

Should we conclude that different therapies are about equally effective? One possibility is that different therapies are about equal in their effects overall but may not be equal in their effects with every patient (Wampold, Mondin, Moody, Stick, et al., 1997). Behaviour therapy, for example, has shown impressive results in treating various types of anxiety disorders, sleep disorders, and sexual dysfunctions and in improving the adaptive functioning of people with schizophrenia and mental retardation. Psychodynamic and humanistic approaches may be more effective in fostering self-insight and personality growth. Cognitive-behavioural therapy has demonstrated impressive results in treating depression and anxiety disorders. By and large, however, the process of determining which treatment, which type of practitioner, and what conditions are most effective for a given client remains a challenge.

Nonspecific factors. Are the benefits of psychotherapy due to nonspecific factors that various psychotherapists share in common, such as the mobilization of hope, the attention and support provided by the therapist, and the development of a good working alliance between the client and therapist? It appears that both specific and nonspecific factors are involved in accounting for therapeutic change.

meta-analysis Statistical technique for combining the results of different studies into an overall average. In psychotherapy research, meta-analysis is used to compute the average benefit or size of effect associated with psychotherapy overall, or with different forms of therapy, in relation to control groups.

nonspecific treatment factors Characteristics that are not specific to any one form of psychotherapy but tend to be shared by psychotherapies, such as the attention a client receives from a therapist and the therapist's encouragement of the client's sense of hope and positive expectancies.

We live in a nation that has become increasingly multi-ethnic and multicultural. The 2001 census listed more than 200 ethnic groups, and Canada now has its largest proportion of foreign-born citizens in 70 years. Almost one in five people is foreign-born, and the same proportion has a mother tongue other than English or French (Statistics Canada, 2003).

In the past, the diagnosis and treatment of psychological disorders was heavily influenced by European and North American thought. But this Western cultural perspective is not universally appropriate for people who hold different cultural beliefs. Cultural learning and values make a difference in what people bring to therapy (Beiser, 2003). Canada's substantial cultural diversity creates serious mental health issues that cannot be ignored, especially at a time when biomedical models of mental health care dominate (Macnaughton, 2000).

Mental health-care practitioners in Canada have become increasingly responsive to the cultural factors that influence the delivery of mental health services. People from different cultural backgrounds often experience and express mental distress in ways that may be open to misinterpretation by someone from another culture. For example, expressions like "I am feeling blue," "I blew my top," "I feel out of sorts," "He's forever changing his mind," and "She is getting on my nerves" are common English idioms that can carry different meanings regarding a person's mental state in a different culture and/or language (Hamid, 2000). In addition, misunderstanding of nonverbal communication can lead to serious mistakes by therapists when a client and therapist have differing cultural traditions and customs (Singh, McKay, & Singh, 1998). This highlights the need to understand culture-specific idioms and nonverbal cues of distress when supporting a person's mental health needs, although the assumptions must be verified in each case to avoid erroneous stereotyping.

There are two broad approaches to the delivery of mental health-care services to Canada's culturally diverse groups. One model calls for the training of culturally skilled practitioners adept at working with clients from various cultural backgrounds (Arthur & Januszkowski, 2001; Lo & Fung, 2003; Macnaughton, 2000). To be culturally skilled, a counsellor must be able to demonstrate competency in self-awareness of how his or her personal world view influences the counselling relationship, knowledge of the history and development of various Canadian cultural groups, intervention skills that address the need to vary the counselling relationship depending on the client's cultural expectations, and advocacy skills that promote cultural sensitivity of mental health problems in organizations and institutions (Arthur & Stewart, 2001).

In many Canadian settings, there are too few culturally skilled practitioners available to meet the high demand for culturally diverse mental health services. Additional methods of responding to the challenge presented by diverse populations are also needed within existing mental health-care settings. The cultural consultation services (CCS) model was designed by Laurence Kirmayer and others at McGill University to work within existing systems. This model made use of a culturally and professionally diverse team including interpreters or culture brokers, community organizations, clinicians with generic cultural competency, and clinicians with expertise in a specific culture or ethnic group. Although the consultants were accessed as needed, there was a core cultural team consisting of psychiatrists, social workers, psychiatric nurses, medical anthropologists, a physician, and a full-time clinical psychologist. A database was used to track the specific skills of each cultural consultant. Benefits of the CCS model included the ability to avoid the pitfall of sweeping generalizations or cultural stereotypes while targeting mental health issues in the context of a person's particular cultural view of the problem. Moreover, there was a greatly reduced language barrier for assessment, diagnosis, and treatment, much improved short- and long-term client functioning, decreased use of mental health services, and increased clinician satisfaction (Kirmayer, Groleau, Guzder, Blake, & Jarvis, 2003).

As a youngster, Edmond Yu showed he had the drive to achieve great things. He was an excellent student, leaving home early for classes and studying in his room late every night. Yet he balanced his rigorous academic work with a variety of hobbies. After emigrating from Hong Kong to Canada, Edmond spent two years at York University in pre-med classes, and later earned a scholarship to study medicine at the University of Toronto.

In his first term, Edmond's marks were excellent. But during the second term, he started to become reclusive; he began studying from home, avoiding campus except for exams or group projects. The initial signs that all was not well were detected an ocean away by his sister, Katherine Yu, who was living in

Hong Kong. She got a phone call saying there had been a serious fight between Edmond and his elder brother. Edmond had been asked to leave the house. There were other calls from Edmond, too, in which he would ramble about someone stealing his wallet at the university. He sounded incoherent, illogical; not himself. "I realized at that point there was something wrong with him," his sister recalls. She flew to Canada.

Things began to quickly spiral downward. Katherine remembers going to his apartment to check up on him. "He said the people in his building, as well as in nearby buildings, were spies," she says. "He believed there were satellites planted in his building—even in his own apartment—watching him." Likely unaware he was suffering from an illness, Edmond rejected Katherine's attempts to get him to seek help.

Katherine went to Edmond, demanding he accept help, see a doctor, take medication. He refused. "I knew there was something wrong with him. He asked me to leave, but I insisted and kept on talking. And then he slapped me in the face." It was painful for Katherine to use the incident against her brother, but she felt his best interests were at stake. The police apprehended Edmond and he was taken to the Clarke Institute of Psychiatry, where he was diagnosed as having paranoid schizophrenia. He was persuaded that, if he accepted treatment, he might still be able to return to medical school. He consented.

At least initially, Edmond tried to stick with the treatment, which consisted of antipsychotic drugs to quell the delusions. Unfortunately, some people experience severe side effects with psychotropic drugs. Edmond was one of them. "When he was on medication, he seemed to be a totally different person," Katherine says. "All he could do was eat and sleep. He was completely non-communicative. His hands were so shaky he couldn't even hold a bowl of soup properly. The soup would always spill."

It was clear to Edmond he would not be able to attend school while on medication. It was equally clear he would not be able to attend school without it. Edmond requested that a doctor certify him fit for medical school. But because he would not take his medication, the doctor refused.

With no classes to attend, no career as a doctor, Edmond flew back to Hong Kong. Within a month, he was picked up by police on a charge of disturbing the peace. Edmond was sent to a psychiatric hospital. The hospital then decided to impose treatment on Edmond—to force medication. When he returned to Canada, he immediately stopped taking the drugs. His non-compliance marked the start of a long struggle with his family over treatment.

Edmond's illness deepened, and his behaviour worsened. He was overtaken by paranoia and suspicion. He would talk non-stop. He felt he had special influence over world affairs. He feared those around him were conspiring to harm him. On occasion, he would be verbally abusive. And he began burning things—clothes, books, photographs. He would take them out on to the driveway and put a match to them. Edmond also started to meditate in front of the family's Scarborough home, sometimes for hours. On two occasions, he threw a knife at a dartboard he set up outside the garage door. Neighbours called police both times. Other times, they just stared from their windows.

Edmond began to drift, from housing to hostels—where he says he was beaten and robbed—to the street. He made the occasional visit home, his deterioration more evident each time. His clothes were becoming ragged. The family later found him living in a public washroom in Grange Park, behind the Art Gallery of Ontario. His family managed to obtain a court order for him to be assessed by a psychiatrist. As a result, he was involuntarily committed to the Clarke Institute of Psychiatry for more than three months. Doctors declared him incapable of making his own treatment decisions, and his mother was appointed a substitute decision-maker. She had the power to authorize forced medication.

Over the next few years, a pattern set in: arrest, often for some form of assault, incarceration, release. The combination of winter, homelessness, and illness was beginning to wear Edmond down. Late one afternoon, he was at the bus loop at the foot of Spadina Ave. Unaccountably, he struck a woman in the face, then boarded a bus. The police were called. The driver ordered everyone off the bus and left Edmond alone with the doors locked. Three police officers boarded the bus and tried to persuade Edmond to leave with them. At one point, he did agree to leave, but then took a hammer out of his jacket.

"I watched while he waggled his right wrist with the hammer in it," said a witness, who watched from an adjacent streetcar. "Then the movement of his wrist stopped, and seconds passed, when I heard what I thought initially was a cap gun. I could see the red flash of the gun, and the body slumped."

Constable Lou Pasquino fired six shots. One hit Edmond in the throat, his head twisting as the shots continued. A second hit his ear and entered the side of his head. The third hit the back of his skull. Edmond was dead before he hit the floor.

Scott Simmie, "Reality is sometimes painful," *Toronto Star*, October 3, 1998.
Reprinted courtesy of the Atkinson Foundation.

The case of Edmond Yu touches on many important issues, including the issue of balancing the rights of the individual with the rights of society. Do people have the right to live on the streets under unsanitary conditions? There are those who argue that a just and humane society has the right and responsibility to care for people who are perceived incapable of protecting their own best interests, even if "care" means involuntarily committing them to a psychiatric institution. Do people who are obviously mentally disturbed have the right to refuse treatment? Do psychiatric institutions have the right to inject them with antipsychotic and other drugs against their will? Should mental patients with a history of disruptive or violent behaviour be hospitalized indefinitely or permitted to live in supervised residences in the community once their conditions are stabilized? When severely disturbed people break the law, should society respond to them with the criminal justice system or with the mental health system?

Mandatory medication? A photograph of Edmond Yu taken at the Scott Mission on Christmas Day, 1996. Yu would be shot by police two months later. Should people suffering from serious mental illnesses, like Edmond Yu, be required to receive treatment?

Methods of Treatment

- **What are the major biological approaches to treating abnormal behaviour patterns?** Biological approaches include drug therapy, electroconvulsive therapy (ECT), repetitive transcranial magnetic stimulation (rTMS), and (rarely) psychosurgery.

- **What is psychotherapy?** Psychotherapy involves a systematic interaction between a therapist and client that incorporates psychological principles to help the client overcome abnormal behaviour, solve problems in living, or develop as an individual.

- **What is psychodynamic therapy?** Psychodynamic therapy originated with psychoanalysis, the approach to treatment developed by Freud. Psychoanalysts use techniques such as free association and dream analysis to help people gain insight into their unconscious conflicts and work through them in the light of their adult personalities. More recent psychodynamic therapies are generally briefer and less intensive.

- **What is behaviour therapy?** Behaviour therapy applies the principles of learning to help people make adaptive behavioural changes. Behaviour therapy techniques include systematic desensitization, gradual exposure, modelling, operant conditioning approaches, and social-skills training.

- **What is humanistic-existential therapy?** Humanistic approaches focus on the client's subjective, conscious experience in the here and now. Rogers's person-centred therapy helps people increase their awareness and acceptance of inner feelings that had met with social condemnation and been disowned. The effective person-centred therapist possesses the qualities of unconditional positive regard, empathy, genuineness, and congruence. Greenberg's approach, emotion-focused therapy (EFT), aims not to eliminate intense or uncomfortable feelings but to transform them into more adaptive feelings.

- **What are three major approaches to cognitive-behavioural therapy?** Cognitive-behavioural therapies focus on modifying the maladaptive cognitions that are believed to underlie emotional problems and self-defeating behaviour. Ellis's rational-emotive behaviour therapy focuses on disputing the irrational beliefs that occasion emotional distress and substituting adaptive behaviour for maladaptive behaviour. Beck's cognitive therapy focuses on helping clients identify, challenge, and replace distorted cognitions, such as tendencies to magnify negative events and minimize personal accomplishments. Meichenbaum's cognitive-behavioural therapy integrates behavioural and cognitive approaches in treatment.

- **What are the general aims of group therapy, family therapy, and marital therapy?** Group therapy provides opportunities for mutual support and shared learning experiences within a group setting to help individuals overcome psychological difficulties and develop more adaptive behaviours. Family therapists work with conflicted families to help them resolve their differences. Family therapists focus on clarifying family communications, resolving role conflicts, guarding against scapegoating individual members, and helping members develop greater autonomy. Marital therapists focus on helping couples improve their communications and resolve their differences.

- **Does psychotherapy work?** Evidence from meta-analyses of psychotherapy outcome studies that compare psychotherapy with control groups supports the value of various approaches to psychotherapy.

- **How are multicultural issues involved in psychotherapy?** Therapists need to take cultural factors into account and become more aware of how their own biases may affect the therapeutic process. Western forms of psychotherapy may be inappropriate in treating members of cultural groups when conflicts in underlying cultural values emerge.

ABNORMAL PSYCHOLOGY AND SOCIETY

Psychiatric Commitment and Patients' Rights

In Canada, legal placement of people in psychiatric institutions against their will is called civil or psychiatric commitment. Through **civil commitment**, individuals deemed to be mentally disordered and a threat to themselves or others may be involuntarily confined to psychiatric institutions to provide them with treatment and help ensure their own safety and that of others. Civil commitment should be distinguished from legal or criminal commitment, in which an individual who has been acquitted of a crime by reason of insanity—that is, found to be "not criminally responsible on account of a mental disorder"—is placed in a psychiatric institution for treatment. In **legal commitment**, a criminal's unlawful act is judged by a court of law to be the result of a mental disorder or defect

civil commitment Legal process involved in placing an individual in a mental institution, even against his or her will. Also called *psychiatric commitment*.

legal commitment Legal process involved in confining a person found "not criminally responsible on account of a mental disorder" in a mental institution. Also called *criminal commitment*.

that should be dealt with by having the individual committed to a psychiatric hospital where treatment can be provided rather than having the individual incarcerated in a prison.

Civil commitment should also be distinguished from voluntary hospitalization, in which a person voluntarily seeks treatment in a psychiatric institution and can, with adequate notice, leave the institution when she or he so desires. Even in such cases, however, when hospital staffers believe that a voluntary patient presents a threat to her or his own welfare or to others, the staff may petition the court to change the patient's legal status from voluntary to involuntary.

Involuntary placement of an individual in a psychiatric hospital usually requires that a petition be filed by a relative or a physician. Psychiatric review panels may be empowered by the court to evaluate the person in a timely fashion. In the event of commitment, the law usually requires periodic legal review and recertification of the patient's involuntary status. The legal process is intended to ensure that people are not indefinitely "warehoused" in psychiatric hospitals. Hospital staff must demonstrate the need for continued inpatient treatment.

Legal safeguards are usually in place to protect people's civil rights in commitment proceedings. Defendants have the right to due process and to be assisted by a lawyer, for example. But when individuals are deemed to present a clear and imminent threat to themselves or others, the court may order immediate hospitalization until a more formal commitment hearing can be held. Such emergency powers are usually limited to a specific period, such as 72 hours. During this time, a formal commitment petition must be filed with the court or the individual has a right to be discharged.

Standards for psychiatric commitment have been tightened over the past generation, and the rights of individuals who are subject to commitment proceedings are more strictly protected. Civil commitment is based on standards that give greater weight to patients' rights. The current criteria for civil commitment differ to some extent across Canadian provinces and territories. However, all require that the person be mentally ill and pose an imminent risk of harm or danger to him- or herself or others (Schuller & Ogloff, 2000). Thus, people cannot be committed or forced to take medication because of their eccentricity. People must be judged mentally ill and to present a clear and present danger to themselves or others in order for them to be psychiatrically committed.

PREDICTING DANGEROUSNESS In order to be psychiatrically committed, people must be judged to be at imminent risk of harming themselves or others. Professionals are thus responsible for making accurate predictions of dangerousness to determine whether people should be involuntarily hospitalized or maintained involuntarily in a hospital. But how accurate are professionals in predicting dangerousness? Do professionals have special skills or clinical wisdom that renders their predictions accurate, or are their predictions no more accurate than those of laypeople?

Unfortunately, psychologists and other mental health professionals who rely on their clinical judgments are not very accurate when it comes to predicting the dangerousness of the people they treat. Mental health professionals tend to overpredict dangerousness—that is, to label many individuals as dangerous when they are not (Monahan, 1981). Clinicians tend to err on the side of caution in overpredicting the potential for dangerous behaviour, perhaps because they believe that failure to predict violence may have more serious consequences than overprediction. The accuracy of predicting violence, especially violence in the long term, is improved if clinicians use the Psychopathy Checklist or similar instruments (H. Bloom, Webster, Hucker, & De Freitas, 2005). The Psychopathy Checklist was developed by psychologist Robert Hare and his colleagues at the University of British Columbia (e.g., Hart, Cox, & Hare, 1995). People with high scores on the checklist are classified as psychopaths. According to Hare (1996b), psychopaths are

> predators who use charm, manipulation, intimidation, and violence to control others and to satisfy their own selfish needs. Lacking in conscience and in feelings for others, they cold-bloodedly take what they want and do as they please, violating social norms and expectations without the slightest sense of guilt or regret (p. 26).

Who is the most dangerous? Is it the apparently drunk driver (A)? Is it the institutionalized psychiatric patient (B)? Or is it the scheming corporate executive Bernie Madoff (C)? Critics of the mental health system, such as psychiatrist Thomas Szasz, point out that drunk drivers account for more injuries and deaths than do people with paranoid schizophrenia, although the latter are more likely to be committed. Others have suggested that corporate executives who knowingly make decisions that jeopardize the health of employees and consumers to maximize profits are guilty of corporate violence that accounts for more deaths and injuries than other types of crime.

How likely is it that truly dangerous people will disclose their intentions to health professionals who are evaluating them or to their own therapists? The client in therapy is not likely to inform a therapist of a clear threat, such as "I'm going to kill ———— next Wednesday morning." Threats are more likely to be vague and nonspecific, as in "I'm so sick of ————; I could kill her," or "I swear he's driving me to murder." In such cases, therapists must infer dangerousness from hostile gestures and veiled threats. Vague, indirect threats of violence are less reliable indicators of dangerousness than specific and direct threats.

As we explore in the Closer Look box on page 90, the problem of predicting dangerousness also arises when therapists need to evaluate the seriousness of threats made by their patients against others.

PATIENTS' RIGHTS We have considered society's right to hospitalize involuntarily people who are judged to be mentally ill and who pose a threat to themselves or others. What happens following commitment, however? Do involuntarily committed patients have the right to receive or demand treatment? Or can society just warehouse them in psychiatric facilities indefinitely without treating them? Consider the opposite side of the coin as well: May people who are involuntarily committed refuse treatment? Such issues fall under the umbrella of patients' rights. Generally speaking, the history of abuses in the mental health system, as highlighted in such popular books and movies as *One Flew Over the Cuckoo's Nest*, have led to a tightening of standards of care and adoption of legal guarantees to protect patients' rights. The legal status of some issues, such as aspects of the right to treatment, remain unsettled, however.

Right to Treatment We might assume that mental health institutions that accept people for treatment will provide them with treatment. However, it is only in the past two decades that Canada has adequately extended civil rights to people in psychiatric hospitals. Patient-advocacy groups and precedent-setting court cases have been required to establish important patient rights, such as the right to treatment in the least restrictive environment (Olley & Ogloff, 1995).

Treatment in the least restrictive environment involves, among other things, not hospitalizing a patient when he or she can be appropriately treated as an outpatient. This is important because it allows the person to continue living in the community. Thus, the state provides mandatory care when necessary, such as involuntary hospitalization, but care must not be unduly restrictive.

One of the most difficult dilemmas a therapist may face is whether or not to disclose confidential information that could protect third parties from harm. Part of the difficulty lies in determining whether the client has made a bona fide threat against another person.

The other part of the dilemma is that the information a client discloses in psychotherapy is generally considered to be confidential. But this right is not absolute. The therapist is obliged to breach confidentiality under certain conditions, such as when there is clear and compelling evidence that an individual poses a serious threat to others. Under such conditions, the therapist could, for example, call the police to prevent the patient from causing harm to him- or herself or others.

In addition, an important Californian case, *Tarasoff v. the Regents of the University of California*, established a basis for the therapist's **duty to warn** the patient's potential victims. In 1969, a graduate student at the University of California at Berkeley, Prosenjit Poddar, a native of India, became depressed when his romantic overtures toward a young woman, Tatiana Tarasoff, were rebuffed. Poddar entered psychotherapy with a psychologist at a student health facility, during the course of which he informed the psychologist that he intended to kill Tatiana when she returned from her summer vacation. The psychologist, concerned about Poddar's potential for violence, first consulted with his colleagues and then notified the campus police. He informed them that Poddar was dangerous and recommended he be taken to a facility for psychiatric treatment.

Poddar was subsequently interviewed by the campus police. They believed he was rational and released him after he promised to keep his distance from Tatiana. Poddar then terminated treatment with the psychologist, and shortly afterward killed Tatiana. He shot her with a pellet gun when she refused to allow him entry to her home and then repeatedly stabbed her as she fled into the street. Poddar was found guilty of the lesser sentence of voluntary manslaughter,

rather than murder, based on testimony of three psychiatrists that Poddar suffered from diminished mental capacity and paranoid schizophrenia. Under California law, his diminished capacity prevented the finding of malice that was necessary for conviction on a charge of first- or second-degree murder.

Does the Tarasoff decision influence Canadian mental health practitioners? Since U.S. court decisions do not apply in Canada, the Tarasoff ruling does not necessarily have sway in this country. Some Canadian civil lawsuits have raised arguments similar to those in the Tarasoff case, but there has yet to be a legal precedent like the Tarasoff ruling (Glancy & Chaimowitz, 2003; Schuller & Ogloff, 2000). Even so, it could be argued that it is ethical for mental health practitioners to warn third parties of impending harm. Accordingly, a duty to warn has been included in the code of ethics for the Canadian Psychological Association (2000). The code states that psychologists should do everything reasonably possible to stop or offset the consequences of actions by others when these actions are likely to cause serious physical harm or death. This may include reporting to appropriate authorities (e.g., the police) or an intended victim, and would be done even when a confidential relationship is involved (p. 19).

Although therapists have difficulty accurately predicting dangerousness, the duty-to-warn provision obliges them to judge whether their clients' disclosures indicate a clear intent to harm others. In the Tarasoff case, the threat was obvious enough to prompt the therapist to breach confidentiality by requesting the help of campus police. In most cases, however, threats are not so clear-cut. There remains a lack of clear criteria for determining whether a therapist "should have known" that a client was dangerous before a violent act occurs (Fulero, 1988). In the absence of guidelines that specify the criteria therapists should use to fulfill their duty to warn, they must rely on their best subjective judgments.

---

duty to warn Obligation imposed on therapists to warn third parties of threats made against them by the therapists' clients. In the U.S., the *Tarasoff* case established the legal basis for duty-to-warn provisions. Although U.S. law does not apply in Canada, the Canadian Psychological Association states that, ethically, therapists have a duty to warn.

A problem in implementing this approach concerns the availability of treatment resources. A person might benefit from either inpatient treatment or a less restricting alternative, such as treatment in a group home in the community. But what happens when the less restrictive alternatives are not available? Even in wealthy countries like Canada, there are insufficient resources for treating patients in the community. Unfortunately, some patients are treated in psychiatric hospitals when they could be living in supervised accommodation in the community.

To make matters more complicated, patients have the right to be treated in the community even when they might be more appropriately treated in a psychiatric hospital. If community resources are unavailable, then the family sometimes assumes the onus of care, even though they may be ill prepared.

Right to Refuse Treatment Consider the following scenario: a person, John Citizen, is involuntarily committed to a psychiatric hospital for treatment. The hospital staff determines that John suffers from a psychotic disorder, paranoid schizophrenia, and should be treated with antipsychotic medication. John, however, decides not to comply with treatment. He claims that the hospital has no right to treat him against his will. The hospital seeks a court order to mandate treatment, arguing it makes little sense to commit people involuntarily unless the hospital is empowered to treat them as the staff deems fit.

Does an involuntary patient like John have the right to refuse treatment? If so, does this right conflict with the rights of the state to commit people to mental institutions to receive treatment for their disorders? One might also wonder whether people who are judged in need of involuntary hospitalization are competent enough to make decisions about which treatments are in their best interests.

Some mental health professionals have raised the concern that involuntarily committed patients who refuse medications would be "rotting with their rights on"—incarcerated but untreated (Appelbaum & Gutheil, 1979). Fortunately, this does not often happen—at least not in Canada. Since the proclamation of the 1982 Canadian Charter of Rights and Freedoms, there has been increasing recognition across the provinces and territories of the right of competent, involuntary patients to refuse treatment (J. E. Gray & O'Reilly, 2005). Today, provincial mental health legislation generally does not allow for institutionalization and compulsory treatment of people who refuse treatment, unless that person poses a threat to him- or herself or to the general public (Canadian Centre for Justice Statistics, 2003). A person like Edmond Yu, from the case study on page 84, would not be involuntarily hospitalized and treated unless he was judged to be at imminent risk of harming himself or others. As we saw earlier, Edmond refused treatment and was generally allowed to do so, even though he was psychotic and would have benefited from treatment. Fortunately, most people in need of psychiatric treatment do not refuse. Fewer than 10% persistently refuse treatment (Gratzer & Matas, 1994).

What are the rights of mental patients? Popular books and films such as *One Flew Over the Cuckoo's Nest*, starring Jack Nicholson, have highlighted many of the abuses of psychiatric hospitals. In recent years, a tightening of standards of care and the adoption of legal safeguards have led to better protection of the rights of patients in psychiatric hospitals.

Mental Illness and Criminal Responsibility

THE INSANITY DEFENCE Our society has long held to the doctrine of free will as a basis for determining responsibility for wrongdoing. The doctrine of free will, as applied to criminal responsibility, requires that people can be held guilty of a crime only if they are judged to have been in control of their actions at the time of committing the crime. Not only must it be determined by a court of law that a defendant has committed a crime beyond a reasonable doubt, but the issue of the individual's state of mind must be considered as well in determining whether the person can be held accountable for his or her crime. Thus, the court must rule not only on whether a crime was committed, but also on whether an individual is held morally responsible and deserving of punishment. The **insanity defence** is based on the belief that when a criminal act derives from a distorted state of mind, and not from the exercise of free will, the individual should not be punished but rather treated for the underlying mental disorder. Historically,

insanity defence Form of legal defence in which a defendant in a criminal case pleads guilty but not criminally responsible on the basis of having a mental disorder.

the consideration of the mental state of the individual at the time of the offence is a relatively recent consideration in cases of criminal behaviour. Changes to Canadian law actually had their inspiration in a famous case in England: the case of Daniel M'Naughten.

In early English law, which formed a basis for Canadian law, the insanity defence was also used. An important legal precedent for modern laws was set in the 1843 legal defence that led to the M'Naughten rule. This was based on a case in England of a Scotsman, Daniel M'Naughten, who had intended to assassinate the prime minister of England, Sir Robert Peel. Instead, he killed Peel's secretary, whom he had mistaken for the prime minister. M'Naughten claimed that the voice of God had commanded him to kill Lord Peel. The English court acquitted M'Naughten on the basis of insanity, finding that the defendant had been "labouring under such a defect of reason, from disease of the mind, as not to know the nature and quality of the act he was doing; or, if he did know it, that he did not know what he was doing was wrong." The M'Naughten rule, as it has come to be called, holds that people do not bear criminal responsibility if, by reason of a mental disease or defect, they either have no knowledge of their actions or are unable to tell right from wrong. A prominent Canadian case that exemplifies this rule of law is the attempted murder of former prime minister Jean Chrétien by André Dallaire, who was found guilty but not criminally responsible.

Armed with a knife, 34-year-old André Dallaire, a thin, bespectacled former convenience-store worker, broke into the home of Prime Minister Jean Chrétien. It was the early hours of November 5, 1995. Dallaire climbed the fence surrounding Chrétien's residence, smashed a window, and entered the house. He intended to cut the prime minister's throat. An inner voice commanded him to kill Chrétien, while another voice told him to stop. Dallaire believed he was a secret agent whose mission was to avenge the "No" side's victory in the Quebec referendum on independence (Fisher, 1996). He believed he would be glorified for liberating Canada from a "traitorous" prime minister.

Outside the bedroom where the prime minister was sleeping, Dallaire encountered Chrétien's wife, Aline. She fled to the bedroom, locked the door, and called the police. The RCMP arrived shortly afterward and took Dallaire into custody. A psychiatric assessment revealed that he was delusional and hallucinating. He had been suffering from paranoid schizophrenia since the age of 16. The judge ruled that Dallaire's intent to kill was the product of a severe mental disorder. Although Dallaire was found guilty of attempted murder, he was not held criminally responsible for his actions because he was suffering from hallucinations and delusions at the time, which prevented him from appreciating the nature and wrongfulness of his actions. Thus, Dallaire was judged to be "not criminally responsible on account of a mental disorder" (**NCRMD**). This is Canada's version of the insanity defence, and is similar to the "not guilty by reason of insanity" defence used in other countries.

How often is the NCRMD defence used? Do people using this defence really "get away with murder" or attempted murder? The defence is not often used, and even when it is used few people are judged to be NCRMD. From 1992 to 1998 in British Columbia, for example, an average of only 46 people per year were found NCRMD (Livingston, Wilson, Tien, & Bond, 2003). People found NCRMD are typically hospitalized until they can safely be released into the community, although some may not be hospitalized if they are no longer suffering from a serious mental disorder.

Before the NCRMD defence came into effect, the 1985 Criminal Code of Canada allowed a person to be found not guilty by reason of insanity (**NGRI**). People found NGRI were automatically placed in a secure psychiatric facility, indefinitely, "until the pleasure of the Lieutenant Governor is known"—meaning that a person was detained until the mental disorder had improved to an extent that would justify release. A person could be detained for longer than he or she would have served in prison if convicted for the crime (J. E. Gray & O'Reilly, 2005). Some people judged to be NGRI were held in psychiatric hospitals without receiving adequate treatment. Later changes to the Criminal Code rectified this problem.

NCRMD Not criminally responsible on account of a mental disorder.

NGRI A person found not guilty by reason of insanity.

Changes came with the case of *R. v. Swain* (1991), which challenged the insanity defence in a number of ways. Owen Swain was charged with aggravated assault after attacking his wife and two children. At the time, he was psychotic; he believed that his family was being attacked by devils and that he had to perform certain rituals to protect them, including physically assaulting them. Swain was hospitalized, successfully treated with antipsychotic medication, and then released on bail. At his trial, the Crown raised the issue of insanity, despite Swain's objections and those of his lawyer. Swain was judged NGRI, which meant that he would be involuntarily placed in a psychiatric hospital. He appealed the decision, arguing that it violated his rights for the Crown to raise the issue of insanity and to automatically incarcerate people judged to be NGRI. Swain's appeal was successful, which led to important reforms in the Canadian version of the insanity defence.

As a result, the Canadian Criminal Code was amended to give the accused person greater procedural and civil rights. The amendment was an attempt to balance the goals of fair and humane treatment of the offender against the safety of the public (R. D. Schneider, Glancy, Bradford, & Seibenmorgen, 2000). Major changes included reductions in how long an accused person could be detained in a psychiatric facility and changes in the procedures for making appeals. The mental disorder defence was also changed, with NGRI being replaced with not criminally responsible on account of a mental disorder (NCRMD). Thus, the Canadian Criminal Code now states that

> no person is criminally responsible for an act committed or an omission made while suffering from a mental disorder that rendered the person incapable of appreciating the nature and quality of the act or omission or of knowing that it was wrong.

Moreover,

> although personality disorders or psychopathic [antisocial] personalities are capable of constituting a disease of the mind, the defence of insanity is not made out where the accused has the necessary understanding of the nature, character and consequences of the act, but merely lacks appropriate feelings for the victim or lacks feelings of remorse or guilt for what he [or she] has done, even though such lack of feeling stems from a disease of the mind. (Greenspan, in Greenspan, Rosenberg, & Henein, 1998, p. 50)

NGRI and NCRMD have many similarities, although there are some important differences. Under NCRMD, for example, the defendant is now considered to be "not criminally responsible" instead of "not guilty." This change more explicitly recognizes that the defendant committed the offence as opposed to being not guilty (S. Davis, 1993).

COMPETENCY TO STAND TRIAL There is a basic rule of law that those who stand accused of crimes must be able to understand the charges and proceedings brought against them and be able to participate in their own defence. The concept of competency to stand trial should not be confused with the legal defence of insanity. A defendant can be held competent to stand trial but still be judged not criminally responsible on account of a mental disorder. A clearly delusional person, for example, may understand the court proceedings and be able to confer with defence counsel but still be acquitted by reason of insanity. On the other hand, a person may be incapable of standing trial at a particular time but be tried and acquitted or convicted at a later time when competency is restored.

In Canada, a judge can order compulsory treatment if the defendant in a criminal trial is found unfit to stand trial due to a mental disorder. It is presumed that every defendant is fit to stand trial unless the court is convinced otherwise. In order to verify the accused's fitness, a psychiatric assessment is needed. The issue of fitness is settled in a separate trial. A defendant is held unfit to stand trial when he or she meets one or more of the following (Bal & Koenraadt, 2000) criteria:

- is not capable of conducting his or her defence
- can't distinguish between available pleas
- doesn't understand the nature and purpose of the proceedings, including the respective roles of the judge, jury, and counsel
- is unable to communicate with counsel rationally or make critical decisions on counsel's advice
- is unable to take the stand to testify if necessary

An accused found unfit to stand trial can be committed to compulsory treatment in a psychiatric hospital. The case is adjourned until the accused has recovered to such an extent that he or she can be found fit. Mentally ill offenders can be committed to a psychiatric hospital on the verdict of unfitness to stand trial for an unlimited time without their criminal case being tried. Consequently, these accused offenders form a relatively large part of the population in psychiatric hospitals (Bal & Koenraadt, 2000).

REVIEW IT

Mental Illness and Criminal Responsibility

- **What are the legal bases of Canada's insanity defence?** The M'Naughten rule, based on a case in England in 1843, treated the failure to appreciate the wrongfulness of one's action as the basis of legal insanity. This rule was adapted and modified over the years to become "not guilty by reason of insanity" (NGRI) and, more recently, "not criminally responsible on account of a mental disorder" (NCRMD). A person found guilty of a crime is judged to be NCRMD if he or she was suffering from a mental disorder that rendered the person incapable of appreciating the nature and quality of the act or omission or of knowing that it was wrong.

- **What is meant by the legal concept of competency to stand trial?** People who are accused of crimes but are incapable of understanding the charges against them or assisting in their own defence can be found incompetent to stand trial and remanded to a psychiatric facility.

Define It

ambulatory, 56
antidepressants, 69
baseline, 53
behavioural assessment, 52
behavioural interview, 52
behavioural rating scale, 54
civil commitment, 87
client-centred therapy, 76
countertransference, 74
culture-bound disorders, 65
deviation IQ, 43
displacement, 73
duty to warn, 90
eclectic orientation, 67
electroconvulsive therapy, 70
electrodermal response, 56
electroencephalograph, 56
electromyograph, 56
forced-choice formats, 47
galvanic skin response, 56
gradual exposure, 75

insanity defence, 91
intelligence quotient, 43
intelligence, 43
legal commitment, 87
mental age, 43
mental status examination, 43
meta-analysis, 83
monoamine oxidase (MAO) inhibitors, 69
NCRMD, 92
neuroleptics, 69
neuropsychological assessment, 51
NGRI, 92
nonspecific treatment factors, 83
objective tests, 47
person-centred therapy, 76
prefrontal lobotomy, 71
psychometric approach, 52
psychopharmacology, 68
psychotherapy, 67

rebound anxiety, 69
reliable, 63
repetitive transcranial magnetic stimulation, 71
selective serotonin-reuptake inhibitors (SSRIs), 69
self-monitoring, 53
semi-structured interview, 42
structured interview, 42
syndromes, 61
systematic desensitization, 75
taijin-kyofu-sho, 65
token economies, 76
tolerance, 68
transference relationship, 73
tricyclics, 69
unconditional positive regard, 76
unstructured interview, 42
validity scales, 47
validity, 63

Think About It

- Can you think of other ways we might classify abnormal behaviour patterns? Which methods of assessment do you feel are most helpful in evaluating people with mental health problems? Explain.

- What type of therapy would you prefer if you were seeking treatment for a psychological disorder? Why? What problems do you see in taking pills to cope with anxiety or depression that may stem from academic or social difficulties?

- Do you think we should abolish the verdict of "not criminally responsible on account of mental disorder"? Should it be replaced with another type of verdict, like "not guilty by reason of insanity"? Why or why not?

Weblinks

CPA Code of Ethics www.cpa.ca/aboutcpa/committees/ethics/codeofethics
Visit this page to read the Canadian Psychological Association's code of ethics for psychologists.

Mental Health Info Source www.cmellc.com/topics
This is a mental health education website. It contains access to e-journals and information on a wide range of mental disorders.

Mental Help Net www.mentalhelp.net
This site has articles and descriptions of psychological disorders. It also provides links to assessment tools and other mental health resources and services.

Psychiatry Online www.priory.com/psych.htm
This site provides an international forum for psychiatry and has links to the latest articles, papers, and journals.

The Section on Clinical Psychology of the Canadian Psychological Association www.cpa.ca/aboutcpa/cpasections/clinicalpsychology
This Canadian Psychological Association site is home to the Section on Clinical Psychology. It is a central source for information about the clinical psychology profession in Canada.

Statistics Canada—Mental Health and the Criminal Justice System www.statcan.gc.ca/pub/85-561-m/2009016/section-a-eng.htm
Information is provided here on mental health and the Canadian criminal justice system, including statistics.

 MySearchLab offers you extensive help with your writing and research projects and provides round-the-clock access to credible and reliable source material. Chapter quizzes and a full electronic version of the text are also provided. Take a tour at www.mysearchlab.com.

Assessment, Classification, and Treatment of Abnormal Behaviour

Methods of Assessment

The Clinical Interview

- The interview involves questions designed to elicit relevant information from people seeking treatment.
- Formats: structured, semi-structured, and unstructured approaches.

Psychological Tests of Intelligence and Personality

- Intelligence tests:
  Stanford-Binet Intelligence Scale
  Wechsler scales
- Self-report personality inventories:
  MMPI-2 and PAI
- Projective personality tests: Rorschach Inkblot Test and the Thematic Apperception Test (TAT)

Neuropsychological Assessment

- These psychological tests are used to indicate possible neurological impairment or brain defects.
  Luria-Nebraska Test Battery.

Behavioural Assessment

- Responses are taken as samples of behaviour rather than as signs of underlying traits or dispositions.
- Types: self-monitoring, analogue or contrived measures, and behavioural rating scales.

Cognitive Assessment

- Focus on measurement of thoughts, beliefs, and attitudes in order to help identify distorted thinking patterns.
- Types: Automatic Thoughts Questionnaire (ATQ) and the Dysfunctional Attitudes Scale (DAS).

Physiological Measurement

- Types: heart rate, blood pressure, galvanic skin response (GSR), muscle tension (EMG), and brainwave activity

Probing the Workings of the Brain

- Methods: EEG, CT scan, PET scan, MRI, fMRI, BEAM, and MEG

Classification of Abnormal Behaviour

Internationally Recognized Diagnostic Systems

1. Diagnostic and Statistical Manual of Mental Disorders (DSM-IV-TR)
2. International Statistical Classification of Diseases and Related Health Problems (ICD-10)

The DSM and Models of Abnormal Behaviour

1. Axis I (Clinical Syndromes)
2. Axis II (Personality Disorders)
3. Axis III (General Medical Conditions)
4. Axis IV (Psychosocial and Environmental Problems)
5. Axis V (Global Assessment of Functioning)

Evaluation of the DSM System

- Certain DSM classes have generally good reliability and validity, but other diagnostic classes, such as personality disorders, are under review.

Advantages and Disadvantages of the DSM System

- Strengths: use of specified diagnostic criteria and a multiaxial system to provide a comprehensive picture of the person's functioning.
- Weaknesses: questions about reliability and validity of certain diagnostic categories, and the adoption of a medical model framework for classifying abnormal behaviour patterns.

Methods of Treatment

Mental Health Professionals

- Three main types in Canada: clinical psychologist, psychiatrists, and social workers.

Biological Therapies

- Psychopharmacology: anti-anxiety drugs, antipsychotic drugs, antidepressants, and lithium.
- Brain Stimulation Techniques: electroconvulsive therapy (ECT), repetitive transcranial magnetic stimulation (rTMS), and deep brain stimulation (DBS).
- Psychosurgery: Early methods, e.g., the prefrontal lobotomy, have given way to more sophisticated psychosurgery techniques.

Behaviour Therapy

- Focus: changing behaviour.
- Methods: systematic desensitization, gradual exposure, modelling, token economies, aversive conditioning, social skills training, and self-control techniques.

Humanistic-Existential Therapies

- Focus: the client's subjective, conscious experiences in the "here and now."
- Methods: person-centred therapy and emotion-focused therapy (EFT).

Cognitive-Behavioural Therapies

- Focus: correcting maladaptive beliefs, automatic types of thinking, and self-defeating attitudes.
- Methods: rational-emotive behaviour therapy (REBT), Beck's cognitive therapy, and Meichenbaum's cognitive-behaviour therapy.

Eclectic Therapy

- Focus: draws upon techniques and teachings of different therapeutic approaches; based on the "best practices" concept.

Group, Family, and Marital Therapy

- Group therapy: provides mutual support and shared learning experiences.
- Family and marital therapy: focus on improving communication and analyzing roles in order to improve relationships.
- Computer assisted therapy.

Evaluating Methods of Treatment

- Psychotherapy outcome studies support the value of various approaches to psychotherapy.
- Nonspecific treatment factors: empathy, support, and attention shown by the therapist; therapeutic alliance; and the working alliance.

Psychiatric Commitment and Patients' Rights

Legal Commitment
- Legal process of confining in a mental institution a person found to be "not criminally responsible on account of a mental disorder."

Civil Commitment
- Legal process involved in placing a person in a mental institution, even against his or her will.

Predicting Dangerousness
- Difficult to predict, although methods such as the psychopathy checklist are useful.
- Duty to warn potential victim.

Patients' Rights
- Right to treatment.
- Right to refuse treatment.

The Insanity Defence

NCRMD—Current Canadian Version of the Insanity Defence
- Not criminally responsible on account of a mental disorder (NCRMD).
- NCRMD means that the person is guilty of the crime but that his or her actions were due to a mental disorder.

Competency to Stand Trial
- A defendant can be competent to stand trial but still be judged NCRMD.
- Competency involves the ability of a defendant to understand the charges against him or her and to participate in his or her defence.

3

Anxiety Disorders

CHAPTER OUTLINE

Types of Anxiety Disorders
Panic Disorder
Agoraphobia
Generalized Anxiety Disorder
Phobic Disorders
Adjustment Disorders
Acute and Posttraumatic Stress Disorders

Theoretical Perspectives
Psychodynamic Perspectives
Behavioural Perspectives
Cognitive Perspectives
Biological Perspectives

Treatment of Anxiety Disorders
Psychodynamic Approaches
Humanistic Approaches
Biological Approaches
Behaviour-Based Approaches

Did You Know That...

- As many as 17% of people will suffer from an anxiety disorder at some point in their lives?

- People experiencing panic attacks are likely to believe they are having heart attacks, even though there is nothing wrong with their hearts?

- Although women are less likely to experience traumatic incidents than men, they are more likely to develop posttraumatic stress disorder (PTSD) at some point in their lives?

- According to one theory, humans may be genetically programmed to more readily acquire fears of snakes than of cuddly animals?

- The same drugs used to treat depression can also help treat anxiety disorders?

Fear is an unpleasant emotion caused by the belief that someone or something is dangerous, likely to cause pain, or a threat. Fear is associated with real or imagined immediate threat, and its manifestation is often fight or flight. Anxiety can be about current concerns or future events, and it is apprehension about something. There is much in our world to be anxious about—our health, social relationships, examinations, careers, international relations, and the condition of the environment are but a few sources of possible concern. It is normal, even adaptive, to be somewhat anxious about these aspects of life. Anxiety serves us when it prompts us to seek regular medical checkups or motivates us to study for tests. Anxiety is an appropriate response to threats, but anxiety can be abnormal when its level is out of proportion to a threat or when it seems to come out of the blue—that is, when it is not in response to environmental changes. In extreme forms, anxiety can impair our daily functioning. Consider the case of Marius:

Slowly, trains snake their way through the city each morning. Most commuters pass the time reading the morning newspapers, sipping coffee, or catching a few last winks. For Marius, the morning commute was an exercise in terror. He noticed perspiration clinging to his shirt, but the air conditioning seemed to be working fine, for a change. So how then was he to account for the sweat? As the train entered the tunnel and darkness shrouded the windows, Marius was gripped by sheer terror. He sensed his heart beating faster, the muscles in his neck tightening. Queasiness soured his stomach. He felt as though he might pass out. Other commuters, engrossed in their morning papers or their private thoughts, paid no heed to Marius, nor did they seem concerned about the darkness that enveloped the train.

Marius had known these feelings all too well before. But now the terror was worse. Other days he could bear it. This time it seemed to start earlier than usual, before the train had entered the tunnel. "Just don't think about it," he told himself, hoping it would pass. "I must think of something to distract myself." He tried humming a song, but the panic grew worse. He tried telling himself that it would be all right, that at any moment the train would enter the station and the doors would open. Not this day, however. On this day, the train came to a screeching halt. The conductor announced a "signalling problem." Marius tried to calm himself: "It's only a short delay. We'll be moving soon." But the train did not start moving soon. More apologies from the conductor. A train had broken down farther ahead in the tunnel. Marius realized it could be a long delay, perhaps hours. Suddenly, he felt the urgent desire to escape. "But how?" he wondered.

Marius felt like he was losing control. Wild imaginings flooded his mind. He saw himself bolting down the aisles in a futile attempt to escape, bowling people over, trying vainly to pry open the doors. He was filled with a sense of doom. Something terrible was about to happen to him. "Is this the first sign of a heart attack?" he wondered anxiously. By now, perspiration had soaked his clothes. His once-neat tie hung awry. His breathing became heavy and laboured, drawing attention from other passengers. "What do they think of me?" he thought. "Will they help me if I need them?"

The train jerked into motion. He realized he would soon be free. "I'm going to be okay," he told himself. "The feelings will pass. I'm going to be myself again." The train pulled slowly into the station, 20 minutes late. The doors opened and the passengers hurried off. Stepping out himself, Marius adjusted his tie and readied himself to start the day. He felt as though he'd been in combat. Nothing that his boss could dish out could hold a candle to what he'd experienced on the 7:30 train.

The Authors' Files

Marius had suffered a panic attack, one of many he experienced before seeking treatment. The attacks varied in frequency. Sometimes they occurred daily, sometimes once a week or so. He never knew whether an attack would occur on a particular day. He knew, however, that he couldn't go on living that way. He feared that one day he would suffer a heart attack on the train. He pictured some passengers trying vainly to revive him while others stared blankly in the detached, distant way that people stare at traffic accidents. He pictured emergency workers rushing onto the train, bearing him on a stretcher to an ambulance. For a while, he considered changing jobs, accepting a less remunerative job closer to home, one that would free him of the need to take the train. He also considered driving to work, but the roads were too thick with traffic. No choice, he figured: either commute by train or switch jobs. His wife, Jill, was unaware of his panic attacks. She wondered why his shirts were heavily stained with perspiration and why he was talking about changing jobs. She worried about making ends meet on a lower income. She had no idea that it was the train ride, and not his job, that Marius was desperate to avoid.

Panic attacks, like the ones suffered by Marius, are a feature of **panic disorder**, a type of **anxiety disorder**. During a panic attack, one's level of anxiety can rise to a level of sheer terror.

Panic attacks are an extreme form of anxiety. Anxiety encompasses many physical features, cognitions, and behaviours, as shown in Table 3.1. Although anxious people need not experience all of them, it is easy to see why anxiety is distressing.

panic disorder Type of anxiety disorder characterized by recurrent episodes of panic.

anxiety disorder Type of psychological disorder in which anxiety is the prominent feature.

TABLE 3.1

Some Features of Anxiety

Physical Features of Anxiety	Behavioural Features of Anxiety	Cognitive Features of Anxiety
Jumpiness, jitteriness	Avoidance and escape behaviours	Worrying about something
Trembling or shaking of the hands or limbs	Clinging, dependent behaviours	A nagging sense of dread or apprehension about the future
Sensations of a tight band around the forehead	Agitated behaviours	Belief that something dreadful is going to happen, with no clear cause
Tightness in the pit of the stomach or chest	Seeking reassurance	Preoccupation with and keen awareness of bodily sensations
Heavy perspiration, sweaty palms	Repeatedly checking that something bad hasn't happened	Thinking things are getting out of hand
Heart pounding or racing		Feeling threatened by people or events that are normally of little or no concern
Light-headedness or faintness		Fear of losing control
Dryness in the mouth or throat		Fear of inability to cope with one's problems
Difficulty talking		Worrying about every little thing
Shortness of breath or shallow breathing		Finding one's thoughts jumbled or confused
Cold fingers or limbs		Thinking the same distrubing thought over and over
Upset stomach or nausea		Thinking that one must either flee crowded places or pass out
Difficulty swallowing, a "lump in the throat"		Not being able to shake off nagging thoughts

TYPES OF ANXIETY DISORDERS

According to a Simon Fraser University review of worldwide research on the prevalence of anxiety disorders, as many as 17% of adults will develop an anxiety disorder at some point in their lives (Somers, Goldner, Waraich, & Hsu, 2006). These disorders may persist for years or decades, especially if the person does not receive treatment.

The anxiety disorders, along with dissociative disorders and somatoform disorders (see Chapter 5, "Dissociative and Somatoform Disorders"), were classified as neuroses throughout most of the 19th century. The term *neurosis* derives from the root meaning "an abnormal or diseased condition of the nervous system." The Scottish physician William Cullen coined it in the 18th century. As the derivation implies, it was assumed that neuroses had biological origins. They were seen as an affliction of the nervous system.

At the beginning of the 20th century, Cullen's organic assumptions were largely replaced by Sigmund Freud's psychodynamic views. Freud maintained that neuroses stem from the threatened emergence of unacceptable, anxiety-evoking ideas into conscious awareness. Various neuroses—anxiety disorders, somatoform disorders, and dissociative disorders—might look different enough on the surface. According to Freud, however, they all represent ways in which the ego attempts to defend itself against anxiety. Freud's assumption of common **etiology**, in other words, united the disorders as neuroses. Freud's concepts were so widely accepted in the early 1900s that they formed the basis for the classification systems found in the first two editions of the *Diagnostic and Statistical Manual of Mental Disorders* (DSM).

etiology Cause or origin; the study of causality.

Since 1980, the DSM has not contained a category termed *neuroses*. The present DSM is based on similarities in observable behaviour and distinctive features rather than on causal assumptions. Many clinicians continue to use the terms *neurosis* and *neurotic* in the manner in which Freud described them, however. Some clinicians use "neuroses" as a convenient means of grouping milder behavioural problems in which people maintain relatively good contact with reality. *Psychoses*, such as schizophrenia, are typified by loss of touch with reality and by the appearance of bizarre behaviour, beliefs, and hallucinations. Anxiety is not limited to the diagnostic categories traditionally termed *neuroses*, moreover. People with adjustment problems, depression, and psychotic disorders may also encounter problems with anxiety.

The DSM-IV recognizes the following specific types of anxiety disorders: panic disorder (with or without agoraphobia), specific phobia, social phobia, generalized anxiety disorder, obsessive-compulsive disorder, and acute and posttraumatic stress disorders. Table 3.2 (on page 102) lists the diagnostic features of anxiety disorders. These are not mutually exclusive—people frequently meet diagnostic criteria for more than one disorder.

Panic Disorder

Panic disorder involves the occurrence of repeated, unexpected panic attacks. Panic attacks are intense anxiety reactions accompanied by physical symptoms such as a pounding heart; rapid respiration, shortness of breath, or difficulty breathing; heavy perspiration; and weakness or dizziness. The attacks are accompanied by feelings of terror, a sense of imminent danger or impending doom, and an urge to escape the situation. They are usually accompanied by thoughts of losing control, going crazy, or dying. People who experience panic attacks tend to be keenly aware of changes in their heart rates (S. Taylor, 2000). They often believe they are having a heart attack even though there is nothing wrong with their heart.

National surveys in Canada and the U.S. reveal that 1% to 5% of people develop panic disorders at some point in their lives (Grant et al., 2006). Panic attacks occur suddenly and quickly reach a peak

Panic. Panic attacks are associated with strong physical reactions, especially cardiovascular symptoms.

TABLE 3.2

Diagnostic Criteria for Anxiety Disorders

Panic Disorder Without Agoraphobia is characterized by recurrent unexpected Panic Attacks about which there is persistent concern.

Panic Disorder With Agoraphobia is characterized by both recurrent unexpected Panic Attacks and Agoraphobia.

Agoraphobia Without History of Panic Disorder is characterized by the presence of Agoraphobia and panic-like symptoms without a history of unexpected Panic Attacks.

Specific Phobia is characterized by clinically significant anxiety provoked by exposure to a specific feared object or situation, often leading to avoidance behavior.

Social Phobia is characterized by clinically significant anxiety provoked by exposure to certain types of social or performance situations, often leading to avoidance behavior.

Obsessive-Compulsive Disorder is characterized by obsessions (which cause marked anxiety or distress) and/or by compulsions (which serve to neutralize anxiety).

Posttraumatic Stress Disorder is characterized by the reexperiencing of an extremely traumatic event accompanied by symptoms of increased arousal and by avoidance of stimuli associated with the trauma.

Acute Stress Disorder is characterized by symptoms similar to those of Posttraumatic Stress Disorder that occur immediately in the aftermath of an extremely traumatic event.

Generalized Anxiety Disorder is characterized by at least 6 months of persistent and excessive anxiety and worry.

Source: Reprinted with permission from the *Diagnostic and Statistical Manual of Mental Disorders*, Fourth Edition, Text Revision, (Copyright ©2000). American Psychiatric Association. p. 429. Note: All of these disorders are coded on Axis I in the DSM-IV.

of intensity, usually in 10 minutes or less. They typically last for about 20 minutes and are associated with a strong sense of uncontrollability. For a diagnosis of panic disorder to be made, there must be recurrent unexpected panic attacks—attacks that are not triggered by specific objects or situations. They seem to come out of the blue. Although the first attacks occur unexpectedly, over time they may become associated with certain situations or cues, such as entering a crowded department store or, like Marius, riding on a subway train.

Panic sufferers are sometimes unaware of subtle changes in their bodily sensations that may precipitate an attack, and so the panic may be perceived as spontaneous because these underlying changes are not detected. If panic sufferers are unable to identify the actual triggers, they may attribute their sensations to more serious causes, such as an impending heart attack or break with reality ("going crazy").

After a panic attack, the person may feel exhausted, as if he or she has survived a truly traumatic experience, as in the following case:

> I was inside a very busy shopping mall and all of a sudden it happened; in a matter of seconds I was like a madwoman. It was like a nightmare, only I was awake: everything went black and sweat poured out of me—my body, my hands, and even my hair got wet through. All of the blood seemed to drain out of me; I went white as a ghost. I felt as if I was going to collapse; it was as if I had no control over my limbs—my back and legs were very weak and I felt as though it was impossible to move. It was as if I had been taken over by some stronger force. I saw all the people looking at me—just faces, no bodies, all merged into one. My heart started pounding in my head and my ears. I thought that my heart was going to stop. I could see black and yellow lights. I could hear the voices of people but from a long way off. I could not think of anything except the way that I was feeling and how I had to get out and run quickly or I would die. I had to escape and get into fresh air. Outside it subsided a little but I felt limp and weak; my legs were like jelly, as though I had run a race and lost. I had a lump in my throat like a golf ball. The incident seemed to me to have lasted hours. I was absolutely drained when I got home and I just broke down and cried. It took until the next day to feel normal again.
>
> Adapted from Hawkrigg, 1975, pp. 1280–1282. Reprinted courtesy of nursingtimes.net.

People often describe panic attacks as the worst experiences of their lives. Their coping abilities are overwhelmed. They may feel they must flee. If flight seems useless, they may freeze. There is a tendency to cling to others for help or support. Some people with panic attacks fear going out alone. Recurrent panic attacks may become so difficult to cope with that sufferers become suicidal. The DSM describes the criteria for the diagnosis of panic disorder in the following way:

> The essential feature of Panic Disorder is the presence of recurrent, unexpected Panic Attacks (see p. 430) followed by at least 1 month of persistent concern about having another Panic Attack, worry about the possible implications or consequences of the Panic Attacks, or a significant behavioral change related to the attacks (Criterion A). The Panic Attacks are not due to the direct physiological effects of a substance (e.g., Caffeine Intoxication) or a general medical condition (e.g., hyperthyroidism) (Criterion C). Finally, the Panic Attacks are not better accounted for by another mental disorder (e.g., Specific or Social Phobia, Obsessive-Compulsive Disorder, Posttraumatic Stress Disorder, or Separation Anxiety Disorder) (Criterion D). (APA, 2000a)

Panic disorder usually begins in late adolescence or the early 20s. Women are two to three times more likely than men to develop panic disorder (APA, 2000a). What little we know about the long course of panic disorder suggests it tends to follow a chronic course that waxes and wanes in severity over time (S. Taylor, 2000).

G. Ron Norton and colleagues at the University of Winnipeg were the first to discover that panic attacks are common among college students and other nonclinical samples. Norton's research and later studies by others showed that these panics are quite common but tend to be milder than those experienced by people with diagnosable panic disorder (Norton, Cox, & Malan, 1992).

Agoraphobia

Panic disorder is often associated with **agoraphobia**. About one third to one half of people with panic disorder also have agoraphobia, and the majority of people with agoraphobia have a history of panic attacks (APA, 2000a). Agoraphobia involves fear of places and situations from which it might be difficult or embarrassing to escape in the event of panicky symptoms or a full-fledged panic attack, or of situations in which help may be unavailable if such problems occur (see Table 3.3 on page 104). People with agoraphobia may fear shopping in crowded stores; walking through crowded streets; crossing bridges; travelling by bus, train, or car; eating in restaurants; or even just leaving the house. They may structure their lives around avoiding exposure to fearful situations and in some cases become housebound for months or even years.

Agoraphobia is more common in women than men (APA, 2000a). It frequently begins in late adolescence or early adulthood. Approximately 2% of adults have experienced agoraphobia at some point in their lives (Grant et al., 2006; R. C. Kessler et al., 2006). Agoraphobia may occur with or without an accompanying panic disorder. In panic disorder with agoraphobia, the person may live in fear of recurrent attacks and avoid public places where attacks have occurred or might occur. Because panic attacks can occur unexpectedly, some people restrict their activities for fear of making public spectacles of themselves or finding themselves without help (S. Taylor, 2000). Others venture outside only with a companion. Still others forge ahead despite intense anxiety.

People with panic disorder who must leave the house to work are less likely than those who do not work or who work from home to develop agoraphobia (Mineka & Zinbarg, 2006). This is because the necessity of leaving the house forces the person to confront his or her feared situations and thereby overcome the fears. In North American culture, it is more acceptable for women than men to stay home and adopt a traditionally feminine role. This might explain why agoraphobia is more common in women than men.

agoraphobia A fear of places and situations from which it might be difficult or embarrassing to escape in the event of panicky symptoms or a full-fledged panic attack, or of situations in which help may be unavailable if such problems occur.

TABLE 3.3

Diagnostic Criteria for Agoraphobia

A. Anxiety about being in places or situations from which escape might be difficult (or embarrassing) or in which help may not be available in the event of having an unexpected or situationally predisposed Panic Attack or panic-like symptoms. Agoraphobic fears typically involve characteristic clusters of situations that include being outside the home alone; being in a crowd or standing in a line; being on a bridge; and traveling in a bus, train, or automobile.

Note: Consider the diagnosis of Specific Phobia if the avoidance is limited to one or only a few specific situations, or Social Phobia if the avoidance is limited to social situations.

B. The situations are avoided (e.g., travel is restricted) or else are endured with marked distress or with anxiety about having a Panic Attack or panic-like symptoms, or require the presence of a companion.

C. The anxiety or phobic avoidance is not better accounted for by another mental disorder, such as Social Phobia (e.g., avoidance limited to social situations because of fear of embarrassment), Specific Phobia (e.g., avoidance limited to a single situation like *elevators*), Obsessive-Compulsive Disorder (e.g., avoidance of dirt in someone with an obsession about contamination), Posttraumatic Stress Disorder (e.g., avoidance of stimuli associated with a severe stressor), or Separation Anxiety Disorder (e.g., avoidance of leaving home or relatives).

Source: Reprinted with permission from the *Diagnostic and Statistical Manual of Mental Disorders*, Fourth Edition, Text Revision, (Copyright ©2000). American Psychiatric Association. p. 433.

People with agoraphobia who have no history of panic disorder may experience mild panicky symptoms, such as dizziness, which lead them to avoid venturing away from places where they feel safe or secure. They, too, tend to become dependent on others for support. The following case of agoraphobia without a history of panic disorder illustrates the dependencies often associated with agoraphobia:

> Carmen, a 59-year-old widow, became increasingly agoraphobic after the death of her husband three years earlier. By the time she came for treatment, she was essentially housebound, refusing to leave her home except under the strongest urging of her daughter, Renata, age 32, and only if Renata accompanied her. Her daughter and 36-year-old son, Peter, did her shopping for her and took care of her other needs as best they could. Yet the burden of caring for their mother, on top of their other responsibilities, was becoming too great for them to bear. They insisted that Carmen begin treatment and she begrudgingly acceded to their demands.
>
> Carmen was accompanied to her evaluation session by Renata. The 59-year-old woman appeared frail when she entered the office clutching Renata's arm, and insisted that Renata stay throughout the interview. Carmen recounted that she had lost her husband and mother within three months of each other; her father had died 20 years earlier. Although she had never experienced a panic attack, she always considered herself an insecure, fearful person. Even so, she had been able to function in meeting the needs of her family until the deaths of her husband and mother left her feeling abandoned and alone. She had now become afraid of "just about everything" and was terrified of being out on her own, lest something bad would happen and she wouldn't be able to cope. Even at home, she was fearful that she might lose Renata and Peter. She needed constant reassurance that they wouldn't abandon her.
>
> The Authors' Files

Generalized Anxiety Disorder

generalized anxiety disorder Type of anxiety disorder characterized by general feelings of dread, foreboding, and heightened states of sympathetic arousal. Formerly referred to as *free-floating anxiety*. Abbreviated *GAD*.

Generalized anxiety disorder (GAD) is characterized by persistent feelings of anxiety that are not triggered by any specific object, situation, or activity but rather seem to be what Freud labelled "free floating." People with GAD are chronic worriers, and

Anxiety: No Panic Disorder	Anxiety: Panic Disorder
Jennifer was a nursing student in her first year at university. She was taking a full course load and beginning some practical training at a local hospital. She had been assigned to work on the cancer unit for a rotation. One day on the unit she was shadowing her supervisor as she usually did. In their interaction with patients, they spent time talking to someone who had just learned that his cancer had spread throughout his body. All of a sudden, Jennifer felt like the room was spinning around her. She had trouble breathing and felt as if there was a heavy weight upon her chest. She asked the supervising nurse if she could take a break. She went to a quiet part of the unit and tried to focus on her breathing. After a few minutes, she rejoined her supervisor and finished her shift, although she felt physically uncomfortable for the rest of the day. Later that night, she told her roommate about the incident and chalked it up to being overwhelmed by her school demands and having interacted with someone who had been given a terminal diagnosis.	Sade was a second-year business student at a local university. She was physically healthy, having never had any major medical issues. Her second-year course load was demanding, such that Sade had little time to spend with friends or her boyfriend. The stress was beginning to get to her. She began to notice heart palpitations while studying, and tried to brush them off as stress. On the day her mid-term schedule was posted, Sade found out that she had three mid-terms in one day. She was already feeling behind in her work. Later that day, while studying, Sade began to have chest pains and felt a tingling sensation in her head and her fingers. Her body felt hot and cold, and she felt droplets of sweat down her back. These symptoms quickly escalated and Sade began feeling panicked that she was dying. She clutched her heart and tried to take her pulse. She felt as though she needed to bolt from the library and get fresh air as quickly as possible. Once she was outside, the symptoms did not abate, and so Sade called 911. Later, at the hospital, the ER doctor explained to her that she likely had a panic attack. Sade wasn't convinced, and began to avoid the library for fear that she would feel this way again.

excessive, uncontrollable worrying is considered the key feature of the disorder (Behar & Borkovec, 2006). They may be excessively worried about life circumstances such as finances, the well-being of their children, social relationships, or even very minor things. Children with generalized anxiety are likely to be worried about academics, athletics, and social aspects of school life. Other related features include restlessness; feeling tense, "keyed up," or "on edge"; becoming easily fatigued; having difficulty concentrating or finding one's mind going blank; irritability; muscle tension; and disturbances of sleep such as difficulty falling asleep, staying asleep, or having restless and unsatisfying sleep (see Table 3.4 on page 106) (APA, 2000a). Not surprisingly, the features of GAD—anxiety, worry, and physical symptoms—cause a significant level of emotional distress or impaired functioning (Craske & Waters, 2005).

Generalized anxiety disorder tends to initially arise in the mid-teens to mid-20s and typically follows a lifelong course. The lifetime prevalence of GAD in the general population is estimated to be about 5% (Block, Kelly, & Carpenter, 2006). The disorder is believed to be twice as common in women as men. GAD frequently occurs together (comorbidly) with other disorders, such as mood disorders, or anxiety disorders such as panic disorder and obsessive-compulsive disorder. The following case illustrates a number of features of GAD.

Rishad was a 52-year-old supervisor at an automobile plant. His hands trembled as he spoke. His cheeks were pale. His face was somewhat boyish, making his hair seem greyed with worry.

He was reasonably successful in his work, although he noted that he was not a "star." His marriage of nearly three decades was in "reasonably good shape," although sexual relations were "less than exciting—I shake so much that it isn't easy to get involved." The mortgage on his house was not a burden and would be paid off within five years, but, Rishad said, "I don't know what it is; I think about money all the time." His three children were doing well. One was employed, one was in college, and one was in high school. But "with everything going on these days, how can you help worrying about them? I'm up for hours worrying about them," Rishad said.

"But it's the strangest thing." Rishad shook his head. "I swear I'll find myself worrying when there's nothing in my head. I don't know how to describe it. It's like I'm worrying first and then there's something in my head to worry about. It's not like I start thinking about this or that and I see it's bad and then I worry. And then the shakes come, and then, of course, I'm worrying about worrying, if you know what I mean. I want to run away; I don't want anyone to see me. You can't direct workers when you're shaking."

Going to work had become a major chore. "I can't stand the noises of the assembly lines. I just feel jumpy all the time. It's like I expect something awful to happen. When it gets bad like that I'll be out of work for a day or two with shakes."

Rishad had been worked up "for everything; my doctor took blood, saliva, urine, you name it. He listened to everything; he put things inside me. He had other people look at me. He told me to stay away from coffee and alcohol. Then from tea. Then from chocolate and Coca-Cola, because there's a little bit of caffeine [in them]. He gave me Valium [a minor tranquillizer] and I thought I was in heaven for a while. Then it stopped working, and he switched me to something else. Then that stopped working, and he switched me back. Then he said he was 'out of chemical miracles' and I better see a shrink or something. Maybe it was something from my childhood."

The Authors' Files

TABLE 3.4

Diagnostic Criteria for Generalized Anxiety Disorder

A. Excessive anxiety and worry (apprehensive expectation), occurring more days than not for at least 6 months, about a number of events or activities (such as work or school performance).

B. The person finds it difficult to control the worry.

C. The anxiety and worry are associated with three (or more) of the following six symptoms (with at least some symptoms present for more days than not for the past 6 months). **Note:** Only one item is required in children.

   (1) restlessness or feeling keyed up or on edge

   (2) being easily fatigued

   (3) difficulty concentrating or mind going blank

   (4) irritability

   (5) muscle tension

   (6) sleep disturbance (difficulty falling or staying asleep, or restless unsatisfying sleep)

D. The focus of the anxiety and worry is not confined to features of an Axis I disorder, e.g., the anxiety or worry is not about having a Panic Attack (as in Panic Disorder), being embarrassed in public (as in Social Phobia), being contaminated (as in Obsessive-Compulsive Disorder), being away from home or close relatives (as in Separation Anxiety Disorder), gaining weight (as in Anorexia Nervosa), having multiple physical complaints (as in Somatization Disorder), or having a serious illness (as in Hypochondriasis), and the anxiety and worry do not occur exclusively during Posttraumatic Stress Disorder.

E. The anxiety, worry, or physical symptoms cause clinically significant distress or impairment in social, occupational, or other important areas of functioning.

F. The disturbance is not due to the direct physiological effects of a substance (e.g., a drug of abuse, a medication) or a general medical condition (e.g., hyperthyroidism) and does not occur exclusively during a Mood Disorder, a Psychotic Disorder, or a Pervasive Developmental Disorder.

Source: Reprinted with permission from the *Diagnostic and Statistical Manual of Mental Disorders,* Fourth Edition, Text Revision, (Copyright ©2000). American Psychiatric Association. p. 476.

Phobic Disorders

The word *phobia* derives from the Greek *phobos*, meaning "fear." The concepts of fear and anxiety are closely related. We already know that **fear** is the feeling of anxiety and agitation in response to a threat. Phobic disorders are persistent fears of objects or situations that are disproportionate to the threats they pose. To experience a sense of gripping fear when your car is about to go out of control is normal because there is an objective basis to the fear. In phobic disorders, however, the fear exceeds any reasonable appraisal of danger. People with a driving phobia, for example, might become fearful even when they are driving well below the speed limit on a sunny, uncrowded highway. Or they might be so afraid they will not drive or even ride in a car. People with phobias are not out of touch with reality; they generally recognize that their fears are excessive or unreasonable.

A curious thing about phobias is that they usually involve fears of the ordinary things in life, not the extraordinary. People with phobias become frightened of ordinary experiences that most people take for granted, such as taking an elevator or driving on a highway. Phobias can become disabling when they interfere with daily tasks such as taking buses, planes, or trains; driving; shopping; or leaving the house. Different types of phobias usually appear at different ages, as noted in Table 3.5. The ages of onset appear to reflect levels of physical and cognitive development and life experiences. Fear of heights, for example, typically emerges when a child learns to crawl or walk and therefore is at risk for falling (B. J. Cox & Taylor, 1999). Let us consider the two types of phobic disorders classified within the DSM system: *specific phobia* and *social phobia* (also known as *social anxiety disorder*).

SPECIFIC PHOBIAS   Specific phobias are persistent, excessive fears of specific objects or situations, such as fear of heights (**acrophobia**), fear of enclosed spaces (**claustrophobia**), or fear of small animals such as mice or snakes and various other "creepy-crawlies." A person experiences high levels of fear and physiological arousal when encountering the phobic object, which prompts strong urges to escape the situation or avoid the feared stimulus. To rise to the level of a psychological disorder, the phobia must make a significant impact on a person's lifestyle or functioning or cause significant distress. You may have a fear of snakes, but unless your fear interferes with your daily life or causes you significant emotional distress, it would not warrant a diagnosis of phobic disorder.

According to the DSM-IV-TR, there are five diagnostic subtypes of specific phobia: (1) animal type (e.g., phobias of dogs or bugs); (2) natural environment type (e.g., phobias of storms, heights, or water); (3) blood-injection-injury type (e.g., phobias of seeing blood or receiving an injection); (4) situational type (e.g., phobias of specific situations, such as enclosed spaces or public transportation); and (5) other types (e.g., phobias of choking or contracting an illness). (Note that the close association between panic disorder and agoraphobia—i.e., most people with agoraphobia have a history of panic or

fear Unpleasant, negative emotion characterized by the perception of a specific threat, sympathetic nervous system activity, and tendencies to avoid the feared object.

specific phobias Persistent but excessive fears of a specific object or situation, such as a fear of heights or of small animals.

acrophobia Excessive fear of heights.

claustrophobia Excessive fear of small, enclosed places.

TABLE 3.5

Typical Age of Onset for Various Phobias

	Mean Age of Onset
Animal phobia	7
Blood phobia	9
Injection phobia	8
Dental phobia	12
Social phobia	16
Claustrophobia	20
Agoraphobia	28

Source: Öst, 1987, pp. 223–229. Copyright the American Psychological Association. Reprinted with permission.

Five diagnostic subtypes of specific phobias. Most phobias fall into five subtypes: (a) animal type, (b) natural environment type, (c) blood-injection-injury type, (d) situational type, and (e) other types (e.g., phobias of choking or contracting an illness).

panic-like episodes—is why agoraphobia is grouped with panic disorder rather than being classified as a subtype of specific phobias.)

Specific phobias often begin in childhood. Many children develop passing fears of specific objects or situations. Some, however, go on to develop chronic clinically significant phobias (Antony & Barlow, 2002). Claustrophobia seems to develop later than most other specific phobias, with a mean age of onset of 20 years (see Table 3.6).

Specific phobias are among the most common psychological disorders, affecting close to 1 in 10 people at some point in their lives (APA, 2000a). They occur more frequently in women than men, perhaps because of cultural factors that socialize women to be dependent on men for protection from threatening objects in the environment (Antony & Barlow, 2002). Clinicians need to be aware of cultural factors when making diagnostic judgments. Fears of magic or spirits are common in some cultures and should not be considered a sign of a phobic disorder unless the fear is excessive in light of the cultural context in which it occurs and leads to significant emotional distress or impaired functioning.

SOCIAL PHOBIA It is not abnormal to experience some fear of social situations such as dating, attending parties or social gatherings, or giving a talk or presentation to a class

TABLE 3.6

Diagnostic Criteria for Specific Phobias

A. Marked and persistent fear that is excessive or unreasonable, cued by the presence or anticipation of a specific object or situation (e.g., flying, heights, animals, receiving an injection, seeing blood).

B. Exposure to the phobic stimulus almost invariably provokes an immediate anxiety response, which may take the form of a situationally bound or situationally predisposed Panic Attack. **Note:** In children, the anxiety may be expressed by crying, tantrums, freezing, or clinging.

C. The person recognizes that the fear is excessive or unreasonable. Note: In children, this feature may be absent.

D. The phobic situation(s) is avoided or else is endured with intense anxiety or distress.

E. The avoidance, anxious anticipation, or distress in the feared situation(s) interferes significantly with the person's normal routine, occupational (or academic) functioning, or social activities or relationships, or there is marked distress about having the phobia.

F. In individuals under age 18 years, the duration is at least 6 months.

G. The anxiety, Panic Attacks, or phobic avoidance associated with the specific object or situation are not better accounted for by another mental disorder. . . .

Source: Reprinted with permission from the *Diagnostic and Statistical Manual of Mental Disorders*, Fourth Edition, Text Revision, (Copyright ©2000). American Psychiatric Association. pp. 449–450.

or group. Yet people with **social phobia** have such an intense fear of social situations that they may avoid them altogether or endure them only with great distress. Underlying social phobia is an excessive fear of negative evaluations from others. As noted by Lynn Alden and colleagues at the University of British Columbia, people with social phobia often worry about their social presentation ("Do I look foolish?") and are frightened of doing or saying something humiliating or embarrassing (Crozier & Alden, 2001; Mellings & Alden, 2000). Research by Martin Antony, currently at Ryerson University, shows that people with social phobia tend to see themselves as not being as good as others (Antony, Rowa, Liss, Swallow, & Swinson, 2005). They tend to be severely critical of their social skills (C. T. Taylor & Alden, 2005) and become absorbed in evaluating their own performance when interacting with others (Woody, 1996). Some even experience full-fledged panic attacks in social situations.

> **social phobia** Excessive fear of engaging in behaviours that involve public scrutiny.

Surveys conducted in Canada and the United States suggest that between 3% and 13% of people develop social phobia at some point in their lives (APA, 2000a; Shields, 2004b).

According to McMaster University psychiatrist and anxiety expert Richard Swinson (2005), there is controversy about whether social phobia is over-diagnosed—that is, controversy about whether psychologists and psychiatrists are confusing ordinary shyness with a psychiatric disorder. Like all psychological disorders, social phobia is diagnosed only when it causes significant suffering or significantly impairs a person's level of functioning in important spheres of life, such as social relationships or performance at work or school.

According to a survey conducted by Statistics Canada, people with social phobia (as diagnosed by rigorous assessment methods), compared to people without the disorder, have lower levels of educational attainment, more employment difficulties, lower income, greater dependence on welfare and social assistance, lower likelihood of marriage, and greater social isolation (Shields, 2004b). To illustrate some of these problems, consider one of our patients, Megan. Megan was on the verge of dropping out of university because she was so anxious about giving presentations in class. She did not simply experience the pre-presentation jitters that we all commonly experience; she felt full-blown terror about giving class presentations, even though she was always well prepared to give her papers.

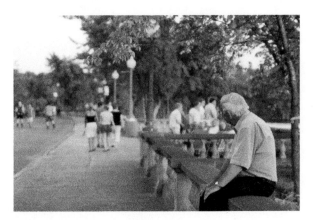

Not just shyness? People with social phobia sometimes experience such high levels of distress that they avoid social situations of all kinds.

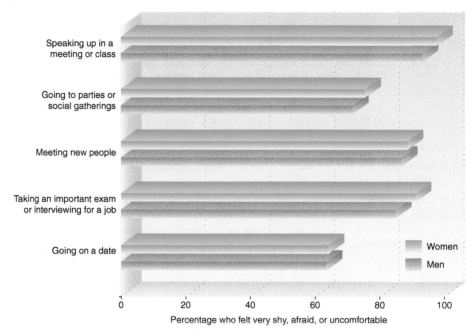

FIGURE 3.1 **Percentage of people with social phobia reporting specific difficulties associated with their fears of social situations.**
More than 90% of people with social phobia feel handicapped by anxiety in their jobs.
Source: Adapted from Statistics Canada, 2004b.

obsession An intrusive, unwanted, and recurrent thought, image, or urge that seems beyond a person's ability to control.

Social phobia is apparently more common among women than men (APA, 2000a; Shields, 2004a), perhaps because of the greater social or cultural pressures placed on young women to please others and earn their approval. People with social phobia may find excuses for declining social invitations. They may eat lunch at their desks to avoid socializing with co-workers. Or they may find themselves in social situations and attempt a quick escape at the first sign of anxiety. Some people with social phobia are unable to order food in a restaurant for fear the server or their companions might make fun of the foods they order or how they pronounce them. Others fear meeting new people and dating (see Figure 3.1). Relief from anxiety negatively reinforces escape behaviour, and escape prevents people with phobias from learning to cope with fear-evoking situations more adaptively. Leaving the scene before anxiety dissipates only strengthens the association between the social situation and anxiety. People with social phobia often turn to tranquillizers or try to "medicate" themselves with alcohol when preparing for social interaction.

The roots of social phobia may begin in childhood. People with social phobia typically report that they were shy as children (Crozier & Alden, 2001; M. B. Stein & Walker, 2002). Consistent with the diathesis-stress model, shyness may represent a diathesis or predisposition that makes one more vulnerable to developing social phobia in the face of stressful experiences, such as traumatic social encounters (e.g., being embarrassed in front of others). Social phobia tends to begin in adolescence and typically follows a chronic and persistent course in life (Antony & Swinson, 2000).

OBSESSIVE-COMPULSIVE DISORDER (OCD) An **obsession** is an intrusive, unwanted, and recurrent thought, image, or urge that seems beyond a person's ability to control. Obsessions can be potent and persistent enough to interfere with daily life and can cause significant distress or anxiety. Obsessions may involve persistent, unwanted doubts; the person may wonder endlessly whether he or she has locked the doors and shut the windows, for example. Some

Phobic disorder. Some people, such as the person shown here, have a fear of germs and becoming infected by them.

sufferers are plagued by personally repugnant images, such as the recurrent thought of a young mother that her children have been run over by traffic on the way home from school.

A **compulsion** is a repetitive behaviour (such as handwashing or checking door locks) or mental act (such as praying, repeating certain words, or counting) that a person feels compelled or driven to perform (APA, 2000a). Compulsions often occur in response to obsessional thoughts and are frequent and forceful enough to interfere with daily life or cause significant distress. A compulsive hand-washer, Corinne, engaged in elaborate handwashing rituals. She spent three to four hours daily at the sink and complained, "My hands look like lobster claws." Some people literally take hours checking and rechecking that all the appliances are off before they leave home, and then still doubts remain.

Most compulsions fall into two categories: checking rituals and cleaning rituals. Rituals can become the focal point of life. Checking rituals, like repeatedly checking that the gas jets are turned off or that doors are securely locked, cause delays and annoy companions; cleaning can occupy several hours a day. Table 3.7 shows some relatively common obsessions and compulsions.

Compulsions often appear to at least partially relieve the anxiety created by obsessional thinking (D. A. Clark, 2004). By washing one's hands 40 or 50 times in a row each time a public doorknob is touched, the compulsive hand-washer may experience some relief from the anxiety engendered by the obsessive thought that germs or dirt still linger in the folds of skin. The person may believe the compulsive act will help prevent some dreaded event from occurring, even though there is no realistic basis to the belief or the behaviour far exceeds what is reasonable under the circumstances.

Obsessive-compulsive disorder (OCD) affects between 2% and 3% of adults during their lifetimes and is typically chronic, waxing and waning in response to life stressors (APA, 2000a). The disorder seems to affect women and men in about equal numbers (APA, 2000a). The DSM diagnoses obsessive-compulsive disorder when people are troubled by recurrent obsessions, compulsions, or both such that they cause marked distress, occupy more than an hour a day, or significantly interfere with normal routines or occupational or social functioning.

The line between obsessions and the firmly held but patently false beliefs that are labelled *delusions*, which are found in schizophrenia, is sometimes less than clear. Obsessions, such as the belief that one is contaminating other people, can, like delusions, become almost unshakable. As noted by internationally recognized OCD expert David Clark, of the University of New Brunswick, although adults with OCD may be uncertain at a given time whether their obsessions or compulsions are unreasonable or excessive,

compulsion A repetitive behaviour or mental act that a person feels compelled or driven to perform.

TABLE 3.7

Examples of Obsessive Thoughts and Compulsive Behaviours

Obsessive Thought Patterns	Compulsive Behaviour Patterns
Thinking that one's hands remain dirty despite repeated washing	Constantly washing one's hands to keep them clean and germ free
Difficulty shaking the thought that a loved one has been hurt or killed	Constantly checking with loved ones to be sure they are alive and well
Repeatedly thinking that one has left the door to the house unlocked; worrying constantly that the gas jets in the house were not turned off	Rechecking that doors are locked or gas jets are switched off before leaving home
Constant concerns with contamination (e.g., fear of dirt, germs, or illness)	Excessive cleaning (e.g., ritualized housecleaning)
Obsessive need for symmetry or exactness	Checking, ordering, and arranging rituals; counting; repeating routine activities (e.g., going in/out of a doorway)
Unacceptable sexual or religious thoughts (e.g., sacrilegious images of Christ)	Mental rituals (e.g., silent recitation of nonsense words to vanquish a horrific image)

they will eventually concede that their concerns are groundless or excessive (D. A. Clark, 2004). True delusions fail to be shaken. Children with OCD may not come to recognize their concerns are groundless, however.

The case of Jack illustrates a checking compulsion:

Jack, a successful chemical engineer, was urged by his wife, Julie, a pharmacist, to seek help for "his little behavioural quirks," which she had found increasingly annoying. Jack was a compulsive checker. When they left the apartment, he would insist on returning to check that the lights or gas jets were off or that the refrigerator doors were shut. Sometimes he would apologize at the elevator and return to the apartment to carry out his rituals. Sometimes the compulsion to check struck him in the garage. He would return to the apartment, leaving Renata fuming. Going on vacation was especially difficult for Jack. The rituals occupied the better part of the morning of their departure. Even then, he remained plagued by doubts.

Renata had also tried to adjust to Jack's nightly routine of bolting out of bed to recheck the doors and windows. Her patience was running thin. Jack realized his behaviour was impairing their relationship as well as causing himself distress, yet he was reluctant to enter treatment. He gave lip service to wanting to be rid of his compulsive habits. However, he also feared that surrendering his compulsions would leave him defenceless against the anxieties they helped ease.

The Authors' Files

adjustment disorders Maladaptive reactions to an identified stressor or stressors that occur shortly following exposure to the stressor(s) and result in impaired functioning or signs of emotional distress that exceed what would normally be expected in the situation. The reaction may be resolved if the stressor is removed or the individual learns to adapt to it successfully.

Adjustment Disorders

Adjustment disorders are among the mildest of psychological disorders. An adjustment disorder is a maladaptive reaction to an identified stressor that develops within a few months of the onset of the stressor. The maladaptive reaction is characterized by significant impairment in social, occupational, or academic functioning or by states of emotional distress that exceed those normally induced by the stressor. For the diagnosis to apply, the stress-related reaction must not be sufficient to meet the diagnostic criteria for

Hassles. One of the major sources of stress in everyday life is common hassles such as traffic jams.

Difficulty in concentrating or adjustment disorder? An adjustment disorder is a maladaptive reaction to a stressful event that may take the form of impaired functioning at school or work, such as having difficulties keeping one's mind on one's studies.

TABLE 3.8

Subtypes of Adjustment Disorders

309.0   With Depressed Mood.   This subtype should be used when the predominant manifestations are symptoms such as depressed mood, tearfulness, or feelings of hopelessness.

309.24   With Anxiety.   This subtype should be used when the predominant manifestations are symptoms such as nervousness, worry, or jitteriness, or, in children, fears of separation from major attachment figures.

309.28   With Mixed Anxiety and Depressed Mood.   This subtype should be used when the predominant manifestation is a combination of depression and anxiety.

309.3   With Disturbance of Conduct.   This subtype should be used when the predominant manifestation is a disturbance in conduct in which there is violation of the rights of others or of major age-appropriate societal norms and rules (e.g., truancy, vandalism, reckless driving, fighting, defaulting on legal responsibilities).

309.4   With Mixed Disturbance of Emotions and Conduct.   This subtype should be used when the predominant manifestations are both emotional symptoms (e.g., depression, anxiety) and a disturbance of conduct (see above subtype).

309.9   Unspecified.   This subtype should be used for maladaptive reactions (e.g., physical complaints, social withdrawal, or work or academic inhibition) to stressors that are not classifiable as one of the specific subtypes of Adjustment Disorder.

Source: Reprinted with permission from the *Diagnostic and Statistical Manual of Mental Disorders*, Fourth Edition, Text Revision, (Copyright ©2000). American Psychiatric Association. pp. 679–680.

other clinical syndromes, such as anxiety disorders or mood disorders. The maladaptive reaction may be resolved if the stressor is removed or the individual learns to cope with it. If the maladaptive reaction lasts for more than six months after the stressor (or its consequences) have been removed, the diagnosis may be changed.

If your relationship with someone comes to an end (an identified stressor) and your grades are falling because you are unable to keep your mind on schoolwork, you may fit the bill for an adjustment disorder. If Uncle Harry has been feeling down and pessimistic since his divorce from Aunt Jane, he too may be diagnosed with an adjustment disorder. So, too, might Cousin Billy, if he has been cutting classes and spraying obscene words on school walls or showing other signs of disturbed conduct. There are several subtypes of adjustment disorders that vary in terms of the type of maladaptive reaction (see Table 3.8).

The concept of an adjustment disorder as a mental disorder highlights some of the difficulties in attempting to define what is normal and what is not. When something important goes wrong in life, we should feel bad about it. If there is a crisis in business, if we are victimized by a crime, if there is a flood or a devastating ice storm, it is understandable that we might become anxious or depressed. There might, in fact, be something more seriously wrong with us if we did not react in a "maladaptive" way, at least temporarily. However, if our emotional reaction exceeds an expectable response or our ability to function is impaired (e.g., avoidance of social interactions, difficulty getting out of bed, or falling behind in our schoolwork), then a diagnosis of adjustment disorder may be indicated. Thus, if you are having trouble concentrating on your schoolwork following the breakup of a romantic relationship, you may have a mild type of psychological disorder—an adjustment disorder.

Acute and Posttraumatic Stress Disorders

In adjustment disorders, people have difficulty adjusting to life stressors—business or marital problems, chronic illness, or bereavement over a loss. Here, we focus on stress-related disorders that arise from exposure to traumatic events. Exposure to traumatic events can produce acute or prolonged stress-related disorders that are labelled, respectively, **acute stress disorder** (ASD) and **posttraumatic stress disorder** (PTSD). Both types of stress disorders have occurred among soldiers exposed to combat, rape survivors, victims of motor vehicle and other accidents, and people who have witnessed the destruc-

acute stress disorder Traumatic stress reaction occurring in the days and weeks following exposure to a traumatic event. Abbreviated *ASD*.

posttraumatic stress disorder Type of anxiety disorder involving impaired functioning following exposure to a traumatic experience, such as combat, physical assault or rape, or natural or technological disasters, in which the person experiences, for at least a month, such problems as reliving or re-experiencing the trauma, intense fear, avoidance of event-related stimuli, generalized numbing of emotional responsiveness, and heightened autonomic arousal. Abbreviated *PTSD*.

tion of their homes and communities by natural disasters such as floods, earthquakes, or tornadoes or who have witnessed or experienced technological disasters such as railroad or airplane crashes.

In these disorders, the traumatic event involves either actual or threatened death or serious physical injury or threat to one's own or another's physical safety (APA, 2000a). The person's response to the threat involves feelings of intense fear, helplessness, or a sense of horror. Children with PTSD may respond to the threat differently, such as by showing confused or agitated behaviour. Exposure to trauma is quite common in the general population, even in countries that are not experiencing civil wars, such as Canada and the U.S. In the latter countries, more than two thirds of people experience some traumatic event in their lives (Galea, Nandi, & Vlahov, 2005). The lifetime prevalence of traumatic stressors is illustrated in Table 3.9, which presents the results from a survey of over 1000 people in Winnipeg (M. B. Stein, Walker, Hazen, & Forde, 1997). As in previous studies, the investigators found that men were generally more likely to experience traumatic stressors, although women were more likely to experience particular stressors such as sexual assault. Although men generally encounter more traumatic experiences, women are more likely to develop PTSD in response to trauma (Tolin & Foa, 2006). In other words, women are at a higher risk for this disorder than men, a consistent finding worth noting. Olff and colleagues (Olff, Langeland, Draijer, & Gersons, 2007) propose that women's increased risk may be due to the type of trauma they experience, their younger age at the time of trauma exposure, their stronger perceptions of threat and loss of control, higher levels of dissociation, insufficient social support resources, and greater use of alcohol to manage trauma-related symptoms such as intrusive memories and psychobiological reactions to trauma.

There are, unfortunately, many different examples of traumatic stressors leading to PTSD. Many Canadian First Nations girls were abused and developed PTSD after being removed from their communities and placed in residential schools (Söchting, 2004). An estimated 19% of U.S. Vietnam War veterans developed PTSD (Dohrenwend et al., 2006). A Canadian government report acknowledged that PTSD is an important problem for the

TABLE 3.9

Lifetime Prevalence of Traumatic Events in a Community Sample of 1000 Winnipeg Residents

Type of Traumatic Event	Women (%)	Men (%)
More common in women		
Rape (at or after age 18)	16	2
Sexual molestation before age 18	19	5
More common in men		
Combat	1	7
Witnessing severe injury or death	19	39
Being threatened with a weapon	12	20
Serious motor vehicle accident	20	29
Equally common in women and men		
Robbery or hold-up	11	13
Physical attack	21	25
Violent death of a friend or family member	35	34
Fire	9	8
Natural disaster	13	14
Other	17	19
Any trauma	74	81

Sample consisted of 524 women and 478 men

Source: Stein, Walker, Hazen, & Forde, 1997. Reprinted with permission from the *American Journal of Psychiatry*, (Copyright 1997). American Psychiatric Association.

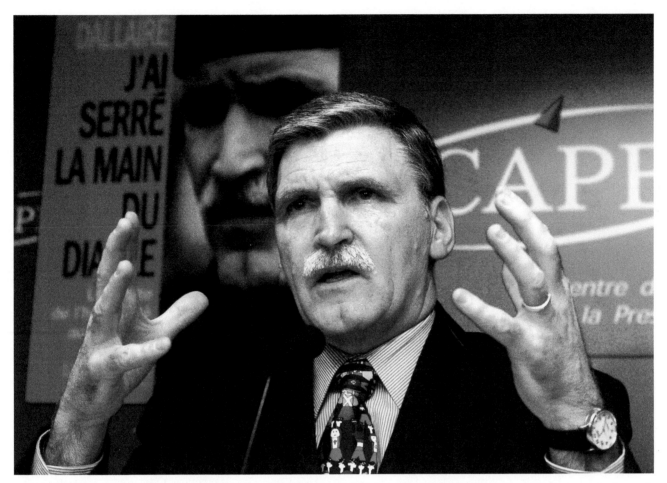

Roméo Dallaire. Dallaire, the former head of the doomed United Nations peacekeeping mission in Rwanda, was discharged from the military for PTSD a few years after the 1994 mission, in which his force tried in vain to stop the slaughter of 800 000 to 1 million Tutsis and moderate Hutus. He attempted suicide several times before learning to cope thanks to medication and therapy. Dallaire says about the effects of PTSD, "Post-traumatic stress disorder hard-wires events in your brain to the extent they will come back in digitally clear detail to your brain. You don't actually remember them. You relive them" ("Dallaire Says," 2007).

Canadian military and that more resources are needed to identify and treat people afflicted with this disorder (Marin, 2001). According to some estimates, as many as 10% to 20% of Canadian armed forces personnel, especially among those stationed in hot spots like Afghanistan, have developed PTSD (Wente, 2006). Some of the survivors of school shootings such as the Columbine High School massacre (1999) and some survivors of the Montreal shootings at École Polytechnique (1989), Concordia University (1992), and Dawson College (2006) also may have developed PTSD, although the precise figures are unknown. After the September 11, 2001, terrorist attacks on New York's World Trade Center, about 8% of Manhattan residents developed PTSD (Galea et al., 2002). Most were traumatized because they were in the vicinity of the towers. The effect of this experience was apparently worsened when these residents saw television images of people falling or jumping from the towers (Ahern et al., 2002). To put a face to these tragedies, consider the following case:

Jennifer Charron, a Canadian-born graphic artist, had studios in World Trade Center's north tower, on the 91st and 92nd floors. Jennifer slept late on the morning of September 11, 2001, planning to go to her studios later in the afternoon. She heard about the first jet on the radio, and rushed to her apartment window just in time to see the unthinkable happen again. "I watched this big plane come across the sky and slam into the south tower," the 30-year-old recalls. "I close my eyes [today] and I can still see it." Jennifer spent the rest of

September 11 on the phone trying to account for co-workers, numbed by the thought of how things might have been for her if the terrorists had struck in mid-afternoon. "You couldn't get away from it. You were constantly reminded," recalls Jennifer. Emotionally exhausted, she quit her job and returned to Ontario. "My favourite part of being back in Canada is that I don't think about it every day."

Gatehouse, 2002, p. 18. Copyright Rogers Communications. Reprinted with permission.

Not everyone who experiences trauma develops traumatic stress reactions. There are many important factors influencing a person's resiliency or vulnerability (Bonnano, 2005; S. Taylor, 2005). Vulnerability factors include a person's degree of neurobiological responsivity to traumatic experiences; the severity of the trauma and degree of exposure; the use of coping responses to stress; the availability of post-trauma social support; and perhaps perceptions of helplessness and leftover emotional effects, such as guilt and depression (S. Taylor, 2005).

To learn more about the vulnerability of certain individuals, researchers have been focusing on the hippocampus in the brain. Researchers have also looked at the size of the hippocampus in people with and without PTSD. They have found that people who have severe, chronic cases of PTSD have smaller hippocampi. The researchers have taken this to suggest that the experience of constant stress as a result of severe and chronic PTSD may ultimately damage the hippocampus, making it smaller (Kolassa & Elbert, 2007).

On the other hand, it has also been proposed that the hippocampus may play a role in determining who is at risk for developing PTSD. Some people may be born with a smaller hippocampus, which could interfere with their ability to recover from a traumatic experience, putting them at risk for developing PTSD. In other words, a smaller hippocampus may be a sign that a person is vulnerable or more likely to develop PTSD after a traumatic experience (Gilbertson et al., 2002).

The risk of being traumatized and developing PTSD is higher for people living in war-torn countries and for those engaging in hazardous activities or occupations. The latter was dramatically illustrated by a recent study of 100 women working as prostitutes in Vancouver (Farley, Lynne, & Cotton, 2005). Ninety percent of these women had been physically assaulted in prostitution. Many reported stabbings and beatings, concussions, and broken bones (e.g., jaws, ribs, collarbones, fingers), as well as cuts, black eyes, and other injuries—often incurred when they refused to perform specific sexual acts. Most of the women (72%) were classified as having PTSD, and 95% said they wanted to leave prostitution but felt unable to do so.

Surveys suggest that about 7% to 9% of Canadian and U.S. adults are affected by PTSD at some point in their lives (Keane, Marshall, & Taft, 2006; Van Ameringen, Mancini, Pipe, & Boyle, 2004). The diagnostic category of acute stress disorder was introduced with the publication of the DSM-IV, and we know little about its prevalence.

Some of the basic features of traumatic stress reactions are re-experiencing the traumatic event, avoiding cues or stimuli associated with the event, a numbing of general or emotional responsiveness, heightened states of bodily arousal, and significant emotional distress or impairment of functioning. In the case of an acute stress reaction, there may be an inability to perform necessary tasks, such as obtaining needed medical or legal assistance, or a failure to mobilize one's resources to obtain support from family as the result of not informing family members about the traumatic experience (APA, 2000a).

Acute stress disorder is further characterized by extreme anxiety and by *dissociation*—feelings of detachment from oneself or one's environment. People with an acute stress disorder may feel they are "in a daze" or that the world seems unreal. The diagnosis of acute stress disorder is applied to a traumatic stress reaction that occurs during the days and weeks immediately following the traumatic experience. Many people with acute stress disorder go on to develop more persistent stress-related problems, leading to a diagnosis of PTSD (A. G. Harvey & Bryant, 2002). In contrast to ASD, PTSD may persist for months, years, or even decades.

ASD frequently occurs in the context of combat or exposure to natural or technological disasters. A soldier may come through a horrific battle not remembering important features of the battle and feeling numb and detached from the environment. People who are injured or who nearly lose their lives in a hurricane, tsunami, or ice storm may walk around "in a fog" for days or weeks afterward; be bothered by intrusive images, flashbacks, and dreams of the disaster; or relive the experience as though it were happening again.

In acute and posttraumatic stress disorders, the traumatic event may be re-experienced in various ways. There can be intrusive memories, recurrent disturbing dreams, or the feeling that the event is indeed recurring (as in "flashbacks" to the event). Exposure to events that resemble the traumatic experience can cause intense psychological distress. People with traumatic stress reactions tend to avoid stimuli that evoke recollections of the trauma. For example, they may not be able to handle a television account or a friend's wish to talk about it. They may have feelings of detachment or estrangement from other people. They may show less responsiveness to the external world after the traumatic event, losing the ability to enjoy previously preferred activities or to have loving feelings.

Have you ever been awakened by a nightmare and been reluctant to return to sleep for fear of re-entering the orb of the dream? Nightmares that are part of traumatic stress reactions often involve the re-experiencing of the traumatic event, which can lead to abrupt awakenings and difficulty falling back to sleep because of fear associated with the nightmare and elevated levels of arousal. Other features of heightened arousal include difficulty falling or staying asleep, irritability or anger outbursts, hypervigilance (being continuously on guard), difficulty concentrating, and an exaggerated startle response (jumping in response to sudden noises or other stimuli) (APA, 2000a).

Although PTSD may wax and wane over time, it can last for years, even decades. Yet there is some good news: people who obtain treatment for PTSD typically recover sooner from its symptoms than those who do not seek help (S. Taylor, 2005).

REVIEW IT

Types of Anxiety Disorders

- **What is an anxiety disorder?** Anxiety, a generalized sense of apprehension or fear, is normal and desirable under some conditions but can become abnormal when it is excessive or inappropriate. Abnormal behaviour patterns in which anxiety is the most prominent feature are labelled *anxiety disorders*.

- **What is panic disorder?** Panic disorder is characterized by repeated panic attacks, which involve intense physical features, notably cardiovascular symptoms, and which may be accompanied by sheer terror and fears of losing control, losing one's mind, or dying. Panic disorder is often associated with agoraphobia.

- **What is generalized anxiety disorder?** Generalized anxiety disorder is a type of anxiety disorder involving persistent anxiety and worry that seems to be "free floating" or not tied to specific situations.

- **What are phobic disorders?** Phobias are excessive fears of specific objects or situations. Phobias involve a behavioural component—avoidance of the phobic stimulus—in addition to physical and cognitive features. Specific pho-

bia are excessive fears of particular objects or situations, such as mice, spiders, tight places, or heights. Social phobia involves an intense fear of being judged negatively by others.

- **What is obsessive-compulsive disorder?** Obsessive-compulsive disorder, or OCD, involves recurrent patterns of obsessions, compulsions, or a combination of the two. Obsessions are nagging, persistent thoughts that create anxiety and seem beyond a person's ability to control. Compulsions are apparently irresistible repetitious urges to perform certain behaviours, such as repeated elaborate handwashing after using a bathroom.

- **What are acute and posttraumatic stress disorders?** Both acute stress disorder and posttraumatic stress disorder involve maladaptive stress reactions that follow exposure to traumatic events. Acute stress disorder occurs in the days and weeks following exposure to a traumatic event. Posttraumatic stress disorder persists for months or even years or decades after the traumatic experience and may not begin until months or years after the event.

THEORETICAL PERSPECTIVES

The anxiety disorders offer something of a theoretical laboratory. Many theories of abnormal behaviour were developed with these disorders in mind. Here, we consider the contributions of these theoretical perspectives to our understanding of anxiety disorders.

Psychodynamic Perspectives

From the psychodynamic perspective, anxiety is a danger signal that threatening impulses of a sexual or aggressive (murderous) nature are nearing the level of awareness. To fend off these threatening impulses, the ego tries to stem or divert the tide by mobilizing its defence mechanisms. For example, with phobias, the defence mechanisms of **projection** and displacement come into play. A phobic reaction is believed to involve the projection of a person's own threatening impulses onto a phobic object. For instance, a fear of knives or other sharp instruments may represent the projection of one's own destructive impulses onto the phobic object. The phobia serves a useful function. Avoiding contact with sharp instruments prevents these destructive wishes from becoming consciously realized or acted on. The threatening impulses remain safely repressed. Similarly, people with acrophobia may harbour unconscious wishes to jump that are controlled by avoiding heights. The phobic object or situation symbolizes or represents these unconscious wishes or desires. The person is aware of the phobia but not of the unconscious impulses that it symbolizes.

Freud's (1909/1959) historic case of "Little Hans," a five-year-old boy who feared he would be bitten by a horse if he left his house, illustrates his principle of displacement. Freud hypothesized that Hans's fear of horses represented the displacement of an unconscious fear of his father. According to Freud's conception of the Oedipus complex, boys have unconscious incestuous desires to possess their mothers and fears of retribution from their fathers, whom they see as rivals in love. Hans's fear of being bitten by horses thus symbolized an underlying fear of castration.

A learning theorist view of Hans's childhood fear would suggest that he "learned" it from being frightened by an accident involving a horse and a transport vehicle, which generalized to a fear of horses. The story of Little Hans has sparked a spirited debate in the psychological annals.

Applying the psychodynamic model to other anxiety disorders, we might hypothesize that in generalized anxiety disorder, unconscious conflicts remain hidden but anxiety leaks through to the level of awareness. The person is unable to account for the anxiety because its source remains shrouded in unconsciousness. In panic disorder, unacceptable sexual or aggressive impulses approach the boundaries of consciousness and the ego strives desperately to repress them, generating high levels of conflict that bring on a full-fledged panic attack. Panic dissipates when the impulse has been safely repressed.

Obsessions are believed to represent the leakage of unconscious impulses into consciousness, and compulsions are acts that help keep these impulses repressed. Obsessive thoughts about contamination by dirt or germs may represent the threatened emergence of unconscious infantile wishes to soil oneself and play with feces. The compulsion (in this case, cleanliness rituals) helps keep such wishes at bay or partly repressed.

The psychodynamic model remains largely speculative, in large part because of the difficulty (some would say impossibility) of arranging scientific tests to determine the existence of the unconscious impulses and conflicts believed to lie at the root of these disorders.

Behavioural Perspectives

From the behavioural perspective, anxiety disorders are acquired through the process of conditioning. According to O. Hobart Mowrer's (1948) **two-factor model**, both classical and operant conditioning are involved in the development of phobias. The fear compo-

---

projection In psychodynamic theory, a defence mechanism in which one's own impulses are attributed to another person.

two-factor model O. Hobart Mowrer's theory that both operant and classical conditioning are involved in the acquisition of phobic responses. The fear component of phobia is acquired by means of classical conditioning (pairing of a previously neutral stimulus with an aversive stimulus), and the avoidance component is acquired by means of operant conditioning (relief from anxiety negatively reinforces avoidance behaviour).

nent of phobia is assumed to be acquired by means of classical conditioning. It is assumed that previously neutral objects and situations gain the capacity to evoke fear by being paired with noxious or aversive stimuli. A child who is frightened by a barking dog may acquire a phobia of dogs. A child who receives a painful injection may develop a phobia of hypodermic syringes. Consistent with this model, evidence shows that many cases of acrophobia, claustrophobia, and blood and injection phobias involve earlier pairings of the phobic object with aversive experiences (B. J. Cox & Taylor, 1999).

As Mowrer pointed out, the avoidance component of phobias is acquired and maintained by operant conditioning. That is, relief from anxiety negatively reinforces avoiding fear-inducing stimuli. A person with an elevator phobia learns to avoid anxiety over taking the elevator by opting for the stairs instead. Avoiding the phobic stimulus thus lessens anxiety, which negatively reinforces the avoidance behaviour. Yet there is a significant cost to avoiding the phobic stimulus. The person is not able to "unlearn" (extinguish) the fear via exposure to the phobic stimulus in the absence of any aversive consequences.

Learning theorists have also noted the role of observational learning in acquiring fears. Modelling (observing parents or others reacting fearfully to a stimulus) and receiving negative information (hearing from others or reading that particular stimuli—spiders, for example—are fearful or disgusting) may also lead to phobias (B. J. Cox & Taylor, 1999).

Some investigators suggest that people may be genetically prepared to acquire phobic responses more readily to certain classes of stimuli than to others (Mineka & Zinbarg, 2006). We're more likely to learn to fear spiders than rabbits, for example. This model, called **prepared conditioning**, suggests that evolutionary forces would have favoured the survival of human ancestors who were genetically predisposed to acquire fears of threatening objects, such as large animals, snakes, and other creepy-crawlies, and of heights, enclosed spaces, and strangers.

Posttraumatic stress disorder may also be explained from a conditioning framework. From a classical conditioning perspective, traumatic experiences function as unconditioned stimuli that become paired with neutral (conditioned) stimuli such as the sights, sounds, and smells associated with the trauma scene—for example, the battlefield or the neighbourhood in which a person has been raped or assaulted (S. Taylor, 2005). Subsequent exposure to similar stimuli evokes the anxiety (a conditioned emotional response) associated with PTSD. The conditioned stimuli that reactivate the conditioned response include visits to the scene and memories or dream images of the trauma. Consequently, the person avoids these stimuli. Avoidance is an operant response, which is reinforced by relief from anxiety. However, avoidance prolongs PTSD because sufferers do not have the opportunity to learn to manage their conditioned reactions. Extinction (gradual weakening or elimination) of conditioned anxiety may only occur when conditioned stimuli (i.e., cues associated with the trauma) are presented in a supportive therapeutic setting in the absence of the troubling unconditioned stimuli.

From a learning perspective, generalized anxiety is precisely that: a product of stimulus generalization. People concerned about broad life themes, such as finances, health, and family matters, are likely to experience their apprehensions in a variety of settings. Anxiety would thus become connected with almost any environment or situation. Similarly, agoraphobia would represent a kind of generalized fear triggered by cues associated with various situations in which it might be hazardous or embarrassing to have a panic attack (such as travelling far from home or being in a shopping mall). Some learning theorists assume that panic attacks, which appear to descend out of nowhere, are triggered by cues that are subtle and not readily identified.

There are challenges to the learning theory account of phobias. For example, many people with phobias insist that they cannot recall painful exposures to the dreaded stimuli. Learning theorists may assume that such memory failures are understandable because many phobias are acquired in early childhood. Yet many phobias, such as social phobia, develop at later ages and appear to involve cognitive processes relating to an exaggerated appraisal of threat in social situations (excessive fears of embarrassment or criticism) rather than the pairing of these situations with aversive experiences.

prepared conditioning Belief that people are genetically prepared to acquire fear responses to certain classes of stimuli, such as fears of large animals, snakes, heights, or strangers. Although the development of such phobias may have had survival value for prehistoric ancestors, such behaviour patterns may be less functional today.

From the learning perspective, compulsive behaviours are operant responses that are negatively reinforced by relief of the anxiety engendered by obsessional thoughts. If a person obsesses that dirt or foreign bodies contaminate other people's hands, shaking hands or turning a doorknob may evoke powerful anxiety. Compulsive handwashing following exposure to a possible contaminant provides some relief from anxiety. The person thus becomes more likely to repeat the obsessive-compulsive cycle the next time he or she is exposed to anxiety-evoking cues such as shaking hands or touching doorknobs.

Cognitive Perspectives

Cognitive theorists and researchers focus on how dysfunctional patterns of thinking may set the stage for anxiety disorders. Here, we examine some of the most common thinking patterns associated with anxiety disorders.

SELF-DEFEATING OR IRRATIONAL BELIEFS Self-defeating thoughts can heighten and perpetuate anxiety disorders. When faced with fear-evoking stimuli, a person may think "I've got to get out of here" or "My heart is going to burst out of my chest" (Antony & Swinson, 2000). Thoughts like these intensify autonomic arousal, disrupt planning, magnify the aversiveness of stimuli, prompt avoidance behaviour, and decrease one's confidence about controlling a situation.

Irrational beliefs may involve exaggerated needs to be approved of by everyone one meets and to avoid any situation in which negative appraisal from others might arise (Antony & Swinson, 1998). The following is one such example: "What if I have an anxiety attack in front of other people? They might think I'm crazy!"

Cognitive theorists relate obsessive-compulsive disorder to tendencies to exaggerate the risk of unfortunate events (D. A. Clark, 2004). Because people with OCD expect terrible things to happen, they engage in rituals to prevent them. An accountant who imagines awful consequences for slight mistakes on a client's tax forms may feel compelled to repeatedly check her or his work. Other irrational beliefs, such as perfectionism, also enter the picture (Antony & Swinson, 1998). The perfectionist exaggerates the consequences of turning in less-than-perfect work and may feel compelled to redo his or her efforts until every detail is flawless.

Cognitive theorists further argue that obsessions arise as a result of trying too hard to control one's thinking (D. A. Clark, 2004). All of us, from time to time, have unwanted, intrusive thoughts. These are the mental flotsam that drifts along the stream of consciousness, which some theorists have called "normal obsessions." Compared to obsessions in OCD, normal obsessions are easier to dismiss, are less frequent, cause less discomfort, and are less likely to lead to compulsions (S. Taylor, Abramowitz, & McKay, 2006). Normal obsessions are extremely common. To illustrate, Table 3.10 shows the frequency of students at the University of New Brunswick who had ever experienced normal obsessions (Purdon & Clark, 1993). Notice that the frequencies are extremely high. Women were more likely to have unwanted harm-related thoughts, whereas men were more likely to have unwanted sexual thoughts. Researchers at the University of Toronto and Northwestern University also reported evidence of normal compulsions; normal individuals are more likely to wash their hands if they believe that they might have behaved immorally (Zhong & Liljenquist, 2006). This suggests that people tend to associate moral impurity with physical dirtiness. This association may be particularly strong in people with OCD.

If nearly everyone experiences normal obsessions, then why do only some people develop more severe and frequent obsessions, such as those characterizing OCD? Part of the answer seems to lie in the way a person appraises his or her unwanted intrusive thoughts (Janeck, Calamari, Riemann, & Heffelfinger, 2003). Irrational beliefs about intrusive thoughts are likely to increase one's odds of developing clinical obsessions. Research by University of Waterloo psychologist Christine Purdon suggests that people with OCD may become particularly upset about their failure to control (suppress) their obsessions, which may make the person anxious and depressed and thereby worsen his or her

TABLE 3.10

Prevalence of Unwanted Intrusive Thoughts ("Normal Obsessions") Among Students Sampled from the University of New Brunswick

Unwanted Intrusive Thoughts	Women (%)	Men (%)
Harm-related thoughts		
Leaving the heat or stove on, resulting in an accident	79	66
Leaving the house unlocked, resulting in a break-in	77	69
Running the car off the road	64	56
Insulting a family member	59	55
Swerving into traffic	55	52
Becoming contaminated by touching a doorknob	35	24
Sexual thoughts		
Seeing strangers naked	51	80
Having sex in public	49	78
Performing a personally repugnant sexual act	43	52
Having sex with an authority figure (e.g., teacher, boss)	38	63

Source: Purdon & Clark, 1993. Copyright 1993 by Elsevier. Reprinted with permission.

OCD (Purdon, Rowa, & Antony, 2005). Similarly, research by Amy Janeck (University of British Columbia) and colleagues reveals that OCD people are excessively preoccupied with their thoughts; they are highly aware of them and monitor them while engaging in "too much thinking about thinking" (Janeck et al., 2003). This may be because people with OCD regard their obsessions as unacceptable and repugnant. To add to the cognitive difficulties experienced by people with OCD, research by investigators including Sean Radomsky at Concordia University has shown that repeated checking undermines memory confidence (Radomsky, Gilchrist, & Dussault, 2006). For example, the more you check and recheck that a stove has been properly switched off by repeatedly turning it on and off, the more uncertain you will be later on about whether you finally did switch off the stove. This is apparently because repeated checking makes it more difficult to visually recall the last check as opposed to previous checks (Radomsky et al., 2006). It is not known whether the same applies to other compulsions such as repeated handwashing.

The distinction between normal and abnormal obsessions is illustrated by two examples from our case files:

Julia was carving a Halloween pumpkin for her young daughter. As she wielded the knife, she had the unwanted intrusive image of stabbing her daughter. This greatly frightened Julia—she believed that "the unwanted image means that, subconsciously, I must want to kill my daughter." Julia desperately tried to push the image out of her mind, and became greatly alarmed when it returned. Because she placed so much significance on it, the image became highly important to her, and therefore kept popping into her mind.

In comparison, one of our colleagues, Sandy, had a similar unwanted image of stabbing her daughter while carving a Halloween pumpkin. Sandy believed the image was "mental garbage." She ignored the image and continued carving. The image held no significance for Sandy and therefore did not return.

The Authors' Files

OVERSENSITIVITY TO THREAT An oversensitivity to threatening cues is a cardinal feature of anxiety disorders (A. T. Beck & Clark, 1997). People with phobias perceive danger in situations that most people consider safe, such as riding in elevators or driving over bridges. We all possess an internal alarm system that is sensitive to cues of threat. This system may have had evolutionary advantages to ancestral humans by increasing the chances of survival in a hostile environment (A. T. Beck & Clark, 1997). Ancestral humans who responded quickly to any sign of threat, such as a rustling sound in a bush that may have indicated a lurking predator about to pounce, may have been better prepared to take defensive action (to fight or flee) than those with less sensitive alarm systems. The emotion of fear is a key element in this alarm system and may have motivated our ancestors to take defensive action, which in turn may have helped them survive. People today who have anxiety disorders may have inherited an acutely sensitive internal alarm that leads them to be overly responsive to cues of threat. Rather than helping them cope effectively with threats, it may lead to inappropriate anxiety reactions in response to a wide range of cues that actually pose no danger to them.

Research led by Michel Dugas at Concordia University suggests that the intolerance of uncertainty plays an important role in GAD (Buhr & Dugas, 2006). This intolerance is a special sort of sensitivity to threat that arises from the belief that it is unacceptable that threatening things occur. People who are intolerant of uncertainty become upset by the possibility of threatening events even when the probability of these events is very small. Considering that daily life is fraught with uncertainties, people who are intolerant of uncertainty are likely to frequently worry and become anxious about threats.

anxiety sensitivity A "fear of fear," or fear that one's emotions or states of bodily arousal will get out of control and lead to harmful consequences.

ANXIETY SENSITIVITY Anxiety sensitivity is a fear of fear. It refers to beliefs that internal emotions or bodily arousal will get out of control, leading to harmful consequences (S. Taylor, 2000). People with a high degree of anxiety sensitivity may be prone to panic when they experience bodily signs of anxiety, such as a racing heart or shortness of breath, because they take these symptoms to be signs of an impending catastrophe, such as a heart attack. Evidence collected at the University of British Columbia and elsewhere suggests that anxiety sensitivity is influenced by a combination of genetic factors and learning experiences. The latter teach people to be afraid of anxiety-related sensations—for example, observing one's parents becoming frightened of sensations such as rapid heartbeat or shortness of breath (S. H. Stewart et al., 2001).

Anxiety sensitivity is an important risk factor for panic attacks, as indicated by longitudinal research (Schmidt, Zvolensky, & Maner, 2006). As we will see next, panic-prone individuals also tend to misattribute changes in their bodily sensations to dire consequences.

MISATTRIBUTIONS OF PANIC SENSATIONS Cognitive models of panic disorder assume that panic attacks involve catastrophic misinterpretations of such bodily sensations as heart palpitations, dizziness, or light-headedness (D. M. Clark, 1986). Rather than attribute changes in physical sensations to more neutral causes, panic-prone people believe they represent the first signs of an impending heart attack or other threatening event such as a loss of control or "going crazy." Changes in bodily sensations in otherwise healthy individuals may be induced by various factors such as unrecognized hyperventilation, temperature changes, or reactions to certain drugs or medications. Or they may be fleeting, normally occurring changes in bodily states that typically go unnoticed by most people.

A cognitive model of panic disorder involving an interaction of cognitive and physiological factors is depicted in Figure 3.2. The model suggests that people with a proneness to panic disorder perceive certain internal bodily cues or external stimuli as unduly threatening or dangerous, perhaps because they are overly sensitive to these cues or have associated them with earlier panic attacks. The sense of threat induces anxiety or feelings of apprehension, which intensify physical sensations by producing an accelerated heart rate, rapid breathing, and sweating, among other bodily symptoms. These changes in bodily sensations, in turn, are misinterpreted as signs of an impending panic attack or, worse, an imminent catastrophe ("I'm having a heart attack!"), which in either case reinforces perceptions of threat, which further heightens anxiety, leading to yet more anxiety-related bodily symptoms, and so on in a vicious cycle that can quickly spiral to a full-fledged panic attack. Thus, catastrophic misinterpretations of bodily cues may set into motion a vicious cycle that brings on panic attacks in panic-prone individuals.

Mounting evidence points to the important role of cognitive factors in anxiety disorders. As the cognitive model would predict, for instance, people with panic disorder do have a greater tendency to misinterpret bodily sensations as signs of impending catastrophe than do people without anxiety disorders or those with other types of anxiety disorders (Mathews & MacLeod, 2005). Studies also show, as the cognitive model would predict, that panic-prone people have greater awareness of and sensitivity to their internal physiological cues, such as heart palpitations (S. Taylor, 1999, 2000). More research is needed, however, to determine the extent to which cognitive factors play a direct causal role in panic disorder or other anxiety disorders.

In addition to irrational beliefs and misinterpretations, other sorts of cognitive factors appear to play an important role in anxiety disorders. Research shows that people with anxiety disorders, compared to people without them, are more likely to selectively attend to threatening information, and there is some evidence that people with anxiety disorders are more likely to selectively remember threatening information (Mathews & MacLeod, 2005). These biases in attention and memory make intuitive sense; if you're anxious or frightened of something—say, spiders—then you're more likely to search for sources of potential threat (e.g., scanning a room for spiders) and you're more likely to recall where you've seen spiders in the past. The biases in attention and memory could be either vulnerability factors or a consequence of anxiety disorders, and they could worsen the disorders by increasing the chances that a person would notice or remember anxiety-provoking things.

FIGURE 3.2 **A cognitive model of panic disorder.** This model involves the interaction of cognitive and physiological factors. In panic-prone people, perceptions of threat from internal or external cues lead to feelings of apprehension or anxiety, which lead to changes in body sensations (e.g., cardiovascular symptoms). These changes lead, in turn, to catastrophic interpretations, thereby intensifying the perception of threat, which further heightens anxiety, and so on in a vicious cycle that may culminate in a full-blown panic attack.

Source: Adapted from D. M. Clark, 1986. Copyright 1986 by Elsevier. Reprinted with permission.

Biological Perspectives

We also have a growing body of evidence that biological factors play a role in anxiety disorders. Many questions remain concerning the interactions of biological and other factors, however.

GENETIC FACTORS   Increasing evidence points to the role of genetic factors in anxiety disorders. Consistent with a genetic contribution, studies of twin pairs reveal higher concordance (agreement) rates between MZ (monozygotic or identical twins) than DZ (dizygotic or fraternal) twins for many anxiety disorders (Kendler & Prescott, 2006). Research conducted at the University of British Columbia, for example, suggests that social anxiety and PTSD symptoms are influenced, at least to some extent, by genes (M. B. Stein, Jang, & Livesley, 2002; M. B. Stein, Jang, Taylor, Vernon, & Livesley, 2002). Table 3.11 on page 124, for example, shows the heritability coefficients for trauma exposure and PTSD symptoms. Findings from the Canadian civilian sample (M. B. Stein, Jang, Taylor, Vernon, & Livesley, 2002) are compared with results from a U.S. Vietnam-era twin registry (Lyons et al., 1993). Heritability coefficients range from 0 to 1, with larger numbers indicating that genes make a greater contribution to the variability of the variable in question. The results in Table 3.11 show two important things: first, genes make a significant but modest contribution to PTSD symptoms in both civilian and Vietnam-era populations; and second, the risk of experiencing a traumatic event is also influenced by genes. For example, the chances of being mugged, beaten up in a bar fight, or sexually assaulted (examples of assaultive trauma) are all moderately heritable. Recent research from UBC suggests that the genes that contribute to assaultive trauma are the same ones that contribute to antisocial personality traits (Jang, Stein, Taylor, Asmundson, &

TABLE 3.11

Heritability Coefficients for Trauma Exposure and PTSD Symptoms

Variable	Canadian Civilian Twin Sample (UBC Twin Study)	U.S. Vietnam-Era Twin Sample
Trauma Exposure		
Assaultive trauma	0.20	—
Volunteered for SEA* service	—	0.36
SEA* service	—	0.35
Combat exposure	—	0.47
Received combat decoration	—	0.54
PTSD Symptoms		
Re-experiencing	0.36	0.25
Avoidance	0.28	0.00
Numbing	0.36	0.28
Hyperarousal	0.29	0.26

*SEA = Southeast Asia. Heritability coefficients range from 0 to 1. The larger the number, the greater the influence of genetic factors on the variability of the variable in question.

Source: Data synthesized from Lyons et al., 1993, Stein et al., 2002, and True et al., 1993.

Livesley, 2003). In other words, if you have antisocial tendencies (as illustrated, for example, by a tendency to engage in criminal behaviour or to hang around with criminals in dangerous parts of town), then your risk increases for being exposed to certain types of traumatic events.

Many different genes are probably involved in the etiology of anxiety disorders, with each gene making a small, additive contribution to a person's risk of developing these disorders (Leonardo & Hen, 2006). There is no single gene for any of them. The process of "gene hunting" is a slow, laborious process, and many initial discoveries are not replicated in later research. So when you read a newspaper announcing that researchers have discovered "the" gene for, say, panic disorder, you need to ask the all-important question of whether the findings have been replicated.

Research replicated in several studies suggests that some genes have narrow effects, influencing a person's risk for developing a particular anxiety disorder. For example, genetic factors for phobias may specifically influence fear conditioning. Other genes have broader effects, influencing the risk for many different types of anxiety disorders as well as the risk for other disorders (Kendler & Prescott, 2006). The genes with broad effects may be the ones linked to **neuroticism**. Neuroticism is not an anxiety disorder but a personality trait characterized by an enduring tendency to experience negative emotional states. People with high levels of neuroticism (also called *negative emotionality* or *internalizing*) tend to cope poorly with stress and frequently experience feelings of anxiety, anger, guilt, and depression. People high on this trait are at increased risk of developing anxiety disorders and other emotional problems (Krueger & Markon, 2006).

A growing body of research suggests that genes exert their influence by interacting with particular environmental events (Moffitt, Caspi, & Rutter, 2006). For example, people possessing a particular form of a gene involved in the serotonin neurotransmitter system (i.e., the "short" version of the serotonin-transporter gene) are more likely than people without this genetic variant to react to stressful life events by developing anxiety or depressive symptoms (Leonardo & Hen, 2006). In other words, both genes and the environment are important; people with genetic vulnerability for developing anxiety disorders appear to be at risk primarily when they experience particular sorts of environmental events.

NEUROTRANSMITTERS The neurotransmitter **gamma-aminobutyric acid (GABA)** is implicated in anxiety. GABA is an inhibitory neurotransmitter, which means it helps

neuroticism Trait describing a general neurotic quality involving such characteristics as anxious, worrisome behaviour, apprehension about the future, and avoidance behaviour.

gamma-aminobutyric acid An inhibitory neurotransmitter believed to play a role in regulating anxiety. Abbreviated *GABA*.

tone down excess activity in the nervous system by preventing neurons from overly excit-ing their neighbours. When the action of GABA is inadequate, neurons can fire exces-sively, possibly bringing about seizures. In less dramatic cases, inadequate action of GABA may contribute to states of anxiety. This view of the role of GABA is supported by the action of the family of anti-anxiety drugs referred to as **benzodiazepines**, which include the well-known Valium and Ativan. Benzodiazepines regulate GABA receptors, thus enhancing GABA's calming (inhibitory) effects (Lydiard, 2003).

Dysfunctions involving serotonin or norepinephrine receptors in the brain have also been implicated in anxiety disorders (D. S. Baldwin, 2006). This may explain why so-called antidepressant drugs that affect these neurotransmitter systems in the brain often have beneficial effects in treating some types of anxiety disorders. Investigators also sus-pect that genes involved in the regulation of serotonin may play a role in determining symptoms of anxiety and depression (Hariri & Brown, 2006).

BIOLOGICAL ASPECTS OF PANIC DISORDER   The strong physical components of panic disorder have led some theorists to speculate that panic attacks have biological underpinnings, perhaps involving an underlying brain dysfunction (J. Gorman, Kent, Sullivan, & Coplan, 2000). Support for a biological basis of panic disorder is found in studies showing that people with panic disorder are more likely than people with-out to experience panicky symptoms in response to certain biological challenges, such as infusion of the chemical sodium lactate or manipulation of carbon dioxide (CO_2) levels in the blood either by intentional **hyperventilation** (which reduces levels of CO_2 in the blood) or inhalation of carbon dioxide (which increases CO_2 levels) (Barlow, 2002).

There appears to be a similarity between (a) the physiological and behavioural con-sequences of response to a conditioned fear stimulus and (b) a panic attack. In animals, these responses are mediated by a "fear network" in the brain that is centred in the amygdala and involves its interaction with the hippocampus and medial prefrontal cortex. Projections from the amygdala to hypothalamic and brain stem sites explain many of the observed signs of conditioned fear responses. It is specu-lated that a similar network is involved in panic disorder. A con-vergence of evidence suggests that both inheritable factors and stressful life events, particularly in early childhood, are responsi-ble for the onset of panic disorder (J. Gorman et al., 2000).

Cognitive theorists propose that cognitive factors may be involved in explaining these biological sensitivities. Theorists point out that biological challenges produce intense physical sen-sations that may be catastrophically misinterpreted by panic-prone people as signs of an impending heart attack or loss of control (Antony, Ledley, Liss, & Swinson, 2006). Perhaps these misinterpretations—not underlying biological sensitivities—may in turn induce panic.

Supportive evidence for the cognitive perspective comes from research showing that cognitive-behavioural therapy, which focuses on changing faulty interpretations of bodily sensations, eliminates CO_2-induced panic in panic disorder patients (Barlow, 2002).

The fact that panic attacks often seem to come out of the blue also seems to support the belief that the attacks are biologically triggered. However, it is possible the cues that set off many panic attacks may be internal, involving changes in bodily sensations, rather than external. Changes in physical cues combined with catastrophic thinking may lead to a spiralling of anxiety that culminates in a full-blown panic attack.

BIOLOGICAL ASPECTS OF OBSESSIVE-COMPULSIVE DISORDER   Another biological model that receives attention suggests that obsessive-compulsive disorder may involve heightened arousal of a particular anxiety circuit, a neural network in the brain involved in signalling danger. In OCD, the brain may be constantly sending messages that some-

benzodiazepines Class of minor tranquillizers that includes Valium and Ativan.

hyperventilation Pattern of overly rapid breathing, sometimes asso-ciated with anxiety, in which the amount of oxygen inhaled is in excess of metabolic require-ments, leading to harmless but sometimes unpleasant sensa-tions such as feeling faint or light-headed.

The fear network. In panic attacks, responses to fear are mediated by the "fear network" centred in the amygdala and involve interaction with the hippocampus and medial prefrontal cortex.

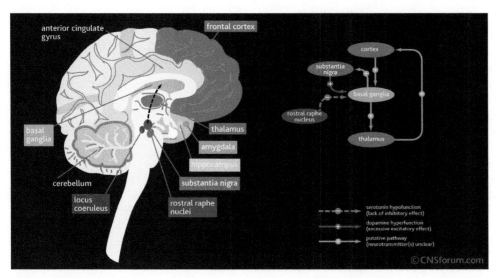

OCD and the brain. Patients with obsessive compulsive disorder (OCD) exhibit increased activity in the neurotransmitter circuits between the cortex, basal ganglia, and thalamus. There seems to be a lack of inhibitory effect on the OCD pathway.

thing is wrong and requires immediate attention, leading to obsessional thoughts and repetitive compulsive behaviours. The compulsive aspects of OCD may also involve disturbances in other brain circuits that usually suppress repetitive behaviours, leading people to feel like they are "stuck in gear" and cannot seek the sense that a particular action (e.g., checking a door lock) has been performed correctly (Szechtman & Woody, 2004). The frontal cortex regulates brain centres in the lower brain that control bodily movement. Perhaps a disruption in these neural pathways is involved in the failure to inhibit the repetitive handwashing and compulsive checking behaviours seen in people with OCD. Evidence also points to differences in brain functioning of people with OCD compared to nonpatient controls (Friedlander & Desrocher, 2006). The significance of these differences in explaining OCD remains unclear, however, and the ability of such models to account for OCD has been called into question (S. Taylor, McKay, & Abramowitz, 2005).

Tying It Together

Unravelling the complex interactions of environmental, physiological, and psychological factors in explaining how anxiety disorders develop remains a challenge (see Figure 3.3). There may be different causal pathways at work. To illustrate, let us offer some possible causal pathways involved in phobic disorders and panic disorder.

Some people may develop phobias by way of classical conditioning—the pairing of a previously neutral stimulus with an unpleasant or traumatic experience. A person may develop a fear of small animals because of experiences in which he or she was bitten or nearly bitten. A fear of riding in elevators may arise from experiences of being trapped in elevators or other enclosed spaces.

Bear in mind that not all people who have traumatic experiences develop related phobias. Perhaps some people have a genetic predisposition that sensitizes them to more readily acquire conditioned responses to stimuli associated with aversive situations. Or perhaps people are more sensitized to these experiences because of an inherited predisposition to respond with greater negative arousal to aversive situations. Whatever factors may be involved in the acquisition of a phobia, people with persistent phobias may have learned to avoid any further contact with the phobic stimulus and so do not avail themselves of opportunities to unlearn the phobia through repeated uneventful contacts with the feared object or situation. Then there are people who acquire phobias without any prior aversive experiences with the phobic stimulus, or at least none they can recall. We can conjecture that cognitive factors, such as observing other people's aversive responses, may play a contributing role in these cases.

Possible causal pathways in panic disorder highlight roles for biological, cognitive, and environmental factors. Some people may inherit a genetic predisposition or diathesis that makes them more likely to panic in response to changes in bodily sensations. This genetic predisposition may involve dysregulations in neurotransmitter systems that control emotional responding. Cognitive factors may also be involved. Bodily sensations such as dizziness, tingling, or numbness may be misconstrued as signs of impending death, insanity, or loss of control. This in turn may lead, like dominoes falling in line, to an anxiety reaction that quickly spirals into a full-fledged panic attack. Whether the anxiety reaction spirals into a state of panic may depend on another vulnerability factor:

Social-Environmental Factors
Threatening or Traumatic Events
Observing Fear Responses in Others
Challenging Demands in New Situations
Cultural Factors Leading to Socialization
  in Passive or Dependent Roles
Lack of Social Support

Biological Factors
Genetic Predisposition
Disturbances in Neurotransmitter Activity
  or Suffocation Alarm System
Abnormalities in Brain Circuits Involved
  in Signalling Danger or Inhibiting
  Repetitive Behaviours

Behavioural Factors
Conditioning Experiences
Lack of Extinction Opportunities

Emotional and Cognitive Factors
Unresolved Psychological Conflicts
  (Freudian or psychodynamic)
Cognitive Factors (anxiety sensitivity,
  self-defeating or irrational thinking,
  catastrophic misinterpretations of
  bodily cues, oversensitivity to threats,
  low self-efficacy)

FIGURE 3.3 Multiple factors in anxiety disorders.

the individual's level of anxiety sensitivity. People with a high level of anxiety sensitivity (extreme fear of their own bodily sensations) may be more likely to panic in response to changes in their physical sensations. In some cases, anxiety sensitivity may be so high that panic ensues even in individuals without a genetic predisposition. Environmental factors may come into play as panic attacks come to be triggered by specific environmental cues, such as stimuli associated with situations (e.g., boarding a subway train or elevator) in which attacks have occurred in the past.

REVIEW IT

Theoretical Perspectives

- **How are anxiety disorders conceptualized within the psychodynamic perspective?** Psychodynamic theorists view anxiety disorders as attempts by the ego to control the conscious emergence of threatening impulses. Feelings of anxiety are warning signals that threatening impulses are nearing awareness. The ego mobilizes defence mechanisms to divert these impulses, thus leading to different anxiety disorders.

- **How do learning/behaviour theorists view anxiety disorders?** Learning and behaviour theorists explain anxiety disorders through conditioning and observational learning. Mowrer's two-factor model incorporates classical and operant conditioning in the explanation of phobias. Phobias, however, appear to be moderated

by cognitive factors, such as irrational beliefs. The principles of reinforcement may help explain patterns of obsessive-compulsive behaviour. People may be genetically predisposed to acquire certain types of phobias that may have had survival value for our prehistoric ancestors. Cognitive factors, such as irrational beliefs and misattributions for panic attacks, may also play a role in anxiety disorders.

- **How does the biological perspective seek to inform our understanding of anxiety disorders?** The biological perspective seeks to uncover the biological underpinnings of anxiety disorders through studying the roles of genetic factors, neurotransmitters, and induction of panic by means of biological challenges.

TREATMENT OF ANXIETY DISORDERS

Each of the major theoretical perspectives has spawned approaches for treating anxiety disorders. Psychological approaches may differ from one another in their techniques and expressed aims, but they seem to have one thing in common: in one way or another, they encourage clients to face rather than avoid the sources of their anxieties. The biological perspective, by contrast, has focused largely on the use of drugs that quell anxiety.

Psychodynamic Approaches

From the psychodynamic perspective, anxieties reflect the energies attached to unconscious conflicts and the ego's efforts to keep them repressed. Traditional psychoanalysis fosters awareness of how clients' anxiety disorders symbolize their inner conflicts, so that the ego can be freed from expending its energy on repression. The ego can thus attend to more creative and enhancing tasks.

More modern psychodynamic therapies also foster clients' awareness of inner sources of conflict. They focus more than traditional approaches on exploring sources of anxiety that arise from current rather than past relationships, however, and they encourage clients to develop more adaptive behaviours. Such therapies are briefer and more directive than traditional psychoanalysis.

Humanistic Approaches

Humanistic theorists believe that many of our anxieties stem from social repression of our genuine selves. Anxiety occurs when the incongruity between one's true inner self and one's social facade draws closer to the level of awareness. A person senses that something bad will happen but is unable to say what it is because the disowned parts of oneself are not directly expressed in consciousness. Because of the disapproval of others, people may fail to develop their individual talents and recognize their authentic feelings. Humanistic therapies thus aim at helping people get in touch with and express their genuine talents and feelings. As a result, clients become free to discover and accept their true selves, rather than reacting with anxiety whenever their true feelings and needs begin to surface.

Biological Approaches

A variety of drugs are used to treat anxiety disorders. Benzodiazepines such as clonazepam (brand name Rivotril) and alprazolam (Xanax) are often used. Although they tend to have a calming effect, physical dependence (addiction) can develop with chronic use of benzodiazepines, leading to withdrawal symptoms when use of the drugs is stopped abruptly. Withdrawal symptoms include rebound anxiety, insomnia, and restlessness (Joffe & Gardner, 2000). These symptoms prompt many patients to return to using the drugs.

Antidepressant drugs are not only effective in treating depression; they have also proven helpful in treating panic disorder, PTSD, social phobia, and obsessive-compulsive disorder (S. Taylor, 2005). Antidepressants may help counter anxiety by normalizing the activity of neurotransmitters in the brain. Antidepressants in common use for treating panic disorder include the tricylics imipramine (Tofranil) and clomipramine (Anafranil) and the selective serotonin reuptake inhibitors (SSRIs) paroxetine (Paxil) and sertraline (Zoloft). However, troublesome side effects may occur, such as heavy sweating and heart palpitations, which lead many patients to prematurely stop using the drugs. Alprazolam can also be helpful in treating panic disorder, social phobia, and generalized anxiety disorder (Cloos, 2005).

Research is ongoing to discover new-generation drugs that help reduce anxiety symptoms. For panic disorder, for example, a newer SNRI (serotonin-norepineprhine reuptake inhibitor) called venlafaxine (Effexor), one of the first and most commonly used, has shown promise during a study with outpatients who suffered from panic attacks. At week 10 of treatment, the percentage of patients who were free from full-symptom panic attacks was 52% in the venlafaxine ER group and 43% in the placebo group—not a massive difference but worth further investigation (Liebowitz, Asnis, Mangano, & Tzanis, 2009).

Obsessive-compulsive disorder often responds to SSRI-type antidepressants—drugs such as fluoxetine (Prozac) and clomipramine (Anafranil) that work specifically on increasing the availability of the neurotransmitter serotonin in the brain (Dell'Osso, Nestadt, Allen, & Hollander, 2006). The effectiveness of these drugs leads researchers to suspect that a problem with serotonin transmission in the brain may be involved in the development of OCD in at least some people with the disorder (Denys, Van Nieuwerburgh, Deforce, & Westenberg, 2006). But as noted by University of Ottawa researchers, some patients fail to respond to these drugs, and among those who do respond, a complete remission of symptoms is uncommon (Blier, Habib, & Flament, 2006). In such cases, neurosurgery is sometimes performed in which connections between brain regions are severed. For example, in a cingulotomy, the cingulate gyrus—a small section of the brain that connects the limbic system and frontal lobes—is severed. Although some neurosurgical studies have found positive results, it is still too early to say whether neurosurgery is safe and effective for people with OCD who have failed to benefit from other treatments (Schruers, Koning, Luermans, Haack, & Griez, 2005).

A potential problem with drug therapy is that patients may attribute clinical improvement to the drugs and not to their own resources. Nor do such drugs produce cures. Relapses are common after patients discontinue medication (Antony & Swinson, 2000). Re-emergence of panic is likely unless cognitive-behavioural treatment is provided to help panic patients modify their cognitive overreactions to bodily sensations (S. Taylor, 2000). Drug therapy is sometimes combined with cognitive-behavioural therapy, although it is currently unclear whether combined treatment is more effective than either treatment alone (Pull, 2007).

Behaviour-Based Approaches

Behavioural treatments based on learning approaches include a variety of techniques aimed at helping individuals confront the objects or situations that elicit their fears and anxieties.

SYSTEMATIC DESENSITIZATION

> Sean has a phobia of receiving injections. His behaviour therapist treats him as he reclines in a comfortable padded chair. In a state of deep muscle relaxation, Sean observes slides projected on a screen. A slide of a nurse holding a needle has just been shown three times, 30 seconds at a time. Each time, Sean has shown no anxiety. So now a slightly more discomforting slide is shown: one of the nurse aiming the needle toward someone's bare arm. After 15 seconds, our armchair adventurer notices twinges of discomfort and raises a finger as a signal (speaking might disturb his relaxation). The projector operator turns off the light, and Sean spends a couple of minutes imagining his "safe scene"—lying on a beach beneath the tropical sun. Then the slide is shown again. This time Sean views it for 30 seconds before feeling anxiety.
>
> Rathus, 2011, p. 481. © 2011 Wadsworth, part of Cengage Learning, Inc. Reproduced by permission. www.cengage.com/permissions

Sean is undergoing systematic desensitization, a fear-reduction procedure originated by psychiatrist Joseph Wolpe (1958). Systematic desensitization is a gradual process. Clients learn to handle progressively more disturbing stimuli while they remain relaxed. About 10 to 20 stimuli are arranged in a sequence or hierarchy—called a **fear-stimulus hierarchy**—according to their capacity to evoke anxiety. By using their imagination or by viewing photos, clients are exposed to the items in the hierarchy,

fear-stimulus hierarchy Ordered series of increasingly fearful stimuli. Used in the behavioural techniques of *systematic desensitization* and *gradual exposure*.

Virtual reality phobia therapy research. Researcher testing a virtual reality therapy system to treat spider phobia (arachnophobia). The system contains eye-tracking software to study a person's response when exposed to virtual spiders in a virtual environment (on screen).

gradually imagining themselves approaching the target behaviour—be it the ability to receive an injection or to remain in an enclosed room or elevator—without undue anxiety.

Joseph Wolpe developed systematic desensitization on the assumption that maladaptive anxiety responses, like other behaviours, are learned or conditioned. He assumed they can be unlearned by counterconditioning. In counterconditioning, a response incompatible with anxiety is made to appear under conditions that usually elicit anxiety. Muscle relaxation is generally used as the incompatible response, and followers of Wolpe usually use the method of progressive relaxation to help clients acquire relaxation skills. For this reason, Sean's therapist is teaching Sean to experience relaxation in the presence of (otherwise) anxiety-evoking slides of needles.

Behaviourally oriented therapists, like Wolpe, explain the benefits of systematic desensitization and similar therapies in terms of principles of counterconditioning. Cognitively oriented therapists note, however, that remaining in the presence of phobic imagery, rather than running from it, is also likely to enhance one's confidence about being able to manage the phobic stimuli without anxiety.

GRADUAL EXPOSURE This method helps people overcome phobias through a step-wise approach of actual exposure to the phobic stimuli. The effectiveness of exposure therapy is well established, making it the treatment of choice for specific phobias (Antony & McCabe, 2005). Here exposure therapy was used in treating a case of claustrophobia:

Claustrophobia (fear of enclosed spaces) is quite common. Cho's claustrophobia took the form of a fear of riding in elevators. Interestingly, Cho worked as an elevator mechanic! He spent his workdays repairing elevators. Unless it was absolutely necessary, however, Cho managed to complete the repairs without riding in the elevator. He would climb the stairs to the floor where an elevator was stuck, make repairs, and hit the down button. He would then race downstairs to see that the elevator had operated correctly. When his work required an elevator ride, panic would seize him as the doors closed. Cho tried to cope by praying for divine intervention to prevent him from passing out before the doors opened.

Cho related the origin of his phobia to an accident three years earlier in which he had been pinned in his overturned car for nearly an hour. He remembered feelings of helplessness and suffocation. Cho developed claustrophobia—a fear of situations from which he could not escape, such as flying in an airplane, driving through a tunnel, taking public transportation, and, of course, riding in an elevator. Cho's fear had become so incapacitating that he was seriously considering switching jobs, although the change would require considerable financial sacrifice. Each night, he lay awake wondering whether he would be able to cope the next day if he were required to test-ride an elevator.

Cho's therapy involved gradual exposure. Gradual exposure, like systematic desensitization, is a step-by-step procedure that involves a fear-stimulus hierarchy. In gradual exposure, however, the target behaviour is approached in actuality rather than symbolically. Moreover, the individual is active rather than relaxed in a recliner.

A typical hierarchy for overcoming a fear of riding in an elevator might include the following steps:

1. Standing outside the elevator
2. Standing in the elevator with the door open
3. Standing in the elevator with the door closed
4. Taking the elevator down one floor
5. Taking the elevator up one floor
6. Taking the elevator down two floors
7. Taking the elevator up two floors
8. Taking the elevator down two floors and then up two floors
9. Taking the elevator down to the basement
10. Taking the elevator up to the highest floor and down again

Clients begin at Step 1 and do not progress to Step 2 until they are able to remain calm on the first. If they become bothered by anxiety, they remove themselves from the situation and regain calmness by practising muscle relaxation or focusing on soothing mental imagery. The encounter is then repeated as often as necessary to reach and sustain feelings of calmness. They then proceed to the next step, repeating the process.

Cho was also trained to practise self-relaxation and talk calmly and rationally to himself to help him remain calm during his exposure trials. Whenever he began to feel even slightly anxious, he would tell himself to calm down and relax. He was able to counter the disruptive belief that he was going to fall apart if he was trapped in an elevator with rational self-statements such as "Just relax. I may experience some anxiety, but it's nothing that I haven't been through before. In a few moments I'll feel relieved."

Cho gradually overcame his phobia but still occasionally experienced some anxiety, which he interpreted as a reminder of his former phobia. He did not exaggerate the importance of these feelings. Now and then it dawned on him that an elevator he was servicing had once occasioned fear. One day following his treatment, Cho was repairing an elevator that serviced a bank vault 30 metres underground. The experience of moving deeper and deeper underground aroused fear, but Cho did not panic. He repeated to himself, "It's only a couple of seconds and I'll be out." By the time he took his second trip down, he was much calmer.

The Authors' Files

COGNITIVE TECHNIQUES The most widely used cognitive technique is Beck's cognitive therapy, which seeks to identify dysfunctional or distorted beliefs and replace them with rational or adaptive alternatives. For example, people with social phobia might think that no one at a party will want to talk with them and that they will wind up lonely and isolated for the rest of their lives. Cognitive therapists help clients recognize the logical flaws in their thinking and assist them in viewing situations rationally. Clients may be asked to gather evidence to test out their beliefs, which may lead them to alter beliefs they find are not grounded in reality. Therapists may encourage clients with social phobia to test their beliefs that they are bound to be ignored, rejected, or ridiculed by others in social gatherings by attending a party, initiating conversations, and monitoring other people's reactions. Therapists may also help clients develop social skills to improve their interpersonal effectiveness and teach them how to handle social rejection, if it should occur, without catastrophizing.

One example of cognitive techniques is **cognitive restructuring**. This involves a process in which therapists help clients pinpoint their self-defeating thoughts and generate rational alternatives so that they learn to cope with anxiety-provoking situations. Cho learned to replace self-defeating thoughts with rational alternatives and to practise speaking

cognitive restructuring Cognitive therapy method that involves replacing irrational or self-defeating thoughts and attitudes with rational alternatives.

rationally and calmly to himself during his exposure trials. Consider the case of Soraya, who also suffered from an elevator phobia:

> Soraya, a 32-year-old writer and mother of two sons, had not been on an elevator in 16 years. Her life revolved around finding ways to avoid appointments and social events on high floors. She had suffered from a fear of elevators since the age of 8, when she had been stuck between floors with her grandmother.
>
> To help overcome her fear of elevators, Soraya imagined herself getting stuck in an elevator and countering the self-defeating thoughts she might experience with rational self-statements. She closed her eyes and reported the thoughts that would come to mind. The psychologist encouraged her to create a rational counterpoint to each of them. She then repeated the exercise in her imagination and practised replacing the self-defeating thoughts with rational alternatives, as in the following examples:

Self-Defeating Thought	Rational Alternative
Oh oh, I'm stuck. I'm going to lose control.	Relax. Just think coolly, what do I have to do next?
I can't take it. I'm going to pass out.	Okay, practise your deep breathing. Help will be coming shortly.
I'm having a panic attack. I can't stand it.	You've experienced all these feelings before. Just let them pass through.
If it takes an hour, that would be horrible.	That would be annoying, but it wouldn't necessarily be horrible. I've gotten stuck in traffic longer than that.
I've got to get out of here.	Stay calm. There's no real danger. I can just sit down and imagine I'm somewhere else until someone comes to help.

The Authors' Files

BEHAVIOURAL TREATMENT OF SOCIAL PHOBIA Exposure therapy is also an effective form of treatment for social phobia (Cottraux, 2005). In exposure therapy, clients are instructed to enter increasingly stressful social situations and to remain in those situations until the urge to escape has lessened. The therapist may help guide them during exposure trials, gradually withdrawing direct support so that clients become capable of handling the situations on their own. Exposure treatment is often combined with (a) cognitive techniques that assist clients in replacing maladaptive anxiety-inducing thoughts with more rational alternatives and (b) behavioural techniques, such as training in conversational skills. The cognitive and behavioural treatments for social phobia have been shown to be effective, and their benefits appear to be durable (Rowa & Antony, 2005).

Flooding is a type of exposure therapy in which subjects are exposed to intensely anxiety-provoking situations. Why? It is believed that anxiety that has been conditioned to a phobic stimulus should extinguish if the individual remains in the phobic situation for a long enough period of time and nothing traumatic occurs. Typically, the phobic individual either avoids the phobic stimulus or beats a hasty retreat at the first opportunity for escape. Thus, no opportunity for unlearning (extinguishing) the fear response occurs. Flooding is just as effective as other forms of cognitive-behavioural treatments but may work faster.

BEHAVIOURAL TREATMENT OF AGORAPHOBIA Evidence shows gradual exposure to fear-inducing stimuli to be more effective than control conditions in reducing avoidance behaviour in people with agoraphobia (S. Taylor, 2000). Treatment is stepwise and gradually exposes the phobic individual to increasingly fearful stimulus situations, such as walking through congested streets or shopping in department stores. A trusted companion or perhaps the therapist may accompany the person during the exposure trials. The

Virtual Therapy

Virtual reality, a computer-generated simulated environment, has become a therapeutic tool. By donning a specialized helmet and gloves that are connected to a computer, a person with a fear of heights, for example, can encounter frightening stimuli in this virtual world, such as riding a glass-enclosed elevator to the 49th floor, peering over a railing on a balcony on the 20th floor, or flying in a helicopter over a war zone (Pull, 2005). Recent findings from Canadian investigators suggest that virtual therapy is also useful for treating driving phobia (Wald & Taylor, 2003). Here, a client practises driving in a simulator under increasingly more challenging situations (e.g., on a quiet street, then in heavy traffic, then in the rain). By a process of exposure to a series of increasingly more frightening virtual stimuli, while progressing only when fears at each preceding step diminish, people learn to overcome fears in much the same way they would had they followed a program of graduated exposure to phobic stimuli in real-life situations. The advantage of virtual reality is that it provides an opportunity to experience situations that might be difficult or impossible to arrange in reality. Virtual therapy is a promising treatment that has been used successfully in helping people overcome many different kinds of phobias, including fears of heights, driving, flying, and spiders (Pull, 2005).

We have only begun to explore the potential therapeutic uses of this new technology. Therapists are experimenting with virtual therapy to help people overcome other types of fears, such as fear of public speaking and agoraphobia. In other applications, virtual therapy may help clients work through unresolved conflicts with significant figures in their lives by allowing them to confront these "people" in a virtual environment.

Self-help therapy modules consisting of compact discs and virtual reality helmets and gloves may even begin to appear on the shelves of your neighbourhood computer software store in the not-too-distant future. With these self-help modules, people may be able in their own living rooms to confront objects or situations they fear, or to learn to stop smoking or lose weight, all with the help and guidance of a "virtual therapist."

Scene from a driving simulator (SimuRide by Aplusb Software Corporation). Virtual-reality therapy using a driving simulator can be useful in treating driving phobia.

---

eventual goal is for the person to be able to handle each situation alone and without discomfort or an urge to escape. The benefits of gradual exposure are typically enduring.

BEHAVIOURAL TREATMENT OF POSTTRAUMATIC STRESS DISORDER Exposure therapy has achieved good results in reducing symptoms of PTSD (National Institute for Clinical Excellence, 2005). Exposure to cues associated with a trauma may involve talking about the trauma, re-experiencing the trauma in one's imagination, viewing related slides or films, or visiting the scene of the event. For combat-related PTSD, homework assignments may involve visiting war memorials or viewing war movies. The person comes to gradually re-experience the traumatic event and accompanying anxiety in a safe setting that is free of negative consequences, which allows extinction to take its course. Exposure therapy is often supplemented with cognitive restructuring that focuses on replacing dysfunctional thoughts with rational alternatives. Training in stress-management skills, such as self-relaxation, may help enhance the client's ability to cope with the troubling features of PTSD, such as heightened arousal and the desire to run away from trauma-related stimuli. Training in anger-management skills may also be helpful, especially with combat veterans who have PTSD (S. Taylor, 2005).

Additional interventions may also be required. Specialist programs may be needed for people with two or more disorders, such as PTSD combined with substance-use disorders (e.g., Najavits, 2002). Some of these programs cater to specific groups, such as the Tsow-Tun Le Lum residential program for Aboriginal adults located in Nanaimo, British Columbia. Other programs need to be very broad in focus in order to address the needs of their clients. Survivors of torture, for example—many of whom have arrived in Canada as refugees—often have PTSD combined with a host of other practical problems, such as the need for housing, education in written and spoken English, and legal aid to help with refugee claims. Organizations such as the Canadian Centre for Victims of Torture, located in Toronto, provide important assistance in these areas.

One controversial but widely used PTSD treatment is eye movement desensitization and reprocessing (EMDR) (F. Shapiro, 2001). The main part of an EMDR intervention requires a patient to recall trauma-related memories while also attending to some form of external oscillatory stimulation. Stimulation is typically induced by the therapist moving a finger from side to side across the patient's field of vision, which induces eye movement. Sets of eye movements are induced until distress is reduced. There are several reasons why EMDR is controversial, including claims by its founder, Francine Shapiro, that EMDR works more rapidly and is more effective than other psychological treatments and that it works in a fundamentally different way from behavioural treatments. These claims have not been supported by research; the most rigorous studies to date indicate that EMDR works no faster and is no more effective than other cognitive-behavioural treatments (Rothbaum, Astin, & Marsteller, 2005; S. Taylor et al., 2003). In fact, Taylor and colleagues (2003) found that behaviour therapy was more effective than EMDR, and other researchers have concluded that EMDR is simply a form of behavioural (exposure) therapy (Rothbaum et al., 2005). Moreover, there is no compelling reason why eye movements would reduce distress. Indeed, research shows that eye movements do not contribute to treatment efficacy (Davidson & Parker, 2001).

BEHAVIOURAL TREATMENT OF OBSESSIVE-COMPULSIVE DISORDER Behaviour therapy has achieved impressive results in treating obsessive-compulsive disorder with a combination of exposure and response prevention within intensive, carefully monitored programs (D. A. Clark, 2004). Exposure involves purposefully placing oneself in situations that evoke obsessive thoughts. For many people, such situations are hard to avoid. Leaving the house, for example, can trigger obsessional thoughts about whether the gas jets are turned off or the windows and doors are locked. Response prevention involves the effort to physically prevent a compulsive behaviour from occurring. Through exposure with response prevention, people with OCD learn to tolerate the anxiety triggered by their obsessive thoughts while they are prevented from performing their compulsive rituals. With repeated exposure, the anxiety eventually subsides and the person feels less compelled to perform the ritual. Extinction, or the weakening of the anxiety response following repeated presentation of the obsessional cues in the absence of any aversive consequences, is believed to underlie the treatment effect. Overall, many people benefit from this treatment (D. A. Clark, 2004). Cognitive therapy is often combined with exposure therapy. The therapist focuses on helping the person correct cognitive distortions such as tendencies to overestimate the likelihood and severity of feared consequences.

It appears that behavioural therapy is at least as effective as drug therapy (use of SSRI-type antidepressants) and may produce more lasting results (Antony & Swinson, 2000; S. Taylor, 2000). Yet it remains to be seen whether a combination of drugs and behaviour therapy is more effective than either approach alone.

Behavioural therapy may also change brain function as well as behaviour. People with obsessive-compulsive disorder who received cognitive-behavioural therapy show changes in their brain functioning, as measured by PET scans (Baxter et al., 2000). A part of the brain that is unusually active in persons with OCD showed a lessening of activity—the same kind of change seen when OCD is treated with the antidepressant Prozac.

COGNITIVE-BEHAVIOURAL TREATMENT OF GENERALIZED ANXIETY Cognitive-behaviour therapists use a combination of techniques to treat generalized anxiety disorder, including relaxation training; substitution of adaptive thoughts for intrusive, anxiety-inducing thoughts; and decatastrophizing (avoiding tendencies to think the worst). Studies from Concordia University, Laval University, and elsewhere indicate that cognitive-behavioural approaches are superior to control conditions and yield equivalent or better effects than alternative drug or psychological therapies (Mitte, 2005).

COGNITIVE-BEHAVIOURAL TREATMENT OF PANIC DISORDER The treatment components in cognitive-behavioural therapy (CBT) for panic disorder include training in skills relating to handling panic attacks without catastrophizing, breathing retraining, exposure to situations linked to panic attacks and to bodily cues associated with panic, and training in relaxation (S. Taylor, 2000).

Therapists help clients think differently about their bodily cues, such as passing sensations of dizziness or heart palpitations. Receiving corrective information that these sensations will subside naturally and are not signs of an impending catastrophe helps clients learn to cope with them without panicking (S. Taylor, 2000). (Persons who complain of cardiovascular symptoms should also be evaluated medically to ensure that they are physically healthy.) On a cognitive level, clients are taught to replace catastrophizing thoughts and self-statements ("I'm having a heart attack") with calming, rational alternatives ("Calm down. These are panicky feelings that will soon pass").

Breathing retraining aims at restoring a normal level of carbon dioxide in the blood by having clients breathe slowly and deeply from the abdomen to avoid the shallow, rapid breathing (hyperventilation) that leads to breathing off too much carbon dioxide. In some treatment programs, people with panic disorder purposefully hyperventilate in the controlled setting of the treatment clinic in order to discover for themselves the relationship between breathing off too much carbon dioxide and cardiovascular sensations. Through these first-hand experiences, they learn to calm themselves down and cope with these sensations rather than overreacting. Some of the common elements of CBT for panic are shown in Table 3.12.

The efficacy of CBT in treating panic disorder is well established (Antony & Swinson, 2000; S. Taylor, 2000). Investigators find that roughly two thirds to four fifths of panic patients treated with CBT become panic-free by the end of treatment, and the gains from CBT appear to be long-lasting (Barlow, 2002). Despite the common belief that panic disorder is best treated with psychiatric drugs, CBT appears to produce even better results than drug treatment with imipramine or benzodiazepines (S. Taylor, 2000).

TABLE 3.12

Elements of Cognitive-Behavioural Programs for Treatment of Panic Disorder

Self-Monitoring	Keeping a log of panic attacks to help determine situational stimuli that might trigger them.
Exposure	A program of gradual exposure to situations in which panic attacks have occurred. During exposure trials, the person engages in self-relaxation and rational self-talk to prevent anxiety from spiraling out of control. In some programs, participants learn to tolerate changes in bodily sensations associated with panic attacks by experiencing these sensations within a controlled setting of the treatment clinic. The person may be spun around in a chair to induce feelings of dizziness, learning in the process that such sensations are not dangerous or signs of imminent harm.
Development of Coping Responses	Developing coping skills to interrupt the vicious cycle in which overreactions to anxiety cues or cardiovascular sensations culminate in panic attacks. Behavioural methods focus on deep, regular breathing and relaxation training. Cognitive methods focus on modifying catastrophic misinterpretations of bodily sensations. Breathing retraining may be used to help the individual avoid hyperventilation during panic attacks.

Coping With a Panic Attack

People who have panic attacks usually feel their hearts pounding such that they are overwhelmed and unable to cope. They typically feel an urge to flee the situation as quickly as possible. If escape is impossible, they may become immobilized and "freeze" until the attack dissipates. What can you do if you suffer a panic attack or an intense anxiety reaction? Let us suggest a few coping responses:

- Don't let your breathing get out of hand. Breathe slowly and deeply.
- "Talk yourself down." Tell yourself to relax. Tell yourself you're not going to die. Tell yourself that no matter how painful the attack is, it is likely to pass soon.

- Find someone to help you through the attack. Telephone someone you know and trust. Talk about anything at all until you regain control.
- Don't fall into the trap of making yourself housebound to avert future attacks.
- If you are uncertain as to whether or not sensations such as pain or tightness in the chest have physical causes, seek immediate medical assistance. Even if you suspect your attack may "only" be one of anxiety, it is safer to have a medical evaluation than to diagnose yourself.

You need not suffer recurrent panic attacks and fears about loss of control. When in doubt, or if attacks are persistent or frightening, consult a professional.

Treatment of Anxiety Disorders

- **How is the treatment of anxiety disorders approached from the major contemporary theoretical perspectives?** Traditional psychoanalysis helps people work through unconscious conflicts that are thought to underlie anxiety disorders. Modern psychodynamic approaches also focus on current disturbed relationships and encourage clients to assume more adaptive behaviour patterns. The biological perspectives have led to the development of various drug therapies to treat anxiety disorders. Learning perspectives encompass a broad range of behavioural and cognitive-behavioural techniques to help people overcome anxiety-related problems. Exposure methods help people with phobias overcome their fears through gradual exposure to the phobic stimuli. Obses-sive-compulsive disorder is often treated with a combination of exposure and response prevention. Relaxation training is often used to help people overcome generalized anxiety. Behavioural treatment of PTSD incorporates progressive exposure to trauma-related cues and training in stress management skills, such as self-relaxation. Cognitive approaches such as rational-emotive therapy and cognitive therapy help people identify and correct cognitive errors that give rise to or maintain anxiety disorders. Cognitive-behavioural approaches to panic disorder focus on helping panic-prone people learn to use deep-breathing skills to tone down their bodily alarm in anxiety-inducing situations and to avoid catastrophizing changes in bodily sensations.

Define It

acrophobia, 107
acute stress disorder, 113
adjustment disorder, 112
agoraphobia, 103
anxiety disorder, 100
anxiety sensitivity, 122
benzodiazepines, 125
claustrophobia, 107
cognitive restructuring, 131

compulsion, 111
etiology, 101
fear, 107
fear-stimulus hierarchy, 129
gamma-aminobutyric acid, 124
generalized anxiety disorder, 104
hyperventilation, 125
neuroticism, 124
obsession, 110

panic disorder, 100
posttraumatic stress disorder, 113
prepared conditioning, 119
projection, 118
social phobia, 109
specific phobias, 107
two-factor model, 118

Think About It

- Anxiety may be a normal emotional reaction in some situations, but not in others. Think of a situation in which you would consider anxiety to be a normal reaction and one in which you would consider it to be a maladaptive reaction. What are the differences? What criteria do you use to draw a line between normal and abnormal?

- Compare and contrast the psychodynamic and learning-based explanations of the classic case of Little Hans. How does this case illustrate the differences between the two models?

- Have you developed any specific phobias, such as fears of small animals, insects, heights, or enclosed spaces? What factors do you think contributed to the development of this phobia (or phobias)? How has the phobia made an impact on your life? How have you coped with it?

- What are the advantages and disadvantages of using anti-anxiety drugs?

Weblinks

Anxiety Treatment and Research Centre
www.stjoes.ca/anxiety
Information on anxiety disorders, including Canadian treatment resources.

Anxiety Disorders Association of Canada
www.anxietycanada.ca
Information and links to provincial anxiety disorder associations.

Anxiety Disorders Association of America
www.adaa.org
The ADAA's website contains information on the nature and treatment of anxiety disorders, as well as links to self-help books and other resources.

International OCD Foundation
www.ocfoundation.org
This nonprofit organization provides information on obsessive-compulsive disorder and its treatment.

National Center for PTSD
www.ptsd.va.gov
This organization's site contains a good deal of useful information on posttraumatic stress reactions and their treatment.

MySearchLab offers you extensive help with your writing and research projects and provides round-the-clock access to credible and reliable source material. Chapter quizzes and a full electronic version of the text are also provided. Take a tour at www.mysearchlab.com.

Anxiety Disorders

Types of Anxiety Disorders

Panic Disorder

- Recurrent, unexpected panic attacks
- With or without agoraphobia

Agoraphobia

- Involves fear of places and situations from which it might be difficult or embarrassing to escape

Generalized Anxiety Disorder

- Excessive anxiety and worry

Phobic Disorders

Specific Phobia
- Severe fear of specific objects or situations

Social Phobia
- Severe fear of social or performance situations

Obsessive-Compulsive Disorder

- Recurrent obsessions and/or compulsions

Adjustment Disorders

Acute and Posttraumatic Stress Disorder
- Persistent symptoms after exposure to trauma
- Re-experiencing, avoidance, emotional numbing, hyperarousal
- maladaptive reaction to an identified stressor

Acute Stress Disorder
- Similar to posttraumatic stress disorder
- Symptoms last only days or weeks after exposure to trauma

Theoretical Perspectives

Psychodynamic

- Anxiety is a signal that threatening sexual or aggressive impulses are nearing the level of awareness.
- Ego mobilizes defence mechanisms to ward off the threatening impulses.

Learning (Behavioural)

- Two-factor model: Fears are acquired by classical conditioning and maintained by operant conditioning.
- Prepared conditioning: People might be genetically predisposed to fear certain types of stimuli.

Cognitive

- Dysfunctional thinking patterns (self-defeating or irrational beliefs)

Biological

- Genetic predisposition (diathesis)
- Dysfunctional neurotransmitter systems (e.g., GABA, serotonin, or norepinephrine systems)

Treatment of Anxiety Disorders

Psychodynamic

- Traditional psychoanalysis: Aims to increase awareness of how anxiety disorders symbolize inner conflicts.
- Modern approaches: Focus more on current relationships and encourage coping skills.

Learning-Based

- Behavioural treatments: Systematic desensitization; gradual exposure
- Cognitive treatments: Rational-emotive behaviour therapy; cognitive theory

Humanistic

- Assumption: Anxiety stems from social repression of the genuine self.
- Goal: To help people get in touch with and express their genuine talents and feelings.

Biological

- Various types of medications. Example: reuptake inhibitors (e.g., sertraline)

Mood Disorders and Suicide

CHAPTER OUTLINE

Types of Mood Disorders
Major Depressive Disorder
Dysthymic Disorder
Bipolar Disorder
Cyclothymic Disorder

Theoretical Perspectives
Stress and Mood Disorders
Psychodynamic Perspectives
Learning Perspectives
Cognitive Perspectives
Biological Perspectives
Tying It Together

Treatment
Psychodynamic Approaches
Behavioural Approaches
Cognitive Approaches
Biological Approaches

Suicide
Who Commits Suicide
Why Do People Commit Suicide?
Theoretical Perspectives
   on Suicide
Predicting Suicide

Did You Know That...

- Feeling depressed is perfectly normal in some circumstances?

- Most people who become severely depressed will suffer additional episodes later in life?

- The bleak light of winter casts some people into a diagnosable state of depression?

- Some people ride an emotional roller coaster, swinging from the heights of elation to the depths of depression without any external cause?

- The ancient Greeks and Romans used a chemical that is still used today to curb turbulent mood swings?

- The most widely used remedy for depression in Germany is not a drug but a herb?

- It is untrue that people who threaten to commit suicide are only seeking attention?

Life has its ups and downs. Most of us feel elated when we have earned high grades, a promotion, or the affections of Ms. or Mr. Right. Most of us feel down or depressed when we are rejected by a date, flunk a test, or suffer financial losses. It is normal and appropriate to be happy about uplifting events. It is just as normal, just as appropriate, to feel depressed by dismal events. It might very well be "abnormal" if we were not depressed by life's miseries.

Our **moods** are enduring states of feeling that colour our psychological lives. Feeling down or depressed is not abnormal in the context of depressing events or circumstances. But people with **mood disorders** experience disturbances in mood that are unusually severe or prolonged and that impair their ability to function in meeting their normal responsibilities. Some people become severely depressed even when things appear to be going well or when they encounter mildly upsetting events that others take in stride. Still others experience extreme mood swings. They ride an emotional roller coaster with dizzying heights and abysmal depths when the world around them remains largely on an even keel.

moods Pervasive qualities of an individual's emotional experience, as in depressed mood, anxious mood, or elated mood.

mood disorders Types of disorders characterized by disturbances of mood, as in depressive disorders (*major depressive disorder* or *dysthymic disorder*) or bipolar disorders (*bipolar disorder* and *cyclothymic disorder*).

TYPES OF MOOD DISORDERS

In this chapter, we focus on several kinds of mood disorders, including two kinds of depressive disorders—major depressive disorder and dysthymic disorder—and two kinds of mood swing disorders—bipolar disorder and cyclothymic disorder (see Table 4.1). Table 4.2 on page 142 lists some of the common features of depression. Using Figure 4.1 on page 142 as a reference point, you can visualize the differences. The depressive disorders are considered **unipolar** because the disturbance lies in only one emotional direction or pole—either in depression, the downward part of the diagram, or in mania, the upward part of the diagram. Disorders that involve mood swings are **bipolar**. They involve excesses of both depression and elation, usually in an alternating pattern, moving from the top of the diagram to the bottom, usually passing through a period of normal balanced mood in the middle.

unipolar Pertaining to a single pole or direction, as in unipolar (depressive) disorders. Contrast with *bipolar disorder*.

bipolar Characterized by opposites, as in *bipolar disorder*.

TABLE 4.1

Types of Mood Disorders

Mood Episodes	Depressive Disorders
Major Depressive Episode	Major Depressive Disorder
Manic Episode	Dysthymic Disorder
Hypomanic Episode	Depressive Disorder Not Otherwise Specified
Mixed Episode	
Bipolar Disorders	**Other Mood Disorders**
Bipolar I Disorder	Mood Disorder Due to . . . (Indicate the General Medical Conditions)
Bipolar II Disorder	
Cyclothymic Disorder	Substance-Induced Mood Disorder
Bipolar Disorder Not Otherwise Specified	Mood Disorder Not Otherwise Specified

Source: Reprinted with permission from the *Diagnostic and Statistical Manual of Mental Disorders*, Fourth Edition, Text Revision, (Copyright ©2000). American Psychiatric Association. pp. 346–347.

TABLE 4.2

Common Features of Depression

Changes in Emotional States	Changes in mood (persistent periods of feeling down, depressed, sad, or blue)
	Tearfulness or crying
	Increased irritability or loss of temper
Changes in Motivation	Feeling unmotivated, or having difficulty getting going in the morning or even getting out of bed
	Reduced level of social participation or interest in social activities
	Loss of enjoyment or interest in pleasurable activities
	Reduced interest in sex
	Failure to respond to praise or rewards
Changes in Functioning and Motor Behaviour	Moving about or talking more slowly than usual
	Changes in sleep habits (sleeping too much or too little, awakening earlier than usual and having trouble getting back to sleep in early morning hours—so-called *early morning awakening*)
	Changes in appetite (eating too much or too little)
	Changes in weight (gaining or losing weight)
	Functioning less effectively than usual at work or school
Cognitive Changes	Difficulty concentrating or thinking clearly
	Thinking negatively about oneself and one's future
	Feeling guilty or remorseful about past misdeeds
	Lack of self-esteem or feelings of inadequacy
	Thinking of death or suicide

major depressive disorder Severe mood disorder characterized by the occurrence of major depressive episodes in the absence of a history of manic episodes. Major depressive disorder is characterized by a range of features such as depressed mood, lack of interest or pleasure in usual activities, lack of energy or motivation, and changes in appetite or sleep patterns.

manic Relating to mania, as in the manic phase of a bipolar disorder.

hypomanic episodes Mild manic episodes.

severe mania

hypomania (mild to moderate mania)

normal/balanced mood

mild to moderate depression

severe depression

FIGURE 4.1 A mood thermometer.
Mood states can be conceptualized as varying along a spectrum or continuum. One end represents severe depression and the other end severe mania, which is a cardinal feature of bipolar disorder. Mild or moderate depression is often called "the blues" but is classified as dysthymia when it becomes chronic. In the middle of the spectrum is normal or balanced mood. Mild or moderate mania is called hypomania, and characterizes cyclothymic disorder.
Source: Adapted from National Institutes of Mental Health.

Many of us, probably most of us, have periods of sadness from time to time. We may feel down in the dumps, cry, lose interest in things, find it hard to concentrate, expect the worst to happen, or even consider suicide. To illustrate the prevalence of sadness and depression, a survey of nearly 5000 high school students in Ontario found that 16% had often felt sad in the preceding seven days and 12% had felt depressed during this period (Adlaf & Paglia, 2001). For most of us, mood changes pass quickly or are not severe enough to interfere with our lifestyle or ability to function.

Among people with mood disorders, including depressive disorders and bipolar disorders, mood changes are more severe or prolonged and affect daily functioning.

Major Depressive Disorder

The diagnosis of **major depressive disorder** (also called *major depression*) is based on the occurrence of one or more major depressive episodes in the absence of a history of **manic** or **hypomanic episodes**. In a major depressive episode, the person experiences either a depressed mood (feeling sad, hopeless, or "down in the dumps") or loss of interest or pleasure in all or virtually all activities for a period of at least two weeks (APA, 2000a). The diagnostic features of a major depressive episode are listed in Table 4.3 on page 143.

Major depression versus bereavement. Major depression is distinguished from a normal grief reaction to the death of a loved one, which is termed bereavement. But major depression may occur in people whose bereavement becomes prolonged or seriously interferes with normal functioning.

TABLE 4.3

Diagnostic Criteria for a Major Depressive Episode

Five (or more) of the following symptoms have been present during the same 2-week period and represent a change from previous functioning; at least one of the symptoms is either (1) depressed mood or (2) loss of interest or pleasure.

Note: Do not include symptoms that are clearly due to a general medical condition, or mood-incongruent delusions or hallucinations.

(1) depressed mood most of the day, nearly every day, as indicated by either subjective report (e.g., feels sad or empty) or observation made by others (e.g., appears tearful)

   Note: In children and adolescents, can be irritable mood.

(2) markedly diminished interest or pleasure in all, or almost all, activities most of the day, nearly every day (as indicated by either subjective account or observation made by others)

(3) significant weight loss when not dieting or weight gain (e.g., a change of more than 5% of body weight in a month), or decrease or increase in appetite nearly every day

   Note: In children, consider failure to make expected weight gains.

(4) insomnia or hypersomnia nearly every day

(5) psychomotor agitation or retardation nearly every day (observable by others, not merely subjective feelings of restlessness or being slowed down)

(6) fatigue or loss of energy nearly every day

(7) feelings of worthlessness or excessive or inappropriate guilt (which may be delusional) nearly every day (not merely self-reproach or guilt about being sick)

(8) diminished ability to think or concentrate, or indecisiveness, nearly every day (either by subjective account or as observed by others)

(9) recurrent thoughts of death (not just fear of dying), recurrent suicidal ideation without a specific plan, or a suicide attempt or a specific plan for committing suicide

Note: The DSM includes separate diagnostic categories for mood disorders due to medical conditions or due to the use of substances such as drugs of abuse.
Source: Reprinted with permission from the *Diagnostic and Statistical Manual of Mental Disorders*, Fourth Edition, Text Revision, (Copyright ©2000). American Psychiatric Association. p. 356.

When are changes in mood considered abnormal? Although changes in mood in response to the ups and downs of everyday life may be quite normal, persistent or severe changes in mood or cycles of extreme elation and depression may suggest the presence of a mood disorder.

People with major depressive disorder may also have poor appetite, lose or gain substantial amounts of weight, and become physically agitated or—at the other extreme—show a marked slowing down in their motor activity. They may lose interest in most of their usual activities and pursuits, have difficulty concentrating and making decisions, have pressing thoughts of death, and attempt suicide. Although depression is a diagnosable psychological disorder, many people polled in surveys perceive it to be a sign of personal weakness (Jorm et al., 2006). Many people don't seem to understand that people who are clinically depressed can't simply "shake it off" or "snap out of it." This attitude may explain why, despite the availability of safe and effective treatments, many people who are clinically depressed remain untreated (C. A. Beck, Patten, et al., 2005). Many people with untreated depression believe that they should be able to handle the problem themselves (Jorm et al., 2006). In fact, it can be very difficult to handle major depression without receiving professional help. Major depressive disorder is the most common type of mood disorder, affecting—at some point in their lives—about 12% of Canadian adults living in the community (Patten et al., 2006). Depression may be even more prevalent in some other countries, such as the United States (Patten et al., 2006). At least 1 in 20 people can be diagnosed with major depression at any given time—it is so common that it's been dubbed the "common cold" of psychological problems. Effective treatment for depression is available and leads not only to psychological improvement but also to increased income, as people are able to return to a more productive level of functioning. In our clinical practices, we have seen college and university students who were on the verge of dropping out of school because of major depression receive effective treatment and become able to complete their degrees.

Major depression, particularly in more severe episodes, may be accompanied by psychotic features, such as delusions that one's body is rotting from illness (Meyers, 2006). People with severe depression may also experience hallucinations, such as "hearing" the voices of others or of demons condemning them for perceived misdeeds or telling them to kill themselves.

Sarah Hamid, an undergraduate at Simon Fraser University in Vancouver, provided the following illustration of some of the features of her unipolar depression:

The symptoms of mental illness crept over Sarah like a cold, damp fog. Cloaked in her dark world, Sarah was sleeping 12 to 16 hours a day. She would weep in class, so much that she'd sneak off to the bathroom so no one could see. "Almost like someone with an addiction," says Sarah, "I was finding places to hide my habit." She ate little and was losing weight. "It got to the point where I was driving home one day and I really wanted to drive the car over the yellow line into oncoming traffic," says Sarah. "I was like, Okay, I really have to tell someone." Her doctor diagnosed severe depression. Now 24, Sarah takes an effective antidepressant, and the crying fits that would overwhelm her for hours once or twice a day now happen only every few months or so and last only maybe 10 minutes.

Hawaleshka, 2002, p. 38. Copyright Rogers Communications. Reprinted with permission.

A major depressive disorder, if left untreated, usually lasts for six months or longer and possibly even two or more years (APA, 2000a). Some people experience a single episode with a full return to previous levels of functioning. However, the majority of people with major depression, at least 50%, have repeated occurrences (Health Canada, 2002b). Given a pattern of repeated occurrences of major depressive episodes and prolonged symptoms, many professionals have come to view major depression as a chronic, indeed lifelong, disorder.

RISK FACTORS FOR MAJOR DEPRESSION Factors that place people at greater risk of developing major depression include age (initial onset is more common among younger adults than older ones), socioeconomic status (people on the lower rungs of the socio-economic ladder are at greater risk than those who are better off), and marital status (people who are not in an intimate relationship tend to be at greater risk than those who are in such a relationship) (Afifi, Cox, & Enns, 2006).

Women are nearly twice as likely as men to develop major depression, although the difference becomes smaller with advancing age (Health Canada, 2002b) (see Figure 4.2 on page 146). Although hormonal or other biologically linked gender differences may be involved, the gender difference may be due to the greater amount of stress women encounter in contemporary life (Hammen, 2005). Women are more likely than men to encounter such stressful life factors as physical and sexual abuse, poverty, single parenthood, and sexism.

Differences in coping styles may also help explain women's greater proneness to depression. Regardless of whether the initial precipitants of depression are biological, psychological, or social, one's coping responses may either worsen or reduce the severity and duration of depressive episodes. Nolen-Hoeksema and Corte (2004) have found that men are more likely to distract themselves when they are depressed, whereas women are more likely to amplify depression by ruminating about their feelings and

NORMAL/ABNORMAL BEHAVIOUR

Sad Mood: No Disorder

Maira is a 28-year-old woman who works as a dental assistant. She had been dating her boyfriend, Brian, for three years when he abruptly broke off their relationship. Maira was shocked, having hoped that they would get married in the next few years. The couple fought periodically, but there were no signs for Maira that Brian was thinking of ending the relationship. For the week after the breakup, Maira constantly felt on the edge of tears, and would start crying if people asked her how she was doing. She had no interest in food and had to force herself to eat a few things through the day. At the end of the week, her pants were a little loose, as she had lost a few pounds. She called in sick to work for three days after the breakup, and spent the majority of the day in bed. She got herself up and dressed later that week when her best friend came over to take her out. Maira and her friend went to see a movie, but Maira was distracted by thoughts about Brian. A few weeks later, Maira still felt sad about the breakup and sometimes cried when things reminded her of Brian. However, she had returned to work and had regained her appetite.

Depression: Disorder

Joaquin is a 39-year-old single man working full-time as a mechanical engineer. He has never been married, though has had several long-term relationships. His last relationship ended over a year ago, when the couple mutually decided to go their separate ways. A few months after that relationship ended, Joaquin began noticing that he was losing interest in his hobbies. He had to force himself to see his friends, and slowly, over the course of a few months, he stopped seeing his friends altogether. He just couldn't get up the energy to do anything but go to work. Work itself became a chore. While Joaquin had once been enthusiastic about his job and his colleagues, he began to have trouble focusing on his work and simply tried to get through the day. Joaquin also began to have trouble sleeping. He was able to get to sleep reasonably but found himself waking up through the night and waking up for the day at 3 or 4 a.m. without being able to get back to sleep. While lying in bed, Joaquin ruminated about how bad he felt and how these feelings were going to last forever. These problems continued on for months until Joaquin began having upsetting thoughts about his own death. These thoughts prompted Joaquin to talk to his family doctor, who immediately suggested that Joaquin might be suffering from a clinical level of depression.

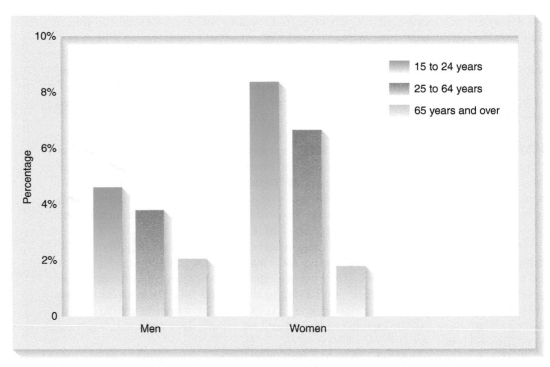

FIGURE 4.2 Prevalence of major depressive disorder, by age and gender, in the past 12 months in Canada.

Source: Adapted from Statistics Canada, 2004a.

Women and depression. Women are more likely to suffer from major depression than men. The higher rates of depression among women may be due to factors such as unhappy marriages, physical and sexual abuse, impoverishment, single parenthood, sexism, hormonal changes, childbirth, and the burden of being a primary caregiver to children.

possible causes. Women may be more likely to sit at home when they are depressed and think about how they feel or try to understand the reasons they feel the way they do, whereas men may try to distract themselves by doing something they enjoy, such as going to a favourite hangout, to get their mind off their feelings. Men often distract themselves by turning to alcohol as a form of self-medication, which can lead to another set of psychological and social problems (Nolen-Hoeksema & Corte, 2004).

Rumination is not limited to women, although they tend to ruminate more than men. Both men and women who repeatedly ruminate about the loss of loved ones or when feeling down or sad are more likely to become depressed and to suffer longer and more severe depression than those who ruminate less (Nolen-Hoeksema & Corte, 2004).

Although the gender gap in depression continues, more men are seeking help for depression. The male ego also seems to be battered by external assaults, from corporate downsizing to growing financial insecurity. While depression has long been viewed by men as a sign of personal weakness, the stigma associated with depression shows signs of lessening, although not disappearing.

Risks of major depression also vary with ethnicity. Aboriginal Canadians (i.e., First Nations, Inuit, and Métis), compared to non-Aboriginal groups, have higher rates of depression and suicide, although there is some fluctuation from one

Aboriginal community to another (Kirmayer, Brass, & Tait, 2000). According to a 2002 Health Canada report (2002a), there are several contributing factors: Because of conflicting messages about the value of their own culture, many Aboriginal people do not have a strong sense of self. Also, cultural instability has led to sexual abuse, family violence, and substance abuse, which are associated with a high risk of depression and suicide. Childhood separation, poverty, and access to firearms are contributing factors as well.

Major depression generally develops in young adulthood (people in their 20s and 30s) (APA, 2000a). It can affect children, but depression is more common in adults (Costello, Erkanli, & Angold, 2006). A multinational study of nine countries,[1] the largest study of its kind so far, showed that rates of major depression have been rising in Canada and elsewhere (Cross-National Collaborative Group, 1992). The greatest increases were found in Florence, Italy, and the least were in Christchurch, New Zealand. In all countries, rates for depression were higher among women than men.

No one knows why depression has been on the rise in many cultures, but speculation focuses on social and environmental changes, such as increasing fragmentation of families due to relocations, exposure to wars and civil conflicts, and increased rates of violent crimes, as well as possible exposure to toxins or infectious agents in the environment that might affect mental as well as physical health (Cross-National Collaborative Group, 1992). One example is the dramatic increase in depression that occurred between 1950 and 1960 in Beirut, Lebanon. This was a period of chaotic political and demographic change in that country. Depression dropped sharply in the following decade, 1960 to 1970, a time of relative prosperity and stability, but increased again between 1970 and 1980 during a time of social upheaval and internal warfare.

SEASONAL AFFECTIVE DISORDER Are you glum on gloomy days? Is your temper short during the brief days of winter? Are you dismal during the dark of long winter nights? Do you feel "up" when the long sunny days of spring and summer return?

Many people report that their moods vary with the weather. For some people, the changing of the seasons from summer into fall and winter leads to a type of depression called *seasonal affective (mood) disorder*—SAD.[2]

The features of SAD include fatigue, excessive sleep, craving for carbohydrates, and weight gain. SAD tends to lift with the early buds of spring. It affects women more often than men and is most common among young adults. SAD possibly occurs in children but not as commonly as in young adults (Magnusson & Partonen, 2005).

Seasonal affective disorder is more prevalent the farther one goes from the equator, because there are greater seasonal variations in daylight hours (Lam & Levitt, 1999). In a survey of a community sample in Toronto, for example, it was found that 11% of people with major depression had the seasonal subtype (Levitt, Boyle, Joffe, & Baumal, 2000). This suggests that seasonal affective disorder is not uncommon.

Although the causes of SAD remain unknown, one possibility is that seasonal changes in light may alter the body's biological rhythms that regulate such processes as body temperature and sleep–wake cycles (Sohn & Lam, 2005). Another possibility is that some parts of the central nervous system may have deficiencies in transmission of the mood-regulating neurotransmitter serotonin during the winter months (Sohn & Lam, 2005). Whatever the underlying cause, a trial of intense light therapy, called *phototherapy*, often helps relieve depression (Lam et al., 2006). Phototherapy typically consists of exposure to a range of 30 minutes to 3 hours of bright artificial light a day. The artificial light supplements the meagre sunlight the SAD-afflicted person

[1]Canada, the United States, Puerto Rico, Italy, France, Germany, Lebanon, Taiwan, and New Zealand.
[2]Seasonal affective disorder is not classified as a diagnostic category in its own right in the DSM-IV but is designated as a specifier of mood disorders in which major depressive episodes occur. For example, major depressive disorder that occurs seasonally would be given a diagnosis of major depressive disorder "with seasonal pattern."

otherwise receives. People can generally carry out some of their daily activities (e.g., eating, reading, writing) during their phototherapy sessions. Improvement typically occurs within several days of phototherapy, but treatment is likely required throughout the course of the winter season. Light directed at the eyes tends to be more successful than light directed at the skin.

We still don't know how phototherapy works. Mobilizing expectations of improvement (a placebo effect) may be involved in explaining at least part of the effect, although research has shown that phototherapy is more effective than a placebo (R. N. Golden et al., 2005; Lam et al., 2006). Phototherapy does not help all people with SAD. Fortunately, however, other treatments are effective. For example, a group of Canadian researchers led by Raymond Lam at the University of British Columbia has shown that SAD can be effectively treated with the antidepressant medication fluoxetine (trade name Prozac) (Lam et al., 2006).

POSTPARTUM DEPRESSION Many, perhaps even most, new mothers experience mood changes, periods of tearfulness, and irritability following the birth of a child. These mood changes are commonly called the "maternity blues," "postpartum blues," or "baby blues." They usually last for a couple of days and are believed to be a normal response to hormonal changes that accompany childbirth. Given these turbulent hormonal shifts, it would be "abnormal" for most women *not* to experience some changes in feeling states shortly following childbirth.

Some mothers, however, undergo severe mood changes that may persist for months or even a year or more. These problems in mood are referred to as **postpartum depression** (PPD). *Postpartum* derives from the Latin roots *post*, meaning "after," and *papere*, meaning "to bring forth." The DSM-IV does not treat postpartum depression as a unique form of depression. Rather, it is recognized as a subtype of major depression affecting women shortly after childbirth. PPD is often accompanied by disturbances in appetite and sleep, low self-esteem, and difficulties in maintaining concentration or attention. The prevalence of PPD is widely believed to be in the range of 10% to 15%, although there are considerable variations across different cultures (Halbreich & Karkun, 2006). This variation could be due to any of a variety of factors, including cultural differences in the stigma associated with depression (which would influence the person's willingness to report depressive symptoms), along with further cultural differences in risk factors for depression, such as the prevalence of stressful life events and the availability of social support (Halbreich & Karkun, 2006). PPD typically remits during the first three months after childbirth—although, as we saw earlier, some cases persist for years (Verkerk, Pop, Van Son, & Van Heck, 2003). Tragically, some women with this disorder commit suicide (Lindahl, Pearson, & Colpe, 2005).

In what is considered to be an especially severe case of postpartum depression, Dr. Suzanne Killinger-Johnson killed herself and her six-month-old baby, Cuyler, by jumping in front of an oncoming subway train. The night before—Thursday, August 10, 2000—Suzanne had been clutching her baby in a Toronto subway station. She stood by the platform for quite some time. Transit officials became concerned, so they called the police. Officers spoke with Suzanne and she left. About 90 minutes later, a similar thing happened at another subway station. This time the police drove her home, leaving her in the care of her husband and relatives. During rush hour the next morning, Suzanne slipped out of the house with her baby and went to yet another subway station. Commuters watched in horror as Suzanne dived in front of an oncoming train, clutching her baby. The infant was killed instantly. Suzanne died several days later.

Although PPD may involve chemical or hormonal imbalances brought on by childbirth (Bloch, Rotenberg, Koren, & Ehud, 2006), psychosocial factors such as financial problems, a troubled marriage, lack of social or emotional support from partners and family members, a history of depression, or an unwanted or sick baby all increase a woman's vulnerability to PPD (Boyce & Hickey, 2005). Having PPD also appears to increase a woman's risk of future depressive episodes (Bloch et al., 2006).

Screening tests for depression, such as the following, are offered annually by the organizers of the National Depression Screening Day (www.mentalhealthscreening.org). Tests like the one below can help you assess whether you are suffering from a serious depression. Such screening tests are not intended for you to diagnose yourself, but rather to raise your awareness of concerns you may want to discuss with a professional.

	Yes	No
1. I feel downhearted, blue, and sad.	____	____
2. I don't enjoy the things that I used to.	____	____
3. I feel that others would be better off if I were dead.	____	____
4. I feel that I am not useful or needed.	____	____
5. I notice that I am losing weight.	____	____
6. I have trouble sleeping through the night.	____	____
7. I am restless and can't keep still.	____	____
8. My mind isn't as clear as it used to be.	____	____
9. I get tired for no reason.	____	____
10. I feel hopeless about the future.	____	____

Rating your responses: If you agree with at least five of the statements, including either item 1 or 2, and if you have had these complaints for at least two weeks, professional help is strongly recommended. If you answered "yes" to statement 3, seek consultation with a professional immediately. If you don't know to whom to turn, contact your college or university counselling centre, neighbourhood mental health centre, or health provider.

Source: Adapted from Brody, 1992b.

Dysthymic Disorder

Major depressive disorder is severe and marked by a relatively abrupt change from one's pre-existing state. In comparison, **dysthymic disorder** (also called *dysthymia*), a milder form of depression, seems to follow a chronic course of development that often begins in childhood or adolescence (APA, 2000a). The term *dysthymia* derives from the Greek roots *dys-*, meaning "bad" or "hard," and *thymos*, meaning "spirit."

Persons with dysthymic disorder feel "bad spirited" or "down in the dumps" most of the time, but they are not so severely depressed as those with major depressive disorder. Whereas major depressive disorder tends to be severe and time limited, dysthymic disorder is relatively mild and nagging, typically lasting for years (Klein & Santiago, 2003).

About 3% to 6% of Canadian adults have dysthymia at some point in their lives (Health Canada, 2002b). Like major depressive disorder, dysthymic disorder is more common in women than men. Similar findings have been reported in other Western countries (Klein & Santiago, 2003).

In dysthymic disorder, complaints of depression may become such a fixture of people's lives that they seem to be part of their personality. The persistence of complaints may lead others to perceive them as whining and complaining. Although dysthymic disorder is less severe than major depressive disorder, persistent depressed mood and low self-esteem can affect a person's occupational and social functioning.

Some people are affected by both dysthymic disorder and major depression at the same time. The term **double depression** applies to those who have a major depressive episode superimposed on a longer-standing dysthymic disorder. Major depressive episodes tend to occur more frequently and to be longer in duration in people with double depression than those with major depression alone (Dunner, 2005).

We noted that major depressive disorder and dysthymic disorder are depressive disorders in the sense that the disturbance of mood is only in one direction—down. Yet some people with mood disorders may have fluctuations in mood in both directions that

dysthymic disorder Mild but chronic type of depressive disorder.

double depression Term applied to persons diagnosed with both *major depressive disorder* and *dysthymic disorder*.

exceed the usual ups and downs of everyday life. These types of disorders are called bipolar disorders. Here, we focus on the two types of bipolar disorder: (1) bipolar disorder and (2) cyclothymic disorder.

Bipolar Disorder

bipolar disorder Disorder characterized by mood swings between states of extreme elation and severe depression. Formerly called *manic depression*.

People with **bipolar disorder** ride an emotional roller coaster, swinging from the heights of elation to the depths of depression without external cause. The first episode may be either manic or depressive. Manic episodes, typically lasting from a few weeks to several months, are generally shorter in duration and end more abruptly than major depressive episodes. More than 90% of people who experience manic episodes eventually experience a recurrence (APA, 2000a). Some people with recurring bipolar disorder attempt suicide "on the way down" from the manic phase. They report that they would do nearly anything to escape the depths of depression they know lie ahead.

The DSM distinguishes between two general types of bipolar disorder, *bipolar I disorder* and *bipolar II disorder* (APA, 2000a). The essential feature of bipolar I disorder is the occurrence of one or more manic episodes. A disorder can thus be labelled "bipolar" even if it consists of manic episodes without any past or present major depressive episodes. In such cases, it is possible that a major depressive disorder will eventually appear or has been overlooked. In a few cases of bipolar I disorder, called the *mixed type*, a manic episode and a major depressive episode occur simultaneously (i.e., rapidly alternating between mania and depression). More frequently, though, cycles of elated and depressed mood states alternate with intervening periods of normal mood.

Bipolar II disorder is associated with a milder form of mania. In bipolar II, the person has experienced one or more major depressive episodes and at least one hypomanic episode, but never a full-blown manic episode. Whether bipolar I and bipolar II represent qualitatively different disorders or different points along a continuum of severity of bipolar disorder remains to be determined.

Bipolar disorder is relatively uncommon, with reported lifetime prevalence rates from community surveys of 0.4% to 2.2% for bipolar I disorder and 0.5% for bipolar II disorder (APA, 2000a). Unfortunately, it appears that many people with bipolar disorder are not adequately treated (C. A. Beck, Williams, et al., 2005).

Unlike major depression, rates of bipolar I disorder appear about equal in men and women, although women tend to have more depressive episodes (Miklowitz & Johnson, 2006). Gender differences in rates of bipolar II disorder are not well established. The typical age of onset of bipolar disorder is in the 20s (Schaffer, Cairney, Cheung, Veldhuizen, & Levitt, 2006), but sometimes the disorder does not appear until a person's 40s or 50s.

Sometimes, cases involve periods of "rapid cycling" in which the individual experiences two or more full cycles of mania and depression within a year without any intervening normal periods. Rapid cycling is associated with an earlier age of onset and is relatively uncommon (Miklowitz & Johnson, 2006).

manic episodes Periods of unrealistically heightened euphoria, extreme restlessness, and excessive activity characterized by disorganized behaviour and impaired judgment. Alternates with major depressive episodes in bipolar disorder.

Manic episodes, or periods of mania, typically begin abruptly, gathering force within days. During a manic episode, the person experiences a sudden elevation or expansion of mood and feels unusually cheerful, euphoric, or optimistic. The full DSM-IV-TR criteria are outlined in Table 4.4. The person seems to have boundless energy and is extremely sociable, although perhaps to the point of becoming overly demanding and overbearing toward acquaintances. Other people recognize the sudden shift in mood to be excessive in light of the person's circumstances. It's one thing to feel elated if you've just won the lottery; it is another to feel euphoric "because" it's Wednesday.

People in a manic episode or phase are excited and may strike others as silly, by carrying jokes too far, for example. They tend to show poor judgment and to become argumentative, sometimes going so far as destroying property. Roommates may find

TABLE 4.4

DSM-IV-TR Criteria for Manic Episode

A. A distinct period of abnormally and persistently elevated, expansive, or irritable mood, lasting at least 1 week (or any duration if hospitalization is necessary).

B. During the period of mood disturbance, three (or more) of the following symptoms have persisted (four if the mood is only irritable) and have been present to a significant degree:

(1) inflated self-esteem or grandiosity

(2) decreased need for sleep (e.g., feels rested after only 3 hours of sleep)

(3) more talkative than usual or pressure to keep talking

(4) flight of ideas or subjective experience that thoughts are racing

(5) distractibility (i.e., attention too easily drawn to unimportant or irrelevant external stimuli)

(6) increase in goal-directed activity (either socially, at work or school, or sexually) or psychomotor agitation

(7) excessive involvement in pleasurable activities that have a high potential for painful consequences (e.g., engaging in unrestrained buying sprees, sexual indiscretions, or foolish business investments)

C. The symptoms do not meet criteria for a Mixed Episode (see p. 365).

D. The mood disturbance is sufficiently severe to cause marked impairment in occupational functioning or in usual social activities or relationships with others, or to necessitate hospitalization to prevent harm to self or others, or there are psychotic features.

E. The symptoms are not due to the direct physiological effects of a substance (e.g., a drug of abuse, a medication, or other treatment) or a general medical condition (e.g., hyperthyroidism).

Note: Manic-like episodes that are clearly caused by somatic antidepressant treatment (e.g., medication, electroconvulsive therapy, light therapy) should not count toward a diagnosis of Bipolar I Disorder.

Source: Reprinted with permission from the *Diagnostic and Statistical Manual of Mental Disorders*, Fourth Edition, Text Revision, (Copyright ©2000). American Psychiatric Association. p. 362.

---

manic people abrasive and avoid them. They tend to speak very rapidly (with **pressured speech**). Their thoughts and speech may jump from topic to topic (in a **rapid flight of ideas**). Others find it difficult to get a word in edgewise. Manic people may also become extremely generous and give away costly possessions or make large charitable contributions they can ill afford. They may not be able to sit still or sleep restfully. They almost always show less need for sleep. They tend to awaken early yet feel well rested and full of energy. They sometimes go for days without sleep and without feeling tired. Although they may have abundant stores of energy, they seem unable to organize their efforts constructively. Their elation impairs their ability to work and maintain normal relationships.

People in a manic episode generally experience an inflated sense of self-esteem that may range from extreme self-confidence to wholesale delusions of grandeur. They may feel capable of solving the world's problems or of composing symphonies despite a lack of any special knowledge or talent. They may spout off about matters on which they know little, such as how to solve world hunger or how to prevent global warming. It soon becomes clear that they are disorganized and incapable of completing their projects. They become highly distractible. Their attention is easily diverted by irrelevant stimuli like the sounds of a ticking clock or of people talking in the next room. They tend to take on multiple tasks, more than they can handle. They may suddenly quit their jobs to enroll in art school, wait tables at night, organize charity drives on weekends, and work on a bestselling novel in their "spare time." They tend to exercise poor judgment and fail to weigh the consequences of their actions. They may get into trouble as a consequence of lavish spending, reckless driving, or sexual escapades. In severe cases,

pressured speech Outpouring of speech in which words seem to surge urgently for expression, as in a manic state.

rapid flight of ideas A characteristic of manic behaviour involving rapid speech and changes of topic.

they may experience disorders of thinking similar to those of people with schizophrenia. They may experience hallucinations or become grossly delusional, believing, for example, that they have a special relationship with God.

The following case provides an account of a manic episode, documented by Toronto psychiatrist Dr. Virginia Edwards:

> Brian began acting quite strangely shortly after his brother's wife had a son. He told his wife, Wanda, he had invented a motor that could run on propane only, and he thought General Motors would buy his invention. He became more and more talkative, with monologues running far into the night, which Wanda found exhausting. Wanda called her father-in-law, who talked quietly to Brian. Brian then broke into tears, rocking back and forth and lamenting what a failure he was. They took Brian to the local hospital and he agreed to be admitted. After he calmed down, he said he felt great, as if his ideas were brilliant. He needed little sleep and his thoughts raced. Brian said that he had never felt so wonderful in his life but that he also felt he was on a roller coaster that he couldn't get off.
>
> Adapted from V. Edwards, 2002, p. 37

Cyclothymic Disorder

Cyclothymia is derived from the Greek *kyklos*, which means "circle," and *thymos*, "spirit." The notion of a circular-moving spirit is an apt description because this disorder involves a chronic cyclical pattern of mood disturbance characterized by mild mood swings of at least two years (one year for children and adolescents). **Cyclothymic disorder** usually begins in late adolescence or early adulthood and persists for years. Few, if any, periods of normal mood last for more than a month or two. Neither the periods of elevated or depressed mood are severe enough to warrant a diagnosis of bipolar disorder, however. Estimates from community studies indicate lifetime prevalence rates for cyclothymic disorder of between 0.4% and 1% (4 to 10 people in 1000), with men and women about equally likely to be affected (APA, 2000a).

The periods of elevated mood are called *hypomanic episodes*, from the Greek prefix *hypo-*, meaning "under" or "less than." Hypomanic episodes are less severe than manic episodes and are not accompanied by the severe social or occupational problems associated with full-blown manic episodes. During hypomanic episodes, people may have an inflated sense of self-esteem, feel unusually charged with energy and alert, and be more restless and irritable than usual. They may be able to work long hours with little fatigue or need for sleep. Their projects may be left unfinished when their moods reverse, however. Then they enter a mildly depressed mood state and find it difficult to summon the energy or interest to persevere. They feel lethargic and depressed, but not to the extent typical of a major depressive episode.

Social relationships may become strained by shifting moods, and work may suffer. Social invitations, eagerly sought during hypomanic periods, may be declined during depressed periods. Phone calls may not be returned as the mood slumps. Sexual interest waxes and wanes with the person's moods.

The boundaries between bipolar disorder and cyclothymic disorder are not yet clearly established. Some forms of cyclothymic disorder may represent a mild, early type of bipolar disorder. About one third of people with cyclothymia go on to develop full-fledged bipolar disorder. People with cyclothymia, compared to other people in the general population, are more likely to have family members who suffer from bipolar disorder. Cyclothymia also responds to similar medications to those used to treat bipolar disorder.

cyclothymic disorder Mood disorder characterized by a chronic pattern of mild mood swings between depression and mania that are not of sufficient severity to be classified as bipolar disorder.

Findings such as these suggest that cyclothymia and bipolar disorder may have etiological factors in common (Akiskal, 2001).

The following case presents an example of the mild mood swings that typify cyclothymic disorder:

> A 29-year-old car salesman was referred by his girlfriend, a psychiatric nurse, who suspected he had a Mood Disorder, even though the patient was reluctant to admit that he might be a "moody" person. According to him, since age 14 he has experienced repeated alternating cycles that he terms "good times and bad times." During a "bad" period, usually lasting 4–7 days, he oversleeps 10–14 hours daily, lacks energy, confidence, and motivation—" just vegetating," as he puts it. Often he abruptly shifts, characteristically upon waking up in the morning, to a 3-day to 4-day. stretch of overconfidence, heightened social awareness, promiscuity, and sharpened thinking ("Things would flash in my mind"), At such times he indulges in alcohol to enhance the experience, but also to help him sleep. Occasionally the "good" periods last 7–10 days, but culminate in irritable and hostile outbursts, which often herald the transition back to another period of "bad" days.

> Reprinted with permission from the *DSM-IV-TR Case Book: A Learning Companion to the Diagnostic and Statistical Manual of Mental Disorders*, Fourth Edition, Text Revision, (Copyright © 2005). American Psychiatric Association. pp. 155–156.

REVIEW IT

Mood Disorders

- **What are mood disorders?** Mood disorders are disturbances in mood that are unusually prolonged or severe and serious enough to impair daily functioning.
- **What are the major types of mood disorders?** There are various kinds of mood disorders, including depressive (unipolar) disorders, such as major depressive disorder and dysthymic disorder, and disorders involving mood swings, such as bipolar disorder and cyclothymic disorder.
- **What are the features associated with major depression?** People with major depressive disorder experience a profound change in mood that impairs their ability to function. There are many associated features of major depressive disorder, including downcast mood; changes in appetite; difficulty sleeping; reduced sense of pleasure in formerly enjoyable activities; feelings of fatigue or loss of energy; sense of worthlessness; excessive or misplaced guilt; difficulties concentrating, thinking clearly, or making decisions; repeated thoughts of death or suicide; attempts at suicide; and even psychotic behaviours (hallucinations and delusions).
- **What is dysthymic disorder?** Dysthymic disorder is a form of chronic depression that is milder than major depressive

disorder but may nevertheless be associated with impaired functioning in social and occupational roles.
- **What are the types of bipolar disorder?** Bipolar I disorder is defined by the occurrence of one or more manic episodes, which generally but not necessarily occur in persons who have experienced major depressive episodes. In bipolar II disorder, depressive episodes occur along with hypomanic episodes but without the occurrence of a full-blown manic episode.
- **What characterizes manic episodes?** Manic episodes are characterized by sudden elevation or expansion of mood and sense of self-importance, feelings of almost boundless energy, hyperactivity, and extreme sociability, which often take a demanding and overbearing form. People in manic episodes tend to exhibit pressured or rapid speech, rapid "flight of ideas," and decreased need for sleep.
- **What is cyclothymic disorder?** Cyclothymic disorder is a type of bipolar disorder characterized by a chronic pattern of mild mood swings that sometimes progresses to bipolar disorder.

THEORETICAL PERSPECTIVES

Multiple factors—biological, psychological, social, and environmental—appear to be involved in the development of mood disorders. In this section, we first consider the relationship between stress and mood disorders and the protective value of social support and particular coping styles. Then we consider psychological and biological perspectives on depression.

Stress and Mood Disorders

Research indicates that there is a robust and causal association between stressful life events and major depressive episodes (Hammen, 2005); major depression is often preceded by stressful events, although not everyone who experiences such events will become depressed. Stressors such as the loss of a loved one, prolonged unemployment, physical illness, marital or relationship problems, economic hardship, pressure at work, racism, and discrimination may all contribute to the development and recurrence of mood disorders, especially major depression (Hammen, 2005; Kendler & Prescott, 2006). To illustrate physical illness as a stressor, results from an Ontario study of 297 people with HIV/AIDS revealed that 54% were currently suffering from clinically significant depression (P. Williams et al., 2005). As we saw earlier, this is much higher than the rate of depression in the general population.

Although stress appears to contribute to the risk of becoming depressed, research indicates that not all cases of major depression are preceded by stressful life events (Kendler & Prescott, 2006). People are also more likely to become depressed when they hold themselves responsible for undesirable events, such as school problems, financial difficulties, unwanted pregnancy, interpersonal problems, and problems with the law (Hammen, 2005). Research by Kate Harkness at Queen's University in Ontario, as well as the work of other investigators, suggests that stressors may interact with one another to influence a person's risk of depression. For example, the experience of childhood abuse and neglect appears to increase the odds that future stressful events (e.g., in adolescence) will lead to depression (Harkness, Bruce, & Lumley, 2006).

People are also more likely to become depressed if they have a particular genetic makeup that leaves them vulnerable to stress. In such a case, a person might possess the short allele (variant) of a gene involved in the regulation of the neurotransmitter serotonin (Caspi & Moffitt, 2006).

To complicate matters, the relationship between stress and depression may cut both ways: stressful life events may contribute to depression, and depressive symptoms in themselves may be stressful or lead to additional sources of stress, such as divorce or loss of employment. When you're depressed, for example, you may find it more difficult to keep up with your work at school or on the job, which can lead to more stress as your work piles up. The closer the stressful event taps the person's core concerns (failing at work or school, for instance), the more likely it is to precipitate a relapse in people who have a history of depression (Hammen, 2005). Stressful events may also play a role in triggering episodes of bipolar disorder (Miklowitz & Johnson, 2006). Some people seem better able to withstand stress or recover from losses than others. Investigators find that psychosocial factors such as social support and coping styles may serve as buffers against depression in times of stress (Hammen, 2005). To illustrate, research conducted at the University of Manitoba and University of Calgary indicates that depression is more prevalent among people who live alone, such as women who are separated or divorced, or elderly men who never married (Afifi et al., 2006; Patten et al., 2006). Close relationships, such as with marital partners, may provide a source of support during times of stress. The availability of social support is also associated with quicker recoveries and better outcomes in cases of major depression (Nasser & Overholser, 2005).

Evidence also shows that people with major depression are less likely to use active problem-solving strategies to alleviate stress than are nondepressed people (Matheson & Anisman, 2003). People with major depression also show deficits in skills needed to solve interpersonal problems with friends, co-workers, or supervisors (Haugh, 2006). People who are better able to solve their problems in daily life are more likely to overcome their depression (Nezu, Wilkins, & Nezu, 2004).

Psychodynamic Perspectives

The classic psychodynamic theory of depression of Freud (1917/1957) and his followers (e.g., Abraham, 1916/1948) holds that depression represents anger directed inward rather than against significant others. Anger may become directed against the self following either the actual or threatened loss of these important others.

Freud believed that **mourning** or normal bereavement is a healthy process by which one eventually comes to psychologically separate oneself from a person who is lost through death, separation, divorce, or other reason. Pathological mourning, however, does not promote healthy separation. Rather, it fosters lingering depression. Pathological mourning is likely to occur in people who hold powerful ambivalent feelings—a combination of positive feelings (love) and negative ones (anger, hostility)—toward the person who has departed or whose departure is feared. Freud theorized that when people lose, or even fear losing, an important figure about whom they feel ambivalent, their feelings of anger toward the other person turn to rage. Yet rage triggers guilt, which in turn prevents the person from venting anger directly at the lost person (called an *object*).

mourning Normal feelings or expressions of grief following a loss. See *bereavement*.

To preserve a psychological connection to the lost object, people introject, or bring inward a mental representation of the object. They thus incorporate the other person into the self. Now anger is turned inward, against the part of the self that represents the inward representation of the lost person. This produces self-hatred, which in turn leads to depression.

While also emphasizing the importance of loss, more recent psychodynamic models focus more on issues relating to the individual's sense of self-worth or self-esteem. One model, called the *self-focusing model*, considers how people allocate their attentional processes after a loss (death of a loved one, a personal failure, and so on) (Pyszczynski & Greenberg, 1992). According to this model, depression-prone people experience a period of intense self-examination (self-focusing) following a major loss or disappointment. They become preoccupied with thoughts about the lost object (loved one) or personal failure and remain unable to surrender hope of somehow regaining it.

Consider a person who must cope with the termination of a failed romantic relationship. It may be clear to all concerned that the relationship is beyond hope of revival. The self-focusing model proposes, however, that the depression-prone individual persists in focusing attention on restoring the relationship, rather than recognizing the futility of the effort and getting on with life. Moreover, the lost partner was someone who was a source of emotional support and upon whom the depression-prone individual had relied to maintain feelings of self-esteem. Following the loss, the depression-prone individual feels stripped of hope and optimism because these positive feelings that had depended on the other person are now lost. The loss of self-esteem and feelings of security, not the loss of the relationship itself, precipitate depression. Similarly, if depression-prone people peg their self-worth to a specific occupational goal, such as success in a modelling career, failure triggers self-focusing and consequent depression. Only by surrendering the object or lost goal and fostering alternative sources of identity and self-worth can the cycle be broken.

Psychodynamic theorists focus on the role of loss in depression. Research does show that the losses of significant others (through death or divorce, for example) are often (but not invariably) associated with the onset of depression (Kendler & Prescott, 2006). Such losses may also lead to other psychological disorders, however. There is yet a lack of research to support Freud's view that repressed anger toward a departed loved one is turned inward in depression.

Research on the utility of the self-focusing model has been mixed. On one hand, people suffering from depression have been shown to engage in higher levels

What happens when we lose our sense of direction? According to the humanistic-existential perspective, depression may result from the inability to find meaning and purpose in one's life.

of self-focusing following failure experiences than others, and in relatively lower levels of self-focusing following successes (Pyszczynski & Greenberg, 1992). On the other hand, self-focused attention has been linked to disorders other than depression, including anxiety disorders, alcoholism, mania, and schizophrenia (Ingram, 1990, 1991). The general linkage between self-focused attention and psychopathology may limit the model's value as an explanation of depression (Ingram, 1991).

Learning Perspectives

Whereas psychodynamic perspectives focus on inner, often unconscious, determinants of mood disorders, learning perspectives dwell more on situational factors, such as the loss of positive reinforcement. We perform best when levels of reinforcement are commensurate with our efforts. Changes in the frequency or effectiveness of reinforcement can shift the balance so that life becomes unrewarding.

REINFORCEMENT AND DEPRESSION Peter Lewinsohn (e.g., Lewinsohn, Sullivan, & Grosscup, 1980) suggested that depression may result when a person's behaviour receives too little reinforcement from the environment. Lack of reinforcement can sap motivation and induce feelings of depression. A vicious cycle may ensue: inactivity and social withdrawal deplete opportunities for reinforcement; lower levels of reinforcement exacerbate withdrawal. The low rate of activity typical of depression may also be a source of secondary reinforcement. Family members and other people may rally around people suffering from depression and release them from their responsibilities. Rather than help people who are struggling with depression regain normal levels of productive behaviour, sympathy may thus backfire and maintain depressed behaviour.

Reduction in reinforcement levels can occur for many reasons. A person who is recuperating at home from a serious illness or injury may find little that is reinforcing to do. Social reinforcement may plummet when people close to us, who were suppliers of reinforcement, die or leave us. People who suffer social losses are more likely to become depressed when they lack the social skills to form new relationships. Some first-year university students are homesick and depressed because they lack the skills to form rewarding new relationships. Widows and widowers may be at a loss as to how to ask someone for a date or start a new relationship.

Changes in life circumstances may also alter the balance of effort and reinforcement. A prolonged layoff may reduce financial reinforcements, which may in turn force painful cutbacks in lifestyle. A disability or an extended illness may also impair one's ability to ensure a steady flow of reinforcements.

Lewinsohn's model is supported by research findings that connect depression to a low level of positive reinforcement. For example, Lewinsohn and Libet (1972) noted a correspondence between depressed moods and lower rates of participation in potentially reinforcing activities. People with depressive disorders were also found to report fewer pleasant activities than nondepressed people (MacPhillamy & Lewinsohn, 1974). It remains unclear, however, whether depression precedes or follows a decline in the level of reinforcement (J. M. Williams, 1984). It may be that people who become depressed lose interest in pleasant activities or withdraw from potentially reinforcing social interactions, and not that inactivity leads to depression. Regardless of the causes of depression, behavioural treatment approaches that encourage people who become depressed to increase their levels of pleasant activities and provide them with the skills to do so are often helpful in alleviating depression (Dimidjian et al., 2006).

INTERACTIONAL THEORY The interactions between depressed persons and other people may help explain the former group's shortfall in positive reinforcement. Interactional theory (Coyne, 1999) proposes that the adjustment to living with a depressed person can become so stressful that the partner or family member becomes progressively less reinforcing toward the depressed person.

Interactional theory is based on the concept of reciprocal interaction. People's behaviour influences and is influenced by the behaviour of others. The theory holds that depression-prone people react to stress by demanding greater social support and reassurance. At first, people who become depressed may succeed in garnering support. Over time, however, their demands and behaviour begin to elicit anger or annoyance. Although loved ones may keep their negative feelings to themselves so as not to further upset the depressed person, these feelings may surface in subtle ways that spell rejection. Depressed people may react to rejection with deeper depression and greater demands, triggering a vicious cycle of further rejection and more profound depression. They may also feel guilty about distressing their family members, which can exacerbate negative feelings about themselves.

Evidence shows that people who become depressed tend to encounter rejection in long-term relationships (Marcus & Nardone, 1992). Family members may find it stressful to adjust to the behaviour of the person who is depressed, especially to such behaviours as withdrawal, lethargy, fretfulness, and despair. Similarly, evidence suggests that people with depressed spouses tend to have negative attitudes toward the spouse if the depressed person is constantly seeking reassurance about his or her self-worth (Van Orden & Joiner, 2006).

All in all, research evidence generally supports Coyne's belief (1999) that people who suffer from depression elicit rejection from others, but there remains a lack of evidence to show that this rejection is mediated by negative emotions (anger and annoyance) that the depressed person induces in others. Rather, a growing body of literature suggests that depressed people may lack effective social skills, which may account for the fact that others often reject them. In some cases, these deficits in social skills may be long-standing (i.e., present even when the person is not depressed), while in other cases the deficits may be present only when the person is depressed (and perhaps a consequence of depression) (Petty, Sachs-Ericsson, & Joiner, 2004). People with major depression tend to be unresponsive, uninvolved, and even impolite when they interact with others. In conversation, for example, they tend to gaze very little at the other person, take an excessive amount of time to respond, show very little approval or validation of the other person, and dwell on their own problems and negative feelings. They dwell on negative feelings even when interacting with strangers. In effect, they turn other people off, setting the stage for rejection.

Whether social skills deficits are a cause or a symptom of depression remains to be determined. Whatever the case, impaired social behaviour likely plays an important role in determining the persistence or recurrence of depression. As we shall see, some psychological approaches to treating depression (e.g., interpersonal psychotherapy and Lewinsohn's social-skills training approach, discussed later) focus on helping people with depression better understand and overcome their interpersonal problems. This may help, in turn, to alleviate depression or perhaps prevent future recurrences.

Cognitive Perspectives

Cognitive theorists relate the origin and maintenance of depression to the ways in which people see themselves and the world around them.

AARON BECK'S COGNITIVE THEORY One of the most influential cognitive theorists, psychiatrist Aaron Beck (A. T. Beck et al., 1979), relates the development of depression to the adoption early in life of a negatively biased or distorted way of thinking—the **cognitive triad of depression** (see Table 4.5 on page 158). The cognitive triad includes negative beliefs about oneself (e.g., "I'm no good"), the environment or the world at large (e.g., "This school is awful"), and the future (e.g., "Nothing will ever turn out right for me"). Cognitive theory holds that people who adopt this negative way of thinking are at greater risk of becoming depressed in the face of stressful or disappointing life experiences, such as getting a poor grade or losing a job.

cognitive triad of depression In Aaron Beck's theory, the view that depression derives from the adoption of negative views of oneself, the world, and the future.

TABLE 4.5

The Cognitive Triad of Depression

Negative view of oneself	Perceiving oneself as worthless, deficient, inadequate, unlovable, and as lacking the skills necessary to achieve happiness.
Negative view of the environment	Perceiving the environment as imposing excessive demands and/or presenting obstacles that are impossible to overcome, leading continually to failure and loss.
Negative view of the future	Perceiving the future as hopeless and believing that one is powerless to change things for the better. All that one expects of the future is continuing failure and unrelenting misery and hardship.

According to Aaron Beck, depression-prone people adopt a habitual style of negative thinking—the so-called cognitive triad of depression.

Source: Adapted from Beck & Young, 2001; Beck et al., 1979. Copyright Guilford Press. Reprinted with permission.

Beck views these negative concepts of the self and the world as mental templates, called *cognitive schemas*, that are adopted in childhood on the basis of early learning experiences. Children may find that nothing they do is good enough to please their parents or teachers. As a result, they may come to regard themselves as basically incompetent and to perceive their future prospects as dim. These beliefs may sensitize them later in life to interpret any failure or disappointment as a reflection of something basically wrong or inadequate about themselves. Minor disappointments and personal shortcomings become "blown out of proportion."

The tendency to magnify the importance of minor failures is an example of an error in thinking that Beck labels a *cognitive distortion*. He believes cognitive distortions set the stage for depression in the face of personal losses or negative life events. Psychiatrist David Burns (1980) enumerated a number of the cognitive distortions associated with depression:

1. *All-or-nothing thinking.* Seeing events in black and white, as either all good or all bad. For example, one may perceive a relationship that ended in disappointment as a totally negative experience, despite any positive feelings or experiences that may have occurred along the way. Perfectionism is an example of all-or-nothing thinking. Perfectionists judge any outcome other than perfect success to be complete failure. They may consider a grade of B+ or even A– to be tantamount to an F. They may feel like abject failures if they fall a few dollars short of their sales quotas or receive a very fine (but less than perfect) performance evaluation. Perfectionism is connected with an increased vulnerability to depression (Flett & Hewitt, 2002).

2. *Overgeneralization.* Believing that if a negative event occurs, it is likely to occur again in similar situations in the future. One may come to interpret a single negative event as foreshadowing an endless series of negative events. For example, receiving a letter of rejection from a potential employer leads one to assume that all other job applications will similarly be rejected.

3. *Mental filter.* Focusing only on negative details of events, thereby rejecting the positive features of one's experiences. Like a droplet of ink that spreads to discolour an entire beaker of water, focusing only on a single negative detail can darken one's vision of reality. Beck called this cognitive distortion **selective abstraction**, meaning the individual selectively abstracts the negative details from events and ignores their positive features. One's self-esteem is thus based on perceived weaknesses and failures rather than on positive features or on a balance of accomplishments and shortcomings. For example, a person receives a job evaluation that contains positive and negative comments but he or she focuses only on the negative.

selective abstraction In Beck's theory, a type of cognitive distortion involving the tendency to focus selectively only on the parts of one's experiences that reflect on one's flaws and to ignore those aspects that reveal one's strengths or competencies.

4. *Disqualifying the positive.* The tendency to snatch defeat from the jaws of victory by neutralizing or denying your accomplishments. An example is dismissal of congratulations for a job well done by thinking and saying, "Oh, it's no big deal. Anyone could have done it." By contrast, taking credit where credit is due may help people overcome depression by increasing their belief that they can make changes that will lead to a positive future (Needles & Abramson, 1990).

5. *Jumping to conclusions.* Forming a negative interpretation of events, despite a lack of evidence. Two examples of this style of thinking are called *mind reading* and the *fortune teller error.* In mind reading, you arbitrarily jump to the conclusion that others don't like or respect you, as in interpreting a friend's not calling for a while as a rejection. The fortune teller error involves the prediction that something bad is always about to happen to oneself. The person believes that the prediction of calamity is factually based even though there is an absence of evidence to support it. For example, the person concludes that a passing tightness in the chest *must* be a sign of heart disease, discounting the possibility of more benign causes.

6. *Magnification and minimization.* Magnification, or *catastrophizing,* refers to the tendency to make mountains out of molehills—to exaggerate the importance of negative events, personal flaws, fears, or mistakes. Minimization is its mirror image, a type of cognitive distortion in which one minimizes or underestimates one's good points.

7. *Emotional reasoning.* Basing reasoning on emotions—thinking, for example, "If I feel guilty, it must be because I've done something really wrong." One interprets feelings and events on the basis of emotions rather than a fair consideration of evidence.

8. *Should statements.* Creating personal imperatives or self-commandments— *should*s or *must*s. For example, "I *should* always get my first serve in!" or "I *must* make Chris like me!" After creating unrealistic expectations, the person may become depressed when he or she falls short.

9. *Labelling and mislabelling.* Explaining behaviour by attaching negative labels to oneself and others. You may explain a poor grade on a test by thinking you were "lazy" or "stupid" rather than simply unprepared for the specific exam or, perhaps, ill. Labelling other people as "stupid" or "insensitive" can engender hostility toward them. Mislabelling involves the use of labels that are emotionally charged and inaccurate, such as calling yourself a "pig" because of a minor deviation from your usual diet.

10. *Personalization.* The tendency to assume you are responsible for other people's problems and behaviour. You may assume your partner or spouse is crying because of something you have done (or not done), rather than recognizing that other causes may be involved.

Consider the errors in thinking illustrated in the following case:

Christie was a 33-year-old real estate sales agent who suffered from frequent episodes of depression. Whenever a deal fell through, she would blame herself: "If only I had worked harder . . . negotiated better . . . talked more persuasively . . . the deal would have been done." After several successive disappointments, each one followed by self-recriminations, she felt like quitting altogether. Her thinking became increasingly dominated by negative thoughts, which further depressed her mood and lowered her self-esteem: "I'm a loser . . . I'll never succeed . . . It's all my fault . . . I'm no good and I'm never going to succeed at anything."

Christie's thinking included cognitive errors such as the following: (1) *personalization* (believing herself to be the sole cause of negative events); (2) *labelling and mislabelling* (labelling herself a loser); (3) *overgeneralization* (predicting a dismal future on the basis of a present disappointment); and (4) *mental filter* (judging her personality entirely on the basis of her disappointments). In therapy, Christie was helped to think more realistically about events and not to jump to conclusions that she was automatically at fault whenever a deal fell through, or to judge her whole personality on the basis of disappointments or perceived flaws within herself. In place of this self-defeating style of thinking, she began to think more realistically when disappointments occurred, such as telling herself, "Okay, I'm disappointed. I'm frustrated. I feel lousy. So what? It doesn't mean I'll never succeed. Let me discover what went wrong and try to correct it the next time. I have to look ahead, not dwell on disappointments in the past."

The Authors' Files

automatic thoughts Thoughts that seem to pop into one's mind. In Aaron Beck's theory, automatic thoughts that reflect cognitive distortions induce negative feelings such as anxiety or depression.

Distorted thinking tends to be experienced as automatic, as if the thoughts had just popped into one's head. These **automatic thoughts** are likely to be accepted as statements of fact rather than opinions or habitual ways of interpreting events.

Supporting Beck's model is evidence linking cognitive distortions (including the magnification of one's shortcomings) and negative thinking to depressive symptoms and clinical depression (R. Beck & Perkins, 2001). People who are depressed also tend to hold more pessimistic views of the future and are more critical of themselves and others (R. Beck & Perkins, 2001). Such pessimistic thinking predicts future development or worsening of depression (Alloy, Abrahamson, Whitehouse, Hogan, Tashman, et al., 1999).

All in all, there is broad research support for many aspects of the theory, including Beck's concept of the cognitive triad of depression and his view that people with depression think more negatively than nondepressed people about themselves, the future, and the world in general. Although dysfunctional cognitions (negative, distorted, or pessimistic thoughts) are more common among people who are depressed, the causal pathways remain unclear. We can't yet say whether dysfunctional or negative thinking causes depression or is merely a feature of depression. Perhaps the causal linkages go both ways. Our thoughts may affect our moods and our moods may affect our thoughts (Kwon & Oei, 1994). Think in terms of a vicious cycle. People who feel depressed may begin thinking in more negative, distorted ways. The more negative and distorted their thinking becomes, the more depressed they feel; the more depressed they feel, the more dysfunctional their thinking becomes. Alternatively, dysfunctional thinking may come first in the cycle, perhaps in response to a disappointing life experience, which then leads to a downcast mood. This in turn may accentuate negative thinking, and so on. We are still faced with the old "chicken or egg" dilemma of determining which comes first in the causal sequence—distorted thinking or depression. Future research may help tease out these causal pathways. Even if it should become clear that distorted cognitions play no direct causal role in the initial onset of depression, the reciprocal interaction between thoughts and moods may play a role in maintaining depression and in determining the likelihood of recurrence (Kwon & Oei, 1994). Fortunately, evidence shows that dysfunctional attitudes tend to decrease with effective treatment for depression (D. A. Clark & Beck, 1999).

learned helplessness In Martin Seligman's model, a behaviour pattern characterized by passivity and perceptions of lack of control that develops because of a history of failure to be able to exercise control over one's environment.

LEARNED HELPLESSNESS (ATTRIBUTIONAL) THEORY The learned helplessness model proposes that people may become depressed because they learn to view themselves as helpless to control the reinforcements in their environments—or to change their lives for the better. The originator of the learned helplessness concept, Martin Seligman (1975), suggests that people learn to perceive themselves as helpless because of their experiences. The learned helplessness model thus straddles the behavioural and the cognitive: situational factors foster attitudes that lead to depression.

Seligman and his colleagues based the learned helplessness model on early laboratory studies of animals. In these studies, dogs exposed to an inescapable electric shock showed the "learned helplessness effect" by failing to learn to escape when the shock was later made escapable (Overmier & Seligman, 1967). Exposure to uncontrollable forces apparently taught the animals they were helpless to change their situation. Animals that developed learned helplessness showed behaviours that were similar to those of people with depression, including lethargy, lack of motivation, and difficulty acquiring new skills (Maier & Seligman, 1976).

Seligman (1975, 1991) proposed that some forms of depression in humans might result from exposure to apparently uncontrollable situations. Such experiences can instill the expectation that future reinforcements will also be beyond the individual's control. A vicious cycle may come into play in many cases of depression. A few failures may produce feelings of helplessness and expectations of further failure. Perhaps you know people who have failed certain subjects, such as mathematics. They may come to believe themselves incapable of succeeding in math. They may thus decide that studying for the quantitative section of the Graduate Record Examinations is a waste of time. They then do poorly, completing the self-fulfilling prophecy by confirming their expectations, which further intensifies feelings of helplessness, leading to lowered expectations and so on, in a vicious cycle.

Although it stimulated much interest, Seligman's model failed to account for the low self-esteem typical of people who are depressed. Nor did it explain variations in the persistence of depression. Seligman and his colleagues (Abramson, Seligman, & Teasdale, 1978) offered a reformulation of the theory to meet such shortcomings. The revised theory held that perception of lack of control over reinforcement alone did not explain the persistence and severity of depression. It was also necessary to consider cognitive factors, especially the ways in which people explain their failures and disappointments to themselves.

Seligman and his colleagues recast the helplessness theory in terms of the social psychology concept of **attributional style**. An attributional style is a personal style of explanation. When disappointments or failures occur, we may explain them in various characteristic ways. We may blame ourselves (an **internal attribution**) or our circumstances (an **external attribution**). We may see bad experiences as typical events (a **stable attribution**) or as isolated events (an **unstable attribution**). We may see them as evidence of broader problems (a **global attribution**) or as evidence of precise and limited shortcomings (a **specific attribution**). The revised helplessness theory—called the *reformulated helplessness theory*—holds that people who explain the causes of negative events (such as failure in work, school, or romantic relationships) according to these three types of attributions are most vulnerable to depression:

1. *internal factors* or beliefs that failures reflect their personal inadequacies, rather than external factors or beliefs that failures are caused by environmental factors;
2. *global factors* or beliefs that failures reflect sweeping flaws in personality, rather than specific factors or beliefs that failures reflect limited areas of functioning; and
3. *stable factors* or beliefs that failures reflect fixed personality factors, rather than unstable factors or beliefs that the factors leading to failures are changeable.

Let us illustrate these attributional styles with the example of a university student who goes on a disastrous date. Afterwards, he shakes his head in wonder and tries to make sense of his experience. An internal attribution for the calamity would involve self-blame, as in "I really messed it up." An external attribution would place the blame elsewhere, as in "Some couples just don't hit it off" or "She must have been in a bad mood." A stable attribution would suggest a problem that cannot be changed, as in "It's my personality." An unstable attribution, on the other hand, would suggest a transient condition, as in "It was probably the head cold." A global attribution for failure magnifies the extent of the problem, as in "I really have no idea what I'm doing when I'm with people." A specific attribution, in contrast, chops the problem down to size, as in "My problem is how to make small talk to get a relationship going."

The revised theory holds that each attributional dimension makes a specific contribution to feelings of helplessness. Internal attributions for negative events are linked to

attributional style Personal style for explaining cause-and-effect relationships between events.

internal attribution In the reformulated helplessness theory, a type of attribution involving the belief that the cause of an event involved factors within oneself. Contrast with *external attribution*.

external attribution In the reformulated helplessness theory, a type of attribution involving the belief that the cause of an event involves factors outside the self. Contrast with *internal attribution*.

stable attribution In the reformulated helplessness theory, a type of attribution involving the belief that the cause of an event involved stable rather than changeable factors. Contrast with *unstable attribution*.

unstable attribution In the reformulated helplessness theory, a type of attribution involving the belief that the cause of an event involved changeable rather than stable factors. Contrast with *stable attribution*.

global attribution In the reformulated helplessness theory, a type of attribution involving the belief that the cause of an event involved generalized rather than specific factors. Contrast with *specific attribution*.

specific attribution In the reformulated helplessness theory, a type of attribution involving the belief that the cause of an event involved specific rather than generalized factors. Contrast with *global attribution*.

Is it me? According to reformulated helplessness theory, the kinds of attributions we make concerning negative events can make us more or less vulnerable to depression. Attributing the breakup of a relationship to internalizing ("It's me"), globalizing ("I'm totally worthless"), and stabilizing ("Things are always going to turn out badly for me") causes can lead to depression.

lower self-esteem. Stable attributions help explain the persistence—or, in medical terms, the *chronicity*—of helplessness cognitions. Global attributions are associated with the generality or pervasiveness of feelings of helplessness following negative events. Attributional style should be distinguished from negative thinking (Gotlib, Lewinsohn, Seeley, Rohde, & Redner, 1993). You may think negatively (pessimistically) or positively (optimistically) but still hold yourself to blame for your perceived failures. An example of pessimistic self-blame for perceived failures would be "I messed up, and this is further evidence that I'm a loser." An example of more optimistic self-blame would be "I messed up, but I can learn from this experience so that it doesn't happen again."

Research is generally but not completely supportive of the reformulated helplessness (attributional) model. There is much evidence that people who are depressed are more likely than nondepressed people to attribute the causes of failures to internal, stable, and global factors (Alloy, Abramson, Walshaw, & Neeren, 2006). Longitudinal studies show that this attributional style, even in people who are currently not depressed, also predicts the person's future risk for the first onset or recurrence of future depressive episodes (Alloy, Abrahamson, Whitehouse, Hogan, Panzarella, & Rose, 2006). Further research, however, is needed to determine whether this attributional style truly causes depression. It could be that some other variable, correlated with depressive attributional style, is the actual causal agent.

Biological Perspectives

Evidence has accumulated pointing to the important role of biological factors, especially genetics and neurotransmitter functioning, in the development of mood disorders. Recent investigations are examining the biological roots of depression at the neurotransmitter level as well as at the genetic, molecular, and cellular levels.

GENETIC FACTORS   A growing body of research implicates genetic factors in mood disorders (Jang, 2005; Kendler & Prescott, 2006). For one thing, we know that mood disorders tend to run in families. Families, however, share environmental similarities as well as genes. Family members may share blue eyes (an inherited attribute) but also a common religion (a cultural attribute). Yet strengthening the genetic link are findings showing that the closer the genetic relationship one shares with a person with a major mood disorder such as major depression or bipolar disorder, the greater the likelihood that one will also suffer from a major mood disorder (Kendler & Prescott, 2006).

Twin studies and adoptee studies provide additional evidence of a genetic contribution. A higher concordance (agreement) rate among monozygotic (MZ) twins than dizygotic (DZ) twins for a given disorder is taken as supportive evidence of genetic factors. Both types of twins share common environments, but MZ twins share 100% of their genes, as compared to approximately 50% for DZ twins. Twin studies suggest that major depression is moderately heritable (Kendler & Prescott, 2006). However, individual depressive symptoms vary widely in their heritabilities. Symptoms such as depressed mood or tearfulness do not appear to be heritable, whereas other symptoms (e.g., loss of libido and appetite) have a heritable basis (Jang, Livesley, Taylor, Stein, & Moon, 2004). Data from twin studies suggest that dysthymic disorder may be relatively less influenced by genetic factors than either major depression or bipolar disorder. Genetic factors are particularly important in bipolar disorder, accounting for roughly 80% of the risk for developing this disorder, although the specific genes remain to be identified (A. Farmer, Elkin, & McGuffin, 2007).

All in all, researchers believe that heredity plays a contributing role in major depression in both men and women (Jang, 2005; Kendler & Prescott, 2006). However, genetics isn't the only, nor is it even the major, determinant of risk of major depression. Environmental factors, such as exposure to stressful life events, appear to play an important role in determining the risk of the disorder (Kendler & Prescott, 2006).

BIOCHEMICAL FACTORS AND BRAIN ABNORMALITIES IN DEPRESSION If there is a genetic component to depression, just what is inherited? Perhaps the genetic vulnerability expresses itself in abnormalities in neurotransmitter activity. These malfunctions may involve either an overabundance or an oversensitivity of receptor sites on receiving (postsynaptic) neurons where neurotransmitters dock. Antidepressant drugs may work by gradually reducing the number and sensitivity of these receptors. Although early speculation focused mainly on the role of norepinephrine in depression, investigators today believe that we also need to take into account irregularities in other neurotransmitters, especially serotonin, in explaining depression (Southwick, Vythilingam, & Charney, 2005).

One line of research uses brain imaging techniques such as the PET scan (to measure metabolic activity) and the MRI (to examine structural differences) that peer into the brains of people with depression. It turns out that the metabolic activity of the prefrontal cortex (the area of the frontal lobes lying in front of the motor areas) is typically lower in clinically depressed groups than in healthy controls (Damasio, 1997; Drevets et al., 1997). The prefrontal cortex is involved in regulating neurotransmitters believed to be involved in mood disorders, including serotonin and norepinephrine, so it is not surprising that evidence points to irregularities in this region of the brain. Abnormalities in the emotional centres of the brain (the limbic system) have also been observed. Other investigators find that MRI scans of the brains of people with bipolar disorder show evidence of structural abnormalities in parts of the brain involved in regulating mood states, such as the limbic system (Miklowitz & Johnson, 2006).

Research, including work done at the University of Toronto, indicates that the brain abnormalities in depression can be corrected with either drugs and/or cognitive therapy. Both treatments can correct the abnormalities in activity in the prefrontal cortex and limbic system (Goldapple et al., 2004).

Gender-related differences in coping styles may also come into play. Men and women may respond differently to feelings of depression. According to Nolen-Hoeksema (2000), women are more likely to ruminate over emotional problems and men are more likely to distract themselves, such as by seeking refuge in a bottle. Differences in coping styles may propel women into longer and more severe bouts of depression while setting the stage for the development of alcohol-related problems in men. As you can see, a complex web of factors may be involved in the development of mood disorders.

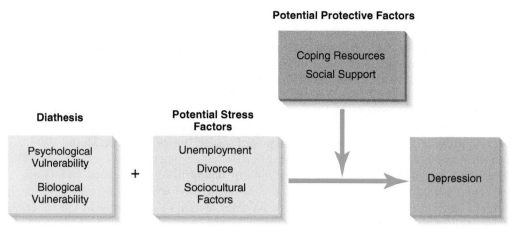

FIGURE 4.3 **Diathesis-stress model of depression.**

Tying It Together

Depression and other mood disorders involve interplay of multiple factors. Consistent with the diathesis-stress model (see Figure 4.3), depression may reflect an interaction of biological factors (such as genetic factors, neurotransmitter irregularities, or brain abnormalities), psychological factors (such as cognitive distortions or learned helplessness), and social and environmental stressors (such as divorce or loss of a job).

Consistent with this formulation, evidence suggests that genes interact with the environment; people with a particular genetic makeup (e.g., a particular version of a gene involved in serotonin regulation) are most likely to become depressed and suicidal in response to stressful life events (Caspi & Moffitt, 2006). In fact, there is a growing body of evidence that many forms of psychological disorder, including major depression, are the result of interactions between genes and the environment (Rutter, 2006). In other words, both genes and environmental events are important in shaping a person's risk for developing major depression and other psychological disorders.

Stressful life events, such as prolonged unemployment or a divorce, may have a depressing effect by reducing neurotransmitter activity in the brain. These biochemical effects may be more likely to occur or be more pronounced in people with a certain genetic predisposition, or *diathesis*, for depression. However, a depressive disorder may not develop, or may develop in a milder form, in people with more effective coping resources for handling stressful situations. For example, people who receive emotional support from others may be better able to withstand the effects of stress than those who have to go it alone. So too may people who make active coping efforts to meet the challenges they face in life.

Sociocultural factors may be major sources of stress that affect the development of mood disorders. These factors include poverty; overcrowding; exposure to racism, sexism, and prejudice; violence in the home or community; unequal stressful burdens placed on women; and family disintegration. These factors may figure prominently in either precipitating mood disorders or accounting for their recurrence. Other sources of stress include negative life events such as the loss of a job, the development of a serious illness, the breakup of a romantic relationship, and the loss of a loved one.

The diathesis for depression may take the form of a psychological vulnerability involving a depressive thinking style, one characterized by tendencies to exaggerate the consequences of negative events, to heap blame on oneself, and to perceive oneself as helpless to effect positive change. This cognitive diathesis may increase the risk of depression in the face of negative life events. These cognitive influences may also interact with a genetically based diathesis to further increase the risk of depression following stressful life events. Then too, the availability of social support from others may help bolster a person's resistance to stress during difficult times. People with more effective social skills may be better able to garner and maintain social reinforcement from others and thus be better able to resist depression than people lacking social skills. But biochemical changes in the brain might make it more difficult for the person to cope effectively and bounce back from stressful life events. Lingering biochemical changes and feelings of depression may exacerbate feelings of helplessness, compound the effects of the initial stressor, and so on.

REVIEW IT

Theoretical Perspectives on Mood Disorders

- **How are mood disorders conceptualized within the psychodynamic model?** In classic psychodynamic theory, depression is viewed in terms of inward-directed anger. People who hold strongly ambivalent feelings toward people they have lost, or whose loss is threatened, may direct unresolved anger toward the inward representations of these people that they have incorporated or introjected within themselves, producing self-loathing and depression. Bipolar disorder is understood in psychodynamic theory in terms of the shifting balances between the ego and superego. More recent psychodynamic models, such as the self-focusing model, incorporate both psychodynamic and cognitive aspects in explaining depression in terms of the continued pursuit of lost love objects or goals that it would be more adaptive to surrender.

- **How do humanistic and learning theorists view depression?** In the existential-humanistic framework, feelings of depression reflect the lack of meaning and authenticity in a person's life. Learning perspectives focus on situational factors in explaining depression, such as changes in the level of reinforcement. When reinforcement is reduced, the person may feel unmotivated and depressed, which can occasion inactivity and further reduce opportunities for reinforcement. Coyne's interactional theory focuses on the negative family interactions that can lead family members of people with depression to become less reinforcing toward them.

- **What are two major cognitive models of depression?** Beck's cognitive model focuses on the role of negative or distorted thinking in depression. Depression-prone people hold negative beliefs about themselves, the environment, and the future. This cognitive triad of depression leads to specific errors in thinking, or cognitive distortions, in response to negative events, which in turn lead to depression.

- **What is the learned helplessness model?** The learned helplessness model is based on the belief that people may become depressed when they come to view themselves as helpless to control the reinforcements in their environment or to change their lives for the better. A reformulated version of the theory holds that the ways in which people explain events—their attributions—determine their proneness toward depression in the face of negative events. The combination of internal, global, and stable attributions for negative events renders one most vulnerable to depression.

- **What role do biological factors play in mood disorders?** Genetic factors appear to play a role in mood disorders, especially in explaining major depressive disorder and bipolar disorder. Imbalances in neurotransmitter activity in the brain appear to be involved in depression and mania. The diathesis-stress model is used as an explanatory framework to illustrate how biological or psychological diatheses may interact with stress in the development of depression.

TREATMENT

Just as theoretical perspectives suggest that many factors may be involved in the development of mood disorders, so too are there various approaches to treatment that derive from psychological and biological models. Here we focus on several of the leading contemporary approaches.

Psychodynamic Approaches

Traditional psychoanalysis aims to help people who become depressed understand their ambivalent feelings toward important people (objects) in their lives whom they have lost or whose loss was threatened. By working through feelings of anger toward these lost objects, they can turn anger outward—through verbal expression of feelings, for example—rather than leave it to fester and turn inward.

Interpersonal psychotherapy (IPT). IPT is a brief, psychodynamic form of therapy that focuses on issues in a person's current interpersonal relationships. Like traditional psychodynamic approaches, IPT assumes that early life experiences are key issues in adjustment, but IPT focuses on the present—the here and now.

interpersonal psychotherapy A brief, psychodynamic form of therapy that focuses on helping people resolve interpersonal problems.

Traditional psychoanalysis can take years to uncover and deal with unconscious conflicts. Modern psychoanalytic approaches also focus on unconscious conflicts, but they are more direct, are relatively brief, and focus on present as well as past conflicted relationships. According to a recent review, patients treated with psychodynamic therapy tended to improve, although most of the research studies had important methodological problems, which makes it difficult to determine whether psychodynamic psychotherapy is any more effective than placebo (Bond, 2006). Eclectic psychodynamic therapists may also use behavioural methods to help clients acquire the social skills they need to develop a broader social network.

Newer models of psychotherapy for depression have emerged from the interpersonal school of psychodynamic therapy derived initially from the work of Harry Stack Sullivan (see Chapter 2) and other neo-Freudians, such as Karen Horney. One contemporary example is **interpersonal psychotherapy** (IPT) (Weissman, Markowitz & Klerman, 2000). IPT is a brief form of therapy (usually no more than 9 to 12 months) that focuses on the client's current interpersonal relationships. The developers of ITP believe that depression occurs within an interpersonal context and that relationship issues need to be emphasized in treatment. IPT has been shown to be an effective treatment for major depression and shows promise in treating other psychological disorders, including dysthymic disorder and bulimia (Markowitz, 2006a, 2006b). Although IPT shares some features with traditional psychodynamic approaches (principally the belief that early life experiences and persistent personality features are important issues in psychological adjustment), it differs from traditional psychodynamic therapy by focusing primarily on clients' current relationships, rather than helping them acquire insight into unconscious internal conflicts of childhood origins. Although unconscious factors and early childhood experiences are recognized, therapy focuses on the present—the here and now.

Interpersonal psychotherapy helps clients deal with unresolved or delayed grief reactions following the death of a loved one as well as role conflicts in present relationships (Weissman, Markowitz, & Klerman, 2000). The therapist helps clients express grief and come to terms with their loss while assisting them in developing new activities and relationships to help renew their lives. The therapist also helps clients identify areas of conflict in their present relationships, understand the issues that underlie them, and consider ways of resolving them. If the problems in a relationship are beyond repair, the therapist helps the client consider ways of ending it and establishing new relationships. In the case of Sal, a 31-year-old television repairman's assistant, depression was associated with marital conflict:

> Sal began to explore his marital problems in the fifth therapy session, becoming tearful as he recounted his difficulty expressing his feelings to his wife because of feelings of being "numb." He felt that he had been "holding on" to his feelings, which was causing him to become estranged from his wife. The next session zeroed in on the similarities between himself and his father, in particular

how he was distancing himself from his wife in a similar way to how his father had kept a distance from him. By session 7, a turning point had been reached. Sal expressed how he and his wife had become "emotional" and closer to one another during the previous week, how he was able to talk more openly about his feelings, and how he and his wife had been able to make a joint decision concerning a financial matter that had been worrying them for some time. When later he was laid off from his job, he sought his wife's opinion rather than picking a fight with her as a way of thrusting his job problems on her. To his surprise he found that his wife responded positively—not "violently," as he had expected— to times when he expressed his feelings. In his last therapy session (session 12), Sal expressed how therapy had led to a "reawakening" within himself with respect to the feelings he had been keeping to himself—an openness that he hoped to create in his relationship with his wife.

Klerman, Weissman, Rounsaville, & Chevron, 1984, pp. 111–113.
Copyright Basic Books. Reprinted with permission.

Behavioural Approaches

Behavioural treatment approaches presume that depressive behaviours are learned and can be unlearned. Behaviour therapists aim to directly modify behaviours rather than seeking to foster awareness of possible unconscious causes of these behaviours. Behaviour therapy has been shown to produce substantial benefits in treating depression in both adults and adolescents (Dimidjian et al., 2006; Hopko, Lejuez, Ruggiero, & Eifert, 2003).

One illustrative behavioural program was developed by Lewinsohn and colleagues (Hops & Lewinsohn, 1995; Lewinsohn, Antonuccio, Steinmetz Breckenridge, & Teri, 1984). It consists of a 12-session, 8-week group therapy program organized as a course—the Coping With Depression (CWD) Course. The course helps clients acquire relaxation skills, increase pleasant activities, and build social skills that enable them to obtain social reinforcement. For example, students learn how to accept rather than deny compliments and how to ask friends to join them in activities to raise the frequency and quality of their social interactions. Participants are taught to generate a self-change plan, to think more constructively, and to develop a lifetime plan for maintaining treatment gains and preventing recurrent depression. The therapist is considered a teacher; the client, a student; the session, a class. Each participant is treated as a responsible adult who is capable of learning. The structure involves lectures, activities, and homework, and each session follows a structured lesson plan.

Another behaviourally based treatment is called Behavioural Activation (BA) and is considered a third-generation behaviour therapy for depression. This treatment is based on operant conditioning models and is often referred to as *applied behavioural analysis*. Research has supported BA as a stand-alone treatment for major depression; an influential and dismantling study found that BA on its own was just as good as cognitive therapy (Jacobson et al., 1996). Here is one example:

Mr. X was a 62-year-old man with chronic treatment-resistant depression and comorbid personality disorder. After 147 days of cognitive therapy (CT), his treatment was switched to behavioural activation (BA) for an additional 147 days. Mood data from each treatment were tracked carefully.

Mr. X met the criteria for major depressive disorder, recurrent, with melancholic features. He and his wife reported that there was a family history of depression and that his difficulties with depression had begun in his mid-20s. At intake, Mr. X reported a lengthy history of treatment with drugs, supportive psychotherapy, and electro-convulsive shock therapy (ECT). He had read about the efficacy of cognitive therapy and specifically requested that it be added to the medication he was already taking. At the time of intake, he was taking venlafaxine HCl, escitalopram, and lorazepam for depression and had received ECT in the past year but had not experienced adequate symptom relief.

Mr. X also displayed several traits of dependent personality disorder, including difficulty making everyday decisions, taking care of his responsibilities, and initiating projects; excessive focus on obtaining nurturance from others; and unrealistic preoccupation with abandonment. His indecisiveness was particularly apparent during assessment: he had so much difficulty deciding between responses on self-report questionnaires and during the interviews that he was often unable to respond at all. His profile, with his limited introspective abilities, his dependent nature, and his longstanding tolerance of personal distress, suggested that he might respond poorly to psychotherapy. The therapist explained to him that treatment would focus more specifically on his behaviours and how his choice of activities affected his mood. The BA model is all about reinforcement. It suggests that life events, including specific trauma or loss, biological predisposition to depression, and the daily hassles of life, lead individuals to experience low levels of positive reinforcement in their lives. Behaviours normally used to cope with negative feelings make many individuals, like Mr. X, feel better in the short run. It is natural for a person who feels sad and no longer finds pleasure in activities he or she previously enjoyed to attempt to cope by withdrawing socially, ceasing to engage in activities, and "shutting down." The problem is that such coping strategies do not help alleviate depression—they make it worse, through negative reinforcement.

To evaluate ongoing treatment progress, Mr. X was initially presented with standardized self-report measures; however, his response style made this impractical, so the therapist instead used a brief measure to monitor his progress. He was asked to track his thoughts and activities and to make a single-item rating of his average daily mood (0 = worst mood ever to 10 = best mood ever).

Over the course of the 147 days in which he received CT, Mr. X appeared to experience limited benefits. His daily mood scores either remained stagnant or dipped lower, reflecting worsening mood, and he continued to report frequent crying spells. He seemed to make little progress in terms of interpersonal functioning or participation in household projects and hobbies. In contrast, during the first 147 days in which he received BA, Mr. X's mood improved, both relative to the CT baseline and across days in this condition.

While this represents one case, Mr. X's story suggests that his response was not merely a result of the effects of time but rather was related to the switch in treatment: during the CT phase, Mr. X's mood actually worsened; his mood began to improve following the introduction of BA.

Adapted from Bottonari, Roberts, Thomas, & Read, 2008

Cognitive Approaches

Cognitive theorists believe that distorted thinking plays a key role in the development of depression. Aaron Beck and his colleagues have developed a multicomponent treatment approach called **cognitive therapy,** which focuses on helping people with depression learn to recognize and change their dysfunctional thinking patterns. Depressed people tend to focus on how they are feeling rather than on the thoughts that may underlie their feeling states. That is, they usually pay more attention to how bad they feel than to the thoughts that may trigger or maintain their depressed moods.

Cognitive therapy, like behaviour therapy, involves a relatively brief therapy format, frequently 14 to 16 weekly sessions. Therapists use a combination of behavioural and cognitive techniques to help clients identify and change dysfunctional thoughts and develop more adaptive behaviours (K. S. Dobson & Khatri, 2002). For example, they assist clients in connecting thought patterns to negative moods by having them monitor the automatic negative thoughts they experience throughout the day by means of a thought

cognitive therapy (1) Name of Aaron Beck's kind of psychotherapy, which challenges the distorted thought patterns that give rise to or exacerbate clients' problems. (2) More generally, a form of psychotherapy that addresses clients' cognitive processes, usually their self-defeating attitudes.

diary or daily record. Clients note when and where negative thoughts occur and how they feel at the time. Once these disruptive thoughts are identified, the therapist helps the client challenge their validity and replace them with more adaptive thoughts. The following case example shows how a cognitive therapist works with a client to dispute the validity of thoughts reflecting the cognitive distortion called *selective abstraction* (the tendency to judge oneself entirely on the basis of specific weaknesses or flaws in character). The client judged herself to be completely lacking in self-control because she ate a single piece of candy while she was on a diet.

Client: I don't have any self-control at all.

Therapist: On what basis do you say that?

C: Somebody offered me candy and I couldn't refuse it.

T: Were you eating candy every day?

C: No, I just ate it this once.

T: Did you do anything constructive during the past week to adhere to your diet?

C: Well, I didn't give in to the temptation to buy candy every time I saw it at the store. . . . Also, I did not eat any candy except that one time when it was offered to me and I felt I couldn't refuse it.

T: If you counted up the number of times you controlled yourself versus the number of times you gave in, what ratio would you get?

C: About 100 to 1.

T: So if you controlled yourself 100 times and did not control yourself just once, would that be a sign that you are weak through and through?

C: I guess not—not *through* and *through* (smiles).

Beck et al., 1979, p. 68. Copyright Guildford Press. Reprinted with permission.

There is ample evidence supporting the effectiveness of cognitive therapy in treating major depression (Hollon, 2006). Depressive symptoms often lift within 8 to 12 sessions. The benefits achieved appear to be at least equal to those achieved from antidepressant medication in treating mild to moderate depression. Questions remain about how effective cognitive or cognitive-behavioural approaches may be in treating severe depression, however (Jacobson & Hollon, 1996). Another open question is whether a combination approach involving antidepressant medication and psychotherapy is preferable to either approach alone (Craighead, Craighead, & Ilardi, 1998). Cognitive therapy or cognitive-behavioural therapy appears to produce about the same level of benefit as interpersonal psychotherapy or antidepressant medications (Hollon, 2006).

There is less research on the psychological treatment of dysthymia, although techniques used in treating major depression, such as cognitive therapy and interpersonal psychotherapy, have shown some promising results (Dunner, 2005). Cognitive theorists suggest that cognitive errors can lead to depression if they are left unchallenged in the individual's mind. Cognitive therapists help assist clients to recognize cognitive distortions and replace them with more rational alternative thoughts.

Table 4.6 on page 170 shows some common examples of automatic thoughts, the types of cognitive distortions they represent, and some rational alternative responses.

Biological Approaches

The most common biological approaches to treating mood disorders involve the use of antidepressant drugs and electroconvulsive therapy for depression and lithium carbonate for bipolar disorder.

ANTIDEPRESSANT DRUGS Drugs used to treat depression include several classes of antidepressants: tricyclic antidepressants (TCAs), monoamine oxidase (MAO) inhibitors,

TABLE 4.6

Cognitive Distortions and Rational Responses

Automatic Thought	Kind of Cognitive Distortion	Rational Response
I'm all alone in the world.	All-or-Nothing Thinking	It may feel like I'm all alone, but there are some people who care about me.
Nothing will ever work out for me.	Overgeneralization	No one can look into the future. Concentrate on the present.
My looks are hopeless.	Magnification	I may not be perfect looking, but I'm far from hopeless.
I'm falling apart. I can't handle this.	Magnification	Sometimes I just feel overwhelmed. But I've handled things like this before. Just take it a step at a time and I'll be okay.
I guess I'm just a born loser.	Labelling and Mislabelling	Nobody is destined to be a loser. Stop talking yourself down.
I've lost only four kilograms on this diet. I should just forget it. I can't succeed.	Negative Focusing/Minimization/ Disqualifying the Positive/ Jumping to Conclusions/ All-or-Nothing Thinking	Four kilograms is a good start. I didn't gain all this weight overnight, and I have to expect that it will take time to lose it.
I know things must really be bad for me to feel this awful.	Emotional Reasoning	Feeling something doesn't make it so. If I'm not seeing things clearly, my emotions will be distorted too.
I know I'm going to flunk this course.	Fortune Teller Error	Give me a break! Just focus on getting through this course, not jumping to negative conclusions.
I know John's problems are really my fault.	Personalization	Stop blaming yourself for everyone else's problems. There are many reasons why John has these problems that have nothing to do with me.
Someone my age should be doing better than I am.	Should Statements	Stop comparing yourself to others. All anyone can be expected to do is their best. What good does it do to compare myself to others? It only leads me to get down on myself rather than getting me motivated.
I just don't have the brains for university.	Labelling and Mislabelling	Stop calling yourself names like "stupid." I can accomplish a lot more than I give myself credit for.
Everything is my fault.	Personalization	There you go again. Stop playing this game of pointing blame at yourself. There's enough blame to go around. Better yet, forget placing blame and try to think through how to solve this problem.
It would be awful if Sue turns me down.	Magnification	It might be upsetting. But it needn't be awful unless I make it so.
If people really knew me, they would hate me.	Mind Reader	What evidence is there for that? More people who get to know me like me than don't like me.
If something doesn't get better soon, I'll go crazy.	Jumping to Conclusions/ Magnification	I've dealt with these problems this long without falling apart. I just have to hang in there. Things are not as bad as they seem.
I can't believe I got another pimple on my face. This is going to ruin my whole weekend.	Mental Filter	Take it easy. A pimple is not the end of the world. It doesn't have to spoil my whole weekend. Other people get pimples and seem to have a good time.

and selective serotonin-reuptake inhibitors (SSRIs). All of these drugs increase levels and, perhaps, the actions of neurotransmitters in the brain. The increased availability of key neurotransmitters in the synaptic cleft may alter the sensitivity of postsynaptic neurons to these chemical messengers. It is not precisely known how antidepressant medications work in relieving depression. Given that there are many different types of these drugs working on various types (and subtypes) of neurotransmitters, it seems likely that there are several different ways in which the various antidepressant medications exert their therapeutic effects. Antidepressants tend to have a delayed effect, typically requiring several weeks of treatment before a therapeutic benefit is achieved. SSRIs not only lift mood, but in many cases also eliminate delusions that may accompany severe depression

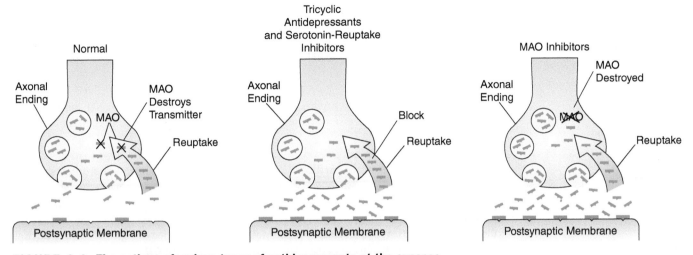

FIGURE 4.4 **The actions of various types of antidepressants at the synapse.**
Tricyclic antidepressants and serotonin-reuptake inhibitors both increase the availability of neurotransmitters by preventing their reuptake by the presynaptic neuron. Tricyclic antidepressants impede the reuptake of both norepinephrine and serotonin. MAO inhibitors work by inhibiting the action of monoamine oxidase, an enzyme that normally breaks down neurotransmitters in the synaptic cleft.

(Zanardi, Franchini, Gasperini, Perez, & Smeraldi, 1996). Antidepressant medication is clearly effective in helping relieve major depression in many cases (Kupfer, 1999). Evidence also shows that antidepressant medication is helpful in treating dysthymia as well (Dunner, 2005).

The different classes of antidepressants increase the availability of neurotransmitters, but in different ways (see Figure 4.4). The tricylics, which include imipramine (trade name Tofranil), amitriptyline (Elavil), desipramine (Norpramin), and doxepin (Sinequan), are so named because of their three-ringed molecular structure. They increase levels in the brain of the neurotransmitters norepinephrine and serotonin by interfering with the reuptake (reabsorption by the transmitting cell) of these chemical messengers. As a result, more of these neurotransmitters remain available in the synapse, which induces the receiving cell to continue to fire, prolonging the volley of nerve impulses travelling through the neural highway in the brain.

The selective serotonin-reuptake inhibitors (SSRIs) (fluoxetine, trade name Prozac, is one) work in a similar fashion but have more specific effects on raising the levels of serotonin in the brain. The MAO inhibitors increase the availability of neurotransmitters by inhibiting the action of monoamine oxidase (MAO), an enzyme that normally breaks down or degrades neurotransmitters in the synaptic cleft. MAO inhibitors are used less widely than other antidepressants because of potentially serious interactions with certain foods and alcoholic beverages.

The potential side effects of tricyclics and MAO inhibitors include dry mouth, constipation, blurred vision, and, less frequently, urinary retention, paralytic ileus (a paralysis of the intestines, which impairs the passage of intestinal contents), confusion, delirium, and cardiovascular complications such as reduced blood pressure. Tricyclics are also highly toxic in very high doses, which raises the prospect of suicidal overdoses if the drugs are used without close supervision.

Compared to the older generation of tricylics, SSRIs such as Prozac and Zoloft have two major advantages: first, they are less toxic and so are less dangerous when taken in very high doses (as in overdose); second, they have fewer of the common side effects (such as dry mouth, constipation, and weight gain) associated with the tricyclics and MAO inhibitors. Still, Prozac and other SSRIs may produce side effects such as upset stomach, headaches, agitation, insomnia, lack of sexual drive, and delayed orgasm. Moreover, SSRIs are only moderately effective in treating depression (S. Taylor & Stein, 2006) and may be less effective than tricyclics (Montgomery, 2006).

Another promising class of medications are the serotonin-noradrenaline reuptake inhibitors (SNRIs), such as Effexor (venlafaxine). SNRIs are similar to tricyclics in that they increase the availability of both serotonin and norepinephrine. Although SNRIs have not been studied as extensively as SSRIs, the evidence so far suggests that in high doses, SNRIs appear to be more effective than SSRIs, but not at low doses (Montgomery, 2006). SNRIs appear to be as effective as tricyclics but with milder side effects (Montgomery, 2006). Patients who fail to respond to a particular SNRI may benefit from another SNRI, or they may benefit from some other medication, such as an SSRI (Blier, 2006).

One issue we need to address in discussing drug therapy is the high rate of relapse following discontinuation of medication. A review of drug withdrawal studies showed relapse rates of 25% to 75% when antidepressants were withdrawn (Petersen, 2006). Continued (maintenance) medication can help reduce the rate of relapse. Psychologically based therapies appear to provide greater protection against a recurrence of depression following termination of treatment, presumably because the learning that occurs during therapy carries past the end of active treatment (Petersen, 2006).

Research, such as studies conducted by Zindel Segal and colleagues at the University of Toronto, suggests that mindfulness-based cognitive therapy (MBCT) is a particularly useful way of preventing and prolonging time to relapse, regardless of whether the patient's depression was first treated with either medication or psychotherapy (Bondolfi et al., 2010; Carney & Segal, 2005). MBCT is a group-based psychosocial intervention that involves training the person in meditation exercises, including exercises that increase awareness of the things in the present (e.g., "What I am doing right now") instead of ruminating about bad things that happened in the past or might happen in the future. MBCT also teaches people to simply observe their unwanted thoughts as they float through the stream of consciousness, without attaching evaluative judgments (e.g., "I've just had the thought 'I'll always fail'—I don't need to get upset about the thought or believe it; all I need to do is to notice that the thought comes and goes") (Segal, Williams, & Teasdale, 2002).

Overall, evidence shows that most people with major depressive disorder will respond favourably to cognitive therapy, cognitive-behavioural therapy, or interpersonal psychotherapy, or to antidepressant medications (APA, 2000b; Hollon & Shelton, 2001). It is currently a matter of debate whether drugs or psychotherapy is most appropriate for severe depression (APA, 2000b; Hollon, 2006), although drugs would be indicated if the depressed person is experiencing delusions and hallucinations. Some people who fail to respond to drug therapy may respond favourably to psychotherapy, and vice versa.

Other interventions can also be useful as adjuncts or alternatives to medication or psychotherapy. For example, research indicates that physical exercise is useful for alleviating depressive symptoms in people with mild to moderate depression (Martinsen, 2005).

LITHIUM The drug lithium carbonate, a powdered form of the metallic element lithium, is the most widely used and one of the most recommended treatments for bipolar disorder (Yatham et al., 2006). It could be said that the ancient Greeks and Romans were among the first to use lithium as a form of chemotherapy. They prescribed mineral water that contained lithium for people with turbulent mood swings.

Lithium is effective in stabilizing moods in people with bipolar disorder and reducing recurrent episodes of mania and depression. People with bipolar disorder may need to use lithium indefinitely to control their mood swings, just as diabetics use insulin continuously to control their illness. Lithium is given orally in the form of a natural mineral salt, lithium carbonate. Despite more than 40 years of use, we still can't say how lithium works, although there is emerging evidence that it influences the communication between neurons (Miklowitz & Johnson, 2006). Lithium treatment must be closely monitored because of potential toxic effects and other side effects. Lithium is not a panacea; many patients fail to respond or cannot tolerate the side effects (e.g., stomach irritation, weight gain, increased thirst). Fortunately, there are other effective medications for bipolar disorder, including some antipsychotic and anticonvulsant medications that happen

St. John's Wort—A Natural "Prozac"?

Might a humble herb be a remedy for depression? The herb, called St. John's wort, or *Hypericum perforatum*, has been used for centuries to help heal wounds. Now people are using it to relieve depression. Nowhere is it more popular than Germany, where high-strength versions of the herb are among the most widely used antidepressants on the market. The benefits of St. John's wort are currently unclear and have been the subject of much debate. Some studies provide support for the benefits of St. John's wort in treating major depressive disorder with fewer reported side effects than medications. For example, Alpert et al. (2005) found that the herb was more effective than fluoxetine (Prozac). Another study found that the herb was at least as effective as the SSRI drug paroxetine (Paxil) in moderate to severe major depression (Szegedi, Kohnen, Dienel, & Kieser, 2005). However, other studies have raised doubts about the herb's efficacy. According to a review of several recent placebo-controlled studies, St. John's wort has minimal beneficial effects on major depression, although it might be useful in treating milder forms of depression

(Linde, Berner, Egger, & Mulrow, 2005). More promising treatments for major depression include cognitive-behaviour therapy or selective serotonin reuptake inhibitors.

Regardless of the effects of St. John's wort on depressive symptoms, the herb appears to increase the levels of serotonin in the brain by interfering with its reabsorption, the same mechanism believed to account for Prozac's benefits. Yet we don't know about the herb's long-term safety. Evidence suggests that it should not be combined with conventional antidepressant medications such as Prozac because St. John's wort interacts with these drugs to produce an excess of serotonin in the brain. This is called the *serotonin syndrome*, and it can progress from dizziness, headaches, and vomiting to coma and death (Vermani, Milosevic, Smith, & Katzman, 2005). St John's wort also should be used with caution in patients receiving anticoagulants (blood thinners), oral contraceptives, or antiviral drugs because it can alter the levels of these medications in the blood by means of its effects on the liver (Vermani et al., 2005).

---

to have mood-stabilizing properties (e.g., Zyprexa, Tegretol) (Yatham et al., 2006). A meta-analysis of placebo-controlled studies revealed that the effect of the newer generation antipsychotics aripiprazole, olanzapine, quetiapine, risperidone, and ziprasidone was superior to placebo in the treatment of bipolar mania (Perlis, 2007). These alternative medications usually cause fewer or less severe side effects than lithium. However, some patients have only a partial response to lithium or other drugs and some fail to respond at all. Thus, there remains a need for alternative treatments or drug strategies to be developed, perhaps involving a combination of these or other drugs.

ELECTROCONVULSIVE THERAPY More commonly called *shock therapy*, electroconvulsive therapy (ECT) continues to evoke controversy. The idea of passing an electric current through someone's brain may seem barbaric. Yet ECT is a generally safe and effective treatment for severe depression, and can help relieve depression in many cases in which alternative treatments have failed.

Electroconvulsive therapy involves the administration of an electrical current to the head. A current of between 70 to 130 volts is used to induce a convulsion that is similar to a grand mal epileptic seizure. ECT is usually administered in a series of 6 to 12 treatments over a period of several weeks. The patient is put to sleep with a brief-acting general anaesthetic and given a muscle relaxant to avoid wild convulsions that might result in injury. As a result, spasms may be barely perceptible to onlookers. The patient awakens soon after the procedure and generally remembers nothing. Although ECT was used earlier in the treatment of a wide variety of psychological disorders, including schizophrenia and bipolar disorder, it is typically used today only to treat major depressive disorder in people who do not respond to antidepressant medication (Pagnin, de Queiroz, Pini, & Cassano, 2004).

ECT results in shorter and less costly hospitalizations for major depression (Olfson, Marcus, Sackeim, Thompson, & Pincus, 1998). Although it often produces a dramatic relief of symptoms, no one knows exactly how ECT works. ECT produces such mammoth chemical and electrical changes in the body that it is difficult to pinpoint the mechanism of therapeutic action. It is possible that ECT may work by normalizing brain levels of certain neurotransmitters (Grover, Mattoo, & Gupta, 2005). Although ECT can be an effective short-term treatment of severe depression, it too is no panacea. Depression often returns at some later point, even among people who continue to be treated with antidepressant medication (Bourgon & Kellner, 2000).

Electroconvulsive therapy may be administered to either both sides of the head (*bilateral ECT*) or to only one (*unilateral ECT*). Unilateral ECT is applied to the nondominant hemisphere of the brain, which, for most people, is the right side. Bilateral ECT tends to produce a somewhat greater clinical benefit than unilateral ECT, but also greater short-term memory impairment (Reisner, 2003).

There is an understandable concern among patients, relatives, and professionals themselves concerning the possible risk of brain damage from ECT. Much of this concern has focused on potential memory loss. The evidence so far suggests that ECT does not result in structural damage to the human brain, and any memory losses suffered as the result of treatment are temporary except for events occurring shortly before or after ECT administration (Reisner, 2003). Earlier memories or those formed weeks after ECT do not appear to be affected. Still, many professionals view ECT as a treatment of last resort, to be used only after other treatment approaches have been tried and failed. Moreover, it is not possible to definitively rule out the possibility that ECT may cause brain damage in a small proportion of people (Reisner, 2003).

In summing up, let us note that experts have described clinical practice guidelines for depression. The guidelines were based on evidence from controlled studies showing the following treatments to be effective in treating depression (APA, 2010a):

- Antidepressant medication (tricyclics, SSRIs, SNRIs)
- Three specific forms of psychotherapy: cognitive therapy, behaviour therapy, and interpersonal psychotherapy
- A combination of one of the recommended forms of psychotherapy and antidepressant medication
- Other specified forms of treatment, including ECT for very severe depression and phototherapy for seasonal depression

Treatments for depression are continually evolving, and researchers have been seeking to identify and investigate new treatments. Combinations of particular medications have been examined. As noted by depression researchers Sidney Kennedy (University of Toronto) and Raymond Lam (University of British Columbia), for patients who have failed to respond to conventional depression treatments, it may be useful to add drugs that are used in the treatment of schizophrenia, such as risperidone (Kennedy & Lam, 2003).

Another promising treatment approach is called *repetitive transcranial magnetic stimulation* (rTMS). This is a noninvasive way of stimulating particular regions of the brain. It involves the use of a device containing a powerful electromagnet, which is placed next to the person's head in order to induce weak electric currents in particular regions of the brain at particular frequencies for a few minutes per day for several days or weeks. It is thought that this can induce enduring changes (i.e., stimulating or calming down) in the activity of particular brain regions (Fitzgerald, Fountain, & Daskalakis, 2006). When used in the treatment of depression, brain regions that are thought to play a role in depression are repeatedly stimulated, typically the left prefrontal cortex. Although there is some preliminary evidence for the benefits of rTMS, more research is needed to evaluate the magnitude of its effects (Mitchell & Loo, 2006). Recent research suggests that rTMS is not as effective as ECT for severe depression (Eranti et al., 2007).

Other innovative methods have also been developed for the treatment of depression, such as deep brain stimulation (involving the placement of electrodes deep within the brain) and vagus nerve stimulation (stimulating the vagus nerve with electrical signals). These methods show promise in the treatment of severely depressed people who have not benefited from other treatments. In one study, for example, 10 patients suffering from very resistant forms of depression (treatment-resistant depression) were given deep brain stimulation. These patients were not responding to pharmacotherapy, psychotherapy, or ECT. Twelve months following initiation of DBS treatment, five patients reached

50% reduction in depressive symptoms and reported significant increases in pleasurable activities (Bewernick et al., 2010).

One of the big challenges—and controversies—in recent years concerns the treatment of depressed children and adolescents. It is widely believed that SSRIs and SNRIs are associated with a worsening of suicidal thoughts and behaviours in children and adolescents. Drug-related suicidal ideation may emerge suddenly, without warning, even in people who have not had a previous episode of suicidal ideation. Agitation and restlessness may be early signs of danger (Simon, 2006). Health Canada and health agencies in other countries such as the United States and United Kingdom have issued warnings about the use of these drugs (Whittington, Kendall, & Pilling, 2005). Health Canada advises that patients (or their caregivers) should consult the treating physician to confirm that the benefits of the drug still outweigh its potential risks. According to a recent review by University of British Columbia psychiatrist E. Jane Garland (2004), there is also evidence suggesting that these medications may not be effective in children and adolescents.

Not all clinicians are convinced that these medications are ineffective and harmful, and so the issue remains controversial (Simon, 2006). Adverse effects, when they do occur, appear to be rare. Alternatives to drugs are available, such as psychotherapies like cognitive-behavioural therapy. These treatments do not have the side effects associated with drugs. However, psychotherapies are only moderately effective in treating depression in children and adolescents (Weisz, McCarty, & Valeri, 2006). Clearly, much more research needs to be done in order to find ways of effectively helping depressed youth. Preliminary evidence suggests that the combination of psychotherapy and SSRIs may be both effective and protective against the increased risk of suicide-related thoughts and behaviours (Whittington et al., 2005).

REVIEW IT

Treatment of Depression

- **What are the approaches taken by the major theoretical perspectives in treating depression?** Psychodynamic treatment of depression has traditionally focused on helping the depressed person uncover and work through ambivalent feelings toward the lost object, thereby lessening the anger directed inward. Modern psychodynamic approaches tend to be more direct and briefer, and they focus more on developing adaptive means of achieving self-worth and resolving interpersonal conflicts. Learning theory approaches focus on helping people with depression increase the frequency of reinforcement in their lives through such means as increasing the rates of pleasant activities in which they participate and assisting them in developing more effective social skills to increase their ability to obtain social reinforcements from others. Cognitive therapists focus on helping the person identify and correct distorted or dysfunctional thoughts and learn more adaptive behaviours. Biological approaches focus on the use of antidepressant drugs and other biological treatments, such as electroconvulsive therapy (ECT). Antidepressant drugs may help normalize neurotransmitter functioning in the brain. Bipolar disorder is commonly treated with lithium.

SUICIDE

Suicidal thoughts are common enough. According to University of Waterloo psychologist Donald Meichenbaum (2005), a practising clinical psychologist will see an average of five patients per month who have suicidal thoughts. Under great stress, many, if not most, people have considered suicide. One Canadian survey found that 10% of men and 13% of women had contemplated suicide at some point in their lives, and 2% of men and 6% of women had attempted suicide (Weissman, Bland, et al., 1999). Thus, most people who have suicidal thoughts do not act on them. Even so, far too many people kill themselves. In 1998, for example, nearly 4000 Canadians took their lives (Health Canada, 2002b). The rates of completed suicide, according to the most recent data, are shown in Figure 4.5 (on page 176), where it can be seen that men are more likely than women to actually kill themselves in suicide attempts.

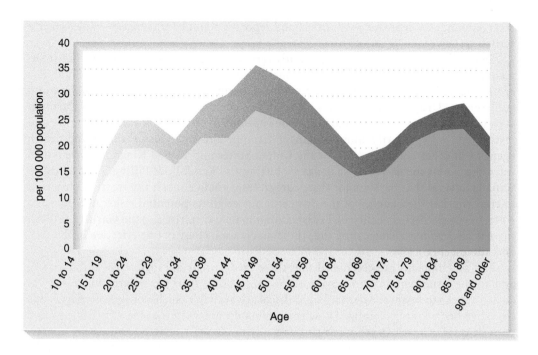

FIGURE 4.5 Suicide rates according to age and gender. Although adolescent suicides may be more widely publicized, adults, especially middle-aged and elderly men, tend to have high suicide rates.

Source: Adapted from Statistics Canada, http://www40.statcan. gc.ca/l01/cst01/hlth66a-eng. htm. Accessed 15/09/11.

Who Commits Suicide

Suicide is one of the leading causes of death in both men and women from adolescence to middle age (Spirito & Esposito-Smythers, 2006; Health Canada, 2002b). Disturbingly, suicide rates among Canadian adolescents have doubled over the past 30 years (Stewart, Manion, & Davidson, 2002). Suicide accounts for 24% of all deaths among 15- to 24-year-olds, and 16% among 25- to 44-year-olds (Statistics Canada, 2011). Although the problem of teenage suicide often grabs the headlines, suicide rates are as high or higher in middle-aged and elderly men (see Figure 4.5).

Despite life-extending advances in medical care, some older adults may find the quality of their lives is less than satisfactory. With longer life, older people are more susceptible to diseases such as cancer and Alzheimer's disease, which can leave them with feelings of helplessness and hopelessness that can give rise to suicidal thinking. Many older adults also suffer a mounting accumulation of losses of friends and loved ones as time progresses, leading to social isolation. These losses, as well as the loss of good health and of a responsible role in the community, may wear down the will to live. Not surprisingly, the highest suicide rates in older men are among those who are widowed or lead socially isolated lives. Whatever the causes, suicide has become an increased risk for elderly people (Szanto et al., 1996). Perhaps society should focus its attention as much on the quality of life that is afforded our elderly as on providing them the medical care that helps make longer life possible.

Although more women than men, by a ratio of 1.5 to 1, attempt suicide, men are four times more likely to "succeed" (Health Canada, 2002b). More males succeed, in large part, because they tend to choose quicker acting and more lethal means, such as firearms or hanging, whereas women are more likely to overdose on pills (Health Canada, 2002b).

Gender differences in suicide risk may mask underlying factors. The common finding that men are more likely to take their own lives may be due to the fact that men are also more likely to have a history of alcohol and drug abuse and less likely to have children in the home. When these two factors were taken into account in one study, gender differences in suicide risk disappeared (Young, Fogg, Scheftner, & Fawcett, 1994).

Why Do People Commit Suicide?

To many lay observers, suicide seems so extreme an act that they believe only "insane" people (meaning people who are out of touch with reality) would commit suicide. How-

Concussions, Depression, and Suicide Among NHLers

The summer of 2011 was a very tough time for hockey fans, with the untimely deaths of three players, Derek Boogaard, Rick Rypien, and Wade Belak. While fans still question the link between concussions, depression, and suicide, the medical field has confirmed this connection time and again. Dr. Robert Cantu, a neurosurgeon and co-director of the Center for the Study of Traumatic Encephalopathy at Boston University, explains that depression, anxiety, and substance abuse are all common in athletes with CTE (chronic traumatic encephalopathy) (Aubry et al., 2009). Sadly, players often fail to report concussive-type injuries and aren't aware that feelings of depression are common in individuals who have suffered a concussion.

Dr. Alain Ptito, neuropsychologist and researcher at the Montreal Neurological Institute at McGill University, has confirmed the connection between depression and concussions:

> Researchers at the Montreal Neurological Institute of McGill University have identified the neurological basis of depression in male athletes with persisting post-concussion symptoms. The study . . . has important clinical implications for the treatment of individuals who have suffered a cerebral concussion. Depression is one of a number of persisting symptoms experienced by athletes following sports concussion. The prevalence of depression in the general population is around 5%, whilst the prevalence of depression in head trauma patients can reach an astounding 40%. "Until now, very little was known about the neurological basis of the depression frequently reported by athletes following concussion," says Dr. Alain Ptito, . . . lead investigator for the study. ("Neurological Basis," 2008)

Concussions, depression, and suicide? Former Toronto Maple Leafs and Calgary Flames tough guy Wade Belak took his own life after suffering with severe depression.

---

ever, suicidal thinking does not necessarily imply loss of touch with reality, deep-seated unconscious conflict, or a personality disorder. Having thoughts about suicide generally reflects a narrowing of the range of options people think are available to them to deal with their problems (Brent & Mann, 2006). That is, they are discouraged by their problems and see no other way out. This is illustrated by the following example:

> Sue Goodwin left work one day with a simple, spontaneous plan: She intended to die. Midway through a regular shift at a regular office, she walked calmly into a Toronto subway station. "I remember standing on the platform, thinking, 'This will show all the people who've hurt me. This will show them what they've done to me.'" The rush of air was coming. The train hurtled toward the station. "And then I jumped." The coma lasted five weeks. "I tried to commit suicide because I thought nobody loved me."

Nunes & Simmie, 2002, pp. 102–103

Many suicides are associated with major depression or bipolar disorder (Miklowitz & Johnson, 2006), which is why we include the topic in this chapter. Attempted or completed suicide is also connected with other psychological disorders such as alcoholism and drug dependence, schizophrenia, and personality disorders, including antisocial personality disorder and borderline personality disorder (Joiner, Brown, & Wingate, 2005).

Stress is also implicated in many suicides (Renaud, Chagnon, Turecki, & Marquette, 2005). Suicide attempts often occur following highly stressful life events, especially "exit events" such as the death of a spouse, close friend, or relative; divorce or separation; a family member's leaving home; or the loss of a close friend. People who consider taking their lives in response to stressful events appear to have poorer problem-solving skills than those who do not consider suicide (Brent & Mann, 2006). People who consider suicide in times of stress may be less able to find alternative ways of coping with the stressors they face.

Theoretical Perspectives on Suicide

The classic psychodynamic model views depression as the turning inward of anger against the internal representation of a lost love object. Suicide thus represents inward-directed anger that turns murderous. Suicidal people, then, do not seek to destroy themselves. Instead, they seek to vent their rage against the internalized representation of the love object. In so doing, they destroy themselves as well, of course. In his later writings, Freud (1920/1987) speculated that suicide may be motivated by the "death instinct," a tendency to return to the tension-free state that preceded birth. Existential and humanistic theorists relate suicide to the perception that life is meaningless and hopeless.

anomie Lack of purpose or identity; aimlessness.

In the 19th century, sociologist Emile Durkheim (1897/1958) noted that people who experience **anomie**—who feel lost, without identity, rootless—are more likely to commit suicide. Sociocultural theorists likewise believe that alienation in today's society may play a role in suicide. In our modern, mobile society, people frequently move hundreds or thousands of kilometres for school and jobs. Executives and their families may be relocated every two years or so. Military personnel and their families may be shifted about yet more rapidly. Many people are thus socially isolated or cut off from their support groups. Moreover, city dwellers tend to limit or discourage informal social contacts because of crowding, overstimulation, and fear of crime. It is thus understandable that many people find few sources of support in times of crisis. In some cases, the availability of family support may not be helpful. Family members may be perceived as part of the problem, not part of the solution.

Learning theorists point to the reinforcing effects of prior suicide threats and attempts and to the effects of stress, especially when combined with inability to solve personal problems. People who threaten or attempt suicide may also receive sympathy and support from loved ones and others, perhaps making future—and more lethal—attempts more likely. This is not to suggest that suicide attempts or gestures should be ignored. It is not the case that people who threaten suicide are merely seeking attention. Although people who threaten suicide might not carry out the act, their threats should be taken seriously. People who commit suicide often tell others of their intentions or leave clues beforehand (Joiner, 2006).

Social-cognitive theorists suggest that suicide may be motivated by positive expectancies and by approving attitudes toward the legitimacy of suicide (Joiner, 2006). People who kill themselves may expect they will be missed or eulogized after death, or that survivors will feel guilty for mistreating them. Suicidal psychiatric patients hold more positive expectancies concerning suicide than do nonsuicidal psychiatric samples. They more often expressed the belief that suicide would solve their problems, for example (Linehan, Camper, Chiles, Strosahl, & Shearin, 1987). Suicide may represent a desperate attempt to deal with one's problems in one fell swoop rather than piecemeal.

Social-cognitive theorists also focus on the potential modelling effects of observing suicidal behaviour in others, especially among teenagers who feel overwhelmed by academic and social stressors. A *social contagion*, or spreading of suicide in a community, may occur in the wake of suicides that receive widespread publicity. Teenagers, who seem to be especially vulnerable to these modelling effects, may even romanticize the suicidal act as one of heroic courage, and may expect their demise to have a profound impact on their community. A suicide of a close friend or sibling does not usually increase the risk of a suicide attempt; such imitation is more likely to be triggered by a suicidal model who is not personally known to the imitator, such as a famous musician, actor, or other celebrity (Brent & Mann, 2006).

Biological factors also appear to be involved in suicide. Evidence shows reduced serotonin activity in people who attempt or commit suicide (Brent & Mann, 2006). Serotonin deficits have been implicated

Teen suicide. Suicidal teenagers may see no other way of handling their life problems. The availability of counselling and support services may help prevent suicide by assisting troubled teens in learning alternative ways of reducing stress and resolving conflicts with others.

in depression, so the relationship with suicide is not surprising. Yet serotonin acts to curb or inhibit nervous system activity, so perhaps decreased serotonin function leads to a disinhibition, or release, of impulsive behaviour that takes the form of a suicidal act in vulnerable individuals. Consistent with this, serotonin deficits have also been linked to impulsive aggression (Brent & Mann, 2006).

Evidence from twin studies suggests that genetic factors influence, to some extent, the risk of suicidal behaviour (Joiner, 2006). Suicidal behaviour that occurs before 25 years of age is highly familial; the greater the number of family members with a history of suicidal behaviour, the earlier the age of the appearance of suicidal acts in offspring (Brent & Mann, 2006).

Suicide is connected with a complex web of factors, and its prediction is not simple. There are, however, common risk factors such as family discord, poor coping skills, and bullying, and protective factors, such as social competence and achievement in school (Table 4.7 on page 180). Yet it is clear that many suicides could be prevented if people with suicidal feelings would receive treatment for the disorders that underlie suicidal behaviour, including depression, schizophrenia, and alcohol and substance abuse (Brent & Mann, 2006; Joiner, 2006).

Predicting Suicide

"I don't believe it. I saw him just last week and he looked fine."
"She sat here just the other day, laughing with the rest of us.
How were we to know what was going on inside her?"
"I knew he was depressed, but I never thought he'd do something like this.
I didn't have a clue."
"Why didn't she just call me?"

Friends and family members often respond to news of a suicide with disbelief or with guilt that they failed to pick up signs of the impending act. Yet even trained professionals find it difficult to predict who is likely to commit suicide.

Evidence points to the role of hopelessness as an important predictor or perhaps contributor to suicidal thinking and behaviour (Brent & Mann, 2006; Joiner, 2006). In one study, psychiatric outpatients with hopelessness scores above a certain cut-off were 11 times more likely to commit suicide than those with scores below the cut-off (A. T. Beck, Brown, Berchick, Stewart, & Steer, 1990). But *when* does hopelessness lead to suicide?

TABLE 4.7

Suicide Risk and Protective Factors

Key Context	Predisposing Factors	Contributing Factors	Precipitating Factors	Protective Factors
Individual	• previous suicide attempt • depression or other mental disorder (e.g., substance use disorder, schizophrenia) • hopelessness • suicidal thoughts	• rigid cognitive style • poor coping skills • gay, lesbian, bisexual or transgendered sexual orientation • impulsivity • aggression • hypersensitivity/anxiety	• personal failure • humiliation • trauma • health crisis	• individual coping and problem-solving skills • willingness to seek help • good physical and mental health • strong cultural identity and spiritual beliefs
Family	• family history of suicidal behaviour/suicide • family history of childhood neglect, sexual or physical abuse • family history of mental disorder • early childhood loss/ separation or deprivation	• family discord • impaired parent–child relationships	• loss of a significant family member • death of a family member, especially by suicide • recent conflict	• family cohesion and warmth • adults modelling healthy adjustment • high and realistic expectations
Peers	• social isolation and alienation	• negative youth attitudes toward seeking adult assistance • peer modelling of maladaptive behaviours	• teasing/cruelty/bullying • interpersonal loss or conflict • rejection • peer death, especially by suicide	• social competence • healthy peer modelling • acceptance and support
School	• long-standing history of negative school experience • lack of meaningful connection to school	• disruption during key transitional periods at school • reluctance/uncertainty among school staff about how to help	• failure • expulsion • disciplinary crisis	• success at school • interpersonal connectedness/belonging
Community	• multiple suicides • community marginalization • political disenfranchisement • socioeconomic deprivation	• sensational media portrayal of suicide • access to firearms or other lethal methods • reluctance/uncertainty among key gatekeepers about how to help • inaccessible community resources	• high profile/celebrity death, especially by suicide • conflict with the law/ incarceration	• opportunities for youth participation • community self-determination • availability of resources • community control over local services

Source: White, 2005, p. 8. Reprinted with the kind permission of the author, Jennifer White; Here to Help, a project of the BC Partners for Mental Health and Addictions Information; and the Ministry of Children and Family Development, British Columbia, Canada.

People who commit suicide tend to signal their intentions, often quite explicitly, such as by telling others about their suicidal thoughts. Some attempt to cloak their intentions. Behavioural clues may still reveal suicidal intent, however. Edwin Shneidman (1994), a leading researcher on suicide, found that 90% of the people who committed suicide had left clear clues, such as disposing of their possessions. People contemplating suicide may also suddenly try to sort out their affairs, as in drafting a will or buying a cemetery plot. They may purchase guns despite lack of prior interest in firearms. When troubled people decide to commit suicide, they may seem to be suddenly at peace; they

Imagine yourself having an intimate conversation with a close campus friend, Chris. You know that things have not been good. Chris's grandfather died six weeks ago, and the two were very close. Chris's grades have been going downhill, and his romantic relationship also seems to be coming apart at the seams. Still, you are unprepared when he says very deliberately, "I just can't take it anymore. Life is just too painful. I don't feel like I want to live anymore. I've decided that the only thing I can do is to kill myself."

When somebody discloses that he or she is contemplating suicide, you may feel bewildered and frightened, as if a great burden has been placed on your shoulders. It has. If someone confides suicidal thoughts to you, your goal should be to persuade him or her to see a professional or to get the advice of a professional yourself as soon as you can. But if the suicidal person declines to talk to another person and you sense you can't break away for such a conference, there are some things you can do then and there (Shneidman, Farberow, & Litman, 1994):

1. *Draw the person out.* Frame questions like "What's going on?" "Where do you hurt?" "What would you like to see happen?" Such questions may prompt people to verbalize thwarted psychological needs and offer some relief. They also grant you the time to appraise the risk and contemplate your next move.
2. *Be sympathetic.* Show that you fathom how troubled the person is. Don't say something like "You're just being silly. You don't really mean it."
3. *Suggest that means other than suicide can be discovered to work out the person's problems*, even if

they are not apparent at the time. Suicidal people can usually see only two solutions to their predicaments—either suicide or some kind of magical resolution. Professionals try to broaden the available alternatives of people who are suicidal.

4. *Ask how the person expects to commit suicide.* People with explicit methods who also possess the means (e.g., a gun or drugs) are at greater risk. Ask if you may hold on to the gun, drugs, or whatever for a while. Sometimes the person will agree.
5. *Propose that the person accompany you to consult a professional right now.* Many campuses have hotlines that you or the suicidal individual can call. Many towns and cities have such hotlines and they can be called anonymously. Other possibilities include the emergency room of a general hospital, a campus health centre or counselling centre, or the campus or local police. If you are unable to maintain contact with the suicidal person, get professional assistance as soon as you separate.
6. *Don't say something like "You're talking crazy."* Such comments are degrading and injurious to the individual's self-esteem.
7. *Don't press the suicidal person to contact specific people, such as parents or a spouse.* Conflict with them may have given rise to the suicidal thoughts.

Above all, keep in mind that your primary goal is to confer with a helping professional. Don't go it alone any longer than you have to.

---

feel relieved of having to contend with life problems. This sudden calm may be misinterpreted as a sign of hope.

The prediction of suicide is not an exact science, even for experienced professionals. Many observable factors, such as hopelessness, do seem to be connected with suicide, but we cannot predict *when* a hopeless person will attempt suicide, if at all.

REVIEW IT

Suicide

- **What are some of the factors linked to suicide?** Mood disorders are often linked to suicide. Although women are more likely to attempt suicide, more men actually succeed, probably because they select more lethal means. The elderly—not the young—are more likely to commit suicide, and the rate of suicide among the elderly appears to be increasing. People who attempt suicide are often depressed, but they are generally in touch with reality. They may, however, lack effective

problem-solving skills and see no way to deal with their life stress other than suicide. A sense of hopelessness figures prominently in suicides.
- **Why should you never ignore a person's threat to commit suicide?** Although certainly not all people who threaten suicide go on to commit the act, many do. People who commit suicide often signal their intentions, by telling others about their suicidal thoughts, for example.

Define It

anomie, 178
attributional style, 161
automatic thoughts, 160
bipolar, 141
bipolar disorder, 150
cognitive therapy, 168
cognitive triad of depression, 157
cyclothymic disorder, 152
double depression, 149
dysthymic disorder, 149

external attribution, 161
global attribution, 161
hypomanic episodes, 142
internal attribution, 161
interpersonal psychotherapy, 166
learned helplessness, 160
major depressive disorder, 142
manic, 142
manic episodes, 150
mood disorders, 141

moods, 141
mourning, 155
postpartum depression, 148
pressured speech, 151
rapid flight of ideas, 151
selective abstraction, 158
specific attribution, 161
stable attribution, 161
unipolar, 141
unstable attribution, 161

Think About It

- Where would you draw the line between a person with a naturally exuberant personality and someone with a bipolar disorder?

- What are the advantages and disadvantages of drug therapy for depression? If you were to become clinically depressed, which course of treatment would you prefer—medication, psychotherapy, or a combination? Explain.

- Did your reading of the text change your ideas about how you might deal with a suicidal threat by a friend or loved one? If so, how?

Weblinks

Mood Disorders Society of Canada
www.mooddisorderscanada.ca
The Mood Disorders Society of Canada is a national, not-for-profit organization that is committed to improving the quality of life for people affected by depression, bipolar disorder, and other related disorders. The site provides information and treatment resources for mood disorders, including major depression and bipolar disorder.

Internet Mental Health
www.mentalhealth.com
A good source of information and numerous links on major depression and bipolar disorder.

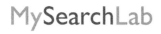 **MySearchLab offers you extensive help with your writing and research projects and provides round-the-clock access to credible and reliable source material. Chapter quizzes and a full electronic version of the text are also provided. Take a tour at www.mysearchlab.com.**

Mood Disorders and Suicide

Types of Mood Disorders

Unipolar

Major Depressive Disorder (MDD)
- Features:
  - One or more major depressive episodes
  - No history of manic or hypomanic episodes
- Lifetime prevalence: 12%
  - More common in women than men
  - Types of MDD include postpartum depression and seasonal affective disorder (SAD)

Dysthymic Disorder
- Features:
  - A chronic pattern of mild depression
  - Typically lasts for many years
- Lifetime prevalence: 3% to 6%
  - More common in women than men

Bipolar

Bipolar Disorder
- Disorder characterized by mood swings between states of extreme elation and severe depression. Formerly called *manic depression*.
- Bipolar I disorder: The occurrence of one or more manic episodes. A disorder can thus be labelled "bipolar"even if it consists of manic episodes without any past or present major depressive episodes.
- Bipolar II disorder: Milder form of mania. In bipolar II, the person has experienced one or more major depressive episodes and at least one hypomanic episode, but never a full-blown manic episode.
- Manic episode: A distinct period of abnormally and persistently elevated, expansive, or irritable mood, lasting at least one week

Cyclothymic Disorder
- Mood disorder characterized by a chronic pattern of mild mood swings between depression and mania that are not of sufficient severity to be classified as bipolar disorder.
- Hypomanic episode: Inflated sense of self-esteem; unusually charged feeling, with energy and alertness; and more restless and irritable than usual episode.
- Less severe than manic episodes and not accompanied by the severe social or occupational problems associated with full-blown manic episodes.

>>

Theoretical Perspectives

Stress and Mood Disorders

- Research indicates that there is a robust and causal association between stressful life events and major depressive episodes, but that not all cases of major depression are preceded by stressful life events.
- Psychosocial factors such as social support and coping styles may serve as buffers against depression in times of stress.

Psychodynamic Perspectives

- Depression represents anger directed inward rather than against significant others. Anger may become directed against the self following either the actual or threatened loss of these important others.
- Recent psychodynamic models focus more on issues relating to the individual's sense of self-worth or self-esteem.

Humanistic Perspectives

- People become depressed when they cannot imbue their existence with meaning and make authentic choices that lead to self-fulfillment.

Learning Perspectives

- Depression may result when a person's behaviour receives too little reinforcement from the environment.

Cognitive Perspectives

- Cognitive theorists relate the origin and maintenance of depression to the ways in which people see themselves and the world around them.
- The learned helplessness model proposes that people may become depressed because they learn to view themselves as helpless to control the reinforcements in their environments.

Biological Perspectives

- Biological perspectives focus on the role of biological factors, especially genetics and neurotransmitter functioning, and brain abnormalities in the development of mood disorders.

Treatment Approaches

Psychodynamic

- Psychotherapies

Behavioural

- Behavioural programs such as Coping With Depression (CWD) and Behavioural Activation (BA)

Cognitive

- Cognitive therapy or cognitive-behavioural therapy

Biological

- Antidepressant drugs (trycyclics, SSRIs, SNRIs)
- ECT, rTMS, deep brain stimulation

5

Dissociative and Somatoform Disorders

CHAPTER OUTLINE

Dissociative Disorders
Dissociative Identity Disorder
Dissociative Amnesia
Dissociative Fugue
Depersonalization Disorder
Theoretical Perspectives
Tying It Together
Treatment of Dissociative Disorders

Somatoform Disorders
Conversion Disorder
Hypochondriasis
Somatization Disorder
Other Somatoform Disorders
Theoretical Perspectives
Treatment of Somatoform Disorders

Did You Know That...

- The term *split personality* is a lay term that refers to multiple personality, not schizophrenia?

- At some time or another, the majority of adults have episodes of feeling detached from their own bodies or thought processes?

- The great majority of people with multiple personalities were physically or sexually abused as children?

- Some people undergo operations even though they know nothing is medically wrong with them?

- Some people who have lost their ability to see or move their legs have displayed a strangely indifferent attitude toward their physical condition?

- There was an epidemic in China in the 1980s affecting more than 3000 people who fell prey to the belief that their genitals were shrinking and retracting into their bodies?

n the Middle Ages, the clergy used rites of exorcism to bring forth demons from people believed to be possessed. Curious incantations were heard during the contests for victims' souls between the exorcist and the demons believed to lurk within.

Curious phrasings were also heard more recently in 20th-century Los Angeles. They were intended to elicit another sort of demon from Kenneth Bianchi, a suspect in an investigation.

At one point, a question was put to Bianchi: "Part, are you the same thing as Ken or are you different?" The interviewer was not a member of the clergy, but a police psychiatrist. The interviewee had been dubbed the "Hillside strangler" by the press. He had terrorized the city, leaving prostitutes dead in the mountains that bank the metropolis.

Under hypnosis—not religious incantations—Bianchi claimed that a hidden personality or "part" named "Steve" had committed the murders. "Ken" knew nothing of them. Bianchi claimed to be suffering from multiple personality disorder (now called *dissociative identity disorder*), one of the intriguing but perplexing psychological disorders we explore in this chapter. Dissociative identity disorder is classified as a dissociative disorder, a type of psychological disorder involving a change or disturbance in the functions of self-identity, memory, or consciousness that make the personality whole. Normally speaking, we know who we are. We may not be certain of ourselves in an existential, philosophical sense, but we know our names, where we live, and what we do for a living. We also tend to remember the salient events of our lives. We may not recall every detail, and we may confuse what we ate for dinner on Tuesday with what we had on Monday, but we generally know what we have been doing for the past days, weeks, and years. Normally speaking, there is a unity to consciousness that gives rise to a sense of self. We perceive ourselves as progressing through space and time. In the dissociative disorders, one or more of these aspects of daily living is disturbed—sometimes bizarrely so.

This chapter also focuses on *somatoform disorders*, a class of psychological disorders involving complaints of physical symptoms that are believed to reflect underlying psychological issues. In some cases there is no apparent medical basis to the physical symptoms, such as in hysterical blindness or numbness (now called *conversion disorder*). In other cases, people may hold an exaggerated view of the meaning of their physical symptoms, believing them to be signs of underlying serious illnesses despite reassurances from their physicians to the contrary.

The dissociative and conversion disorders were grouped with the anxiety disorders in earlier versions of the diagnostic manual under the more general category of "neurosis." The common grouping was based on the psychodynamic model, which held that these various disorders involve maladaptive ways of managing anxiety. In the anxiety disorders, the appearance of disturbing levels of anxiety was expressed directly in behaviour, such as in a phobia where a person would avoid a feared object or situation. But the role of anxiety in the dissociative and somatoform disorders was inferred from rather than expressed in behaviour. Persons with dissociative disorders may show no signs of overt anxiety. However, they manifest other psychological problems, such as loss of memory or changes in identity, that are theorized within the psychodynamic model to serve the purpose of keeping the underlying sources of anxiety out of awareness. Likewise, people with conversion disorder often show a strange indifference to physical problems (e.g., loss of vision). Here, too, it was theorized that the "symptoms" mask unconscious sources of anxiety. Some theorists interpret indifference to symptoms to mean there is an underlying benefit to them; that is, they help prevent anxiety from intruding into consciousness. But, as we will see later, this interpretation has been recently challenged.

The DSM now separates the anxiety disorders from the other categories of neuroses—the dissociative and somatoform disorders—with which they were historically linked. Yet many practitioners continue to use the broad conceptualization of neuroses as a framework for classifying the anxiety, dissociative, and somatoform disorders.

DISSOCIATIVE DISORDERS

The major dissociative disorders include dissociative identity disorder, dissociative amnesia, dissociative fugue, and depersonalization disorder. In each case, there is a disruption or dissociation ("splitting off") of the functions of identity, memory, or consciousness—functions that normally combine to make us whole.

Dissociative Identity Disorder

In response to a newspaper inquiry, Nancy came forth to tell her story about her struggles with a dissociative identity disorder. Nancy, who resides in Ontario, gave the following account of her problems, how they arose, and how she has worked to overcome them:

> The piano has a place of honour in Nancy's living room. It's a red mahogany Lesage made in Quebec. But Nancy fears that piano. She will play it only if the doors are locked or if her husband, Hugh, is around. When she was a girl, she loved to play the classics every day—sonatinas, rondos, and allegros by Mozart. She concentrated so hard. She shut herself off from her surroundings. "I felt I was inside the music." And while Nancy played, her father and sometimes other men molested her. Her father touched her; he masturbated. From the time she was a toddler, he had abused her. It could happen anywhere in the house. At the piano, she had the music to take her away. But wherever she was, Nancy had grown skilled at using her mind to float away from her father's grasp. She could peel off a piece of herself, so she hardly felt the pain. That ability saved her then. But now it's a problem.
>
> She got therapy and soon even started a self-help group. "I found out it's okay to talk about what happened, to say it out loud. I realized it really wasn't my fault." After a few years, she left the group. "I thought I was doing quite well. I'd learned to handle the flashbacks and the memories." But she started getting sick a lot again. There was something that had bothered Nancy for years—the voices inside her. And by this point, they seemed awfully persistent. "There's a saying that it's okay to talk to yourself and as long as you don't answer, you're not crazy." But Nancy noticed she was waking up at night, hearing herself talking and answering. She had said something to her husband years before: "Hughie, I think I'm going crazy. I hear all these voices. They're talking, fighting, arguing." The arguments that rattled through her head could be about something as simple as whether to serve a chicken dinner with baked potatoes or rice. Or whether to go to the mall. "It was like Siamese twins who constantly talk back and forth because they can't do anything without each other." And there was amnesia, confusion, lost time. Nancy was sure she had invited that couple to dinner. They were puzzled why she got angry when they didn't show up.

We all dissociate. We all daydream; we cruise along a straight stretch of highway and later we don't really remember the details at all. But for someone like Nancy, those moments of lost time were deeper, more frequent. Her earliest memory of abuse is from when she was about three years old. The abuse continued until she was 18, when she got married. Hugh showed up in Nancy's life and helped her. She told him about some of the past. "You need to talk about this," he told her. Nancy said she was fine. She was married, to the right man. And she was a nurse, which she'd always wanted to be. But that fell apart one night at work. Nancy went to walk into the medication room and walked into the wall instead. She collapsed. She was sick for months. She couldn't drive, couldn't climb stairs. She vomited and had severe headaches. Nancy underwent many tests. Maybe it was a brain tumour. Or an inner-ear problem. Finally, a neurologist said, "Nancy, is it possible you've been under stress?" "It was like a light being turned on," she says. "And I said, 'Yes, I'm 36 and I've been under stress for 33 years.'"

She was then sent to two psychiatrists. Both made the diagnosis of dissociative identity disorder. There appear to be eight different parts to Nancy's personality. In her mind, each has its own physical appearance. She pictures them with different hair, different glasses. There is Malveen. She's shy, introverted, overwhelmed with guilt. This part of Nancy stopped growing when she was a teenager and met Hugh. There's Dorothy, well organized, able to do ten things at once. There's another part that's all anger. And there is Just Me, that persistent part she always argued with. Good therapy and the right medication sent that personality away. Nancy continues to work on her recovery.

Six years earlier, one of the men who abused her was convicted of assault, gross indecency, and sexual intercourse with a female under 14. The judge called the crimes abhorrent. But because of the way that the judge addressed the jury, the man was granted a new trial. He died before it took place. Nancy's mother and father, both abused as children, are gone now. Mother, a nurse, died 13 years ago in Nancy's home. Father, a postal worker then city employee, died seven years ago. Nancy had been looking after him, cleaning his apartment, getting his groceries. She had confronted him and wrung out an apology. He was about to be charged when he died.

Therapy has been hard and slow, but Nancy is not discouraged. "Each of these parts of me was beneficial. They helped me to survive. But it would be good for me now to merge these parts. It would be good to become one healthy person."

P. Wilson, 2000. Reprinted courtesy of
The Hamilton Spectator.

dissociative identity disorder Dissociative disorder in which a person has two or more distinct or alternate personalities.

Nancy was diagnosed with multiple personality disorder, which is now called **dissociative identity disorder**. In this disorder, sometimes referred to as *split personality*, two or more personalities—each with well-defined traits and memories—"occupy" one person. They may or may not be aware of one another. There are many variations. Sometimes two personalities vie for control. Sometimes there is one dominant or core personality and several subordinate ones. Themes of sexual ambivalence (sexual openness versus inhibition) and shifting sexual orientations are particularly common. It is as if conflicting internal impulses cannot coexist or achieve dominance. As a result, each is expressed as the cardinal or steering trait of an alternate personality. The clinician can sometimes bring forth alternate personalities by inviting them to make themselves known, as in asking, "Is there another part of you that wants to say something to me?"

The case of Margaret illustrates the purported emergence of an alternate personality:

[Margaret explained that] she often "heard a voice telling her to say things and do things." It was, she said, "a terrible voice" that sometimes threatened to "take over completely." When it was finally suggested to [Margaret] that she let the voice "take over," she closed her eyes, clenched her fists, and grimaced for a few moments during which she was out of contact with those around her. Suddenly she opened her eyes and one was in the presence of another person. Her name, she said, was "Harriet." Whereas Margaret had been paralyzed, and complained of fatigue, headache and backache, Harriet felt well, and she at once proceeded to walk unaided around the interviewing room. She spoke scornfully of Margaret's religiousness, her invalidism, and her puritanical life, professing that she herself liked to drink and "go partying" but that Margaret was always going to church and reading the Bible. "But," she said impishly and proudly, "I make her miserable—I make her say and do things she doesn't want to." At length, at the interviewer's suggestion, Harriet reluctantly agreed to "bring Margaret back," and after more grimacing and fist clenching, Margaret reappeared, paralyzed, complaining of her headache and backache, and completely amnesiac for the brief period of Harriet's release from prison.[*]

[*]I am indebted to Dr. F. H. Frankel for permission to use these observations.

Nemiah, 1978, pp. 179–180. Copyright 1978 by
The Belknap Press of Harvard University Press. Used by permission.

As with Margaret, the dominant personality is often unaware of the existence of the alternate personalities. This seems to suggest that the mechanism of dissociation is controlled by unconscious processes. Although the dominant personality lacks insight into the existence of the other personalities, she or he may vaguely sense that something is amiss. There may even be interpersonality rivalry, in which one personality aspires to do away with another, usually in blissful ignorance of the fact that this would result in the death of all.

Celebrated cases of multiple personality have been depicted in the popular media. One became the subject of the film *The Three Faces of Eve*. In the film, Eve White is a timid housewife who harbours two other personalities: Eve Black, a sexually provocative, antisocial personality, and Jane, a balanced, developing personality who can reconcile her sexual needs with the demands of social acceptability. The three faces eventually merge into one—Jane, providing a "happy ending." The real-life Eve, whose name was Chris Sizemore, failed to maintain this integrated personality. Her personality split into 22 subsequent personalities, purportedly after she learned that another famous case—Sybil—had 16 personalities (Kihlstrom, 2005). As for the celebrated case of Sybil, which was also made into a movie, recent evidence, including tape recordings of sessions with a psychiatrist who claimed to have elicited Sybil's multiple personalities, indicates that Sybil was highly suggestible to the psychiatrist's suggestions that there were multiple personalities but is unlikely to have had genuine multiple personality disorder (Rieber, Takoosian, & Iglesias, 2002).

The diagnostic criteria for dissociative identity disorder are listed in Table 5.1 on page 190.

The 1970s witnessed an "epidemic" of dissociative identity disorder cases. The number of alter egos reported by patients has also risen over time. It was almost as if there was some kind of contest to determine who could have (or be) the patient with the greatest number of alternate personalties (Kihlstrom, 2005). In the 1980s and 90s, it also became common for multiple-personality patients to talk with their therapists about previously unheard-of phenomena: alters of races or sexes different from the hosts; alters of different species, including cats, dogs, panthers, gorillas, and lobsters; and alters of demons, angels, and even God (Piper & Merskey, 2004).

The three faces of Eve. In the film *The Three Faces of Eve*, a timid housewife, Eve White, harbours two alternate personalities: Eve Black, an antisocial personality, and Jane, an integrated personality who can accept her sexual and aggressive urges but still engage in socially appropriate behaviour. The 1957 film is reportedly based on the life of Christine Costner Sizemore, who suffered with dissociative identity disorder and was a patient of Hervey M. Cleckley and Corbett H. Thigpen.

Although dissociative identity disorder is generally considered rare, the very existence of the disorder continues to arouse debate. The DSM cautions that the disorder has lately become overdiagnosed in people who are highly suggestible, leading them to be overly compliant with suggestions that they might have it (APA, 2000a). Increased public attention paid to the disorder in recent years may also account for the perception that its prevalence is greater than was previously believed.

The disorder does appear to be culture-bound and largely restricted to North America (Spanos, 2001). Very few cases have been reported elsewhere (Piper & Merskey, 2004)—and even in North America, few psychologists and psychiatrists have ever encountered a case of multiple personality. Most cases of multiple personality are reported by a relatively small number of investigators and clinicians who strongly believe in the existence of the disorder. Surveys in Canada and the United States reveal that many mental health professionals are skeptical of the validity of the concept of dissociative identity disorder (e.g., Lalonde, Hudson, Gigante, & Pope, 2001). Critics such as the University of Western Ontario's Harold Merskey and colleagues wonder whether some overzealous clinicians might be helping to manufacture that which they are seeking (Piper & Merskey, 2004).

Some other leading authorities agree, most notably the late psychologist Nicholas Spanos, who worked at Carleton University. To Spanos and other psychologists (e.g., Lilienfeld & Lynn, 2003), multiple personality is not a distinct disorder but a form of role-playing in which individuals first come to construe themselves as having multiple selves and then begin to act in ways that are consistent with their conception of the disorder. Eventually, their role-playing becomes so ingrained that it becomes a reality to them. Perhaps their therapists or counsellors, maybe unintentionally, first planted the idea in their minds that their confusing welter of emotions and behaviours may represent different personalities at work. Impressionable people may have learned how to enact the role of persons with the disorder by watching others perform the role on television and in the movies. Films like *The Three Faces of Eve* and *Sybil* have given detailed examples of the behaviours that characterize multiple personalities (Spanos, 2001). Or perhaps therapists provided cues about the features of multiple personality, enough for clients to enact the role convincingly.

Many reinforcers may become contingent on enacting the role of a multiple personality type. Receiving attention from others and evading accountability for unacceptable

---

TABLE 5.1

Criteria for Dissociative Identity Disorder (Formerly Multiple Personality Disorder)

A. The presence of two or more distinct identities or personality states (each with its own relatively enduring pattern of perceiving, relating to, and thinking about the environment and self).

B. At least two of these identities or personality states recurrently take control of the person's behavior.

C. Inability to recall important personal information that is too extensive to be explained by ordinary forgetfulness.

D. The disturbance is not due to the direct physiological effects of a substance (e.g., blackouts or chaotic behavior during Alcohol Intoxication) or a general medical condition (e.g., complex partial seizures). **Note:** In children, the symptoms are not attributable to imaginary playmates or other fantasy play.

Source: Reprinted with permission from the *Diagnostic and Statistical Manual of Mental Disorders*, Fourth Edition, Text Revision, (Copyright ©2000). American Psychiatric Association. p. 529.

behaviour are two possible sources of reinforcement (Spanos, 2001). This is not to suggest that people with multiple personalities are "faking" any more than it would be to suggest you are faking your behaviour when you perform daily roles as a student, spouse, or worker. You may enact the role of a student (e.g., sitting attentively in class, raising your hand when you wish to talk, etc.) because you have learned to organize your behaviour according to the nature of the role and because you have been rewarded for doing so. People with multiple personalities may have come to identify so closely with the role that it becomes real for them.

In support of their belief that multiple personality represents a form of role-playing, Spanos and his colleagues showed that with proper cues, college students in a laboratory simulation of the Bianchi-type interrogation could easily enact a multiple-personality role, even attributing the blame to an alternate personality for a murder they were accused of committing (Spanos, 2001). Perhaps the manner in which the Bianchi interrogation was conducted had cued Bianchi to enact the multiple-personality role in order to evade criminal responsibility. (It didn't work, as he was eventually convicted.)

Kenneth Bianchi, the so-called Hillside strangler. Did the police psychiatrist who interviewed Bianchi suggest to him that he could role-play a person with multiple personalities?

Relatively few cases of multiple personality involve criminal behaviour, in which enactment of a multiple-personality role might relieve individuals of criminal responsibility for their behaviour. But even in more typical cases, there may be more subtle incentives for enacting the role of a multiple personality, such as a therapist's expression of interest and excitement at discovering a multiple personality. People with multiple personalities were often highly imaginative during childhood. Accustomed to playing games of "make-believe," they may readily adopt alternate identities—especially if they learn how to enact the multiple-personality role and there are external sources of validation such as a clinician's interest and concern.

The social-reinforcement model may help to explain why some clinicians seem to "discover" many more cases of multiple personality than others. These clinicians may be "multiple personality magnets." They may unknowingly cue clients to enact the multiple-personality role and may reinforce the performance with extra attention and concern. With the right set of cues, certain clients may adopt the role of a multiple personality to please their clinicians.

The role-playing model has been challenged by some researchers (e.g., Gleaves, Hernandez, & Warner, 2003), and it remains to be seen how many cases of the disorder in clinical practice the model can explain. Whether multiple personality is a real phenomenon or a form of role-playing, there is no question that people who display this behaviour have serious emotional and behavioural difficulties.

Multiple personality, which is often called *split personality* by laypeople, should not be confused with schizophrenia. The term *split personality* refers to multiple personality, not schizophrenia. *Schizophrenia* (which comes from roots that mean "split brain") occurs much more commonly than multiple personality, and involves the "splitting" of cognition, affect, and behaviour (see Chapter 10). Thus, there may be little agreement between thoughts and emotions or between the individual's perception of reality and what is truly happening. The person with schizophrenia may become giddy when told of disturbing events or may experience hallucinations or delusions. In people with multiple personalities, the personality apparently divides into two or more personalities, but each of them usually shows more integrated functioning on cognitive, emotional, and behavioural levels than is true of people with schizophrenia.

Dissociative Amnesia

Dissociative amnesia is another controversial diagnostic category (Kihlstrom, 2005). *Amnesia* derives from the Greek roots *a-*, meaning "not," and *mnasthai*, meaning "to

dissociative amnesia Type of dissociative disorder in which a person experiences memory losses in the absence of any identifiable organic cause. General knowledge and skills are usually retained.

remember." In **dissociative amnesia** (formerly called *psychogenic amnesia*), a person becomes unable to recall important personal information usually involving material relating to traumatic or stressful experiences that cannot be accounted for by simple forgetfulness. Nor can the memory loss be attributed to a particular organic cause, such as a blow to the head or a particular medical condition, or to the direct effects of drugs or alcohol. Unlike some progressive forms of memory impairment (such as dementia associated with Alzheimer's disease), the memory loss in dissociative amnesia is reversible, although it may last for days, weeks, or even years. Recall of dissociated memories may happen gradually but often occurs suddenly and spontaneously, as when a soldier who has no recall of a battle for several days afterward suddenly recalls the experience after being transported to a hospital away from the battlefield.

Most types of dissociative amnesia involve localized amnesia, which means that events occurring during a specific time period are lost to memory. For example, a person cannot recall events for a number of hours or days after a stressful or traumatic incident, as in warfare or a case where there's an uninjured survivor of an accident. Other forms of dissociative amnesia include selective amnesia and generalized amnesia. In selective amnesia, people forget only the disturbing particulars that take place during a certain time period. Some people may recall the period of life during which they conducted an extramarital affair, but not the guilt-arousing affair itself. A soldier may recall most of a battle, but not the death of his or her compatriot. In generalized amnesia, people forget their entire lives—who they are, what they do, where they live, and with whom they live. This form of amnesia is very rare, although you wouldn't think so if you watch daytime soap operas. Persons with generalized amnesia cannot recall personal information but tend to retain their habits, tastes, and skills. If you had generalized amnesia, you would still know how to read, although you would not recall your elementary-school teachers. You would still prefer french fries to broccoli, or vice versa. People with dissociative amnesia usually forget events or periods of life that were traumatic—ones that generated strong negative emotions such as horror or guilt.

Some researchers argue that true dissociative amnesia is exceedingly rare, and that many cases of so-called dissociative amnesia are actually caused by brain injury or disease (Kihlstrom, 2005). In some cases, this explanation is quite plausible. For example, forgetting what happened during a severe motor vehicle accident may not be dissociative amnesia; it may simply reflect the fact that you had a mild brain injury (concussion) that temporarily disrupted the brain's ability to form and retain memories. However, other cases, particularly dissociative amnesia purportedly involving the loss of one's identity (as the person's only problem), are typically very different from the memory problems caused by brain damage or disease. People with this type of amnesia have seemingly lost the most deeply ingrained of all their memories—those of who they are—while they are able to readily recall other more recent things, such as what they had for breakfast in the hospital that morning. Other cognitive functions such as reasoning skills are also unaffected. In comparison, people with brain damage or disease often have difficulty recalling recent events—even for patients with dementia associated with Alzheimer's disease, one of the last things they forget is who they are (Lezak, 2004). A simple concussive blow to the head might wipe out your memory of events in the hours or days before the concussion, but you'll likely still remember who you are and recognize friends and family.

People sometimes claim they cannot recall certain events of their lives, such as criminal acts, promises made to others, and so forth. Falsely claiming amnesia as a way of escaping responsibility is called **malingering**, and involves the attempt to fake symptoms or make false claims for personal gain. It can be sometimes be very difficult to determine whether a person's reported memory loss is dissociative amnesia, malingering, or some other problem.

malingering Faking illness so as to avoid or escape work or other duties, or to obtain benefits.

dissociative fugue Type of dissociative disorder in which one suddenly flies from one's life situation, travels to a new location, assumes a new identity, and has amnesia for past personal material. The person usually retains skills and other abilities and may appear to others in the new environment to be leading a normal life.

Dissociative Fugue

Fugue derives from the Latin *fugere*, meaning "flight." The word *fugitive* has the same origin. Fugue is like amnesia "on the run." In **dissociative fugue** (formerly called *psychogenic fugue*), a person travels suddenly and unexpectedly from his or her home or place of work, is unable to recall past personal information, and either becomes confused about his or her identity or assumes a new identity (either partially or completely) (APA, 2000a). Despite these odd behaviours, the person may appear "normal" and show no other signs of mental disturbance. The person may not think about the past, or may report a past filled with false memories but not recognize them as false.

Whereas people with amnesia appear to wander aimlessly, people in a fugue state act more purposefully. Some stick close to home. They spend the afternoon in the park or in a theatre, or they spend the night at a hotel under another name, usually having little if any contact with others during the fugue state. But the new identity is incomplete and fleeting and the individual's former sense of self soon returns, in a matter of hours or a few days. Less common is a pattern in which the fugue state lasts for months or years and involves travel to distant cities or foreign lands and assumption of a new identity. These individuals may assume an identity that is more spontaneous and sociable than their former selves, which were typically "quiet" and "ordinary." They may establish new families and successful businesses. Although these cases may sound rather bizarre, the fugue state is not considered psychotic because people with the disorder can think and behave quite normally—in their new lives, that is. Then one day, quite suddenly, their awareness of their past identity returns to them, and they are flooded with old memories. After this, they typically do not recall the events that occurred during the fugue state. The new identity and the new life—including all its involvements and responsibilities—vanish from recollection.

Fugue, like amnesia, is rare, and believed to affect only about 2 people in 1000 among the general population (APA, 2000a). It is most likely to occur in the wake of an extremely stressful event such as a disaster. The underlying notion is that dissociation in the fugue state protects one from traumatic memories or other sources of emotionally painful experiences or conflict (Isaac & Chand, 2006), but the evidence favouring this hypothesis is plagued by poor methodology (Kihlstrom, 2005). Fugue can also be difficult to distinguish from malingering. That is, a number of persons who were dissatisfied with their former lives could claim to be amnesic when they are uncovered in their new locations and new identities.

Depersonalization Disorder

Depersonalization involves a temporary loss or change in the usual sense of our own reality. In a state of depersonalization, people may feel detached from their minds or bodies. They may have the sense of living in a dream or a movie, or acting like a robot (Holmes et al., 2005).

Derealization—a sense of unreality about the external world involving strange changes in perception of surroundings or in the sense of the passage of time—may also be present. People and objects may seem to change in size or shape; they may sound different. All these feelings can be associated with feelings of anxiety, including dizziness and fears of going insane, or with depression.

Although these sensations are strange, people with depersonalization maintain contact with reality. They can distinguish reality from unreality, even during the depersonalization episode. In contrast to people experiencing generalized amnesia and fugue, they know who they are. Their memories are intact and they know where they are—even if they do not like their present state. Feelings of depersonalization usually come on suddenly and fade gradually.

depersonalization Feelings of unreality or detachment from one's self or one's body, as if one were a robot, or functioning on automatic pilot, or observing oneself from outside.

derealization Loss of the sense of reality of one's surroundings, experienced in terms of strange changes in one's environment (e.g., people or objects changing size or shape) or in the sense of the passage of time.

Derealization. Episodes of derealization are characterized by the sense that one's surroundings have become strange or unreal—for example, colours may seem washed out or very bright—and time may seem to be oddly slowed down or sped up.

What is even more unusual about all this is that we have thus far described only normal feelings of depersonalization. According to the DSM, single brief episodes of depersonalization are experienced by about half of all adults, usually during times of extreme stress. Estimates are that 80% to 90% of people go through dissociative experiences at one time or another (Gershuny & Thayer, 1999).

Consider Dimitry's experience:

> "We went to Orlando with the children after school let out. I had also been driving myself hard, and it was time to let go. We spent three days 'doing' Disney World, and it got to the point where we were all wearing shirts with mice and ducks on them and singing Disney songs like 'Yo ho, yo ho, a pirate's life for me.' On the third day, I began to feel unreal and ill at ease while we were watching these teenagers singing and dancing in front of Cinderella's Castle. The day was finally cooling down, but I broke into a sweat. I became shaky and dizzy and sat down on the cement next to the four-year-old's stroller without giving [my wife] an explanation. There were strollers and kids and [adults'] legs all around me, and for some strange reason I became fixated on the pieces of popcorn strewn on the ground. All of a sudden it was like the people around me were all silly mechanical creatures, like the dolls in the It's a Small World [exhibit] or the animals on the Jungle Cruise. Things sort of seemed to slow down, the way they do when you've smoked marijuana, and there was this invisible wall of cotton between me and everyone else.
>
> "Then the concert was over and my wife was like, 'What's the matter?' and did I want to stay for the Electrical Parade and the fireworks or was I sick? Now I was beginning to wonder if I was going crazy and I said I was sick, that my wife would have to take me by the hand and drive us back to the Sonesta Village [motel]. Somehow, we got back to the monorail and turned in the strollers. I waited in the herd [of people] at the station like a dead person, my eyes glazed over, looking out over kids with Mickey Mouse ears and Mickey Mouse balloons. The mechanical voice on the monorail almost did me in and I got really shaky.
>
> "I refused to go back to the Magic Kingdom. I went with the family to Sea-World, and on another day I dropped [my wife] and the kids off at the Magic Kingdom and picked them up that night. My wife thought I was goldbricking or something, and we had a helluva fight about it, but we had a life to get back to and my sanity had to come first."
>
> The Authors' Files

depersonalization disorder Disorder characterized by persistent or recurrent episodes of depersonalization.

Dimitry's depersonalization experience was limited to the one episode and would not qualify for a diagnosis of **depersonalization disorder**. Depersonalization disorder is diagnosed only when such experiences are persistent or recurrent and cause marked distress (APA, 2000a). The DSM diagnoses depersonalization disorder according to the criteria shown in Table 5.2.

In terms of observable behaviour and associated features, depersonalization may be more closely related to disorders such as phobias and panic than to dissociative disorders (Holmes et al., 2005). Unlike other forms of dissociative disorders that seem to protect the self from anxiety, depersonalization can lead to anxiety and in turn to avoidance behaviour, as we saw in the case of Dimitry.

Theoretical Perspectives

The dissociative disorders are fascinating and perplexing phenomena. How can one's sense of personal identity become so distorted that one develops multiple personalities, blots out large chunks of personal memory, or develops a new self-identity? Although these disorders remain in many ways mysterious, clues have emerged that provide insights into their origins.

Depersonalization: No Disorder

Depersonalization: Disorder

Alex is a 44-year-old man who had worked in the bank industry for over 15 years. Recently, he was laid off and found himself needing to go back on the job market. His strong résumé and job experience made him a good candidate for several jobs, and he began going on job interviews. At this first interview, he was mildly nervous, being out of practice at job interviews. It went fairly well, but he wasn't interested in the job. At his second interview, several weeks later, Alex quickly realized that this was a desirable position for him and he felt his anxiety about doing well in the interview increase. During the interview, Alex met with two of the company's staff members. They were friendly and encouraging, and seemed to feel that Alex might be a good fit with their staff. During one conversation, Alex noticed that the room appeared strange around him. It was as if things were moving a bit slower than normal and people were talking slower than usual. He also felt the odd sensation that his arms and legs did not belong to him. Although he felt unusual, he was able to answer questions. After the interview he returned home and told his wife about his experience. By dinner, these strange feelings had gone away.

Cheng is a 30-year-old man who works as a bus driver. Through the years, he has had ups and downs with some anxiety, but nothing that kept him from working or managing his responsibilities. He is married with two small children, and is very involved with their activities. About a year ago, Cheng began having periods in which he felt "spaced out," especially during times of anxiety. These episodes became progressively worse, to the point that he now feels "spacey" almost all day. He began to question whether he was really alive or not, or if what he was experiencing was a dream. He described watching the world as if there was a layer of Saran Wrap between him and reality. He constantly did things to "check" if things around him were real. This included touching objects that looked odd and asking his wife whether he was really alive or not. These feelings were very upsetting for Cheng, to the point that he began to withdraw from his family and call in sick to work on a regular basis. Driving had become a great source of stress for Cheng, as he constantly wondered if he was capable of driving a bus with these symptoms. He wondered, "How can I be responsible for a bus full of people when I don't even know if things around me are real?" After six months of these symptoms, Cheng stopped going to work and spent most of the day in bed. He still feels like there is something between him and "reality."

Psychodynamic theorists believe that dissociative disorders involve the massive use of repression, which leads to the "splitting off" from consciousness of unacceptable impulses and painful memories. In dissociative amnesia and fugue, the ego protects itself from becoming flooded with anxiety by blotting out disturbing memories or by dissociating threatening impulses of a sexual or aggressive nature. In multiple personality, people may express these unacceptable impulses through the development of alternate personalities. In depersonalization, people stand outside themselves—safely distanced from the emotional turmoil within.

Learning and cognitive theorists view dissociation as a learned response that involves *not thinking* about disturbing acts or thoughts in order to avoid feelings of guilt and shame evoked by such experiences. The habit of not thinking about these matters is

TABLE 5.2

Diagnostic Criteria for Depersonalization Disorder

A. Persistent or recurrent experiences of feeling detached from, and as if one is an outside observer of, one's mental processes or body (e.g., feeling like one is in a dream).

B. During the depersonalization experience, reality testing remains intact.

C. The depersonalization causes clinically significant distress or impairment in social, occupational, or other important areas of functioning.

D. The depersonalization experience does not occur exclusively during the course of another mental disorder, such as Schizophrenia, Panic Disorder, Acute Stress Disorder, or another Dissociative Disorder, and is not due to the direct physiological effects of a substance (e.g., a drug of abuse, a medication) or a general medical condition (e.g., temporal lobe epilepsy).

Source: Reprinted with permission from the *Diagnostic and Statistical Manual of Mental Disorders,* Fourth Edition, Text Revision, (Copyright ©2000). American Psychiatric Association. p. 532.

Brief dissociative experiences, such as momentary feelings of depersonalization, are quite common. The great majority of us experience them at least some of the time (Simeon & Abugel, 2006). Dissociative disorders, by contrast, involve more persistent and severe dissociative experiences. Researchers have developed a measure, the Dissociative Experiences Scale (DES), to offer clinicians a way of measuring dissociative experiences that occur both in the general population and among people with dissociative disorders (E. M. Bernstein & Putnam, 1986). Fleeting dissociative experiences are quite common, but those reported by people with dissociative disorders are more frequent and problematic than those in the general population.

The following is a listing of some of the types of dissociative experiences drawn from the Dissociative Experiences Scale that many people encounter from time to time. Bear in mind that transient experiences like these are reported by both normal and abnormal groups in varying frequencies. Let us also suggest that if these experiences become persistent or commonplace, or cause you concern or distress, it might be worthwhile to discuss them with a professional.

Have you ever experienced the following?

_____ 1. Suddenly realizing, when you are driving the car, that you don't remember what has happened during all or part of the trip.

_____ 2. Suddenly realizing, when you are listening to someone talk, that you did not hear part or all of what the person said.

_____ 3. Finding yourself in a place and having no idea how you got there.

_____ 4. Finding yourself dressed in clothes that you don't remember putting on.

_____ 5. Experiencing a feeling that seemed as if you were standing next to yourself or watching yourself do something and actually seeing yourself as if you were looking at another person.

_____ 6. Looking in a mirror and not recognizing yourself.

_____ 7. Feeling sometimes that other people, objects, and the world around you are not real.

_____ 8. Remembering a past event so vividly that it seems like you are reliving it in the present.

_____ 9. Having the experience of being in a familiar place but finding it strange and unfamiliar.

_____ 10. Becoming so absorbed in watching television or a movie that you are unaware of other events happening around you.

_____ 11. Becoming so absorbed in a fantasy or daydream that it feels as though it were really happening to you.

_____ 12. Talking out loud to yourself when you are alone.

_____ 13. Finding that you act so differently in a particular situation compared with another that it feels almost as if you were two different people.

_____ 14. Finding that you cannot remember whether or not you have just done something or perhaps had just thought about doing it (e.g., not knowing whether you have just mailed a letter or have just thought about mailing it).

_____ 15. Feeling sometimes as if you were looking at the world through a fog such that people and objects appear far away or unclear.

Source: Bernstein & Putnam, 1986. Copyright 1986 by Wolters Kluwer Health. Reprinted with permission.

---

negatively reinforced by relief from anxiety or by removal of feelings of guilt or shame. Some social cognitive theorists, such as Spanos (2001) and others (e.g., Lilienfeld & Lynn, 2003), propose that dissociative identity disorder is a form of role-playing acquired by means of observational learning and reinforcement. This is not quite the same as pretending or malingering; people can honestly come to organize their behaviour patterns according to particular roles they have observed. They might also become so absorbed in role-playing that they "forget" they are enacting a role.

Tying It Together

A widely held view of dissociative identity disorder is that it represents a means of coping with and surviving severe childhood abuse (C. A. Ross, 2001). It is possible that in some cases, severely abused children may retreat into alter personalities as a psychological defence against unbearable abuse. The construction of alter personalities may allow these children to escape psychologically or distance themselves from their suffering. Dissociation may offer a means of escape when no other means is available. In the face of repeated abuse, these alter personalities may become stabilized, making it difficult for the person to maintain a unified personality. In adulthood, people with multiple personalities may use their alter personalities to block out traumatic childhood memories and their emotional reactions to them—wiping the slate clean and beginning life anew in the guise of alter personalities (C. A. Ross, 2001). The alter identities or personalities may also serve as a way of coping with stressful situations or of expressing deep-seated resentments that the individual is unable to integrate within his or her primary personality. Although this theory is popular with many clinicians, the evidence comes largely from methodologically weak studies (Kihlstrom, 2005).

The great majority of people with multiple personalities report being physically or sexually abused as children, although most people abused as children do not develop multiple personalities (Piper & Merskey, 2004). Similarly, the vast majority of people exposed to trauma do not develop dissociative disorders (Kihlstrom, 2005).

Consistent with the diathesis-stress model, only certain individuals may be predisposed to develop dissociative disorders when exposed to severe stress. Certain personality traits, such as a proneness to fantasize, a high ability to be hypnotized, and an openness to altered states of consciousness, may predispose individuals to develop dissociative experiences in the face of extreme stress caused by events such as traumatic abuse (Isaac & Chand, 2006). These personality traits themselves do not lead to dissociative disorders, but they might increase the risk that people who experience severe trauma will develop dissociative phenomena as a survival mechanism.

Perhaps most of us can divide our consciousness so that we become unaware—at least temporarily—of those events we normally focus on. Perhaps most of us can thrust the unpleasant from our minds and enact various roles—parent, child, lover, business person, soldier—that help us meet the requirements of our situations. Perhaps the marvel is *not* that attention can be splintered, but that human consciousness is normally integrated into a meaningful whole.

Treatment of Dissociative Disorders

Dissociative amnesia and fugue are usually fleeting experiences that end abruptly. Episodes of depersonalization can be recurrent and persistent, and they are most likely to occur when people are undergoing periods of mild anxiety or depression. In such cases, clinicians usually focus on managing the anxiety or the depression. Much of the attention in the research literature has focused on dissociative identity disorder and specifically on bringing together an integration of the alter personalities into a cohesive personality structure.

Traditional psychoanalysis aims at helping people with dissociative identity disorder to uncover and learn to cope with early childhood traumas. The analyst can work with whatever personality dominates the therapy session. Any and all personalities can be asked to talk about their memories and dreams as best they can. Any and all personalities can be assured that the therapist will help them to make sense of their anxieties and to safely "relive" traumatic experiences and make them conscious. If therapy is successful, the self will be able to work through the traumatic memories and will no longer need to escape into alternate "selves" to avoid the anxiety associated with the trauma. Thus, reintegration of the personality becomes possible.

Does this sort of therapy work? Coons (1986) followed 20 "multiples" aged 14 to 47 at time of intake for an average of 39 months. Only five of the subjects showed a complete reintegration of their personalities. Other therapists report significant improvement in measures of dissociative and depressive symptoms in treated patients (Ellason & Ross, 1997), but these studies have been criticized for methodological problems (Kihlstrom, 2005). Reports of the effectiveness of other forms of therapy, such as cognitive-behavioural therapy, rely largely on uncontrolled case studies. Nor do we have evidence showing psychiatric drugs or other biological approaches to be effective in bringing about an integration of various alternate personalities. Accordingly, it is not possible to draw firm conclusions about the safety and efficacy of psychoanalytic or other treatments for dissociative identity disorder.

Little is known about the treatment of other forms of dissociative disorder. The relative infrequency of these disorders has hampered efforts to conduct controlled experiments that compare different forms of treatment with one another and with control groups. However, preliminary evidence suggests that cognitive-behavioural therapy and some types of medication may be helpful in treating depersonalization disorder (Hunter, Baker, Phillips, Sierra, & David, 2005; Simeon & Abugel, 2006).

A CLOSER LOOK

A Recovered-Memory Controversy

A high-level business executive's comfortable life fell apart one day when his 19-year-old daughter accused him of having repeatedly molested her throughout her childhood. He lost his marriage as well as his $400 000-a-year job. But he fought back against the allegations that he insisted were untrue. He sued his daughter's therapists who had assisted her in recovering these memories. A jury sided with the father, awarding him $500 000 in damages from the two therapists.

In the Canadian case of *R. v. François* (1994), Lorne François was convicted of repeatedly raping a 13-year-old girl in 1985. The only evidence was the girl's testimony. She said that she had repressed memories of the sexual assaults but that the recollections returned in 1990. At the time of the recollections, the police suggested that if she thought long enough about her past, she might recall something in a "flashback." The girl reported that the flashbacks occurred while doing this. The conviction was later overturned by the Supreme Court of Canada.

These are just two of many cases involving allegations made by adults who claim to have only recently become aware of memories of being sexually abused during childhood. Hundreds of people throughout North America have been brought to trial on the basis of recovered memories of childhood abuse, with many of these cases resulting in convictions and long jail sentences, even in the absence of any corroborating evidence. Recovered memories of sexual abuse in childhood may occur following suggestive probing by a therapist or hypnotist (Loftus & Davis, 2006). The issue of recovered memories continues to be hotly debated in psychology and the broader community (Prout & Dobson, 1998). At the heart of the debate is the question, "Are recovered memories believable?" No one doubts that child sexual abuse is a major problem confronting our society. But should recovered memories be taken at face value?

Several lines of evidence lead us to question the validity of recovered memories. Research evidence shows, for example, that under some circumstances, people who are given plausible but false information about their childhoods may come to believe the information to be true. To illustrate, consider the research by psychologist Stephen Porter, who with his colleagues at the University of British Columbia demonstrated that some people can create false memories of emotional childhood events (Porter et al., 2000; Porter, Yuille, & Lehman, 1999). Participants in this research were university students. The parents of the students were asked to provide information about six emotional events (e.g., serious accidents, medical procedures, animal attacks) that the student may or may not have experienced as a child. This information enabled the researchers to construct, for a given student, a fabricated childhood event that could form the basis of a false memory. The experiment consisted of three interviews over two weeks. In the first interview, students were interviewed about a real and a false event, with both introduced to the student as true. In the second and third interviews, students were re-interviewed about the false event. Interviewers attempted to elicit a false memory in each student, using methods such as guided imagery (e.g., asking the student to repeatedly imagine the fictitious event), mild social pressure that the event actually occurred, and the encouragement of repeated attempts to recover the memory. Porter, Yuille, and Lehman (1999) found that 26% of students created a false memory, 30% created a partial false memory (e.g., the student was unsure about whether the false event had occurred), and 44% created no false memory. Further results suggested that false memories are most likely to occur in people with dissociative tendencies (i.e., high scores on the Dissociative Experiences Scale) and when the interviewer is engaging, persuasive, and confident (Porter et al., 2000).

Underscoring the importance of findings such as these, a leading memory expert, psychologist Elizabeth Loftus, wrote of the dangers of taking recovered memories at face value:

> After developing false memories, innumerable "patients" have torn their families apart, and more than a few innocent people have been sent to ➤

prison. This is not to say that people cannot forget horrible things that have happened to them; most certainly they can. But there is virtually no support for the idea that clients presenting for therapy routinely have extensive histories of abuse of which they are completely unaware, and that they can be helped only if the alleged abuse is resurrected from their unconscious. (Loftus, 1996, p. 356)

Should we conclude, then, that all recovered memories are bogus? Not necessarily. It is possible for people in adulthood to recover memories of childhood, including memories of abuse (Chu, Frey, & Ganzel, 1999). There is little doubt that abuse can be forgotten and later remembered, although ordinary forgetting and remembering—rather than a special

mechanism such as repression—seem more than adequate to account for this (Loftus & Davis, 2006). Some recovered memories may be true; others may not. Unfortunately, we don't have the tools to distinguish the true memory from the false one. A "memory" report's being detailed or a person's expressing it with confidence and emotion does not mean the event actually happened (Loftus & Davis, 2006).

We shouldn't think of the brain as a kind of mental camera that stores snapshots of events as they actually happened in the form of memories. Memory is more of a reconstructive process, in which bits of information are pieced together in ways that can sometimes lead to a distorted recollection of events, even though the person may be convinced the memory is accurate.

REVIEW IT

Dissociative Disorders

- **What are dissociative disorders?** Dissociative disorders involve changes or disturbances in identity, memory, or consciousness that affect the ability to maintain an integrated sense of self. They include dissociative identity disorder, dissociative amnesia, dissociative fugue, and depersonalization disorder.

- **What is the major feature of dissociative identity disorder?** In dissociative identity disorder, two or more distinct personalities, each possessing well-defined traits and memories, exist within a person and repeatedly take control of the person's behaviour.

- **What are the clinical features associated with dissociative amnesia, dissociative fugue, and depersonalization disorder?** Dissociative amnesia involves loss of memory for personal information that cannot be accounted for by organic causes. In dissociative fugue, a person travels suddenly away from home or place of work, shows a loss of memory for his or her personal past, and experiences identity confusion or takes on a new identity. Depersonalization disorder involves persistent or recurrent episodes of depersonalization that are of sufficient severity to cause significant distress or impairment in functioning.

- **How do psychodynamic theorists conceptualize dissociative disorders?** Psychodynamic theorists view dissociative disorders as involving a form of psychological defence by which the ego defends itself against troubling memories and unacceptable impulses by blotting them out of consciousness.

- **How do learning and cognitive theorists account for these disorders?** To learning and cognitive theorists, dissociative experiences involve ways of learning not to think about certain troubling behaviours or thoughts that might lead to feelings of guilt or shame. Relief from anxiety negatively reinforces this pattern of dissociation. Some social-cognitive theorists suggest that multiple personality may represent a form of role-playing behaviour.

- **How has dissociative identity disorder been treated?** Most therapeutic approaches help the person with dissociative identity disorder uncover and cope with dissociated painful experiences from childhood. Biological approaches focus on the use of drugs to treat the anxiety and depression often associated with the disorder, but drugs have not been able to bring about reintegration of the personality.

SOMATOFORM DISORDERS

somatoform disorders Disorders in which people complain of physical (somatic) problems although no physical abnormality can be found. See *conversion disorder, hypochondriasis,* and *somatization disorder.*

The word *somatoform* derives from the Greek *soma,* meaning "body." In the **somatoform disorders,** people have physical symptoms suggestive of physical disorders, but no organic abnormalities can be found to account for them. Moreover, there is evidence or some reason to believe that the symptoms reflect psychological factors. Some people complain of problems in breathing or swallowing or of a "lump in the throat." Problems such as these can reflect overactivity of the sympathetic branch of the autonomic nervous system, which can be related to anxiety. Sometimes the symptoms take more unusual forms, as in a "paralysis" of a hand or leg that is inconsistent with the workings of the nervous system. In yet other cases, people are preoccupied with the belief that they have a serious disease, yet no evidence of a physical abnormality can be found. We consider several forms of somatoform disorders, including *conversion disorder*, *hypochondriasis*, and *somatization disorder*.

Somatoform disorders are distinguished from malingering or purposeful fabrication of symptoms for obvious gain (such as avoiding work). They are also distinguished from a **factitious disorder**, the most common form of which is **Münchausen syndrome**. Münchausen syndrome is a form of feigned illness in which people either fake being ill or make themselves ill (by ingesting toxic substances such as rat poison or injecting themselves with bacteria, for example). Münchausen syndrome is named after the fictional accounts published by Rudolf Erich Raspe (e.g., 1860) about Baron Münchausen, an 18th-century German army officer.

Some Münchausen patients go through unnecessary surgeries, even though they know there is nothing wrong with them. Yet unlike in malingering, there is no apparent purpose to the fakery, save for the attention the person receives from medical professionals. A rare and potentially very harmful variant of this disorder is Münchausen by proxy syndrome (MBPS), where the parent feigns or induces illness in a child (Ayoub, 2006). For example, the parent may attempt to poison the child in order for the child (and, by proxy, the parent) to receive medical attention. Thus, MBPS can be associated with severe and sometimes deadly child abuse.

Malingering is motivated by external incentives, and so it is not considered a psychological disorder within the DSM framework. In factitious disorders, however, the symptoms are not connected with obvious gains. The absence of external incentives in these disorders suggests that they serve a psychological need; hence, they are considered psychological disorders.

Why do patients with Münchausen syndrome feign illness or sometimes put themselves at grave risk by causing themselves to be sick or injured? This syndrome represents an extreme need for nurturance or attention (Slovenko, 2006), although the underlying reasons for this need are unclear. Perhaps enacting the sick role in the protected hospital environment provides a sense of security that was lacking in childhood. Perhaps the hospital becomes a stage on which patients can act out resentments against doctors and parents, resentments that have been brewing since childhood. Perhaps they are trying to identify with a parent who was often sick. Or perhaps they learned to enact a sick role in childhood to escape repeated sexual abuse or other traumatic experiences and continue to enact the role to escape stressors in their adult lives (Trask & Sigmon, 1997). No one is really sure, and the disorder remains one of the more puzzling forms of abnormal behaviour.

Now let's consider several of the major types of somatoform disorder.

factitious disorder Type of psychological disorder characterized by the intentional fabrication of psychological or physical symptoms for no apparent gain.

Münchausen syndrome Type of factitious disorder characterized by the feigning of medical symptoms for no apparent purpose other than getting admitted to or remaining in hospital.

Tall Tales. Baron Münchausen, who, according to the fictional accounts published by Rudolf Erich Raspe, regaled his friends with tales of his incredible feats. In one of his tall tales, depicted here, he claimed that he had fallen asleep inside a cannon and was inadvertently shot across the Thames River.

TABLE 5.3

Diagnostic Criteria for Conversion Disorder

A. One or more symptoms or deficits affecting voluntary motor or sensory function that suggest a neurological or other general medical condition.

B. Psychological factors are judged to be associated with the symptom or deficit because the initiation or exacerbation of the symptom or deficit is preceded by conflicts or other stressors.

C. The symptom or deficit is not intentionally produced or feigned (as in Factitious Disorder or Malingering).

D. The symptom or deficit cannot, after appropriate investigation, be fully explained by a general medical condition, or by the direct effects of a substance, or as a culturally sanctioned behavior or experience.

E. The symptom or deficit causes clinically significant distress or impairment in social, occupational, or other important areas of functioning or warrants medical evaluation.

F. The symptom or deficit is not limited to pain or sexual dysfunction, does not occur exclusively during the course of Somatization Disorder, and is not better accounted for by another mental disorder.

Source: Reprinted with permission from the *Diagnostic and Statistical Manual of Mental Disorders*, Fourth Edition, Text Revision, (Copyright ©2000). American Psychiatric Association. p. 498.

Conversion Disorder

Conversion disorder is characterized by a major change in or loss of physical functioning, although there are no medical findings to support the physical symptoms or deficits (see Table 5.3). The symptoms are not intentionally produced. The person is not malingering. The physical symptoms usually come on suddenly in stressful situations. A soldier's hand may become "paralyzed" during intense combat, for example. The fact that conversion symptoms first appear in the context of or are aggravated by conflicts or stressors the individual encounters gives credence to the view that they relate to psychological factors (APA, 2000a).

Conversion disorder is so named because of the psychodynamic belief that it represents the channelling, or *conversion*, of repressed sexual or aggressive energies into physical symptoms. Conversion disorder was formerly called *hysteria* or *hysterical neurosis* and played an important role in Freud's development of psychoanalysis (see Chapter 1). Hysterical or conversion disorders seem to have been more common in Freud's day but are relatively rare today.

According to the DSM, conversion symptoms mimic neurological or general medical conditions involving problems with voluntary motor (movement) or sensory functions. Some of the "classic" symptom patterns involve paralysis, epilepsy, problems in coordination, blindness and tunnel vision, loss of the sense of hearing or of smell, or loss of feeling in a limb (anaesthesia). The bodily symptoms found in conversion disorders often do not match the medical conditions they suggest. For example, conversion epileptics, unlike true epileptic patients, may maintain control over their bladders during an attack. People whose vision is supposedly impaired may wend their way through the physician's office without bumping into the furniture. People who become "incapable" of standing or walking may nevertheless perform other leg movements normally. Nonetheless, there are some cases in which hysteria or conversion disorder was incorrectly diagnosed in people who turned out to have underlying medical conditions that went unrecognized and untreated.

If you suddenly lost your vision, or if you could no longer move your legs, you would probably be very upset. But some people with conversion disorders, like those with dissociative amnesia, show a remarkable indifference to their symptoms, a phenomenon termed *la belle indifférence* ("beautiful indifference"). This was once thought to be an important feature that distinguished conversion disorders from real

conversion disorder Type of somatoform disorder characterized by loss or impairment of physical function in the absence of any organic causes that might account for the changes. Formerly called *hysteria* or *hysterical neurosis*.

la belle indifférence French term describing the lack of concern over one's symptoms displayed by some people with conversion disorder but also by people with real physical disorders.

Faking or real? People with hypochondriasis do not consciously fake their symptoms but fear their symptoms are due to a real illness. Feeling resentful toward their own doctor, they often go "doctor shopping."

physical disorders. However, accumulating evidence shows that many people cope with real physical disorders by denying their pain or concern, which provides the semblance of indifference and relieves anxieties—at least temporarily. In fact, people with conversion disorder are no more likely than people with real physical disorders to display *la belle indifférence*, suggesting that this feature is of little diagnostic value (J. Stone, Smyth, Carson, Warlow, & Sharpe, 2006).

Hypochondriasis

The core feature of hypochondriasis is a preoccupation or fear that one's physical symptoms are due to an underlying serious illness, such as cancer or a heart problem. The fear persists despite medical reassurances that it is groundless (see Table 5.4).

People with hypochondriasis do not consciously fake their physical symptoms. They generally experience physical discomfort, often involving the digestive system or an assortment of aches and pains. Unlike conversion disorder, hypochondriasis does not involve the loss or distortion of physical function. Unlike the attitude of indifference toward one's symptoms that is sometimes found in conversion disorders, people who develop hypochondriasis are very concerned, indeed unduly concerned, about their symptoms and what they fear they may represent. About 1% to 5% of the population develop hypochondriasis at some point in their lives (APA, 2000a). The disorder appears to be about equally common in men and women. It most often begins between the ages of 20 and 30, although it can begin at any age.

People with hypochondriasis may be overly sensitive to slight changes in heartbeat and minor aches and pains. Anxiety about physical symptoms can produce its own physical sensations, however—for example, heavy sweating and dizziness, even fainting. Thus, a vicious cycle may ensue. People with hypochondriasis may become resentful when their doctors tell them how their own fears may be causing their physical symptoms. They frequently go "doctor shopping" in the hope that a competent and

---

TABLE 5.4

Diagnostic Criteria for Hypochondriasis

A. Preoccupation with fears of having, or the idea that one has, a serious disease based on the person's misinterpretation of bodily symptoms.

B. The preoccupation persists despite appropriate medical evaluation and reassurance.

C. The belief in Criterion A is not of delusional intensity (as in Delusional Disorder, Somatic Type) and is not restricted to a circumscribed concern about appearance (as in Body Dysmorphic Disorder).

D. The preoccupation causes clinically significant distress or impairment in social, occupational, or other important areas of functioning.

E. The duration of the disturbance is at least 6 months.

F. The preoccupation is not better accounted for by Generalized Anxiety Disorder, Obsessive-Compulsive Disorder, Panic Disorder, a Major Depressive Episode, Separation Anxiety, or another Somatoform Disorder.

Source: Reprinted with permission from the *Diagnostic and Statistical Manual of Mental Disorders*, Fourth Edition, Text Revision, (Copyright ©2000). American Psychiatric Association. p. 507.

sympathetic physician will heed them before it is too late. Physicians, too, can develop hypochondriasis, as we see in the following case example:

A 38-year-old radiologist is evaluated after returning from a 10-day stay at a famous out-of-state diagnostic center to which he had been referred by a local gastroenterologist after "he reached the end of the line" with the radiologist. The patient reports that he underwent extensive physical and laboratory examinations, X-ray examinations of the entire gastrointestinal tract, esophagoscopy, gastroscopy, and colonoscopy at the center. Although he was told that the results of the examinations were negative for significant physical disease, he appears resentful and disappointed rather than relieved at the findings. He was seen briefly for a "routine" evaluation by a psychiatrist at the diagnostic center, but had difficulty relating to the psychiatrist on more than a superficial level.

On further inquiry concerning the patient's physical symptoms, he describes occasional twinges of mild abdominal pain, sensations of "fullness," "bowel rumblings," and a "firm abdominal mass" that he can sometimes feel in his left lower quadrant. Over the last few months he has gradually become more aware of these sensations and convinced that they may be the result of a carcinoma of the colon. He tests his stool for occult blood weekly and spends 15–20 minutes every 2–3 days carefully palpating his abdomen as he lies in bed at home. He has secretly performed several X-ray studies on himself in his own office after hours.

Although he is successful in his work, has an excellent attendance record, and is active in community life, the patient spends much of his leisure time at home alone in bed. His wife, an instructor at a local school of nursing, is angry and bitter about this behavior, which she describes as "robbing us of what we've worked so hard and postponed so much for." Although she and the patient share many values and genuinely love each other, his behavior causes a real strain on their marriage.

When the patient was 13, a heart murmur was detected on a school physical exam. Because a younger brother had died in early childhood of congenital heart disease, the patient was removed from gym class until the murmur could be evaluated. The evaluation proved the murmur to be benign, but the patient began to worry that the evaluation might have "missed something" and considered the occasional sensations of "skipping a beat" as evidence that this was so. He kept his fears to himself; they subsided over the next 2 years, but never entirely left him.

As a second-year medical student he was relieved to share some of his health concerns with his classmates, who also worried about having the diseases they were learning about in pathology. He realized, however, that he was much more preoccupied with and worried about his health than they were. Since graduating from medical school, he has repeatedly experienced a series of concerns, each following the same pattern: noticing a symptom, becoming increasingly preoccupied with what it might mean, and having a negative physical evaluation. At times he returns to an "old" concern, but is too embarrassed to pursue it with physicians he knows, as when he discovered a "suspicious" nevus only 1 week after he had persuaded a dermatologist to biopsy one that proved to be entirely benign.

The patient tells his story with a sincere, discouraged tone, brightened only by a note of genuine pleasure and enthusiasm as he provides a detailed account of the discovery of a genuine, but clinically insignificant, urethral anomaly as the result of an intravenous pyelogram he had ordered himself. Near the end of the interview, he explains that his coming in for evaluation now is largely at his own insistence, precipitated by an encounter with his 9-year-old son. The boy had accidentally walked in while he was palpating his own abdomen for "masses" and asked, "What do you think it is this time, Dad?" As he describes his shame and anger (mostly at himself) about this incident, his eyes fill with tears.

Source: Reprinted with permission from the *DSM-IV-TR Case Book: A Learning Companion to the Diagnostic and Statistical Manual of Mental Disorders,* Fourth Edition, Text Revision, (Copyright ©2005). American Psychiatric Association. pp. 88–90.

People who develop hypochondriasis have more health worries, have more psychiatric symptoms, and perceive their health to be worse than do other people. They are also more likely than other psychiatric patients to report being sick as children, having missed school because of health reasons, and having experienced childhood trauma, such as sexual abuse or physical violence. Hypochondriasis may fluctuate in severity over time or it may persist in a severe form for many years (Strassnig, Stowell, First, & Pincus, 2006; S. Taylor & Asmundson, 2004). Many people with this disorder also have other psychological disorders, especially major depression and anxiety disorders (S. Taylor & Asmundson, 2004).

Somatization Disorder

somatization disorder Type of somatoform disorder involving recurrent multiple complaints that cannot be explained by any clear physical causes. Formerly called *Briquet's syndrome*.

Somatization disorder, formerly known as *Briquet's syndrome*, is characterized by multiple and recurrent somatic complaints that begin prior to the age of 30 (most commonly during the teen years), persist for at least several years, and result in the seeking of medical attention and a significant impairment in fulfilling social or occupational roles. Complaints usually involve various organ systems (Hiller, Rief, & Brähler, 2006). Seldom does a year pass without some physical complaint that prompts a trip to the doctor. People with somatization disorder are heavy users of medical services; people with somatization symptoms use twice as many inpatient and outpatient medical services as non-somatizing patients, resulting in twice the annual medical costs (Strassnig et al., 2006). The complaints cannot be explained by physical causes or exceed what would be expected from a known physical problem. Complaints seem vague or exaggerated, and the person frequently receives medical care from a number of physicians, sometimes at the same time.

Somatization disorder usually begins in adolescence or young adulthood and appears to be a lifelong disorder involving major disability (Kirmayer & Looper, 2006). It usually occurs in the context of other psychological disorders, especially anxiety disorders and depressive disorders (APA, 2000a). Estimates are that 1 person in 1000 is affected by somatization disorder, with 10 times as many cases found among women as among men (APA, 2000a). Not much is known of the childhood background of people with somatization disorder. Although a number of studies found high rates of childhood sexual abuse among patients with somatoform disorders, several recent studies found that other aspects of negative parenting style have a stronger association with somatization, such as childhood physical and emotional abuse and an unsupportive (e.g., hostile and rejecting/neglectful) family environment (Kirmayer & Looper, 2006).

The essential feature of hypochondriasis is fear of disease, of what bodily symptoms may portend. Persons with somatization disorder, by contrast, are pestered by the symptoms themselves. Both diagnoses may be given to the same individual if the diagnostic criteria for both disorders are met.

Other Somatoform Disorders

Two other somatoform disorders, which we will briefly mention, are *body dysmorphic disorder* and *pain disorder*. Body dysmorphic disorder is diagnosed when a person is preoccupied with some imagined defect in his or her appearance. The person is typically preoccupied with a facial feature, and may become highly upset about some minor feature ("My lips are too thin" or "My ears aren't symmetrical"). In some cases, this preoccupation can lead the person to repeatedly seek plastic surgery. The preoccupation with the body part far exceeds normal worries about physical imperfections. People with body dysmorphic disorder may endlessly worry about their bodies and be considerably distressed as a result. Preoccupation can also interfere with work, school, or social functioning (e.g., by avoiding social gatherings because of imagined ugliness, or failing to get work assignments done because the person is spending too much time checking his or her appearance in the mirror).

Pain disorder is characterized by a preoccupation with pain in cases in which a physical cause cannot adequately explain the persistence of the person's pain. Psychological factors are judged to play an important role in creating or intensifying the person's chronic pain. For example, receiving sympathy and attention from others can motivate the person to focus on and complain excessively of pain. In other cases, complaints of pain may be reinforced because they enable the person to get out of arduous or boring tasks (e.g., household chores). Such incentives often perpetuate pain complaints. Stressful life events may also contribute to the pain experienced in people diagnosed with pain disorder. This can arise because stressors can lead the person to experience prolonged muscle tension, resulting in muscle cramps or headaches.

Theoretical Perspectives

Conversion disorder, or *hysteria*, was known to Hippocrates, who attributed the strange bodily symptoms to a wandering uterus, which created internal chaos. The term *hysterical* derives from the Greek *hystera*, meaning "uterus." Hippocrates noticed that these complaints were less common among married women. He prescribed marriage as a "cure" on the basis of these observations, and also on the theoretical assumption that pregnancy would satisfy uterine needs and fix the organ in place. Pregnancy fosters hormonal and structural changes that are of benefit to some women with menstrual complaints, but Hippocrates's belief in the "wandering uterus" has contributed throughout the centuries to degrading interpretations of complaints by women of physical problems. Despite Hippocrates's belief that hysteria is exclusively a female concern, it also occurs in men.

Modern theoretical accounts of the somatoform disorders, like those of the dissociative disorders, have most often sprung from psychodynamic and learning theories. Although not much is known about the biological underpinnings of somatoform disorders, evidence indicates that somatization disorder tends to run in families. A recent twin study conducted at the University of British Columbia indicates that hypochondriacal features—such as excessive health-related worry and the unfounded belief that one has a serious, undiagnosed disease—are caused by a combination of environmental and genetic factors (S. Taylor, Thordarson, Jang, & Asmundson, 2006). Environmental factors include learning experiences such as episodes of childhood illness that teach the child that he or she is sickly and frail (S. Taylor & Asmundson, 2004). Such experiences can give rise to unrealistic beliefs (e.g., "My health is in constant jeopardy"), which can cause people to focus their attention on their bodies and thereby notice and misinterpret the significance of minor bodily aches and pains or other bodily changes (Marcus, Gurley, Marchi, & Bauer, 2007). Such factors also appear to play a role in somatization (R. J. Brown, 2004). Thus, an accumulating body of research supports learning theories of hypochondriasis and other somatoform disorders, although the results indicate that biological factors such as genes also play a role (Kirmayer & Looper, 2006; Rief & Barsky, 2005; S. Taylor, Thordarson, Jang, & Asmundson, 2006).

Hysterical disorders provided an arena for some of the debate between the psychological and biological theories of the 19th century. The alleviation—albeit often temporary—of hysterical symptoms through hypnosis by Charcot, Josef Breuer, and Freud contributed to the belief that hysteria was rooted in psychological rather than physical causes and led Freud to the development of a theory of the unconscious mind. Freud held that the ego manages to control unacceptable or threatening sexual and aggressive impulses arising from the id through defence mechanisms such as repression. Such control prevents the outbreak of anxiety that would occur if the person were to become aware of them. In some cases, the leftover emotion or energy that is "strangulated" or cut off from the threatening impulses becomes converted into a physical symptom, such as hysterical paralysis or blindness. Although the early psychodynamic formulation of hysteria is still widely held, empirical evidence has been lacking. One problem with the Freudian view is

What to take? Hypochondriasis involves persistent concerns or fears that one is seriously ill, although no organic basis can be found to account for the person's physical complaints. People with this disorder frequently medicate themselves with over-the-counter preparations and find little, if any, reassurance in doctors' assertions that their health is not in jeopardy.

primary gains In psychodynamic theory, the relief from anxiety obtained through the development of a neurotic symptom.

secondary gains Side benefits associated with neuroses or other disorders, such as expressions of sympathy and increased attention from others and release from ordinary responsibilities.

Koro syndrome Culture-related somatoform disorder, found primarily in China, in which people fear that their genitals are shrinking and retracting into the body.

Dhat syndrome Usually diagnosed among young Indian men who describe an intense fear or anxiety over the loss of semen.

that it does not explain how energies left over from unconscious conflicts become transformed into physical symptoms (E. Miller, 1987). A further problem is that psychodynamic theory does not consider the role of learning factors (e.g., sympathy or other forms of positive reinforcement for expressing symptoms) or biological factors in the disorder (Stonnington, Barry, & Fisher, 2006; Wald, Taylor, & Scamvougeras, 2004).

According to psychodynamic theory, hysterical symptoms are functional: they allow the person to achieve **primary gains** and **secondary gains**. The primary gains consist of allowing the individual to keep internal conflicts repressed. The person is aware of the physical symptom, but not of the conflict it represents. In such cases, the "symptom" is symbolic of, and provides the person with a "partial solution" of, the underlying conflict. For example, the hysterical paralysis of an arm might symbolize and also prevent the individual from acting on repressed unacceptable sexual (e.g., masturbatory) or aggressive (e.g., murderous) impulses. Repression occurs automatically, so the individual remains unaware of the underlying conflicts. *La belle indifférence*, first noted by Charcot, is believed to occur because the physical symptoms help relieve rather than cause anxiety. From the psychodynamic perspective, conversion disorders, like dissociative disorders, serve a purpose.

Secondary gains may allow the individual to avoid burdensome responsibilities and to gain the support—rather than condemnation—of those around them. For example, soldiers sometimes experience sudden "paralysis" of their hands, which prevents them from firing their guns in battle. They may then be sent to recuperate at a hospital rather than face enemy fire. The symptoms in such cases are not considered contrived, as would

---

FOCUS ON DIVERSITY

Koro and Dhat Syndromes: Asian Somatoform Disorders?

In Canada, it is common for people who develop hypochondriasis to be troubled by the idea that they have serious illnesses, such as cancer. The Koro and Dhat syndromes of East Asia and India, respectively, share some clinical features with hypochondriasis. Although these syndromes may seem strange to most North American readers, they are each connected through folklore within their cultures.

KORO SYNDROME

Koro syndrome is a culture-bound syndrome found primarily in China and some other East Asian countries, although Koro-like cases have also been described in Africa, India, and Western countries, including Canada (Dzokoto & Adams, 2005). People with Koro fear that their genitals are shrinking and retracting into the body and believe that this will result in death (Cheng, 1996). The syndrome, which tends to be short-lived, has been identified mainly in young men, although some cases have also been reported in women, who fear that their genitals or breasts are shrinking or retracting into the body (Chowdhury, 1996; Dzokoto & Adams, 2005). Physiological signs of anxiety that approach panic proportions are common, including profuse sweating, breathlessness, and heart palpitations. Men who suffer from Koro have been known to use mechanical devices such as chopsticks to try to prevent the penis from retracting into the body (Cheng, 1996).

Epidemics involving hundreds or thousands of people have been reported in parts of Asia such as China, Singapore, Thailand, and India (Dzokoto & Adams, 2005). For example, in southern China an epidemic of Koro involving more than 3000 people occurred during 1984–1985, with incidence in the most severely afflicted villages ranging from 6% to 19% (Cheng, 1996). People who fall victim to Koro tend to be poorly educated, lacking in proper sex information, and accepting of Koro-related folk beliefs (such as the belief that shrinkage of the penis will be lethal) (Cheng, 1996; Chowdhury, 1996; Dzokoto & Adams, 2005). Medical reassurance that such fears are unfounded often quell Koro episodes. Similar reassurance generally fails to dent the concerns of Westerners who develop hypochondriasis, however (S. Taylor & Asmundson, 2004). Koro episodes among those who do not receive corrective information tend to pass with time but may recur.

Koro has been classified in various ways—as a form of anxiety disorder, depersonalization, body-image disturbance, or an atypical somatoform disorder (Chowdhury, 1996; Dzokoto & Adams, 2005).

DHAT SYNDROME

Dhat[1] **syndrome** is found among young males in India and involves excessive fears over the loss of seminal fluid during nocturnal emissions (Ranjith & Mohan, 2006). Some men with this syndrome also believe (incorrectly) that semen mixes with urine and is excreted through urination. Men with Dhat syndrome may roam from physician to physician seeking help to prevent nocturnal emissions or the (imagined) loss of semen mixed with excreted urine. There is a widespread belief within Indian culture (and in other Eastern cultures) that the loss of semen is harmful because it depletes the body of physical and mental energy (Ranjith & Mohan,

---

[1]The word *Dhat* can be loosely translated as "the elixir of life."

be the case in malingering. A number of World War II bomber pilots suffered hysterical "night blindness" that prevented them from carrying out dangerous nighttime missions. In the psychodynamic view, their "blindness" may have achieved a primary gain of shielding them from guilt associated with dropping bombs on civilian areas. It may also have achieved a secondary purpose of helping them avoid dangerous missions.

Psychodynamic theory and learning theory concur that the symptoms in conversion disorders relieve anxiety, but psychodynamic theorists seek the causes of anxiety in unconscious conflicts. However, there is little evidence to support psychodynamic theories that propose that medically unexplained symptoms such as those found in somatoform disorders are the expression of unconscious psychological conflicts (R. J. Brown, 2004).

Learning theorists focus on the more direct reinforcing properties of the symptom and its secondary role in helping the individual avoid or escape uncomfortable or anxiety-evoking situations. From the learning perspective, the symptoms in conversion and other somatoform disorders may also carry the benefits or reinforcing properties of the "sick role" (Speed & Mooney, 1997). Persons with conversion disorders may be relieved of chores and responsibilities such as going to work or performing household tasks. Being sick also usually earns sympathy and support. People who received such reinforcers during past illnesses are likely to learn to adopt a sick role even when they are not ill. We are not suggesting that people with conversion disorders are fakers. We are merely pointing out that people may learn to adopt roles that lead to reinforcing consequences, regardless of whether they deliberately seek to enact these roles.

Dhat syndrome. Found principally in India, Dhat syndrome afflicts young men with an intense fear or anxiety over the loss of semen.

2006). Like other culture-bound syndromes, Dhat must be understood within its cultural context. Based on the cultural belief in the life-preserving nature of semen, it is not surprising that some Indian males experience extreme anxiety over the involuntary loss of the fluid through nocturnal emissions.

According to Ranjith and Mohan (2006), Dhat is a form of health anxiety similar to hypochondriasis: under stress, people who are predisposed to worry about their health may focus their attention on bodily products or changes, such as turbidity of urine and tiredness. And, in light of widely held beliefs in their community, they may misattribute these bodily products or changes to loss of semen.

Culture-bound disorders such as Koro and Dhat are unlikely to remain static. The prevalence and features of such disorders probably shift along with changes in the pertinent cultures. In recent years, there have been several reports of cases of Dhat in various countries, including Western countries, which raise doubt about whether we should still consider Koro and Dhat to be culture-bound syndromes (Chandrashekar & Math, 2006).

CULTURE-BOUND DISSOCIATIVE CONDITIONS
Commonalities also exist between the Western concept of dissociative disorders and certain culture-bound syndromes found in other parts of the world. For example, *amok* is a culture-bound syndrome occurring primarily in Southeast Asian and Pacific island cultures that describes a trancelike state in which a person suddenly becomes highly excited and violently attacks other people or destroys objects. People who "run amok" may later claim to have no memory of the episode or recall feeling as if they were acting like a robot. Another example is *zar*, a term used in North African and Middle Eastern countries to describe spirit possession in people who experience dissociative states during which they engage in unusual behaviour, ranging from shouting to banging their heads against a wall. The behaviour itself is not deemed abnormal, because it is believed to be controlled by spirits.

A leading cognitive explanation of hypochondriasis focuses on the role of distorted thinking (Marcus et al., 2007; S. Taylor & Asmundson, 2004). People who develop hypochondriasis have a tendency to "make mountains out of molehills" by exaggerating the importance of their physical complaints. They misinterpret relatively minor physical complaints as signs of a serious illness, creating anxiety and leading them to chase down one doctor after another in an attempt to uncover the dreaded disease they fear they have. The anxiety itself may lead to unpleasant physical symptoms, which are likewise exaggerated in importance, leading to more worrisome thoughts.

Cognitive theorists have recently speculated that hypochondriasis and panic disorder, which often occur concurrently, may share a common cause, namely a cognitive bias to misinterpret changes in bodily cues or sensations as signs of catastrophic harm (Salkovskis & Clark, 1993). Differences between the two disorders may hinge on whether the misinterpretation of bodily cues carries a perception of imminent threat leading to a rapid spiralling of anxiety (panic disorder) or of a longer-range threat in the form of an underlying disease process (hypochondriasis). Research into cognitive processes involved in hypochondriasis deserves further study. Given the linkages that may exist between hypochondriasis and anxiety disorders such as panic disorder and OCD, it remains unclear whether hypochondriasis should be classified as a somatoform disorder or an anxiety disorder.

Treatment of Somatoform Disorders

The treatment approach that Freud pioneered—psychoanalysis—began with the treatment of hysteria, which is now termed *conversion disorder*. Psychoanalysis seeks to uncover and bring unconscious conflicts that originated in childhood into conscious awareness. Once the conflict is aired and worked through, the symptom is no longer needed as a "partial solution" to the conflict and should disappear. The psychoanalytic method is supported by case studies, some reported by Freud and others by his followers. However, the infrequency of conversion disorders in contemporary times has made it difficult to mount controlled studies of the psychoanalytic technique.

The behavioural approach to treating conversion disorders and other somatoform disorders may focus on removing sources of secondary reinforcement (or secondary gain) that may become connected with physical complaints. Family members and others, for example, often perceive individuals with somatization disorder as sickly and infirm and as incapable of carrying normal responsibilities. Other people may be unaware of how they reinforce dependent and complaining behaviours when they relieve the sick person of responsibilities. The behaviour therapist may teach family members to reward attempts to assume responsibility and ignore nagging and complaining. The behaviour therapist may also work more directly with the person who has a somatoform disorder, for example, helping the person to learn more adaptive ways of handling stress or anxiety through relaxation and cognitive restructuring (e.g., Wald et al., 2004). A lack of controlled studies in this area limits any general conclusions about the effectiveness of behavioural methods. A growing number of studies, however, indicates that cognitive-behavioural therapy (CBT) is effective in treating hypochondriasis and somatization disorder (Greeven et al., 2007; Janca, 2005; S. Taylor, Asmundson, & Coons, 2005). CBT is used to help modify the exaggerated illness-related beliefs of patients with the disorder.

Attention has recently turned to the use of antidepressants, especially SSRI medications such as fluoxetine (Prozac) and paroxetine (Paxil), in treating some types of somatoform disorder. Interestingly, both CBT and paroxetine were similarly effective for hypochondriasis in an 18-month follow-up study (Greenven et al., 2009). Although we lack specific drug therapies for conversion disorder, several studies suggest that hypochondriasis can be successfully treated with SSRI medications (Greeven et al., 2007; S. Taylor, Asmundson, & Coons, 2005). We lack any systematic studies of approaches to treating factitious disorder (Münchausen syndrome) and are limited to a few isolated case examples; for the most part, Münchausen syndrome is extremely difficult to treat and the prognosis is poor (Huffman & Stern, 2003; Slovenko, 2006).

In addition to the more formal treatment of these disorders, several self-help books are aimed at people suffering with health anxiety or hypochondriases. Two good examples are Asmundson and Taylor's *It's Not All in Your Head: How Worrying About Your Health Could Be Making You Sick—And What You Can Do About It* (2005) and Owens and Antony's *Overcoming Health Anxiety: Letting Go of Your Fear of Illness* (2011).

The dissociative and somatoform disorders remain among the most intriguing and least-understood patterns of abnormal behaviour.

REVIEW IT

Somatoform Disorders

- **What are somatoform disorders?** In somatoform disorders, there are physical complaints that cannot be accounted for by organic causes. Thus, the symptoms are theorized to reflect psychological rather than organic factors. Three types of somatoform disorders are considered: conversion disorder, hypochondriasis, and somatization disorder.

- **What are the major features of conversion disorder, hypochondriasis, and somatization disorder?** In conversion disorder, symptoms or deficits in voluntary motor or sensory functions occur that suggest an underlying physical disorder, but no apparent medical basis for the condition can be found. Hypochondriasis is a preoccupation with the fear of having or the belief that one has a serious medical illness, but no medical basis for the complaints can be found, and fears of illness persist despite medical reassurances. Formerly known as *Briquet's syndrome*, somatization disorder involves multiple and recurrent complaints of physical symptoms that persist for many years and usually begin prior to the age of 30—most typically during adolescence.

- **How are somatoform disorders conceptualized by the various theoretical perspectives?** The psychodynamic view holds that conversion disorders represent the conversion into physical symptoms of the leftover emotion or energy cut off from unacceptable or threatening impulses that the ego has prevented from reaching awareness. The symptom is functional, allowing the person to achieve both primary gains and secondary gains. Learning theorists focus on reinforcements that are associated with conversion disorders, such as the reinforcing effects of adopting a "sick role." Cognitive factors in hypochondriasis include unrealistic beliefs about health and disease.

- **How is the treatment of conversion disorder approached by the various theoretical perspectives?** Psychodynamic therapists attempt to uncover and bring to the level of awareness the unconscious conflicts, originating in childhood, that are believed to be at the root of the problem. Once the conflict is uncovered and worked through, the symptoms should disappear because they are no longer needed as a partial solution to the underlying conflict. Behavioural approaches focus on removing underlying sources of reinforcement that may be maintaining the abnormal behaviour pattern. More generally, behaviour therapists assist people with somatoform disorders to learn to handle stressful or anxiety-arousing situations more effectively.

Define It

la belle indifférence, 201
conversion disorder, 201
depersonalization, 193
depersonalization disorder, 194
derealization, 193
Dhat syndrome, 206

dissociative amnesia, 192
dissociative fugue, 192
dissociative identity disorder, 188
factitious disorder, 200
Koro syndrome, 206

malingering, 192
Münchausen syndrome, 200
primary gains, 206
secondary gains, 206
somatization disorder, 204
somatoform disorders, 199

Think About It

- Why is conversion disorder considered a treasure trove in the annals of abnormal psychology? What role did the disorder play in the development of psychological models of abnormal behaviour?

- How might you apply the diathesis-stress model in accounting for the development of dissociative identity disorder?

- Do you believe that people with dissociative identity disorder are playing a role? Why or why not?

Weblinks

Sidran Institute   www.sidran.org
The Sidran Institute's website contains information on dissociative disorders, including links to books and educational materials.

Imaginary Crimes   http://members.shaw.ca/imaginarycrimes/repressedmemory.htm
Information and links on repressed memory.

Recovered Memories   http://psych.athabascau.ca/html/aupr/psyclaw.shtml#Recovered_Memories
Contains useful links on recovered memories.

False Memory Syndrome Foundation
www.fmsonline.org
Further useful information on repressed and recovered memories and dissociative disorders.

Psychology Works for Intense Illness Concern (Hypochondriasis)   www.cpa.ca/cpasite/userfiles/Documents/factsheets/hypo.pdf
Fact sheet and links on hypochondriasis from the Canadian Psychological Association.

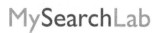

MySearchLab offers you extensive help with your writing and research projects and provides round-the-clock access to credible and reliable source material. Chapter quizzes and a full electronic version of the text are also provided. Take a tour at www.mysearchlab.com.

Dissociative and Somatoform Disorders

Dissociative Disorders

Dissociative Identity Disorder (formerly called Multiple Personality Disorder)

Features
- At least two distinct personalities
- Different personalities repeatedly take control
- Failure to recall important personal information
- Not due to drugs, alcohol, or medical condition

Theories
- Psychodynamic: Massive repression
- Diathesis-stress model
- Spanos's theory: Disorder is a form of well-ingrained role-playing, reinforced by others.

Treatments
- Psychodynamic: Goal of uncovering trauma and reintegrating personalities
- Effectiveness of any treatment remains to be established

Other important points
- Existence of disorder is controversial.
- Suggestible individuals may be led to "reveal" multiple personalities by hypnosis or by leading questions from overzealous therapists.

Dissociative Amnesia

Features
- Unable to recall important personal information
- Usually triggered by traumatic or stressful experiences
- Not due to simple forgetfulness
- Not due to drugs, alcohol, or medical condition

Theories
- Psychodynamic: Massive repression
- Learning theory: Learned avoidance
- Diathesis-stress model

Treatments
- Amnesia is usually short-lived and so treatment is usually unnecessary.

Other important points
- Amnesia can be selective or generalized.
- Can be difficult to distinguish dissociative amnesia from malingering.

Dissociative Fugue

Features
- Dissociative amnesia "on the run"
- Person travels suddenly and unexpectedly away from home and assumes new identity
- Amnesia for past identity

Theories
- Psychodynamic: Massive repression
- Learning theory: Learned avoidance
- Diathesis-stress model

Treatments
- Amnesia is usually short-lived and so treatment is usually unnecessary.

Other important points
- Flight is purposeful, not aimless wandering.
- Person is not psychotic.
- Disorder often spontaneously ends.
- Malingering must be ruled out.

Depersonalization Disorder

Features
- Recurrent/persistent depersonalization
- Reality testing is intact
- Depersonalization causes distress or impairment
- Not due to drugs, alcohol, or medical condition

Theories
- Psychodynamic: Massive repression
- Learning theory: Learned avoidance
- Diathesis-stress model

Treatments
- Cognitive-behavioural treatments and some medications show promise

Other important points
- Depersonalization may be associated with derealization.
- Isolated episodes of depersonalization and derealization are common experiences in normal people.

>>

Somatoform Disorders

Conversion Disorder (formerly called Hysteria)

Features
- Symptoms/deficits suggesting a physical disorder
- Psychological factors are judged to contribute to the disorder
- Not due to purposefully producing the symptoms
- Not due to other factors (e.g., not a physical disorder)
- Symptoms cause significant distress/impairment

Theories
- Psychodynamic: Expression of unconscious conflict
- Learning theory: Reinforcement for sick role

Treatments
- Psychodynamic, cognitive-behavioural, and other treatments, although little is known about the efficacy of these interventions

Other important points
- Not due to malingering or factitious disorder or to an undiagnosed physical disorder such as a neurological disease

Hypochondriasis

Features
- Persistent fear/preoccupation that one has a serious illness
- Fear/preoccupation persists despite medical reassurance
- Causes significant distress/impairment
- Not due to some other disorder

Theories
- Psychodynamic: Expression of unconscious conflict
- Learning theory: Reinforcement for sick role
- Cognitive theory: Role of dysfunctional beliefs and misinterpretations of harmless bodily sensations

Treatments
- Cognitive-behavioural therapy
- Particular medications such as SSRIs

Other important points
- Not due to malingering or factitious disorder

Somatization Disorder (formerly called Briquet's Syndrome)

Features
- Multiple, recurrent, medically unexplained physical symptoms involving multiple organ systems
- Persists for many years
- Causes significant distress/impairment and frequent medical consultations

Theories
- Psychodynamic: Expression of unconscious conflict
- Learning theory: Reinforcement for sick role
- Cognitive theory: Role of dysfunctional beliefs and misinterpretations of harmless bodily sensations

Treatments
- Cognitive-behavioural therapy
- Particular medications such as SSRIs

Other important points
- Not due to malingering or factitious disorder

6

Personality Disorders

CHAPTER OUTLINE

Types of Personality Disorders
Personality Disorders Characterized by Odd or
    Eccentric Behaviour
Personality Disorders Characterized by Dramatic,
    Emotional, or Erratic Behaviour
Personality Disorders Characterized by Anxious
    or Fearful Behaviour
Problems with the Classification of Personality
    Disorders

Theoretical Perspectives
Psychodynamic Perspectives
Learning Perspectives
Family Perspectives
Cognitive-Behavioural Perspectives
Biological Perspectives
Sociocultural Views

Treatment
Psychodynamic Approaches
Behavioural Approaches
Biological Approaches
Canadian Treatment Services

Did You Know That...

- Warning signs of personality disorders may begin appearing in childhood, even during the preschool years?

- People with schizoid personalities may develop stronger attachments to animals than to people?

- Not all people with psychopathic personalities are lawbreakers; some are very successful in their chosen, lawful occupations?

- Many notable figures in history, from Lawrence of Arabia to Adolf Hitler and even Marilyn Monroe, have been depicted as borderline personalities?

- Adults with dependent personalities may have such difficulty making independent decisions that they allow their parents to decide whom they will or will not marry?

- It is often difficult to draw the line between normal variations in behaviour and personality disorders?

- The conceptualization of certain types of personality disorders may be sexist?

- Despite a veneer of self-importance, people with narcissistic personalities may harbour deep feelings of insecurity?

- Identical twins reared apart show remarkable similarity in psychopathic traits?

A ll of us have particular styles of behaviour and ways of relating to others. Some of us are orderly; others, sloppy. Some of us prefer solitary pursuits; others are more social. Some of us are followers; others, leaders. Some of us seem immune to rejection by others, whereas others avoid social initiatives for fear of getting shot down. When behaviour patterns become so inflexible or maladaptive that they cause significant personal distress or impair people's social or occupational functioning, they may be diagnosed as personality disorders.

TYPES OF PERSONALITY DISORDERS

In most of us by the age of thirty, the character has set like plaster, and will never soften again.

—William James

personality disorders Types of abnormal behaviour patterns involving excessively rigid patterns of behaviour or ways of relating to others that ultimately become self-defeating because their rigidity prevents adjustment to external demands.

ego syntonic Behaviour or feelings that are perceived as natural or compatible parts of the self.

ego dystonic Behaviour or feelings that are perceived to be foreign or alien to one's self-identity.

Personality disorders are excessively rigid patterns of behaviour or ways of relating to others. Their rigidity prevents people from adjusting to external demands; thus, they ultimately become self-defeating. Disordered personality traits become evident by adolescence or early adulthood and continue through much of adult life, becoming so deeply ingrained that they are highly resistant to change. The warning signs of personality disorders may be detected during childhood, even in the troubled behaviour of preschoolers. Children with childhood behaviour problems such as conduct disorder, depression, anxiety, and immaturity are at greater than average risk of developing personality disorders during adolescence (D. P. Bernstein, Cohen, Skodol, Bezirganian, & Brook, 1996).

Despite the self-defeating consequences of their behaviour, people with personality disorders do not generally perceive a need to change. Using psychodynamic terms, the DSM notes that people with personality disorders tend to perceive their traits as **ego syntonic**—as natural parts of themselves. As a result, persons with personality disorders are more likely to be brought to the attention of mental health professionals by others than to seek services themselves. In contrast, persons with anxiety disorders or mood disorders tend to view their disturbed behaviour as **ego dystonic**. They do not see their behaviour as parts of their self-identities and are thus more likely to seek help to relieve the distress caused by it.

The DSM groups clinical syndromes on Axis I and personality disorders on Axis II. Both clinical syndromes and personality disorders may thus be diagnosed in clients whose behaviours meet the criteria for both classes of disorders. A person may have an Axis I mood disorder, for example, such as major depression, and also show the more enduring characteristics associated with an Axis II personality disorder.

The DSM groups personality disorders into three clusters:

Cluster A: People who are perceived as odd or eccentric. This cluster includes paranoid, schizoid, and schizotypal personality disorders.

Cluster B: People whose behaviour is overly dramatic, emotional, or erratic. This grouping consists of antisocial, borderline, histrionic, and narcissistic personality disorders.

Cluster C: People who often appear anxious or fearful. This cluster includes avoidant, dependent, and obsessive-compulsive personality disorders.

Personality Disorders Characterized by Odd or Eccentric Behaviour

This group of personality disorders includes paranoid, schizoid, and schizotypal disorders. People with these disorders often have difficulty relating to others, or may show little or no interest in developing social relationships.

The DSM-5, due in May 2013, will include significant changes in personality disorder assessment. The reviewers have proposed a revised definition for personality disorder, reduced the number of disorders from 10 to 6, updated criteria based on core impairments in personality functioning and pathological personality traits, and introduced a new measure of dysfunction called the Levels of Personality Functioning Scale.

DEFINITION CHANGE

The current definition of a personality disorder, one already referred to in this text, speaks of a pervasive and problematic pattern of thinking, emotions, and behaving. In the DSM-5, the definition will focus on personality traits that contribute to a failure to adapt, an impaired sense of self-identity, and/or a failure to develop effective interpersonal functioning. This is closer to definitions of Axis I disorders in that it refers to a failure to adapt to the demands of everyday life.

SIX PERSONALITY DISORDERS

Instead of the current 10 personality disorders, in the DSM-5 there will be 6: antisocial/psychopathic, avoidant, borderline, narcissistic, obsessive-compulsive, and schizotypal types. A clinician will now have a rating system of 1 to 5 to indicate how closely the individual matches the description (1 = not at all, 5 = extremely).

TRAITS AND FACETS

Based on the well-researched Five-Factor Model of Personality, the DSM-5 will include six personality "trait domains" in addition to the six personality disorders: negative emotionality, introversion, antagonism, disinhibition, compulsivity, and schizotypy. Again, clinicians will be asked to rate each of the six domains on a scale of 0 to 3, depending on how descriptive each is of the patient. Next, the level of disturbance of each trait domain will be measured by the Levels of Personality Functioning Scale. This will help to determine the individual's impairment in self-functioning as a result of an identified trait domain.

PARANOID PERSONALITY DISORDER   The defining trait of **paranoid personality disorder** is pervasive suspiciousness—the tendency to interpret other people's behaviour as deliberately threatening or demeaning. People with the disorder are excessively mistrustful of others, and their relationships suffer for it. They may be suspicious of co-workers and supervisors but can generally maintain employment.

The following case illustrates the unwarranted suspicion and reluctance to confide in others that typifies people with paranoid personalities:

paranoid personality disorder
Type of personality disorder characterized by persistent suspiciousness of the motives of others, but not to the point of holding clear-cut delusions.

An 85-year-old man is seen by a social worker at a senior citizens' center for evaluation of health-care needs for himself and his bedridden wife. He is apparently healthy, with no evidence of impairment in thinking or memory. He has been caring for his wife, but has been reluctantly persuaded to seek help because her condition has deteriorated, and his strength and energy have decreased with age.

A history is obtained from the subject and his daughter. He has never been treated for mental illness and in fact has always claimed to be "immune to psychological problems" and to act only on the basis of "rational" thought. He had a moderately successful career as a lawyer and businessman. He has been married for 60 years, and his wife is the only person for whom he has ever expressed tender feelings and is probably the only person he has ever trusted. He has always been extremely careful about revealing anything of himself to others, assuming that they are out to take something away from him. He refuses obviously sincere offers of help from acquaintances because he suspects their motives. He never reveals his identity to a caller without first questioning him as to the nature of his business. Throughout his life there have been numerous occasions on which he has displayed exaggerated suspiciousness, sometimes of almost delusional proportions (e.g., storing letters from a client in a secret safe deposit box so that he could use them as evidence in the event that the client attempted to sue him for mismanagement of an estate).

He has always involved himself in "useful work" during his waking hours and claims never to have time for play, even during the 20 years he has been retired. He spends many hours monitoring his stock market investments and has changed brokers several times when he suspected that minor errors on monthly statements were evidence of the brokers' attempt to cover up fraudulent deals.

Source: Reprinted with permission from the *DSM-IV-TR Case Book: A Learning Companion to the Diagnostic and Statistical Manual of Mental Disorders*, Fourth Edition, Text Revision, (Copyright ©2005). American Psychiatric Association. pp. 211–213.

People who have paranoid personalities tend to be overly sensitive to criticism, whether real or imagined. They take offence at the smallest slight. They are readily angered and hold grudges when they think they have been mistreated. They are unlikely to confide in others because they believe that personal information may be used against them. They question the sincerity and trustworthiness of friends and associates. A smile or a glance may be viewed with suspicion. As a result, they have few friends and intimate relationships. When they do form an intimate relationship, they may suspect infidelity, although there is no evidence to back up their suspicions. They tend to remain hypervigilant, as if they must be on the lookout against harm. They deny blame for misdeeds, even when warranted, and are perceived by others as cold, aloof, scheming, devious, and humourless. They tend to be argumentative and may launch repeated lawsuits against those who they believe have mistreated them.

Clinicians need to weigh cultural and sociopolitical factors when arriving at a diagnosis of paranoid personality disorder. They may find members of immigrant or ethnic minority groups, political refugees, or people from other cultures to be guarded or defensive in their behaviour. This behaviour may, however, reflect unfamiliarity with the language, customs, or rules and regulations of the majority culture or a cultural mistrust arising from a history of neglect or oppression. Such behaviour should not be confused with paranoid personality disorder (APA, 2000a).

Although the suspicions of people with paranoid personality disorder are exaggerated and unwarranted, there is an absence of the outright paranoid delusions that characterize the thought patterns of people with paranoid schizophrenia (e.g., believing the RCMP are out to get them). People who have paranoid personalities are unlikely to seek treatment for themselves; they see others as causing their problems. The reported prevalence of paranoid personality disorder in the general population ranges from 0.5% to 2.5% (APA, 2000a). The disorder is diagnosed in clinical samples more often in men than women.

schizoid personality disorder
Type of personality disorder characterized by a persistent lack of interest in social relationships, flattened affect, and social withdrawal.

Schizoid personality. It is normal to be reserved about displaying one's feelings, especially when one is among strangers, but people with schizoid personalities rarely express emotions and are distant and aloof. Yet the emotions of people with schizoid personalities are not as shallow or blunted as they are in people with schizophrenia.

SCHIZOID PERSONALITY DISORDER Social isolation is the cardinal feature of **schizoid personality disorder**. Often described as a loner or an eccentric, the person with a schizoid personality lacks interest in social relationships. The emotions of persons with schizoid personalities appear shallow or blunted, but not to the degree found in schizophrenia (see Chapter 10, "Schizophrenia"). People with this disorder seem to rarely, if ever, experience strong anger, joy, or sadness. They look distant and aloof. Their faces tend to show no emotional expression, and they rarely exchange social smiles or nods. They seem indifferent to criticism or praise and appear to be wrapped up in abstract ideas rather than in thoughts about people. Although they prefer to remain distant from others, they maintain better contact with reality than do people with schizophrenia. The prevalence of the disorder in the general population remains unknown. Men with schizoid personality disorder rarely date or marry. Women who have it are more likely to accept romantic advances passively and marry, but they seldom initiate relationships or develop strong attachments to their partners.

Akhtar (1987, 2003) claims there may be discrepancies between outer appearances and the inner lives of people with schizoid personalities. Although they may appear to have little appetite for sex, for example, they may harbour voyeuristic wishes and become attracted to pornography. Akhtar also suggests that the distance and social aloofness of people with schizoid personalities could be somewhat superficial. They may also harbour exquisite sensitivity, deep curiosities about people, and wishes for love that they cannot express. In some cases, sensitivity is expressed in deep feelings for animals rather than people.

SCHIZOTYPAL PERSONALITY DISORDER Schizotypal personality disorder usually becomes evident by early adulthood. The diagnosis applies to people who have difficulties forming close relationships and whose behaviour, mannerisms, and thought patterns are peculiar or odd but not disturbed enough to merit a diagnosis of schizophrenia. They may be especially anxious in social situations, even when interacting with familiar people. Their social anxieties seem to be associated with paranoid thinking (e.g., fears that others mean them harm) rather than concerns about being rejected or evaluated negatively by others (APA, 2000a).

Schizotypal personality disorder is believed to be slightly more common in males and is thought to affect about 3% of the general population (APA, 2000a). Clinicians need to be careful not to label certain behaviour patterns that reflect culturally determined beliefs or religious rituals as schizotypal, such as beliefs in voodoo and other magical beliefs.

The eccentricity associated with the schizoid personality is limited to a lack of interest in social relationships. Schizotypal personality disorder refers to a wider range of odd behaviour, beliefs, and perceptions. Persons with the disorder may experience unusual perceptions or illusions, such as feeling the presence of a deceased family member in the room. They realize, however, that the person is not actually there. They may become unduly suspicious of others or paranoid in their thinking. They may develop **ideas of reference**, such as the belief that other people are talking about them. They may engage in "magical thinking," such as believing they possess a "sixth sense" (i.e., can foretell the future) or that others can sense their feelings. They may attach unusual meanings to words. Their own speech may be vague or unusually abstract but not so much that it becomes incoherent or filled with the loose associations that characterize schizophrenia. They may appear unkempt, display unusual mannerisms, and engage in unusual behaviour such as talking to themselves in the presence of others. Their faces may register little emotion. Like people with schizoid personalities, they may fail to exchange smiles with or nod at others. They may appear silly and smile and laugh at the wrong times. They tend to be socially withdrawn and aloof, with few if any close friends or confidants. They seem to be especially anxious around unfamiliar people.

Some of these features are found in the case of Nisar:

Nisar, a 27-year-old auto mechanic, had few friends and preferred science fiction novels to socializing with other people. He seldom joined in conversations. At times, he seemed to be lost in his thoughts, and his co-workers would have to whistle to get his attention when he was working on a car. He often showed a "queer" expression on his face. Perhaps the most unusual feature of his behaviour was his reported intermittent experience of "feeling" his deceased mother standing nearby. These illusions were reassuring to him, and he looked forward to their occurrence. Nisar realized they were not real. He never tried to reach out to touch the apparition, knowing it would disappear as soon as he drew closer. It was enough, he said, to feel her presence.

The Authors' Files

schizotypal personality disorder Type of personality disorder characterized by eccentricities or oddities of thought and behaviour but without clearly psychotic features.

ideas of reference Form of delusional thinking in which a person reads personal meaning into the behaviour of others or external events that are completely independent of the person.

Despite the DSM's grouping of schizotypal behaviour with personality disorders, the schizotypal behaviour pattern may fall within a spectrum of schizophrenia-related disorders that also includes paranoid and schizoid personality disorders, schizoaffective disorder (discussed in Chapter 10), and schizophrenia itself. Schizotypal personality disorder may actually share a common genetic basis with schizophrenia (Kendler & Walsh, 1995; Siever & Davis, 2004). Let us note, however, that schizotypal personality disorder tends to follow a chronic course, and relatively few people diagnosed with the disorder go on to develop schizophrenia or other psychotic disorders (APA, 2000a). Perhaps the emergence of schizophrenia in persons with this shared genetic predisposition is determined by such factors as stressful early family relationships.

Personality Disorders Characterized by Dramatic, Emotional, or Erratic Behaviour

This cluster of personality disorders includes the antisocial, borderline, histrionic, and narcissistic types. The behaviour patterns of these types are excessive, unpredictable, or self-centred. People with these disorders have difficulty forming and maintaining relationships.

Much of our attention in this section focuses on antisocial personality disorder. Historically, it is the personality disorder that has been most extensively studied by scholars and researchers.

antisocial personality disorder
Type of personality disorder characterized by a chronic pattern of antisocial and irresponsible behaviour and lack of remorse. Abbreviated *APD*.

ANTISOCIAL PERSONALITY DISORDER (AND PSYCHOPATHY) People with **antisocial personality disorder** (APD) persistently violate the rights of others and often break the law. They disregard social norms and conventions, are impulsive, and fail to live up to interpersonal and vocational commitments. Yet they often show a superficial charm and are at least average in intelligence (Cleckley, 1976). Perhaps the features that are most striking about them are their low levels of anxiety in threatening situations and their lack of guilt or remorse following wrongdoing. Punishment seems to have little if any effect on their behaviour. Although parents and others have usually punished them for their misdeeds, they persist in leading irresponsible and impulsive lives.

Men are more likely than women to receive diagnoses of APD (Cale & Lilienfeld, 2002). The prevalence rate for the disorder in Canada is estimated to be about 1.7% to 3.7% (Bland, Newman, & Orn, 1988; Bland, Orn, & Newman, 1988; Offord et al., 1996) (see Table 6.1). In a study of psychiatric disorders in Ontario, Offord and colleagues (1996) found a one-year prevalence rate of 2.9% in males and 0.5% in females. Although the prevalence of the disorder has been rising in both genders in recent years, it has been climbing even more sharply among women (APA, 2000a). For a diagnosis of APD to be applied, the person must be at least 18 years of age. The alternative diagnosis of conduct disorder is used for younger people (see Chapter 11, "Abnormal Behaviour Across the Lifespan"). Many children with conduct disorders do not continue to show antisocial behaviour as adults.

TABLE 6.1

Estimates of Lifetime Prevalence of Antisocial Personality Disorder in the Canadian General and Forensic Populations (percentage with disorder)

	Males		Females	
General Population	**General Population**	**Incarcerated**	**General Population**	**Incarcerated**
1.7% to 3.7%	3%	37.8% to 56.9% (meets stringent criteria)	1.0% to 1.2%	29.0% to 36.8% (meets stringent criteria)

Sources: Blanchette, 1996; Bland, Newman, & Orn, 1988; Bland, Orn, & Newman, 1988; Correctional Services Canada, 2002b; Gove, 1979; Motiuk & Porporino, 1991; Offord et al., 1996.

We once used terms like *psychopath* and *sociopath* to refer to the type of people who are commonly classified as having antisocial personalities—people whose behaviour is amoral and asocial, impulsive, and lacking in remorse and shame. The roots of the word *psychopath* focus on the idea that something is amiss (pathological) in the individual's psychological functioning. The roots of sociopathy centre on the person's social deviance. The DSM criteria for APD focus more on elements of criminal actions (e.g., those that involve antisocial behaviour and social deviance) than on the traditional elements of **psychopathy** that emphasize emotional (e.g., callousness and a lack of the normal pangs of guilt, anxiety, and remorse) and interpersonal traits (e.g., superficial charm and manipulative behaviour) (Hare, 1996a, 1996b; Harpur & Hare, 1994). The pattern of behaviour that characterizes both APD and psychopathic personality begins in childhood or adolescence and extends into adulthood.

With the widespread clinical use of the DSM-IV-TR, the traditional conception of the personality construct psychopathy was overshadowed (Hare, Hart, & Harpur, 1991). University of British Columbia psychologist Robert Hare devised the Psychopathy Checklist–Revised (PCL-R), which is used to identify and diagnose psychopaths and determine their degree of psychopathy. The PCL-R measures interpersonal and affective traits such as callousness, selfishness, and the remorseless use of others (known as Factor 1 subfactors, which are closely related to the traditional concept of psychopathy). It also measures impulsive lifestyle and antisocial behaviour traits (known as Factor 2 subfactors, which are associated with the concept of the antisocial personality). Although the two factors are related, they have important distinctions that have significant implications for mental health treatment and recidivism rates of dangerous criminal offenders (Hare, 1996a, 1996b; Serin, 1998).

Profile of the Antisocial Personality Common features of people with APD include failure to conform to social norms, irresponsibility, aimlessness and lack of long-term goals or plans, impulsive behaviour, outright lawlessness, violence, chronic unemployment, marital problems, lack of remorse or empathy, substance abuse, a history of alcoholism, and a disregard for the truth and for the feelings and needs of others (Patrick, Cuthbert, & Lang, 1994; Robins, Tipp, & Przybeck, 1991; S. S. Smith & Newman, 1990). Irresponsibility may be seen in a personal history dotted by repeated, unexplained absences from work, abandonment of jobs without having other job opportunities to fall back on, or long stretches of unemployment despite available job opportunities. Irresponsibility extends to financial matters, where there may be repeated failure to repay debts, pay child support, or meet other financial responsibilities to one's family and dependants. The diagnostic features of APD, as defined in the DSM, are shown in Table 6.2 on page 220.

Profile of the Psychopathic Personality Hervey Cleckley (1941) showed that the characteristics defining the psychopathic personality—self-centredness, irresponsibility, impulsivity, and insensitivity to the needs of others—exist not only among criminals but also among many respected members of the community, including doctors, lawyers, politicians, and business executives. Hare's Psychopathy Checklist–Revised has been shown to be a valid and reliable predictor of psychopathy in both criminal and noncriminal populations (Hare, 1996a; Hart & Hare, 1997; Hare, Hart, & Harpur, 1991). The PCL-R measures the main aspects of psychopathy, and it was found that the Factor 1 personality traits associated with psychopathy seem to remain stable across a lifespan. In contrast, the Factor 2 antisocial behaviours that are more closely associated with APD as diagnosed by the DSM criteria tend to decline with age and may actually disappear by the time a person reaches the age of 40 (Harpur & Hare, 1994).

Antisocial personality. Serial killer Paul Bernardo killed without feeling or remorse and displayed some of the superficial charm seen in some people with antisocial personality disorder.

psychopathy Type of personality pattern characterized by affective and interpersonal traits, such as shallow emotions, selfishness, arrogance, superficial charm, deceitfulness, manipulativeness, irresponsibility, sensation seeking, and a lack of empathy, anxiety, and remorse, combined with persistent violations of social norms, a socially deviant and nomadic lifestyle, and impulsiveness.

TABLE 6.2

Diagnostic Criteria for Antisocial Personality Disorder

A. There is a pervasive pattern of disregard for and violation of the rights of others occurring since age 15 years, as indicated by three (or more) of the following:

   (1) failure to conform to social norms with respect to lawful behaviors as indicated by repeatedly performing acts that are grounds for arrest

   (2) deceitfulness, as indicated by repeated lying, use of aliases, or conning others for personal profit or pleasure

   (3) impulsivity or failure to plan ahead

   (4) irritability and aggressiveness, as indicated by repeated physical fights or assaults

   (5) reckless disregard for safety of self or others

   (6) consistent irresponsibility, as indicated by repeated failure to sustain consistent work behavior or honor financial obligations

   (7) lack of remorse, as indicated by being indifferent to or rationalizing having hurt, mistreated, or stolen from another

B. The individual is at least age 18 years.

C. There is evidence of Conduct Disorder (see p. 98) with onset before age 15 years.

D. The occurrence of antisocial behavior is not exclusively during the course of Schizophrenia or a Manic Episode.

Source: Reprinted with permission from the *Diagnostic and Statistical Manual of Mental Disorders*, Fourth Edition, Text Revision, (Copyright ©2000). American Psychiatric Association. p. 706.

Antisocial Behaviour, Psychopathy, and Criminality   We may tend to think of psychopathic behaviour as synonymous with criminal behaviour. Although there is a strong relationship between the two, not all criminals show signs of psychopathy and only a minority of people with psychopathic personalities become criminals (Hare, 1996b; Lilienfeld & Andrews, 1996). Many psychopaths are law-abiding and quite successful in their chosen occupations, yet they possess a personality style characterized by a callous disregard of the interests and feelings of others.

Investigators have begun to view psychopathic personality as composed of two somewhat independent factors. The first is a personality factor. It consists of such traits as superficial charm, selfishness, lack of empathy, and callous and remorseless use of others and disregard of their feelings and welfare. This psychopathic personality factor applies to people who have these kinds of psychopathic traits but generally manage to avoid coming into contact with the law. In one study, Hart and Hare (1989) estimated that only 12.5% of a Canadian correctional population sample was rated as psychopathic, in comparison to 50% who were diagnosed with APD. In fact, psychopathic individuals possess those very qualities that allow them to charm and take advantage of co-workers on their way to the top chief executive positions in business, politics, and other social institutions (Babiak, 1995; Hare 1996b). In recent years, media accounts have abounded trying to explain how a number of top corporate executives could have arrived at the point where they fraudulently reaped millions, and in some cases billions, of dollars from their own companies, which not only devastated employees, shareholders, and other stakeholders, but undermined the world economy. A common question is whether, or to what extent, these corrupt albeit exceedingly wealthy leaders were psychopathic (English 2002; Gettler, 2003; Hercz, 2001).

The second factor is considered a behavioural dimension. It is characterized by the adoption of an unstable and antisocial lifestyle, including frequent problems with the law, poor employment history, and unstable relationships, and is more closely aligned with APD (Hare, Hart, & Harpur, 1991). These two factors are not entirely separate—many psychopathic individuals show evidence of both sets of traits.

We should also note that people may become criminals or delinquents not because of a disordered personality but because they were reared in environments or subcultures that encouraged and rewarded criminal behaviour (Hare, 1986b). The criminal behaviour of a professional thief or drug pusher, although antisocial, does not in itself justify a diagnosis of APD. Canadian studies indicate that criminal and aggressive behaviour have multiple causes and represent many personality styles in both male and female offenders (Laishes, 2002). Although the behaviour of criminals is deviant to society at large, it may be normal by the standards of their subcultures. We should also recognize that lack of remorse, a cardinal feature of APD, does not characterize all criminals. Some criminals regret their crimes, and evidence of remorse is considered when a sentence is passed.

Nearly twice as many males as females are diagnosed with APD in Canadian prisons (see Table 6.1 on page 218). Proportionally, far fewer psychopaths than APD individuals are imprisoned. Psychopaths who do enter the correctional system, such as Clifford Olson, Paul Bernardo, and Karla Homolka, are much more likely to have committed serious, violent, cold-blooded serial offences (Hare, 1996b; Hare, Hart, & Harpur, 1991). It should not come as a surprise that psychopaths are overrepresented in maximum-security penitentiaries in Canada (Motiuk & Porporino, 1991). In addition, psychopaths who scored high on the PCL-R had the highest rates of both recidivism (80%) and violent recidivism (25%). They reoffended within an average span of 30 months (Correctional Services Canada, 2002b).

Sociocultural Factors and Antisocial Personality Disorder   Antisocial personality disorder cuts across all racial and ethnic groups. Researchers find no evidence of ethnic or racial differences in the rates of the disorder (Robins, Tipp, & Przybeck, 1991). The disorder is more common, however, among people with lower socioeconomic status (SES). One explanation is that people with APD may drift downward occupationally, perhaps because their antisocial behaviour makes it difficult for them to hold steady jobs or progress upward. It is possible, too, that people from lower SES levels are more likely to have been reared by parents who themselves modelled antisocial behaviour. However, it is also possible that the diagnosis is misapplied to people living in hard-pressed communities who may engage in seemingly antisocial behaviour as a type of defence strategy in order to survive (APA, 2000a).

Psychophysiological and Biological Factors Associated with Antisocial Personality and Psychopathy   There are several psychophysiological and biological factors that are related to antisocial personality and psychopathy:

1. *Lack of emotional responsiveness.* People with antisocial personalities can maintain their composure in stressful situations that would induce anxiety in most people (Cleckley, 1976). Lack of anxiety in response to threatening situations may help explain the failure of punishment to induce antisocial people to relinquish their behaviour. For most of us, the fear of getting caught and being punished is sufficient to inhibit antisocial impulses. People with antisocial personalities, however, often fail to inhibit behaviour that has led to punishment in the past (P. A. Arnett, Smith, & Newman, 1997). They may not learn to inhibit antisocial or aggressive behaviour because they experience little if any fear or anticipatory anxiety about being caught and punished.

   In an early classic study, Lykken (1957) showed that prison inmates with antisocial personalities performed more poorly than normal controls on a shock-avoidance task, although their general learning ability did not differ from that of normals. The shock-avoidance task involved learning responses to avoid getting a mild electric shock. Lykken reasoned that the inmates who had antisocial personalities were less able to learn avoidance responses because they experienced unusually low levels of anxiety in anticipation of the shock.

   When people get anxious, their palms tend to sweat. This skin response, called the galvanic skin response (GSR), is a sign of activation of the sympathetic branch of the autonomic nervous system (ANS). In an early study, Hare (1965) showed that people with antisocial personalities had lower GSR levels when they were expecting painful stimuli than did normal controls. Apparently, people with antisocial personalities experienced little anxiety in anticipation of impending pain.

   Hare's findings of a weaker GSR response in anticipation of an aversive stimulus in people with antisocial personalities has been replicated a number of times (e.g., P. A. Arnett, 1997; Patrick et al., 1994). Other research generally supports the view that people with antisocial personalities are generally less aroused than others both at times of rest and in situations in which they are faced with stress (Fowles, 1993). This lack of emotional responsivity may help explain why the threat of punishment seems to have little effect on deterring their antisocial behaviour. It is conceivable that the autonomic nervous systems of people with antisocial personalities are underresponsive to threatening stimuli.

2. *The craving-for-stimulation model.* Other investigators have attempted to explain the antisocial personality's lack of emotional response in terms of the levels of stimulation necessary to maintain an **optimum level of arousal.** Our optimum levels of arousal are the degrees of arousal at which we feel best and function most efficiently.

Psychopathic individuals appear to have exaggerated cravings for stimulation (P. A. Arnett et al., 1997). Perhaps they require a higher-than-normal threshold of stimulation to maintain an optimum state of arousal (Quay, 1965). That is, they may need more stimulation than other people to function normally.

A need for higher levels of stimulation may explain why people with psychopathic traits tend to become bored more easily than other people and more often gravitate to more stimulating but potentially dangerous activities, such as the use of intoxicants (such as drugs or alcohol), motorcycling, skydiving, high-stakes gambling, or sexual adventures. A higher-than-normal threshold for stimulation would not directly cause antisocial or criminal behaviour; after all, part of the "right stuff" of respected astronauts includes sensation seeking. However, threat of boredom and inability to tolerate monotony may influence some sensation seekers to drift into crime or reckless behaviour (S. B. Smith, 1983).

3. *Lack of restraint on impulsivity.* Other research on brainwave functions shows lower levels of activity in the frontal lobes of the cerebral cortex in men with APD (Deckel, Hesselbrock, & Bauer, 1996). The frontal cortex plays a key role in inhibiting impulsive behaviour, which may help explain why people with antisocial personalities have difficulty controlling impulsive or aggressive behaviour. Some theorists have speculated that the cerebral cortex may mature more slowly in people with antisocial personalities (Reid, 1986).

4. *Limbic abnormalities.* As described above, one of the distinguishing features of psychopathic personalities is a dysfunctional processing of emotional information. A recent study of the brain's limbic system using magnetic resonance imaging (MRI) compared both criminal nonpsychopaths and noncriminal control participants with criminal psychopaths while they performed an affective memory task (Kiehl et al., 2001). Results revealed that criminal psychopaths showed significantly less brain activity in the emotional parts of the brain found within the limbic system but showed overstimulation in areas of the frontal-temporal lobes that are associated with processing and regulating emotional information. This suggests that the emotional irregularities found in psychopathic offenders may be tied to diminished input from brain structures within the limbic system.

BORDERLINE PERSONALITY DISORDER Borderline personality disorder (BPD) is primarily characterized by a pervasive pattern of instability in relationships, self-image, and mood and a lack of control over impulses. People with BPD tend to be uncertain about their values, goals, loyalties, careers, choices of friends, and perhaps even sexual orientations. This instability in self-image or identity leaves them with persistent feelings of emptiness and boredom. They cannot tolerate being alone and will make desperate attempts to avoid feelings of abandonment (Gunderson, 1996).

optimum level of arousal Level of arousal associated with peak performance and maximum feelings of well-being.

borderline personality disorder Type of personality disorder characterized by abrupt shifts in mood, lack of a coherent sense of self, and unpredictable, impulsive behaviour. Abbreviated *BPD*.

Borderline personality disorder. World War II dictator Adolf Hitler lived—and died—by the Nazi principle of "death before dishonour"—arguably a form of the "all-or-nothing" thinking characteristic of BPD.

Fear of abandonment renders them clinging and demanding in their social relationships, but their clinging often pushes away the people on whom they depend. Signs of rejection may enrage them, straining their relationships further. Their feelings toward others are consequently intense and shifting. They alternate between extremes of adulation (when their needs are met) and loathing (when they feel neglected). They tend to view other people as all good or all bad, shifting abruptly from one extreme to the other. As a result, they may flit from partner to partner in a series of brief and stormy relationships. People they had idealized are treated with contempt when relationships end or when they feel the other person fails to meet their needs (Gunderson, 2001).

Many notable figures have been described as having personality features associated with borderline personality disorder, including Marilyn Monroe, T. E. Lawrence (Lawrence of Arabia), Adolf Hitler, and the philosopher Søren Kierkegaard (Sass, 1982). Some theorists believe we live in highly fragmented and alienating times that tend to create the problems in forming cohesive identities and stable relationships that characterize people with borderline personalities (Sass, 1982). "Living on the edge" or border can be seen as

QUESTIONNAIRE

The Sensation-Seeking Scale

Do you crave stimulation or seek sensation? Are you satisfied by reading or watching television, or must you ride the big wave or bounce your motorbike over desert dunes? Zuckerman (1980) finds four factors related to sensation seeking: (1) pursuit of thrill and adventure, (2) disinhibition (that is, proclivity to express impulses), (3) pursuit of experience, and (4) susceptibility to boredom. Although some sensation seekers get involved with drugs or encounter trouble with the law, many are law-abiding and limit their sensation seeking to sanctioned activities. Thus, sensation seeking should not be interpreted as criminal or antisocial in itself.

Zuckerman developed several sensation-seeking scales that assess the levels of stimulation people seek in order to feel their best and function efficiently. A brief form of one of them follows. To assess your own sensation-seeking tendencies, pick the choice, A or B, that best depicts you. Then compare your responses to those on page 246.

1. A. I would like a job that requires a lot of travel.
   B. I would prefer a job in one location.
2. A. I am invigorated by a brisk, cold day.
   B. I can't wait to get indoors on a cold day.
3. A. I get bored seeing the same old faces.
   B. I like the comfortable familiarity of everyday friends.
4. A. I would prefer to live in an ideal society in which everyone is safe, secure, and happy.
   B. I would have preferred living in the unsettled days of our history.
5. A. I sometimes like to do things that are a little frightening.
   B. A sensible person avoids activities that are dangerous.

6. A. I would not like to be hypnotized.
   B. I would like to have the experience of being hypnotized.
7. A. The most important goal in life is to live it to the fullest and experience as much as possible.
   B. The most important goal in life is to find peace and happiness.
8. A. I would like to try parachute jumping.
   B. I would never want to try jumping out of a plane, with or without a parachute.
9. A. I enter cold water gradually, giving myself time to get used to it.
   B. I like to dive or jump right into the ocean or a cold pool.
10. A. When I go on a vacation, I prefer the change of camping out.
    B. When I go on a vacation, I prefer the comfort of a good room and bed.
11. A. I prefer people who are emotionally expressive, even if they are a bit unstable.
    B. I prefer people who are calm and even-tempered.
12. A. A good painting should shock or jolt the senses.
    B. A good painting should give one a feeling of peace and security.
13. A. People who ride motorcycles must have some kind of unconscious need to hurt themselves.
    B. I would like to drive or ride a motorcycle.

Source: Zuckerman, 2007, pp. 1303–1305. Copyright Elsevier. Reprinted with permission.

a metaphor for an unstable society. Borderline personality disorder is believed to occur in about 2% of the general population (APA, 2000a). Although it is diagnosed more often (about 75% of the time) in women, gender differences in prevalence rates for BPD in the general population remain undetermined.

The term *borderline personality* was originally used to refer to individuals whose behaviour appeared to be on the border between neuroses and psychoses. People with BPD generally maintain better contact with reality than people with psychoses, although they may show transient psychotic behaviour during times of stress. Generally speaking, they seem to be more severely impaired than most people with neuroses but not as dysfunctional as those with psychotic disorders.

Borderline personality disorder may actually lie closer to mood disorders than psychotic disorders. Many individuals diagnosed with BPD also meet diagnostic criteria for mood disorders, such as major depression and bipolar disorder. Some researchers, however, find weaker links between borderline personality and depression, so connections remain somewhat muddled (Gunderson & Phillips, 1991). Many people with BPD also meet criteria for other personality disorders. University of Toronto researcher Paul Links and his colleagues conducted a seven-year follow-up study of a Canadian sample of BPD patients. They found that those patients with persistent symptoms of the disorder were more likely to have coexisting personality disorders than those patients who were in remittance for BPD, including avoidant (59.2%), self-defeating (40.7%), passive-aggressive (37%), dependent (33.3%), and histrionic (25.9%) symptoms (Links, Heslegrave, & van Reekum, 1998). Other investigators have found that in addition to meeting the DSM criteria for a variety of personality disorders, patients with BPD share the personality dimensions of neuroticism, impulsivity, anxiousness, affective liability, and insecure attachment (Skodol, Gunderson, et al., 2002; Skodol, Siever, et al., 2002).

Instability of moods is a central characteristic of borderline personality disorder. Moods run the gamut from anger and irritability to depression and anxiety, and may shift frequently and abruptly (Koenigsberg et al., 2002). Other features of BPD are ongoing anger, loneliness, boredom, a deep sense of emptiness, and impulsivity (Hochhausen, Lorenz, & Newman, 2002; Zanarini, Frankenburg, Hennen, & Silk, 2003). People with BPD have difficulty controlling anger and are prone to fights or smashing things. They often act on impulse, like eloping with someone they have just met. This impulsive and unpredictable behaviour can often be self-destructive and is linked to a risk of suicidal attempts and gestures (e.g., Sanislow, Grilo, & McGlashan, 2000). It may also involve spending sprees, gambling, drug abuse, engaging in unsafe sexual activity, reckless driving, binge eating, or shoplifting. People with BPD sometimes partake in impulsive acts of self-mutilation, such as scratching their wrists or burning cigarettes on their arms, as in this young woman's case:

> Client: I've got such repressed anger in me; what happens is ... I can't feel it; I get anxiety attacks. I get very nervous, smoke too many cigarettes. So what happens to me is I tend to explode. Into tears or hurting myself or whatever ... because I don't know how to contend with all those mixed up feelings.
>
> Interviewer: What was the more recent example of such an explosion?
>
> Client: I was alone at home a few months ago; I was frightened! I was trying to get in touch with my boyfriend and I couldn't.... He was nowhere to be found. All my friends seemed to be busy that night and I had no one to talk to.... I just got more and more nervous and more and more agitated. Finally, bang!—I took out a cigarette and lit it and stuck it into my forearm. I don't know why I did it because I didn't really care for him all that much. I guess I felt I had to do something dramatic....
>
> M. H. Stone, 1980, p. 400. Copyright 1980 by The McGraw-Hill Companies. Reprinted with permission.

Self-mutilation is sometimes carried out as an expression of anger or a means of manipulating others. Such acts may be intended to counteract self-reported feelings of "numbness," particularly in times of stress. Not surprisingly, frequent self-mutilation among people with BPD is associated with an increased risk of suicidal thinking (Dulit, Fyer, Leon, Brodsky, & Frances, 1994).

Individuals with BPD tend to have very troubled relationships with their families of origin and others. Commonly, BPD patients remember traumatic childhood experiences, ranging from their parents being neglectful or abusive to parental losses or separations (Liotti & Pasquini 2000; Paris & Frank, 1989). Additionally, there is an association between documented childhood sexual abuse and the later development of BPD (J. G. Johnson, Cohen, Brown, Smailes, & Bernstein, 1999). Patients with BPD tend to view their relationships as rife with hostility and to perceive others as rejecting and abandoning (Benjamin & Wonderlich, 1994). They also tend to be difficult to work with in psychotherapy, demanding a great deal of support from therapists and calling them at all hours or acting suicidal to elicit support. They tend to drop out early from psychotherapy (Aronson, 1989), but those who have a coexisting mood disorder are more amenable to treatment (Pope, Jones, Hudson, Cohen, & Gunderson, 1983). Their behaviour toward therapists, as toward other people, undergoes rapid alterations between adulation and outrage. These abrupt shifts in feelings are interpreted by psychoanalysts as signs of "splitting," or an inability to reconcile the positive and negative aspects of one's experiences of oneself and others.

From the modern psychodynamic perspective, borderline individuals cannot synthesize positive and negative elements of personality into complete wholes. They therefore fail to achieve fixed self-identities or images of others. Rather than viewing important figures in their lives as sometimes loving, sometimes rejecting, they shift back and forth between viewing them as all good or all bad, between idealization and abhorrence. The psychoanalyst Otto Kernberg, a leading authority on borderline personality, tells of a woman in her 30s whose attitude toward him vacillated in such a way. According to Kernberg, the woman would respond to him in one session as if he was the most wonderful therapist, feeling that all her problems were solved. But several sessions later, she would turn against him and accuse him of being unfeeling and manipulative, become very dissatisfied with the treatment she was receiving, and threaten to drop out and never come back (Sass, 1982). A review by a leading BPD researcher, psychiatrist Joel Paris of McGill University (2005), found that structured psychodynamic therapies as well as a range of other interpersonal and cognitive therapies are more effective in the long-term treatment of BPD than are pharmacological interventions.

Paris conducted an extensive review of 170 recent articles on BPD and determined that about 1 in 10 BPD patients commits suicide (Paris, 2002a). Another study found that early death from all causes approaches a rate of 1 in 5 (Paris, 2002b). As for the persistence of the disorder, Paris followed up the long-term outcomes of 64 patients with BPD at 15- and 27-year time periods. He found that in the long term, a slight majority of BPD patients no longer met the full criteria for the disorder. Moreover, most BPD patients showed improvement leading up to and beyond the ages of 40 and 50 (Paris & Zweig-Frank, 2001).

HISTRIONIC PERSONALITY DISORDER Histrionic personality disorder involves excessive emotionality and the necessity to be the centre of attention. The term is derived from the Latin *histrio*, which means "actor." People with histrionic personality disorder tend to be dramatic and emotional, but their emotions seem shallow, exaggerated, and volatile. The disorder was formerly called hysterical personality. The supplanting of hysterical with histrionic and the associated exchange of the roots *hystera* (meaning "uterus") and *histrio* allow professionals to distance themselves from the notion that the disorder is intricately bound up with being female. The disorder is diagnosed more frequently in women than men, however (Hartung & Widiger, 1998). Some studies, using structured interview methods, find similar rates of occurrence among men and women (APA, 2000a). Whether the gender discrepancy in clinical practice reflects true differences in the underlying rates of the disorder, diagnostic biases, or other unseen factors remains something of an open question (Corbitt & Widiger, 1995).

histrionic personality disorder
Type of personality disorder characterized by excessive need to be the centre of attention and to receive reassurance, praise, and approval from others. Such persons often appear overly dramatic and emotional in their behaviour.

Despite a long-standing belief among clinicians that histrionic personality is closely related to conversion disorder, research has not borne out this connection (Kellner, 1992). People with conversion disorder are actually more likely to show features of dependent personality disorder than histrionic personality disorder.

People with histrionic personalities may become unusually upset by news of a sad event and cancel plans for the evening, inconveniencing their friends. They may exude exaggerated delight when they meet someone or become enraged when someone fails to notice their new hairstyle. They may faint at the sight of blood or blush at a slight faux pas. They tend to demand that others meet their needs for attention and play the victim when others fall short. If they feel a touch of fever, they may insist that others drop everything to rush them to a doctor. They tend to be self-centred and intolerant of delays of gratification; they want what they want when they want it. They grow quickly restless with routine and crave novelty and stimulation. They are drawn to fads. Others may see them as putting on airs or play-acting, although they may show a certain charm. They may enter a room with a flourish and embellish their experiences with flair. When pressed for details, however, they fail to colour in the specifics of their tales. They tend to be flirtatious and seductive but are too wrapped up in themselves to develop intimate relationships or have deep feelings toward others. As a result, their associations tend to be stormy and ultimately ungratifying. They tend to use their physical appearance as a means of drawing attention to themselves. Men with the disorder may act and dress in an overly "macho" manner to draw attention to themselves; women may choose very frilly, feminine clothing. Glitter supersedes substance.

People with histrionic personalities may be attracted to professions like modelling or acting, where they can hog the spotlight. Despite outward successes, they may lack self-esteem and strive to impress others to boost their self-worth. If they suffer setbacks or lose their place in the limelight, depressing inner doubts may emerge. The case of Marcella shows some of these features:

> Marcella was a 36-year-old attractive but overly made-up woman who was dressed in tight pants and high heels. Her hair was in a bird's nest of the type that had been popular when she was a teenager. Her social life seemed to bounce from relationship to relationship, from crisis to crisis. Marcella sought help from a psychologist at this time because her 17-year-old daughter, Natasha, had just been hospitalized for cutting her wrists. Natasha lived with Marcella and her mother's current boyfriend, Morris, and there were constant arguments in the apartment. Marcella recounted the disputes that took place with high drama, waving her hands, clanging the bangles that hung from her wrists, and clutching her breast. It was difficult having Natasha live at home, because Natasha had expensive tastes, was "always looking for attention," and flirted with Morris as a way of "flaunting her youth." Marcella saw herself as a doting mother and denied any possibility that she was in competition with her daughter.
>
> Marcella came for a handful of sessions, during which she basically vented her feelings and was encouraged to make decisions that might lead to a reduction of some of the pressures on her and her daughter. At the end of each session, she said, "I feel so much better," and thanked the psychologist profusely. At termination of "therapy," she took the psychologist's hand and squeezed it endearingly. "Thank you so much, doctor," she said, and made her exit.
>
> The Authors' Files

Marcella also showed a number of features of narcissism, which we discuss next.

NARCISSISTIC PERSONALITY DISORDER Narkissos was a handsome youth who, according to Greek myth, fell in love with his reflection in a spring. Because of his excessive self-love, in one version of the myth, he was transformed by the gods into the flower we know as the narcissus.

Persons with **narcissistic personality disorder** have an inflated or grandiose sense of themselves and an extreme need for admiration. They brag about their accomplishments

narcissistic personality disorder Type of personality disorder characterized by the adoption of an inflated self-image and demands for constant attention and admiration, among other features.

and expect others to shower them with praise and notice their special qualities, even when their accomplishments are ordinary. Narcissists enjoy basking in the light of adulation; they are self-absorbed and tend to lack empathy for others. Although they share certain features with histrionic personalities, such as demanding to be the centre of attention, they have a much more inflated view of themselves and are less melodramatic than people with histrionic personality disorder. The label of borderline personality disorder is sometimes applied to them, but people with narcissistic personality disorder are generally better able to organize their thoughts and actions. They tend to be more successful in their careers and better able to rise to positions of status and power. Their relationships tend to be more stable than those of people with BPD.

Narcissistic personality disorder is believed to occur in less than 1% of the general population (APA, 2000a). Although more than half of the people diagnosed with the disorder are men, we cannot say whether there is an underlying gender difference in the prevalence rates of the general population. A certain degree of narcissism or self-aggrandizement may represent a healthful adjustment to insecurity, a shield from criticism and failure, or a motive for achievement (Goleman, 1988). Excessive narcissistic qualities can become unhealthy, especially when cravings for adulation are insatiable. Table 6.3 compares "normal" self-interest with self-defeating extremes of narcissism. Up to a point, self-interest fosters success and happiness. In more extreme cases, as with narcissism, it can compromise relationships and careers.

People with narcissistic personalities tend to be preoccupied with fantasies of success and power, ideal love, or recognition for brilliance or beauty. They, like people with histrionic personalities, may gravitate toward careers in which they can receive adulation, such as modelling, acting, or politics. Although they tend to exaggerate their accomplishments and abilities, many people with narcissistic personalities are quite successful in their occupations but envy those who

Narkissos. According to one version of the Greek myth, Narkissos fell in love with his reflection in a spring. Because of his excessive self-love, the gods transformed him into a flower—the narcissus.

TABLE 6.3

Healthy Narcissism and Destructive Narcissism

Healthy Narcissism	Destructive Narcissism
Has healthy confidence and self-esteem but does not value him- or herself more than others.	Tends to exaggerate achievements or talents; believes he or she is special.
Is assertive yet takes into consideration others' perspectives.	Expects constant praise and admiration from others.
Shares in the emotional lives of others.	Has great difficulty receiving any sort of criticism; has fragile self-esteem.
May enjoy positions of power but does not think he or she is better than others.	Believes he or she is better than others; relationships are self-serving.
After failure, feels dissatisfied but not worthless.	Experiences of failure are felt as extremely degrading.
Being criticized prompts self-evaluation but does not shake emotional stability.	Criticism produces excessive aggravation and self-focus.

achieve even greater success. Insatiable ambition may prompt them to devote themselves tirelessly to work. They are driven to succeed, not so much for money as for the adulation that attends success.

Their interpersonal relationships are invariably strained by the demands they impose on others and by their lack of empathy with and concern for other people. They seek the company of flatterers and are often superficially charming and friendly and able to draw people to them. But their interest in people is one-sided: they seek people who will serve their interests and nourish their sense of self-importance (Goleman, 1988). They have a sense of entitlement that leads them to exploit others. They treat sex partners as devices for their own pleasure or to brace their self-esteem.

The case of Devon illustrates several features of the narcissistic personality:

> Most people agreed that Devon, a 35-year-old investment banker, had a certain charm. He was bright, articulate, and attractive. He possessed a keen sense of humour that drew people to him at social gatherings. He would always position himself in the middle of the room, where he could be the centre of attention. The topics of conversation invariably focused on his "deals," the "rich and famous" people he had met, and his outmanoeuvring of opponents. His next project was always bigger and more daring than the last. Devon loved an audience. His face would light up when others responded to him with praise or admiration for his business successes, which were always inflated beyond their true measure. But when the conversation shifted to other people, he would lose interest and excuse himself to make a drink or to call his answering machine. When hosting a party, he would urge guests to stay late and feel hurt if they had to leave early; he showed no sensitivity to or awareness of the needs of his friends.
>
> The few friends he had maintained over the years had come to accept Devon on his own terms. They recognized that he needed to have his ego fed or that he would become cool and detached.
>
> Devon had also had a series of romantic relationships with women who were willing to play the adoring admirer and make the sacrifices that he demanded—for a time. But they inevitably tired of the one-sided relationship or grew frustrated by Devon's inability to make a commitment or feel deeply toward them. Lacking empathy, Devon was unable to recognize other people's feelings and needs. His demands for constant attention from willing admirers derived not from selfishness but from a need to ward off underlying feelings of inadequacy and diminished self-esteem. It was sad, his friends thought, that Devon needed so much attention and adulation from others and that his many achievements were never enough to calm his inner doubts.
>
> The Authors' Files

Personality Disorders Characterized by Anxious or Fearful Behaviour

This cluster of personality disorders includes the avoidant, dependent, and obsessive-compulsive types. Although the features of these disorders differ, they share a component of fear or anxiety.

avoidant personality disorder
Type of personality disorder characterized by avoidance of social relationships due to fears of rejection.

AVOIDANT PERSONALITY DISORDER Persons with **avoidant personality disorder** are so terrified of rejection and criticism that they are generally unwilling to enter relationships without ardent reassurances of acceptance. As a result, they may have few close relationships outside their immediate families. They also tend to avoid group occupational or recreational activities for fear of rejection. They prefer to eat lunch alone at their desks. They shun company picnics and parties, unless they are perfectly sure of acceptance. Avoidant personality disorder, which appears to be equally common in men and women, is believed to affect between 0.5% and 1.0% of the general population (APA, 2000a).

Unlike people with schizoid qualities, with whom they share the feature of social withdrawal, individuals with avoidant personalities have interest in and feelings of warmth toward other people. However, fear of rejection prevents them from striving to meet their needs for affection and acceptance. In social situations, they tend to hug the walls and avoid conversing with others. They fear public embarrassment—the thought that others might see them blush, cry, or act nervously. They tend to stick to their routines and exaggerate the risks or effort involved in trying new things. They may refuse to attend a party that is an hour away on the pretext that the late drive home would be too taxing.

The case of Jamie illustrates several of the features of the avoidant personality:

Jamie, a 24-year-old accounting clerk, had dated only a few women, and he had met them through family introductions. He never felt confident enough to approach a woman on his own. Perhaps it was his shyness that first attracted Loren. A 22-year-old secretary, she worked alongside Jamie and asked him if he would like to get together some time after work. At first Jamie declined, claiming some excuse, but when Loren asked again a week later, Jamie agreed, thinking she must really like him if she were willing to pursue him. The relationship developed quickly, and soon they were dating virtually every night. The relationship was strained, however. Jamie interpreted any slight hesitation in her voice as a lack of interest. He repeatedly requested reassurance that she cared about him and evaluated every word and gesture for evidence of her feelings. If Loren said she could not see him because of fatigue or illness, Jamie assumed she was rejecting him and sought reassurance. After several months, Loren decided she could no longer accept Jamie's nagging, and the relationship ended. Jamie assumed that Loren had never truly cared for him.

The Authors' Files

There is a good deal of overlap between avoidant personality disorder and social phobia, particularly with a severe subtype of social phobia that involves a generalized pattern of social phobia (excessive, irrational fear of most social situations) (Herbert, Hope, & Bellack, 1992; Turner, Beidel, & Townsley, 1992; Widiger, 1992). Although research evidence shows that many cases of generalized social phobia occur in the absence of avoidant personality disorder (Holt, Heimberg, & Hope, 1992), relatively fewer cases of avoidant personality occur in the absence of generalized social phobia (Widiger, 1992). Thus, avoidant personality disorder may represent a more severe form of social phobia (Hofman, Newman, Ehlers, & Roth, 1995). Still, the scientific jury is out on the question of whether avoidant personality disorder should be considered a severe form of generalized social phobia or a distinct diagnostic category, as it is presently classified.

DEPENDENT PERSONALITY DISORDER Dependent personality disorder describes people who have an excessive need to be taken care of by others. This leads them to be overly submissive and clinging in their relationships and extremely fearful of separation. People with this disorder find it very difficult to do things on their own. They seek advice in making even the smallest decision. Children or adolescents with the problem may look to their parents to select their clothes, diets, schools or universities, even their friends. Adults with the disorder allow others to make important decisions for them. Sometimes, they are so dependent on others for making decisions that they allow their parents to determine whom they will or will not marry, as in the case of Matthew:

Matthew is a 34-year-old single man who lives with his mother and works as an accountant. He is seeking treatment because he is very unhappy after having just broken up with his girlfriend. His mother had disapproved of his marriage plans, ostensibly because the woman was of a different religion. Matthew felt trapped and forced to choose between his mother and his girlfriend, and

dependent personality disorder
Type of personality disorder characterized by difficulties making independent decisions and by overly dependent behaviour.

because "blood is thicker than water," he had decided not to go against his mother's wishes. Nonetheless, he is angry at himself and at her and believes that she will never let him marry and is possessively hanging on to him. His mother "wears the pants" in the family and is a very domineering woman who is used to getting her way. Matthew is afraid of disagreeing with his mother for fear that she will not be supportive of him and he will then have to fend for himself. He criticizes himself for being weak, but also admires his mother and respects her judgment—"Maybe Carol wasn't right for me after all." He alternates between resentment and a "Mother knows best" attitude. He feels that his own judgment is poor.

Matthew works at a job several grades below what his education and talent would permit. On several occasions he has turned down promotions because he didn't want the responsibility of having to supervise other people or make independent decisions. He has worked for the same boss for 10 years, gets on well with him, and is, in turn, highly regarded as a dependable and unobtrusive worker. He has two very close friends whom he has had since early childhood. He has lunch with one of them every single workday and feels lost if his friend is sick and misses a day.

Matthew is the youngest of four children and the only boy. He was "babied and spoiled" by his mother and elder sisters. He had considerable separation anxiety as a child—he had difficulty falling asleep unless his mother stayed in the room, mild school refusal, and unbearable homesickness when he occasionally tried "sleepovers." As a child he was teased by other boys because of his lack of assertiveness and was often called a baby. He has lived at home his whole life except for 1 year of college, from which he returned because of homesickness. His heterosexual adjustment has been normal except for his inability to leave his mother in favor of another woman.

Source: Reprinted with permission from the *DSM-IV-TR Case Book: A Learning Companion to the Diagnostic and Statistical Manual of Mental Disorders*, Fourth Edition, Text Revision, (Copyright ©2005). American Psychiatric Association. pp. 179–180.

After marriage, people with dependent personality disorder may rely on their spouses to make decisions such as where they should live, which neighbours they should befriend, how they should discipline their children, what jobs they should take, how they should budget money, and where they should vacation. Like Matthew, individuals with dependent personality disorder avoid positions of responsibility. They turn down challenges and promotions and work beneath their potential. They tend to be overly sensitive to criticism and are preoccupied with fears of rejection and abandonment. They may be devastated by the end of a close relationship or by the prospect of living on their own. Because of a fear of rejection, they often subordinate their wants and needs to those of others. They may agree with outlandish statements about themselves and do degrading things in order to please others.

Although dependent personality disorder is diagnosed more frequently in women (APA, 2000a; Bornstein, 1997), it is not clear that there is an underlying difference in the prevalence of the disorder between men and women (Corbitt & Widiger, 1995). The diagnosis is often applied to women who, for fear of abandonment, tolerate husbands who openly cheat on them, abuse them, or gamble away family resources. Underlying feelings of inadequacy and helplessness discourage them from taking effective action. In a vicious circle, their passivity encourages further abuse, leading them to feel yet more inadequate and helpless. The diagnosis of women with this disorder is controversial and may be seen as unfairly "blaming the victim" because women in our society are often socialized into more dependent roles. A panel convened by the American Psychological Association noted that women also encounter greater stress than men in contemporary life (Goleman, 1990). Women are more likely than men to be subjected to second-class citizenship, which may set the stage for dependency.

Dependent personality disorder has been linked to other psychological disorders, including major depression, bipolar disorder, and social phobia, and to physical problems such as hypertension, cancer, and gastrointestinal disorders such as ulcers and colitis (Bornstein, 1999). There also appears to be a link between dependent personality and what psychodynamic theorists refer to as "oral" behaviour problems, such as smoking, eating disorders, and alcoholism (Bornstein, 1993, 1999). Psychodynamic writers trace dependent behaviour to the utter dependence of a newborn baby and the baby's seeking of nourishment through oral means (suckling). From infancy, they suggest, people associate provision of food with love. Food may come to symbolize love, and persons with dependent personalities may overeat to symbolically ingest love (R. P. Greenberg & Bornstein, 1988a, 1988b).

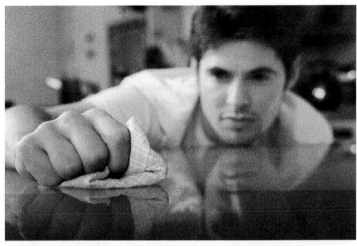

"A place for everything, and everything in its place"? People with obsessive-compulsive personalities may have invented this maxim. Many such people have excessive needs for orderliness in their environment.

Research shows that people with dependent personalities are more reliant on other people for support and guidance than the average person (R. P. Greenberg & Bornstein, 1988a). People with dependent personalities often attribute their problems to physical rather than emotional causes and seek support and advice from medical experts rather than psychologists or counsellors (R. P. Greenberg & Bornstein, 1988b).

OBSESSIVE-COMPULSIVE PERSONALITY DISORDER The defining features of **obsessive-compulsive personality disorder** involve an excessive degree of orderliness, perfectionism, rigidity, difficulty coping with ambiguity, difficulties expressing feelings, and meticulousness in work habits. About 1% of people in community samples are diagnosed with the disorder (APA, 2000a). The disorder is about twice as common in men than women. Unlike obsessive-compulsive anxiety disorder, people with obsessive-compulsive personality disorder do not necessarily experience outright obsessions or compulsions. If they do, both diagnoses may be deemed appropriate.

Persons with obsessive-compulsive personality disorder are so preoccupied with perfection that they cannot complete things in a timely fashion. Their efforts inevitably fall short of their expectations and they force themselves to redo their work. Or they may ruminate about how to prioritize their assignments and never seem to get started working. They focus on details that others perceive as trivial. As the saying goes, they often fail to see the forest for the trees. Their rigidity impairs their social relationships; they insist on doing things their way rather than compromising. Their zeal for work keeps them from participating in or enjoying social and leisure activities. They tend to be stingy with money. They find it difficult to make decisions and postpone or avoid them for fear of making the wrong choice. They tend to be overly rigid in issues of morality and ethics because of inflexibility in personality rather than deeply held convictions. They tend to be overly formal in relationships and find it difficult to express feelings. It is hard for them to relax and enjoy pleasant activities; they worry about the costs of such diversions.

Consider the case of Andrew:

> Andrew, a 34-year-old systems analyst, was perfectionistic, overly concerned with details, and rigid in his behaviour. Andrew was married to Teja, a graphic artist. He insisted on scheduling their free time hour by hour and became unnerved when they deviated from his agenda. He would circle a parking lot repeatedly in search of just the right parking spot to ensure that another car would not scrape his car. He refused to have the apartment painted for over a year because he couldn't decide on the colour. He had arranged all the books on their bookshelf alphabetically and insisted that every book be placed in its proper position.

obsessive-compulsive personality disorder Type of personality disorder characterized by rigid ways of relating to others, perfectionistic tendencies, lack of spontaneity, and excessive attention to details.

Andrew never seemed to be able to relax. Even on vacation, he was bothered by thoughts of work that he had left behind and by fears that he might lose his job. He couldn't understand how people could lie on a beach and let all their worries evaporate in the summer air. Something can always go wrong, he figured, so how can people let themselves go?

The Authors' Files

Problems With the Classification of Personality Disorders

Questions remain about the reliability and validity of the diagnostic categories for personality disorders. There may be too much overlap among the diagnoses to justify so many different categories. Agreement between raters on personality disorder diagnoses remains modest at best (Coolidge & Segal, 1998). The classification system also seems to blur the distinctions between normal and abnormal variations in personality. Moreover, some categories of personality disorder may be based on sexist presumptions.

UNDETERMINED RELIABILITY AND VALIDITY   The present DSM system sought to remove ambiguities in the diagnostic criteria of personality disorders in earlier editions by providing descriptive criteria that more tightly define particular disorders. The reliability and validity of the definitions used in DSM-IV remains to be fully tested, however (Livesley, 2001).

PROBLEMS DISTINGUISHING AXIS I FROM AXIS II DISORDERS   Some commentators on the DSM system question whether there is sufficient justification for placing personality disorders and clinical syndromes on separate axes—Axis I and Axis II, respectively (R. F. Farmer, 2000). University of British Columbia psychiatrist John Livesley, a leading expert on personality disorders, questions the assumption that personality

NORMAL/ABNORMAL BEHAVIOUR

Normal Perfectionism: No Disorder	OCPD: Disorder
Carley had always been a high achiever. She got straight A's in high school, played on several sports teams, and was student council president. Her parents told her stories of how she had been a high achiever even as a small child. For example, if she went out of the lines while colouring, she would start the picture over. She always spent a lot of time on her school work, making sure she had completed it properly and had done her best. Her quality of work was rewarded—teachers were always thrilled to have Carley in their classes and regularly praised her neat and thorough work. At university, Carley continued to have high expectations for herself. She often prioritized her school work and readings over socializing, making sure that her assignments were done before she went out. At the beginning of university, Carley would often rewrite lecture notes to make them neater, but soon realized that she did not have enough time to do this for all lectures. Instead, she decided to bring her laptop to lectures so that her notes would be neatly typed. Her room in residence was the neatest room on the floor, and her friends in residence often teased her about how everything in her room was "perfect." Carley was able to laugh at herself and identified with being a "perfectionist."	Danish is a 50-year-old divorced man who lives in a small house by himself. He works as an accountant. He and his former wife divorced 15 years ago after having years of relationship stress. The couple would constantly fight about their different styles—Julia being laid back and relaxed, Danish being uptight and perfectionistic. At first, Julia would tease Danish about his stubbornness and need for things to be done "his way." However, this gentle teasing soon gave way to real frustration and resentment. Danish would often start projects around the house but was unable to finish them after getting stuck on a detail. For example, it took Danish two months to install a closet organization system because he wanted to ensure that all the screws were even and installed "properly." "Properly" to Danish meant that things were done his way. A huge source of frustration between the two was Danish's judgmental style. He had a strict moral code, and often made snide judgmental remarks about things Julia had said or done. Since the couple divorced, Danish continued to have difficulty in relationships, and so had stopped dating. He had few friends, as many of his old friends found him to be inflexible and judgmental toward them.

disorders are discriminable from clinical syndromes such as anxiety or depressive disorders (Livesley, 2001). First, for example, it may be difficult to distinguish in actual practice between obsessive-compulsive disorder and obsessive-compulsive personality disorder. Second, clinical syndromes are believed to be variable over time, whereas personality disorders are held to be generally more enduring patterns of disturbance. Yet evidence indicates that features of personality disorders may vary over time with changes in circumstances. On the other hand, some Axis I clinical syndromes (dysthymia, for example) follow a more or less chronic course.

OVERLAP AMONG DISORDERS Psychologists Brian O'Connor of Lakehead University and Jamie Dyce of Concordia University College of Alberta contend that not only are the diagnostic criteria for any given category of personality disorder broader than they are for other psychological disorders, but there is also a high degree of overlap among the personality disorders. Moreover, a person does not have to satisfy all the diagnostic criteria in order to be diagnosed with a personality disorder (O'Connor & Dyce, 2001). Overlap undermines the DSM's conceptual clarity or purity by increasing the number of cases that seem to fit two or more diagnostic categories (Livesley, 2001). Although some personality disorders have distinct features, many appear to share common traits. For example, the same person may have traits suggestive of dependent personality disorder (inability to make decisions or initiate activities independently) and of avoidant personality disorder (extreme social anxiety and heightened sensitivity to criticism). One study found that as many as 25% of people with schizoid personality disorders could also be diagnosed as having avoidant personality disorder (Reich & Noyes, 1986). Another reported that in a sample of people with borderline personality disorder, nearly one in four (23%) also met criteria for APD (Hudziak et al., 1996). Overall, roughly two out of three people with personality disorders meet diagnostic criteria for more than one type of personality disorder (Widiger, 1991). The high degree of overlap suggests that the personality disorders included in the DSM system may not be sufficiently distinct from one another (Westen & Shedler, 1999). Some so-called disorders may thus represent different aspects of the same disorder, not separate diagnostic categories. To account for this lack of distinction, the updated version—the DSM-5—will reduce the number of personality disorders from 10 to 6.

DIFFICULTY IN DISTINGUISHING BETWEEN VARIATIONS IN NORMAL BEHAVIOUR AND ABNORMAL BEHAVIOUR Another problem with the diagnosis of personality disorders is that they involve traits that, in lesser degrees, describe the behaviour of most normal individuals. Feeling suspicious now and then does not mean you have a paranoid personality disorder. The tendency to exaggerate your own importance does not mean you are narcissistic. You may avoid social interactions for fear of embarrassment or rejection without having an avoidant personality disorder, and you may be especially conscientious in your work without having an obsessive-compulsive personality disorder. Because the defining attributes of these disorders are commonly occurring personality traits, clinicians should apply these diagnostic labels only when the patterns are so pervasive that they interfere with the individual's functioning or cause significant personal distress. Yet it can be difficult to know where to draw the line between normal variations in behaviour and personality disorders. We continue to lack the data to more precisely determine the point at which a trait becomes sufficiently inflexible or maladaptive to justify a personality disorder diagnosis (Livesley, 2001).

Livesley and his colleagues (Livesley, Jang, & Vernon, 1998) provide evidence that personality traits sit on a continuum and that the extremes of some personality dimensions may signal dysfunction or maladjustment. From this dimensional perspective, disordered patterns of personality are considered variations of normal personality patterns. But it's not just extremeness that distinguishes normal from disordered personality patterns. For instance, being extremely sociable may not be such a bad thing. Livesley (1998) suggests that the definition of personality disorder should also include measurable dysfunctions in one or more of the following three domains: the self system (the stable and integrated sense of oneself and others), interpersonal relationships (intimate relationships and affiliation with others), and societal relationships (prosocial behaviours and co-operative relationships).

SEXIST BIASES The construction of certain personality disorders may have sexist under-pinnings. For example, diagnostic criteria for personality disorders label stereotypical feminine behaviour as pathological with greater frequency than is the case with stereotypical masculine behaviour. The concept of the histrionic personality seems a caricature of the traditional stereotype of the feminine personality: flighty, emotional, shallow, seductive, attention seeking. But if the feminine stereotype corresponds to a mental disorder, shouldn't we also have a diagnostic category that reflects the masculine stereotype of the "macho male"? It may be possible to show that overly masculinized traits are associated with significant distress or impairment in social or occupational functioning in certain males. Highly masculinized males often get into fights and experience difficulties working for female bosses. There is no personality disorder that corresponds to the macho male stereotype, however.

The diagnosis of dependent personality disorder may also unfairly stigmatize women who are socialized into dependent roles as having a "mental disorder." Women may be at a greater risk of receiving diagnoses of histrionic or dependent personality disorders because clinicians perceive these patterns as existing more commonly among women or because women are more likely than men to be socialized into these behaviour patterns. Clinicians may also be biased in favour of perceiving women as having histrionic personality disorder and men as having antisocial personality disorder even when the men and women in question do not differ in symptomatology (Garb, 1997).

Clinicians may also have a gender bias when it comes to diagnosing borderline personality disorder. In one study, researchers presented a hypothetical case example to a sample of 311 psychologists, social workers, and psychiatrists (Becker & Lamb, 1994). Half of the sample was presented with a case identified as a female; the other half read the identical case except that it was identified as male. Clinicians more often diagnosed the case identified as female as having borderline personality disorder.

All in all, personality disorders are convenient labels for identifying common patterns of ineffective and ultimately self-defeating behaviour, but labels do not explain their causes. Still, the development of an accurate descriptive system is an important step toward scientific explanation. The establishment of reliable diagnostic categories sets the stage for valid research into causation and treatment.

REVIEW IT

Types of Personality Disorders

- **What are personality disorders?** Personality disorders are maladaptive or rigid behaviour patterns or personality traits associated with states of personal distress that impair a person's ability to function in social or occupational roles. People with personality disorders do not generally recognize a need to change themselves.

- **What are the classes of personality disorders within the DSM system?** The DSM categorizes personality disorders according to the following clusters of characteristics: odd or eccentric behaviour; dramatic, emotional, or erratic behaviour; anxious or fearful behaviour.

- **What are the features associated with personality disorders characterized by odd or eccentric behaviour?** People with paranoid personality disorder are unduly suspicious and mistrustful of others, to the point that their relationships suffer. But they do not hold the more flagrant paranoid delusions typical of schizophrenia. Schizoid personality disorder describes people who have little if any interest in social relationships, show a restricted range of emotional expression, and appear distant and aloof. People with

schizotypal personalities appear odd or eccentric in their thoughts, mannerisms, and behaviour, but not to the degree found in schizophrenia.

- **What are the features associated with personality disorders characterized by dramatic, emotional, or erratic behaviour?** Antisocial personality disorder describes people who persistently engage in behaviour that violates social norms and the rights of others and who tend to show no remorse for their misdeeds. The psychopathic personality includes affective and interpersonal traits that when combined with criminality are often associated with persistent, senseless, and violent behaviour. Borderline personality disorder is defined in terms of instability in self-image, relationships, and mood. People with borderline personality disorder often engage in impulsive acts, which are frequently self-destructive. People with histrionic personality disorder tend to be highly dramatic and emotional in their behaviour, whereas people diagnosed with narcissistic personality disorder have an inflated or grandiose sense of self and, like those with histrionic personalities, demand to be the centre of attention.

- **What are the features associated with personality disorders characterized by anxious or fearful behaviour?** Avoidant personality disorder describes people who are so terrified of rejection and criticism that they are generally unwilling to enter relationships without unusually strong reassurances of acceptance. People with dependent personality disorder are overly dependent on others and have extreme difficulty acting independently or making even the smallest decisions on their own. People with obsessive-compulsive personality disorder have various traits such as orderliness, perfectionism, rigidity,

and excessive attention to detail but are without the true obsessions and compulsions associated with obsessive-compulsive (anxiety) disorder.

- **What are some problems associated with the classification of personality disorders?** Various controversies and problems attend the classification of personality disorders, including a lack of demonstrated reliability and validity, too much overlap among the categories, difficulty in distinguishing between variations in normal behaviour and abnormal behaviour, and underlying sexist biases in certain categories.

THEORETICAL PERSPECTIVES

In this section, we consider the theoretical perspectives on personality disorders. Many of the theoretical accounts of disturbed personality derive from the psychodynamic model. We thus begin with a review of traditional and modern psychodynamic models.

Psychodynamic Perspectives

Traditional Freudian theory focused on problems arising from the Oedipus complex as the foundation for many abnormal behaviours, including personality disorders. Freud (1905/1962) believed that children normally resolve the Oedipus complex by forsaking incestuous wishes for the parent of the opposite gender and identifying with the parent of the same gender. As a result, they incorporate the parent's moral principles in the form of a personality structure called the *superego*. Many factors may interfere with appropriate identification, however, such as having a weak or absent father or an antisocial parent. These factors may sidetrack the normal developmental process, preventing children from developing the moral constraints that prevent antisocial behaviour and the feelings of guilt or remorse that normally follow behaviour that is hurtful to others.

More recent psychodynamic theories have generally focused on the earlier, pre-Oedipal period of about 18 months to 3 years of age, during which infants are theorized to begin to develop their identities as separate from those of their parents. These recent advances in psychodynamic theory focus on the development of the sense of self in explaining such disorders as narcissistic and borderline personality disorders.

HEINZ KOHUT One of the principal shapers of modern psychodynamic concepts was Heinz Kohut (1913–1981), whose views are labelled **self psychology**. Kohut focused much of his attention on the development of the narcissistic personality.

Kohut (1966) believed that people with narcissistic personalities may mount a facade of self-importance to cover up deep feelings of inadequacy. Kohut maintained that early childhood is characterized by a normal stage of "healthful narcissism." Infants feel powerful, as though the world revolves around them. Infants also normally perceive older people, especially parents, as idealized towers of strength and wish to be one with them to share their power. Empathic parents reflect their children's inflated perceptions by making them feel that anything is possible and by nourishing their self-esteem (e.g., telling them how terrific and precious they are). Even empathic parents are critical from time to time, however, and puncture their children's grandiose sense of self. Or they fail to measure up to their children's idealized views of them. Gradually, unrealistic expectations dissolve and are replaced by more realistic appraisals. This process of childhood narcissism that eventually gives way to more realistic appraisals of self and others is perfectly normal. Earlier grandiose self-images form the basis for assertiveness later in childhood and set the stage for ambitious striving in adulthood. In adolescence, childhood idealization is transformed into realistic admiration for parents, teachers, and friends. In adulthood, these ideas develop into a set of internal ideals, values, and goals.

self psychology Hans Kohut's theory that describes processes that normally lead to the achievement of a cohesive sense of self or, in narcissistic personality disorder, to a grandiose but fragile sense of self.

Lack of parental empathy and support, however, sets the stage for pathological narcissism in adulthood. Children who are not prized by their parents may fail to develop a sturdy sense of self-esteem. They may be unable to tolerate even slight blows to their self-worth. They develop damaged self-concepts and feel incapable of being loved and admired because of perceived inadequacies or flaws. Pathological narcissism involves the construction of a grandiose facade of self-perfection that is merely a shell to cloak perceived inadequacies. The facade always remains on the brink of crumbling, however, and must be continually shored up by a constant flow of reassurance that one is special and unique. This leaves the person vulnerable to painful blows to self-esteem following failure to achieve social or occupational goals. Being so needy of constant approval, a person with a narcissistic personality may fly into a rage when he or she feels slighted in any way.

OTTO KERNBERG Modern psychodynamic views of the borderline personality also trace the disorder to difficulties in the development of the self in early childhood. Kernberg (1975), a leading psychodynamic theorist (born 1928), views borderline personality in terms of a pre-Oedipal failure to develop a sense of constancy and unity in one's image of the self and others. Kernberg proposes that childhood failure to synthesize these contradictory images of good and bad results in a failure to develop a consistent self-image and in tendencies toward **splitting**—shifting back and forth between viewing oneself and other people as "all good" or "all bad."

In Kernberg's view, parents, even excellent parents, invariably fail to meet all their children's needs. Infants therefore face the early developmental challenge of reconciling images of the nurturing, comforting "good mother" with those of the withholding, frustrating "bad mother." Failure to reconcile these opposing images into a realistic, unified, and stable parental image may fixate children in the pre-Oedipal period. As adults, then, they may retain these rapidly shifting attitudes toward their therapists and others.

MARGARET MAHLER Mahler (1897–1985), another influential modern psychodynamic theorist, explained borderline personality disorder in terms of childhood separation from the mother figure. Mahler and her colleagues (Mahler & Kaplan, 1977) believed that during the first year, an infant develops a **symbiotic** attachment to his or her mother. *Symbiosis* is a biological term derived from the Greek root meaning "to live together"; it describes life patterns in which two species lead interdependent lives. In psychology, symbiosis is likened to a state of oneness in which a child's identity is fused with his or her mother's. Normally, children gradually differentiate their own identities or senses of self from their mothers. The process is called **separation-individuation**. Separation involves developing a separate psychological and biological identity from the mother. Individuation involves recognizing the personal characteristics that define one's self-identity. Separation-individuation may be a stormy process. Children may vacillate between seeking greater independence and moving closer to, or "shadowing," their mother, which is seen as a wish for reunion. The mother may disrupt normal separation-individuation by refusing to let go of the child or by too quickly pushing the child toward independence. The tendencies of people with borderline personalities to react to others with ambivalence and to alternate between love and hate are suggestive to Mahler of earlier ambivalences during the separation-individuation process. Borderline personality disorder may arise from a failure to master this developmental challenge.

Further on in this chapter, we underscore the links between abuse in childhood and the later development of personality disorders. These linkages suggest that failure to form close-bonding relationships with parental caregivers in childhood plays a critical role in developing many of the maladaptive personality patterns classified as personality disorders.

Learning Perspectives

Learning theorists tend to focus more on the acquisition of behaviour than on the notion of enduring personality traits. Similarly, they think more in terms of maladaptive behaviour than of disorders of "personality" or "personality traits." Trait theorists believe that personality traits steer behaviour, providing a framework for consistent behaviour in

splitting Term describing the inability of some persons (especially people with borderline personalities) to reconcile the positive and negative aspects of themselves and others into a cohesive integration, resulting in sudden and radical shifts between strongly positive and strongly negative feelings.

symbiotic (1) In biology, the living together of two different but interdependent organisms. (2) In Margaret Mahler's object-relations theory, the term used to describe the state of oneness that normally exists between a mother and infant in which the infant's identity is fused with the mother's.

separation-individuation In Margaret Mahler's theory, the process by which young children come to separate psychologically from their mothers and to perceive themselves as separate and distinct persons.

What are the origins of antisocial personality disorder? Are youth who develop antisocial personalities largely unsocialized because early learning experiences lack the consistency and predictability that help other children connect their behaviour with rewards and punishments? Or are they very "socialized"—but socialized to imitate the behaviour of other antisocial youth? Are we confusing antisocial behaviour with antisocial personality disorder? To what extent does criminal behaviour or membership in gangs overlap with antisocial personality disorder? Can environmental factors explain how people with antisocial personality disorder maintain their composure (their relatively low levels of arousal) under circumstances that would induce anxiety in most of us?

diverse situations. Many critics (e.g., Mischel, 1979), however, argue that behaviour is actually less consistent across situations than trait theorists would suggest. Behaviour may depend more on situational demands than on inherent traits. For example, we may describe a person as lazy and unmotivated. But is this person always lazy and unmotivated? Aren't there some situations in which the person may be energetic and ambitious? What differences in these situations may explain differences in behaviour? Learning theorists are generally interested in defining the learning histories and situational factors that give rise to maladaptive behaviour and the reinforcers that maintain them.

Learning theorists suggest that in childhood, many important experiences occur that shape the development of the maladaptive habits of relating to others that constitute personality disorders. For example, children who are regularly discouraged from speaking their minds or exploring their environments may develop a dependent personality behaviour pattern. Obsessive-compulsive personality disorder may be connected with excessive parental discipline or overcontrol in childhood. Theodore Millon (1981) suggests that children whose behaviour, even slight transgressions, is rigidly controlled and punished by parents may develop inflexible, perfectionistic standards. As these children mature, they may strive to develop in an area in which they excel, such as school work or athletics, as a way of avoiding parental criticism or punishment. But excessive attention to a single area of development may prevent them from becoming well rounded. They may thus squelch spontaneity and avoid new challenges or risks. They may also place perfectionistic demands on themselves so as to avoid any risk of punishment or rebuke, and develop other behaviour associated with the obsessive-compulsive personality pattern.

Millon suggests that histrionic personality disorder may be rooted in childhood experiences in which social reinforcers, such as parental attention, are connected to a child's appearance and willingness to perform for others, especially in cases where reinforcers are dispensed inconsistently. Inconsistent attention teaches children not to take approval for granted and to strive for it continually. People with histrionic personalities may also have identified with parents who are dramatic, emotional, and attention-seeking. Extreme sibling rivalry would further heighten motivation to perform for attention from others.

Behaviour theories emphasize the role of reinforcement in explaining the origins of antisocial behaviour. Ullmann and Krasner (1975) proposed, for example, that people with antisocial personalities may have failed to learn to respond to other people as potential reinforcers. Most children learn to treat others as reinforcing agents because others reinforce them with praise when they behave appropriately and punish them for misbehaviour. Reinforcement and punishment provide feedback (information about social expectations) that helps children modify their behaviour to maximize the chances of future rewards and minimize the risks of future punishment. As a consequence, children become socialized. They become sensitive to the demands of powerful others, usually parents and teachers, and learn to regulate their behaviour accordingly. They thus adapt to social expectations. They learn what to do and what to say, how to dress and how to act to obtain social reinforcement or approval from others.

People with antisocial personalities, by contrast, may not have become socialized because their early learning experiences lacked the consistency and predictability that helped other children connect their behaviour with rewards and punishments. Perhaps they were sometimes rewarded for doing the "right thing" but just as often not. They may have borne the brunt of harsh physical punishments that depended more on parental whims than on their own conduct. As adults they may not place much value on what other people expect because there was no clear connection between their own behaviour and reinforcement in childhood. They may have learned as children that there was little they could do to prevent punishment and so perhaps lost the motivation to try. Although Ullmann and Krasner's views may account for some features of antisocial personality disorder, they may not adequately address the development of the "charming" type of antisocial personality, which describes people who are skilful at reading social cues produced by other people and using them for personal advantage.

Family Perspectives

Many theorists have argued that disturbances in family relationships underlie the development of personality disorders. Researchers find that people with borderline personality disorder remember their parents as having been more controlling and less caring than do reference subjects with other psychological disorders (Zweig-Frank & Paris, 1991), which is consistent with psychodynamic formulations. When people with borderline personality disorder recall their earliest memories, they are more likely than other people to paint significant others as malevolent or evil. They portray their parents and others close to them as having been more likely to injure them deliberately or to fail to help them escape injuries by others (Nigg, Lohr, Western, Gold, & Silk, 1992).

A number of researchers have linked a history of physical or sexual abuse or neglect in childhood to the development of personality disorders, including borderline personality disorder, in adulthood (e.g., Zanarini et al., 1997). Perhaps the "splitting" observed in people with the disorder is a function of having learned to cope with unpredictable and harsh behaviour from parental figures or other caregivers.

Again consistent with psychodynamic theory, family factors such as parental overprotection and authoritarianism have been implicated in the development of dependent personality traits that may hamper the development of independent behaviour (Bornstein, 1992). Extreme fears of abandonment may also be involved, perhaps resulting from a failure to develop secure bonds with parental attachment figures in childhood due to parental neglect, rejection, or death. Subsequently, a chronic fear of being abandoned by other people with whom one has close relationships may develop, leading to the clinginess that typifies dependent personality disorder. Theorists also suggest that obsessive-compulsive personality disorder may emerge within a strongly moralistic and rigid family environment, which does not permit even minor deviations from expected roles or behaviour (e.g., Oldham, 1994).

As in the case of borderline personality disorder, researchers find that childhood abuse or neglect is a risk factor in the development of antisocial personality disorder in adulthood (Luntz & Widom, 1994). In a view that straddles the psychodynamic and learning theories, the McCords (McCord & McCord, 1964) focus on the role of parental rejection or neglect in the development of antisocial personality disorder. They suggest that children normally learn to associate parental approval with conformity to parental practices and values, and disapproval with disobedience. When tempted to transgress, children feel anxious for fear of losing parental love.

Anxiety serves as a signal that encourages a child to inhibit antisocial behaviour. Eventually, the child identifies with parents and internalizes these social controls in the form of a conscience. When parents do not show love for their children, this identification does not occur. Children do not fear loss of love because they have never had it. The anxiety that might have served to restrain antisocial and criminal behaviour is absent.

Children who are rejected or neglected by their parents may not develop warm feelings of attachment to others. They may lack the ability to empathize with the feelings and needs of others, developing instead an attitude of indifference. Or perhaps they still retain a wish to develop loving relationships but lack the ability to experience genuine feelings.

Although family factors may be implicated in some cases of antisocial personality disorder, many neglected children do not later show antisocial or other abnormal behaviour. We are left to develop other explanations to predict which deprived children will develop antisocial personalities or other abnormal behaviour and which will not.

Cognitive-Behavioural Perspectives

Social-cognitive theorist Albert Bandura (1973, 1986) has studied the role of observational learning in aggressive behaviour, which is one of the common components of antisocial behaviour. He and his colleagues (e.g., Bandura, Ross, & Ross, 1963) have shown that children acquire skills, including aggressive skills, by observing the behaviour of others. Exposure to aggression may come from watching violent television programs or observing parents who act violently toward one another. Bandura does not believe that children and adults display aggressive behaviour in a mechanical way, however. Rather, people usually do not imitate aggressive behaviour unless they are provoked and believe they are more likely to be rewarded than punished for it. When models get their way with others by acting aggressively, children may be more likely to imitate them. Children may also acquire antisocial behaviour such as cheating, bullying, or lying by direct reinforcement if they find such behaviour helps them avoid blame or manipulate others.

Cognitive-behaviour–oriented psychologists have shown that the ways in which people with personality disorders interpret their social experiences influence their behaviour. Antisocial adolescents, for example, tend to incorrectly interpret other people's behaviour as threatening (Dodge, Laird, Lochman, & Zelli, 2002). Perhaps because of family and community experiences, they tend to presume that others intend them ill when they do not. In a promising cognitive therapy method based on such findings—**problem-solving therapy**—antisocial adolescent boys have been encouraged to reconceptualize their social interactions as problems to be solved rather than as threats to be responded to with aggression (Kazdin & Whitley, 2003). They then generate nonviolent solutions to social confrontations and, like scientists, test out the most promising ones. In the section on biological perspectives, we also see that the antisocial personality's failure to profit from punishment is connected with a cognitive factor: the meaning of the aversive stimulus.

problem-solving therapy Form of therapy that focuses on helping people develop more effective problem-solving skills.

Biological Perspectives

Our knowledge about biological factors in most personality disorders has progressed rapidly in recent years with advances in genetics and neuroimaging technologies. We have suggestive evidence of genetic factors based in part on findings that the first-degree biological relatives (parents and siblings) of people with certain personality disorders, especially antisocial, schizotypal, and borderline types, are more likely to be diagnosed with these disorders than are members of the general population (APA, 2000a). Recent studies using fMRI technology have also provided evidence for neurological differences in personality traits (J. R. Gray and Braver, 2002; Reuter et al., 2004).

GENETIC FACTORS The establishment of well-defined criteria or dimensions is considered the essential first step in the search for the genetic underpinnings of personality disorders (Jang, Livesley, & Vernon, 2002). To that end, Kerry Jang and John Livesley initiated the UBC Twin Project in 1991 to help build valid diagnostic systems and measurements for major forms of personality disorders. With over 1000 adult twin pairs, it is Canada's largest twin study and the only one dedicated to the study of psychiatric disorders.

Studies of familial transmission are limited because family members share common environments as well as genes. Hence, researchers have turned to twin and adoptee studies to tease out genetic and environmental effects. Evidence from twin studies suggests that dimensions of personality associated with particular personality disorders may have an inherited component (Livesley, Jang, Jackson, & Vernon, 1993). Researchers examined the genetic contribution to 18 dimensions that underlie various personality disorders, including callousness, identity problems, anxiousness, insecure attachment, narcissism, social avoidance, self-harm, and oppositionality (negativity) (Livesley, Jang, Jackson, & Vernon, 1993). Genetic influences were suggested by findings of greater correlations of a given trait among identical (monozygotic, or MZ) twins than among fraternal (dizygotic, or DZ) twins. A statistical measure of heritability, reflecting the percentage of variability in a given trait that is accounted for by genetics, was computed for each personality dimension. The results showed that 12 of the 18 dimensions had heritabilities in the range of 40% to 60%, indicating a substantial genetic contribution to these characteristics. The highest heritabilities were for narcissism (64%) and identity problems (59%), and the lowest were for conduct problems (0%) and submissiveness (25%).

The findings suggest that genetics play a role in varying degrees in the development of the traits that underlie personality disorders. Certainly, not all people possessing these traits develop personality disorders. It is possible, however, that people with a genetic predisposition for these traits may be more vulnerable to developing personality disorders if they encounter certain environmental influences, such as being reared in a dysfunctional family.

In fact, it may be the case that genetically based behaviour dictates what environments and situations a person will seek out (Jang, Vernon, & Livesley, 2001). Jang and his colleagues at UBC argue that people do not just passively respond to nor are merely shaped by their environment, but that personality plays a role in the kinds of environments that will be actively sought out. For instance, a person with a genetic predisposition for sensation seeking may gravitate toward exhilarating situations such as bungee jumping, heli-skiing/boarding, or street racing. In this regard, genetic personality traits and the environment act cyclically (e.g., thrill seekers gravitate to thrilling environments and thrilling environments serve to reinforce the thrill seeking), and thus the person's personality becomes self-reinforcing and well ingrained. The question remains: to what extent is the influence of the environment dependent upon pre-existing genetic factors?

Evidence from adoption studies shows that biological and adopted children of people with antisocial personality disorder are more likely to develop the disorder themselves, which is consistent with the view that both genetics and environment play a role in its development (APA, 2000a). Consistent with a genetic contribution, evidence shows striking similarities between identical twins reared apart on some personality dimensions, including a psychopathic personality dimension (D. L. DiLalla, Carey, Gottesman, & Bouchard, 1996). A Danish study found four to five times greater incidence of psychopathy among the biological relatives of antisocial adoptees than among the adoptive relatives (Schulsinger, 1972). However, the size of the genetic contribution was relatively small. Environmental influences also contribute to antisocial behaviour. Evidence from adoption studies links criminal behaviour to genetics, although environmental factors also play a role (G. Carey, 1992; L. F. DiLalla & Gottesman, 1991).

NEUROPSYCHOLOGICAL FACTORS The neuroscience theory of personality can be traced back to physiologist Ivan Pavlov, who introduced the concept of nervous system excitation (e.g., a conditioned pleasure response) and inhibition (e.g., a conditioned fear response)

(Corr, 2004; Corr & Perkins, 2005). Later, personality theorist Hans Eysenck (Eysenck & Eysenck, 1985) incorporated Pavlov's ideas of excitatory and inhibitory processes into his theory of personality and suggested that extroverts—active, socially outgoing people—differ from introverts—socially withdrawn, introspective people—with respect to differences in cortical arousal sensitivity. Eysenck believed that extroverts have a lower level of arousal and seek out stimulating activity to increase their arousal. In contrast, introverts have higher levels of arousal and are more easily aroused, and thus seek to avoid sensory stimulation. Because social behaviour is arousing, in social situations you may expect an extrovert to be the "life of the party," whereas an introvert may prefer to avoid parties altogether.

Over a 40-year period, theorist Jeffrey Gray has woven the theories of Pavlov and Eysenck into what is now known as reinforcement sensitivity theory (RST) (Corr, 2004). Gray's RST has evolved into a biological personality theory that focuses on three distinct neuropsychological systems: (1) the behavioural approach system (BAS), (2) the fight-flight-freeze system (FFFS), and (3) the behavioural inhibition system (BIS) (J. A. Gray, 1970; J. A. Gray & McNaughton, 2003). New evidence supporting the neurological basis of personality comes from a growing body of molecular genetics (Canli et al., 2006; Caspi et al., 2003; Ebstein, Benjamin, & Belmaker, 2003), as well as neuroimaging research studies (Reuter et al., 2004; Schaefer et al., 2006).

Gray suggests that each neuropsychological system functions in a unique way. The BAS, for instance, is sensitive to and anticipates rewards; it acts to seek out pleasure. It has been linked with personality traits characterized by positive affect, extroversion, and impulsivity, but it may also underlie addictive behaviours, hypomania, and mania (Segarra et al., 2007; Smits & Boeck, 2006). The FFFS is a fear response to punishing stimuli; it acts to avoid pain. The FFFS is tied to defensive escape (panic) and avoidance (fear) behaviours and is linked to panic disorders and phobias (Corr, 2004). The BIS is sensitive to potential conflicts caused by the expected rewards and punishments in a situation. When there is a goal conflict, the BIS is activated to resolve any potential or anticipated threat and to bring the person back to a nonconflict state.

Let's say, for example, that you and your friends are vacationing in a foreign country and you are excited (BAS activation) about going to a raucous nightclub that is quite a distance from your hotel. Although you are out to have a fun time, you may initially tend to be alert to your surroundings, looking for potential danger in this novel situation (BIS activation). If all goes well, the BIS relaxes and you and your extroverted friends are free to enjoy the evening's events (BAS activity). If someone were actually to threaten you, however, the FFFS would immediately kick in and you would be ready to respond to the danger. As for any introverted friends among your group, chances are they'd be on high alert before, during, and even after your night out on the town. Thus, as you can see from this illustration, the BIS acts as an alarm signal and is characterized by risk assessment, worry, rumination, and vigilance. Traits associated with the BIS include negative affect, neuroticism, low self-esteem, and anxiety (Segarra et al., 2007) and conditions such as generalized anxiety and obsessive-compulsive disorder (Corr & Perkins, 2006).

Sociocultural Views

The sociocultural perspective leads us to examine the social conditions that may contribute to the development of the behaviour patterns identified as personality disorders. For instance, a Canadian study found that socioeconomic status (SES) risk factors, such as low family income, teenage-parent family, lone-parent family, low parental education, and family dysfunction, are associated with an increased vulnerability to one or more behavioural problems in young children, especially when the children are exposed to hostile or ineffective parenting (Landy & Tam, 1998). Because antisocial personality disorder is reported more frequently among people from lower socioeconomic classes, we might examine the role that the kinds of stressors encountered by disadvantaged families play in developing problem behaviour patterns. Some Canadian neighbourhoods and communities are beset by social problems such as alcohol and drug abuse, teenage pregnancy, and disorganized and disintegrating families. These stressors are associated with an increased likelihood of child abuse and neglect, which may in turn contribute to lower self-esteem and breed feelings of anger and resentment in children. Neglect and abuse may be translated into the lack of empathy and callous disregard for the welfare of others that are associated with antisocial personalities.

Little information is available about the rates of personality disorders outside North America. One initiative in this direction involved a joint program sponsored by the World Health Organization (WHO) and the Alcohol, Drug Abuse, and Mental Health Administration (ADAMHA) of the U.S. government. The goal of the program was to develop and standardize diagnostic instruments that could be used to arrive at psychiatric diagnoses worldwide. The result of this effort was the development of the International Personality Disorder Examination (IPDE), a semistructured interview protocol for diagnosing personality disorders (Loranger et al., 1994). The IPDE was pilot-tested by psychiatrists and clinical psychologists in 11 countries (India, Switzerland, the Netherlands, the United Kingdom, Luxembourg, Germany, Kenya, Norway, Japan, Austria, and the United States). The interview protocol had reasonably good reliability for diagnosing personality disorders among the different languages and cultures that were sampled. Although more research is needed to determine the rates of particular personality disorders in other parts of the world, investigators found borderline and avoidant types to be the most frequently diagnosed. Perhaps the characteristics associated with these personality disorders reflect some dimensions of personality disturbance that are commonly encountered throughout the world.

REVIEW IT

Theoretical Perspectives

- **How do traditional Freudian concepts of disturbed personality development compare with more recent psychodynamic approaches?** Traditional Freudian theory focused on unresolved Oedipal conflicts in explaining normal and abnormal personality development. More recent psychodynamic theorists have focused on the pre-Oedipal period in explaining the development of such personality disorders as narcissistic and borderline personality.

- **How do learning theorists view personality disorders?** Learning theorists view personality disorders in terms of maladaptive patterns of behaviour rather than personality traits. Learning theorists seek to identify the early learning experiences and present reinforcement patterns that may explain the development and maintenance of personality disorders.

- **What is the role of family relationships in personality disorders?** Many theorists have argued that disturbed family relationships play a formative role in the development of many personality disorders. For example, theorists have connected antisocial personality to parental rejection or neglect and parental modelling of antisocial behaviour.

- **How do cognitive encoding strategies of antisocial adolescents differ from those of their peers?** Antisocial adolescents are more likely to interpret social cues as provocations or intentions of ill will. This cognitive bias may lead them to be confrontative in their relationships with peers.

- **What roles might biological factors play in personality disorders?** To varying degrees, genetics play a role in the development of traits that underlie personality disorders. Some people with a genetic predisposition for these traits may be more vulnerable to developing personality disorders if they encounter certain environmental influences. In others, genetically based behaviour can dictate what environments a person will seek out. Reinforcement sensitivity theory (RST), backed up by genetic and neuropsychological evidence, helps explain and describe the psychophysiological basis of personality differences.

- **What role do sociocultural factors play in the development of personality disorders?** The effects of poverty, urban blight, and drug abuse can lead to family disorganization and disintegration, making it less likely that children will receive the nurturance and support they need to develop more socially adaptive behaviour patterns. Sociocultural theorists believe that such factors may underlie the development of personality disorders, especially antisocial personality disorder.

TREATMENT

We began the chapter with a quotation from the eminent psychologist William James (1842–1910), who suggested that people's personalities seem to be "set in plaster" by a certain age. His view may be especially applicable to many people with personality disorders, who are typically highly resistant to change.

People with personality disorders usually see their behaviour, even maladaptive, self-defeating behaviour, as natural parts of themselves. Although they may be unhappy and distressed, they are unlikely to perceive their own behaviour as causative. Like Marcella on page 226, whom we described as showing features of a histrionic personality disorder, they may condemn others for their problems and believe that others, not themselves, need to change. Thus, they usually do not seek help on their own. Or, they begrudgingly acquiesce to treatment at the urging of others but drop out or fail to cooperate with a therapist. Or they may go for help when they feel overwhelmed by anxiety or depression and terminate treatment as soon as they find some relief rather than probing more deeply for the underlying causes of their problems. People with personality disorders also tend to respond more poorly to treatment of problems such as depression than others, perhaps because of the negative influence of their maladaptive behaviour patterns (Shea, Widiger, & Klein, 1992). For many reasons, observers have widely believed that personality disorders have been difficult to treat, yet recent evidence suggests that both psychodynamic and cognitive-behavioural therapies are equally effective in producing long-term improvement in personality disorders (Leichsenring, Hiller, Weissberg, & Leibing, 2006).

Psychodynamic Approaches

Psychodynamic approaches are often used to help people with personality disorders become more aware of the roots of their self-defeating behaviour patterns and learn more adaptive ways of relating to others. Progress in therapy may be hampered by difficulties in working therapeutically with people who have personality disorders, especially clients with borderline and narcissistic personality disorders. Psychodynamic therapists often report that people with borderline personality disorder tend to have turbulent relationships with them, sometimes idealizing them, sometimes denouncing them as uncaring. Case studies suggest that therapists feel manipulated and exploited by borderline clients' needs to test their approval, such as by calling them at all hours or threatening suicide. Such clients can be exhausting and frustrating, although some successes have been reported among therapists who can handle clients' demands.

Promising results have been reported based on a brief, structured form of psychodynamic therapy pioneered at New York's Beth Israel Medical Center (Svartberg, Stiles, & Seltzer, 2004). There, researchers reported that a relatively brief form of psychodynamically oriented psychotherapy that averaged 40 weeks of treatment resulted in significant improvement in symptom complaints and social adjustment of people with personality disorders (Winston et al., 1994). The treatment emphasized interpersonal behaviour and used a more active, confrontational style in addressing clients' defences than is the case in traditional psychoanalysis.

Behavioural Approaches

Behaviour therapists see their task as changing clients' behaviour rather than their personality structures. Many behaviour theorists do not think in terms of clients' "personalities" at all, but rather in terms of acquired maladaptive behaviour that is maintained by reinforcement contingencies. Behaviour therapists therefore focus on attempting to replace maladaptive behaviour with adaptive behaviour through techniques such as extinction, modelling, and reinforcement. If clients are taught behaviour likely to be reinforced by other people, the new behaviour may well be maintained.

Behavioural marital therapists, for example, may encourage clients not to reinforce their spouse's histrionic behaviour. Techniques for treating social phobia, such as those described in Chapter 3, have also been of benefit in treating people with avoidant personality disorder (Renneberg, Goldstein, Phillips, & Chambless, 1990). This may include social-skills training to help clients function more effectively in social situations, such as dating and meeting new people. Cognitive methods may be incorporated to help socially avoidant individuals offset catastrophizing beliefs, such as the exaggerated fear of being shot down or rejected by dates.

Despite the difficulties in treating borderline personality disorder, two groups of therapists headed by Aaron Beck (e.g., A. T. Beck, Freeman, Davis, & Associates, 2004) and Marsha Linehan (Koerner & Linehan, 2002; Linehan, 1993) report promising results using cognitive-behavioural techniques specifically adapted to the problems encountered in working with clients with borderline personality disorder. Beck's approach focuses on helping the individual correct cognitive distortions that underlie tendencies to see oneself and others as either all good or all bad. Linehan's technique, called dialectical behaviour therapy (DBT), combines behaviour therapy and supportive psychotherapy.

DBT involves several modules, including (1) mindfulness techniques, through which individuals are taught to pay attention to the present moment in a nonjudgmental way; (2) distress tolerance, where individuals learn to tolerate strong emotions and their decisions; (3) emotion regulation strategies, which include identifying and labelling emotions, taking opposite action from what the emotion is telling you, and being mindful of current emotions; and (4) interpersonal effectiveness.

One component of distress tolerance is

IMPROVE the Moment

This skill is used in moments of distress to help one relax. The acronym stands for

Imagery: Imagine relaxing scenes, things going well, or other things that please you.

Meaning: Find some purpose or meaning in what you are feeling.

Prayer: Either pray to whomever you worship or, if not religious, chant a personal mantra.

Relaxation: Relax your muscles, breathe deeply; use with Self Soothing.

One thing in the moment: Focus your entire attention on what you are doing right now. Keep yourself in the present.

Vacation (brief): Take a break from it all for a short period of time.

Encouragement: Cheer-lead yourself. Tell yourself you can make it through this.

Dialectical Behaviour Therapy (DBT) seems to help the lives of those with borderline personality disorder. A recent study led by a psychologist with Toronto's Centre for Addiction and Mental Health (CAMH), Shelley McMain, found that DBT and active psychiatric management were similarly helpful in reducing suicidal and self-injurious episodes, reducing health-care use, and improving BPD symptoms (McMain et al., 2009).

Behaviour techniques are used to help clients develop more effective social skills and problem-solving skills, which can help improve their relationships with others and their ability to cope with negative events. Because people with borderline personality disorder tend to be overly sensitive to even the slightest cues of rejection, therapists provide continuing acceptance and support, even when clients push the limits by becoming manipulative or overly demanding.

Biological Approaches

Drug therapy does not directly treat personality disorders. Antidepressants or anti-anxiety drugs are sometimes used to treat the emotional distress that individuals with personality disorders may encounter, however. Drugs do not alter the long-standing patterns of maladaptive behaviour that may give rise to distress. However, a study indicates that the antidepressant Prozac can reduce aggressive behaviour and irritability in impulsive and aggressive individuals with personality disorders (Rivas-Vazquez & Blais, 2002). Researchers suspect that impulsive aggressive behaviour may be related to serotonin deficiencies. Prozac and similar drugs act to increase the availability of serotonin in the synaptic connections in the brain.

Canadian Treatment Services

Paris (1998) takes the approach that personality disorders are clusters of traits that can be viewed as amplifications of normal personality traits. The therapy implications of this premise are as follows: First, psychotherapy should focus on reducing the extremeness of the traits in part by identifying maladaptive behavioural patterns and bringing them to the attention of the patient. Second, the maladaptive behaviours should be given some historical perspective so that the patient can see how his or her behaviour is shaped by past experiences more than current realities and how this leads to inappropriate consequences. Third, treatment involves change. Patients are given the skills to practise alternative and more adaptive behaviour patterns. Still, the treatment goals for patients with personality disorders remain modest, and therapy sessions should be spaced out because these disorders' chronic nature precludes quick change.

Because of the diversity of problems associated with personality disorders, no single therapy modality works with all patients. Added to this are the cost-containment constraints on mental health services across Canada and the need for service-delivery mechanisms that must be comprehensive and flexible yet efficient and effective (Links, 1998). Livesley (2005) suggests that just such a system of care for personality-disordered patients needs to be grounded in evidence-based therapies and requires an integrated and systematic approach. Treatment phases would focus on safety and crisis support (e.g., telephone and mobile crisis support and hospital emergency support), containment of psychological distress through continuing care (e.g., outpatient treatment, daycare, and community-based care), control and regulation (e.g., improving self-management skills, coping skills, and problem-solving skills), exploration and change (e.g., changing maladaptive beliefs and interpersonal behaviours), and long-term treatment that focuses on the integration of clear boundaries between self and others (e.g., through goal-setting and experimenting with new behaviours).

One fairly low-cost alternative to traditional treatment is the use of well-designed self-help books. For example, for individuals dealing with obsessive-compulsive personality traits, a great resource is *When Perfect Isn't Good Enough*, by Dr. Marty Antony, a psychologist at Ryerson University, and Dr. Richard Swinson, medical director of the Anxiety Treatment and Research Centre at St. Joseph's Healthcare in Hamilton, Ontario (1998). Research has revealed that using this book as a self-help module leads to significant decreases in perfectionism in individuals coping with obsessive traits, though the participants were not formally diagnosed with OCPD (Pleva & Wade, 2006).

Much remains to be learned about working with people who have personality disorders. The major challenges involve recruiting people who do not see themselves as being disordered into treatment and prompting them to develop insight into their self-defeating or injurious behaviour. Current efforts to help such people are too often reminiscent of an old couplet:

> He that complies against his will,
> Is of his own opinion still.
> SAMUEL BUTLER, *HUDIBRAS*

In this chapter, we have considered a number of problems in which people act out on maladaptive impulses yet fail to see how their behaviour is disrupting their lives. In the next chapter, we explore other maladaptive behaviours that are frequently connected with lack of self-insight: behaviours involving substance abuse.

REVIEW IT

Treatment of Personality Disorders

- **How do therapists approach the treatment of personality disorders?** Experts from different schools of therapy try to assist people with personality disorders to gain better awareness of their self-defeating behaviour patterns and learn more adaptive ways of relating to others. Despite the difficulties in working therapeutically with these clients, promising results are emerging from the use of relatively short-term psychodynamic therapy and cognitive-behaviour treatment approaches. The delivery of mental health services across Canada needs to be comprehensive and flexible yet efficient and effective.

Define It

antisocial personality
   disorder, 218
avoidant personality
   disorder, 228
borderline personality
   disorder, 222
dependent personality
   disorder, 229
ego dystonic, 214
ego syntonic, 214

histrionic personality
   disorder, 225
ideas of reference, 217
narcissistic personality
   disorder, 226
obsessive-compulsive personality
   disorder, 231
optimum level of arousal, 226
paranoid personality
   disorder, 215

personality disorders, 214
problem-solving therapy, 239
psychopathy, 219
schizoid personality disorder, 216
schizotypal personality
   disorder, 217
self psychology, 235
separation-individuation, 236
splitting, 236
symbiotic, 236

Think About It

- Have you known people whose personality traits or styles caused continuing difficulties in their relationships with others? Did their personalities relate to any one of the types of personality disorders discussed in this chapter? Did they ever seek help from a mental health professional? If so, what was the outcome? If not, why not?

- Have you known anyone who you believe might fit the profile of an antisocial personality? What factors do you believe may have shaped this individual's personality development? How did the individual's personality affect his or her relationships with others?

- What factors make it difficult to treat people with personality disorders? If you were a therapist, how might you attempt to overcome these difficulties?

Key for Sensation-Seeking Scale (page 223)

Because this is an abbreviated version of a questionnaire, no norms are applicable. However, answers that agree with the following key are suggestive of sensation seeking:

1. A	5. A	9. B	13. B
2. A	6. B	10. A	
3. A	7. A	11. A	
4. B	8. A	12. A	

Weblinks

Personality Disorders   www.phac-aspc.gc.ca/
publicat/miic-mmac/pdf/chap_5_e.pdf
A chapter on personality disorders from Health Canada's *A Report on Mental Illness in Canada* (2002b).

Internet Mental Health
http://mentalhealth.com/p20-grp.html
This site includes a list of personality disorders linked to relevant information about description, diagnosis, treatment, and research.

MentalHelp.Net
mentalhelp.net/poc/center_index.php?id=8
This site includes a list of personality disorders linked to information about symptoms and treatment.

Borderline Personality Disorder Clinic, CAMH
www.camh.net/About_CAMH/
Guide_to_CAMH/Mental_Health_Programs/
General_Psychiatry_Program/guide_cats_bpd.html
This is an example of a treatment program for borderline personality disorder, run through the Centre for Addiction and Mental Health.

Personality Disorders

Types of Personality Disorders

Types of abnormal behaviour patterns involving excessively rigid patterns of behaviour or ways of relating to others that ultimately become self-defeating because their rigidity prevents adjustment to external demands.

Personality Disorders Characterized by Odd or Eccentric Behaviour

Paranoid Personality Disorder
- Persistent suspiciousness of the motives of others, but not to the point of holding clear-cut delusions

Schizoid Personality Disorder
- Persistent lack of interest in social relationships, flattened affect, and social withdrawal

Schizotypal Personality Disorder
- Eccentricities or oddities of thought and behaviour but without clearly psychotic features

Personality Disorders Characterized by Dramatic, Emotional, or Erratic Behaviour

Antisocial Personality Disorder
- Chronic pattern of antisocial and irresponsible behaviour and lack of remorse

Borderline Personality Disorder
- Abrupt shifts in mood, lack of a coherent sense of self, and unpredictable, impulsive behaviour

Histrionic Personality Disorder
- Excessive need to be the centre of attention and to receive reassurance, praise, and approval from others. Such persons often appear overly dramatic and emotional in their behaviour.

Narcissistic Personality Disorder
- Adoption of an inflated self-image and demands for constant attention and admiration, among other features

Personality Disorders Characterized by Anxious or Fearful Behaviour

Avoidant Personality Disorder
- Avoidance of social relationships due to fears of rejection

Dependent Personality Disorder
- Difficulties making independent decisions; overly dependent behaviour

Obsessive-Compulsive Personality Disorder
- Rigid ways of relating to others, perfectionistic tendencies, lack of spontaneity, and excessive attention to details

Problems With the Classification of Personality Disorders

Undetermined Reliability and Validity
- The reliability and validity of the definitions used in the DSM-IV remains to be fully tested.

Problems Distinguishing Axis I From Axis II Disorders
- The assumption that personality disorders are discriminable from clinical syndromes like anxiety or depressive disorders is questionable.

Overlap Among Disorders
- Although some personality disorders have distinct features, many appear to share common traits.

Difficulty in Distinguishing Between Variations in Normal Behaviour and Abnormal Behaviour
- Personality disorders involve traits that, in lesser degrees, describe the behaviour of most normal individuals.

Sexist Bias
- Diagnostic criteria for personality disorders label stereotypical feminine behaviour as pathological with greater frequency than is the case with stereotypical masculine behaviour.

>>

Theoretical Perspectives

Psychodynamic Perspectives

- *Self psychology:* Heinz Kohut's theory that describes processes that normally lead to the achievement of a cohesive sense of self.
- *Object-relations theory:* Margaret Mahler used the term *symbiotic* to describe the state of oneness that normally exists between mother and infant in which the infant's identity is fused with the mother's. Mahler's *separation-individuation* is the process by which young children come to separate psychologically from their mothers and to perceive themselves as separate and distinct persons.

Learning Perspectives

- Focus more on the acquisition of behaviour than on the notion of enduring personality traits. Many important experiences occur in childhood that shape the development of the maladaptive habits of relating to others that constitute personality disorders.

Family Perspectives

- Disturbances in family relationships underlie the development of personality disorders.

Cognitive-Behavioural Perspectives

- Albert Bandura noted that children acquire skills, including aggressive skills, by observing the behaviour of others. The ways in which people with personality disorders interpret their social experiences influence their behaviour.

Biological Perspectives

- Genetics plays a role in varying degrees in the development of traits that underlie personality disorders.
- Jeffrey Gray's reinforcement sensitivity theory is based on the behavioural approach system (BAS), the fight-flight-freeze system (FFFS), and the behavioural inhibition system (BIS).

Sociocultural Views

- Social conditions contribute to the development of the behaviour patterns identified as personality disorders.

Treatment

Psychodynamic Approaches

- Help people with personality disorders become more aware of the roots of their self-defeating behaviour patterns and learn more adaptive ways of relating to others.

Behaviour Approaches

- Focus on replacing maladaptive behaviour with adaptive behaviour through techniques such as extinction, modelling, and reinforcement. If clients are taught behaviours that are likely to be reinforced by other people, the new behaviour may well be maintained.

Biological Approaches

- Drug therapy does not directly treat personality disorders. Antidepressants or anti-anxiety drugs are sometimes used to treat the emotional distress that individuals with personality disorders may encounter.

Canadian Treatment Services

- John Livesley proposes a systematic, integrated, multi-perspective, evidence-based treatment approach.

7

Substance Abuse and Dependence

CHAPTER OUTLINE

Classification of Substance-Related Disorders
Substance Abuse and Dependence
Addiction, Physiological Dependence, and
  Psychological Dependence
Pathways to Drug Dependence

Drugs of Abuse
Depressants
Stimulants
Hallucinogens
Inhalants

Theoretical Perspectives
Biological Perspectives
Learning Perspectives
Cognitive Perspectives
Psychodynamic Perspectives
Sociocultural Perspectives
Tying It Together

Treatment
Biological Approaches
Nonprofessional Support Groups
Residential Approaches
Psychodynamic Approaches
Behavioural Approaches
Relapse-Prevention Training

Did You Know That...

- You can become psychologically dependent on a drug without becoming physically addicted?

- Alcohol "goes to women's heads" more rapidly than men's?

- Light to moderate alcohol intake is associated with a reduced risk of heart disease and lower death rates?

- Coca-Cola originally contained cocaine?

- Habitual smoking is a form of physical addiction, not just a bad habit?

- Being able to "hold your liquor" better than most people may put you at risk of developing a drinking problem?

- A widely used treatment for heroin addiction involves the substitution of another addictive drug?

The planet is a supermarket of psychoactive chemicals or drugs. The Western world is flooded with substances that alter the mood and twist perceptions—substances that lift you up, cool you down, and turn you upside down. Many people use these substances because their friends do. Some adolescents use them because their parents and authority figures tell them not to. Some users are seeking pleasure or temporary relief from emotional pain. Others are searching for inner truth.

Throughout North America, psychoactive drugs are widely used. A recent Ontario survey revealed that 45% of people aged 15 and older had used marijuana at some point in their lives, and 79% had used alcohol (Adlaf, Begin, & Sawka, 2005). According to the survey, compared to marijuana and alcohol, the lifetime use of other substances is less common: hallucinogens, 11%; cocaine, 11%; amphetamines (speed), 6%; MDMA (ecstasy), 4%; and heroin, 1%. Some people consume multiple substances, which is called *polydrug use*. To illustrate, consider the following study conducted by members of Robert Pihl's research group at McGill University (Barrett, Gross, Garand, & Pihl, 2005). Pihl is an internationally acclaimed substance-abuse researcher. He and his colleagues conducted a survey of drug use of 186 people who attended "raves" in Montreal. Most participants were in their early 20s. About 80% reported using multiple psychoactive substances (excluding tobacco) at the most recent rave they attended. Cannabis, alcohol, ecstasy, amphetamines, cocaine, ketamine (Special K), and GHB (gamma-hydroxybutyrate) were the most frequently used. Frequent rave attendees tended to use more of these substances than infrequent attendees. Later in this chapter, we will discuss the brain damage and other harmful effects of these drugs, especially when used repeatedly and in large quantities.

The old standby, alcohol, is the most popular drug on campus—whether the campus is a high school or a university. In fact, 90% of Canadian university students report using alcohol within the past year, as compared to an estimated 25% to 33% who report using any illicit drug (Canadian Centre on Substance Abuse [CCSA] & Centre for Addiction and Mental Health [CAMH], 1999; Gliksman, Adlaf, Demers, Newton-Taylor, & Schmidt, 2000). Under certain conditions, the use of substances that affect mood and behaviour is normal enough, at least as gauged by statistical frequency and social standards. It is normal to start the day with caffeine in the form of coffee or tea, to take wine or coffee with meals, to meet friends for a drink after work, and to end the day with a nightcap. Many of us take prescription drugs that calm us down or ease our pain. Flooding the bloodstream with nicotine by means of smoking is normal in the sense that about one in five Canadians smoke (Health Canada, 2001a). Some psychoactive substances are illegal and are used illicitly, such as cocaine, marijuana, and heroin. Others are available by prescription, such as minor tranquillizers, amphetamines, and opiate analgesics. Still others are available without prescription or over the counter, such as tobacco (which contains nicotine, a mild stimulant) and alcohol (which is a depressant). The most widely and easily accessible substances—tobacco and alcohol—cause more deaths through sickness and accidents than all other illicit drugs combined.

Table 7.1 shows recent results, separated by gender, from the Centre for Addiction and Mental Health's longest ongoing survey of substance use in Canada. Such surveys suggest that the prevalence of illicit drug use has remained roughly stable over the past two decades (e.g., CCSA & CAMH, 1999), although the prevalence of marijuana use may increase if the drug is legalized.

TABLE 7.1

Drug Use Among Men and Women (percentages)

	Men	Women
Alcohol		
Drank alcohol (past 12 months)	80.9%	77.4%
Drank daily		
Total sample	10.1%	4.7%*
Drinkers	12.5%	6.1%*
Average number of drinks consumed weekly (mean), by drinkers	6.5	2.8*
Exceeded low risk drinking guidelines		
Total sample	29.3%	14.3%*
Drinkers	36.3%	18.7%*
Consumed 5 or more drinks on a single occasion weekly (weekly binge drinking)		
Total sample	11.4%	3.1%*
Drinkers	14.1%	4.0%*
Reported hazardous or harmful drinking (AUDIT 8+)		
Total sample	19.0%	7.5%*
Drinkers	23.7%	9.7%*
Tobacco		
Currently smoke cigarettes	21.2%	16.2%
Daily	17.0%	12.2%
Average number of cigarettes smoked daily (mean), by smokers	14.9	11.4
Daily smokers reporting high smoking dependence	16.0%	13.2%
Cannabis		
Have used cannabis		
Lifetime	44.8%	34.8%*
Past 12 months	17.4%	9.5%*
Reported moderate or high risk of cannabis problems (ASSIST-CIS 4+)		
Total sample	9.4%	4.5%*
Users	54.2%	47.9%
Cocaine[a]		
Have used cocaine		
Lifetime	9.8%	5.1%*
Past 12 months	<1.0%	<1.0%
Prescription Opioids		
Reported any use of prescription-type opioid pain relievers (past 12 months)	19.4%	23.0%
Reported use for nonmedical purposes (past 12 months)	2.4%	1.0%
Driving[b]		
Drivers who drove after drinking (past 12 months)	11.6%	2.3%*
Drivers who drove after using cannabis (past 12 months)	3.3%	<1.0%*

Note: [a] Estimates for cocaine are based on data from the 2008 CAMH Monitor cycle; [b] estimates for driving are based on licensed drivers; * indicates a discernible sex difference ($p < .05$) after controlling for other demographic factors.
Source: Ialomiteanu, Adlaf, Mann, & Rehm, 2011. Reprinted with permission.

The prevalence of tobacco use has declined to some extent over the past few decades (CCSA & CAMH, 1999; Health Canada, 2001a). To illustrate, in 1965 a total of 61% of men and 38% of women were smokers. In 2001, these figures dropped to 25% and 20% respectively (Health Canada, 2001a). From 1999 to 2009 we saw a further overall decline, to 17% (Health Canada, 2009). The decline is likely due to a range of factors, including government legislation banning smoking in various public places, restrictions on the sale of tobacco to minors, warnings on tobacco packages, and public health campaigns emphasizing the harmful effects of smoking.

Although there has been some decline in overall alcohol consumption over the years (CCSA & CAMH, 1999), problem drinking, especially binge drinking, remains widespread on university campuses and elsewhere in society. A binge drinker is someone who reports consuming five or more drinks (for men) or four or more drinks (for women) on one occasion during the preceding two-week period. A 2004 survey of Canadian universities (the sample of 6282 undergraduates averaged 22 years of age and included 2248 men and 4034 women) found that undergraduates display diverse drinking patterns.

Two drinking types represent more than half of students: light-infrequent drinking (indicated by the usual consumption of fewer than five drinks daily and less than weekly drinking), reported by 35.8%, and light-frequent drinking (indicated by the usual consumption of fewer than five drinks on the days they drink and weekly drinking), reported by 22.1%.

Almost one third of students reported a heavy pattern of drinking, including 16.1% who reported heavy-frequent drinking (indicated by the usual consumption of more than five drinks on the days they drink and weekly drinking) and 11.7% who reported heavy-infrequent drinking (indicated by the usual consumption of more than five drinks on the days they drink and less than weekly drinking).

The prevalence of binge drinking is higher in male than female students (Adler, 1994; H. Wechsler, Davenport, Dowdall, Moeykens, & Castillo, 1994). The prevalence of alcohol dependence appears to be rising, due largely to increases in adolescent alcohol abuse leading eventually to outright dependence (Nelson, Heath, & Kessler, 1998).

CLASSIFICATION OF SUBSTANCE-RELATED DISORDERS

substance-use disorders Patterns of maladaptive behaviour involving the use of a psychoactive substance. Substance-use disorders include substance-abuse disorders and substance-dependence disorders.

substance-induced disorders Disorders induced by the use of psychoactive substances, including intoxication, withdrawal syndromes, mood disorders, delirium, and amnesia.

psychoactive Describing chemical substances or drugs that have psychological effects.

intoxication State of drunkenness.

The DSM-IV classifies substance-related disorders into two major categories: **substance-use disorders** and **substance-induced disorders**. Substance-use disorders involve maladaptive use of **psychoactive** substances. These types of disorders include substance abuse and substance dependence. Substance-induced disorders involve disorders that can be induced by using psychoactive substances, such as intoxication, withdrawal syndromes, mood disorders, delirium, dementia, amnesia, psychotic disorders, anxiety disorders, sexual dysfunctions, and sleep disorders. Different substances have different effects, so some of these disorders may apply to one, a few, or nearly all substances.

Substance **intoxication** is a state of drunkenness or "being high." These effects largely reflect the chemical actions of the psychoactive substances. The particular features of intoxication depend on which drug is ingested, the dose, the user's biological reactivity, and—to some degree—the user's expectations. Signs of intoxication often include confusion, belligerence, impaired judgment, inattention, and impaired motor and spatial skills. Extreme intoxication from the use of alcohol, cocaine, opiates, and PCP (phencyclidine) can even result in death (yes, you can die from an alcohol overdose), either because of the substance's biochemical effects or because of behaviour patterns—such as suicide—that are connected with psychological pain or impaired judgment brought on by use of the drug.

Substance Abuse and Dependence

Where does substance use end and abuse begin? According to the DSM, substance abuse involves a pattern of recurrent use that leads to damaging consequences. Damaging consequences may involve failing to meet one's major role responsibilities (e.g., as a student, worker, or parent), putting oneself in situations where substance use is physically dangerous (e.g., combining driving with substance use), encountering repeated problems with the law arising from substance use (e.g., multiple arrests for substance-related behaviour), or having recurring social or interpersonal problems because of substance use (e.g., repeatedly getting into fights when drinking).

When people repeatedly miss school or work because they are drunk or "sleeping it off," their behaviour may fit the definition of **substance abuse**. A single incident of excessive drinking at a friend's wedding would not qualify. Nor would regular consumption of low to moderate amounts of alcohol be considered abusive, so long as it is not connected with any impairment in functioning. Neither the amount nor the type of drug ingested, nor whether the drug is illicit, is key to defining substance abuse according to the DSM. Rather, the determining feature of substance abuse is whether a pattern of drug-using behaviour becomes repeatedly linked to damaging consequences.

Substance abuse may continue for a long period of time or progress to **substance dependence**, a more severe type of substance-use disorder in which abuse is associated with physiological signs of dependence (tolerance or withdrawal) and/or compulsive use of a substance. People who are compulsive users lack control over their drug use. They may be aware of how their drug use is disrupting their lives or damaging their health but feel helpless or powerless to stop using drugs, even though they may want to. By the time they become dependent on a given drug, they've given over much of their lives to obtaining and using it. The diagnostic criteria for substance dependence are listed in Table 7.2.

substance abuse Continued use of a psychoactive drug despite the knowledge that it is causing or contributing to a persistent or recurrent social, occupational, psychological, or physical problem.

substance dependence Impaired control over the use of a psychoactive drug and continued or even increased use despite awareness that the substance is disrupting one's life. Substance dependence is often characterized by physiological dependence.

TABLE 7.2

Diagnostic Criteria for Substance Dependence

A maladaptive pattern of substance use, leading to clinically significant impairment or distress, as manifested by three (or more) of the following, occurring at any time in the same 12-month period:

(1) tolerance, as defined by either of the following:

    (a) a need for markedly increased amounts of the substance to achieve intoxication or desired effect

    (b) markedly diminished effect with continued use of the same amount of the substance

(2) withdrawal, as manifested by either of the following:

    (a) the characteristic withdrawal syndrome for the substance (refer to Criteria A and B of the criteria sets for Withdrawal from the specific substances)

    (b) the same (or a closely related) substance is taken to relieve or avoid withdrawal symptoms

(3) the substance is often taken in larger amounts or over a longer period than was intended

(4) there is a persistent desire or unsuccessful efforts to cut down or control substance use

(5) a great deal of time is spent in activities necessary to obtain the substance (e.g., visiting multiple doctors or driving long distances), use the substance (e.g., chain-smoking), or recover from its effects

(6) important social, occupational, or recreational activities are given up or reduced because of substance use

(7) the substance use is continued despite knowledge of having a persistent or recurrent physical or psychological problem that is likely to have been caused or exacerbated by the substance (e.g., current cocaine use despite recognition of cocaine-induced depression, or continued drinking despite recognition that an ulcer was made worse by alcohol consumption)

Source: Reprinted with permission from the *Diagnostic and Statistical Manual of Mental Disorders*, Fourth Edition, Text Revision, (Copyright ©2000). American Psychiatric Association. p. 197.

withdrawal syndrome Characteristic cluster of withdrawal symptoms following the sudden reduction or abrupt cessation of use of a psychoactive substance after physiological dependence has developed.

tachycardia Abnormally rapid heartbeat.

delirium tremens Withdrawal syndrome that often occurs following a sudden decrease or cessation of drinking in chronic alcoholics that is characterized by extreme restlessness, sweating, disorientation, and hallucinations. Abbreviated *DTs*.

delirium (1) State of mental confusion, disorientation, and extreme difficulty in focusing attention. (2) A syndrome occurring among the elderly that typically involves confusion, problems with concentration, and cognitive dysfunction.

disorientation State of mental confusion or lack of awareness with respect to time, place, or the identity of oneself or others.

Repeated use of a substance may alter the body's physiological reactions, leading to the development of tolerance or a physical **withdrawal syndrome** (see Table 7.2 on page 253). Tolerance is a state of physical habituation to a drug such that with frequent use, higher doses are needed to achieve the same effect. A withdrawal syndrome (also called an *abstinence syndrome*) involves a characteristic cluster of withdrawal symptoms that occur when a dependent person abruptly stops using a particular substance following a prolonged period of heavy use. People who experience a withdrawal syndrome often return to using the substance in order to relieve the discomfort associated with withdrawal, which serves to maintain the addictive pattern. Withdrawal symptoms vary with the particular type of drug. With alcohol dependence, typical withdrawal symptoms include dryness in the mouth, nausea or vomiting, weakness, **tachycardia**, anxiety and depression, headaches, insomnia, elevated blood pressure, and fleeting hallucinations.

In some cases of chronic alcoholism, withdrawal produces a state of **delirium tremens,** or "the DTs." The DTs are usually limited to chronic, heavy users of alcohol who dramatically lower their intake of alcohol after many years of steady drinking. The DTs involve intense autonomic hyperactivity (profuse sweating and tachycardia) and **delirium**— a state of mental confusion characterized by incoherent speech, **disorientation**, and extreme restlessness. Terrifying hallucinations—frequently of creepy-crawly animals (worms, snakes, etc.)—may also be present. Substances that tend to lead to withdrawal syndromes include alcohol, opiates, cocaine, amphetamines, sedatives and barbiturates, nicotine, and anti-anxiety agents (minor tranquillizers). Marijuana and hallucinogens such as LSD are not recognized as producing a withdrawal syndrome because of a lack of evidence that abrupt withdrawal from these substances reliably produces clinically significant withdrawal effects (APA, 2000a).

Tolerance and withdrawal syndromes are often, but not necessarily, associated with substance dependence. Substance dependence sometimes involves a pattern of compulsive use without the development of the physiological features of dependence (tolerance and/or a withdrawal syndrome). For example, people may become compulsive users of marijuana, especially when they come to rely on the drug to help them cope with the stresses of daily life. Yet they may not require larger amounts of the substance to get "high" or experience distressing withdrawal symptoms when they cease using it. In most cases, however, substance dependence and physiological features of dependence occur together. Despite the fact that the DSM considers substance abuse and dependence to be distinct diagnostic categories, the boundary between the two is not always clear.

Two of the many faces of alcohol use—and abuse. Alcohol is our most widely used—and abused—drug. Many people use alcohol to celebrate achievements and happy occasions, as in the photograph on the left. Unfortunately, like the man in the photograph on the right, some people use alcohol to drown their sorrows, which may only worsen their problems. Where does substance use end and abuse begin? According to the DSM, use becomes abuse when it leads to damaging consequences.

TABLE 7.3

Lifetime Prevalence of Drug Dependence by Type of Drug (in percentages)

Drug	Edmonton Survey (Russell et al., 1994)	Estimates From Canada and U.S. (APA, 2000)
Tobacco	—	up to 25.0
Alcohol	16.5	15.0
Marijuana	5.9	5.0
Amphetamines	1.5	1.5
Opiates	0.7	0.7
Barbiturates or sedatives	0.7	< 1.0
Hallucinogens	0.5	0.6
Cocaine	0.5	2.0

— Not assessed.

Source: Based on J. M. Russell, S. C. Newman, & R. C. Bland, 1994. Copyright 1994 by John Wiley & Sons. Used by permission; American Psychiatric Association, 2000a. *Diagnostic and Statistical Manual of Mental Disorders*, Fourth Edition, Text Revision.

One of the most reliable estimates of the prevalence of substance dependence comes from the DSM-IV (APA, 2000a), which synthesizes data from the United States, Canada, and other countries. Estimates from the DSM-IV and elsewhere suggest that about 15% of adults in Canada and the United States have a history of alcohol dependence (APA, 2000a; H. E. Ross, 1995). Up to 25% have developed nicotine dependence through the repeated use of tobacco products, usually cigarettes (APA, 2000a). About 7.5% have developed a dependence on an illicit drug, inhalant, or nonprescription use of tranquilizers or other psychiatric (psychotropic) drugs. Table 7.3 gives the lifetime prevalence of drug dependence for other types of drugs. The table shows the estimates from the DSM-IV (APA, 2000a) and, for comparison purposes, the results from one of the most extensive epidemiologic surveys done in Canada: Roger Bland's Edmonton survey. The results of this survey are quite similar to the estimates in the DSM-IV, although the prevalence of cocaine dependence is lower in the Edmonton survey, corresponding to the lower prevalence of cocaine problems in Canada compared to the United States (APA, 2000a; CCSA & CAMH, 1999).

People can abuse or become dependent on more than one psychoactive substance at the same time. People who abuse or become dependent on heroin, for instance, may also abuse or become dependent on other drugs, such as alcohol, cocaine, or stimulants—simultaneously or successively. In fact, surveys from Canada and elsewhere indicate that most illicit users of opioids such as heroin are polydrug users involved in the intensive co-use of crack or cocaine (or both) (Fischer & Rehm, 2006). People who engage in these patterns of polydrug abuse face increased potential of harmful overdoses when drugs are used in combination. Moreover, "successful" treatment of one form of abuse may not affect, and in some cases could even exacerbate, abuse of other drugs.

Addiction, Physiological Dependence, and Psychological Dependence

The DSM uses the terms *substance abuse* and *substance dependence* to classify people whose use of these substances impairs their functioning. It does not use the term *addiction* to describe these problems, yet the concept of addiction is widespread among professionals and laypeople alike. But what is meant by *addiction*?

People define **addiction** in different ways. For our purposes, we define it as the habitual or compulsive use of a drug accompanied by evidence of physiological dependence. **Physiological dependence** means that one's body has changed as a result of the regular

addiction Impaired control over the use of a chemical substance accompanied by physiological dependence.

physiological dependence State of physical dependence on a drug in which the user's body comes to depend on a steady supply.

use of a psychoactive drug such that it comes to depend on a steady supply of the substance. The major signs of physiological dependence involve the development of tolerance and/or an abstinence syndrome. A **psychological dependence** involves a pattern of compulsive use associated with impaired control over the use of a drug.

Although physical addiction is generally associated with substance dependence, some cases of dependence involve compulsive patterns of using drugs without physical signs of addiction (Schuckit et al., 1999). You can become psychologically dependent on a drug without developing a physiological dependence or addiction.

On the other hand, people may become physiologically dependent on a drug but not become compulsive users or psychologically dependent. For example, people recuperating from surgery are often given narcotics derived from opium as painkillers. Some may develop signs of physiological dependence—such as tolerance and a withdrawal syndrome—but they likely will not become habitual users or show a lack of control over the use of these drugs.

In recent years, the concept of addiction has been extended beyond the abuse of chemical substances to apply to many habitual forms of maladaptive behaviour, such as pathological gambling (Ladouceur, 2002). In the vernacular, we hear of people being "addicted to" love or shopping or almost anything. There have even been suggestions that people can become addicted to the Internet (Beard, 2005), whereby people (usually males) lose sleep, miss meals, experience social isolation, and fail to attend classes or neglect work responsibilities because of excessive use of the Internet, such as for the purpose of using chat rooms, playing online games, or visiting gambling or sexual websites (Chou, Condron, & Belland, 2005). These people are excessively preoccupied with using the Internet, to the exclusion of everything else in their lives, and they seem to experience symptoms of withdrawal (anxiety, depression) when they are separated from it (Niemz, Griffiths, & Banyard, 2005). Preoccupation with the Internet and other so-called addictions do not involve physiological dependence on a chemical substance. In this chapter, we limit the term *addiction* to the habitual use of substances that produce physiological dependence.

Pathways to Drug Dependence

Although the progression to substance dependence varies from person to person, some common pathways can be described according to the following stages (R. D. Weiss, Mirin, & Bartel, 1994):

1. *Experimentation.* During the stage of experimentation, or occasional use, the drug temporarily makes users feel good, even euphoric. Users feel in control and believe they can stop at any time.
2. *Routine use.* During the next stage, a period of routine use, people begin to structure their lives around the pursuit and use of drugs. Denial plays a major role at this stage, as users mask the negative consequences of their behaviour to themselves and others. Values change. What had formerly been important, such as family and work, comes to matter less than the drugs.

   As routine drug use continues, problems mount. Users devote more of their resources to drugs. Family bank accounts are emptied, "temporary" loans are sought from friends and relatives for trumped-up reasons, and family heirlooms and jewellery are sold to pawnbrokers for a fraction of their value. Lying and manipulation become a way of life to cover up the drug use. The husband sells the television set to a pawnbroker and forces the front door open to make it look like a burglary. The wife claims to have been robbed at knifepoint to explain the disappearance of a gold chain or engagement ring. Family relationships become strained as the mask of denial shatters and the consequences of drug abuse become apparent: days lost from work, unexplained absences from home, rapid mood shifts, depletion of family finances, failure to pay bills, stealing from family members, and absence from family gatherings or children's birthday parties.

3. *Addiction or dependence.* Routine use becomes addiction or dependence when users feel powerless to resist drugs, either because they want to experience their effects or to avoid the consequences of withdrawal. Little or nothing else matters at this stage, as seen in the case of Eugene, a 41-year-old architect, who related the following conversation with his wife: "She had just caught me with cocaine again after I had managed to convince her that I hadn't used in over a month. Of course I had been tooting (snorting) almost every day, but I had managed to cover my tracks a little better than usual. So she said to me that I was going to have to make a choice—either cocaine or her. Before she finished the sentence, I knew what was coming, so I told her to think carefully about what she was going to say. It was clear to me that there wasn't a choice. I love my wife, but I'm not going to choose anything over cocaine. It's sick, but that's what things have come to. Nothing and nobody comes before my coke." (R. D. Weiss et al., 1994, p. 55)

REVIEW IT

Classification of Substance-Related Disorders

- **How does the DSM distinguish between substance-abuse disorders and substance-dependence disorders?** According to the DSM, substance-abuse disorders involve a pattern of recurrent use of a substance that repeatedly leads to damaging consequences. Substance-dependence disorders involve impaired control over the use of a substance and often include features of physiological dependence on the substance, as manifested by the development of tolerance or an abstinence syndrome.

- **What are meant by the terms *addiction* and *psychological dependence*?** Although various people use the term *addiction* differently, it is employed here to refer to the habitual or compulsive use of a substance together with the development of physiological dependence. Psychological dependence involves compulsive use of a substance, with or without the development of physiological dependence.

DRUGS OF ABUSE

Drugs of abuse are generally classified into three major groupings: (1) depressants, such as alcohol and opiates; (2) stimulants, such as amphetamine and cocaine; and (3) hallucinogens.

Depressants

A **depressant** is a drug that slows down or curbs the activity of the central nervous system. It reduces feelings of tension and anxiety, causes our movements to become sluggish, and impairs our cognitive processes. In high doses, depressants can arrest vital functions and cause death. The most widely used depressant, alcohol, can lead to death when taken in large amounts because of its depressant effects on respiration (breathing). Other effects are specific to the particular kind of depressant. For example, some depressants, such as heroin, produce a "rush" of pleasure. Here we will consider several of the major types of depressants.

ALCOHOL You may not have thought of alcohol as a drug, perhaps because it is so popular, or maybe because it is ingested by drinking rather than by smoking or injection. But alcoholic beverages such as wine, beer, and hard liquor contain a depressant called *ethyl alcohol* (or *ethanol*). The concentration of the drug varies with the type of beverage (wine and beer have less pure alcohol per ounce than distilled spirits such as whisky, gin, or vodka). Alcohol is classified as a depressant drug because it has biochemical effects similar to those of a class of minor tranquillizers, the benzodiazepines, which include the well-known drugs diazepam (Valium) and chlordiazepoxide (Librium). We can think of alcohol as a type of over-the-counter tranquillizer.

depressant Drug that lowers the level of activity of the central nervous system.

Alcohol is used in many ways. It is our mealtime relaxant, our party social facilitator, our bedtime sedative. We observe holy days, laud our achievements, and express joyful wishes with alcohol. Adolescents assert their maturity with alcohol. Pediatricians used to swab the painful gums of teething babies with alcohol. Alcohol even deals the death blow to germs on surface wounds and is the active ingredient in some antiseptic mouthwashes. In Western countries such as Canada, most adults drink alcohol at least occasionally. Most people who drink do so in moderation, but many develop significant problems with alcohol use (Adlaf, Begin, & Sawka, 2005). Alcohol is the most widely abused substance in the world. Many lay and professional people use the term *alcoholism* to refer to problems of alcohol dependence. Although definitions of alcoholism vary, we use the term to refer to a state of physical dependence on or addiction to alcohol that is characterized by impaired control over the use of the drug.

The personal and social costs of alcoholism are considerable. In Canada, the economic costs of alcoholism—based on days lost from work, health problems associated with alcoholism, and costs resulting from motor vehicle accidents involving alcohol use—are staggering, amounting to more than $7.5 billion annually according to a 1992 estimate (Dingle, Samtani, Kraatz, & Solomon, 2002). Alcohol abuse is connected with lower productivity, loss of jobs, and downward movement in socioeconomic status. Estimates are that over 20% of homeless people suffer from alcohol dependence (M. Farrell et al., 2003). Alcohol also plays a part in about 27% of all male suicides and 17% of all female suicides in Canada (Dingle et al., 2002). It is a leading cause of death of young people. Approximately 40% of Canadian teens killed in motor vehicle accidents have alcohol in their systems (Centre for Addictions Research, BC, 2006).

Alcohol, not cocaine or other drugs, is the drug of choice among young people today, and the leading drug of abuse (CCSA & CAMH, 1999; Gliksman et al., 2000). Drinking is so integrated into university life that it has become essentially normative, as much a part of the experience as attending a weekend hockey or basketball game.

Despite the popular image of alcoholics as skid-row drunks, the truth is that only a small minority of people with alcoholism fit that stereotype. The great majority of alcoholics are the type of people you're likely to see every day—your neighbours, co-workers, friends, and members of your own family. They are found in all walks of life and every social and economic class. Many have families, hold good jobs, and live fairly comfortably. Yet alcoholism can have just as devastating an effect on the well-to-do as the indigent, leading to wrecked careers and ruined marriages, motor vehicle and other accidents, and severe, life-threatening physical disorders, as well as exacting an enormous emotional toll.

No single drinking pattern is exclusively associated with alcoholism. Some people with alcoholism drink heavily every day; others binge only on weekends. Still others can abstain for lengthy periods of time but periodically "go off the wagon" and engage in episodes of binge drinking that may last for days, weeks, or months.

Risk Factors for Alcoholism   Investigators have identified a number of factors that place people at increased risk for developing alcoholism and alcohol-related problems. These include:

1. *Gender.* The lifetime prevalence of alcohol dependence among women and men is similar, according to some studies. For example, a Canadian survey reported that the lifetime prevalence among women and men was 11% and 12% respectively (Lukassen & Beaudet, 2005). However, other studies have found that alcohol abuse and dependence is more common in men (APA, 2000a). The conflicting results may have to do with when the studies were conducted; the gender gap in the prevalence of alcoholism is narrowing, with women catching up to men (Zilberman, Tavares, & el-Guebaly, 2003). This seems to be partly because social drinking has become more acceptable for women. In general, women start drinking several years later than men, but once alcohol abuse or dependence develops in women, the disorder progresses somewhat more rapidly. But in general, the clinical course of alcohol dependence is more similar than different (APA, 2000a).

Alcohol seems to "go to women's heads" more rapidly than men's. This is apparently because women metabolize less alcohol in the stomach than men do. Why? It appears that women have less of an enzyme that metabolizes alcohol in the stomach (Frezza et al., 1990). Alcohol then reaches women's circulatory systems and brains relatively intact. This means that gram for gram, women drinkers absorb more alcohol into their bloodstreams than their male counterparts. It is almost as if women were injecting alcohol intravenously. It is not a substance to be trifled with.

2. *Age.* The great majority of cases of alcohol dependence develop in young adulthood, before age 40. The typical age of onset is late adolescence (Sher, Grekin, & Williams, 2005). Although alcohol-use disorders tend to develop somewhat later in women than men, women who develop these problems experience health, social, and occupational problems by middle age just as their male counterparts do. Although many people who develop alcohol problems "grow out" of them, a significant number of people have lifelong problems (Sher et al., 2005).

3. *Antisocial personality disorder.* Antisocial behaviour in adolescence or adulthood increases the risk of later alcoholism (Sher et al., 2005).

4. *Family history.* The best predictor of problem drinking in adulthood appears to be a family history of alcohol abuse. Family members who drink may act as models and "set a poor example." Moreover, the biological relatives of people with alcohol dependence may also inherit a predisposition that makes them more likely to develop problems with alcohol (Söderpalm, Gordh, & Söderpalm, 2011).

5. *Sociodemographic factors.* Alcohol problems are more common among people of lower income and educational levels and among people living alone (CCSA & CAMH, 1999; Khan, Murray, & Barnes, 2002). In Canada, alcohol and drug dependence are more common among Aboriginal than non-Aboriginal people (Tjepkema, 2002). We further examine ethnic group differences in alcohol use and abuse in the accompanying feature, "Focus on Diversity: Ethnicity and Alcohol Abuse," on page 260.

QUESTIONNAIRE

How Do You Know If You're Hooked?

Are you dependent on alcohol? If you shake and shiver and feel tormented when you go without a drink for a while, the answer is clear enough. Sometimes the clues are more subtle, however.

The following self-test can shed some light on the question. Simply place a che ck mark in the yes or no column for each item. Then refer to the key on page 259.

	Yes	No
1. Do you sometimes go on drinking binges?	___	___
2. Do you tend to keep away from your family or friends when you are drinking?	___	___
3. Do you become irritated when your family or friends talk about your drinking?	___	___
4. Do you feel guilty now and then about your drinking?	___	___
5. Do you often regret the things you have said or done when you have been drinking?	___	___
6. Do you find that you fail to keep the promises you make about controlling or cutting down on your drinking?	___	___
7. Do you eat irregularly or not at all when you are drinking?	___	___
8. Do you feel low after drinking?	___	___
9. Do you sometimes miss work or appointments because of drinking?	___	___
10. Do you use more and more to get drunk or high?	___	___

Source: Adapted from "Addictive Personalities" (1989, February 20), *Newsweek,* p. 52.

Striking cultural differences in alcohol use and abuse have long been evident. Chinese and Jewish populations, for example, are considerably less susceptible to alcohol problems than Irish people and some Aboriginal groups (Prince, 2000). In Canada, the Aboriginal population consists of three broad groups: First Nations, Métis, and Inuit people. They encompass a diverse range of smaller groups, differing from one another in history, culture, and traditions (Tjepkema, 2002). Surveys of people living in First Nations communities reveal that more than 70% of respondents believe alcohol abuse is an important problem in their community (Rodgers & Abas, 1988; Statistics Canada, 1993). Alcohol abuse in Aboriginal communities is often associated with other forms of drug abuse, such as inhalant abuse (Gfellner & Hundelby, 1995). Alcohol-related health problems, such as liver disease, are also significantly higher in Aboriginal populations (Scott, 1994).

Taken as a group, Aboriginal Canadians, compared to their non-Aboriginal counterparts, do not have more of a tendency to drink alcohol. But those who do consume alcohol are likely to drink more heavily, even when socioeconomic status is taken into consideration (Haggarty, Cernovsky, Kermeen, & Merskey, 2000; Lavallée & Bourgault, 2000; Tjepkema, 2002). Tjepkema, for example, assessed "heavy drinking" (defined as five or more drinks in a single sitting) among off-reserve Aboriginal and non-Aboriginal Canadians. Fewer Aboriginal than non-Aboriginal people were weekly drinkers (27% versus 38%). The groups did not differ in the proportion of people who were light or abstinent drinkers (both 50%), but the Aboriginal group had more heavy drinkers (23% versus 16%). The same pattern was found regardless of whether the respondents lived in urban or rural areas. Similar findings were obtained in a study of women in northern Quebec: alcohol consumption was less frequent among Aboriginal women, but those who did drink consumed higher quantities of alcohol (Lavallée & Bourgault, 2000).

Group differences in alcohol use and abuse have been attributed to psychosocial factors such as cultural or religious attitudes toward drinking. The cultural traditions concerning the use of alcohol in family, religious, and social settings, particularly during childhood, can influence the risk for later alcohol problems (APA, 2000a). Jewish people, for example, tend to expose children to the ritual use of wine within a religious context and to impose strong cultural restraints on excessive and underage drinking.

Psychosocial factors within cultures also may influence drinking patterns. To illustrate, Gfellner and Hundelby (1990) investigated the predictors of drug and alcohol use in a small urban community in Manitoba. The number of a person's friends who used alcohol or drugs was the strongest predictor of alcohol or drug use for both Aboriginal and non-Aboriginal students. Peer attitudes about drug or alcohol use was also a predictor for Aboriginal students (Gfellner & Hundelby, 1990).

Many writers see the prevalence of alcoholism among Aboriginal people as a consequence of the forced attempt by European colonists to eradicate tribal language and culture, leading to a loss of cultural identity that sets the stage for alcoholism, drug abuse, and depression. Kahn (1982) explains the greater incidence of psychopathology among Aboriginal people in terms of the disruption in traditional culture caused by the appropriation of their lands by European powers and the attempts to sever them from their cultural traditions while denying them full access to the dominant Western culture. Aboriginal people have since lived in severe cultural and social disorganization that has resulted in high rates of psychopathology and substance abuse. Beset by such problems, Aboriginal adults are prone to child abuse and neglect. Abuse and neglect contribute to feelings of hopelessness and depression among adolescents, who then seek to escape their feelings through alcohol and other drugs (Berlin, 1987).

Conceptions of Alcoholism: Disease, Moral Defect, or Behaviour Pattern? According to the medical perspective, alcoholism is a disease. E. M. Jellinek (1960), a leading proponent of the disease model, believed that alcoholism is a permanent, irreversible condition. Jellinek believed that once a person with alcoholism takes a drink, the biochemical effects of the drug on the brain create an irresistible physical craving for more. Jellinek's ideas have contributed to the view that "once an alcoholic, always an alcoholic." Alcoholics Anonymous (AA), which adopted Jellinek's concepts, views people who suffer from alcoholism as either drinking or "recovering." In other words, alcoholism is never cured. Jellinek's concepts have also supported the idea that "just one drink" will cause the person with alcoholism to "fall off the wagon." In this view, the sole path to recovery is abstinence.

Although the disease model has achieved prominence and gained wide acceptance, the nature of alcoholism continues to be debated. For most of history, immoderate drinking was seen as a moral defect. Alcoholism was first considered a disease in the

Research into the acculturation hypothesis suggests that alcohol and drug abuse is greatest among Aboriginal youths who identify least closely with traditional values. Bicultural youth, consisting of those who felt comfortable within both their traditional culture and the larger society, showed the lowest levels of abuse of alcohol and other drugs ("Acculturation," 2004). These findings would suggest that the best adjustment (meaning the lowest levels of culture-related stress) is found among youth who have adapted to both cultures. Other factors, such as the poverty faced by many Aboriginal people, may also contribute to stress and alcohol and drug abuse.

Biological factors also appear to contribute to ethnic differences in alcohol use and abuse. The low rates of alcohol problems in Asian countries appear to be related to a lack in some Asians of the enzyme aldehyde dehydrogenase, which is involved in the metabolizing of alcohol in the body. Roughly 50% of Asians are at least partially missing the enzyme, compared to only 5% to 15% of Caucasians (APA, 2000a; Prince, 2000). The enzyme may be partially or totally absent—an estimated 10% of Asian people completely lack the enzyme. When they drink alcohol, they experience a flushed face and palpitations, and sometimes nausea, dizziness, and headaches. This reaction can be so intense that it sometimes leads the person to abstain altogether from drinking. The other 40% of Asian people with a relative deficiency of the enzyme have less intense reactions but still are less likely to develop an alcohol problem (APA, 2000a). The flushing response is evident even in infants (Prince, 2000) and can be a deterrent to alcohol use and abuse. However, the flushing response provides only a modest defence against excessive drinking. Among the Japanese, for example, alcohol abuse has increased considerably in recent years, despite their susceptibility to the flushing response (Prince, 2000).

Alcohol and ethnic diversity. The damaging effects of alcohol abuse appear to be taking the heaviest toll on Canada's First Nations people. Jewish people have relatively low incidences of alcohol-related problems, perhaps because they tend to expose children to the ritual use of wine in childhood and impose strong cultural restraints on excessive drinking. Asian people tend to drink less heavily than most other Canadians, in part because of cultural constraints and possibly because they have less biological tolerance of alcohol, as shown by a greater flushing response.

1960s. Since that time, the campaign to instill this view has been so pervasive that most people now endorse it.

Yet not all professionals regard alcoholism as a medical disease. To some, the term is used as a label to describe a harmful pattern of alcohol ingestion and related behaviours. In this view, the "just-one-drink" hypothesis is not a biochemical inevitability. For these observers, it is instead a common self-fulfilling prophecy, as we see later in the chapter.

Psychological Effects of Alcohol   The effects of alcohol or other drugs vary from person to person. By and large, they reflect the interaction of (1) the physiological effects of the substances, and (2) our interpretations of those effects. What do most people expect from alcohol? People frequently hold stereotypical expectations that alcohol will reduce states of tension, enhance pleasurable experiences, wash away their worries, and enhance their social skills. But what does alcohol actually do?

At a physiological level, alcohol, like the benzodiazepines, appears to heighten the sensitivity of the gamma-aminobutyric acid (GABA) receptor sites (Suzdak et al., 1986). Because GABA is an inhibitory neurotransmitter, increasing the action of GABA reduces overall nervous system activity, producing feelings of relaxation. As people drink, their senses become clouded, and balance and co-ordination suffer. Still higher doses act on the parts of the brain that regulate involuntary vital functions such as heart rate, respiration rate, and body temperature.

People may do many things when drinking that they would not do when sober, in part because of expectations concerning the drug, and in part because of the drug's effects on the brain. For example, they may become more flirtatious or sexually aggressive or say or do things they later regret. Their behaviour may reflect their expectation that alcohol has liberating effects and provides an external excuse for questionable behaviour. Later they can claim, "It was the alcohol, not me." The drug may impair the brain's ability to curb impulsive behaviour, perhaps by interfering with information-processing functions (Steele & Southwick, 1985). Although alcohol may make them feel more relaxed and self-confident, it may prevent them from exercising good judgment, which can lead them to make choices they would ordinarily reject, such as engaging in risky sex (Gordon & Carey, 1996). One of the lures of alcohol is that it induces short-term feelings of euphoria and elation that can drown self-doubts and self-criticism. Alcohol may also make people less capable of perceiving the unfortunate consequences of their behaviour. Chronic use, however, may deepen feelings of depression. Alcohol dependence and other substance-use disorders are strongly correlated with depression (Currie et al., 2005; Lukassen & Beaudet, 2005). This correlation exists for various reasons, as described later in this chapter.

Alcohol in increasing amounts can dampen sexual arousal or excitement and impair our ability to perform sexually. As an intoxicant, alcohol also hampers co-ordination and motor ability and slurs speech. These effects help explain why alcohol use is implicated in so many road fatalities, other accidents, and violent crimes (see Figure 7.1).

In a more general sense, Health Canada reports that in 2010, 14.6% of Canadians reported experiencing at least one harm in their lifetime as a result of their alcohol use. The prevalence of lifetime harm due to alcohol use for males (20.4%) was double that reported by females (9.2%). *Harm* is defined by Health Canada as problems occurring in any of the following eight areas: physical health; friendships and social life; financial position; home life or marriage; work, studies, or employment opportunities; legal issues; learning ability; and housing.

Physical Health and Alcohol   Chronic, heavy alcohol use affects virtually every organ and body system either directly or indirectly. Heavy alcohol use is linked to a higher risk of various forms of cancer, such as cancer of the throat, esophagus, larynx, stomach, colon, liver, and possibly cancer of the bowel and breast (Fuchs et al., 1995). Heavy drinking is also linked to coronary heart disease, ulcers, hypertension, gout, and pancreatitis

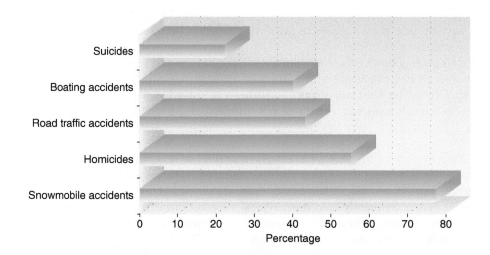

FIGURE 7.1 Estimated percentages of deaths in Canada from various causes connected with the use of alcohol.
Alcohol is a factor in over half of the homicides in Canada.
Source: Adapted from Dingle, Samtani, Kraatz, & Solomon, 2002.

(painful inflammation of the pancreas) (CCSA & CAMH, 1999; U.S. Department of Health and Human Services [USDHHS], 2001). The linkages noted here are based on a statistical association or correlation between heavy drinking on the one hand and health problems on the other. These linkages are strongly suggestive of the damaging effects of heavy drinking. However, because they are based on correlational evidence, we cannot conclude they are necessarily causal.

Heavy drinking clearly does damage the liver, the organ that serves as the primary site of alcohol metabolism. Chronic, heavy consumption of alcohol is a leading cause of illness and death from liver disease (USDHHS, 2001). Two of the major forms of alcohol-related liver disease are alcoholic hepatitis, a serious and potentially life-threatening inflammation of the liver, and cirrhosis of the liver, a potentially fatal liver disease in which healthy liver cells are replaced with scar tissue. To a great extent, the health risks of alcohol consumption depend on the amount and duration of use. Some people may also be genetically more susceptible to the harmful effects of heavy alcohol use than others.

Habitual drinkers tend to be malnourished, which can put them at risk of complications arising from nutritional deficiencies. Chronic drinking is thus associated with nutritionally linked disorders such as cirrhosis of the liver (linked to protein deficiency) and **alcohol-induced persisting amnestic disorder** (connected with vitamin B deficiency). Alcohol-induced persisting amnestic disorder (also known as **Korsakoff's syndrome**) is characterized by glaring confusion, disorientation, and memory loss regarding recent events.

All told, it is estimated that in 1995 over 6500 Canadians lost their lives as a result of alcohol consumption, with motor vehicle accidents, liver cirrhosis, and suicide as the primary causes (CCSA & CAMH, 1999). Each year, it is estimated that thousands of Canadians die because of alcohol. After tobacco, alcohol is the second leading cause of premature death in our society. Men who drink heavily stand nearly twice the risk of dying before the age of 65 as men who abstain; women who drink heavily are more than three times as likely to die before age 65 as are women who abstain ("NIAAA Report," 1990).

Mothers who drink during pregnancy put their fetuses at risk for infant mortality, birth defects, central nervous system dysfunctions, and later academic problems (H. E. Jones, 2006). Many children whose mothers drank during pregnancy develop fetal alcohol syndrome (FAS), a syndrome characterized by facial features such as a flattened nose, widely spaced eyes, an underdeveloped upper jaw, and mental retardation. Research from all over the world suggests FAS is disturbingly common, affecting 1 in 100 babies (Mukherjee, Hollins, & Turk, 2006).

We don't know whether a minimum amount of alcohol is needed to produce FAS. Some children of mothers who drank as little as two ounces of alcohol a day during their first trimesters have been found to have FAS (Astley, Clarren, Little, Sampson, & Daling, 1992). Although the question of whether there is any safe dose of alcohol during pregnancy continues to be debated, the fact remains that FAS is an entirely preventable birth defect. The safest course for women who know or suspect they are pregnant is to not drink. Period. The same applies, of course, to other substances, such as cocaine and heroin. Even tobacco smoking during pregnancy can have harmful effects, including low birth weight and sudden infant death syndrome (SIDS) (H. E. Jones, 2006).

Moderate Drinking: Is There a Health Benefit? According to the Canadian guidelines for low-risk drinking, weekly intake should not exceed 14 drinks for men and 9 for women, and daily consumption should not exceed 2 drinks for both women and men (Adlaf et al., 2005). Despite the above list of adverse effects associated with heavy drinking, growing evidence links light-to-moderate use of alcohol with reduced risk of heart attacks and lower death rates ("Alcohol and the Heart," 1996; Thun et al., 1997). Researchers suspect that alcohol may help prevent blood clots from forming that can clog arteries and lead to heart attacks. Alcohol also appears to increase the levels of HDL cholesterol—the so-called good cholesterol—that sweeps away fatty deposits along artery walls (Ochs, 1998). Although light to moderate use of alcohol (about one drink per day) may have a protective effect on the heart, public health officials caution that promoting the possible health benefits of alcohol may backfire by increasing the risks of alcohol abuse and dependence (Brody, 1994). Alcohol use is also linked to an increased

alcohol-induced persisting amnestic disorder See *Korsakoff's syndrome.*

Korsakoff's syndrome Form of brain damage associated with chronic thiamine deficiency. The syndrome is associated with chronic alcoholism and characterized by memory loss, disorientation, and the tendency to invent memories to replace lost ones (confabulation). Also called *alcohol-induced persisting amnestic disorder.*

Alcohol Use: No Disorder	Alcohol Abuse: Disorder
Navleen is a 25-year-old manager of a retail store. She recently moved into an apartment with a roommate after living with her parents through university. She is enjoying her newfound freedom, especially the freedom to stay out late with her friends. Her closest friends are all single and they enjoy going to nightclubs to dance. Navleen goes out at least three nights per week, and often has several glasses of wine when out. Her friends also drink when they are out, and they plan ahead to share taxis home. Every once in a while, Navleen has more than a few glasses of wine. For example, a few weeks ago, Navleen was celebrating a friend's birthday and ended up drinking several cocktails and shooters. She hadn't intended to drink that much but got caught up in the celebration. The next morning, she could not get out of bed and ended up calling in sick. Once she felt better, she reminded herself to drink less at the next birthday celebration. At the next outing, she stuck with a few glasses of wine and felt much better the next day.	Jenelle lives on her own and works at a local bank. She is single and enjoys partying with her other single friends. She goes out two or three nights per week, and often consumes a number of drinks when out. Although she goes out regularly, Jenelle does not plan for how she will get home. On numerous occasions, she has accepted a ride home from men she has just met who have also been drinking. Fortunately, she has not been in a car accident yet, though she recognizes, after the fact, that she has put herself in danger a number of times. Recently, Jenelle had a very frightening experience. After a night of partying and drinking, she accepted a ride home from a man she met that evening. Instead of taking her home, he began driving toward a remote end of the city. Jenelle did not realize this immediately, but when she did she became fearful about what this man might do to her. She began to cry and beg him to take her home. Luckily, he turned around and took her home, but Jenelle realized that she had narrowly escaped a horrible situation. She realized that her judgment was grossly impaired by her drinking.

risk of some forms of cancer, including breast cancer (Smith-Warner et al., 1998). Heavy drinking is clearly damaging to the heart and other organs, and any level of alcohol intake by a pregnant woman may be harmful to a developing fetus. Health-promotion efforts might be better directed toward finding safer ways of achieving the health benefits associated with moderate drinking (such as by quitting smoking, lowering dietary fat and cholesterol, and exercising more regularly) than by encouraging alcohol consumption (Gaziano et al., 1993).

BARBITURATES Estimates indicate that almost 1% of the adult population meet the criteria for a substance-abuse or dependence disorder involving the use of barbiturates, sleep medication (hypnotics), or anti-anxiety agents at some point in their lives (APA, 2000a; J. M. Russell, Newman, & Bland, 1994). **Barbiturates** such as amobarbital, pentobarbital, phenobarbital, and secobarbital are depressants or **sedatives** with several medical uses, including alleviation of anxiety and tension, anaesthetization of pain, treatment of epilepsy and high blood pressure, and short-term treatment of insomnia. Barbiturate use quickly leads to psychological dependence and physiological dependence in the form of both tolerance and the development of a withdrawal syndrome.

In contrast to the profiles of young cocaine or narcotic abusers, most barbiturate addicts are middle-aged people who initially used sedatives to combat anxiety or insomnia and then got hooked. Because of concerns about abuse, physicians today prescribe other drugs for the temporary relief of anxiety and tension, such as minor tranquillizers like Valium and Librium. However, it is now recognized that minor tranquillizers can also create physiological dependence. Moreover, regular use of these drugs fails to help people alter the sources of stress in their lives.

Barbiturates are also popular street drugs because they are relaxing and produce a mild state of euphoria or "high." High doses of barbiturates, like alcohol, produce drowsiness, slurred speech, motor impairment, irritability, and poor judgment—a particularly deadly combination of effects when their use is combined with the operation of a motor vehicle. The effects of barbiturates last from three to six hours.

Because of synergistic effects, a mixture of barbiturates and alcohol is about four times as powerful as either drug used by itself (Aston & Cullumbine, 1959). A combination

barbiturates Types of depressant drugs that are sometimes used to relieve anxiety or induce sleep but that are highly addictive.

sedatives Types of depressant drugs that reduce states of tension and restlessness and induce sleep.

of barbiturates and alcohol was implicated in the deaths of the entertainers Marilyn Monroe and Judy Garland. Even such widely used anti-anxiety drugs as Valium and Librium, which have a wide margin of safety when used alone, can be dangerous and lead to overdose when their use is combined with alcohol (APA, 2000a).

Physiologically dependent people need to be withdrawn from sedatives, barbiturates, and anti-anxiety agents carefully and only under medical supervision. Abrupt withdrawal can produce states of delirium that can be life-threatening (APA, 2000a). Delirium may involve visual, tactile, or auditory hallucinations and disturbances in thinking processes and consciousness. The longer the period of use and the higher the doses used, the greater the risk of severe withdrawal effects. Grand mal epileptic seizures and even death may occur if the individual undergoes untreated, abrupt withdrawal.

OPIATES Opiates are **narcotics,** a term applied to addictive drugs that have pain-relieving and sleep-inducing properties. They are derived from the poppy plant and include such derivatives as morphine, heroin, and codeine. Synthetic opiates such as Demerol and Percodan are manufactured in a laboratory to have effects similar to natural opiates. The major medical application of opiates—natural or synthetic—is the relief of pain; that is, **analgesia.** Opiates produce a rush or intense feelings of pleasure, which is the primary reason for their popularity as street drugs. They also dull awareness of one's personal problems, which is attractive to people seeking a mental escape from stress.

The medical use of opiates is carefully regulated because overdoses can lead to comas and even death, although prescription opiates are, unfortunately, readily available on the street—and through the Internet. Street use of these drugs is associated with many fatal overdoses and accidents. Estimates are that about 0.7% of the adult population (7 people in 1000) currently have or have had an opiate abuse or dependence disorder (APA, 2000a; J. M. Russell et al., 1994). Once dependence sets in, it usually follows a chronic course, although periods of temporary abstinence are frequent (APA, 2000a).

Opiates become drugs of abuse because they are capable of producing a euphoric state of pleasure or rush. They produce pleasurable effects apparently because they stimulate brain centres that regulate sensations of pleasure and pain (USDHHS, 1986). It appears that the brain has its own natural opiate system. Two revealing discoveries were made in the 1970s. One was that neurons in the brain have receptor sites into which opiates fit—like a key in a lock. The second was that the human body produces substances similar to opiates in chemical structures that dock at those same receptor sites (A. Goldstein, 1976). Some of these natural substances are labelled **endorphins,** which is short for *endogenous morphine*—that is, morphine coming from within. Endorphins appear to play a role in regulating states of pleasure and pain. Opiates mimic the actions of endorphins by docking at receptor sites intended for them, which in turn stimulates the brain centres that produce pleasurable sensations.

The opiate heroin is usually injected either directly beneath the skin ("skin popping") or into a vein ("mainlining"). You may be surprised to learn that heroin is not the most widely abused opiate. Studies from Canada and the United States indicate that prescription opiates, often illicitly obtained, such as oxycodone (OxyContin) and hydrocodone (Vicodin), are more widely abused than heroin (Kuehn, 2007).

The positive effects of opiates are immediate. In the case of heroin, there is a powerful rush that lasts for 5 to 15 minutes and a state of satisfaction, euphoria, and well-being that lasts for 3 to 5 hours. In this state, all positive drives seem satisfied. All negative feelings of guilt, tension, and anxiety disappear. With prolonged usage, addiction can develop. Many physiologically dependent people support their habits through dealing (selling heroin), prostitution, or selling stolen goods. Heroin is a depressant, however, and its chemical effects do not directly stimulate criminal or aggressive behaviour.

The withdrawal syndrome associated with dependence on opiates can be severe. It begins within four to six hours after the last dose. Flu-like symptoms are accompanied by anxiety, feelings of restlessness, irritability, and cravings for the drug. Within a few days, symptoms progress to rapid pulse, high blood pressure, cramps, tremors, hot and cold flashes, fever, vomiting, insomnia, and diarrhea, among other symptoms. Although these symptoms can be uncomfortable, they are usually not devastating, especially when

opiates Types of depressant drugs with strong addictive properties that are derived from the opium poppy; provide feelings of euphoria and relief from pain.

narcotics Drugs, such as opiates, that are used for pain relief and treatment of insomnia, but which have strong addictive potential.

analgesia State of relief from pain without loss of consciousness.

endorphins Natural substances that function as neurotransmitters in the brain and are similar in their effects to morphine.

other drugs are prescribed to relieve them. Moreover, unlike withdrawal from barbiturates, the withdrawal syndrome rarely results in death.

Stimulants

Stimulants such as amphetamines and cocaine are psychoactive substances that increase the activity of the nervous system. Effects vary somewhat from drug to drug, but some stimulants contribute to feelings of euphoria and self-confidence. Stimulants such as amphetamines, cocaine, and even caffeine (the stimulant found in coffee) increase the availability in the brain of the neurotransmitters norepinephrine and dopamine. High levels of these neurotransmitters, therefore, remain available in the synaptic gaps between neurons, which maintains high levels of nervous system activity and states of high arousal.

amphetamines Types of synthetic stimulants, such as Dexedrine and Benzedrine. Abuse can trigger an amphetamine psychosis that mimics acute episodes of schizophrenia.

AMPHETAMINES The **amphetamines** are a class of synthetic stimulants. Street names for stimulants include speed, uppers, bennies (for amphetamine sulfate; trade name Benzedrine), dexies (dextroamphetamine; trade name Dexedrine), and meth (for methamphetamine, a street drug).

Amphetamines are used in high doses for their euphoric rush. They are often taken in pill form or smoked in a relatively pure form called "ice" or "crystal meth." The most potent form of amphetamine, liquid methamphetamine, is injected directly into the veins and produces an intense and immediate rush. Some users inject methamphetamine for days on end to maintain an extended high. Eventually, such highs come to an end. People who have been on extended highs sometimes "crash" and fall into a deep sleep or depression, and may suffer from brain damage (Maxwell, 2005). Some people commit suicide on the way down. High doses can cause restlessness, irritability, hallucinations, paranoid delusions, loss of appetite, and insomnia.

Physiological dependence can develop, leading to an abstinence syndrome characterized most often by depression and fatigue as well as unpleasant, vivid dreams, insomnia or hypersomnia (excessive sleeping), increased appetite, and either a slowing down of motor behaviour or agitation (APA, 2000a). Psychological dependence is seen most often in people who use amphetamines as a way of coping with stress or depression.

amphetamine psychosis Psychotic state induced by ingestion of amphetamines.

Violent behaviour may occur in the context of amphetamine dependence, especially when the drug is smoked or injected intravenously (APA, 2000a). The hallucinations and delusions of the **amphetamine psychosis** mimic the features of paranoid schizophrenia, which has encouraged researchers to study the chemical changes induced by amphetamines as possible causes of schizophrenia.

cocaine Stimulant derived from coca leaves.

COCAINE It might surprise you to learn that the original formula for Coca-Cola contained an extract of **cocaine**. In 1906, however, the company withdrew cocaine from its secret formula. The beverage was originally described as a "brain tonic and intellectual beverage," in part because of its cocaine content. Cocaine is a natural stimulant extracted from the leaves of the coca plant—the plant from which the soft drink obtained its name. Coca-Cola is still flavoured with an extract from the coca plant, but one that is not known to be psychoactive.

It was long believed that cocaine was not physically addicting. However, evidence supports the addictive properties of the drug in producing a tolerance effect and an identifiable withdrawal syndrome, consisting of depression, inability to experience pleasure, and intense cravings for the drug (APA, 2000a). Withdrawal symptoms are usually brief in duration and may involve a "crash" or period of intense depression and exhaustion following a cocaine binge.

crack Hardened, smokable form of cocaine.

Cocaine is brewed from coca leaves as a "tea," breathed in ("snorted") in powder form, and injected ("shot up") in liquid form. The rise in the use of **crack**, a hardened form of cocaine suitable for smoking that may contain more than 75% pure cocaine, has made cocaine—once the toy of the well-to-do—available to adolescents. Crack "rocks"— so called because they look like small white pebbles—are available in small ready-to-smoke amounts and are considered the most habit-forming street drug available. Crack produces a prompt and potent rush that wears off in a few minutes. The rush from snorting cocaine is milder and takes a while to develop, but it tends to linger longer than the rush of crack.

Freebasing also intensifies the effects of cocaine. Cocaine in powder form is heated with ether, freeing the psychoactive chemical base of the drug, and then smoked. Ether, however, is highly flammable.

Cocaine is most commonly used by young adults, although even in Canada it is not widely used—a 1994 survey found that 1.7% of young adults had tried cocaine in the previous 12 months (CCSA & CAMH, 2008). The lifetime prevalence of cocaine dependence in Canada is about 0.5%, which is lower than in the United States (2%) (APA, 2000a; J. M. Russell et al., 1994). It is unclear whether Canada will eventually catch up to the United States.

Cocaine abuse is characterized by periodic binges lasting perhaps 12 to 36 hours, which are then followed by 2 to 5 days of abstinence, during which time the abuser may experience cravings that prompt another binge (Gawin & Ellinwood, 1989). According to one estimate, between 10% and 15% of people who try snorting cocaine eventually develop cocaine abuse or dependence (Gawin, 1991).

Cocaine increases the availability in the brain of the neurotransmitter dopamine, producing a pleasurable "high" (Volkow et al., 1997). The drug produces a sudden rise in blood pressure, constricts blood vessels (with associated reduction of the oxygen supply to the heart), and accelerates the heart rate. Overdoses can produce restlessness, insomnia, headaches, nausea, convulsions, tremors, hallucinations, delusions, and even sudden death. Death may result from respiratory or cardiovascular collapse. Although intravenous use of cocaine carries the greatest risk of a lethal overdose, other forms of use can also be fatal. Table 7.4 on page 268 summarizes a number of the health risks of cocaine use.

Repeated and high-dose use of cocaine can lead to depression and anxiety (R. D. Weiss et al., 1994). Depression may be severe enough to prompt suicidal behaviour. Both initial and routine users report episodes of "crashing" (feelings of depression after a binge), although crashing is more common among long-term high-dose users. Psychotic behaviours, which can be induced by cocaine use as well as by use of amphetamines, tend to become more severe with continued use. Cocaine psychosis is usually preceded by a period of heightened suspiciousness, depressed mood, compulsive behaviour, fault finding, irritability, and increasing paranoia (R. D. Weiss et al., 1994). Psychosis may also include visual and auditory hallucinations and delusions of persecution.

NICOTINE Habitual smoking is not just a bad habit. It is also a form of physical addiction to a stimulant drug, nicotine, found in tobacco products including cigarettes, cigars, and smokeless tobacco (D. A. Kessler et al., 1997). Smoking (or other tobacco use) is the means of administering the drug to the body.

More than 30 000 lives in Canada are lost each year from smoking-related causes, mostly from lung cancer, cardiovascular disease, and chronic obstructive lung disease (CCSA & CAMH, 1999). Smoking is implicated in one in three cancer deaths (American Cancer Society, 2003). Smokers overall stand twice the risk of dying from cancer as nonsmokers; among heavy smokers, the risk is four times as great (Bartecchi, MacKenzie, & Schrier, 1994; Peto, Lopez, Boreham, & Thun, 2006).

The World Health Organization estimates that a billion people worldwide smoke, and more than three million die each year from smoking-related causes. Smoking is expected to become the world's leading cause of death by the year 2020 ("Smoking," 1996).

Largely because of health concerns, the percentage of Canadians who smoke declined from 61% of men and 38% of women in 1965 to 18.6% overall in 2009 (Health Canada, 2010). Teenage smoking has not decreased as dramatically. Young adults aged 20 to 24 still have the highest smoking rate of any age group, at 32%. The younger that people start to smoke, the more difficulty they have in quitting (Health Canada, 2001a).

Cigarette smoking causes cancer of the larynx, oral cavity, esophagus, and lungs and may contribute to cancer of the bladder, pancreas, and kidneys. Pregnant women who smoke risk miscarriage, premature birth, and birth defects in their offspring. Smokers

Crack. Crack "rocks" resemble small white pebbles. Crack produces a powerful, prompt rush when smoked. Small, ready-to-smoke doses are available at prices that make them affordable to adolescents.

freebasing Method of ingesting cocaine by means of heating the drug with ether to separate its most potent component (its "free base") and then smoking the extract.

TABLE 7.4

Health Risks of Cocaine Use

Physical Effects and Risks

Effects	Risks
Increased heart rate	Accelerated heart rate may give rise to heart irregularities that can be fatal, such as ventricular tachycardia (extremely rapid contractions) or ventricular fibrillation (irregular, weakened contractions).
Increased blood pressure	Rapid or large changes in blood pressure may place too much stress on a weak-walled blood vessel in the brain, which can cause it to burst, producing cerebral hemorrhage or stroke.
Increased body temperature	Can be dangerous to some individuals.
Possible grand mal seizures (epileptic convulsions)	Some grand mal seizures are fatal, particularly when they occur in rapid succession or while driving a car.
Respiratory effects	Overdoses can produce gasping or shallow irregular breathing that can lead to respiratory arrest.
Dangerous effects in special populations	Various special populations are at greater risk from cocaine use or overdose. People with coronary heart disease have died because their heart muscles were taxed beyond the capacity of their arteries to supply oxygen.

Medical Complications of Cocaine Use

Nasal problems	When cocaine is administered intranasally (snorted), it constricts the blood vessels serving the nose, decreasing the supply of oxygen to these tissues, leading to irritation and inflammation of the mucous membranes, ulcers in the nostrils, frequent nosebleeds, and chronic sneezing and nasal congestion. Chronic use may lead to tissue death of the nasal septum, the part of the nose that separates the nostrils, requiring plastic surgery.
Lung problems	Freebase smoking may lead to serious lung problems within three months of initial use.
Malnutrition	Cocaine suppresses the appetite so that weight loss, malnutrition, and vitamin deficiencies may accompany regular use.
Seizures	Grand mal seizures, typical of epileptics, may occur due to irregularities in the electrical activity of the brain. Repeated use may lower the seizure threshold, described as a type of "kindling" effect.
Sexual problems	Despite the popular belief that cocaine is an aphrodisiac, frequent use can lead to sexual dysfunctions, such as impotence and failure to ejaculate among males, and decreased sexual interest in both sexes. Although some people report initial increased sexual pleasure with cocaine use, they may become dependent on cocaine for sexual arousal or lose the ability to enjoy sex for extended periods following long-term use.
Other effects	Cocaine use may increase the risk of miscarriage among pregnant women. Sharing of infected needles is associated with transmission of hepatitis, endocarditis (infection of the heart valve), and HIV. Repeated injections often lead to skin infections as bacteria are introduced into the deeper levels of the skin.

Source: Adapted from Weiss & Mirin, 1994.

have twice the risk of developing Alzheimer's disease and other forms of dementia as nonsmokers ("Extinguishing Alzheimer's," 1998). Lung cancer, which in 90% of cases is caused by smoking, has now surpassed breast cancer as the leading killer of women. Although quitting smoking clearly has health benefits, it unfortunately does not reduce the risks to normal (nonsmoking) levels. The lesson is clear: if you don't smoke, don't start. But if you do smoke, quit.

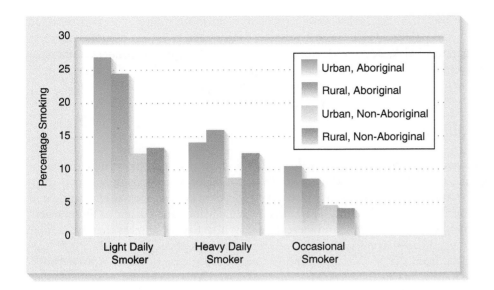

FIGURE 7.2 **Smoking prevalence among people 15 years of age and older, according to off-reserve Aboriginal status and geographic region, Canada.**
Source: Based on Tjepkema, 2002.

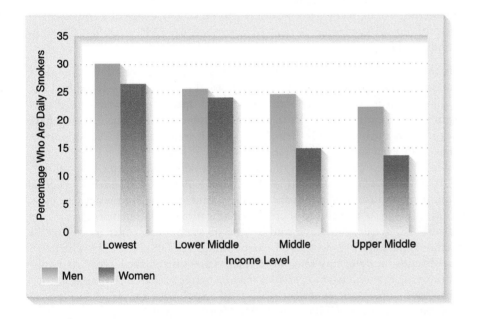

FIGURE 7.3 **Cigarette smoking in Canada, according to income status.**
Smoking is most prevalent among poorer (and less educated) members of society.
Source: Adapted from Canadian Centre on Substance Abuse and Centre for Addiction and Mental Health, 1999.

The prevalence of smoking among adults is higher among Aboriginal than non-Aboriginal people, regardless of whether they live in rural or urban environments (see Figure 7.2). Smoking is becoming increasingly concentrated among the poorer and less well-educated segments of the population (CCSA & CAMH, 1999; Health Canada, 2001a) (see Figure 7.3).

Nicotine is delivered to the body through the use of tobacco products. As a stimulant, it increases alertness but can also give rise to cold, clammy skin, nausea and vomiting, dizziness and faintness, and diarrhea—all of which account for the discomforts of novice smokers. Nicotine also stimulates the release of epinephrine, a hormone that generates a rush of autonomic activity including rapid heartbeat and release of stores of sugar into the blood. Nicotine quells the appetite and provides a sort of psychological "kick" (Grunberg, 1991). Nicotine also leads to the release of endorphins, opiate-like hormones produced in the brain. This may account for the pleasurable feelings associated with tobacco use.

Habitual use of nicotine leads to a physiological dependence on the drug (Lichtenstein & Glasgow, 1992). Nicotine dependence is associated with both tolerance (intake rises to a level of a pack or two a day before levelling off) and a characteristic withdrawal syndrome. The withdrawal syndrome for nicotine includes such features as lack of energy, depressed mood, irritability, frustration, nervousness, impaired concentration, light-headedness and dizziness, drowsiness, headaches, fatigue, irregular bowels, insomnia, cramps, lowered heart rate, heart palpitations, increased appetite, weight gain, sweating, tremors, and craving for cigarettes (APA, 2000a; Klesges et al., 1997). It is nicotine dependence, not cigarette smoking per se, that is classifiable as a psychological disorder in the DSM system. Between 80% and 90% of regular smokers have nicotine dependence (APA, 2000a).

Hallucinogens

hallucinogens Substances that give rise to hallucinations.

psychedelics Class of drugs that induce sensory distortions or hallucinations. Also called *hallucinogens*.

Hallucinogens, also known as **psychedelics,** are a class of drugs that produce sensory distortions or hallucinations. Hallucinations involve major alterations in colour perception and hearing. Hallucinogens may also have additional effects, such as relaxation and euphoria or, in some cases, panic. The hallucinogens include such drugs as lysergic acid diethylamide (LSD), psilocybin, and mescaline. Psychoactive substances that are similar in effect to psychedelic drugs are marijuana (cannabis) and phencyclidine (PCP). Mescaline is derived from the peyote cactus and has been used for centuries by Native Americans in the southwest United States, Mexico, and Central America in religious ceremonies, as has psilocybin, which is derived from certain mushrooms. LSD, PCP, and marijuana are more commonly used in North America.

Although tolerance to hallucinogens may develop, we lack evidence of a consistent or characteristic withdrawal syndrome associated with their use (APA, 2000a). Cravings following withdrawal may occur, however.

LSD A powerful hallucinogenic drug. LSD is the acronym for *lysergic acid diethylamide.*

LSD   LSD is the acronym for *lysergic acid diethylamide,* a synthetic hallucinogenic drug. In addition to the vivid parade of colours and visual distortions produced by LSD, users have claimed that it "expands consciousness" and opens new worlds—as if they were looking into some reality beyond the usual reality. Sometimes they believe they have achieved great insights during an LSD "trip," but when it wears off they usually cannot follow through on or even summon up these discoveries.

LSD apparently decreases the action of serotonin, a neurotransmitter that inhibits neural firing. It may also increase utilization of dopamine. Because LSD curbs the action of an inhibiting neurotransmitter and increases dopamine activity, brain activity escalates, in this case giving rise to a flurry of colourful sensations or hallucinations.

The effects of LSD are unpredictable and depend on the amount taken as well as the user's expectations, personality, mood, and surroundings (USDHHS, 1992). The user's prior experiences with the drug may also play a role, as users who have learned to handle the effects of the drug through past experience may be better prepared than new users.

flashbacks (1) Vivid re-experiencings of a past event, which may be difficult to distinguish from current reality. (2) Experiences of sensory distortions or hallucinations occurring days or weeks after use of LSD or another hallucinogenic drug that mimic the drug's effects.

Some users have unpleasant experiences or "bad trips" with the drug. Feelings of intense fear or panic may occur (USDHHS, 1992). Users may fear losing control or sanity. Some experience terrifying fears of death. Fatal accidents have sometimes occurred during LSD trips. **Flashbacks,** typically involving a re-experiencing of some of the perceptual distortions of the trip, may occur days, weeks, or even years afterward. Flashbacks tend to occur suddenly and often without warning. They may stem from chemical changes in the brain caused by the prior use of the drug. Triggers for flashbacks include entry into darkened environments, use of various drugs, anxiety or fatigue states, and stress (APA, 2000a). Psychological factors, such as underlying personality problems, may also be involved in explaining why some users experience flashbacks. In some cases, a flashback may involve an imagined re-enactment of the LSD experience (Matefy, 1980).

PHENCYCLIDINE (PCP)   Phencyclidine, or PCP—referred to as "angel dust" on the street—was developed as an anaesthetic in the 1950s but was discontinued as such when its hallucinatory side effects were discovered. A smokable form of PCP became popular as a street drug in the 1970s because it was readily manufactured and relatively inexpensive. By the mid-1980s, more than one in five young people in the 18-to-25 age range had used PCP (USDHHS, 1986). However, its popularity has since waned, largely because of its unpredictable effects.

The effects of PCP, like most drugs, are dose-related. In addition to causing hallucinations, PCP accelerates the heart rate and blood pressure and causes sweating, flushing, and numbness. PCP is classified as a deliriant—a drug capable of producing states of delirium. It also has dissociating effects, causing users to feel as if there is some sort of invisible barrier or wall between themselves and their environments. Dissociation can be experienced as pleasant, engrossing, or frightening, depending on the user's expectations, mood, setting, and so on. Overdoses can give rise to drowsiness and a blank stare, convulsions, and, now and then, coma; paranoia and aggressive behaviour; and tragic accidents resulting from perceptual distortion or impaired judgment during states of intoxication.

MARIJUANA **Marijuana** is produced from the *Cannabis sativa* plant. Marijuana sometimes produces mild hallucinations, so is regarded as a minor hallucinogen. The psychoactive substance in marijuana is **delta-9-tetrahydrocannabinol**, or THC, which is found in the plant's branches and leaves but is highly concentrated in the resin of the female plant. **Hashish**, or "hash," is also derived from the resin. Although it is more potent than marijuana, hashish has similar effects.

Marijuana dependence is the most common form of dependence on illicit drugs in North America, affecting an estimated 5% to 6% of the adult population at some point in their lives (APA, 2000a; J. M Russell et al., 1994). Males are more likely than females to develop a marijuana-use disorder (either abuse or dependence), and the rates of these disorders are greatest among young people aged 18 to 30 (APA, 2000a).

Low doses of the drug can produce relaxing feelings similar to drinking a highball of liquor. Some users report that at low doses the drug makes them feel more comfortable in social gatherings. Higher doses, however, often lead users to withdraw into themselves. Some users believe the drug increases their capacity for self-insight or creative thinking, although the insights or thoughts achieved under its influence may not seem so insightful or creative once the drug's effects have passed. People may turn to marijuana, as to other drugs, to help them cope with life problems or to help them function when they are under stress. Strongly intoxicated people perceive time as passing more slowly; a song of a few minutes may seem to last an hour. There is increased awareness of bodily sensations, such as heartbeat. Smokers also report that strong intoxication heightens sexual sensations. Visual hallucinations may occur.

Strong intoxication can cause smokers to become disoriented. If their moods are euphoric, disorientation may be construed as harmony with the universe. Yet some smokers find strong intoxication disturbing. An accelerated heart rate and sharpened awareness of bodily sensations cause some smokers to fear their hearts will "run away" from them. Some smokers are frightened by disorientation and fear they will not "come back." High levels of intoxication now and then induce nausea and vomiting.

marijuana A mild or minor hallucinogen derived from the *Cannabis sativa* plant.

delta-9-tetrahydrocannabinol Major active ingredient in marijuana. Abbreviated *THC*.

hashish Drug derived from the resin of the marijuana plant, *Cannabis sativa*.

Marijuana. The proportion of marijuana users in Canada is much higher among young adults than in the population as a whole.

Marijuana dependence is associated more with patterns of compulsive use or psychological dependence than with physiological dependence. Although tolerance to many of the drug's effects may occur with chronic use, some users report reverse tolerance or sensitization. A withdrawal syndrome has not been reliably demonstrated (APA, 2000a). However, research with animals points to some disturbing similarities between marijuana and addictive drugs such as heroin and cocaine (Wickelgren, 1997). In one study, researchers found that withdrawal from marijuana activated the same brain circuits involved in withdrawal from opiates, alcohol, and cocaine (Rodríguez de Fonseca, Carrera, Navarro, Koob, & Weiss, 1997). These brain circuits are also involved in producing feelings of anxiety when an animal or person is under stress (Blakeslee, 1997). In another study, researchers determined that marijuana activated the same reward circuits in the brain as heroin (Tanda, Pontieri, & Di Chiara, 1997). Although these studies were conducted with animals, researchers believe that the underlying biological mechanisms may apply to humans as well (Blakeslee, 1997).

University students who are heavy users of marijuana show evidence of cognitive impairment, including diminished ability in tasks requiring attention, abstraction, and mental flexibility (Pope & Yurgelun-Todd, 1996). However, it is unclear whether these deficits are due to the drug or are characteristic of people who become heavy users (T. H. Lee, 1997).

We do know that marijuana impairs perception and motor co-ordination and thus makes driving and the operation of other machines dangerous. It also impairs short-term memory and retards learning ability. Although it induces positive mood changes in many users, some people report anxiety and confusion; there are also occasional reports of psychotic reactions. Marijuana elevates the heart rate to about 140 to 150 beats per minute and, in some people, raises blood pressure. These changes may be especially dangerous to people with heart conditions or hypertension. Finally, marijuana smoke contains carcinogenic hydrocarbons, so chronic users risk lung cancer and other respiratory diseases.

Inhalants

Many different kinds of substances fall into the category of inhalants. Substances commonly used in inhalant abuse include adhesives, aerosols, anaesthetics, benzene, carbon dioxide, cleaning fluids, correction fluid, deodorants and deodorizers, disinfectants, ether, fingernail polish, refrigeration and air conditioner coolant, lighter fluid, fuels, whiteboard markers, paint and paint removers, styrene, toluene, and transmission fluid. In cases of inhalant abuse, these substances are typically used by soaking a cloth with the substance and then either holding the cloth near the face to inhale fumes or putting the cloth in a bag and inhaling from the bag. An alternative is to pour the substance into a bag or balloon and then inhale the fumes. Inhalants can induce feelings of intoxication and euphoria. The reinforcing effects of inhalants occur mainly through their effects on GABA and dopamine neurotransmitter systems. Inhalant abuse is a serious and dangerous problem—it is associated with impairments in learning and memory. The use of inhalants, even on a single occasion, increases the risk of serious medical illness and even death (Ridenour, 2005).

REVIEW IT

Drugs of Abuse

- **What are depressants?** Depressants are drugs that depress or slow nervous system activity. They include alcohol, sedatives and minor tranquillizers, and opiates. Their effects include intoxication, impaired coordination, slurred speech, and impaired intellectual functioning. Chronic alcohol abuse is linked to alcohol-induced persisting amnestic disorder (Korsakoff's syndrome), cirrhosis of the liver, fetal alcohol syndrome, and other physical health problems. Barbiturates are depressants or sedatives that have been used medically for relief of anxiety and short-term insomnia, among other uses. Opiates such as morphine and heroin are derived from the opium poppy. Others are synthesized. Used medically for relief of pain, they are strongly addictive.

- **What are stimulants?** Stimulants increase the activity of the nervous system. Amphetamines and cocaine are stimulants that increase the availability of neurotransmitters in the brain, leading to heightened states of arousal and pleasurable feelings. High doses can produce psychotic reactions that mimic features of paranoid schizophrenia. Habitual cocaine use can lead to a variety of health problems, and an overdose can cause sudden death. Repeated use of nicotine, a mild stimulant found in cigarettes, leads to physiological dependence.

- **What are hallucinogens?** They are drugs that distort sensory perceptions and can induce hallucinations. They include lysergic acid diethylamide (LSD), psilocybin, and mescaline. Other drugs with similar effects are cannabis (marijuana) and phencyclidine (PCP). There is little evidence that these drugs induce physiological dependence, although psychological dependence may occur.

THEORETICAL PERSPECTIVES

People begin using psychoactive substances for various reasons. Some adolescents start using drugs because of peer pressure or because they believe drugs make them seem more sophisticated or grown up. Some use drugs as a way of rebelling against their parents or society at large. Regardless of why people get started with drugs, they continue to use them because of their pleasurable effects or because they find it difficult to stop. Most adolescents drink alcohol to "get high," not to establish that they are adults. Many people smoke cigarettes for the pleasure they provide. Others smoke to help them relax when they are tense and, paradoxically, to give them a kick or a lift when they are tired. Many would like to quit but find it difficult to break their addiction.

People who are anxious about their jobs or social lives may be drawn to the calming effects of alcohol, marijuana (in certain doses), tranquillizers, and sedatives. People with low self-confidence and self-esteem may be drawn to the ego-boosting effects of amphetamines and cocaine. Many poor young people attempt to escape the poverty, anguish, and tedium of inner-city life through using heroin and similar drugs. More well-to-do adolescents may rely on drugs to manage the transition from dependence on their parents to independence and major life changes concerning jobs, university, and lifestyles. In the next sections, we consider several major theoretical perspectives on substance abuse and dependence.

Biological Perspectives

We are beginning to learn more about the biological underpinnings of addiction. Much of the recent research has focused on neurotransmitters, especially dopamine, and on the role of genetic factors.

NEUROTRANSMITTERS A common pathway in the brain involving the neurotransmitter dopamine may explain the pleasure-inducing effects of many drugs. Researchers suspect that drugs such as nicotine, alcohol, heroin, cocaine, and even marijuana produce pleasurable effects by increasing the levels of the neurotransmitter dopamine—the brain's "reward and reinforcing" agent (L. Chang & Haning, 2006).

We know that laboratory rats will work for injections of cocaine by repetitively pressing a lever. They will continue to work for cocaine injections even if the neural pathways that use norepinephrine are destroyed. Their work effort plummets when the neural pathways for dopamine are destroyed (R. D. Weiss et al., 1994). With repeated drug use over time, the brain's ability to make dopamine on its own can diminish, leading to cravings for drugs that will provide a steady supply of dopamine (Blakeslee, 1997). This may explain the intense cravings and anxiety that accompany drug withdrawal and the difficulty people with chemical dependencies have maintaining abstinence.

Other neurotransmitters are also believed to be involved in drug use and abuse. Evidence points to the neurotransmitter serotonin playing a role in activating the brain's pleasure or reward circuits in response to use of cocaine and other drugs (Blakeslee, 1998; Rocha et al., 1998). We also know that a group of neurotransmitters called *endorphins* have pain-blocking properties similar to opiates such as heroin. Endorphins and opiates dock at the same receptor sites in the brain. Normally, the brain produces a certain level of endorphins that maintains a sort of psychological steady state of comfort and potential to experience pleasure. However, when the body becomes habituated to a supply of opiates, it may stop producing endorphins. This makes the user dependent on opiates for feelings of comfort, relief from pain, and feelings of pleasure. When the habitual user stops using heroin or other opiates, feelings of discomfort and little aches and pains may be magnified until the body resumes adequate production of endorphins. This discomfort might account, at least in part, for the unpleasant withdrawal symptoms experienced by opiate addicts when they attempt to quit using. However, this model remains speculative, and more research is needed to document direct relationships between endorphin production and withdrawal symptoms.

GENETIC FACTORS Increasing evidence points to genetic factors in substance abuse and dependence. We know that alcoholism runs in families. People with a family history of alcoholism are about three or four times more likely to develop problems of alcohol abuse or dependence than others (APA, 2000a; Schuckit & Smith, 1996). The closer the genetic relationship, the greater the risk. Familial patterns provide only suggestive evidence of genetic factors because families share common environments as well as common genes. More definitive evidence comes from twin and adoptee studies.

Monozygotic (MZ) twins have identical genes, whereas fraternal or dizygotic (DZ) twins share only half of their genes. If genetic factors are involved, we would expect MZ twins to have higher concordance (agreement) rates for alcoholism than DZ twins. The evidence for higher concordance rates for alcoholism among MZ twins than DZ twins is stronger for male twin pairs than female twin pairs, which indicates that genetic factors may be more strongly involved in alcoholism in males than females (Jang, Livesley, & Vernon, 1997; Kendler & Prescott, 2006). To illustrate, research conducted at the University of British Columbia found that alcohol and drug problems were due to a combination of environmental and genetic factors in men but were entirely due to environmental factors in women (Jang et al., 1997). Future research may help clarify these apparent gender differences.

Other evidence points to a genetic contribution in other forms of substance abuse, including opiate, marijuana, cocaine, and nicotine dependence (Jang et al., 1997; Kendler & Prescott, 2006). An emerging body of research suggests the importance of gene–environment interactions in the development of substance-use disorders, where people with a particular genetic makeup are most likely to develop drug abuse or dependence when exposed to substances such as alcohol, cocaine, or nicotine under particular environmental conditions (e.g., highly stressful conditions) (Caspi & Moffitt, 2006).

If alcoholism or other forms of substance abuse and dependence are influenced by genetic factors, what is it that is inherited? Some clues have begun to emerge. Researchers have linked alcoholism, nicotine dependence, and opiate addiction to genes involved in determining the structure of dopamine receptors in the brain (Kotler et al., 1997). We've mentioned that dopamine is involved in regulating states of pleasure, which leads researchers to suspect that genetic factors enhance feelings of pleasure derived from alcohol, which in turn may increase cravings for the drug (Altman, 1990). In all likelihood there is not one "alcoholism gene" but a set of genes that interact with each other and with environmental factors to increase the risk of alcoholism (Kendler & Prescott, 2006).

Evidence also suggests that a genetic vulnerability to alcoholism may involve a combination of at least two factors (Sher et al., 2005). First, genetic factors influence the ability to rapidly metabolize alcohol (some people, such as many people from Asian backgrounds, are genetically predisposed to have difficulty metabolizing alcohol, thereby leading to flushing and nausea when they drink). People who metabolize alcohol relatively quickly can tolerate larger doses and are less likely to develop upset stomachs, dizziness, and headaches when they drink. Unfortunately, a lower sensitivity to the unpleasant effects of alcohol may make it difficult to know when to say "when." Thus, people who are better able to "hold their liquor" may be at greater risk of developing drinking problems. They may need to rely on other cues, such as counting their drinks, to learn to limit their drinking. People whose bodies more readily "put the brakes" on excess drinking may be less likely to develop problems in moderating their drinking than those with better tolerance. Second, genetic factors influence the degree of reinforcement (enjoyment) obtained from consuming alcohol (Sher et al., 2005).

Despite the role of genetic factors in alcoholism, environmental factors are also important. For example, there is evidence that some types of family experiences, such as drinking at home and particular types of parenting, promote the development of alcohol problems, especially in genetically vulnerable individuals (Sher et al., 2005).

Learning Perspectives

Learning theorists propose that substance-related behaviours are largely learned and can, in principle, be unlearned. They focus on the roles of operant and classical conditioning and observational learning. Substance abuse problems are regarded not as symptoms of diseases but rather as problem habits. Although learning theorists do not deny that genetic or biological factors may be involved in the genesis of substance-abuse problems, they place a greater emphasis on the role of learning in the development and maintenance of these problem behaviours (McCrady, 1993, 1994).

Drug use may become habitual because of the pleasure or positive reinforcement that drugs produce. In the case of drugs like cocaine, which appear capable of directly stimulating pleasure mechanisms in the brain, the reinforcement is direct and powerful.

OPERANT CONDITIONING In animal studies, injection of psychoactive drugs like cocaine has been made contingent on the performance of various tasks, such as pressing a lever (R. D. Weiss et al., 1994). Laboratory animals will learn to press a lever repeatedly for cocaine. Researchers can estimate the reinforcing power of drugs by comparing the rates at which animals perform operant responses such as pressing a lever to receive them. Animals will perform to receive a wide range of drugs, including amphetamines, nicotine, barbiturates, opiates, alcohol, and PCP. Performance rates are most dramatic for cocaine, however. Rhesus monkeys will work continuously for cocaine until they die (R. D. Weis et al., 1994).

People may initially use a drug because of social influence, trial and error, or social observation. In the case of alcohol, they learn that the drug can produce reinforcing effects, such as feelings of euphoria and reductions in states of anxiety and tension. Alcohol may also release behavioural inhibitions. Alcohol can thus be reinforcing when it is used to combat depression (by producing euphoric feelings, even if short-lived), to combat tension (by functioning as a tranquillizer), or to help people sidestep moral conflicts (e.g., by dulling awareness of moral prohibitions against sexual behaviour or aggression). Social reinforcers are also made available by substance abuse, such as the approval of drug-abusing companions and, in the cases of depressants and stimulants, the (temporary) overcoming of social shyness.

ALCOHOL AND TENSION REDUCTION Learning theorists have long maintained that one of the primary reinforcers for using alcohol is relief from states of tension. The tension-reduction theory proposes that the more often one drinks to reduce tension or anxiety, the stronger or more habitual the habit becomes. Viewed in this way, alcohol use can be likened to a form of self-medication—a way of easing psychological pain, at least temporarily.

Laboratory studies have provided inconsistent support for the tension-reduction theory (Pihl & Smith, 1983), although the stressors induced in those studies tended to be mild (for ethical reasons). The occurrence of more severe stressful events, such as physical or sexual assault, is associated with an increased risk of alcohol abuse (S. H. Stewart, 1996). Thus, there is some support for the tension-reduction theory, although many other factors aside from tension reduction appear to play a role in alcohol use and abuse.

Drugs, including nicotine from cigarette smoking, may also be used as a form of self-medication for depression (Breslau, Peterson, Schultz, Chilcoat, & Andreski, 1998). Stimulants such as nicotine temporarily elevate the mood, whereas depressants such as alcohol quell anxiety. Although nicotine, alcohol, and other drugs may temporarily alleviate emotional distress, they cannot resolve underlying personal or emotional problems. Rather than learning to resolve these problems, people who use drugs as forms of self-medication often find themselves facing additional substance-related problems.

NEGATIVE REINFORCEMENT AND WITHDRAWAL   Once people become physiologically dependent, negative reinforcement comes into play in maintaining a drug habit. In other words, people may resume using drugs to gain relief from unpleasant withdrawal symptoms. In operant conditioning terms, the resumption of drug use is negatively reinforced by relief from unpleasant withdrawal symptoms that occur following cessation of drug use. For example, the addicted smoker who quits cold turkey may shortly return to smoking to fend off the discomfort of withdrawal. Smokers who are able to quit and maintain abstinence are occasionally bothered by urges to smoke but have learned to manage them.

THE CONDITIONING MODEL OF CRAVINGS   Principles of classical conditioning may help explain the cravings for drugs experienced by people with drug dependencies. Repeated exposure to cues associated with drug use (such as the sight or aroma of an alcoholic beverage or the sight of a needle and syringe) may elicit conditioned responses in the form of alcohol or drug cravings (Drummond & Glautier, 1994). Although drug cravings may have a biological basis involving a bodily need to restore levels of the addictive substance, they may also become conditioned responses triggered by a wide range of cues (conditioned stimuli) that were previously associated with use of the substance. For example, socializing with certain companions (drinking buddies) or even passing a liquor store may elicit conditioned cravings for alcohol. Sensations of anxiety or depression that were paired with use of alcohol or drugs may also elicit cravings. The following case illustrates conditioned cravings to environmental cues:

> A 29-year-old man was hospitalized for the treatment of heroin addiction. After four weeks of treatment, he returned to his former job, which required him to ride the subway past the stop at which he had previously bought his drugs. Each day, when the subway doors opened at this location, [he] experienced an enormous craving for heroin, accompanied by tearing, a runny nose, abdominal cramps, and gooseflesh. After the doors closed, his symptoms disappeared, and he went on to work.
>
> Weiss & Mirin, 1987, p. 71. Reprinted with permission from *Cocaine*, (Copyright ©1987). American Psychiatric Association.

Similarly, some people are primarily "stimulus smokers." They reach for a cigarette in the presence of smoking-related stimuli such as seeing someone smoke or smelling smoke. Smoking becomes a strongly conditioned habit because it is paired repeatedly with many situational cues—watching television, finishing dinner, driving in the car, studying, drinking or socializing with friends, sex, and, for some, using the bathroom. Environmental stimuli associated with substance use (e.g., being in a bar or seeing someone smoke) can influence tolerance, elicit withdrawal symptoms, and trigger relapse of substance use (S. Siegel, 2005). The conditioning model of craving is strengthened by research showing that people with alcoholism tend to salivate more than others to the sight and smell of alcohol (Monti et al., 1987). In Pavlov's classic experiment, a salivation response was conditioned in dogs by repeatedly pairing the sound of a bell (a neutral or conditioned stimulus) with the presentation of food powder (an unconditioned stimulus). Salivation among people who develop alcoholism can also be viewed as a conditioned response to alcohol-related cues. Whereas salivating to a bell may be harmless, salivating at a bottle of scotch or at a picture of a bottle in a magazine ad can throw the person who suffers from alcoholism and is trying to remain abstinent into a tailspin. People with drinking problems who show the greatest salivary response to alcohol cues may be at the highest risk of relapse. They may also profit from treatments designed to extinguish their responses to alcohol-related cues.

One such treatment, called **cue-exposure training**, holds promise in the treatment of alcohol dependence and other forms of addictive behaviour (Drummond & Glautier, 1994; Monti et al., 1994). In cue-exposure treatment, a person is repeatedly seated in front of drug- or alcohol-related cues, such as open alcoholic beverages, while being prevented from using the drug. This pairing of the cue (alcohol bottle) with nonreinforcement (by dint of preventing drinking) may lead to extinction of the conditioned craving. Cue-exposure treatment may be combined with coping-skills training to help people with substance-abuse problems learn to cope with drug-use urges without resorting to drug use (Monti et al., 1994). It has also been applied to helping nondependent problem drinkers learn to stop drinking after two or three drinks (Sitharthan, Sitharthan, Hough, & Kavanagh, 1997).

OBSERVATIONAL LEARNING The role of modelling or observational learning may in part explain the increased risk of alcoholism among people with a family history of alcoholism. Teens who say their fathers imbibe more than two drinks a day have about a 75% greater risk of developing substance-abuse problems than do teens with fathers who are light drinkers or abstainers ("Teens Who Have Problems," 1999). Researchers also find that young men from families with a history of alcoholism were more strongly affected by exposure to others who modelled excessive drinking than were men without familial alcoholism (Chipperfield & Vogel-Sprott, 1988). Perhaps their parents had modelled excessive drinking and they learned to regulate their own intake by observing the drinking behaviour of others. When their drinking companions drink to excess, they may be more likely to follow their lead.

Cognitive Perspectives

Evidence supports the role of various cognitive factors in substance abuse and dependence, including expectancies, attitudes, beliefs, decision-making processes, and self-awareness.

OUTCOME EXPECTANCIES, DECISION MAKING, AND SUBSTANCE ABUSE The beliefs and expectancies you hold concerning the effects of alcohol and other drugs clearly influence your decision to use them or not. People who hold positive expectancies about the effects of a drug not only are more likely to use the drug (Schafer & Brown, 1991) but also are more likely to use larger quantities of it (A. R. Baldwin, Oei, & Young, 1994). One of the key factors in predicting problem alcohol use in adolescents is the degree to which their friends hold positive attitudes toward alcohol use (Scheier, Botvin, & Baker, 1997). Similarly, students in grades five and seven who hold more positive impressions of smokers (e.g., seeing them as cool, independent, or good looking) were more likely than their peers to become smokers by the time they reached grade nine (Dinh, Sarason, Peterson, & Onstad, 1995). Smoking prevention programs may need to focus on changing the image that young people hold of smokers long before they ever light up a cigarette themselves. Positive alcohol expectancies also appear in children even before drinking begins.

Among the most widely held positive expectancies concerning alcohol is that it reduces tension, helps divert attention from one's problems, heightens pleasure, lessens anxiety in social situations, and makes one more socially adept (MacLatchy-Gaudet & Stewart, 2001). In one study, alcohol expectancies were stronger predictors of the likelihood of drinking among adolescents than family drinking history (Christiansen & Goldman, 1983). The belief that alcohol helps make a person more socially adept (more relaxed, outgoing, assertive, and carefree in social interactions) appears to be an especially important factor in prompting drinking in adolescents and university students (Burke & Stephens, 1999; G. T. Smith, Goldman, Greenbaum, & Christiansen, 1995).

From a decision-making perspective, people choose whether to use drugs according to their weighing of the expected positive and negative consequences. Consider people with drinking problems who face the choice to drink or not to drink every day. They may

cue-exposure training Treatment used for people with substance dependence; it involves exposure to cues associated with ingestion of drugs or alcoholic beverages in a controlled situation in which the person is prevented from using the drug.

be aware of the eventual negative consequences of drinking (e.g., getting fired or divorced or incurring serious health troubles), but expectations of immediate relief from anxiety and feelings of pleasure may be more prominent at a given moment (Cox & Klinger, 1988). They may well decide, then, to drink. The person with a drinking problem may or may not be aware of such decisions, or of decisions to engage in the chain of behaviours that lead to problem drinking—such as whether to take a route from work that runs past a favourite watering hole.

SELF-EFFICACY EXPECTANCIES Part of the appeal of substances such as alcohol lies in their ability to enhance self-efficacy expectancies (beliefs in our ability to accomplish tasks) either directly (by enhancing feelings of energy, power, and well-being) or indirectly (by reducing stressful states of arousal, such as anxiety). Cocaine also enhances self-efficacy expectancies, an outcome sought in particular by performance-conscious athletes. People may therefore come to rely on substances in challenging situations in which they doubt their abilities. Alcohol can also help protect one's sense of self-efficacy by shunting criticism for socially unacceptable behaviour from the self to the alcohol. People who "screw up" while drinking can maintain their self-esteem by attributing their misdeeds to alcohol.

CAN YOU HAVE JUST ONE DRINK? According to the disease model of alcoholism, abstainers who binge after just one drink do so largely for biochemical reasons. Experimental research, however, suggests that cognitive factors may be more important. In fact, the one-drink hypothesis may be explained by the drinker's expectancies rather than the biochemical properties of alcohol.

Studies of the one-drink hypothesis, like many other studies on alcohol, are made possible by the fact that the taste of vodka can be cloaked by tonic water. In a classic study by Marlatt, Demming, and Reid (1973), subjects were led to believe they were participating in a taste test. Alcohol-dependent subjects and social drinkers who were informed they were sampling an alcoholic beverage (vodka) drank significantly more than counterparts who were informed they were sampling a nonalcoholic beverage. The expectations of the alcohol-dependent subjects and the social drinkers alike turned out to be the crucial factors that predicted the amount consumed (see Figure 7.4). The actual content of the beverages was immaterial.

Marlatt (1978) explains the one-drink effect as a self-fulfilling prophecy. If people with alcohol-related problems believe just one drink will cause a loss of control, they perceive the outcome as predetermined when they drink. Their drinking—even taking one drink—may thus escalate into a binge. When individuals who were formerly physiologically dependent on alcohol share this belief—which is propounded by many groups, including AA—they may interpret "just one drink" as "falling off the wagon." Marlatt's point is that the "mechanism" of falling off the wagon due to one drink is cognitive, reflecting one's expectations about the effects of the drink, and not physiological. This expectation is an example of what Aaron Beck refers to as *absolutist thinking* (A. T. Beck et al., 1979). When we insist on seeing the world in black and white rather than shades of grey, we may interpret one bite of dessert as proof we are off our diets, or one cigarette as proof we are hooked again. Rather than telling ourselves, "Okay, I goofed, but that's it—I don't have to have more," we encode our lapses as catastrophes and transform them into full-blown relapses. Still, alcohol-dependent people who believe they may go on a drinking binge if they have just one drink are well advised to abstain rather than place themselves in situations they feel they may not be able to manage.

Psychodynamic Perspectives

According to traditional psychodynamic theory, alcoholism reflects certain features of what is termed an *oral-dependent personality*. Alcoholism is, by definition, an oral behaviour pattern. Psychodynamic theory also associates excessive alcohol use with other oral traits, such as dependence and depression, and traces the origins of these traits to fixation in the oral stage of psychosexual development. Excessive drinking in adulthood symbolizes efforts to attain oral gratification.

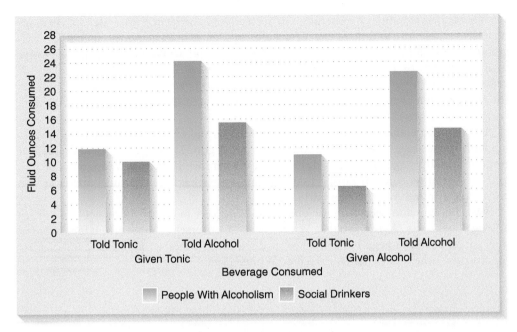

FIGURE 7.4 Must people who develop alcoholism fall off the wagon if they have one drink?

It is widely believed that people who develop alcoholism will "lose control" if they have just one drink. Will they? If so, why? Laboratory research by Marlatt and his colleagues (1973) suggests that the tendency of people who suffer from alcoholism to drink to excess following a first drink may be the result of a self-fulfilling prophecy rather than a craving. Like the dieter who eats a piece of chocolate, people who develop alcoholism may assume that they have lost control because they have fallen off the wagon, and then go on a binge. This figure shows that people with alcoholism who participated in the Marlatt study drank more when they were led to believe that the beverage contained alcohol, regardless of its actual content. It remains unclear, however, whether binge drinking by people with alcohol-related problems in real-life settings can be explained as a self-fulfilling prophecy.
Source: Marlatt, Demming, & Reid, 1973, pp. 233–241.

Psychodynamic theorists also view smoking as an oral fixation, although they have not been able to predict who will or will not smoke. Sigmund Freud smoked upward of 20 cigars a day despite several attempts to desist. Although he contracted oral cancer and had to have painful jaw surgery, he would still not surrender his "oral fixation." He eventually succumbed to cancer of the mouth in 1939 at the age of 83, after years of agony.

Research support for these psychodynamic concepts is mixed. Although people who develop alcoholism often show dependent traits, it is unclear whether dependence contributes to or stems from problem drinking. Chronic drinking, for example, is connected with loss of employment and downward movement in social status, both of which would render drinkers more reliant on others for support. Moreover, an empirical connection between dependence and alcoholism does not establish that alcoholism represents an oral fixation that can be traced to early development.

Then too, many—but certainly not all—people who suffer from alcoholism have antisocial personalities characterized by independence-seeking as expressed through rebelliousness and rejection of social and legal codes (Graham & Strenger, 1988). All in all, there doesn't appear to be a single alcoholic personality (Sher & Trull, 1994).

Sociocultural Perspectives

Cultural and religious factors are also related to consumption of alcohol and drugs. Rates of alcohol abuse vary across ethnic and religious groups (see the earlier "Focus on Diversity" box, page 260). Let us note some other sociocultural factors. Church attendance, for example, is generally connected with abstinence from alcohol. Perhaps people who are more willing to engage in culturally sanctioned activities, such as church-going, are also more likely to adopt culturally sanctioned prohibitions against excessive drinking. Rates of alcohol use also vary across cultures. For example, alcohol use is greater in Germany than in Canada, apparently because of a cultural tradition that makes the consumption of alcohol, especially beer, normative in German society (Cockerham, Kunz, & Lueschen, 1989).

Use of alcohol and drugs often occurs within a group or social setting. We go drinking with friends or entertain over drinks at home. A good wine list is a sign of class in a restaurant. Drinking is determined, in part, by where we live, with whom we worship, and the social or cultural norms that regulate our behaviour. Cultural attitudes can encourage or discourage problem drinking.

Peer pressure and peer drug use play important roles in the use of alcohol and drugs among adolescents (A. D. Farrell & White, 1998). Conversely, support from family members can reduce the negative influence of drug-using peers on an adolescent's use of tobacco and other drugs (A. D. Farrell & White, 1998).

Tying It Together

Substance abuse and dependence are complex patterns of behaviour that involve an interplay of biological, psychological, and environmental factors. Genetic factors and the early home environment may give rise to predispositions (diatheses) to abuse and dependence. In adolescence and adulthood, positive expectations concerning drug use, together with social pressures and a lack of cultural constraints, affect drug-use decisions and tendencies toward abuse. When physiological dependence occurs, people may use a substance to avoid withdrawal symptoms.

Genetic factors may create an inborn tolerance for certain drugs, such as alcohol, which can make it difficult to regulate usage or to know "when to say when." Some individuals may have genetic tendencies that lead them to become unusually tense or anxious. Perhaps they turn to alcohol or other drugs to quell their nervousness. Genetic predispositions may interact with environmental factors that increase the potential for drug abuse and dependence—factors such as pressure from peers to use drugs, parental modelling of excessive drinking or drug use, and family disruption that results in a lack of effective guidance or support. Cognitive factors, especially positive drug expectancies (e.g., beliefs that using drugs will enhance one's social skills or sexual prowess), may also raise the potential for alcohol or drug problems.

Sociocultural factors need to be taken into account in this matrix of factors, such as the availability of alcohol and other drugs, presence or absence of cultural constraints that might curb excessive or underage drinking, the glamorizing of drug use in popular media, and inborn tendencies (such as among Asians) to flush more readily following alcohol intake.

Learning factors also play important roles. Drug use may be positively reinforced by the pleasurable effects associated with its use (mediated perhaps by release of dopamine in the brain or by activation of endorphin receptors). It may also be negatively reinforced by the reduction of states of tension and anxiety that depressant drugs such as alcohol, heroin, and tranquillizers can produce. Sadly, people who become dependent on drugs often continue to use them solely because of the relief from withdrawal symptoms and cravings they encounter when they go without the drug.

Problems of substance abuse and dependence are best approached by investigating the distinctive constellation of factors that apply to each individual case. No single model or set of factors will explain each case, which is why we need to understand each individual's unique characteristics and personal history.

Theoretical Perspectives

- **How are problems of substance abuse and dependence conceptualized within the major theoretical perspectives?** Biological perspectives focus on uncovering the biological pathways that may explain the mechanisms of physiological dependence. The disease model is a prominent biological perspective that treats problems of substance abuse and dependence as disease processes. Learning perspectives view substance-abuse disorders as learned patterns of behaviour, with roles for classical and operant conditioning and observational learning. Cognitive perspectives focus on the roles of attitudes, beliefs, and expectancies in accounting for substance use and abuse. Sociocultural perspectives emphasize the cultural, group, and social factors that underlie drug-use patterns, including the role of peer pressure in determining adolescent drug use. Psychodynamic theorists view problems of substance abuse, such as excessive drinking and habitual smoking, as signs of an oral fixation.

TREATMENT

There have been and remain a vast array of nonprofessional, biological, and psychological approaches to substance abuse and dependence. However, treatment has often been a frustrating endeavour. In many, perhaps most, cases, people with drug dependencies really do not want to discontinue the substances they are abusing. Most people who abuse cocaine, for example, like most abusers of alcohol and other drugs, do not seek treatment on their own. Those who do not seek treatment tend to be heavy abusers who deny the negative impact of cocaine on their lives and dwell within a social milieu that fails to encourage them to get help. When people do come for treatment, helping them through a withdrawal syndrome is usually straightforward enough, as we shall see. However, helping them pursue a life devoid of their preferred substances is more problematic. Moreover, treatment takes place in a setting—such as a therapist's office, support group, residential centre, or hospital—in which abstinence is valued and encouraged. Then the individual returns to the work, family, or street settings in which abuse and dependence were instigated and maintained. The problem of returning to abuse and dependence following treatment—that is, of relapse—can thus be more troublesome than the problems involved in initial treatment. For this reason, recent treatment efforts have focused on relapse prevention (Brandon, Vidrine, & Litvin, 2007). Given the difficulties encountered in treating people with substance-abuse problems, it is no wonder there is much variability in the outcomes achieved in substance-abuse treatment, regardless of the types of clients, treatments, or measures of outcome used (McLellan et al., 1994). One consistent finding that does emerge is that people with more severe alcohol- and drug-use problems preceding treatment tend to have poorer outcomes in controlling their substance use following treatment.

Another complication is that many people with substance-abuse problems also have psychological disorders and vice versa (APA, 2000a; Currie et al., 2005). Most clinics and treatment programs focus on the drug or alcohol problem, or the other psychological disorders, rather than treating all these problems simultaneously, however. This narrow focus results in poorer treatment outcomes, including more frequent rehospitalizations among those with these dual diagnoses.

Biological Approaches

An increasing range of biological approaches is used in treating problems of substance abuse and dependence. For people with chemical dependencies, biological treatment typically begins with **detoxification**—that is, helping them through withdrawal from addictive substances.

DETOXIFICATION   Detoxification is often carried out in a hospital setting to provide the support needed to help the person withdraw safely from the addictive substance. In the case of addiction to alcohol or barbiturates, hospitalization allows medical personnel to

detoxification Process of ridding the system of alcohol or drugs under supervised conditions in which withdrawal symptoms can be monitored and controlled.

monitor the development of potentially dangerous withdrawal symptoms, such as convulsions. The tranquillizing agents called *benzodiazepines*, such as Valium, may help block more severe withdrawal symptoms such as seizures and delirium tremens (Mayo-Smith, 1997). Behavioural treatment using monetary rewards for abstinent behaviour (judged by clean urine samples) may help improve outcomes during detoxification from opiates (Bickel, Amass, Higgins, Badger, & Esch, 1997). Detoxification from alcohol takes about a week. When tranquillizers are used to cope with subsequent urges to drink, however, people can be caught up in a game of "musical drugs."

Next, we consider other drugs used to treat people with chemical dependencies.

DISULFIRAM The drug disulfiram (brand name Antabuse) discourages alcohol consumption because the combination of the two produces a strong aversive reaction consisting of nausea, sweating, flushing, rapid heart rate, reduced blood pressure, and vomiting. In some extreme cases, drinking alcohol while taking disulfiram can lead to such a dramatic drop in blood pressure that the individual goes into shock and may even die. Although disulfiram has been used widely in alcoholism treatment, its effectiveness is limited because many patients who want to continue drinking simply stop using the drug. Others stop taking the drug in the belief that they can maintain abstinence without it. Unfortunately, many return to uncontrolled drinking. Another drawback is that the drug has toxic effects in people with liver disease, a frequent ailment of people who suffer from alcoholism. Little evidence supports the efficacy of the drug in the long run (Garbutt, West, Carey, Lohr, & Crews, 1999).

ANTIDEPRESSANTS Antidepressants have shown some promise in reducing cravings for cocaine following withdrawal from the drug. These drugs may stimulate neural processes that regulate feelings of pleasure derived in everyday experiences. If pleasure can be more readily derived from non-drug-related activities, cocaine-addicted patients may be less likely to return to using the drug to induce pleasurable feelings. However, antidepressants have thus far failed to produce consistent results in reducing relapse rates for cocaine dependence, so it is best to withhold judgment concerning their efficacy (O'Brien, 1996). Of all the medications tested to date, disulfiram (Antabuse) has demonstrated the most consistent effect in reducing cocaine use (Vocci & Elkashef, 2005). Other medications that look promising according to controlled studies include baclofen, modafinil, tiagabine, and topiramate. All pharmacotherapy trials in cocaine-dependent patients include behaviour therapy. Therefore, these trials essentially evaluate whether the medications add to the effect of behavioural interventions (Vocci & Elkashef, 2005).

Researchers suspect that deficiencies of the neurotransmitter serotonin may underlie alcohol desires or cravings (Anton, 1994). Research is underway focusing on whether the appetite for alcohol can be curbed by using serotonin-reuptake inhibitors (e.g., Prozac), which increase the availability of serotonin in the brain. The use of these drugs in the early stages of abstinence may help people who are alcohol dependent to maintain sobriety and continue in treatment. In one clinical trial, Prozac improved the moods and reduced the drinking of people with coexisting (comorbid) alcohol dependence and depression (Cornelius et al., 1997). The actions of another neurotransmitter, dopamine, may account for the pleasurable or euphoric effects of alcohol. Drugs that mimic dopamine may be helpful in blocking the pleasurable reinforcing effects of alcohol.

NICOTINE REPLACEMENT THERAPY One promising development in the pharmacological treatment of cigarette smoking is nicotine-replacement therapy in the form of prescription gum (brand name Nicorette), transdermal (skin) patches, and a nasal spray (Hurt et al., 1998). Many regular smokers, perhaps the great majority, are nicotine dependent. The use of nicotine replacements helps avert withdrawal symptoms following

Is the path to abstinence from smoking skin deep? Forms of nicotine-replacement therapy—such as nicotine transdermal (skin) patches and chewing gum that contains nicotine—allow people to continue to receive nicotine when they quit smoking. Though nicotine-replacement therapy is more effective than a placebo in helping people quit smoking, it does not address the behavioural components of addiction to nicotine, such as the habit of smoking while drinking alcohol. For this reason, nicotine-replacement therapy may be more effective if it is combined with behaviour therapy that focuses on changing smoking habits.

smoking cessation. After quitting smoking, ex-smokers can gradually wean themselves from the nicotine replacement.

Nicotine-chewing-gum treatment and the nicotine patch have been shown to be effective aids in quitting smoking (e.g., O'Brien & McKay, 1998). The jury is still out on nicotine nasal sprays. However, although nicotine patches and gum may help quell the physiological components of withdrawal, they have no effect on the behavioural components of the addiction, such as the habit of smoking while drinking alcohol. As a result, nicotine replacement may be ineffective in promoting long-term changes unless it is combined with behavioural therapy that focuses on changing smoking habits ("Last Draw," 1996).

A non-nicotine-based antismoking drug, an antidepressant called bupropion (trade name Zyban), has been shown to be more effective than a placebo in helping smokers quit (Hurt et al., 1997). This is the first drug that works on reducing cravings for nicotine, in much the same way that other antidepressants are being used to treat cocaine cravings.

METHADONE MAINTENANCE PROGRAMS Methadone, a synthetic opiate, is widely used in treating heroin addiction. Although methadone treatment for opioid dependence gained its popularity through studies in the United States, it was first experimentally practised in the late 1950s by Dr. Robert Halliday and his addiction-treatment team in Vancouver (Fischer & Rehm, 2006). Methadone satisfies cravings for heroin and prevents the intense withdrawal symptoms that people addicted to heroin suffer upon withdrawal (O'Brien, 1996). Methadone does not produce the intense high or the stuporous state associated with heroin use, so people using it can hold jobs (O'Brien & McKay, 1998). However, like other opiates, methadone is highly addictive. For this reason, people treated with methadone can be conceptualized as swapping dependence on one drug for dependence on another. Yet methadone programs are usually publicly financed and so relieve people who are addicted to heroin of the need to engage in criminal activity to support their dependence. Although methadone can be taken indefinitely, individuals may be weaned from it without returning to using heroin.

For maximum effectiveness, methadone treatment must be combined with psychological counselling (O'Brien, 1996). Although methadone treatment produces clear benefits in improved daily functioning, not everyone succeeds with methadone, even with counselling (O'Brien & McKay, 1998). Some addicts turn to other drugs such as cocaine to get high, or they return to using heroin.

NALOXONE AND NALTREXONE Naloxone and naltrexone are sister drugs that block the high produced by heroin and other opiates. By blocking the opiate's effects, they may be useful in helping addicts avoid relapsing following opiate withdrawal.

Naltrexone (brand name ReVia) blocks the high from alcohol as well as from opiates, and has been approved in Canada for the treatment of alcoholism (Gianoulakis, 2001). In a double-blind placebo-control study, naltrexone in combination with behavioural treatment cut the relapse rates in people treated for alcoholism by more than half (Volpicelli, Alternman, Hayashida, & O'Brien, 1992; Volpicelli, Clay, Watson, & Volpicelli, 1994). Naltrexone doesn't prevent the person from taking a drink, but seems to blunt cravings for the drug (O'Brien & McKay, 1998). By blocking the pleasure produced by alcohol, the drug can help break the vicious cycle in which one drink creates a desire for another, leading to episodes of binge drinking.

A nagging problem with drugs such as naltrexone, naloxone, disulfiram, and methadone is that people with substance-abuse problems may simply stop using them and return to their substance-abusing behaviour. Nor do such drugs provide alternative sources of positive reinforcement that can replace the pleasurable states produced by drugs of abuse. Drugs such as these are only effective in the context of a broader treatment program, consisting of psychological counselling and other treatment components such as job training and stress-management training—treatments designed to help people with substance-abuse problems attain the skills they need to embark on a life in the mainstream culture (W. R. Miller & Brown, 1997).

methadone Artificial narcotic that lacks the rush associated with heroin and that is used to help people addicted to heroin abstain without incurring an abstinence syndrome.

naloxone Drug that prevents users from becoming high if they subsequently take heroin. Some people are placed on naloxone after being withdrawn from heroin to prevent return to heroin.

naltrexone Chemical cousin of naloxone that blocks the high from alcohol as well as opiates and is now approved for use in treating alcoholism.

Nonprofessional Support Groups

Despite the complexity of the factors contributing to substance abuse and dependence, these problems are frequently handled by laypeople or nonprofessionals. Such people often have or had the problems themselves. For example, self-help group meetings are sponsored by organizations such as Alcoholics Anonymous (AA), Narcotics Anonymous, and Cocaine Anonymous. These groups promote abstinence and provide members with an opportunity to discuss their feelings and experiences in a supportive group setting. More experienced group members ("sponsors") support newer members during periods of crisis or potential relapse. The meetings are sustained by nominal voluntary contributions.

The most widely used nonprofessional program, Alcoholics Anonymous, is based on the belief that alcoholism is a disease, not a sin. AA assumes that people who suffer from alcoholism are never "cured," regardless of how long they abstain from alcohol or how well they control their drinking. Instead of being cured, people who suffer from alcoholism are seen as "recovering." It is also assumed that people who suffer from alcoholism cannot control their drinking and need help in order to stop. There are more than 50 000 chapters of AA in North America ("Treatment of Drug Abuse," 1995). AA is so deeply embedded in the consciousness of health-care professionals that many of them automatically refer newly detoxified people to AA as a follow-up agency. About half of AA members have problems with illicit drugs as well as alcohol.

The AA experience is part spiritual, part group-supportive, part cognitive. AA follows a 12-step approach in which the beginning steps deal with acceptance of one's powerlessness over alcohol and turning one's will and life over to a higher power. This spiritual component may be helpful to some participants but not to others who prefer not to appeal for divine support. (Other lay organizations, such as Rational Recovery, do not adopt a spiritual approach.) The later steps focus on examining one's character flaws, admitting one's wrongdoings, being open to God's help in overcoming character defects, making amends to others, and, at the 12th step, bringing the AA message to other people suffering from alcoholism (McCrady, 1994). Prayer and meditation are urged on members to help them get in touch with their higher power. The meetings themselves provide group support. So does the buddy or sponsoring system, which encourages members to call each other for support when they feel tempted to drink.

Alcoholics Anonymous claims to have a high success rate—in the neighbourhood of 75% (Wallace, 1985). Critics note that percentages this high are based on personal testimonies rather than on careful surveys or experiments. Moreover, such estimates include only persons who attend meetings for extended periods. The dropout rate is high, with as many as 70% of members dropping out within 10 meetings, according to one survey. Even AA estimates that 50% of its members drop out after three months ("Treatment of Alcoholism," 1996). It has been difficult to conduct controlled studies because AA does not keep records of its members in order to protect their anonymity and because of an inability to conduct randomized clinical trials in AA settings (McCaul & Furst, 1994). On the other hand, the greater the involvement with AA, researchers find, the better the outcome in terms of days not drinking or using drugs (Morgenstern, Langenbucher, Labouvie, & Miller, 1997). Yet we can't say for certain whether regular participation in AA or the personal motivation that may contribute to both use of AA and change in substance-use behaviour is responsible for better outcomes. In all likelihood, success is due to both factors. Nor can we say who is likely to succeed in AA and who is not.

Al-Anon, begun in 1951, is a spin-off of AA that supports the families and friends of people suffering from alcoholism. Another spin-off of AA, Alateen, provides support to children whose parents have alcoholism, helping them see they are not to blame for their parents' drinking and are thus undeserving of the guilt they may feel.

Al-Anon Organization sponsoring support groups for family members of people with alcoholism.

Residential Approaches

A residential approach to treatment involves a stay in a hospital or therapeutic residence. Hospitalization may be recommended when substance abusers cannot exercise self-control in their usual environments or cannot tolerate withdrawal symptoms, and when their behaviour is self-destructive or dangerous to others. Outpatient treatment is less costly and often indicated when withdrawal symptoms are less severe, clients are committed to changing their behaviour, and environmental support systems, such as families, strive to help clients make the transition to a drug-free lifestyle. The great majority (nearly 90%) of people treated for alcoholism are helped on an outpatient basis (McCaul & Furst, 1994).

When alcoholism was first considered a disease in the 1960s, only a few medically based treatment programs existed. Many other residential programs have since come into being, with some facilities, such as the Betty Ford Clinic, receiving a great deal of media attention. Most inpatient programs use an extended 28-day detoxification or drying-out period. Clients are helped through withdrawal symptoms in a few days. Then the emphasis shifts to counselling about the destructive effects of alcohol and combating distorted ideas or rationalizations. Consistent with the disease model, the goal of abstinence is urged (Desmond, 1987).

Researchers find that most people with alcohol-use disorders do not require hospitalization, although some certainly do. Studies comparing outpatient and inpatient programs reveal no overall difference in relapse rates (W. R. Miller & Hester, 1986). However, medical insurance may not cover outpatient treatment, which may encourage many people who may benefit from outpatient treatment to admit themselves for inpatient treatment.

A number of residential therapeutic communities are also in use. Some of them have part- or full-time professional staffs. Others are run entirely by laypeople. Residents are expected to remain free of drugs and take responsibility for their actions. They are often confronted about their excuses for failing to take responsibility for themselves and about their denial of the damage being done by their drug abuse. They share their life experiences to help one another develop productive ways of handling stress. As with AA, we lack evidence from controlled studies demonstrating the efficacy of residential treatment programs. Also like AA, therapeutic communities have high numbers of early dropouts. Moreover, many former members of residential treatment programs who remain substance free during their time in residence relapse upon returning to the world outside. Evidence suggests that a day-treatment therapeutic community may be as effective as a residential treatment facility (Guydish, Werdegar, Sorensen, Clark, & Acampora, 1998).

Psychodynamic Approaches

Psychoanalysts view substance abuse and dependence as symptomatic of conflicts that are rooted in childhood experiences. Focusing on substance abuse or dependence per se is seen to offer, at most, a superficial type of therapy. It is assumed that if the underlying conflicts are resolved, abusive behaviour will also subside as more mature forms of gratification are sought. Traditional psychoanalysts also assume that programs directed solely at abusive behaviour will be of limited benefit because they fail to address the underlying psychological causes of abuse. Although there are many reports of successful psychodynamic case studies of people with substance-abuse problems, there is a dearth of controlled and replicable research studies. The effectiveness of psychodynamic methods for treating substance abuse and dependence thus remains unsubstantiated.

Behavioural Approaches

The use of behaviour therapy or behaviour modification in treating substance abuse and dependence focuses on modifying abusive and dependent behaviour patterns. The issue to many behaviourally oriented therapists is not whether substance abuse and dependence are diseases but whether abusers can learn to change their behaviour when they are faced with temptation.

SELF-CONTROL STRATEGIES   Self-control training focuses on helping abusers develop skills they can use to change their abusive behaviour. Behaviour therapists focus on three components of substance abuse:

1. The antecedent cues or stimuli (As) that prompt or trigger abuse,
2. The abusive behaviours (Bs) themselves, and
3. The reinforcing or punishing consequences (Cs) that maintain or discourage abuse.

Table 7.5 shows the kinds of strategies used to modify the "ABCs" of substance abuse.

TABLE 7.5

Self-Control Strategies for Modifying the "ABCs" of Substance Abuse

1. Controlling the A's (Antecedents) of Substance Abuse

People who abuse or become dependent on psychoactive substances become conditioned to a wide range of external (environmental) and internal stimuli (body states). They may begin to break these stimulus-response connections by

Removing drinking and smoking paraphernalia from the home—all alcoholic beverages, beer mugs, carafes, ashtrays, matches, cigarette packs, lighters, etc.

Restricting the stimulus environment in which drinking or smoking is permitted. Using the substance only in a stimulus-deprived area of their homes, such as the garage, bathroom, or basement. All other stimuli that might be connected to using the substance are removed—there is no television, reading material, radio, or telephone. In this way, substance abuse becomes detached from many controlling stimuli.

Not socializing with others with substance-abuse problems, by avoiding situations linked to abuse—bars, the street, bowling alleys, etc.

Frequenting substance-free environments—lectures or concerts, gyms, museums, evening classes—by socializing with nonabusers, sitting in nonsmoking cars of trains, eating in restaurants without liquor licences.

Managing the internal triggers for abuse. By practising self-relaxation or meditation and not taking the substance when tense; by expressing angry feelings by writing them down or self-assertion, not by taking the substance; and by seeking counselling for prolonged feelings of depression, not alcohol, pills, or cigarettes.

2. Controlling the B's (Behaviours) of Substance Abuse

People can prevent and interrupt substance abuse by

Using response prevention—breaking abusive habits by physically preventing them from occurring or making them more difficult—by not bringing alcohol home or cigarettes to the office.

Using competing responses when tempted, by being prepared to handle substance-related situations with appropriate ammunition—mints, sugarless chewing gum, etc.—and by taking a bath or shower, walking the dog, walking around the block, taking a drive, calling a friend, spending time in a substance-free environment, practising meditation or relaxation, or exercising when tempted rather than using the substance.

Making abuse more laborious—buying one can of beer at a time; storing matches, ashtrays, and cigarettes far apart; wrapping cigarettes in foil to make smoking more cumbersome; pausing for 10 minutes when struck by the urge to drink, smoke, or use another substance and asking oneself, "Do I really need this one?"

3. Controlling the C's (Consequences) of Substance Abuse

Substance abuse has immediate positive consequences such as pleasure, relief from anxiety and withdrawal symptoms, and stimulation. People can counter these intrinsic rewards and alter the balance of power in favour of nonabuse by

Rewarding themselves for nonabuse and punishing themselves for abuse.

Switching to brands of beer and cigarettes they don't like.

Setting gradual substance-reduction schedules and rewarding themselves for sticking to them.

Punishing themselves for failing to meet substance-reduction goals. People with substance-abuse problems can assess themselves at, say, 10 cents for each slip, and donate the cash to an unpalatable cause, such as a brother-in-law's birthday present.

Rehearsing motivating thoughts or self-statements—like writing reasons for quitting smoking on index cards. For example,

Each day I don't smoke adds another day to my life.

Quitting smoking will help me breathe deeply again.

Foods will smell and taste better when I quit smoking.

Think how much money I'll save by not smoking.

Think how much cleaner my teeth and fingers will be by not smoking.

I'll be proud to tell others that I kicked the habit.

My lungs will become clearer each and every day I don't smoke.

Smokers can carry a list of 20 to 25 such statements and read several of them at various times throughout the day. The statements can become parts of their daily routine, a constant reminder of their goals.

AVERSIVE CONDITIONING In **aversive conditioning**, painful or aversive stimuli are paired with substance-abuse or abuse-related stimuli to make abuse less appealing. In the case of problem drinking, tastes of different alcoholic beverages are usually paired with chemically induced nausea and vomiting or with electric shock. As a consequence, alcohol may come to elicit an aversive conditioned response, such as fear or nausea, that inhibits drinking. Relief from aversive responses then negatively reinforces avoidance of alcohol.

SOCIAL-SKILLS TRAINING Social-skills training helps people develop effective interpersonal responses in social situations that prompt substance abuse. Assertiveness training, for example, may be used to teach people with alcohol-related problems how to fend off social pressures to drink. Behavioural marital therapy seeks to improve marital communication and a couple's problem-solving skills to relieve marital stresses that can trigger abuse. Couples may learn how to use written behavioural contracts. One such contract might stipulate that the person with a substance-abuse problem agrees to abstain from drinking or to start taking Antabuse, and his or her spouse agrees to refrain from making comments about past drinking and the probability of future lapses. The available evidence supports the utility of social-skills training and behavioural marital therapy approaches in treating alcoholism (Finney & Monahan, 1996; O'Farrell et al., 1996).

Relapse-Prevention Training

The word **relapse** derives from Latin roots meaning "to slide back." From 50% to 90% of people who are successfully treated for substance-abuse problems eventually relapse (Leary, 1996). Relapses often occur in response to negative mood states such as depression or anxiety, to interpersonal conflict, or to social pressures to resume drinking (Cooney, Litt, Morse, Bauer, & Gaupp, 1997). People with drinking problems who relapse are more likely than those who do not to have encountered stress, such as the loss of a loved one or economic problems. They are also more likely than those who maintain sobriety to rely on avoidance methods of coping, such as denial. Successful abstainers from alcohol tend to have more social and family resources and support to draw on in handling stress (Havassy, Hall, & Wasserman, 1991).

Because of the prevalence of relapse, behaviourally oriented therapists have devised a number of methods referred to as **relapse-prevention training**. Such training helps people with substance abuse problems cope with temptations and high-risk situations to prevent lapses—that is, slips—from becoming full-blown relapses (Marlatt & Gordon, 1985). High-risk situations include negative mood states, such as depression, anger, or anxiety; interpersonal conflict, such as marital problems or conflicts with employers; and socially conducive situations, such as "the guys getting together." Participants learn to cope with these situations by, for example, learning self-relaxation skills to counter anxiety and learning to resist social pressures to resume use of the substance. Trainees are also taught to avoid practices that might prompt a relapse, such as keeping alcohol on hand for friends.

Although it contains many behavioural strategies, relapse-prevention training is a cognitive-behavioural technique in that it also focuses on the person's interpretations of any lapses or slips that may occur, such as smoking a first cigarette or taking a first drink following quitting. Clients are taught how to avoid the so-called **abstinence-violation effect** (AVE)—the tendency to overreact to a lapse—by learning to reorient their thinking about lapses and slips. People who have a slip may be more likely to relapse if they attribute their slip to personal weakness and experience shame and guilt rather than to an external or transient event (Curry, Marlatt, & Gordon, 1987). For example, consider a skater who slips on the ice. Whether or not the skater gets back up and continues to perform depends largely on whether he or she sees the slip as an isolated and correctable event or as a sign of complete failure (Marlatt & Gordon, 1985). Evidence shows that the best predictor of progression from a first to a second lapse among ex-smokers was the feeling of giving up after the first lapse (Shiffman et al., 1996). But those who responded to a first lapse by using coping strategies were more likely to succeed in averting a subsequent lapse on the same day.

aversive conditioning Behaviour therapy technique in which a maladaptive response is paired with exposure to an aversive stimulus, such as electric shock or nausea, so that a conditioned aversion develops toward the stimuli associated with the maladaptive response. Also termed *aversion therapy*.

relapse Recurrence of a problem behaviour or disorder.

relapse-prevention training Cognitive-behavioural technique used in the treatment of addictive behaviours that involves the use of behavioural and cognitive strategies to resist temptations and prevent lapses from becoming relapses.

abstinence-violation effect Tendency in people trying to maintain abstinence from a substance, such as alcohol or cigarettes, to overreact to a lapse with feelings of guilt and a sense of resignation that may then trigger a full-blown relapse. Abbreviated *AVE*.

The disease model of alcoholism contends that people who suffer from alcoholism who have just one drink will lose control and go on a binge. Some professionals, however, such as Linda and Mark Sobell, have argued that behaviour modification self-control techniques can teach many people who abuse alcohol or have a dependence to engage in **controlled social drinking**—to have a drink or two without necessarily falling off the wagon.

The contention that people who develop alcoholism can learn to drink moderately remains controversial. The proponents of the disease model of alcoholism, who have wielded considerable political strength, stand strongly opposed to attempts to teach controlled social drinking.

To support their contention, the Sobells, who did a good deal of their research at Toronto's Addiction Research Foundation, published the results of an experiment in which people who suffered from alcoholism either were taught to control their drinking or were encouraged to abstain from alcohol. The Sobells (M. B. Sobell & Sobell, 1973, 1976, 1984) reported that 85% of their 20 controlled-drinking subjects remained in control of their drinking at a two-year follow-up. However, a research group critical of the Sobells (Pendery, Maltzman, & West, 1982) published its own 10-year follow-up of the Sobells' subjects. The group claimed that only 1 in 20 people remained successful at controlled social drinking. Most had returned to uncontrolled drinking on many occasions, and 4 of the group had died from alcohol-related causes.

Despite the controversy it caused, Pendery et al.'s study was flawed. The researchers reported results for only the controlled drinking group without reporting data for the Sobells' control group (the abstinence-based treatment condition). Without some kind of control group, it is impossible to assess the effects of controlled drinking. A 10-year follow-up of the Sobells' study reported by Dickens, Doob, Warwick, and Winegard (1982) found that there were more deaths in the abstinence group (30%) than in the controlled drinking group (20%).

Other investigators have found that controlled social drinking is a reasonable treatment goal for younger people with problem drinking who are less alcohol dependent but are headed on the road toward chronic alcoholism (e.g., W. R. Miller & Muñoz, 1983; Sanchez-Craig, Annis, Bornet, & MacDonald, 1984; Sanchez-Craig & Wilkinson, 1986/1987). Evidence supporting controlled social drinking programs for people with chronic alcoholism, however, remains lacking. Interest in controlled social drinking programs has also waned, largely because of strong opposition from professionals and lay organizations committed to the abstinence model. Nevertheless, as noted by University of Calgary psychologist David Hodgins (2006), controlled drinking is feasible for some people, and so we should consider how best to integrate it into our treatment systems. Controlled-drinking programs may be best suited for younger people with early-stage alcoholism or problem drinking, those who reject goals of total abstinence or have failed in programs requiring abstinence, and those who do not show severe withdrawal symptoms (Marlatt, Larimer, Baer, & Quigley, 1993; Rosenberg, 1993; Sobell, Toneatto, & Sobell, 1990). Researchers also find that women tend to do better than men in controlled-drinking programs (Marlatt et al., 1993). By offering moderation as a treatment goal, controlled-drinking programs may also reach many people with alcohol-use disorders who might otherwise go untreated because they refuse to participate in abstinence-only treatment programs (Marlatt et al., 1993).

Controlled-drinking programs may actually represent a pathway to abstinence for people who would not otherwise enter abstinence-only treatment programs (Marlatt et al., 1993). That is, treatment in a controlled-drinking program may be the first step in the direction of giving up drinking completely. A large percentage—about one out of four in one study (Miller et al., 1993)—enter with the goal of achieving controlled drinking but become abstinent by the end of treatment. On the other hand, controlled social drinking may not be appropriate for people with established alcohol dependence and those who are taking medications that interact with alcohol or have other medical risks that might be aggravated by alcohol (Lawson, 1983; "Treatment of Alcoholism," 1996).

controlled social drinking Controversial approach to treating problem drinkers in which the goal of treatment is the maintenance of controlled social drinking in moderate amounts, rather than total abstinence.

In contrast to the disease model, which contends that people who suffer from alcoholism automatically lose control if they take a single drink, the relapse-prevention model assumes that whether a lapse becomes a relapse depends on the person's interpretation of the lapse (Marlatt & Gordon, 1985). Self-defeating attributions such as "What's the use? I'm just doomed to fail" trigger depression, resignation, and resumption of problem drinking. Participants in relapse-prevention training programs are encouraged to view lapses as temporary setbacks that provide opportunities to learn what kinds of situations lead to temptation and how they can avoid or cope with such situations. If they can learn to think "Okay, I had a slip, but that doesn't mean all is lost unless I believe it is," they are less likely to catastrophize lapses and subsequently relapse. Other relapse-prevention techniques focus on training smokers' spouses or partners to be more helpful in maintaining abstinence. Social support appears to play a key role in determining relapse in abstinence-based programs for alcoholism, drug abuse, and cigarette smoking (e.g., Nides et al., 1995).

All in all, efforts to treat people with substance abuse and dependence problems have been mixed at best. Many abusers really do not want to discontinue use of these substances, although they would prefer, if possible, to avoid their negative consequences. The more effective substance-abuse treatment programs involve intensive, multiple treatment approaches that address the wide range of problems that people with substance-abuse disorders frequently present, including co-occurring (comorbid) psychiatric problems such as depression (R. A. Brown, Evans, Miller, Burgess, & Mueller, 1997). Comorbidity of substance-use disorders and other psychiatric disorders has become the rule in treatment facilities rather than the exception (Brems & Johnson, 1997). Substance abusers who have comorbid disorders or more severe psychological problems typically fare more poorly in treatment for their drug or alcohol problems (Simpson, Joe, Fletcher, Hubbard, & Anglin, 1999). For people with alcoholism and other substance abuse problems, a number of different therapies, including 12-step and cognitive-behavioural approaches, often work well (Breslin, Li, Sdao-Jarvie, Tupker, & Ittig-Deland, 2002).

The major problem is that many people with alcohol-use disorders have no contact whatsoever with alcohol treatment programs or self-help organizations (Institute of Medicine, 1990). Clearly, more needs to be done to help people whose use of alcohol and other drugs puts them at risk. In the case of inner-city youth who have become trapped in a milieu of street drugs and hopelessness, the availability of culturally sensitive counselling and job-training opportunities would be of considerable benefit in helping them assume more productive social roles. The challenge is clear: to develop cost-effective ways of helping people recognize the negative effects of substances and forgo the powerful and immediate reinforcements they provide.

REVIEW IT

Treatment

- **What treatment approaches are used to help people overcome problems of substance abuse and dependence?** Biological approaches to substance-abuse disorders include detoxification; the use of drugs such as disulfiram, methadone, naloxone, naltrexone, and antidepressants; and nicotine replacement therapy. Residential-treatment approaches include hospitals and therapeutic residences. Nonprofessional support groups, such as Alcoholics Anonymous, promote abstinence within a supportive group setting. Psychodynamic therapists focus on uncovering the inner conflicts, originating in childhood, that are believed to be at the root of substance-abuse problems. Behavioural therapists focus on helping people with substance-related problems change problem behaviours through such techniques as self-control training, aversive conditioning, and skills training. Regardless of the initial success of a treatment technique, relapse remains a pressing problem in treating people with substance-abuse problems. Relapse-prevention training employs cognitive-behavioural techniques to help ex-abusers cope with high-risk situations and to prevent lapses from becoming relapses by helping participants interpret lapses in less damaging ways.

Define It

abstinence-violation effect, 287
addiction, 255
Al-Anon, 284
alcohol-induced persisting
    amnestic disorder, 263
amphetamine psychosis, 266
amphetamines, 266
analgesia, 265
aversive conditioning, 287

barbiturates, 264
cocaine, 266
controlled social drinking, 288
crack, 266
cue-exposure training, 277
delirium tremens, 254
delirium, 254
delta-9-tetrahydrocannabinol, 271
depressant, 257

detoxification, 281
disorientation, 254
endorphins, 265
flashbacks, 270
freebasing, 267
hallucinogens, 270
hashish, 271
intoxication, 252
Korsakoff's syndrome, 263

LSD, 270
marijuana, 271
methadone, 283
naloxone, 283
naltrexone, 283
narcotics, 265
opiates, 265

physiological dependence, 255
psychedelics, 270
psychoactive, 252
psychological dependence, 256
relapse, 287
relapse-prevention training, 287
sedatives, 264

substance abuse, 253
substance dependence, 253
substance-induced disorders, 252
substance-use disorders, 252
tachycardia, 254
withdrawal syndrome, 254

Think About It

- What is the basis for determining when drug use becomes abuse or dependence? Have you or someone you know crossed the line between use and abuse?

- Many teenagers today have parents who themselves smoked marijuana or used other drugs when they were younger. If you were one of those parents, what would you tell your kids about drugs?

- What do you think of the concept of using methadone, a narcotic drug, to treat problems of addiction to another narcotic drug, heroin? What are the advantages and disadvantages of this approach? Do you believe the government should support methadone maintenance programs? Why or why not?

- Do you use alcohol? How does it affect you physically and mentally? Have you consumed alcohol and driven? How do you feel about that? Have you ever done anything under the influence of alcohol that you later regretted? What? Why?

Key for "How Do You Know If You're Hooked?" Questionnaire (page 259)

Any "yes" answer suggests you may be dependent on alcohol. If you have answered any of these questions in the affirmative, we suggest you seriously examine what your drinking means to you.

Weblinks

Centre for Addiction and Mental Health (CAMH)   www.camh.net
This is a public hospital providing direct patient care for people with mental health and addiction problems. CAMH is also a research facility, an education and training institute, and a community-based organization providing health promotion and prevention services across Ontario.

Canadian Centre on Substance Abuse   www.ccsa.ca
This website provides statistics and other information on substance use disorders.

Alcoholics Anonymous
www.alcoholics-anonymous.org
AA's website provides information on the nature and treatment of alcohol problems.

Mothers Against Drunk Driving (MADD)
www.madd.ca
MADD's Canadian site provides information on the prevalence and cost of alcohol abuse.

National Council on Alcohol and Drug Dependence
www.ncadd.org
This site contains numerous links providing information on the nature and treatment of substance use disorders.

FASworld   www.fasworld.com
A Canadian-based website providing information about fetal alcohol spectrum (FAS) disorders.

 MySearchLab offers you extensive help with your writing and research projects and provides round-the-clock access to credible and reliable source material. Chapter quizzes and a full electronic version of the text are also provided. Take a tour at www.mysearchlab.com.

Substance Abuse and Dependence

Classification of Substance-Related Disorders

Substance-Use Disorders

Substance Abuse
- Features
  - Pattern of repeated drug-using behaviour that has damaging consequences
  - May develop into substance dependence

Substance Dependence
- Features
  - Physiological signs of dependence (tolerance or withdrawal) and/or
  - Compulsive use of substance (e.g., lack of control over substance use)

Substance-Induced Disorders

- When induced by psychoactive substances:
  - Intoxication
  - Withdrawal syndromes
  - Mood disorders, anxiety disorders, psychotic disorders
  - Delirium, dementia, amnesia
  - Sexual dysfunction, sleep disorders

Pathways to Drug Dependence

- Experimentation
- Routine use
- Addiction or dependence

Drugs of Abuse

Depressants

- Alcohol
- Barbiturates (sedatives; e.g., amobarbital)
- Opiates (narcotics; e.g., heroin)

Hallucinogens

- LSD ("acid" or lysergic acid diethylamide)
- PCP ("angel dust" or phencyclidine)
- Marijuana (e.g., "hash")

Stimulants

- Amphetamines (e.g., "meth," or methamphetamine)
- Cocaine (e.g., "crack")
- Nicotine

Inhalants

- Diverse group of substances (e.g., aerosols)

>>

Theoretical Perpectives

Biological

- Recent research focuses on neu-rotransmitters (dopamine) and genetic factors like vulnerability to alcoholism.

Psychodynamic

- Alcoholism reflects features of an oral-dependent personality; fixation in the oral stage of psychosexual development.

Learning-Based

- Proposes that substance-related behaviours can be unlearned.
- Substance abuse and dependence is maintained by principles of operant conditioning and reinforcement.

Sociocultural

- Cultural and religious factors are related to consumption of alcohol and drugs.
- Peer drug use plays a role in use of alcohol and drugs among adolescents.

Cognitive

- Expectancies, attitudes, beliefs, and decision-making processes play a role in substance abuse.
- Outcome expectancies and self-efficacy expectancies influence decision making.

Treatment

Biological

- Detoxification
- Disulfiram
- Antidepressants
- Nicotine replacement therapy
- Methadone maintenance programs
- Naxalone and Naltrexone

Psychodynamic

- Substance abuse/dependence is viewed as stemming from unresolved inner conflicts.
- Effectiveness of this approach is unsubstantiated.

Nonprofessional Support Groups

- Self-help group meetings promote abstinence in a supportive setting.

Behavioural

- Self-control strategies
- Aversive conditioning
- Social-skills training

Residential

- Hospital stay, therapeutic residence, or outpatient treatment

8

Eating Disorders and Sleep Disorders

CHAPTER OUTLINE

Eating Disorders
Anorexia Nervosa
Bulimia Nervosa
Causes of Anorexia and Bulimia
Treatment of Anorexia Nervosa and Bulimia Nervosa
Binge-Eating Disorder

Sleep Disorders
Dyssomnias
Parasomnias
Treatment of Sleep Disorders

Did You Know That...

- Although others see them as "skin and bones," young women with anorexia nervosa still see themselves as too fat?

- Some bulimic women force themselves to vomit after every meal?

- Drugs used to treat depression may also help curb bulimic binges?

- Nutrition management and psychoeducational programs are important in the treatment of eating disorders?

- Some people have sleep attacks in which they suddenly fall asleep without any warning?

- Some people literally gasp for breath hundreds of times during sleep without realizing it?

- Sleeping pills are only a short-term solution for the treatment of sleeping disorders and can actually worsen insomnia?

J essica was a 20-year-old communications major when she consulted a psychologist for the first time. For years she had kept a secret from everyone, including her fiancé, Ken. She and Ken were planning to get married in three months. She had decided that it was time to finally confront her problem. She told the psychologist she didn't want to bring the problem into the marriage with her, that it wouldn't be fair to Ken. She said, "I don't want him to have to deal with this. I want to stop this before the marriage." Jessica went on to describe her problem: "I go on binges and then throw it all up. It makes me feel like I'm in control, but really I'm not." To conceal her secret, she would lock herself in the bathroom, run the water in the sink to mask the sounds, and induce vomiting. She would then clean up after herself and spray an air freshener to mask any telltale odours. "The only one who suspects," she said with embarrassment, "is my dentist. He said my teeth are beginning to decay from stomach acid."

Jessica had bulimia nervosa, an eating disorder characterized by recurrent cycles of bingeing and purging. Eating disorders such as bulimia nervosa and anorexia nervosa often affect young people of high school or university age, especially young women. Although rates of diagnosable eating disorders in college and university students are not as high as you might think, chances are you have known people with anorexia or bulimia or with disturbed eating patterns that fall within a spectrum of eating-related disorders, such as repeated binge eating or excessive dieting.

Another class of psychological disorders that commonly affects young adults is sleep disorders. The most common form of sleep disorder, chronic insomnia, affects many young people who are making their way in the world and tend to bring their worries and concerns to bed with them.

EATING DISORDERS

eating disorders Psychological disorders involving disturbed eating patterns and maladaptive ways of controlling body weight.

anorexia nervosa Eating disorder, primarily affecting young women, characterized by maintenance of an abnormally low body weight, distortions of body image, intense fears of gaining weight, and, in females, amenorrhea.

bulimia nervosa Eating disorder characterized by a recurrent pattern of binge eating followed by self-induced purging and accompanied by persistent overconcern with body weight and shape.

In a nation of plenty, some people literally starve themselves—sometimes to death. They are obsessed with their weight and desire to achieve an exaggerated image of thinness. Others engage in repeated cycles in which they binge on food and then attempt to purge their excess eating, such as by inducing vomiting. These dysfunctional patterns are the two major types of **eating disorders: anorexia nervosa** and **bulimia nervosa**, respectively. Eating disorders are characterized by disturbed patterns of eating and maladaptive ways of controlling body weight. Like many other psychological disorders, anorexia and bulimia are often accompanied by other forms of psychopathology, including mood, anxiety, impulse-control, and substance-use disorders (Hudson, Hiripi, Pope, & Kessler, 2007; Milos, Spindler, & Schnyder, 2004).

Anorexia nervosa and bulimia nervosa were once considered very rare, but they are becoming increasingly common in Canada and other developed countries. Hospitalization rates for Canadian women with eating disorders increased 20% between 1987 and 1999 (Health Canada, 2002b). The great majority of cases (about 90%) occur among women, especially young women (HealthyOntario.com, 2003). Canadian sources indicate that although these disorders may develop in middle or even late adulthood, they typically begin during adolescence or early adulthood, when the pressures to be thin are the strongest (Jilek, 2001; National Institute of Nutrition, 2001). As these social pressures have increased, so too have the rates of eating disorders. Estimates are that between 1% and 2% of female adolescents and young adults in Canada develop anorexia and 3% to 10% develop bulimia (Canadian Mental Health Association, 2003). Rates of anorexia and bulimia among young Canadian males are much lower, estimated at roughly 0.3% (Woodside et al., 2001).

A much larger percentage of young women show bulimic behaviours (occasional bingeing and purging) or excessive dieting, but not to the point that they would warrant a diagnosis of an eating disorder. In one large study, researchers found that almost one quarter of Ontario high school females were dieting to lose weight and that 27% showed symptoms of an eating disorder along with reported bingeing and purging. It was also found that disordered eating attitudes and behaviours increased significantly with age. Among younger females (aged 12 to 15), 18.8% had binged or purged, while the reported incidence increased to 26.3% in females aged 15 and older (J. M. Jones, Bennett, Olmsted, Lawson, & Rodin, 2001). These figures are disturbing because these eating attitudes and behaviours put females at risk for developing full-blown eating disorders (Fairburn, Cooper, Doll, & Davies, 2005).

Anorexia Nervosa

Nairi was the 22-year-old daughter of a renowned English professor. She had begun her college career full of promise at the age of 17, but two years ago, after "social problems" occurred, she returned to live at home and took progressively lighter course loads at a local college. Nairi had never been overweight, but about a year ago her mother noticed that she seemed to be gradually "turning into a skeleton."

Nairi spent literally hours every day shopping at the supermarket, butcher, and bakeries, conjuring up gourmet treats for her parents and younger siblings. Arguments over her lifestyle and eating habits divided the family into two camps. The camp led by her father called for patience; that headed by her mother demanded confrontation. Her mother feared that Nairi's father would "protect her right into her grave" and wanted Nairi placed in residential treatment "for her own good." The parents finally compromised on an outpatient evaluation.

At an even five feet, Nairi looked like a prepubescent 11-year-old. Her nose and cheekbones protruded crisply. Her lips were full, but the redness of her lipstick was unnatural, as if too much paint had been dabbed on a corpse for a funeral. Nairi weighed only 78 pounds, but she dressed in a stylish silk blouse, scarf, and baggy pants so that not one inch of her body was revealed.

Nairi vehemently denied that she had a problem. Her figure was "just about where I want it to be" and she engaged in aerobic exercise daily. A deal was struck in which outpatient treatment would be tried as long as Nairi lost no more weight and showed steady gains back to at least 90 pounds. Treatment included a day hospital with group therapy and two meals a day. But word came back that Nairi was artfully toying with her food—cutting it up, sort of licking it, and moving it about her plate—rather than eating it. After three weeks Nairi had lost another pound. At that point, her parents were able to persuade her to enter a residential treatment program, where her eating behaviour could be more carefully monitored.

The Authors' Files

Anorexia derives from the Greek roots *an-*, meaning "without," and *orexis*, meaning "a desire for." Thus, *anorexia* means "without desire for [food]," which is something of a misnomer because loss of appetite is rare among people with anorexia nervosa. However, they may be repelled by food and refuse to eat more than is absolutely necessary to maintain a minimal weight for their ages and heights. Often, they starve themselves to the point where they become dangerously emaciated. By and large, anorexia nervosa develops in early to late adolescence, between the ages of 12 and 18, although earlier and later onsets are sometimes found.

The clinical features listed in Table 8.1 on page 296 are used to diagnose anorexia nervosa. Although reduced body weight is the most obvious sign, the most prominent clinical feature is an intense fear of obesity. One common pattern of anorexia begins after menarche, when a girl notices added weight and insists it must come off. Extreme dieting and, often, excessive exercise continue unabated after the initial weight-loss goal is achieved, however—even after the girls' families and others express concern. Another common pattern occurs among young women when they leave home to attend university or college and

Diagnostic Criteria for Anorexia Nervosa

A. Refusal to maintain body weight at or above a minimally normal weight for age and height (e.g., weight loss leading to maintenance of body weight less than 85% of that expected; or failure to make expected weight gain during period of growth, leading to body weight less than 85% of that expected).

B. Intense fear of gaining weight or becoming fat, even though underweight.

C. Disturbance in the way in which one's body weight or shape is experienced, undue influence of body weight or shape on self-evaluation, or denial of the seriousness of the current low body weight.

D. In postmenarcheal females, amenorrhea, i.e., the absence of at least three consecutive menstrual cycles. (A woman is considered to have amenorrhea if her periods occur only following hormone, e.g., estrogen, administration.)

Specify type:

Restricting Type: during the current episode of Anorexia Nervosa, the person has not regularly engaged in binge-eating or purging behavior (i.e., self-induced vomiting or the misuse of laxatives, diuretics, or enemas)

Binge-Eating/Purging Type: during the current episode of Anorexia Nervosa, the person has regularly engaged in binge-eating or purging behavior (i.e., self-induced vomiting or the misuse of laxatives, diuretics, or enemas)

Source: Reprinted with permission from the *Diagnostic and Statistical Manual of Mental Disorders*, Fourth Edition, Text Revision, (Copyright ©2000). American Psychiatric Association. p. 589.

encounter difficulties adjusting to the demands of college life and independent living. Anorexia is also more common among young women involved in ballet or modelling, in which there is often a strong emphasis on maintaining an unrealistically thin body shape.

Adolescent girls and women with anorexia almost always deny that they are losing too much weight or wasting away. They may argue that their ability to engage in stressful exercise demonstrates their fitness. Women with eating disorders are more likely than normal women to view themselves as heavier than they are (Horne, Van Vactor, & Emerson, 1991). Others may see them as nothing but "skin and bones," but anorexic women have a distorted body image and may still see themselves as too fat. Although they literally starve themselves, they may spend much of the day thinking and talking about food, and even preparing elaborate meals for others (Rock & Curran-Celentano, 1996).

Although anorexia is far more common in women than in men, an increasing number of young men are presenting with anorexia. Many are involved in sporting activities, such as wrestling and gymnastics, in which they have experienced pressure to maintain a lower weight classification. In this regard, it seems that young men and women experience similar pressures to achieve weight loss and leanness (Ricciardelli & McCabe, 2004).

SUBTYPES OF ANOREXIA Due to the earlier work of Canadian eating disorder authorities Garfinkel, Moldofsky, and Garner (1980), the DSM diagnosis of anorexia now includes two general subtypes of anorexia: a binge-eating/purging type and a restrictive type. The first type is characterized by frequent episodes of binge eating and purging; the second type is not. Although repeated cycles of binge eating and purging occur in bulimia, bulimic individuals do not reduce their weight to anorexic levels. The distinction between the subtypes of anorexia is supported by differences in personality patterns. Individuals with the eating/purging type tend to have problems related to impulse control, which, in addition to binge-eating episodes, may involve substance abuse or stealing (Garner, 1993). They tend to alternate between periods of rigid control and impulsive behaviour. Those with the restrictive type tend to be rigidly, even obsessively, controlled about their diet and appearance.

Who's at risk? Competitive activities that emphasize endurance, aesthetics, and weight levels put athletes at risk for developing an eating disorder. Runners, wrestlers, swimmers, and dancers are among the athletes who have a high occurrence of eating disorders.

MEDICAL COMPLICATIONS OF ANOREXIA University of Toronto psychiatrists Allan Kaplan and Blake Woodside (1987) concluded that anorexia can lead to serious medical complications that in extreme cases can be fatal. Weight losses of as much as 35% of body weight may occur and anemia may develop. Females suffering from anorexia are also likely to encounter dermatological problems such as dry, cracking skin; fine, downy hair; even a yellowish discoloration that may persist for years after weight is regained. Cardiovascular complications include heart irregularities, hypotension (low blood pressure), and associated dizziness upon standing, sometimes causing blackouts. Decreased food ingestion can cause gastrointestinal problems such as constipation, abdominal pain, and obstruction or paralysis of the bowels or intestines. Menstrual irregularities are common, and **amenorrhea** (absence or suppression of menstruation) is part and parcel of the clinical definition of anorexia in females. Muscular weakness and abnormal growth of bones may occur, causing loss of height and **osteoporosis.**

The death rate from anorexia is estimated at 5% to 8% over a 10-year period, with most deaths due to suicide or medical complications associated with severe weight loss (Goleman, 1995). Some studies show that people with eating disorders may have a sixfold increase in death compared to the normal population (Crisp, Callender, Halek, & Hsu, 1992).

Bulimia Nervosa

I think of how many people would like to have more than one cookie out of the bag they bring home from the supermarket. Some of them do have several cookies, savour them, then place the rest of the bag in the cupboard. Others have a harder time doing that; they eat too many cookies, half the package perhaps, then feel repentant and disgusted with themselves. But imagine ratcheting that urge up further. Imagine that you are unable to sleep because of the cookies in your cupboard, that you can't work or read or leave the house knowing the uneaten cookies are there. That feeling of anxiety begins to build in you, a desperation and a kind of anger, until you break down and cram the cookies into your mouth several at a time, devouring them until you throw up. If, after you throw up, there are still some cookies left in the bag, you have to keep eating them, even though by then you are sick of their taste and texture. If there are 10 bags of cookies and no way that you can eat them all, you will have to bury the rest of them immediately at the bottom of the garbage pail—first crushing them and soaking them in water, say, to prevent your retrieving them later—in order to be rid of them.

Lau, 2001, pp. 81–82. Reprinted with permission of the publisher.

Canadian writer Evelyn Lau describes her bulimic urges at a time in her life when she suffered from bulimia nervosa. *Bulimia* derives from the Greek roots *bous*, meaning "ox" or "cow," and *limos*, meaning "hunger." The unflattering picture inspired by the origin of the term is one of continuous eating, like a cow chewing its cud. Bulimia nervosa is an eating disorder characterized by recurrent episodes of gorging on large quantities of food followed by use of inappropriate ways to prevent weight gain, such as purging by means of self-induced vomiting or by using laxatives, diuretics, or enemas; fasting; or engaging in excessive exercise (see Table 8.2 on page 298). Two or more strategies may be used for purging, such as both vomiting and use of laxatives (Tobin, Johnson, & Dennis, 1992). Although people with anorexia are extremely thin, bulimic individuals are usually of normal weight. However, they have an excessive concern about their shape and weight.

Bulimic individuals typically gag themselves to induce vomiting. Most attempt to conceal their behaviour. Fear of gaining weight is a constant factor. Although an overconcern with body shape and weight is a cardinal feature of both bulimia and anorexia, bulimic individuals do not pursue the extreme thinness characteristic of anorexia. Their ideal weights are similar to those of women who do not suffer from eating disorders (Fairburn, Cooper, & Cooper, 1986).

amenorrhea Absence of menstruation—a symptom of anorexia nervosa.

osteoporosis Physical disorder caused by calcium deficiency that is characterized by extreme brittleness of the bones (from the Greek *osteon*, meaning "bone," and the Latin *porus*, meaning "pore").

TABLE 8.2

Diagnostic Criteria for Bulimia Nervosa

A. Recurrent episodes of binge eating. An episode of binge eating is characterized by both of the following:

    (1) eating, in a discrete period of time (e.g., within any 2-hour period), an amount of food that is definitely larger than most people would eat during a similar period of time and under similar circumstances

    (2) a sense of lack of control over eating during the episode (e.g., a feeling that one cannot stop eating or control what or how much one is eating)

B. Recurrent inappropriate compensatory behavior in order to prevent weight gain, such as self-induced vomiting; misuse of laxatives, diuretics, enemas, or other medications; fasting; or excessive exercise.

C. The binge eating and inappropriate compensatory behaviors both occur, on average, at least twice a week for 3 months.

D. Self-evaluation is unduly influenced by body shape and weight.

E. The disturbance does not occur exclusively during episodes of Anorexia Nervosa.

Specify type:

Purging Type: during the current episode of Bulimia Nervosa, the person has regularly engaged in self-induced vomiting or the misuse of laxatives, diuretics, or enemas

Nonpurging Type: during the current episode of Bulimia Nervosa, the person has used other inappropriate compensatory behaviors, such as fasting or excessive exercise, but has not regularly engaged in self-induced vomiting or the misuse of laxatives, diuretics, or enemas

Source: Reprinted with permission from the *Diagnostic and Statistical Manual of Mental Disorders*, Fourth Edition, Text Revision, (Copyright ©2000). American Psychiatric Association. p. 594.

The binge itself usually occurs in secret and most commonly at home during unstructured afternoon or evening hours (Guertin, 1999). A binge typically lasts from 30 to 60 minutes and involves consumption of forbidden foods that are generally sweet and rich in fat. Binge eaters typically feel they lack control over their bingeing and may consume 5000 to 10 000 calories at a sitting. One young woman described eating everything available in the refrigerator, even to the point of scooping out margarine from its container with her finger (Guertin, 1999). The episode continues until the binger is spent or exhausted, suffers painful stomach distension, induces vomiting, or runs out of food. Drowsiness, guilt, and depression usually ensue, but bingeing is initially pleasant because of release from dietary constraints.

The age range for onset of bulimia is the late teens, when concerns about dieting and dissatisfaction with bodily shape or weight are at their height (APA, 2000a).

MEDICAL COMPLICATIONS OF BULIMIA Bulimia is also associated with many medical complications (A. S. Kaplan & Woodside, 1987). Many of these stem from repeated vomiting. There may be irritations of the skin around the mouth (due to frequent contact with stomach acid), blockage of salivary ducts, decay of tooth enamel, and dental cavities. The acid from the vomit may damage taste receptors on the palate, which might make the person less sensitive to the taste of vomit with repeated purgings (J. Rodin, Bartoshuk, Peterson, & Schank, 1990). Decreased sensitivity to the aversive taste of vomit may play a role in maintaining the purging behaviour (J. Rodin et al., 1990). Cycles of bingeing and vomiting may cause abdominal pain, hiatal hernia, and other abdominal complaints. Stress on the pancreas may produce pancreatitis (inflammation), which is a medical emergency. Disturbed menstrual function is found in as many as 50% of normal-weight women with bulimia (Weltzin, Cameron, Berga, & Kaye, 1994). Excessive use of laxatives may cause bloody diarrhea and laxative dependency, so the person cannot have normal bowel movements without laxatives. In the extreme, the bowel can lose its reflexive eliminatory response to pressure from waste material. Bingeing on large quantities of salty food may cause convulsions and swelling. Repeated vomiting or abuse of laxatives can lead to potassium deficiency, producing muscular weakness, cardiac irregularities, even sudden death—especially when diuretics are used. As with anorexia, menstruation may come to a halt.

Sophia is a beautiful 41-year-old woman who has struggled with her weight for over 20 years. At five foot six inches, she weighs 140 pounds, and this has fluctuated plus or minus 10 pounds over these last 20 years. She is unhappy with her body shape, feeling that her hips are too big and her stomach is not flat enough. When she was in her 20s, she tried a bunch of fad diets but was never able to sustain any weight loss. She now eschews diets but is always trying to be "careful" about what she eats. She reads food labels and tries not to eat takeout or fast food too often. When she does feel like she's indulged too much, she is a bit stricter with her food intake the following day. For example, she recently had two helpings of dinner at a friend's dinner party and compensated the following day with a smaller breakfast and lunch, and also made sure to go on a brisk walk. Although Sophia still thinks about her weight and shape more than she'd like, it doesn't consume her. She is able to wear a bathing suit in front of others, she doesn't mind clothes shopping, and she still enjoys desserts now and then.

Jiao has always struggled with eating and body image. She was an athlete in high school, excelling in track and cross-country running. Although her body type was not that of a typical runner, she kept herself in excellent condition and trained extensively. Once Jiao graduated from high school, she did not run as often as before and noticed that this led to changes in her body shape and a weight gain of about five pounds. She was annoyed with the change in her weight, and became obsessed with the small folds of skin on her stomach, calling them "disgusting" even when her friends told her they couldn't even see what she was talking about. Though not competing as a runner anymore, Jiao picked up her training schedule again to match what she used to do. After several weeks, she could not see any changes in the shape of her stomach, so she upped her efforts. She began training even more vigorously, running 10 kilometres or more daily. She also reduced her food intake, gradually getting her intake down to 900 kCals per day. She refused to eat before she'd exercised. Jiao's weight dropped dramatically. After a few months of this, she became obsessed with food. She dreamed about food, watched cooking shows, and thought about food all day long. Finally, one afternoon she gave in and ate everything she had been denying herself—cookies, chocolate, peanut butter, french fries. . . . She ate until she couldn't eat anymore. Afterwards, she felt disgusted with herself and vowed to run even more the next day. This began a cycle of starvation and bingeing for Jiao.

Causes of Anorexia and Bulimia

Like other psychological disorders, anorexia and bulimia involve a complex interplay of a host of biopsychosocial factors. Increasingly, researchers are finding that eating disorders arise when underlying genetic and neurobiological vulnerabilities interact with the social pressures felt by young people that lead them to put a high value on their physical appearance, especially their weight (Steiger, 2007).

SOCIOCULTURAL FACTORS   Evidence shows that eating disorders are less common, even rare, in non-Western countries (Ricciardelli, McCabe, Williams, & Thompson, 2007). Sociocultural theorists point to societal pressures and expectations placed on young men and, to an even greater extent, women in our society as contributing to the development of eating disorders (Ricciardelli et al., 2007). The pressure to achieve an unrealistic standard of thinness, combined with the importance attached to appearance in defining the female role in our society, can lead young women to strive toward an unrealistically thin ideal and to develop an overriding fear of gaining weight that can put them at risk of developing eating disorders. Additionally, University of Toronto psychologists Janet Polivy and Peter Herman (2002) suggest that in our culture, thinness acts as a point of focus for women's dissatisfaction and distress, and its pursuit serves as an ineffective problem-solving strategy.

The media plays an important role in promoting cultural values and has been shown to exert its influence on both women's and men's reactions to thinness. For example, Canadian female university students participated in a study that examined how they responded to pictures of fashion models who represented the thin ideal. The researchers discovered that the women who viewed the pictures of models were significantly more depressed and angry

Wanting to be Barbie. The Barbie doll has long been a symbol of the busty but thin feminine form that has become idealized in our culture. If women were proportioned like the classic Barbie doll, they would resemble the woman in the photograph on the right. To achieve this idealized form, the average woman would need to grow nearly 30 centimetres in height, reduce her waist by about 13 centimetres, and add 10 centimetres to her bustline. What message do you think the Barbie doll figure conveys to young girls?

than the women who viewed pictures that did not contain human figures. This study demonstrates that viewing idealized female models has an immediate negative emotional impact and arguably gives credence to the role media images play in the development of disordered eating attitudes and behaviours (Pinhas, Toner, Ali, Garfinkel, & Stuckless, 1999).

A recent study found that the more time adolescent girls spend on Facebook, the greater their chances of developing a negative body image and various eating disorders, such as anorexia, bulimia, and exaggerated dieting ("Facebook Users," 2011). A similar direct link was found between viewing gossip- and leisure-related television programs (the likes of *Gossip Girl*) and eating disorders in adolescent girls. The study also revealed that the level of personal empowerment in these girls is negatively linked to eating disorders, such that the higher the level of empowerment, the more positive the physical self-image and the lower the chances of developing an eating disorder.

Men, too, are experiencing greater dissatisfaction with their body image. They are under increasing media influence to look leaner and more muscular (Leit, Gray, & Pope, 2002). The authors of one Canadian study, for example, have suggested that more males are participating in weight training and bodybuilding in an attempt to achieve the media-endorsed image of the ideal body shape (Goldfield, Blouin, & Woodside, 2006). One side effect of this trend is that male bodybuilders exhibit many eating-related characteristics of men with bulimia nervosa. Competitive bodybuilders show even higher rates of unhealthy eating and weight-control practices than do recreational bodybuilders and may be at risk of developing bulimia nervosa.

Despite the widespread belief that eating disorders, especially anorexia nervosa, are more common among affluent people, Canadian research (J. M. Jones et al., 2001) supports evidence that shows no strong linkage between socioeconomic status and eating disorders (Gard & Freeman, 1996). Beliefs that eating disorders are associated with high socioeconomic status may reflect the likelihood that affluent patients find treatment more accessible. Alternatively, it may be that the social pressures on young women to strive to achieve an ultra-thin ideal have now generalized across all socioeconomic levels.

PSYCHOSOCIAL FACTORS   Although cultural pressures to conform to an ultra-thin female ideal play a major role in eating disorders, the great majority of young women exposed to these pressures do not develop the disorders. Other factors must be involved. One likely factor involved in bulimic cases is a history of rigid dieting (Patton, Selzer, Coffey, Carlin, & Wolfe, 1999). Women with bulimia typically engage in extreme dieting characterized by very strict rules about what they can eat, how much they can eat, and how often they can eat (Drewnowski, Yee, Kurth, & Krahn, 1994). Not surprisingly, they tend to spend more time thinking about their weight than nonbulimic women (Zotter & Crowther, 1991).

Bulimic women tend to have been slightly overweight preceding the development of bulimia, and the initiation of the binge–purge cycle usually follows a period of strict dieting to lose weight. In a typical scenario, the rigid dietary controls fail, which prompts initial bingeing. This sets in motion a chain reaction in which bingeing leads to fear of weight gain, which prompts self-induced vomiting or excessive exercise to reduce any added weight. Some bulimic women become so concerned about possible weight gain that they resort to vomiting after every meal (Lowe, Gleaves, & Murphy-Eberenz, 1998). Purging is negatively reinforced by producing relief, or at least partial relief, from anxiety over gaining weight.

Body dissatisfaction is another important factor in eating disorders (Heatherton, Mahamedi, Striepe, Field, & Keel, 1997). Body dissatisfaction may lead to maladaptive attempts—through self-starvation and purging—to attain a desired body weight or shape. Bulimic and anorexic women tend to be extremely concerned about their body weight and shape (Jacobi, Hayward, de Zwaan, Kraemer, & Agras, 2004).

Cognitive factors are also involved. University of Toronto researchers have found that women with anorexia often have significantly higher perfectionistic attitudes in comparison to healthy controls, and the higher the perfectionism score, the poorer the outcome (Sutandar-Pinnock, Woodside, Carter, Olmsted, & Kaplan, 2003). Perfectionists tend to get down on themselves when they fail to meet the high standards they set, including their rigid dieting standards. Their extreme dieting may give them a sense of control and independence that they may feel they lack in other aspects of their lives. Bulimic women tend to be both perfectionistic and dichotomous ("black or white") in their thinking patterns (Fairburn, Welch, Doll, Davies, & O'Connor, 1997). Thus, they expect themselves to adhere perfectly to their rigid dietary rules and judge themselves as complete failures when they deviate even slightly. They also judge themselves harshly for episodes of binge eating and purging. These cognitive factors influence each other, as illustrated in Figure 8.1. In addition, women with bulimic tendencies tend to have a dysfunctional cognitive style that may lead to exaggerated beliefs about the negative consequences of gaining weight (Poulakis & Wertheim, 1993).

Researchers have also noted linkages between bulimia and problems in interpersonal relationships. Bulimic women tend to be shy and to have few, if any, close friends (Fairburn et al., 1997). One study of 21 college women with bulimia and a matched control group of 21 nonbulimic women found that those with bulimia had more social problems. They believed that less social support was available to them and reported more social conflict, especially with family members (Grissett & Norvell, 1992). They also rated themselves, and were judged by others, as less socially skilful than the control group. Although causal links between a lack of social skills and eating disorders remain to be substantiated fully, it is possible that enhancing the social skills of women with bulimia may increase the quality of their relationships and perhaps reduce their tendencies to use food in maladaptive ways.

Young women with bulimia also tend to have more psychological problems and lower self-esteem than other dieters (Jacobi et al., 2004). Canadian researchers have found that anorexia and bulimia often occur together with many kinds of psychological disorders, including affective disorders such as major depression and dysthymic disorder; anxiety disorders such as obsessive-compulsive disorder, panic disorder, phobia, generalized anxiety disorder, and posttraumatic stress disorder; and disorders found in children and adolescents such as oppositional defiant disorder and conduct disorder (Geist, Davis, & Heinmaa, 1998). Perhaps some forms of binge eating involve attempts at self-medication for emotional problems. Consistent with this view is evidence that bulimic women are more likely than other women to have experienced childhood sexual and physical abuse (Kent & Waller, 2000). Bulimia may develop in some cases as an ineffective means of coping with abuse.

Negative Self-Evaluation

Characteristic Extreme Concerns About Shape and Weight

Perfectionism and Dichotomous Thinking

Intense and Rigid Dieting

Perfectionism and Dichotomous Thinking

Binge Eating — Negative Affect

Self-Induced Vomiting/Laxative Misuse

FIGURE 8.1 A cognitive model of bulimia nervosa.
Source: Fairburn, 1997, pp. 209–241. Copyright 1997 by Oxford University Press. Reprinted with permission.

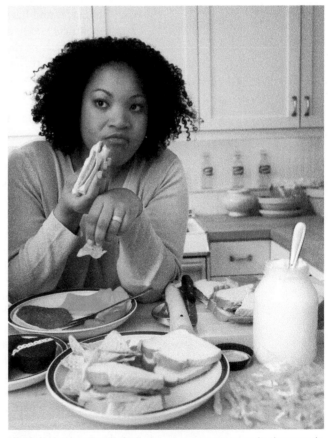

Bingeing. People with bulimia nervosa may cram in thousands of calories during a single binge and then attempt to purge what they have consumed by forcing themselves to vomit.

What we have gained from this research is the understanding that bulimia often develops within a context of extreme, rigid dieting overlaying psychological, interpersonal, and cognitive factors.

FAMILY FACTORS AND EATING DISORDERS Eating disorders frequently develop against a backdrop of family conflicts (Fairburn et al., 1997). Some theorists focus on the brutal effect of self-starvation on parents. They suggest that some adolescents use their refusal to eat to punish parents for feelings of loneliness and alienation they experience in the home. One related study compared the mothers of adolescent girls with eating disorders to the mothers of other girls. Mothers of the adolescents with eating disorders were more likely to be unhappy about their families' functioning, to have their own problems with eating and dieting, to believe their daughters ought to lose weight, and to regard their daughters as unattractive (Pike & Rodin, 1991). Moreover, mothers of daughters with eating disorders showed high levels of perfectionism and an overconcern about shape and weight (Woodside et al., 2002). Is binge eating, as suggested by Humphrey (1986), a metaphoric effort to gain the nurturance and comfort that the mother is denying her daughter? Does purging represent the symbolic upheaval of negative feelings toward the family?

Families of young women with eating disorders tend to be more often conflicted while at the same time less cohesive and nurturing and more overprotective and critical than reference groups (Fairburn et al., 1997). The parents seem less capable of promoting independence in their daughters (Strober & Humphrey, 1987). Conflicts with parents over issues of autonomy are often implicated in the development of both anorexia nervosa and bulimia (Ratti, Humphrey, & Lyons, 1996). Yet it remains uncertain whether these family patterns contribute to the initiation of eating disorders or whether eating disorders go on to disrupt family life. The truth probably lies in an interaction between the two.

systems perspective View that problems reflect the systems (family, social, school, ecological, etc.) in which they are embedded.

From the **systems perspective**, families are systems that regulate themselves in ways that minimize the open expression of conflict and reduce the immediate need for overt change. Within this perspective, girls who develop anorexia may be seen as helping maintain the shaky balances and harmonies found in dysfunctional families by displacing attention from family conflicts and marital tensions onto themselves (Minuchin, Rosman, & Baker, 1978). The girl may become the identified patient although the family unit is actually dysfunctional.

Regardless of the factors that initiate eating disorders, social reinforcers may maintain them. Young women with eating disorders may quickly become the focus of attention of their families and receive attention from their parents that might otherwise be lacking.

BIOLOGICAL FACTORS Interest in the biological underpinnings of eating disorders, especially bulimia, has largely focused on the role of the neurotransmitter serotonin. Serotonin is involved in regulating mood and appetite, especially appetite for carbohydrates.

Decreased serotonin activity or responsivity may be involved in prompting binge eating in bulimic individuals, especially carbohydrate bingeing (Levitan, Kaplan, Joffe, Levitt, & Brown, 1997). This line of thinking is buttressed by evidence that antidepressants such as Prozac, which increase serotonin activity, can decrease binge-eating episodes in bulimic women (Walsh, Fairburn, Mickley, Sysko, & Parides, 2004). We also know that many women with eating disorders are depressed or have a history of depression, and imbalances of serotonin are implicated in depressive disorders. It may be that bulimia is related to depression, perhaps at a genetic level.

Recent reseach has also implicated another common neurotransmitter, dopamine, and the reward circuitry in the brain with bulimia. Dopamine helps regulate behaviour such as learning and motivation. Frank, Reynolds, Shott, and O'Reilly (2011) found that weakened responses in the brain regions implicated in reward were related to the frequency of binge/purge episodes. This might indicate that overeating and purging episodes cause this weaker response and set off a vicious cycle of altered brain function.

Before now, the dopamine–bulimia connection had not been fully explored. The research described here confirms that bulimic behaviour affects the brain's reward function; however, at this point it is uncertain whether these alterations return to normal with recovery. Future developments might include specific medication to alter brain dopamine action.

Another interesting finding related to brain function in those with bulimia was that individuals with bulimia were more impulsive than others during psychological testing.

Rachel Marsh and her colleagues (2009) at Columbia University and the New York State Psychiatric Institute compared the performance on a task by 20 women with bulimia nervosa with that by 20 healthy women who served as controls. During the testing, the women's brain functioning was monitored by means of functional magnetic resonance imaging (fMRI). The task was the Simon Spatial Incompatibility task, in which participants must indicate the direction an arrow is pointing regardless of where it appears on a screen. The task is easier when the arrow direction matches the side of the screen but more difficult when, for instance, an arrow that points left appears on the right-hand side of the screen. Ignoring the side of the screen to focus on the arrow direction requires regulating behaviour, by fighting the tendency to respond automatically and resolving conflicting messages.

Marsh and colleagues (2009) found differences in how the two groups responded. The women with bulimia responded faster and made more errors on conflict trials that required self-regulatory control to respond correctly. They responded faster on congruent trials following incorrect conflict trials, suggesting impulsive responding even immediately after having committed an error. When patients with bulimia did respond correctly on trials in which the arrow side and direction did not match, their frontostriatal circuits did not activate (as should happen) to the same degree as did those of women in the control group.

"These group differences in performance and patterns of brain activity suggest that individuals with bulimia nervosa do not activate frontostriatal circuits appropriately, perhaps contributing to impulsive responses to conflict stimuli that normally require both frontostriatal activation and the exercise of self-regulatory control to generate a correct response," the authors conclude. "We speculate that this inability to engage frontostriatal systems also contributes to their inability to regulate binge-type eating and other impulsive behaviors" (Marsh et al., 2009).

Evidence also supports a genetic link with eating disorders (Lamberg, 2003). A large-scale study of more than 2000 female twins showed a much higher concordance rate for bulimia nervosa—23% versus 9%—among monozygotic (MZ) twins than among dizygotic (DZ) twins (Kendler et al., 1991). Greater concordance for anorexia is also found among MZ than DZ twins—50% versus 5%—suggesting that genetics plays a role in anorexia as well (Holland, Sicotte, & Treasure, 1988). Eating disorders also tend to run in families, which is further suggestive of a genetic component. However, genetic factors cannot fully account for the development of eating disorders. Eating disorder researchers Howard Steiger and Kenneth Bruce (2007) of the McGill University–affiliated Douglas Hospital Research Centre propose that, as in the diathesis-stress model, a genetic predisposition involving a dysfunction of neurotransmitter activity interacts with family, social, cultural, and environmental pressures, thereby leading to the development of eating disorders.

Canadian studies have also shown that adolescent girls with type-1 diabetes were twice as likely to develop eating disorders as their nondiabetic peers (Frankenfield, 2000). A long-term follow-up of young diabetic women with eating disorders found that they had a threefold higher risk of developing diabetic retinopathy (a potentially blinding complication of diabetes that damages the eye's retina) compared to other diabetic women (G. Rodin et al., 2002). It was recommended that young women with diabetes who have poor metabolic control and who are concerned about their shape and weight should be monitored for a potential eating disorder.

Treatment of Anorexia Nervosa and Bulimia Nervosa

Eating disorders are difficult to treat, and treatment efforts are often met with ongoing denial and resistance by patients with such disorders, especially anorexia (A. S. Kaplan & Garfinkel, 1999). People with anorexia may be hospitalized, especially when weight loss is severe or body weight is falling rapidly. In a hospital, they are usually placed on a closely monitored re-feeding regimen. Dalhousie University philosopher Chris MacDonald (2002) alerts us to the ethical dilemma that results when caregivers are confronted with patients who resist treatment. It forces caregivers to decide which interventions, such as tube feeding or chemical restraints, justify a violation of the patient's autonomy and right to refuse treatment, especially when the patient's well-being is at stake.

The fear of becoming fat is a prime factor underlying eating disorders such as anorexia and bulimia. The Goldfarb Fear of Fat Scale (Goldfarb, Dykens, & Gerrard, 1985) measures the degree to which people fear becoming fat. The scale may help identify individuals at risk of developing eating disorders. It differentiates between anorexic and normal women and between bulimic and nonbulimic women. Dieters, however, also score higher on the scale than nondieters.

To complete the Fear of Fat Scale, read each of the following statements and write in the number that best represents your own feelings and beliefs. Then check the key on page 307.

1 = very untrue
2 = somewhat untrue
3 = somewhat true
4 = very true

_____ 1. My biggest fear is becoming fat.

_____ 2. I am afraid to gain even a little weight.

_____ 3. I believe there is a real risk that I will become overweight someday.

_____ 4. I don't understand how overweight people can live with themselves.

_____ 5. Becoming fat would be the worst thing that could happen to me.

_____ 6. If I stopped concentrating on controlling my weight, chances are I would become very fat.

_____ 7. There is nothing that I can do to make the thought of gaining weight less painful and frightening.

_____ 8. I feel like all my energy goes into controlling my weight.

_____ 9. If I eat even a little, I may lose control and not stop eating.

_____ 10. Staying hungry is the only way I can guard against losing control and becoming fat.

Source: Goldfarb, Dykens, & Gerrard, 1985, pp. 329–332. Copyright Taylor & Francis. Reprinted with permission.

Allan Kaplan (2002) contends that psychotherapy is still a common treatment for anorexia, but by itself, its efficacy remains in question. The best outcomes result from treatment that involves psychotherapy combined with nutritional management and family interventions (A. S. Kaplan, 2002). Cognitive analytic therapy has been shown to benefit anorexic patients (Treasure & Ward, 1997). Behaviour therapy has also been shown to be effective in promoting weight gain in anorexic patients (W. G. Johnson, Tsoh, & Varnado, 1996). Behaviour therapy is commonly used with rewards made contingent on adherence to the re-feeding protocol (Rock & Curran-Celentano, 1996). Individual or family therapy following hospitalization has also shown favourable long-term benefits (Eisler et al., 1997). Family therapy may also be employed to help resolve underlying family conflicts. Family group psychoeducation (FGP) has been shown to be a cost-effective alternative to family therapy during the first months of treatment for severely anorexic teens (Geist, Heinmaa, Stephens, Davis, & Katzman, 2000). FGP provides patients and parents with information about the nature of eating disorders, developmental issues, and weight-regulation issues, and also provides them with opportunities to discuss the information.

Hospitalization may also be used to help break the binge–purge cycle in bulimia, but it appears to be necessary only in cases in which eating behaviours are clearly out of control and outpatient treatment has failed or where there is evidence of severe medical complications, suicidal thoughts or attempts, or substance abuse (APA, 2000a).

Cognitive-behavioural therapy (CBT) is useful in helping bulimic individuals challenge self-defeating thoughts and beliefs, such as unrealistic, perfectionistic expectations regarding dieting and body weight (Wilson & Fairburn, 1998). Another common dysfunctional thinking pattern is dichotomous (all-or-nothing) thinking, which predisposes bulimic individuals to purge when they slip even a little from their rigid diets. CBT also challenges tendencies to overemphasize appearance in determining self-worth. To eliminate self-induced vomiting, therapists may use the behavioural technique of exposure with response prevention, developed for treatment of people with obsessive-compulsive disorder. In this technique, the bulimic patient is exposed to eating forbidden foods while the therapist stands by to prevent vomiting until the urge to purge passes. Bulimic individuals thus learn to tolerate violations of their dietary rules without resorting to purging.

Another psychologically based treatment, interpersonal psychotherapy, has also shown good success and may be used as an alternative treatment in cases where CBT proves unsuccessful (Wilson & Fairburn, 1998). Interpersonal therapy focuses on resolving interpersonal problems in the belief that more effective interpersonal functioning will lead to healthier food habits and attitudes.

Canadian studies have also found that brief therapy interventions are effective for reducing symptoms in bulimic patients. For instance, as a first step in their treatment, Carter et al. (2003) found that bulimic patients who were not well informed about bulimia, had more problems with intimacy, and had higher compulsivity scores benefited from self-help manuals that provided information about the disorder or focused on self-assertion skills. In another study, it was shown that group psychoeducation by itself provided therapeutic benefits in five sessions (R. Davis, Olmsted, Rockert, Marques, & Dolhanty, 1997).

The pharmacological treatment of eating disorders has generally been disappointing (Zhu & Walsh, 2002). Antidepressant drugs have been shown to provide short-term therapeutic benefits in treating bulimia but have not been very successful in treating anorexia (Zhu & Walsh, 2002). They are believed to work by decreasing the urge to binge through normalizing serotonin—the brain chemical involved in regulating appetite.

A review of the available evidence suggests that CBT is more effective than antidepressant medication in treating bulimia nervosa and carries a lower rate of relapse (Zhu & Walsh, 2002). It appears that CBT should be the first treatment choice for bulimia, followed by use of antidepressant medication if psychological treatment is not successful (Compas, Haaga, Keefe, Leitenberg, & Williams, 1998; Wilson & Fairburn, 1998). Studies examining whether a combined CBT–medication treatment approach is more effective than either treatment component alone have thus far produced inconsistent results (Walsh et al., 1997).

Treatment of eating disorders in Canada has moved away from relying on long-term hospitalization, psychotherapy, and drugs that have risky side effects. Treatment has progressed toward a team approach that focuses on nutritional stabilization along with brief forms of psychotherapy, group and family psychoeducation, and outpatient care that is tailored to different stages of recovery (Health Canada, 2002b). Although progress has been made in treating eating disorders (Health Canada, 2002b), there is considerable room for improvement. Even with CBT, about half of treated patients show continued evidence of bulimic behaviour (Compas et al., 1998; Wilson & Fairburn, 1998). Eating disorders can be a tenacious and enduring problem, especially when excessive fears of body weight and distortions of body image are maintained. A recent study reported that 10 years after an initial presentation with bulimia, approximately 30% of women still showed recurrent binge-eating or purging behaviours (Keel, Mitchell, Miller, Davis, & Crow, 1999). Recovery from anorexia also tends to be a long process. A recent study of 88 German patients with anorexia showed that 50% of the patients did not recover sooner than 6 years after their first hospitalization (Herzog, Schellberg, & Deter, 1997).

On a more positive note, research has recently shown that involving parents in treatment of bulimia doubles the success rate. The first randomized controlled study of those dealing with bulimia nervosa took place in 2007 and was run by a team based at the University of Chicago Medical Center ("Involving Parents," 2011). They found that, immediately following treatment, almost 40% of individuals who included their family in the treatment stopped bingeing and purging, while only about 18% of those who participated in the usual treatment, psychotherapy, stopped. Even more encouraging was that six months after the end of their treatment, about 30% of the family-included treatment group were still abstinent (not bingeing and purging), compared to only 10% of the group that received only psychotherapy.

Binge-Eating Disorder

People with **binge-eating disorder** (BED) have recurrent eating binges but do not purge themselves of the excess food afterwards. Binge-eating disorder is classified in the DSM as a potential disorder requiring further study. The proposed changes in the DSM-5

binge-eating disorder Proposed psychological disorder characterized by repeated episodes in which binge eating occurs but is not followed by purging.

Many other disordered conditions that involve food, eating, and body image have been identified. Some have a formal diagnosis, while others are somewhat controversial.

Feeding and eating problems associated with infancy and childhood include the following:

- *Pica.* The persistent craving or eating of items that are not food, such as clay, dirt, stones, feces, paint chips, or plastic.
- *Rumination disorder.* Characterized by repeated eating, regurgitation, and then re-chewing and re-eating of food.

Bigorexia. People with muscle dysmorphia, also known as *reverse anorexia nervosa*, are preoccupied with the belief that they are not muscular enough, and will go to extreme lengths to build muscle.

- *Feeding disorder of infancy or early childhood.* Persistent failure to consume foods that provide adequate nutrition, which results in weight loss or a failure to gain weight appropriately for development.
- *Prader-Willi syndrome.* A disorder of chromosome 15 characterized by a severe loss of muscle tone and feeding difficulties in early infancy, followed in later childhood by an insatiable appetite, excessive eating, and gradual development of life-threatening obesity.
- *Cyclic vomiting syndrome* (also known as *abdominal migraine*). Characterized by recurrent bouts of severe nausea and vomiting that last for hours or even days and alternate with longer periods without symptoms.

Eating and body-image disorders associated with adolescents and adults include the following:

- *Anorexia athletica.* Exercising for an amount of time or at an intensity that is well beyond normal (in association with an obsessive preoccupation with diet and weight).
- *Muscle dysmorphia* (also known as *bigorexia* or *reverse anorexia nervosa*). Common in bodybuilders, a chronic preoccupation with the belief and insecurity that one is not muscular enough, accompanied by a variety of muscle-bulking strategies.
- *Orthexia nervosa.* Obsession with eating "pure" or "superior" foods and with "proper" food preparation to the point that it interferes with a person's life.
- *Night-eating syndrome.* A form of compulsive eating whereby more than half the person's daily food intake is consumed after dinner and before breakfast, accompanied by feelings of anxiety and guilt.
- *Nocturnal sleep-related eating disorder.* A rare type of sleepwalking disorder characterized by recurrent episodes of eating during sleep; it can lead to significant weight gain.
- *Gourmand syndrome.* An eating disorder linked to damage of the right hemisphere of the brain that results in the person becoming obsessed with shopping for specialty foods and engaging in elaborate food preparation and dining rituals associated with gourmet food.

include binge-eating disorder as a separate category, a free-standing diagnosis. At this time, however, BED is under great scrutiny.

The available evidence indicates that unlike bulimia, BED is more commonly found among obese individuals (Spitzer et al., 1992). It is frequently associated with people suffering from depression who have a history of unsuccessful attempts at losing excess weight and keeping it off. People with BED tend to be older than those with anorexia or bulimia (Arnow, Kenardy, & Agras, 1992). Like other eating disorders, BED is found more frequently among women, although of all the eating disorders, men are most likely to experience BED (Health Canada, 2002b). Overall, about 2% of the population report frequent eating binges; it is the most common eating disorder, at about 3.5% of women and 2% of men at some point in their lives.

People with BED are often described as "compulsive overeaters." During a binge, they feel a loss of control over their eating. BED may fall within a broader domain of compulsive behaviours characterized by impaired control over maladaptive behaviours, such as pathological gambling and substance-abuse disorders. A history of dieting may play a role in some cases of BED, although it appears to be a less important factor in BED than in bulimia (Howard & Porzelius, 1999).

Cognitive-behavioural techniques have shown some positive effects in treating binge-eating disorder (Carter & Fairburn, 1998). Antidepressants, especially antidepressants of the SSRI family, may also reduce the frequency of binge-eating episodes by helping regulate serotonin levels in the brain (Hudson et al., 1998).

Behaviour modification leads to modest weight losses that are generally well maintained for at least a year after treatment (Brownell & Wadden, 1992). However, a look at longer-term outcomes reveals a dimmer picture. As many as 90% to 95% of people who lose weight by dieting or behaviour modification return to their baseline weight levels within five years (Wilson, 1994). The problem appears to be that the changes in diet, exercise patterns, and eating habits that led to the initial weight loss do not generally carry over into changes in lifestyles that would promote long-term maintenance of weight loss. Clearly, to maintain weight losses, people need to make healthy changes in dietary and exercise patterns a part of their lifestyle.

REVIEW IT

Eating Disorders

- **What are the major types of eating disorders?** There are two major types of eating disorders included in the DSM: anorexia nervosa and bulimia nervosa. Anorexia nervosa involves maintenance of weight at least 15% below normal levels, intense fears of becoming overweight, distorted body image, and, in females, amenorrhea. In comparison, people with bulimia nervosa are usually of normal weight, but because of a preoccupation with weight control and body shape, they engage in repeated binges and regular purging to keep weight down. Another type of eating disorder, binge-eating disorder, is listed as a potential disorder requiring further study.

- **What are some of the factors involved in these types of eating disorders?** They tend to begin in adolescence and affect many more females than males. They both involve preoccupations with weight control and maladaptive ways of trying to keep weight down. Many factors have been implicated in their development, including social pressures on young women to adhere to unrealistic standards of thinness, issues of control, underlying psychological problems, and conflict within the family—especially over issues of autonomy. People with binge-eating disorder tend to be older than those with anorexia or bulimia and to suffer from obesity.

Norms for the Fear of Fat Scale

Comparative scores are available for women only. You may compare your own score on the Fear of Fat Scale to those obtained by the following groups:

Group	Number	Mean
Non-dieting college women (women satisfied with their weight)	49	17.30
General female college population	73	18.33
College women who are dissatisfied with their weight and have been on three or more diets during the past year	40	23.90
Bulimic college women (actively bingeing and purging)	32	30.00
Anorexic women in treatment	7	35.00

Source of data: Goldfarb, L. A., Dykens, E. M., & Gerrard, M. (1985). The Goldfarb fear of fat scale. *Journal of Personality Assessment, 49,* 329–332. Reprinted with permission.

Keep the following in mind as you interpret your score:

1. The Goldfarb samples are quite small.
2. A score at a certain level does not place you in that group; it merely means that you report an equivalent fear of fat. In other words, a score of 33.00 does not indicate you have bulimia or anorexia. It means that your self-reported fear of fat approximates those reported by bulimic and anorexic women in the Goldfarb study.

SLEEP DISORDERS

Sleep is a biological function that remains in many ways a mystery. We know that sleep is restorative and that most of us need at least seven or more hours of sleep a night to function at our best. Yet we cannot identify the specific biochemical changes occurring during sleep that account for its restorative function. We also know that many of us are troubled by sleep problems, although the causes of some of these problems remain obscure. Sleep problems of sufficient severity and frequency that lead to significant personal distress or impaired functioning in social, occupational, or other roles are classified in the DSM system as **sleep disorders.**

Highly specialized diagnostic facilities, called *sleep disorders centres*, have been established throughout Canada to provide a more comprehensive assessment of sleep problems. The Canadian Sleep Society provides a list of about 130 sleep centres across Canada (see www.canadiansleepsociety.com). People with sleep disorders typically spend a few nights at a sleep centre, where they are wired to devices that track their physiological responses during sleep or attempted sleep—brainwaves, heart and respiration rates, and so on. This form of assessment is termed **polysomnographic (PSG) recording,** because it involves simultaneous measurement of diverse physiological response patterns, including brainwaves, eye movements, muscle movements, and respiration. Information obtained from physiological monitoring of sleep patterns is combined with that obtained from medical and psychological evaluations, subjective reports of sleep disturbance, and sleep diaries (daily logs compiled by the problem sleeper that track the length of time between retiring to bed and falling asleep, number of hours slept, nightly awakenings, daytime naps, and so on). Multidisciplinary teams of physicians and psychologists in sleep centres sift through this information to arrive at a diagnosis and suggest treatment approaches to address the presenting problem.

The DSM groups sleep disorders into two major categories: **dyssomnias** and **parasomnias.**

Dyssomnias

Dyssomnias are characterized by disturbances in the amount, quality, or timing of sleep. There are five specific types of dyssomnias: primary insomnia, primary hypersomnia, narcolepsy, breathing-related sleep disorder, and circadian rhythm sleep disorder.

INSOMNIA The word **insomnia** derives from the Latin *in-*, meaning "not" or "without," and, of course, *somnus*, meaning "sleep." Occasional bouts of insomnia, especially during times of stress, are not abnormal. All the same, more than an estimated 3.3 million Canadians aged 15 and older suffer from insomnia, averaging just 6.5 hours of sleep a night—a full hour less than those who don't have insomnia (Tjepkema, 2005). Although chronic insomnia affects older people in greater numbers, young people usually complain that it takes too long to get to sleep whereas older people are more likely to complain of waking frequently during the night or of waking too early in the morning. Many seniors also have more chronic health problems that interfere with their sleep patterns (Tjepkema, 2005). Overall, there are a host of factors that can have a negative impact on the odds of Canadians getting a good night's sleep, including, for example, high levels of life stress; shift work; heavy drinking or cannabis use; obesity; being divorced, separated, or widowed; being female; and lower levels of education and income (Tjepkema, 2005).

Chronic insomnia lasting a month or longer is often a sign of an underlying physical problem or of a psychological disorder such as depression. If the underlying problem is treated successfully, chances are that normal sleep patterns will be restored. Chronic insomnia that cannot be accounted for by another psychological or physical disorder or by the effects of drugs or medications is classified as a sleep disorder called *primary insomnia.* People with primary insomnia have persistent difficulty falling asleep, remaining asleep, or achieving restorative sleep (sleep that leaves the person feeling refreshed and alert) for a period of a month or longer. The sleep disturbance or associated daytime

sleep disorders Diagnostic category representing persistent or recurrent sleep-related problems that cause significant personal distress or impaired functioning.

polysomnographic (PSG) recording The simultaneous measurement of multiple physiological responses during sleep or attempted sleep.

dyssomnias Category of sleep disorders involving disturbances in the amount, quality, or timing of sleep.

parasomnias Category of sleep disorders involving the occurrence of abnormal behaviours or physiological events during sleep or at the transition between wakefulness and sleep.

insomnia Term applying to difficulties falling asleep, remaining asleep, or achieving restorative sleep.

fatigue causes significant levels of personal distress or difficulties performing usual social, occupational, student, or other roles. Not surprisingly, there is a high rate of comorbidity (co-occurrence) between insomnia and other psychological problems, especially anxiety and depression (Morin, LeBlanc, Daley, Gregoire, & Merette, 2006; Toward Optimized Practice, 2007). Although the prevalence of primary insomnia is unknown, it is considered the most common form of sleep disturbance.

Psychological factors play a prominent role in primary insomnia. For example, University of Ottawa psychologists found that high levels of anxiety were associated with moderate to severe sleep-onset chronic insomnia (Viens, De Koninck, Mercier, St-Onge, & Lorrain, 2003). People troubled by primary insomnia tend to bring their anxieties and worries to bed with them, which raises their bodily arousal to a level that prevents natural sleep. Then they worry about not getting enough sleep, which only compounds their sleep difficulties. They may try to force themselves to sleep, which tends to backfire by creating more anxiety and tension, making sleep even less likely to occur. Sleep cannot be forced. Trying to make yourself fall asleep is likely to backfire. We can set the scene for sleep only by retiring when we are tired and relaxed and allowing sleep to occur naturally.

HYPERSOMNIA The word **hypersomnia** is derived from the Greek *hyper*, meaning "over" or "more than normal," and the Latin *somnus*, meaning "sleep." Primary hypersomnia involves a pattern of excessive sleepiness during the day that continues for a period of a month or longer. The excessive sleepiness (sometimes referred to as "sleep drunkenness") may take the form of difficulty awakening following a prolonged sleep period (typically 8 to 12 hours). Or, there may be a pattern of daytime sleep episodes occurring virtually every day in the form of intended or unintended napping (such as inadvertently falling asleep while watching television). Despite the fact that daytime naps often last an hour or more, the person does not feel refreshed upon awakening. The disorder is considered primary because it cannot be accounted for by inadequate amounts of sleep during the night due to insomnia, by another psychological or physical disorder, by drug or medication use, or by other factors (such as loud neighbours keeping the person up).

Although many of us feel sleepy during the day from time to time, and may even drift off occasionally while reading or watching television, the person with primary hypersomnia has more persistent and severe periods of sleepiness that typically lead to difficulties in daily functioning, such as missing important meetings because of difficulty awakening. Although the prevalence of the disorder is unknown, surveys of the general population show complaints related to daytime sleepiness affecting between 0.5% and 5% of the adult population (APA, 2000a).

NARCOLEPSY The word **narcolepsy** derives from the Greek *narke*, meaning "stupor," and *lepsis*, meaning "an attack." People with narcolepsy experience sleep attacks in which they suddenly fall asleep without any warning at various times during the day. They remain asleep for an average period of about 15 minutes. The person can be in the midst of a conversation at one moment and slump to the floor fast asleep a moment later. The diagnosis is made when sleep attacks occur daily for a period of three months or longer and are combined with the presence of one or both of the following conditions: (1) **cataplexy** (a sudden loss of muscular control) and (2) intrusions of **REM sleep** in the transitional state between wakefulness and sleep (APA, 2000a). REM, or rapid eye movement, sleep is the stage of sleep associated with dreaming. It is so named because the sleeper's eyes tend to dart about rapidly under their closed lids. Narcoleptic attacks are associated with an almost immediate transition into REM sleep from a state of wakefulness. In normal sleep, REM typically follows several stages of non-REM sleep.

Cataplexy typically follows a strong emotional reaction such as joy or anger. It can range from a mild weakness in the legs to a complete loss of muscle control that results in the person suddenly collapsing (J. M. Siegel, 2004). People with narcolepsy may also experience sleep paralysis, a temporary state following awakening in which the person feels incapable of moving or talking. The person may also report frightening hallucinations, called *hypnagogic hallucinations*, which occur just before the onset of sleep and tend to involve visual, auditory, tactile, and kinesthetic (body movement) sensations.

hypersomnia Condition relating to a pattern of excessive sleepiness during the day.

narcolepsy Sleep disorder characterized by sudden, irresistible episodes of sleep (sleep attacks).

cataplexy Brief, sudden loss of muscular control, typically lasting from a few seconds to as long as two minutes.

REM sleep REM (rapid eye movement) sleep is the stage of sleep associated with dreaming that is characterized by the appearance of rapid eye movements under closed eyelids.

Narcolepsy affects men and women equally and is a relatively uncommon disorder, affecting an estimated 0.02% (2 in 10 000) to 0.16% (16 in 10 000) people within the general adult population (APA, 2000a). Unlike hypersomnia, in which daytime sleep episodes follow a period of increasing sleepiness, narcoleptic attacks occur abruptly, without prior sleepiness. The attacks can be dangerous and frightening, especially if they occur when the person is driving or using heavy equipment or sharp implements. About two out of three people with narcolepsy have fallen asleep while driving, and four out of five have fallen asleep on the job (Aldrich, 1992). Household accidents resulting from falls are also common (Cohen, Ferrans, & Eshler, 1992). Not surprisingly, the disorder is associated with a lower quality of life in terms of general health and daily functioning (Ferrans, Cohen, & Smith, 1992). Scientists have recently discovered that narcolepsy with cataplexy is related to low levels of a **neuropeptide**, hypocretin, in the cerebrospinal fluid in the brain (Baumann, Khatami, Werth, & Bassetti, 2006). The hypocretin deficiency is due to a loss of hypocretin-producing neurons, but the exact cause of that loss remains unknown.

BREATHING-RELATED SLEEP DISORDER   People with a **breathing-related sleep disorder** experience repeated disruptions of sleep due to respiratory problems (APA, 2000a). These frequent disruptions of sleep result in insomnia or excessive daytime sleepiness.

The subtypes of the disorder are distinguished in terms of the underlying causes of the breathing problem. The most common type is obstructive sleep apnea, which involves repeated episodes of either complete or partial obstruction of breathing during sleep (Canadian Lung Association, 2006). The word **apnea** derives from the Greek prefix *a-*, meaning "not" or "without," and *pneuma*, meaning "breath." The breathing difficulty results from the blockage of airflow in the upper airways, often due to a structural defect, such as an overly thick palate or enlarged tonsils or adenoids. In cases of complete obstruction, the sleeper may literally stop breathing for periods of 15 to 90 seconds as many as 30 times an hour, or more in severe cases (APA, 2000a; Fleetham et al., 2006). When these lapses of breathing occur, the sleeper may suddenly sit up, gasp for air, take a few deep breaths, and fall back asleep without awakening or realizing that breathing was interrupted. The narrowing of the air passages also produces loud snoring, which alternates with these momentary silences when breathing is suspended (Phillipson, 1993).

Although a biological reflex kicks in to force a gasping breath after these brief interruptions of breathing, the frequent disruptions of normal sleep resulting from apneas can leave people feeling sleepy the following day, making it more difficult for them to function effectively. Obstructive sleep apnea is a relatively common problem, affecting an estimated 2% to 4% of the adult population (Banno, Walld, & Kryger, 2005). The disorder is more common in younger men than women, but the rates increase and become more similar in both men and women as they approach age 50 (Bardwell, Moore, Ancoli-Israel, & Dimsdale, 2003). It is also much more common among people who are obese (e.g., because of a narrowing of the upper airways due to an enlargement of soft tissue); along with rising obesity rates in people across North America, we are now seeing an associated rise in the incidence of sleep apnea (Banno et al., 2005). Alcohol use before bedtime can also cause snoring due to a narrowing of the breathing passageways into outright blockages, resulting in sleep apneas (Phillipson, 1993).

People with sleep apnea may gasp for breath hundreds of times during the night without realizing it. They may become aware of the problem only when it is diagnosed or when their bed partners point it out to them. The person's bed partner is usually very aware of the problem because the loudness of the person's snoring can reach levels associated with industrial noise pollution (Caffier et al., 2007). Bed partners commonly look for other sleeping places to obtain a good night's sleep. Not surprisingly, people who have sleep apnea report a

neuropeptide An amino acid found in cerebrospinal fluid that plays a role in neuronal transmission and the modulation of brain circuits or regions.

breathing-related sleep disorder Sleep disorder in which sleeping is repeatedly disrupted due to difficulties breathing normally.

apnea Temporary cessation of breathing.

Sleep apnea. Loud snoring may be a sign of obstructive sleep apnea, a breathing-related sleep disorder in which a person may temporarily stop breathing as many as 500 times during a night's sleep. Loud snoring, described by bed partners as reaching levels of industrial noise pollution, may alternate with momentary silences when breathing is suspended.

poorer quality of life than unaffected people; they are vulnerable to excessive daytime sleepiness, impaired intellectual and memory functioning, and depression—factors that can contribute to the loss of employment, marriage breakups, and accidents at work and on the road (Banno & Kryger, 2007). Sleep apnea is also associated with an increased risk of high blood pressure, heart attacks, strokes, and even sudden death.

Not only does obstructive sleep apnea result in personal suffering; there is also a high cost to the health-care system when it goes undiagnosed. Meir Kryger and others at Winnipeg's St. Boniface General Hospital Research Centre, North America's first sleep-disorder breathing lab, tracked medical system usage by sleep apnea patients before and after treatment (Kryger, 2001). In studies that looked at the 2-year and 10-year time spans preceding diagnosis, it was shown that sleep apnea patients used about two times the medical resources as the general population (Ronald et al., 1999). Prior to diagnosis for apnea, patients were being treated for cardiovascular diseases, chronic obstructive airways disease, and depression, which accounted for most of the increased medical resource utilization (R. Smith et al., 2002). The good news is that once apnea patients are diagnosed and they follow a treatment regime, there is a significant reduction in medical care costs (Bahammam et al., 1999). Toronto Western Hospital psychiatrists conducted a review of the sleep apnea literature and concluded that the disorder has serious medical, socioeconomic, and psychological consequences, although it remains largely undiagnosed (Chung, Jairam, Hussain, & Shapiro, 2002). They contend that by detecting and treating obstructive sleep apnea, morbidity and mortality rates and health-care costs associated with the disorder will be reduced. Consequently, they strongly recommend that primary-care physicians be prepared to screen patients who have symptoms of obstructive sleep apnea and refer them for an overnight (polysomnographic) assessment at a sleep clinic.

CIRCADIAN RHYTHM SLEEP DISORDER Most bodily functions follow a cycle or an internal rhythm—called a circadian rhythm—that lasts about 24 hours. Even when people are relieved of scheduled activities and work duties and placed in environments that screen the time of day, they usually follow relatively normal sleep–wake schedules. Our circadian rhythm appears to be partially genetically based—we tend to be either morning people (early risers who are more alert early in the day) or evening people (late risers who are more alert at night) (Hur, 2007).

In **circadian rhythm sleep disorder**, this rhythm becomes grossly disturbed because of a mismatch between the sleep schedule demands imposed on the person and the person's internal sleep–wake cycle. The disruption in normal sleep patterns caused by the mismatch can lead to insomnia or hypersomnia. Like other sleep disorders, the mismatch must be persistent and severe enough to cause significant levels of distress or impair one's ability to function in social, occupational, or other roles. The jet lag that can accompany travel between time zones does not qualify because it is usually transient. However, frequent changes of time zones and frequent changes of work shifts (as encountered, for example, by nursing personnel) can induce more persistent or recurrent problems adjusting sleep patterns to scheduling demands, resulting in a circadian rhythm sleep disorder. Treatment may involve a program of making gradual adjustments in the sleep schedule to allow the person's circadian system to become aligned with changes in the sleep–wake schedule (Dahl, 1992).

circadian rhythm sleep disorder
Sleep disorder characterized by disruption of sleep due to a mismatch in sleep schedules between the body's internal sleep–wake cycle and the demands of the environment. Formerly called *sleep–wake schedule disorder*.

Parasomnias

The parasomnias involve abnormal behaviours or physiological events taking place during sleep or at the threshold between wakefulness and sleep. Among the more common parasomnias are nightmare disorder, sleep terror disorder, and sleepwalking disorder.

NIGHTMARE DISORDER Nightmare disorder involves recurrent awakenings from sleep because of frightening dreams (nightmares). The nightmares are typically lengthy, story-like dreams that involve threats of imminent physical danger to the individual, such as being chased, attacked, or injured. The nightmare is usually recalled vividly upon awakening.

Although alertness is regained quickly after awakening, anxiety and fear may linger and prevent a return to sleep. In a major poll, nearly one in five Canadians reported that

nightmare disorder Sleep disorder characterized by recurrent awakenings from sleep due to the occurrence of frightening nightmares. Formerly called *dream anxiety disorder*.

Nightmares. Although frightening dreams are common in people of all ages, they occur more frequently during times of stress.

they often (3.6%) or sometimes (14.7%) have nightmares that disturb their sleep (Leger Marketing, 2002). The actual percentage of people having the intense, recurrent nightmares that produce the kind of emotional distress or difficulties in functioning that would lead to a diagnosis of nightmare disorder remains unknown (APA, 2000a).

Nightmares are often associated with traumatic experiences and are generally more frequent when the individual is under stress. Supporting the general link between trauma and nightmares, researchers report that the incidence of nightmares was greater among survivors of the 1989 San Francisco earthquake in the weeks following the quake than among comparison groups (Wood, Bootzin, Rosenham, Nolen-Hoeksema, & Jourden, 1992). An increased frequency of nightmares was also observed among children who were exposed to the 1994 Los Angeles earthquake (Kolbert, 1994).

Nightmares generally occur during REM sleep. REM tends to become longer and the dreams occurring during REM more intense in the latter half of sleep, so nightmares usually occur late at night or toward morning. Although nightmares may contain great motor activity, as in fleeing from an assailant, dreamers show little muscle activity. The same biological processes that activate dreams—including nightmares—inhibit body movement, causing a type of paralysis. This is indeed fortunate, as it prevents the dreamer from jumping out of bed and running into a dresser or a wall in an attempt to elude the pursuing assailants from a dream.

SLEEP TERROR DISORDER It typically begins with a loud, piercing cry or scream in the night. Even the most soundly asleep parent will be summoned to their child's bedroom as if shot from a cannon. The child (most cases involve children) may be sitting up, appear frightened, and show signs of extreme arousal—profuse sweating with rapid heartbeat and respiration. The child may start talking incoherently or thrash about wildly but remain asleep. If the child awakens fully, he or she may not recognize the parent or may attempt to push the parent away. After a few minutes, the child falls back into a deep sleep and upon awakening in the morning remembers nothing of the experience. These terrifying attacks, called *sleep terrors*, are more intense than ordinary nightmares. Unlike nightmares, sleep terrors tend to occur during the first third of nightly sleep and during deep non-REM sleep (Dahl, 1992).

sleep terror disorder Sleep disorder characterized by repeated episodes of sleep terror resulting in abrupt awakenings.

A **sleep terror disorder** involves repeated episodes of sleep terrors resulting in abrupt awakenings that begin with a panicky scream (APA, 2000a). If awakening occurs during a sleep terror episode, the person will usually appear confused and disoriented for a few minutes. The person may feel a vague sense of terror and be able to report some fragmentary dream images, but not the sort of detailed dreams typical of nightmares. Most of the time the person falls back to sleep and remembers nothing of the experience the following morning.

Sleep terror disorder in children is typically outgrown during adolescence. More boys than girls are affected by the disorder, but among adults the gender ratio is about even. In adults, the disorder tends to follow a chronic course during which the frequency and intensity of the episodes waxes and wanes over time. Prevalence data on the disorder are lacking, but episodes of sleep terror are estimated to occur in 1% to 6% of children but in fewer than 1% of adults (APA, 2000a). The cause of sleep terror disorder remains a mystery.

sleepwalking disorder Type of sleep disorder involving repeated episodes of sleepwalking.

SLEEPWALKING DISORDER Sleepwalking disorder involves repeated episodes in which the sleeper arises from bed and walks about the house while remaining fully asleep. Because these episodes tend to occur during the deeper stages of sleep, when there is an absence of dreaming, it does not appear that a sleepwalking episode involves the enactment of a dream. In sleepwalking disorder, the occurrence of repeated episodes of sleepwalking are of sufficient severity to cause significant levels of personal distress or impaired functioning. Sleepwalking disorder is more common in children, affecting between 1% and 5%, according to some estimates (APA, 2000a). Between 10% and 30% of children are believed to have had at least one episode of sleepwalking. The prevalence of the disorder among adults is unknown, as are its causes. However, perhaps as many as 7% of adults have experienced occasional sleepwalking episodes (APA, 2000a). The causes of sleepwalking remain obscure, although both genetic and environmental factors are believed to be involved (Hublin, Kaprio, Partinen, Heikkila, & Koskenvuo, 1997).

Although sleepwalkers typically avoid walking into things, accidents occasionally happen. Sleepwalkers tend to have a blank stare on their faces during these episodes. They are generally unresponsive to others and difficult to awaken. When they do awaken the following morning, they typically have little if any recall of the experience. If they are awakened during the episode, they may be disoriented or confused for a few minutes (as is the case with sleep terrors), but full alertness is soon restored. There is no basis to the belief that it is harmful to sleepwalkers to awaken them during episodes.

Isolated incidents of violent behaviour have been associated with sleepwalking, but these are rare occurrences and may well involve other forms of psychopathology. For instance, Canadian psychiatrists describe a distinct parasomnia for which they have coined the name *sexsomnia* (C. M. Shapiro, Trajanovic, & Fedoroff, 2003). The researchers suggest that sexsomnia is distinct from pure sleepwalking and involves complex sexual behaviour, which can include sexual activity with other people, while asleep. Look at the case of D. W.:

D. W. is a 43-year-old divorced police officer. He has an extensive sleep history of parasomnias. A few years earlier, he had stood trial for impaired driving and driving under the influence of alcohol. His defence was parasomnia, based on a previous history of sleepwalking and sleep talking that had intensified in the two years prior to his offence. Many features surrounding the case supported the parasomnia (sleepwalking) claim.

Subsequently, it was discovered that Mr. W. had another manifestation of his parasomnia, namely sexsomnia. This emerged at a "routine" follow-up in which the [interviewer] commented to Mr. W. that his "sleep-driving" was being rivalled as the most unusual of parasomnias. A description of sexsomnia was given, and Mr. W. responded by saying, "Oh, but I do that." The disingenuous response by the interviewer—"But you never told me"—was followed by Mr. W. saying, "But you never asked." Mr. W.'s two current girlfriends independently confirmed that he frequently engages in sexual behaviour while asleep. One described him as a "different person" during these activities—apparently, he is a more amorous and gentle lover and more oriented toward satisfying his partner when he is asleep.

Shapiro, Trajanovic, & Federoff, 2003, pp. 311–317

Treatment of Sleep Disorders

The most common pharmacologic method for treating sleep disorders in Canada is the use of sleep medications called **anxiolytics**. However, because of problems associated with these drugs, nonpharmacological treatment approaches, principally cognitive-behavioural therapy, have come to the fore.

BIOLOGICAL APPROACHES Various anxiolytic (anti-anxiety) drugs are frequently used to treat insomnia, including a class of minor tranquillizers called benzodiazepines (e.g., Dalmane, Halcion, and Restoril) and, to a lesser extent, barbiturates (e.g., Seconal, Nembutal, and Amytal) (Health Canada, 2000). (These drugs are also widely used in the treatment of anxiety disorders, as we saw in Chapter 3.) When Canadians were polled in 2002, the results indicated that nearly 1 in 10 takes a sleeping pill to help with sleep (Leger Marketing, 2002). The use of sleeping pills by Canadians increases with age, and two-thirds more women than men use them (Health Canada, 1995). However, McMaster University researchers caution that the overall benefit of anxiolytic drugs in comparison to a placebo is relatively minor (Holbrook, Crowther, Lotter, Cheng, & King, 2000). Prudent use of these drugs is recommended, as they can produce adverse side effects as well as dependence if used regularly over time.

anxiolytics Drugs, such as sedatives and anaesthetics, that induce partial or complete unconsciousness and are commonly used in the treatment of sleep disorders.

When used for the short-term treatment of insomnia, anxiolytics are generally effective in reducing the time it takes to get to sleep, increasing total length of sleep, and reducing nightly awakenings (Nowell, Buysse, Morin, Reynolds, & Kupfer, 1998). They work by reducing arousal and inducing feelings of calmness, thereby making the person more receptive to sleep. However, as many as 10% of sleep disorder patients take sleeping pills for months or years, despite a lack of evidence from controlled studies supporting their long-term efficacy.

A number of problems are associated with using drugs to combat insomnia (Ramakrishnan & Scheid, 2007). Sleep-inducing drugs tend to suppress REM sleep, which may interfere with some of the restorative functions of sleep. They can also lead to a carryover or "hangover" the following day, which is associated with daytime sleepiness and reduced performance. Rebound insomnia can follow discontinuation of the drug, causing worse insomnia than was originally the case. Rebound insomnia may be lessened, however, by tapering off the drug rather than abruptly discontinuing it. These drugs quickly lose their effectiveness at a given dosage level, so progressively larger doses must be used to achieve the same effect. High doses can be dangerous, especially if they are mixed with alcoholic beverages at bedtime. Regular use can also lead to physical dependence (addiction). Once dependence is established, withdrawal symptoms following cessation of use may occur, including agitation, tremors, nausea, headaches, and, in severe cases, delusions or hallucinations.

Users can also become psychologically dependent on sleeping pills. That is, they can develop a psychological need for the medication and assume they will not be able to get to sleep without it. Because worry about going without drugs heightens bodily arousal, such self-doubts are likely to become self-fulfilling prophecies. Moreover, users may attribute their success in falling asleep to the pill and not to themselves, which strengthens reliance on the drugs and makes it harder to forgo using them.

Not surprisingly, there is little evidence of long-term benefits of drug therapy after withdrawal (Morin & Wooten, 1996). Relying on sleeping pills does nothing to resolve the underlying cause of the problem or help the person learn more effective ways of coping with it. If anxiolytic drugs like benzodiazepines are to be prescribed at all for sleep problems, they should be used only for a brief period of time (a few weeks at most) and at the lowest possible dose (Holbrook et al., 2000). The aim should be to provide a temporary respite so that the clinician can help the client find effective ways of handling the sources of stress and anxiety that contribute to insomnia.

Minor tranquillizers of the benzodiazepine family and tricyclic antidepressants are also used to treat the deep-sleep disorders—sleep terrors and sleepwalking. They seem to have a beneficial effect by decreasing the length of deep sleep and reducing partial arousals between sleep stages (Dahl, 1992). Use of sleep medications for these disorders, as for primary insomnia, also incurs the risk of physiological and psychological dependence and thus should be used only in severe cases and only as a temporary means of breaking the cycle.

Narcolepsy is predominantly a neurological disorder, and sleep apnea involves physiological factors. Thus, both disorders are commonly treated using medical interventions. The excessive daytime sleepiness that accompanies narcolepsy is commonly treated with psychostimulants, such as Modafinil, but prospective new therapies are emerging (e.g., hypocretin gene therapy and stem cell transplantation) (Thorpy, 2007). Treatments for sleep apnea range from the use of medical assistive devices (e.g., continuous positive airway pressure—a technique of delivering pressurized air via a face mask to prevent the airway from collapsing—or oral appliances that expand the size of the upper airway) to lifestyle changes (e.g., weight loss, avoiding alcohol and sleeping pills, and a regular sleep routine) to, in some cases, surgery (e.g., to expand the upper airway by removing excess tissue from inside the roof of the mouth) (Banno & Kryger, 2007; Canadian Lung Association, 2006).

PSYCHOLOGICAL APPROACHES Psychological approaches have by and large been limited to treatment of primary insomnia. Overall, cognitive-behavioural treatment approaches have produced substantial benefits in treating chronic insomnia, as measured by both reductions in sleep latency and improvement of perceived sleep quality (Viens et al., 2003). As many as 60% to 80% of patients respond favourably. Still, only about a third become good sleepers.

Many of us have difficulty from time to time falling asleep or remaining asleep. Although sleep is a natural function and cannot be forced, we can develop more adaptive sleep habits that help us become more receptive to sleep. However, if insomnia or other sleep-related problems persist or become associated with difficulties functioning during the day, it would be worthwhile to have the problem checked out with a professional. Here are some techniques to help you acquire more adaptive sleep habits:

1. Retire to bed only when you feel sleepy.
2. Limit your activities in bed as much as possible to sleeping. Avoid watching television or reading in bed.
3. If after 10 to 20 minutes of lying in bed you are unable to fall asleep, get out of bed, leave the bedroom, and put yourself in a relaxed mood by reading, listening to calming music, or practising self-relaxation.
4. Establish a regular routine. Sleeping late to make up for lost sleep can throw off your body clock. Set your alarm for the same time each morning and get up, regardless of how many hours you have slept.
5. Avoid naps during the daytime. You'll feel less sleepy at bedtime if you catch Zs during the afternoon.
6. Avoid ruminating in bed. Don't focus on solving your problems or organizing the rest of your life as you're attempting to sleep. Tell yourself that you'll think about tomorrow tomorrow. Help yourself enter a more sleepful frame of mind by engaging in a mental fantasy or mind trip, or just let all thoughts slip away from consciousness. If an important idea comes to you, don't rehearse it in your mind. Jot it down on a handy pad so you won't lose it. But if thoughts persist, get up and follow them elsewhere.
7. Put yourself in a relaxed frame of mind before sleep. Some people unwind before bed by reading; others prefer watching television or just resting quietly. Do whatever you find most relaxing. You may find it helpful to incorporate into your regular bedtime routine techniques for lowering your level of arousal, such as meditation or progressive relaxation.
8. Establish a regular daytime exercise schedule. Regular exercise during the day (not directly before bedtime) can help induce sleepiness upon retiring.
9. Avoid use of caffeinated beverages, such as coffee and tea, in the evening or late afternoon. Also, avoid drinking alcoholic beverages. Alcohol can interfere with normal sleep patterns (reduced total sleep, REM sleep, and sleep efficiency) even when consumed six hours before bedtime.

Is your bed a cue for sleeping? People who use their beds for many activities, including eating, reading, and watching television, may find that lying in bed loses its association with sleeping. Behaviour therapists use stimulus control techniques to help people with insomnia create a stimulus environment associated with sleeping.

10. Practise rational restructuring. Substitute rational alternatives for self-defeating thoughts. Here are some examples:

Self-Defeating Thoughts	Rational Alternatives
"I must fall asleep right now or I'll be a wreck tomorrow."	"I may feel tired, but I've been able to get by with little sleep before. I can make up for it tomorrow by getting to bed early."
"What's the matter with me that I can't seem to fall asleep? "	"Stop blaming yourself. You can't control sleep. Just let whatever happens happen."
"If I don't get to sleep right now, I won't be able to concentrate tomorrow on the exam (conference, meeting, etc.)."	"My concentration may be off a bit, but I'm not going to fall apart. There's no point blowing things out of proportion. I might as well get up for a while and watch a little television rather than lie here ruminating."

Cognitive-behavioural techniques are short term in emphasis and focus on directly lowering states of physiological arousal, modifying maladaptive sleeping habits, and changing dysfunctional thoughts. Cognitive-behavioural therapists typically use a combination of techniques, including stimulus control, relaxation training, and anxiety-management training. Stimulus control involves changing the stimulus environment associated with sleeping. Under normal conditions, we learn to associate stimuli relating to lying down in bed with sleeping, so that exposure to these stimuli comes to induce feelings of sleepiness. But when people use their beds for many other activities—such as eating, reading, and watching television—the bed may lose its association with sleepiness. Moreover, the longer the person with insomnia lies in bed tossing and turning, the more the bed becomes associated with cues related to anxiety and frustration. Stimulus control techniques attempt to strengthen the connection between the bed and sleep by restricting as much as possible the activities spent in bed to sleeping and by limiting the time spent in bed trying to fall asleep to 10 or 20 minutes at a time. If sleep does not occur within the designated time period, the person is instructed to leave the bed and go to another room to restore a relaxed frame of mind before returning to bed, such as by sitting quietly, reading, watching television, or practising relaxation exercises.

In their practical book *Quiet Your Mind and Get to Sleep: Solutions to Insomnia for Those With Depression, Anxiety, or Chronic Pain* (2009), Dr. Colleen Carney and Rachel Manber recommend CBT for insomnia that involves setting a rise time when people have to get up and out of bed, no matter what their night of sleep was like.

Relaxation techniques, such as the Jacobson progressive relaxation approach, may be practised before bedtime to help reduce the level of physiological arousal. Biofeedback training may also be used as a way of teaching self-relaxation skills. Based on a meta-analysis of outcome studies, it does not appear that the combination of stimulus control and relaxation training produces any larger benefit than either approach alone (Murtagh & Greenwood, 1995).

Cognitive restructuring involves substituting rational alternatives for self-defeating, maladaptive thoughts or beliefs (see the Closer Look box on page 315 for examples). The belief that failing to get a good night's sleep will lead to unfortunate, even disastrous, consequences the next day reduces the chances of falling asleep because it raises the level of anxiety and can lead the person to try unsuccessfully to force sleep to happen. Most of us do reasonably well if we lose sleep or even miss a night of sleep, even though we might like more.

Recent research supports the use of a cognitive-behavioural intervention for insomnia delivered online that can significantly improve insomnia in adults (Ritterband et al., 2009). Ritterband and colleagues at the American Academy of Sleep Medicine found that sleep improved significantly for those who received a cognitive-behavioural intervention for insomnia via the Internet over a period of six weeks, whereas control participants showed no change during the treatment period. Ritterband reports that all patients with improved sleep after using the Internet intervention maintained these improvements six months after the study's completion. This potentially opens up help to a much wider group of individuals dealing with this very difficult problem.

REVIEW IT

Sleep Disorders

- **What are the major types of sleep disorders?** Sleep disorders are classified into two major categories: dyssomnias and parasomnias. Dyssomnias involve disturbances in the amount, quality, or timing of sleep. They include five specific types: primary insomnia, primary hypersomnia, narcolepsy, breathing-related sleep disorder, and circadian rhythm sleep disorder. Parasomnias involve disturbed behaviours or abnormal physiological responses occurring either during sleep or at the threshold between wakefulness and sleep. They include three major types: nightmare disorder, sleep terror disorder, and sleepwalking disorder.

- **What are the major forms of treatment for sleep disorders?** The most common form of treatment for sleep disorders involves the use of anxiolytic drugs. However, use of these drugs should be time limited because of the potential for psychological and/or physical dependence, among other problems associated with their use. Cognitive-behavioural interventions have produced substantial benefits in helping people with chronic insomnia.

Define It

amenorrhea, 297
anorexia nervosa, 294
anxiolytics, 313
apnea, 310
binge-eating disorder, 305
breathing-related sleep
    disorder, 310
bulimia nervosa, 294
cataplexy, 309

circadian rhythm sleep
    disorder, 311
dyssomnias, 308
eating disorders, 294
hypersomnia, 309
insomnia, 308
narcolepsy, 309
neuropeptide, 310
nightmare disorder, 311

osteoporosis, 297
parasomnias, 308
polysomnographic (PSG)
    recording, 308
REM sleep, 309
sleep disorders, 308
sleep terror disorder, 312
sleepwalking disorder, 312
systems perspective, 302

Think About It

- How are sociocultural factors related to the development of eating disorders? How might we as a society change the social influences that lead many young women to develop disordered eating habits?

- Do you believe that high-risk anorexic patients who resist or refuse treatment should be forced to accept medical intervention? Why or why not?

- Do your sleep habits help or hinder your sleeping patterns? Explain.

- What are the drawbacks of relying on sleep medications to combat chronic insomnia? Do you get enough sleep? If not, what can you do about it?

Weblinks

Eating Disorders www.phac-aspc.gc.ca/publicat/
miic-mmac/pdf/chap_6_e.pdf
This site links to the chapter on eating disorders from Health Canada's *A Report on Mental Illness in Canada* (2002b).

Internet Mental Health
http://mentalhealth.com/dis/p20-et01.html
The Internet Mental Health site has links to information about anorexia nervosa and bulimia.

Bulimia Anorexia Nervosa Association
www.bana.ca
This site offers Canadian-focused information and support for eating disorders.

National Eating Disorder Information Centre (NEDIC) www.nedic.ca
This site provides Canadian information and resources on eating disorders and weight preoccupation.

Canadian Sleep Society (CSS)
www.canadiansleepsociety.com
The CSS's website has information on research and links to treatment centres.

Sleepnet.com www.sleepnet.com
A comprehensive sleep disorder site that includes a sleep test.

MySearchLab offers you extensive help with your writing and research projects and provides round-the-clock access to credible and reliable source material. Chapter quizzes and a full electronic version of the text are also provided. Take a tour at www.mysearchlab.com.

Eating Disorders and Sleep Disorders

Eating Disorders
Disorders involving disturbed eating patterns and maladaptive ways of controlling body weight

Anorexia Nervosa

- Maintenance of an abnormally low body weight
- Distortions of body image
- Intense fears of gaining weight
- Amenorrhea in females

Medical Complications of Anorexia
- Menstrual irregularities
- Muscular weakness
- Abnormal growth of bones
- Estimated 5% to 8% mortality rate

Bulimia Nervosa

- Recurrent pattern of binge eating followed by self-induced purging
- Persistent overconcern with body weight and shape

Medical Complications of Bulimia

- Irritations of the skin around the mouth due to frequent contact with stomach acid
- Blockage of salivary ducts
- Decay of tooth enamel and dental cavities
- Pancreatitis and muscular weakness
- Cardiac irregularities
- Sudden death

Causes of Anorexia and Bulimia

Sociocultural
- Pressure to achieve an unrealistic standard of thinness or an ideal body shape

Psychosocial
- High perfectionistic attitudes and comorbidity with psychological disorders

Family
- Family conflicts and issues of autonomy

Biological
- Genetic predisposition

Treatment of Anorexia Nervosa and Bulimia Nervosa

- Nutritional management
- Family interventions
- Cognitive-behavioural therapy
- Interpersonal psychotherapy

Binge-Eating Disorder

- Repeated episodes in which binge eating occurs but is not followed by purging

Sleep Disorders

Dyssomnias
Disturbances in the amount, quality, or timing of sleep

Insomnia
- Difficulties falling asleep, remaining asleep, or achieving restorative sleep

Hypersomnia
- Pattern of excessive sleepiness during the day

Narcolepsy
- Sudden, irresistible episodes of sleep (sleep attacks)

Breathing-Related Sleep Disorder
- Breathing difficulties that disrupt sleep

Circadian Rhythm Sleep Disorder
- Mismatch in sleep schedules between the body's internal sleep–wake cycle and the demands of the environment

Parasomnias
Occurrence of abnormal behaviours or physiological events occurring during sleep or at the transition between wakefulness and sleep

Nightmare Disorder
- Recurrent awakenings from sleep due to the occurrence of frightening nightmares

Sleep Terror Disorder
- Repeated episodes of sleep terror resulting in abrupt awakenings

Sleepwalking Disorder
- Repeated episodes of sleepwalking

Treatment of Sleep Disorders

Biological Approaches
- Anxiolytic drugs for insomnia
- Stimulant drugs for narcolepsy
- Surgery and assistive devices for sleep apnea

Psychological Approaches
- Focus on directly lowering states of physiological arousal
- Modifying maladaptive sleeping habits
- Changing dysfunctional thoughts

9

Gender Identity Disorder, Paraphilias, and Sexual Dysfunctions

CHAPTER OUTLINE

Gender Identity Disorder
Theoretical Perspectives

Paraphilias
Types of Paraphilias
Fetishism
Theoretical Perspectives
Treatment of Paraphilias
Sexual Assault

Sexual Dysfunctions
Types of Sexual Dysfunctions
Theoretical Perspectives
Sex Therapy
Biological Treatments of Male Sexual
    Dysfunctions

Did You Know That...

- Unlike people with gender identity disorder, gay and lesbian people do not perceive themselves as members of the opposite sex?

- Homosexuality is no longer considered a psychological disorder?

- Professional strippers are not classified as exhibitionists?

- Becoming sexually aroused by watching your partner disrobe or viewing an X-rated movie is not a form of voyeurism?

- Some people cannot become sexually aroused unless others subject them to pain or humiliation?

- In most cases of sexual assault, the woman was acquainted with the assailant?

- Orgasm is a reflex?

- Premature ejaculation affects about one out of three men?

- Both men and women have the male sex hormone testosterone circulating in their bodies?

- The drug Viagra, used in the treatment of erectile dysfunction, became the fastest-selling drug in history when it was introduced?

Off the fog-bound shore of Ireland lies the isle of Inis Beag.[1] From the air it is an emerald jewel, warm and enticing. From the ground, the perspective is different.

The inhabitants of Inis Beag believe that normal women do not have orgasms and that those who do must be deviant (Messenger, 1971). Premarital sex is virtually unknown. Women participate in sexual relations in order to conceive children and pacify their husbands' lustful urges. They need not be concerned about being called on for frequent performances because the men of Inis Beag believe, groundlessly, that sex saps their strength. Relations on Inis Beag take place in the dark—literally and figuratively, and with nightclothes on. Consistent with local standards of masculinity, the man ejaculates as quickly as he can. Then he rolls over and goes to sleep, without concern for his partner's satisfaction. Women do not complain, however, as they are reared to believe it is abnormal for them to experience sexual pleasure.

If Inis Beag is not your cup of tea, perhaps the ambience of the island of Mangaia will strike you as more congenial. Mangaia is a Polynesian pearl; languidly, it lifts out of the azure waters of the Pacific. Inis Beag and Mangaia are on opposite sides of the world—literally and figuratively.

From childhood, Mangaian children are expected to explore their sexuality through masturbation (D. Marshall, 1971). Mangaian teenagers are encouraged by their elders to engage in sexual relations. They are often found on hidden beaches or beneath the sheltering fronds of palms, industriously practising skills acquired from their elders. Mangaian women usually reach orgasm numerous times before their partners do. Young men vie to see who is more skilful in helping their partner attain multiple orgasms.

The inhabitants of Mangaia and Inis Beag have identical anatomic features and the same hormones pulsing through their bodies. Their attitudes and cultural values about what is normal and abnormal differ vastly, however. Their attitudes affect their sexual behaviour and the enjoyment they attain—or do not attain—from sex. In sex, as in other areas of behaviour, the lines between normal and abnormal are not always drawn precisely. Sex, like eating, is a natural function. Yet this natural function has been profoundly affected by cultural, religious, and moral beliefs, customs, folklores, and superstitions.

Even in Canada today, we find attitudes as diverse as those on Inis Beag and Mangaia. Some people feel guilty about any form of sexual activity and thus reap little if any pleasure from sex. Others, who see themselves as sexually liberated, may worry about whether they have become free enough or skilful enough in their sexual activity.

In the realm of sexual behaviour, our conceptions of what is normal and what is not are clearly influenced by sociocultural factors. Various patterns of sexual behaviour that might be considered abnormal in Inis Beag, such as masturbation, premarital intercourse, and oral-genital sex, are normal in Western society from the standpoint of statistical frequency. For example, a survey of a representative sample of 3432 males and females between the ages of 18 and 59 found that 63% of adult men and 42% of adult women questioned reported that they had masturbated during the previous year (Laumann, Gagnon, Michael, & Michaels, 1994). It is likely that many more practised masturbation but were hesitant to admit so to interviewers.

---

[1]"Inis Beag" is a pseudonym for an actual small Irish community studied by cultural anthropologist John Cowan Messenger between 1958 and 1966.

Behaviour may be labelled abnormal because it deviates from the norms of one's society. For example, kissing is a highly popular form of mild petting in Western cultures but is considered deviant behaviour in some societies, such as among the Sirionó of Bolivia and the Thonga of Africa. The Thonga tribesmen were shocked when they first observed European visitors kissing, and one man exclaimed, "Look at them—they eat each other's saliva and dirt."

Sexual behaviour may also be considered abnormal if it is self-defeating, harms others, causes personal distress, or interferes with one's ability to function. The disorders we feature in this chapter—gender identity disorder, paraphilias, and sexual dysfunctions—meet one or more of the criteria of abnormality. In exploring these disorders, we touch on questions that probe the boundaries between abnormality and normality. For example, is gay or lesbian sexual orientation a psychological disorder? Are some instances of voyeurism or exhibitionism normal and others abnormal? When is it considered abnormal to have difficulty becoming sexually aroused or reaching orgasm?

GENDER IDENTITY DISORDER

gender identity One's psychological sense of being female or being male.

gender identity disorder Disorder in which an individual believes that her or his anatomic gender is inconsistent with her or his psychological sense of being female or male.

Our **gender identity** is our sense of being male or female. Gender identity is normally based on anatomic gender, and in the normal run of things, our gender identity is consistent with our anatomic gender. In **gender identity disorder**, however, there is a conflict between one's anatomic gender and one's gender identity. In the upcoming DSM-5, the term *gender identity disorder* will be replaced with *gender dysphoria*, which may be less stigmatizing.

The terms with which and ways in which transgender people are talked about in popular culture, academia, and science change, particularly as individuals' awareness, knowledge, and openness about transgender people evolves. According to the American Psychological Association (n.d.), *transgender* is an umbrella term for persons whose gender identity, gender expression, or behaviour does not conform to that typically associated with the sex to which they were assigned at birth. *Gender identity* refers to a person's internal sense of being male, female, or something else. Under the more general term *transgender* falls the more specific category called *transsexual*, referring to people whose gender identity is different from their assigned sex. Some individuals who are transsexual are dissatisfied with the disconnect between their assigned sex and their gender identity. This is called **gender dysphoria**, which means incongruity between one's genital anatomy and one's gender identity or role. Those who suffer with intense distress may wish to alter their bodies through hormones, surgery, and other means to make their bodies as congruent as possible with their gender identities. This process of transition through medical intervention is often referred to as *sex reassignment* or *gender reassignment*, but more recently is also referred to as *gender affirmation*.

gender dysphoria Incongruity between one's genital anatomy and one's gender identity or role.

It must be clearly noted that being transgendered is not always considered a mental disorder. A disorder exists only if a condition causes significant distress or disability. A good portion of transgendered people do not find their gender distressing. Finding the necessary support to express their gender identity and minimize discrimination is their focus, not a mental disorder. It should also be noted that the diagnosis of gender identity disorder is full of controversy, as some contend it inappropriately pathologizes gender noncongruence.

Gender identity disorder may begin in childhood. Children with the disorder find their anatomic gender to be a source of persistent and intense distress. The diagnosis is not used simply to label "tomboyish" girls and "sissyish" boys. It is applied to children who persistently repudiate their anatomic traits (girls might insist on urinating standing up or assert that they do not want to grow breasts; boys may find their penis and testes

TABLE 9.1

Diagnostic Criteria for Gender Identity Disorder

A. A strong and persistent cross-gender identification (not merely a desire for any perceived cultural advantages of being the other sex).

    In children, the disturbance is manifested by four (or more) of the following:

(1) repeatedly stated desire to be, or insistence that he or she is, the other sex

(2) in boys, preference for cross-dressing or simulating female attire; in girls, insistence on wearing only stereotypical masculine clothing

(3) strong and persistent preferences for cross-sex roles in make-believe play or persistent fantasies of being the other sex

(4) intense desire to participate in the stereotypical games and pastimes of the other sex

(5) strong preference for playmates of the other sex

    In adolescents and adults, the disturbance is manifested by symptoms such as a stated desire to be the other sex, frequent passing as the other sex, desire to live or be treated as the other sex, or the conviction that he or she has the typical feelings and reactions of the other sex.

B. Persistent discomfort with his or her sex or sense of inappropriateness in the gender role of that sex.

    In children, the disturbance is manifested by any of the following: in boys, assertion that his penis or testes are disgusting or will disappear or assertion that it would be better not to have a penis, or aversion toward rough-and-tumble play and rejection of male stereotypical toys, games, and activities; in girls, rejection of urinating in a sitting position, assertion that she has or will grow a penis, or assertion that she does not want to grow breasts or menstruate, or marked aversion toward normative feminine clothing.

    In adolescents and adults, the disturbance is manifested by symptoms such as preoccupation with getting rid of primary and secondary sex characteristics (e.g., request for hormones, surgery, or other procedures to physically alter sexual characteristics to simulate the other sex) or belief that he or she was born the wrong sex.

C. The disturbance is not concurrent with a physical intersex condition.

D. The disturbance causes clinically significant distress or impairment in social, occupational, or other important areas of functioning.

Source: Reprinted with permission from the *Diagnostic and Statistical Manual of Mental Disorders*, Fourth Edition, Text Revision, (Copyright ©2000). American Psychiatric Association. p. 581.

revolting) or who are preoccupied with clothing or activities that are stereotypic of the other gender (see Table 9.1).

About five times as many boys as girls have gender identity disorder (Zucker & Green, 1992). With an estimated worldwide lifetime prevalence of 0.001% to 0.002%, gender identity disorder is rare (Roberto, 1983). The disorder takes many paths. It can

Gender reassignment. Chastity Bono, left; Chaz Bono, right, in 2011. Bono has gender identity disorder and has undergone hormone and surgical procedures to transition from female to male.

come to an end or abate markedly by adolescence, with the child becoming more accepting of her or his gender identity. It may persist into adolescence or adulthood. The child may also develop a gay or lesbian sexual orientation at about the time of adolescence (Zucker & Green, 1992).

In surgical construction procedures, surgeons attempt to construct external genitalia that are as close as possible to those of the opposite gender. People who undergo these operations can engage in sexual activity, even achieve orgasm, yet they are incapable of conceiving or bearing children because they lack the internal reproductive organs of their reconstructed gender.

Men seeking gender reassignment outnumber female applicants. Recent clinical studies show generally favourable psychological outcomes following gender reassignment surgery (Y. L. S. Smith, Van Goozen, Kuiper, & Cohen-Kettenis, 2005), especially when safeguards are taken to restrict surgical treatment to the most appropriate candidates. In one recent study of 162 postoperative transsexuals, the majority were found to be functioning well socially and psychologically, with only 2 expressing regrets about the procedure (Y. L. S. Smith et al., 2005). Unfavourable outcome was predicted by being a nonhomosexual male-to-female transsexual who also had other significant psychological problems.

Gender identity should not be confused with sexual orientation. Gay and lesbian individuals have erotic interest in members of their own gender, but their gender identity (sense of being male or female) is consistent with their anatomic sex. They do not desire to become members of the opposite gender or despise their own genitalia, as we may find in people with gender identity disorder. Nor is homosexuality any longer considered a psychological disorder. In 1973, it was dropped from the DSM listing of psychological disorders. Yet people who are persistently distressed or confused about their sexual orientation, whether they are gay, bisexual, or heterosexual, may continue to be diagnosed with a definable type of sexual disorder called *sexual disorder not otherwise specified*.[2] In practice, however, this diagnosis has been applied almost exclusively to people with a gay, lesbian, or bisexual sexual orientation.

Unlike a gay or lesbian sexual orientation, gender identity disorder is very rare. People with gender identity disorder who are sexually attracted to members of their own anatomic gender are unlikely to consider themselves gay or lesbian, however. Nature's gender assignment is a mistake in their eyes. From their perspective, they are trapped in bodies of the wrong gender.

Theoretical Perspectives

No one knows what causes gender identity disorder (Zucker, 2005). Psychodynamic theorists point to extremely close mother–son relationships, parents with empty relationships, and fathers who were absent or detached (Stoller, 1969). These family circumstances may foster strong identification with the mother in young males, leading to a reversal of expected gender roles and identity. Girls with weak, ineffectual mothers and strong, masculine fathers may overly identify with their fathers and develop a psychological sense of themselves as "little men."

Learning theorists similarly point to father absence in the case of boys—to the unavailability of a strong male role model. Socialization patterns might have affected children who were reared by parents who had wanted children of the other gender and who strongly encouraged cross-gender dressing and patterns of play.

---

[2]We refer to *gay* and *lesbian* people rather than *homosexuals*. There are several problems with the label *homosexual*: (1) since it has been historically associated with concepts of deviance and mental illness, it may perpetuate negative stereotypes of gay men and lesbians; (2) the term is often used to refer to men only, thus rendering lesbians invisible; and (3) it is often ambiguous in meaning—that is, does it refer to sexual behaviour or to sexual orientation?

Gender Dissatisfaction: No Disorder

Maya had always been a tomboy. Her mother remembers Maya gravitating toward her older brother's toys even as a small child. While Maya's sister was playing "house," Maya preferred to smash cars into each other and run around outside. When Maya turned seven, she asked her mother if she could cut her hair more like a boy's. Maya's mother complied, and Maya wore her hair short for several years. She dressed in jogging pants and T-shirts, which she found much more comfortable than dresses and tights. These clothes also made it easier for her to play with the boys at recess, climbing and horsing around. A few times, she complained to her mother that it would be easier to be a boy—boys don't ever have to wear dresses, and they can pee standing up. Other than this, Maya never complained about being a girl. She identified as a girl, and ended up having both female and male friends throughout school. Even as a teenager, however, Maya still liked sports and wearing comfortable clothes, but she found that lots of other girls felt the same way she did.

Gender Dissatisfaction: Gender Identity Disorder

From a very young age, Renato's mother felt that Renato was different from other little boys. At first, she thought it was cute that he preferred dolls and liked to play dress-up with his older sister and her friends. In fact, when they were older, his sister's friends always asked if Renato would come to play with them, and they loved dressing him up, putting makeup on him, and having him do a "show" for his parents. But Renato's mom started to worry when Renato was four years old. At that point, Renato expressed a strong preference for dresses and girls' clothes. Renato's mother didn't want to make a big deal of this, so would let him dress in girls' clothes at home. But when it came time for Renato to start school, she was concerned about what the teacher and other kids would say. She told Renato that he would have to wear pants to school, and that sent him into a tantrum. He also told his mother than he hated his penis and wished that he could cut it off. He began refusing to stand when urinating, and said that he wanted to go to the bathroom like a girl. This continued for the next several years, and Renato never wavered in his desire to be a girl. In fact, he began to talk about feeling that he really was a girl and that there'd been a mistake when he was born.

Learning history or childhood rearing experiences are probably insufficient by themselves to shape gender identity or to produce gender identity disorder. This point is underscored by the case of a Winnipeg boy, originally known as Bruce, who was raised as a girl (Colapinto, 2000). When he was eight months old, his doctor badly botched a circumcision, resulting in the loss of Bruce's penis. The family was persuaded by the leading sexologist John Money to raise Bruce as a girl. Even though Bruce received hormones to promote a female appearance, the results were disastrous. Renamed Brenda and wearing a dress, he was clearly masculine in his appearance, interests, and behaviour, and he always felt that he was really a boy. "She" was teased at school because of his masculine appearance and behaviour, and life was miserable. At age 14, he was told of the botched operation, and shortly thereafter he changed his name to David and began living in the male role. He later married and adopted three children. Thus, years of socialization into the female gender role were unsuccessful in altering his gender identity. But even life as a male was not easy for him. David suffered from marital difficulties and bouts of depression. Tragically, he committed suicide in 2004, at age 38.

The great majority of people with the type of family histories described here by psychodynamic and learning theorists do not develop gender identity disorder. Perhaps family factors play a role in combination with a biological predisposition. We know that people with gender identity disorder often showed cross-gender preferences in toys, games, and clothing very early in childhood. If there are critical early learning experiences in gender identity disorder, they may occur very early in life. Prenatal hormonal imbalances may also be involved. Perhaps the brain is "masculinized" or "feminized" by sex hormones during certain stages of prenatal development. The brain could become differentiated as to gender identity in one direction while the genitals develop in the other direction (Money, 1987). Researchers suspect that gender identity disorders may develop as the result of an interaction in utero between the developing brain and the release of sex hormones (Zhou, Hofman, Gooren, & Swaab, 1995). Yet speculations about the origins of gender identity disorder remain unsubstantiated by hard evidence.

REVIEW IT

Gender Identity Disorder

- **What is gender identity disorder?** People with gender identity disorder find their anatomic gender to be a source of persistent and intense distress. People with the disorder may seek to change their sex organs to resemble those of the opposite gender, and many undergo gender reassignment surgery to accomplish this purpose.
- **How is gender identity disorder different from sexual orientation?** Gender identity disorder involves a mismatch between one's psychological sense of being male or female and one's anatomic sex. Sexual orientation relates to the direction of one's sexual attraction—toward members of one's own or the opposite gender. Unlike people with gender identity disorder, people with a gay or lesbian sexual orientation have a gender identity consistent with their anatomic gender.

PARAPHILIAS

paraphilias Sexual deviations or types of sexual disorders in which a person experiences recurrent sexual urges and sexually arousing fantasies involving nonhuman objects (such as articles of clothing), inappropriate or nonconsenting partners (e.g., children), or situations producing humiliation or pain to oneself or one's partner. The person has either acted upon such urges or is strongly distressed by them.

The word *paraphilia* was coined from the Greek roots *para*, meaning "to the side of," and *philos*, meaning "loving." In the **paraphilias**, people show sexual arousal ("loving") in response to atypical stimuli ("to the side of" normally arousing stimuli). According to the DSM-IV, paraphilias involve recurrent, powerful sexual urges and fantasies lasting six months or longer that centre on (1) nonhuman objects such as underwear, shoes, leather, or silk; (2) humiliation or experience of pain in oneself or one's partner; or (3) children and other persons who do not or cannot grant consent. Although acting on paraphilic urges is not required for a diagnosis (the person might be distressed by the urges but not act on them), people with paraphilias often engage in overt paraphilic behaviours like exhibitionism and voyeurism.

In the new DSM-5, due out in 2013, there will be a clearer separation between a paraphilia (according to the nature of the urges, fantasies, or behaviours) and a diagnosed paraphilic disorder (on the basis of distress and impairment). In other words, having a paraphilia will be a necessary but not a sufficient condition for having a paraphilic disorder (American Psychological Association, n.d.) and the addition of "disorder" to the diagnosis confirms this separation of non-normal and pathological. This approach assumes the possibility of non-normal sexual behaviour that is not pathological.

Some people who receive the diagnosis of paraphilia can function sexually in the absence of paraphilic stimuli or fantasies. Others resort to paraphilic stimuli under stress. Still others cannot become sexually aroused unless these stimuli are used, in actuality or in fantasy. For some individuals, the paraphilia is their exclusive means of attaining sexual gratification.

The majority of people with paraphilias are men (APA, 2000a). However, studies in Canada, England, and the United States have identified women who have paraphilias (Litman, 2003) and raise the possibility that paraphilias in women may have been previously overlooked by researchers and clinicians. Little is known about the prevalence of paraphilias in women, although they are probably rare. According to the Canadian Centre for Justice Statistics (1999), in 1999 only 2% of convicted sex offenders were women.

Some paraphilias are relatively harmless and victimless. Among these are fetishism and transvestic fetishism. Others, such as exhibitionism and pedophilia, have unwilling victims. A most harmful paraphilia is sexual sadism when acted out with a nonconsenting partner. Voyeurism falls somewhere in between because the "victim" does not typically know he or she is being watched.

Types of Paraphilias

EXHIBITIONISM Exhibitionism involves recurrent, powerful urges to expose one's genitals to an unsuspecting stranger in order to surprise, shock, or sexually arouse the victim. The person may masturbate while fantasizing about or actually exposing himself. Almost all cases involve men (Freund & Blanchard, 1986). The victims are almost always women.

According to Toronto investigators Ron Langevin and Reuben Lang (1987), most exhibitionists are married and have generally satisfactory relationships with women. The person diagnosed with exhibitionism is typically not interested in actual sexual contact with the victim and therefore is not usually dangerous. Nevertheless, victims may believe themselves in great danger and may be traumatized by the act. Victims are probably best advised to show no reaction to people who expose themselves but to just continue on their way, if possible. It would be unwise to insult the person who exposed himself, lest it provoke a violent reaction. Nor do we recommend an exaggerated show of shock or fear—it tends to reinforce the person for the act of exposing himself.

Some researchers view exhibitionism as a means for perpetrators to indirectly express hostility toward women, perhaps because of perceptions of having been wronged by women in the past or of not being noticed or taken seriously by them (J. K. P. Lee, Jackson, Pattison, & Ward, 2002). Men with this disorder tend to be shy, dependent, and lacking in social and sexual skills—even socially inhibited (Allen et al., 2004). Some doubt their masculinity and harbour feelings of inferiority (Blair & Lanyon, 1981). Their victims' revulsion or fear boosts their sense of mastery of the situation and heightens their sexual arousal. Consider the case of Devon:

> Devon was a 26-year-old, handsome, boyish-looking married male with a 3-year-old daughter. He had spent about a quarter of his life in reform schools and prison. As an adolescent, he had been a fire-setter. As a young adult, he had begun to expose himself. He came to the clinic without his wife's knowledge because he was exposing himself more and more often—up to three times a day—and was afraid he would eventually be arrested and thrown into prison again.
>
> Devon said he liked sex with his wife, but it wasn't as exciting as exposing himself. He couldn't prevent his exhibitionism, especially now, when he was between jobs and worried about where the family's next month's rent was coming from. He loved his daughter more than anything and couldn't stand the thought of being separated from her.
>
> Devon's method of operation was as follows: He would look for slender adolescent females, usually near the junior and senior high schools. He would take his penis out of his pants and play with it while he drove up to a girl or a small group of girls. He would lower the car window, continuing to play with himself, and ask them for directions. Sometimes the girls didn't see his penis. That was okay. Sometimes they saw it and didn't react. That was okay, too. When they saw it and became flustered and afraid, that was best of all. He would start to masturbate harder, and now and then he managed to ejaculate before the girls had departed.
>
> Devon's history was unsettled. His father had left home before he was born, and his mother had drunk heavily. He was in and out of foster homes throughout his childhood. Before he was 10 years old he was involved in sexual activities with neighbourhood boys. Now and then, the boys forced neighbourhood girls into petting, and Devon had mixed feelings when the girls got upset. He felt bad for them, but he also enjoyed it. A couple of times girls seemed horrified at the sight of his penis, and it made him "really feel like a man. To see that look, you know, with a girl, not a woman, but a girl—a slender girl—that's what I'm after."
>
> The Authors' Files

Exhibitionism. Exhibitionism is a type of paraphilia that characterizes people who seek sexual arousal or gratification through exposing themselves to unsuspecting victims. People with this disorder are usually not interested in actual sexual contact with their victims.

exhibitionism Type of paraphilia almost exclusively occurring in males in which the man experiences persistent and recurrent sexual urges and sexually arousing fantasies involving the exposure of his genitals to a stranger and either has acted on these urges or feels strongly distressed by them.

Wearing revealing bathing suits is not a form of exhibitionism in the clinical sense of the term. Nearly all people diagnosed with exhibitionism disorder are men, and they are motivated by the wish to shock and dismay unsuspecting observers, not to show off the attractiveness of their bodies. Nor do professional strippers typically meet the clinical criteria for exhibitionism. Although they may seek to show off the attractiveness of their bodies, they are generally not motivated by the desire to expose themselves to unsuspecting strangers in order to arouse them or shock them. The chief motive of the stripper, of course, may simply be to earn a living.

Fetishism

The French *fetiche* is thought to derive from the Portuguese *feitico*, referring to a "magic charm." In this case, the "magic" lies in the object's or situation's ability to sexually arouse. The object or situation of interest is called the *fetish*, the person a *fetishist* who has a *fetish* for that object or situation. The chief feature of **fetishism** is recurrent, powerful sexual urges and arousing fantasies involving inanimate objects, such as an article of clothing (bras, panties, hosiery, boots, shoes, leather, silk, and the like), a body part (e.g., feet), or situations. It is normal for men to like the sight, feel, and smell of their lovers' undergarments. Men with fetishism, however, may prefer the object to the person and may not be able to become sexually aroused without it. They often experience sexual gratification by masturbating while fondling the object, rubbing or smelling it, or by having their partners wear it during sexual activity.

The origins of fetishism can sometimes be traced to early childhood experiences; fetishism is thought to be a type of conditioning or imprinting, like a pathological association. But although research suggests that early learning experiences may be important, the origin of fetishes is likely to be more complex, involving an interplay of learning experiences and various biological (e.g., hormonal) factors (Quinsey, 2003). Winnicott (1953) described a fetish as a specific object or type of object, dating from an experience during the period in which the mother gradually pulls back as an immediate provider of satisfaction of the child's desires, that persists as a characteristic in adult sexual life. Another, newer possible explanation comes from the field of neuroscience. The neuroscientists Ramachandran and Hubbard (2001) stated that the region processing sensory input from the feet lies immediately next to the region processing sexual stimulation and could possibly be an explanation for certain types of fetishes of the feet.

TRANSVESTIC FETISHISM The chief feature of **transvestic fetishism** is recurrent, powerful urges and related fantasies involving cross-dressing for purposes of sexual arousal. Other people with fetishes can be satisfied by handling objects such as women's clothing while they masturbate; people with transvestic fetishism want to wear them. They may wear full feminine attire and makeup or favour one particular article of clothing, such as women's stockings. Men with transvestic fetishism are typically heterosexual. Typically, the man cross-dresses in private and imagines himself to be a woman whom he is stroking as he masturbates. Some men frequent transvestite clubs or become involved in transvestic subcultures.

Gay men may cross-dress to attract other men or because it is fashionable to masquerade as women in some social circles, not because they are sexually aroused by cross-dressing. Males with gender identity disorder cross-dress because of gender discomfort associated with wearing men's clothing. Because cross-dressing among gay men and men with gender identity disorder is performed for reasons other than sexual arousal or gratification, it is not considered a form of transvestic fetishism. Nor are female impersonators who cross-dress for theatrical purposes considered to have a form of transvestism. For reasons such as these, the diagnosis is usually limited to heterosexuals.

fetishism Type of paraphilia in which a person uses an inanimate object or a body part (*partialism*) as a focus of sexual interest and as a source of arousal.

transvestic fetishism Type of paraphilia in heterosexual males characterized by recurrent sexual urges and sexually arousing fantasies involving dressing in female clothing, in which the person has either acted on these urges or is strongly distressed by them. Also termed *transvestism*.

Most men with transvestism are married and engage in sexual activity with their wives, but they seek additional sexual gratification through dressing as women, as in the case of Mario:

Mario was a 55-year-old plumber who had been cross-dressing for many years. There was a time when he would go out in public as a woman, but as his prominence in the community grew, he became more afraid of being discovered in public. His wife, Myrna, knew of his "peccadillo," especially since he borrowed many of her clothes, and she also encouraged him to stay at home, offering to help him with his "weirdness." For many years, his paraphilia had been restricted to the home.

The couple came to the clinic at the urging of the wife. Myrna described how Mario had imposed his will on her for 20 years. Mario would wear her undergarments and masturbate while she told him how disgusting he was. (The couple also regularly engaged in "normal" sexual intercourse, which Myrna enjoyed.) The cross-dressing situation had come to a head because a teenaged daughter had almost walked into the couple's bedroom while they were acting out Mario's fantasies.

With Myrna out of the consulting room, Mario explained that he had grown up in a family with several older sisters. He described how underwear had been perpetually hanging all around the one bathroom to dry. As an adolescent, Mario experimented with rubbing against articles of underwear, then with trying them on. On one occasion a sister walked in while he was modelling panties before the mirror. She told him he was one of the "dregs of society" and he straightaway experienced unparalleled sexual excitement. He masturbated when she left the room, and his orgasm was the strongest of his young life.

Mario did not think that there was anything wrong with wearing women's undergarments and masturbating. He was not about to give it up, regardless of whether his marriage was destroyed as a result. Myrna's main concern was finally separating herself from Mario's "sickness." She didn't care what he did anymore, so long as he did it by himself. "Enough is enough," she said.

That was the compromise the couple worked out in marital therapy. Mario would engage in his fantasies by himself. He would choose times when Myrna was not at home, and she would not be informed of his activities. He would also be very, very careful to choose times when the children would not be around.

Six months later the couple was together and content. Mario had replaced Myrna's input into his fantasies with transvestic-sadomasochistic magazines. Myrna said, "I see no evil, hear no evil, smell no evil." They continued to have sexual intercourse. After a while, Myrna even forgot to check to see which underwear had been used.

The Authors' Files

Transvestic fetishism should be distinguished from gender identity disorder. Transvestic fetishists do not consider themselves to be women, and transsexuals are not sexually aroused by cross-dressing. Even so, the two disorders appear to be connected; transvestic fetishism sometimes develops into gender identity disorder, if the individual is already predisposed toward gender identity disorder. In fact, transsexualism is often preceded by transvestic fetishism (Zucker & Blanchard, 1997). According to Ray Blanchard, the head of the Clinical Sexology Program at the University of Toronto and a leading researcher in the subject, gender identity disorders may be uncommon in women because one precursor—transvestic fetishism—is rare in women (Blanchard, 1989). Although gender identity disorders seem to be more common in children than adults, they occur in only 3% of boys and 1% of girls (Green & Blanchard, 1995).

voyeurism Type of paraphilia characterized by recurrent sexual urges and sexually arousing fantasies involving the act of watching unsuspecting others who are naked, in the act of undressing, or engaging in sexual activity, in which the person has either acted on these urges or is strongly distressed by them.

VOYEURISM The chief feature of **voyeurism** is either acting on or being strongly distressed by recurrent, powerful sexual urges and related fantasies involving watching unsuspecting people, generally strangers, who are undressed, disrobing, or engaging in sexual activity. The purpose of watching or "peeping" is to attain sexual excitement. The person who engages in voyeurism does not typically seek sexual activity with the person or persons being observed.

Are the acts of watching one's partner disrobe or viewing sexually explicit films forms of voyeurism? The answer is no. The people who are observed know they are being observed by their partners or will be observed by film audiences. Voyeuristic acts involve watching unsuspecting persons disrobing or engaging in sexual activities. Note that feelings of sexual arousal while watching our partners undress or observing sex scenes in R- and X-rated films fall within the normal spectrum of human sexuality.

During voyeuristic acts, the person usually masturbates while watching or fantasizing about watching. Peeping may be the person's exclusive sexual outlet. Some people engage in voyeuristic acts in which they place themselves in risky situations—the prospect of being found out or injured apparently heightens the excitement.

frotteurism Type of paraphilia characterized by recurrent sexual urges or sexually arousing fantasies involving bumping and rubbing against nonconsenting victims for sexual gratification. The person has either acted on these urges or is strongly distressed by them.

FROTTEURISM The French word *frottage* refers to the artistic technique of making a drawing by rubbing against a raised object. The chief feature of the paraphilia of **frotteurism** is recurrent, powerful sexual urges and related fantasies involving rubbing against or touching a nonconsenting person. Frotteurism, or "mashing," generally occurs in crowded places, such as subway cars, buses, or elevators. It is the rubbing or touching, not the coercive aspect of the act, that is sexually arousing. Almost all people diagnosed with frotteurism are male. The man may imagine himself enjoying an exclusive, affectionate sexual relationship with the victim. Because the physical contact is brief and furtive, people who commit frotteuristic acts stand only a small chance of being caught by authorities. Even the victims may not realize at the time what has happened or register much protest (Spitzer et al., 1994).

pedophilia Type of paraphilia involving sexual attraction to children.

PEDOPHILIA The word **pedophilia** derives from the Greek *paidos*, meaning "child." The chief feature of pedophilia is recurrent, powerful sexual urges and related fantasies involving sexual activity with prepubescent children (typically 13 years old or younger). Some pedophiles may not have actually molested children, because the diagnosis can be made on the basis of recurrent fantasies without the person necessarily acting on those fantasies (Barbaree & Seto, 1997). To be diagnosed with pedophilia, the person must be at least 16 years of age and at least 5 years older than the child or children toward whom he or she is sexually attracted or whom he or she has victimized. In some cases of pedophilia, the person is attracted only to children. In other cases, the person is attracted to adults as well.

Although some persons with pedophilia restrict their pedophilic activity to looking at or undressing children, others engage in exhibitionism, kissing, fondling, oral sex, anal intercourse, and, in the case of girls, vaginal intercourse (Knudsen, 1991). Not being worldly wise, children are often exploited by molesters who inform them that they are "educating" them, "showing them something," or doing something they will "like." Some men with pedophilia limit their sexual activity with children to incestuous relations with family members; others molest children only outside the family. Not all child molesters have pedophilia, however. The clinical definition of pedophilia is brought to bear only when sexual attraction to children is recurrent and persistent. Some molesters engage in these acts or experience pedophilic urges only occasionally or during times of opportunity.

Despite the stereotype, most cases of pedophilia do not involve "dirty old men" who hang around schoolyards in raincoats. Men with this disorder are usually (otherwise) law-abiding, respected citizens in their 30s or 40s. Most are married or divorced and have children of their own. They are usually well acquainted with their victims, who are typically either relatives or friends of the family. Many cases of pedophilia are not isolated incidents. They may be a series of acts that begin when children are very young and continue for many years until they are discovered or the relationship is broken off (Finkelhor, Hotaling, Lewis, & Smith, 1990).

Nearly all pedophiles are men, although the disorder is occasionally seen in women (Seto, 2004). In recent years, there have been a number of widely publicized newspaper and television reports of female high school teachers in their late 20s, 30s, or older having affairs with adolescent students (e.g., Denov, 2001). Such reports have come from schools in British Columbia, Ontario, and elsewhere. Some of these may be cases of pedophilia, especially where the female teacher persistently seeks sexual encounters with young students.

The origins of pedophilia are complex and varied. Some cases fit the stereotype of a weak, shy, socially inept, and isolated person who is threatened by mature relationships and turns to children for sexual gratification because children are less critical and demanding (Ames & Houston, 1990). In other cases, it may be that childhood sexual experiences with other children were so enjoyable that the person, as an adult, is attempting to recapture the excitement of earlier years. Or perhaps in some cases of pedophilia, people who were sexually abused in childhood by adults may now be reversing the situation in an effort to establish feelings of mastery. Consistent with the latter possibility, research indicates that pedophilic men, compared to other kinds of sex offenders, are more likely to have been sexually abused as children (W. L. Marshall, Serran, & Cortoni, 2000; Seto, 2004). This suggests that early sex-related experiences may be somehow linked to pedophilia. Seto's (2008) developmental theory of persistent sexual offending against children proposes two pathways: antisociality, stemming from psychopathy or adverse disadvantages, and sexual attraction to prepubescent children (pedophilia). When both are present, offending against children is especially likely (Seto, 2008). (See Figure 9.1 for details.) Men whose pedophilic acts involve incestuous relationships with their own children tend to fall at one extreme or the other on the dominance spectrum, either being very dominant or passive (Ames & Houston, 1990).

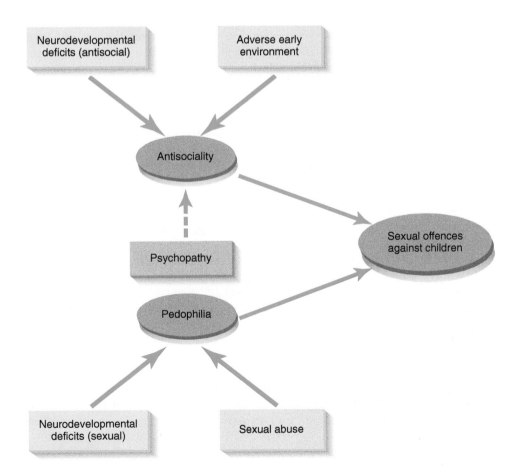

FIGURE 9.1 Developmental theory of persistent sexual offending against children
The developmental theory proposes two pathways: antisociality, stemming from psychopathy or adverse disadvantages, and sexual attraction to prepubescent children (pedophilia). When both are present, offending against children is especially likely (Seto, 2008).
Source: Serin et al., 2011, pp. 112–113. Reprinted with permission by Pearson Canada Inc.

Effects of Child Sexual Abuse   Child survivors of sexual abuse are more likely than nonabused children to develop psychological problems, including anxiety, depression, anger and aggressive behaviour, eating disorders, premature sexual behaviour or promiscuity, drug abuse, self-destructive behaviour such as suicide attempts, lack of trust, low self-esteem, social withdrawal, psychosomatic problems such as stomach aches and headaches, and symptoms of posttraumatic stress disorder (PTSD) (Boney-McCoy & Finkelhor, 1996). Regressive behaviours in the form of thumb-sucking or recurrences of childhood fears, such as fear of the dark or of strangers, are not uncommon. Although the effects of child sexual abuse are more similar than not between boys and girls (e.g., both genders tend to experience fears and sleep disturbances), there are some important differences. The clearest gender difference is that boys tend to develop "externalized" behaviour problems, such as excessive aggressive behaviour, whereas girls tend to experience "internalized" problems, such as depression (Finkelhor et al., 1990).

Late adolescence and early adulthood is a particularly difficult time for survivors of child sexual abuse because unresolved feelings of anger and guilt and a deep sense of mistrust can prevent survivors from developing intimate relationships (Jackson, Calhoun, Amick, Maddever, & Habif, 1990). Research and scientific reviews conducted throughout the world, including at universities in Ontario and Manitoba, indicate that there are many serious long-term consequences of childhood sexual abuse (Abdulrehman & De Luca, 2001). Adult survivors of childhood sexual abuse, compared to people who were never abused, are more likely to have psychological disorders (e.g., anxiety disorders, mood disorders, suicidal behaviour, substance abuse, and antisocial behaviour), relationship problems, fewer friends, more social adjustment problems, and greater problems in sexual functioning. Martin Kruze is a tragic case in point. He, along with many other young hockey players, was sexually abused by men working in Toronto's Maple Leaf Gardens from the 1970s to the 1990s (Vine & Challen, 2002). Many boys were traumatized. Kruze, who as an adult blew the whistle on the abuse, later committed suicide.

SEXUAL MASOCHISM   Sexual masochism derives its name from the Austrian novelist Leopold von Sacher-Masoch (1835–1895), who wrote stories and novels about men who sought sexual gratification from women by having the women inflict pain on them, often in the form of flagellation (being beaten or whipped). Sexual masochism involves strong, recurrent urges and fantasies relating to sexual acts that involve being humiliated, bound, flogged, or made to suffer in other ways. The urges are either acted on or cause significant personal distress. In some cases of sexual masochism, the person cannot attain sexual gratification in the absence of pain or humiliation.

In some cases, sexual masochism involves binding or mutilating oneself during masturbation or sexual fantasies. In others, a partner is engaged to restrain (bondage), blindfold (sensory bondage), paddle, or whip the person. Some partners are prostitutes; others are consensual partners who are asked to perform the sadistic role. In some cases, the person may desire, for purposes of sexual gratification, to be urinated or defecated on or subjected to verbal abuse.

A most dangerous expression of masochism is **hypoxyphilia** (also known as *autoerotic asphyxiation*), in which participants are sexually aroused by being deprived of oxygen—for example, by using a noose, plastic bag, chemical, or pressure on the chest during a sexual act, such as masturbation. The oxygen deprivation is usually accompanied by fantasies of asphyxiating or being asphyxiated by a lover. People who engage in this activity generally discontinue it before they lose consciousness, but occasional deaths due to suffocation have resulted from miscalculations (Blanchard & Hucker, 1991).

To illustrate the nature of this paraphilia, an Alberta study of 19 cases of death due to hypoxyphilia revealed that the person is often a single male aged 15 to 29 years who performed the act repetitively and when alone. Accidental death typically occurred when

sexual masochism Type of paraphilia characterized by sexual urges and sexually arousing fantasies involving receiving humiliation or pain, in which the person has either acted on these urges or is strongly distressed by them.

hypoxyphilia Paraphilia in which a person seeks sexual gratification by being deprived of oxygen by means of using a noose, plastic bag, chemical, or pressure on the chest.

there was a failure of the "safety" mechanism designed to restore oxygen (Tough, Butt, & Sanders, 1994). According to Stephen Hucker, a Toronto psychiatrist and expert on paraphilias, people who engage in hypoxyphilia also tend to practise other forms of sexual masochism, such as self-administered electrical shocks (Hucker, 1985).

SEXUAL SADISM   Sexual sadism is named after the infamous Marquis de Sade, the 18th-century Frenchman who wrote stories about the pleasures of achieving sexual gratification by inflicting pain or humiliation on others. Sexual sadism is the flip side of sexual masochism. It involves recurrent, powerful urges and related fantasies of engaging in acts in which the person is sexually aroused by inflicting physical suffering or humiliation on another person. People with this paraphilia either act out their fantasies or are disturbed by them. They may recruit consenting partners, who may be lovers or wives with a masochistic streak, or prostitutes. Still others—known as *sadistic rapists*—stalk and assault nonconsenting victims and become aroused by inflicting pain or suffering on them. The experience of power and control may be as important as inflicting pain (Hucker, 1997). Most rapists, however, do not seek to become sexually aroused by inflicting pain on their victims; they may even lose sexual interest when they see their victims in pain.

Many people have occasional sadistic or masochistic fantasies or engage in sex play involving simulated or mild forms of **sadomasochism** with their partners. *Sadomasochism* describes a mutually gratifying sexual interaction involving both sadistic and masochistic acts. Simulation may take the form of using a feather brush to strike one's partner, so that no actual pain is administered. People who engage in sadomasochism frequently switch roles during their encounters or from one encounter to another. The clinical diagnosis of sexual masochism or sadism is not usually brought to bear unless such people become distressed by their behaviour or fantasies or act them out in ways that are harmful to themselves or others.

S & M paraphernalia. Some of the devices used by people who engage in sadomasochism.

sexual sadism Type of paraphilia or sexual deviation characterized by recurrent sexual urges and sexually arousing fantasies involving inflicting humiliation or physical pain on sex partners, in which the person has either acted on these urges or is strongly distressed by them.

sadomasochism Sexual activities between partners involving the attainment of gratification by means of inflicting and receiving pain and humiliation.

OTHER PARAPHILIAS   There are many other paraphilias. These include making obscene phone calls (telephone scatologia); necrophilia (sexual urges or fantasies involving sexual contact with corpses); partialism (sole focus on part of the body); zoophilia (sexual urges or fantasies involving sexual contact with animals); and sexual arousal associated with feces (coprophilia), enemas (klismaphilia), and urine (urophilia).

Theoretical Perspectives

Psychodynamic theorists see many paraphilias as defences against leftover castration anxiety from the Oedipal period. The thought of the penis disappearing into the vagina is unconsciously equated with castration.

The man who develops a paraphilia may avoid this threat of castration anxiety by displacing sexual arousal into other activities—for example, undergarments, children, or watching others. By sequestering his penis under women's clothes, the man with transvestic fetishism engages in a symbolic act of denial that women do not have penises, which eases castration anxiety by unconsciously providing evidence of women's (and his own) safety. The shock and dismay shown by the victim of a man who exposes himself provides unconscious reassurance that he does, after all, have a penis. Sadism involves an unconscious identification with the man's father—the "aggressor" of his Oedipal fantasies—and relieves anxiety by giving him the opportunity to enact the role of the castrator. Some psychoanalytic theorists see masochism as a way of coping with conflicting feelings about sex. Basically, the man feels guilty about sex but is able to enjoy it so long as he is being punished for it. Others view masochism as the redirection inward of aggressive impulses originally aimed at the powerful, threatening father. Like the child who is relieved when his inevitable punishment is over, the man gladly accepts bondage and flagellation in place of castration. These views remain speculative and controversial. We lack any direct evidence that men with paraphilias are handicapped by unresolved castration anxiety.

Learning theorists explain paraphilias in terms of conditioning and observational learning (Pfaus, Kippin, & Centeno, 2001; Seto, 2004). Some object or activity becomes inadvertently associated with sexual arousal. The object or activity then gains the capacity to elicit sexual arousal. For example, a boy who glimpses his mother's stockings on the towel rack while he is masturbating may go on to develop a fetish for stockings (Breslow, 1989). Orgasm in the presence of the object reinforces the erotic connection, especially when it occurs repeatedly. Yet if fetishes were acquired by mechanical association, we would expect people to develop fetishes for stimuli that are inadvertently and repeatedly connected with sexual activity, such as bedsheets, pillows, even ceilings (Breslow, 1989; W. L. Marshall & Eccles, 1993). Such is not the case. The meaning of the stimulus also apparently plays a role. Perhaps the development of fetishes depends on people's ability to eroticize certain types of stimuli (like women's undergarments) and incorporate them into their erotic and masturbatory fantasies. Fetishes can often be traced to experiences in early childhood. Like other patterns of abnormal behaviour, paraphilias may involve multiple biological, psychological, and sociocultural factors. Money and Lamacz (1990) hypothesize a multifactorial model that traces the development of paraphilias to childhood. They suggest that childhood experiences etch a pattern or "lovemap" that can be likened to a software program in the brain that determines the kinds of stimuli and behaviours that come to arouse people sexually. In the case of paraphilias, lovemaps become "vandalized" by early traumatic experiences, such as incest, physical abuse, or neglect, and excessively harsh antisexual child-rearing. Yet not all children who undergo such experiences develop paraphilias. Nor do all people with paraphilias have such traumatic experiences. Perhaps some children are more vulnerable to developing distorted lovemaps than others. The precise nature of such vulnerability remains to be defined.

Origins of fetishism? The conditioning model of the origins of fetishism suggests that men who develop fetishisms involving women's undergarments may have had experiences in childhood in which sexual arousal was repeatedly paired with exposure to their mother's undergarments. The developing fetish may have been strengthened by the boy incorporating the object into his erotic fantasies or masturbatory activity.

Treatment of Paraphilias

Therapists of various theoretical persuasions have attempted to treat clients with paraphilias. Psychoanalysts, for example, attempt to bring childhood sexual conflicts (typically of an Oedipal nature) into awareness so that they can be resolved in the light of the individual's adult personality. Favourable results from individual case studies appear in the literature from time to time, but there is a dearth of controlled investigations to support the efficacy of psychodynamic treatment of paraphilias.

Behaviour therapists have used aversive conditioning to induce a negative emotional reaction to paraphilic stimuli or fantasies. In aversive conditioning, the stimulus that elicits sexual arousal (e.g., panties) is paired repeatedly with an aversive stimulus (e.g., electric shock) in the belief that the stimulus will acquire aversive properties. A basic limitation of aversive conditioning is that it does not help the individual acquire more adaptive behaviours in place of maladaptive response patterns. This may explain why researchers find that a broad-based, cognitive-behavioural program for treating exhibitionism that emphasizes the development of adaptive thoughts, the building of social skills, and the development of stress-management skills is more effective than an alternative program based on aversion therapy (W. L. Marshall, Eccles, & Barbaree, 1991).

Maletzky (1991, 1998; Maletzky & Steinhauser, 2002) reported on the success rates of the largest treatment program study to date, based on more than 7000 cases of rapists and sex offenders with paraphilias. Treatment procedures incorporated a variety of behavioural techniques, including aversive and nonaversive methods, that were tailored to the particular type of paraphilia. Success rates for treatment of various paraphilias are reported in Table 9.2. Two cautions are advised in interpreting these data, however. First, criteria for success were at least partly dependent on self-reports of an absence of deviant sexual interests or behaviour, and self-reports may be biased, especially in offender groups. Second, with the lack of a control group, we cannot discount the possibility that other factors, such as fears of legal consequences or nonspecific factors unrelated to the specific behavioural techniques used, influenced the outcome. Nonetheless, these data are among the strongest sources of evidence supporting the effectiveness of behavioural techniques in treating paraphilias.

Some promising results are also reported in using selective serotonin reuptake inhibitors (SSRIs) such as Prozac in treating voyeurism and fetishism (D. M. Greenberg & Bradford, 1997). Why SSRIs? These medications have been used effectively in treating obsessive-compulsive disorder (see Chapter 3), and researchers speculate that paraphilias may fall within an obsessive-compulsive spectrum (Kruesi, Fine, Valladares, Phillips, & Rapoport, 1992). Many people with paraphilias report feeling compelled to carry out paraphilic acts in much the same way that people with obsessive-compulsive disorder feel driven to perform compulsive acts. Paraphilias also tend

TABLE 9.2

Percentages of Sex Offenders Successfully Treated

Paraphilia	No. of Cases Treated	% of Cases Treated Successfully
Situational pedophilia (heterosexual)	3012	95.6
Predatory pedophilia (heterosexual)	864	88.3
Situational pedophilia (homosexual)	717	91.8
Predatory pedophilia (homosexual)	596	80.1
Exhibitionism	1130	95.4
Rape	543	75.5
Voyeurism	83	93.9
Public masturbation	77	94.8
Frotteurism	65	89.3
Fetishism	33	94.0
Transvestic fetishism	14	78.6
Obscene telephoning	29	93.1
Zoophilia	23	95.6

A treatment success was defined as an offender who completed all treatment sessions, reported no covert or overt deviant sexual behaviour at the end of treatment or at any follow-up session, demonstrated no deviant sexual arousal at the end of treatment or at any follow-up session, and had no repeat legal charges for any sexual crime at the end of treatment or at any follow-up session.

Source: Maletzky, 1998. Copyright 2002 by Oxford University Press. Reprinted with permission.

Correctional Service Canada's National Moderate Intensity Sex Offender Program

NATIONAL MODERATE INTENSITY SEX OFFENDER PROGRAM

The National Sex Offender Program is a cognitive-behavioural intervention that is designed to be a therapeutic rather than solely a didactic or psychoeducational program. It is based on empirical research and best practice in the provision of services to sex offenders, and the principles of social learning, adult learning, group processes, therapeutic rapport and alliance, motivational enhancement, overlearning, and skills development.

The National Sex Offender Program targets criminogenic needs and known risk factors for sexual offending. The format of the National Sex Offender Program uses a "menu" approach based on criminogenic needs and known risk factors associated with individual offenders' patterns of sexual offending behaviour. In the National Sex Offender Program, the client is regarded as the "expert" about his own behaviour and, as such, the role of the service provider is to assist the client to develop, through guided learning, an awareness of the dynamics and motivations of his sexual offending behaviour and to develop a self-management plan to avoid re-offending. The National Sex Offender Program also incorporates both group and individual work, and recognizes learning that occurs outside the formal treatment venue.

REFERRAL CRITERIA

The Sex Offender Program is intended for all federal offenders who:

- Have been convicted of a sex offence or;
- Have been convicted of a sexually motivated crime or;
- Have admitted to a sex offence for which they have not been convicted.

AND

- Offenders having a moderate risk to re-offend relative to other sex offenders, as assessed using a sex offender–specific actuarial assessment instrument such as the Static-99
- Offenders who have moderate to high criminogenic needs as assessed using a sex offender–specific measure of dynamic risk factors such as the Stable-2007 (moderate to high need levels refers to the number, type, and extent of entrenchment of dynamic risk factors).

Source: Adapted from Correctional Services Canada, Moderate Intensity Sex Offender Program, www.csc-scc.gc.ca/text/prgm/sexoff-eng.shtml. Accessed 15/09/11.

---

to have an obsessional quality. The person experiences intrusive, repetitive urges to engage in paraphilic acts or thoughts that relate to the paraphilic object or situation. However, Maletzky (1998) cautions that these drugs may act to reduce sexual drives rather than specifically target deviant sexual fantasies.

Sexual Assault

sexual assault Nonconsensual bodily contact for a sexual purpose.

Although **sexual assault** is not a diagnosable psychological disorder, it certainly meets several of the criteria used to define abnormal behaviour. Sexual assault, like pedophilia, is socially unacceptable, violates social norms, and is grievously harmful to its victims. Sexual assault may also be associated with some clinical syndromes, especially some forms of sexual sadism.

The term *sexual assault* has particular legal meaning:

aggravated sexual assault Sexual assault in which the victim is maimed or disfigured or has his or her life endangered.

Sexual assault has replaced *rape* as the term used in the Canadian legal system. There are three levels of sexual assault. Level 1 encompasses any non-consensual bodily contact for a sexual purpose, including touching, kissing, and oral, vaginal, and anal sex. Bodily contact can involve any part of the accused's body or an object. Level 2 is sexual assault with a weapon, in which the weapon is used to threaten or injure the victim. Level 3 is **aggravated sexual assault**, in which the victim is maimed or disfigured or has her or his life endangered. The central issue in determining whether an assault has occurred is whether consent was freely given. The person has to be capable of giving consent; therefore a person who is drunk, under the influence of drugs, unconscious, fearful, or underage is unable to give consent. (Rathus, Nevid, Fichner-Rathus, & Herold, 2010, p. 336. Reprinted with permission by Pearson Canada Inc.)

INCIDENCE OF SEXUAL ASSAULT Sexual assault is disturbingly common. To illustrate, a Winnipeg survey of 551 women revealed that "about a quarter of all women in North America" reported being sexually assaulted (e.g., unwanted touching) at some point in their lives (Brickman & Briere, 1984). In a later and larger survey of students from colleges and universities across Canada, 28% of women reported being sexually abused in the previous year and 11% of men reported having victimized a female dating partner in this way during the same period (DeKeseredy, 1997). Similar results have been reported from campuses in the United States (e.g., Gross, Winslett, Roberts, & Gohm, 2006). In 2002, 8800 sexual assaults against children and youth were reported to a subset of 94 police departments in Canada. This included 2863 sexual assaults against children and youth by family members. In the Canadian population in general, it has been estimated that more than 30% of men and over 50% of women have been sexually assaulted (Committee on Sexual Offences Against Children and Youth, 1984).

In over 80% of sexual assault cases overall, the woman is acquainted with the assailant (Cole, 2006). Sexual assault is the most common violent crime on campus. Most sexual assaults occur in social situations, such as at a party or when students study together in a dormitory room, and roughly half of perpetrators and sexual assault survivors are drinking alcohol at the time of the assault (Cole, 2006). Some men may use alcohol intoxication as an excuse for sexual assault, and some men perceive women who drink alcohol to be more sexually available and therefore appropriate targets for sexual aggression. Regardless of the motives or perceptions of a man or a woman, sexual assault is never justified. Although sexual assaults on males do occur, especially in prisons, the great majority of cases involve women as the victim.

THEORETICAL PERSPECTIVES There is no single kind of perpetrator of sexual assault. Sexual assailants are no more likely than other offenders to have the kinds of psychological disorders coded on Axis I of the DSM-IV (Polaschek, Ward, & Hudson, 1997). Sexual assault has more to do with violent impulses and issues of power and control than with sexual gratification. According to DeKeseredy's (1997) survey of Canadian undergraduates, men who had sexually abused tended to hold beliefs that women should be obedient, respectful, dependent, and sexually submissive toward men. Such beliefs may increase the odds that a man will become sexually abusive. Many sex offenders were sexually abused themselves as children (Seto, 2004). Some rapists who were abused as children may humiliate women as a way of expressing anger and power over them and of taking revenge. For still other rapists, violent cues appear to enhance sexual arousal, so they are motivated to combine sex with aggression (W. L. Marshall & Moulden, 2001). Sadistic sexual assaults frequently employ torture and **bondage**, merging sex and aggression. Sadistic rapists are most likely to mutilate their victims.

William L. Marshall, a psychologist at Queen's University and an expert on paraphilias, argues that the risk of committing sexual offences is increased by early learning experiences that cause the person to have low self-confidence and poor social skills. Possessing poor social skills means that the person has difficulty attracting dating partners. Sexual offences involve the domination or humiliation of victims, and thereby may give a sense of power to men who are otherwise lacking in power and self-confidence. Offensive sexual behaviours are maladaptive attempts to achieve intimacy through sex. These efforts are invariably unsuccessful and self-defeating; they merely serve to isolate the person further from society. Paradoxically, the pattern may become deeply ingrained because it results in the momentary pleasure associated with orgasm and because it offers the illusory hope of eventually achieving intimacy with another person. These and other factors are implicated in Marshall's theory (see, for example, W. L. Marshall, 2001).

Marshall and others emphasize the role of attachment problems in sexual offenders (Beech & Mitchell, 2005; W. L. Marshall, 2001). Many sexual offenders report having had sexually or physically abusive childhood experiences; they also in many cases did not have safe, loving relationships (bondings) with one or both parents, because the parents were abusive, rejecting, or emotionally cold. These experiences are thought to increase

bondage Form of sadomasochism involving the binding of the arms or legs of oneself or one's partner during sexual activity.

the chances that a child will as an adult either seek out intimate, sexual attachments with children, perhaps confusing sex with intimacy, or become sexually aggressive with women (Beech & Mitchell, 2005).

Does pornography lead to sexual aggression? Given the seriousness of sexual assault and the growing size of the pornography industry, it is important to understand the role of pornography and sex offending. Psychologist Michael Seto and colleagues from the Centre for Addiction and Mental Health in Toronto reviewed the evidence regarding this important question (Seto, Maric, & Barbaree, 2001). They concluded that the existing evidence suggests that people who are already predisposed to sexually offend are most likely to show an effect of pornography exposure (e.g., to be stimulated or encouraged by violent pornography or more likely to engage in sexual violence). Subsequent research lends support for this conclusion (e.g., Carr & VanDeusen, 2004).

Sociocultural factors also need to be considered. Although many rapists show evidence of psychopathology on psychological tests, especially psychopathic traits (Beech & Mitchell, 2005), many do not (S. L. Brown & Forth, 1997). The very normality of many rapists on psychological instruments suggests that socialization factors play an important role. Some sociocultural theorists argue that our culture actually breeds rapists by socializing men into sexually dominant and aggressive roles associated with stereotypical concepts of masculinity (G. C. Hall & Barongan, 1997). Sexually coercive college men tend to have an excessively masculinized personality orientation, adhere more strictly to traditional gender roles, view women as adversaries in the "mating game," and hold more accepting attitudes toward the use of violence against women than do noncoercive men (Polaschek et al., 1997). They are also more prone to blame sexual assault survivors over rapists and to become sexually aroused by portrayals of sexual assault than are men who hold less rigid stereotypes. Sociocultural influences also reinforce themes that may underlie sexual assault, such as the cultural belief that a masculine man is expected to be sexually assertive and overcome a woman's resistance until she "melts" in his arms (Stock, 1991).

Date sexual assault is a form of acquaintance sexual assault. College and university men on dates frequently perceive their dates' protests as part of an adversarial sex game. One male undergraduate said, "Hell, no," when asked whether a date had consented to sex. He added, "But she didn't say no, so she must have wanted it, too. It's the way it works" (Celis, 1991). Consider the case of William, a man who sexually assaulted a woman he had met online:

> William met Sarah two months ago in a chat room on the Internet. They were drawn to each other's comments and quickly began talking just between the two of them. After a few weeks of online chatting, William called Sarah. They hit it off on the phone as well and planned to meet up for dinner. Sarah seemed really interested in William—she laughed at all his jokes and complimented him throughout dinner. After dinner, he invited her to his apartment. He was thrilled that she said yes. They started watching a movie, but soon began kissing instead. When William went to remove Sarah's dress, she hesitated. He thought she was just being shy, so he tried again. This time she pulled his hand away. But William knew that she really liked him, and had come to his apartment, so she must want to have sex as much as he did. He ignored her protests, thinking that sometimes women had to resist a bit to protect their reputations. Afterwards, he couldn't understand why she was crying. She'd given him all the right signs that she was into him, and it wasn't like they'd just met. He was surprised when Sarah didn't return his calls in the following days.

Let us rebut these beliefs. Accepting a date is not the equivalent of consenting to intercourse. Accompanying a man to his room or apartment is not the equivalent of consenting to intercourse. Kissing and petting are not the equivalent of consenting to intercourse. When a woman fails to consent or says no, the man must take no for an answer.

EFFECTS OF SEXUAL ASSAULT Women who are sexually assaulted suffer more than the assault itself. They report loss of appetite, headaches, irritability, anxiety and depression, and menstrual irregularity in the wake of a sexual assault. Some become sullen, withdrawn, and mistrustful. In some cases, women show an unrealistic composure, which often gives

Given the incidence of sexual assault, it is important to be aware of strategies that may prevent it. By listing strategies for sexual assault prevention, we do not mean to imply that sexual assault survivors are somehow responsible for falling prey to an attack. The responsibility for any act of sexual violence lies with the perpetrator, not with the person who is assaulted, and perhaps with society for fostering attitudes that underlie sexual violence. On a societal level, we need to do a better job of socializing young men to acquire prosocial and respectful attitudes toward women. Exposing them to feminist, egalitarian, and multicultural education, as well as educating them about the often devastating impact of sexual assault on the person who is assaulted, may help promote more respectful attitudes in young men (Foubert & Perry, 2007; Hall & Barongan, 1997; Kershner, 1996).

PREVENTING STRANGER SEXUAL ASSAULT

- Establish signals and plans with other women in the building or neighbourhood.
- List only first initials in the phone directory and on the mailbox.
- Use deadbolt locks.
- Lock windows and install iron grids on first-floor windows.
- Keep doorways and entries well lit.
- Have keys handy for the car or the front door.
- Do not walk by yourself after dark.
- Avoid deserted areas.
- Do not allow strange men into the apartment or the house without checking their credentials.
- Keep the car door locked and the windows up.
- Check out the back seat of the car before getting in.
- Don't live in a risky building.
- Don't give rides to hitchhikers (that includes female hitchhikers).

- Don't converse with strange men on the street.
- Shout "Fire!" not "Rape!" People flock to fires but circumvent scenes of violence.

PREVENTING "DATE RAPE"

- Avoid getting into secluded situations until you know your date very well.
- Be wary when a date attempts to control you in any way, such as frightening you by driving rapidly or taking you some place you would rather not go.
- Stay sober. We often do things we would not otherwise do—including engaging in sexual activity with people we might otherwise reject—when we have had too many drinks. Be aware of your limits. And if you do drink, don't leave your drink unattended. Many women have been sexually assaulted as a result of their drinks being spiked with drugs.
- Be very assertive and clear concerning your sexual intentions. Some rapists, particularly date rapists, tend to misinterpret women's wishes. If their dates begin to implore them to stop during kissing or petting, they construe pleading as "female game playing." So if kissing or petting is leading where you don't want it to go, speak up.
- When dating a person for the first time, try to date in a group.
- Encourage your college or university to offer educational programs about date sexual assault.
- Talk to your date about his attitudes toward women. If you get the feeling that he believes men are in a war with women, or that women try to "play games" with men, you may be better off dating someone else.

Source: Adapted from Nevid, Jeffrey S., Fichner-Rathus, Lois, & Rathus, Spencer A. *Human Sexuality in a World of Diversity,* 2nd ed. © 1995. Reprinted and electronically reproduced by permission of Pearson Education, Inc., Upper Saddle River, New Jersey.

way to venting of feelings later on. Because of society's tendency to blame the victim for the assault, some survivors also have misplaced feelings of guilt, shame, and self-blame. Survivors often develop sexual dysfunctions such as lack of sexual desire and difficulty becoming sexually aroused (Letourneau, Resnick, Kilpatrick, Saunders, & Best, 1996). Many survivors show signs of PTSD, including intrusive memories of the sexual assault, nightmares, emotional numbing, and heightened autonomic arousal (Taylor, 2005).

Psychological problems experienced by sexual assault survivors often continue through at least the first year following the sexual assault (Kimerling & Calhoun, 1994). About one in four sexual assault survivors continues to encounter psychological problems such as depression and anxiety for a number of years after the attack (Calhoun & Atkeson, 1991; Koss et al., 1994).

TREATMENT OF SEXUAL ASSAULT SURVIVORS Treatment of sexual assault survivors is often a two-phase process that first assists women in coping with the immediate aftermath of sexual assault and then helps them with their long-term adjustment. Crisis intervention provides women with emotional support and information to help them see to their immediate needs as well as to help them develop strategies for coping with the trauma (S. Taylor, 2005). Longer-term treatment may be designed to help sexual assault survivors cope with undeserved feelings of guilt and shame, lingering feelings of anxiety and depression, and the interpersonal and sexual problems they may develop with the men in their lives. Unfortunately, most sexual assault survivors do not seek help from mental health professionals, sexual assault crisis centres, or sexual assault survivor assistance programs (Kimerling & Calhoun, 1994). The cultural stigma associated with seeking help for mental health problems may discourage a fuller utilization of psychological services.

REVIEW IT

Paraphilias

- **What are paraphilias?** Paraphilias are sexual deviations involving patterns of arousal to stimuli such as nonhuman objects (e.g., shoes or clothes), humiliation, the experience of pain in oneself or one's partner, or children.
- **What are the major types of paraphilia?** Paraphilias include exhibitionism, fetishism, transvestic fetishism, voyeurism, frotteurism, pedophilia, sexual masochism, and sexual sadism. Although some paraphilias are essentially harmless (such as fetishism), others, such as pedophilia and sexual sadism, often harm nonconsenting victims.
- **What causes paraphilias, and what makes them so difficult to treat?** Paraphilias may be caused by the interaction of biological, psychological, and social factors. Efforts

to treat paraphilias are compromised by the fact that most people with these disorders do not wish to change.
- **What factors underlie tendencies to sexually assault?** The desires to dominate women or express hatred toward them may be more prominent motives for sexual assault than is sexual desire. Although some men who sexually assault show clear evidence of underlying psychopathology, many do not. Sexual assault has more to do with violent impulses and issues of power than with pursuit of sexual gratification. From a sociocultural perspective, we should examine cultural attitudes, such as stereotypes of male aggressiveness and social dominance, that underlie propensities to sexually assault.

SEXUAL DYSFUNCTIONS

sexual dysfunctions Psychological disorders involving persistent difficulties with sexual interest, arousal, or response.

Sexual dysfunctions involve problems with sexual interest, arousal, or response. Sexual dysfunctions are widespread in our society, affecting over 40% of women and roughly 33% of men (Hayes, Bennett, Fairley, & Dennerstein, 2006; Laumann, Paik, & Rosen, 1999). They are often significant sources of distress to the affected person and his or her partner. There are various types of sexual dysfunctions, but they tend to share some common features, as outlined in Table 9.3. Table 9.4 shows the estimated rates of several major types of sexual dysfunction based on community samples.

TABLE 9.3

Common Features of Sexual Dysfunction

Fear of failure	Fears relating to failure to achieve or maintain erection or failure to reach orgasm.
Assumption of a spectator role rather than a performer role	Monitoring and evaluating your body's reactions during sex.
Diminished self-esteem	Thinking less of yourself for failure to meet your standard of normality.
Emotional effects	Guilt, shame, frustration, depression, anxiety. Avoiding sexual contacts for fear of failure to perform adequately; making excuses to your partner.
Avoidance behaviour	Fears relating to failure to achieve or maintain erection or failure to reach orgasm.

Source: Adapted from Nevid, Jeffrey S., Fichner-Rathus, Lois, & Rathus, Spencer A. *Human Sexuality in a World of Diversity,* 2nd ed. © 1995. Reprinted and electronically reproduced by permission of Pearson Education, Inc., Upper Saddle River, New Jersey.

TABLE 9.4

Estimated Prevalence of Various Current Sexual Dysfunctions (percentage of respondents reporting any problem)

Premature ejaculation	36–38
Erectile dysfunction	4–9
Male orgasmic disorder	4–10
Female orgasmic disorder	5–10

Source: Spector & Carey, 1990, pp. 389–408. Copyright Springer. Reprinted with the kind permission of Springer Science+Business Media B.V.

Some cases of sexual dysfunction have existed throughout the individual's lifetime, and are thus labelled lifelong dysfunctions. In the case of acquired dysfunctions, the problem begins following a period (or at least one occurrence) of normal functioning. In the case of a situational dysfunction, the problem occurs in some situations (e.g., with one's spouse) but not in others (e.g., with a lover or when masturbating), or at some times but not others. In the case of a generalized dysfunction, the problem occurs in all situations and whenever the individual engages in sexual activity.

Types of Sexual Dysfunctions

The DSM-IV groups most sexual dysfunctions into the following categories:

1. Sexual desire disorders
2. Sexual arousal disorders
3. Orgasm disorders
4. Sexual pain disorders

The first three categories correspond to the first three phases of the sexual response cycle.

SEXUAL DESIRE DISORDERS Sexual desire disorders involve disturbances in sexual appetite or an aversion to genital sexual activity. People with **hypoactive sexual desire disorder** have an absence or lack of sexual interest or desire. Typically, there is either a complete or virtual absence of sexual fantasies. However, clinicians have not reached any universally agreed upon criteria for determining the level of sexual desire that is considered normal. Individual clinicians must weigh various factors in reaching a diagnosis in cases of low sexual desire, such as the client's lifestyle (e.g., a lack of sexual energy or interest in parents contending with the demands of infants or young children is to be expected), sociocultural factors (e.g., culturally restrictive attitudes may restrain sexual desire or interest), the quality of the relationship between the client and her or his partner (declining sexual interest or activity may reflect relationship problems rather than diminished drive), and the client's age (desire normally declines but does not disappear with increasing age). Couples usually seek help when one or both partners recognize that the level of sexual activity in the relationship is deficient or has waned to the point that little desire or interest remains. Sometimes the lack of desire is limited to one partner. In other cases, both partners may feel sexual urges but anger and conflict concerning other issues inhibit sexual interaction. Although problems in sexual desire were first included in the DSM in 1980, hypoactive sexual desire disorder has become one of the most commonly diagnosed sexual dysfunctions in women today (Hayes et al., 2006). Giving lie to the myth that men are always ready for sex, the number of men presenting with hypoactive sexual desire disorder appears to be on the rise (Letourneau & O'Donohue, 1993). However, premature ejaculation is still the most common sexual dysfunction in men (Hellstrom, Nehra, Shabsigh, & Sharlip, 2006).

People with **sexual aversion disorder** have a strong aversion to genital sexual contact and avoid all or nearly all genital contact with a partner. They may, however, desire and

hypoactive sexual desire disorder Persistent or recurrent lack of sexual interest or sexual fantasies.

sexual aversion disorder Type of sexual dysfunction characterized by aversion to, and avoidance of, genital sexual contact.

enjoy affectionate contact or nongenital sexual contact. Their disgust with any form of genital contact may stem from childhood sexual abuse, sexual assault, or other traumatic experiences. In other cases, deep-seated feelings of sexual guilt or shame may impair sexual response. In men, the diagnosis is often connected with a history of erectile failures. Such men may associate sexual opportunities with failure and shame. Their partners may also develop aversions to sexual contact because their sexual contacts have been so frustrating or emotionally painful.

SEXUAL AROUSAL DISORDERS Disorders of sexual arousal comprise an inability to achieve or maintain the physiological responses involved in sexual arousal or excitement— vaginal lubrication in the woman or penile erection in the man—that are needed to allow completion of sexual activity.

In women, sexual arousal is characterized by lubrication of the vaginal walls that makes entry by the penis possible. In men, sexual arousal is characterized by erection. Almost all women now and then have difficulty becoming or remaining lubricated. Almost all men have occasional difficulty attaining or maintaining an erection through intercourse. The diagnoses of **female sexual arousal disorder** and **male erectile disorder** (also called *sexual impotence* or *erectile dysfunction*) are reserved for persistent or recurrent problems in becoming genitally aroused.

female sexual arousal disorder
Type of sexual dysfunction in women involving difficulties becoming sexually aroused, as defined by a lack of vaginal lubrication or failure to maintain sufficient lubrication to complete the sexual act or lack of sexual excitement or pleasure during sexual activity.

male erectile disorder Sexual dysfunction in males characterized by difficulty in achieving or maintaining erection during sexual activity.

A CLOSER LOOK

A New View of Women's Sexual Dysfunctions?

The classification of sexual dysfunctions in *the Diagnostic and Statistical Manual of Mental Disorders* (American Psychiatric Association, 2000) is based on the Human Sexual Response Cycle model of Masters and Johnson (1966). This classification has been criticized because of (1) the specific wording of these sexual dysfunction criteria, and (2) the overall taxonomic system for classifying sexual dysfunctions in women. These criticisms resulted in attempts to establish new classification systems. Yet these revisions continued to use the Masters and Johnson medical model, which is symptom-focused on problems relating to desire, arousal, orgasm, and pain.

Leonore Tiefer, a clinical psychologist and activist, convened a group of feminist social scientists in 2000 to propose a new diagnostic system that was intended to be free of the pharmaceutical conflicts of interest and the medical model on which they are based. Specifically, there was concern over the creation of a "Female Sexual Dysfunction (FSD)" diagnosis by pharmaceutical companies that would then be in a profitable position to develop and market a drug to treat this "disease." Thus, the "New View Campaign" was formed.

The New View classification system is a radical departure from the existing American Psychiatric Association's (DSM-IV) taxonomic structure. It is based on feminist theories attributing women's sexual problems to cultural and relational factors (Tiefer, 2001). The system deliberately avoids specifying any particular "normal" pattern of sexual response. Instead, the resulting four-part classification system focuses on the causes of sexual problems, defined as "discontent or dissatisfaction with any emotional, physical, or relational aspect of sexual experience." It does not differentiate among the problematic symptoms of desire, arousal, orgasm, or other sexual complaints.

The causes of women's sexual problems are classified by Tiefer (2001) into four main groupings:

- Sexual problems due to sociocultural, political, or economic factors
- Sexual problems relating to a partner or a relationship
- Sexual problems due to psychological factors
- Sexual problems due to medical factors

The New View classification is an improvement over the DSM-IV perspective on sexual response, which is based on a medical model of men's sexuality. However, empirical data supporting the usefulness and validity of the new classification system has not been collected. Moreover, this radical departure from the DSM-IV system means that there is no continuity of research between the two systems. Also, an overriding question exists: Is it useful to diagnose sexual dysfunction on the basis of causes rather than on the basis of symptoms? Moreover, with a new system, we need to start all over again in determining the prevalence of sexual difficulties. What we previously knew about the rates of sexual desire, arousal, orgasm, and genital pain complaints would thus be lost.

Lori A. Brotto, PhD, is an assistant professor in the Department of Obstetrics and Gynaecology at the University of British Columbia.

Source: Rathus, Nevid, Fichner-Rathus, & Herold, 2010, p. 366. Reprinted with permission by Pearson Canada Inc.

ORGASM DISORDERS Orgasm, or sexual climax, is an involuntary reflex that results in rhythmic contractions of the pelvic muscles and is usually accompanied by feelings of intense pleasure. In men, these contractions are accompanied by expulsion of semen. There are three specific types of orgasm disorders: **female orgasmic disorder, male orgasmic disorder,** and **premature ejaculation.**

Orgasmic disorder refers to persistent or recurrent delay in reaching orgasm or the absence of orgasm following a normal level of sexual interest and arousal. The clinician needs to make a judgment about whether there is an "adequate" amount and type of stimulation to achieve an orgasmic response. There is a broad range of normal variation in sexual response that needs to be considered. Many women, for example, require direct clitoral stimulation (by means of stimulation by her own hand or her partner's) in order to achieve orgasm during vaginal intercourse. This should not be considered abnormal, because the clitoris, not the vagina, is the woman's most erotically sensitive organ.

In men, recurrent or persistent difficulty achieving orgasm following a normal pattern of sexual interest and excitement is termed *male orgasmic disorder*. This disorder is relatively rare and has received very little attention in the clinical literature (Rosen & Leiblum, 1995). Men with this problem can usually reach orgasm through masturbation but not through intercourse.

Premature ejaculation is defined as a recurrent or persistent pattern of ejaculation with minimal sexual stimulation. It can occur prior to, upon, or shortly after penetration, but before the man desires it. Note the subjective elements. In making the diagnosis, the clinician weighs the man's age, the novelty of the partner, and the frequency of sexual activity. Occasional experiences of rapid ejaculation, such as when the man is with a new partner, has had infrequent sexual contacts, or is very highly aroused, fall within the normal spectrum. More persistent patterns of premature ejaculation would occasion a diagnosis of the disorder. About one in three men experience premature ejaculation (Hellstrom et al., 2006).

SEXUAL PAIN DISORDERS In **dyspareunia,** sexual intercourse is associated with recurrent pain in the genital region. The pain cannot be explained fully by an underlying medical condition and so is believed to have a psychological component. However, many, perhaps even most, cases of pain during intercourse are traceable to an underlying medical condition, such as insufficient lubrication or a urinary tract infection. The DSM classifies these cases under a different diagnostic label, "Sexual Dysfunction Due to Medical Condition."

Dyspareunia can occur in both men and women but is more common in women (Meana & Binik, 1994). Women who seek treatment for this disorder are often afraid of intercourse and vaginal penetration (Reissing, Binik, & Khalifé, 1999). McGill University psychologist Yitzchak Binik and colleagues argue that dyspareunia is primarily a pain syndrome rather than a sexual dysfunction (Binik, 2005).

Vaginismus involves an involuntary spasm of the muscles surrounding the vagina when vaginal penetration is attempted, making sexual intercourse painful or impossible.

Theoretical Perspectives

As emphasized by internationally renowned University of British Columbia sexologist Rosemary Basson (2001, 2005), sexual dysfunctions, like most psychological disorders, reflect a complex interplay of biological, psychological, and other factors.

BIOLOGICAL PERSPECTIVES Deficient testosterone production and thyroid overactivity or underactivity are among the many biological conditions that can lead to impaired sexual desire (Kresin, 1993). Medical conditions can also impair sexual arousal in both men and women (Graber, 1993). Diabetes, for instance, is the most common organic cause of erectile dysfunction, with estimates indicating that half of diabetic men eventually suffer some degree of erectile dysfunction (Thomas & LoPiccolo, 1994). Diabetes may also impair sexual response in women, with decreased vaginal lubrication being the most common consequence.

female orgasmic disorder Type of sexual dysfunction in women involving difficulties achieving orgasm.

male orgasmic disorder Type of sexual dysfunction in men involving persistent difficulties achieving orgasm.

premature ejaculation Type of sexual dysfunction involving a persistent or recurrent pattern of ejaculation occurring during sexual activity at a point before the man desires it.

dyspareunia Persistent or recurrent pain experienced during or following sexual intercourse.

vaginismus Type of sexual dysfunction characterized by the recurrent or persistent contraction of the muscles surrounding the vaginal entrance, making penile entry while attempting intercourse difficult or impossible.

Biological factors may play a prominent role in as many as 70% to 80% of cases of erectile dysfunction (Brody, 1995). Other biological factors that can impair sexual desire, arousal, and orgasm include nerve-damaging conditions such as multiple sclerosis, lung disorders, kidney disease, circulatory problems, damage caused by sexually transmitted diseases, and side effects of various drugs (Brody, 1995; Segraves, 1988). Yet even in cases of sexual dysfunction that are traced to physical causes, emotional problems such as anxiety, depression, and marital conflict can compound the problem.

The male sex hormone testosterone plays a pivotal role in sexual interest and functioning in women as well as men (both genders produce testosterone in varying amounts) (Meston & Bradford, 2006). Men with deficient production of testosterone may lose sexual interest and the capacity for erections (Kresin, 1993). The adrenal glands and ovaries are the sites of testosterone production in women. Women who have these organs surgically removed because of invasive disease no longer produce testosterone and may gradually lose sexual interest and the capacity for sexual response. Although hormonal deficiencies may play a role in sexual dysfunction in such cases, researchers find that most men and women with sexual dysfunctions have normal hormone levels (Schreiner-Engel, Schiavi, White, & Ghizzani, 1989; F. M. Stuart, Hammond, & Pett, 1987).

Many temporary physical conditions can lead to problems in desire, arousal, and orgasm—even to sexual pain. Fatigue impairs sexual response and can lead to genital pain if the couple persists in attempting intercourse. Depressants such as tranquillizers, alcohol, and narcotics can lessen sexual response (Segraves, 1988). These effects are normally isolated unless people do not recognize their causes and attach too much meaning to them. That is, if you are intoxicated and do not know that alcohol can suppress your sexual response, you may wonder whether there is something wrong with you. Biological factors may thus interact with psychological factors in leading to the development of a persistent problem. Because of your concern, you may try to bear down during your next sexual opportunity, causing anxiety that may further interfere with normal sexual response. A second failure may strengthen self-doubts, creating more anxiety, which in turn stems performance, which may lead to a vicious cycle resulting in repeated failure experiences.

PSYCHODYNAMIC PERSPECTIVES Psychodynamic hypotheses generally involve conflicts of the phallic stage (Fenichel, 1945). Mature genital sexuality is believed to require successful resolution of the Oedipus and Electra complexes. Men with sexual dysfunctions are presumed to suffer from unconscious castration anxiety. Sexual intercourse elicits an unconscious fear of retaliation by the father, rendering the vagina unsafe. Erectile dysfunction "saves" the man from having to enter the vagina. Premature ejaculation allows him to "escape" rapidly and may also represent unconscious hatred of women (H. S. Kaplan, 1974). Orgasmic disorder prevents him from completing the act and unconsciously minimizes his guilt and fear. Rapid ejaculation serves the unconscious purpose of expressing hatred through soiling the woman and denying her sexual pleasure.

In women, unresolved penis envy engenders hostility toward men. The woman who remains fixated in the phallic stage punishes her partner for having a penis by not permitting the organ to bring her pleasure, as in female sexual arousal disorder. The clamping down of the vaginal muscles in vaginismus may express an unconscious wish to castrate her partner (H. S. Kaplan, 1974). In orgasmic disorder, she has failed to overcome penis envy and to develop mature sexuality, which involves transferring erotic feelings from the clitoris to the vagina. She thus prevents orgasm from occurring through intercourse. It is difficult to test the validity of the psychoanalytic concepts because they involve unconscious conflicts, like castration anxiety and penis envy, that cannot be scientifically observed. Evidence for these views relies on case studies

When a source of pleasure becomes a source of anxiety.
Sexual dysfunctions can be a source of intense personal distress and lead to friction between partners. Problems in communication can give rise to or exacerbate sexual dysfunctions.

that involve interpretation of patients' histories. Case-study accounts are open to rival interpretations. We can say with certainty, however, that despite the traditional psychoanalytic conception, clitoral stimulation remains a key part of the woman's erotic response as she matures and is not a sign of an immature fixation.

LEARNING PERSPECTIVES Learning theorists focus on the role of conditioned anxiety in the development of sexual dysfunctions. The occurrence of physically or psychologically painful experiences associated with sexual activity may cause a person to respond to sexual encounters with anxiety that is strong enough to counteract sexual pleasure and performance. A history of sexual abuse or sexual assault plays a role in many cases in women with sexual arousal disorder, sexual aversion disorder, orgasmic disorder, or vaginismus. People who were sexually traumatized earlier in life may find it difficult to respond sexually when they develop intimate relationships. They may be flooded with feelings of helplessness, unresolved anger, or misplaced guilt, or experience flashbacks of the abusive experiences when they engage in sexual relations with their partners, preventing them from becoming sexually aroused or achieving orgasm.

Sexual fulfillment is also based on learning sexual skills. Sexual skills or competencies, like other types of skills, are acquired through opportunities for new learning. We learn about how our bodies and our partners' bodies respond sexually in various ways, including trial and error with our partners, learning about our own sexual response through self-exploration (as in masturbation), reading about sexual techniques, and perhaps by talking to others or viewing sex films or videos. Yet those who have been raised to feel guilty or anxious about sex may have lacked such opportunities to develop sexual knowledge and skills. Consequently, they may respond to sexual opportunities with feelings of anxiety and shame rather than arousal and pleasure.

COGNITIVE PERSPECTIVES Irrational beliefs and attitudes may contribute to sexual dysfunctions (Meston & Bradford, 2006). Consider the irrational beliefs that we must have the approval at all times of everyone who is important to us and we must be thoroughly competent at everything we do. If we cannot accept the occasional disappointment of others, we may catastrophize the significance of a single frustrating sexual episode. If we insist that every sexual experience must be perfect, we set the stage for inevitable failure.

Helen Singer Kaplan (1974) noted problems that can occur with our ability to regulate our levels of sexual arousal. Men who ejaculate prematurely, for example, may have difficulty gauging their level of sexual arousal. As a consequence, they may not be able to temporarily suspend stimulation in time to delay ejaculation. Most men respond to sexual arousal with positive emotions, such as joy and warmth. But for men with sexual dysfunctions, sexual arousal becomes disconnected from positive emotions (Rowland, Cooper, & Slob, 1996). Psychologist David Barlow (1986) proposed that anxiety may have inhibiting or arousing effects on sexual response depending on the man's thought processes (see Figure 9.2 on page 346). For men with sexual dysfunctions, anxiety has inhibiting effects. Perhaps because they expect to fail in sexual encounters, their thoughts are focused on anticipated feelings of shame and embarrassment rather than on erotic stimuli. Concerns about failing increase autonomic arousal or anxiety, which leads men to focus even more attention on the consequences of failure, which in turn leads to dysfunctional performance. Failure experiences in turn lead to avoidance of sexual encounters because these situations have become encoded as opportunities for repeated failure, frustration, and self-defeat. Functional men, by contrast, expect to succeed and focus their attention on erotic stimuli, not on fears of failure. Their erotic attentional focus increases autonomic arousal or anxiety, but not to the point that it interferes with their sexual response. Mild anxiety may actually enhance their sexual arousal. By focusing on erotic cues, functional men become more aroused, successfully engage in sexual activity, and heighten their expectations of a future successful performance—all leading to increased approach tendencies.

The cognitive model formulated by Barlow highlights the role of interfering cognitions in sexual dysfunctions. Interfering cognitions include expectancies of failure that are evoked by performance demands. They heighten anxiety to the point of impairing

FIGURE 9.2 Barlow's model of erectile dysfunction. In this model, past experience with erectile dysfunction leads men to expect that they will fail again. They consequently focus on anticipated feelings of shame and embarrassment when they engage in sexual relations rather than on erotic stimuli. These concerns heighten their anxiety, impairing their performance and distracting them from erotic cues. Functional men, by contrast, expect to succeed and focus more of their attention on erotic stimuli, which heightens their sexual response. Although they too may experience anxiety, it is not severe enough to distract them from erotic cues or impair their performance. *Source:* Barlow, 1986, pp. 140–148.

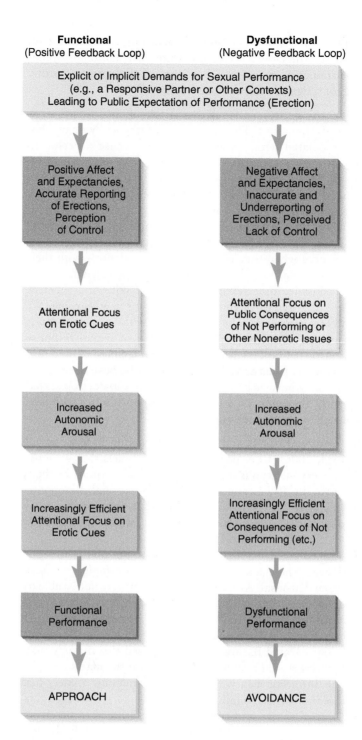

Functional (Positive Feedback Loop) — Dysfunctional (Negative Feedback Loop)

Explicit or Implicit Demands for Sexual Performance (e.g., a Responsive Partner or Other Contexts) Leading to Public Expectation of Performance (Erection)

Positive Affect and Expectancies, Accurate Reporting of Erections, Perception of Control | Negative Affect and Expectancies, Inaccurate and Underreporting of Erections, Perceived Lack of Control

Attentional Focus on Erotic Cues | Attentional Focus on Public Consequences of Not Performing or Other Nonerotic Issues

Increased Autonomic Arousal | Increased Autonomic Arousal

Increasingly Efficient Attentional Focus on Erotic Cues | Increasingly Efficient Attentional Focus on Consequences of Not Performing (etc.)

Functional Performance | Dysfunctional Performance

APPROACH | AVOIDANCE

sexual performance. In a vicious cycle, the more people focus on these interfering cognitions, the more difficult it will be for them to perform sexually—and the more likely it is that they will focus on interfering cognitions in the future. Although the model was derived from research on men, Barlow believes it may also help explain sexual dysfunctions in women.

PROBLEMS IN RELATIONSHIPS "It takes two to tango," as they say. Sexual relations are usually no better than other facets of relationships or marriages (Perlman & Abramson, 1982). Couples who harbour resentments toward each other may choose the sexual arena for combat. Communication problems, moreover, are linked to general marital dissatisfaction. Couples who find it difficult to communicate their sexual desires may lack the means to help their partners become more effective lovers.

SOCIOCULTURAL PERSPECTIVES At around the turn of the last century, an English-woman was quoted as saying she would "close her eyes and think of England" when her husband engaged her in sexual relations. This old-fashioned stereotype suggests how sexual pleasure was once considered exclusively a male preserve—for women, sex was primarily a duty. Mothers usually informed their daughters of the conjugal duties before the wedding, and girls encoded sex as just one of the ways in which women serviced the needs of others. Women who harbour such stereotypical attitudes toward female sexuality may be unlikely to become aware of their sexual potentials. In addition, sexual anxieties may transform negative expectations into self-fulfilling prophecies. Sexual dysfunctions in men, too, may be linked to severely restricted sociocultural beliefs and sexual taboos.

Modern psychodynamic theorists recognize that anger and other negative feelings women may hold toward men can lead to sexual dysfunctions. Yet they believe that these negative emotions stem from sociocultural factors rather than penis envy. Women in our society are often socialized to sacrifice for and submit to their husbands, which may engender rebellion through becoming sexually unresponsive.

Sociocultural factors also play an important role in erectile dysfunction. Investigators find a greater incidence of erectile dysfunction in cultures with more restrictive sexual attitudes toward premarital sex among females, sex in marriage, and extramarital sex (Welch & Kartub, 1978). Men in these cultures may be prone to developing sexual anxiety or guilt that may interfere with sexual performance.

PSYCHOLOGICAL FACTORS Various psychological factors such as depression, anxiety, guilt, and low self-esteem can impair sexual interest or performance. One principal culprit is **performance anxiety**, a type of anxiety that involves an excessive concern about whether we will be able to perform successfully. People troubled by performance anxiety become spectators during sex rather than performers. Their attention is focused on how their bodies are responding (or not responding) to sexual stimulation and on concerns they have about the negative consequences of failing to perform adequately, rather than absorbing themselves in their erotic experiences. Men with performance anxiety may have difficulty achieving or maintaining an erection or may ejaculate prematurely; women may fail to become adequately aroused or have difficulty achieving orgasm. A vicious cycle may ensue in which each failure experience instills deeper doubts, which lead to more anxiety during sexual encounters, which occasions repeated failure, and so on.

In Western cultures, the connection between a man's sexual performance and his sense of manhood is deeply ingrained. The man who repeatedly fails to perform sexually may suffer a loss of self-esteem, become depressed, or feel he is no longer a man (M. P. Carey, Wincze, & Meisler, 1998). He may see himself as a total failure, despite other accomplishments in life. Sexual opportunities are construed as tests of his manhood, and he may respond to them by bearing down and trying to will (force) an erection. Willing an erection may backfire because erection is a reflex that cannot be forced. With so much of his self-esteem riding on the line whenever he makes love, it is little wonder that anxiety about the quality of his performance—performance anxiety—may mount to a point that it inhibits erection. The erectile reflex is controlled by the parasympathetic branch of the autonomic nervous system. Activation of the sympathetic nervous system, which occurs when we are anxious, can block parasympathetic control, preventing the erectile reflex from occurring. Ejaculation, in contrast, is under sympathetic nervous system control, so heightened levels of arousal, as in the case of performance anxiety, can trigger premature ejaculation.

One client who suffered erectile dysfunction described his feelings of sexual inadequacy this way:

I always felt inferior, like I was on probation, having to prove myself. I felt like I was up against the wall. You can't imagine how embarrassing this was. It's like you walk out in front of an audience that you think is a nudist convention and it turns out to be a tuxedo convention.

The Authors' Files

performance anxiety Fear relating to the threat of failing to perform adequately.

Another man described how performance anxiety led him to prepare for sexual relations as though he were psyching himself up for a big game:

> At work I have control over what I do. With sex, you don't have control over your sex organ. I know that my mind can control what my hands do. But the same is not true of my penis. I had begun to view sex as a basketball game. I used to play in college. When I would prepare for a game, I'd always be thinking, "Who was I guarding that night?" I'd try to psych myself up, sketching out in my mind how to play this guy, thinking through all possible moves and plays. I began to do the same thing with sex. If I were dating someone, I'd be thinking the whole evening about what might happen in bed. I'd always be preparing for the outcome. I'd sketch out in my mind how I was going to touch her, what I'd ask her to do. But all the time, right through dinner or the movies, I'd be worrying that I wouldn't get it up. I kept picturing her face and how disappointed she'd be. By the time we did go to bed, I was paralyzed with anxiety.
>
> The Authors' Files

Women, too, may equate their self-esteem with their ability to reach frequent and intense orgasms. Yet when men and women try to bear down to will arousal or lubrication or to force an orgasm, they may find that the harder they try, the more these responses elude them. Forty years ago the pressures concerning sex often revolved around the issue "Should I or shouldn't I?" Today, however, the pressures for both men and women are often based more on achieving performance goals relating to proficiency at reaching orgasm and satisfying one's partner's sexual needs.

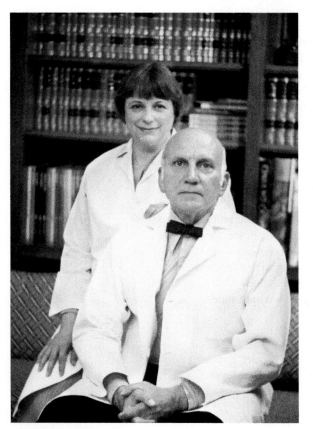

Masters and Johnson. Sex therapists William Masters and Virginia Johnson.

Sex Therapy

Until the groundbreaking work of sex researchers William Masters and Virginia Johnson in the 1960s, there was no effective treatment for most sexual dysfunctions. Psychoanalytic forms of therapy approached sexual dysfunctions indirectly, for example. It was assumed that sexual dysfunctions represented underlying conflicts and that the dysfunctions might abate if the underlying conflicts—the presumed causes of the dysfunctions—were resolved through psychoanalysis. A lack of evidence that psychoanalytic approaches reversed sexual dysfunctions led clinicians and researchers to develop other approaches that would focus more directly on the sexual problems themselves.

Most contemporary sex therapists assume that sexual dysfunctions can be treated by directly modifying a couple's sexual interactions. Pioneered by Masters and Johnson, sex therapy employs a variety of relatively brief, cognitive-behavioural techniques that centre on enhancing self-efficacy expectancies, improving a couple's ability to communicate, fostering sexual competencies (sexual knowledge and skills), and reducing performance anxiety. Therapists may also work with couples to help them iron out problems in their relationship that may impede sexual functioning. When feasible, both sex partners are involved in therapy. In some cases, however, individual therapy may be preferable, as we shall see.

Significant changes have occurred in the treatment of sexual dysfunctions in the past 20 years. There is greater emphasis now on the role of biological or organic factors in the development of sexual problems and greater use of medical treatments, such as the use of the drugs Viagra, Cialis, and Levitra, in treating male erectile dysfunction. But even men whose erectile problems can be traced to physical causes can benefit from sex therapy along with medical intervention (Bach, Barlow, & Wincze, 2004).

Let us briefly survey some of the more common sex-therapy techniques for particular types of disorders.

SEXUAL DESIRE DISORDERS Sex therapists may try to help people with low sexual desire kindle their sexual appetite through the use of self-stimulation (masturbation) exercises together with erotic fantasies (Leiblum, 2006). Or, in working with couples, the therapist might prescribe mutual pleasuring exercises the couple could perform at home or encourage them to expand their sexual repertoire in order to add novelty and excitement to their sex life. When a lack of sexual desire is connected with depression, the treatment would probably focus on relieving the underlying depression in the hope that sexual interest would rebound when the depression lifts. When problems of low sexual desire or sexual aversion appear to be rooted in deep-seated causes, sex therapist Helen Singer Kaplan (1987) has recommended the use of insight-oriented approaches to help uncover and resolve underlying issues. Some cases of hypoactive sexual desire involve hormonal deficiencies, especially lack of testosterone. Testosterone replacement is effective only in the relatively few cases in which production of the hormone is truly deficient (Simpkins & Van Meter, 2005). A lack of sexual desire may also reflect relationship problems that may need to be addressed through couples therapy. Couples therapy might also be used when sexual dysfunction develops from problems in the relationship (McCarthy & Bodnar, 2005). In other cases of sexual aversion, a program of mutual pleasuring, beginning with partner stimulation in nongenital areas and gradually progressing to genital stimulation, may help desensitize fears about sexual contact.

DISORDERS OF AROUSAL Women who have difficulty becoming sexually aroused and men with erectile problems are first educated to the fact that they need not "do" anything to become aroused. As long as their problems are psychological, not organic, they need only experience sexual stimulation under relaxed, nonpressured conditions, so that disruptive cognitions and anxiety do not inhibit reflexive responses.

Masters and Johnson have the couple counter performance anxiety by engaging in **sensate focus exercises**. These are nondemand sexual contacts—sensuous exercises that do not demand sexual arousal in the form of vaginal lubrication or erection. Partners begin by massaging each other without touching the genitals. The partners learn to "pleasure" each other and to "be pleasured" by means of following and giving verbal instructions and by guiding each other's hands. The method fosters both communication and sexual skills and countermands anxiety because there is no demand for sexual arousal. After several sessions, direct massage of the genitals is included in the pleasuring exercise. Even when obvious signs of sexual excitement are produced (lubrication or erection), the couple does not straightaway engage in intercourse, because intercourse might create performance demands. After excitement is achieved consistently, the couple engages in a relaxed sequence of other sexual activities, culminating eventually in intercourse.

A number of similar sex-therapy methods were employed in the case of Victor P.:

sensate focus exercises In sex therapy, mutual pleasuring activities between partners that are focused on the partners taking turns giving and receiving physical pleasure.

Victor P., a 44-year-old concert violinist, was eager to show the therapist reviews of his concert tour. A solo violinist with a distinguished orchestra, Victor's life revolved around practice, performances, and reviews. He dazzled audiences with his technique and the energy of his performance. As a concert musician, Victor had exquisite control over his body, especially his hands. Yet he could not control his erectile response in the same way. Since his divorce seven years earlier, Victor had been troubled by recurrent episodes of erectile failure. Time and time again he had become involved in a new relationship, only to find himself unable to perform sexually. Fearing repetition, he would sever the relationship. He was unable to face an audience of only one. For a while, he dated casually, but then he met Michelle.

Michelle was a writer who loved music. They were a perfect match because Victor, the musician, loved literature. Michelle, a 35-year-old divorcée, was exciting, earthy, sensual, and accepting. The couple soon grew inseparable. He would practise while she would write—poetry mostly, but also short magazine pieces. Unlike some women Victor met who did not know Bach from Bartok, Michelle held her own in conversations with Victor's friends and fellow musicians over a late-night dinner. They kept their own apartments; Victor needed his own space and solitude for practice.

In the nine months of their relationship, Victor was unable to perform on the stage that mattered most to him—his canopied bed. It was just so frustrating. He said, "I would become erect and then just as I approach her to penetrate, pow! It collapses on me." Victor's history of nocturnal erections and erections during light petting suggested that he was basically suffering from performance anxiety. He was bearing down to force an erection, much as he might try to learn the fingering of a difficult violin piece. Each night became a command performance in which Victor served as his own harshest critic. Victor became a spectator to his own performance, a role that Masters and Johnson refer to as **self-spectatoring**. Rather than focusing on his partner, his attention was riveted on the size of his penis. As noted by the late great pianist Vladimir Horowitz, the worst thing a pianist can do is watch his fingers. Perhaps the worst thing a man with erectile problems can do is watch his penis.

To break the vicious cycle of anxiety, erectile failure, and more anxiety, Victor and Michelle followed a sex-therapy program (Rathus & Nevid, 1977) modelled after the Masters and Johnson–type treatment. The aim was to restore the pleasure of sexual activity, unfettered by anxiety. The couple was initially instructed to abstain from attempts at intercourse to free Victor from any pressure to perform. The couple progressed through a series of steps:

1. Relaxing together in the nude without any touching, such as when reading or watching television together.
2. Sensate focus exercises.
3. Genital stimulation of each other manually or orally to orgasm.
4. Nondemand intercourse (intercourse performed without any pressure on the man to satisfy his partner). The man may afterward help his partner achieve orgasm by using manual or oral stimulation.
5. Resumption of vigorous intercourse (intercourse involving more vigorous thrusting and use of alternative positions and techniques that focus on mutual satisfaction). The couple is instructed not to catastrophize occasional problems that may arise.

The therapy program helped Victor overcome his erectile disorder. Victor was freed of the need to prove himself by achieving erection on command. He surrendered his post as critic. Once the spotlight was off the bed, he became a participant and not a spectator.

The Authors' Files

self-spectatoring Tendency to observe one's behaviour as if one were a spectator of oneself. People with sexual dysfunctions often become self-spectators in the sense of focusing their attention during sexual activity on the response of their sex organs rather than on their partners or the sexual stimulation itself.

DISORDERS OF ORGASM Women with orgasmic disorder often harbour underlying beliefs that sex is dirty or sinful. They may have been taught not to touch themselves. They are often anxious about sex and have not learned, through trial and error, what kinds of sexual stimulation will arouse them and help them reach orgasm. Treatment in these cases includes modification of negative attitudes toward sex. When orgasmic disorder reflects the woman's feelings about, or relationship with, her partner, treatment requires working through these feelings or enhancing the relationship.

In either case, Masters and Johnson work with the couple and first use sensate focus exercises to lessen performance anxiety, open channels of communication, and help the couple acquire pleasuring skills. Then during genital massage and, later, during intercourse, the woman directs her partner to use caresses and techniques that stimulate her. By taking charge, the woman becomes psychologically freed from the stereotype of the passive, submissive female role.

Many researchers find that a program of directed masturbation is most effective in helping preorgasmic women—women who have never achieved orgasm through any means (Baucom, Shoham, Mueser, Daiuto, & Stickle, 1998; Heiman & LoPiccolo, 1987; LoPiccolo & Stock, 1986). Masturbation provides a chance to learn about one's own body and give oneself pleasure without reliance on a partner or need to attend to a partner's needs. Directed masturbation programs educate women about their sexual anatomy and encourage them to experiment with self-caresses in the privacy of their own homes. Women proceed at their own pace and are encouraged to incorporate sexual fantasies and imagery during self-stimulation exercises designed to heighten their level of sexual arousal. They gradually learn to bring themselves to orgasm, sometimes with the help of a vibrator. Once women can masturbate to orgasm, additional couples-oriented treatment can facilitate but does not guarantee transference to orgasm with a partner (Heiman & LoPiccolo, 1987; LoPiccolo & Stock, 1986).

Although scant attention in the scientific literature has been focused on male orgasmic disorder, the standard treatment, barring any underlying organic problem, focuses on increasing sexual stimulation and reducing performance anxiety (LoPiccolo, 1990; LoPiccolo & Stock, 1986).

The most widely used approach to treating premature ejaculation, called the *stop–start* or *stop-and-go technique*, was introduced in 1956 by the urologist James Semans. The man and his partner just suspend sexual activity when he is about to ejaculate and then resume stimulation when his sensations subside. Repeated practice enables the man to regulate ejaculation by sensitizing him to the cues that precede the ejaculatory reflex (making him more aware of his "point of no return," the point at which the ejaculatory reflex is triggered).

VAGINISMUS AND DYSPAREUNIA Vaginismus is a conditioned reflex involving the involuntary constriction of the vaginal opening. It involves a psychologically based fear of penetration, rather than a physical defect or disorder (LoPiccolo & Stock, 1986). Treatment for vaginismus involves a combination of cognitive-behavioural exercises, such as relaxation techniques, and the use of vaginal dilators to gradually desensitize the vaginal musculature. The woman herself regulates the insertion of dilators (plastic rods) of increasing diameter, always proceeding at her own pace to avoid any discomfort (LoPiccolo & Stock, 1986). The method is generally successful as long as it is unhurried. Because women with vaginismus often have histories of sexual molestation or sexual assault, psychotherapy may be part of the treatment program in order to deal with the psychological consequences of traumatic experiences (LoPiccolo & Stock, 1986). In cases of painful intercourse or dyspareunia, treatment focuses on attempting to resolve the underlying psychological or medical conditions that give rise to the pain.

Research from McGill University supports the value of cognitive-behavioural therapy for dyspareunia but also suggests that a surgical intervention called *vestibulectomy* may be very effective (Bergeron et al., 2001). Vestibulectomy involves the surgical removal of the vulvar tissue that appears to be the source of pain in dyspareunia.

EVALUATION OF SEX THERAPY Success rates for sex therapy have been more impressive for some disorders than others. High levels of success are reported in treating vaginismus in women and premature ejaculation in men (J. G. Beck, 1993; O'Donohue, Letourneau, & Geer, 1993). Reported success rates in treating vaginismus have ranged as high as 80% (Hawton & Catalan, 1990) to 100% (Masters & Johnson, 1970). Success rates in treating premature ejaculation with the stop–start or squeeze procedures have been reported as high as 95%, but relapse rates tend to be high (Segraves & Althof, 1998). Success rates in treating erectile dysfunction with sex therapy techniques are more variable (Rosen, 1996), and we still lack the methodologically sound studies needed to support the effectiveness of these techniques (O'Donohue, Swingen, Dopke, & Regev, 1999). Outcomes of treatment for male orgasmic disorder also vary and are often disappointing (Dekker, 1993).

How Do You Find a Qualified Sex Therapist?

How would you locate a sex therapist if you had a sexual dysfunction? Since provinces do not regulate use of the term sex *therapist,* it is essential to determine that a sex therapist is a member of a recognized profession (such as psychology, social work, medicine, or marriage and family counselling) and has had training and supervision in sex therapy. Professionals are usually licensed or certified by their provinces. (All provinces require licensing of psychologists and physicians, but some provinces do not license social workers or marriage counsellors.) Only physicians are permitted to bill their provincial health plans for providing sex therapy services.

If you are uncertain how to locate a qualified sex therapist in your area, try your university or college psychology department, health department, or counselling centre; a medical or psychological association; a marriage and family therapy association; a family physician; or your instructor.

Relatively few people in Canada have been trained as specialists in sex therapy. The only Canadian organization that certifies sex therapists is the Board of Examiners in Sex Therapy and Counselling in Ontario (BESTCO), comprising professionals from diverse backgrounds with clinical expertise in human sexual concerns.

Some Canadian therapists are also certified by American-based organizations such as the American Association of Sex Educators, Counselors, and Therapists (AASECT) and the Society for Sex Therapy and Research (SSTAR).

Ethical professionals are not annoyed or embarrassed if you ask them (1) what their profession is, (2) where they earned their advanced degree, and (3) whether they are licensed or certified, or if you inquire about (4) their fees, (5) their plans for treatment, and (6) their training in human sexuality and sex therapy. These questions are important because there is such a wide diversity in the professional background and training of sex therapists. Accordingly, the type of treatments and services that are available vary enormously (Kleinplatz, 2003). If the therapist becomes uncomfortable, asks why you are asking such questions, or fails to provide a direct answer, beware.

Professionals are also prohibited, by the ethical principles of their professions, from engaging in unethical practices, such as sexual relations with their clients. Any therapist who makes a sexual overture toward a client, or tries to persuade a client to engage in sexual relations, is acting unethically.

Source: Rathus, Nevid, Fichner-Rathus, & Herold, 2010, p. 375. Reprinted with permission by Pearson Canada Inc.

Although some progress has been made in treating sexual desire disorders, we would benefit from new treatment methods because current techniques often fail to resolve the problem (J. G. Beck, 1995; Hawton, 1991). Better results are generally reported from directed masturbation programs for preorgasmic women, with success rates measured as the percentage of women achieving orgasm reported in a range of 70% to 90% (Rosen & Leiblum, 1995). However, much lower rates are reported when measured in terms of percentages of women reporting orgasm during sexual intercourse with their partners (Segraves & Althof, 1998). Some researchers believe that the final determination of the effectiveness of directed masturbation as a treatment alternative remains to be made (O'Donohue, Dopke, & Swingen, 1997).

Biological Treatments of Male Sexual Dysfunctions

Biological treatments of erectile disorder have included silicone implants, hormonal treatments, injections of muscle relaxants, vascular surgery, and medications that promise to help men with erectile dysfunction achieve erections. The popularity of penile implants (semirigid or inflatable silicone rods) has fallen off over the years because of their invasiveness and potential complications and because less intrusive treatments are now available (Rosen, 1996). In 1998, the first drug was approved for the treatment of erectile dysfunction (Morrow, 1998). Called Viagra, the drug expands blood vessels in the penis, which increases the flow of blood to the penis and in turn causes erection (I. Goldstein et al., 1998). Taken about an hour before sexual relations, the drug has helped 70% to 80% of patients achieve erections. Similar findings have been reported with related drugs such as Cialis and Levitra. In the first few weeks following its release to the public, Viagra became the fastest-selling new drug in history. Viagra and some related drugs have also been tried to help women with sexual dysfunctions, but so far the results suggest that they are no better than placebos (Basson, McInnes, Smith, Hodgson, & Koppiker, 2002; Meston & Bradford, 2006).

Hormone treatments may be helpful for men with abnormally low levels of male sex hormones but not for those whose hormone levels are within normal limits (Simpkins & Van Meter, 2005). Because hormone treatments can have side effects, such as liver damage, they should not be undertaken lightly.

Vascular surgery may be effective in rare cases in which blockage in the blood vessels prevents blood from swelling the penis or in which the penis is structurally defective (Mohr & Beutler, 1990).

Evidence indicates that SSRI-type antidepressant drugs may also help delay ejaculation in men with premature ejaculation (Kim & Seo, 1998). These drugs affect the availability of neurotransmitters that may play a role in the brain's regulation of the ejaculatory reflex.

All in all, the success rates reported for treating sexual dysfunctions through psychological or biological approaches are quite encouraging, especially when we remember that only a generation or two ago there were no effective treatments available.

REVIEW IT

Sexual Dysfunctions

- **What are the major types of sexual dysfunctions?** Sexual dysfunctions include sexual desire disorders (hypoactive sexual desire disorder and sexual aversion disorder), sexual arousal disorders (female sexual arousal disorder and male erectile disorder), orgasm disorders (female and male orgasmic disorders and premature ejaculation), and sexual pain disorders (dyspareunia and vaginismus).
- **What causes sexual dysfunctions?** Sexual dysfunctions can stem from biological factors (such as disease or the effects of alcohol and other drugs), psychological factors (such as performance anxiety, unresolved conflicts, or lack of sexual competencies), and sociocultural factors (such as sexually restrictive cultural learning).
- **What are the major goals of sex therapy?** Sex therapists help people overcome sexual dysfunctions by enhancing self-efficacy expectancies, teaching sexual competencies, improving sexual communication, and reducing performance anxiety.

Define It

aggravated sexual assault, 336
bondage, 337
dyspareunia, 343
exhibitionism, 327
female orgasmic disorder, 343
female sexual arousal
    disorder, 342
fetishism, 328
frotteurism, 330
gender dysphoria, 322
gender identity, 322

gender identity disorder, 322
hypoactive sexual desire
    disorder, 341
hypoxyphilia, 332
male erectile disorder, 342
male orgasmic disorder, 343
paraphilias, 326
pedophilia, 330
performance anxiety, 347
premature ejaculation, 343
sadomasochism, 333

self-spectatoring, 350
sensate focus exercises, 349
sexual assault, 336
sexual aversion disorder, 341
sexual dysfunctions, 340
sexual masochism, 332
sexual sadism, 333
transvestic fetishism, 328
vaginismus, 343
voyeurism, 330

Think About It

- Do you believe that how children are reared by their parents plays a causative role in the development of gender identity disorder? Why or why not?

- Do you think our culture is to blame for socializing boys and young men into sexually aggressive roles? Why or why not?

- Do you believe that exhibitionists, voyeurs, and pedophiles should be punished, treated, or both? Explain.

- When does a sexual problem become a sexual dysfunction?

Weblinks

SexualityandU.ca   www.sexualityandu.ca
One of the best sources of sexuality information for young adults in Canada. Includes information for young people, parents, and physicians. Includes current research.

Notes on Gender Role Transition   www.avitale.com
This website contains information on gender identity disorder and some paraphilias.

The Lesbian, Gay, Bisexual, and Transgender Community Center   www.gaycenter.org
This site provides information on gender identity disorder.

Gender Identity Clinic   www.camh.net/About_CAMH/ Guide_to_CAMH/Mental_Health_Programs/ General_Psychiatry_Program/gid_guide_to_camh.html

This site describes treatment options for gender dysphoria from Toronto's Centre for Addiction and Mental Health.

Board of Examiners in Sex Therapy & Counselling in Ontario   www.bestco.info
The BESTCO organization set standards for the granting of registered status in sex therapy. It also identifies clinicians who have expertise in sex therapy.

Sexual Counselling   www.sexualcounselling.com
This site offers answers to a range of questions about sex, and specific questions can be submitted online.

 MySearchLab offers you extensive help with your writing and research projects and provides round-the-clock access to credible and reliable source material. Chapter quizzes and a full electronic version of the text are also provided. Take a tour at www.mysearchlab.com.

Gender Identity Disorder, Paraphilias, and Sexual Dysfunctions

Gender Identity Disorder

Theoretical Perspectives

Psychodynamic Perspective
- Overly close mother–son relationships, parents with empty relationships, and detached fathers lead to over-identifying with opposite-sex parent.

Learning Perspective
- For boys, unavailability of strong male role model; socialization patterns in families where parent wanted child of other gender.

Biological Perspective
- Interaction in utero between the developing brain and release of sex hormones.

Paraphilias

Exhibitionism

- Recurrent, powerful urges to expose genitals to unsuspecting strangers
- Intended to shock, surprise, or arouse victim

Fetishism

- Recurrent, powerful urges and arousing fantasies involving either inanimate objects or a particular body part

Transvestic Fetishism

- Recurrent, powerful sexual urges and fantasies involving cross-dressing
- Not to be confused with gender identity disorder (transsexualism)

Voyeurism

- Acting on or being strongly distressed by recurrent, powerful sexual urges and fantasies about watching unsuspecting people undressing or engaging in sex

Frotteurism

- Recurrent, powerful sexual urges and fantasies involving rubbing against or touching a nonconsenting person

Pedophilia

- Recurrent, powerful sexual urges and fantasies involving sexual activity with prepubescent children

Sexual Masochism

- Recurrent, powerful sexual urges and fantasies about sexual acts involving humiliation or suffering

Sexual Sadism

- Recurrent, powerful sexual urges and fantasies involving the humiliation or suffering of others

>>

Sexual Dysfunctions

Sexual Desire Disorders

- Hypoactive sexual desire disorder
- Sexual aversion disorder

Sexual Arousal Disorders

- Female sexual arousal disorder
- Male erectile disorder

Orgasm Disorders

- Female orgasmic disorder
- Male orgasmic disorder
- Premature ejaculation

Sexual Pain Disorders

- Dyspareunia
- Vaginismus

10

Schizophrenia

CHAPTER OUTLINE

Clinical Features of Schizophrenia
Historical Contributions to Concepts of Schizophrenia
Prevalence and Costs of Schizophrenia
Phases of Schizophrenia
Major Features of Schizophrenia
Subtypes of Schizophrenia
Categorical Model

Theoretical Perspectives
Psychodynamic Perspectives
Learning Perspectives
Biological Perspectives
The Diathesis-Stress Model
Family Theories

Treatment
Biological Approaches
Psychoanalytic Approaches
Learning-Based Approaches
Psychosocial Rehabilitation
Family-Intervention Programs
Early-Intervention Programs

Did You Know That...

- You cannot be diagnosed with schizophrenia until months have passed, even though you show all the signs of the disorder?

- Despite wide differences in cultures, the rate of schizophrenia is similar in both developed and developing nations throughout the world?

- Auditory hallucinations may be a form of inner speech?

- Some people with schizophrenia maintain unusual, seemingly uncomfortable positions for hours during which they will not respond to questions or communicate with others?

- Even if you have two parents with schizophrenia, your chances of developing the disorder are less than 1 in 2?

- Living in a family environment that is hostile, critical, and unsupportive increases the risk of relapse among people with schizophrenia?

- Drugs can help control but cannot cure schizophrenia?

Schizophrenia is perhaps the most puzzling and disabling clinical syndrome. It is the psychological disorder that best corresponds to popular conceptions of madness or lunacy. It often elicits fear, misunderstanding, and condemnation rather than sympathy and concern. Accordingly, social stigma is an important problem associated with schizophrenia. The disorder strikes at the heart of a person, stripping the mind of the intimate connections between thoughts and emotions and filling it with distorted perceptions, false ideas, and illogical conceptions, as in the case of Marilyn:

For someone who lives in total isolation, Marilyn R. has a lot of company. She's got the Cabir brothers. All five of them, all abusive, callous and unrelenting in their insults. Marilyn recalls a beating she suffered at the hands of a Cabir: "He just went crazy and said, 'I hate you.' And he grabbed an ashtray and just—pow!—hit me over the head with it. Put his teeth in my face and was going for the knife. . . ."

Marilyn starts to weep. It's a memory so vivid, so real, that the Cabirs' place of residence comes as a shock. "They're all in the wall. They just stand there and keep giving me slurs all the time. They say am I ever ugly, say 'I can't stand the sight of her,'" she explains. "Strange, isn't it?"

Marilyn finds a bi-weekly injection she gets at a downtown Toronto drop-in centre helps quiet the Cabirs. But it doesn't make them go away. They're in the walls every day and every night. They even follow her on the bus. The Cabirs—very real to Marilyn but invisible to a visitor—are only part of the story. The room she lives in is just as surreal—and far more frightening. It is crawling with cockroaches.

A swarm of hatchlings has taken over the table—probing every square millimetre of the surface. Marilyn sits, flyswatter in hand, trying to get as many as she can. Her conversation is interrupted frequently by the slap of her weapon. "I wish they'd go away," she says of the Cabirs. (Swat!) "He just stands there in the wall. He just stands there with his hands on his hips. He's there now. The whole family's there." (Swat!) In addition to the cockroaches, Marilyn has caught nine mice in her room. Scattered rodent droppings dot the thick shag carpet, a rug so heavily infested with insects, a visitor is grateful the room is partially dark.

The date is December 17. Marilyn has no plans for Christmas. And despite her appalling living conditions, she has no hope of finding anything better. She's been there five years. "I guess I'll be here the rest of my life," she says. In the spring of the following year, however, the City of Toronto got a look at 136 Jones Ave.—a look that convinced inspectors it was unfit for human habitation.

Marilyn was hooked up with a mental health worker, a woman who was astonished at the conditions in which she lived. The worker helped find her a new place; a considerable feat in a city where people like Marilyn languish on waiting lists for up to five years. Marilyn moved to a self-contained subsidized apartment in the Sherbourne–Dundas Street area. Not exactly prime real estate, but conditions are a world apart from her old place. "It was awful. Unbearable. I left a lot behind because those cockroaches used to get in my clothes." For her new apartment, Marilyn pays $300 a month—$30 less than her old place. And, she says, the surroundings have made a tremendous improvement in her mental health. "Oh, 100 per cent better!" she smiles. And she's still got company. "The Cabirs are here," she says. "There's five of them in the wall."

From S. Simmie (Oct. 4, 1998), "I'd sit in the kitchen and just shake,"
Toronto Star. Reprinted courtesy of the Atkinson Foundation.

Schizophrenia touches every facet of an affected person's life. Acute episodes of schizophrenia are characterized by delusions, hallucinations, illogical thinking, incoherent speech, and bizarre behaviour. Between acute episodes, people with schizophrenia may still be unable to think clearly and may lack appropriate emotional responses to people and events in their lives. They may speak in a flat tone and show little if any facial expressiveness. Although researchers are immersed in probing the psychological and biological foundations of schizophrenia, the disorder remains in many ways a mystery. In this chapter, we examine how research has illuminated our understanding of schizophrenia.

CLINICAL FEATURES OF SCHIZOPHRENIA

Although various forms of "madness" have afflicted people throughout the course of history, no one knows how long the behaviour pattern we now label **schizophrenia** existed before it was first described as a medical syndrome by Emil Kraepelin in 1893. Modern conceptualizations of schizophrenia have been largely shaped by the contributions of Kraepelin, Eugen Bleuler, and Kurt Schneider.

Historical Contributions to Concepts of Schizophrenia

Emil Kraepelin (1856–1926), one of the fathers of modern psychiatry, called the disorder we recognize today as schizophrenia *dementia praecox*. The term was derived from the Latin *dementis*, meaning "out" (*de-*) of one's "mind" (*mens*), and the roots that form the word *precocious*, meaning "before" one's level of "maturity." *Dementia praecox* thus refers to premature impairment of mental abilities. Kraepelin believed that dementia praecox was a disease process caused by specific, although unknown, pathology in the body.

Kraepelin wrote that dementia praecox involves the "loss of the inner unity of thought, feeling, and acting." The syndrome begins early in life, and the course of deterioration eventually results in complete "disintegration of the personality" (Kraepelin, 1909–1913, p. 943). Kraepelin's description of dementia praecox includes delusions, hallucinations, and odd motor behaviours—things that typically characterize the disorder today.

In 1911, the Swiss psychiatrist Eugen Bleuler (1857–1939) renamed dementia praecox *schizophrenia*, from the Greek *schistos*, meaning "cut" or "split," and *phren*, meaning "brain." In doing so, Bleuler focused on the major characteristic of the syndrome: the splitting of the brain functions that give rise to cognition, feelings or affective responses, and behaviour. A person with schizophrenia, for example, might giggle inappropriately when discussing an upsetting event, or might show no emotional expressiveness in the face of tragedy.

Although Bleuler accepted Kraepelin's description of the symptoms of schizophrenia, he did not accept Kraepelin's views that schizophrenia necessarily begins early in life and inevitably follows a deteriorating course. Bleuler proposed that schizophrenia follows a more variable course. In some cases, acute episodes occur intermittently. In others, there might be limited improvement rather than inevitable deterioration. Bleuler believed that schizophrenia could be recognized on the basis of four primary features or symptoms. Today, we refer to them as the **four As**:

1. **Associations.** Associations or relationships among thoughts become disturbed. We now call this type of disturbance *thought disorder* or *looseness of associations*. Looseness of associations means that ideas are strung together with little or no relationship among them, and the speaker does not appear to be aware of the lack of connectedness. The person's speech appears to others to become rambling and confused.

schizophrenia Enduring psychosis that involves failure to maintain integrated personality functioning, impaired reality testing, and disturbances in thinking. Common features of schizophrenia include delusions, hallucinations, flattened or inappropriate affect, and bizarre behaviour.

four As In Bleuler's view, the primary characteristics of schizophrenia: loose *associations*, blunted or inappropriate *affect*, *ambivalence*, and *autism*.

associations Linkages or relationships among thoughts or utterances.

affect Emotion or feeling state that is attached to objects, ideas, or life experiences. Pronounced *AF-fect*.

ambivalence A state in which a person holds conflicting feelings toward others, such as loving and hating a person at the same time.

autism (1) An absorption into daydreaming and fantasy. (2) A disorder in childhood characterized by failure to relate to others, lack of speech, disturbed motor behaviours, intellectual impairment, and demands for sameness in the environment. Also one of Bleuler's *Four As*, describing one of the primary symptoms of schizophrenia.

first-rank symptoms In Kurt Schneider's view, the primary features of schizophrenia, such as hallucinations and delusions, that distinctly characterize the disorder.

second-rank symptoms In Schneider's view, symptoms associated with schizophrenia that also occur in other psychological disorders.

2. **Affect.** Affect or emotional response becomes flattened or inappropriate. The individual may show a lack of response to upsetting events or burst into laughter upon hearing that a family member or friend has died.

3. **Ambivalence.** People with schizophrenia hold ambivalent or conflicting feelings toward others, such as loving and hating them at the same time.

4. **Autism.** Autism is withdrawal into a private fantasy world that is not bound by principles of logic. (Note that autism, as a feature of schizophrenia, is different from the disorder of childhood known as autism, which is discussed in Chapter 11.)

In Bleuler's view, hallucinations and delusions represent "secondary symptoms" that accompany the primary symptoms but do not define the disorder.

Another influential developer of modern concepts of schizophrenia was German psychiatrist Kurt Schneider (1887–1967). Schneider believed that Bleuler's criteria (his four As) were too vague for diagnostic purposes and that they failed to distinguish schizophrenia adequately from other disorders. Schneider (1957) distinguished between two sets of symptoms: **first-rank symptoms**, which he believed are central to diagnosis, and **second-rank symptoms**, which he believed are found not only in schizophrenia but also in other psychoses and in some nonpsychotic disorders such as personality disorders. In contrast to Bleuler, Schneider proposed that hallucinations and delusions are key or first-rank features of schizophrenia (K. Schneider, 1957). He considered disturbances in mood and confused thinking to be second-rank symptoms because they are also found in other disorders. Although Schneider's ranking of disturbed behaviours helped distinguish schizophrenia from other disorders, we now know that first-rank symptoms are sometimes found among people with other disorders, especially bipolar disorder. Although first-rank symptoms are clearly associated with schizophrenia, they are not unique to it.

Today, the contributions of Kraepelin, Bleuler, and Schneider are expressed in modified form in the present DSM diagnostic system. However, the diagnostic code for schizophrenia is not limited, as Kraepelin had proposed, to cases in which there is a course of progressive deterioration. The present code is also tighter than earlier conceptualizations; it separates into other diagnostic categories cases in which there are disturbances of mood combined with psychotic behaviour or that involve schizophrenic-like thinking but without overt psychotic behaviour (schizotypal personality disorder). The DSM-IV criteria for schizophrenia also require that psychotic behaviours be present at some point during the course of the disorder and that signs of the disorder be present for at least six months. People with briefer forms of psychosis are placed in diagnostic categories that may be connected with more favourable outcomes. Table 10.1 describes the major clinical criteria for schizophrenia.

Prevalence and Costs of Schizophrenia

According to the best estimates, about 1% of the adult Canadian population suffers from schizophrenia at some point in their lives (Health Canada, 2006a). The rates of schizophrenia appear to be similar in both developed and developing countries (APA, 2000a; Jablensky et al., 1992). Schizophrenia is the fifth leading cause of disability worldwide and the most common diagnosis of people who are involuntarily hospitalized (Bland, 1998; Health Canada, 2006a). Although some people with schizophrenia have healthy relationships, most (60% to 70%) do not marry, and most have limited social contacts (Health Canada, 2006a). The chronic course of the disorder contributes

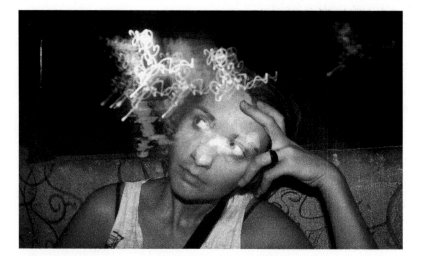

Hallucinations. According to Kurt Schneider, hallucinations and delusions are numbered among the first-rank symptoms of schizophrenia—that is, the symptoms of schizophrenia that are central to the diagnosis. So-called second-rank symptoms are found in other disorders as well. Schneider considered confusion and disturbances in mood to be second-rank symptoms.

Diagnostic Criteria for Schizophrenia

A. *Characteristic symptoms:* Two (or more) of the following, each present for a significant portion of time during a 1-month period (or less if successfully treated):
  (1) delusions
  (2) hallucinations
  (3) disorganized speech (e.g., frequent derailment or incoherence)
  (4) grossly disorganized or catatonic behavior
  (5) negative symptoms, i.e., affective flattening, alogia, or avolition

Note: Only one Criterion A symptom is required if delusions are bizarre or hallucinations consist of a voice keeping up a running commentary on the person's behavior or thoughts, or two or more voices conversing with each other.

B. *Social/occupational dysfunction:* For a significant portion of the time since the onset of the disturbance, one or more major areas of functioning such as work, interpersonal relations, or self-care are markedly below the level achieved prior to the onset (or when the onset is in childhood or adolescence, failure to achieve expected level of interpersonal, academic, or occupational achievement).

C. *Duration:* Continuous signs of the disturbance persist for at least 6 months. This 6-month period must include at least 1 month of symptoms (or less if successfully treated) that meet Criterion A (i.e., active-phase symptoms) and may include periods of prodromal or residual symptoms. During these prodromal or residual periods, the signs of the disturbance may be manifested by only negative symptoms or two or more symptoms listed in Criterion A present in an attenuated form (e.g., odd beliefs, unusual perceptual experiences).

D. *Schizoaffective and Mood Disorder exclusion:* Schizoaffective Disorder and Mood Disorder With Psychotic Features have been ruled out because either (1) no Major Depressive, Manic, or Mixed Episodes have occurred concurrently with the active-phase symptoms; or (2) if mood episodes have occurred during active-phase symptoms, their total duration has been brief relative to the duration of the active and residual periods.

E. *Substance/general medical condition exclusion:* The disturbance is not due to the direct physiological effects of a substance (e.g., a drug of abuse, a medication) or a general medical condition.

Source: Reprinted with permission from the *Diagnostic and Statistical Manual of Mental Disorders*, Fourth Edition, Text Revision, (Copyright ©2000). American Psychiatric Association. p. 312.

to ongoing social problems, so people with schizophrenia are greatly overrepresented in prison and homeless populations. About 40% to 60% of people with schizophrenia attempt suicide, and about 10% die from suicide. They are between 15 and 25 times more likely than the general population to die from a suicide attempt (Health Canada, 2006a).

Phases of Schizophrenia

Schizophrenia usually afflicts young people, and often does so at the very time that they are making their way from the family into the outside world (APA, 2000a). People who develop schizophrenia become increasingly disengaged from society. They fail to function in the expected roles of student, worker, or spouse, and their families and communities grow intolerant of their deviant behaviour. The disorder typically develops in the late teens or early 20s, a time at which the brain is reaching full maturation (Andreasen, 1999). In about three quarters of cases, the first signs of schizophrenia appear by the age of 25 (Keith, Regier, & Rae, 1991). Men and women are affected equally by schizophrenia but men usually develop the disorder earlier (Health Canada, 2006a).

In some cases, the onset of the disorder is acute. It occurs suddenly, within a few weeks or months. The individual may have been well adjusted and may have shown few if any signs of behavioural disturbance. Then a rapid transformation in personality and behaviour leads to an acute psychotic episode.

In most cases, however, there is a slower, more gradual decline in functioning. It may take years before psychotic behaviours emerge, although early signs of deterioration may

prodromal phase (1) Stage in which the early features or signs of a disorder become apparent. (2) In schizophrenia, the period of decline in functioning that precedes the development of the first acute psychotic episode.

residual phase In schizophrenia, the phase of the disorder that follows an acute phase, characterized by a return to a level of functioning typical of the prodromal phase.

be observed. This period of deterioration is called the **prodromal phase**. It is characterized by waning interest in social activities and increasing difficulty in meeting the responsibilities of daily living. At first, such people seem to take less care of their appearance. They fail to bathe regularly or they wear the same clothes repeatedly. Over time, their behaviour may become increasingly odd or eccentric. There are lapses in job performance or schoolwork. Their speech may become increasingly vague and rambling. These changes in personality may start out so gradually that they raise little concern among friends and families. They may be attributed to "a phase" that the person is passing through. But as behaviour becomes more bizarre—like hoarding food, collecting garbage, or talking to oneself on the street—the acute phase of the disorder begins. Finally, psychotic symptoms such as wild hallucinations, delusions, and increasingly bizarre behaviour develop.

Following acute episodes, people who develop schizophrenia may enter the **residual phase,** in which their behaviour returns to the level that was characteristic of the prodromal phase. Although flagrant psychotic behaviours may be absent during the residual phase, the person may continue to be impaired by a deep sense of apathy, difficulties in thinking or speaking clearly, and the harbouring of unusual ideas, such as beliefs in telepathy or clairvoyance. Such patterns of behaviour make it difficult for the person to meet expected social roles as wage earners, marital partners, or students. Full return to normal behaviour is uncommon but may occur. More commonly, a chronic pattern characterized by occasional relapses and continued impairment between acute episodes may develop (Wiersma, Nienhuis, Slooff, & Giel, 1998).

The chronic course of the disorder contributes to ongoing social problems. As a result, people with schizophrenia are greatly overrepresented in prison and homeless populations. Up to 80% of people with schizophrenia abuse substances at some point in their lives. Substance abuse in people with schizophrenia is associated with poorer functional adjustment, suicidal behaviour, and violence (Health Canada, 2006a). However, because of their behavioural problems (such as odd or socially inappropriate behaviour), people with schizophrenia are more often the victims than the perpetrators of violence (Health Canada, 2006a).

Public misunderstanding and fear contribute to the serious stigma associated with schizophrenia. Contrary to popular opinion, most people with the disorder are withdrawn and not violent. In fact, when adequately treated, people with the disorder are no more violent than the general population. Even so, the stigma of violence interferes with schizophrenics' ability to acquire housing, employment, and treatment, and also makes it difficult for them to make friends or enter intimate relationships. The stigma associated with schizophrenia also adds to the burden of the people caring for the person with the disorder, such as families and caregivers (Health Canada, 2006a; Sartorius & Schulze, 2005). Public education about the nature of schizophrenia is an important step toward reducing the stigma associated with the disorder.

Major Features of Schizophrenia

Schizophrenia is a pervasive disorder that affects a wide range of psychological processes involving cognition, affect, and behaviour. People with schizophrenia show a marked decline in occupational and social functioning. They may have difficulty holding a conversation, forming friendships, holding a job, or taking care of their personal hygiene. Yet no single behaviour pattern is unique to schizophrenia, nor is any one behaviour pattern invariably present among people with schizophrenia. People with schizophrenia may exhibit delusions, problems with associative thinking, and hallucinations at one time or another, but not necessarily all at once. There are also different kinds or types of schizophrenia, characterized by different behaviour patterns.

Let us consider how schizophrenia affects thinking, speech, attentional and perceptual processes, emotional processes, and voluntary behaviour.

DISTURBANCES OF THOUGHT AND SPEECH Schizophrenia is characterized by disturbances in thinking and in the expression of thoughts through coherent, meaningful speech. Disturbances in thinking may be found in both the content and form of thought.

Disturbances in the Content of Thought   The most prominent disturbance in the content of thought involves delusions, or false beliefs that remain fixed in the person's mind despite their illogical bases and lack of supporting evidence. They tend to remain unshakable even in the face of disconfirming evidence. Delusions may take many forms, including delusions of persecution (e.g., "The police are out to get me"), delusions of reference ("People on the bus are talking about me," or "People on television are making fun of me"), delusions of being controlled (believing that one's thoughts, feelings, impulses, or actions are controlled by external forces, such as agents of the devil), and delusions of grandeur (believing oneself to be Jesus or to be on a special mission, or having grand but illogical plans for saving the world). People with delusions of persecution may think they are being pursued by the Mafia, terrorists, the RCMP, or some other group. A woman we treated who had delusions of reference believed that television news correspondents were broadcasting coded information about her. A man with delusions of this type expressed the belief that his neighbours had bugged the walls of his house. Other delusions include beliefs that one has committed unpardonable sins or is rotting from some horrible disease. Common delusions include thought broadcasting (believing that one's thoughts are somehow transmitted to the external world so that others can overhear them), thought insertion (believing that one's thoughts have been planted in one's mind by an external source), and thought withdrawal (believing that thoughts have been removed from one's mind).

Mellor (1970) offers the following examples of thought broadcasting, thought insertion, and thought withdrawal:

Thought Broadcasting: A 21-year-old student reported, "As I think, my thoughts leave my head on a type of mental ticker-tape. Everyone around has only to pass the tape through their mind and they know my thoughts" (p. 17).

Thought Insertion: A 29-year-old housewife reported that when she looks out of the window, she thinks, "The garden looks nice and the grass looks cool, but the thoughts of [a man's name] come into my mind. There are no other thoughts there, only his. . . . He treats my mind like a screen and flashes his thoughts on it like you flash a picture" (p. 17).

Thought Withdrawal: A 22-year-old woman experienced the following: "I am thinking about my mother, and suddenly my thoughts are sucked out of my mind by a phrenological vacuum extractor, and there is nothing in my mind, it is empty" (pp. 16–17).

Disturbances in the Form of Thought   Unless we are engaged in daydreaming or purposefully letting our thoughts wander, our thoughts tend to be tightly knit together. The connections (or associations) between our thoughts tend to be logical and coherent. People with schizophrenia, however, tend to think in a disorganized, illogical fashion. In schizophrenia, the form or structure of thought processes as well as their content is often disturbed. Clinicians label this type of disturbance a **thought disorder**.

Thought disorder is recognized by a breakdown in the organization, processing, and control of thoughts. Looseness of associations, which we now regard as a chief sign of thought disorder, was one of Bleuler's four As. The speech pattern of people with schizophrenia is often disorganized or jumbled, with parts of words combined incoherently or words strung together to make meaningless rhymes. Their speech may jump from one topic to another but show little interconnectivity between the ideas or thoughts that are expressed. People with thought disorder are usually unaware that their thoughts and behaviour appear abnormal. In severe cases, their speech may become completely incoherent or incomprehensible.

Another common sign of thought disorder is poverty of speech; that is, speech that is coherent but is so limited in production or vague that little informational value is conveyed. Less commonly occurring signs include **neologisms** (words made up by the speaker that have little or no meaning to others), **perseveration** (inappropriate but persistent repetition of the same words or train of thought), **clanging** (stringing together of words or sounds on the basis of rhyming, such as, "I know who I am but I don't know Sam"), and **blocking** (involuntary abrupt interruption of speech or thought). Disconnected speech is more common and more severe among younger patients; poverty of speech is found more often and is more severe among older patients (P. D. Harvey et al., 1997).

thought disorder Disturbances in thinking characterized by various features, especially a breakdown in logical associations between thoughts.

neologisms Type of disturbed thinking associated with schizophrenia involving the coining of new words.

perseveration Persistent repetition of the same thought or train of thought.

clanging In people with schizophrenia, the tendency to string words together because they rhyme or sound alike.

blocking (1) Disruption of self-expression of threatening or emotionally laden material. (2) In people with schizophrenia, a condition of suddenly becoming silent with loss of memory for what they have just discussed.

Many but not all people with schizophrenia show evidence of thought disorder. Some appear to think and speak coherently but have disordered content of thought as seen by the presence of delusions. Nor is disordered thought unique to schizophrenia; it has even been found in milder form among people without psychological disorders (Bachman & Cannon, 2005), especially when they are tired or under stress. Disordered thought is also found among other diagnostic groups, such as persons with mania. Thought disorders in people experiencing a manic episode tend to be short-lived and reversible, however. In those with schizophrenia, thought disorder tends to be more persistent or recurrent—it occurs most often during acute episodes but may linger into residual phases. Thought disorders that persist beyond acute episodes are connected with poorer prognoses, perhaps because lingering thought disorders reflect more severe disorders (Marengo & Harrow, 1997).

ATTENTIONAL DEFICIENCIES To read this book, you must screen out background noises and other environmental stimuli. The ability to focus on relevant stimuli is basic to learning and thinking. Kraepelin and Bleuler suggested that schizophrenia involves a breakdown in the processes of attention. People with schizophrenia appear to have difficulty filtering out irrelevant distracting stimuli, a deficit that makes it nearly impossible for them to focus their attention and organize their thoughts (Q. Wang et al., 2007).

The mother of a son who had schizophrenia provided the following illustration of her son's difficulties in filtering out extraneous sounds:

> [H]is hearing is different when he's ill. One of the first things we notice when he's deteriorating is his heightened sense of hearing. He cannot filter out anything. He hears each and every sound around him with equal intensity. He hears the sounds from the street, in the yard, and in the house, and they are all much louder than normal. (Anonymous, 1985, p. 1; cited in Freedman et al., 1987, p. 670)

People with schizophrenia also appear to be hypervigilant or acutely sensitive to extraneous sounds, especially during the early stages of the disorder. During acute episodes, they may become flooded by these stimuli, overwhelming their ability to make sense of their environments. Through measuring involuntary brainwave responses to auditory stimuli, researchers have found that the brains of people with schizophrenia are less able than those of other people to inhibit or screen out responses to distracting sounds (Bergida & Lenzenweger, 2006).

Investigators suspect that attentional deficits associated with schizophrenia are, to a certain extent, inherited (Goldberg et al., 2006). Although the underlying mechanism is not entirely clear, attentional deficits may be related to dysfunction in the subcortical parts of the brain that regulate attention to external stimuli, such as the basal ganglia (Cornblatt & Keilp, 1994). Scientists suspect there may be a "gating" mechanism in the brain responsible for filtering extraneous stimuli, much like how the closing of a gate in a road can stem the flow of traffic (de Bruin, van Luijtelaar, Cools, & Ellenbroek, 2003). Evidence suggests that training in attention skills may help reduce attentional deficits in schizophrenia patients (Medalia, Aluma, Tryon, & Merriam, 1998).

PERCEPTUAL DISTURBANCES

> Every so often during the interview, Sara would look over her right shoulder in the direction of the office door and smile gently. When asked why she kept looking at the door, she said that the voices were talking about the two of us just outside the door and she wanted to hear what they were saying. "Why the smile?" Sara was asked. "They were saying funny things," she replied, "like maybe you thought I was cute or something."
>
> Alex was flailing his arms wildly in the hall of the psychiatric unit. Sweat seemed to pour from his brow, and his eyes darted about with agitation. He was subdued and injected with haloperidol (brand name Haldol) to reduce his

agitation. When he was about to be injected he started shouting, "Father, forgive them for they know not . . . forgive them . . . father . . ." His words became jumbled. Later, after he had calmed down, he reported that the ward attendants had looked to him like devils or evil angels. They were red and burning, and steam issued from their mouths.

The Authors' Files

Hallucinations, the most common form of perceptual disturbance in schizophrenia, are images perceived in the absence of external stimulation. They are difficult to distinguish from reality. For Sara, the voices coming from outside the consulting room were real enough, even though no one was there. Hallucinations may involve any of the senses. Auditory hallucinations ("hearing voices") are most common. Tactile hallucinations (such as tingling, electrical, or burning sensations) and somatic hallucinations (feeling like snakes are crawling inside one's belly) are also common. Visual hallucinations (seeing things that are not there), gustatory hallucinations (tasting things that are not present), and olfactory hallucinations (sensing odours that are not present) are rarer.

Auditory hallucinations occur in over 60% of cases of schizophrenia (Cleghorn et al., 1992; Rector & Seeman, 1992). In auditory hallucinations, the voices may be experienced as female or male and as originating inside or outside one's head (APA, 2000a). When hallucinating, schizophrenic people may hear voices conversing about them in the third person, debating their virtues or faults.

Some people with schizophrenia experience command hallucinations, voices that instruct them to perform certain acts, such as harming themselves or others. Joanne, for example, was instructed by "devils" to commit suicide, and so she attempted to jump from a bridge. People with schizophrenia who experience command hallucinations are often hospitalized for fear they may harm themselves or others. There is a good reason for this. One study found that four out of five people with command hallucinations reported obeying them, with nearly half reporting they had obeyed commands to harm themselves during the past month (Kasper, Rogers, & Adams, 1996). Yet command hallucinations often go undetected by professionals because command hallucinators deny them or are unwilling to discuss them.

Hallucinations of Other Types Hallucinations are not unique to schizophrenia. People with major depression and mania sometimes experience hallucinations. Nor are hallucinations invariably a sign of psychopathology. Cross-cultural evidence shows they are common and socially valued in some developing countries (Bentall, 1990). Even in developed countries, about 5% of respondents in nonpatient samples report experiencing hallucinations during the preceding year, mostly auditory hallucinations (Honig et al., 1998). Hallucinations in people without psychiatric conditions are often triggered by unusually low levels of sensory stimulation (lying in the dark in a soundproof room for an extended time) or low levels of arousal (Teunisse, Cruysberg, Hoefnagels, Verbeek, & Zitman, 1996). Unlike psychotic individuals, these people realize their hallucinations are not real and feel in control of them.

People who are free of psychological disorders sometimes experience hallucinations during the course of a religious experience or ritual (Asaad & Shapiro, 1986). Participants in such experiences may report fleeting trancelike states with visions or

***The Cat* by Louis Wain (1860–1939).** This is one of the later paintings by a Victorian artist who developed schizophrenia. The painting depicts his withdrawal from reality to fantasy, a hallmark of schizophrenia.

other perceptual aberrations. All of us hallucinate nightly, if we consider dreams to be a form of hallucination (perceptual experience in the absence of external stimuli).

Hallucinations may occur in response to hallucinogenic drugs, such as LSD. They may also occur during grief reactions, when images of the deceased may appear, and in other stressful conditions. In most cases, grief-induced hallucinations can be differentiated from psychotic ones in that the individual can distinguish the former type from reality. Bentall (1990) views the hallucinations of psychiatric patients as involving the lack of ability to distinguish between real and imaginary events. That is, these individuals tend to confuse real and imaginary (hallucinatory) events.

Drug-induced hallucinations tend to be visual and often involve abstract shapes, such as circles or stars, or flashes of light. Schizophrenic hallucinations, in contrast, tend to be more fully formed and complex. Hallucinations (e.g., of bugs crawling on one's skin) are common during delirium tremens, which often occurs as part of the withdrawal syndrome for chronic alcoholism. Hallucinations may also occur as side effects of medications or in neurological disorders, such as Parkinson's disease.

Causes of Hallucinations   The causes of psychotic hallucinations remain unknown, but speculations abound. Disturbances in brain chemistry are suspected of playing a role. The neurotransmitter dopamine has been implicated because antipsychotic drugs that block dopamine activity also tend to reduce hallucinations. Conversely, drugs that lead to increased production of dopamine tend to induce hallucinations. Because hallucinations resemble dreamlike states, it is also possible that hallucinations are types of daytime dreams connected with a failure of brain mechanisms that normally prevent dream images from intruding on waking experiences.

Hallucinations may also represent a type of subvocal inner speech (Stephane, Barton, & Boutros, 2001). Many of us talk to ourselves from time to time, although we usually keep our mutterings beneath our breath (subvocal) and recognize the voice as our own. Might auditory hallucinations that occur among people with schizophrenia be projections of their own internal voices or self-speech onto external sources? In one experiment, 14 of 18 hallucinators who suffered from schizophrenia reported that the voices disappeared when they engaged in a procedure that prevented them from talking to themselves under their breath (Bick & Kinsbourne, 1987). Similar results were obtained for 18 of 21 normal subjects who reportedly experienced hallucinations in response to hypnotic suggestions.

Researchers found that activity in Broca's area, a part of the brain involved in controlling speech, was greater in people with schizophrenia when they were hearing voices than at a later time when they were no longer hallucinating (McGuire, Shah, & Murray, 1993). This same area is known to become active when people engage in inner speech (Paulesu, Frith, & Frackowiak, 1993). Researchers have also found evidence of similar electrical activity in the auditory cortex of the brain during auditory hallucinations and in response to hearing real sounds (Stephane et al., 2001). This evidence supports the view that auditory hallucinations may be a form of inner speech (silent self-talk) that for some unknown reason is attributed to external sources rather than to one's own thoughts (Johns, Gregg, Allen, & McGuire, 2006).

Even if theories linking subvocal speech to auditory hallucinations stand up to further scientific inquiry, however, they cannot account for hallucinations in other sensory modalities, such as visual, tactile, and olfactory hallucinations (Larøi, 2006).

The brain mechanisms responsible for hallucinations are likely to involve a number of interconnected brain systems. One intriguing possibility is that defects in deeper brain structures may lead the brain to create its own reality, which goes unchecked because of a failure of the higher thinking centres in the brain, located in the frontal lobes of the cerebral cortex, to perform a reality check on these images to determine whether they are real, imagined, or hallucinated (Collerton, Perry, & McKeith, 2005). Consequently, people may misattribute their own internally generated voices to outside sources. As we'll see later, evidence from other brain-imaging studies points to abnormalities in the frontal and temporal lobes in at least some people with schizophrenia.

EMOTIONAL DISTURBANCES Disturbances of affect or emotional response in schizophrenia are typified by blunted affect—also called *flat affect*—and by inappropriate affect. Flat affect is inferred from the absence of emotional expression in the face and voice. People with schizophrenia may speak in a monotone and maintain an expressionless face, or "mask." They may not experience a normal range of emotional response to people and events. Or their emotional responses may be inappropriate, like giggling at bad news.

It is not fully clear, however, whether emotional blunting in people with schizophrenia is a disturbance in their ability to express emotions, to report the presence of emotions, or to actually experience emotions (Berenbaum & Oltmanns, 2005). They may, in other words, experience emotions even if their experiences are not communicated to the world outside through such means as facial expression. Support along these lines is found in research showing that people with schizophrenia displayed less facial expression of positive and negative emotions when viewing emotion-eliciting films than did control subjects but reported experiencing as much positive or negative emotion (Kring, Kerr, Smith, & Neale, 1993). It may be that people with schizophrenia experience emotions internally but lack the capacity to express them outwardly (Kring & Neale, 1996).

OTHER TYPES OF IMPAIRMENT People who suffer from schizophrenia may become confused about their personal identities—the cluster of attributes and characteristics that

NORMAL/ABNORMAL BEHAVIOUR

Unusual Experiences: No Disorder

Ahmed is a 17-year-old high school student. He does not drink or do drugs. With his family, Ahmed belongs to a local church that holds very particular views about religion and Christianity. He has been attending this church since he was a baby. Most members of the church hold strong beliefs about spirits and the afterlife. It is a commonplace experience at church for people to talk about communicating with spirits, and no one finds this unusual or frightening. In fact, the congregation values these experiences, and the stories are told and retold to other members. Ahmed has had a few experiences that he's shared with his congregation. For example, while falling asleep he sometimes feels a "presence" near him. He never sees anything, but he has a very strong sensation of someone being near him. He feels that this is the presence of a spirit, and he welcomes these experiences. When he told a friend outside of the congregation, the friend thought that this sounded "weird." Ahmed realized that other people do not share his beliefs about spirits, so he decided to share these experiences only with his fellow churchgoers from now on rather than his school friends.

Unusual Experiences: Psychotic Disorder

Dejuan is a 20-year-old college student studying marketing. He has a family history of mental illness, with his paternal uncle having been diagnosed with schizophrenia when he was a young man. Dejuan has been having a series of unusual experiences for a few years that he has not told anyone about. It started with hearing sounds and words that other people could not hear. Dejuan would be standing in a room and feel as though he heard someone calling his name. When he would look, no one would be there. He chalked this up as an unusual experience, and didn't think about it much further. However, these experiences had begun to intensify more recently. Dejuan began hearing a voice talking to him even when no one was around. This voice would comment on what he was doing and give him suggestions for things he should do. At first, the voice was pleasant and simply made observations. More recently, the voice had become more critical and demanding. Although Dejuan felt a lot of anxiety about the voice, he began to take it more and more seriously, trying to appease it in the way he acted. Dejuan's family became increasingly worried about him, as they noticed odd expressions on his face, his seeming distracted from others, and his beginning to withdraw from his friends and family. At one point, Dejuan began talking back to the voices and his parents overheard. They immediately took him to the emergency room at their local hospital.

A person diagnosed with disorganized schizophrenia. One of the features of disorganized schizophrenia is grossly inappropriate affect, as shown by this young man who continuously giggles, laughs, and makes facial grimaces for no apparent reason.

A person diagnosed with catatonic schizophrenia. People with catatonic schizophrenia may remain in unusual, difficult positions for hours, even though their limbs become stiff or swollen. They may seem oblivious to their environment, even to people who are talking to them. Yet they may later say that they heard what was being said. Periods of stupor may alternate with periods of agitation.

stupor State of relative or complete unconsciousness in which a person is not generally aware of or responsive to the environment, as in a catatonic stupor.

define them as individuals and give meaning and direction to their lives. They may fail to recognize themselves as unique individuals and be unclear as to how much of what they experience is part of themselves. In psychodynamic terms, this phenomenon is sometimes referred to as *loss of ego boundaries*. They may also have difficulty adopting a third-party perspective and fail to perceive their own behaviour and verbalizations as socially inappropriate in a given situation because they are unable to see things from another person's point of view (Penn, Combs, & Mohamed, 2001).

Disturbances of volition are most often seen in the residual or chronic state and are characterized by loss of initiative to pursue goal-directed activities. People with schizophrenia may be unable to carry out plans and may lack interest or drive. Apparent ambivalence toward choosing courses of action may block goal-directed activities.

People with schizophrenia may show highly excited or wild behaviour or slow to a state of **stupor**. They may exhibit odd gestures and bizarre facial expressions, or become unresponsive and curtail spontaneous movement. In extreme cases, as in catatonic schizophrenia, the person may seem unaware of the environment or maintain a rigid posture. Or the person may move about in an excited but seemingly purposeless manner.

People with schizophrenia also tend to show significant impairment in their interpersonal relationships. They tend to withdraw from social interactions and become absorbed in private thoughts and fantasies. Or they cling so desperately to others that they make them uncomfortable. They may become so dominated by their own fantasies that they essentially lose touch with the outside world. They also tend to have been introverted and peculiar even before the appearance of psychotic behaviour (Metsänen et al., 2004). These early signs may be associated with a vulnerability to schizophrenia, at least in people with a genetic risk of developing the disorder.

Subtypes of Schizophrenia

The belief that there are different forms or types of schizophrenia traces back to Kraepelin, who listed three types of schizophrenia: paranoid, catatonic, and hebephrenic (now called *disorganized type*). The DSM-IV also lists these three specific types of schizophrenia: disorganized, catatonic, and paranoid. People with schizophrenia who display active psychotic features, such as hallucinations, delusions, incoherent speech, or confused or disorganized behaviour, but who do not meet the specifications of the other types are considered to be of an *undifferentiated type*. Others who have no prominent psychotic features at the time of evaluation but have some residual features (e.g., social withdrawal, peculiar behaviour, blunted or inappropriate affect, and strange beliefs or thoughts) are classified as having a *residual type* of schizophrenia.

Let us consider the specific types of schizophrenia recognized by the DSM system.

DISORGANIZED TYPE The **disorganized type** is associated with such features as confused behaviour; incoherent speech; vivid, frequent hallucinations; flattened or inappropriate affect; and disorganized delusions that often involve sexual or religious themes. Social impairment is frequent among people with disorganized schizophrenia. They also display silliness and giddiness of mood, giggling and talking nonsensically. They often neglect their appearance and hygiene and lose control of their bladder and bowel.

CATATONIC TYPE The **catatonic type** is a subtype of schizophrenia characterized by markedly impaired motor behaviour and a slowing down of activity that progresses to a stupor but may switch abruptly into an agitated phase. People with catatonic schizophrenia may show unusual mannerisms or grimacing or maintain bizarre, apparently strenuous postures for hours, even though their limbs become stiff or swollen. A striking but less common feature is **waxy flexibility**, which involves the adoption of a fixed posture into which they have been positioned by others. They will not respond to questions or comments during these periods, which can last for hours. Later, they may report they heard what others were saying at the time.

> A 24-year-old man had been brooding about his life. He professed that he did not feel well, but could not explain his bad feelings. While hospitalized, he initially sought contact with people, but a few days later was found in a statuesque position, his legs contorted in an awkward-looking position. He refused to talk to anyone and acted as if he couldn't see or hear anything. His face was an expressionless mask. A few days later, he began to talk, but in an echolalic or mimicking way. For example, he would respond to the question, "What is your name?" by saying, "What is your name?" He could not care for his needs and required to be fed by spoon.
>
> Arieti, 1974, p. 40. Copyright Basic Books. Reprinted with permission.

Although catatonia is associated with schizophrenia, it may also occur in other physical and psychological disorders, including brain disorders, states of drug intoxication, metabolic disorders, and mood disorders (Moskowitz, 2004).

PARANOID TYPE The paranoid type is characterized by preoccupations with one or more delusions or with the presence of frequent auditory hallucinations (APA, 2000a). The behaviour and speech of those with paranoid schizophrenia do not show the marked disorganization typical of the disorganized type, nor is there a prominent display of flattened or inappropriate affect or catatonic behaviour. Their delusions often involve themes of grandeur, persecution, or jealousy. They may believe, for example, that their spouse or lover is unfaithful despite a lack of evidence. They may also become highly agitated, confused, and fearful.

> Myra, a 25-year-old woman, was visibly frightened. She was shaking badly and had the look of someone who feared that she might be attacked at any moment. The night before, she had been found cowering in a corner of the local bus station, mumbling to herself incoherently, having arrived in town minutes earlier on a bus. The station manager had called the police, who took her to the hospital. She told the interviewer that she had to escape because the Mafia was closing in

disorganized type Subtype of schizophrenia characterized by disorganized behaviour, bizarre delusions, and vivid hallucinations. Formerly *hebephrenic schizophrenia*.

catatonic type Subtype of schizophrenia characterized by gross disturbances in motor activity, such as catatonic stupor.

waxy flexibility Feature of catatonic schizophrenia in which a person's limbs are moved into a certain posture or position that the person then rigidly maintains for a lengthy period of time.

on her. She was a schoolteacher, she explained, at least until the voices started bothering her. The voices would tell her she was bad and had to be punished. Sometimes the voices were in her head; sometimes they spoke to her through the electrical wires in her apartment. The voices told her that someone from the Mafia would come to kill her. She felt that one of her neighbours, a shy man who lived down the hall, was in league with the Mafia. She felt the only hope she had was to escape. To go somewhere, anywhere. So she hopped on the first bus leaving town, heading nowhere in particular, except away from home.

The Authors' Files

Categorical Model

positive symptoms The more flagrant features of schizophrenia characterized by the *presence* of abnormal behaviour, such as hallucinations, delusions, thought disorder, disorganized speech, and inappropriate affect.

negative symptoms Features of schizophrenia characterized by the *absence* of normal behaviour. Negative symptoms are deficits or behavioural deficiencies, such as social-skills deficits, social withdrawal, flattened affect, poverty of speech and thought, psychomotor retardation, and failure to experience pleasure in pleasant activities.

premorbid functioning Level of functioning before the onset of a disorder.

Some investigators have gone beyond the DSM typology in proposing other ways of categorizing schizophrenia. One alternative typology distinguishes between two basic types of schizophrenia: Type I and Type II (Crow, 1980a, 1980b, 1980c). Type I schizophrenia is characterized by more flagrant symptoms called **positive symptoms,** such as hallucinations, delusions, and looseness of associations, as well as by an abrupt onset, preserved intellectual ability, and a more favourable response to antipsychotic medication (Penn, 1998). Type II schizophrenia corresponds to a pattern consisting largely of deficit or **negative symptoms** of schizophrenia, such as flat affect, low motivation, loss of pleasure in activities, social withdrawal, and poverty of speech. Type II is also characterized by a more gradual onset, intellectual impairment, and poorer response to antipsychotic drugs (Selten, Gernaat, Nolen, Wiersma, & van den Bosch, 1998).

One intriguing possibility is that Type I and Type II schizophrenia represent different pathological processes. The Type I pattern may involve a defect in the inhibitory (blocking) mechanisms in the brain that would normally control excessive or distorted behaviours. Underlying this malfunction may be a disturbance in the supply or regulation of dopamine in the brain; antipsychotic drugs that regulate dopamine function generally have a favourable impact on positive symptoms. The negative symptoms associated with Type II schizophrenia represent the more enduring or persistent characteristics of schizophrenia. The Type II pattern is associated with poorer **premorbid functioning** and with a more progressive decline in functioning leading to enduring disability (Earnst & Kring, 1997). One possibility is that Type II schizophrenia is caused by structural damage or atrophy in the brain.

The Type I–Type II distinction remains controversial, because evidence does not clearly support the existence of two distinct behaviour patterns in schizophrenia. Some investigators (e.g., Kay, 1990; Mortimer, Lund, & McKenna, 1990) find that only a minority of people with schizophrenia can be classified as exhibiting either predominantly positive or negative symptoms. Positive and negative symptoms may define not distinct subtypes of schizophrenia but rather separate dimensions that can coexist in the same individual.

Perhaps, as other research suggests, a three-dimensional model is most appropriate for grouping schizophrenic symptoms (Liddle, 1999). One dimension, a *psychotic dimension,* consists of delusional thinking and hallucinations. A *negative*

On the run? People with paranoid schizophrenia hold systematized delusions that commonly involve themes of persecution and grandeur. They usually do not show the degree of confusion, disorganization, or disturbed motor behaviour seen in people with disorganized or catatonic schizophrenia. This man may have features of both paranoid and disorganized types. Unless they are discussing the areas in which they are delusional, their thought processes may appear to be relatively intact.

dimension comprises negative symptoms such as flat affect and poverty of speech and thought. The third dimension, labelled a *disorganized dimension*, includes inappropriate affect and thought disorder (disordered thought and speech). Although schizophrenic symptoms seem to cluster into these three dimensions, there is considerable overlap. Thus, it does not appear that these dimensions represent distinct subtypes of schizophrenia. Still, it remains an open question whether different underlying neurobiological processes give rise to different constellations of symptoms.

REVIEW IT

Clinical Features of Schizophrenia

- **What is schizophrenia, and how prevalent is it?** Schizophrenia is a chronic psychotic disorder characterized by acute episodes involving a break with reality, as manifested by such features as delusions, hallucinations, illogical thinking, incoherent speech, and bizarre behaviour. Residual deficits in cognitive, emotional, and social areas of functioning persist between acute episodes. Schizophrenia is believed to affect about 1% of the population.

- **What key historical figures in psychiatry influenced our conceptions of schizophrenia?** Emil Kraepelin was the first to describe the syndrome we identify as schizophrenia. He labelled the disorder *dementia praecox* and believed that it was a disease that develops early in life and follows a progressively deteriorating course. Eugen Bleuler renamed the disorder *schizophrenia* and believed that its course is more variable. He also distinguished between primary symptoms (the four As) and secondary symptoms. Kurt Schneider distinguished between first-rank symptoms that define the disorder and second-rank symptoms that occur in schizophrenia and other disorders.

- **What are the major phases of schizophrenia?** Schizophrenia usually develops in late adolescence or early adulthood. Its onset may be abrupt or gradual. The period of deterioration preceding the onset of acute symptoms is called the *prodromal phase*. An acute episode involves the emergence of clear psychotic features. A level of functioning that was typical of the prodromal phase characterizes the residual phase.

- **What are the most prominent features of schizophrenia?** Among the more prominent features of schizophrenia are disorders in the content of thought (delusions) and form of thought (thought disorder), as well as the presence of perceptual distortions (hallucinations) and emotional disturbances (flattened or inappropriate affect). There are also dysfunctions in the brain processes that regulate attention to the external world.

- **What are the various subtypes of schizophrenia?** The disorganized type describes a version of schizophrenia associated with grossly disorganized behaviour and thought processes. The catatonic type describes a version of the disorder associated with grossly impaired motor behaviours, such as maintenance of fixed postures and muteness for long periods of time. The paranoid type involves the presence of paranoid delusions or frequent auditory hallucinations. The undifferentiated type is a catch-all category that applies to cases involving schizophrenic episodes that don't clearly fit the other types. The residual type is that found in individuals who do not have prominent psychotic behaviours at the time of evaluation. Researchers have also distinguished between two general types of schizophrenia: Type I, characterized by positive symptomatology, more abrupt onset, better response to antipsychotic medication, and better preserved intellectual ability; and Type II, characterized by negative symptomatology, more gradual onset, poorer response to antipsychotic medication, and greater cognitive impairment.

THEORETICAL PERSPECTIVES

The understanding of schizophrenia has been approached from each of the major theoretical perspectives. Although the underlying causes of schizophrenia have not been identified, they are presumed to involve biological abnormalities in combination with psychosocial and environmental influences.

Psychodynamic Perspectives

According to the psychodynamic perspective, schizophrenia represents the overwhelming of the ego by primitive sexual or aggressive drives or impulses arising from the id. These impulses threaten the ego and give rise to intense intrapsychic conflict. Under such a threat, the person regresses to an early period in the oral stage, referred to as *primary narcissism*. In this period, the infant has not yet learned that it and the world are distinct entities. Because the ego mediates the relationship between the self and the outer world, this breakdown in ego functioning accounts for the detachment from reality that is typical of schizophrenia. Input from the id causes fantasies to become mistaken for reality, giving rise to hallucinations and delusions. Primitive impulses may also carry more weight than social norms and be expressed in bizarre, socially inappropriate behaviour.

Freud's followers, such as Erik Erikson and Harry Stack Sullivan, placed more emphasis on interpersonal than intrapsychic factors. Sullivan (1962), for example, who devoted much of his life's work to schizophrenia, emphasized the importance of impaired mother–child relationships, arguing that they can set the stage for gradual withdrawal from other people. In early childhood, anxious and hostile interactions between the child and parent lead the child to take refuge in a private fantasy world. A vicious cycle ensues: the more the child withdraws, the less opportunity there is to develop a sense of trust in others and the social skills necessary to establish intimacy. Then the weak bonds between the child and others prompt social anxiety and further withdrawal. This cycle continues until young adulthood. Then, faced with increasing demands at school or work and in intimate relationships, the person becomes overwhelmed with anxiety and withdraws completely into a world of fantasy.

Critics of Freud's views point out that schizophrenic behaviour and infantile behaviour are not much alike, so that schizophrenia cannot be explained by regression. Freud's detractors and modern psychodynamic theorists note that psychodynamic explanations are post hoc or retrospective. Early child–adult relationships are recalled from the vantage point of adulthood rather than observed longitudinally. Psychoanalysts have not been able to demonstrate that hypothesized early childhood experiences or family patterns lead to schizophrenia.

Learning Perspectives

Although learning theory may not account for schizophrenia, the principles of conditioning and observational learning may play a role in the development of some forms of schizophrenic behaviour. From this perspective, people may learn to "emit" schizophrenic behaviours when they are more likely to be reinforced than normal behaviour.

Ullmann and Krasner (1975) focused on the reinforcement value of social stimulation. Children who later develop schizophrenia may grow up in nonreinforcing environments because of disturbed family patterns or other environmental influences. Thus, they never learn to respond appropriately to social stimuli. Instead, as Sullivan (1962) also argued, they increasingly attend to private or idiosyncratic stimuli. Other people perceive them as strange, and they suffer social rejection. In a vicious cycle, rejection spurs feelings of alienation; alienation, in turn, engenders more bizarre behaviour. Patterns of bizarre behaviour may be maintained by the unintentional reinforcement they receive from some people in the form of attention and expressions of sympathy.

Support for this view is found in operant conditioning studies in which bizarre behaviour is shaped by reinforcement. Experiments involving people with schizophrenia show, for example, that reinforcement affects the frequency of bizarre versus normal verbalizations and that hospital patients can be shaped into performing odd behaviours. In a classic case example, Haughton and Ayllon (1965) conditioned a 54-year-old woman with chronic schizophrenia to cling to a broom. A staff member gave her the broom to hold, and when she did, another staff member gave her a cigarette. This pattern was repeated several times. Soon, the woman could not be parted from the broom. But the fact that reinforcement can influence people to engage in peculiar behaviour does not demonstrate that bizarre behaviours characterizing schizophrenia are learned behaviours determined by reinforcement.

There are other shortcomings to these behavioural explanations. For example, many of us grow up in harsh or punishing circumstances but do not retreat into private worlds of fantasy or display bizarre behaviour. Also, many people with schizophrenia grow up in homes that are supportive and socially reinforcing. Moreover, schizophrenic behaviours fall into patterns that are unlikely to occur by chance and then be reinforced to the point that they become learned habits.

Social-cognitive theorists suggest that modelling of schizophrenic behaviour can occur within mental hospitals. In that setting, patients may begin to model themselves after fellow patients who act strangely. Hospital staff may inadvertently reinforce schizophrenic behaviour by paying more attention to those patients who exhibit more bizarre behaviour. This understanding is consistent with the observation that schoolchildren who disrupt class garner more attention from their teachers than do well-behaved children.

Perhaps some forms of schizophrenic behaviour can be explained by the principles of modelling and reinforcement. However, many people come to display schizophrenic behaviour patterns without prior exposure to other people with schizophrenia. In fact, the onset of schizophrenic behaviour patterns is more likely to lead to hospitalization than to result from it.

Biological Perspectives

Although we still have much to learn about the biological underpinnings of schizophrenia, most investigators today recognize that biological factors play a determining role.

GENETIC FACTORS We now have compelling evidence that schizophrenia is strongly influenced by genetic factors (DeLisi & Fleischhaker, 2007). One source of evidence of genetic factors is based on familial studies. Schizophrenia, like many other disorders, tends to run in families. Overall, people with biological relatives with schizophrenia have about a tenfold greater risk of developing the disorder than do members of the general population (APA, 2000a).

Further supporting a genetic linkage, evidence shows that the closer the genetic relationship between people diagnosed with schizophrenia and their family members, the greater the likelihood (or concordance rate) of schizophrenia in their relatives. Figure 10.1 on page 374 shows the pooled results of European studies on family incidence of schizophrenia conducted from 1920 to 1987. However, the fact that families share common environments as well as common genes requires that we dig deeper to examine the genetic underpinnings of schizophrenia.

More support for a genetic contribution to schizophrenia is found in twin studies, which show the concordance rate for the disorder among identical or monozygotic (MZ) twins to be more than twice the rate found among fraternal or dizygotic (DZ) twins (Kendler & Prescott, 2006).

We should be careful, however, not to overinterpret the results of twin studies. MZ twins not only share 100% genetic similarity, but they may also be treated more alike than DZ twins. Thus, environmental factors may play a role in explaining the higher concordance rates found among MZ twins. To help sort out environmental from genetic factors, investigators have turned to adoption studies in which high-risk (HR) children (children of one or more biological parents with schizophrenia) were adopted away shortly after birth and reared apart from their biological parents.

Adoption studies provide stronger evidence for a genetic contribution to schizophrenia (Gottesman, McGuffin, & Farmer, 1987). In perhaps the best-known example, researchers in Denmark examined official registers and found 39 high-risk (HR) adoptees who had been reared apart from their biological mothers who had schizophrenia (Rosenthal et al., 1968, 1975). Three of the 39 HR adoptees (8%) were diagnosed with schizophrenia, as compared to none of a reference group of 47 adoptees whose biological parents had no psychiatric history.

Other investigators have approached the question of heredity in schizophrenia from the opposite direction. Kety and colleagues (Kety, Rosenthal, Wender, & Schulsinger, 1968; Kety, Rosenthal, Wender, Schulsinger, & Jacobsen, 1975, 1978) used official records to

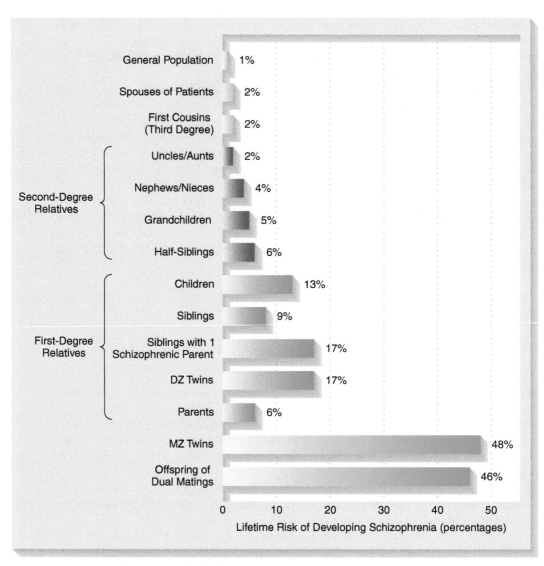

FIGURE 10.1 The familial risk of schizophrenia.
Generally speaking, the more closely one is related to people who have developed schizophrenia, the greater the risk of developing the disorder oneself. Monozygotic (MZ) twins, whose genetic heritages overlap fully, are much more likely than dizygotic (DZ) twins, whose genes overlap by 50%, to be concordant for schizophrenia.

Source: Adapted from Gottesman, McGuffin, & Farmer, 1987.

cross-fostering study Method of determining heritability of a trait or disorder by examining differences in prevalence among adoptees reared by either adoptive parents or biological parents who possessed the trait or disorder in question. Evidence that the disorder followed biological rather than adoptive parentage favours the heritability of the trait or disorder.

find 33 index cases of children in Copenhagen, Denmark, who had been adopted early in life and were later diagnosed with schizophrenia. They compared the rates of diagnosed schizophrenia in the biological and adoptive relatives of the index cases with those of the relatives of a matched reference group that consisted of adoptees with no psychiatric history. The results strongly supported the genetic explanation. The incidence of diagnosed schizophrenia was greater among the biological relatives of the adoptees who had schizophrenia than among the biological relatives of the control adoptees. Adoptive relatives of both the index and control cases showed similar low rates of schizophrenia. Similar results were found in later research that extended the scope of the investigation to the rest of Denmark (Kety et al., 1994). It thus appears that family linkages in schizophrenia follow shared genes, not shared environments.

Still another approach, the **cross-fostering study**, has yielded additional evidence of genetic factors in schizophrenia. In this approach, investigators compare the incidence of schizophrenia among children whose biological parents either had or didn't have schizophrenia and who were reared by adoptive parents who either had or didn't have schizophrenia. Another Danish study, by Wender and colleagues (Wender, Rosenthal, Kety, Schulsinger, & Welner, 1974), found that the incidence of schizophrenia related to the presence of the disorder in the children's biological parents but not in their adoptive parents. High-risk children (children whose biological parents had schizophrenia) were almost twice as likely to develop schizophrenia as children of nonschizophrenic biological parents, regardless of whether they were reared by a parent with schizophrenia. It is also notable that adoptees whose biological parents did not suffer from schizophrenia were at no greater risk of developing the disorder if reared by an adoptive parent with schizophrenia than if reared by a nonschizophrenic parent. In sum, a genetic relationship with a person with schizophrenia seems to be the most prominent risk factor for developing the disorder.

Although it is recognized that genetic factors play an important role in schizophrenia, the mode of genetic transmission remains unknown. Evidence points to an interaction of multiple genes involved in determining risk for schizophrenia (Kendler & Prescott, 2006). Researchers have identified several chromosomes, including chromosomes 6, 8, 13, 15, and 22, that appear to contain genes linked to the disorder (Detera-Wadleigh & McMahon, 2006; Vazza et al., 2007).

York University psychologist R. Walter Heinrichs (2001, 2005) argued that *schizophrenia* may be an umbrella term for several different disorders, each arising from different mechanisms manifesting themselves primarily in cognitive disturbances. It is possible that there are several different sets of genetic aberrations, with each independently causing schizophrenia. Preliminary findings support this idea. For example, Anne Bassett and her colleagues at the University of Toronto have found that one form of schizophrenia seems to be associated with abnormalities specifically on chromosome 22 (Bassett & Chow, 1999; Chow, Watson, Young, & Bassett, 2006). About 25% of people with this genetic abnormality develop a psychotic disorder such as schizophrenia. These people also tend to have unusual facial features (e.g., long, narrow face, prominent nose, small ears and mouth) and congenital defects (e.g., heart defects).

Genetics alone does not determine risk of schizophrenia. For one thing, people may carry a high genetic risk of schizophrenia and not develop the disorder. For another, the rate of concordance among MZ twins, as noted earlier, is well below 100%, even though identical twins carry identical genes. The prevailing view today, which we discuss later, is the diathesis-stress model, which holds that schizophrenia involves a complex interplay of genetic and environmental factors.

BIOCHEMICAL FACTORS Contemporary biological investigations of schizophrenia have focused on the role of the neurotransmitter dopamine. The **dopamine theory** posits that schizophrenia involves an overreactivity of dopamine receptors in the brain—the receptor sites on postsynaptic neurons into which molecules of dopamine lock (Abi-Dargham, 2004).

dopamine theory Biochemical theory of schizophrenia that proposes that schizophrenia involves the action of dopamine.

People with schizophrenia do not appear to produce more dopamine. Instead, they appear to use more of it. But why? Research suggests that people with schizophrenia may have a greater than normal number of dopamine receptors in their brains or have receptors that are overly sensitive to dopamine (Gur & Pearlson, 1993; Seeman & Kapur, 2001).

The major source of evidence for the dopamine model is found in the effects of antipsychotic drugs called *major tranquillizers* or *neuroleptics*. The most widely used neuroleptics belong to a class of drugs called *phenothiazines*, which includes such drugs as Largactil and Mellaril. Neuroleptic drugs block dopamine receptors, thereby reducing the level of dopamine activity (Kane, 1996). As a consequence, neuroleptics inhibit excessive transmission of neural impulses that may give rise to schizophrenic behaviour.

Another source of evidence supporting the role of dopamine in schizophrenia is based on the actions of amphetamines, a class of stimulant drugs. These drugs increase the concentration of dopamine in the synaptic cleft by blocking its reuptake by presynaptic neurons. When given in large doses to normal people, these drugs can lead to abnormal behaviour states that mimic paranoid schizophrenia.

Overall, evidence points to irregularities in schizophrenia patients in the neural pathways in the brain that utilize dopamine (Meador-Woodruff et al., 1997; Seeman & Kapur, 2001). The specific nature of this abnormality remains unclear. We can't yet say whether the abnormality involves overreactivity of particular dopamine pathways or more complex interactions among dopamine systems. One possibility is that overreactivity of dopamine receptors may be involved in producing more flagrant behaviour patterns (positive symptoms) but not the negative symptoms or deficits associated with schizophrenia. Decreased rather than increased dopamine reactivity may be connected with some of the negative symptoms of schizophrenia (Earnst & Kring, 1997). We should also note that other neurotransmitters, such as norepinephrine, serotonin, and GABA, also appear to be involved in the disorder (Busatto et al., 1997).

VIRAL INFECTIONS Might schizophrenia be caused by a slow-acting virus that attacks the developing brain of a fetus or newborn child? Prenatal rubella (German measles), a viral infection, is a cause of later mental retardation. Could another virus give rise to schizophrenia?

Viral infections are more prevalent in the winter months. Viral infection during pregnancy or infancy could account for findings of an excess number of people with schizophrenia being born in the winter (Müller, 2004). However, we have yet to find an identified viral agent we can link to schizophrenia. Moreover, there is some evidence to suggest that many different sorts of infectious agents—not just viruses—are linked to schizophrenia, raising the possibility that some cases of schizophrenia are the result of a reaction by the immune system of a developing child (Müller, 2004). But such infections probably account for only a fraction of the number of cases of schizophrenia (Müller, 2004).

BRAIN ABNORMALITIES Despite the widely held belief that schizophrenia is a brain disease, researchers are still asking, "Where is the pathology?" They are trying to find an answer by using modern brain-imaging techniques, including PET scans, EEGs, CT scans, and MRIs, to probe the inner workings of the brains of people with schizophrenia. Evidence from these types of studies shows various abnormalities in the brains of people with schizophrenia.

The most prominent finding involves enlargements of brain ventricles (the hollow spaces in the brain) (Dwork, 1997; Lauriello et al., 1997). Ventricular enlargement is a sign of structural damage involving loss of brain cells. It is found in about three out of four schizophrenia patients (Coursey, Alford, & Safarjan, 1997). Still, not all people with schizophrenia show evidence of enlarged ventricles or other signs of brain damage. Research conducted at the University of Toronto and York University, for example, shows that only some people with schizophrenia seem to have abnormalities in the frontal or temporal lobes (Zakzanis, Poulin, Hansen, & Jolic, 2000). This leads researchers to suspect that there may be several forms of schizophrenia that have different causal processes. Perhaps one form involves a degenerative loss of brain tissue (Knoll et al., 1998).

Structural damage to the brains of some schizophrenia patients may have occurred long before the initial onset of the disorder, most probably either prenatally or very early in life (Akbarian et al., 1996; Gur et al., 1998). One theory points to prenatal complications occurring during the period of 13 to 15 weeks in fetal development, when certain brain structures are forming (J. O. Davis & Bracha, 1996). Consistent with this possibility, a cross-national group of Canadian investigators have found that schizophrenia tends to be associated with poor fetal growth, premature birth, and low birth weight (G. N. Smith et al., 1999).

The source of brain damage in schizophrenia remains an open question. Among the suspected causes are prenatal infections, birth complications such as anoxia (oxygen deprivation), brain traumas suffered early in life or during prenatal development, environmental influences in childhood, or genetic defects leading to abnormal brain development (van Os, Krabbendam, Myin-Germeys, & Delespaul, 2005).

Another line of research points to possible neurotransmitter disturbances. By tracking blood flow in the brain and using brain-imaging techniques such as PET scans, EEGs, and MRIs, researchers find evidence that some people with schizophrenia have reduced brain activity in the frontal lobes, specifically in the prefrontal cortex, the area of the

CONTROLS

SCHIZOPHRENICS

FIGURE 10.2 **PET scans of people with schizophrenia versus normals.** Positron emission tomography (PET scan) evidence of the metabolic processes of the brain shows relatively less metabolic activity (indicated by less yellow and red) in the frontal lobes of the brains of people with schizophrenia. PET scans of the brains of four normal people are shown in the top row, and PET scans of the brains of four people with schizophrenia are shown below.

frontal lobes in the cerebral cortex that lies in front of the motor cortex (Zakzanis & Heinrichs, 1999) (see Figure 10.2). The prefrontal cortex is involved in performing various cognitive and emotional functions, the kinds of functions that are often impaired in people with schizophrenia. One function of the prefrontal cortex is to serve as a kind of mental clipboard for holding information needed to guide organized behaviour (Casanova, 1997). Abnormalities in the complex circuitry of the frontal lobes may explain why people with schizophrenia have difficulty organizing their thoughts and behaviour and performing higher-level cognitive tasks, such as formulating concepts, prioritizing information, and formulating goals and plans (Barch, 2005). Imbalances in neurotransmitter functioning in these neural pathways may be involved in explaining disturbed brain circuitry (Goldman-Rakic & Selemon, 1997). The prefrontal cortex is also involved in regulating attention, so findings of reduced activity coincide with research evidence of deficits in attention among people with schizophrenia. These are intriguing findings that may provide clues as to the biological bases of schizophrenia.

Other evidence points to defects in brain circuitry involving brain regions lying below the cortex, especially the **hippocampus** and **amygdala**, two structures in the limbic system (Boos, Aleman, Cahn, Hulshoff Pol, & Kahn, 2007). The limbic system plays a key role in regulating emotions and higher mental functions, including memory. These structures send projections to the prefrontal cortex, which interprets information received from lower brain centres. Imbalances in neurotransmitter function may also be involved in disrupting these brain circuits.

hippocampus One of a pair of structures in the limbic system that are involved in processes of memory.

amygdala One of a pair of almond-shaped structures in the limbic system that are involved in emotion and memory.

The Diathesis-Stress Model

In 1962, psychologist Paul Meehl proposed an integrative model that led to the development of the diathesis-stress model. Meehl suggested that certain people possess a genetic predisposition to schizophrenia that is expressed behaviourally only if they are reared in stressful environments (Meehl, 1962, 1972).

Later, Zubin and Spring (1977) formulated the diathesis-stress model, which views schizophrenia in terms of the interaction or combination of a diathesis in the form of a genetic predisposition to develop the disorder with environmental stress that exceeds the individual's stress threshold or coping resources. Environmental stressors may include psychological factors such as family conflict, child abuse, emotional deprivation, or loss

FIGURE 10.3 Diathesis-stress model of schizophrenia.

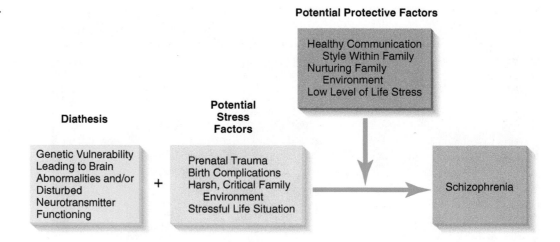

of supportive figures, as well as physical environmental influences, such as early brain trauma or injury. On the other hand, if environmental stress remains below the person's stress threshold, schizophrenia may never develop—even in persons at genetic risk (see Figure 10.3).

More recently, University of Western Ontario psychologist Richard W. J. Neufeld developed a comprehensive dynamic vulnerability model, which posits that genetic factors and environmental stressors interact in complex, mutually reinforcing ways (Neufeld, Vollick, Carter, Boksman, & Jetté, 2002). According to this model, genetic vulnerability to schizophrenia influences the person's ability to cope and affects the way she or he appraises (interprets) stressful events. In turn, coping is said to influence the genetically mediated vulnerability to developing schizophrenia symptoms. To illustrate, a genetic predisposition leads to odd behaviour and thinking problems, which leads to environmental stress (e.g., school failure, rejection by peers). This then creates distress for the person, which impairs coping and worsens schizophrenic symptoms.

What is the biological basis for the diathesis? No one has yet been able to find any specific brain abnormality present in all individuals who receive a schizophrenia diagnosis (Jablensky, 2006). Perhaps it shouldn't surprise us that a "one-size-fits-all" model doesn't apply. Schizophrenia is a complex disorder characterized by different subtypes and symptom complexes. There may be different causal processes in the brain explaining different forms of schizophrenia or even different schizophrenias (Jablensky, 2006).

We noted two possible causal processes, with one involving structural damage to brain tissue, and the other involving disturbed neurotransmitter functioning that disrupts complex brain circuits involved in thought, perception, emotions, and attention. The wealth of confusing thoughts and perceptions, social withdrawal, and bizarre behaviour that characterizes schizophrenia may be the result of this disturbed neurotransmitter functioning in brain circuits involving the prefrontal cortex and its connections to lower brain regions (Barch, 2005; Weinberger, 1997). These neural networks are involved in processing information efficiently and turning it into meaningful thoughts and behaviour. A defect in this circuitry may be involved in explaining the more flagrant, positive features of schizophrenia such as hallucinations, delusions, and thought disorder.

Another potential causal process involves structural damage to the brain, as evidenced by the presence of enlarged ventricles. Ventricular enlargement may play a greater role in explaining negative symptoms and chronic cognitive impairment than the more flagrant features of the disorder (Antonova, Sharma, Morris, & Kumari, 2004).

RESEARCH EVIDENCE SUPPORTING THE DIATHESIS-STRESS MODEL Several lines of evidence support the diathesis-stress model. Evidence suggests that stress predicts the initial onset of schizophrenia occurring in genetically vulnerable individuals (van Os et al., 2005). Sources of stress may involve sociocultural factors associated with poverty, such as overcrowding, poor diet and sanitation, impoverished housing, and inadequate health care (Selten, Cantor-Graae, & Kahn, 2007). Research from several countries, including Canada, has shown that the incidence of schizophrenia is higher among immigrants than among those who are native-born. The high rate of schizophrenia among immigrants is thought to be a result of the stress that is often associated with immigration, such as discrimination, difficulty coping because of language problems, and feeling isolated within one's new community (G. N. Smith et al., 2006). Such stressors appear to trigger schizophrenia in genetically vulnerable individuals.

Research on gene–environment interactions provides further support for the diathesis-stress model. To illustrate, consider the research on cannabis use and schizophrenia (Caspi & Moffitt, 2006). Here, cannabis use can be considered to be an environmental stimulus. People who possess particular forms of the COMT gene are liable to develop psychotic symptoms (delusions and hallucinations) when they use cannabis, and sometimes these symptoms persist to the point that the person develops schizophrenia. In comparison, people with other forms of the COMT gene do not experience these reactions to cannabis. COMT genes are involved in the regulation of dopamine. Thus, an environmental stimulus (cannabis use) may trigger schizophrenia only in genetically vulnerable individuals. In other words, there is a gene–environment interaction.

Perhaps the strongest support for the diathesis-stress model comes from longitudinal studies of "high-risk" (HR) children who are at increased genetic risk of developing the disorder by virtue of having one or more parents with schizophrenia. Longitudinal studies of HR children support the central tenet of the diathesis-stress model that heredity interacts with environmental influences in determining vulnerability to schizophrenia. Longitudinal studies track individuals over extended periods of time. Ideally, they begin before the emergence of the disorder or behaviour pattern in question and follow its course. In this way, investigators may identify early characteristics that predict the later development of a particular disorder, such as schizophrenia. These studies require a commitment of many years and substantial cost. Because schizophrenia occurs in only about 1% of the general population, researchers have focused on HR children, who are more likely to develop the disorder. Children with one schizophrenic parent have about a 10% to 25% chance of developing schizophrenia, and those with two schizophrenic parents have about a 45% risk (Erlenmeyer-Kimling et al., 1997). Still, children who have two biological parents with schizophrenia stand a better than even chance of not developing the disorder themselves.

Finnish researchers followed 112 HR children, index cases who were adopted away at birth (Tienari et al., 1987, 1990; Tienari, Wahlberg, & Wynne, 2006). These index cases, who were compared with a reference group of 135 cases, matched adopted children of non-schizophrenic biological parents. Evidence showed a much higher rate of schizophrenia in the index cases than the control cases, 5% versus 1% respectively (Tienari, 1991, 1992).

Consistent with the diathesis-stress model, environmental factors appear to have played a role in the Finnish study. Disturbed rearing in adoptive families predicted the development of schizophrenia (Tienari et al., 2006). Moreover, index children reared by disturbed adoptive families were more likely to have developed other serious psychological problems, such as borderline personality, than those reared by more functional families. Some of the disturbed families were rigid and tended to cope with family conflict by denying it. Others were chaotic; they showed low levels of trust and high levels of anxiety. The evidence from the Finnish study indicates that a combination of genetic factors and a disruptive family environment increases the risk of schizophrenia. A drawback of the Finnish study, however, was that it was not possible to determine whether disturbed family relationships represented the reaction of the families to the emergence of behavioural problems in their troubled offspring or, instead, were a contributing factor in their own right (Kendler & Prescott, 2006; Miklowitz, 2004).

Researchers have also compared HR children and other children to search for factors or markers that may predispose HR children to schizophrenia (e.g., Szymanski, Kane, & Lieberman, 1991). If we understand these early indicators, we may be able to understand the processes that lead to schizophrenia. We may also be able to identify children at greatest risk and devise intervention programs that might prevent the development of the disorder.

Protective factors in high-risk children. A supportive and nurturing environment may reduce the likelihood of developing schizophrenia among high-risk children.

The best-known longitudinal study of HR children was undertaken by Sarnoff Mednick and his colleagues in Denmark. In 1962, the Mednick group identified 207 HR children (those whose mothers had schizophrenia) and 104 reference subjects who were matched for factors such as gender, social class, age, and education but whose mothers did not have schizophrenia (Mednick, Parnas, & Schulsinger, 1987). The children from both groups ranged in age from 10 to 20 years, with a mean of 15 years. None showed signs of disturbance when first interviewed.

Later, at an average age of 20, the children were re-examined. By then, 20 of the HR children were found to have demonstrated abnormal behaviour, although not necessarily a schizophrenic episode (Mednick & Schulsinger, 1968). The children who showed abnormal behaviour, referred to as the HR "sick" group, were then compared with a matched group of 20 HR children from the original sample who remained well functioning (an HR "well" group) and a matched group of 20 low-risk (LR) subjects. It turned out that the mothers of the HR "well" offspring had experienced easier pregnancies and deliveries than those of the HR "sick" group or the LR group. Seventy percent of the mothers of the HR "sick" children had serious complications during pregnancy or delivery. Perhaps, consistent with the diathesis-stress model, complications during pregnancy or childbirth or shortly after birth cause brain damage (a stress factor) that in combination with a genetic vulnerability leads to severe psychological disorders in later life. A study in Finland provided a supportive link in showing an association between fetal and postnatal abnormalities and the development of schizophrenia in adulthood (P. B. Jones, Rantakallio, Hartikainen, Isohanni, & Sipila, 1998). The low rate of complications during pregnancy and birth in the HR "well" group in the Danish study suggests that normal pregnancies and births may actually help protect HR children from developing abnormal behaviour patterns (Mednick et al., 1987).

Evaluation of these same HR subjects in the late 1980s, when they averaged 42 years of age and had passed through the period of greatest risk for development of schizophrenia, showed a significantly higher percentage of schizophrenia in the HR group than the LR comparison group— 16% versus 2% respectively (Parnas et al., 1993). These results, like those of the Finnish study, show a strong familial association for schizophrenia between mothers and their children. An Israeli study paralleled the Danish and Finnish studies in finding a significantly greater risk of schizophrenia in a sample of HR children (8% with diagnosed schizophrenia) as compared to LR controls (0%) by the age of 30 (Ingraham, Kugelmass, Frenkel, Nathan, & Mirsky, 1995).

Evidence from longitudinal studies of HR children indicates that environmental factors, including quality of parenting and possible complications occurring prenatally or shortly after birth, may interact with genetic factors in the causal pathway leading to schizophrenia. Certain environmental factors, such as good parenting, may actually have a protective role in preventing the development of the disorder in people at increased genetic risk. In support of the role of early environmental influences, Mednick and his colleagues found that HR children who developed schizophrenia had poorer relationships with their parents than did HR children who did not go on to develop the disorder (Mednick et al., 1987). The presence of childhood behaviour problems may also be a marker for the later development of schizophrenia-related disorders in HR children (Amminger et al., 1999).

In the next section, we go on to consider the role of family factors in schizophrenia.

Family Theories

Disturbed family relationships have long been regarded as playing a role in the development and course of schizophrenia (Miklowitz, 2004). Early family theories of schizophrenia focused on the role of a "pathogenic" family member, such as the schizophrenogenic mother (Fromm-Reichmann, 1948, 1950). In what some feminists view as historical psychiatric sexism, the schizophrenogenic mother was described as cold, aloof, overprotective, and domineering. She was characterized as stripping her children of self-esteem, stifling their independence, and forcing them into dependency on her. Children reared by such mothers were believed to be at special risk for developing schizophrenia if their fathers were passive and failed to counteract the pathogenic influences of the mother. Despite extensive research, however, mothers of people who develop schizophrenia do not fit the stereotypical picture of the schizophrenogenic mother (Neill, 1990).

schizophrenogenic mother Type of mother, described as cold but also overprotective, who was believed to be capable of causing schizophrenia in her children. Research has failed to support the validity of this concept.

In the 1950s, family theorists began to focus on the role of disturbed communications in the family. One of the more prominent theories, put forth by Gregory Bateson and his colleagues (Bateson, Jackson, Haley, & Weakland, 1956), was that **double-bind communications** contributed to the development of schizophrenia. A double-bind communication transmits two mutually incompatible messages. In a double-bind communication with a child, a mother might freeze up when the child approaches her and then scold the child for keeping a distance. Whatever the child does, she or he is wrong. With repeated exposure to such double binds, the child's thinking may become disorganized and chaotic. The double-binding mother prevents discussion of her inconsistencies because she cannot admit to herself that she is unable to tolerate closeness. Note this vignette:

double-bind communications Pattern of communication involving the transmission of contradictory or mixed messages without acknowledgment of the inherent conflict; posited by some theorists to play a role in the development of schizophrenia.

> A young man who had fairly well recovered from an acute schizophrenic episode was visited in the hospital by his mother. He was glad to see her and impulsively put his arm around her shoulders whereupon she stiffened. He withdrew his arm and she asked, "Don't you love me anymore?" He then blushed and she said, "Dear, you must not be so easily embarrassed and afraid of your feelings." The patient was able to stay with her only a few minutes more and following her departure he assaulted an aide.
>
> Bateson, Jackson, Haley, & Weakland, 1956, pp. 251–264. Copyright John Wiley & Sons.

Perhaps double-bind communications serve as a source of family stress that increases the risk of schizophrenia in genetically vulnerable individuals. In more recent years, investigators have broadened the investigation of family factors in schizophrenia by viewing the family in terms of a system of relationships among the members, rather than singling out mother–child or father–child interactions. Research has begun to identify stressful factors in the family that may interact with a genetic vulnerability in leading to the development of schizophrenia. Two principal sources of family stress that have been studied are patterns of deviant communications and negative emotional expression in the family.

COMMUNICATION DEVIANCE Communication deviance describes a pattern characterized by unclear, vague, disruptive, or fragmented parental communication and by parental inability to focus in on what the child is saying (Kymalainen, Weisman, Resales, & Armesto, 2006). Parents high in communication deviance tend to attack their children personally rather than offer constructive criticism and may subject them to double-bind communications. They also tend to interrupt the child with intrusive, negative comments. They are prone to telling the child what she or he "really" thinks rather than allowing the child to formulate her or his own thoughts and feelings. Parents of people with schizophrenia show higher levels of communication deviance than parents of people without schizophrenia (Kymalainen et al., 2006).

Communication deviance may be one of the stress-related factors that increase the risk of development of schizophrenia in genetically vulnerable individuals (Kymalainen et al., 2006). Then, too, the causal pathway may work in the opposite direction. Perhaps communication deviance is a parental reaction to the behaviour of disturbed children. Parents may learn to use odd language as a way of coping with

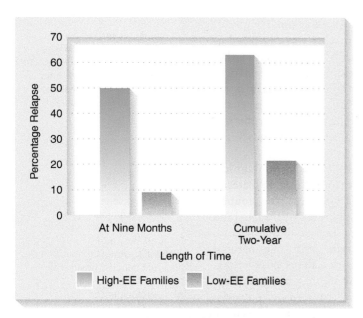

FIGURE 10.4 Relapse rates of people with schizophrenia in high- and low-EE families.
People with schizophrenia whose families are high in expressed emotion (EE) are at greater risk of relapse than those whose families are low in EE. Whereas low-EE families may help protect the family member with schizophrenia from environmental stressors, high-EE families may impose additional stress.

Source: Adapted from Leff & Vaughn (1981).

children who continually interrupt and confront them (Miklowitz, 2004). Or perhaps parents and children share genetic traits that become expressed as disturbed communications and increased vulnerability toward schizophrenia, without there being a causal link between the two.

EXPRESSED EMOTION Another measure of disturbed family communications is called *expressed emotion* (EE). EE involves the tendency of family members to be hostile, critical, and unsupportive of their schizophrenic family members. People with schizophrenia whose families are high in EE tend to show poorer adjustment and have higher rates of relapse following release from the hospital than those with more supportive families (Miklowitz, 2004). Expressed emotion in relatives is also associated with a greater risk of relapse from other disorders, such as major depression and eating disorders (Butzlaff & Hooley, 1998).

Low-EE families may actually serve to protect or buffer the family member with schizophrenia from the adverse impact of outside stressors and help prevent recurrent episodes (Strachan, 1986) (see Figure 10.4). Yet family interactions are a two-way street. Family members and patients influence each other and are influenced in turn. Disruptive behaviours by the schizophrenic family member frustrate other members of the family, prompting them to respond to the person in a less supportive and more critical and hostile way. This in turn can exacerbate the schizophrenia patient's disruptive behaviour (Miklowitz, 2004).

Families of people with schizophrenia tend to have little if any preparation or training for coping with the stressful demands of caring for them. Rather than focusing so much on the negative influence of high-EE family members, we should learn to better understand the negative day-to-day interactions between people with schizophrenia and their family members that lead to high levels of expressed emotion. Recent evidence shows that families can be helped to reduce the level of expressed emotion (Miklowitz, 2004).

Research on expressed emotion and family stress factors helps focus attention on the need for family-intervention programs that help prepare families for the burdens of caregiving and assist them in learning more adaptive ways of relating to one another. This, in turn, may reduce the stress imposed on the family member with schizophrenia and improve family harmony.

FAMILY FACTORS IN SCHIZOPHRENIA: CAUSES OR SOURCES OF STRESS? No evidence supports the belief that family factors, such as negative family interactions, lead to schizophrenia in children who do not have a genetic vulnerability. What then is the role of family factors in schizophrenia? In the diathesis-stress model, disturbed patterns of emotional interaction and communication in the family represent a source of potential stress that may increase the risks of developing schizophrenia among people with a genetic predisposition for the disorder. Perhaps these increased risks can be minimized or eliminated if families are taught to handle stress and to be less critical and more supportive of the members of their families with schizophrenia. Counselling programs that help family members of people with chronic schizophrenia learn to express their feelings without attacking or criticizing the person with the disorder may prevent family conflicts that damage the person's adjustment (Miklowitz, 2004). The family member with schizophrenia may also benefit from efforts to reduce the level of contact with relatives who fail to respond to family interventions.

Theoretical Perspectives

- **How is schizophrenia conceptualized in traditional psychodynamic theory and learning perspectives?** In the traditional psychodynamic model, schizophrenia represents a regression to a psychological state corresponding to early infancy in which the proddings of the id produce bizarre, socially deviant behaviour and give rise to hallucinations and delusions. Learning theorists propose that some forms of schizophrenic behaviour may result from a lack of social reinforcement, which leads to gradual detachment from the social environment and increased attention to an inner world of fantasy. Modelling and selective reinforcement of bizarre behaviour may explain some schizophrenic behaviours in a hospital setting.

- **What do we know about the biological bases of schizophrenia?** Compelling evidence for a strong genetic component in schizophrenia comes from studies of family patterns of schizophrenia, twin studies, and adoption studies. The mode of genetic transmission remains unknown.

Most researchers believe the neurotransmitter dopamine plays a role in schizophrenia, especially in the more flagrant features of the disorder. Viral factors may also be involved, but definite proof of viral involvement is lacking. Evidence of brain dysfunctions and structural damage in schizophrenia is accumulating, but researchers are uncertain about causal pathways.

- **How is schizophrenia conceptualized in the diathesis-stress model?** The diathesis-stress model posits that schizophrenia results from an interaction of a genetic predisposition (the diathesis) and environmental stressors (e.g., family conflict, child abuse, emotional deprivation, loss of supportive figures, and early brain trauma).

- **How are family factors related to the development and course of schizophrenia?** Family factors such as communication deviance and expressed emotion (EE) may act as sources of stress that increase the risk of development or recurrence of schizophrenia among people with a genetic predisposition.

TREATMENT

There is no cure for schizophrenia. Treatment of schizophrenia is generally multifaceted, incorporating pharmacological, psychological, and rehabilitative approaches. Most people treated for schizophrenia in organized mental health settings receive some form of antipsychotic medication, which is intended to control more flagrant behaviour patterns such as hallucinations and delusions and decrease the risk of recurrent episodes.

Biological Approaches

The advent in the 1950s of antipsychotic drugs—also referred to as *major tranquillizers* or *neuroleptics*—revolutionized the treatment of schizophrenia and provided the impetus for large-scale releases of mental patients into the community (deinstitutionalization). The first of these drugs, chlorpromazine (Largactil), was introduced to North America by McGill University psychiatrist Heinz Lehmann (Lehmann & Hanrahan, 1954). Antipsychotic medication helped control the more flagrant behaviour patterns of schizophrenia and reduced the need for long-term hospitalization when taken on a maintenance basis (Sheitman, Kinon, Ridgway, & Lieberman, 1998). Yet for many chronic schizophrenia patients today, entering a hospital is like going through a revolving door. That is, they are repeatedly admitted and discharged within a relatively brief time frame. Many are simply discharged to the streets once they are stabilized on medication and receive little if any follow-up care or available housing. This often leads to a pattern of chronic homelessness punctuated by brief stays in the hospital. Only a small proportion of people with schizophrenia who are discharged from long-term care facilities are successfully reintegrated into the community (Bellack & Mueser, 1990).

Commonly used antipsychotic drugs include the phenothiazines chlorpromazine (Largactil), thioridazine (Mellaril), trifluoperazine (Stelazine), and fluphenazine (Moditen), as well as haloperidol (Haldol), which is chemically distinct from the phenothiazines but produces similar effects.

Although we can't say with certainty how these drugs work, it appears they derive their therapeutic effect from blocking dopamine receptors in the brain. This reduces dopamine activity, which seems to quell the more flagrant signs of schizophrenia such as hallucinations and delusions. The effectiveness of antipsychotic drugs has been repeatedly demonstrated in double-blind, placebo-controlled studies (Kane, 1996). Yet a substantial minority of people with schizophrenia receive little benefit from traditional neuroleptics, and no clear-cut factors determine who will best respond (Kane & Marder, 1993).

The major risk of long-term treatment with neuroleptic drugs (possibly excluding clozapine and other new-generation drugs) is a potentially disabling side effect called **tardive dyskinesia** (TD). TD is an involuntary movement disorder that can affect any body part (Hansen, Casey, & Hoffman, 1997). It is irreversible in many cases, even when the neuroleptic medication is withdrawn. It occurs most often in patients who are treated with neuroleptics for six months or longer. TD can take different forms, the most common of which is frequent eye blinking. Common signs of the disorder include involuntary chewing and eye movements, lip smacking and puckering, facial grimacing, and involuntary movements of the limbs and trunk. In some cases, the movement disorder is so severe that patients have difficulties breathing, talking, or eating. Overall, about one in four people receiving long-term treatment with neuroleptics eventually develop TD (Jeste & Caligiuri, 1993).

Tardive dyskinesia is more common among older people and women (Hansen et al., 1997). Unfortunately, we lack a safe and effective treatment for TD (Sheitman et al., 1998). Although TD tends to improve gradually or stabilize over a period of years, many people with TD remain persistently and severely disabled.

The risk of these potentially disabling side effects requires physicians to carefully weigh the risks and benefits of long-term treatment with these drugs. Investigators have altered drug regimens in an attempt to reduce the risk of TD, such as by stopping medication in stable outpatients and starting it again when early symptoms reappear. However, intermittent medication schedules are associated with a twofold increase in the risk of relapse and have not been shown to lower the risk of TD (Kane, 1996).

A new generation of drugs, called *atypical antipsychotic drugs* (clozapine, risperidone, and olanzapine are examples), have been introduced and offer the promise of controlling schizophrenic symptoms with fewer neurological side effects than conventional antipsychotics (Kapur & Remington, 2001). They may also be more effective in treating negative symptoms of schizophrenia than conventional antipsychotics. One of these atypical antipsychotics, clozapine, is the only known drug that carries a minimal risk of TD (Conley & Buchanan, 1997; Kane, 1996). Clozapine appears to be more effective than conventional antipsychotics in reducing the symptoms of schizophrenia patients, including patients who have failed to respond to other antipsychotics (Breier et al., 1999; Wahlbeck, Cheine, Essali, & Adams, 1999). However, other side effects limit its use, especially the risk of agranulocytosis, a potentially lethal disorder in which the body produces inadequate supplies of white blood cells. The disorder affects 1% to 2% of patients who use the drug (Kane & Marder, 1993). There are also promising findings that olanzapine may reduce the risk of TD relative to conventional antipsychotics (Tollefson, Beasley, Tamura, Tran, & Potvin, 1997). Recent research has shown olanzapine to be helpful, but most people with schizophrenia show only a partial response to this drug (Stauffer et al., 2011).

A panel of Canadian experts on schizophrenia (psychologists and psychiatrists) published a set of clinical practice guidelines on the treatment of the disorder (Working Group for the Canadian Psychiatric Association and Canadian Alliance for Research on Schizophrenia, 1998). The guidelines, based on the current state of knowledge, are similar to those of other countries. According to the guidelines, antipsychotic medications are the most effective treatment available, especially when combined with psychoeducational interventions. Antipsychotic drugs help control the more flagrant or bizarre features of schizophrenia, but they are not a cure. Updates to the original guidelines re-emphasize the use of antipsychotics as an essential part of the treatment plan and emphasize that the medication must be individualized due to the wide range of responses ("Clinical Practice Guidelines," 2005).

tardive dyskinesia Movement disorder characterized by involuntary movements of the face, mouth, neck, trunk, or extremities caused by long-term use of antipsychotic medications. Abbreviated *TD*.

People with chronic schizophrenia typically receive maintenance doses of antipsychotic drugs once their flagrant symptoms abate. The working group notes that the relapse rate may be as high as 90% in the first year after hospital discharge if the patient discontinues medication. Staying on medication can reduce the relapse rate to about 40% (Hogarty, 1993). Still, not all people with schizophrenia require antipsychotic medication to maintain themselves in the community. Unfortunately, no one can yet predict which patients can manage effectively without continued medication.

Drug therapy needs to be supplemented with psychoeducational programs that help schizophrenia patients develop better social skills and adjust to the demands of community living. A wide array of treatment components are needed within a comprehensive model of care, including such elements as antipsychotic medication, medical care, family therapy, social-skills training, crisis intervention, rehabilitation services, and housing and other social services (Marder et al., 1996; Penn & Mueser, 1996). Programs also need to ensure a continuity of care between the hospital and the community.

Psychoanalytic Approaches

Freud did not believe traditional psychoanalysis to be well suited to the treatment of schizophrenia. The withdrawal into a fantasy world that typifies schizophrenia prevents the individual with schizophrenia from forming a meaningful relationship with the psychoanalyst. The techniques of classical psychoanalysis, Freud wrote, must "be replaced by others; and we do not know yet whether we shall succeed in finding a substitute" (Arieti, 1974, p. 532).

Other psychoanalysts such as Harry Stack Sullivan and Frieda Fromm-Reichmann adapted psychoanalytic techniques specifically for the treatment of schizophrenia. However, research has failed to demonstrate the effectiveness of psychoanalytic or psychodynamic therapy for schizophrenia. In light of negative findings, some critics have argued that further research on the use of psychodynamic therapies for treating schizophrenia is not warranted (e.g., Klerman, 1984).

Learning-Based Approaches

Although few behaviour therapists believe that faulty learning causes schizophrenia, learning-based interventions have been shown to be effective in modifying schizophrenic behaviour and assisting people with the disorder in developing more adaptive behaviours that can help them adjust more effectively to living in the community. Therapy methods include techniques such as (1) selective reinforcement of behaviour (e.g., providing attention for appropriate behaviour while extinguishing bizarre verbalizations through withdrawal of attention); (2) the token economy, in which individuals on inpatient units are rewarded for appropriate behaviour with tokens, such as plastic chips, that can be exchanged for tangible reinforcers such as desirable goods or privileges; and (3) social-skills training, in which clients are taught conversational skills and other appropriate social behaviours through coaching, modelling, behaviour rehearsal, and feedback.

TOKEN-ECONOMY SYSTEMS Promising results have emerged from studies applying intensive learning-based approaches in hospital settings. A classic study by Paul and Lentz (1977) showed that a psychosocial treatment program based on a token-economy system improved adaptive behaviour in the hospital, decreased need for medication, and lengthened community tenure following release in relation to a traditional, custodial-type treatment condition with a milieu approach that emphasized patient participation in decision making (see Figure 10.5 on page 386).

Overall, token economies have proven to be more effective than intensive milieu treatment and traditional custodial treatment in improving social functioning and reducing psychotic behaviour (Mueser & Liberman, 1995). However, the many prerequisites

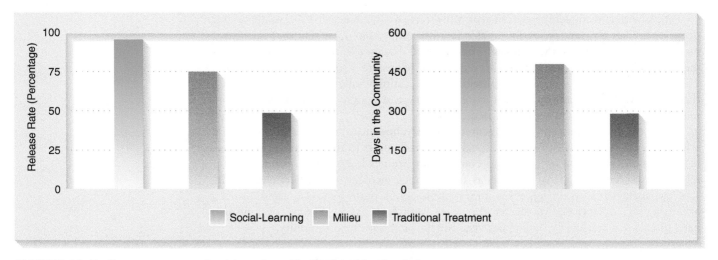

FIGURE 10.5 Some measures of outcome from the Paul and Lentz study.
This figure shows the release rates and community tenure (days in the community) of people with schizophrenia in the three conditions studied by Paul and Lentz: (1) social-learning-based treatment, (2) milieu treatment, and (3) traditional hospital treatment. Nearly all of the subjects in the social-learning program (97.5%) were able to be discharged and to remain in the community for a minimum of 90 days, as compared to 71% of the milieu-therapy participants and 45% of the control (standard treatment) participants. Subjects in the social-learning program also remained in the community longer than subjects who received the other conditions.

Source: Glynn & Mueser, 1986.

may limit the applicability of this approach. Such programs require strong administrative support, skilled treatment leaders, extensive staff training, and continuous quality control (Glynn & Mueser, 1986).

SOCIAL-SKILLS TRAINING   Social-skills training (SST) involves programs that help individuals acquire a range of social and vocational skills. People with schizophrenia are often deficient in basic social skills, including skills involving assertiveness, interview skills, and general conversational skills—skills that may be needed to adjust successfully to community living. Controlled studies have shown that SST can improve a wide range of social skills, increase social adjustment, reduce psychiatric symptoms in persons with schizophrenia, and improve community functioning (Penn, 1998). Social-skills training has also been shown to reduce relapse rates during the first year following treatment (Bellack & Mueser, 1993). Researchers in Calgary found that the benefits of a short (nine-week) social-skills training program tended to be lost over time (D. J. G. Dobson, McDougall, Busheikin, & Aldous, 1995), suggesting that long-term programs may be required, at least for some people with schizophrenia. It remains to be seen whether social-skills training can produce a substantial payoff in helping patients adapt to community living (Dilk & Bond, 1996; Penn, 1998).

Although different approaches to skills training have been developed, the basic model uses role-playing exercises in a group format. Participants practise skills such as starting or maintaining conversations with new acquaintances and receive feedback and reinforcement from the therapist and other group members. The first step might be a dry run in which the participant role-plays the targeted behaviour, such as asking strangers for bus directions. The therapist and other group members then praise the effort and provide constructive feedback. Role-playing is augmented by techniques such as modelling (observation of the therapist or other group members enacting the desired behaviour), direct instruction (specific directions for enacting the desired behaviour), shaping (reinforcement for successive approximations to the target behaviour), and coaching (therapist's use of verbal or nonverbal prompts to elicit a particular desired behaviour in the role play). Participants are given homework assignments to practise the behaviours in the settings in which they live, such as on the hospital ward or in the community. The aim is to enhance generalization or transfer of training to other settings. Training sessions may also be run in stores, restaurants, schools, and other real-life settings.

CBT WITH SOCIAL-SKILLS TRAINING Multifaceted cognitive-behavioural interventions, which can include social-skills training and other techniques, appear to be helpful (Rector & Beck, 2001). Cognitive-behavioural interventions can include teaching patients skills for managing the stress in their lives and showing them ways of managing their symptoms. For example, they can include helping patients identify triggers that make their symptoms worse (e.g., anxiety, family conflicts) and teaching them skills for dealing with the triggers (e.g., relaxation training, cognitive restructuring, skills training for conflict negotiating). Recently, cognitive-behavioural interventions have been targeted to reduce particular symptoms, such as hallucinations, along with social functioning. Cognitive-behavioural therapy combined with social-skills training has shown significant long-term improvements on psychotic effects and social functioning. In a naturalistic study (Wiersma, Jenner, van de Willige, Spakman, & Nienhuis, 2001), patients were assessed at two and four years post-treatment. The combined treatments improved the overall burden of "hearing voices"; 60% of the individuals showed improvement with regard to fear, loss of control, disturbance of thought, and interference with thinking. Complete disappearance of hallucinations occurred in 18% of the patients. It appears that CBT with coping training can improve both overall symptomatology and quality of life, even over longer periods of time.

Psychosocial Rehabilitation

People with schizophrenia typically have difficulties functioning in social and occupational roles. These problems limit their ability to adjust to community life even in the absence of overt psychotic behaviour. Many older, long-hospitalized individuals who have been resettled in the community are particularly ill prepared to handle the tasks of daily living, such as cooking, shopping, or travelling around town. Many younger individuals with schizophrenia have markedly deficient social skills, even though they have spent only short periods of time in mental hospitals (Anthony & Liberman, 1986). As a result, a number of self-help groups and more structured psychosocial rehabilitation centres have sprung up to help people with schizophrenia find a place in society. Many centres were launched by nonprofessionals or by people with schizophrenia themselves, largely because mental health agencies often failed to provide comparable services (Anthony & Liberman, 1986). This, combined with family-intervention programs and community programs, can reduce the risk of relapse (Rathod & Turkington, 2005).

Community programs typically offer services such as housing, as well as job and educational opportunities. These programs often make use of skills-training approaches to help clients learn how to handle money, resolve disputes with family members, develop friendships, take buses, cook their own meals, shop, and so on.

The rehabilitation model teaches that people with emotional or physical disabilities can achieve their potentials if they are given the support and structure they need and if the expectations and demands placed on them are consistent with their capabilities. Both the client and the family should be helped to adjust their expectations to attainable levels (Anthony & Liberman, 1986).

Family-Intervention Programs

Family conflicts and negative family interactions can heap stress on family members with schizophrenia, increasing the risk of recurrent episodes (Addington, Collins, McCleery, & Addington, 2005). Researchers and clinicians have worked with families of people with schizophrenia to help them cope with the burdens of care and assist them in developing more co-operative, less confrontational ways of relating to others. The specific components involved in family interventions vary from program to program, but they tend to share certain common features, such as a focus on the practical aspects of everyday living, educating family members about schizophrenia, teaching them how to relate in a less hostile way to family members with schizophrenia, improving communication in the family, and fostering effective problem-solving and coping skills for handling family problems and disputes.

Structured family-intervention programs have been shown to reduce rates of relapse among schizophrenia patients (Addington et al., 2005). However, the benefits appear to be modest and questions remain about whether recurrences are prevented or merely delayed. We should also note that not all people with schizophrenia live with their families. Perhaps similar psychoeducational programs can be applied to nonfamily environments in which people live with schizophrenia, such as foster-care homes or board-and-care homes.

In sum, no single treatment approach meets all the needs of people with schizophrenia. The conceptualization of schizophrenia as a lifelong disability underscores the need for long-term treatment interventions involving antipsychotic medication, family interventions, psychological interventions, vocational training, and social-system support such as provision of decent housing. These interventions should be co-ordinated and integrated within a comprehensive model of treatment to be most effective in helping the individual achieve maximal social adjustment (Coursey et al., 1997). Treatment services are also more likely to improve client functioning in certain areas, such as improving work or independent living, when they are specifically targeted toward those areas (Brekke, Long, Nesbitt, & Sobel, 1997). This model may consist of drug therapy, hospitalization as needed, inpatient learning-based programs, family-intervention programs, skills-training programs, social self-help clubs, and rehabilitation programs.

A CLOSER LOOK

Psychosis Sucks! Early Psychosis Intervention Programs

Have you experienced unusual sensitivity to noise, light, and colour? Appetite changes, loss of energy, and withdrawal from friends? Do you hear voices that no one else hears? Do your thoughts seem to be sped up or slowed down? Do you feel just generally confused? Do you have periods of feeling spacey or disoriented, difficulty concentrating or remembering things? Are you suspicious of others? If you were experiencing any of these things, would you seek help? Often friends and family members are the first to notice these changes. And some might say these signs are just typical teenage experiences, when in fact these are potentially early signs of psychosis.

You can understand why, out of fear, a young person might not seek help, but early intervention makes a difference.

While the whole field of early intervention for psychosis is still growing, there is good research that shows intervention can help prevent the full development of acute psychosis (Perkins, 2005). In addition, it seems that the duration of time before intervention influences how well the person responds to medication and other forms of treatment. It's important to treat these early symptoms—within the first three to five years—with medication, psychosocial interventions, stress management, and family support (Birchwood, Todd, & Jackson, 1988). According to the Canadian Mental Health Association (2000), "In most cases, psychosis will not go away on its own. Early detection and appropriate treatment offer the best chance for full recovery and reduction in relapse rates" (Bertelsen, Jeppesen, & Petersen, et al., 2008).

WHY GET HELP EARLY?

According to the Canadian Mental Health Association, the benefits of early intervention can include

- reduced disruption of activities
- reduced disruption of family and social relationships
- reduced likelihood of hospitalization
- reduced disability and fewer relapses
- reduced risk of suicide
- improved capacity to maintain self-identity and self-esteem
- faster and more complete recovery

At this point Canada has well-established early psychosis intervention (EPI) clinics. However, many communities still lack ready access to comprehensive services, so the type of treatment really does depend on where your family lives. To find an EPI service close to where you live, check the Canadian Early Psychosis Intervention Clinical Programs list: www.telecarecorp.com/articles1-278/EarlyIntervention ProgramsinCanada.

RESOURCES WORTH NOTING

Psychosis Sucks
www.psychosissucks.ca
An Early Psychosis Intervention Program.
PEPP: Prevention and Early Intervention Program for Psychoses
www.pepp.ca
Support for friends and family members of those suffering with psychosis.

Early-Intervention Programs

The treatment approaches described so far in this chapter were all intended for people with full-blown schizophrenia. More recently, there have been important developments in treating symptoms before they become very severe. Such programs are important because the earlier a person receives treatment, the better the outcome in terms of reducing symptoms and improving daily functioning (Killackey & Yung, 2007). There are two main forms of early intervention. The first is to initiate treatment as early as possible once the person has developed schizophrenia, using the treatments described above. The second is to intervene before the onset of schizophrenia (i.e., prevention programs). This involves accurately identifying people at high risk for schizophrenia, as suggested by (a) a high-risk age (late teens or early 20s), (b) recent deterioration in social functioning, and (c) a family history of psychosis. Such high-risk people are then offered treatment—typically cognitive-behaviour therapy or antipsychotic medication (Killackey & Yung, 2007).

Research suggests that treating the symptoms as early as possible is important in improving outcomes (Malla, Norman, & Joober, 2005). However, further studies are needed to fully evaluate the benefits of treatments aimed at preventing schizophrenia (Killackey & Yung, 2007; Malla et al., 2005).

REVIEW IT

Treatment Approaches

- **How does the treatment of schizophrenia involve a multifaceted approach?** Contemporary treatment approaches tend to be multifaceted, incorporating pharmacological and psychosocial approaches. Antipsychotic medication is not a cure, but it tends to stem the more flagrant aspects of the disorder and to reduce the need for hospitalization and the risk of recurrent episodes.
- **What types of psychosocial interventions have shown promising results?** These are principally learning-based approaches, such as token-economy systems and social-skills training. They help increase the adaptive behaviour of schizophrenia patients. Psychosocial-rehabilitation approaches help people with schizophrenia adapt more successfully to occupational and social roles in the community. Family-intervention programs help families cope with the burdens of care, communicate more clearly, and learn more helpful ways of relating to the patient.

Define It

affect, 360
ambivalence, 360
amygdala, 377
associations, 359
autism, 360
blocking, 363
catatonic type, 369
clanging, 363
cross-fostering study, 374
disorganized type, 369

dopamine theory, 375
double-bind communications, 381
first-rank symptoms, 360
four As, 359
hippocampus, 377
negative symptoms, 370
neologisms, 363
perseveration, 363
positive symptoms, 370
premorbid functioning, 370

prodromal phase, 362
residual phase, 362
schizophrenia, 359
schizophrenogenic mother, 381
second-rank symptoms, 360
stupor, 368
tardive dyskinesia, 384
thought disorder, 363
waxy flexibility, 369

Think About It

- The authors state that schizophrenia is perhaps the most disabling type of mental or psychological disorder. What makes it so?
- What are the relative risks and benefits of antipsychotic medication? Do you believe that people with schizophrenia should be treated indefinitely with these drugs? Why or why not?
- What might you say to critics who claim that schizophrenia is not a disease because no one has yet found any specific disease process in the brain that accounts for it?

Weblinks

Schizophrenia Society of Canada
www.schizophrenia.ca
This site offers information in English and French
about the causes and treatments of schizophrenia. It
contains a number of useful links.

Schizophrenia www.nimh.nih.gov/health/topics/
schizophrenia/index.shtml
The National Institute of Mental Health's schizophrenia
page provides useful information on the disorder.

Schizophrenia.com www.schizophrenia.com
Another informationally rich website, containing
many links and discussion forums concerning
schizophrenia.

Schizoaffective Disorder www.noah-health.org/en/
mental/disorders/schizo.html
This website provides information on schizoaffective
disorder.

Early Psychosis Intervention www.cmha.ca/bins/
content_page.asp?cid=3-105-107&lang=1
Information from the CAMH on early diagnosis of
psychosis.

MySearchLab offers you extensive help with your writing and research projects
and provides round-the-clock access to credible and reliable source material.
Chapter quizzes and a full electronic version of the text are also provided.
Take a tour at www.mysearchlab.com.

Schizophrenia

Main Types of Schizophrenia Symptoms
(Organized according to the three-dimensional model)

Psychotic Dimension

Examples
- Hallucinations
- Delusions

Negative Dimension

Examples
- Flat affect
- Poverty of speech and thought

Disorganized Dimension

Examples
- Inappropriate affect
- Disordered thought and speech

Subtypes of Schizophrenia

Paranoid Type

- Preoccupation with one or more delusions, or preoccupation with frequent auditory hallucinations
- Does not have disorganized behaviour or flat or inappropriate affect

Disorganized Type

- Confused behaviour, incoherent speech, hallucinations, disorganized delusions, inappropriate (e.g., silly) affect

Catatonic Type

- Markedly impaired motor behaviour, stupor, mannerisms, bizarre postures, waxy flexibility

Undifferentiated Type

- Fails to meet specifications for any of single one of the above three types, or has features of more than one of the above types

Residual Type

- No prominent psychotic features but still has features of a previous episode of schizophrenia (e.g., blunted affect)

Theoretical Perspectives

Psychodynamic

- Schizophrenia is the overwhelming of the ego by the id, producing intrapsychic conflict and regression to an early period called *primary narcissism*.

Family Theories

Communication Deviance
- Patterns of communication characterized by unclear, vague, disruptive, or fragmented parental communication

Expressed Emotion
- Tendency of family members to be hostile, critical, and unsupportive of schizophrenic family members

Learning-Based

- People may learn to "emit" schizophrenic behaviours and never learn to respond appropriately to social stimuli.

Biological

Genetic Factors
- Evidence is compelling that schizophrenia is strongly influenced by and specifically points to the interaction of multiple genes.

Biochemical Factors
- The "dopamine theory" proposes that people with schizophrenia have a greater than normal number of dopamine receptors and/or these receptors are overly sensitive to dopamine.

Brain Abnormalities
- Less activity in frontal lobes, enlarged ventricles, degeneration of brain tissue

>>

Treatment

Biological

- Major tranquillizers or neuroleptics have revolutionized treatment.
- New-generation drugs—atypical antipsychotic drugs—control symptoms with fewer neurological side effects.

Psychoanalytic

- Psychodynamic therapies for treating schizophrenia are not warranted; patient cannot form meaningful relationship with therapist.

Learning-Based

- Interventions have been shown effective in modifying schizophrenic behaviour and improving social functioning.

Psychosocial Rehabilitation

- Social-skills training combined with cognitive-behavioural treatment shows improved adjustment to community life.

Family Intervention Programs

- Family intervention programs focusing on the practical aspects of everyday living have been shown to reduce relapse among schizophrenic patients.

Early Intervention Programs

- Two main types: (1) initiate treatment as early as possible once schizophrenia has developed or (2) intervene before the onset of schizophrenia.

11

Abnormal Behaviour Across the Lifespan

CHAPTER OUTLINE

Pervasive Development Disorders
Autism

Mental Retardation
Causes of Mental Retardation
Intervention

Learning Disorders
Types of Learning Disorders
Intervention

Attention-Deficit and Disruptive Behaviour Disorder
Attention-Deficit/Hyperactivity Disorder
Conduct Disorder
Oppositional Defiant Disorder

Anxiety and Depression in Childhood and Adolescence
Separation Anxiety Disorder
Perspectives on Anxiety Disorders in Childhood
Depression in Childhood and Adolescence

Delirium
Clinical Picture
Diagnosis
Treatment and Outcomes

Dementia
Clinical Picture
Neuropathy
Causes and Diagnosis
Treatment and Outcomes

Did You Know That...

- Many behaviour patterns considered normal for children would be considered abnormal in adults?

- Maternal smoking during pregnancy may contribute to the development of attention-deficit/hyperactivity disorder (ADHD) in children?

- Some people can recall verbatim every story they read in a newspaper?

- Most children with ADHD are given stimulants to help calm them down?

- Major depression can occur in young children?

- A specific protein in spinal fluid can be used to diagnose Alzheimer's disease?

- In the elderly, delirium-like symptoms can sometimes occur as early signs of infection or heart problems, making accurate delirium diagnosis problematic?

P sychological problems in childhood and adolescence often have a special poignancy. They affect children at ages when they have little capacity to cope. The same could be said for some diseases that are more likely to occur later in life. Contrary to images and messages we get from our current culture that aging is equated with disease and decline, most older people are physically and mentally healthy, living happy and productive lives. In fact, psychological disorders in general are lower among older people than younger people. Here we'll focus on the 10% to 20% of people over the age of 65 who have psychological problems that could be severe enough to warrant diagnosis and treatment, disorders such as delirium and dementia disorder. We'll come to these at the end of this chapter.

Some psychological problems in childhood and adolescence mirror the types of problems found in adults—problems such as mood and anxiety disorders. In some cases, such as separation anxiety, the problems are unique to childhood; in others, such as attention-deficit/hyperactivity disorder (ADHD), the problems manifest differently in childhood than in adulthood.

To determine what is normal and abnormal among children and adolescents, not only do we consider the criteria outlined in earlier chapters, we also weigh what is to be expected given a child's age, gender, and family and cultural background, as well as the sundry developmental transformations that are taking place. Many problems are first identified when a child enters school. They may have existed earlier but were tolerated or unrecognized as problematic in the home. Sometimes, the stress of starting school contributes to their onset. Keep in mind, however, that what is socially acceptable at one age, such as intense fear of strangers at about nine months, may be socially unacceptable at more advanced ages. Many behaviour patterns that would be considered abnormal among adults—such as intense fear of strangers and lack of bladder control—are perfectly normal for children at certain ages.

Just how common are mental health problems among Canada's children and adolescents? Although we lack nationwide statistics, University of British Columbia researchers reviewed studies from Ontario, Quebec, the United States, and the United Kingdom that indicated that about 14% of children and adolescents have a mental disorder (Waddell, McEwan, Shepherd, Offord, & Hua, 2005; Waddell & Shepherd, 2002). The four most common categories—anxiety disorders, conduct disorders, ADHD, and depressive disorders—account for nearly 90% of those mental disorders.

Despite the prevalence of psychological disorders among the young, fewer than a quarter of children and youth with mental disorders receive specialized clinical services (Waddell et al., 2005; Waddell, Offord, Shepherd, Hua, & McEwan, 2002). Children who have internalized problems, such as anxiety and depression, are at higher risk of going untreated than are children with externalized problems (problems involving acting out or aggressive behaviour), which tend to be disruptive or annoying to others.

In this chapter we first examine a number of psychological disorders affecting children and adolescents, and then focus on two of the most frequent cognitive disorders found among the elderly: delirium and dementia. Delirium develops quickly and can be described as a confused state, while dementia is the gradual worsening of memory and cognitive function. We examine the features of these disorders, their causes, and the treatments used.

PERVASIVE DEVELOPMENTAL DISORDERS

Pervasive developmental disorders (PDDs), which are also referred to as *autistic spectrum disorders* (Alberta Learning, 2003), involve markedly impaired behaviour or functioning in multiple areas of development. These disorders generally become evident in the first few years of life and are often associated with mental retardation (APA, 2000a). They were generally classified as forms of psychoses in early editions of the DSM, and were thought to reflect childhood forms of adult psychoses, such as schizophrenia, because they share features such as social and emotional impairment, oddities of communication, and stereotyped motor behaviours. Research has shown that they are distinct from schizophrenia and other psychoses, however, and PDDs are now classified separately from psychotic disorders. The label of schizophrenia with childhood onset is reserved for the relatively rare instances in which schizophrenia develops in childhood (Jacobsen et al., 1997).

McGill University child research psychiatrist Eric Fombonne (2005) estimates that the prevalence of all forms of PDDs is 0.6% to 0.7%. The DSM (APA, 2000a) includes the following PDDs: autistic disorder, Rett's disorder, childhood disintegrative disorder, Asperger's disorder, and pervasive developmental disorder not otherwise specified. The major type of pervasive developmental disorder, and our focus here, is autism, or autistic disorder.

pervasive developmental disorders Disorders involving markedly impaired behaviour or functioning in multiple areas of development. Abbreviated *PDDs*. Also called *autistic spectrum disorders*.

Autism

Mahin nursed eagerly, sat, and walked at the expected ages. Yet some of his behaviour made us vaguely uneasy. He never put anything in his mouth. Not his fingers nor his toys—nothing. . . . More troubling was the fact that Mahin didn't look at us, or smile, and wouldn't play the games that seemed as much a part of babyhood as diapers. He rarely laughed, and when he did, it was at things that didn't seem funny to us. He didn't cuddle, but sat upright in my lap, even when I rocked him. But children differ and we were content to let Mahin be himself. We thought it hilarious when my brother, visiting us when Mahin was eight months old, observed "That kid has no social instincts whatsoever." Although Mahin was a first child, he was not isolated. I frequently put him in his playpen in front of the house, where the schoolchildren stopped to play with him as they passed. He ignored them, too.

It was Natasha, a personality kid, born two years later, whose responsiveness emphasized the degree of Mahin's difference. When I went into her room for the late feeding, her little head bobbed up and she greeted me with a smile that reached from her head to her toes. And the realization of that difference chilled me more than the wintry bedroom. Mahin's babbling had not turned into speech by the time he was three. His play was solitary and repetitious. He tore paper into long thin strips, bushel baskets of it every day. He spun the lids from my canning jars and became upset if we tried to divert him. Only rarely could I catch his eye, and then saw his focus change from me to the reflection in my glasses. . . .

[Mahin's] adventures in our suburban neighbourhood had been unhappy. He had disregarded the universal rule that sand is to be kept in sandboxes, and the children themselves had punished him. He walked around a sad and solitary figure, always carrying a toy airplane, a toy he never played with. At that time, I had not heard the word that was to dominate our lives, to hover over every conversation, to sit through every meal beside us. That word was autism.

Adapted from Eberhardy, 1967

autism Disorder characterized by pervasive deficits in the ability to relate to and communicate with others, and by a restricted range of activities and interests. Children with autistic disorder lack the ability to relate to others and seem to live in their own private worlds.

Autism, or *autistic disorder*, is one of the severest disorders of childhood. It is a chronic, lifelong condition. Children with autism, like Mahin, seem utterly alone in the world, despite parental efforts to bridge the gulf that divides them.

Autism. Autism, one of the most severe childhood disorders, is characterized by pervasive deficits in the ability to relate to and communicate with others, and by a restricted range of activities and interests. Children with autistic disorder lack the ability to relate to others and seem to live in their own private worlds.

autistic thinking The tendency to view oneself as the centre of the universe, to believe that external events somehow refer to oneself.

Autism derives from the Greek *autos*, meaning "self." The term *autism* was first used in 1906 by Swiss psychiatrist Eugen Bleuler to refer to a peculiar style of thinking among people with schizophrenia. (Autism is one of Bleuler's four As.) **Autistic thinking** is the tendency to view oneself as the centre of the universe, to believe that external events somehow refer to oneself. In 1943, another psychiatrist, Leo Kanner, applied the diagnosis "early infantile autism" to a group of disturbed children who seemed unable to relate to others, as if they lived in their own private worlds. Unlike children suffering from mental retardation, children with autism seemed to shut out any input from the outside world, creating a kind of "autistic aloneness" (Kanner, 1943).

Autism is a lifelong condition that spans all socioeconomic levels (Fombonne, 2005). It typically becomes evident in toddlers between 18 and 30 months of age (Rapin, 1997), and is four times more common in boys (Fombonne, 2005).

FEATURES OF AUTISM Perhaps the most poignant feature of autism is the child's utter aloneness (see Table 11.1). Other features include language and communication problems and ritualistic or stereotyped behaviour. The child may also be mute, or if some language skills are present, they may be characterized by peculiar usage, as in echolalia (parroting back what the child has heard in a high-pitched monotone); pronoun reversals (using "you" or "he" instead of "I"); use of words that have meaning only to those who have intimate knowledge of the child; and tendencies to raise the voice at the end of sentences, as if asking a question. Nonverbal communication may also be impaired or absent. For example, children with autistic disorder may not engage in eye contact or display facial expressions. Although these children may be unresponsive to others, researchers find them to be capable of displaying strong emotions, especially strong negative emotions such as anger, sadness, and fear (Capps, Kasari, Yirmiya, & Sigman, 1993).

A primary feature of autism is interminable, repeated, purposeless, stereotyped movements—twirling, flapping the hands, or rocking back and forth with the arms around the knees. Some children with autism mutilate themselves, even as they cry out in pain. They may bang their head, slap their face, bite their hands and shoulders, or pull out their hair. They may also throw sudden tantrums or panics. Another feature of autism is an aversion to environmental changes—a feature termed "preservation of sameness." When familiar objects are moved even slightly from their usual places, children with autism may throw tantrums or cry continually until their placement is restored. Children with autistic disorder may also insist on eating the same food every day.

Children with autism are bound by ritual. The teacher of one five-year-old girl with autistic disorder learned to greet her every morning by saying, "Good morning, Lily, I am very, very glad to see you" (Diamond, Balvin, & Diamond, 1963). Although Lily would not respond to the greeting, she would shriek if the teacher omitted even one of the *very*s.

Children who develop autism appear to have failed to develop a differentiated self-concept—a sense of themselves as distinct individuals (Toichi et al., 2002). Despite their unusual behaviour, autistic children are often quite attractive and can have an "intelligent look" about them. However, as measured by scores on standardized tests, their intellectual development tends to lag below the norm. International studies indicate that 30% of autistic subjects have mild to moderate levels of mental retardation and 40% have severe to profound levels (Fombonne, 2005). Even those who function at an average level of intelligence show deficits in activities requiring the ability to symbolize, such as recognize emotions, engage in symbolic play, and problem solve conceptually (Yirmiya & Sigman, 1991). They also display difficulty in attending to tasks that involve interacting with other people.

THEORETICAL PERSPECTIVES Early views of autism focused on pathological family relationships. Kanner and his colleagues (e.g., Kanner & Eisenberg, 1955) suggested that children with autism were reared by cold, detached parents who were dubbed "emotional

TABLE 11.1

Diagnostic Criteria for Autistic Disorder

A. A total of six (or more) items from (1), (2), and (3), with at least two from (1), and one each from (2) and (3):

  (1) qualitative impairment in social interaction, as manifested by at least two of the following:

    (a) marked impairment in the use of multiple nonverbal behaviors such as eye-to-eye gaze, facial expression, body postures, and gestures to regulate social interaction

    (b) failure to develop peer relationships appropriate to developmental level

    (c) a lack of spontaneous seeking to share enjoyment, interests, or achievements with other people (e.g., by a lack of showing, bringing, or pointing out objects of interest)

    (d) lack of social or emotional reciprocity

  (2) qualitative impairments in communication as manifested by at least one of the following:

    (a) delay in, or total lack of, the development of spoken language (not accompanied by an attempt to compensate through alternative modes of communication such as gesture or mime)

    (b) in individuals with adequate speech, marked impairment in the ability to initiate or sustain a conversation with others

    (c) stereotyped and repetitive use of language or idiosyncratic language

    (d) lack of varied, spontaneous make-believe play or social imitative play appropriate to developmental level

  (3) restricted repetitive and stereotyped patterns of behavior, interests, and activities, as manifested by at least one of the following:

    (a) encompassing preoccupation with one or more stereotyped and restricted patterns of interest that is abnormal either in intensity or focus

    (b) apparently inflexible adherence to specific, nonfunctional routines or rituals

    (c) stereotyped and repetitive motor mannerisms (e.g., hand or finger flapping or twisting, or complex whole-body movements)

    (d) persistent preoccupation with parts of objects

B. Delays or abnormal functioning in at least one of the following areas, with onset prior to age 3 years: (1) social interaction, (2) language as used in social communication, or (3) symbolic or imaginative play.

C. The disturbance is not better accounted for by Rett's Disorder or Childhood Disintegrative Disorder.

Source: Reprinted with permission from the *Diagnostic and Statistical Manual of Mental Disorders*, Fourth Edition, Text Revision, (Copyright ©2000). American Psychiatric Association. p. 75.

---

refrigerators." Psychoanalyst Bruno Bettelheim (1967) also focused on the family by suggesting that extreme self-absorption is the child's defence against parental rejection. The parents rear the child in an emotionally and socially desolate atmosphere in which the child's efforts to develop language and social skills wither. The child surrenders efforts to develop mastery over the external world and withdraws into a world of fantasy. The pathological insistence on preservation of sameness represents the child's rigid, defensive efforts to impose order and predictability.

Research, however, has not supported the devastating assumption that parents of autistic children are frosty and remote (Hoffmann & Prior, 1982). Of course, there is truth to the notion that children with autism and their parents do not relate to one another very well, but causal connections are clouded. Rather than rejecting their children and thus fostering autism, parents may grow somewhat aloof because their efforts to relate to their children repeatedly meet with failure. Aloofness then becomes a result of autism, not a cause.

Psychologist O. Ivar Lovaas and his colleagues (Lovaas, Koegel, & Schreibman, 1979) offer a cognitive-behavioural perspective on autism. They suggest that children with autism have perceptual deficits that limit them to processing only one stimulus at a time. As a result, they are slow to learn by means of classical conditioning (association of stimuli). From the learning theory perspective, children become attached to their primary caregivers because they are associated with primary reinforcers such as food and hugging. Children with autism, however, attend either to the food or to the cuddling and do not connect it with the parent.

Cognitive theorists have focused on the kinds of cognitive deficits shown by children with autism and the possible relationships among these deficits. Children with autism appear to have difficulty integrating information from various senses (Rutter, 1983). At times, they seem hypersensitive to stimulation. At other times they are so insensitive that

theory of mind The ability to appreciate that other people have a mental state that is different from one's own.

an observer might wonder whether they are deaf. Perceptual and cognitive deficits seem to diminish their capacity to make use of information—to comprehend and apply social rules. This may impede the development of what psychologists call a **theory of mind**. Theory of mind is the ability to appreciate that other people have a mental state that is different from one's own. Autistic children show deficits in their ability to infer beliefs, intentions, and emotions in others (Baron-Cohen, 1995, 1998). Not being able to readily see the world from another person's perspective interferes with the normal give and take of social relationships.

But what is the basis of these perceptual and cognitive deficits? Canadian experts who have reviewed the research into the causes of autism have concluded that the many impairments associated with autism, including mental retardation, communications deficits, repetitive bizarre motor behaviour, and even seizures, suggest an underlying neurobiological basis (Nicolson & Szatmari, 2003). MRI scans show that compared to normal children, autistic children have a period of overgrowth of brain size early in postnatal development, especially in the frontal regions. This period is followed by significantly slowed growth resulting in a brain volume smaller than average for children aged 5 to 16. The brain tissue that connects the two halves of the brain, the corpus callosum, is smaller than normal in autistic patients, which may affect **lateralization** of brain function. The area of the brain that regulates motor function, the cerebellum, also shows abnormal development in autistic individuals.

lateralization The developmental process by which the left hemisphere specializes in verbal and analytic functions and the right hemisphere specializes in nonverbal, spatial functions.

Nicolson and Szatmari's (2003) review of the research indicates that there is substantial support for the suggestion that genetics plays a significant role in the neurodevelopment of autistic children, with susceptible genes on chromosomes 2 and 7 in particular. It may be that multiple genes are involved and that they interact with other factors, possibly environmental or biological in origin, leading to autism (McIntosh, 1999).

Recently, researchers have found that the mirror neurons—circuits that activate in similar ways when we perform actions or watch other people perform the same actions—in those with autism are not as fully developed and may be the reason for social deficits (Bastiaansen et al., 2011). Also, brain scans are revealing autism's characteristic signature. Researchers from Yale University have identified three distinct neural signatures: trait markers, which are brain regions with reduced activity in children with autism and their unaffected siblings; state markers, which are brain areas with reduced activity found only in children with autism; and compensatory activity, which is enhanced activity seen only in unaffected siblings. The enhanced brain activity may reflect a developmental process by which these children overcome a genetic predisposition to develop autism (Kaiser et al., 2010). This discovery may lead to earlier diagnosis of autism. Early diagnosis tools are crucial to early intervention programs ("Children With Autism," 2011; "New Research Tool," 2008).

The Early Autism Study, led by Mel Rutherford at McMaster University, is developing an early diagnosis tool using eye-tracker technology that measures eye direction while babies look at faces, eyes, and bouncing balls on a computer screen. These researchers are finding that they can distinguish between a group of siblings with autism from a group with no autism at 9 months and 12 months ("New Research Tool," 2008).

Still, the cause of autism remains unknown, and some recent controversial but scientifically plausible ideas are being examined. Some ideas point to the immune system, to viruses, and to an overload of hormones.

Establishing contact. One of the principal therapeutic tasks in working with autistic children is the establishment of interpersonal contact. Behaviour therapists use reinforcers to increase adaptive social behaviours, such as paying attention to the therapist and playing with other children. Behaviour therapists may also use punishments to suppress self-mutilative behaviour.

TREATMENT Although there is no cure for autism, structured treatment programs have yielded the best results. The most effective treatment programs focus on behavioural, educational, and communication deficits and are highly intensive and structured, offering a great deal of individual instruction (Rapin,

1997). In a classic study conducted by Lovaas (1987) at UCLA, children suffering from autism received more than 40 hours of one-to-one behaviour modification each week for at least two years. Significant intellectual and educational gains were reported for 9 of the 19 children (47%) in the program. The children who improved achieved normal IQ scores and were able to succeed in grade 1. Only 2% of a control group that did not receive the intensive treatment achieved similar gains. Treatment gains were well maintained at the time of a follow-up when the children were 11 years old (McEachin, Smith, & Lovaas, 1993).

These psychological intervention programs are effective for many children with autism, but the key point is that any intervention must begin early. Research continues to support the necessity of early intervention programs; the more intense or comprehensive the therapy, the better it is in terms of helping children improve social and communication skills. Those who received therapy, including behavioural, speech, and occupational therapy, had the best outcomes in a recent study of over 1000 children with autism (Mazurek, Kanne, & Miles, 2012). Children who are better functioning at the start of treatment typically gain the most.

Learning to recognize emotions through computer programs. An interactive computer game called FaceSay™, by Symbionica, helps children with autism learn where to look for clues to emotions on faces and thereby learn how to recognize emotions in others.

Biological approaches have had only limited impact in the treatment of autism. One line of research has focused on drugs normally used to treat schizophrenia, such as Haldol, which blocks dopamine activity. Several controlled studies show Haldol to be helpful in many cases in reducing social withdrawal and repetitive motor behaviour (such as rocking), aggression, hyperactivity, and self-injurious behaviour (McCracken et al., 2002). We have not seen drugs lead to consistent improvement in cognitive and language development in children with autism, however.

An interactive computer program called FaceSay™, by Symbionica, LLC, has been shown to improve the ability of children with autism spectrum disorders to recognize faces, facial expressions, and emotions, according to the results of a study conducted by psychologists at the University of Alabama at Birmingham (Hopkins et al., 2011). FaceSay™ features interactive games that let children with autism practise recognizing the facial features and expressions of an avatar, or software "puppet." Specifically, the computer program teaches the children where to look for facial cues such as an eye gaze or a facial expression.

Autistic traits generally continue into adulthood to one degree or another. Yet some autistic children do go on to achieve college and university degrees and are able to function independently (Rapin, 1997). Others need continuing treatment throughout their lives, even institutionalized care. Even the highest-functioning adults with the disorder manifest deficient social and communication skills and a highly limited range of interests and activities (APA, 2000a).

REVIEW IT

Pervasive Developmental Disorders

- **What are pervasive developmental disorders?** Pervasive developmental disorders involve marked deficiencies in multiple areas of development. They develop within the first years of life and are often associated with mental retardation. Autistic disorder is the most prominent type of pervasive developmental disorder.

- **What are the clinical features of autism?** Children with autism shun affectionate behaviour, engage in stereotyped behaviour, attempt to preserve sameness, and tend to have peculiar speech habits such as echolalia, pronoun reversals, and idiosyncratic speech. The causes of autism remain unknown, but gains in academic and social functioning have been obtained through the use of early intensive behaviour therapy.

MENTAL RETARDATION

Mental retardation involves a broad delay in the development of cognitive and social functioning. The course of development of children with mental retardation is variable. Many improve over time, especially if they receive support, guidance, and enriched educational opportunities. Children with mental retardation who are reared in impoverished environments may fail to improve or may deteriorate further in relation to other children.

Mental retardation is generally assessed by a combination of formal intelligence tests and observation of adaptive functioning. The DSM-IV-TR uses three criteria in diagnosing mental retardation: (1) an IQ score of approximately 70 or below on a test like the Wechsler Intelligence Scale for Children (WISC) or the Stanford-Binet, (2) evidence of impaired functioning in adaptive behaviour, and (3) onset of the disorder before age 18. People whose behaviour is impaired fail to meet the standards of behaviour that are expected of someone of the same age within a given cultural setting. They do not develop comparable social and communication skills or become adequately independent and self-sufficient. For infants, task-related judgments of subaverage intellectual functioning may be used in place of IQ scores because tests of infant intelligence either do not yield reliable IQ scores or do not yield any IQ scores at all.

The DSM-IV-TR classifies mental retardation according to level of severity. Table 11.2 provides a description of the deficits and abilities associated with various degrees of mental retardation. Children with mild mental retardation are generally capable of meeting basic academic demands such as learning to read simple passages. As adults, they are generally capable of independent functioning, although they may require some guidance and support.

A 2002 study of adolescents conducted in the Niagara Region found results comparable to earlier Canadian and international studies (Bradley, Thompson, & Bryson, 2002). The researchers identified the overall prevalence of mental retardation as 7.18 in 1000. Using broad criteria, they found that the prevalence for mild mental retardation (MMR; IQ = 50–75) was 3.54 in 1000; for severe mental retardation (SMR; IQ under 50), it was 3.64 in 1000. Although the overall rates of mild and severe mental retardation in adolescents were nearly equivalent, the number of individuals with MMR declined slightly with age, whereas the rates of SMR remained constant. The authors caution that

TABLE 11.2

Classifications of Developmental Delay

Classification	Range of IQ Scores	Adaptive Limitations	Percentage of Developmentally Delayed Population
Mild	55–70	Can reach grade 6 skill level. Capable with training of living independently and being self-supporting.	90%
Moderate	40–55	Can reach grade 2 skill level. Can work and live in sheltered environments with supervision.	6%
Severe	25–40	Can learn to talk and perform basic self-care but needs constant supervision.	3%
Profound	Below 25	Very limited ability to learn; may only be able to learn very simple tasks; poor language skills and limited self-care.	1%

Source: Ciccarelli, Harrigan, & Fritzley, 2010, p. 339. Reprinted with permission by Pearson Canada Inc.

the lower-than-expected rate of MMR may be related to Ontario's integration policy for education, which has made individuals with MMR less visible as they adapt to the mainstream classroom, albeit with a modified program of study. Moreover, once formal schooling is completed, people with MMR blend into the community much more readily than people with SMR. Males in the study outnumbered females by a ratio of 1.3 to 1.0, but more females fell in the range of SMR.

Not all systems of classification of mental retardation are based on level of severity. The American Association on Intellectual and Developmental Disabilities, formerly the American Association on Mental Retardation (AAMR), an organization composed of leading professionals in the field, classifies mental retardation according to the intensity of support needed by the individual in various areas of functioning (AAMR, 1992). Some individuals need only intermittent support that varies in intensity from time to time on an as-needed basis, whereas others require more constant or pervasive support involving extensive commitment of staff and resources. This system of classification attempts to match the level of support needed to the individual's ability to function in work, school, and home environments.

Causes of Mental Retardation

In many cases, mental retardation can be traced to biological causes, including chromosomal and genetic disorders, infectious diseases, and brain damage. Specifically, where the retardation is due to genes, geneticists have uncovered several genes that have been identified to cause this disorder. However, it is not one or two genes that cause mental retardation but spontaneous mutations in the genes, as demonstrated in new research by Dutch geneticists. The majority of mental retardation is caused by spontaneous mutations in paternal sperm or maternal egg cells (Vissers et al., 2010). To be clear, mental retardation is not transmitted from one generation to the next but occurs through spontaneously genetic changes such as deletions and duplications (Webber et al., 2009). The gene in which the child has a defect still shows a normal function in both parents.

Unexplained cases might involve cultural or familial causes, such as being raised in an impoverished home environment, or perhaps they involve an interaction of environmental and genetic factors, the nature of which remains poorly understood (Thapar, Gottesman, Owen, O'Donovan, & McGuffin, 1994).

DOWN SYNDROME AND OTHER CHROMOSOMAL ABNORMALITIES The most common chromosomal abnormality resulting in mental retardation is **Down syndrome**, which is characterized by an extra or third chromosome on the 21st pair of chromosomes, resulting in 47 chromosomes rather than the normal complement of 46. Down syndrome occurs in about 1 in 800 births. It usually occurs when the 21st pair of chromosomes in either the egg or the sperm fails to divide normally, resulting in an extra chromosome. Chromosomal abnormalities become more likely as parents age, so expectant couples in their mid-30s or older often undergo prenatal genetic tests to detect Down syndrome and genetic abnormalities. Down syndrome can be traced to a defect in the mother's chromosomes in about 95% of cases (Antonarakis & Down Syndrome Collaborative Group, 1991), with the remainder attributable to defects in the father's sperm.

People with Down syndrome are recognizable by certain physical features, such as a round face; broad, flat nose; and small, downward-sloping folds of skin at the inside corners of the eyes that give the impression of slanted eyes. Children with Down syndrome are also characterized by a protruding tongue;

Down syndrome Condition caused by a chromosomal abnormality involving an extra chromosome on the 21st pair (trisomy 21); it is characterized by mental retardation and various physical abnormalities. Formerly called *mongolism* and *Down's syndrome* in Canada.

Lauren Potter. Lauren Potter plays Becky Jackson in the hit television series *Glee*.

small, squarish hands and short fingers; a curved fifth finger; and disproportionately small arms and legs in relation to their bodies. Nearly all of these children have mental retardation, and many suffer from physical problems, such as malformations of the heart and respiratory difficulties. Sadly, most die by middle age. In their later years, they tend to suffer memory losses and experience childish emotions that represent a form of senility.

Children with Down syndrome suffer various deficits in learning and development. They tend to be unco-ordinated and to lack proper muscle tone, which makes it difficult for them to carry out physical tasks and engage in play activities like other children. Down syndrome children suffer memory deficits, especially for information presented verbally, which makes it difficult for them to learn in school. They also have difficulty following instructions from teachers and expressing their thoughts or needs clearly in speech. Despite their disabilities, most can learn to read, write, and perform simple arithmetic if they receive appropriate schooling and the right encouragement.

Although less common than Down syndrome, chromosomal abnormalities on the sex chromosome may also result in mental retardation, such as in Klinefelter's syndrome and Turner's syndrome. Klinefelter's syndrome, which occurs only in males, is characterized by the presence of an extra X sex chromosome, resulting in an XXY sex chromosomal pattern rather than the XY pattern that men normally have. Estimates of the prevalence of Klinefelter's syndrome range from 1 in 500 to 1 in 1000 male births (Brody, 1993). Men with this XXY pattern fail to develop appropriate secondary sex characteristics, resulting in small, underdeveloped testes; low sperm production; enlarged breasts; poor muscular development; and infertility. Mild retardation or learning disabilities frequently occur among these men. Men with Klinefelter's syndrome often don't discover they have the condition until they undergo tests for infertility.

Turner's syndrome is found exclusively in females and is characterized by the presence of a single X sex chromosome instead of the normal two. Although such girls develop normal external genitals, their ovaries remain poorly developed, producing reduced amounts of estrogen. As women, they tend to be shorter than average and infertile. They also tend to show evidence of mild retardation, especially in skills relating to math and science.

FRAGILE X SYNDROME AND OTHER GENETIC ABNORMALITIES Fragile X syndrome is the most common type of inherited (genetic) mental retardation. It is the second most common form of retardation overall after Down syndrome ("Blood Test Can Detect Retardation," 1993; Plomin, Owen, & McGuffin, 1994). The disorder is believed to be caused by a mutated gene on the X sex chromosome (Huber, Gallagher, Warren, & Bear, 2002). The defective gene is located in an area of the chromosome that appears fragile, hence the name *fragile X syndrome*. Fragile X syndrome causes mental retardation in about 1 in every 1000 to 1500 males and (generally less severe) mental handicaps in about 1 in every 2000 to 2500 females (Angier, 1991b; Rousseau et al., 1991). The effects of fragile X syndrome range from mild learning disabilities to retardation so profound that those affected can hardly speak or function.

Females normally have two X sex chromosomes, whereas males have only one. For females, having two X sex chromosomes seems to provide some protection against the disorder if the defective gene turns up on one of the two chromosomes (Angier, 1991b). This may explain why the disorder usually has more profound effects on males than on females. Yet the mutation does not always manifest itself. Many males and females carry the fragile X mutation but show no clinical evidence of it. Nevertheless, they can pass along the syndrome to their offspring.

A genetic test can detect the presence of the mutation by direct DNA analysis and may help prospective parents who seek out genetic counselling. Prenatal testing of the fetus is also available. Although there is no treatment for fragile X syndrome, identifying the defective gene is the first step toward understanding how the protein produced by the gene functions to create the disability—which may lead to the development of treatments (Huber et al., 2002).

Phenylketonuria (PKU) is a genetic disorder that occurs in 1 in 10 000 births (Plomin et al., 1994). It is caused by a recessive gene that prevents the child from metabolizing the amino acid phenylalanine (Phe), which is found in many foods. Consequently, phenylalanine and its derivative, phenylpyruvic acid, accumulate in the body, causing damage to the central nervous system that results in mental retardation and emotional disturbance. PKU can be detected in newborns by analyzing blood or urine samples. Although there is no cure for PKU, children with the disorder may suffer less damage or develop normally if they are placed on a diet low in phenylalanine soon after birth (Brody, 1990). Such children receive protein supplements that compensate for their nutritional loss.

University of Toronto researchers Mary Lou Smith and her colleagues tested children with PKU who had either high or low levels of Phe (M. L. Smith, Klim, & Hanley, 2000). They found that PKU children with low Phe levels were indistinguishable from non-PKU controls on several cognitive tasks. In contrast, however, the higher the levels of Phe in school-aged children with PKU, the greater the impairment in cognitive performance on specific problem-solving and verbal memory tasks.

Tay-Sachs disease is caused by recessive genes on chromosome 15. A fatal degenerative disease of the central nervous system, it mostly afflicts Jews of Eastern European ancestry and French Canadians of the Gaspé region of Quebec (Triggs-Raine, Richard, Wasel, Prence, & Natowicz, 1995). About 1 in 14 French Canadians in Eastern Quebec is a carrier of the recessive gene responsible for the disorder (Chodirker et al., 2001; Kaback et al., 1993). Children afflicted by Tay-Sachs suffer gradual loss of muscle control, deafness and blindness, retardation, and paralysis, and usually die before the age of five.

Today, various prenatal diagnostic tests can detect the presence of chromosomal abnormalities and genetic disorders. In amniocentesis, which is usually conducted about 14 to 15 weeks following conception, a sample of amniotic fluid is drawn with a syringe from the amniotic sac that contains the fetus. With chorionic villus sampling (CVS), cells are extracted from the placenta outside the sac where the fetus develops. CVS is best performed between 10 and 12 weeks into a woman's pregnancy. Depending upon the procedure, cells from the fetus or the placenta can then be examined for abnormalities, including Down syndrome, X-linked disorders, PKU, Smith-Lemli-Optiz syndrome, and Tay-Sachs.

In the future, it may be possible to control the impact of defective genes during prenatal development. For now, expectant couples rely on genetic counselling. It offers a complete and accurate view of the options available and can assist couples in making informed decisions about terminating a pregnancy or, alternatively, help them prepare for a baby who has congenital defects.

PRENATAL FACTORS Some cases of mental retardation are caused by maternal infections or substance abuse during pregnancy. Rubella (German measles) in the mother, for example, can be passed along to the unborn child, causing brain damage that results in retardation, and may play a role in autism. Although the mother might experience only mild symptoms or none at all, the effects on the fetus can be tragic. Other maternal diseases that can cause retardation in the child include syphilis, **cytomegalovirus**, and genital herpes.

Widespread programs that immunize women against rubella before pregnancy and tests for syphilis during pregnancy have reduced the risk of transmission of these infections to children. Most children who contract genital herpes from their mothers do so during delivery by coming into contact with the herpes simplex virus that causes the disease in the birth canal. Caesarean sections (C-sections) reduce the risk of the baby's coming into contact with the virus during outbreaks.

Drugs the mother ingests during pregnancy are able to pass through the placenta to the child. Some can cause severe birth deformities and mental retardation. Children whose mothers drink alcohol during pregnancy are often born with fetal alcohol syndrome (FAS). FAS is among the most prominent causes of mental retardation. Maternal smoking during pregnancy has also been linked to the development of

phenylketonuria Genetic disorder that prevents the metabolization of phenylpyruvic acid, leading to mental retardation. Abbreviated *PKU*.

Tay-Sachs disease Disease of lipid metabolism that is genetically transmitted and usually results in death in early childhood.

cytomegalovirus Maternal disease of the herpes virus group that carries a risk of mental retardation to the unborn child.

attention-deficit/hyperactivity disorder in children (Milberger, Biederman, Faraone, Chen, & Jones, 1996).

Birth complications, such as oxygen deprivation or head injuries, place children at increased risk for neurological disorders, including mental retardation. Prematurity also places children at risk of retardation and other developmental problems. Brain infections, such as encephalitis and meningitis, or traumas during infancy and early childhood can cause mental retardation and other health problems. Children who ingest toxins, such as paint chips containing lead, may also suffer brain damage that produces mental retardation.

CULTURAL-FAMILIAL CAUSES   Children with mental retardation fall mainly into the mild range of severity, and there is no apparent biological cause or distinguishing physical feature that sets these children apart from other children. Psychosocial factors, such as an impoverished home, a social environment that is not intellectually stimulating, or parental neglect or abuse, may play a causal or contributing role in the development of mental retardation in such children. Supporting a family linkage is evidence from a study in Atlanta in which mothers who failed to finish high school were four times more likely than better-educated mothers to have children with mild retardation (Drews, Yeargin-Allsopp, Decouflé, & Murphy, 1995).

These cases are considered **cultural-familial retardation**. Children in impoverished families may lack toys, books, or opportunities to interact with adults in intellectually stimulating ways. Consequently, they may fail to develop appropriate language skills or become unmotivated to learn the skills that are valued in contemporary society. Economic burdens, such as the need to hold multiple jobs, may prevent the parents from spending time reading to them, talking to them at length, and exposing them to creative play or trips to museums and parks. Children may spend most of their days glued to the television set. The parents, most of whom were also reared in poverty, may lack the reading or communication skills to help shape the development of these skills in their children. A vicious cycle of poverty and impoverished intellectual development may be repeated from generation to generation.

Children with this form of developmental delay may respond dramatically when provided with enriched learning experiences, especially at earlier ages. For example, the Health Canada–funded Aboriginal Head Start (AHS) program was instituted in 114 urban centres and northern communities across Canada to promote education and school readiness, Aboriginal culture and language, parental involvement, health, nutrition, and social support (Health Canada, 2002a). To date, the AHS program has been highly successful and has exceeded program expectations as major gains have been achieved in all areas of children's development (Health Canada, 2000a; Indian and Northern Affairs, 2003; Ottawa Aboriginal Head Start Program, 1998).

Intervention

The services that children with mental retardation require to meet the developmental challenges they face depend in part on the type of retardation and the level of severity (Dykens & Hodapp, 1997; Snell, 1997). With appropriate training, children with mild retardation may approach a grade 6 level of competence. They can acquire vocational skills that allow them to support themselves minimally through meaningful work. In Canada, most mildly mentally retarded children are integrated into the regular classroom, typically with a modified curriculum. Children with more severe forms of retardation, on the other hand, may be placed in special schools or classes if the caregiver prefers (Bradley et al., 2002).

Controversy remains over the **mainstreaming** of children with mental retardation into regular classes. Although some children with mild retardation may achieve better when they are mainstreamed, others may not do so well in regular classes. Some of these children find regular classes overwhelming and they withdraw from their schoolmates.

cultural-familial retardation Milder form of mental retardation that is believed to result, or at least be influenced by, impoverishment in the child's home environment.

mainstreaming The practice of having all students with disabilities included in the regular classroom. Also referred to as *integration* or *inclusion*.

Got a minute? Try the following:

1. Without referring to a calendar, calculate the day of the week that March 15, 2079, will fall on.
2. List the prime numbers between 1 and 1 billion. (Hint: The list starts 1, 2, 3, 5, 7, 11, 13, 17, . . .)
3. Repeat verbatim the newspaper stories you read over coffee this morning.
4. Sing accurately every note played by the first violin in Beethoven's Ninth Symphony.

These tasks are impossible for all but a very few. Ironically, people who are most likely to be able to accomplish these feats suffer from autism, mental retardation, or both. Such a person is commonly called an idiot savant. The term *savant* is derived from the French *savoir*, meaning "to know." The label *savant syndrome* is preferable to the pejorative *idiot savant* in referring to someone with severe mental deficiencies who possesses some remarkable mental abilities. The prevalence of savant syndrome among people with mental retardation is estimated at about 0.06%, or about 1 case in 2000 (Hill, 1987). The emergence of savant syndrome is also closely linked to infantile autism (L. K. Miller, 1999). Most people with savant syndrome, like most people with autism, are male (Treffert, 1988). Among a sample of 5400 people with autism, 531 cases (9.8%) were reported by parents to have savant syndrome (Rimland, 1978). Because they want to think of their children as special, however, parents might overreport the incidence of savant syndrome.

The savant syndrome phenomenon occurs more frequently in males by a ratio of roughly 6 to 1. The special skills of people with savant syndrome tend to appear out of the blue and may disappear as suddenly. Some people with the syndrome engage in lightning calculations. Thomas Fuller, a 19th-century enslaved man in Virginia, "was able to calculate the number of seconds in 70 years, 17 days, and 12 hours in a minute and one half, taking into account the 17 leap years that would have occurred in the period" (S. B. Smith, 1983). There are also cases of persons with the syndrome who were blind but could play back any musical piece, no matter how complex, or repeat long passages of foreign languages without losing a syllable.

Various theories have been presented to explain savant syndrome (Treffert, 1988). Some experts believe that children with savant syndrome have unusually well-developed memories that allow them to record and scan vast amounts of information. It has been suggested that people with savant syndrome may inherit two sets of hereditary factors, one for retardation and the other for special abilities. Perhaps it is coincidental that their special abilities and their mental handicaps were inherited in common. Other theorists suggest that the left and right hemispheres of their cerebral cortex are organized in an unusual way. This latter belief is supported by research suggesting that the special abilities these individuals possess often involve skills associated with right hemisphere functioning. Still other theorists suggest that they learn special skills to compensate for their lack of more general skills, perhaps as a means of coping with their environment or of earning social reinforcements. It could be that their skills in concrete functions, such as calculation, compensate for their lack of abstract thinking ability. Perhaps, as the neurologist Oliver Sacks speculates, the brain circuits of some people with savant syndrome are wired with a "deep arithmetic"—an innate structure for perceiving mathematical relationships that is analogous to the prewiring that allows people to perceive and produce language.

Some earlier research has pointed to possible gender-linked left hemisphere damage occurring prenatally or congenitally. Compensatory right hemisphere development might then take place, establishing specialized brain circuitry that processes concrete and narrowly defined kinds of information (Treffert, 1988). An environment that reinforces savant abilities and provides opportunities for practice and concentration would give further impetus to the development of these unusual abilities. As it stands, savant syndrome remains a mystery.

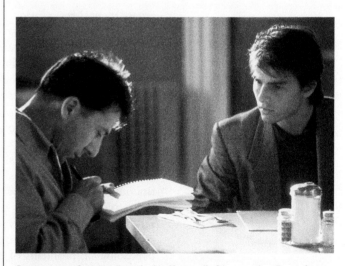

Savant syndrome. Dustin Hoffman (left) won the Best Actor Oscar for his portrayal in the 1988 film *Rain Man* of a man with autism who showed a remarkable capacity for numerical calculation. Tom Cruise played his brother. Hoffman was able to capture a sense of emotional detachment and isolation in his character.

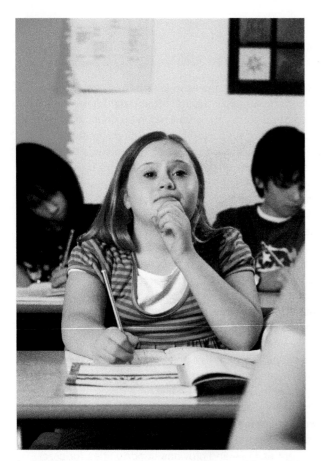

Inclusion. Across Canada, most children with special learning needs remain in regular classrooms and are provided with educational programs that meet their individual needs.

There has also been a trend in Canada and the United States toward deinstitutionalization of people with more severe mental retardation, a policy shift motivated in large part by public outrage over the appalling conditions that existed in many institutions serving this population.

People with mental retardation who are capable of functioning in the community have the right to receive less restrictive care than is provided in large institutions. Many are capable of living outside an institution and have been placed in supervised group homes. Residents typically share household responsibilities and are encouraged to participate in meaningful daily activities, such as training programs or sheltered workshops. Others live with their families and attend structured day programs. Adults with mild retardation often work in outside jobs and live in their own apartments or share apartments with other persons who have mild retardation. Behavioural approaches can be used to teach persons with more severe retardation such basic hygienic behaviours as toothbrushing, self-dressing, and hair combing. In demonstrating toothbrushing, the therapist might first define the component parts of the targeted behaviour (picking up the toothbrush, wetting the toothbrush, taking the cap off the tube, putting the paste on the brush, and so on) (Kissel, Whitman, & Reid, 1983). The therapist might then shape the desired behaviour by using such techniques as verbal instruction (e.g., "Jim, pick up the toothbrush"), physical guidance (physically guiding the client's hand in performing the desired response), and reward (use of positive verbal reinforcement) for successful completion of the desired response ("That's really good, Jim"). Such behavioural techniques have been shown to be effective in teaching a simple but remunerative vocational skill (for example, stamping return addresses on envelopes) to a group of adult women with such severe mental retardation that they were essentially nonverbal (Schepis, Reid, & Fitzgerald, 1987). These techniques may also help people with severe mental retardation develop adaptive capacities that can enable them to perform more productive roles.

Other behavioural treatment techniques include social-skills training, which focuses on increasing the individual's ability to relate co-operatively with others, and anger-management training to help individuals develop more effective ways of handling conflicts than aggressively acting out (Huang & Cuvo, 1997).

Children with mental retardation stand perhaps a three to four times greater chance of developing other psychological disorders, such as attention-deficit/hyperactivity disorder (ADHD), depression, or anxiety disorders (Borthwick-Duffy, 1994). Mental health professionals have been slow to recognize the prevalence of mental health problems among people with mental retardation, perhaps because of a long-held conceptual distinction between emotional impairment on the one hand and intellectual deficits on the other (Nezu, 1994). Many professionals even assumed (wrongly) that people with mental retardation were worry free and somehow immune to psychological problems (Nezu, 1994). Given these commonly held beliefs, it is perhaps not surprising that many of the psychological problems of people with mental retardation have gone unrecognized and untreated (Reiss & Valenti-Hein, 1994).

Children and adults with mental retardation may need psychological counselling to help them adjust to life in the community. Many have difficulty making friends and may become socially isolated. Problems with self-esteem are also common, especially because people who have mental retardation are often demeaned and ridiculed. Supportive counselling may be supplemented with behavioural techniques to help those with developmental disabilities acquire skills in areas such as personal hygiene, work, and social relationships.

Mental Retardation

- **What is mental retardation, and how is it assessed?** Mental retardation is a general delay in the development of intellectual and adaptive abilities. It is assessed through evaluation of performance on intelligence tests and measures of functional ability. Most cases fall in the range of mildly retarded.
- **What are the causes of mental retardation?** There are many causes of mental retardation, including chromosomal abnormalities such as Down syndrome; genetic disorders such as fragile X syndrome, phenylketonuria, and Tay-Sachs disease; prenatal factors such as maternal diseases and alcohol (and other drug) use; and familial/cultural factors associated with intellectually impoverished home environments.

LEARNING DISORDERS

Many famous scientists, leaders, and celebrities have been thought to have what are now considered learning disorders. Among their number are Albert Einstein, Alexander Graham Bell, Winston Churchill, Agatha Christie, and Tom Cruise. These highly creative and successful people suffered from **dyslexia** and related disorders. The term *dyslexia* is derived from the Greek roots *dys-*, meaning "bad," and *lexikon*, meaning "of words." Dyslexia is the most common type of **learning disorder** (also called a *learning disability*) (Shaywitz, 1998). It accounts for roughly 80% of learning-disability cases. People with learning disorders have average or higher intelligence, and may even be gifted, but show inadequate development in reading, math, or writing skills that impairs school performance or daily activities (see the Closer Look box on page 408 for a Canadian definition of *learning disabilities*).

About 12% of children in Canadian schools are identified as having a learning disorder (Lipps & Frank, 1997). Learning disorders tend to run a chronic course and are the most common long-term conditions of children up to age 14 (Cossette & Duclos, 2002). The more severe the problem is in childhood, the more likely it is to affect adult development (Spreen, 1988). Children with learning disorders tend to perform poorly in school; about half of all children who received remedial education were identified as having a learning disability (Lipps & Frank, 1997).

dyslexia Type of learning disorder characterized by impaired reading ability that may involve difficulty with the alphabet or spelling.

learning disorder Deficiency in a specific learning ability noteworthy because of the individual's general intelligence and exposure to learning opportunities.

Types of Learning Disorders

The several types of learning disorders include mathematics disorder, disorder of written expression, and reading disorder.

MATHEMATICS DISORDER   Mathematics disorder characterizes children with deficiencies in arithmetic skills. They may have problems understanding basic mathematical terms or operations, such as addition or subtraction; decoding mathematical symbols (+, =, etc.); or learning sequential facts, such as multiplication tables, by rote memory. The problem may become apparent as early as grade 1 (age 6) but is not generally recognized until about grade 3 (age 8).

DISORDER OF WRITTEN EXPRESSION   Disorder of written expression—dysgraphia— characterizes children with grossly deficient writing skills and occurs regardless of the ability to read. It is not related to intellectual impairment. The deficiency may be characterized by errors in spelling, grammar, or punctuation or by difficulty in composing sentences and paragraphs. Severe writing difficulties generally become apparent by age 7 (grade 2), although milder cases may not be recognized until age 10 (grade 5) or later. Dysgraphia is known as one of the most common learning disabilities, with a prevalence of 4% to 10%. It often overlaps with other learning disabilities such as speech impairment, ADHD, or developmental co-ordination disorder (Nicolson & Fawcett, 2011; Nicolson & Szatmari, 2003).

On January 30, 2002, after years of deliberation, the Learning Disabilities Association of Canada (LDAC) adopted an official definition of learning disabilities that is the culmination of a thorough review of learning disabilities research and input from hundreds of individuals in all provinces and territories by the LDAC National Legal Committee and the LDAC "Think Tank" (Learning Disabilities Association of Canada, 2002):

Learning disabilities refer to a number of disorders that may affect the acquisition, organization, retention, understanding, or use of verbal or nonverbal information. These disorders affect learning in individuals who otherwise demonstrate at least average abilities essential for thinking and/or reasoning. As such, learning disabilities are distinct from global intellectual deficiency.

Learning disabilities result from impairments in one or more processes related to perceiving, thinking, remembering, or learning. These include but are not limited to: language processing; phonological processing; visual spatial processing; processing speed; memory and attention; and executive functions (e.g., planning and decision-making).

Learning disabilities range in severity and may interfere with the acquisition and use of one or more of the following:

- oral language (e.g., listening, speaking, understanding);
- reading (e.g., decoding, phonetic knowledge, word recognition, comprehension);
- written language (e.g., spelling and written expression); and
- mathematics (e.g., computation, problem solving).

Learning disabilities may also involve difficulties with organizational skills, social perception, social interaction, and perspective taking.

Learning disabilities are lifelong. The way in which they are expressed may vary over an individual's lifetime, depending on the interaction between the demands of the environment and the individual's strengths and needs. Learning disabilities are suggested by unexpected academic under-achievement or achievement that is maintained only by unusually high levels of effort and support.

Learning disabilities [occur] due to genetic and/or neurobiological factors or injury that alters brain functioning in a manner that affects one or more processes related to learning. These disorders are not due primarily to hearing and/or vision problems, socio-economic factors, cultural or linguistic differences, lack of motivation, or ineffective teaching, although these factors may further complicate the challenges faced by individuals with learning disabilities. Learning disabilities may co-exist with various conditions including attentional, behavioural, and emotional disorders, sensory impairments, or other medical conditions.

For success, individuals with learning disabilities require early identification and timely specialized assessments and interventions involving home, school, community, and workplace settings. The interventions need to be appropriate for each individual's learning disability subtype and, at a minimum, include the provision of:

- specific skill instruction;
- accommodations;
- compensatory strategies; and
- self-advocacy skills.

Source: Learning Disabilities Association of Canada, 2002. Reprinted with the kind permission of the Learning Disabilities Association of Canada.

READING DISORDER Reading disorder—dyslexia—characterizes children who have poorly developed skills in recognizing letters and words and comprehending written text. Children with dyslexia may read slowly, with difficulty, and may distort, omit, or substitute words when reading aloud. They may have trouble decoding letters. They may perceive letters upside down (*w* for *m*) or reversed (*b* for *d*). Dyslexia is usually apparent by the age of 7, coinciding with grade 2, but it is sometimes recognized in 6-year-olds. Although it was earlier believed that the problem affected mostly boys, more recent studies find similar rates among boys and girls (APA, 2000a; Shaywitz, 1998). Yet boys with dyslexia are more likely than girls to exhibit disruptive behaviour and so are more likely to be referred for evaluation. Children and adolescents with dyslexia tend to be more prone than their peers to depression, to have lower self-worth and feelings of competence in their academic work, and to have signs of ADHD (Boetsch, Green, & Pennington, 1996).

THEORETICAL PERSPECTIVES Canadian neuropsychologists contend that learning disorders originate primarily from neurobiological factors (Fiedorowicz, 1999; Fiedorowicz et al., 1999, 2002). Many children with learning disorders have problems with visual or auditory sensation and perception. They may lack the capacity to copy words or to discriminate geometric shapes. Other children have short attention spans or show hyperactivity, which is also suggestive of an underlying brain abnormality.

Much of the research on learning disorders has focused on dyslexia. Mounting evidence points to underlying brain dysfunctions (Shaywitz et al., 1998). Cross-cultural language research has now shown that dyslexia is a universal neuroanatomical disorder that causes the same reading disabilities (Paulesu et al., 2001). There is evidence of impaired visual processing in people with dyslexia that would be consistent with a defect in a major visual relay station in the brain involved in sequencing the flow of visual information from the retina to the visual cortex (Livingstone, Rosen, Drislane, & Galaburda, 1991). Inspection of the autopsied brains of people who had dyslexia showed that this relay station was smaller and less well organized than in other people. As a result, the brains of people with dyslexia are not likely to be able to decipher a rapid succession of visual stimuli, such as those involved in decoding letters and words. Words may thus become blurry, fuse together, or seem to jump off the page—all problems reported by people with dyslexia (Blakeslee, 1991).

Dysfunctions in other sensory pathways involving the sense of hearing and even the sense of touch may also be involved in learning disorders. For example, research suggests that some forms of dyslexia may be traceable to an abnormality in the brain circuits responsible for processing rapidly flowing auditory infor-

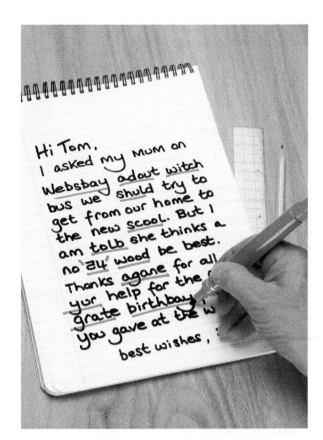

Dyslexia. Children with dyslexia have difficulty decoding words. Note the misspelled words in this person's message.

mation (Blakeslee, 1994). This flaw in brain circuitry may make it difficult to understand rapidly occurring speech sounds, such as the sounds corresponding to the letters *b* and *p* in syllables like *ba* and *pa*. Problems discerning the differences between many basic speech sounds can make it difficult for people with dyslexia to learn to speak correctly and later, perhaps, to learn to read. They continue to have problems distinguishing between words like *boy* and *toy* or *pet* and *bet* in rapid speech. If defects in brain circuitry responsible for relaying and processing sensory data are involved in learning disorders, as the evidence suggests, it may lead the way to the development of specialized treatment programs to help children adjust to their sensory capabilities.

Genetic factors appear to be involved in brain abnormalities associated with dyslexia (Fiedorowicz et al., 1999, 2002). People whose parents have dyslexia are at greater risk themselves (see Figure 11.1 on page 410) (Vogler, DeFries, & Decker, 1985). Moreover, higher rates of concordance (agreement) for dyslexia are found between identical (MZ) than fraternal (DZ) twins—70% versus 40% (Plomin et al., 1994). Suspicion has focused on the role that particular genes may play in causing subtle defects in the brain circuitry involved in reading.

Intervention

With the growing recognition of the neurobiological nature of learning disabilities, our approach to treatment in Canada now involves support and intervention strategies that focus on a child's information processing style and academic strengths. The support aspect focuses on bolstering the child's self-esteem and increasing motivation, developing close teacher–parent partnerships, and, in older children, developing effective self-advocacy skills. Once an **individual education plan** (IEP) is in place, intervention can be accomplished through language re-education; a variety of mixed-ability teaching methods; academic accommodations such as alternative learning

individual education plan A contractual document that contains learning and behavioural outcomes for a student, a description of how the outcomes will be achieved, and a description of how the outcomes will be evaluated. Abbreviated *IEP*.

FIGURE 11.1 **Familial risk of developmental reading disorder (dyslexia).**
Boys are at greater risk than girls of developing dyslexia, and children of both genders whose parents have dyslexia are at relatively greater risk. Although these data are consistent with a genetic explanation of the etiology of dyslexia, it is also possible that parents with dyslexia do not provide their children with the types of stimulation that foster reading skills, such as books and the reading of bedtime stories.

Source: Adapted from Vogler, DeFries, & Decker, 1985, pp. 419–421. Copyright Sage Publications. Reprinted with permission.

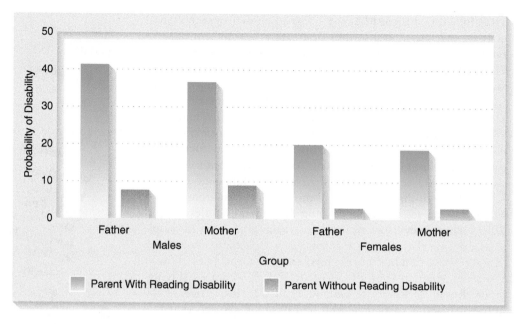

and testing methods; development of compensatory skills; and the use of assistive technologies such as computers, spell checkers, and calculators (Learning Disabilities Association of Canada, 2003a, 2003b).

REVIEW IT

Learning Disorders

- **What are learning disorders?** Learning disorders (also called *learning disabilities*) are specific deficits in the development of arithmetic, writing, or reading skills.
- **What are the causes of learning disorders and approaches to treatment?** The causes remain under study but most probably involve underlying neurobiological brain dysfunctions that make it difficult to process or decode visual and auditory information. Intervention focuses mainly on the remediation and accommodation of specific skill deficits.

ATTENTION-DEFICIT AND DISRUPTIVE BEHAVIOUR DISORDERS

The category of attention-deficit and disruptive behaviour disorders encompasses a diverse range of problem behaviours, including attention-deficit/hyperactivity disorder (ADHD), conduct disorder (CD), and oppositional defiant disorder (ODD). These disorders are socially disruptive and usually more upsetting to other people than to the children who receive the diagnoses. Although there are differences among these disorders, the rate of comorbidity (co-occurrence) among them is very high (Jensen, Martin, & Cantwell, 1997).

Attention-Deficit/Hyperactivity Disorder

Many parents believe their children are not attentive toward them—that they run around on whim and do things in their own way. Some inattention, especially in early childhood, is normal enough. In **attention-deficit/hyperactivity disorder** (ADHD), however, children display degrees of impulsivity, inattention, and **hyperactivity** that are considered inappropriate to their developmental levels.

ADHD is divided into three subtypes: a predominantly inattentive type, a predominantly hyperactive or impulsive type, and a combination type characterized by high

attention-deficit/hyperactivity disorder Behaviour disorder of childhood characterized by excessive motor activity and inability to focus one's attention. Abbreviated *ADHD*.

hyperactivity Abnormal behaviour pattern found most often in young boys that is characterized by extreme restlessness and difficulty maintaining attention.

levels of both inattention and hyperactivity-impulsivity (APA, 2000a). The disorder is usually first diagnosed during elementary school, when problems with attention or hyperactivity-impulsivity make it difficult for the child to adjust to school. Although signs of hyperactivity are often observed earlier, many overactive toddlers do not go on to develop ADHD.

ADHD is far from rare. Canadian studies have found the prevalence rates of ADHD to be between 5% and 10% in children aged 6 to 14 (Romano, Baillargeon, & Tremblay, 2002). Boys were two to three times more likely than girls to be identified as having ADHD, and 6- to 8-year-olds had higher rates than 12- to 14-year-olds. Although inattention appears to be the basic problem, there are associated problems such as an inability to sit still for more than a few moments, bullying, temper tantrums, stubbornness, and failure to respond to punishment (see Table 11.3).

TABLE 11.3

Diagnostic Criteria for Attention-Deficit/Hyperactivity Disorder (ADHD)

A. Either (1) or (2):

   (1) six (or more) of the following symptoms of **inattention** have persisted for at least 6 months to a degree that is maladaptive and inconsistent with developmental level:

Inattention

     (a) often fails to give close attention to details or makes careless mistakes in schoolwork, work, or other activities

     (b) often has difficulty sustaining attention in tasks or play activities

     (c) often does not seem to listen when spoken to directly

     (d) often does not follow through on instructions and fails to finish schoolwork, chores, or duties in the workplace (not due to oppositional behavior or failure to understand instructions)

     (e) often has difficulty organizing tasks and activities

     (f) often avoids, dislikes, or is reluctant to engage in tasks that require sustained mental effort (such as schoolwork or homework)

     (g) often loses things necessary for tasks or activities (e.g., toys, school assignments, pencils, books, or tools)

     (h) is often easily distracted by extraneous stimuli

     (i) is often forgetful in daily activities

   (2) six (or more) of the following symptoms of **hyperactivity-impulsivity** have persisted for at least 6 months to a degree that is maladaptive and inconsistent with developmental level:

Hyperactivity

     (a) often fidgets with hands or feet or squirms in seat

     (b) often leaves seat in classroom or in other situations in which remaining seated is expected

     (c) often runs about or climbs excessively in situations in which it is inappropriate (in adolescents or adults, may be limited to subjective feelings of restlessness)

     (d) often has difficulty playing or engaging in leisure activities quietly

     (e) is often "on the go" or often acts as if "driven by a motor"

     (f) often talks excessively

Impulsivity

     (g) often blurts out answers before questions have been completed

     (h) often has difficulty awaiting turn

     (i) often interrupts or intrudes on others (e.g., butts into conversations or games)

B. Some hyperactive-impulsive or inattentive symptoms that caused impairment were present before age 7 years.

C. Some impairment from the symptoms is present in two or more settings (e.g., at school [or work] and at home).

Source: Reprinted with permission from the *Diagnostic and Statistical Manual of Mental Disorders*, Fourth Edition, Text Revision, (Copyright ©2000). American Psychiatric Association. p. 92.

Attention Issues: No Disorder

Attention Issues: ADHD

Kai is a seven-year-old boy in grade 2. His parents describe him as an active and energetic boy who sometimes seems like he has "ants in his pants." He is especially excitable in new situations that are full of stimulation. For example, his teacher has had to talk to him a few times because of his excitability during gym class. He sometimes gets too rough when playing games with his classmates, though his intentions are never aggressive. When he's excited about something, Kai has trouble focusing on anything else. His mom says that it's virtually impossible to get his attention when he's waiting for a friend to come over, or just before a birthday party. Sometimes she worries about leaving him at a friend's house in case he gets out of hand. Luckily, this hasn't happened and Kai continues to be invited on playdates and to parties. Kai's teacher has remarked that he has the ability to focus on lots of things at school, especially activities where he has something to do with his hands. Kai's parents also note that he is able to sit and listen to stories or watch kids' movies.

Behzad is a nine-year-old boy who lives with his parents and two younger siblings. He is in grade 4 at school and is struggling. He has been identified by his teacher as having attention and behaviour problems at school. On a regular basis, Behzad is removed from the regular classroom due to being disruptive. He constantly interrupts the teacher and other children, he has trouble staying in his seat, and he cannot finish classroom assignments. Behzad's parents have had similar concerns at home. Behzad is very physical with his siblings and sometimes accidentally hurts them. He is especially aggressive when he's frustrated, and it seems that he is increasingly frustrated even when doing things he likes. He has trouble sitting through television shows and is not able to sit and read books. He can sometimes focus on a video game for a sustained period of time, but this seems to be one of the only activities that can consume his attention. Behzad's parents are very worried because his disruptive behaviour and trouble focusing appears to be having a negative impact on his achievement at school. They are also worried that the teachers are beginning to think of him as a "problem" and are removing him from the classroom rather than looking at ways of helping him focus.

Activity and restlessness impair the ability of children with ADHD to function in school. They seem incapable of sitting still. They fidget and squirm in their seats, butt into other children's games, have outbursts of temper, and may engage in dangerous behaviour, such as running into the street without looking. All in all, they can drive parents and teachers to despair.

Where does "normal" age-appropriate overactivity end and hyperactivity begin? Assessment of the degree of hyperactive behaviour is crucial, because many normal children are called "hyper" from time to time. Some critics of the ADHD diagnosis argue that it merely labels children who are difficult to control as mentally disordered or sick. Most children, especially boys, are highly active during the early school years. Proponents of the diagnosis counter that there is a difference in quality between normal overactivity and ADHD. Normally overactive children are goal directed and can exert voluntary control over their own behaviour. But children with ADHD appear hyperactive without reason and do not seem to be able to conform their behaviour to the demands of teachers and parents. Put it another way: most children can sit still and concentrate for a while when they want to; children with ADHD seemingly cannot.

Children with ADHD tend to do more poorly in school than their peers despite being, for the most part, of average or above average intelligence. They may fail to follow or remember instructions and complete assignments. They are more likely than their peers to have learning disabilities, to repeat grades, and to be placed in special-education classes (Faraone et al., 1993; Leibson, Katusic, Barbaresi, Ransom, & O'Brien, 2001). They also stand a greater risk of having mood disorders, anxiety disorders, and problems getting along with family members (Biederman et al., 1996). They are frequently disruptive in the classroom and tend to get into fights (especially the boys). Not surprisingly, they are frequently unpopular with their classmates. Although

ADHD symptoms tend to decline with age, the disorder can persist into adolescence and adulthood (Asherson, Chen, Craddock, & Taylor, 2007; M. Weiss & Murray, 2003).

THEORETICAL PERSPECTIVES Although the causes of ADHD are not known, both biological and environmental influences are believed to be involved (Arnold, O'Leary, & Edward, 1997). Increasing evidence points to a complex genetic vulnerability to ADHD wherein multiple genes have a singularly small, albeit additive, impact (Faraone & Khan, 2006). Hereditary evidence comes from findings of higher concordance rates for ADHD among monozygotic (MZ) twins than dizygotic (DZ) twins, supporting a genetic linkage (Sherman, McGue, & Ianoco, 1997).

Neuropsychological testing, EEG studies, and MRI studies of children and adolescents with ADHD point to abnormalities in the areas of the brain involved in regulating the processes of attention, inhibition of motor (movement) behaviour, and executive control (i.e., the ability to focus, plan, and act) (Bush, Valera, & Seidman, 2005; Castellanos, Glaser, & Gerhardt, 2006; Seidman, Valera, & Makris, 2005; Serene, Ashtari, Szeszko, & Kumra, 2007). We shall also see that the effects of stimulants on children with ADHD offer some support to the hypothesis of organic causes. Despite evidence suggestive of biological factors, we lack a definitive biological explanation of ADHD. In fact, some theorists suggest that the mounting evidence from neuropsychological studies challenges the long-held belief that ADHD is a single coherent clinical entity (Stefanatos & Baron, 2007).

ADHD has also been linked with exposure to environmental toxins. Children who have ADHD were found to be 2.5 times more likely than other children to have had prenatal exposure to environmental tobacco smoke (ETS) (Braun, Khan, Froehlich, Auinger, & Lanphear, 2006). Moreover, a significant dose–response relationship was found: the greater the exposure to ETS, the higher the risk of ADHD, especially for girls. These researchers also found a significant dose–response relationship between higher levels of lead in the blood and ADHD.

Attention-deficit/hyperactivity disorder (ADHD).
ADHD is more common in boys than girls and is characterized by attentional difficulties, restlessness, impulsivity, excessive motor behaviour (continuous running around or climbing), and temper tantrums.

TREATMENT It seems odd that the drugs used to help ADHD children calm down and attend better in school belong to a class of stimulants that include Ritalin (methylphenidate) and longer-acting variants, such as Ritalin SR and Concerta. These stimulants have a paradoxical effect of calming down children with ADHD and increasing their attention spans. Although the use of stimulant medication is not without criticism, it is clear that these drugs can help many children with ADHD calm down and concentrate better on tasks and schoolwork, perhaps for the first time in their lives (L. S. Goldman, Genel, Bezman, & Slanetz, 1998). These drugs not only improve attention in ADHD children but also reduce impulsivity, overactivity, and disruptive, annoying, or aggressive behaviour (Gillberg et al., 1997; Hinshaw, 1992). Stimulant medication appears to be safe and effective when carefully monitored, and successful in helping about three out of four children with ADHD ("Attention Deficit Disorder," 1995; Hinshaw, 1992; Spencer et al., 1996). Improvements are noted at home as well as in school. The normal (voluntary) high activity levels shown in physical education classes and on weekends are not disrupted, however.

We do not know what accounts for the seemingly paradoxical effects of stimulants in calming children with ADHD, although it is suspected that these drugs work on neurotransmitter systems in the brain ("Attention Deficit Disorder," 1995). Although the precise mechanisms are not well understood, we know that these drugs heighten dopamine and norepinephrine activity in the prefrontal cortex of the brain, the area that regulates attention and control of impulsive behaviour (Faraone, 2003a, 2003b). Thus, the drugs may help ADHD children focus their attention and avoid acting out impulsively. Stimulant medication has become so popular that its use increased more than sevenfold during the 1990s (Gibbs, 1998). Currently, an estimated 82 in 1000 Canadian children are using these types of drugs as treatment for ADHD (Romano, Baillargeon, Fortier, et al., 2005). The rate of usage climbs from 0.58% in 4- to 5-year-old boys to a peak of 6.31% in 10- to 11-year-old boys. By comparison, girls are much less likely to use these drugs; their highest usage is at age 8 to 9 (1.09%).

Although stimulant medication can help reduce restlessness and increase attention, it is hardly a panacea. Canadian pediatric researchers caution that although Ritalin has a significant short-term effect on the symptoms of ADHD, there is a lack of evidence that demonstrates its usefulness beyond four weeks of treatment. Research is needed to determine its long-term effectiveness (Schachter, Pham, King, Langford, & Moher, 2001). Moreover, no solid evidence has shown that stimulant medication improves academic performance or leads to better outcomes in adulthood.

Then there is the question of side effects. Although short-term side effects (e.g., loss of appetite or insomnia) usually subside within a few weeks of treatment or may be eliminated by lowering the dose, concerns have been raised about whether stimulants might retard a child's growth. Although these drugs do slow growth for a few years, researchers found that the drug delays but does not stunt a youngster's growth (Gorman, 1998). Recently, Health Canada (2006b) posted a drug advisory warning Canadians with high blood pressure, heart disease, and cardiovascular conditions or an overactive thyroid to avoid any stimulant drugs to manage symptoms of ADHD. In rare cases, these drugs can result in cardiac arrest, stroke, or sudden death. A subsequent Health Canada (2006c) information update also indicated the potential for adverse psychiatric effects, such as agitation and hallucinations in children who use ADHD drugs.

With so many children on Ritalin and similar drugs, critics claim we are too ready to seek a "quick fix" for problem behaviour in children rather than examining other factors contributing to the child's problem, such as dysfunctions in the family (Gibbs, 1998). As one pediatrician put it, "It takes time for parents and teachers to sit down and talk to kids. . . . It takes less time to get a child a pill" (Hancock, 1996, p. 52). Whatever the benefits of stimulant medication, medication alone typically fails to bring the social and academic behaviour of children with ADHD into a normal range (Hinshaw, 1992). Drugs cannot teach new skills. Thus, attention has focused on whether a combination of stimulant medication and behavioural or cognitive-behavioural techniques can produce greater benefits than either approach alone. Cognitive-behavioural treatment of ADHD combines behaviour modification, typically based on the use of reinforcement (e.g., a teacher praising the child with ADHD for sitting quietly) and cognitive modification (e.g., training the child to silently talk himself or herself through the steps involved in solving challenging academic problems). Thus far, the evidence favours a combination approach. A McMaster University–based review of 14 studies involving nearly 1400 participants found that a combination of medication and behavioural interventions yielded better outcomes than either type of treatment alone (Schachar et al., 2002).

Conduct Disorder

conduct disorder Pattern of abnormal behaviour in childhood characterized by disruptive, antisocial behaviour.

Although they both involve disruptive behaviour, **conduct disorder** differs in important ways from ADHD. Whereas children with ADHD seem literally incapable of controlling their behaviour, children with conduct disorders purposefully engage in patterns of antisocial behaviour that violate social norms and the rights of others. Whereas children with ADHD throw temper tantrums, children diagnosed as conduct disordered are intentionally aggressive and cruel. Like antisocial adults, many conduct-disordered children are callous and apparently do not experience guilt or remorse for their misdeeds.

The prevalence of conduct disorder in Canadian children and youth is estimated to be 3.3% (Waddell & Shepherd, 2002). Conduct disorders are much more common among boys than girls, especially the childhood-onset type in which characteristic features of the disorder appear before age 10 (APA, 2000a). Conduct disorder typically takes a somewhat different form in boys than girls. In boys, it is more likely to be manifested in stealing, fighting, vandalism, or disciplinary problems at school, whereas in girls the disorder is more likely to involve lying, truancy, running away, substance use, and prostitution (APA, 2000a). Although there are differences between ADHD and conduct disorder, some children with conduct disorder also display a pattern of short attention span and hyperactivity that may justify a double diagnosis.

Conduct disorder is typically a chronic or persistent disorder (Lahey et al., 1995). Longitudinal studies show that Canadian elementary schoolchildren with conduct disorders are more likely than other children to engage in delinquent acts as early adolescents (Tremblay et al., 1992). Another form of conduct disorder may involve a cluster of personality traits that have different origins than antisocial behaviour (Wootton, Frick, Shelton, & Silverthorn, 1997). These traits include callousness (uncaring, mean, and cruel behaviour) and an unemotional way of relating to others.

oppositional defiant disorder
Disorder in childhood or adolescence characterized by excessive oppositionality or tendencies to refuse requests from parents and others.

Oppositional Defiant Disorder

Debate continues among professionals over the issue of whether conduct disorder (CD) and **oppositional defiant disorder** (ODD) are separate disorders or variations of a common disruptive behaviour disorder (Rey, 1993). Or perhaps ODD is a precursor or milder form of conduct disorder (Abikoff & Klein, 1992; Biederman et al., 1996). Currently, the two disorders are conceptualized as related but separate disorders. ODD is more closely related to nondelinquent (negativistic) conduct disturbance, and conduct disorder involves more outright delinquent behaviour in the form of truancy, stealing, lying, and aggressiveness (Rey, 1993). University of British Columbia researchers have found a strong association between oppositional defiant disorder symptoms and generalized anxiety symptoms in preadolescent children (Garland & Garland, 2001). However, they noted reluctance on the part of clinicians to give a diagnosis of ODD to children with anxiety disorders. This reluctance can have an impact on treatment and outcomes.

Children with ODD tend to be negativistic or oppositional. They are defiant of authority, which is exhibited by their tendency to argue with parents and teachers and refuse to follow requests or directives from adults. They may deliberately annoy other people, become easily angered or lose their temper, become touchy or easily annoyed, blame others for their mistakes or misbehaviour, feel resentful toward others,

Oppositional defiant disorder (ODD). A common childhood disorder that engenders a "no-win" situation for everyone concerned.

or act in spiteful or vindictive ways toward others (Angold & Costello, 1996; APA, 2000a). The disorder typically begins before age eight and develops gradually over a period of months or years. It typically starts in the home environment but may extend to other settings, such as school.

ODD is one of the most common diagnoses among children (Doll, 1996). Studies show that among children diagnosed with a psychological disorder, about one in three are judged to meet the criteria for ODD (Rey, 1993). An estimated 6% to 12% of school-aged children display ODD (Frick & Silverthorn, 2001). ODD is more common overall among boys than girls. However, this overall effect masks a gender shift over age. Among children 12 years of age or younger, ODD appears to be more than twice as common among boys; yet among adolescents, a higher prevalence is reported in girls (Rey, 1993). By contrast, most studies find conduct disorder to be more common in boys than girls across all age groups.

THEORETICAL PERSPECTIVES The causal factors in ODD remain obscure. Some theorists believe that oppositionality is an expression of an underlying child temperament described as the "difficult-child" type (Rey, 1993). Learning theorists view oppositional behaviours as arising from parental use of inappropriate reinforcement strategies. In this view, parents may inappropriately reinforce oppositional behaviour by "giving in" to the child's demands whenever the child refuses to comply with the parents' wishes, which can become a pattern.

McMaster University researchers have found that family and parenting factors are implicated in the development of disruptive behaviour disorders such as oppositional defiant disorder and conduct disorder (Cunningham & Boyle, 2002). Some forms of disruptive behaviour disorders appear to be linked to unassertive and ineffective parenting styles, such as failure to provide positive reinforcement for appropriate behaviour and use of harsh and inconsistent discipline for misbehaviour. Families of children with CD tend to be characterized by negative, coercive interactions (Dadds, Sanders, Morrison, & Rebgetz, 1992). Children with CD are often very demanding and noncompliant in relating to their parents and other family members. Family members often reciprocate by using negative behaviours, such as threatening or yelling at the child or using physical means of coercion. Parental aggression against children with conduct behaviour problems is common, including pushing, grabbing, slapping, spanking, hitting, or kicking (Jouriles, Mehta, McDonald, & Francis, 1997). Parents of children with oppositional defiant disorders or severe conduct disorder display high rates of antisocial personality disorder and substance abuse (Frick et al., 1992). It's not too much of a stretch to speculate that parental modelling of antisocial behaviours can lead to antisocial conduct in their children.

Some investigations focus on the ways in which children with disruptive behaviour disorders process information. For example, children who are overly aggressive in their behaviour tend to be biased in their processing of social information: they may assume that others intend them ill when they do not (Lochman & Dodge, 1994). They usually blame others for the scrapes they get into. They believe they are misperceived and treated unfairly. They may believe that aggression will lead to favourable results (Dodge, Lochman, Hamish, Bates, & Pettit, 1997). They are also less able than their peers to generate alternative (nonviolent) responses to social conflicts (Lochman & Dodge, 1994).

Genetic factors may interact with family or other environmental factors in the development of conduct disorder in children and antisocial behaviour in adolescence (Slutske et al., 1997, 1998). Genetic factors may also be involved in the development of oppositional defiant disorder.

TREATMENT The treatment of conduct disorders remains a challenge. Although there is not an established pharmacological treatment approach, Toronto psychiatrist Lindley Bassarath (2003) reviewed recent studies that indicate that certain antipsychotic and stimulant drugs may be effective in reducing antisocial behaviour in CD children and adolescents. Psychotherapy has not generally been shown to help disruptive children change their behaviour. Placing children with conduct disorders in programs or treatment settings with explicit rules and clear rewards for obeying them may offer greater promise (Henggeler et al., 1986). Such programs usually rely on operant conditioning procedures that involve systematic use of rewards and punishments.

Many children with conduct disorders, especially boys, display aggressive behaviour and have problems controlling their anger. Many can benefit from programs designed to help them learn anger-coping skills that they can use to handle conflict situations without resorting to violent behaviour. Cognitive-behavioural therapy has been used to teach boys who engage in antisocial and aggressive behaviour to reconceptualize social provocations as problems to be solved rather than as challenges to their manhood that must be answered with violence. They have been trained to use calming self-talk to inhibit impulsive behaviour and control anger whenever they experience social taunts or provocations and to generate and try out nonviolent solutions to social conflicts (Lochman & Lenhart, 1993). Other programs present child models on video demonstrating skills of anger control. The results of these programs appear promising (Kazdin & Weisz, 1998; Webster-Stratton & Hammond, 1997). Sometimes the disruptive child's parents are brought into the treatment process (Kazdin & Whitley, 2003).

The following example illustrates the involvement of the parents in the behavioural treatment of a case of oppositional defiant disorder:

> Dimitry was a seven-year-old second-grader referred by his parents. The family relocated frequently because the father was in the navy. Dimitry usually behaved when his father was taking care of him, but he was noncompliant with his mother and yelled at her when she gave him instructions. His mother was incurring great stress in the effort to control Dimitry, especially when her husband was at sea.
>
> Dimitry had become a problem at home and in school during grade 1. He ignored and violated rules in both settings. Dimitry failed to carry out his chores and frequently yelled at and hit his younger brother. When he acted up, his parents would restrict him to his room or the yard, take away privileges and toys, and spank him. But all of these measures were used inconsistently. He also played on the railroad tracks near his home and twice the police had brought him home after he had thrown rocks at cars.
>
> A home observation showed that Dimitry's mother often gave him inappropriate commands. She interacted with him as little as possible and showed no verbal praise, physical closeness, smiles, or positive facial expressions or gestures. She paid attention to him only when he misbehaved. When Dimitry was noncompliant, she would yell back at him and then try to catch him to force him to comply. Dimitry would then laugh and run from her.
>
> Dimitry's parents were informed that the child's behaviour was a product of inappropriate cueing techniques (poor directions), a lack of reinforcement for appropriate behaviour, and lack of consistent sanctions for misbehaviour. They were taught the appropriate use of reinforcement, punishment, and **time out**. The parents then charted Dimitry's problem behaviours to gain a clearer idea of what triggered and maintained them. They were shown how to reinforce acceptable behaviour and use time out as a contingent punishment for misbehaviour. Dimitry's mother was also taught relaxation training to help desensitize her to Dimitry's disruptions. Biofeedback was used to enhance the relaxation response.
>
> During a 15-day baseline period, Dimitry behaved in a noncompliant manner about four times per day. When treatment was begun, Dimitry showed an immediate drop to about one instance of noncompliance every two days. Follow-up data showed that instances of noncompliance were maintained at a bearable level of about one per day. Fewer behavioural problems in school were also reported, even though they had not been addressed directly.

S. J. Kaplan, 1986, pp. 227–230. Reprinted with the kind permission of Springer Science+Business Media B.V.

time out Behavioural technique in which an individual who emits an undesired behaviour is removed from an environment in which reinforcers are available and placed in an unreinforcing environment for a period of time as a form of punishment. Time out is frequently used in behavioural programs for modifying behaviour problems in children, in combination with positive reinforcement for desirable behaviour.

In Canada, as in most other industrialized nations, the emphasis is more on treatment than prevention. This usually means that by the time a conduct-disordered youth gets into care, his or her problem behaviour is well established and therefore more resistant and more expensive to treat. A failure to implement effective prevention programs may have more to do with short-sighted political agendas and rigid service-delivery systems than it does with program costs or a lack of desire to serve long-term needs to prevent future conduct-disordered youth (Moretti et al., 1997).

REVIEW IT

Attention-Deficit and Disruptive Behaviour Disorders

- **What are attention-deficit and disruptive behaviour disorders?** This category includes attention-deficit/hyperactivity disorder (ADHD), conduct disorder, and oppositional defiant disorder. ADHD is characterized by impulsivity, inattention, and hyperactivity. Children with conduct disorders intentionally engage in antisocial behaviour. Children with ODD show negativistic or oppositional behaviour but not outright delinquent or antisocial behaviour characteristic of conduct disorder.

However, ODD may represent an early stage of development of conduct disorder.

- **How are these disorders treated?** Stimulant medication is generally effective in reducing hyperactivity, but has not led to general academic gains. Behaviour therapy may help ADHD children adapt better to school. Behaviour therapy may also be helpful in modifying behaviours of children with conduct disorders and oppositional defiant disorder.

ANXIETY AND DEPRESSION IN CHILDHOOD AND ADOLESCENCE

Anxieties and fears are a normal feature of childhood, just as they are a normal feature of adult life. Childhood fears—of the dark or of small animals—are commonplace and are usually outgrown naturally. Anxiety is considered abnormal, however, when it is excessive and interferes with normal academic or social functioning or becomes troubling or persistent. Children, like adults, may suffer from different types of diagnosable anxiety disorders, including specific phobias, social phobias, and generalized anxiety disorder (GAD). Although these disorders may develop at any age, we will consider a type of anxiety disorder that typically develops during early childhood: separation anxiety disorder.

Children may also show a more general pattern of avoidance of social interactions that characterizes avoidant personality disorder. Although children who are socially avoidant or have social phobias may have warm relationships with family members, they tend to be shy and withdrawn around others. Their avoidance of people outside the family interferes with their development of social relationships with their peers. Their distress at being around other children at school can also impede their academic progress. Such problems tend to develop after normal fear of strangers fades, at age two and a half or later.

Despite the stereotype of a happy childhood, clinical depression is found in children and adolescents. Estimates indicate that slightly more than 2% of Canadian children experience a depressive disorder (Waddell & Shepherd, 2002). Major depression has even been found, although rarely, among preschoolers. Although there is no discernible gender difference in the risk of depression in childhood, a prominent gender difference appears after the age of 15, with adolescent girls becoming about twice as likely to become depressed as adolescent boys (Hankin et al., 1998). Nationwide surveys have revealed that, of Canadian youth aged 15 to 19 years, 12% of the females and 3% to 6% of the males have had a major depressive episode (Shaw & Grenier, 2001).

Separation Anxiety Disorder

It is normal for children to show anxiety when they are separated from their caregivers (Ainsworth & Bowlby, 1991). Mary Ainsworth (1989), who has chronicled the development of attachment behaviours, notes that separation anxiety is a normal feature of the child–caregiver relationship and begins during the first year of life. The sense of security normally provided by bonds of attachment apparently encourages children to explore their environments and become progressively independent of their caregivers (Bowlby, 1988).

Separation anxiety disorder is diagnosed when separation anxiety is persistent and excessive or inappropriate for the child's developmental level. That is, three-year-olds ought to be able to attend preschool without nausea and vomiting brought on by anxiety. Six-year-olds ought to be able to attend grade 1 without persistent dread that something awful will happen to themselves or their parents. Children with this disorder tend to cling to their parents and follow them around the house. They may voice concerns about death and dying and insist that someone stay with them while they are falling asleep. Other features of the disorder include nightmares, stomach aches, nausea and vomiting when separation is anticipated (as on school days), pleading with parents not to leave, or throwing tantrums when parents are about to depart. Children may refuse to attend school for fear that something will happen to their parents while they are away. The disorder affects about 4% of children and young adolescents and occurs more frequently, according to community-based studies, among females (APA, 2000a). The disorder may persist into adulthood, leading to an exaggerated concern about the well-being of one's children and spouse and difficulty tolerating any separation from them.

The development of separation anxiety disorder frequently follows a stressful life event, such as illness, the death of a relative or pet, or a change of schools or homes. Richa's problems followed the death of her grandmother:

> Richa's grandmother died when Richa was seven years old. Her parents decided to permit her request to view her grandmother in the open coffin. Richa took a tentative glance from her father's arms across the room, then asked to be taken out of the room. Her five-year-old sister took a leisurely close-up look, with no apparent distress.
>
> Richa had been concerned about death for two or three years by this time, but her grandmother's passing brought on a new flurry of questions: "Will I die?" "Does everybody die?" and so on. Her parents tried to reassure her by saying, "Grandma was very, very old, and she also had a heart condition. You are very young and in perfect health. You have many, many years before you have to start thinking about death."
>
> Richa also could not be alone in any room in her house. She pulled one of her parents or her sister along with her everywhere she went. She also reported nightmares about her grandmother and, within a couple of days, insisted on sleeping in the same room with her parents. Fortunately, Richa's fears did not extend to school. Her teacher reported that Richa spent some time talking about her grandmother, but her academic performance was apparently unimpaired.
>
> Richa's parents decided to allow Richa time to "get over" the loss. Richa gradually talked less and less about death, and by the time three months had passed, she was able to go into any room in her house by herself. She wanted to continue to sleep in her parents' bedroom, however, so her parents "made a deal" with her. They would put off the return to her own bedroom until the school year had ended (a month away), if Richa would agree to return to her own bed at that time. As a further incentive, a parent would remain with her until she fell asleep for the first month. Richa overcame the anxiety problem in this fashion with no additional delays.
>
> The Authors' Files

separation anxiety disorder
Childhood disorder characterized by extreme fears of separation from parents or others on whom the child is dependent.

Perspectives on Anxiety Disorders in Childhood

Theoretical understandings of excessive anxiety in children to some degree parallel explanations of anxiety disorders in adults. Psychoanalytic theorists argue that childhood anxieties and fears, like their adult counterparts, symbolize unconscious conflicts. Cognitive theorists focus on the role of cognitive biases underlying anxiety reactions. In support of the cognitive model, investigators find that highly anxious children show cognitive biases in processing information, such as interpreting ambiguous situations as threatening, expecting negative outcomes, thinking poorly of themselves and of their ability to cope, and engaging in negative self-talk (Weems, Costa, Watts, Taylor, & Cannon, 2007). Expecting the worst, combined with low self-confidence, encourages avoidance of feared activities—with friends, in school, and elsewhere. Negative expectations may also heighten feelings of anxiety to the point where they impede performance. Learning theorists suggest that the occurrence of generalized anxiety may touch on broad themes, such as fears of rejection or failure, that carry across situations. Underlying fears of rejection or self-perceptions of inadequacy may generalize to most areas of social interaction and achievement.

Depression in Childhood and Adolescence

The basic features of depression in children and adolescents are similar to those in adults (Kovacs, 1996). Depressed children and adolescents typically show a greater sense of hopelessness, display more cognitive errors and negative attributions (e.g., blaming themselves for negative events), have lower perceived competence or self-efficacy, and have lower self-esteem than do their nondepressed peers (Lewinsohn, Rohde, & Seeley, 1994). They often report episodes of sadness, crying, and apathy as well as insomnia, fatigue, and poor appetite. They may refuse to attend school, express fears of their parents' dying, and cling to their parents or retreat to their rooms. They may have suicidal thoughts or attempt suicide.

Is this child too young to be depressed? Although we tend to think of childhood as the happiest and most carefree time of life, depression is actually quite common among children and adolescents. Depressed children may report feelings of sadness and lack of interest in previously enjoyable activities. Many, however, do not report, or are not aware of, feelings of depression, even though they may look depressed to observers. Depression may also be masked by other problems such as conduct/school-related problems, physical complaints, and overactivity.

Moderate levels of depression may persist for years, severely impacting school performance and social functioning (Nolen-Hoeksema & Girgus, 1994). Adolescent depression is associated with an increased risk of future major depressive episodes and suicide attempts in adulthood (M. M. Weissman, Wolk, et al., 1999). About three out of four children who become depressed from age 8 to 13 have a recurrence later in life (Goleman, 1994).

Children who experience depression may also lack skills in various domains, including academic performance, social acceptance by peers, and athletic performance (Seroczynski, Cole, & Maxwell, 1997). They may find it hard to concentrate in school and may suffer from impaired memory, making it difficult for them to keep their grades up (Goleman, 1994).

Childhood depression rarely occurs by itself (Hammen & Compas, 1994). Depressed children typically experience other psychological disorders, especially anxiety disorders and conduct or oppositional defiant disorders (Hammen & Compas, 1994). Eating disorders are also common among depressed adolescents, at least among females (Rohde, Lewinsohn, & Seeley, 1991). Overall, childhood depression increases the chances that a child will develop another psychological disorder by at least twentyfold (Angold & Costello, 1993).

We should recognize that depressed children or adolescents may fail to label what they are feeling as depression. Further, conduct disorders, academic problems, physical complaints, and even hyperactivity may stem now and then from unrecognized depression. Among adolescents, aggressive and sexual acting out may also be signs of underlying depression.

CORRELATES AND TREATMENT OF DEPRESSION IN CHILDHOOD AND ADOLESCENCE As children mature and their cognitive abilities increase, however, cognitive factors, such as attributional styles, appear to play a stronger role in the development of depression. Older children (in grades 6 and 7) who adopt a more helpless or pessimistic explanatory style (attributing negative events to internal, stable, and global causes and attributing positive events to external, unstable, and specific causes) are more likely than children with a more optimistic explanatory style to develop depression (Nolen-Hoeksema, Girgus, & Seligman, 1992). Researchers also find that adolescents who are depressed tend to hold more dysfunctional attitudes and to adopt a more helpless explanatory style than their nondepressed peers (Lewinsohn et al., 1994).

Genetic factors also appear to play a role in explaining depressive symptoms, at least among adolescents (O'Connor, McGuire, Reiss, Hetherington, & Plomin, 1998). The role of genetics in childhood depression requires further study, however (Kovacs, Devlin, Pollock, Richards, & Mukerji, 1997).

Adolescent girls may face a greater risk of depression because they tend to face more social challenges than boys during adolescence—challenges such as pressures to narrow their interests and pursue feminine-typed activities (Nolen-Hoeksema & Girgus, 1994). It may be that girls who adopt a more passive, ruminative style of coping as children may be at greatest risk of becoming depressed when they face socially restrictive attitudes that devalue their accomplishments and abilities in relation to those of boys, when they face restrictions placed on the social roles and activities deemed appropriate for their gender, and when they encounter sexual pressures or abuse.

Accumulating evidence supports the effectiveness of cognitive-behavioural therapy (CBT) in treating depression in childhood and adolescence (Braswell & Kendall, 2001; Lewinsohn & Clarke, 1999). Although individual approaches vary, CBT usually involves a coping-skills model in which children or adolescents receive social-skills training (e.g., learning how to start a conversation or make friends) to increase the likelihood of obtaining social reinforcement (Kazdin & Weisz, 1998). In addition, family therapy may be useful in helping families resolve underlying conflicts and reorganize their relationships in ways that members can become more supportive of each other.

The earlier generation of antidepressants failed to show superior results to placebos in treating childhood or adolescent depression (Rutter, 1997). We cannot assume drugs that may be effective with adults will work as well or be as safe when used with children (Vitello & Jensen, 1997). However, the drug Prozac, one of the new generation of SSRI antidepressants, has been shown in at least one study to produce better results than a placebo control in relieving severe and persistent depression in children and adolescents (Emslie et al., 1997). Still, the complete elimination of depressive symptoms was rare.

SUICIDE AMONG CHILDREN AND ADOLESCENTS Suicide is relatively uncommon among children under the age of 10 in Canada. However, for youth aged 10 to 19 years, Health Canada (1999a) reports that after traffic fatalities, suicide is the second leading cause of death, accounting for almost one in five deaths. The rates of suicide climb with age, rising from 2.0 in 100 000 between the ages of 10 and 14 years to 11.5 between the ages of 15 and 19. Males are about three and a half times as likely as females to complete a suicide. These official statistics only account for reported suicide; some apparently accidental deaths may be suicides as well.

Despite the commonly held view that children and adolescents who talk about suicide are only venting their feelings, young people who do intend to kill themselves may very well talk about it beforehand (Brody, 1992a). In fact, those who discuss their plans are the ones most likely to carry them out. Moreover, children and adolescents who have survived suicide attempts are most likely to try again (Brody, 1992a). Unfortunately, parents tend not to take their children's suicidal talk seriously. They often refuse treatment for their children or terminate treatment prematurely.

Several factors are associated with an increased risk of suicide among children and adolescents (Levy, Jurkovic, & Spirito, 1995; Lewinsohn et al., 1994; Neiger & Hopkins, 1988):

1. *Gender.* Girls, like women, are three times more likely than boys to attempt suicide. Boys, like men, are more likely to succeed, however, perhaps because boys, like men, are more apt to use lethal means, such as guns. The presence of a loaded handgun in the house turns out to be the greatest risk factor for completed suicide among children, even those as young as five (Brody, 1992a).
2. *Age.* Young people in late adolescence or early adulthood (ages 15 to 24) are at greater risk than younger adolescents.
3. *Ethnicity.* The suicide rate for Canadian Aboriginal youth is three to four times higher than for youth in the general population (Health Canada, 1999a). The rates of suicide in some First Nations communities are among the highest in the world ("Federal Paternalism," 1999).
4. *Depression and hopelessness.* Depression and hopelessness, especially when combined with low self-esteem, are major risk factors for suicide among adolescents, as for adults.
5. *Previous suicidal behaviour.* A quarter of adolescents who attempt suicide are repeaters. More than 80% of adolescents who take their lives have talked about it before doing so. Suicidal teenagers may carry lethal weapons, talk about death, make suicide plans, or engage in risky or dangerous behaviour. A family history of suicide also increases risk of teenage suicide (Mann, Underwood, & Arango, 1996).
6. *Family problems.* Family problems are present among about 75% of adolescent suicide attempters. Problems include family instability and conflict, physical or sexual abuse, loss of a parent due to death or separation, and poor parent–child communication (Asarnow, Carlson, & Guthrie, 1987; Wagner, 1997).
7. *Stressful life events.* Many suicides among young people are directly preceded by stressful or traumatic events, such as the breakup of a relationship with a girlfriend or boyfriend, unwanted pregnancy, getting arrested, having problems at school, moving to a new school, or having to take an important test.
8. *Substance abuse.* Addiction in the adolescent's family or by the adolescent is a factor.
9. *Social contagion.* Adolescent suicides sometimes occur in clusters, especially when a suicide or a group of suicides receives widespread publicity (R. C. Kessler, Downey, Milavsky, & Stipp, 1988; Phillips & Carstensen, 1986). Adolescents may romanticize suicide as a heroic act of defiance. There are often suicides or attempts among the siblings, friends, parents, or adult relatives of suicidal adolescents. Note the case of Alexandra:

Alexandra was an exceptionally attractive 17-year-old who was hospitalized after cutting her wrists.

"Before we moved to [an upper-middle-class U.S. town in Westchester County]," she told the psychologist, "I was the brightest girl in the class. Teachers loved me. If we had had a yearbook, I'd have been the most likely to succeed. Then we moved, and suddenly I was hit with it. Everybody was bright, or tried to be. Suddenly I was just another ordinary student planning to go to college.

"Teachers were good to me, but I was no longer special, and that hurt. Then we all applied to college. Do you know that 90% of the kids in the high school go on to college? I mean four-year colleges? And we all knew—or suspected—that the good schools had quotas on kids from here. I mean you can't have 30 kids from our senior class going to Yale or Princeton or Wellesley, can you? You're better off applying from Utah.

"Then Carmen got her early-acceptance rejection from Brown. Carmen was number one in the class. Nobody could believe it. Her father had gone to Brown and Carmen had scored almost 1500 on her SATs. Carmen was out of commission for a few days—I mean she didn't come to school or anything—and then, boom, she was gone. She offed herself, kaput, no more, the end. Then Brian was rejected from Cornell. A few days later, he was gone, too. And I'm like, 'These kids were better than me.' I mean their grades and their SATs were higher than mine, and I was going to apply to Brown and Cornell. I'm like, 'What chance do I have? Why bother?'"

The Authors' Files

You can identify how catastrophizing cognitions can play a role in such tragic cases. Consistent with the literature on suicide among adults, suicidal children and adolescents make less use of active problem-solving strategies in handling stressful situations. They may see no other way out of their perceived failures or stresses. As with adults, one approach to working with suicidal children and adolescents involves helping them challenge distorted thinking and generate alternative strategies for handling the problems and stressors they face.

REVIEW IT

Anxiety and Depression

- **What types of anxiety disorders affect children?** Anxiety disorders that occur commonly among children and adolescents include specific phobias, social phobia, and generalized anxiety disorder. Children may also show separation anxiety disorder, which involves excessive anxiety at times when they are separated from their parents. Cognitive biases such as expecting negative outcomes, negative self-talk, and interpreting ambiguous situations as threatening figure prominently in anxiety disorders in children and adolescents, as they often do among adults.
- **What are the distinguishing features of depression in childhood and adolescence?** Depressed children, especially younger children, may not report or be aware of feeling depressed. Depression may also be masked by seemingly unrelated behaviours, such as conduct disorders. Depressed children also tend to show cognitive biases associated with depression in adulthood, such as adoption of a pessimistic explanatory style and distorted thinking. Although rare, suicide in children does occur and threats should be taken seriously. Risk factors for adolescent suicide include gender, age, geography, race, depression, past suicidal behaviour, strained family relationships, stress, substance abuse, and social contagion.

DELIRIUM

Perhaps you have experienced a state of delirium upon waking and not knowing where you were, or experienced strange hallucinations and weird symptoms during a high fever or after an injury. The following picture of delirium is much like that experience: a temporary state in which there is a clouding of consciousness and the person has a feeling of being unaware of what is happening around them. It's a frightening state for those experiencing it and for those observing. It is really a state of brain failure, in which one lies between normal wakefulness and stupor or coma.

Clinical Picture

Delirium is a commonly occurring syndrome among the elderly that typically involves confusion, problems with concentration, and cognitive dysfunction such as memory disturbances (see Table 11.4 on page 424). The elderly are particularly at risk due to the brain changes that are associated with normal aging (Trzepacz, Meagher, & Wise, 2002) and because older adults are more prone to falls and are more susceptible to adverse reactions from medications (Chan, Nicklason, & Vial, 2001), experiences that can provoke a state of

Diagnostic Criteria for Delirium

A. Disturbance of consciousness (i.e., reduced clarity of awareness of the environment) with reduced ability to focus, sustain, or shift attention.

B. A change in cognition (such as memory deficit, disorientation, language disturbance) or the development of a perceptual disturbance that is not better accounted for by a preexisting, established, or evolving dementia.

C. The disturbance develops over a short period of time (usually hours to days) and tends to fluctuate during the course of the day.

Source: Reprinted with permission from the *Diagnostic and Statistical Manual of Mental Disorders*, Fourth Edition, Text Revision, (Copyright ©2000). American Psychiatric Association. p. 143.

delirium. Impaired attention is considered the core cognitive disturbance. Most patients also experience a variety of other symptoms, including problems with orientation, language skills, mood, thinking, perception, and motor behaviour and the disruption of sleep–wake cycles.

For each individual the symptoms vary, but the patterns of symptoms are common. There are three typical patterns seen: acute onset (sometimes abrupt, but often over hours or days), fluctuant course (symptoms tend to wax and wane over any 24-hour period and typically worsen at night), and transient nature (in most cases, delirium resolves within days or weeks). With so many symptoms, it can easily be mistaken for other psychiatric or medical disorders. For example, in the elderly, delirium and the corresponding changes in mental state are often the early signs of infection or heart problems (Wahlund & Bjorlin, 1999). Knowing the pattern of onset and symptoms can also help distinguish delirium from dementia.

Before delirium becomes acute, it almost always involves a prodromal phase over two to three days of discontent, restlessness, poor concentration, anxiety, irritability, sleep disturbance, and, for some, nightmares. The course of the disorder is not always typical but does seem to follow general trends such as rapid onset, development over a period of days, and brevity; rarely does it last for more than a month.

Psychomotor, or body movement, disturbances might be either hyperactive, manifesting in restless or agitated behaviour, or hypoactive, slowing down movements. For some there is a shift from one extreme to the other (APA, 2000a).

Diagnosis

In order to properly diagnose delirium, typically several measures are used. Initially, cognitive impairment is identified with instruments such as the Mini–Mental State Examination (MMSE) (Folstein, Folstein, & McHugh, 1975) (see Table 11.5 for sample questions used in this exam). Following this, a rating scale is used to determine the actual symptoms experienced and the type of onset of these symptoms. Formal delirium diagnosis requires documentation of acute onset and fluctuant course. The Delirium Rating Scale (DRS) (Trzepacz, Baker, & Greenhouse, 1998) is the most widely used scale to date, and although it requires interpretation by a skilled clinician, it has the significant advantage of distinguishing between the disturbances of depression, delirium, and dementia (see Table 11.6 for further details on distinguishing delirium and dementia). The DRS is performed by a skilled clinician who then also applies the DSM or ICD criteria for the full picture of dysfunction.

Treatment and Outcomes

Since most cases of delirium are reversible, the underlying causes, whether medical or injury, must be identified immediately. Treatment typically involves medication, environment changes, and family support (APA, 2000a). The medications most widely used are neuroleptics (Fricchione et al., 2008).

Sample Items from the Mini Mental State Examination

Orientation to Time
"What is the date?"

Registration
"Listen carefully. I am going to say three words. You say them back after I stop.
Ready? Here they are . . .
APPLE (pause), PENNY (pause), TABLE (pause). Now repeat those words back to me." [Repeat up
to 5 times, but score only the first trial.]

Naming
"What is this?" [Point to a pencil or pen.]

Reading
"Please read this and do what it says." [Show examinee the words on the stimulus form.]
CLOSE YOUR EYES

Reproduced with special permission of the Publisher, Psychological Assessments Resources, Inc., 16204 North
Florida Avenue, Lutz, Florida 33549, from the Mini Mental State Examination, by Marshal Folstein and Susan Folstein,
Copyright 1975, 1998, 2001 by Mini Mental LLC, Inc. Published 2001 by Psychological Assessment Resources, Inc.
Further reproduction is prohibited without permission of PAR, Inc. The MMSE can be purchased from PAR, Inc. by
calling (813) 968-3003.

Distinguishing Features of Depression, Dementia, and Delirium

Features	Depression	Delirium	Dementia
Onset	Weeks to months (rapid)	Hours to days (acute)	Months to years (slow, indefinite)
Duration	Short	Variable	Long/lifetime
Mood	Consistent	Labile	Fluctuation
Disabilities	Recognizes	New disabilities appear (acute)	May conceal deficits
Answers	"Don't know"	May be incoherent (acute)	Offers response but not correct, but may be close to correct
MMSE	Performance fluctuates	Acute fluctuations	Fairly stable with downward trajectory over time
Progression	Resolves with treatment	Resolves with treatment	Ongoing

Source: Insel & Badger, 2002, p. 363. Copyright John Wiley & Sons. Reprinted with permission.

In some cases the individual recovers naturally, without intervention. In others, treatment is effective or the individual develops a progressive neurological deficit or dies from an underlying physical condition.

REVIEW IT

Delirium

- **Cognitive problems are seen in anxiety and dementia. What are the differences between these types of symptoms in anxiety and dementia?** In anxiety, cognitive problems, such as catastrophizing or ruminating, and more subtle changes in thinking can play a role in causing and maintaining the disorder. In dementia, the cognitive problems are the main defining feature.

- **How are delirium and dementia different?** The onset, characteristic, and pattern of symptoms are different in delirium and dementia. With delirium, the onset is sudden, depending on the cause; with dementia, the onset is insidious, slow, and often unrecognized. In delirium, the symptoms typically include disorganized, distorted, or fragmented speech with possible delusions or hallucinations; with dementia, there is a general impoverishment of thoughts, with words difficult to find yet misperceptions or hallucinations usually absent.

DEMENTIA

dementia A form of cognitive impairment involving generalized progressive deficits in a person's memory and learning of new information, ability to communicate, judgment, and motor co-ordination.

While delirium has a sudden onset, with symptoms that come and go, **dementia** has quite a gradual onset and is a gradual decline from previous levels of functioning. Dementia is a form of cognitive impairment involving generalized progressive deficits in a person's memory and learning of new information, ability to communicate, judgment, and motor co-ordination (APA, 2000a) (see Table 11.7). You can imagine that this would have a significant impact on how an individual functions in his or her environment and with other people.

Clinical Picture

Beginning with mild yet annoying symptoms like forgetfulness, the person's symptoms become increasingly obvious and distressing. As the condition progresses, their capacity to care for themselves and for staying in touch with their surroundings gradually worsens.

Memory loss and disturbance of executive function (abstract thinking, organizing, and planning) are two major losses with dementia. In fact, the first sign of dementia is memory loss. As the memory loss becomes more pronounced, individuals become unable to remember even basic facts about themselves and their lives.

Generally, deterioration continues downward over the course of months and years. A Canadian study confirmed that the average duration of life after the individual contacts a doctor for memory problems is about 3.3 years (Wolfson et al., 2001). This contradicts the duration of 7 to 10 years that was taught for many years.

Neuropathy

amyloid plaques Hallmarks of Alzheimer's disease: the accumulation of protein fragments, normally broken down in healthy brains, that accumulate to form hard, insoluble plaques between nerve cells (neurons) in the brain.

There are a number of brain abnormalities now known to be characteristic of dementia: amyloid plaques, neurofibrillary tangles, reduction in neurotransmitters involved in memory, and inflammation of the brain. Plaques and tangles are also found in healthy brains but are found in far greater numbers in people with Alzheimer's disease.

The **amyloid plaques** are made largely of protein, called *beta amyloid*, or *A-beta*, and are split from a much larger protein molecule known as APP. Both APP and A-beta

---

TABLE 11.7

Diagnostic Criteria for Dementia of the Alzheimer's Type

A. The development of multiple cognitive deficits manifested by both

   (1) memory impairment (impaired ability to learn new information or to recall previously learned information)

   (2) one (or more) of the following cognitive disturbances:

      (a) aphasia (language disturbance)

      (b) apraxia (impaired ability to carry out motor activities despite intact motor function)

      (c) agnosia (failure to recognize or identify objects despite intact sensory function)

      (d) disturbance in executive functioning (i.e., planning, organizing, sequencing, abstracting)

B. The cognitive deficits in Criteria A1 and A2 each cause significant impairment in social or occupational functioning and represent a significant decline from a previous level of functioning.

C. The course is characterized by gradual onset and continuing cognitive decline.

Source: Reprinted with permission from the *Diagnostic and Statistical Manual of Mental Disorders*, Fourth Edition, Text Revision, (Copyright ©2000). American Psychiatric Association. p. 157.

are present in normal brains. The key problem in Alzheimer's disease is that abnormally high amounts of A-beta accumulate in the brain, overwhelming the enzymes and other molecules whose job it is to clear it away (Cummings, 2004). As well, the clearing away process itself appears to be defective.

The **neurofibrillary tangles** are made of a protein called *tau*, which, like amyloid, occurs in normal nerve cells. In Alzheimer's disease, tau becomes chemically altered and piles up as thread-like tangles, impairing the protein's key roles in nerve cells. One of these roles is in nerve sprouting, an important feature of self-repair in the nervous system.

The third very important alteration in the brain concerns the neurotransmitter **acetylcholine** (Ach), which is important in memory. It seems that one of the areas affected the earliest and most severely is in the base of the forebrain involved in Ach release. The depletion of Ach contributes significantly to the memory deficits (Schliebs & Arendt, 2006). Drugs that inhibit the breakdown of the already-reduced levels of Ach can be beneficial for patients.

Another common characteristic of the disease is inflammation of the brain. Whenever and wherever the body suffers trauma or is attacked by some kind of potentially threatening influence, such as an infection or a toxin, it defends itself in part by mounting an inflammatory response. This immune response also occurs in the Alzheimer's brain.

Causes and Diagnosis

The diagnosis of dementia involves a thorough physical and psychological assessment to evaluate symptoms such as aphasia (difficulty remembering words or being completely unable to speak, read, or write), apraxia (loss of the ability to execute or carry out learned purposeful movements), and other memory loss.

There are at least 50 disorders known to cause dementia (Bondi & Lange, 2001), including degenerative diseases such as Huntington's and Parkinson's. Other causes are severe head injury; inhalation of toxic substances; oxygen deprivation; strokes; infectious diseases such as syphilis, meningitis, and AIDS; intracranial tumours; and certain dietary deficiencies, especially of the B vitamins. The most common cause of dementia, accounting for about 56% of all cases, is **Alzheimer's disease**, a fatal neurodegenerative disorder (Selkoe, 1993). The prevalence of Alzheimer's disease is often inaccurately reported; only 5% to 7% of the over-65 population suffer with this disorder (Hy & Keller, 2000).

People who have a mother with Alzheimer's disease appear to be at higher risk for getting the disease than those individuals whose fathers are afflicted. In a new study (Mosconi et al., 2010), researchers set out to evaluate Alzheimer's risk in healthy, cognitively normal individuals by measuring their cerebrospinal fluid proteins, which are known to be altered in Alzheimer's. They compared individuals with a maternal or paternal history of Alzheimer's to individuals with no family history. They found that only individuals whose mothers had Alzheimer's showed altered levels of a protein called amyloid, a major hallmark of Alzheimer's pathology. In contrast, individuals whose fathers had Alzheimer's and those with no family history had protein levels within normal range. The prevailing hypothesis is that the protein clumps together into plaques, which damage the brain's nerve cells, causing the characteristic symptoms of Alzheimer's. Thus, while a person might have a family history of Alzheimer's disease, which significantly increases the risk for developing this disorder, which of that person's parents has the disease is very important in determining the risk.

The diagnosis of Alzheimer's is often given only after all other potential causes of dementia are ruled out. Only in the past decade have reliable screening and diagnostic tools been available. Researchers have discovered a previously unknown substance in spinal fluid that can be used to diagnose Alzheimer's disease: a beta-amyloid protein called Abeta16 ("New Marker," 2009). Independent studies show that Alzheimer's

neurofibrillary tangles Pathological protein aggregates (or brain lesions) found within brain cells (in the cerebral cortex and hippocampus) in patients with Alzheimer's disease and thought to contribute to the degradation of neurons in the brain.

acetylcholine A neurotransmitter important in memory. Abbreviated *Ach*.

Alzheimer's disease Fatal neurogenerative disorder that accounts for the majority of dementia cases.

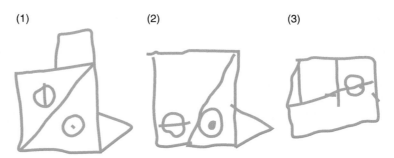

FIGURE 11.2 Neuropsychological test performance.
These drawings represent part of the neuropsychological test performance of a 59-year-old woman with a diagnosis of Alzheimer's disease. The figure at the left (1) was drawn by the psychologist, who then handed the piece of paper to the patient and asked her to make an exact copy of the figure next to the original. After the patient had completed her replica (2), the piece of paper was turned over and she was asked to draw the figure again, this time from memory. The figure that she drew based on memory is presented at the right (3).

Source: Oltmanns, Thomas F. & Emery, Robert E. *Abnormal Psychology*, 6th ed. © 2010. Reprinted and electronically reproduced by permission of Pearson Education, Inc., Upper Saddle River, New Jersey.

patients have higher levels of the protein in their spinal fluid than do healthy individuals (Fukumoto et al., 2010). Researchers are proposing that the discovery of the new protein could be used to diagnose patients with Alzheimer's and also help determine which medications are most effective for the disease.

In fact, researchers at Purdue University are in the early stages of designing a molecule to stop the debilitating symptoms of Alzheimer's disease. It has been shown in its first phase of clinical trials to be safe and to reduce biomarkers, like the beta-amyloid protein, for the disease ("New Alzheimer's Treatment," 2008).

Detecting Alzheimer's disease early in the process is ideal. Tools such as brain scans and memory tests, like the neuropsychological memory test in Figure 11.2, currently appear to predict best whether a person with cognitive problems might develop Alzheimer's disease. In 2010, the American Academy of Neurology reported on tests performed on 85 people with mild cognitive impairment (MCI) who were part of a larger study called the Alzheimer's Disease Neuroimaging Initiative (Landau et al., 2010). Several techniques were used in assessing the subjects in the study, including MRI brain scans, to measure the size of a participant's hippocampus, the part of the brain responsible for learning and memory; measurement of amyloid proteins (such as those discussed above); and PET brain scans, to detect metabolic abnormalities in the brain that might signal Alzheimer's disease. People who showed abnormal results on both PET scans and episodic memory tests were nearly 12 times more likely to develop Alzheimer's disease than those who scored normally on both measures (Landau et al., 2010). In other words, the PET scans and the memory tests best predicted later development of Alzheimer's disease.

When Alzheimer's disease is diagnosed, the clinician also specifies one of the following subtypes, depending on the prominent features presented: (1) with delirium, (2) with delusions, (3) with depressed mood, or (4) uncomplicated (for cases where none of these other characteristics apply) (APA, 2000a).

Treatment and Outcomes

Currently, there is no cure for Alzheimer's disease, but some medications can slow down the decline of memory, language, and thinking abilities. Aricept, Exelon, and Reminyl have been approved for use in Canada to treat symptoms in people with mild to moderate Alzheimer's disease. For those with moderate to advanced Alzheimer's disease, Ebixa (memantine hydrochloride) has been conditionally approved. All are cholinesterase inhibitors, drugs that inhibit the breakdown of acetylcholine.

Another line of treatment research is focused on developing vaccines that might help clear away any accumulated plaques.

Dementia

- **Is memory impairment the only indication that a person is developing dementia?** No, memory impairment is not the only sign. Decline in executive functioning is another sign that is often revealed through difficulty performing familiar tasks. There might also be problems with language and difficulties with orientation of time and space as well as decreased judgment and changes in mood or behaviour.

Define It

acetylcholine, 427
Alzheimer's disease, 427
amyloid plaques, 426
attention-deficit/hyperactivity disorder, 410
autism, 395
autistic thinking, 396
conduct disorder, 414
cultural-familial retardation, 404

cytomegalovirus, 403
dementia, 426
Down syndrome, 401
dyslexia, 407
hyperactivity, 410
individual education plan, 409
lateralization, 398
learning disorder, 407
mainstreaming, 404
neurofibrillary tangles, 427

oppositional defiant disorder, 415
pervasive developmental disorders, 395
phenylketonuria, 403
separation anxiety disorder, 419
Tay-Sachs disease, 403
theory of mind, 398
time out, 417

Think About It

- Have you known anyone with autism or worked with children who have the disorder? What were the most prominent features of the disorder? What, if any, interventions were helpful?

- Do you think children with mental retardation should be mainstreamed into regular classes? Why or why not?

- Do you think people with learning disorders should be given special consideration when given standardized tests (e.g., provincial achievement tests), such as having extra time? Why or why not?

- What are the risks and benefits of using stimulant medication such as Ritalin in treating ADHD in children?

- Do you know someone with Alzheimer's disease? Were there signs of memory loss early on? What interventions are helpful?

Weblinks

Autism Society Canada   http://autismsocietycanada.ca
This website is a primary source for Canadian information about autism spectrum disorders, services, and resources.

Canadian Association for Community Living
www.cacl.ca
This site provides information about Canadian community supports and services for persons of all ages who have intellectual disabilities.

Special Olympics Canada   www.specialolympics.ca
Homepage for Special Olympics Canada, a nonprofit organization dedicated to enriching the lives of Canadians with intellectual disabilities.

Learning Disabilities Association of Canada (LDAC)
www.ldac-taac.ca
This site is Canada's central repository for information about learning disabilities, resources, and supports.

Children and Adults with Attention Deficit Disorders (CHADD)   www.chadd.org
This Canadian site is dedicated to the support, education, and betterment of the lives of children and adults with attention deficit disorders.

Children and Youth
www.ontario.cmha.ca/children_and_youth.asp
This page from the Canadian Mental Health Association provides information about a wide range of mental and emotional problems of children and youth.

Alzheimer Society   **www.alzheimer.ca**
The Alzheimer Society is a leading national not-for-profit health organization. Its aim is to improve the quality of life for Canadians affected by Alzheimer's

disease and related dementias and advance the search for the cause and cure.

Canadian Dementia Action Network
www.cdan.ca/aboutus.html
CDAN brings together Canada's world-class biomedical researchers and clinicians for the purpose of quickly identifying promising treatments for Alzheimer's disease and related dementias (ADRD).

MySearchLab

MySearchLab offers you extensive help with your writing and research projects and provides round-the-clock access to credible and reliable source material. Chapter quizzes and a full electronic version of the text are also provided. Take a tour at www.mysearchlab.com.

Abnormal Behaviour Across the Lifespan

Pervasive Developmental Disorders

Autism
One of the most severe disorders of childhood, autism is a chronic lifelong condition, the causes of which are mostly unknown.

Features
- Impaired social communications and social interactions
- Restricted, repetitive, and stereotyped behaviour patterns

Treatment
- Early intervention is important
- Intensive behavioural treatment (IBT)

Mental Retardation
Broad delay in the development of cognitive and social functioning

Causes of Mental Retardation
- Chromosomal and genetic disorders
- Prenatal infectious diseases and brain injuries
- Cultural or familial causes, such as being raised in an impoverished home environment

Intervention
- Mainstreaming: having all students with disabilities included in the regular classroom
- Behavioural techniques that help children and adults acquire skills in areas such as personal hygiene, work, and social relationships

Learning Disorders
Average or higher intelligence, but shows inadequate development in reading, math, or writing skills that impairs school performance or daily activities

Types of Learning Disorders
- Mathematics disorder
- Disorder of written expression
- Reading disorder (dyslexia is most common)

Intervention
- Remediation and accommodation of specific skill deficits
- Target information processing style and academic strengths
- Individual education plan (IEP): learning and behaviour outcomes contract

Theoretical Perspectives
- Neurobiological problems with visual or auditory sensation and perception
- Genetic factors in dyslexia

>>

Anxiety and Depression

Separation Anxiety Disorder
- Characterized by extreme fears of separation from parents or others on whom the child is dependent

Perspectives on Anxiety Disorders in Childhood
- Psychoanalytic theorists: anxiety symbolizes unconscious conflicts
- Cognitive model: expecting negative outcomes, negative self-talk, and interpreting ambiguous situations as threatening
- Learning (anxiety-control) and cognitive-behavioural therapy

Depression in Childhood and Adolescence
- Sense of hopelessness, displays cognitive errors and negative attributions, lower perceived competence or self-efficacy, and lower self-esteem
- Episodes of sadness, crying, and apathy, as well as insomnia, fatigue, and poor appetite

Correlates and Treatment of Depression in Childhood and Adolescence
- Frequently related to family problems and conflicts
- Cognitive-behavioural and family therapy

Attention-Deficit and Disruptive Behaviour Disorders

Attention-Deficit/Hyperactivity Disorder (ADHD)
Characterized by excessive motor activity and inability to focus one's attention

Theoretical Perspectives
- Brain abnormalities involved in regulating the processes of attention, inhibition of motor (movement) behaviour, and executive control
- Neuropsychological studies challenge the long-held belief that ADHD is a single coherent clinical entity.

Intervention
- Cognitive-behavioural treatment combined with medication

Conduct Disorder
Pattern of purposeful antisocial behaviour that violates social norms and the rights of others

Oppositional Defiant Disorder
Characterized by excessive oppositionality or tendencies to refuse requests from parents and others

Theoretical Perspectives
- Family and parenting factors
- Biased processing of social information

Treatment
- Multisystemic therapy (MST) approach
- Cognitive-behavioural therapy

Cognitive Disorders of Aging

Delirium
Commonly occurring syndrome among the elderly that typically involves confusion, problems with concentration, and cognitive dysfunction such as memory disturbances

Clinical Picture
- Problems with orientation, language skills, mood, thinking, perception, and motor behaviour and the disruption of sleep–wake cycles
- Acute onset, fluctuant course, and transient

Treatment and Outcomes
- Medication (neuroleptics), environment changes, and family support

Dementia
A form of cognitive impairment involving generalized progressive deficits in a person's memory and learning of new information, ability to communicate, judgment, and motor co-ordination.

Clinical Picture
- Memory loss and disturbance of executive function (abstract thinking, organizing, and planning) are two major losses with dementia.

Alzheimer's Disease
- Fatal neurogenerative disorder that accounts for the majority of dementia cases

APPENDIX

RESEARCH METHODS IN ABNORMAL PSYCHOLOGY

Abnormal psychology is a branch of the scientific discipline of psychology, which means that the pursuit of knowledge in the field is based on the application of the scientific method. Here, we examine how researchers apply the scientific method in investigating abnormal behaviour.

Let us begin by asking you to imagine that you're in your first psychology class and the professor enters the room carrying a small wire-mesh cage with a white rat. She smiles and sets the cage on her desk. The professor removes the rat from the cage and places it on the desk. She asks the class to observe its behaviour. As a serious student, you attend closely. The animal moves to the edge of the desk, pauses, peers over, and seems to jiggle its whiskers at the floor below. It manoeuvres along the edge, tracking the perimeter. Now and then it pauses and vibrates its whiskers downward in the direction of the floor.

The professor picks up the rat and returns it to the cage. She asks the class to describe the animal's behaviour.

A student responds, "The rat seems to be looking for a way to escape."

The professor writes each response on the blackboard. Another student raises her hand. "The rat is making a visual search of the environment," she says. "Maybe it's looking for food."

The professor prompts other students for their descriptions.

"It's looking around," says one.

"Trying to escape," says another.

Your turn arrives. Trying to be scientific, you say, "We can't say what its motivation might be. All we know is that it's scanning its environment."

"How so?" the professor asks.

"Visually," you reply, confidently.

The professor writes the response and then turns to the class, shaking her head. "Each of you observed the rat," she said, "but none of you described its behaviour. Each of you made certain inferences, that the rat was 'looking for a way down' or 'scanning its environment' or 'looking for food,' and the like. These are not unreasonable inferences, but they are inferences, not descriptions. They also happen to be wrong. You see, the rat is blind. It's been blind since birth. It couldn't possibly be looking around, at least not in a visual sense."

Description, Explanation, Prediction, and Control: The Objectives of Science

Description is one of the primary objectives of science. To understand abnormal behaviour, we must first learn to describe it. Description allows us to recognize abnormal behaviour and provides the basis for explaining it.

description In science, the representation of observations without interpretation or inferences as to their nature or meaning. Contrast with *inference*, which is the process of drawing conclusions based on observations.

inference Conclusion that is drawn from data.

theories (1) Plausible or scientifically defensible explanations of events. (2) Formulations of the relationships underlying observed events. Theories are helpful to scientists because they provide a means of organizing observations and lead to predictions about future events.

Descriptions should be clear, unbiased, and based on careful observation. Our anecdote about the blind rat illustrates the point that our observations and our attempts to describe them can be influenced or biased by our expectations. Our expectations reflect our models of behaviour, and they may incline us to perceive events—such as the rat's movements and other people's behaviour—in certain ways. Describing the rat in the classroom as "scanning" and "looking" for something is an **inference** or conclusion we draw from our observations based on our model of how animals explore their environments. Description would involve a precise accounting of the animal's movements around the desk, measuring how far in each direction it moves, how long it pauses, how it bobs its head from side to side, and so on.

Inference is also important in science, however. Inference allows us to jump from the particular to the general—to suggest laws and principles of behaviour that can be woven into models and **theories** of behaviour. In Chapter 1, we considered the major theoretical perspectives or models of abnormal behaviour. Let us note here that without a way of organizing our descriptions of phenomena in terms of models and theories, we would be left with a buzzing confusion of unconnected observations. The crucial issue is to distinguish between description and inference—to recognize when we jump from a description of events to an inference based on an interpretation of events. For example, we do not describe a person's behaviour as "schizophrenic"; rather, we interpret behaviour as schizophrenic on the basis of our model of schizophrenia. To do otherwise would be to affix ourselves to a given label or model and lose the intellectual flexibility needed to revise our inferences in the light of new evidence or ways of conceptualizing information.

Theories help scientists explain puzzling behaviour and predict future behaviour. Prediction entails the discovery of factors that anticipate the occurrence of events. Geology, for example, seeks clues in the forces affecting the earth that can forecast natural events such as earthquakes and volcanic eruptions. Scientists who study abnormal behaviour seek clues in overt behaviour, biological processes, family interactions, and so forth to predict the development of abnormal behaviours as well as factors that might predict response to various treatments. It is not sufficient for theoretical models to help us explain or make sense of events or behaviours that have already occurred. Useful theories must allow us to predict the occurrence of particular behaviours.

The idea of controlling human behaviour—especially the behaviour of people with serious problems—is controversial. The history of societal response to abnormal behaviours, including abuses such as exorcism and cruel forms of physical restraint, render the idea particularly distressing. Within science, however, the word *control* need not imply that people are coerced into doing the bidding of others like puppets dangling on strings. Psychologists, for example, are committed to the dignity of the individual, and the concept of human dignity requires that people be free to make decisions and exercise choices. Within this context, controlling behaviour means using scientific knowledge to help people shape their own goals and more efficiently use their resources to accomplish them. Today, in Canada, even when helping professionals restrain people who are violently disturbed, their goal is to assist them to overcome their agitation and regain the ability to exercise meaningful choices in their lives.[1] Ethical standards prohibit the use of injurious techniques in research or practice.

Psychologists and other scientists use the scientific method to advance the description, explanation, prediction, and control of abnormal behaviour.

The Scientific Method

The scientific method involves systematic attempts to test our assumptions and theories about the world through gathering objective evidence. Various means are used in applying

[1]Here we are talking about violently confused and disordered behaviour, not criminal behaviour. Both criminals and disturbed people may be dangerous to others, but with criminals the intention of restraint is usually limited to protecting society.

the scientific method, including observational and experimental methods. Here, let us focus on the basic steps involved in using the scientific method in experimentation:

1. *Formulating a research question.* Scientists derive research questions from their observations and theories of events and behaviour. For instance, based on their clinical observations and understandings of the underlying mechanisms in depression, they may formulate questions about whether certain experimental drugs or particular types of psychotherapy can help people overcome depression.

2. *Framing the research question in the form of a hypothesis.* A **hypothesis** is a precise prediction about behaviour examined through research. For example, scientists might hypothesize that people who are clinically depressed will show greater improvement on measures of depression if they are given an experimental drug than if they receive an inert placebo ("sugar pill").

3. *Testing the hypothesis.* Scientists test hypotheses through carefully controlled observation and experimentation. They might test the hypothesis about the experimental drug by setting up an experiment in which one group of people with depression is given the experimental drug and another group is given the placebo. They would then administer tests to see if the people who received the active drug showed greater improvement over a period of time than those who received the placebo.

4. *Drawing conclusions about the hypothesis.* In the final step, scientists draw conclusions from their findings about the correctness of their hypotheses. Psychologists use statistical methods to determine the likelihood that differences between groups are **significant** as opposed to chance fluctuations. Psychologists are reasonably confident that group differences are significant—that is, not due to chance—when the probability that chance alone can explain the difference is less than 5%. When well-designed research findings fail to bear out hypotheses, scientists can modify the theories from which the hypotheses are derived. Research findings often lead to modifications in theory, new hypotheses, and, in turn, subsequent research.

We will consider the major research methods used by psychologists and others in studying abnormal behaviour: the naturalistic-observation, correlational, experimental, epidemiological, kinship, and case-study methods. Before we do so, however, let us consider some of the principles that guide ethical conduct in research.

Ethics in Research

Ethical principles are designed to protect the rights of people, respect the dignity and integrity of the individual, impart responsible caring, protect human welfare, and preserve scientific integrity. Psychological practitioners, researchers, and scientists follow ethical standards that address the following major concerns: psychologists are prohibited from using methods that cause psychological or physical harm to subjects or clients; psychologists must inform participants and obtain a signed consent form stating they are aware of risks of participation; they must ensure confidentiality; and they must aim to maximize what is of benefit to subjects or clients (CPA, 2000). Psychologists also must follow ethical guidelines that protect animal subjects in research.

Institutions such as universities and hospitals have review committees, often called research ethics boards (REBs), that review proposed research studies in light of ethical guidelines (National Council on Ethics in Human Research, 2002). Investigators must receive approval before they are permitted to begin their studies. Two of the major principles on which ethical research guidelines are based are (1) informed consent and (2) confidentiality.

The principle of **informed consent** requires that people be free to choose whether they wish to participate in research studies. They must be given sufficient information in advance about the study's purposes, methods, risks, and benefits, to allow them to make an informed decision about their participation. Subjects must also be free to withdraw

hypothesis Assumption that is tested through experimentation.

significant In statistics, a magnitude of difference that is taken as indicating meaningful differences between groups because of the low probability that it occurred by chance.

informed consent Agreement by individuals to participate in research based on a prior disclosure of information about the study's purposes, methods, risks, and benefits sufficient to allow subjects to make informed decisions about their participation.

from a study at any time without penalty. In some cases, researchers may withhold certain information until all the data are collected. For instance, subjects in placebo control studies of experimental drugs are told that they may receive an inert placebo rather than the active drug. After the study is concluded, participants who received the placebo are given the option of receiving the active treatment. In studies in which information was withheld or deception was used, subjects must be **debriefed** afterwards. That is, they must receive an explanation of the true methods and purposes of the study and why it was necessary to keep them in the dark.

Subjects also have a right to expect that their identities will not be revealed. Investigators are required to protect their **confidentiality** by keeping the records of their participation secure and by not disclosing their identities to others.

The Naturalistic-Observation Method

The **naturalistic-observation method** is used to observe behaviour in the field, where it happens. Anthropologists have lived in preliterate societies in order to study human diversity. Sociologists have followed the activities of adolescent gangs in inner cities. Psychologists have spent weeks observing the behaviour of homeless people in train stations and bus terminals. They have even observed the eating habits of slender and overweight people in fast-food restaurants, searching for clues to obesity.

Scientists take every precaution to ensure their naturalistic observations are **unobtrusive** so as to prevent any interference with the behaviour they observe. Otherwise, the presence of the observer may distort the observed behaviour. Over the years, naturalistic observers have sometimes found themselves in controversial situations. For example, they have allowed sick or injured apes to die when medicine could have saved them. Observers of substance abuse and other criminal behaviour have allowed illicit behaviour to go unreported to authorities. In such cases, the ethical trade-off is that unobtrusive observation can yield information of benefit to all.

Naturalistic observation provides a good deal of information on how subjects behave, but it does not necessarily reveal why they behave as they do. Men who frequent bars and drink, for example, are more likely to get into fights than men who do not. But such observations do not show that alcohol causes aggression. As we see in the following pages, questions of cause and effect are best approached by means of controlled experiments.

Correlation

Correlation is a statistical measure of the relationship between two factors or **variables.** In the naturalistic-observation study that occurred in the fast-food restaurant, eating behaviours were related—or correlated—to patrons' weights. They were not directly manipulated. In other words, the investigators did not manipulate the weights or eating rates of their subjects, but merely measured the two variables in some fashion and examined whether they were statistically related to each other. When one variable (weight level) increases as the second variable (rate of eating) increases, there is a **positive correlation** between them. If one variable decreases as the other increases, there is a **negative correlation** between the variables.

Although correlational research reveals whether there is a statistical relationship between variables, it does not prove the variables are causally related. Causal connections sometimes work in unexpected directions, and sometimes there is no causal connection between variables that are merely correlated. There are correlations between depression and negative thoughts, and it may seem logical that depression is caused by such thoughts. However, it is also possible that feelings of depression give rise to negative thoughts. Perhaps the direction of causality works both ways, with negative thinking contributing to depression and depression in turn influencing negative thinking. Moreover, depression and negative thinking may both reflect a common causative factor, such as stress, and not be causally related to each other at all.

---

debriefed Providing research participants with a fuller accounting of a study's aims and purposes after their participation, including information about any deception that may have been used or other information that may have been withheld.

confidentiality The principle of safeguarding information so that it remains secret and is not disclosed to other parties.

naturalistic-observation method Method of scientific research in which the behaviour of subjects is carefully and unobtrusively observed and measured in their natural environments.

unobtrusive Not interfering.

correlation Relationship or association between two or more variables. A correlation between variables may suggest, but does not prove, that a causal relationship exists between them.

variables Conditions that are measured (dependent variables) or manipulated (independent variables) in scientific studies.

positive correlation Statistical relationship between two variables such that increases in one variable are associated with increases in the other.

negative correlation Statistical relationship between two variables such that increases in one variable are associated with decreases in the other.

Although correlational research does not reveal cause and effect, it can be used to serve the scientific objective of prediction. When two variables are correlated, we can use one to predict the other. Knowledge of correlations among alcoholism, family history, and attitudes toward drinking helps us predict which adolescents are at great risk of developing problems with alcohol, although causal connections are complex and somewhat nebulous. But knowing which factors predict future problems may help us direct preventive efforts toward these high-risk groups to help prevent problems from developing.

THE LONGITUDINAL STUDY   One type of correlational study is the **longitudinal study,** in which subjects are studied at periodic intervals over lengthy periods, perhaps for decades. By studying people over time, researchers can investigate the events associated with the onset of abnormal behaviour and, perhaps, learn to identify factors that predict the development of such behaviour. However, such research is time-consuming and costly. It requires a commitment that may literally outlive the original investigators. Therefore, long-term longitudinal studies are relatively uncommon. In Chapter 10, "Schizophrenia," we examine one of the best-known longitudinal studies, the Danish high-risk study that has tracked since 1962 the development of a group of children whose mothers had schizophrenia and so were at increased risk of developing the disorder (Mednick, 1970).

> **longitudinal study** Research study in which subjects are followed over time. Longitudinal studies have helped researchers identify factors in early life that may predict the later development of disorders such as schizophrenia.

Prediction is based on the correlation between events or factors that are separated in time. As in other forms of correlational research, we must be careful not to infer causation from correlation. A **causal relationship** between two events involves a time-ordered relationship in which the second event is the direct result of the first. We need to meet two strict conditions to posit a causal relationship between two factors:

> **causal relationship** Relationship between two factors or events in which one is necessary and sufficient to bring about the other. Also called a *cause-and-effect relationship.*

1. The effect must follow the cause in a time-ordered sequence of events.
2. Other plausible causes of the observed effects (rival hypotheses) must be eliminated.

Through the experimental method, scientists seek to demonstrate causal relationships by first manipulating the causal factor and then measuring its effects under controlled conditions that minimize the risk of possible rival hypotheses.

The Experimental Method

The term *experiment* can cause some confusion. Broadly speaking, an experiment is a trial or test of a hypothesis. From this vantage point, any method that actually seeks to

TABLE A.1

Examples of Independent and Dependent Variables in Experimental Research

Independent Variables	Dependent Variables
Type of treatment: for example, different types of drug treatments or psychological treatments	Behavioural variables: for example, measures of adjustment, activity levels, eating behaviour, smoking behaviour
Treatment factors: for example, brief vs. long-term treatment, inpatient vs. outpatient treatment	Physiological variables: for example, measures of physiological responses such as heart rate, blood pressure, and brain wave activity
Experimental manipulations: for example, type of beverage consumed (alcoholic vs. nonalcoholic)	Self-report variables: for example, measures of anxiety, mood, or marital or life satisfaction

experimental method Scientific method that aims to discover cause-and-effect relationships by means of manipulating the independent variable(s) and observing their effects on the dependent variable(s).

independent variable Factor in an experiment that is manipulated so that its effects can be measured or observed.

dependent variables Measures of outcome in a scientific study that is assumed to be dependent on the effects of the independent variable.

test a hypothesis could be considered experimental—including naturalistic observation and correlational studies. But investigators usually limit the use of the term **experimental method** to refer to studies in which researchers seek to uncover cause-and-effect relationships by manipulating possible causal factors directly.

The factors or variables hypothesized to play a causal role are manipulated or controlled by the investigator in experimental research. A manipulated or controlled factor is called an **independent variable.** The observed effects are labelled **dependent variables,** because changes in them are believed to depend on the independent or manipulated variable. Dependent variables are observed and measured, not manipulated, by the experimenter. Examples of independent and dependent variables of interest to investigators of abnormal behaviour are shown in Table A.1.

In an experiment, subjects are exposed to an independent variable, for example, the type of beverage (alcoholic versus nonalcoholic) they consume in a laboratory setting. They are then observed or examined to determine whether the independent variable makes a difference in their behaviour, or, more precisely, whether the independent variable affects the dependent variable—in this case, whether they behave more aggressively if they consume alcohol.

experimental subjects (1) In an experiment, subjects receiving a treatment or intervention, in contrast to *control subjects*. (2) More generally, persons who participate in an experiment.

control subjects Subjects who do not receive the experimental treatment or manipulation but for whom all other conditions are held constant.

EXPERIMENTAL AND CONTROL SUBJECTS Well-controlled experiments assign subjects to experimental and control groups at random. **Experimental subjects** are given the experimental treatment. **Control subjects** are not. Care is taken to hold other conditions constant for each group. By using random assignment and holding other conditions constant, experimenters can be reasonably confident that the experimental treatment, and not uncontrolled factors such as room temperature or differences between the types of subjects in the experimental and control groups, brought about the differences in outcome between the experimental and control groups.

When experimenters use random assignment to ensure that subject characteristics are randomly distributed across groups, it is reasonable to assume that differences between groups involve the treatments they receive, rather than differences in the types of subjects making up the groups. Still, it is possible that apparent treatment effects stem from subjects' expectancies about the treatments they receive rather than from the active components in the treatments themselves. For example, knowing you are being given an alcoholic beverage to drink might affect your behaviour, quite apart from the alcoholic content of the beverage itself.

blind In the context of research design, a state of being unaware of whether or not one has received a treatment.

CONTROLLING FOR SUBJECT EXPECTANCIES In order to control for subject expectancies, experimenters rely on procedures that render subjects **blind**, or uninformed, as to what treatments they are receiving. For example, the taste of an alcoholic beverage such as vodka may be masked by mixing it with tonic water in certain amounts to keep subjects blind as to whether the drinks they receive contain alcohol or tonic water only. In this way, subjects who truly receive alcohol should have no expectations different from those receiving the nonalcoholic control beverage. Similarly, drug-treatment studies are often designed to control for subjects' expectations by keeping subjects in the dark as to whether they are receiving the experimental drug or an inert placebo control.

placebo (*pluh-SEE-bo*) Inert medication or form of bogus treatment intended to control for the effects of expectancies. Sometimes referred to as a "sugar pill."

The term **placebo** derives from the Latin for "I shall please," referring to the fact that belief in the effectiveness of a treatment (its pleasing qualities) may inspire hopeful expectations that help people mobilize themselves to overcome their problems, regardless of whether the substance they receive is chemically active or inert. In medical research on chemotherapy, a placebo—also referred to as a "sugar pill"—is an inert substance that physically resembles an active drug. By comparing the effects of the active drug with those of the placebo, the experimenter can determine whether the drug has specific effects beyond those accounted for by expectations.

In a single-blind placebo-control study, subjects are randomly assigned to treatment conditions in which they receive an active drug (experimental condition) or a placebo (placebo-control condition) but are kept blind, or uninformed, about which drug they are receiving. It is also helpful to keep the dispensing researchers blind as to which substances the subjects are receiving, lest the researchers' expectations come to affect the results. So in the case of a double-blind placebo design, neither the researcher nor the subject is told whether an active drug or a placebo is being administered. Of course, this approach assumes that the subjects and the experimenters cannot "see through" the blind. In some cases, however, telltale side effects or obvious drug effects may break the blind (Basoglu, Marks, Livanou, & Swinson, 1997). Still, the double-blind placebo control is among the strongest and most popular experimental designs, especially in drug-treatment research.

Placebo-control groups have also been used in psychotherapy research in order to control for subject expectancies. Assume you were to study the effects of therapy method A on mood. It would be inadequate to assign the experimental group to therapy method A randomly and the control group to a no-treatment waiting list. The experimental group might show improvement because of group participation, not because of therapy method A. Participation might raise expectations of success, and these expectations might be sufficient to engender improvement. Changes in control subjects placed on the "waiting list" would help to account for effects due to the passage of time, but they would not account for placebo effects, such as the benefits of therapy that result from instilling a sense of hope.

An attention-placebo *control group design* can be used to separate the effects of a particular form of psychotherapy from placebo effects. In an attention-placebo group, subjects are exposed to a believable or credible treatment that contains the nonspecific factors that therapies share—such as the attention and emotional support of a therapist—but not the specific ingredients of therapy represented in the active treatment. Attention-placebo treatments commonly substitute general discussions of participants' problems for the specific ingredients of therapy contained in the experimental treatment. Unfortunately, although attention-placebo subjects may be kept blind as to whether they are receiving the experimental treatment, the therapists themselves are generally aware of which treatment is being administered. Therefore, the attention-placebo method may not control for therapists' expectations.

The Epidemiological Method

The **epidemiological method** studies the rates of occurrence of abnormal behaviour in various settings or population groups. One type of epidemiological study is the **survey method,** which relies on interviews or questionnaires. Surveys are used to ascertain the rates of occurrence of various disorders in the population as a whole and in various subgroups classified according to such factors as race, ethnicity, gender, or social class. Rates of occurrence of a given disorder are expressed in terms of **incidence,** or the number of new cases of a disorder occurring during a specific period of time, and **prevalence** (recall Table 1.1 on page 2), which refers to the overall number of cases of a disorder existing in a population during a given period of time. Prevalence rates, then, include both new and continuing cases.

Epidemiological studies may point to potential causal factors in illnesses and disorders, even though they lack the power of experiments. By finding that illnesses or disorders cluster in certain groups or locations, researchers may be able to identify certain distinguishing characteristics that place these groups or regions at higher risk. Yet such

epidemiological method Method of research involved in tracking the rates of occurrence of particular disorders among different groups.

survey method Method of scientific research in which large samples of people are questioned by the use of a survey instrument.

incidence Number of new cases of a disorder occurring within a specific period of time.

prevalence Overall number of cases of a disorder existing in a population during a given period of time.

epidemiological studies cannot control for selection factors—that is, they cannot rule out rival hypotheses that other unrecognized factors might play a causal role in putting a certain group at greater risk. Therefore, they must be considered suggestive of possible causal influences that must be tested further in experimental studies.

SAMPLES AND POPULATIONS   In the best of possible worlds, we would conduct surveys in which every member of the **population** of interest would participate. In that way, we could be sure the survey results accurately represent the population we wish to study. In reality, unless the population of interest is rather narrowly defined (for example, designating the population of interest as the students living on your dormitory floor), chances are it is extremely difficult, if not impossible, to survey every member of a given population. Even census takers can't count every head in the general population. Consequently, most surveys are based on a **sample** or subset of a population. Researchers take steps when constructing a sample to ensure that it represents the target population. A researcher who sets out to study smoking rates in a local community by interviewing people drinking coffee in late-night cafés will probably overestimate its true prevalence.

One method of obtaining a representative sample is **random sampling.** A random sample is drawn in such a way that each member of the population of interest has an equal probability of selection. Epidemiologists sometimes construct random samples by surveying at random a given number of households within a target community. By repeating this process in a random sample of Canadian communities, the overall sample can approximate the general Canadian population, based on even a tiny percentage of the overall population. In fact, a representative nationwide sample of about 1500 eligible voters may be more accurate in predicting an election result than a haphazard sample of millions.

Random sampling is often confused with random assignment. *Random sampling* refers to the process of randomly choosing individuals within a target population to participate in a survey or research study. By contrast, *random assignment* refers to a process by which members of a research sample are assigned at random to different experimental conditions or treatments.

Kinship Studies

Kinship studies attempt to disentangle the roles of heredity and environment in determining behaviour. Heredity plays a critical role in determining a wide range of traits. The structures we inherit make our behaviour possible (humans can walk and run) and at the same time place limits on us (humans cannot fly without artificial equipment). Heredity plays a role in determining not only our physical characteristics (hair colour, eye colour, height, and the like) but also many of our psychological characteristics. The science of heredity is called **genetics.** Human behavioural genetics is the study of the interactive effect of genetic and environmental factors on behaviour, especially personality patterns and psychological disorders.

Genes are the basic building blocks of heredity. They are the structures that regulate the development of traits. Some traits, such as blood type, are transmitted by a single pair of genes, one of which is derived from each parent. Other traits, referred to as **polygenic,** are determined by complex combinations of genes. **Chromosomes,** the rod-shaped structures that house our genes, are found in the nuclei of the body's cells. Each consists of more than a thousand genes. A normal human cell contains 46 chromosomes, organized into 23 pairs. Chromosomes consist of large complex molecules of deoxyribonucleic acid (DNA). Genes occupy various segments along the length of chromosomes. There are about 20 000 to 25 000 genes in every cell in our bodies.

The set of traits specified by our genetic code is referred to as our **genotype.** Our appearance and behaviour are not determined by our genotype alone. We are also influenced by environmental factors such as nutrition, exercise, accident and illness, learning, and culture. The constellation of our actual or expressed traits is called our **phenotype.** Our phenotype represents the interaction of genetic and environmental influences. People who possess genotypes for particular psychological disorders are said

population Total group of people, other organisms, or events.

sample Part of a population.

random sampling Drawing samples in such a way that every member of a population has an equal probability of being selected.

genetics Science of heredity.

genes Units found on chromosomes that carry heredity.

polygenic Traits or characteristics that are determined by more than one gene.

chromosomes Structures found in the nuclei of cells that carry the units of heredity, or *genes.*

genotype (1) Genetic constitution of an individual or a group. (2) Sum total of traits that one inherits from one's parents.

phenotype Representation of the total array of traits of an organism, as influenced by the interaction of nature (genetic factors) and nurture (environmental factors).

to have a genetic predisposition that makes them more likely to develop the disorder in response to stress or other factors, such as physical or psychological trauma.

The more closely people are related, the more genes they have in common. Children receive half their genes from each parent. There is thus a 50% overlap in genetic heritage between each parent and his or her offspring. Siblings (brothers and sisters) similarly share half their genetic heritage. Aunts and uncles related by blood to their nephews and nieces have a 25% overlap; first cousins, a 12.5% overlap (see Figure A.1).

In order to determine whether a pattern of abnormal behaviour has a genetic basis, researchers locate one case of a person with the disorder and then study how the disorder is distributed among that person's family members. The case first diagnosed is referred to as the index case, or **proband**. If the distribution of the disorder among family members of the proband approximates their degree of kinship, there may be a genetic involvement in the disorder. However, the closer their kinship, the more likely people also are to share environmental backgrounds. For this reason, twin and adoptee studies are of particular value.

TWIN STUDIES Sometimes a fertilized egg cell (or *zygote*) divides into two cells that separate, so that each develops into a separate person. In such cases, there is a 100% overlap in genetic makeup, and the offspring are known as identical or **monozygotic (MZ) twins.** Sometimes a woman releases two egg cells, or ova, in the same month, and they are both fertilized. In such cases, the zygotes (fertilized egg cells) develop into fraternal or **dizygotic (DZ) twins.** DZ twins overlap 50% in their genetic heritage, just as other siblings do.

Identical or MZ twins are important in the study of the relative influences of heredity and environment because differences between MZ twins are the result of environmental rather than genetic influences. MZ twins look more alike and are closer in height than DZ twins. In twin studies, researchers identify probands for a given disorder who are members of MZ or DZ twin pairs and then study the other twins in the pairs. A role for genetic factors is suggested when MZ twins are more likely than DZ twins to share a disorder. Differences in the rates of **concordance** (agreement for the given trait or disorder) for MZ versus DZ twins are found for some forms of abnormal behaviour, such as schizophrenia and bipolar disorder. Even among MZ twins, though, environmental influences cannot be ruled out. Parents and teachers, for example, often encourage MZ twins to behave in similar ways. Put it another way: if one twin does *x*, everyone expects the other to do *x* also. Expectations have a way of influencing behaviour and making for self-fulfilling prophecies. We should also note that twins might not be typical of the general population, so we need to be cautious when generalizing the results of twin studies to the larger population. Twins tend to have had shorter gestational periods, lower birth weights, and a greater frequency of congenital malformations than non-twins (Kendler & Prescott, 2006). Perhaps differences in prenatal experiences influence their later development in ways that set them apart from non-twins.

ADOPTEE STUDIES **Adoptee studies** can provide powerful arguments for or against genetic factors in the appearance of psychological traits and disorders. Assume that children are reared by adoptive parents from a very early age—perhaps from birth. The children share environmental backgrounds with their adoptive parents but not their genetic heritages. Then assume we compare the traits and behaviour patterns of these children to those of their biological parents and their adoptive parents. If the children show a greater similarity to their biological parents than their adoptive parents on certain traits or disorders, we have strong evidence indeed for genetic factors in these traits and disorders.

proband Initial diagnosed case of a given disorder. Also called an *index case*.

monozygotic (MZ) twins Twins who develop from the same fertilized egg and therefore share identical genes. Also called *identical twins*. Abbreviated *MZ twins*. Contrast with fraternal or *dizygotic (DZ) twins*.

dizygotic (DZ) twins Twins who develop from separate fertilized eggs. Also called *fraternal twins*. Abbreviated *DZ twins*. Often contrasted with *monozygotic (MZ) twins* in studies of heritability of particular traits or disorders.

concordance Agreement.

adoptee studies Studies of adopted-away children that examine whether their behaviour patterns and psychological functioning more closely resemble those of their biological parents or adoptive parents.

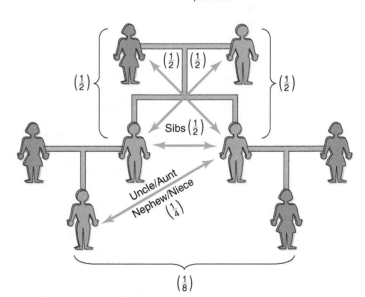

FIGURE A.1 A family tree showing the proportion of shared inheritance among relatives.
The more closely people are related, the more genes they have in common. Kinship studies, including twin studies and adoptee studies, afford researchers insight into the heritability of various patterns of abnormal behaviour.

Although adoptee studies may represent the strongest source of evidence for genetic factors in explaining abnormal behaviour patterns, we should recognize that adoptees, like twins, may not be typical of the general population. In this book we explore how adoptee and other kinship studies add to our understanding of genetic and environmental influences in many psychological disorders.

The Case-Study Method

Case studies have been important influences in the development of theories and treatment of abnormal behaviour. Freud developed his theoretical model primarily on the basis of case studies, such as that of Anna O. Therapists representing other theoretical viewpoints have also reported cases studies.

TYPES OF CASE STUDIES **Case studies** involve intensive studies of individuals. Some case studies are based on historical material, involving subjects who have been dead for hundreds of years. Freud, for example, conducted a case study of the Renaissance artist and inventor Leonardo da Vinci. More commonly, case studies reflect an in-depth analysis of an individual's course of treatment. They typically include detailed histories of the subject's background and response to treatment. The therapist attempts to glean information from a particular client's experience in therapy that may be of help to other therapists treating similar clients.

Despite the richness of clinical material that case studies can provide, they are much less rigorous as research designs than experiments. There are bound to be distortions or gaps in memory when people discuss historical events, especially those of their childhoods. Some people may intentionally colour events to make a favourable impression on the interviewer; others aim to shock the interviewer with exaggerated or fabricated recollections. Interviewers themselves may unintentionally guide subjects into slanting the histories they report in ways that are compatible with their own theoretical perspectives.

SINGLE-CASE EXPERIMENTAL DESIGNS The lack of control available in the traditional case-study method led researchers to develop more sophisticated methods, called **single-case experimental designs,** in which subjects are used as their own controls. One of the most common forms of the single-case experimental design is the A-B-A-B or **reversal design** (see Figure A.2). The reversal design consists of the repeated measurement of clients' behaviour across four successive phases:

1. *A baseline phase (A).* The baseline phase, which occurs prior to the inception of treatment, is characterized by repeated measurement of the target problem behaviours at periodic intervals. This measurement allows the experimenter to establish a **baseline** rate for the behaviour before treatment begins.
2. *A treatment phase (B).* Now the target behaviours are measured as the client undergoes treatment.
3. *A second baseline phase (A, again).* Treatment is now temporarily withdrawn or suspended. This is the reversal in the reversal design, and it is expected that the positive effects of treatment should now be reversed because the treatment has been withdrawn.
4. *A second treatment phase (B, again).* Treatment is reinstated and the target behaviours are reassessed.

case studies Carefully drawn biographies that are typically constructed on the basis of clinical interviews, observations, psychological tests, and, in some cases, historical records.

single-case experimental designs Type of case study in which the subject (case) is used as his or her own control by varying the conditions to which the subject is exposed (by use of a reversal phase) or by means of a multiple-baseline design.

reversal design An A-B-A-B type of experimental single-subject design in which treatment is instituted following a baseline phase and then withdrawn (reversal phase) so as to examine effects on behaviour.

baseline Period of time preceding the implementation of a treatment. Used to gather data regarding the rate of occurrence of the target behaviour before treatment is introduced.

Baseline (A) → Treatment (B) → Baseline (Reversal) (A) → Treatment (B)

FIGURE A.2 **Diagram of an A-B-A-B reversal design.**

Clients' target behaviours or response patterns are compared from one phase to the next in order to determine the effects of treatment. The experimenter looks for evidence of a correspondence between the subject's behaviour and the particular phase of the design to determine whether the independent variable (that is, the treatment) has produced the intended effects. If the behaviour improves whenever treatment is introduced (during the first and second treatment phases) but returns (or is reversed) to baseline levels during the reversal phase, the experimenter can be reasonably confident that the treatment had the intended effect.

The method is illustrated by a case in which Azrin and Peterson (1989) used a controlled blinking treatment to eliminate a severe eye tic—a form of squinting in which the subject's eyes shut tightly for a fraction of a second—in a nine-year-old girl. The tic occurred about 20 times a minute when the girl was at home. In the clinic, the rate of eye tics or squinting was measured for 5 minutes during a baseline period (A). Then the girl was prompted to blink her eyes softly every 5 seconds (B). The experimenters reasoned that voluntary "soft" blinking would activate motor (muscle) responses incompatible with those producing the tic, thereby suppressing it. As seen in Figure A.3, the tic was virtually eliminated in just a few minutes of practising the incompatible or competing response ("soft" blinking), but returned to near baseline levels during the reversal phase (A) when the competing response was withdrawn. The positive effects were quickly reinstated during the second treatment period (B). The child was also taught to practise the blinking response at home during scheduled three-minute practice periods and whenever the tic occurred or she felt an urge to squint. The tic was completely eliminated during the first six weeks of the treatment program and remained absent at a follow-up evaluation two years later.

Although reversal designs offer better controls than traditional treatment case studies, it is not always possible or ethical to reverse certain behaviours or treatment effects. For example, participants in a stop-smoking program who reduce or quit smoking during treatment are not advised to revert to their baseline smoking rates when treatment is temporarily withdrawn during a reversal phase.

modelling In behaviour therapy, a technique for helping a client acquire new behaviour by means of having the therapist or members of a therapy group demonstrate a target behaviour that is then imitated by a client.

rehearsal In behaviour therapy, a practice opportunity in which a person enacts a desired response and receives feedback from others.

feedback Information about one's behaviour.

FIGURE A.3 Treatment results from the Azrin and Peterson study.
Notice how the target response, eye tics per minute, decreased when the competing response was introduced in the first "B" phase. It then increased to near baseline levels when the competing response was withdrawn during the second "A" phase. It decreased again when the competing response was reinstated in the second "B" phase.
Source: Azrin, N. H., & Peterson, A. L. (1989). Reduction of an eye tic controlled by blinking. *Behavior Therapy, 20*, 467–473. Copyright 1989 by the Association for Advancement of Behavior Therapy. Reprinted by permission of the publisher.

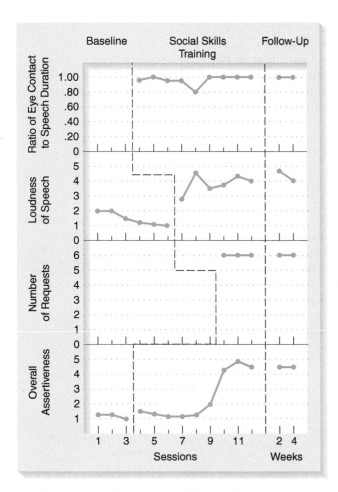

FIGURE A.4 Treatment results from the study by Bornstein, Bellack, and Hersen.
The blue dotted line shows the point at which social-skills training was applied to each of the targeted behaviours. Here we see that the targeted behaviours (eye contact, loudness of speech, and number of requests) improved only when they were subject to the treatment approach (social-skills training). We thus have evidence that the treatment—and not another, unidentified factor—accounted for the results. The section on the bottom shows ratings of Jane's overall level of assertiveness during the baseline assessment period, the social-skills training program, and the follow-up period.

Source: M. R. Bornstein, Bellack, & Hersen (1977).

The multiple-baseline design is a type of single-case experimental design that does not require a reversal phase. In a multiple-baseline design across behaviours, treatment is applied, in turn, to two or more behaviours following a baseline period. A treatment effect is inferred if changes in each of these behaviours corresponded to the time at which each was subjected to treatment. Because no reversal phase is required, many of the ethical and practical problems associated with reversal designs are avoided.

A multiple-baseline design was used to evaluate the effects of a social-skills training program in the treatment of a shy, unassertive seven-year-old girl named Jane (M. R. Bornstein, Bellack, & Hersen, 1977). The program taught Jane to maintain eye contact, speak more loudly, and make requests of other people through **modelling** (therapist demonstration of the target behaviour), **rehearsal** (practice), and therapist **feedback** regarding the effectiveness of practice. However, the behaviours were taught sequentially, not simultaneously. Measurement of each behaviour and an overall rating of assertiveness were obtained during a baseline period from observations of Jane's role-playing of social situations with other children, such as playing social games at school and conversing in class. As shown in Figure A.4, Jane's performance of each behaviour improved following treatment. The rating of overall assertiveness showed more gradual improvement as the number of behaviours included in the program increased. Treatment gains were generally maintained at a follow-up evaluation.

To show a clear-cut treatment effect, changes in target behaviours should occur only when those behaviours are subjected to treatment. In some cases, however, changes in the treated behaviours may lead to changes in the yet untreated behaviours, apparently because of generalization of the effect. Fortunately, though, generalization effects have tended to be the exception, rather than the rule, in experimental research (Kazdin, 1992).

No matter how tightly controlled the design or how impressive the results, single-case designs suffer from weak external validity because they do not show whether a treatment effective for one person is effective for others. Replication with other individuals can help strengthen external validity. If these results prove encouraging, they may lead to controlled experiments to provide even more convincing evidence of treatment effectiveness.

Critical Thinking

critical thinking A style of thinking characterized by the adoption of a questioning attitude and careful weighing of available evidence to determine if claims made by others stand up to scrutiny.

Scientists may use different methods to study phenomena of interest to them, but they have in common a skeptical, hard-nosed way of thinking called **critical thinking**. Critical thinking involves a willingness to challenge the conventional wisdom and common knowledge that many of us take for granted. It also means finding reasons to support beliefs, rather than relying on feelings or gut impressions. When people think critically, they maintain open minds. They suspend their beliefs until they have obtained and evaluated evidence that either supports or refutes them. In "A Closer Look: Thinking Critically About Abnormal Psychology," we examine the features of critical thinking and how they can be applied in our study of abnormal psychology.

We are exposed to a flood of information about our mental health that comes streaming down to us through a variety of media—television, radio, Internet, and print media including books, magazines, and newspapers. We may hear a news report touting a new drug as a "breakthrough" in the treatment of anxiety, depression, or obesity, only to learn some time later that the so-called breakthrough doesn't live up to expectations or carries serious side effects. Some reports in the media are accurate and reliable; others are misleading, biased, or contain half-truths, exaggerated claims, or unsupported conclusions. The situation is compounded when even reputed experts disagree with one another. How are we to know what to believe?

To sort through the high volume of sometimes confusing information, we need to arm ourselves with skills of critical thinking, which involves adopting a questioning attitude toward information we hear and read. Critical thinkers carefully weigh available evidence to see if claims people make can stand up to scrutiny. Becoming a critical thinker means never taking claims at face value. It means looking carefully at both sides of an argument. Sad to say, most of us take certain "truths" for granted. Critical thinkers, however, never say, "This is true because so-and-so says it is true." They seek to evaluate assertions and claims for themselves.

We encourage you to apply critical thinking skills to questions posed in the "Think About It" sections in each chapter. We will now review some general principles of critical thinking.

FEATURES OF CRITICAL THINKING

Critical thinkers adopt a skeptical attitude toward information they receive. They carefully examine the definitions of terms, evaluate the logical bases of arguments, and evaluate claims in light of available evidence. Here are some key features of critical thinking:

1. Maintain a skeptical attitude. Don't take anything at face value, not even claims made by respected scientists or textbook authors. Consider evidence yourself and seek additional information to help you evaluate claims made by others.

2. Consider the definitions of terms. Statements may be true or false depending on how the terms that are used are defined. Consider the statement "Stress is bad for you." If we define stress in terms of hassles and work or family pressures that stretch our ability to cope to the max, then there is perhaps substance to the statement. However, if we define stress more broadly to include any factors that impose a demand on us to adjust, including events such as a new marriage or the birth of a child, then perhaps certain types of stress can be positive, even if they are stressful. Perhaps we all need some amount of stress to be active and alert.

3. Weigh the assumptions or premises on which arguments are based. Consider a case in which we are comparing differences in the rates of psychological disorders across racial or ethnic groups in our society. Assuming we find differences, should we conclude that ethnicity or racial identity accounts for these differences? This conclusion might be valid if we can assume all other factors that distinguish one racial or ethnic group from another are held constant. However, ethnic or racial minorities in Canada and the United States are disproportionately represented among the poor, and the poor are more apt to develop more severe psychological disorders. Differences among racial or ethnic groups may thus be a function of poverty, not race or ethnicity per se. These differences may also be due to negative stereotyping of racial minorities by clinicians in making diagnostic judgments, rather than to differences in underlying rates of the disorder.

4. Bear in mind that correlation is not causation. Critical thinkers recognize that correlation is not causation. Consider the relationship between depression and stress. Evidence shows a positive correlation between these variables, which means depressed people tend to have higher levels of stress in their lives (Hammen, 2005; Pianta & Egeland, 1994). But does stress cause depression? Perhaps it does. Or perhaps depression leads to greater stress. After all, depressive symptoms may be stressful in themselves and may lead to additional stress as the person finds it increasingly difficult to meet life responsibilities, such as keeping up with work at school or on the job. It is also possible that the two variables are not causally linked at all but are linked through a third variable, perhaps an underlying genetic factor. It is conceivable that people inherit clusters of genes that make them more prone to encounter both depression and stress.

5. Consider the kinds of evidence on which conclusions are based. Some conclusions, even seemingly "scientific" conclusions, are based on anecdotes and personal endorsements. They are not founded on sound research. For example, there is much controversy today about so-called recovered memories that may suddenly arise in adulthood, usually during the course of psychotherapy or hypnosis, and usually involving incidents of sexual abuse committed during childhood by the person's parents or family members. Are such memories accurate? Or might they be tales spun of imaginary thread? (See Chapter 5, "Dissociative and Somatoform Disorders.")

6. Do not oversimplify. Consider the statement "Alcoholism is inherited." In Chapter 7, "Substance Abuse and Dependence," we review evidence suggesting that genetic factors may create a predisposition to alcoholism, at least in males. But the origins of alcoholism, as well as of schizophrenia, depression, and physical health problems such as cancer and heart disease, are more complex, reflecting a complicated interplay of biological and environmental factors. In only a few cases are diseases the direct result of a single defective gene or genes. People may even inherit a predisposition to the development of a particular psychological or physical disorder but avoid developing it if they are raised in a supportive family environment and learn to manage stress effectively.

7. Do not overgeneralize. In Chapter 5, we consider evidence showing that a history of severe abuse in childhood figures prominently in the great majority of cases of people who later develop multiple personalities. Does this mean that all (or even most) abused children go on to develop multiple personalities? Actually, very few do.

THINKING CRITICALLY ABOUT ONLINE INFORMATION

With today's online services, a world of information is literally at your fingertips. If you have access to the Internet, you can obtain information relating to the following:

- Listings and abstracts (brief descriptions) of scientific studies published in leading psychology journals. Much of this information is provided free of charge.
- Do-it-yourself psychology quizzes and questionnaires.
- Access to online encyclopedias containing hundreds if not thousands of entries relating to psychological issues.
- Access to homepages of leading psychology organizations, such as the Canadian Psychological Association, the Canadian Mental Health Association (CMHA), and the Canadian Alliance on Mental Illness and Mental Health (CAMIMH), that provide information about professional psychology and topics in psychology of general interest to the lay public.
- Forums and chat lines that bring together people who share similar concerns, such as people who have suffered loss of loved ones and people with family members who have psychological disorders.
- Information on topics relating to psychology provided by federal health agencies, including Health Canada's Mental Health Site and the Canadian Health Network (CHN).

The Internet holds a vast repository of health-related information. Anyone can post information online, so the casual browser may not know how to distinguish accurate, scientifically based information from misinformation. The beauty—and the risk—of the Internet is that it is freely available to anyone to post just about anything, from credible scientific information to advertising hype to complete malarkey. Don't believe everything you read online: think critically!

1. Check out the credentials of the source. Who is posting the material? Is it a well-respected medical or scientific institution, or is it an individual or group of individuals with no scientific credentials or perhaps even with a grudge against the scientific establishment? The most reliable sources are scientific journals that are subject to peer review, a process by which other scientists carefully scrutinize each potential contributor's work before publication. In addition to scientific journals, the more reliable sources of health and medical information are those that are frequently updated, such as websites maintained by government agencies such as Health Canada and its many divisions, as well as those sponsored by leading psychology organizations, including the Canadian Psychological Association and the Canadian Psychiatric Association.

2. Look for citations. Scientists back up what they say with citations of original scientific sources. The references listed at the end of this book, for example, represent the sources your authors used in preparing these chapters. If online authors cite findings from scientific literature, you should expect them to supply some of the references they use, such as noting the journals or other periodicals in which the studies were published (including the year, volume, and page numbers). Having this information allows the reader to check the original sources to see if the statements made are accurate. In some cases, however, scientific organizations such as the CMHA and scholarly organizations such as the Canadian Psychological Association prepare information for the general public that is no less reliable, although it may not be annotated with source notes or references.

3. Beware of any product claims. Many commercial organizations use the Internet to tout or sell services and products. Don't assume that product claims are scientifically valid. Think of them as electronic advertising, basically an Internet version of a television commercial. Be skeptical (and keep a tight grip on your wallet). Don't be misled by the offer of a money-back guarantee. These are not guarantees that the product will work as advertised. Rather, they guarantee you'll get your money back if they don't succeed (although often there are strings attached).

Research Methods in Abnormal Psychology

- **What are the basic objectives of the scientific method and the steps involved in applying it?** The scientific approach focuses on four general objectives: description, explanation, prediction, and control. There are four steps to the scientific method: formulating a research question, framing the research question in the form of a hypothesis, testing the hypothesis, and drawing conclusions about the correctness of the hypothesis.

- **How are ethical standards applied in conducting research?** Psychologists follow the ethical principles of the profession that govern research with human and nonhuman subjects. Two of the key ethical provisions in research with humans are informed consent and confidentiality. Psychologists conducting research in institutional settings are required to obtain approval from institutional review boards to ensure that their methods meet ethical standards.

- **What are the methods used by psychologists to study abnormal behaviour?** The naturalistic-observation method allows scientists to measure behaviour under naturally occurring conditions. Correlational research explores the relationship between variables, which may help predict future behaviour and suggest possible underlying causes. But correlational research does not directly test cause-and-effect relationships. Longitudinal research is a type of correlational design that involves the study of selected subjects at periodic intervals over long periods of time, sometimes spanning decades. Research samples need to be representative of a target population.

In the experimental method, the investigator directly controls or manipulates the independent variable under controlled conditions in order to demonstrate cause-and-effect relationships. Experiments use random assignment as the basis for determining which subjects (called *experimental subjects*) receive an experimental treatment and which others (called *control subjects*) do not. Researchers use various methods to attempt to control for subjects' and researchers' expectations, including single-blind placebo-control, double-blind placebo-control, and attention-placebo control group designs.

The epidemiological method examines the rates of occurrence of abnormal behaviour in various population groups or settings. Evidence of how disorders cluster in certain groups or geographic areas may reveal underlying causes. Kinship studies attempt to disentangle the contributions of environment and heredity.

Case-study methods can provide a richness of clinical material, but they are limited by the difficulties of obtaining accurate and unbiased client histories, by possible therapist biases, and by a lack of control groups. Single-case experimental designs are intended to help researchers overcome some of the limitations of the case-study method.

Define It

adoptee studies, 441
baseline, 442
blind, 438
case studies, 442
causal relationship, 437
chromosomes, 440
concordance, 441
confidentiality, 436
control subjects, 438
correlation, 436
critical thinking, 444
debriefed, 436
dependent variables, 438
description, 433
dizygotic (DZ) twins, 441
epidemiological method, 439
experimental method, 438

experimental subjects, 438
feedback, 443
genes, 440
genetics, 440
genotype, 440
hypothesis, 435
incidence, 439
independent variable, 438
inference, 434
informed consent, 435
longitudinal study, 437
modelling, 443
monozygotic (MZ) twins, 441
naturalistic-observation
  method, 436
negative correlation, 436
phenotype, 440

placebo, 438
polygenic, 440
population, 440
positive correlation, 436
prevalence, 439
proband, 441
random sampling, 440
rehearsal, 443
reversal design, 442
sample, 440
significant, 435
single-case experimental
  designs, 442
survey method, 439
theories, 434
unobtrusive, 436
variables, 436

Think About It

- Why should we not assume that because two variables are correlated they are causally linked?

- Why should experimenters assign subjects to experimental and control groups at random?

- How do investigators attempt to separate out the effects of heredity and environment?

- What are the limitations of the case study in drawing cause-and-effect relationships?

A

abnormal psychology Branch of psychology that deals with the description, causes, and treatment of abnormal behaviour patterns, p. 2.

abstinence-violation effect Tendency in people trying to maintain abstinence from a substance, such as alcohol or cigarettes, to overreact to a lapse with feelings of guilt and a sense of resignation that may then trigger a full-blown relapse. Abbreviated *AVE*, p. 287.

acetylcholine A neurotransmitter important in memory. Abbreviated *Ach*, p. 427.

acrophobia Excessive fear of heights, p. 107.

acute stress disorder Traumatic stress reaction occurring in the days and weeks following exposure to a traumatic event. Abbreviated *ASD*, p. 113.

addiction Impaired control over the use of a chemical substance accompanied by physiological dependence, p. 255.

adjustment disorders Maladaptive reactions to an identified stressor or stressors that occur shortly following exposure to the stressor(s) and result in impaired functioning or signs of emotional distress that exceed what would normally be expected in the situation. The reaction may be resolved if the stressor is removed or the individual learns to adapt to it successfully, p. 112.

adoptee studies Studies of adopted-away children that examine whether their behaviour patterns and psychological functioning more closely resemble those of their biological parents or adoptive parents, p. 441.

affect Emotion or feeling state that is attached to objects, ideas, or life experiences. Pronounced *AF-fect*, p. 360.

aggravated sexual assault Sexual assault in which the victim is maimed or disfigured or has his or her life endangered, p. 336.

agoraphobia Excessive, irrational fear of open places, p. 5.

Al-Anon Organization sponsoring support groups for family members of people with alcoholism, p. 284.

alcohol-induced persisting amnestic disorder See *Korsakoff's syndrome*, p. 263.

Alzheimer's disease Progressive brain disease characterized by gradual loss of memory and intellectual functioning, personality changes, and eventual loss of ability to care for oneself, p. 21.

ambivalence A state in which a person holds conflicting feelings toward others, such as loving and hating a person at the same time, p. 360.

ambulatory Able to walk about on one's own, p. 56.

amenorrhea Absence of menstruation—a symptom of anorexia nervosa, p. 297.

amphetamine psychosis Psychotic state induced by ingestion of amphetamines, p. 266.

amphetamines Types of synthetic stimulants, such as Dexedrine and Benzedrine. Abuse can trigger an amphetamine psychosis that mimics acute episodes of schizophrenia, p. 266.

amygdala One of a pair of almond-shaped structures in the limbic system that are involved in emotion and memory, p. 377.

amyloid plaques Hallmarks of Alzheimer's disease: the accumulation of protein fragments, normally broken down in healthy brains, that accumulate to form hard, insoluble plaques between nerve cells (neurons) in the brain, p. 426.

analgesia State of relief from pain without loss of consciousness, p. 265.

anomie Lack of purpose or identity; aimlessness, p.178.

anorexia nervosa Eating disorder, primarily affecting young women, characterized by maintenance of an abnormally low body weight, distortions of body image, intense fears of gaining weight, and, in females, amenorrhea, p. 294.

antidepressants Types of drugs that act to relieve depression. Tricyclics, MAO inhibitors, and selective serotonin-reuptake inhibitors are the major classes of antidepressants, p. 69.

antisocial personality disorder Type of personality disorder characterized by a chronic pattern of antisocial and irresponsible behaviour and lack of remorse. Abbreviated *APD*, p. 218.

anxiety disorder Type of psychological disorder in which anxiety is the prominent feature, p. 100.

anxiety sensitivity A "fear of fear," or fear that one's emotions or states of bodily arousal will get out of control and lead to harmful consequences, p. 122.

anxiolytics Drugs, such as sedatives and anaesthetics, that induce partial or complete unconsciousness and are commonly used in the treatment of sleep disorders, p. 313.

apnea Temporary cessation of breathing, p. 310.

associations Linkages or relationships among thoughts or utterances, p. 359.

attention-deficit/hyperactivity disorder Behaviour disorder of childhood characterized by excessive motor activity and inability to focus one's attention. Abbreviated *ADHD*, p. 410.

attributional style Personal style for explaining cause-and-effect relationships between events, p. 161.

autism Disorder characterized by pervasive deficits in the ability to relate to and communicate with others, and by a restricted range of activities and interests. Children with autistic disorder lack the ability to relate to others and seem to live in their own private worlds, p. 395.

autistic thinking The tendency to view oneself as the centre of the universe, to believe that external events somehow refer to oneself, p. 396.

automatic thoughts Thoughts that seem to pop into one's mind. In Aaron Beck's theory, automatic thoughts that reflect cognitive distortions induce negative feelings such as anxiety or depression, p. 160.

aversive conditioning Behaviour therapy technique in which a maladaptive response is paired with exposure to an aversive stimulus, such as electric shock or nausea, so that a conditioned aversion develops toward the stimuli associated with the maladaptive response. Also termed *aversion therapy*, p. 287.

avoidant personality disorder Type of personality disorder characterized by avoidance of social relationships due to fears of rejection, p. 228.

axon Long, thin part of a neuron along which nervous impulses travel, p. 20.

B

barbiturates Types of depressant drugs that are sometimes used to relieve anxiety or induce sleep but that are highly addictive, p. 264.

baseline Period of time preceding the implementation of a treatment. Used to gather data regarding the rate of occurrence of the target behaviour before treatment is introduced, p. 53.

behaviour therapy A learning-based model of therapy, p. 28.

behavioural assessment Approach to clinical assessment that focuses on the objective recording or description of problem behaviour rather than on inferences about personality traits, p. 52.

behavioural interview Approach to clinical interviewing that focuses on relating

problem behaviour to antecedent stimuli and reinforcement consequences, p. 52.

behavioural rating scale Method of behavioural assessment that involves the use of a scale to record the frequency of occurrence of target behaviours, p. 54.

behaviourism School of psychology that defines psychology as the study of observable or overt behaviour and focuses on investigating the relationships between stimuli and responses, p. 25.

benzodiazepines Class of minor tranquillizers that includes Valium and Ativan, p. 125.

binge-eating disorder Proposed psychological disorder characterized by repeated episodes in which binge eating occurs but is not followed by purging, p. 305.

biopsychosocial model A conceptual model that emphasizes that human behaviour is linked to complex interactions among biological, psychological, and sociocultural factors, p. 35.

bipolar Characterized by opposites, as in *bipolar disorder*, p. 141.

bipolar disorder Disorder characterized by mood swings between states of extreme elation and severe depression. Formerly called *manic depression*, p. 150.

blind In the context of research design, a state of being unaware of whether or not one has received a treatment, p. 438.

blocking (1) Disruption of self-expression of threatening or emotionally laden material. (2) In people with schizophrenia, a condition of suddenly becoming silent with loss of memory for what they have just discussed, p. 363.

bondage Form of sadomasochism involving the binding of the arms or legs of oneself or one's partner during sexual activity, p. 337.

borderline personality disorder Type of personality disorder characterized by abrupt shifts in mood, lack of a coherent sense of self, and unpredictable, impulsive behaviour. Abbreviated *BPD*, p. 222.

breathing-related sleep disorder Sleep disorder in which sleeping is repeatedly disrupted due to difficulties breathing normally, p. 310.

bulimia nervosa Eating disorder characterized by a recurrent pattern of binge eating followed by self-induced purging and accompanied by persistent overconcern with body weight and shape, p. 294.

C

case studies Carefully drawn biographies that are typically constructed on the basis of clinical interviews, observations, psychological tests, and, in some cases, historical records, p. 442.

cataplexy Brief, sudden loss of muscular control, typically lasting from a few seconds to as long as two minutes, p. 309.

catastrophize To exaggerate or magnify the negative consequences of events; to "blow things out of proportion," p. 30.

catatonic type Subtype of schizophrenia characterized by gross disturbances in motor activity, such as catatonic stupor, p. 369.

causal relationship Relationship between two factors or events in which one is necessary and sufficient to bring about the other. Also called a *cause-and-effect relationship*, p. 437.

choleric Having or showing bad temper, p. 9.

chromosomes Structures found in the nuclei of cells that carry the units of heredity, or *genes*, p. 440.

circadian rhythm sleep disorder Sleep disorder characterized by disruption of sleep due to a mismatch in sleep schedules between the body's internal sleep–wake cycle and the demands of the environment. Formerly called *sleep–wake schedule disorder*, p. 311.

civil commitment Legal process involved in placing an individual in a mental institution, even against his or her will. Also called *psychiatric commitment*, p. 87.

clanging In people with schizophrenia, the tendency to string words together because they rhyme or sound alike, p. 363.

claustrophobia Excessive fear of small, enclosed places, p. 107.

client-centred therapy Another name for Carl Rogers's *person-centred therapy*, p. 76.

clinical psychologist Person with graduate training in psychology who specializes in abnormal behaviour. He or she must be registered and licensed with a provincial psychological regulatory body in order to provide psychological services in that province, p. 2.

cocaine Stimulant derived from coca leaves, p. 266.

cognitive restructuring Cognitive therapy method that involves replacing irrational or self-defeating thoughts and attitudes with rational alternatives, p. 131.

cognitive therapy (1) Name of Aaron Beck's kind of psychotherapy, which challenges the distorted thought patterns that give rise to or exacerbate clients' problems. (2) More generally, a form of psychotherapy that addresses clients' cognitive processes, usually their self-defeating attitudes, p. 168.

cognitive triad of depression In Aaron Beck's theory, the view that depression derives from the adoption of negative views of oneself, the world, and the future, p. 157.

compulsion A repetitive behaviour or mental act that a person feels compelled or driven to perform, p. 111.

concordance Agreement, p. 441.

conditioned response (1) In classical conditioning, a learned or acquired response to a previously neutral stimulus. (2) A response to a conditioned stimulus. Abbreviated *CR*, p. 26.

conditioned stimulus Previously neutral stimulus that comes to evoke a conditioned response following repeated pairings with a stimulus (unconditioned stimulus) that had already evoked that response. Abbreviated *CS*, p. 26.

conduct disorder Pattern of abnormal behaviour in childhood characterized by disruptive, antisocial behaviour, p. 414.

confidentiality The principle of safeguarding information so that it remains secret and is not disclosed to other parties, p. 436.

conscious Aware, p. 23.

control subjects Subjects who do not receive the experimental treatment or manipulation but for whom all other conditions are held constant, p. 438.

controlled social drinking Controversial approach to treating problem drinkers in which the goal of treatment is the maintenance of controlled social drinking in moderate amounts, rather than total abstinence, p. 288.

conversion disorder Type of somatoform disorder characterized by loss or impairment of physical function in the absence of any organic causes that might account for the changes. Formerly called *hysteria* or *hysterical neurosis*, p. 201.

correlation Relationship or association between two or more variables. A correlation between variables may suggest, but does not prove, that a causal relationship exists between them, p. 436.

countertransference In psychoanalysis, the transfer of feelings that the analyst holds toward other persons in her or his life onto the client, p. 74.

crack Hardened, smokable form of cocaine, p. 266.

critical thinking A style of thinking characterized by the adoption of a questioning attitude and careful weighing of available evidence to determine if claims made by others stand up to scrutiny, p. 444.

cross-fostering study Method of determining heritability of a trait or disorder by examining differences in prevalence among adoptees reared by either adoptive parents or biological parents who possessed the trait or disorder in question. Evidence that the disorder followed biological rather than adoptive parentage favours the heritability of the trait or disorder, p. 374.

cue-exposure training Treatment used for people with substance dependence; it involves exposure to cues associated with ingestion of drugs or alcoholic beverages in a controlled situation in which the person is prevented from using the drug, p. 277.

cultural-familial retardation Milder form of mental retardation that is believed to result, or at least be influenced by, impoverishment in the child's home environment, p. 404.

culture-bound disorders Patterns of behaviour that are found within only one or a few cultural contexts, p. 65.

cyclothymic disorder Mood disorder characterized by a chronic pattern of mild mood swings between depression and mania that are not of sufficient severity to be classified as bipolar disorder, p. 152.

cytomegalovirus Maternal disease of the herpes virus group that carries a risk of mental retardation to the unborn child, p. 403.

D

debriefed Providing research participants with a fuller accounting of a study's aims and purposes after their participation, including information about any deception that may have been used or other information that may have been withheld, p. 436.

defence mechanisms In psychodynamic theory, the reality-distorting strategies used by the ego to shield itself from conscious awareness of anxiety-evoking or troubling material, p. 25.

deinstitutionalization Practice of discharging large numbers of hospitalized mental patients to the community and of reducing the need for new admissions through the development of alternative treatment approaches such as halfway houses and crisis intervention services, p. 13.

delirium (1) State of mental confusion, disorientation, and extreme difficulty in focusing attention. (2) A syndrome occurring among the elderly that typically involves confusion, problems with concentration, and cognitive dysfunction, p. 254.

delirium tremens Withdrawal syndrome that often occurs following a sudden decrease or cessation of drinking in chronic alcoholics and that is characterized by extreme restlessness, sweating, disorientation, and hallucinations. Abbreviated *DTs*, p. 254.

delta-9-tetrahydrocannabinol Major active ingredient in marijuana. Abbreviated *THC*, p. 271.

delusions Firmly held but inaccurate beliefs that persist despite evidence that they have no basis in reality, p. 5.

dementia A form of cognitive impairment involving generalized progressive deficits in a person's memory and learning of new information, ability to communicate, judgment, and motor coordination, p. 426.

dementia praecox Term given by Emil Kraepelin to the disorder we now call *schizophrenia*, p. 14.

demonological model The model that explains abnormal behaviour in terms of supernatural forces, p. 9.

dendrites Root-like structures at the end of a neuron that receive nerve impulses from other neurons, p. 20.

dependent personality disorder Type of personality disorder characterized by difficulties making independent decisions and by overly dependent behaviour, p. 229.

dependent variables Measures of outcome in a scientific study that is assumed to be dependent on the effects of the independent variable, p. 438.

depersonalization Feelings of unreality or detachment from one's self or one's body, as if one were a robot, or functioning on automatic pilot, or observing oneself from outside, p. 193.

depersonalization disorder Disorder characterized by persistent or recurrent episodes of depersonalization, p. 194.

depressant Drug that lowers the level of activity of the central nervous system, p. 257.

derealization Loss of the sense of reality of one's surroundings, experienced in terms of strange changes in one's environment (e.g., people or objects changing size or shape) or in the sense of the passage of time, p. 193.

description In science, the representation of observations without interpretation or inferences as to their nature or meaning. Contrast with *inference*, which is the process of drawing conclusions based on observations, p. 433.

detoxification Process of ridding the system of alcohol or drugs under supervised conditions in which withdrawal symptoms can be monitored and controlled, p. 281.

deviation IQ Intelligence quotient derived by determining the deviation between the individual's score and the norm (mean), p. 43.

Dhat syndrome Usually diagnosed among young Indian men who describe an intense fear or anxiety over the loss of semen, p. 206.

diathesis A predisposition or vulnerability, p. 35.

diathesis-stress model Model of abnormal behaviour that posits that abnormal behaviour patterns, such as schizophrenia, involve the interaction of genetic and environmental influences. In this model, a genetic or acquired predisposition, or *diathesis*, increases an individual's vulnerability to developing the disorder in response to stressful life circumstances. If, however, the level of stress is kept under the person's particular threshold, the disorder may never develop, even among people with the predisposition, p. 35.

disorganized type Subtype of schizophrenia characterized by disorganized behaviour, bizarre delusions, and vivid hallucinations. Formerly *hebephrenic schizophrenia*, p. 369.

disorientation State of mental confusion or lack of awareness with respect to time, place, or the identity of oneself or others, p. 254.

displacement In psychodynamic theory, a type of defence mechanism that involves the transferring of impulses toward threatening or unacceptable objects onto more acceptable or safer objects, p. 73.

dissociative amnesia Type of dissociative disorder in which a person experiences memory losses in the absence of any identifiable organic cause. General knowledge and skills are usually retained, p. 192.

dissociative fugue Type of dissociative disorder in which one suddenly flies from one's life situation, travels to a new location, assumes a new identity, and has amnesia for past personal material. The person usually retains skills and other abilities and may appear to others in the new environment to be leading a normal life, p. 192.

dissociative identity disorder Dissociative disorder in which a person has two or more distinct or alternate personalities, p. 188.

dizygotic (DZ) twins Twins who develop from separate fertilized eggs. Also called *fraternal twins*. Abbreviated *DZ twins*. Often contrasted with *monozygotic (MZ) twins* in studies of heritability of particular traits or disorders, p. 441.

DNA Deoxyribonucleic acid is a double-strand complex molecule of helical structure that contains the genetic instructions for building and maintaining living organisms, p. 18.

dopamine Neurotransmitter of the catecholamine class that is believed to play a role in schizophrenia, p. 22.

dopamine theory Biochemical theory of schizophrenia that proposes that schizophrenia involves the action of dopamine, p. 375.

double depression Term applied to persons diagnosed with both *major depressive disorder* and *dysthymic disorder*, p. 149.

double-bind communications Pattern of communication involving the transmission of contradictory or mixed messages without acknowledgment of the inherent conflict; posited by some theorists to play a role in the development of schizophrenia, p. 381.

Down syndrome Condition caused by a chromosomal abnormality involving an extra chromosome on the 21st pair (trisomy 21); it is characterized by mental retardation and various physical abnormalities. Formerly called *mongolism* and *Down's syndrome* in Canada, p. 401.

downward drift hypothesis The belief that people with psychological problems may drift downward in socioeconomic status, p. 34.

duty to warn Obligation imposed on therapists to warn third parties of threats made against them by the therapists' clients. In the U.S., the *Tarasoff* case established the legal basis for duty-to-warn provisions. Although U.S. law does not apply in Canada, the Canadian Psychological Association states that, ethically, therapists have a duty to warn, p. 90.

dyslexia Type of learning disorder characterized by impaired reading ability that may involve difficulty with the alphabet or spelling, p. 407.

dyspareunia Persistent or recurrent pain experienced during or following sexual intercourse, p. 343.

dyssomnias Category of sleep disorders involving disturbances in the amount, quality, or timing of sleep, p. 308.

dysthymic disorder Mild but chronic type of depressive disorder, p. 149.

E

eating disorders Psychological disorders involving disturbed eating patterns and maladaptive ways of controlling body weight, p. 294.

eclectic orientation Adoption of principles or techniques from various systems or theories, p. 67.

ego In psychodynamic theory, the psychic structure corresponding to the concept of the self. The ego is governed by the reality principle and is responsible for finding socially acceptable outlets for the urgings of the id. The ego is characterized by the capacity to tolerate frustration and delay gratification, p. 24.

ego dystonic Behaviour or feelings that are perceived to be foreign or alien to one's self-identity, p. 214.

ego ideal In Freud's view, the configuration of higher social values and moral ideals embodied in the superego, p. 24.

ego syntonic Behaviour or feelings that are perceived as natural or compatible parts of the self, p. 214.

electroconvulsive therapy Induction of a convulsive seizure by means of passing an electric current through the head; used primarily in the treatment of severe depression. Abbreviated *ECT*, p. 70.

electrodermal response Changes in the electrical conductivity of the skin following exposure to a stimulus, p. 56.

electroencephalograph Instrument for measuring the electrical activity of the brain (brainwaves). Abbreviated *EEG*, p. 56.

electromyograph Instrument often used in biofeedback training for measuring muscle tension. Abbreviated *EMG*, p. 56.

emotional intelligence "The ability to perceive emotions, to access and generate emotions so as to assist thought, to understand emotions and emotional knowledge, and to reflectively regulate emotions so as to promote emotional and intellectual growth" (Mayer & Salovey, 1997), p. 29.

endorphins Natural substances that function as neurotransmitters in the brain and are similar in their effects to morphine, p. 265.

epidemiological method Method of research involved in tracking the rates of occurrence of particular disorders among different groups, p. 439.

epigenetics The study of the heritable and acquired changes in gene regulation (phenotype) that occur without affecting DNA sequence (genotype), p. 18.

epigenome The sum total of inherited and acquired molecular variations to the genome that lead to changes in gene regulation without changing the DNA sequence of the genome itself, p. 18.

etiology Cause or origin; the study of causality, p. 101.

exhibitionism Type of paraphilia almost exclusively occurring in males in which the man experiences persistent and recurrent sexual urges and sexually arousing fantasies involving the exposure of his genitals to a stranger and either has acted on these urges or feels strongly distressed by them, p. 327.

exorcism Ritual intended to expel demons or evil spirits from a person believed to be possessed, p. 10.

expectancies In social-cognitive theory, a personal variable describing people's predictions of future outcomes, p. 32.

experimental method Scientific method that aims to discover cause-and-effect relationships by means of manipulating the independent variable(s) and observing their effects on the dependent variable(s), p. 438.

experimental subjects (1) In an experiment, subjects receiving a treatment or intervention, in contrast to *control subjects*. (2) More generally, persons who participate in an experiment, p. 438.

external attribution In the reformulated helplessness theory, a type of attribution involving the belief that the cause of an event involves factors outside the self. Contrast with *internal attribution*, p. 161.

F

factitious disorder Type of psychological disorder characterized by the intentional fabrication of psychological or physical symptoms for no apparent gain, p. 200.

fear Unpleasant, negative emotion characterized by the perception of a specific threat, sympathetic nervous system activity, and tendencies to avoid the feared object, p. 107.

fear-stimulus hierarchy Ordered series of increasingly fearful stimuli. Used in the behavioural techniques of *systematic desensitization* and *gradual exposure*, p. 129.

feedback Information about one's behaviour, p. 443.

female orgasmic disorder Type of sexual dysfunction in women involving difficulties achieving orgasm, p. 343.

female sexual arousal disorder Type of sexual dysfunction in women involving difficulties becoming sexually aroused, as defined by a lack of vaginal lubrication or failure to maintain sufficient lubrication to complete the sexual act or lack of sexual excitement or pleasure during sexual activity, p. 342.

fetishism Type of paraphilia in which a person uses an inanimate object or a body part (*partialism*) as a focus of sexual interest and as a source of arousal, p. 328.

first-rank symptoms In Kurt Schneider's view, the primary features of schizophrenia, such as hallucinations and delusions, that distinctly characterize the disorder, p. 360.

flashbacks (1) Vivid re-experiencings of a past event, which may be difficult to distinguish from current reality. (2) Experiences of sensory distortions or hallucinations occurring days or weeks after use of LSD or another hallucinogenic drug that mimic the drug's effects, p. 270.

forced-choice formats Method of structuring test questions that requires respondents to select among a set number of possible answers, p. 47.

four As In Bleuler's view, the primary characteristics of schizophrenia: loose *associations*, blunted or inappropriate *affect*, *ambivalence*, and *autism*, p. 359.

freebasing Method of ingesting cocaine by means of heating the drug with ether to separate its most potent component (its "free base") and then smoking the extract, p. 267.

frotteurism Type of paraphilia characterized by recurrent sexual urges or sexually arousing fantasies involving bumping and rubbing against nonconsenting victims for sexual gratification. The person has either acted on these urges or is strongly distressed by them, p. 330.

G

galvanic skin response Measure of the change in electrical activity of the skin caused by increased activity of the sweat glands that accompanies states of sympathetic nervous system arousal, such as when a person is anxious. Abbreviated *GSR*, p. 56.

gamma-aminobutyric acid An inhibitory neurotransmitter believed to play a role in regulating anxiety. Abbreviated *GABA*, p. 124.

gender dysphoria Incongruity between one's genital anatomy and one's gender identity or role, p. 322.

gender identity One's psychological sense of being female or being male, p. 322.

gender identity disorder Disorder in which an individual believes that her or his anatomic gender is inconsistent with her or his psychological sense of being female or male, p. 322.

gene expression The process by which a gene sequence becomes activated ("turned on") and is translated into the proteins that determine the structure and functions of body cells, p. 18.

gene silencing The process of preventing or suppressing ("switching off") a gene sequence from being translated into proteins, p. 18.

general paresis Degenerative brain disorder that occurs during the final stage of syphilis, p. 15.

generalized anxiety disorder Type of anxiety disorder characterized by general feelings of dread, foreboding, and heightened states of sympathetic arousal. Formerly referred to as *free-floating anxiety*. Abbreviated *GAD*, p. 105.

genes Units found on chromosomes that carry heredity, p. 440.

genetics Science of heredity, p. 440.

genotype (1) Genetic constitution of an individual or a group. (2) Sum total of traits that one inherits from one's parents, p. 440.

global attribution In the reformulated helplessness theory, a type of attribution involving the belief that the cause of an event involved generalized rather than specific factors. Contrast with *specific attribution*, p. 161.

gradual exposure In behaviour therapy, a method of overcoming fears through a stepwise process of direct exposure to increasingly fearful stimuli, p. 75.

H

hallucinations Perceptions that occur in the absence of an external stimulus that are confused with reality, p. 3.

hallucinogens Substances that give rise to hallucinations, p 270.

hashish Drug derived from the resin of the marijuana plant, *Cannabis sativa*, p. 271.

hippocampus One of a pair of structures in the limbic system that are involved in processes of memory, p. 377.

histrionic personality disorder Type of personality disorder characterized by excessive need to be the centre of attention and to receive reassurance, praise, and approval from others. Such persons often appear overly dramatic and emotional in their behaviour, p. 225.

humours Four fluids in the body: phlegm, black bile, blood, and yellow bile. Hippocrates believed that the health of the body and mind depended on their balance, p. 9.

hyperactivity Abnormal behaviour pattern found most often in young boys that is characterized by extreme restlessness and difficulty maintaining attention, p. 410.

hypersomnia Condition relating to a pattern of excessive sleepiness during the day, p. 309.

hyperventilation Pattern of overly rapid breathing, sometimes associated with anxiety, in which the amount of oxygen inhaled is in excess of metabolic requirements, leading to harmless but sometimes unpleasant sensations such as feeling faint or light-headed, p. 125.

hypnosis Trancelike state, induced by suggestion, in which one is generally passive and responsive to the commands of the hypnotist, p. 15.

hypoactive sexual desire disorder Persistent or recurrent lack of sexual interest or sexual fantasies, p. 341.

hypomanic episodes Mild manic episodes, p 142.

hypothesis Assumption that is tested through experimentation, p. 435.

hypoxyphilia Paraphilia in which a person seeks sexual gratification by being deprived of oxygen by means of using a noose, plastic bag, chemical, or pressure on the chest, p. 332.

hysteria Former term for *conversion disorder*, p. 15.

I

id In psychodynamic theory, the unconscious psychic structure that is present at birth. The id contains instinctual drives and is governed by the pleasure principle, p. 23.

ideas of persecution A form of delusional thinking characterized by false beliefs that one is being persecuted or victimized by others, p. 5.

ideas of reference Form of delusional thinking in which a person reads personal meaning into the behaviour of others or external events that are completely independent of the person, p. 217.

identification (1) In psychodynamic theory, the process of incorporating the personality or behaviour of others. (2) In social learning theory, a process of imitation by which children acquire behaviours similar to those of role models, p. 24.

incidence Number of new cases of a disorder occurring within a specific period of time, p. 439.

independent variable Factor in an experiment that is manipulated so that its effects can be measured or observed, p. 438.

individual education plan A contractual document that contains learning and behavioural outcomes for a student, a description of how the outcomes will be achieved, and a description of how the outcomes will be evaluated. Abbreviated *IEP*, p. 409.

inference Conclusion that is drawn from data, p. 434.

informed consent Agreement by individuals to participate in research based on a prior disclosure of information about the study's purposes, methods, risks, and benefits sufficient to allow subjects to make informed decisions about their participation, p. 435.

insanity defence Form of legal defence in which a defendant in a criminal case pleads guilty but not criminally responsible on the basis of having a mental disorder, p. 91.

insomnia Term applying to difficulties falling asleep, remaining asleep, or achieving restorative sleep, p. 308.

intelligence (1) Global capacity to understand the world and cope with its challenges. (2) Trait or traits associated with successful performance on intelligence tests, p. 43.

intelligence quotient Measure of intelligence derived on the basis of scores on an intelligence test. Called a *quotient* because it was originally derived by dividing a respondent's mental age by her or his actual age. Abbreviated *IQ*, p. 43.

internal attribution In the reformulated helplessness theory, a type of attribution involving the belief that the cause of an event involved factors within oneself. Contrast with *external attribution*, p. 161.

interpersonal psychotherapy A brief, psychodynamic form of therapy that focuses on helping people resolve interpersonal problems, p. 166.

intoxication State of drunkenness, p. 252.

K

knobs Swollen endings of axon terminals, p. 21.

Koro syndrome Culture-related somatoform disorder, found primarily in China, in which people fear that their genitals are shrinking and retracting into the body, p. 206.

Korsakoff's syndrome Form of brain damage associated with chronic thiamine deficiency. The syndrome is associated with chronic alcoholism and characterized by memory loss, disorientation, and the tendency to invent memories to replace lost ones (confabulation). Also called *alcohol-induced persisting amnestic disorder*, p. 263.

L

la belle indifférence French term describing the lack of concern over one's symptoms displayed by some people with conversion disorder but also by people with real physical disorders, p. 201.

lateralization The developmental process by which the left hemisphere specializes in verbal and analytic functions and the right hemisphere specializes in nonverbal, spatial functions, p. 398.

learned helplessness In Martin Seligman's model, a behaviour pattern characterized by passivity and perceptions of lack of control that develops because of a history of failure to be able to exercise control over one's environment, p. 160.

learning disorder Deficiency in a specific learning ability noteworthy because of the individual's general intelligence and exposure to learning opportunities, p. 407.

legal commitment Legal process involved in confining a person found "not criminally responsible on account of a mental disorder" in a mental institution. Also called *criminal commitment*, p. 87.

longitudinal study Research study in which subjects are followed over time. Longitudinal studies have helped researchers identify factors in early life that may predict the later development of disorders such as schizophrenia, p. 437.

LSD A powerful hallucinogenic drug. LSD is the acronym for *lysergic acid diethylamide*, p. 270.

M

Münchausen syndrome Type of factitious disorder characterized by the feigning of medical symptoms for no apparent purpose other than getting admitted to or remaining in hospitals, p. 200.

mainstreaming The practice of having all students with disabilities included in the regular classroom. Also referred to as *integration* or *inclusion*, p. 404.

major depressive disorder Severe mood disorder characterized by the occurrence of major depressive episodes in the absence of a history of manic episodes. Major depressive disorder is characterized by a range of features such as depressed mood, lack of interest or pleasure in usual activities, lack of energy or motivation, and changes in appetite or sleep patterns, p. 142.

male erectile disorder Sexual dysfunction in males characterized by difficulty in achieving or maintaining erection during sexual activity, p. 342.

male orgasmic disorder Type of sexual dysfunction in men involving persistent difficulties achieving orgasm, p. 343.

malingering Faking illness so as to avoid or escape work or other duties, or to obtain benefits, p. 192.

manic Relating to mania, as in the manic phase of a bipolar disorder, p. 142.

manic episodes Periods of unrealistically heightened euphoria, extreme restlessness, and excessive activity characterized by disorganized behaviour and impaired judgment. Alternates with major depressive episodes in bipolar disorder, p. 150.

marijuana A mild or minor hallucinogen derived from the *Cannabis sativa* plant, p. 271.

medical model Biological perspective in which abnormal behaviour is viewed as symptomatic of underlying illness, p. 2.

melancholia State of severe depression, p. 9.

mental age Age equivalent that corresponds to the person's level of intelligence, as measured by performance on the Stanford-Binet Intelligence Scale. Abbreviated *MA*, p. 43.

mental status examination Structured clinical evaluation to determine various aspects of a client's mental functioning, p. 43.

meta-analysis Statistical technique for combining the results of different studies into an overall average. In psychotherapy research, meta-analysis is used to compute the average benefit or size of effect associated with psychotherapy overall, or with different forms of therapy, in relation to control groups, p. 83.

methadone Artificial narcotic that lacks the rush associated with heroin and that is used to help people addicted to heroin abstain without incurring an abstinence syndrome, p. 283.

modelling In behaviour therapy, a technique for helping a client acquire new behaviour by means of having the therapist or members of a therapy group demonstrate a target behaviour that is then imitated by a client, p. 443.

monoamine oxidase (MAO) inhibitors Antidepressants that act to increase the availability of neurotransmitters in the brain by inhibiting the actions of an enzyme, monoamine oxidase, that normally breaks down or degrades neurotransmitters (norepinephrine and serotonin) in the synaptic cleft, p. 69.

monozygotic (MZ) twins Twins who develop from the same fertilized egg and therefore share identical genes. Also called *identical twin*s. Abbreviated *MZ twins*. Contrast with fraternal or *dizygotic (DZ) twins*, p. 441.

mood disorders Types of disorders characterized by disturbances of mood, as in depressive disorders (*major depressive disorder* or *dysthymic disorder*) or bipolar disorders (*bipolar disorder* and *cyclothymic disorder*), p. 141.

moods Pervasive qualities of an individual's emotional experience, as in depressed mood, anxious mood, or elated mood, p. 141.

moral principle In psychodynamic theory, the principle that governs the superego to set moral standards and enforce adherence to them, p. 24.

moral therapy A 19th-century treatment philosophy that emphasized that hospitalized mental patients should be treated with care and understanding in a pleasant environment, not shackled in chains, p. 12.

mourning Normal feelings or expressions of grief following a loss. See *bereavement*, p. 155.

N

naloxone Drug that prevents users from becoming high if they subsequently take heroin. Some people are placed on naloxone after being withdrawn from heroin to prevent return to heroin, p. 283.

naltrexone Chemical cousin of naloxone that blocks the high from alcohol as well as opiates and is now approved for use in treating alcoholism, p. 283.

narcissistic personality disorder Type of personality disorder characterized by the adoption of an inflated self-image and demands for constant attention and admiration, among other features, p. 226.

narcolepsy Sleep disorder characterized by sudden, irresistible episodes of sleep (sleep attacks), p. 309.

narcotics Drugs, such as opiates, that are used for pain relief and treatment of insomnia, but which have strong addictive potential, p. 265.

naturalistic-observation method Method of scientific research in which the behaviour of subjects is carefully and unobtrusively observed and measured in their natural environments, p. 436.

NCRMD Not criminally responsible on account of a mental disorder, p. 92.

negative correlation Statistical relationship between two variables such that increases in one variable are associated with decreases in the other, p. 436.

negative reinforcers Reinforcers whose removal increases the frequency of an operant behaviour. Anxiety, pain, and social disapproval often function as negative reinforcers; that is, their removal tends to increase the rate of the immediately preceding behaviour. Contrast with *positive reinforcer*, p. 27.

negative symptoms Features of schizophrenia characterized by the *absence* of normal behaviour. Negative symptoms are deficits or behavioural deficiencies, such as social-skills deficits, social withdrawal, flattened affect, poverty of speech and thought, psychomotor retardation, and failure to experience pleasure in pleasant activities, p. 370.

neo-Freudians Term used to describe the "second generation" of theorists who followed in the Freudian tradition. On the whole, neo-Freudians (such as Jung, Adler, Horney, and Sullivan) placed greater emphasis on the importance of cultural and social influences on behaviour and lesser importance on sexual impulses and the functioning of the id, p. 25.

neologisms Type of disturbed thinking associated with schizophrenia involving the coining of new words, p. 363.

neurofibrillary tangles Pathological protein aggregates (or brain lesions) found within brain cells (in the cerebral cortex and hippocampus) in patients with Alzheimer's disease and thought to contribute to the degradation of neurons in the brain, p. 427.

neuroleptics Group of antipsychotic drugs used in the treatment of schizophrenia, such as the phenothiazines (e.g., Thorazine), p. 69.

neurons Nerve cells, p. 20.

neuropeptide An amino acid found in cerebrospinal fluid that plays a role in neuronal transmission and the modulation of brain circuits or regions, p. 310.

neuropsychological assessment Methods of psychological assessment used to detect signs of underlying neurological damage or brain defects, p. 51.

neuroticism Trait describing a general neurotic quality involving such characteristics as anxious, worrisome behaviour, apprehension about the future, and avoidance behaviour, p. 124.

neurotransmitters Chemical substances that serve as a type of messenger by transmitting neural impulses from one neuron to another, p. 21.

NGRI A person found not guilty by reason of insanity, p. 92.

nightmare disorder Sleep disorder characterized by recurrent awakenings from sleep due to the occurrence of frightening nightmares. Formerly called *dream anxiety disorder*, p. 311.

nonspecific treatment factors Characteristics that are not specific to any one form of psychotherapy but tend to be shared by psychotherapies, such as the attention a client receives from a therapist and the therapist's encouragement of the client's sense of hope and positive expectancies, p. 83.

norepinephrine Type of neurotransmitter of the catecholamine class, p. 21.

O

objective tests Tests that allow a limited, specified range of response options or answers so that they can be scored objectively, p. 47.

obsession An intrusive, unwanted, and recurrent thought, image, or urge that seems beyond a person's ability to control, p. 110.

obsessive-compulsive personality disorder Type of personality disorder characterized by rigid ways of relating to others, perfectionistic tendencies, lack of spontaneity, and excessive attention to details, p. 231.

opiates Types of depressant drugs with strong addictive properties that are derived from the opium poppy; provide feelings of euphoria and relief from pain, p. 265.

oppositional defiant disorder Disorder in childhood or adolescence characterized by excessive oppositionality or tendencies to refuse requests from parents and others, p. 415.

optimum level of arousal Level of arousal associated with peak performance and maximum feelings of well-being, p. 222.

osteoporosis Physical disorder caused by calcium deficiency that is characterized by extreme brittleness of the bones (from the Greek *osteon*, meaning "bone," and the Latin *porus*, meaning "pore"), p. 297.

P

panic disorder Type of anxiety disorder characterized by recurrent episodes of panic, p. 100.

paranoid Having irrational suspicions, p. 4.

paranoid personality disorder Type of personality disorder characterized by persistent suspiciousness of the motives of others, but not to the point of holding clear-cut delusions, p. 215.

paraphilias Sexual deviations or types of sexual disorders in which a person experiences recurrent sexual urges and sexually arousing fantasies involving nonhuman objects (such as articles of clothing), inappropriate or nonconsenting partners (e.g., children), or situations producing humiliation or pain to oneself or one's partner. The person has either acted upon such urges or is strongly distressed by them, p. 326.

parasomnias Category of sleep disorders involving the occurrence of abnormal behaviours or physiological events during sleep or at the transition between wakefulness and sleep, p. 308.

pedophilia Type of paraphilia involving sexual attraction to children, p. 330.

performance anxiety Fear relating to the threat of failing to perform adequately, p. 347.

perseveration Persistent repetition of the same thought or train of thought, p. 363.

person-centred therapy Carl Rogers's method of psychotherapy, emphasizing the establishment of a warm, accepting therapeutic relationship that frees clients to engage in a process of self-exploration and self-acceptance, p. 76.

personality disorders Types of abnormal behaviour patterns involving excessively rigid patterns of behaviour or ways of relating to others that ultimately become self-defeating because their rigidity prevents adjustment to external demands, p. 214.

pervasive developmental disorders Disorders involving markedly impaired behaviour or functioning in multiple areas of development. Abbreviated *PDDs*. Also called *autistic spectrum disorders*, p. 395.

phenothiazines Group of antipsychotic drugs or "major tranquillizers" used in the treatment of schizophrenia, p. 12.

phenotype Representation of the total array of traits of an organism, as influenced by the interaction of nature (genetic factors) and nurture (environmental factors), p. 440

phenylketonuria Genetic disorder that prevents the metabolization of phenylpyruvic acid, leading to mental retardation. Abbreviated *PKU*, p. 403.

phlegmatic Slow and stolid, p. 403.

physiological dependence State of physical dependence on a drug in which the user's body comes to depend on a steady supply, p. 255.

placebo (*pluh-SEE-bo*) Inert medication or form of bogus treatment intended to control for the effects of expectancies. Sometimes referred to as a "sugar pill," p. 438.

pleasure principle In psychodynamic theory, the governing principle of the id, involving the demands for immediate gratification of instinctual needs, p. 23.

polygenic Traits or characteristics that are determined by more than one gene, p. 440.

polysomnographic (PSG) recording The simultaneous measurement of multiple physiological responses during sleep or attempted sleep, p. 308.

population Total group of people, other organisms, or events, p. 440.

positive correlation Statistical relationship between two variables such that increases in one variable are associated with increases in the other, p. 436.

positive reinforcers Types of reinforcers that increase the frequency of a behaviour when they are presented. Food and social approval are generally, but not always, positive reinforcers. Contrast with *negative reinforcer*, p. 27.

positive symptoms The more flagrant features of schizophrenia characterized by the *presence* of abnormal behaviour, such as hallucinations, delusions, thought disorder, disorganized speech, and inappropriate affect, p. 370.

possession In demonology, a type of superstitious belief in which abnormal behaviour is taken as a sign that the individual has become possessed by demons or the devil, usually as a form of retribution or the result of making a pact with the devil, p. 9.

postpartum depression Persistent and severe mood changes that occur following childbirth. Abbreviated *PPD*, p. 148.

posttraumatic stress disorder Type of anxiety disorder involving impaired functioning following exposure to a traumatic experience, such as combat, physical assault or rape, or natural or technological disasters, in which the person experiences, for at least a month, such problems as reliving or re-experiencing the trauma, intense fear, avoidance of event-related stimuli, generalized numbing of emotional responsiveness, and heightened autonomic arousal. Abbreviated *PTSD*, p. 113.

preconscious In psychodynamic theory, descriptive of material that lies outside of present awareness but that can be brought into awareness by focusing attention. See also *unconscious*, p. 23.

prefrontal lobotomy Form of psychosurgery in which certain neural pathways in the brain are severed in the attempt to control disturbed behaviour, p. 71.

premature ejaculation Type of sexual dysfunction involving a persistent or recurrent pattern of ejaculation occurring during sexual activity at a point before the man desires it, p. 343.

premorbid functioning Level of functioning before the onset of a disorder, p. 370.

prepared conditioning Belief that people are genetically prepared to acquire fear

responses to certain classes of stimuli, such as fears of large animals, snakes, heights, or strangers. Although the development of such phobias may have had survival value for prehistoric ancestors, such behaviour patterns may be less functional today, p. 119.

pressured speech Outpouring of speech in which words seem to surge urgently for expression, as in a manic state, p. 151.

prevalence Overall number of cases of a disorder existing in a population during a given period of time, p. 439.

primary gains In psychodynamic theory, the relief from anxiety obtained through the development of a neurotic symptom, p. 206.

primary process thinking In psychodynamic theory, the mental process in infancy by which the id seeks gratification of primitive impulses by means of imagining it possesses what it desires. Thinking that is illogical and magical, and fails to discriminate between reality and fantasy, p. 24.

primary reinforcers Natural reinforcers or stimuli that have reinforcement value without learning. Water, food, warmth, and relief from pain are examples of primary reinforcers. Contrast with *secondary reinforcers*, p. 28.

proband Initial diagnosed case of a given disorder. Also called an *index case*, p. 441.

problem-solving therapy Form of therapy that focuses on helping people develop more effective problem-solving skills, p. 239.

prodromal phase (1) Stage in which the early features or signs of a disorder become apparent. (2) In schizophrenia, the period of decline in functioning that precedes the development of the first acute psychotic episode, p. 362.

projection In psychodynamic theory, a defence mechanism in which one's own impulses are attributed to another person, p. 118.

proteins Organic compounds consisting of amino acids that perform most life functions and make up the majority of cellular structures, p. 18.

psychedelics Class of drugs that induce sensory distortions or hallucinations. Also called *hallucinogens*, p. 270.

psychiatrist Physician who specializes in the diagnosis and treatment of mental disorders, p. 2.

psychic (1) Relating to mental phenomena. (2) A person who claims to be sensitive to supernatural forces, p. 23.

psychoactive Describing chemical substances or drugs that have psychological effects, p. 252.

psychoanalytic theory Theoretical model of personality developed by Freud. Also called *psychoanalysis*, p. 22.

psychodynamic model Theoretical model of Freud and his followers in which behaviour is viewed as the product of clashing forces within the personality, p. 15.

psychological dependence Reliance, as on a substance, although one may not be physiologically dependent, p. 256.

psychological disorders Disturbances of psychological functioning or behaviour associated with states of personal distress or impaired social, occupational, or interpersonal functioning. Also called *mental disorders*, p. 2.

psychometric approach Method of psychological assessment that seeks to use psychological tests to identify and measure the reasonably stable traits in an individual's personality that are believed to largely determine his or her behaviour, p. 52.

psychopathy Type of personality pattern characterized by affective and interpersonal traits, such as shallow emotions, selfishness, arrogance, superficial charm, deceitfulness, manipulativeness, irresponsibility, sensation seeking, and a lack of empathy, anxiety, and remorse, combined with persistent violations of social norms, a socially deviant and nomadic lifestyle, and impulsiveness, p. 219.

psychopharmacology Field of study that examines the effects of drugs on behaviour and psychological functioning and explores the use of psychoactive drugs in the treatment of emotional disorders, p. 68.

psychosis Type of major psychological disorder in which people show impaired ability to interpret reality and difficulties in meeting the demands of daily life. Schizophrenia is a prominent example of a psychotic disorder. Plural: *psychoses*, p. 25.

psychotherapy Method of helping involving a systematic interaction between a therapist and a client that brings psychological principles to bear on influencing the client's thoughts, feelings, or behaviours in order to help that client overcome abnormal behaviour or adjust to problems in living, p. 67.

punishments Unpleasant stimuli that suppress the frequency of the behaviours they follow, p. 28.

R

random sampling Drawing samples in such a way that every member of a population has an equal probability of being selected, p. 440.

rapid flight of ideas A characteristic of manic behaviour involving rapid speech and changes of topics, p. 151.

reality principle In psychodynamic theory, the governing principle of the ego that involves consideration of what is socially acceptable and practical in gratifying needs, p. 24.

rebound anxiety Occurrence of strong anxiety following withdrawal from a tranquillizer, p. 69.

receptor site Part of a dendrite on the receiving neuron that is structured to receive a neurotransmitter, p. 21.

reciprocal determinism The ongoing process of two-way interactions among personal factors (cognitive abilities—expectancies, values, attitudes, and beliefs—as well as affective and biological characteristics), behaviours (skills, talents, habits, and interpersonal relations), and environmental factors (physical surroundings and other people), p. 32.

rehearsal In behaviour therapy, a practice opportunity in which a person enacts a desired response and receives feedback from others, p. 443.

reinforcement Stimulus that increases the frequency of the response it follows. See *positive* and *negative* and *primary* and *secondary* reinforcers, p. 27.

relapse Recurrence of a problem behaviour or disorder, p. 287.

relapse-prevention training Cognitive-behavioural technique used in the treatment of addictive behaviours that involves the use of behavioural and cognitive strategies to resist temptations and prevent lapses from becoming relapses, p. 287.

reliable In psychological assessment, the consistency of a measuring instrument, such as a psychological test or rating scale. There are various ways of measuring reliability, such as test-retest reliability, internal consistency, and interrater reliability. Also see *validity*, p. 63.

REM sleep REM (rapid eye movement) sleep is the stage of sleep associated with dreaming that is characterized by the appearance of rapid eye movements under closed eyelids, p. 309.

repetitive transcranial magnetic stimulation A procedure that uses strong magnetic pulses to stimulate the brain. Abbreviated *rTMS*, p. 309.

repression In psychodynamic theory, a type of defence mechanism involving the ejection from awareness of anxiety-provoking ideas, images, or impulses, without the conscious awareness that one has done so, p. 25.

residual phase In schizophrenia, the phase of the disorder that follows an acute phase, characterized by a return to a level of functioning typical of the prodromal phase, p. 362.

reversal design An A-B-A-B type of experimental single-subject design in which treatment is instituted following a baseline phase and then withdrawn (reversal phase) so as to examine effects on behaviour, p. 442.

S

sadomasochism Sexual activities between partners involving the attainment of gratification by means of inflicting and receiving pain and humiliation, p. 333.

sample Part of a population, p. 440.

sanguine Cheerful, p. 9.

schizoid personality disorder Type of personality disorder characterized by a persistent lack of interest in social relationships, flattened affect, and social withdrawal, p. 216.

schizophrenia Enduring psychosis that involves failure to maintain integrated personality functioning, impaired reality testing, and disturbances in thinking. Common features of schizophrenia include delusions, hallucinations, flattened or inappropriate affect, and bizarre behaviour, p. 359.

schizophrenogenic mother Type of mother, described as cold but also overprotective, who was believed to be capable of causing schizo-

phrenia in her children. Research has failed to support the validity of this concept, p. 381.

schizotypal personality disorder Type of personality disorder characterized by eccentricities or oddities of thought and behaviour but without clearly psychotic features, p. 217.

second-rank symptoms In Schneider's view, symptoms associated with schizophrenia that also occur in other psychological disorders, p. 360.

secondary gains Side benefits associated with neuroses or other disorders, such as expressions of sympathy and increased attention from others and release from ordinary responsibilities, p. 206.

secondary process thinking In psychodynamic theory, the reality-based thinking processes and problem-solving activities of the ego, p. 24.

secondary reinforcers Stimuli that gain reinforcement value through their association with established reinforcers. Money and social approval are typically secondary reinforcers. Contrast with *primary reinforcers*, p. 28.

sedatives Types of depressant drugs that reduce states of tension and restlessness and induce sleep, p. 264.

selective abstraction In Beck's theory, a type of cognitive distortion involving the tendency to focus selectively only on the parts of one's experiences that reflect on one's flaws and to ignore those aspects that reveal one's strengths or competencies, p. 158.

selective serotonin-reuptake inhibitors (SSRIs) Type of antidepressant medication that prevents serotonin from being taken back up by the transmitting neuron, thus increasing its action, p. 69.

self Centre of consciousness that organizes sensory impressions and governs one's perceptions of the world. The sum total of a person's thoughts, sensory impressions, and feelings, p. 24.

self psychology Hans Kohut's theory that describes processes that normally lead to the achievement of a cohesive sense of self or, in narcissistic personality disorder, to a grandiose but fragile sense of self, p. 235.

self-monitoring In behavioural assessment, the process of recording or observing one's own behaviour, thoughts, or emotions, p. 53.

self-spectatoring Tendency to observe one's behaviour as if one were a spectator of oneself. People with sexual dysfunctions often become self-spectators in the sense of focusing their attention during sexual activity on the response of their sex organs rather than on their partners or the sexual stimulation itself, p. 350.

semi-structured interviews Type of clinical interview in which interviewers are guided by a general outline but are free to modify the order in which questions are asked and to branch off in other directions, p. 42.

sensate focus exercises In sex therapy, mutual pleasuring activities between partners that are focused on the partners taking turns giving and receiving physical pleasure, p. 349.

separation anxiety disorder Childhood disorder characterized by extreme fears of separation from parents or others on whom the child is dependent, p. 419.

separation-individuation In Margaret Mahler's theory, the process by which young children come to separate psychologically from their mothers and to perceive themselves as separate and distinct persons, p. 236.

serotonin Type of neurotransmitter, imbalances of which have been linked to mood disorders and anxiety, p. 22.

sexual assault Nonconsensual bodily contact for a sexual purpose, p. 336.

sexual aversion disorder Type of sexual dysfunction characterized by aversion to, and avoidance of, genital sexual contact, p. 341.

sexual dysfunctions Psychological disorders involving persistent difficulties with sexual interest, arousal, or response, p. 340.

sexual masochism Type of paraphilia characterized by sexual urges and sexually arousing fantasies involving receiving humiliation or pain, in which the person has either acted on these urges or is strongly distressed by them, p. 332.

sexual sadism Type of paraphilia or sexual deviation characterized by recurrent sexual urges and sexually arousing fantasies involving inflicting humiliation or physical pain on sex partners, in which the person has either acted on these urges or is strongly distressed by them, p. 333.

significant In statistics, a magnitude of difference that is taken as indicating meaningful differences between groups because of the low probability that it occurred by chance, p. 435.

single-case experimental designs Type of case study in which the subject (case) is used as his or her own control by varying the conditions to which the subject is exposed (by use of a reversal phase) or by means of a multiple-baseline design, p. 442.

sleep disorders Diagnostic category representing persistent or recurrent sleep-related problems that cause significant personal distress or impaired functioning, p. 308.

sleep terror disorder Sleep disorder characterized by repeated episodes of sleep terror resulting in abrupt awakenings, p. 312.

sleepwalking disorder Type of sleep disorder involving repeated episodes of sleep-walking, p. 312.

social phobia Excessive fear of engaging in behaviours that involve public scrutiny, p. 109.

social-cognitive theory A broader view of learning theory that emphasizes both situational determinants of behaviour (reinforcements and punishments) and cognitive factors (expectancies, values, attitudes, beliefs, etc.), p. 32.

soma Cell body, p. 20.

somatization disorder Type of somatoform disorder involving recurrent multiple complaints that cannot be explained by any clear physical causes. Formerly called *Briquet's syndrome*, p. 204.

somatoform disorders Disorders in which people complain of physical (somatic) problems although no physical abnormality can be found. See *conversion disorder*, *hypochondriasis*, and *somatization disorder*, p. 199.

specific attribution In the reformulated helplessness theory, a type of attribution involving the belief that the cause of an event involved specific rather than generalized factors. Contrast with *global attribution*, p. 161.

specific phobias Persistent but excessive fears of a specific object or situation, such as a fear of heights or of small animals, p. 107.

splitting Term describing the inability of some persons (especially people with borderline personalities) to reconcile the positive and negative aspects of themselves and others into a cohesive integration, resulting in sudden and radical shifts between strongly positive and strongly negative feelings, p. 236.

stable attribution In the reformulated helplessness theory, a type of attribution involving the belief that the cause of an event involved stable rather than changeable factors. Contrast with *unstable attribution*, 161.

structural hypothesis In Freud's theory, the belief that the clashing forces within the personality could be divided into three psychic structures: the id, the ego, and the superego, p. 23.

structured interviews Means by which an interviewer obtains clinical information from a client by asking a fairly standard series of questions concerning such issues as the client's presenting complaints or problems, mental state, life circumstances, and psychosocial or developmental history, p. 42.

stupor State of relative or complete unconsciousness in which a person is not generally aware of or responsive to the environment, as in a catatonic stupor, p. 368.

substance abuse Continued use of a psychoactive drug despite the knowledge that it is causing or contributing to a persistent or recurrent social, occupational, psychological, or physical problem, p. 253.

substance dependence Impaired control over the use of a psychoactive drug and continued or even increased use despite awareness that the substance is disrupting one's life. Substance dependence is often characterized by physiological dependence, p. 253.

substance-induced disorders Disorders induced by the use of psychoactive substances, including intoxication, withdrawal syndromes, mood disorders, delirium, and amnesia, p. 252.

substance-use disorders Patterns of maladaptive behaviour involving the use of a psychoactive substance. Substance-use disorders include substance-abuse disorders and substance-dependence disorders, p. 252.

superego In psychodynamic theory, the psychic structure that represents the incorporation of the moral values of the parents and important others and floods the ego with guilt and shame when it falls short of meeting those standards. The superego is governed by the moral principle and consists of two parts: the conscience and the ego ideal, p. 24.

survey method Method of scientific research in which large samples of people are questioned by the use of a survey instrument, p. 439.

symbiotic (1) In biology, the living together of two different but interdependent organisms. (2) In Margaret Mahler's object-relations theory, the term used to describe the state of oneness that normally exists between a mother and infant in which the infant's identity is fused with the mother's, p. 236.

synapse Junction between the terminal knob of one neuron and the dendrite or soma of another, through which nerve impulses pass, p. 21.

syndromes Clusters of symptoms that are characteristic of particular disorders, p. 61.

systematic desensitization Behaviour therapy technique for overcoming phobias by means of exposure (in imagination or by means of slides) to progressively more fearful stimuli while one remains deeply relaxed, p. 75.

systems perspective View that problems reflect the systems (family, social, school, ecological, etc.) in which they are embedded, p. 302.

T

tachycardia Abnormally rapid heartbeat, p. 254.

taijin-kyofu-sho Psychiatric syndrome found in Japan that involves excessive fear of offending or causing embarrassment to others. Abbreviated *TKS*, p. 65.

tardive dyskinesia Movement disorder characterized by involuntary movements of the face, mouth, neck, trunk, or extremities caused by long-term use of antipsychotic medications. Abbreviated *TD*, p. 384.

Tay-Sachs disease Disease of lipid metabolism that is genetically transmitted and usually results in death in early childhood, p. 403.

terminals In neuropsychology, the small branching structures found at the tips of axons, p. 21.

theories (1) Plausible or scientifically defensible explanations of events. (2) Formulations of the relationships underlying observed events. Theories are helpful to scientists because they provide a means of organizing observations and lead to predictions about future events, p. 434.

theory of mind The ability to appreciate that other people have a mental state that is different from one's own, p. 398.

thought disorder Disturbances in thinking characterized by various features, especially a breakdown in logical associations between thoughts, p. 363.

time out Behavioural technique in which an individual who emits an undesired behaviour is removed from an environment in which reinforcers are available and placed in an unreinforcing environment for a period of time as a form of punishment. Time out is frequently used in behavioural programs for modifying behaviour problems in children, in combination with positive reinforcement for desirable behaviour, p. 417.

token economies Behavioural treatment programs, in institutional settings, in which a controlled environment is constructed such that people are reinforced for desired behaviours by receiving tokens (such as poker chips) that may be exchanged for desired rewards or privileges, p. 76.

tolerance Physical habituation to a drug so that with frequent usage, higher doses are needed to attain similar effects, p. 68.

transference relationship In psychoanalysis, a client's transfer or generalization to the analyst of feelings and attitudes the client holds toward important figures in his or her life, p. 73.

transvestic fetishism Type of paraphilia in heterosexual males characterized by recurrent sexual urges and sexually arousing fantasies involving dressing in female clothing, in which the person has either acted on these urges or is strongly distressed by them. Also termed *transvestism*, p. 328.

trephining Harsh prehistoric practice of cutting a hole in a person's skull, possibly as an ancient form of surgery for brain trauma, or possibly as a means of releasing the demons that prehistoric people may have believed caused abnormal behaviour in the afflicted persons, p. 9.

tricyclics Group of antidepressant drugs that increase the activity of norepinephrine and serotonin in the brain by interfering with the reuptake of these neurotransmitters by transmitting neurons. Also called *TCAs* (tricyclic antidepressants), p. 69.

two-factor model O. Hobart Mowrer's theory that both operant and classical conditioning are involved in the acquisition of phobic responses. The fear component of phobia is acquired by means of classical conditioning (pairing of a previously neutral stimulus with an aversive stimulus), and the avoidance component is acquired by means of operant conditioning (relief from anxiety negatively reinforces avoidance behaviour), p. 118.

U

unconditional positive regard In Carl Rogers's view, the expression of unconditional acceptance of another person's basic worth as a person, regardless of whether one approves of all of the behaviour of the other person. The ability to express unconditional positive regard is considered a quality of an effective person-centred therapist, p. 76.

unconditioned response Unlearned response or a response to an unconditioned stimulus. Abbreviated *UR* or *UCR*, p. 26.

unconditioned stimulus Stimulus that elicits an instinctive or unlearned response from an organism. Abbreviated *US* or *UCS*, p. 26.

unconscious (1) In psychodynamic theory, pertaining to impulses or ideas that are not readily available to awareness, in many instances because they are kept from awareness by means of *repression*. (2) Also in psychodynamic theory, the part of the mind that contains repressed material and primitive urges of the id. (3) More generally, a state of unawareness or loss of consciousness, p. 23.

unipolar Pertaining to a single pole or direction, as in unipolar (depressive) disorders. Contrast with *bipolar disorder*, p. 141.

unobtrusive Not interfering, p. 436.

unstable attribution In the reformulated helplessness theory, a type of attribution involving the belief that the cause of an event involved changeable rather than stable factors. Contrast with *stable attribution*, p. 161.

unstructured interviews Type of clinical interview in which interviewers determine which questions to ask rather than following a standard interview format, p. 42.

vaginismus Type of sexual dysfunction characterized by the recurrent or persistent contraction of the muscles surrounding the vaginal entrance, making penile entry while attempting intercourse difficult or impossible, p. 343.

validity (1) With respect to tests, the degree to which a test measures the traits or constructs that it purports to measure. (2) With respect to experiments, the degree to which an experiment yields scientifically accurate and defensible results, p. 63.

validity scales Groups of test items that serve to detect whether the results of a particular test are valid or whether a person responded in a random manner or in a way intended to create a favourable or unfavourable impression, p. 47.

variables Conditions that are measured (dependent variables) or manipulated (independent variables) in scientific studies, p. 436.

voyeurism Type of paraphilia characterized by recurrent sexual urges and sexually arousing fantasies involving the act of watching unsuspecting others who are naked, in the act of undressing, or engaging in sexual activity, in which the person has either acted on these urges or is strongly distressed by them, p. 330.

W

waxy flexibility Feature of catatonic schizophrenia in which a person's limbs are moved into a certain posture or position that the person then rigidly maintains for a lengthy period of time, p. 369.

withdrawal syndrome Characteristic cluster of withdrawal symptoms following the sudden reduction or abrupt cessation of use of a psychoactive substance after physiological dependence has developed, p. 254.

world view Prevailing view of the times. (English translation of the German *Weltanschauung*), p. 9.

A

Abdulrehman, R. Y., & De Luca, R. V. (2001). The implications of childhood sexual abuse on adult social behavior. *Journal of Family Violence, 16*, 193–203.

Abi-Dargham, A. (2004). Do we still believe in the dopamine hypothesis? New data bring new evidence. *International Journal of Neuropsychopharmacology, 7*(Suppl. 1), S1–S5.

Abikoff, H., & Klein, R. G. (1992). Attention-deficit hyperactivity and conduct disorder: Comorbidity and implications for treatment. *Journal of Consulting and Clinical Psychology, 60*, 881–892.

Aboriginal Planet. (2002). *Aboriginal Planet—who are we?* Ottawa: Department of Foreign Affairs and International Trade. Retrieved February 9, 2003, from http://www.dfait-maeci.gc.ca/foreign_policy/aboriginal/talk/talk-en.asp

Abraham, K. (1948). The first pregenital stage of the libido. In D. Bryan & A. Strachey (Trans.), *Selected papers of Karl Abraham, M.D.* (pp. 248–279). London: Hogarth Press. (Original work published 1916)

Abramson, L. T., Seligman, M. E. P., & Teasdale, J. D. (1978). Learned helplessness in humans: Critique and reformulation. *Journal of Abnormal Psychology, 87*, 49–74.

Acculturation increases risk for substance use by foreign-born youth. (2004, January–February). *SAMHSA News, 12*(1). Retrieved November 1, 2011 from http://www.samhsa.gov/samhsa_news/VolumeXII_1/article2.htm

Achenbach, T. M., & Rescorla, L. A. (2001). *Manual for the ASEBA school-age forms and profiles: An integrated system multi-informant assessment.* Burlington: University of Vermont, Research Center for Children, Youth, and Families.

Addictive personalities. (1989, February 20). *Newsweek.*

Addington, J., Collins, A., McCleery, A., & Addington, D. (2005). The role of family work in early psychosis. *Schizophrenia Research, 79*, 77–83.

Adlaf, E. M., Begin, P., & Sawka, E. (Eds.). (2005). *Canadian addiction survey (CAS): A national survey of Canadians' use of alcohol and other drugs.* Ottawa: Health Canada, Canadian Executive Council on Addictions, & Canadian Centre on Substance Abuse.

Adlaf, E. M., & Paglia, A. (2001). *The mental health and well-being of Ontario students 1991–1999: Findings from the OSDUS.* CAMH Research Documents Series 7. Toronto: Centre for Addiction and Mental Health.

Adler, J. (1994, December 18). The endless binge. *Newsweek,* 72–73.

Afifi, T. O., Cox, B. J., & Enns, M. W. (2006). Mental health profiles among married, never-married, and separated/divorced mothers in a nationally representative sample. *Social Psychiatry and Psychiatric Epidemiology, 41*, 122–129.

Ahern, J., Galea, S., Resnick, H., Kilpatrick, D., Bucuvalas, M., Gold, J., & Vlahov, D. (2002). Television images and psychological symptoms after the September 11 terrorist attacks. *Psychiatry: Interpersonal and Biological Processes, 65*, 289–300.

Ainsworth, M. D. (1989). Attachments beyond infancy. *American Psychologist, 44*, 709–716.

Ainsworth, M. D. S., & Bowlby, J. (1991). An ethological approach to personality development. *American Psychologist, 46*, 333–341.

Akbarian, S., Kim, J. J., Potkin, S. G., Hetrick, W. P., Bunney, W. E., Jr., & Jones, E. G. (1996). Maldistribution of interstitial neurons in prefrontal white matter of the brains of schizophrenic patients. *Archives of General Psychiatry, 53*, 425–436.

Akhtar, S. (1987). Schizoid personality disorder: A synthesis of developmental, dynamic, and descriptive features. *American Journal of Psychotherapy, 41*, 499–518.

Akhtar, S. (2003). Things: Developmental, psychopathological, and technical aspects of inanimate objects. *Canadian Journal of Psychoanalysis, 11*(1), 1–44.

Akiskal, H. S. (2001). Dysthymia and cyclothymia in psychiatric practice a century after Kraepelin. *Journal of Affective Disorders, 62*, 17–31.

Alberta Learning. (2003). *Teaching students with autism spectrum disorders.* Edmonton: Author.

Alcohol and the heart: Consensus emerges. (1996, January). *Harvard Heart Letter, 6*(5).

Aldrich, M. S. (1992). Narcolepsy. *Neurology, 42*(7, Suppl. 6), 34–43.

Allderidge, P. (1979). Hospitals, madhouses and asylums: Cycles in the care of the insane. *British Journal of Psychiatry, 134*, 321–324.

Allen, M., Bourhis, J., Sahlstein, E., Laskowski, K., Falato, W. L., Ackerman, J., . . . Cashman, L. (2004). A meta-analysis of the relationship between social skills and sexual offenders. *Communication Reports, 17*, 1–10.

Alloy, L. B., Abramson, L. Y., Walshaw, P. D., & Neeren, A. M. (2006). Cognitive vulnerability to unipolar and bipolar mood disorders. *Journal of Social and Clinical Psychology, 25*, 726–754.

Alloy, L. B., Abramson, L. Y., Whitehouse, W. G., Hogan, M. E., Panzarella, C., & Rose, D. T. (2006). Prospective incidence of first onsets and recurrences of depression in individuals at high and low cognitive risk for depression. *Journal of Abnormal Psychology, 115*, 145–156.

Alloy, L. B., Abramson, L. Y., Whitehouse, W. G., Hogan, M. E., Tashman, N. A., Steinberg, D. L, . . . Donovan, P. (1999). Depressogenic cognitive styles: Predictive validity, information processing and personality characteristics, and developmental origins. *Behaviour Research and Therapy, 37*, 503–531.

Alpert, J., Nierenberg, A. A., Mischoulon, D., Otto, M. W., Zajecka, J., Murck, H., & Rosenbaum, J. F. (2005). A double-blind, randomized trial of St John's wort, fluoxetine, and placebo in major depressive disorder. *Journal of Clinical Psychopharmacology, 25*, 441–447.

Altman, L. K. (1990, April 18). Scientists see a link between alcoholism and a specific gene. *The New York Times,* pp. A1, A18.

American Association on Mental Retardation. (1992). *Mental retardation: Definition, classification, and systems of supports* (9th ed.). Washington, DC: Author.

American Cancer Society. (2003). *Cancer facts and figures 2003.* Atlanta, GA: Author.

American Psychiatric Association. (2000a). *Diagnostic and statistical manual of mental disorders* (4th ed., text revision). Washington, DC: Author.

American Psychiatric Association. (2000b). Practice guideline for major depressive disorder in adults. *American Journal of Psychiatry, 150*(Suppl. 4), 1–26.

American Psychiatric Association. (2010a). *Practice guideline for the treatment of patients with major depressive disorder* (3rd ed.). Washington, DC: Author.

American Psychiatric Association. (2010b). *Proposed draft revisions to DSM disorders and criteria.* Retrieved October 10, 2011, from http://www.dsm5.org/ProposedRevision/Pages/Default.aspx

American Psychological Association. (n.d.). Answers to your questions about transgender people, gender identity, and gender expression. Retrieved November 9, 2011, from http://www.apa.org/topics/sexuality/transgender.aspx

Ames, M. A., & Houston, D. A. (1990). Legal, social, and biological definitions of pedophilia. *Archives of Sexual Behavior, 19*, 333–342.

Amminger, G. P., Pape, S., Rock, D., Roberts, S. A., Ott, S. L., Squires-Wheeler, E., . . . Erlenmeyer-Kimling, L. (1999). Relationship between childhood behavioral disturbance and later schizophrenia in the New York High-Risk Project. *American Journal of Psychiatry, 156,* 525–530.

Andreasen, N. C. (1999). Understanding the causes of schizophrenia. *New England Journal of Medicine, 340,* 645–647.

Angier, N. (1991, August 4). Kids who can't sit still. *The New York Times,* Section 4A, pp. 30–33.

Angold, A., & Costello, E. J. (1993). Depressive comorbidity in children and adolescents: Empirical, theoretical, and methodological issues. *American Journal of Psychiatry, 150,* 1779–1791.

Angold, A., & Costello, E. J. (1996). Toward establishing an empirical basis for the diagnosis of oppositional defiant disorder. *Journal of the American Academy of Child and Adolescent Psychiatry, 35,* 1205–1212.

Anonymous. (1985, June 13). Schizophrenia—A mother's agony over her son's pain. *Chicago Tribune,* pp. 5:1–3.

Anthony, W. A., & Liberman, R. P. (1986). The practice of psychiatric rehabilitation: Historical, conceptual, and research base. *Schizophrenia Bulletin, 12,* 542–559.

Anton, R. F. (1994). Medications for treating alcoholism. *Alcohol Health and Research World, 18,* 265–271.

Antonarakis, S. E., and Down Syndrome Collaborative Group. (1991). Parental origin of the extra chromosome in trisomy 21 as indicated by analysis of DNA polymorphisms. *New England Journal of Medicine, 324,* 872–876.

Antonova, E., Sharma, T., Morris, R., & Kumari, V. (2004). The relationship between brain structure and neurocognition in schizophrenia: A selective review. *Schizophrenia Research, 70,* 117–145.

Antony, M. M., & Barlow, D. H. (2002). Specific phobias. In D. H. Barlow, *Anxiety and its disorders: The nature and treatment of anxiety and panic* (2nd ed., pp. 380–417). New York: Guilford.

Antony, M. M., Ledley, D. R., Liss, A., & Swinson, R. P. (2006). Responses to symptom induction exercises in panic disorder. *Behaviour Research and Therapy, 44,* 85–98.

Antony, M. M., & McCabe, R. E. (2005). *Overcoming animal and insect phobias: How to conquer fear of dogs, snakes, rodents, bees, spiders, and more.* Oakland, CA: New Harbinger.

Antony, M. M., Rowa, K., Liss, A., Swallow, S. R., & Swinson, R. P. (2005). Social comparison processes in social phobia. *Behavior Therapy, 36,* 65–75.

Antony, M. M., & Swinson, R. P. (1998). *When perfect isn't good enough: Strategies for coping with perfectionism.* Oakland, CA: New Harbinger.

Antony, M. M., & Swinson, R. P. (2000). *Phobic disorders and panic in adults: A guide to assessment and treatment.* Washington, DC: American Psychological Association.

Anway, M. D., Cupp, A. S., Uzumcu, M., & Skinner, M. K. (2005). Epigenetic trans-generational actions of endocrine disruptors and male fertility. *Science, 308,* 1466–1469.

Appelbaum, P. S., & Gutheil, T. G. (1979). "Rotting with their rights on": Constitutional theory and clinical reality in drug refusal by psychiatric patients. *Bulletin of the American Academy of Psychiatry and the Law, 7,* 306–315.

Arieti, S. (1974). *Interpretation of schizophrenia* (2nd ed.). New York: Basic Books.

Arnett, J. L. (2006). Psychology and health. *Canadian Psychology, 47*(1), 19–32.

Arnett, P. A. (1997). Autonomic responsivity in psychopaths: A critical review and theoretical proposal. *Clinical Psychology Review, 17,* 903–936.

Arnett, P. A., Smith, S. S., & Newman, J. P. (1997). Approach and avoidance motivation in psychopathic criminal offenders during passive avoidance. *Journal of Personality and Social Psychology, 72,* 1413–1428.

Arnold, E. H., O'Leary, S. G., & Edward, G. H. (1997). Father involvement and self-reported parenting of children with attention deficit-hyperactivity disorder. *Journal of Consulting and Clinical Psychology, 65,* 337–342.

Arnow, B., Kenardy, J., & Agras, W. S. (1992). Binge eating among the obese: A descriptive study. *Journal of Behavioral Medicine, 15,* 155–170.

Aronson, T. A. (1989). A critical review of psychotherapeutic treatments of the borderline personality: Historical trends and future directions. *Journal of Nervous and Mental Disease, 177,* 511–528.

Arthur, N., & Januszkowski, T. (2001). The multicultural counselling competencies of Canadian counsellors. *Canadian Journal of Counselling, 35*(1), 36–48.

Arthur, N., & Stewart, J. (2001). Multicultural counselling in the new millennium: Introduction to the special theme issue. *Canadian Journal of Counselling, 35*(1), 3–14.

Asaad, G., & Shapiro, B. (1986). Hallucinations: Theoretical and clinical overview. *American Journal of Psychiatry, 143,* 1088–1097.

Asarnow, J. R., Carlson, G. A., & Guthrie, D. (1987). Coping strategies, self-perceptions, hopelessness, and perceived family environments in depressed and suicidal children. *Journal of Consulting and Clinical Psychology, 55,* 361–366.

Asherson, P., Chen, W., Craddock, B., & Taylor, E. (2007). Adult attention-deficit hyperactivity disorder: Recognition and treatment in general adult psychiatry. *British Journal of Psychiatry, 190,* 4–5.

Asmundson, G. J. G., & Taylor, S. (2005). *It's not all in your head: How worrying about your health could be making you sick— and what to do about it.* New York: Guilford.

Astley, S. J., Clarren, S. K., Little, R. E., Sampson, P. D., & Daling, J. R. (1992). Analysis of facial shape in children gestationally exposed to marijuana, alcohol, and/or cocaine. *Pediatrics, 89,* 67–77.

Aston, R., & Cullumbine, H. (1959). Studies on the nature of the joint action of ethanol and barbiturates. *Toxicology and Applied Pharmacology, 1,* 65–72.

Attention deficit disorder—Part II. (1995, May). *The Harvard Mental Health Letter, 11*(11), 1–3.

Aubry, M., Cantu, R., Dvorak, J., Johnston, K., McCrory, P., Meeuwisse, W., & Molloy, M. (2009). Consensus statement on concussion in sport: The 3rd International Conference on Concussion in Sport held in Zurich, November 2008. *British Journal of Sports Medicine, 43,* i76–i84.

Ayoub, C. C. (2006). Munchausen by proxy. In T. G. Plante (Ed.), *Mental disorders of the new millennium: Vol. 3. Biology and function* (pp. 173–193). Westport, CT: Praeger.

Azrin, N. H., & Peterson, A. L. (1989). Reduction of an eye tic by controlled blinking. *Behavior Therapy, 20,* 467–473.

B

Babiak, P. (1995). When psychopaths go to work: A case study of an industrial psychopath. *International Journal of Applied Psychology, 44*(2), 171–188.

Bach, A. K., Barlow, D. H., & Wincze, J. P. (2004). The enhancing effects of manualized treatment for erectile dysfunction among men using sildenafil: A preliminary investigation. *Behavior Therapy, 35,* 55–73.

Bachman, P., & Cannon, T. D. (2005). Cognitive and neuroscience aspects of thought disorder. In K. J. Holyoak & R. G. Morrison (Eds.), *Cambridge handbook of thinking and reasoning* (pp. 493–526). New York: Cambridge University Press.

Baer, L., Rauch, S. L., Ballantine, H. T., Jr., Martuz, R., Cosgrove, R., Cassein, E., . . . Jenike, M. A. (1995). Cingulotomy for intractable obsessive-compulsive disorder: Prospective long-term follow-up of 18 patients. *Archives of General Psychiatry, 52,* 384–392.

Bagby, R. M., Nicholson, R., & Buis, T. (1998). Utility of the Deceptive-Subtle items in the detection of malingering. *Journal of Personality Assessment, 70,* 405–415.

Bahammam, A., Delaive, K., Ronald, J., Manfreda, J., Roos, L., & Kryger, M. H. (1999). Health care utilization in males with obstructive sleep apnea syndrome two years after diagnosis and treatment. *Sleep, 22,* 740–747.

Baker, R. C., & Kirschenbaum, D. S. (1993). Self-monitoring may be necessary for successful weight control. *Behavior Therapy, 24,* 377–394.

Bal, P., & Koenraadt, F. (2000). Criminal law and mentally ill offenders in comparative perspective. *Psychology, Crime and Law, 6,* 219–250.

Baldwin, A. R., Oei, T. P. S., & Young, R. (1994). To drink or not to drink: The differential role of alcohol expectancies and drinking refusal self-efficacy in quantity and frequency of alcohol consumption. *Cognitive Therapy and Research, 17,* 511–530.

Baldwin, D. S. (2006). Serotonin noradrenaline reuptake inhibitors: A new generation of treatment for anxiety disorders. *International Journal of Psychiatry in Clinical Practice, 67*(Suppl. 6), 9–15.

Bandura, A. (1973). *Aggression: A social learning analysis.* Englewood Cliffs, NJ: Prentice-Hall.

Bandura, A. (1986). *Social foundations of thought and action: A social cognitive theory.* Englewood Cliffs, NJ: Prentice-Hall.

Bandura A. (1989). Social cognitive theory. In R. Vasta (Ed.), *Annals of child development: Vol. 6. Six theories of child development* (pp. 1–60). Greenwich, CT: JAI Press.

Bandura, A. (2001). Social cognitive theory: An agentic perspective. *Annual Review of Psychology, 52*(2), 1–26.

Bandura, A., Blanchard, E. B., & Ritter, B. (1969). The relative efficacy of desensitization and modeling approaches for inducing behavioral, affective, and cognitive changes. *Journal of Personality and Social Psychology, 13,* 173–199.

Bandura, A., Jeffery, R. W., & Wright, C. L. (1974). Efficacy of participant modeling as a function of response induction aids. *Journal of Abnormal Psychology, 83,* 56–64.

Bandura, A., Ross, D., & Ross, S. A. (1963). Imitation of film-mediated aggressive models. *Journal of Abnormal and Social Psychology, 66,* 3–11.

Banno, K., & Kryger, M. H. (2007). Sleep apnea: Clinical investigations in humans. *Sleep Medicine, 8*(4), 402–426.

Banno, K., Walld, R., & Kryger, M. H. (2005). Increasing obesity trends in patients with sleep-disordered breathing referred to a sleep disorders center. *Journal of Clinical Sleep Medicine, 1,* 364–366.

Barbaree, H. E., & Seto, M. C. (1997). Pedophilia: Assessment and treatment. In D. R. Laws & W. T. O'Donohue (Eds.), *Sexual deviance: Theory, assessment, and treatment* (pp. 175–193). New York: Guilford.

Barch, D. M. (2005). The cognitive neuroscience of schizophrenia. *Annual Review of Clinical Psychology, 1,* 321–353.

Bardwell, W. A., Moore, P., Ancoli-Israel, S., & Dimsdale, J. E. (2003). Fatigue in obstructive sleep apnea: Driven by depressive symptoms instead of apnea severity? *The American Journal of Psychiatry, 160,* 350–355.

Barlow, D. H. (1986). Causes of sexual dysfunction: The role of anxiety and cognitive interference. *Journal of Consulting and Clinical Psychology, 54,* 140–148.

Barlow, D. H. (2002). *Anxiety and its disorders: The nature and treatment of anxiety and panic* (2nd ed.). New York: Guilford.

Baron-Cohen, S. (1995). *Mindblindness: An essay on autism and theory of mind.* Cambridge, MA: MIT Press.

Baron-Cohen, S. (1998). *Autism and "theory of mind": An introduction and review.* International Symposium on Autism 1998. Toronto: Geneva Centre for Autism. Retrieved October 11, 2003, from http://www.autism.net/html/baron-cohen.html

Barrett, S. P., Gross, S. R., Garand, I., & Pihl, R. O. (2005). Patterns of simultaneous polysubstance use in Canadian rave attendees. *Substance Use & Misuse, 40,* 1525–1537.

Bartecchi, C. E., MacKenzie, T. D., & Schrier, R. W. (1994). The human costs of tobacco use. *New England Journal of Medicine, 330,* 907–912.

Basch, M. F. (1980). *Doing psychotherapy.* New York: Basic Books.

Basoglu, M., Marks, I., Livanou, M., & Swinson, S. (1997). Double-blindness procedures, rater blindness, and ratings of outcome. *Archives of General Psychiatry, 54,* 744–748.

Bassarath, L. (2003). Medication strategies in childhood aggression: A review. *Canadian Journal of Psychiatry, 48,* 367–373.

Bassett, A. S., & Chow, E. W. C. (1999). 22q11 deletion syndrome: A genetic subtype of schizophrenia. *Biological Psychiatry, 46,* 882–891.

Basson, R. (2001). Human sex-response cycles. *Journal of Sex & Marital Therapy, 27,* 33–43.

Basson, R. (2005). Women's sexual dysfunction: Revised and expanded definitions. *Canadian Medical Association Journal, 172,* 1327–1333.

Basson, R., McInnes, R., Smith, M. D., Hodgson, G., & Koppiker, N. (2002). Efficacy and safety of sildenafil citrate in women with sexual dysfunction associated with female sexual arousal disorder. *Journal of Women's Health & Gender-Based Medicine, 11,* 367–377.

Bastiaansen, J. A., Thioux, M., Nanetti, L., van der Gaag, C., Ketelaars, C., Minderaa, R., & Keysers, C. (2011). Age-related increase in inferior frontal gyrus activity and social functioning in autism spectrum disorder. *Biological Psychiatry, 69,* 832–838.

Bateson, G. D., Jackson, D., Haley, J., & Weakland, J. (1956). Toward a theory of schizophrenia. *Behavioral Science, 1,* 251–264.

Baucom, D. H., Shoham, V., Mueser, K. T., Daiuto, A. D., & Stickle, T. (1998). Empirically supported couple and family interventions for marital distress and adult mental health problems. *Journal of Consulting and Clinical Psychology, 66,* 53–88.

Baumann, C. R., Khatami, R., Werth, E., & Bassetti, C. L. (2006). Hypocretin (orexin) deficiency predicts severe objective excessive daytime sleepiness in narcolepsy with cataplexy. *Journal of Neurology, Neurosurgery, and Psychiatry, 77,* 402–404.

Baxter, L. R., Ackerman, R. F., Swerdlow, N. R., Brody, A., Saxena, S., Schwartz, J. M., . . . Phelps, M. E. (2000). Specific brain system mediation of obsessive-compulsive disorder responsive to either medication or behavior therapy. In W. K. Goodman, M. V. Rudorfer, & J. D. Maser (Eds.), *Obsessive-compulsive disorder: Contemporary issues in treatment* (pp. 573–609). Mahwah, NJ: Erlbaum.

Baylis, P. J. (2002). Promoting resilience: A review of the literature. Retrieved April 23, 2003, from http://www.amhb.ab.ca/chmh/resources/page.cfm?pg=Promoting%20Resilience%20

Beard, K. W. (2005). Internet addiction: A review of current assessment techniques and potential assessment questions. *CyberPsychology & Behavior, 8,* 7–14.

Bebbington, P. (1993). Transcultural aspects of affective disorders. *International Review of Psychiatry, 5,* 145–156.

Beck, A. T. (1976). *Cognitive therapy and the emotional disorders.* New York: International Universities Press.

Beck, A. T., Brown, G., Berchick, R. J., Stewart, B. L., & Steer, R. A. (1990). Relationship between hopelessness and ultimate suicide: A replication with psychiatric outpatients. *American Journal of Psychiatry, 147,* 190–195.

Beck, A. T., & Clark, D. A. (1997). An information processing model of anxiety: Automatic and strategic processes. *Behaviour Research and Therapy, 35,* 49–58.

Beck, A. T., Freeman, A., Davis, D. D., & Associates. (2004). *Cognitive therapy of personality disorders* (2nd ed.). Guilford Clinical Psychology and Psychopathology Series. New York: Guilford Press.

Beck, A. T., Rush, A. J., Shaw, B. F., & Emery, G. (1979). *Cognitive therapy of depression.* New York: Guilford.

Beck, A. T., & Young, J. E. (1985). Depression. In D. H. Barlow (Ed.), *Clinical handbook of psychological disorders: A step-by-step treatment manual* (pp. 206–244). New York: Guilford.

Beck, C. A., Patten, S. B., Williams, J. V. A., Wang, J. L., Currie, S. R., Maxwell, C. J., & el-Guebaly, N. (2005). Antidepressant utilization in Canada. *Social Psychiatry and Psychiatric Epidemiology, 40,* 799–807.

Beck, C. A., Williams, J. V. A., Wang, J. L., Kassam, A., el-Guebaly, N., Currie, S. R., . . . Patten, S. B. (2005). Psychotropic medication use in Canada. *Canadian Journal of Psychiatry, 50,* 605–613.

Beck, J. G. (1993). Vaginismus. In W. O'Donohue & J. H. Geer (Eds.), *Handbook of sexual dysfunctions: Assessment and treatment* (pp. 381–397). Boston: Allyn & Bacon.

Beck, J. G. (1995). Hypoactive sexual desire disorder: An overview. *Journal of Consulting and Clinical Psychology, 63,* 919–927.

Beck, R., & Perkins, T. S. (2001). Cognitive content-specificity for anxiety and depression: A meta-analysis. *Cognitive Therapy and Research, 25,* 651–663.

Becker, D., & Lamb, S. (1994). Sex bias in the diagnosis of borderline personality disorder and posttraumatic stress disorder. *Professional Psychology: Research and Practice, 25,* 55–61.

Beech, A. R., & Mitchell, I. J. (2005). A neurobiological perspective on attachment problems in sexual offenders and the role of selective serotonin re-uptake inhibitors in the treatment of such problems. *Clinical Psychology Review, 25,* 153–182.

Behar, E., & Borkovec, T. D. (2006). The nature and treatment of generalized anxiety disorder. In B. O. Rothbaum (Ed.), *Pathological anxiety: Emotional process-*

ing in etiology and treatment (pp. 181–196). New York: Guilford.

Beidel, D. C., & Turner, S. M. (1986). A critique of the theoretical bases of cognitive behavioral theories and therapy. *Clinical Psychology Review, 6,* 177–199.

Beiser, M. (2003). Culture and psychiatry, or "the tale of the hole and the cheese." *Canadian Journal of Psychiatry, 48*(3), 143–144.

Beitman, B. D., Goldfried, M. R., & Norcross, J. C. (1989). The movement toward integrating the psychotherapies: An overview. *American Journal of Psychiatry, 146,* 138–147.

Bellack, A. S., & Mueser, K. T. (1990). Schizophrenia. In A. S. Bellack, M. Hersen, & A. E. Kazdin (Eds.), *International handbook of behavior modification and therapy* (2nd ed., pp. 353–370). New York: Plenum.

Bellack, A. S., & Mueser, K. T. (1993). Psychosocial treatment for schizophrenia. *Schizophrenia Bulletin, 19,* 317–336.

Benjamin, L. S., & Wonderlich, S. A. (1994). Social perceptions and borderline personality disorder: The relation to mood disorders. *Journal of Abnormal Psychology, 103,* 610–624.

Bentall, R. P. (1990). The illusion of reality: A review and integration of psychological research on hallucinations. *Psychological Bulletin, 107,* 82–95.

Berenbaum, H., & Oltmanns, T. F. (2005). Emotional experience and expression in schizophrenia and depression. In P. Ekman & E. L. Rosenberg (Eds.), *What the face reveals: Basic and applied studies of spontaneous expression using the Facial Action Coding System (FACS)* (2nd ed., pp. 441–458). New York: Oxford University Press.

Bergeron, S., Binik, Y. M., Khalifé, S., Pagidas, K., Glazer, H. I., Meana, M., & Amsel, R. (2001). A randomized comparison of group cognitive-behavioral therapy, surface electromyographic biofeedback, and vestibulectomy in the treatment of dyspareunia resulting from vulvar vestibulitis. *Pain, 91,* 297–306.

Bergida, H., & Lenzenweger, M. F. (2006). Schizotypy and sustained attention: Confirming evidence from an adult community sample. *Journal of Abnormal Psychology, 115,* 545–551.

Berlim, M. T., & Turecki, G. (2007). Definition, assessment, and staging of treatment-resistant refractory major depression: A review of current concepts and methods. *Canadian Journal of Psychiatry, 52,* 46–54.

Berlin, I. N. (1987). Suicide among American Indian adolescents: An overview. *Suicide and Life-Threatening Behavior, 17,* 218–232.

Bernstein, D. P., Cohen, P., Skodol, A., Bezirganian, S., & Brook, J. S. (1996). Childhood antecedents of adolescent personality disorders. *American Journal of Psychiatry, 153,* 907–913.

Bernstein, E. M., & Putnam, F. W. (1986). Development, reliability, and validity of a dissociation scale. *Journal of Nervous and Mental Disease, 174,* 727–735.

Bertelsen, M., Jeppesen, P., Petersen, L., Thorup, A., Øhlenschlaeger, J., le Quach, P., . . . Nordentoft, M. (2008). Five-year follow-up of a randomized multicenter trial of intensive early intervention vs standard treatment for patients with a first episode of psychotic illness: The OPUS trial. *Archives of Geneneral Psychiatry, 65,* 762–771.

Bettelheim, B. (1967). *The empty fortress: Infantile autism and the birth of the self.* New York: Free Press.

Bewernick, B. H., Hurlemann, R., Matusch, A., Kayser, S., Grubert, C., Hadrysiewicz, B., . . . Schlaepfer, T. E. (2010). Nucleus accumbens deep brain stimulation decreases ratings of depression and anxiety in treatment-resistant depression. *Biological Psychiatry, 67,* 110–116.

Bibby, R. W. (2006). *The boomer factor: What Canada's most famous generation is leaving behind.* Toronto: Bastian Books.

Bick, P. A., & Kinsbourne, M. (1987). Auditory hallucinations and subvocal speech in schizophrenic patients. *American Journal of Psychiatry, 144,* 222–225.

Bickel, W. K., Amass, L., Badger, G. J., & Esch, R. A. (1997). Effects of adding behavioral treatment to opioid detoxification with buprenorphine. *Journal of Consulting and Clinical Psychology, 65,* 803–810.

Biederman, J., Faraone, S. V., Milberger, S., Garcia Jetton, J., Chen, L., Mick, E., . . . Russell, R. L. (1996). Is childhood oppositional defiant disorder a precursor to adolescent conduct disorder? Findings from a four-year follow-up study of children with ADHD. *Journal of the American Academy of Child and Adolescent Psychiatry, 35,* 1193–1204.

Binder, J. L., & Strupp, H. H. (1997). "Negative process": A recurrently discovered and underestimated facet of therapeutic process and outcome in the individual psychotherapy of adults. *Clinical Psychology: Science and Practice, 4,* 121–139.

Binik, Y. M. (2005). Should dyspareunia be retained as a sexual dysfunction in DSM-V? A painful classification decision. *Archives of Sexual Behavior, 34,* 11–21.

Biran, M. (1988). Cognitive and exposure treatment for agoraphobia: Reexamination of the outcome research. *Journal of Cognitive Psychotherapy: An International Quarterly, 2*(3), 165–178.

Birchwood, M., Tood, P., & Jackson, C. (1988). Early intervention in psychosis: The critical period hypothesis. *British Journal of Psychiatry (Supplement), 33,* 53–59.

Blair, C. D., & Lanyon, R. I. (1981). Exhibitionism: Etiology and treatment. *Psychological Bulletin, 89,* 439–463.

Blakeslee, S. (1991, September 15). Study ties dyslexia to brain flaw affecting vision and other senses. *The New York Times,* pp. A1, A30.

Blakeslee, S. (1994, August 16). New clue to cause of dyslexia seen in mishearing of fast sounds. *The New York Times,* pp. C1, C10.

Blakeslee, S. (1997, June 27). Brain studies tie marijuana to other drugs. *The New York Times,* p. A16.

Blakeslee, S. (1998, May 14). Two studies shed new light on cocaine's effect on brain. *The New York Times,* p. A20.

Blanchard, R. (1989). The classification and labeling of nonhomosexual gender dysphorias. *Archives of Sexual Behavior, 18,* 315–334.

Blanchard, R., & Hucker, S. J. (1991). Age, transvestism, bondage, and concurrent paraphilic activities in 117 fatal cases of autoerotic asphyxia. *British Journal of Psychiatry, 159,* 371–377.

Blanchette, K. (1996). *The relationships between criminal history, mental disorder, and recidivism among federally sentenced female offenders,* Unpublished master's thesis, Carleton University, Ottawa.

Bland, R. C. (1998). Psychiatry and the burden of mental illness. *Canadian Journal of Psychiatry, 43,* 801–810.

Bland, R. C., Newman, S. C., & Orn, H. (1988a). Period prevalence of psychiatric disorders in Edmonton. *Acta Psychiatrica Scandinavica, 77* (Suppl. 338), 24–32.

Bland, R. C., Orn, H., & Newman, S. C. (1988b). Lifetime prevalence of psychiatric disorders in Edmonton. *Acta Psychiatrica Scandinavica, 77* (Suppl. 338), 33–42.

Blankstein, K. R., & Segal, Z. V. (2001). Cognitive assessment: Issues and methods. In K. S. Dobson (Ed.), *Handbook of cognitive-behavioral therapies* (2nd ed., pp. 40–85). New York: Guilford.

Blier, P. (2006). Dual serotonin and noradrenaline reuptake inhibitors: Focus on their differences. *International Journal of Psychiatry in Clinical Practice, 10*(Suppl. 2), 22–32.

Blier, P., Habib, R., & Flament, M. F. (2006). Pharmacotherapies in the management of obsessive-compulsive disorder. *Canadian Journal of Psychiatry, 51,* 417–430.

Bloch, M., Rotenberg, N., Koren, D., & Ehud, K. (2006). Risk factors for early postpartum depressive symptoms. *General Hospital Psychiatry, 28,* 3–8.

Block, D. R., Kelly, M. M., & Carpenter, L. L. (2006). Generalized anxiety disorder: Diagnostic and treatment issues. *Directions in Psychiatry, 26,* 171–181.

Blood test can detect retardation. (1993, October 6). *The New York Daily News,* p. 10.

Bloom, B. L. (1992). Computer-assisted psychological intervention: A review and commentary. *Clinical Psychology Review, 12,* 169–197.

Bloom, H., Webster, C., Hucker, S., & De Freitas, K. (2005). The Canadian contribution to violence risk assessment: History and implications for current psychiatric practice. *Canadian Journal of Psychiatry, 50,* 3–11.

Boetsch, E. A., Green, P. A., & Pennington, B. F. (1996). Psychosocial correlates of dyslexia across the lifespan. *Development and Psychopathology, 8,* 539–562.

Bond, M. (2006). Psychodynamic psychotherapy in the treatment of mood disorders. *Current Opinion in Psychiatry, 19,* 40–43.

Bondi, M. W., & Lange, K. L. (2001). Alzheimer's disease. In H. S. Friedman (Ed.), *The disorders: Specialty articles from the Encyclopedia of mental health*. San Diego: Academic Press.

Bondolfi, G., Jermann, F., Van der Linden, M., Gex-Fabry, M., Bizzini, L., Rouget, B. W., ... Bertschy, G. (2010). Depression relapse prophylaxis with Mindfulness-Based Cognitive Therapy: Replication and extension in the Swiss health care system. *Journal of Affective Disorders, 122*, 224–231.

Boney-McCoy, S., & Finkelhor, D. (1996). Is youth victimization related to trauma symptoms and depression after controlling for prior symptoms and family relationships? A longitudinal, prospective study. *Journal of Consulting and Clinical Psychology, 64*, 1406–1416.

Bonnano, G. A. (2005). Resilience in the face of potential trauma. *Current Directions in Psychological Science, 14*, 135–138.

Boos, H. B., Aleman, A., Cahn, W., Hulshoff Pol, H., & Kahn, R. S. (2007). Brain volumes in relatives of patients with schizophrenia: A meta-analysis. *Archives of General Psychiatry, 64*, 297–304.

Bornstein, R. F. (1992). The dependent personality: Developmental, social, and clinical perspectives. *Psychological Bulletin, 112*, 3–23.

Bornstein, R. F. (1993). *The dependent personality*. New York: Guilford.

Bornstein, R. F. (1997). Dependent personality disorder in the DSM-IV and beyond. *Clinical Psychology: Science and Practice, 4*, 175–187.

Bornstein, R. F. (1999). Dependent and histrionic personality disorders. In T. Millon & P. H. Blaney (Eds.), *Oxford textbook of psychopathology* (pp. 535–554). New York: Oxford University Press.

Bornstein, M. R., Bellack, A. S., & Hersen, M. (1977). Social-skills training for unassertive children: A multiple-baseline analysis. *Journal of Applied Behavior Analysis, 10*, 183–195.

Borthwick-Duffy, S. A. (1994). Epidemiology and prevalence of psychopathology in individuals with mental retardation. *Journal of Consulting and Clinical Psychology, 62*, 17–27.

Bottonari, K. A., Roberts, J. E., Thomas, S. N., & Read, J. P. (2008). Stop thinking and start doing: Switching from cognitive therapy to behavioral activation in a case of chronic treatment-resistant depression. *Cognitive and Behavioral Practice, 15*, 376–386.

Bouchard, S., Paquin, B., Payeur, R., Allard, M., Rivard, V., Fournier, T., ... Lapierre, J. (2004). Delivering cognitive-behavior therapy for panic disorder with agoraphobia in videoconference. *Telemedicine Journal and E-Health, 10*(1), 13–25.

Bourgon, L. N., & Kellner, C. H. (2000). Relapse of depression after ECT: A review. *Journal of ECT, 16*, 19–31.

Bowers, T. G., & Clum, G. A. (1988). Relative contribution of specific and nonspecific treatment effects: Meta-analysis of placebo-controlled behavior therapy research. *Psychological Bulletin, 103*, 315–323.

Bowlby, J. (1988). *A secure base: Clinical applications of attachment theory*. New York: Basic Books.

Boyce, P., & Hickey, A. (2005). Psychosocial risk factors to major depression after childbirth. *Social Psychiatry and Psychiatric Epidemiology, 40*, 605–612.

Bradley, E. A., Thompson, A., & Bryson, S. E. (2002). Mental retardation in teenagers: Prevalence data from the Niagara Region, Ontario. *Canadian Journal of Psychiatry, 47*, 652–659.

Brandon, T. H., Vidrine, J. I., & Litvin, E. B. (2007). Relapse and relapse prevention. *Annual Review of Clinical Psychology, 3*, 258–284.

Braswell, L., & Kendall, P. C. (2001). Cognitive-behavioral therapy with children. In K. Dobson (Ed.), *Handbook of cognitive-behavioral therapies* (2nd ed., pp. 246–294). New York: Guilford.

Braun, J. M., Kahn, R. S., Froehlich, T., Auinger, P., & Lanphear, B. P. (2006). Exposures to environmental toxicants and attention deficit hyperactivity disorder in U.S. children. *Environmental Health Perspectives, 114*, 1904–1909.

Braxton, L. E., Calhoun, P. S., Williams, J. E., & Boggs, C. D. (2007). Validity rates of the Personality Assessment Inventory and the Minnesota Multiphasic Personality Inventory–2 in a VA medical center setting. *Journal of Personality Assessment, 88*(1), 5–15.

Breier, A. F., Malhotra, A. K., Su, T.-P., Pinals, D. A., Elman, I., Adler, C. M., ... Pickar, D. (1999). Clozapine and risperidone in chronic schizophrenia: Effects on symptoms, Parkinsonian side effects, and neuroendocrine response. *American Journal of Psychiatry, 156*, 294–298.

Brekke, J., Long, J. D., Nesbitt, N., & Sobel, E. (1997). The impact of service characteristics on functional outcomes from community support programs for persons with schizophrenia: A growth curve analysis. *Journal of Consulting and Clinical Psychology, 65*, 464–475.

Brems, C., & Johnson, M. E. (1997). Clinical implications of the co-occurrence of substance use and other psychiatric disorders. *Professional Psychology: Research and Practice, 28*, 437–447.

Brennand, K. J., Simone, A., Jou, J., Gelboin-Burkhart, C., Tran, N., Sangar, S., ... Gage, F. H. (2011). Modelling schizophrenia using human induced pluripotent stem cells. *Nature, 473*, 221–225.

Brent, D. A., & Mann, J. J. (2006). Familial pathways to suicidal behavior—Understanding and preventing suicide among adolescents. *New England Journal of Medicine, 355*, 2719–2721.

Breslau, N., Peterson, E. L., Schultz, L. R., Chilcoat, H. D., & Andreski, P. (1998). Major depression and stages of smoking: A longitudinal investigation. *Archives of General Psychiatry, 55*, 161–166.

Breslin, C., Li, S., Sdao-Jarvie, K., Tupker, E., & Ittig-Deland, V. (2002). Brief treatment for young substance abusers: A pilot study in an addiction treatment setting. *Psychology of Addictive Behaviors, 16*, 10–16.

Breslow, N. (1989). Sources of confusion in the study and treatment of sadomasochism. *Journal of Social Behavior and Personality, 4*, 263–274.

Brickman, J., & Briere, J. (1984). Incidence of rape and sexual assault in an urban Canadian population. *International Journal of Women's Studies, 7*, 195–206.

Brody, J. E. (1990, June 7). A search to bar retardation in a new generation. *The New York Times*, p. B9.

Brody, J. E. (1992a, June 16). Suicide myths cloud efforts to save children. *The New York Times*, pp. C1, C3.

Brody, J. E. (1992b, September 30). Myriad masks hide an epidemic of depression. *The New York Times*, p. C12.

Brody, J. E. (1993, December 15). Living with a common genetic abnormality. *The New York Times*, p. C17.

Brody, J. E. (1994, December 28). Wine for the heart: Overall, risks may outweigh benefits. *The New York Times*, p. C10.

Brody, J. E. (1995, August 2). With more help available for impotence, few men seek it. *The New York Times*, p. C9.

Brown, R. A., Evans, D. M., Miller, I. W., Burgess, E. S., & Mueller, T. I. (1997). Cognitive-behavioral treatment for depression in alcoholism. *Journal of Consulting and Clinical Psychology, 65*, 715–726.

Brown, R. J. (2004). Psychological mechanisms of medically unexplained symptoms: An integrative conceptual model. *Psychological Bulletin, 130*, 793–812.

Brown, S. L., & Forth, A. E. (1997). Psychopathy and sexual assault: Static risk factors, emotional precursors, and rapist subtypes. *Journal of Consulting and Clinical Psychology, 65*, 848–857.

Brown, T. A., Di Nardo, P. A., Lehman, C. L., & Campbell, L. A. (2001). Reliability of DSM-IV anxiety and mood disorders: Implications for the classification of emotional disorders. *Journal of Abnormal Psychology, 110*(1), 49–58.

Brownell, K. D., & Wadden, T. A. (1992). Etiology and treatment of obesity: Understanding a serious, prevalent, and refractory disorder. *Journal of Consulting and Clinical Psychology, 60*, 505–517.

Buhr, K., & Dugas, M. J. (2006). Investigating the construct validity of intolerance of uncertainty and its unique relationship with worry. *Journal of Anxiety Disorders, 20*, 222–236.

Burke, R. S., & Stephens, R. S. (1999). Social anxiety and drinking in college students: A social cognitive theory analysis. *Clinical Psychology Review, 19*, 513–530.

Burns, D. D. (1980). *Feeling good: The new mood therapy*. New York: Morris.

Burns, D. D., & Beck, A. T. (1978). Modification of mood disorders. In J. P. Foreyt & D. P. Rathjen (Eds.), *Cognitive behavior therapy: Research and application* (pp. 109–134). New York: Plenum Press.

Busatto, G. F., Pilowsky, L. S., Costa, D. C., Ell, P. J., David, A. S., Lucey, J. V., & Kerwin, R.W. (1997). Correlation between reduced in vivo benzodiazepine receptor binding and severity of psychotic symptoms in schizophrenia. *American Journal of Psychiatry, 154,* 56–63.

Bush, G., Valera, E. M., & Seidman, L. J. (2005). Functional neuroimaging of attention-deficit/hyperactvity disorder: A review and suggested future directions. *Biological Psychiatry, 57,* 1273–1284.

Butzlaff, R. L., & Hooley, J. M. (1998). Expressed emotion and psychiatric relapse: A meta-analysis. *Archives of General Psychiatry, 55,* 547–552.

C

Caffier, P. P., Berl, J. C., Muggli, A., Reinhardt, A., Jakob, A., Möser, M., Fietze, I., . . . Hölzl, M. (2007). Snoring noise pollution—the need for objective quantification of annoyance, regulatory guidelines and mandatory therapy for snoring. *Physiological Measurement, 28,* 25–40.

Cale, E. M., & Lilienfeld, S. O. (2002). Sex differences in psychopathology and antisocial personality disorder: A review and integration. *Clinical Psychology Review, 22,* 1179–1207.

Calhoun, K. S., & Atkeson, B. M. (1991). *Treatment of rape victims: Facilitating psychosocial adjustment.* New York: Pergamon.

Callinan, P. A., & Feinberg, A. P. (2006). The emerging science of epigenomics. *Human Molecular Genetics, 15*(Suppl. 1), R95–R101.

Camara, W. J., Nathan, J. S., & Puente, A. E. (2000). Psychological test usage: Implications in professional psychology. *Professional Psychology: Research and Practice, 31*(2), 141–154.

Canadian Alliance on Mental Illness and Mental Health. (2000). *A call for action: Building consensus for a national action plan on mental illness and mental health: A discussion paper.* Ottawa: Author.

Canadian Centre for Justice Statistics. (1999). Crime statistics in Canada. *Juristat, 20*(5).

Canadian Centre for Justice Statistics. (2003). *Special study on mentally disordered accused in the criminal justice system* (Catalogue No. 85-559-XIE). Ottawa: Statistics Canada.

Canadian Centre on Substance Abuse & Centre for Addiction and Mental Health. (1999). *Canadian profile: Alcohol, tobacco and other drugs.* Ottawa: Author.

Canadian Health Network. (1999). *Is mental illness related to poverty?* Retrieved April 20, 2003, from http://www.canadian-health-network.ca/faq-faq/mental_health-sante_mentale/7e.html

Canadian Institute for Health Information. (2001). *The Canadian enhancement of ICD-10 (international statistical classification of diseases and related health problems, tenth revision): Final report.* Ottawa: Author.

Canadian Lung Association. (2006). Sleep apnea. Ottawa: Author. Retrieved May 4, 2007, from http://www.lung.ca/diseases-maladies/apnea-apnee_e.php

Canadian Mental Health Association. (2000). Early psychosis intervention. Retrieved October 15, 2011, from http://www.cmha.ca/bins/content_page.asp?cid=3-105-107

Canadian Mental Health Association. (2003). *Eating disorders.* Retrieved July 31, 2003, from http://www.cmha.ca/english/info_centre/mh_pamphlets/mh_pamphlet_ed.pdf

Canadian Psychological Association. (2000). *Canadian code of ethics for psychologists* (3rd ed.). Ottawa: Author.

Canadian Psychological Association. (2002). *The clinical psychologist in Canada: How can we help?* Retrieved October 2, 2011, from http://www.cpa.ca/cpasite/userfiles/Documents/sections/clinical/brochureE.pdf

Canadian Sleep Society (n.d.). Sleep centres in Canada. Retrieved November 10, 2011, from http://www.canadiansleepsociety.com/centers.html

Canli, T., Qiu, M., Omura, K., Congdon, E., Haas, B. W., Amin, Z., . . . Lesch, K. P. (2006). Neural correlates of epigenesis. *Proceedings of the National Academy of Sciences of the United States of America, 103,* 16033–16038.

Capps, L., Kasari, C., Yirmiya, N., & Sigman, M. (1993). Parental perception of emotional expressiveness in children with autism. *Journal of Consulting and Clinical Psychology, 61,* 475–484.

Carey, G. (1992). Twin imitation for antisocial behavior: Implications for genetic and family environment research. *Journal of Abnormal Psychology, 101,* 18–25.

Carey, M. P., Wincze, J. P., & Meisler, A. W. (1998). Sexual dysfunction: Male erectile disorder. In D. H. Barlow (Ed.), *Clinical handbook for psychological disorders: A step-by-step treatment manual* (pp. 442–480). New York: Guilford.

Carney, C. E., & Manber, R. (2009). *Quiet your mind and get to sleep: Solutions to insomnia for those with depression, znxiety, or chronic pain.* Oakland, CA: New Harbinger.

Carney, C. E., & Segal, Z. V. (2005). Mindfulness-Based Cognitive Therapy for depression. In L. VandeCreek (Ed.), *Innovations in clinical practice: Focus on adults* (pp. 5–17). Sarasota, FL: Professional Resource Press.

Carr, J. L., & VanDeusen, K. M. (2004). Risk factors for male sexual aggression on college campuses. *Journal of Family Violence, 19,* 279–289.

Carter, J. C., & Fairburn, C. G. (1998). Cognitive-behavioral self-help for binge eating disorder: A controlled effectiveness study. *Journal of Consulting and Clinical Psychology, 66,* 616–623.

Carter, J. C., Olmsted, M. P., Kaplan, A. S., McCabe, R. E., Mills, J. S., & Aimé, A. (2003). Self-help for bulimia nervosa: A randomized control trial. *American Journal of Psychiatry, 160,* 973–978.

Casanova, M. R. (1997). Functional and anatomical aspects of prefrontal pathology in schizophrenia. *Schizophrenia Bulletin, 23,* 517–519.

Caspi, A., & Moffitt, T. E. (2006). Gene-environment interactions in psychiatry: Joining forces with neuroscience. *Nature Reviews: Neuroscience, 7,* 583–590.

Caspi, A., Sugden, K., Moffitt, T. E., Taylor, A., Craig, I. W., Harrington, H., . . . Poulton, R. (2003). Influence of life stress on depression: Moderation by a polymorphism in the 5-HTT gene. *Science, 301,* 386–389.

Castellanos, F. X., Glaser, P. E., & Gerhardt, G. A. (2006). Towards a neuroscience of attention-deficit/hyperactivity disorder: Fractionating the phenotype. *Journal of Neuroscience Methods, 151*(1), 1–4.

Castelnuovo, G., Gaggioli, A., Mantovani, F., & Riva, G. (2003). New and old tools in psychotherapy: The use of technology for the integration of traditional clinical treatments. *Psychotherapy: Theory, Research, Practice, Training, 40*(1/2), 33–44.

Celis, W. (1991, January 2). Students trying to draw line between sex and an assault. *The New York Times,* pp. 1, B8.

Centre for Addictions Research, BC. (2006). *Responding to your teen's alcohol use.* Victoria, BC: Author.

Chan, M., Nicklason, F., & Vial, J. H. (2001). Adverse drug events as a cause of hospital admission in the elderly. *Internal Medicine Journal, 31,* 199–205.

Chandrashekar, C. R., & Math, S. B. (2006). Psychosomatic disorders in developing countries: Current issues and future challenges. *Current Opinion in Psychiatry, 19,* 201–206.

Chang, L., & Haning, W. (2006). Insights from recent positron emission tomographic studies of drug abuse and dependence. *Current Opinion in Psychiatry, 19,* 246–252.

Chang, S. C. (1984). [Review of the book *Taijin-kyofu,* by I. Yamashita]. *Transcultural Psychiatric Research Review, 21,* 283–288.

Charney, D. S., Nemeroff, C. B., Lewis, L., Laden, S. K., Gorman, J. M., Laska, E. M., . . . Solomon, S. (2002). National depressive and manic-depressive association consensus statement on the use of placebo in clinical trials of mood disorders. *Archives of General Psychiatry, 59,* 262–270.

Cheng, S. T. (1996). A critical review of Chinese Koro. *Culture, Medicine and Psychiatry, 20,* 67–82.

Children with autism benefit from early, intensive therapy. (2011, September 28). *ScienceDaily.* Retrieved from October 30, 2011, http://www.sciencedaily.com/releases/2011/09/110928125418.htm

Chipperfield, B., & Vogel-Sprott, M. (1988). Family history of problem drinking among young male social drinkers: Modeling effects on alcohol consumption. *Journal of Abnormal Psychology, 97,* 423–428.

Chodirker, B. N., Cadrin, C., Davies, G. A. L., Summers, A. M., Wilson, R. D., Winsor, E. J. T., & Young, D. (2001). Canadian guidelines for prenatal diagnosis: Genetic indications for prenatal diagnosis. *JOGC: Journal of Obstetrics and Gynaecology Canada, 105*(6), 1–7.

Chou, C., Condron, L., & Belland, J. C. (2005). A review of the research on Internet addiction. *Educational Psychology Review, 17,* 363–388.

Chow, E. W. C., Watson, M., Young, D. A., & Bassett, A. S. (2006). Neurocognitive profile in 22q11 deletion syndrome and schizophrenia. *Schizophrenia Research, 87,* 270–278.

Chowdhury, A. N. (1996). The definition and classification of Koro. *Culture, Medicine and Psychiatry, 20,* 41–65.

Christiansen, B. A., & Goldman, M. S. (1983). Alcohol-related expectancies versus demographic/background variables in the prediction of adolescent drinking. *Journal of Consulting and Clinical Psychology, 52,* 249–257.

Chu, J. A., Frey, L. M., Ganzel, B. L., & Matthews, J. A. (1999). Memories of childhood abuse: Dissociation, amnesia, and corroboration. *American Journal of Psychiatry, 156,* 749–755.

Chung, S. A., Jairam, S., Hussain, M. R., & Shapiro, C. M. (2002). How, what, and why of sleep apnea. Perspectives for primary care physicians. *Canadian Family Physician, 48,* 1073–1080.

Ciccarelli, S. K., Harrigan, T. R., & Fritzley, V. H. (2010). *Psychology,* Canadian ed., Toronto: Pearson Education Canada.

Clark, D. A. (2004). *Cognitive-behavioral therapy for OCD.* New York: Guilford.

Clark, D. A. & Beck, A. T. (with Alford, B. A.). (1999). *Scientific foundations of cognitive theory and therapy of depression.* New York: Wiley.

Clark, D. M. (1986). A cognitive approach to panic. *Behaviour Research and Therapy, 24*(4), 461–470.

Cleckley, H. (1941). *The mask of sanity: An attempt to reinterpret the so-called psychopathic personality.* St. Louis, MO: Mosby.

Cleckley, H. (1976). *The mask of sanity: An attempt to clarify some issues about the so-called psychopathic personality* (5th ed.). St. Louis, MO: Mosby.

Cleghorn, J. M., Franco, S., Szechtman, B., Kaplan, R. D., Szechtman, H., Brown, . . . Garnett, E. S. (1992). Toward a brain map of auditory hallucinations. *American Journal of Psychiatry, 149,* 1062–1069.

Clinical practice guidelines: Treatment of schizophrenia [Special issue]. (2005). *Canadian Journal of Psychiatry, 50*(Suppl. 1).

Cloos, J.-M. (2005). The treatment of panic disorder. *Current Opinion in Psychiatry, 18,* 45–50.

Cockerham, W. C., Kunz, G., & Lueschen, G. (1989). Alcohol use and psychological distress: A comparison of Americans and West Germans. *International Journal of the Addictions, 24,* 951–961.

Cohen, F. L., Ferrans, C. E., & Eshler, B. (1992). Reported accidents in narcolepsy. *Loss, Grief and Care, 5*(3/4), 71–80.

Colapinto, J. (2000). *As nature made him: The boy who was raised as a girl.* New York: HarperCollins.

Cole, T. B. (2006). Rape at US colleges often fueled by alcohol. *JAMA: Journal of the American Medical Association, 296,* 504–505.

Collerton, D., Perry, E., & McKeith, I. (2005). Why people see things that are not there: A novel Perception and Attention Deficit model for recurrent complex visual hallucinations. *Behavioral and Brain Sciences, 28,* 737–794.

Committee on Sexual Offences Against Children and Youths (Canada). (1984). *Sexual offences against children: Report of the Committee on Sexual Offences Against Children and Youths.* Ottawa: Ministry of Supply and Services Canada.

Compas, B. E., Haaga, D. A., Keefe, F. J., Leitenberg, H., & Williams, D. A. (1998). Sampling of empirically supported psychological treatments from health psychology: Smoking, chronic pain, cancer, and bulimia nervosa. *Journal of Consulting and Clinical Psychology, 66,* 89–112.

Conley, R. R., & Buchanan, R. W. (1997). Evaluation of treatment-resistant schizophrenia. *Schizophrenia Bulletin, 23,* 663–674.

Coolidge, F. L., & Segal, D. L. (1998). Evolution of personality disorder diagnosis in the Diagnostic and Statistical Manual of Mental Disorders. *Clinical Psychology Review, 18,* 585–599.

Cooney, N. L., Litt, M. D., Morse, P. A., Bauer, L. O., & Gaupp, L. (1997). Alcohol cue reactivity, negative-mood reactivity, and relapse in treated alcoholic men. *Journal of Abnormal Psychology, 106,* 243–250.

Coons, P. M. (1986). Treatment progress in 20 patients with multiple personality disorder. *Journal of Nervous and Mental Disease, 174,* 715–721.

Corbitt, E. M., & Widiger, T. A. (1995). Sex differences among the personality disorders: An exploration of the data. *Clinical Psychology: Science and Practice, 2,* 225–238.

Cordes, C. (1985). Common threads found in suicide. *APA Monitor, 16*(10), 11.

Cornblatt, B. A., & Keilp, J. G. (1994). Impaired attention, genetics, and the pathophysiology of schizophrenia. *Schizophrenia Bulletin, 20,* 31–46.

Cornelius, J. R., Salloum, I. M., Ehler, J. G., Jarrett, P. J., Cornelius, M. D., Perel, J. M., . . . Black, A. (1997). Fluoxetine in depressed alcoholics: A double-blind, placebo-controlled trial. *Archives of General Psychiatry, 54,* 700–705.

Corr, P. J. (2004). Reinforcement sensitivity theory and personality. *Neuroscience and Biobehavioral Reviews, 28,* 317–332.

Corr, P. J., & Perkins, A. M. (2006). The role of theory in the psychophysiology of personality: From Ivan Pavlov to Jeffrey Gray. *International Journal of Psychophysiology, 62,* 367–376.

Correctional Services Canada. (2002a). *A mental health profile of federally sentenced offenders.* Ottawa: Author. Retrieved July 16, 2003, from http://www.csc-scc.gc.ca/text/pblct/forum/e02/e021d_e.shtml

Correctional Services Canada. (2002b). *Recidivism.* Ottawa: Author. Retrieved July 16, 2003, from http://www.csc-scc.gc.ca/text/pblct/forum/e052/e052h_e.shtml

Correctional Services Canada. (2009). Correctional programs: Sexual offender programs. Retrieved October 18, 2011, from http://www.csc-scc.gc.ca/text/prgrm/sexoff-eng.shtml

Cossette, L., & Duclos, E. (2002). *A profile of disability in Canada, 2001* (Catalogue No. 89-577-XIE). Ottawa: Statistics Canada. Retrieved August 13, 2007, from http://www.statcan.gc.ca/english/freepub/89-577-XIE/pdf/89-577-XIE01001.pdf

Costello, E. J., Erkanli, A., & Angold, A. (2006). Is there an epidemic of child or adolescent depression? *Journal of Child Psychology and Psychiatry, 47,* 1263–1271.

Cottraux, J. (2005). Recent developments in research and treatment for social phobia (social anxiety disorder). *Current Opinion in Psychiatry, 18,* 51–54.

Coursey, R. D., Alford, J., & Safarjan, B. (1997). Significant advances in understanding and treating serious mental illness. *Professional Psychology: Research and Practice, 28,* 205–216.

Cox, B. J., & Taylor, S. (1999). Anxiety disorders: Panic and phobias. In T. Millon & P. Blaney (Eds.), *Oxford textbook of psychopathology* (pp. 81–113). Oxford: Oxford University Press.

Cox, W. M., & Klinger, E. (1988). A motivational model of alcohol use. *Journal of Abnormal Psychology, 97,* 168–180.

Coyne, J. C. (1999). Thinking interactionally about depression: A radical restatement. In T. Joiner & J. C. Coyne (Eds.), *The interactional nature of depression: Advances in interpersonal approaches* (pp. 365–392). Washington, DC: American Psychological Association.

Craighead, W. E., Craighead, L. W., & Ilardi, S. S. (1998). Psychosocial treatments for major depressive disorder. In P. E. Nathan & J. M. Gorman (Eds.), *A guide to treatments that work* (pp. 226–239). New York: Oxford University Press.

Craske, M. G., & Waters, A. M. (2005). Panic disorder, phobias, and generalized anxiety disorder. *Annual Review of Clinical Psychology, 1,* 197–225.

Crisp, A. H., Callender, J. S., Halek, C., & Hsu, L. K. (1992). Long-term mortality in anorexia nervosa: A 20-year follow-up of the St George's and Aberdeen cohorts. *British Journal of Psychiatry, 161*(1), 104–107.

Cross-National Collaborative Group. (1992). The changing rate of major depression: Cross-national comparisons. *JAMA: Journal of the American Medical Association, 268,* 3098–3105.

Crow, T. J. (1980a). Molecular pathology of schizophrenia: More than one disease process? *British Medical Journal, 280,* 66–68.

Crow, T. J. (1980b). Positive and negative schizophrenic symptoms and the role of dopamine: A debate. *British Journal of Psychiatry, 137,* 379–383.

Crozier, W. R., & Alden, L. E. (Eds.). (2001). *International handbook of social anxiety: Concepts, research, and interventions relating to the self and shyness.* New York: Wiley.

Cummings, J. L. (2004). Alzheimer's disease. *New England Journal of Medicine, 351,* 56–67.

Cunningham C. E., & Boyle, M. H. (2002). Preschoolers at risk for attention-deficit hyperactivity disorder and oppositional defiant disorder: Family, parenting, and behavioral correlates. *Journal of Abnormal Child Psychology, 30,* 555–569.

Currie, S. R., Patten, S. B., Williams, J. V. A., Wang, J., Beck, C. A., el-Guebaly, N., & Maxwell, C. (2005). Comorbidity of major depression with substance use disorders. *Canadian Journal of Psychiatry, 50,* 660–666.

Curry, S., Marlatt, G. A., & Gordon, J. R. (1987). Abstinence violation effect: Validation of an attributional construct with smoking cessation. *Journal of Consulting and Clinical Psychology, 55,* 145–149.

D

Dadds, M. R., Sanders, M. R., Morrison, M., & Rebgetz, M. (1992). Childhood depression and conduct disorder: II. An analysis of family interaction patterns in the home. *Journal of Abnormal Psychology, 101,* 505–513.

Dahl, R. E. (1992). The pharmacologic treatment of sleep disorders. *Psychiatric Clinics of North America, 15,* 161–178.

Dallaire says PTSD seared genocide in his memory. (2007, October 3). CBC News. Retrieved September 15, 2011, from http://www.cbc.ca/news/canada/montreal/story/2007/10/03/qc-dallaire1003.html

Damasio, A. R. (1997). Neuropsychology: Towards a neuropathology of emotion and mood. *Nature, 386,* 769–770.

Davidson, P. R., & Parker, K. C. H. (2001). Eye movement desensitization and reprocessing (EMDR): A meta-analysis. *Journal of Consulting and Clinical Psychology, 69,* 305–316.

Davis, J. O., & Bracha, H. S. (1996). Prenatal growth markers in schizophrenia: A monozygotic co-twin control study. *American Journal of Psychiatry, 153,* 1166–1172.

Davis, R., Olmsted, M., Rockert, W., Marques, T., & Dolhanty, J. (1997). Group psychoeducation for bulimia nervosa with and without additional psychotherapy process sessions. *International Journal of Eating Disorders, 22*(1), 25–34.

Davis, S. (1993). Changes to the Criminal Code provisions for mentally disordered offenders and their implications for Canadian psychiatry. *Canadian Journal of Psychiatry, 38,* 122–126.

de Bruin, N. M., van Luijtelaar, E. L., Cools, A. R., & Ellenbroek, B. A. (2003). Filtering disturbances in schizophrenic patients: Gating of auditory evoked potentials and prepulse inhibition of the acoustic startle response compared. Emphasis on the role of dopamine. *Current Neuropharmacology, 1,* 47–87.

Deckel, A. W., Hesselbrock, V., & Bauer, L. (1996). Antisocial personality disorder, childhood delinquency, and frontal brain functioning: EEG and neuropsychological findings. *Journal of Clinical Psychology, 52,* 639–650.

DeKeseredy, W. S. (1997). Measuring sexual abuse in Canadian university/college dating relationships: The contributions of a national representative sample survey. In M. D. Schwartz (Ed.), *Researching sexual violence against women* (pp. 43–53). Thousand Oaks, CA: Sage.

Dekker, J. (1993). Inhibited male orgasm. In W. O'Donohue & J. H. Geer (Eds.), *Handbook of sexual dysfunctions: Assessment and treatment* (pp. 279–301). Boston: Allyn & Bacon.

DeLisi, L. E., & Fleischhaker, W. (2007). Schizophrenia research in the era of the genome, 2007. *Current Opinion in Psychiatry, 20,* 109–110.

Dell'Osso, B., Nestadt, G., Allen, A., & Hollander, E. (2006). Serotoin-norepinephrine reuptake inhibitors in the treatment of obsessive-compulsive disorder: A critical review. *Journal of Clinical Psychiatry, 67,* 600–610.

Denov, M. S. (2001). A culture of denial: Exploring professional perspectives on female sex offending. *Canadian Journal of Criminology, 43,* 303–329.

Denys, D., Van Nieuwerburgh, F., Deforce, D., & Westenberg, H. G. M. (2006). Association between serotonergic candidate genes and specific phenotypes of obsessive compulsive disorder. *Journal of Affective Disorders, 91,* 39–44.

Depression Guideline Panel. (1993). *Depression in primary care: Vol. 2. Treatment of major depression.* Clinical Practice Guideline 5. AHCPR publication No. 93-0551. Rockville, MD: US Department of Health and Human Services, Public Health Service, Agency for Health Care Policy and Research.

Desmond, E. W. (1987, November). Out in the open: Changing attitudes and new research give fresh hope to alcoholics. *Time,* pp. 80–90.

Detera-Wadleigh, S. D., & McMahon, F. J. (2006). G72/G30 in schizophrenia and bipolar disorder: Review and meta-analysis. *Biological Psychiatry, 60,* 106–114.

Devanand, D. P., Dwork, A. J., Hutchinson, E. R., Bolwig, T. G., & Sackeim, H. A. (1994). Does ECT alter brain structure? *American Journal of Psychiatry, 151,* 957–970.

Diamond, S., Balvin, R., & Diamond, F. R. (1963). *Inhibition and choice: A neurobehavioral approach to problems of plasticity in behavior.* New York: Harper & Row.

Dickens, B. M., Doob, A. N., Warwick, O. H., & Winegard, W. C. (1982). *Report of the Committee of Enquiry into Allegations Concerning Drs. Linda and Mark Sobell.* Toronto: Addiction Research Foundation.

DiLalla, D. L., Carey, G., Gottesman, I. I., & Bouchard, T. J., Jr. (1996). Heritability of MMPI personality indicators of psychopathology in twins reared apart. *Journal of Abnormal Psychology, 105,* 491–499.

DiLalla, L. F., & Gottesman, I. I. (1991). Biological and genetic contributors to violence: Widom's untold tale. *Psychological Bulletin, 109,* 125–129.

Dilk, M. N., & Bond, G. R. (1996). Meta-analytic evaluation of skills training research for individuals with severe mental illness. *Journal of Consulting and Clinical Psychology, 64,* 1337–1346.

Dimidjian, S., Hollon, S. D., Dobson, K. S., Schmaling, K. B., Kohlenberg, R. J., Addis, M. E.,... Jacobson, N. S. (2006). Randomized trial of behavioral activation, cognitive therapy, and antidepressant medication in the acute treatment of adults with major depression. *Journal of Consulting and Clinical Psychology, 74,* 658–670.

Dingle, G., Samtani, P., Kraatz, J., & Solomon, R. (2002). *The real facts on alcohol use, injuries and deaths.* Mississauga, ON: MADD.

Dinh, K. T., Sarason, I. G., Peterson, A. V., & Onstad, L. E. (1995). Children's perceptions of smokers and nonsmokers: A longitudinal study. *Health Psychology, 14,* 32–40.

Dix, D. L. (1999). *Asylum, prison, and poorhouse: The writings and reform of Dorothea Dix in Illinois.* (D. L. Lightner, Ed.). Carbondale: Southern Illinois University Press.

Dobson, D. J. G., McDougall, G., Busheikin, J., & Aldous, J. (1995). Effects of social skills training and social milieu treatment on symptoms of schizophrenia. *Psychiatric Services, 46,* 376–380.

Dobson, K. S., & Dozois, D. J. A. (2001). Historical and philosophic bases of the cognitive-behavioral therapies. In K. S. Dobson (Ed.), *Handbook of cognitive-behavioral therapies* (2nd ed., pp. 3–39). New York: Guilford.

Dobson, K. S., & Khatri, N. (2002). Major depressive disorder. In M. Hersen (Ed.), *Clinical behavior therapy: Adults and children* (pp. 37–51). New York: Wiley.

Dodge, K. A., Laird, R., Lochman, J. E., & Zelli, A. (2002). Multidimensional latent-construct analysis of children's social information processing patterns: Correlations with aggressive behavior problems. *Psychological Assessment, 14*(1), 60–73.

Dodge, K. A., Lochman, J. E., Hamish, J. D., Bates, J. E., & Pettit, G. S. (1997). Reactive and proactive aggression in school children and psychiatrically impaired chronically assaultive youth. *Journal of Abnormal Psychology, 106,* 37–51.

Dohrenwend, B. P., Turner, J. B., Turse, N. A., Adams, B. G., Koenen, K. C., & Marshall, R. (2006). The psychological risks of Vietnam for U.S. veterans: A revisit with new data and methods. *Science, 313,* 979–982.

Doll, B. (1996). Prevalence of psychiatric disorders in children and youth: An agenda for advocacy by school psychology. *School Psychology Quarterly, 11,* 20–46.

Dozois, D., & Firestone, P. (2010). *Abnormal psychology: Perspectives* (4th ed.). Toronto: Pearson.

Drevets, W. C., Price, J. L., Simpson, J. R., Todd, R. D., Reich, T., Vannier, M., & Raichle, M. E. (1997). Subgenual prefrontal cortex abnormalities in mood disorders. *Nature, 386,* 824–827.

Drewnowski, A., Yee, D. K., Kurth, C. L., & Krahn, D. D. (1994). Eating pathology and DSM-III-R bulimia nervosa: A continuum of behavior. *American Journal of Psychiatry, 151,* 1217–1219.

Drews, C. D., Yeargin-Allsopp, M., Decouflé, P., & Murphy, C. C. (1995). Variation in the influence of selected sociodemographic risk factors for mental retardation. *American Journal of Public Health, 85,* 329–334.

Drummond, D. C., & Glautier, S. (1994). A controlled trial of cue exposure treatment in alcohol dependence. *Journal of Consulting and Clinical Psychology, 62,* 809–817.

Dryden, J., Johnson, B. R., Howard, S., & McGuire, A. (1998, April 13–17). *Resiliency: A comparison arising from conversations with 9–12-year-old children and their teachers.* Paper presented at the Annual Meeting of the American Educational Research Association, San Diego.

Dryden, W. (1984). *Rational-emotive therapy: Fundamentals and innovations.* London: Croom Helm.

Dulit, R. A., Fyer, M. R., Leon, A. C., Brodsky, B. S., & Frances, A. J. (1994). Clinical correlates of self-mutilation in borderline personality disorder. *American Journal of Psychiatry, 151,* 1305–1311.

Dunner, D. L. (2005). Dysthymia and double depression. *International Review of Psychiatry, 17,* 3–8.

Durkheim, E. (1958). *Suicide: A study in sociology* (J. A. Spaulding & G. Simpson, Trans.). New York: Free Press.

Dwork, A. J. (1997). Postmortem studies of the hippocampal formation in schizophrenia. *Schizophrenia Bulletin, 23,* 385–402.

Dykens, E. M., & Hodapp, R. M. (1997). Treatment issues in genetic mental retardation syndromes. *Professional Psychology: Research and Practice, 28,* 263–270.

Dzokoto, V. A., & Adams, G. (2005). Understanding genital-shrinking epidemics in West Africa: Koro, Juju, or mass psychogenic illness? *Culture, Medicine and Psychiatry, 29,* 53–78.

E

Earnst, K. S., & Kring, A. M. (1997). Construct validity of negative symptoms: An empirical and conceptual review. *Clinical Psychology Review, 17,* 167–189.

Eberhardy, F. (1967). The view from "the couch." *Journal of Child Psychology and Psychiatry, 8*(3–4), 257–263.

Ebstein, R. H., Benjamin, J., & Belmaker, R. H. (2003). Behavioral genetics, genomics, and personality. In R. Plomin, J. C. DeFries, I. W. Craig, & P. McGuffin (Eds.), *Behavioral genetics in the postgenomic era.* Washington, DC: American Psychological Association.

Edwards, H. P. (2000, January 4). Regulatory requirements for registration in psychology across Canada: A comparison of acts, regulations, by-laws and guidelines in view of the AIT. Ottawa. Retrieved August 15, 2011, from http://www.cpa.ca/documents/PSWAIT%20Report.pdf

Edwards, V. (2002). *Depression and bipolar disorders: Everything you need to know.* Toronto: Key Porter.

Eisler, I., Dare, C., Russell, G. F., Szmukler, G., le Grange, D., & Dodge, E. (1997). Family and individual therapy in anorexia nervosa: A 5-year follow-up. *Archives of General Psychiatry, 54,* 1025–1030.

Elkin, I. (2010). Depression severity and effect of antidepressant medications. *JAMA: Journal of the American Medical Association, 303,* 1596.

Ellason, J. W., & Ross, C. A. (1997). Two-year follow-up of inpatients with dissociative identity disorder. *American Journal of Psychiatry, 154,* 832–839.

Ellerby, J. H., McKenzie, J., McKay, S., Gariépy, G. J., & Kaufert, J. M. (2000). Bioethics for clinicians: 18. Aboriginal culture. *Canadian Medical Association Journal, 163,* 845–850.

Elliot, R., Watson, J. C., Goldman, R. N., & Greenberg, L. S. (2004). *Learning emotion-focused therapy: The process-experiential approach to change.* Washington, DC: American Psychological Association.

Ellis, A. (1977). *How to live with—and without—anger.* New York: Reader's Digest.

Ellis, A. (1993). Reflections on rational-emotive therapy. *Journal of Consulting and Clinical Psychology, 61,* 199–201.

Ellis, A. (2003). Early theories and practices of rational emotive behavior theory and how they have been augmented and revised during the last three decades. *Journal of Rational-Emotive & Cognitive-Behavior Therapy, 21*(3/4), 219–243.

Ellis, A., & Dryden, W. (1987). *The practice of rational emotional therapy (RET).* New York: Springer.

Ellis, A., Young, J., & Lockwood, G. (1987). Cognitive therapy and rational-emotive therapy: A dialogue. *Journal of Cognitive Psychotherapy, 1,* 205–255.

Emslie, G. J., Rush, A. J., Weinberg, W. A., Kowatch, R. A., Hughes, C. W., Carmody, T., & Rintelmann, J. (1997). A double-blind, randomized, placebo-controlled trial of fluoxetine in children and adolescents with depression. *Archives of General Psychiatry, 54,* 1031–1037.

Engelsmann, F. F. (2000). Transcultural psychiatry: Goals and challenges. *Canadian Journal of Psychiatry, 45,* 429–430.

English, S. (2002, October 29). Psycho at the top? *The Age.* Retrieved from http://www.theage.com.au/articles/2002/10/28/1035683360087.html

Eranti, S., Mogg, A., Pluck, G., Landau, S., Purvis, R., Brown, R. G., . . . McLoughlin, D. M. (2007). A randomized, controlled trial with 6-month follow-up of repetitive transcranial magnetic stimulation and electroconvulsive therapy for severe depression. *American Journal of Psychiatry, 164,* 73–81.

Erlenmeyer-Kimling, L., Adamo, U. H., Rock, D., Roberts, S. A., Bassett, A. J., Squires-Wheeler, E., . . . Gottesman, I. I. (1997). The New York High-Risk Project: Prevalence and comorbidity of Axis I disorders in offspring of schizophrenic parents at 25-year follow-up. *Archives of General Psychiatry, 54,* 1096–1102.

Everett, B. (2002, December 5). Mental health reform. *Canadian Mental Health Association.* Retrieved February 6, 2003, from http://www.ontario.cmha.ca/content/policy_and_action/everett_20021205.asp

Everett, B. (2006). *Stigma: The hidden killer: Background paper and literature review.* Mood Disorders Society of Canada. Retrieved from http://www.mooddisorderscanada.ca/documents/Publications/Stigma%20the%20hidden%20killer.pdf

Exner, J. E. (1991). *The Rorschach: A comprehensive system: Vol. 2. Interpretation* (2nd ed.). New York: Wiley.

Exner, J. E. (1993). *The Rorschach: A comprehensive system: Vol. 1. Basic foundations* (3rd ed.). New York: Wiley.

Extinguishing Alzheimer's. (1998, June 23). *The New York Times,* p. F7.

Eysenck, H. J., & Eysenck, M. W. (1985). *Personality and individual differences: A natural science approach.* New York: Plenum.

F

Facebook users more prone to developing eating disorders, study finds. (2011, February 7). *ScienceDaily.* Retrieved November 10, 2011, from http://www.sciencedaily.com/releases/2011/02/110207091754.htm

Fairburn, C. G. (1997). Eating disorders. In D. M. Clark & C. G. Fairburn (Eds.), *Science and the practice of cognitive behaviour therapy* (pp. 209–241), New York: Oxford University Press.

Fairburn, C. G., Cooper, Z., & Cooper, P. J. (1986). The clinical features and maintenance of bulimia nervosa. In K. D. Brownell & J. P. Foreyt (Eds.), *Handbook of eating disorders: Physiology, psychology, and treatment of obesity, anorexia, and bulimia* (pp. 389–404). New York: Basic Books.

Fairburn, C. G., Cooper, Z., Doll, H. A., & Davies, B. A. (2005). Identifying dieters who will develop an eating disorder: A prospective, population-based study. *The American Journal of Psychiatry, 162*(12), 2249–2255.

Fairburn, C. G., Welch, S. L., Doll, H. A., Davies, B. A., & O'Connor, M. E. (1997). Risk factors for bulimia nervosa: A community-based case-control study. *Archives of General Psychiatry, 54,* 509–517.

Faraone, S. V. (2003a, August). *ADHD: Facts and fiction.* Paper presented at the meeting of the American Psychological Association, Toronto.

Faraone, S. V. (2003b, August). *The persistence of attention-deficit/hyperactivity disorder through adolescence and adulthood.* Paper presented at the meeting of the American Psychological Association, Toronto.

Faraone, S. V., Biederman, J., Lehman, B. K., Spencer, T., Norman, D., Seidman, L. J., . . . Tsuang, M. T. (1993). Intellectual performance and school failure in children with attention deficit hyperactivity disorder and their siblings. *Journal of Abnormal Psychology, 102,* 616–623.

Faraone, S. V., & Khan. S. A. (2006). Candidate gene studies of attention-deficit/hyperactivity disorder. *Journal of Clinical Psychiatry, 67*(Suppl. 8), 13–20.

Farber, B. A., Brink, D. C., & Raskin, P. M. (Eds.). (1996). *The psychotherapy of Carl Rogers: Cases and commentary.* New York: Guilford.

Farberman, R. K. (1997). Public attitudes about psychologists and mental health care: Research to guide the American Psychological Association public education campaign. *Professional Psychology: Research and Practice, 28,* 128–136.

Farley, M., Lynne, J., & Cotton, A. J. (2005). Prostitution in Vancouver: Violence and the colonization of First Nations women. *Transcultural Psychiatry, 42,* 242–271.

Farmer, A., Elkin, A., & McGuffin, P. (2007). The genetics of bipolar affective disorder. *Current Opinion in Psychiatry, 20,* 8–12.

Farmer, R. F. (2000). Issues in the assessment and conceptualization of personality disorders. *Clinical Psychology Review, 20,* 823–851.

Farrell, A. D., Camplair, P. S., & McCullough, L. (1987). Identification of target complaints by computer interview: Evaluation of the Computerized Assessment System for Psychotherapy Evaluation and Research. *Journal of Consulting and Clinical Psychology, 55,* 691–700.

Farrell, A. D., & White, K. S. (1998). Peer influences and drug use among urban adolescents: Family structure and parent-adolescent relationship as protective factors. *Journal of Consulting and Clinical Psychology, 66,* 248–258.

Farrell, M., Howes, S., Taylor, C., Lewis, G., Jenkins, R., Bebbington, P., . . . Meltzer, H. (2003). Substance misuse and psychiatric comorbidity: An overview of the OPCS National Psychiatric Morbidity Survey. *International Review of Psychiatry, 15,* 43–49.

Federal paternalism angers Pikangikum. (1999). *Canadian Aboriginal News.* Retrieved October 24, 2001, from http://www.canadianaboriginal.com/news/news131a.htm

Fenichel, O. (1945). *The psychoanalytic theory of neurosis.* New York: Norton.

Ferrans, C. E., Cohen, F. L., & Smith, K. M. (1992). The quality of life of persons with narcolepsy. *Loss, Grief and Care, 5,* 23–32.

Fiedorowicz, C. (1999). Neurobiological basis of learning disabilities: An overview. In E. Lowe (Ed.), *Linking research to practice: Second Canadian forum: November 25–27, 1999: Proceedings report* (pp. 64–67). Ottawa: Canadian Child Care Federation.

Fiedorowicz, C., Benezra, E., MacDonald, G. W., McElgunn, B., & Wilson, A. (1999). *Neurobiological basis of learning disabilities.* Ottawa: Learning Disabilities Association of Canada.

Fiedorowicz, C., Benezra, E., MacDonald, G. W., McElgunn, B., Wilson, A., & Kaplan, B. (2002). The neurobiological basis of learning disabilities: An update. *Learning Disabilities: A Multidisciplinary Focus, 11*(2), 61–73.

Fiez, J. A. (2001). Bridging the gap between neuroimaging and neuropsychology: Using working memory as a case-study. *Journal of Clinical & Experimental Neuropsychology, 23*(1), 19–31.

Finkelhor, D., Hotaling, G., Lewis, I. A., & Smith, C. (1990). Sexual abuse in a national survey of adult men and women: Prevalence, characteristics, and risk factors. *Child Abuse and Neglect, 14,* 19–28.

Finney, J. W., & Monahan, S. C. (1996). The cost-effectiveness of treatment for alcoholism: A second approximation. *Journal of Studies on Alcohol, 57,* 229–243.

Fischer, B., & Rehm, J. (2006). Illicit opioid use and treatment for opioid dependence: Challenges for Canada and beyond. *Canadian Journal of Psychiatry, 51,* 621–623.

Fisher, L. (1996). Bizarre right from Day 1. *Maclean's,* p. 14.

Fitzgerald, P. B., Benitez, J., de Castella, A., Daskalakis, Z. J., Brown, T. L., & Kulkarni, J. (2006). A randomized, controlled trial of sequential bilateral repetitive transcranial magnetic stimulation for treatment-resistant depression. *American Journal of Psychiatry, 163,* 88–94.

Fitzgerald, P. B., Fountain, S., & Daskalakis, Z. J. (2006). A comprehensive review of the effects of rTMS on motor cortical excitability and inhibition. *Clinical Neurophysiology, 117,* 2584–2596.

Fitzgerald, P. B., Huntsman, S., Gunewardene, R., Kulkarni, J., & Daskalakis, Z. J. (2006). A randomized trial of low-frequency right-prefrontal-cortex transcranial magnetic stimulation as augmentation in treatment-resistant major depression. *International Journal of Neuropsychopharmacology, 9,* 655–666.

Fleetham, J., Ayas, N., Bradley, D., Ferguson, K., Fitzpatrick, M., George, C., . . . CTS Sleep Disordered Breathing Committee. (2006). Canadian Thoracic Society guidelines: Diagnosis and treatment of sleep disordered breathing in adults. *Canadian Respiratory Journal: Journal of the Canadian Thoracic Society, 13*(7), 387–392.

Flett, G. L., & Hewitt, P. L. (Eds.). (2002). *Perfectionism: Theory, research, and treatment.* Washington, DC: American Psychological Association.

Folstein, M. F., Folstein, S. E., & McHugh, P. R. (1975). "Mini-Mental State": A practical method for grading the cognitive state of patients for the clinician. *Journal of Psychiatric Research, 12,* 189–98.

Fombonne, E. (2005). Epidemiology of autistic disorder and other pervasive developmental disorders. *The Journal of Clinical Psychiatry, 66*(Suppl. 10), 3–8.

Foster, S. L., & Cone, J. D. (1986). Design and use of direct observation procedures. In A. R. Ciminero, K. S. Calhoun, & H. E. Adams (Eds.), *Handbook of behavioral assessment* (2nd ed., pp. 253–324). New York: Wiley.

Foubert, J. D., & Perry, B. C. (2007). Creating lasting attitude and behavior change in fraternity members and male student athletes: The qualitative impact of an empathy-based rape prevention program. *Violence Against Women, 13,* 70–86.

Fowles, D. C. (1993). Electrodermal activity and antisocial behavior: Empirical findings and theoretical issues. In J.-C. Roy, W. Boucsein, D. Fowles, & J. Gruzelier (Eds.), *Progress in electrodermal research* (pp. 223–237). London: Plenum.

Frank G. K. W., Reynolds, J. R., Shott, M. E., & O'Reilly, M. E. (2011). Altered temporal difference learning in bulimia nervosa. *Biological Psychiatry, 70,* 728–735.

Frankenfield, G. (2000). Eating disorders more likely in diabetic girls. *WebMD.* Retrieved July 31, 2003, from http://my.webmd.com/content/Article/26/1728_58622.htm

Fraser, F. (1994). The participation of aboriginal and other cultural minorities in cultural development. *Canadian Journal of Communications, 19*(3).

Freedman, R., Adler, L. E., Gerhardt, G. A., Waldo, M., Baker, N., Rose, G. M., . . . Franks, R. (1987). Neurobiological studies of sensory gating in schizophrenia. *Schizophrenia Bulletin, 13,* 669–678.

Freud, S. (1957). Mourning and melancholia. In J. Rickman (Ed.), *A general selection from the works of Sigmund Freud.* Garden City, NY: Doubleday. (Original work published 1917)

Freud, S. (1959). Analysis of a phobia in a 5-year-old boy. In A. Strachey & J. Strachey (Ed. & Trans.), *Collected papers* (Vol. 3). New York: Basic Books. (Original work published 1909)

Freud, S. (1962). *Three essays on the theory of sexuality* (J. Strachey, Trans.). New York: Basic Books. (Original work published 1905)

Freud, S. (1964). New introductory lectures. In J. Strachey (Ed. and Trans.), *Standard edition of the complete psychological works of Sigmund Freud* (Vol. 22). London: Hogarth Press. (Original work published in 1933)

Freud, S. (1987). Beyond the pleasure principle. In J. Strachey (Trans.), *On metapsychology: The theory of psychoanalysis.* Middlesex, UK: Penguin, p. 316. (Original work published 1920)

Freund, K., & Blanchard, R. (1986). The concept of courtship disorder. *Journal of Sex and Marital Therapy, 12,* 79–92.

Frezza, M., di Padova, C., Pozzato, G., Terpin, M., Baraona, E., & Lieber, C. S. (1990). High blood alcohol levels in women: The role of decreased gastric alcohol dehydrogenase activity and first-pass metabolism. *New England Journal of Medicine, 322,* 95–99.

Fricchione, G. L., Nejad, S. H., Esses, J. A., Cummings, T. J., Querques, J., Cassem, N. H., & Murray, G. B. (2008). Postoperative delirium. *American Journal of Psychiatry, 165,* 803–812.

Frick, P. J., Lahey, B. B., Loeber, R., Stouthamer-Loeber, M., Christ, M. A., & Hanson, K. (1992). Familial risk factors to oppositional defiant disorder and conduct disorder: Parental psychopathology and maternal parenting. *Journal of Consulting and Clinical Psychology, 60,* 49–55.

Frick, P. J., & Silverthorn, P. (2001). Psycho-pathology in children. In H. E. Adams & P. B. Sutker (Eds.), *Comprehensive handbook of psychopathology* (3rd ed., pp. 881–919). New York: Plenum.

Friedlander, L., & Desrocher, M. (2006). Neuroimaging studies of obsessive-compulsive disorder in adults and children. *Clinical Psychology Review, 26,* 32–49.

Fromm-Reichmann, F. (1948). Notes on the development of treatment of schizophrenics by psychoanalytic psychotherapy. *Psychiatry, 11,* 263–273.

Fromm-Reichmann, F. (1950). *Principles of intensive psychotherapy.* Chicago: University of Chicago Press.

Fuchs, C. S., Stampfer, M. J., Colditz, G. A., Giovannucci, E. L., Manson, J. E., Kawachi, I., . . . Rosner, B. (1995). Alcohol consumption and mortality among women. *New England Journal of Medicine, 332,* 1245–1250.

Fukumoto, H., Tokuda, T., Kasai, T., Ishigami, N., Hidaka, H., Kondo, M., . . . Nakagawa, M. (2010). High-molecular-weight β-amyloid oligomers are elevated in cerebrospinal fluid of Alzheimer patients. *FASEB Journal: The Journal of the Federation of American Societies for Experimental Biology, 24,* 2716–2726.

Fulero, S. M. (1988). Tarasoff: 10 years later. *Professional Psychology: Research and Practice, 19,* 184–190.

G

Galea, S., Ahern, J., Resnick, H., Kilpatrick, D., Bucuvalas, M., Gold, J., . . . Vlahov, D. (2002). Psychological sequelae of the September 11 terrorist attacks in New York City. *New England Journal of Medicine, 346,* 982–987.

Galea, S., Nandi, A., & Vlahov, D. (2005). The epidemiology of post-traumatic stress disorder after disasters. *Epidemiologic Reviews, 27,* 78–91.

Garb, H. N. (1997). Race bias, social class bias, and gender bias in clinical judgment. *Clinical Psychology: Science and Practice, 4,* 99–120.

Garbutt, J. C., West, S. L., Carey, T. S., Lohr, K. N., & Crews, F. T. (1999). Pharmacological treatment of alcohol dependence. *JAMA: Journal of the American Medical Association, 281,* 1318–1325.

Gard, M. C., & Freeman, C. P. (1996). The dismantling of a myth: A review of eating disorders and socio-economic status. *International Journal of Eating Disorders, 20,* 1–12.

Garfield, S. L. (1994). Eclecticism and integration in psychotherapy: Development and issues. *Clinical Psychology: Science and Practice, 1,* 123–137.

Garfinkel, P. E., Moldofsky, H., & Garner, D. M. (1980). The heterogeneity of anorexia nervosa: Bulimia as a distinct subgroup. *Archives of General Psychiatry, 37,* 1036–1040.

Garland, E. J. (2004). Facing the evidence: Antidepressant treatment in children and adolescents. *Canadian Medical Association Journal, 170,* 490–491.

Garland, E. J., & Garland, O. M. (2001). Correlation between anxiety and oppositionality in a children's mood and anxiety disorder clinic. *Canadian Journal of Psychiatry, 46,* 953–958.

Garner, D. M. (1993). Binge eating in anorexia nervosa. In C. G. Fairburn & G. T. Wilson (Eds.), *Binge eating: Nature, assessment, and treatment* (pp. 50–76). New York: Guilford.

Gatehouse, J. (2002, September 16). The echoes of terror. *Maclean's,* p. 18.

Gauthier, J. G. (1999). Bridging the gap between biological and psychological perspectives in the treatment of anxiety disorders. *Canadian Psychology, 40*(1), 1–11.

Gawin, F. H. (1991). Cocaine addiction: Psychology and neurophysiology. *Science, 251,* 1580–1586.

Gawin, F. H., & Ellinwood, E. H. (1989). Cocaine dependence. *Annual Review of Medicine, 40,* 149–161.

Gaziano, J. M., Buring, J. E., Breslow, J. L., Goldhaber, S. Z., Rosner, B., VanDenburgh, M., . . . Hennekens, C. H. (1993). Moderate alcohol intake, increased levels of high-density lipoprotein and its subfractions, and decreased risk of myocardial infarction. *New England Journal of Medicine, 329,* 1829–1834.

Geist, R., Davis, R., & Heinmaa, M. (1998). Binge/purge symptoms and comorbidity in adolescents with eating disorders. *Canadian Journal of Psychiatry, 43,* 507–512.

Geist, R., Heinmaa, M., Stephens, D., Davis, R., & Katzman, D. K. (2000). Comparison of family therapy and family group psychoeducation in adolescents with anorexia nervosa. *Canadian Journal of Psychiatry, 45,* 173–178.

Gershuny, B. S., & Thayer, J. F. (1999). Relations among psychological trauma, dissociative phenomena, and trauma- related distress: A review and integration. *Clinical Psychology Review, 19,* 631–657.

Gettler, L. (2003, February 21). Psychopath in a suit. *The Age.* Retrieved from http://www.theage.com.au/articles/2003/02/20/1045638423969.html

Gfellner, B. M., & Hundelby, J. D. (1990). Family and peer predictors of substance use among Aboriginal and non-Aboriginal adolescents. *Canadian Journal of Native Studies, 10,* 267–294.

Gfellner, B. M., & Hundelby, J. D. (1995). Patterns of drug use among Native and white adolescents: 1990–1993. *Canadian Journal of Public Health, 86,* 95–97.

Gianoulakis, C. (2001). Influence of the endogenous opioid system on high alcohol consumption and genetic predisposition to alcoholism. *Journal of Psychiatry and Neuroscience, 26,* 304–318.

Gibbs, N. (1998, November 30). The age of Ritalin. *Time,* pp. 84–94.

Gilbertson, M. W., Shenton, M. E., Ciszewski, A., Kasai, K., Lasko, N. B., Orr, S. P., & Pitman, R. K. (2002). Smaller hippcampal volume predicts pathologic vulnerability to psychological trauma. *Nature Neuroscience, 5,* 1242–1247.

Gillberg, C., Melander, H., von Knorring, A. L., Janols, L. O., Thernlund, G., Hägglöf, B., . . . Kopps, S. (1997). Long-term stimulant treatment of children with attention-deficit hyperactivity disorder symptoms: A randomized, double-blind, placebo-controlled trial. *Archives of General Psychiatry, 54,* 857–864.

Glancy, G. D., & Chaimowitz, G. (2003). [Letter]. *Journal of the American Academy of Psychiatry and the Law, 31,* 524–525.

Gleaves, D. H., Hernandez, E., & Warner, M. S. (2003). The etiology of dissociative identity disorder: Reply to Gee, Allen and Powell (2003). *Professional Psychology: Research and Practice, 34,* 116–118.

Gliksman, L., Adlaf, E., Demers, A., Newton-Taylor, B., & Schmidt, K. (2000). *Canadian campus survey.* Toronto: Centre for Addiction and Mental Health.

Glynn, S., & Mueser, K. T. (1986). Social learning for chronic mental inpatients. *Schizophrenia Bulletin, 12,* 648–668.

Goldapple, K., Segal, Z., Garson, C., Lau, M., Bieling, P., Kennedy, S., & Mayberg, H. (2004). Modulation of cortical-limbic pathways in major depression. *Archives of General Psychiatry, 61,* 34–41.

Goldberg, T. E., Straub, R. E., Callicott, J. H., Hariri, A., Mattay, V. S., Bigelow, L., . . . Weinberger, D. R. (2006). The G72/G30 gene complex and cognitive abnormalities in schizophrenia. *Neuropsychopharmacology, 31,* 2022–2032.

Golden, C. J., Hammeke, T. A., & Purisch, A. D. (1980). *The Luria-Nebraska Neuropsychological Battery: Manual.* Los Angeles: Western Psychological Services.

Golden, R. N., Gaynes, B. N., Ekstrom, R. D., Hamer, R. M., Jacobsen, F. M., Suppes, T., . . . Nemeroff, C. B. (2005). The efficacy of light therapy in the treatment of mood disorders: A review and meta-analysis of the evidence. *American Journal of Psychiatry, 162,* 656–662.

Goldfarb, L. A., Dykens, E. M., & Gerrard, M. (1985). The Goldfarb Fear of Fat Scale. *Journal of Personality Assessment, 49,* 329–332.

Goldfield, G. S., Blouin, A. G., & Woodside, D. B. (2006). Body image, binge eating, and bulimia nervosa in male bodybuilders. *Canadian Journal of Psychiatry, 51*(3), 160–168.

Goldman, L. S., Genel, M., Bezman, R. J., & Slanetz, P. J. (1998). Diagnosis and treatment of attention-deficit/hyperactivity disorder in children and adolescents. *JAMA: Journal of the American Medical Association, 279,* 1100–1107.

Goldman-Rakic, P. S., & Selemon, L. D. (1997). Functional and anatomical aspects of prefrontal pathology in schizophrenia. *Schizophrenia Bulletin, 23,* 437–458.

Goldstein, A. (1976). Opioid peptides (endorphins) in pituitary and brain. *Science, 193,* 1081–1086.

Goldstein, I., Lue, T. F., Padma-Nathan, H., Rosen, R. C., Steers, W. D., & Wicker, P. A. (1998). Oral sildenafil in the treatment of erectile dysfunction. *New England Journal of Medicine, 338,* 1397–1404.

Goleman, D. (1988, November 1). Narcissism looming larger as root of personality woes. *The New York Times,* pp. C1, C16.

Goleman, D. (1990, December 6). Women's depression rate is higher. *The New York Times.*

Goleman, D. (1994, January 11). Childhood depression may herald adult ills. *The New York Times,* pp. C1, C10.

Goleman, D. (1995, October 4). Eating disorder rates surprise the experts. *The New York Times,* p. C11.

Gordon, C. M., & Carey, M. P. (1996). Alcohol's effects on requisites for sexual risk reduction in men: An initial experimental investigation. *Health Psychology, 15,* 56–60.

Gorman, C. (1998, November 30). How does it work? *Time,* p. 92.

Gorman, J., Kent, J. M., Sullivan, G. M., & Coplan, J. D. (2000). Neuroanatomical hypothesis of panic disorder, revised. *American Journal of Psychiatry, 157,* 493–505.

Gotlib, I. H., Lewinsohn, P. M., Seeley, J. R., Rohde, P., & Redner, J. E. (1993). Negative cognitions and attributional style in depressed adolescents: An examination of stability and specificity. *Journal of Abnormal Psychology, 102,* 607–615.

Gottesman, I. I., McGuffin, P., & Farmer, A. E. (1987). Clinical genetics as clues to the "real" genetics of schizophrenia (A decade of modest gains while playing for time). *Schizophrenia Bulletin, 13*(1), 23–47.

Gove, W. (1979). Sex differences in the epidemiology of mental disorder: Evidence and explanations. In E. L. Gomberg & V. Franks (Eds.), *Gender and disordered behavior: Sex differences in psychopathology.* New York: Brunner/Mazel.

Graber, B. (1993). Medical aspects of sexual arousal disorders. In W. O'Donohue & J. H. Geer (Eds.), *Handbook of sexual dysfunctions: Assessment and treatment* (pp. 103–156). Boston: Allyn & Bacon.

Graham, J. R., & Strenger, V. E. (1988). MMPI characteristics of alcoholics: A review. *Journal of Consulting and Clinical Psychology, 56,* 197–205.

Grant, B. F., Hasin, D. S., Stinson, F. S., Dawson, D. A., Goldstein, R. B., Huang, B., & Saha, T. D. (2006). The epidemiology of DSM-IV panic disorder and agoraphobia in the United States: Results from the National Epidemiologic Survey on alcohol and related conditions. *Journal of Clinical Psychiatry, 67,* 363–374.

Gratzer, T. G., & Matas, M. (1994). The right to refuse treatment: Recent Canadian developments. *Bulletin of the American Academy of Psychiatry and Law, 22,* 249–256.

Gray, J. A. (1970). The psychophysiological basis of introversion-extraversion. *Behaviour Research & Therapy, 8,* 249–266.

Gray, J. A., & McNaughton, N. (2003). *The neuropsychology of anxiety: An enquiry into the functions of the septo-hippocampal system* (2nd ed.). Oxford: Oxford University Press.

Gray, J. E., & O'Reilly, R. L. (2005). Canadian compulsory community treatment laws: Recent reforms. *International Journal of Law and Psychiatry, 28,* 13–22.

Gray, J. R., & Braver, T. S. (2002). Personality predicts working-memory-related activation in the caudal anterior cingulate cortex. *Cognitive and Affective Behavioral Neuroscience, 2*(1), 64–75.

Green, R., & Blanchard, R. (1995). Gender identity disorders. In H. I. Kaplan & B. J. Sadock (Eds.), *Comprehensive textbook of psychiatry* (6th ed., pp. 1345–1360). Baltimore, MD: Williams & Wilkins.

Greenberg, D. M., & Bradford, J. M. W. (1997). Treatment of the paraphilic disorders: A review of the role of selective serotonin reuptake inhibitors. *Sexual Abuse: Journal of Research and Treatment, 9,* 349–360.

Greenberg, L. (2006). Emotion-focused therapy: A synopsis. *Journal of Contemporary Psychotherapy, 36*(2), 87–93.

Greenberg, L. S. (2002a). *Emotion-focused therapy: Coaching clients to work through their feelings.* Washington, DC: American Psychological Association.

Greenberg, L. S. (2002b). Integrating an emotion-focused approach to treatment into psychotherapy integration. *Journal of Psychotherapy Integration, 12*(2), 154–189.

Greenberg, R. P., & Bornstein, R. F. (1988a). The dependent personality: I. Risk for physical disorders. *Journal of Personality Disorders, 2,* 126–135.

Greenberg, R. P., & Bornstein, R. F. (1988b). The dependent personality: II. Risk for psychological disorders. *Journal of Personality Disorders, 2,* 136–143.

Greenberg, R. P., Bornstein, R. F., Greenberg, M. D., & Fisher, S. (1992). A meta-analysis of antidepressant outcome under "blinder" conditions. *Journal of Consulting and Clinical Psychology, 60,* 664–669.

Greenberg, R. P., Bornstein, R. F., Zborowski, M. J., Fisher, S., & Greenberg, M. D. (1994). A meta-analysis of fluoxetine outcome in the treatment of depression. *Journal of Nervous and Mental Disease, 182,* 547–551.

Greenspan, E. L., Rosenberg, M., & Henein, M. (Annotators). (1998). *Martin's Criminal Code.* Aurora, ON: Canada Law Book.

Greeven, A., van Balkom, A. J., Visser, S., Merkelbach, J. W., van Rood, Y. R., Van der Does, A. J., . . . Spinhoven, P. (2007). Cognitive behavior therapy and paroxetine in the treatment of hypochondriasis: A randomized controlled trial. *American Journal of Psychiatry, 164,* 91–99.

Griffin, J. D. (1993, December). A historical oversight. *Newsletter of the Ontario Psychiatric Association,* pp. 9–10.

Griffiths, M. (2005). Online therapy for addictive behaviors. *CyberPsychology and Behavior, 8,* 555–561.

Grissett, N. I., & Norvell, N. K. (1992). Perceived social support, social skills, and quality of relationships in bulimic women. *Journal of Consulting and Clinical Psychology, 60,* 293–299.

Gross, A. M., Winslett, A., Roberts, M., & Gohm, C. L. (2006). An examination of sexual violence against college women. *Violence Against Women, 12,* 288–300.

Grover, S., Mattoo, S. K., & Gupta, N. (2005). Theories on mechanism of action of electroconvulsive therapy. *German Journal of Psychiatry, 8,* 70–84.

Grunberg, N. E. (1991). Smoking cessation and weight gain. *New England Journal of Medicine, 324,* 768–769.

Guertin, T. L. (1999). Eating behavior of bulimics, self-identified binge eaters, and non-eating disordered individuals: What differentiates these populations? *Clinical Psychology Review, 19,* 1–24.

Gunderson, J. G. (1996). The borderline patient's intolerance of aloneness: Insecure attachments and therapist availability. *American Journal of Psychiatry, 153,* 752–758.

Gunderson, J. G. (2001). *Borderline personality disorder: A clinical guide.* Washington, DC: American Psychiatric Press.

Gunderson, J. G., & Phillips, K. A. (1991). A current view of the interface between borderline personality disorder and depression. *American Journal of Psychiatry, 148,* 967–975.

Gur, R. E., Cowell, P., Turetsky, B. I., Gallacher, F., Cannon, T., Bilker, W., & Gur, R. C. (1998). A follow-up magnetic resonance imaging study of schizophrenia: Relationship of neuroanatomical changes to clinical and neurobehavioral measures. *Archives of General Psychiatry, 55,* 145–152.

Gur, R. E., & Pearlson, G. D. (1993). Neuroimaging in schizophrenia research. *Schizophrenia Bulletin, 19,* 337–353.

Guydish, J., Werdegar, D., Sorensen, J. L., Clark, W., & Acampora, A. (1998). Drug abuse day treatment: A randomized clinical trial comparing day and residential treatment programs. *Journal of Consulting and Clinical Psychology, 66,* 280–289.

H

Haggarty, J., Cernovsky, Z., Kermeen, P., & Merskey, H. (2000). Psychiatric disorders in an Arctic community. *Canadian Journal of Psychiatry, 45,* 357–362.

Halbreich, U., & Karkun, S. (2006). Cross-cultural and social diversity of prevalence of postpartum depression and depressive symptoms. *Journal of Affective Disorders, 91,* 97–111.

Hall, G. C., & Barongan, C. (1997). Prevention of sexual aggression: Sociocultural risk and protective factors. *American Psychologist, 52,* 5–14.

Hall, T. M. (2011). *Index of culture-bound syndromes: By culture.* Retrieved November 22, 2011, from http://homepage.mac.com/mccajor/cbs_cul.html

Hamid, S. (2000). Culture-specific syndromes: It's all relative. *Visions: BC's Mental Health Journal, 9*(Winter), 5–8.

Hammen, C. (2005). Stress and depression. *Annual Review of Clinical Psychology, 1,* 293–319.

Hammen, C., & Compas, B. E. (1994). Unmasking unmasked depression in children and adolescents: The problem of comorbidity. *Clinical Psychology Review, 14,* 585–603.

Hancock, L. (1996, March 18). Mother's little helper. *Newsweek,* pp. 51–56.

Hankin, B. L., Abramson, L. Y., Moffitt, T. E., Silva, P. A., McGee, R., & Angell, K. E. (1998). Development of depression from preadolescence to young adulthood: Emerging gender differences in a 10-year longitudinal study. *Journal of Abnormal Psychology, 107,* 128–140.

Hansen, T. E., Casey, D. E., & Hoffman, W. F. (1997). Neuroleptic intolerance. *Schizophrenia Bulletin, 23,* 567–582.

Hare, R. D. (1965). Temporal gradient of fear arousal in psychopaths. *Journal of Abnormal Psychology, 70,* 442–445.

Hare, R. D. (1996a). Psychopathology and antisocial personality disorder: A case of diagnostic confusion. *Psychiatric Times, 13*(2), 39–40.

Hare, R. D. (1996b). Psychopathy: A clinical construct whose time has come. *Criminal Justice and Behavior, 23,* 25–54.

Hare, R. D., Hart, S. D., & Harpur, T. J. (1991). Psychopathy and the DSM-IV criteria for antisocial personality disorder. *Journal of Abnormal Psychology, 100,* 391–398.

Hariri, A. R., & Brown, S. M. (2006). Images in neuroscience: Serotonin. *American Journal of Psychiatry, 163,* 12.

Harkness, K. L., Bruce, A. E., & Lumley, M. N. (2006). The role of childhood abuse and neglect in the sensitization to stressful life events in adolescent depression. *Journal of Abnormal Psychology, 115,* 730–741.

Harpur, T. J., & Hare, R. D. (1994). Assessment of psychopathy as a function of age. *Journal of Abnormal Psychology, 103,* 604–609.

Harris, S., Davies, M. F., & Dryden, W. (2006). An experimental test of a core REBT hypothesis: Evidence that irrational beliefs lead to physiological as well as psychological arousal. *Journal of Rational-Emotive & Cognitive-Behaviour Therapy, 24*(2), 101–111.

Hart, S. D., Cox, D. N., & Hare, R. D. (1995). *The Hare Psychopathy Checklist: Screening version.* Toronto: Multi-Health Systems.

Hart, S. D., & Hare, R. D. (1989). Discriminant validity of the Psychopathy Checklist in a forensic psychiatric population. *Psychological Assessment: A Journal of Consulting and Clinical Psychology, 1,* 211–218.

Hart, S. D., & Hare, R. D. (1997). Psychopathy: Assessment and association with criminal conduct. In D. M. Stoff, J. Breiling, & J. D. Maser (Eds.), *Handbook of antisocial behavior* (pp. 22–35). New York: Wiley.

Hartung, C. M., & Widiger, T. A. (1998). Gender differences in the diagnosis of mental disorders: Conclusions and controversies

of the DSM-IV. *Psychological Bulletin, 123,* 260–278.

Harvey, A. G., & Bryant, R. A. (2002). Acute stress disorder: A synthesis and critique. *Psychological Bulletin, 128,* 886–902.

Harvey, P. D., Lombardi, J., Leibman, M., Parrella, M., White, L., Powchik, P., . . . Davis, K. L. (1997). Age-related differences in formal thought disorder in chronically hospitalized schizophrenic patients: A cross-sectional study across nine decades. *American Journal of Psychiatry, 154,* 205–210.

Haugh, J. A. (2006). Specificity and social problem-solving: Relation to depressive and anxious symptomatology. *Journal of Social and Clinical Psychology, 25,* 392–403.

Haughton, E., & Ayllon, T. (1965). Production and elimination of symptomatic behavior. In L. P. Ullmann & L. Krasner (Eds.), *Case studies in behavior modification.* New York: Holt, Rinehart and Winston.

Havassy, B. E., Hall, S. M., & Wasserman, D. A. (1991). Social support and relapse: Commonalities among alcoholics, opiate users, and cigarette smokers. *Addictive Behaviors, 16,* 235–246.

Hawaleshka, D. (2002, October 21). New national survey data shows that many health problems are getting worse. *Maclean's,* p. 38.

Hawkrigg, J. J. (1975). Agoraphobia. *Nursing Times, 71,* 1280–1282.

Hawton, K. (1991). Sex therapy. *Behavioural Psychotherapy, 19,* 131–136.

Hawton, K., & Catalan, J. (1990). Sex therapy for vaginismus: Characteristics of couples and treatment outcomes. *Sexual and Marital Therapy, 5,* 39–48.

Hayes, R. D., Bennett, C. M., Fairley, C. K., & Dennerstein, L. (2006). What can prevalence studies tell us about female sexual difficulty and dysfunction? *Journal of Sexual Medicine, 3,* 589–595.

Health Canada. (1995). *Canada's alcohol and other drugs survey* (Catalogue No. H39-338/1995E). Ottawa: Author. Retrieved November 1, 2011, from http://dsp-psd.pwgsc.gc.ca/Collections/H39-338-1995E.pdf

Health Canada. (1999a). *Measuring up: A health surveillance update on Canadian children and youth.* Ottawa: Author, Retrieved November 1, 2011, from http://www.phac-aspc.gc.ca/publicat/meas-haut

Health Canada. (1999b). *Toward a healthy future: Second report on the health of Canadians* (Catalogue No. H39-468/1999E). Ottawa: Minister of Public Works and Government Services Canada. Retrieved November 1, 2011, from http://dsp-pds.pwgsc.gc.ca/Collection/H39-468-1999E.pdf

Health Canada. (2000). *Straight facts about drugs & drug abuse* (Catalogue No. H39-65/2000E). Ottawa: Author. Retrieved November 1, 2011, from http:/dsp-psd.pwgsc.gc.ca/Collection/H39-65-2000E.pdf

Health Canada. (2001a). *Canadian tobacco use monitoring survey (CTUMS) 2001.* Retrieved November 1, 2011, from http://www.hc-sc.gc.ca/hc-ps/tobac-tabac/research-recherche/stat/_ctums-esutc_2001/ar-rpa-2001-eng.php

Health Canada. (2001b, June 26). *Centres of excellence for children's well being.* Retrieved April 26, 2003, from http://www.hc-sc.gc.ca/hppb/childhood-youth/centres/index2.html

Health Canada. (2002a). *Aboriginal Head Start in urban and northern communities.* Ottawa: Author. Retrieved October 18, 2003, from http://www.hc-sc.gc.ca/dca-dea/programs-mes/ahs_overview_e.html#top

Health Canada. (2002b). *A report on mental illnesses in Canada* (Catalogue No. 0-662-32817-5). Ottawa: Health Canada Editorial Board Mental Illnesses in Canada. Retrieved November 1, 2011, from http://www.phac-aspc.gc.ca/publicat/miic-mmac/pdf/men_ill_e.pdf

Health Canada. (2006a). New cautions regarding rare heart-related risks for all ADHD drugs: Advisory. Ottawa: Author. Retrieved from http://www.hc-sc.gc.ca/ahc-asc/media/advisories-avis/2006/2006_35_e.html

Health Canada. (2006b). *The human face of mental health and mental illness in Canada 2006* (Catalogue No. HP5-19/2006E). Ottawa: Minister of Public Works and Government Services. Retrieved November 1, 2011, from http://www.phac-aspc.gc.ca/publicat/human-humain06/

Health Canada. (2006c). New information regarding uncommon psychiatric adverse events for all ADHD drugs: Advisory. Ottawa: Author. Retrieved from http://www.hc-sc.gc.ca/ahc-asc/media/advisories-avis/2006/2006_91_e.html

Health Canada. (2010). *Canadian tobacco use monitoring survey (CTUMS).* Ottawa: Author. Retrieved November 1, 2011, from http://www.hc-sc.gc.ca/tobac-tabac/research-recherche/stat/ctums-esutc_2010-eng.php

HealthyOntario.com. (2003). *Eating disorders: The facts.* Retrieved July 31, 2003, from http://www.healthyontario.com/english/printVersion.asp?which=features&text_id=91&channel_id=0

Heatherton, T. F., Mahamedi, F., Striepe, M., Field, A. E., & Keel, P. (1997). A 10-year longitudinal study of body weight, dieting, and eating disorder symptoms. *Journal of Abnormal Psychology, 106,* 117–125.

Hebb, D. O. (2002). *The organization of behavior: A neuropsychological theory.* Mahwah, NJ: Erlbaum. (Original work published 1949)

Heiman, J. R., & LoPiccolo, J. (1987). *Becoming orgasmic: A sexual and personal growth program for women* (2nd ed.). Englewood Cliffs, NJ: Prentice Hall.

Heinrichs, R. W. (2001). *In search of madness: Schizophrenia and neuroscience.* London: Oxford University Press.

Heinrichs, R. W. (2005). The primacy of cognition in schizophrenia. *American Psychologist, 60,* 229–242.

Hellstrom, W. J. G., Nehra, A., Shabsigh, R., & Sharlip, I. D. (2006). Premature ejaculation: The most common male sexual dysfunction. *Journal of Sexual Medicine, 3*(Suppl. S1), 1–3.

Henggeler, S. W., Rodick, J. D., Borduin, C. M., Hanson, C. L., Watson, S. M., & Urey, J. R. (1986). Multisystemic treatment of juvenile offenders: Effects on adolescent behavior and family interaction. *Developmental Psychology, 22,* 132–141.

Herbert, J. D., Hope, D. A., & Bellack, A. S. (1992). Validity of the distinction between generalized social phobia and avoidant personality disorder. *Journal of Abnormal Psychology, 101,* 332–339.

Hercz, R. (2001, September 8). Psychopaths among us. *Saturday Night.*

Herzog, W., Schellberg, D., & Deter, H. C. (1997). First recovery in anorexia nervosa patients in the long-term course: A discrete-time survival analysis. *Journal of Consulting and Clinical Psychology, 65,* 169–177.

Hill, A. L. (1987). Idiot savants: The rate of incidence. *Perceptual and Motor Skills, 44,* 161–162.

Hiller, W., Rief, W., & Brähler, E. (2006). Somatization in the population: From mild bodily misperceptions to disabling symptoms. *Social Psychiatry and Psychiatric Epidemiology, 41,* 704–712.

Hinshaw, S. P. (1992). Academic underachievement, attention deficits, and aggression: Comorbidity and implications for intervention. *Journal of Consulting and Clinical Psychology, 60,* 893–903.

Hochhausen, N. M., Lorenz, A. R., & Newman, J. P. (2002). Specifying the impulsivity of female inmates with borderline personality disorder. *Journal of Abnormal Psychology, 111,* 495–501.

Hodgins, D. (2006). Can patients with alcohol use disorders return to social drinking? Yes, so what should we do about it? *Canadian Journal of Psychiatry, 50,* 264–265.

Hoffmann, W. L., & Prior, M. R. (1982). Neuropsychological dimensions of autism in children: A test of the hemispheric dysfunction hypothesis. *Journal of Clinical Neuropsychology, 4,* 27–42.

Hofmann, S. G., Newman, M. G., Ehlers, A., & Roth, W. T. (1995). Psychophysiological differences between subgroups of social phobia. *Journal of Abnormal Psychology, 104,* 224–231.

Hogarty, G. E. (1993). Prevention of relapse in chronic schizophrenic patients. *Journal of Clinical Psychiatry, 54*(Suppl.), 18–23.

Holbrook, A. M., Crowther, R., Lotter, A., Cheng, C., & King, D. (2000). The diagnosis and management of insomnia in clinical practice: A practical evidence-based approach. *CMAJ: Canadian Medical Association Journal, 162,* 216–220.

Holland, A. J., Sicotte, N., & Treasure, J. (1988). Anorexia nervosa: Evidence for a genetic basis. *Journal of Psychosomatic Research, 32,* 561–571.

Hollon, S. D. (2006). Cognitive therapy in the treatment and prevention of depression. In T. E. Joiner, J. S. Brown, & J. Kistner (Eds.), *The interpersonal, cognitive, and social nature of depression* (pp. 133–151). Mahwah, NJ: Erlbaum.

Hollon, S. D., & Kendall, P. C. (1980). Cognitive self-statements in depression: Development of an automatic thoughts questionnaire. *Cognitive Therapy and Research, 4*(4), 383–395.

Hollon, S. D., & Shelton, R. C. (2001). Treatment guidelines for major depressive disorder. *Behavior Therapy, 32,* 235–258.

Holmes, E. A., Brown, R. J., Mansell, W., Fearon, R. P., Hunter, E. C. M., Frasquilho, F., & Oakley, D. A. (2005). Are there two qualitatively distinct forms of dissociation? A review and some clinical implications. *Clinical Psychology Review, 25,* 1–23.

Holt, C. S., Heimberg, R. G., & Hope, D. A. (1992). Avoidant personality disorder and the generalized subtype of social phobia. *Journal of Abnormal Psychology, 101,* 318–325.

Honig, A., Romme, M., Ensink, B., Escher, S., Pennings, M., & deVries, M. W. (1998). Auditory hallucinations: A comparison between patients and nonpatients. *Journal of Nervous and Mental Disease, 186,* 646–651.

Hopkins, I. M., Gower, M. W., Perez, T. A., Smith, D. S., Amthor, F. R., Wimsatt, F. C., & Biasini, F. J. (2011). Avatar assistant: Improving social skills in students with an ASD through a computer-based intervention. *Journal of Autism and Developmental Disorders, 41,* 1443–1455.

Hopko, D. R., Lejuez, C. W., Ruggiero, K. J., & Eifert, G. H. (2003). Contemporary behavioral activation treatments for depression: Procedures, principles and progress. *Clinical Psychology Review, 23,* 699–717.

Hops, H., & Lewinsohn, P. M. (1995). A course for the treatment of depression among adolescents. In K. D. Craig & K. S. Dobson (Eds.), *Anxiety and depression in adults and children* (pp. 230–245). Thousand Oaks, CA: Sage.

Horne, L. R., Van Vactor, J. C., & Emerson, S. (1991). Disturbed body image in patients with eating disorders. *American Journal of Psychiatry, 148,* 211–215.

Howard, C. E., & Porzelius, L. K. (1999). The role of dieting in binge eating disorder: Etiology and treatment implications. *Clinical Psychology Review, 19,* 25–44.

Huang, W., & Cuvo, A. J. (1997). Social skills training for adults with mental retardation in job-related settings. *Behavior Modification, 21,* 3–44.

Huber, K. M., Gallagher, S. M., Warren, S. T., & Bear, M. F. (2002). Altered synaptic plasticity in a mouse model of fragile X mental retardation. *Proceedings of the National Academy of Sciences of the United States of America, 99,* 7746–7750.

Hublin, C., Kaprio, J., Partinen, M., Heikkila, K., & Koskenvuo, M. (1997). Prevalence and genetics of sleepwalking: A population-based twin study. *Neurology, 48*(1), 177–181.

Hucker, S. J. (1985). Self-harmful sexual behavior. *Psychiatric Clinics of North America, 8,* 323–327.

Hucker, S. J. (1997). Sexual sadism: Theory and psychopathology. In D. R. Laws & W. T. O'Donohue (Eds.), *Sexual deviance: Theory, assessment, and treatment.* New York: Guilford.

Hudson, J. I., McElroy, S. L., Raymond, N. C., Crow, S., Keck, P. E., Jr., Carter, W. P., . . . Jonas, J. M. (1998). Fluvoxamine in the treatment of binge-eating disorder: A multicenter placebo-controlled, double-blind trial. *American Journal of Psychiatry, 155,* 1756–1762.

Hudziak, J. J., Boffeli, T. J., Kreisman, J. J., Battaglia, M. M., Stanger, C., & Guze, S. B. (1996). Clinical study of the relation of borderline personality disorder to Briquet's syndrome (hysteria), somatization disorder, antisocial personality disorder, and substance abuse disorders. *American Journal of Psychiatry, 153,* 1598–1606.

Huffman, J. C., & Stern, T. A. (2003). The diagnosis and treatment of Munchausen's syndrome. *General Hospital Psychiatry, 25,* 358–363.

Humphrey, L. L. (1986). Family dynamics in bulimia. *Adolescent Psychiatry, 13,* 315–331.

Hunter, E. C., Baker, D., Phillips, M. L., Sierra, M., & David, A. S. (2005). Cognitive-behaviour therapy for depersonalization disorder: An open study. *Behaviour Research and Therapy, 43,* 1121–1130.

Hur, Y.-M. (2007). Stability of genetic influence on morningness-eveningness: A cross-sectional examination of South Korean twins from preadolescence to young adulthood. *Journal of Sleep Research, 16*(1), 17–23.

Hurd, H. M., Drewry, W. F., Dewey, R., Pilgrim, C. W., Blumer, G. A., & Burgess, T. J. W. (1916). *The institutional care of the insane in the United States and Canada* (Vols. 1–3). Baltimore, MD: The Johns Hopkins Press.

Hurt, R. D., Dale, L. C., Croghan, G. A., Croghan, I. T., Gomez-Dahl, L. C., & Offord, K. P. (1998). Nicotine nasal spray for smoking cessation: Pattern of use, side effects, relief of withdrawal symptoms, and cotinine levels. *Mayo Clinic Proceedings, 73,* 118–125.

Hurt, R. D., Sachs, D. P., Glover, E. D., Offord, K. P., Johnston, J. A., Dale, L. C., . . . Sullivan, P. M. (1997). A comparison of sustained-release bupropion and placebo for smoking cessation. *New England Journal of Medicine, 337,* 1195–1202.

Hwang, S. W. (2001). Homelessness and health. *CMAJ: Canadian Medical Association Journal, 164,* 229–233.

Hy, L. X., & Keller, D. M. (2000). Prevalence of AD among whites: A summary by levels of severity. *Neurology, 55,* 198–204.

Ialomiteanu, A. R., Adlaf, E. M., Mann, R. E., & Rehm, J. (2011). *CAMH monitor eReport: Addiction and mental health indicators among Ontario adults, 1977–2009* (CAMH Research Document Series No. 31). Toronto: Centre for Addiction and Mental Health. Retrieved October 25, 2011, from http://www.camh.net/Research/camh_monitor.html

Indian and Northern Affairs Canada. (2003). Statement by Mr. Keith Conn, delegation of Canada to the second session of the UN Permanent Forum on Indigenous Issues on agenda item: Health. Ottawa: Author. Retrieved October 18, 2003, from http://www.ainc-inac.gc.ca/nr/spch/unp/hea_e.html

Ingraham, L. J., Kugelmass, S., Frenkel, E., Nathan, M., & Mirsky, A. F. (1995). Twenty-five year follow-up of the Israeli High-Risk Study: Current and lifetime psychopathology. *Schizophrenia Bulletin, 21,* 183–192.

Ingram, R. E. (1990). Self-focused attention in clinical disorders: Review and a conceptual model. *Psychological Bulletin, 107,* 156–176.

Ingram, R. E. (1991). Tilting at windmills: A response to Pyszczynski, Greenberg, Hamilton, and Nix. *Psychological Bulletin, 110,* 544–550.

Insel, K. C., and Badger, T. A. (2002), Deciphering the 4 D's: Cognitive decline, delirium, depression and dementia—a review. *Journal of Advanced Nursing, 38*(4), 360–368.

Institute of Medicine. (1990). *Broadening the base of treatment for alcohol problems: Report of a study by a committee of the Institute of Medicine, Division of Mental Health and Behavioral Medicine.* Washington, DC: National Academy Press.

Involving parents in therapy doubles success rates for bulimia treatment. (2007, September 7). *ScienceDaily.* Retrieved November 18, 2011, from http://www.sciencedaily.com/releases/2007/09/070903204931.htm

Irle, E., Exner, C., Thielen, K., Weniger, G., & Rüther, E. (1998). Obsessive-compulsive disorder and ventromedial frontal sessions: Clinical and neuropsychological findings. *American Journal of Psychiatry, 155,* 255–263.

Isaac, M., & Chand, P. K. (2006). Dissociative and conversion disorders: Defining boundaries. *Current Opinion in Psychiatry, 19,* 61–66.

J

Jablensky, A. (2006). Subtyping schizophrenia: Implications for genetic research. *Molecular Psychiatry, 11,* 815–836.

Jablensky, A., Sartorius, N., Ernberg, G., Anker, M., Korten, A., Cooper, J. E., . . . Bertelsen, A. (1992). Schizophrenia: Manifestations, incidence and course in different cultures: A World Health Organization ten-country study. *Psychological Medicine, 20*(Monograph Suppl.), 1–97.

Jackson, J., Calhoun, K. S., Amick, A. E., Maddever, H. M., & Habif, V. L. (1990). Young adult women who report childhood intrafamilial sexual abuse: Subsequent adjustment. *Archives of Sexual Behavior, 19,* 211–221.

Jacobi, C., Hayward, C., de Zwaan, M., Kraemer, H. C., & Agras, W. S. (2004). Coming to terms with risk factors for eating disorders: Application of risk terminology and suggestions for a general taxonomy. *Psychological Bulletin, 130,* 19–65.

Jacobson, N. S., Dobson, K. S., Truax, P. A., Addis, M. E., Koerner, K., Gollan, J. K., . . . Prince, S. E. (1996). A component analysis of cognitive-behavioral treatment for depression. *Journal of Consulting and Clinical Psychology, 64,* 295–304.

Jacobson, N. S., & Hollon, S. D. (1996). Cognitive-behavior therapy versus pharmacotherapy: Now that the jury's returned its verdict, it's time to present the rest of the evidence. *Journal of Consulting and Clinical Psychology, 64,* 74–80.

Janca, A. (2005). Rethinking somatoform disorders. *Current Opinion in Psychiatry, 18,* 65–71.

Janeck, A. S., Calamari, J. E., Riemann, B. C., & Heffelfinger, S. K. (2003). Too much thinking about thinking? Metacognitive differences in obsessive-compulsive disorder. *Journal of Anxiety Disorders, 17,* 181–195.

Jang, K. L. (2005). *The behavioral genetics of psychopathology: A clinical guide.* Mahwah, NJ: Erlbaum.

Jang, K. L., Livesley, W. J., Taylor, S., Stein, M. B., & Moon, E. C. (2004). Heritability of individual depressive symptoms. *Journal of Affective Disorders, 80,* 125–133.

Jang, K. L., Livesley, W. J., & Vernon, P. A. (1997). Gender-specific etiological differences in alcohol and drug problems: A behavioural genetic analysis. *Addiction, 92,* 1265–1276.

Jang, K. L., Livesley, W. J., & Vernon, P. A. (2002). The etiology of personality function: The University of British Colombia Twin Project. *Twin Research, 5*(5), 342–346.

Jang, K. L., Stein, M. B., Taylor, S., Asmundson, G. J., & Livesley, W. J. (2003). Exposure to traumatic events and experiences: Aetiological relationships with personality function. *Psychiatry Research, 120,* 61–69.

Jang, K. L., Vernon, P. A., & Livesley, W. J. (2001). Behavioural-genetic perspectives on personality function. *Canadian Journal of Psychiatry, 46,* 234–244.

Jellinek, E. M. (1960). *The disease concept of alcoholism.* New Haven, CT: Hillhouse.

Jensen, P. S., Martin, D., & Cantwell, D. P. (1997). Comorbidity in ADHD: Implications for research, practice, and DSM-V. *Journal of the American Academy of Child and Adolescent Psychiatry, 36,* 1065–1079.

Jeste, D. V., & Caligiuri, M. P. (1993). Tardive dyskinesia. *Schizophrenia Bulletin, 19,* 303–315.

Jilek, W. G. (2001, July). *Anorexia nervosa: Cultural factors in psychiatric disorders.* Paper presented at the 26th Congress of the World Federation for Mental Health, Vancouver. Retrieved July 31, 2003, from http://www.mentalhealth.com/mag1/wolfgangex.html

Joffe, R. T., & Gardner, D. M. (2000). *The Canadian psychotropic handbook.* Mississauga, ON: Sudler & Hennessey.

Johns, L. C., Gregg, L., Allen, P., & McGuire, P. K. (2006). Impaired verbal self-monitoring in psychosis: Effects of state, trait and diagnosis. *Psychological Medicine, 36,* 465–474.

Johnson, J. G., Cohen, P., Brown, J., Smailes, E. M., & Bernstein, D. P. (1999). Childhood maltreatment increases risk for personality disorders during early adulthood. *Archives of General Psychiatry, 56,* 600–606.

Johnson, P. A. (1989). *Wellness behaviour specialist program proposal for the Ontario Ministry of Colleges and Universities.* Unpublished manuscript. Confederation College, Thunder Bay, ON.

Johnson, W. G., Tsoh, J. Y., & Varnado, P. J. (1996). Eating disorders: Efficacy of pharmacological and psychological interventions. *Clinical Psychology Review, 16,* 457–478.

Joiner, T. E. (2006). *Why people die by suicide.* Cambridge, MA: Harvard University Press.

Joiner, T. E., Jr., Brown, J. S., & Wingate, L. R. (2005). The psychology and neurobiology of suicidal behavior. *Annual Review of Psychology, 56,* 287–314.

Jones, E. (1953). *The life and work of Sigmund Freud.* New York: Basic Books.

Jones, H. E. (2006). Drug addiction during pregnancy: Advances in maternal treatment and understanding child outcomes. *Current Directions in Psychological Science, 15,* 126–130.

Jones, J. M., Bennett, S., Olmsted, M. P., Lawson, M. L., & Rodin, G. (2001). Disordered eating attitudes and behaviours in teenaged girls: A school-based study. *CMAJ: Canadian Medical Association Journal, 165,* 547–552.

Jones, P. B., Rantakallio, P., Hartikainen, A.-L., Isohanni, M., & Sipila, P. (1998). Schizophrenia as a long-term outcome of pregnancy, delivery, and perinatal complications: A 28-year follow-up of the 1966 North Finland general population birth cohort. *American Journal of Psychiatry, 155,* 355–364.

Jouriles, E. N., Mehta, P., McDonald, R., & Francis, D. J. (1997). Psychometric properties of family members' reports of parental physical aggression toward clinic-referred children. *Journal of Consulting and Clinical Psychology, 65,* 309–318.

K

Kaback, M., Lim-Steele, J., Dabholkar, D., Brown, D., Levy, N., & Zeiger, K. (1993). Tay-Sachs disease: Carrier screening, prenatal diagnosis, and the molecular era. *JAMA: Journal of the American Medical Association, 270,* 2307–2315.

Kahan, B., & Goodstadt, M. (2002, April). *The IDM manual for using the Interactive Domain Model approach to health promotion.* Centre for Health Promotion, University of Toronto. Retrieved April 20, 2003, from http://www.utoronto.ca/chp/download

Kahn, M. W. (1982). Cultural clash and psychopathology in three aboriginal cultures. *Academic Psychology Bulletin, 4,* 553–561.

Kaiser, M. D., Hudac, C. M., Shultz, S., Lee, S. M., Cheung, C., Berken, A. M., . . . Pelphrey, K. A. (2010). Neural signatures of autism. *Proceedings of the National Academy of Sciences of the United States of America, 107,* 21223–21228.

Kane, J. M. (1996). Drug therapy: Schizophrenia. *New England Journal of Medicine, 334,* 34–41.

Kane, J. M., & Marder, S. R. (1993). Psychopharmalogic treatment of schizophrenia. *Schizophrenia Bulletin, 19,* 287–302.

Kanner, L. (1943). Autistic disturbances of affective content. *Nervous Child, 2,* 217–240.

Kanner, L., & Eisenberg, L. (1955). Notes on the follow-up studies of autistic children. In P. H. Hoch & J. Zubin (Eds.), *Psychopathology of childhood: The proceedings of the forty-fourth annual meeting of the American Psychopathological Association, held in New York City, June 1954.* New York: Grune & Stratton.

Kaplan, A. S. (2002). Psychological treatments for anorexia nervosa: A review of published studies and promising new directions. *Canadian Journal of Psychiatry, 47,* 235–242.

Kaplan, A. S., & Garfinkel, P. E. (1999). Difficulties in treating patients with eating disorders: A review of patient and clinical variables. *Canadian Journal of Psychiatry, 44,* 665–670.

Kaplan, A. S., & Woodside, D. B. (1987). Biological aspects of anorexia nervosa and bulimia nervosa. *Journal of Consulting and Clinical Psychology, 55,* 645–653.

Kaplan, H. S. (1974). *The new sex therapy: Active treatment of sexual dysfunctions.* New York: Brunner/Mazel.

Kaplan, H. S. (1987). *Sexual aversion, sexual phobias, and panic disorder.* New York: Brunner/Mazel.

Kaplan, S. J. (1986). *The private practice of behavior therapy: A guide for behavioral practitioners.* New York: Plenum Press.

Kapur, S., & Remington, G. (2001). Atypical antipsychotics: New directions and new challenges in the treatment of schizophrenia. *Annual Review of Medicine, 52,* 503–517.

Kasper, M. E., Rogers, R., & Adams, P. A. (1996). Dangerousness and command hallucinations: An investigation of psychotic inpatients. *Bulletin of the American Academy of Psychiatry and the Law, 24,* 219–224.

Kay, S. R. (1990). Significance of the positive-negative distinction in schizophrenia. *Schizophrenia Bulletin, 16,* 635–652.

Kazdin, A. E. (1992). *Research design in clinical psychology* (2nd ed.). Boston: Allyn & Bacon.

Kazdin, A. E., & Weisz, J. R. (1998). Identifying and developing empirically supported child and adolescent treatments. *Journal of Consulting and Clinical Psychology, 66,* 19–36.

Kazdin, A. E., & Whitley, M. K. (2003). Treatment of parental stress to enhance therapeutic change among children referred for aggressive and antisocial behavior. *Journal of Consulting and Clinical Psychology, 71,* 504–515.

Keane, T. M., Marshall, A. D., & Taft, C. T. (2006). Posttraumatic stress disorder: Etiology, epidemiology, and treatment outcome. *Annual Review of Clinical Psychology, 2,* 161–197.

Kearins, J. M. (1981). Visual spatial memory in Australian Aboriginal children in desert regions. *Cognitive Psychology, 13,* 434–460.

Keel, P. K., Mitchell, J. E., Miller, K. B., Davis, T. L., & Crow, S. J. (1999). Long-term outcome of bulimia nervosa. *Archives of General Psychiatry, 56,* 63–69.

Keiller, S. W., & Graham, J. R. (1993). The meaning of low scores on MMP-2 clinical scales of normal subjects. *Journal of Personality Assessment, 62,* 211–223.

Keith, S. J., Regier, D. A., & Rae, D. S. (1991). Schizophrenic disorders. In L. N. Robins & D. A. Regier (Eds.), *Psychiatric disorders in America: The Epidemiologic Catchment Area Study* (pp. 33–52). New York: Free Press.

Kellner, R. (1992). Diagnosis and treatment of hypochondriacal syndromes. *Psychosomatics, 33,* 278–289.

Kendell, R., & Jablensky, A. (2003). Distinguishing between the validity and utility of psychiatric diagnoses. *American Journal of Psychiatry, 160,* 4–12.

Kendler, K. S., & Gardner, C. O., Jr. (1998). Boundaries of major depression: An evaluation of DSM-IV criteria. *American Journal of Psychiatry, 155,* 172–177.

Kendler, K. S., MacLean, C., Neale, M., Kessler, R., Heath, A., & Eaves, L. (1991). The genetic epidemiology of bulimia nervosa. *American Journal of Psychiatry, 148,* 1627–1637.

Kendler, K. S., & Prescott, C. A. (2006). *Genes, environment, and psychopathology: Understanding the causes of psychiatric and substance use disorders.* New York: Guilford.

Kendler, K. S., & Walsh, D. (1995). Schizotypal personality disorder in parents and the risk for schizophrenia in siblings. *Schizophrenia Bulletin, 21,* 47–52.

Kennedy, S. H., & Lam, R. W. (2003). Enhancing outcomes in the management of treatment resistant depression: A focus on atypical antipsychotics. *Bipolar Disorders, 5*(Suppl. 2), 36–47.

Kennedy, S. H., Lam, R. W., Cohen, N. L., Ravindran, A. V., & CANMAT Depression Work Group. (2001). Clinical guidelines for the treatment of depressive disorders: IV. Medications and other biological treatments. *Canadian Journal of Psychiatry, 46*(Suppl. 1), 38S–58S.

Kent, A., & Waller, G. (2000). Childhood emotional abuse and eating psychopathology. *Clinical Psychology Review, 20,* 887–903.

Kernberg, O. F. (1975). *Borderline conditions and pathological narcissism.* New York: Aronson.

Kershner, R. (1996). Adolescent attitudes about rape. *Adolescence, 31,* 29–33.

Kessler, D. A., Barnett, P. S., Witt, A., Zeller, M. R., Mande, J. R., & Schultz, W. B. (1997). The legal and scientific basis for FDA's assertion of jurisdiction over cigarettes and smokeless tobacco. *JAMA: Journal of the American Medical Association, 277,* 405–409.

Kessler, R. C., Berglund, P., Demler, O., Jin, R., Merikangas, K. R., & Walters, E. E. (2005). Lifetime prevalence and age-of-onset distributions of DSM-IV disorders in the National Comorbidity Survey Replication, *Archives of General Psychiatry, 62*(6), 593–602.

Kessler, R. C., Chiu, W. T., Demler, O., & Walters, E. E. (2005). Prevalence, severity, and comorbidity of 12-month DSM-IV disorders in the National Comorbidity Survey Replication. *Archives of General Psychiatry, 62*(6), 617–627.

Kessler, R. C., Chiu, W. T., Jin, R., Ruscio, A. M., Shear, K., & Walters, E. E. (2006). The epidemiology of panic attacks, panic disorder, and agoraphobia in the National Comorbidity Survey Replication. *Archives of General Psychiatry, 63,* 415–424.

Kessler, R. C., Downey, G., Milavsky, J. R., & Stipp, H. (1988). Clustering of teenage suicides after television news stories about suicides: A reconsideration. *American Journal of Psychiatry, 145*(11), 1379–1383.

Kety, S. S., Rosenthal, D., Wender, P. H., & Schulsinger, F. (1968). The types and prevalence of mental illness in the biological and adoptive families of adopted schizophrenics. In D. Rosenthal & S. S. Kety (Eds.), *The transmission of schizophrenia: Proceedings of the second research conference of the Foundations' Fund for Research in Psychiatry, Dorado, Puerto Rico, 26 June to 1 July 1967.* Oxford: Pergamon.

Kety, S. S., Rosenthal, D., Wender, P. H., Schulsinger, F., & Jacobsen, B. (1975). Mental illness in the biological and adoptive families of adoptive individuals who have become schizophrenic: A preliminary report based on psychiatric interviews. In R. R. Fieve, D. Rosenthal, & H. Brill (Eds.), *Genetic research in psychiatry: Proceedings of the sixty-third annual meeting of the American Psychopathological Association.* Baltimore, MD: Johns Hopkins University Press.

Kety, S. S., Rosenthal, D., Wender, P. H., Schulsinger, F., & Jacobsen, B. (1978). The biological and adoptive families of adopted individuals who become schizophrenic. In L. C. Wynne, R. L. Cromwell, & S. Mathysse (Eds.), *The nature of schizophrenia: New approaches to research and treatment* (pp. 25–37). New York: Wiley.

Khan, S., Murray, R. P., & Barnes, G. E. (2002). A structural equation model of the effect of poverty and unemployment on alcohol abuse. *Addictive Behaviors, 27,* 405–423.

Kiehl, K. A., Smith, A. M., Hare, R. D., Mendrek, A., Forste, B. B., Brink, J., & Liddle, P. F. (2001). Limbic abnormalities in affective processing by criminal psychopaths as revealed by functional magnetic resonance imaging. *Biological Psychiatry, 50,* 678–684.

Kihlstrom, J. K. (2005). Dissociative disorders. *Annual Review of Clinical Psychology, 1,* 227–253.

Killackey, E., & Yung, A. R. (2007). Effectiveness of early intervention in psychosis. *Current Opinion in Psychiatry, 20,* 121–125.

Kim, S. C., & Seo, K. K. (1998). Efficacy and safety of fluoxetine, sertraline, and clomipramine in patients with premature ejaculation: A double-blind, placebo-controlled study. *Journal of Urology, 159,* 425–427.

Kimerling, R., & Calhoun, K. S. (1994). Somatic symptoms, social support, and treatment seeking among sexual assault victims. *Journal of Consulting and Clinical Psychology, 62,* 333–340.

Kirby, M. J. L., & Keon, W. J. (2004). *Mental health, mental illness and addiction: Overview of policies and programs in Canada. Interim report of the Standing Senate Committee on Social Affairs, Science and Technology.* Ottawa: Senate of Canada. Retrieved from http://www.parl.gc.ca/Content/SEN/Committee/381/soci/rep/report1/repintnov04vol1-e.pdf

Kirby, M. J. L., & Keon, W. J. (2006). *Out of the shadows at last: Transforming mental health, mental illness and addiction services in Canada.* Ottawa: Senate of Canada, Standing Senate Committee on Social Affairs, Science and Technology. Retrieved from http://www.parl.gc.ca/Content/SEN/Committee/391/soci/rep/rep02may06-e.htm

Kirmayer, L. J. (2001). Cultural variations in the clinical presentation of depression and anxiety: Implications for diagnosis and treatment. *Journal of Clinical Psychiatry, 62*(Suppl. 13), 22–28.

Kirmayer, L. J., Brass, G. M., & Tait, C. L. (2000). The mental health of Aboriginal peoples: Transformations of identity and community. *Canadian Journal of Psychiatry, 45,* 607–616.

Kirmayer, L. J., Groleau, D., Guzder, J., Blake, C., & Jarvis, E. (2003). Cultural consultation: A model of mental health service for multicultural societies. *Canadian Journal of Psychiatry, 48,* 145–153.

Kirmayer, L. J., & Looper, K. J. (2006). Abnormal illness behaviour: Physiological, psychological and social dimensions of coping with distress. *Current Opinion in Psychiatry, 19,* 54–60.

Kirmayer, L. J., & Minas, H. (2000). The future of cultural psychiatry: An international perspective. *Canadian Journal of Psychiatry, 45,* 438–446.

Kissel, R. C., Whitman, T. L., & Reid, D. H. (1983). An institutional staff training and self-management program for developing multiple self-care skills in severely/profoundly retarded individuals. *Journal of Applied Behavior Analysis, 16,* 395–415.

Klein, D. N., & Santiago, N. J. (2003). Dysthymia and chronic depression: Introduction, classification, risk factors, and course. *Journal of Clinical Psychology, 59,* 807–816.

Kleinman, A. (1987). Anthropology and psychiatry: The role of culture in cross-cultural research on illness. *British Journal of Psychiatry, 151,* 447–454.

Kleinplatz, P. J. (2003). What's new in sex therapy? From stagnation to fragmentation. *Sexual and Relationship Therapy, 18,* 95–106.

Klepinger, D. H., Billy, J. O., Tanfer, K., & Grady, W. R. (1993). Perceptions of AIDS risk and severity and their association with risk-related behavior among U.S. men. *Family Planning Perspectives, 25*(2), 74–82.

Klerman, G. L. (1984). Ideology and science in the individual psychotherapy of schizophrenia. *Schizophrenia Bulletin, 10,* 608–612.

Klerman, G. L., Weissman, M. M., Rounsaville, B. J., & Chevron, E. S. (1984). *Interpersonal psychotherapy of depression.* New York: Basic Books.

Klesges, R. C., Winders, S. E., Meyers, A. W., Eck, L. H., Ward, K. D., Hultquist, C. M., . . . Shadish, W. R. (1997). How much weight gain occurs following smoking cessation? A comparison of weight gain using both continuous and point prevalence abstinence. *Journal of Consulting and Clinical Psychology, 65,* 286–291.

Knoll, J. L., IV, Garver, D. L., Ramberg, J. E., Kingsbury, S. J., Croissant, D., & McDermott, B. (1998). Heterogeneity of the psychoses: Is there a neurodegenerative psychosis? *Schizophrenia Bulletin, 24,* 365–379.

Knudsen, D. D. (1991). Child sexual coercion. In E. Grauerholz & M. A. Koralewski (Eds.), *Sexual coercion: A sourcebook on its nature, causes, and prevention* (pp. 17–28). Lexington, MA: Lexington.

Kobak, K. A., Greist, J. H., Jefferson, J. W., & Katzelnick, D. J. (1996). Computer-administered clinical rating scales: A review. *Psychopharmacology, 127,* 291–301.

Kobak, K. A., Taylor, L. H., Dotti, S. L., Geist, J. H., Jefferson, J. W., Burroughs, D., . . . Serlin, R. C. (1997). A computer-administered telephone interview to identify mental disorders. *JAMA: Journal of the American Medical Association, 278,* 905–910.

Koenigsberg, H. W., Harvey, P. D., Mitropoulou, V., Schmeidler, J., New, A. S., Goodman, M., . . . Siever, L. J. (2002). Characterizing affective instability in borderline personality disorder. *American Journal of Psychiatry, 159,* 784–788.

Koerner, K., & Linehan, M. M. (2002). Research on dialectical behavior therapy for patients with borderline personality disorder. *Psychiatric Clinics of North America, 23*(1), 151–167.

Kohut, H. (1966). Forms and transformations of narcissism. *Journal of the American Psychoanalytic Association, 14,* 243–272.

Kolassa, I.-T., & Elbert, T. (2007). Structural and functional neuroplasticity in relation to traumatic stress. *Current Directions in Psychological Science, 16,* 321–325.

Kolbert, E. (1994, January 21). Demons replace dolls and bicycles in world of children of the quake. *The New York Times,* p. A19.

Koss, M. P., Goodman, L. A., Browne, A., Fitzgerald, L. F., Keita, G. P., & Russo, N. F. (1994). *No safe haven: Male violence against women at home, at work, and in the community.* Washington, DC: American Psychological Association.

Kotler, M., Cohen, H., Segman, R., Gritsenko, I., Nemanov, L., Lerer, B., . . . Ebstein, R. P. (1997). Excess dopamine D4 receptor (D4DR) exon III seven repeat allele in opioid-dependent subjects. *Molecular Psychiatry, 2,* 251–254.

Kovacs, M. (1996). Presentation and course of major depressive disorder during childhood and later years of the lifespan. *Journal of American Academy of Children and Adolescent Psychiatry, 35,* 705–715.

Kovacs, M., Devlin, B., Pollock, M., Richards, C., & Mukerji, P. (1997). A controlled family history study of childhood-onset depressive disorder. *Archives of General Psychiatry, 54,* 613–623.

Kraepelin, E. (1909–1913). *Psychiatrie* (8th ed.). Leipzig: Barth.

Kresin, D. (1993). Medical aspects of inhibited sexual desire disorder. In W. O'Donohue & J. H. Geer (Eds.), *Handbook of sexual dysfunctions: Assessment and treatment* (pp. 15–52). Boston: Allyn & Bacon.

Kring, A. M., Kerr, S. L., Smith, D. A., & Neale, J. M. (1993). Flat affect in schizophrenia does not reflect diminished subjective experience of emotion. *Journal of Abnormal Psychology, 102,* 507–517.

Kring, A. M., & Neale, J. M. (1996). Do schizophrenic patients show a disjunctive relationship among expressive, experiential, and psychophysiological components of emotion? *Journal of Abnormal Psychology, 105,* 249–257.

Krueger, R. F., & Markon, K. E. (2006). Reinterpreting comorbidity: A model-based approach to understanding and classifying psychopathology. *Annual Review of Clinical Psychology, 2,* 111–133.

Kruesi, M. J., Fine, S., Valladares, L., Phillips, R. A., Jr., & Rapoport, J. L. (1992). Paraphilias: A double-blind cross-over comparison of clomipramine versus desipramine. *Archives of Sexual Behavior, 21,* 587–593.

Kryger, M. H. (2001). Waking up to the consequences of sleep disorders. Winnipeg, MB: St. Boniface General Hospital Research Centre. Retrieved August 3, 2003, from http://www.sbrc.umanitoba.ca/framekryger.htm

Kryger, M. H., Roth, T., & Dement, W. C. (Eds.). (2005). *Principles and practice of sleep medicine* (4th ed.). Toronto: Saunders.

Kuehn, B. M. (2007). Opiod prescriptions soar. *JAMA: Journal of the American Medical Association, 297,* 249–251.

Kupfer, D. J. (1999). Research in affective disorders comes of age [Editorial]. *American Journal of Psychiatry, 156,* 165–167.

Kurtz, J. E., & Blais, M. A. (2007). Introduction to the special issue on the Personality Assessment Inventory. *Journal of Personality Assessment, 88*(1), 1–4.

Kwon, S.-M., & Oei, T. P. S. (1994). The roles of two levels of cognitions in the development, maintenance, and treatment of depression. *Clinical Psychology Review, 14,* 331–358.

Kymalainen, J. A., Weisman, A. G., Resales, G. A., & Armesto, J. C. (2006). Ethnicity, expressed emotion, and communication deviance in family members of patients with schizophrenia. *Journal of Nervous and Mental Disease, 194,* 391–396.

L

Ladouceur, R. (2002). *Understanding and treating the pathological gambler.* New York: Wiley.

Lahey, B. B., Loeber, R., Hart, E. L., Frick, P. J., Applegate, B., Zhang, Q., . . . Russo, M. F. (1995). Four-year longitudinal study of conduct disorder in boys: Patterns and predictors of persistence. *Journal of Abnormal Psychology, 104,* 83–93.

Laishes, J. (2002). *The 2002 mental health strategy for women offenders.* Ottawa: Correctional Services Canada. Retrieved from http://www.csc-scc.gc.ca/text/prgrm/fsw/mhealth/toc-eng.shtml

Lakhan, S. E., & Callaway, H. (2010). Deep brain stimulation for obsessive-compulsive disorder and treatment-resistant depression: Systematic review. *BMC Research Notes, 3*(1), 60.

Lalonde, J. K., Hudson, J. I., Gigante, R. A., & Pope, H. G., Jr. (2001). Canadian and American psychiatrists' attitudes toward dissociative disorders diagnoses. *Canadian Journal of Psychiatry, 46,* 407–412.

Lam, R. W., & Levitt, A. J. (1999). *Canadian consensus guidelines for the treatment of seasonal affective disorder.* Vancouver: Clinical and Academic Publishing.

Lam, R. W., Levitt, A. J., Levitan, R. D., Enns, M. W., Morehouse, R., Michalak, E. E., & Tam, E. M. (2006). The CAN-SAD study: Randomized controlled trial of the effectiveness of light therapy and fluoxetine in patients with winter seasonal affective disorder. *American Journal of Psychiatry, 163,* 805–812.

Lamberg, L. (2003). Advances in eating disorders offer food for thought. *JAMA: Journal of the American Medical Association, 290,* 1437–1442.

Lambert, M. J., & Bergin, A. E. (1994). The effectiveness of psychotherapy. In A. E. Bergin & S. L. Garfield (Eds.), *Handbook of psychotherapy and behavior change* (4th ed., pp. 72–113). New York: Wiley.

Landau, S. M., Harvey, D., Madison, C. M., Reiman, E. M., Foster, N. L., Aisen, P. S., . . . Jagust, W. J. (2010). Comparing predictors of conversion and decline in mild cognitive impairment. *Neurology, 75,* 230–238.

Landy, S., & Tam, K. K. (1998). *Understanding the contribution of multiple risk factors on child development at various ages* (Catalogue No. MP32-28/98-22E). Ottawa: Human Resources Development Canada. Retrieved from http://publications.gc.ca/pub?id=81774&sl=0

Lang, P. J. (1968). Fear reduction and fear behavior: Problems in treating a construct. In J. M. Schlien (Ed.), *Research in psychotherapy* (Vol. 3, pp. 90–102). Washington, DC: American Psychological Association.

Langevin, R., & Lang, R. (1987). The courtship disorders. In G. D. Wilson (Ed.), *Variant sexuality: Research and theory* (pp. 202–228). London: Croom Helm.

Larøi, F. (2006). The phenomenological diversity of hallucinations: Some theoretical and clinical implications. *Psychologica Belgica, 46,* 163–183.

The last draw for smokers. (1996, October). *UC Berkeley Wellness Letter, 13,* 2–3.

Lau, E. (2001). More and more. In L. Crozier & P. Lane (Eds.), *Addicted: Notes from the belly of the beast* (pp. 73–84). Vancouver: Greystone Books, an imprint of Douglas & McIntyre Publishers Inc.

Laumann, E. O., Gagnon, J. H., Michael, R. T., & Michaels, S. (1994). *The social organization of sexuality: Sexual practices in the United States.* Chicago: University of Chicago Press.

Laumann, E. O., Paik, A., & Rosen, R. C. (1999). Sexual dysfunction in the United States: Prevalence and predictors. *JAMA: Journal of the American Medical Association, 281,* 537–544.

Lauriello, J., Hoff, A., Wieneke, M. H., Blankfeld, H., Faustman, W. O., Rosenbloom, M., . . . Pfefferbaum, A. (1997). Similar extent of brain dysmorphology in severely ill women and men with schizophrenia. *American Journal of Psychiatry, 154,* 819–825.

Lavallée, C., & Bourgault, C. (2000). The health of Cree, Inuit and southern Quebec women: Similarities and differences. *Canadian Journal of Public Health, 91,* 212–216.

Lawson, D. M. (1983). Alcoholism. In M. Hersen (Ed.), *Outpatient behavior therapy: A clinical guide* (pp. 143–172). New York: Grune & Stratton.

Learning Disabilities Association of Canada. (2002). Official definition of learning disabilities. Ottawa: Author. Retrieved November 22, 2011, from http://www.ldac-acta.ca/en/learn-more/ld-defined/official-definition-of-learning-disabilities.html

Learning Disabilities Association of Canada. (2003a). *Advocating for your child with learning disabilities: IV. Programming plans, placement options.* Ottawa: Author. Retrieved October 18, 2003, from http://www.ldac-taac.ca/english/indepth/advocacy/yorchild/6.htm

Learning Disabilities Association of Canada. (2003b). *Fact Sheet. Assistive technology and learning disabilities.* Ottawa: Author. Retrieved October 18, 2003, from http://www.ldac-taac.ca/english/indepth/assistiv/ATandLD.pdf

Leary, W. E. (1996, December 18). Responses of alcoholics to therapies seem similar. *The New York Times,* p. A17.

Lee, J. K. P., Jackson, H. J., Pattison, P., & Ward, T. (2002). Developmental risk factors for sexual offending. *Child Abuse & Neglect, 26,* 73–92.

Lee, S. (2001). From diversity to unity: The classification of mental disorders in 21st-century China. *Psychiatric Clinics of North America, 24,* 421–431.

Lee, T. H. (1997, May). Marijuana's cognitive effects persist. *Journal Watch for Psychiatry, 2*(5), 41.

Leff, J., & Vaughn, C. (1981). The role of maintenance therapy and relatives' expressed emotion in relapse of schizophrenia: A two-year follow-up. *British Journal of Psychiatry, 139,* 102–104.

Lefley, H. P. (1990). Culture and chronic mental illness. *Hospital and Community Psychiatry, 41,* 277–286.

Leger Marketing. (2002). *Canadians and sleep: Report.* Retrieved August 3, 2003, from http://www.legermarketing.com/documents/spclm/020121eng.pdf

Lehmann, H. E., & Hanrahan, G. E. (1954). Chlorpromazine: New inhibiting agent for psychomotor excitement and manic states. *Archives of Neurology and Psychiatry, 71,* 227–237.

Leiblum, S. R. (2006). *Principles and practice of sex therapy* (4th ed.). New York: Guilford.

Leibson, C. L., Katusic, S. K., Barbaresi, W. J., Ransom, J., & O'Brien, P. C. (2001). Use and costs of medical care for children and adolescents with and without attention-deficit/hyperactivity disorder. *JAMA: Journal of the American Medical Association, 285,* 60–66.

Leichsenring, F., Hiller, W., Weissberg, M., & Leibing, E. (2006). Cognitive-behavioral therapy and psychodynamic psychotherapy: Techniques, efficacy, and indications. *American Journal of Psychotherapy, 60,* 233–259.

Leichsenring, F., & Rabung, S. (2008). Effectiveness of long-term psychodynamic psychotherapy: A meta-analysis. *JAMA: Journal of the American Medical Association, 300,* 1551–1565.

Leit, R. A., Gray, J. J., & Pope, H. G., Jr. (2002). The media's representation of the ideal male body: A cause for muscle dysmorphia? *International Journal of Eating Disorders, 31,* 334–338.

Leonardo, E. D., & Hen, R. (2006). Genetics of affective and anxiety disorders. *Annual Review of Psychology, 57,* 117–137.

Leszcz, M., MacKenzie, R., el-Guebaly, N., Atkinson, M. J., & Wiesenthal, S. (2002). Part V: Canadian psychiatrists' use of psychotherapy. *Canadian Psychiatric Association: The Bulletin, 34*(5), 28–31.

Letendre, A. D. (2002). Aboriginal traditional medicine: Where does it fit? *Crossing Boundaries—An Interdisciplinary Journal, 1*(2), 78–87.

Letourneau, E., & O'Donohue, W. (1993). Sexual desire disorders. In W. O'Donohue & J. H. Geer (Eds.), *Handbook of sexual dysfunctions: Assessment and treatment* (pp. 53–81). Boston: Allyn & Bacon.

Letourneau, E. J., Resnick, H. S., Kilpatrick, D. G., Saunders, B. E., & Best, C. L. (1996). Comorbidity of sexual problems and posttraumatic stress disorder in female crime victims. *Behavior Therapy, 27,* 321–336.

Levitan, R. D., Kaplan, A. S., Joffe, R. T., Levitt, A. J., & Brown, G. M. (1997). Hormonal and subjective responses to intravenous metachlorophenylpiperazine in bulimia nervosa. *Archives of General Psychiatry, 54,* 521–527.

Levitt, A. J., Boyle, M. H., Joffe, R. T., & Baumal, Z. (2000). Estimated prevalence of the seasonal subtype of major depression in a Canadian community sample. *Canadian Journal of Psychiatry, 45,* 650–654.

Levy, S. R., Jurkovic, G. L., & Spirito, A. (1995). A multisystems analysis of adolescent suicide attempters. *Journal of Abnormal Child Psychology, 23,* 221–234.

Lewinsohn, P. M., Antonuccio, D. O., Steinmetz Breckenridge, J., & Teri, L. (1984). *The Coping with Depression course: A psychoeducational intervention for unipolar depression.* Eugene, OR: Castalia.

Lewinsohn, P. M., & Clarke, G. N. (1999). Psychosocial treatments for adolescent depression. *Clinical Psychology Review, 19,* 329–342.

Lewinsohn, P. M., & Libet, J. M. (1972). Pleasant events, activity schedules, and depressions. *Journal of Abnormal Psychology, 79,* 291–295.

Lewinsohn, P. M., Rohde, P., & Seeley, J. R. (1994). Psychosocial risk factors for future adolescent suicide attempts. *Journal of Consulting and Clinical Psychology, 62,* 297–305.

Lewinsohn, P. M., Sullivan, J. M., & Grosscup, S. J. (1980). Changing reinforcing events: An approach to the treatment of depression. *Psychotherapy: Theory, Research, & Practice, 17,* 322–334.

Lewinsohn, P. M., Teri, L., & Wasserman, D. (1983). Depression. In M. Hersen (Ed.), *Outpatient behavior therapy: A practical guide* (pp. 81–108). New York: Grune & Stratton.

Lezak, M. D., Howieson, D. B., & Loring, D. W. (2004). *Neuropsychological assessment* (4th ed.). New York: Oxford University Press.

Lichtenstein, E., & Glasgow, R. E. (1992). Smoking cessation: What have we learned over the past decade? *Journal of Consulting and Clinical Psychology, 60,* 518–527.

Liddle, P. F. (1999). The multidimensional phenotype of schizophrenia. In C. A. Tamminga (Ed.), *Schizophrenia in a molecular age* (pp. 1–28). Washington, DC: American Psychiatric Press.

Liebowitz, M. R., Asnis, G., Mangano, R., & Tzanis, E. (2009). A double-blind, placebo-controlled, parallel-group, flexible-dose study of venlafaxine extended release capsules in adult outpatients with panic disorder. *Journal of Clinical Psychiatry, 70,* 550–561.

Lilienfeld, S. O., & Andrews, B. P. (1996). Development and preliminary validation of a self-report measure of psychopathic personality traits in noncriminal populations. *Journal of Personality Assessment, 66,* 488–524.

Lilienfeld, S. O., & Lynn, S. J. (2003). Dissociative identity disorder: Multiple personalities, multiple controversies. In S. O. Lilienfeld, S. J. Lynn, & J. M. Lohr (Eds.), *Science and pseudoscience in clinical psychology* (pp. 109–142). New York: Guilford.

Lilienfeld, S. O., & Marino, L. (1995). Mental disorder as a Roschian concept: A critique of Wakefield's "harmful dysfunction" analysis. *Journal of Abnormal Psychology, 104,* 411–420.

Lindahl, V., Pearson, J. L., & Colpe, L. (2005). Prevalence of suicidality during pregnancy and the postpartum. *Archives of Women's Mental Health, 8,* 77–87.

Linde, K., Berner, M., Egger, M., & Mulrow, C. (2005). St John's wort for depression: Meta-analysis of randomised controlled trials. *British Journal of Psychiatry, 186,* 99–107.

Linehan, M. M. (1993). *Cognitive-behavioral treatment of borderline personality disorder.* New York: Guilford.

Linehan, M. M., Camper, P., Chiles, J. A., Strosahl, K., & Shearin, E. (1987). Interpersonal problem solving and parasuicide. *Cognitive Therapy and Research, 11,* 1–12.

Links, P. S. (1998). Developing effective services for patients with personality disorders. *Canadian Journal of Psychiatry, 43,* 251–259.

Links, P. S., Heslegrave, R., & van Reekum, R. (1998). Prospective follow-up study of borderline personality disorder: Prognosis, prediction of outcome, and Axis II comorbidity. *Canadian Journal of Psychiatry, 43,* 265–270.

Liotti, G., & Pasquini, P. (2000). Predictive factors for borderline personality disorder: Patients' early traumatic experiences and losses suffered by the attachment figure. *Acta Psychiatrica Scandinavica, 102*(4), 282–289.

Lipps, G., & Frank, J. (1997). The National Longitudinal Survey of Children and Youth, 1994–1995: Initial results from the school component (Catalogue no. 81-003-XPB). *Education Quarterly Review, Statistics Canada, 4*(2), 43–57.

Litman, L. C. (2003). Sexual sadism with lust-murder proclivities in a female? *Canadian Journal of Psychiatry, 48,* 127.

Livesley, W. J. (1998). Suggestions for a framework for an empirically based classification of personality disorder. *Canadian Journal of Psychiatry, 43,* 137–147.

Livesley, W. J. (2001). Conceptual and taxonomic issues. In W. J. Livesley (Ed.), *Handbook of personality disorders: Theory, research, and treatment* (pp. 3–38). New York: Guilford.

Livesley, W. J. (2005). Principles and strategies for treating personality disorder. *Canadian Journal of Psychiatry, 50,* 442–450.

Livesley, W. J., Jang, K. L., Jackson, D. N., & Vernon, P. A. (1993). Genetic and environmental contributions to dimensions of personality disorder. *American Journal of Psychiatry, 150,* 1826–1831.

Livesley, W. J., Jang, K. L., & Vernon, P. A. (1998). Phenotypic and genetic structure of traits delineating personality disorders. *Archives of General Psychiatry, 55,* 941–948.

Livingston, J. D., Wilson, D., Tien, G., & Bond, L. (2003). A follow-up study of persons found not criminally responsible on account of mental disorder in British Columbia. *Canadian Journal of Psychiatry, 48,* 408–415.

Livingstone, M. S., Rosen, G. D., Drislane, F. W., & Galaburda, A. M. (1991). Physiological and anatomical evidence for a magnocellular defect in developmental dyslexia. *Proceedings of the National Academy of Sciences, 88,* 7943–7947.

Lo, H. T., & Fung, K. P. (2003). Culturally competent psychotherapy. *Canadian Journal of Psychiatry, 48,* 161–170.

Lochman, J. E., & Dodge, K. A. (1994). Social-cognitive processes of severely violent, moderately aggressive, and nonaggressive boys. *Journal of Consulting and Clinical Psychology, 62,* 366–374.

Lochman, J. E., & Lenhart, L. A. (1993). Anger coping intervention for aggressive children: Conceptual models and outcome effects. *Clinical Psychology Review, 13,* 785–805.

Loftus, E. F. (1996). The myth of repressed memory and the realities of science. *Clinical Psychology: Science and Practice, 3,* 356–365.

Loftus, E. F., & Davis, D. (2006). Recovered memories. *Annual Review of Clinical Psychology, 2,* 469–498.

LoPiccolo, J. (1990). Sexual dysfunction. In A. S. Bellack, M. Hersen, & A. E. Kazdin (Eds.), *International handbook of behavior modification and therapy* (2nd ed., pp. 575–564). New York: Plenum.

LoPiccolo, J., & Stock, W. E. (1986). Treatment of sexual dysfunction. *Journal of Consulting and Clinical Psychology, 54,* 158–167.

Loranger, A. W., Sartorius, N., Andreoli, A., Berger, P., Buchheim, P., Channabasavanna, S. M., . . . Regier, D. A. (1994). The International Personalty Disorder Examination: The World Health Organization/Alcohol, Drug, Abuse and Mental Health Administration International Pilot Study of Personality Disorders. *Archives of General Psychiatry, 51,* 215–224.

Lovaas, O. I. (1987). Behavioral treatment and normal educational and intellectual functioning in young autistic children. *Journal of Consulting and Clinical Psychology, 55,* 3–9.

Lovaas, O. I., Koegel, R. L., & Schreibman, L. (1979). Stimulus overselectivity in autism: A review of the research. *Psychological Bulletin, 86,* 1236–1254.

Lowe, M. R., Gleaves, D. H., & Murphy-Eberenz, K. P. (1998). On the relation of dieting and bingeing in bulimia nervosa. *Journal of Abnormal Psychology, 107,* 263–271.

Lukassen, J., & Beaudet, M. P. (2005). Alcohol dependence and depression among heavy drinkers in Canada. *Social Science & Medicine, 61,* 1658–1667.

Luntz, B. K., & Widom, C. S. (1994). Antisocial personality disorder in abused and neglected children grown up. *American Journal of Psychiatry, 151,* 670–674.

Luthar, S. S., & Cicchetti, D. (2000). The construct of resilience: Implications for interventions and social policies. *Development and Psychopathology, 12,* 857–885.

Lydiard, R. B. (2003). The role of GABA in anxiety disorders. *Journal of Clinical Psychiatry, 64*(Suppl. 3), 21–27.

Lykken, D. T. (1957). A study of anxiety in the sociopathic personality. *Journal of Abnormal and Social Psychology, 55,* 6–10.

Lyons, M. J., Goldberg, J., Eisen, S. A., True, W., Tsuang, M. T., Meyer, J. M., & Henderson, W. G. (1993). Do genes influence exposure to trauma? A twin study of combat. *American Journal of Medical Genetics, 48,* 22–27.

M

MacDonald, C. (2002). Treatment resistance in anorexia nervosa and the pervasiveness of ethics in clinical decision making. *Canadian Journal of Psychiatry, 47,* 267–270.

Mackay, A. V. (1980). Positive and negative schizophrenic symptoms and the role of dopamine. *British Journal of Psychiatry, 137,* 383–386.

MacLatchy-Gaudet, H. A., & Stewart, S. H. (2001). The context-specific positive alcohol outcome expectancies of university women. *Addictive Behaviors, 26,* 31–49.

Macnaughton, E. (2000). Cultural competence and "the knowledge resource base." *Visions: BC's Mental Health Journal,* 9(Winter), 14–15.

MacPhillamy, D. J., & Lewinsohn, P. M. (1974). Depression as a function of levels of desired and obtained pleasure. *Journal of Abnormal Psychology, 83,* 651–657.

Magnusson, A., & Partonen, T. (2005). The diagnosis, symptomatology, and epidemiology of seasonal affective disorder. *CNS Spectrums, 10,* 625–634.

Maher, W. B., & Maher, B. A. (1985). Psychopathology: I. From ancient times to the eighteenth century. In G. A. Kimble & K. Schlesinger (Eds.), *Topics in the history of psychology* (Vol. 2). Hillsdale, NJ: Erlbaum.

Mahler, M., & Kaplan, L. (1977). Developmental aspects in the assessment of narcissistic and so-called borderline personalities. In P. Hartocollis (Ed.), *Borderline personality disorders: The concept, the syndrome, the patient* (pp. 71–85). New York: International Universities Press.

Maier, S. F., & Seligman, M. E. P. (1976). Learned helplessness: Theory and evidence. *Journal of Experimental Psychology (General), 105,* 3–46.

Maletzky, B. M. (1991). *Treating the sexual offender.* Newbury Park, CA: Sage.

Maletzky, B. M. (1998). The paraphilias: Research and treatment. In P. E. Nathan & J. M. Gorman (Eds.), *A guide to treatments that work* (pp. 472–500). New York: Oxford University Press.

Maletzky, B. M., & Steinhauser, C. (2002). A 25-year follow-up of cognitive/behavioral therapy with 7,275 sexual offenders. *Behavior Modification, 26,* 123–147.

Malla, A. K., Norman, R. M. G., & Joober, R. (2005). First-episode psychosis, early intervention, and outcome: What have we learned? *Canadian Journal of Psychiatry, 50,* 881–891.

Mann, J. J., Underwood, M. D., & Arango, V. (1996). Postmortem studies of suicide victims. In S. J. Watson (Ed.), *Biology of schizophrenia and affective disease* (pp. 179–221). Washington, DC: American Psychiatric Press.

Marcus, D. K., Gurley, J. R., Marchi, M. M., & Bauer, C. (2007). Cognitive and perceptual variables in hypochondriasis and health anxiety: A systematic review. *Clinical Psychology Review, 27,* 127–139.

Marcus, D. K., & Nardone, M. E. (1992). Depression and interpersonal rejection. *Clinical Psychology Review, 12,* 433–449.

Marder, S. R., Wirshing, W. C., Mintz, J., McKenzie, J., Johnston, K., Eckman, T. A., . . . Liberman, R. P. (1996). Two-year outcome of social skills training and group psychotherapy for outpatients with schizophrenia. *American Journal of Psychiatry, 153,* 1585–1592.

Marengo, J. T., & Harrow, M. (1997). Longitudinal courses of thought disorder in schizophrenia and schizoaffective disorder. *Schizophrenia Bulletin, 23,* 273–285.

Marin, A. (2001). *Report to the Minister of National Defence: Systematic treatment of CF members with PTSD.* Ottawa: Department of National Defence.

Markowitz, J. C. (2006a). Adaptations of interpersonal psychotherapy. *Psychiatric Annals, 36,* 559–563.

Markowitz, J. C. (2006b). Interpersonal psychotherapy for depression and dysthymic disorder. In D. J. Stein, D. J. Kupfer, & A. F. Schatzberg (Eds.), *American Psychiatric Publishing textbook of mood disorders* (pp. 373–388). Washington, DC: American Psychiatric Publishing.

Marlatt, G. A. (1978). Craving for alcohol, loss of control, and relapse: A cognitive-behavioral analysis. In P. E. Nathan, G. A. Marlatt, & T. Løberg (Eds.), *Alcoholism: New directions in behavioral research and treatment* (pp. 271–314). New York: Plenum.

Marlatt, G. A., Demming, B., & Reid, J. B. (1973). Loss of control drinking in alcoholics: An experimental analogue. *Journal of Abnormal Psychology, 81,* 233–241.

Marlatt, G. A., & Gordon, J. R. (Eds.). (1985). *Relapse prevention: Maintenance strategies in the treatment of addictive behaviors.* New York: Guilford.

Marlatt, G. A., Larimer, M. E., Baer, J. S., & Quigley, L. A. (1993). Harm reduction for alcohol problems: Moving beyond the controlled drinking controversy. *Behavior Therapy, 24,* 461–504.

Marsh, R., Steinglass, J. E., Gerber, A. J., O'Leary, K. G., Wang, Z., Murphy, D., . . . Peterson, B. S. (2009). Deficient activity in the neural systems that mediate self-regulatory control in bulimia nervosa. *Archives of General Psychiatry, 66,* 51–63.

Marshall, D. (1971). Sexual behavior on Mangaia. In D. S. Marshall & R. C. Suggs (Eds.), *Human sexual behavior: Variations in the ethnographic spectrum.* Englewood Cliffs, NJ: Prentice Hall.

Marshall, W. L. (2001). Attachment problems in the etiology and treatment of sexual offenders. In W. Everaerd, E. Laan, & S. Both (Eds.), *Sexual appetite, desire and motivation: Energetics of the sexual system* (pp. 135–143). Amsterdam: Royal Netherlands Academy of the Arts and Sciences.

Marshall, W. L., & Eccles, A. (1993). Pavlovian conditioning processes in adolescent sex offenders. In H. E. Barbaree, W. L. Marshall, & S. M. Hudson (Eds.), *The juvenile sex offender* (pp. 118–142). New York: Guilford.

Marshall, W. L., Eccles, A., & Barbaree, H. E. (1991). The treatment of exhibitionists: A focus on sexual deviance versus cognitive and relationship features. *Behaviour Research and Therapy, 29,* 129–135.

Marshall, W. L., & Moulden, H. (2001). Hostility toward women and victim empathy of rapists. *Sexual Abuse: A Journal of Research and Treatment, 13,* 249–255.

Marshall, W. L., Serran, G. A., & Cortoni, F. A. (2000). Childhood attachments, sexual abuse, and their relationship to adult coping in child molesters. *Sexual Abuse: Journal of Research and Treatment, 12,* 17–26.

Martin, R. L., Cloninger, C. F., Guze, S. B., & Clayton, P. J. (1985). Mortality in a follow-up of 500 psychiatric outpatients: I. Total mortality. *Archives of General Psychiatry, 42,* 47–54.

Martinsen, E. W. (2005). Exercise and depression. *International Journal of Sport and Exercise Psychology, 3,* 469–483.

Masten, A. S. (2001). Ordinary magic: Resilience processes in development. *American Psychologist, 56(3),* 227–238.

Masters, W. H., & Johnson, V. E. (1970). *Human sexual inadequacy.* Boston: Little, Brown.

Matefy, R. (1980). Role-play theory of psychedelic drug flashbacks. *Journal of Consulting and Clinical Psychology, 48,* 551–553.

Matheson, K., & Anisman, H. (2003). Systems of coping associated with dysphoria, anxiety and depressive illness: A multivariate profile perspective. *Stress: The International Journal on the Biology of Stress, 6,* 223–234.

Mathews, A., & MacLeod, C. (2005). Cognitive vulnerability to emotional disorders. *Annual Review of Clinical Psychology, 1,* 167–195.

Maxwell, J. C. (2005). Emerging research on methamphetamine. *Current Opinion in Psychiatry, 18,* 235–242.

Mayer, J. D., & Salovey, P. (1997). What is emotional intelligence? In P. Salovey & D. Sluyter (Eds.), *Emotional development and emotional intelligence: Educational implications* (pp. 3–31). New York: Basic Books.

Mayo-Smith, M. F. (1997). Pharmacological management of alcohol withdrawal. A meta-analysis and evidence-based practice guideline. American Society of Addiction Medicine Working Group on Pharmacological Management of Alcohol Withdrawal. *JAMA: Journal of the American Medical Association, 278,* 144–151.

Mazurek, M. O., Kanne, S. M., Miles, J. H. (2012). Predicting improvement in social-communication symptoms of autism spectrum disorders using retrospective treatment data. *Research in Autism Spectrum Disorders, 6,* 535–545.

McCarthy, B. W., & Bodnar, L. E. (2005). Couple sex therapy: Assessment, treatment, and relapse prevention. In J. L. Lebow (Ed.), *Handbook of clinical family therapy* (pp. 464–493). New York: Wiley.

McCaul, M. E., & Furst, J. (1994). Alcoholism treatment in the United States. *Alcohol Health & Research World, 18,* 253–260.

McCord, W., & McCord, J. (1964). *The psychopath: An essay on the criminal mind.* New York: Van Nostrand.

McCormick, R. M. (2000). Aboriginal traditions in the treatment of substance abuse. *Canadian Journal of Counselling, 34*(1), 25–32.

McCracken, J. T., McGough, J., Shah, B., Cronin, P., Hong, D., Aman, M. G., . . . McMahon, D. (2002). Risperidone in children with autism and serious behavioral problems. *New England Journal of Medicine, 347,* 314–321.

McCrady, B. S. (1993). Alcoholism. In D. H. Barlow (Ed.), *Clinical handbook of psychological disorders* (2nd ed., pp. 362–393). New York: Guilford.

McCrady, B. S. (1994). Alcoholics Anonymous and behavior therapy: Can habits be treated as diseases? Can diseases be treated as habits? *Journal of Consulting and Clinical Psychology, 62,* 1159–1166.

McEachin, J. J., Smith, T., & Lovaas, O. I. (1993). Long-term outcome for children with autism who received early intensive behavioral treatment. *American Journal on Mental Retardation, 97,* 359–372.

McGuire, P. K., Shah, G. M. S., & Murray, R. M. (1993). Increased blood flow in Broca's area during auditory hallucinations in schizophrenia. *Lancet, 342,* 703–706.

McIntosh, D. E. (1999). Identifying at-risk preschoolers: The discriminant validity of the Differential Ability Scales. *Psychology in the Schools, 36,* 1–10.

McLellan, A. T., Alterman, A. I., Metzger, D. S., Grissom, G. R., Woody, G. E., Luborsky, L., & O'Brien, C. P. (1994). Similarity of outcome predictors across opiate, cocaine, and alcohol treatments: Role of treatment services. *Journal of Consulting and Clinical Psychology, 62,* 1141–1158.

McMain, S. F., Links, P. S., Gnam, W. H., Guimond, T., Cardish, R. J., Korman, L., & Streiner, D. L. (2009.) A randomized trial of dialectical behavior therapy versus general psychiatric management for borderline personality disorder. *American Journal of Psychiatry, 166,* 1365–1374.

McNally, R. J., Cassiday, K. L., & Calamari, J. E. (1990). Taijin-kyofu-sho in a Black American woman: Behavioral treatment of a "culture-bound" anxiety disorder. *Journal of Anxiety Disorders, 4,* 83–87.

Mead, M. (1935). *Sex and temperament in three primitive societies.* New York: Morrow.

Meador-Woodruff, J. H., Haroutunian, V., Powchik, P., Davidson, M., Davis, K. L., & Watson, S. J. (1997). Dopamine receptor transcript expression in striatum and prefrontal and occipital cortex: Focal abnormalities in orbitofrontal cortex in schizophrenia. *Archives of General Psychiatry, 54,* 1089–1095.

Meana, M., & Binik, Y. M. (1994). Painful coitus: A review of female dyspareunia. *Journal of Nervous and Mental Disease, 182,* 264–272.

Medalia, A., Aluma, M., Tryon, W., & Merriam, A. E. (1998). Effectiveness of attention training in schizophrenia. *Schizophrenia Bulletin, 24,* 147–152.

Mednick, S. A. (1970). Breakdown in individuals at high risk for schizophrenia: Possible predispositional perinatal factors. *Mental Hygiene, 54,* 50–63.

Mednick, S. A., Parnas, J., & Schulsinger, F. (1987). The Copenhagen High-Risk project, 1962–86. *Schizophrenia Bulletin, 13,* 485–495.

Mednick, S. A., & Schulsinger, F. (1968). Some pre-morbid characteristics related to breakdown in children with schizophrenic mothers. In D. Rosenthal & S. S. Kety (Eds.), *The transmission of schizophrenia: Proceedings of the second research conference of the Foundations' Fund for Research in Psychiatry, Dorado, Puerto Rico, 26 June to 1 July 1967* (pp. 267–291). New York: Pergamon.

Meehl, P. E. (1962). Schizotaxia, schizotypy, schizophrenia. *American Psychologist, 17,* 827–838.

Meehl, P. E. (1972). A critical afterword. In I. I. Gottesman & J. Shields (Eds.), *Schizophrenia and genetics: A twin study vantage point* (pp. 367–415). New York: Academic.

Meichenbaum, D. (1976). Toward a cognitive theory of self-control. In G. Schwartz & D. Shapiro (Eds.), *Consciousness and self-regulation: Advances in research, volume 1.* New York: Plenum.

Meichenbaum, D. (1977). *Cognitive-behavior modification: An integrative approach.* New York: Plenum.

Meichenbaum, D. (1993). Changing conceptions of cognitive behavior modification: Retrospect and prospect. *Journal of Consulting and Clinical Psychology, 61,* 202–204.

Meichenbaum, D. (2005). 35 years of working with suicidal patients: Lessons learned. *Canadian Psychology, 46,* 64–72.

Mellings, T. M. B., & Alden, L. E. (2000). Cognitive processes in social anxiety: The effects of self-focus, rumination and anticipatory processing. *Behaviour Research and Therapy, 38,* 243–257.

Mellor, C. S. (1970). First rank symptoms of schizophrenia. *British Journal of Psychiatry, 177,* 15–23.

Mental Health Promotion. (2003). Frequently asked questions. Retrieved April 23, 2003, from http://www.hc-sc.gc.ca/hppb/mental-health/mhp/faq.html

Messenger, J. (1971). Sex and repression in an Irish folk community. In D. S. Marshall & R. C. Suggs (Eds.), *Human sexual behavior: Variations in the ethnographic spectrum.* Englewood Cliffs, NJ: Prentice Hall.

Meston, C. M., & Bradford, A. (2006). Sexual dysfunctions in women. *Annual Review of Clinical Psychology, 3,* 81–104.

Metsänen, M., Wahlberg, K.-E., Saarento, O., Tarvainen, T., Miettunen, J., Koistinen, P., . . . Tienari, P. (2004). Early presence of thought disorder as a prospective sign of mental disorder. *Psychiatry Research, 125,* 193–203.

Meyers, B. S. (2006). Psychotic depression. *Psychiatric Annals, 36,* 7–9.

Miklowitz, D. J. (2004). The role of family systems in severe and recurrent psychiatric disorders: A developmental psychopathology view. *Development and Psychopathology, 16,* 667–688.

Miklowitz, D. J., & Johnson, S. L. (2006). The psychopathology and treatment of bipolar disorder. *Annual Review of Clinical Psychology, 2,* 199–235.

Milberger, S., Biederman, J., Faraone, S. V., Chen, L., & Jones, J. (1996). Is maternal smoking during pregnancy a risk factor for attention deficit hyperactivity disorder in children? *American Journal of Psychiatry, 153,* 1138–1142.

Miller, E. (1987). Hysteria: Its nature and explanation. *British Journal of Clinical Psychology, 26,* 163–173.

Miller, L. K. (1999). The savant syndrome: Intellectual impairment and exceptional skills. *Psychological Bulletin, 125,* 31–46.

Miller, W. R., & Brown, S. A. (1997). Why psychologists should treat alcohol and drug problems. *American Psychologist, 52,* 1269–1279.

Miller, W. R., & Hester, R. K. (1986). Inpatient alcoholism treatment: Who benefits? *American Psychologist, 41,* 794–805.

Miller, W. R., & Muñoz, R. F. (1983). *How to control your drinking* (2nd ed.). Albuquerque: University of New Mexico Press.

Millon, T. (1981). *Disorders of personality: DSM-III, Axis II.* New York: Wiley.

Milner, P. (2006). Trains of neural thought. *Canadian Psychology/Psychologie canadienne, 47*(1), 36–43.

Milos, G., Spindler, A., & Schnyder, U. (2004). Psychiatric comorbidity and Eating Disorder Inventory (EDI) profiles in eating disorder patients. *Canadian Journal of Psychiatry, 49,* 179–184.

Milstone, C. (1995). *The mentally ill and the criminal justice system: Innovative community-based programs.* Ottawa: Health Canada, Mental Health Division, Health Services Directorate, Health Programs and Services.

Mineka, S., & Zinbarg, R. (2006). A contemporary learning theory perspective on the etiology of anxiety disorders. *American Psychologist, 61,* 10–26.

Minuchin, S. (1974). *Families & family therapy.* Cambridge, MA: Harvard University Press.

Minuchin, S., Rosman, B. L., & Baker, L. (1978). *Psychosomatic families: Anorexia nervosa in context.* Cambridge, MA: Harvard University Press.

Miron, J. (2006). "Open to the public": Touring Ontario asylums in the nineteenth century. In D. Wright and J. E. Moran (Eds.), *Mental health and Canadian society: Historical perspectives*. Montreal: McGill-Queen's University Press.

Mischel, W. (1979). On the interface of cognition and personality: Beyond the person-situation debate. *American Psychologist, 34,* 740–754.

Mitchell, P. B., & Loo, C. K. (2006). Transcranial magnetic stimulation for depression. *Australian and New Zealand Journal of Psychiatry, 40,* 406–413.

Mitte, K. (2005). Meta-analysis of cognitive-behavioral treatments for generalized anxiety disorder: A comparison with pharmacotherapy. *Psychological Bulletin, 131,* 785–795.

Moffitt, T. E., Caspi, A., & Rutter, M. (2006). Measured gene-environment interactions in psychopathology: Concepts, research strategies, and implications for research, intervention, and public understanding of genetics. *Perspectives on Psychological Science, 1,* 5–27.

Mohr, D. C., & Beutler, L. E. (1990). Erectile dysfunction: A review of diagnostic and treatment procedures. *Clinical Psychology Review, 10,* 123–150.

Monahan, J. (1981). *A clinical prediction of violent behavior.* (DHHS Publication No. ADM. 81-921). Rockville, MD: National Institute of Mental Health.

Money, J. (1987). Sin, sickness, or status? Homosexual gender identity and psychoneuroendocrinology. *American Psychologist, 42,* 384–399.

Money, J., & Lamacz, M. (1990). *Vandalized lovemaps: Paraphilic outcome of seven cases in pediatric sexology.* Buffalo, NY: Prometheus.

Montgomery, S. (2006). Serotonin noradrenaline reuptake inhibitors: Logical evolution of antidepressant development. *International Journal of Psychiatry in Clinical Practice, 10*(Suppl. 2), 5–11.

Monti, P. M., Rohsenow, D. J., Rubenois, A. V., Niaura, R. S., Sirota, A. D., Colby, S. M., . . . Abrams, D. B. (1994). Cue exposure with coping skills treatment for male alcoholics: A preliminary investigation. *Journal of Consulting and Clinical Psychology, 61,* 1011–1019.

Moore, B. A., Fazzino, T., Garnet, B., Cutter, C. J., & Barry, D. T. (2011). Computer-based treatments for drug abuse and dependence: A systematic review. *Journal of Substance Abuse Treatment, 40,* 215–223.

Moretti, M. M., Emmrys, C., Grizenko, N., Holland, R., Moore, K., Shamsie, J., & Hamilton, H. (1997). The treatment of conduct disorder: Perspectives from across Canada. *Canadian Journal of Psychiatry, 42,* 637–648.

Morgenstern, J., Langenbucher, J., Labouvie, E., & Miller, K. J. (1997). The comorbidity of alcoholism and personality disorders in a clinical population: Prevalence rates and relation to alcohol typology variables. *Journal of Abnormal Psychology, 106,* 74–84.

Morin, C. M., LeBlanc, M., Daley, M., Gregoire, J. P., & Merette, C. (2006). Epidemiology of insomnia: Prevalence, self-help treatments, consultations, and determinants of help-seeking behaviors. *Sleep Medicine, 7*(2), 123–130.

Morin, C. M., & Wooten, V. (1996). Psychological and pharmacological approaches to treating insomnia: Critical issues in assessing their separate and combined effects. *Clinical Psychology Review, 16,* 521–542.

Morrow, D. J. (1998, April 21). Pfizer drug for impotence leads market. *The New York Times,* pp. D1, D4.

Mortimer, A. M., Lund, C. E., & McKenna, P. J. (1990). The positive:negative dichotomy in schizophrenia. *British Journal of Psychiatry, 157,* 41–49.

Mosconi, L., Glodzik, L., Mistur, R., McHugh, P., Rich, K. E., Javier, E., . . . de Leon, M. J. (2010). Oxidative stress and amyloid-beta pathology in normal individuals with a maternal history of Alzheimer's. *Biological Psychiatry, 68,* 913–921.

Moskowitz, A. K. (2004). "Scared stiff": Catatonia as an evolutionary-based fear response. *Psychological Review, 111,* 984–1002.

Motiuk, L. L., & Porporino, F. J. (1991). *The prevalence, nature and severity of mental health problems among federal male inmates in Canadian penitentiaries* (Catalogue No. R-24). Ottawa: Correctional Service of Canada, Research and Statistics Branch.

Mowrer, O. H. (1948). Learning theory and the neurotic paradox. *American Journal of Orthopsychiatry, 18,* 571–610.

Muckle, W., & Turnbull, J. (2006). Sheltering the homeless. *CMAJ: Canadian Medical Association Journal, 175,* 1177.

Mueser, K. T., & Liberman, R. P. (1995). Behavior therapy in practice. In B. Bongar & L. E. Beutler (Eds.), *Comprehensive textbook of psychotherapy: Theory and practice* (pp. 84–110). New York: Oxford University Press.

Mukherjee, R. A. S., Hollins, S., & Turk, J. (2006). Psychiatric comorbidity in foetal alcohol syndrome. *Psychiatric Bulletin, 30,* 194–195.

Müller, N. (2004). Immunological and infectious aspects of schizophrenia. *European Archives of Psychiatry and Clinical Neuroscience, 254,* 1–3.

Murray, H. A. (1943). *Thematic Appperception Test manual.* Cambridge, MA: Harvard University Press.

Murstein, B. I., & Mathes, S. (1996). Projection on projective techniques and pathology: The problem that is not being addressed. *Journal of Personality Assessment, 66,* 337–349.

Murtagh, D. R. R., & Greenwood, K. M. (1995). Identifying effective psychological treatments for insomnia: A meta-analysis. *Journal of Consulting and Clinical Psychology, 63,* 79–89.

N

Najavits, L. M. (2002). *Seeking safety: A treatment manual for PTSD and substance abuse.* New York: Guilford.

Nasser, E. H., & Overholser, J. C. (2005). Recovery from major depression: The role of support from family, friends, and spiritual beliefs. *Acta Psychiatrica Scandinavica, 111,* 125–132.

National Council on Ethics in Human Research. (2002). Who we are. Retrieved February 15, 2003, from http://ncehr-cnerh.org/english/mstr_frm.html

National Institute for Clinical Excellence. (2005). *Post-traumatic stress disorder (PTSD): The management of PTSD in adults and children in primary and secondary care.* London: Royal College of Psychiatrists and British Psychological Society.

National Institute of Nutrition. (2001). Giving adolescents a fighting chance against eating disorders. Retrieved July 31, 2003, from http://www.nin.ca/public_html/Publications

Needles, D. J., & Abramson, L. Y. (1990). Positive life events, attributional style, and hopefulness: Testing a model of recovery from depression. *Journal of Abnormal Psychology, 99,* 156–165.

NCS Pearson, Inc. (1997). *Wechsler Adult Intelligence Scale* (WAIS-III) (3rd ed.). Bloomington, MN: Author.

Neiger, B. L., & Hopkins, R. W. (1988). Adolescent suicide: Character traits of high-risk teenagers. *Adolescence, 23,* 469–475.

Neill, J. (1990). Whatever became of the schizophrenogenic mother? *American Journal of Psychotherapy, 44,* 499–505.

Nelson, C. B., Heath, A. C., & Kessler, R. C. (1998). Temporal progression of alcohol dependence symptoms in the U.S. household population: Results from the National Comorbidity Survey. *Journal of Consulting and Clinical Psychology, 66,* 474–483.

Nemiah, J. C. (1978). Psychoneurotic disorders. In A. M. Nicholi, Jr. (Ed.), *Harvard guide to modern psychiatry.* Cambridge, MA: Belknap Press.

Neufeld, R. W. J., Vollick, D., Carter, J. R., Boksman, K., & Jetté, J. (2002). Application of stochastic modeling to the assessment of group and individual differences in cognitive functioning. *Psychological Assessment, 14,* 279–298.

Neugebauer, R. (1979). Medieval and early modern theories of mental illness. *Archives of General Psychiatry, 36,* 477–483.

Neurological basis of depression following sports concussion found. (2008, January 21). *ScienceDaily.* Retrieved November 10, 2011, from http://www.sciencedaily.com/releases/2008/01/080118115428.htm

Nevid, J. S., Fichner-Rathus, L., & Rathus, S. A. (1995). *Human sexuality in a world of diversity* (2nd ed.). Boston: Allyn & Bacon.

New Alzheimer's treatment completes first phase of testing. (2008, January 23). *ScienceDaily.* Retrieved November 25, 2011, from http://www.sciencedaily.com/releases/2008/01/080123101629.htm

New marker for Alzheimer's discovered. (2009, September 14). *ScienceDaily.* Retrieved November 25, 2011, from http://www.sciencedaily.com/releases/2009/09/090914131906.htm

New research tool can detect autism at 9 months of age. (2008, May 20). *Science-Daily*. Retrieved October 20, 2011, from http://www.sciencedaily.com/releases/2008/05/080520112133.htm

Nezu, A. M. (1994). Introduction to special section: Mental retardation and mental illness. *Journal of Consulting and Clinical Psychology, 62*, 4–5.

Nezu, A. M., Wilkins, V. M., & Nezu, C. M. (2004). Social problem solving, stress, and negative affect. In E. C. Chang, T. J. D'Zurilla, & L. J. Sanna (Eds.), *Social problem solving: Theory, research, and training* (pp. 49–65). Washington, DC: American Psychological Association.

NIAAA report links drinking and early death. (1990, October). *The Addiction Letter, 6*, 5.

Niaura, R., Todaro, J. F., Stroud, L., Spiro, A., III, Ward, K. D., & Weiss, S. (2002). Hostility, the metabolic syndrome, and incident coronary heart disease. *Health Psychology, 21*, 588–593.

Nicholson, I. R., & Neufeld, R. W. J. (1992). A dynamic vulnerability perspective on stress and schizophrenia. *American Journal of Orthopsychiatry, 62*, 117–130.

Nicholson, R. A., Mouton, G. J., Bagby, R. M., Buis, T., Peterson, S. A., & Buigas, R. A. (1997). Utility of MMPI-2 indicators of response distortion: Receiver operating characteristic analysis. *Psychological Assessment, 9*, 471–479.

Nicolson, R. I., & Fawcett, A. J. (2011). Dyslexia, dysgraphia, procedural learning and the cerebellum. *Cortex, 47*(1), 117–127.

Nicolson, R., & Szatmari, P. (2003). Genetic and neurodevelopmental influences in autistic disorder. *Canadian Journal of Psychiatry, 48*, 526–537.

Nides, M. A., Rakos, R. F., Gonzales, D., Murray, R. P., Tashkin, D. P., Bjornson-Benson, W. M., . . . Connett, J. E. (1995). Predictors of initial smoking cessation and relapse through the first 2 years of the Lung Health Study. *Journal of Consulting and Clinical Psychology, 63*, 60–69.

Niemz, K., Griffiths, M., & Banyard, P. (2005). Prevalence of pathological Internet use among university students and correlations with self-esteem, the General Health Questionnaire (GHQ), and disinhibition. *Cyber-Psychology & Behavior, 8*, 562–570.

Nigg, J. T., Lohr, N. E., Western, D., Gold, L. J., & Silk, K. R. (1992). Malevolent object representations in borderline personality disorder and major depression. *Journal of Abnormal Psychology, 101*, 61–67.

Nolen-Hoeksma, S. (2000). The role of rumination in depressive disorders and mixed anxiety/depressive symptoms. *Journal of Abnormal Psychology, 109*, 504–511.

Nolen-Hoeksema, S., & Corte, C. (2004). Gender and self-regulation. In R. F. Baumeister & K. D. Vohs (Eds.), *Handbook of self-regulation: Research, theory, and applications* (pp. 411–421). New York: Guilford.

Nolen-Hoeksema, S., & Girgus, J. S. (1994). The emergence of gender differences in depression during adolescence. *Psychological Bulletin, 115*, 424–443.

Nolen-Hoeksema, S., Girgus, J. S., & Seligman, M. E. (1992). Predictors and consequences of childhood depressive symptoms: A 5-year longitudinal study. *Journal of Abnormal Psychology, 101*, 405–422.

Norton, G. R., Cox, B. J., & Malan, J. (1992). Nonclinical panickers: A critical review. *Clinical Psychology Review, 12*, 121–139.

Nowell, P. D., Buysse, D. J., Morin, C., Reynolds, C F., III, & Kupfer, D. J. (1998). Effective treatments for selected sleep disorders. In P. E. Nathan & J. M. Gorman (Eds.), *A guide to treatments that work* (pp. 531–543). New York: Oxford University Press.

Nunes, J., & Simmie, S. (2002). *Beyond crazy: Journeys through mental illness*. Toronto: McClelland & Stewart.

O

O'Brien, C. P. (1996). Recent developments in the pharmacotherapy of substance abuse. *Journal of Consulting and Clinical Psychology, 64*, 677–686.

O'Brien, C. P., & McKay, J. (1998). Psychopharmacological treatments of substance use disorders. In P. E. Nathan & J. M. Gorman (Eds.), *A guide to treatments that work* (pp. 127–155). New York: Oxford University Press.

Ochs, R. (1998, March 9). Alcohol: Sorting the contradictions. *Newsday*.

O'Connor, B. P., & Dyce, J. A. (2001). Personality disorders. In M. Hersen & V. B. Van Hasselt (Eds.), *Advanced abnormal psychology* (2nd ed., pp. 399–417). New York: Kluwer Academic/Plenum.

O'Donohue, W., Dopke, C. A., & Swingen, D. N. (1997). Psychotherapy for female sexual dysfunction: A review. *Clinical Psychology Review, 17*, 537–566.

O'Donohue, W., Letourneau, E., & Geer, J. H. (1993). Premature ejaculation. In W. O'Donohue & J. H. Geer (Eds.), *Handbook of sexual dysfunctions: Assessment and treatment* (pp. 303–333). Boston: Allyn & Bacon.

O'Donohue, W., Swingen, D. N., Dopke, C. A., & Regev, L. G. (1999). Psychotherapy for male sexual dysfunction: A review. *Clinical Psychology Review, 19*, 591–630.

O'Farrell, T. J., Choquette, K. A., Cutter, H. S. G., Floyd, F. J., Bayog, R., Brown, E. D., . . . Deneault, P. (1996). Cost-benefit and cost-effectiveness analyses of behavioral marital therapy as an addition to outpatient alcoholism treatment. *Journal of Substance Abuse, 8*, 145–166.

Offord, D. R., Boyle, M. H., Campbell, D., Goering, P., Lin, E., Wong, M., & Racine, Y. A. (1996). One-year prevalence of psychiatric disorders in Ontarians 15 to 64 years of age. *Canadian Journal of Psychiatry, 41*(9), 559–563.

Oldham, J. M. (1994). Personality disorders: Current perspectives. *JAMA: Journal of the American Medical Association, 272*, 1770–1776.

Olesen, J., & Goadsby, P. J. (2000). Synthesis of migraine mechanisms. In J. Olesen, P. Tfelt-Hansen, & K. M. A. Welch (Eds.), *The headaches* (2nd ed., pp. 331–336). Philadelphia: Lippincott Williams & Wilkins.

Olff, M., Langeland, W., Draijer, N., & Gersons, B. P. (2007). Gender differences in posttraumatic stress disorder. *Psychological Bulletin, 133*, 183–204.

Olfson, M., Marcus, S., Sackeim, H. A., Thompson, J., & Pincus, H. A. (1998). Use of ECT for the inpatient treatment of recurrent major depression. *American Journal of Psychiatry, 155*, 22–29.

Olley, M. C., & Ogloff, J. R. P. (1995). Patients' rights advocacy: Implications for program design and implementation. *Journal of Mental Health Administration, 22*, 368–376.

Oltmanns, Thomas F., & Emery, Robert E. (2010). *Abnormal Psychology* (6th ed.). Upper Saddle River, NJ: Prentice Hall.

O'Neill, P. (2004). The ethics of problem definition. *Canadian Psychology/Psychologie canadienne, 46*(1), 13–20.

Osborne, L. (2001, May 6). Regional disturbances. *The New York Times Magazine*, 98–102.

Öst, L. (1992). Blood and injection phobia: Background and cognitive, physiological, and behavioral variables. *Journal of Abnormal Psychology, 101*, 68–74.

Öst, L-G. (1987). Age of onset in different phobias. *Journal of Abnormal Psychology, 96*(3), 223–229.

Ottawa Aboriginal Head Start Program (1998). *Evaluation Report 1997–1998*. Ottawa: Author. Retrieved October 18, 2003, from http://www.aboriginalcanada.com/headstart/docs/report2c.pdf

Overmier, J. B. L., & Seligman, M. E. (1967). Effect of inescapable shock upon subsequent escape and avoidance learning. *Journal of Comparative and Physiological Psychology, 63*, 28–33.

Owens, K. M. B., & Antony, M. M. (2011). *Overcoming health anxiety: Letting go of your fear of illness*. Oakland, CA: New Harbinger.

P

Pagnin, D., de Queiroz, V., Pini, S., & Cassano, G. B. (2004). Efficacy of ECT in depression: A meta-analytic review. *Journal of ECT, 20*, 13–20.

Paris, J. (1998). Psychotherapy for personality disorders: Working with traits. *Bulletin of the Menninger Clinic, 62*, 287–297.

Paris, J. (2002a). Chronic suicidality among patients with borderline personality disorder. *Psychiatric Services, 53*, 738–742.

Paris, J. (2002b). Implications of long-term outcomes research for the management of patients with borderline personality disorder. *Harvard Review of Psychiatry, 10*, 315–323.

Paris, J. (2005). Recent advances in the treatment of borderline personality disorder. *Canadian Journal of Psychiatry, 50*, 435–441.

Paris, J., & Frank, H. (1989). Perceptions of parental bonding in borderline patients. *American Journal of Psychiatry, 146*, 1498–1499.

Paris, J., & Zweig-Frank, H. (2001). A 27-year follow-up of patients with borderline personality disorder. *Comprehensive Psychiatry, 42,* 482–487.

Parnas, D. J., Cannon, T. D., Jacobsen, B., Schulsinger, H., Schulsinger, F., & Mednick, S. A. (1993). Lifetime DSM-III-R diagnostic outcomes in the offspring of schizophrenic mothers: Results from the Copenhagen High-Risk Study. *Archives of General Psychiatry, 50,* 707–714.

Patrick, C. J., Cuthbert, B. N., & Lang, P. J. (1994). Emotion in the criminal psychopath: Fear image processing. *Journal of Abnormal Psychology, 103,* 523–534.

Patten, S. B., Wang, J. L., Williams, J. V. A., Currie, S., Beck, C. A., Maxwell, C. J., & el-Guebaly, N. (2006). Descriptive epidemiology of major depression in Canada. *Canadian Journal of Psychiatry, 51,* 84–90.

Patton, G. C., Selzer, R., Coffey, C., Carlin, J. B., & Wolfe, R. (1999). Onset of adolescent eating disorders: Population based cohort study over 3 years. *British Medical Journal, 318,* 765–768.

Paul, G. L., & Lentz, R. J. (1977). *Psychosocial treatment of chronic mental patients: Milieu versus social-learning programs.* Cambridge, MA: Harvard University Press.

Paulesu, E., Demonet, J. F., Fazio, F., McCrory, E., Chanoine, V., Brunswick, N., . . . Frith, U. (2001). Dyslexia: Cultural diversity and biological unity. *Science, 291,* 2165–2167.

Paulesu, E., Frith, C. D., & Frackowiak, R. S. J. (1993). The neural correlates of the verbal component of working memory. *Nature, 362,* 342–344.

Pendery, M. L., Maltzman, I. M., & West, L. J. (1982). Controlled drinking by alcoholics? New findings and a reevaluation of a major affirmative study. *Science, 217,* 169–174.

Penn, D. L. (1998). Assessment and treatment of social dysfunction in schizophrenia. *Clinician's Research Digest, Supplemental Bulletin, 18,* 1–2.

Penn, D. L., Combs, D., & Mohamed, S. (2001). Social cognition and social functioning in schizophrenia. In P. W. Corrigan & D. L. Penn (Eds.), *Social cognition and schizophrenia* (pp. 97–121). Washington, DC: American Psychological Association.

Penn, D. L., & Mueser, K. T. (1996). Research update on the psychosocial treatment of schizophrenia. *American Journal of Psychiatry, 153,* 607–617.

Perkins, D. O., Gu, H., Boteva, K., Lieberman, J. A. (2005). Relationship between duration of untreated psychosis and outcome in first-episode schizophrenia: A critical review and meta-analysis. *American Journal of Psychiatry, 162,* 1785–1804.

Perlis, R. (2007). Review: Adding second generation antipsychotics to mood stabilisers reduces acute mania symptoms. *Evidence-Based Mental Health, 10*(4), 111.

Perlman, S. D., & Abramson, P. R. (1982). Sexual satisfaction among married and cohabitating individuals. *Journal of Consulting and Clinical Psychology, 50,* 458–460.

Petersen, T. J. (2006). Enhancing the efficacy of antidepressants with psychotherapy. *Journal of Psychopharmacology, 30*(Suppl. 3), 19–28.

Peto, R., Lopez, A. D., Boreham, J., & Thun, M. (2006). *Mortality from smoking in developed countries 1950–2000* (2nd ed.). Oxford: Oxford University Press. Retrieved November 20, 2011, from http://www.ctsu.ox.ac.uk/deathsfromsmoking/publications.html

Petty, S. C., Sachs-Ericsson, N., & Joiner, T. E., Jr. (2004). Interpersonal functioning deficits: Temporary or stable characteristics of depressed individuals? *Journal of Affective Disorders, 81,* 115–122.

Pfaus, J. G., Kippin, T. E., & Centeno, S. (2001). Conditioning and sexual behavior: A review. *Hormones and Behavior, 40,* 291–321.

Phillips, D. P., & Carstensen, L. S. (1986). Clustering of teenage suicide after television news stories about suicide. *New England Journal of Medicine, 315,* 685–689.

Phillipson, E. A. (1993). Sleep apnea—a major public health problem [Editorial]. *New England Journal of Medicine, 328,* 1271–1273.

Pianta, R. C., & Egeland, B. (1994). Relation between depressive symptoms and stressful life events in a sample of disadvantaged mothers. *Journal of Consulting and Clinical Psychology, 62,* 1229–1234.

Pihl, R. O., & Smith, S. (1983). Of affect and alcohol. In L. A. Pohorecky & J. Brick (Eds.), *Stress and alcohol use: Proceedings of the First International Symposium on Stress and Alcohol Use, held June 9–11, 1982, at Rutgers University, New Brunswick, New Jersey, U.S.A.* (pp. 203–228). New York: Elsevier.

Pike, K. M., & Rodin, J. (1991). Mothers, daughters, and disordered eating. *Journal of Abnormal Psychology, 101,* 198–204.

Pine, D. S., Alegria, M., Cook. E. H., Jr., Costello, E. J., Dahl, R. E., Koretz, D., . . . Vitiello, B. (2002). Advances in Developmental Science and DSM-V. In D. J. Kupfer, M. B. First, & D. A. Regier (Eds.), *A research agenda for DSM-V* (pp. 85–122). Washington, DC: American Psychiatric Association.

Pinhas, L., Toner, B. B., Ali, A., Garfinkel, P. E., & Stuckless, N. (1999). The effects of the ideal of female beauty on mood and body satisfaction. *International Journal of Eating Disorders, 25*(2), 223–226.

Piotrowski, C. (2000). How popular is the Personality Assessment Inventory in practice and training? *Psychological Reports, 86*(1), 65–66.

Piper, A., & Merskey, H. (2004). The persistence of folly: A critical examination of dissociative identity disorder. Part I. The excesses of an improbable concept. *Canadian Journal of Psychiatry, 49,* 592–600.

Pleva, J., & Wade, T. D. (2006). Guided self-help versus pure self-help for perfectionism: A randomised controlled trial. *Behaviour Research and Therapy, 45,* 849–861.

Plomin, R., Owen, M. J., & McGuffin, P. (1994). The genetic basis of complex human behaviors. *Science, 264,* 1733–1739.

Podymow, T., Turnbull, J., Tadic, V., & Muckle, W. (2006). Shelter-based convalescence for homeless adults. *Canadian Journal of Public Health, 97,* 379–383.

Polaschek, D. L. L., Ward, T., & Hudson, S. M. (1997). Rape and rapists: Theory and treatment. *Clinical Psychology Review, 17,* 117–144.

Polivy, J., & Herman, C. P. (2002). Causes of eating disorders. *Annual Review of Psychology, 53,* 187–213.

Poonwassie, A., & Charter, A. (2001). An Aboriginal worldview of helping: Empowering approaches. *Canadian Journal of Counselling, 35*(1), 63–73.

Pope, H. G., Jr., Jones, J. M., Hudson, J., Cohen, B. M., & Gunderson, J. G. (1983). The validity of DSM-III borderline personality disorder: A phenomenological, family history, treatment response, and long-term follow-up study. *Archives of General Psychiatry, 40,* 23–30.

Pope, H. G., Jr., & Yurgelun-Todd, D. (1996). The residual cognitive effects of heavy marijuana use in college students. *JAMA: Journal of the American Medical Association, 275,* 521–527.

Porter, S., Birt, A. R., Yuille, J. C., & Lehman, D. R. (2000). Negotiating false memories: Interviewer and rememberer characteristics relate to memory distortion. *Psychological Science, 11,* 507–510.

Porter, S., Yuille, J. C., & Lehman, D. R. (1999). The nature of real, implanted, and fabricated childhood emotional events: Implications for the recovered memory debate. *Law and Human Behavior, 23,* 517–537.

Poulakis, Z., & Wertheim, E. H. (1993). Relationships among dysfunctional congitions, depressive symptoms, and bulimic tendencies. *Cognitive Therapy and Research, 17,* 549–559.

Power, M. (2000). Freud and the unconscious. *The Psychologist, 13,* 612–614.

Prevention-Dividend Project. (2003). *Encouraging the understanding, and use, of economic evaluations in Canada's non-profit and public sectors.* Retrieved April 23, 2003, from http://prevention-dividend.com/en/welcome

Prince, R. H. (2000). Transcultural psychiatry: Personal experiences and Canadian perspectives. *Canadian Journal of Psychiatry, 45*(2), 195–196.

Prout, P. I., & Dobson, K. S. (1998). Recovered memories of childhood sexual abuse: Searching for the middle ground in clinical practice. *Canadian Psychology, 39,* 257–265.

Psychological Assessment Resources (PAR) Inc. (2001). *Mini-mental state examination,* (2nd ed.). Lutz, FL: Author.

Pull, C. B. (2005). Current status of virtual reality exposure therapy in anxiety disorders. *Current Opinion in Psychiatry, 18,* 7–14.

Pull, C. B. (2007). Combined pharmacotherapy and cognitive-behavioural therapy for anxiety disorders. *Current Opinion in Psychiatry, 20,* 30–35.

Purdon, C., & Clark, D. A. (1993). Obsessive intrusive thoughts in nonclinical subjects. Part I. Content and relation with depressive, anxious and obsessional symptoms. *Behaviour Research and Therapy, 31*(8), 713–720.

Purdon, C., Rowa, K., & Antony, M. M. (2005). Thought suppression and its effects on thought frequency, appraisal and mood state in individuals with obsessive-compulsive disorder. *Behaviour Research and Therapy, 43,* 93–108.

Pyszczynski, T., & Greenberg, J. (1992). *Hanging on and letting go: Understanding the onset, progression, and remission of depression.* New York: Springer.

Q

Quay, H. C. (1965). Psychopathic personality as pathological stimulation seeking. *American Journal of Psychiatry, 122,* 180–183.

Quinsey, V. L. (2003). The etiology of anomalous sexual preference in men. *Annals of the New York Academy of Sciences, 989,* 105–117.

R

R. v. François (1994) 2 S.C.R. 827.

R. v. Swain (1991) 63 C.C.C. (3d) 481 (S.C.C.).

Rabheru, K. (2001). The use of electroconvulsive therapy in special patient populations. *Canadian Journal of Psychiatry, 46,* 710–719.

Radomsky, A. S., Gilchrist, P. T., & Dussault, D. (2006). Repeated checking really does cause memory distrust. *Behaviour Research and Therapy, 44,* 305–316.

Ramachandran, V. S., & Hubbard, E. M. (2001). Synaesthesia—A window into perception, thought and language. *Journal of Consciousness Studies, 8*(12), 3–34.

Ramakrishnan, K., & Scheid, D. C. (2007). Treatment options for insomnia. *American Family Physician, 76,* 517–526.

Ranjith, G., & Mohan, R. (2006). Dhat syndrome as a functional somatic syndrome: Developing a sociosomatic model. *Psychiatry, 69,* 142–150.

Rapin, I. (1997). Autism. *New England Journal of Medicine, 337,* 97–104.

Rapoport, M. J., Mamdani, M., & Herrmann, N. (2006). Electroconvulsive therapy in older adults: 13-year trends. *Canadian Journal of Psychiatry, 51,* 616–619.

Raspe, R. E. (1860). *Baron Munchausen's narrative of his marvelous travels.* New York: Hurst.

Rathod, S., & Turkington, D. (2005). Cognitive-behaviour therapy for schizophrenia: A review. *Current Opinion in Psychiatry, 18,* 159–163.

Rathus, S. A. (1996). *Psychology in the new millennium.* (6th ed.). Fort Worth, TX: Harcourt Brace Jovanovich.

Rathus, S. A. (2011). *Psychology: Concepts and Connections,* Brief Version (10th ed). Florence, KY: Cengage.

Rathus, S. A., & Nevid, J. S. (1977). *BT: Behavior therapy: Strategies for solving problems.* Garden City, NY: Doubleday.

Rathus, S. A., Nevid, J. S., Fichner-Rathus, L., & Herold, E. S. (2010). *Human sexuality in a world of diversity* (3rd Canadian ed.). Toronto: Pearson Education Canada.

Ratti, L. A., Humphrey, L. L., & Lyons, J. S. (1996). Structural analysis of families with

a polydrug-dependent, bulimic, or normal adolescent daughter. *Journal of Consulting & Clinical Psychology, 64,* 1255–1262.

Rector, N. A., & Beck, A. T. (2001). Cognitive behavioral therapy for schizophrenia: An empirical review. *Journal of Nervous and Mental Disease, 189,* 278–287.

Rector, N. A., & Seeman, M. V. (1992). Auditory hallucinations in women and men. *Schizophrenia Research, 7,* 233–236.

Reich, J., & Noyes, R. (1986). Differentiating schizoid and avoidant personality disorders [Letter to the editor]. *American Journal of Psychiatry, 143,* 1061–1063.

Reid, W. J. (1986). Antisocial personality. In R. Michels & J. O. Cavenar, Jr. (Eds.), *Psychiatry* (Vol. 1). New York: Basic Books.

Reisner, A. D. (2003). The electroconvulsive therapy controversy: Evidence and ethics. *Neuropsychology Review, 13,* 199–219.

Reiss, S., & Valenti-Hein, D. (1994). Development of a psychopathology rating scale for children with mental retardation. *Journal of Consulting and Clinical Psychology, 62,* 28–33.

Reissing, E. D., Binik, Y. M., & Khalifé, S. (1999). Does vaginismus exist? A critical review of the literature. *Journal of Nervous and Mental Disease, 187,* 261–274.

Renaud, J., Chagnon, F., Turecki, G., & Marquette, C. (2005). Completed suicides in a youth centres population. *Canadian Journal of Psychiatry, 50,* 690–694.

Renneberg, B., Goldstein, A. J., Phillips, D., & Chambless, D. J. (1990). Intensive behavioral group treatment of avoidant personality disorder. *Behavior Therapy, 21,* 363–377.

Renner, M. J., & Mackin, R. S. (1998). A life stress instrument for classroom use. *Teaching of Psychology, 25*(1), 46–48.

Reuter, M., Stark, R., Hennig, J., Walter, B., Kirsch, P., Schienle, A., & Vaitl, D. (2004). Personality and emotion: Test of Gray's personality theory by means of an fMRI study. *Behavioral Neuroscience, 118,* 462–469.

Rey, J. M. (1993). Oppositional defiant disorder. *American Journal of Psychiatry, 150,* 1769–1778.

Ricciardelli, L. A., & McCabe, M. P. (2004). A biopsychosocial model of disordered eating and the pursuit of muscularity in adolescent boys. *Psychological Bulletin, 130*(2), 179–205.

Ricciardelli, L. A., McCabe, M. P., Williams, R. J., & Thompson, J. K. (2007). The role of ethnicity and culture in body image and disordered eating among males. *Clinical Psychology Review, 27,* 582–606.

Ridenour, T. A. (2005). Inhalants: Not to be taken lightly anymore. *Current Opinion in Psychiatry, 18,* 243–247.

Rieber, R. W., Takooshian, H., & Iglesias, H. (2002). The case of Sybil in the teaching of psychology. *Journal of Social Distress and the Homeless, 11,* 355–360.

Rief, W., & Barsky, A. J. (2005). Psychobiological perspectives on somatoform disorders. *Psychoneuroendocrinology, 30,* 996–1002.

Rimland, B. (1978). The savant capabilities of autistic children and their cognitive impli-

cations. In G. Serban (Ed.), *Cognitive defects in the development of mental illness.* New York: Brunner/Mazel.

Ritterband, L. M., Thorndike, F. P., Gonder-Frederick, L. A., Magee, J. C., Bailey, E. T., Saylor, D. K., & Morin, C. M. (2009). Efficacy of an Internet-based behavioral intervention for adults with insomnia. *Archives of General Psychiatry, 66,* 692–698.

Rivas-Vazquez, R. A., & Blais, M. A. (2002). Pharmacologic treatment of personality disorder. *Professional Psychology: Research and Practice, 33*(1), 104–107.

Roberto, L. G. (1983). Issues in diagnosis and treatment of transsexualism. *Archives of Sexual Behavior, 12,* 445–473.

Robins, L. N., Tipp, J., & Przybeck, T. (1991). Antisocial personality. In L. N. Robins & D. A. Regier (Eds.), *Psychiatric disorders in America: The Epidemiologic Catchment Area Study* (pp. 258–290). New York: Free Press.

Rocha, B. A., Scearce-Levie, K., Lucas, J. J., Hiroi, N., Castonon, N., Nestler, E. J., & Hen, R. (1998). Increased vulnerability to cocaine in mice lacking the serotonin-1B receptor [Letter]. *Nature, 393,* 175.

Rochlen, A. B., Zack, J. S., & Speyer, C. (2004). Online therapy: Review of relevant definitions, debates, and current empirical support. *Journal of Clinical Psychology, 60,* 269–283.

Rock, C. L., & Curran-Celentano, J. (1996). Nutritional management of eating disorders. *The Psychiatric Clinics of North America, 19,* 701–713.

Rodgers, D. D., & Abas, N. (1988). A survey of Native mental health needs in Manitoba. *Arctic Medical Research, 47*(Suppl. 1), 576–580.

Rodin, G., Olmsted, M. P., Rydall, A. C., Maharaj, S. I., Colton, P. A., Jones, J. M., . . . Daneman, D. (2002). Eating disorders in young women with type 1 diabetes mellitus. *Journal of Psychosomatic Research, 53,* 943–949.

Rodin, J., Bartoshuk, L., Peterson, C., & Schank, D. (1990). Bulimia and taste: Possible interactions. *Journal of Abnormal Psychology, 99,* 32–39.

Rodríguez de Fonseca, F., Carrera, M. R. A., Navarro, M., Koob, G. F., & Weiss, F. (1997). Activation of corticotropin-releasing factor in the limbic system during cannabinoid withdrawal. *Science, 276,* 2050–2054.

Rohde, P., Lewinsohn, P. M., & Seeley, J. R. (1991). Comorbidity of unipolar depression: II. Comorbidity with other mental disorders in adolescents and adults. *Journal of Abnormal Psychology, 101,* 214–222.

Romano, E., Baillargeon, R. H., Fortier, I., Hong-Wu, X., Robaey, P., Zoccolillo, M., & Tremblay, R. E. (2005). Individual change in methylphenidate use in a national sample of children aged 2 to 11 years. *Canadian Journal of Psychiatry, 50,* 144–152.

Romano, E., Baillargeon, R. H., & Tremblay, R. E. (2002). *Prevalence of hyperactivity-impulsivity and inattention among Canadian children: Findings from the first data* collection cycle (1994–1995) of the *National Longitudinal Survey of Children and Youth* (Catalogue No. RH63-1/561-01-03E). Ottawa: Human Resources Development Canada.

Ronald, J., Delaive, K., Roos, L., Manfreda, J., Bahammam, A., & Kryger, M. H. (1999). Health care utilization in the 10 years prior to diagnosis in obstructive sleep apnea syndrome patients. *Sleep, 22*(2), 225–229.

Rosa, M. A., Gattaz, W. F., Pascual-Leone, A., Fregni, F., Rosa, M. O., Rumi, D. O., . . . Marcolin, M. A. (2006). Comparison of repetitive transcranial magnetic stimulation and electroconvulsive therapy in unipolar non-psychotic refractory depression: A randomized, single-blind study. *International Journal of Neuropsychopharmacology, 9,* 667–676.

Rosen, R. C. (1996). Erectile dysfunction: The medicalization of male sexuality. *Clinical Psychology Review, 16,* 497–519.

Rosen, R. C., & Leiblum, S. R. (1995). Treatment of sexual disorders in the 1990s: An integrated approach. *Journal of Consulting and Clinical Psychology, 63,* 877–890.

Rosenberg, H. (1993). Prediction of controlled drinking by alcoholics and problem drinkers. *Psychological Bulletin, 113,* 129–130.

Rosenthal, D., Wender, P. H., Kety, S. S., Schulsinger, F., Welner, J., & Ostergaard, L. (1968). Schizophrenics' offspring reared in adoptive homes. In D. Rosenthal & S. S. Kety (Eds.), *The transmission of schizophrenia: Proceedings of the second research conference of the Foundations' Fund for Research in Psychiatry, Dorado, Puerto Rico, 26 June to 1 July 1967.* Oxford: Pergamon.

Rosenthal, D., Wender, P. H., Kety, S. S., Schulsinger, F., Welner, J., & Rieder, R. O. (1975). Parent–child relationships and psychopathological disorder in the child. *Archives of General Psychiatry, 32,* 466–476.

Ross, C. A. (2001). *Dissociative identity disorder: Diagnosis, clinical features, and treatment of multiple personality* (2nd ed.). New York: Wiley.

Ross, H. E. (1995). DSM-III-R alcohol abuse and dependence and psychiatric comorbidity in Ontario: Results from the Mental Health Supplement to the Ontario Health Survey. *Drug and Alcohol Dependence, 39,* 111–128.

Rothbaum, B. O., Astin, M. C., & Marsteller, F. (2005). Prolonged exposure versus eye movement desensitization and reprocessing (EMDR) for PTSD rape victims. *Journal of Traumatic Stress, 18,* 607–616.

Rotter, J. B. (1972). Beliefs, social attitudes, and behavior: A social learning analysis. In J. B. Rotter, J. E. Chance, & E. J. Phares (Eds.), *Applications of a social learning theory of personality.* New York: Holt, Rinehart and Winston.

Rousseau, F., Heitz, D., Biancalana, V., Blumenfeld, S., Kretz, C., Boué, J., . . . Mandel, J.-L. (1991). Direct diagnosis by DNA analysis of the fragile X syndrome of mental retardation. *New England Journal of Medicine, 325,* 1673–1681.

Rowa, K., & Antony, M. M. (2005). Psychological treatments for social phobia. *Canadian Journal of Psychiatry, 50,* 308–316.

Rowland, D. L., Cooper, S. E., & Slob, A. K. (1996). Genital and psychoaffective response to erotic stimulation in sexually functional and dysfunctional men. *Journal of Abnormal Psychology, 105,* 194–203.

Ruskin, P. E., Silver-Aylaian, M., Kling, M. A., Reed, S. A., Bradham, D. D., Hebel, J. R., . . . Hauser, P. (2004). Treatment outcomes in depression: Comparison of remote treatment through telepsychiatry to in-person treatment. *American Journal of Psychiatry, 161,* 1471–1476.

Russell, J. M., Newman, S. C., & Bland, R. C. (1994). Drug abuse and dependence. *Acta Psychiatric Scandinavica, 89*(Suppl. 376), 54–62.

Russell, L. B., Hubley, A., & Palepu, A. (2005). *What is important to the quality of life of homeless or hard-to-house Canadian adults and street youth? A multi-site study.* Poster presented at Canadian Conference on Homelessness, May 17–20, 2005, Toronto. Retrieved from http://educ.ubc.ca/faculty/hubley/pdfs/CCH_poster_text.pdf

Rutter, M. (1983). Cognitive deficits in the pathogenesis of autism. *Journal of Child Psychology and Psychiatry, 24,* 513–531.

Rutter, M. (1997). Implications of genetic research for child psychiatry. *Canadian Journal of Psychiatry, 42,* 569–576.

Rutter, M. (1999). Resilience concepts and findings: Implications for family therapy. *Journal of Family Therapy, 21*(2), 119–144.

Rutter, M. (2006). *Genes and behavior: Nature–nurture interplay examined.* Malden, MA: Blackwell.

S

Sachdev, P., & Hay, P. (1996). Site and size of lesion and psychosurgical outcome in obsessive-compulsive disorder: A magnetic resonance imaging study. *Biological Psychiatry, 39,* 739–742.

Salkovskis, P. M., & Clark, D. M. (1993). Panic disorder and hypochondriasis. *Advances in Behaviour Research and Therapy, 15,* 23–48.

Sanchez-Craig, M., Annis, H. M., Bornet, A. R., & MacDonald, K. R. (1984). Random assignment to abstinence or controlled drinking: Evaluation of a cognitive-behavioral program for problem drinkers. *Journal of Consulting and Clinical Psychology, 52,* 390–403.

Sanchez-Craig, M., & Wilkinson, D. A. (1986/1987). Treating problem drinkers who are not severely dependent on alcohol. In M. B. Sobell & L. C. Sobell (Eds.), *Moderation as a goal or outcome of treatment for alcohol problems: A dialogue* (pp. 39–67). New York: Haworth.

Sanislow, C. A., Grilo, C. M., & McGlashan, T. H. (2000). Factor analysis of the DSM-III-R borderline personality disorder criteria in psychiatric inpatients. *American Journal of Psychiatry, 157,* 1629–1633.

Sartorius, N., & Schulze, H. (2005). *Reducing the stigma of mental illness: A report from a global programme of the World Psychi-*

atric Association. New York: Cambridge University Press.

Sass, L. (1982, August 22). The borderline personality. *The New York Times Magazine,* pp. 12–15, 66–67.

Satir, V. (1967). *Conjoint family therapy: A guide to theory and technique* (rev. ed.). Palo Alto, CA: Science and Behavior Books.

Schachar, R., Jadad, A. R., Gauld, M., Boyle, M., Booker, L., Snider, A., . . . Cunningham, C. (2002). Attention-deficit hyperactivity disorder: Critical appraisal of extended treatment studies. *Canadian Journal of Psychiatry, 47,* 337–348.

Schachter, H. M., Pham, B., King, J., Langford, S., & Moher, D. (2001). How efficacious and safe is short-acting methylphenidate for the treatment of attention-deficit disorder in children and adolescents? A meta-analysis. *CMAJ: Canadian Medical Association Journal, 165,* 1475–1488.

Schaefer, A., Braver, T. S., Reynolds, J. R., Burgess, G. C., Yarkoni, T., & Gray, J. R. (2006). Individual differences in amygdala activity predict response speed during working memory. *Journal of Neuroscience, 26,* 10120–10128.

Schafer, J., & Brown, S. (1991). Marijuana and cocaine effect expectancies and drug use patterns. *Journal of Consulting and Clinical Psychology, 59,* 558–565.

Schaffer, A., Cairney, J., Cheung, A., Veldhuizen, S., & Levitt, A. (2006). Community survey of bipolar disorder in Canada: Lifetime prevalence and illness characteristics. *Canadian Journal of Psychiatry, 51,* 9–16.

Scheier, L. M., Botvin, G. J., & Baker, E. (1997). Risk and protective factors as predictors of adolescent alcohol involvement and transitions in alcohol use: A prospective analysis. *Journal of Studies on Alcohol, 58,* 652–667.

Schepis, M. M., Reid, D. H., & Fitzgerald, J. R. (1987). Group instruction with profoundly retarded persons: Acquisition, generalization, and maintenance of a remunerative work skill. *Journal of Applied Behavior Analysis, 20,* 97–105.

Schliebs, R., & Arendt, T. (2006). The significance of the cholinergic system in the brain during aging and in Alzheimer's disease. *Journal of Neural Transmission, 113,* 1625–1644.

Schmidt, N. B., Zvolensky, M. J., & Maner, J. K. (2006). Anxiety sensitivity: Prospective prediction of panic attacks and Axis I pathology. *Journal of Psychiatric Research, 40,* 691–699.

Schneider, K. (1957). Primäre und sekundäre Symptome bei der Schizophrenia. *Fortschritte der Neurologie Psychiatrie, 25,* 487–490.

Schneider, R. D., Glancy, G. D., Bradford, J. M., & Seibenmorgen, E. (2000). Canadian landmark case, *Winko v. British Columbia:* Revisiting the conundrum of the mentally disordered accused. *Journal of the American Academy of Psychiatry and Law, 28,* 206–212.

Schoeneman, T. J. (1984). The mentally ill witch in textbooks of abnormal psychology: Current status and implications of a fallacy. *Professional Psychiatry, 15*, 299–314.

Schreiner-Engel, P., Schiavi, R. C., White, D., & Ghizzani, A. (1989). Low sexual desire in women: The role of reproductive hormones. *Hormones and Behavior, 23*, 221–234.

Schruers, K., Koning, K., Luermans, J., Haack, M. J., & Griez, E. (2005). Obsessive-compulsive disorder: A critical review of therapeutic perspectives. *Acta Psychiatrica Scandinavica, 111*, 261–271.

Schuckit, M. A., Daeppen, J.-B., Danko, G. P., Tripp, M. L., Smith, T. L., Li, T.-K., . . . Bucholz, K. K. (1999). Clinical implications for four drugs of the DSM-IV distinction between substance dependence with and without a physiological component. *American Journal of Psychiatry, 156*, 41–49.

Schuckit, M. A., & Smith, T. L. (1996). An 8-year follow-up of 450 sons of alcoholic and control subjects. *Archives of General Psychiatry, 53*, 202–210.

Schuller, R. A., & Ogloff, J. R. P. (2000). *Introduction to psychology and law: Canadian perspectives*. Toronto: University of Toronto Press.

Schulsinger, F. (1972). Psychopathy: Heredity and environment. *International Journal of Mental Health, 1*, 190–206.

Schulze, B., & Angermeyer, M. C. (2003). Subjective experiences of stigma. A focus group study of schizophrenic patients, their relatives and mental health professionals. *Social Science and Medicine, 56*, 299–312.

Schulze-Rauschenbach, S. C., Harms, U., Schlaepfer, T. E., Maier, W., Falkai, P., & Wagner M. (2005). Distinctive neurocognitive effects of repetitive transcranial magnetic stimulation and electroconvulsive therapy in major depression. *British Journal of Psychiatry, 186*, 410–416.

Schumacher, A., & Petronis, A. (2006). Epigenetics of complex diseases: From general theory to laboratory experiments. *Current Topics in Microbiology and Immunology, 310*, 81–115.

Scott, K. (1994). Substance use among indigenous Canadians. In D. McKenzie (Ed.), *Aboriginal substance use: Research issues*. Ottawa: Canadian Centre on Substance Abuse.

Sealy, P., & Whitehead, P. C. (2004). Forty years of deinstitutionalization of psychiatric services in Canada: An empirical assessment. *Canadian Journal of Psychiatry, 49*, 249–257.

Seeman, P., & Kapur, S. (2001). The dopamine receptor basis of psychosis. In A. Breier, P. V. Tran, J. M. Herrea, G. D. Tollefson, & F. P. Bymaster (Eds.), *Current issues in the psychopharmacology of schizophrenia* (pp. 73–84). Philadelphia, PA: Lippincott Williams & Wilkins.

Segal, Z. V., Williams, M. G., & Teasdale, J. D. (2002). *Mindfulness-based cognitive therapy for depression: A new approach to preventing relapse*. New York: Guilford.

Segarra, P., Ross, S. R., Pastor, M. C., Montañés, S., Poy, R., & Moltó, J. (2007).

MMPI-2 predictors of Gray's two-factor reinforcement sensitivity theory. *Personality and Individual Differences, 43*, 437–448.

Segerstrom, S. C., Taylor, S. E., Kemeny, M. E., & Fahey, J. L. (1998). Optimism is associated with mood, coping, and immune change in response to stress. *Journal of Personality and Social Psychology, 74*, 1646–1655.

Segraves, R. (1988). Drugs and desire. In S. R. Leiblum & R. C. Rosen (Eds.), *Sexual desire disorders*. New York: Guilford.

Segraves, R. T., & Althof, S. (1998). Psychotherapy and pharmacotherapy of sexual dysfunctions. In P. E. Nathan & J. M. Gorman (Eds.), *A guide to treatments that work* (pp. 447–471). New York: Oxford University Press.

Seidman, L. J., Valera, E. M., & Makris, N. (2005). Structural brain imaging of attention deficit/hyperactivity disorder. *Biological Psychiatry, 57*, 1263–1272.

Selkoe, D. J. (1993). Aging brain, aging mind. *Scientific American, 267*(3), 134–142.

Seligman, M. E. P. (1975). *Helplessness: On depression, development, and death*. San Francisco: Freeman.

Seligman, M. E. P. (1991). *Learned optimism*. New York: Knopf.

Selten, J.-P., Cantor-Graae, E., & Kahn, R. S. (2007). Migration and schizophrenia. *Current Opinion in Psychiatry, 20*, 111–115.

Selten, J.-P., Gernaat, H. B., Nolen, W. A., Wiersma, D., van den Bosch, R. J. (1998). Experience of negative symptoms: Comparisons of schizophrenic patients to patients with a depressive disorder and to normal subjects. *American Journal of Psychiatry, 155*, 350–354.

Serene, J. A., Ashtari, M., Szeszko, P. R., & Kumra, S. (2007). Neuroimaging studies of children with serious emotional disturbances: A selective review. *Canadian Journal of Psychiatry, 52*, 135–145.

Serin, R. C. (1998). Treatment responsivity, intervention, and reintegration: A conceptual model. *Forum on Corrections Research, 10*, 29–32.

Serin, R., Forth, A., Brown, A., Nunes, K., Bennell, C., & Pozzulo, J. (2011). *Psychology of criminal behaviour: A Canadian perspective*. Toronto: Pearson Education Canada.

Seroczynski, A. D., Cole, D. A., & Maxwell, S. E. (1997). Cumulative and compensatory effects of competence and incompetence on depressive symptoms in children. *Journal of Abnormal Psychology, 106*, 586–597.

Seto, M. C. (2004). Pedophilia and sexual offenses against children. *Annual Review of Sex Research, 15*, 321–361.

Seto, M. C. (2008). *Pedophilia and sexual offending against children: Theory, assessment, and intervention*. Washington, DC: American Psychological Assocation.

Seto, M. C., Maric, A., & Barbaree, H. E. (2001). The role of pornography in the etiology of sexual aggression. *Aggression and Violent Behavior, 6*, 35–53.

Shapiro, C. M., Trajanovic, N. N., & Fedoroff, J. P. (2003). Sexsomnia—A new parasomnia? *Canadian Journal of Psychiatry, 48*(5), 311–317.

Shapiro, F. (2001). *Eye movement desensitization and reprocessing (EMDR): Basic principles, protocols, and procedures* (2nd ed.). New York: Guilford.

Shaw, E., & Grenier, D. (2001). Taking the pulse of Canadian children—A health report card for the millennium. *Paediatrics & Child Health, 6*(4), 181–183. Retrieved October 20, 2003, from http://www.pulsus.com/Paeds/06_04/shaw_ed.htm

Shaywitz, S. E. (1998). Dyslexia. *New England Journal of Medicine, 338*, 307–312.

Shaywitz, S. E., Shaywitz, B. A., Pugh, K. R., Fulbright, R. K., Constable, R. T., Mencl, W. E., . . . Gore, J. C. (1998). Functional disruption in the organization of the brain for reading in dyslexia. *Proceedings of the National Academy of Sciences of the United States of America, 95*, 2636–2641.

Shea, M. T., Widiger, T. A., & Klein, M. H. (1992). Comorbidity of personality disorders and depression: Implications for treatment. *Journal of Consulting and Clinical Psychology, 60*, 857–868.

Sheitman, B. B., Kinon, B. J., Ridgway, B. A., & Lieberman, J. A. (1998). Pharmacological treatments of schizophrenia. In P. E. Nathan & J. M. Gorman (Eds.), *A guide to treatments that work* (pp. 167–189). New York: Oxford University Press.

Sher, K. J., Grekin, E. R., & Williams, N. A. (2005). The development of alcohol use disorders. *Annual Review of Clinical Psychology, 1*, 493–523.

Sher, K. J., & Trull, T. J. (1994). Personality and disinhibitory psychopathology: Alcoholism and antisocial personality disorder. *Journal of Abnormal Psychology, 103*, 92–102.

Sherman, D. K., McGue, M. K., & Ianoco W. G. (1997). Twin concordance for attention deficit hyperactivity disorder: A comparison of teachers' and mothers' reports. *American Journal of Psychiatry, 154*(4), 532–535.

Shields, M. (2004a). Social anxiety disorder—beyond shyness (Catalogue No. 82-003-SIE2004000). *Health Reports, 15*(Suppl.), 47–81.

Shields, M. (2004b). *Stress, health and the benefit of social support* (Catalogue No. 82-003-XPE). *Health Reports, 15*(1), 9–38.

Shiffman, S., Hickcox, M., Paty, J. A., Gnys, M., Kasiel, J. D., & Richards, T. J. (1996). Progression from a smoking lapse to relapse: Prediction from abstinence violation effects, nicotine dependence, and lapse characteristics. *Journal of Consulting and Clinical Psychology, 64*, 993–1002.

Shneidman, E. S. (1994). Clues to suicide, reconsidered. *Suicide and Life-Threatening Behavior, 24*, 395–397.

Shneidman, E. S., Farberow, N. L., & Litman, R. E. (1994). *The psychology of suicide: A clinician's guide to evaluation and treatment*. Northvale, NJ: Aronson.

Siegel, J. M. (2004). Hypocretin (orexin): Role in normal behavior and neuropathology. *Annual Review of Psychology, 55,* 125–148.

Siegel, S. (2005). Drug tolerance, drug addiction, and drug anticipation. *Current Directions in Psychological Science, 14,* 296–300.

Siever, L. J., & Davis, K. L. (2004). The pathophysiology of schizophrenia disorders: Perspectives from the spectrum. *American Journal of Psychiatry, 161,* 398–413.

Simeon, D., & Abugel, J. (2006). *Feeling unreal: Depersonalization disorder and the loss of the self.* New York: Oxford University Press.

Simmie, S. (1998, October 4). I'd sit in the kitchen and just shake. *Toronto Star.*

Simmie, S. (1998, October 3). Reality is sometimes painful. *Toronto Star.*

Simmons, H. G. (1987). Psychosurgery and the abuse of psychiatric authority in Ontario. *Journal of Health Politics, Policy and Law, 12,* 537–550.

Simon, G. E. (2006). The antidepressant quandary—considering suicide risk when treating adolescent depression. *New England Journal of Medicine, 355,* 2722–2723.

Simpkins, J. W., & Van Meter, R. (2005). Potential testosterone therapy for hypogonadal sexual dysfunction in women. *Journal of Women's Health, 14,* 449–451.

Simpson, D. D., Joe, G. W., Fletcher, B. W., Hubbard, R. L., & Anglin, M. D. (1999). A national evaluation of treatment outcomes for cocaine dependence. *Archives of General Psychiatry, 57,* 507–514.

Singh, N. N., McKay, J. D., & Singh, A. N. (1998). Culture and mental health: Nonverbal communication. *Journal of Child and Family Studies, 7,* 403–409.

Sitharthan, T., Sitharthan, G., Hough, M. J., & Kavanagh, D. J. (1997). Cue exposure in moderation drinking: A comparison with cognitive-behavior therapy. *Journal of Consulting and Clinical Psychology, 65,* 878–882.

Skodol, A. E., Gunderson, J. G., Pfohl, B., Widiger, T. A., Livesley, W. J., & Siever, L. J. (2002). The borderline diagnosis I: Psychopathology, comorbidity, and personality structure. *Biological Psychiatry, 51,* 936–950.

Skodol, A. E., Siever, L. J., Livesley, W. J., Gunderson, J. G., Pfohl, B., & Widiger, T. A. (2002). The borderline diagnosis II: Biology, genetics, and clinical course. *Biological Psychiatry, 51,* 951–963.

Slovenko, R. (2006). Patients who deceive. *International Journal of Offender Therapy and Comparative Criminology, 50,* 241–244.

Slutske, W. S., Heath, A. C., Dinwiddie, S. H., Madden, P. A. F., Bucholz, K. K., Dunne, M. P., . . . Martin, N. G. (1997). Modeling genetic and environmental influences in the etiology of conduct disorder: A study of 2,682 adult twin pairs. *Journal of Abnormal Psychology, 106,* 266–279.

Slutske, W. S., Heath, A. C., Dinwiddie, S. H., Madden, P. A., Bucholz, K. K., Dunne,

M. P., . . . Martin, N. G. (1998). Common genetic risk factors for conduct disorder and alcohol dependence. *Journal of Abnormal Psychology, 107,* 363–374.

Smith, D. (1982). Trends in counseling and psychotherapy. *American Psychologist, 37,* 802–809.

Smith, D. B., & Morrissette, P. J. (2001). The experiences of white male counsellors who work with First Nations clients. *Canadian Journal of Counselling, 35*(1), 74–88.

Smith, G. N., Boydell, J., Murray, R. M., Flynn, S. McKay, K., Sherwood, M., & Honer, W. G. (2006). The incidence of schizophrenia in European immigrants to Canada. *Schizophrenia Research, 87,* 205–211.

Smith, G. N., Flynn, S. W., McCarthy, N., Meistrich, B., Ehmann, T. S., MacEwan, G. W., . . . Honer, W. G. (1999). Low birth-weight in schizophrenia: Prematurity or poor fetal growth? *Schizophrenia Research, 47,* 177–184.

Smith, G. T., Goldman, M. S., Greenbaum, P. E., & Christiansen, B. A. (1995). Expectancy for social facilitation from drinking: The divergent paths of high-expectancy and low-expectancy adolescents. *Journal of Abnormal Psychology, 104,* 32–40.

Smith, M. L., & Glass, G. V. (1977). Meta-analysis of psychotherapy outcome studies. *American Psychologist, 32,* 752–760.

Smith, M. L., Glass, G. V., & Miller, T. I. (1980). *The benefits of psychotherapy.* Baltimore, MD: Johns Hopkins University Press.

Smith, M. L., Klim, P., & Hanley, W. B. (2000). Executive function in school-aged children with phenylketonuria. *Journal of Developmental and Physical Disabilities, 12,* 317–332.

Smith, R., Ronald, J., Delaive, K., Walld, R., Manfreda, J., & Kryger, M. H. (2002). What are obstructive sleep apnea patients being treated for prior to this diagnosis? *Chest, 121*(1), 164–172.

Smith, S. B. (1983). *The great mental calculators: The psychology, methods, and lives of calculating prodigies, past and present.* New York: Columbia University Press.

Smith, S. S., & Newman, J. P. (1990). Alcohol and drug abuse-dependence disorders in psychopathic and nonpsychopathic criminal offenders. *Journal of Abnormal Psychology, 99,* 430–439.

Smith, V. (2003, January 4). I never fit well as a girl. *The Globe and Mail.*

Smith, Y. L. S., Van Goozen, S. H. M., Kuiper, A. J., & Cohen-Kettenis, P. T. (2005). Sex reassignment: Outcomes and predictors of treatment for adolescent and adult transsexuals. *Psychological Medicine, 35,* 89–99.

Smith-Warner, S. A., Spiegelman, D., Yaun, S.-S., van den Brandt, P. A., Folsom, A. R., Goldbohm, A., . . . Hunter, D. J. (1998). Alcohol and breast cancer in women: A pooled analysis of cohort studies. *JAMA: Journal of the American Medical Association, 279,* 535–540.

Smits, D. J. M., & Boeck, P. D. (2006). From BIS/BAS to the Big Five. *European Journal of Personality, 20,* 255–270.

Smoking will be world's biggest killer. (1996, September 17). *Newsday,* p. A21.

Snell, M. E. (1997). Teaching children and young adults with mental retardation in school programs: Current research. *Behaviour Change, 14,* 73–105.

Sobell, L. C., Toneatto, A., & Sobell, M. B. (1990). Behavior therapy. In A. S. Bellack & M. Hersen (Eds.), *Handbook of comparative treatments for adult disorders* (pp. 479–505). New York: Wiley.

Sobell, M. B., & Sobell, L. C. (1973). Alcoholics treated by individualized behavior therapy: One year treatment outcome. *Behaviour Research and Therapy, 11,* 599–618.

Sobell, M. B., & Sobell, L. C. (1976). Second year treatment outcome of alcoholics treated by individualized behavior therapy: Results. *Behaviour Research and Therapy, 14,* 195–215.

Sobell, M. B., & Sobell, L. C. (1984). The aftermath of heresy: A response to Pendery et al.'s critique of "Individualized behavior therapy for alcoholics." *Behaviour Research and Therapy, 22,* 413–440.

Söchting, I. (2004). Painful pasts: Post-traumatic stress in women survivors of Canada's Indian residential schools. *Visions: BC's Mental Health and Addictions Journal, 2*(4), 13–14.

Social Services Ottawa. (1999). *Homelessness in Ottawa-Carleton.* Ottawa: Ottawa-Carleton, Policy, Planning and Performance Management Services Branch Strategic and Operational Support Directorate Social Services. Retrieved February 6, 2003, from http://ottawa.ca/city_services/housing/pdf/12_2_2_en.pdf

Söderpalm Gordh, A. H. V., & Söderpalm, B. (2011). Healthy subjects with a family history of alcoholism show increased stimulative subjective effects of alcohol. *Alcoholism: Clinical and Experimental Research, 35,* 1426–1434.

Sohn, C.-H., & Lam, R. W. (2005). Update on the biology of seasonal affective disorder. *CNS Spectrums, 10,* 635–646.

Somers, J. M., Goldner, E. M., Waraich, P., & Hsu, L. (2006). Prevalence and incidence studies of anxiety disorders: A systematic review of the literature. *Canadian Journal of Psychiatry, 51,* 100–113.

Southwick, S. M., Vythilingam, M., & Charney, D. S. (2005). The psychobiology of depression and resilience to stress: Implications for prevention and treatment. *Annual Review of Clinical Psychology, 1,* 255–291.

Spanos, N. P. (1978). Witchcraft in histories of psychiatry: A critical analysis and an alternative conceptualization. *Psychological Bulletin, 85,* 417–439.

Spanos, N. P. (1996). *Multiple identities and false memories: A sociocognitive perspective.* Washington, DC: American Psychological Association.

Spector, I. P., & Carey, M. P. (1990). Incidence and prevalence of the sexual dysfunctions: A critical review of the empirical literature. *Archives of Sexual Behavior, 19*(4), 389–408.

Speed, J., & Mooney, G. (1997). Rehabilitation of conversion disorders: An operant approach. *Neurorehabilitation, 8,* 175–181.

Spencer, T., Biederman, J., Wilens, T., Harding, M., O'Donnell, D., & Griffin, S. (1996). Pharmacotherapy of attention-deficit hyperactivity disorder across the life cycle. *Journal of the American Academy of Child and Adolescent Psychiatry, 35,* 409–432.

Spirito, A., & Esposito-Smythers, C. (2006). Attempted and completed suicide in adolescence. *Annual Review of Clinical Psychology, 2,* 237–266.

Spitzer, R. L., Devlin, M. J., Walsh, B. T., Hasin, D., Wing, R. R., Marcus, M. D., . . . Nonas, C. (1992). Binge eating disorder: A multisite field trial of the diagnostic criteria. *International Journal of Eating Disorders, 11*(3), 191–203.

Spitzer, R. L., Gibbon, M., Skodol, A. E., Williams, J. B. W., & First, M. B. (1989). *DSM-III-R casebook: A learning companion to the Diagnostic and Statistical Manual of Mental Disorders (third edition, revised).* Washington, DC: American Psychiatric Press.

Spitzer, R. L., Gibbon, M., Skodol, A. E., Williams, J. B. W., & First, M. B. (1994). *DSM-IV casebook: A learning companion to the Diagnostic and Statistical Manual of Mental Disorders, fourth edition.* Washington, DC: American Psychiatric Press.

Spreen, O. (1988). Prognosis of learning disability. *Journal of Consulting and Clinical Psychology, 56,* 836–842.

Statistics Canada. (1993). *Language, tradition, health, lifestyle and issues: 1991 Aboriginal Peoples Survey* (Catalogue No. 89-533-XPB). Ottawa: Author.

Statistics Canada. (2002). How healthy are Canadians? Annual report 2002 (Catalogue No. 82-003-S2002001). *Health Reports, 13*(Suppl.), 73–88.

Statistics Canada. (2003). *2001 Census: Analysis series. Aboriginal peoples of Canada: A demographic profile* (Catalogue No. 96F0030XIE2001007). Ottawa: Author. Retrieved from http://www12.statcan.ca/english/census01/products/analytic/companion/abor/pdf/96F0030XIE2001007.pdf

Statistics Canada. (2004a, September 9). *Canadian community health survey: Mental health and well-being* (Catalogue 82-617-XIE). Ottawa: Author.

Statistics Canada. (2004b, December 24). *Social anxiety disorder—beyond shyness.* (Health Reports – Supplement, 82-003-S/E2004000 vol. 15, December 2004. http://www.statscan.gc.ca/bsolc/olc-cel/olc-cel?catno=82-003-S/E&lang=eng#

Statistics Canada (2011). Suicides and suicide rate, by sex and age group. CANSIM, Table 102-0551 (Catalogue No. 84F0209X). Ottawa: Author. Retrieved November 15, 2011, from htttp://www40.statcan.gc.ca/l01/cst01/hlth66-eng.htm

Stauffer, V., Case, M., Kollack-Walker, S., Ascher-Svanum, H., Ball, T., Kapur, S., & Kinon, B. J. (2011). Trajectories of response to treatment with atypical antipsychotic medication in patients with schizophrenia pooled from 6 double-blind,

randomized clinical trials. *Schizophrenia Research, 130,* 11–19.

Steele, C. M., & Southwick, L. (1985). Alcohol and social behavior: I. The psychology of drunken excess. *Journal of Personality and Social Psychology, 48,* 18–34.

Stefanatos, G. A., & Baron, I. S. (2007). Attention-deficit/hyperactivity disorder: A neuropsychological perspective towards DSM-V. *Neuropsychology Review, 17*(1), 5–38.

Steiger, H. (2007). Eating disorder paradigms for the new millennium: Do "attachment" and "culture" appear on brain and genome scans? *Canadian Journal of Psychiatry, 52,* 209–211.

Steiger, H., & Bruce, K. R. (2007). Phenotypes, endophenotypes, and genotypes in bulimia spectrum eating disorders. *Canadian Journal of Psychiatry, 52,* 220–227.

Stein, D. J., Solms, M., & van Honk, J. (2006). The cognitive-affective neuroscience of the unconscious. *CNS Spectrums, 11,* 580–583.

Stein, M. B., Jang, K. L., & Livesley, W. J. (2002). Heritability of social anxiety-related concerns and personality characteristics: A twin study. *Journal of Nervous and Mental Disease, 190,* 219–224.

Stein, M. B., Jang, K. L., Taylor, S., Vernon, P. A., & Livesley, W. J. (2002). Genetic and environmental influences on trauma exposure and posttraumatic stress disorder symptoms: A general population twin study. *American Journal of Psychiatry, 159,* 1675–1681.

Stein, M. B., & Walker, J. R. (2002). *Triumph over shyness: Conquering shyness and social anxiety.* New York: McGraw-Hill.

Stein, M. B., Walker, J. R., Hazen, A. L., & Forde, D. R. (1997). Full and partial posttraumatic stress disorder: Findings from a community survey. *American Journal of Psychiatry, 154*(8), 1114–1119.

Stephane, M., Barton, S., & Boutros, N. N. (2001). Auditory verbal hallucinations and dysfunction of neural substrates of speech. *Schizophrenia Research, 50,* 61–78.

Stephens, T., Dulberg, C., & Joubert, N. (1999). Mental health of the Canadian population: A comprehensive analysis. *Chronic Diseases in Canada, 20,* 118–126.

Stephens, T., & Joubert, N. (2001). The economic burden of mental health problems in Canada. *Chronic Diseases in Canada, 22,* 18–23.

Stewart, S. E., Manion, I. G., & Davidson, S. (2002). Emergency management of the adolescent suicide attempter: A review of the literature. *Journal of Adolescent Health, 30,* 312–325.

Stewart, S. H. (1996). Alcohol abuse in individuals exposed to trauma: A critical review. *Psychological Bulletin, 120,* 83–112.

Stewart, S. H., Taylor, S., Jang, K. L., Cox, B. J., Watt, M. C., Fedoroff, I. C., & Borger, S. C. (2001). Causal modeling of relations among learning history, anxiety sensitivity, and panic attacks. *Behaviour Research and Therapy, 39,* 443–456.

Stock, W. E. (1991). Feminist explanations: Male power, hostility, and sexual coercion. In E. Grauerholz & M. A. Koralewski

(Eds.), *Sexual coercion: A sourcebook on its nature, causes, and prevention* (pp. 61–73). Lexington, MA: Lexington.

Stoller, R. J. (1969). Parental influences in male transexualism. In R. Green & J. Money (Eds.), *Transsexualism and Sex Reassignment.* Baltimore, MD: Johns Hopkins Press.

Stone, J., Smyth, R., Carson, A., Warlow, C., & Sharpe, M. (2006). *La belle indifférence* in conversion symptoms and hysteria: Systematic review. *British Journal of Psychiatry, 188,* 204–209.

Stone, M. H. (1980). *The borderline syndromes: Constitution, personality, and adaptation.* New York: McGraw-Hill.

Stonnington, C. M., Barry, J. J., & Fisher, R. S. (2006). Conversion disorder. *American Journal of Psychiatry, 163,* 1510–1517.

Strachan, A. M. (1986). Family intervention for the rehabilitation of schizophrenia: Toward protection and coping. *Schizophrenia Bulletin, 12,* 678–698.

Strassnig, M., Stowell, K. R., First, M. B., & Pincus, H. A. (2006). General medical and psychiatric perspectives on somatoform disorders: Separated by an uncommon language. *Current Opinion in Psychiatry, 19,* 194–200.

Stricker, G., & Gold, J. R. (1999). The Rorschach: Toward a nomothetically based, idiographically applicable configurational model. *Psychological Assessment, 11,* 240–250.

Strober, M., & Humphrey, L. L. (1987). Familial contributions to the etiology and course of anorexia nervosa and bulimia. *Journal of Consulting and Clinical Psychology, 55,* 654–659.

Strupp, H. H. (1992). The future of psychodynamic psychotherapy. *Psychotherapy: Theory, Research, Practice, Training, 29,* 21–27.

Stuart, F. M., Hammond, D. C., & Pett, M. A. (1987). Inhibited sexual desire in women. *Archives of Sexual Behavior, 16,* 91–106.

Stuart, H. L. (2005). Fighting stigma and discrimination is fighting for mental health. *Canadian Public Policy, 31* (Suppl.), 21–28. Retrieved from http://economics.ca/cgi/jab?journal=cpp&view=v31s1/CPPv31s1p021.pdf

Stuart, H. L., & Arboleda-Florez, J. (2000). Homeless shelter users in the postdeinstitutionalization era. *Canadian Journal of Psychiatry, 45,* 55–62.

Sullivan, H. S. (1962). *Schizophrenia as a human process.* New York: Norton.

Sulloway, F. J. (1983). *Freud: Biologist of the mind: Beyond the psychoanalytic legend.* New York: Basic Books.

Sussman, S. (1998). The first asylums in Canada: A response to neglectful community care and current trends. *Canadian Journal of Psychiatry, 43,* 260–264.

Sussman, S. (1999). *Dr. Ruth Kajander: A pioneer of Canadian psychiatry.* London, ON: Sussco Publishing Company.

Sutandar-Pinnock, K., Woodside, D. B., Carter, J. C., Olmsted, M. P., & Kaplan, A. S. (2003). Perfectionism in anorexia nervosa: A 6–24-month follow-up. *International Journal of Eating Disorders, 33*(2), 225–229.

Suzdak, P. D., Glowa, J. R., Crawley, J. N., Schwartz, R. D., Skolnick, P., & Paul, S. M. (1986). A selective imidazobenzodiazepine antagonist of ethanol in the rat. *Science, 225*, 1243–1247.

Svartberg, M., Stiles, T. C., & Seltzer, M. H. (2004). Randomized, controlled trial of the effectiveness of short-term dynamic psychotherapy and cognitive therapy for cluster C personality disorders. *American Journal of Psychiatry, 161*, 810–817.

Swinson, R. P. (2005). Social anxiety disorder. *Canadian Journal of Psychiatry, 50*, 305–307.

Szanto, K., Reynolds, C. F., Frank, E., Stack, J., Fasiczka, A. L., Miller, M., . . . Kupfer, D. J. (1996). Suicide in elderly depressed patients. Is active vs. passive suicidal ideation a clinically valid distinction? *American Journal of Geriatric Psychiatry, 4*, 197–207.

Szasz, T. S. (1961). *The myth of mental illness: Foundations of a theory of personal conduct.* New York: Hoeber-Harper.

Szechtman, H., & Woody, E. Z. (2004). Obsessive-compulsive disorder as a disturbance of security motivation: Constraints on comorbidity. *Psychological Review, 111*, 111–127.

Szegedi, A., Kohnen, R., Dienel, A., & Kieser, M. (2005). Acute treatment of moderate to severe depression with hypericum extract WS 5570 (St John's wort): Randomised controlled double blind non-inferiority trial versus paroxetine. *British Medical Journal, 330*, 503–509.

Szyf, M. (2006). Letter from the editor. *Epigenetics, 1*(1), i.

Szymanski, S., Kane, J. M., & Lieberman, J. A. (1991). A selective review of biological markers in schizophrenia. *Schizophrenia Bulletin, 17*, 99–111.

T

Talbot, J. D., & McMurray, L. (2004). Combining cognitive-behavioural therapy and pharmacotherapy in the treatment of anxiety disorders. *Canadian Psychiatric Association Bulletin, 36*(1), 20–22.

Tanda, G., Pontieri, F. E., & DiChiara, G. (1997). Cannabinoid and heroin activation of mesolimbic dopamine transmission by a common μ_1 opioid receptor mechanism. *Science, 276*, 2048–2050.

Taylor, C. T., & Alden, L. E. (2005). Social interpretation bias and generalized social phobia: The influence of developmental experiences. *Behaviour Research and Therapy, 43*, 759–777.

Taylor, S. (2000). *Understanding and treating panic disorder: Cognitive-behavioural approaches.* New York: Wiley.

Taylor, S. (2005). *Clinician's guide to PTSD: A cognitive-behavioral approach.* New York: Guilford.

Taylor, S., Abramowitz, J. S., & McKay, D. (2006). Cognitive-behavioral models of obsessive-compulsive disorder. In M. M. Antony, C. Purdon, & L. Summerfeldt (Eds.), *Psychological treatment of obsessive-compulsive disorder: Fundamentals and beyond* (pp. 9–29). Washington, DC: American Psychological Association.

Taylor, S., & Asmundson, G. J. G. (2004). *Treating health anxiety: A cognitive-behavioral approach.* New York: Guilford.

Taylor, S., Asmundson, G. J. G., & Coons, M. J. (2005). Current directions in the treatment of hypochondriasis. *Journal of Cognitive Psychotherapy, 19*, 285–304.

Taylor, S., McKay, D., & Abramowitz, J. S. (2005). Is obsessive-compulsive disorder a disturbance of security motivation? *Psychological Review, 112*, 650–657.

Taylor, S., & Stein, M. B. (2006). The future of selective serotonin reuptake inhibitors (SSRIs) in psychiatric treatment. *Medical Hypotheses, 66*, 14–21.

Taylor, S., Thordarson, D. S., Jang, K. L., & Asmundson, G. J. G. (2006). Genetic and environmental origins of health anxiety: A twin study. *World Psychiatry, 5*, 47–50.

Taylor, S., Thordarson, D. S., Maxfield, L., Fedoroff, I. C., Lovell, K., & Ogrodniczuk, J. (2003). Comparative efficacy, speed, and adverse effects of three treatments for PTSD: Exposure therapy, EMDR, and relaxation training. *Journal of Consulting and Clinical Psychology, 71*, 330–338.

Teens who have problems with fathers use drugs more. (1999, August 30). CNN. Retrieved from http://www.cnn.com/US/9908/30/teen.drugs.02/index.html

Teichner, G., Golden, C. J., Bradley, J. D. D., & Crum, T. A. (1999). Internal consistency and discriminant validity of the Luria Nebraska Neuropsychological Battery-III. *International Journal of Neuroscience, 98*, 141–152.

Teunisse, R. J., Cruysberg, J. R., Hoefnagels, W. H., Verbeek, A. I., & Zitman, F. G. (1996). Visual hallucinations in psychologically normal people: Charles Bonnet's syndrome. *Lancet, 347*, 794–797.

Thapar, A., Gottesman, I. I., Owen, M. J., O'Donovan, M. C., & McGuffin, P. (1994). The genetics of mental retardation. *British Journal of Psychiatry, 164*, 747–758.

Thomas, A. M., & LoPiccolo, J. (1994). Sexual functioning in persons with diabetes: Issues in research, treatment, and education. *Clinical Psychology Review, 14*, 61–86.

Thorpy, M. (2007). Therapeutic advances in narcolepsy. *Sleep Medicine, 8*, 427–440.

Thun, M. J., Peto, R., Lopez, A. D., Monaco, J. H., Henley, S. J., Heath, C. W., & Doll, R. (1997). Alcohol consumption and mortality among middle-aged and elderly U.S. adults. *New England Journal of Medicine, 337*, 1705–1714.

Tiefer, L. (2001). Arriving at a "new view" of women's sexual problems: Background, theory, and activism. In E. Kachak & L. Tiefer (Eds.), *A new view of women's sexual problems* (pp. 63–98). New York: Haworth.

Tienari, P. (1991). Interaction between genetic vulnerability and family environment: The Finnish adoptive family study of schizophrenia. *Acta Psychiatrica Scandinavica, 84*, 460–465.

Tienari, P. (1992). Implications of adoption studies on schizophrenia. *British Journal of Psychiatry, 161*(Suppl. 18), 52–58.

Tienari, P., Lahti, L., Sorri, A., Naarala, M., Moring, J., Kaleva, M., . . . Wynne, L. C. (1990). Adopted-away offspring of schizophrenics and controls: The Finnish adoptive family study of schizophrenia. In L. N. Robbins & M. Rutter (Eds.), *Straight and devious pathways from childhood to adulthood.* New York: Cambridge University Press.

Tienari, P., Sorri, A., Naarala, M., Wahlberg, K.-E., Moring, J., Pohjola, J., . . . Wynne, L. C. (1987). Genetic and psychosocial factors in schizophrenia: The Finnish Adoptive Family Study. *Schizophrenia Bulletin, 13*, 477–484.

Tienari, P., Wahlberg, K.-E., & Wynne, L. C. (2006). Finnish adoption study of schizophrenia: Implications for family interventions. *Families, Systems, and Health, 24*, 442–451.

Tjepkema, M. (2002). Health of the off-reserve Aboriginal population. *Health Reports, 13*(Suppl.), 73–86.

Tjepkema, M. (2005). Insomnia. *Health Reports, 17*(1), 9–25.

Tobin, D. L., Johnson, C. L., & Dennis, A. B. (1992). Divergent forms of purging behavior in bulimia nervosa patients. *International Journal of Eating Disorders, 11*, 17–24.

Toichi, M., Kamio, Y., Okada, T., Sakihama, M., Youngstrom, E. A., Findling, R. L., & Yamamoto, K. (2002). A lack of self-consciousness in autism. *American Journal of Psychiatry, 159*, 1422–1424.

Tolin, D. F., & Foa, E. B. (2006). Sex differences in trauma and posttraumatic stress disorder: A quantitative review of 25 years of research. *Psychological Bulletin, 132*, 959–992.

Tollefson, G. D., Beasley, C. M., Tamura, R. N., Tran, P. V., & Potvin, J. H. (1997). Blind, controlled, long-term study of the comparative incidence of treatment-emergent tardive dyskinesia with olanzapine or haloperidol. *American Journal of Psychiatry, 154*, 1248–1254.

Tolomiczenko, G. S., & Goering, P. N. (1998). Pathways into homelessness: Broadening the perspective. *Psychiatry Rounds, 2*(8), 1–6.

Tough, S. C., Butt, J. C., & Sanders, G. L. (1994). Autoerotic asphyxial deaths: Analysis of nineteen fatalities in Alberta, 1978 to 1989. *Canadian Journal of Psychiatry, 39*, 157–160.

Toward Optimized Practice. (2007). Adult primary insomnia: Assessment to diagnosis. Edmonton, AB: Author. Retrieved from http://www.topalbertadoctors.org/download/439/insomnia_management_guideline.pdf

Trask, P. C., & Sigmon, S. T. (1997). Munchausen syndrome: A review and new conceptualization. *Clinical Psychology: Science and Practice, 4*, 346–358.

Treasure, J., & Ward, A. (1997). Cognitive analytical therapy in the treatment of anorexia nervosa. *Clinical Psychology & Psychotherapy, 4*(1), 62–71.

Treatment of alcoholism—Part II. (1996, September). *The Harvard Mental Health Letter, 13,* 1–5.

Treatment of drug abuse and addiction—Part I. (1995, August). *The Harvard Mental Health Letter, 12,* 1–4.

Treffert, D. A. (1988). The idiot savant: A review of the syndrome. *American Journal of Psychiatry, 145,* 563–572.

Tremblay, R. E., Masse, B., Perron, D., Leblanc, M., Schwartzman, A. E., & Ledingham, J. E. (1992). Early disruptive behavior, poor school achievement, delinquent behavior, and delinquent personality: Longitudinal analyses. *Journal of Consulting and Clinical Psychology, 60,* 64–72.

Trenton State College. (1991, Spring). *Sexual Assault Victim Education and Support Unit (SAVES-U) Newsletter.* Ewing, NJ: Author.

Trigger, B. G., & Swagerty, W. R. (1996). Entertaining strangers: North America in the sixteenth century. In B. G. Trigger and W. E. Washburn (Eds.), *The Cambridge History of the Native Peoples of the Americas: Vol. 1. North America, Part 1* (pp. 325–398). New York: Cambridge University Press.

Triggs-Raine, B., Richard, M., Wasel, N., Prence, E. M., & Natowicz, M. R. (1995). Mutational analyses of Tay-Sachs disease: Studies on Tay-Sachs carriers of French Canadian background living in New England. *American Journal of Human Genetics, 56,* 870–879.

Trimble, J. E., Manson, S. E., Dinges, N. G., & Medicine, B. (1984). American Indian concepts of mental health: Reflections and directions. In P. B. Pederson, N. Sartorius, & A. J. Marsella (Eds.), *Mental health services: The cross-cultural context* (pp. 199–220). Beverly Hills, CA: Sage.

True, W. R., Rice, J., Eisen, S. A., Heath, A. C., Goldberg, J., Lyons, M. J., & Nowak, J. (1993). A twin study of genetic and environmental contributions to liability for posttraumatic stress symptoms. *Archives of General Psychiatry, 50,* 257–265.

Trull, T. J., Tragesser, S. L., Solhan, M., & Schwartz-Mette, R. (2007). Dimensional models of personality disorder: Diagnostic and Statistical Manual of Mental Disorders Fifth Edition and beyond. *Current Opinion in Psychiatry, 20,* 52–56.

Trzepacz, P. T., Baker, R. W., Greenhouse, J. (1988). A symptom rating scale for delirium. *Psychiatry Research, 23,* 89–97.

Trzepacz, P. T., Meagher, D. J., & Wise, M. G. (2002). Neuropsychiatric aspects of delirium. In S. C. Yudofsky & R. E. Hales (Eds.), *The American Psychiatric Publishing textbook of neuropsychiatry and clinical neurosciences* (pp. 525–564). Washington, DC: American Psychiatric Publishing.

Turnbull, J., Muckle, W., & Tadic, V. (2004). *Promoting Social Inclusion through a Harm Reduction Approach.* Presentation at A Community Forum on Homelessness: Linking Ottawa Research With Action and Policy, Ottawa, November 22. Retrieved from http://www.endhomelessnessottawa.ca/pdf/Research_at_Alliance_Forum_Nov_22_2004.pdf

Turner, S. M., Beidel, D. C., Dancu, C. V., & Keys, D. J. (1986). Psychopathology of social phobia and comparison to avoidant personality disorder. *Journal of Abnormal Psychology, 95,* 389–394.

Turner, S. M., Beidel, D. C., & Townsley, R. M. (1992). Social phobia: A comparison of specific and generalized subtypes and avoidant personality disorder. *Journal of Abnormal Psychology, 101,* 326–331.

Tyhurst, J. S., Chalke, F. C. R., Lawson, F. S., McNeel, B. H., Roberts, C. A., Taylor, G. C., . . . Griffin, J. D. (1963). *More for the mind: A study of psychiatric services in Canada.* Toronto: Canadian Mental Health Association.

U

U.S. Department of Health and Human Services. (1986). *NIDA Capsules: Designer drugs.* No. 10. U.S. Department of Health and Human Services (USDHSS), Public Health Service, Alcohol, Drug Abuse, and Mental Health Administration, National Institute on Drug Abuse. Rockville, MD: National Institute on Drug Abuse.

U.S. Department of Health and Human Services. (1992). *NIDA Capsules: LSD (Lysergic acid diethylamide)* No. 39. U.S. Department of Health and Human Services, Public Health Service, Alcohol, Drug Abuse, and Mental Health Administration, National Institute on Drug Abuse. Rockville, MD: National Institute on Drug Abuse.

U.S. Department of Health and Human Services. (2001). *Healthy people 2000: National health promotion and disease prevention objectives.* Washington, DC: U.S. Government Printing Office.

Ullmann, L. P., & Krasner, L. (1975). *A psychological approach to abnormal behavior* (2nd ed.). Englewood Cliffs, NJ: Prentice-Hall.

V

Van Ameringen, M., Mancini, C., Pipe, B., & Boyle, M. (2004, October). *Canadian PTSD epidemiology study.* Paper presented at the annual convention of the Canadian Psychiatric Association, Montreal.

Van Orden, K. A., & Joiner, T. E. (2006). The inner and outer turmoil of excessive reassurance seeking: From self-doubts to social rejection. In K. D. Vohs & E. J. Finkel (Eds.), *Self and relationships: Connecting intrapersonal and interpersonal processes* (pp. 104–129). New York: Guilford.

van Os, J., Krabbendam, L., Myin-Germeys, I., & Delespaul, P. (2005). The schizophrenia envirome. *Current Opinion in Psychiatry, 18,* 141–145.

Vazza, G., Bertolin, C., Scudellaro, E., Vettori, A., Boaretto, F., Rampinelli, S., . . . Mostacciuolo, M. L. (2007). Genome-wide scan supports the existence of a susceptibility locus for schizophrenia and bipolar disorder on chromosome 15q26. *Molecular Psychiatry, 12,* 87–93.

Verkerk, G. J. M., Pop, V. J. M., Van Son, M. J. M., & Van Heck, G. L. (2003). Prediction of depression in the postpartum period: A longitudinal follow-up study in high-risk and low-risk women. *Journal of Affective Disorders, 77,* 159–166.

Vermani, M., Milosevic, I., Smith, F., & Katzman, M. A. (2005). Herbs for mental illness: Effectiveness and interaction with conventional medicines. *Journal of Family Practice, 54,* 789–800.

Viens, M., De Koninck, J., Mercier, P., St-Onge, M., & Lorrain, D. (2003). Trait anxiety and sleep-onset insomnia. Evaluation of treatment using anxiety management training. *Journal of Psychosomatic Research, 54(1),* 31–37.

Vine, C., & Challen, P. (2002). *Gardens of shame: The tragedy of Martin Kruze and the sexual abuse at Maple Leaf Gardens.* Vancouver: Greystone.

Vissers, L. E. L. M., de Ligt, J., Gilissen, C., Janssen, I., Steehouwer, M., de Vries, P., . . . Veltman, J. A. (2010). A *de novo* paradigm for mental retardation. *Nature Genetics, 42,* 1109–1112.

Vitello, B., & Jensen, P. S. (1997). Medication development and testing in children and adolescents: Current problems, future directions. *Archives of General Psychiatry, 54,* 871–876.

Vocci, F. J., & Elkashef, A. (2005). Pharmacotherapy and other treatments for cocaine abuse and dependence. *Current Opinion in Psychiatry, 18,* 265–270.

Vogler, G. P., DeFries, J. C., & Decker, S. N. (1985). Family history as an indicator of risk for reading disability. *Journal of Learning Disabilities, 18,* 419–421.

Volkow, N. D., Wang, G. J., Fischman, M. W., Foltin, R. W., Fowler, J. S., Abumrad, N. N., . . . Shea, C. E. (1997). Relationship between subjective effects of cocaine and dopamine transporter occupancy. *Nature, 386,* 827–830.

Volpicelli, J. R., Alterman, A. I., Hayashida, M., & O'Brien, C. P. (1992). Naltrexone in the treatment of alcohol dependence. *Archives of General Psychiatry, 49,* 876–880.

Volpicelli, J. R., Clay, K. L., Watson, N. T., & Volpicelli, L. A. (1994). Naltrexone and the treatment of alcohol dependence. *Alcohol Health & Research World, 18,* 272–278.

W

Waddell, C., McEwan, K., Shepherd, C. A., Offord, D. R., & Hua, J. M. (2005). A public health strategy to improve the mental health of Canadian children. *Canadian Journal of Psychiatry, 50,* 226–233.

Waddell, C., Offord, D. R., Shepherd, C. A., Hua, J. M., & McEwan, K. (2002). Child psychiatric epidemiology and Canadian public policy-making: The state of the science and the art of the possible. *Canadian Journal of Psychiatry, 47,* 825–832.

Waddell, C., & Shepherd, C. (2002). *Prevalence of mental disorders in children and youth: A research update prepared for the British Columbia Ministry of Children* and *Family Development, October 2002.* Vancouver: The University of British Columbia.

Wagner, B. M. (1997). Family risk factors for child and adolescent suicidal behavior. *Psychological Bulletin, 121,* 246–298.

Wahlbeck, K., Cheine, M., Essali, A., & Adams, C. (1999). Evidence of clozapine's effectiveness in schizophrenia: A systematic review and meta-analysis of randomized trials. *American Journal of Psychiatry, 156,* 990–999.

Wahlund, L. A. & Bjorlin, G. A. (1999). Delirium in clinical practice: Experiences from a specialized delirium ward. *Dementia and Geriatric Cognitive Disorders, 10,* 389–392.

Wakefield, J. C. (1992a). The concept of mental disorder: On the boundary between biological facts and social values. *American Psychologist, 47,* 373–388.

Wakefield, J. C. (1992b). Disorder as harmful dysfunction: A conceptual critique of DSM-III-R's definition of mental disorder. *Psychological Review, 99,* 232–247.

Wakefield, J. C. (1997). Normal inability versus pathological disability: Why Ossorio's definition of mental disorder is not sufficient. *Clinical Psychology: Science and Practice, 4,* 249–258.

Wakefield, J. C. (2001). Evolutionary history versus current causal role in the definition of disorder: Reply to McNally. *Behaviour Research and Therapy, 39,* 347–366.

Wald, J., & Taylor, S. (2003). Preliminary research on the efficacy of virtual reality exposure therapy to treat driving phobia. *CyberPsychology and Behavior, 6,* 459–465.

Wald, J., Taylor, S., & Scamvougeras, A. (2004). Cognitive behavioural and neuropsychiatric treatment of posttraumatic conversion disorder: A case study. *Cognitive Behaviour Therapy, 33,* 12–20.

Waldram, J. B. (2001). The problem of "culture" and the counseling of Aboriginal peoples. In L. J. Kirmayer, M. E. MacDonald, & G. M. Brass (Eds.), *The mental health of indigenous peoples: Proceedings of the Advanced Study Institute* (pp. 145–158). Montreal: McGill Summer Program in Social & Cultural Psychiatry.

Waldram, J. B. (2004). *Revenge of the Windigo: The construction of the mind and mental health of North American Aboriginal peoples.* Toronto: University of Toronto Press.

Wallace, J. (1985). The alcoholism controversy. *American Psychologist, 40,* 372–373.

Walsh, B. T., Fairburn, C. G., Mickley, D., Sysko, R., & Parides, M. K. (2004). Treatment of bulimia nervosa in a primary care setting. *American Journal of Psychiatry, 161,* 556–561.

Walsh, B. T., Wilson, G. T., Loeb, K. L., Devlin, M. J., Pike, K. M., Roose, S. P., . . . Waternaux, C. (1997). Medication and psychotherapy in the treatment of bulimia nervosa. *American Journal of Psychiatry, 154,* 523–531.

Wampold, B. E., Mondin, G. W., Moody, M., & Ahn, H. (1997). The flat earth as a metaphor for the evidence for uniform efficacy of bona fide psychotherapies: Reply to Crits-Christoph (1997) and Howard et al. (1997). *Psychological Bulletin, 122,* 226–230.

Wampold, B. E., Mondin, G. W., Moody, M., Stick, F., Benson, K., & Ahn, H. (1997). A meta-analysis of outcome studies comparing bona fide psychotherapies: Empirically, "All must have prizes." *Psychological Bulletin, 122,* 203–215.

Wang, Q., Chan, R., Sun, J., Yao, J., Deng, W., Sun, X., . . . Li, T. (2007). Reaction time of the continuous performance test is an endophenotypic marker for schizophrenia: A study of first-episode neuroleptic-naïve schizophrenia, their non-psychotic first-degree relatives and healthy population controls. *Schizophrenia Research, 89,* 293–298.

Warme, G. (2006). *Daggers of the mind: Psychiatry and the myth of mental disease.* Toronto: House of Anansi Press.

Wasylenki, D. (2001). The paradigm shift from institution to community. In Q. Rae-Grant (Ed.), *Psychiatry in Canada: 50 years* (pp. 95–110). Ottawa: Canadian Psychiatric Association.

Watson, J. B. & Rayner, R. (1920). Conditioned emotional reactions. *Journal of Experimental Psychology, 3*(1), 1–14.

Webber. C., Hehir-Kwa, J. Y., Nguyen, D.-Q., de Vries, B. B. A., Veltman, J. A., & Ponting, C. P. (2009). Forging links between human mental retardation–associated CNVs and mouse gene knockout models. *PLoS Genetics, 5*(6), e10000531. Retrieved from http://www.plosgenetics.org/article/info:doi/10.1371/journal.pgen.1000531

Webster-Stratton, C., & Hammond, M. (1997). Treating children with early-onset conduct problems: A comparison of child and parent training interventions. *Journal of Consulting and Clinical Psychology, 65,* 93–109.

Wechsler, D. (1975). Intelligence defined and undefined: A relativistic appraisal. *American Psychologist, 30,* 135–139.

Wechsler, H., Davenport, A., Dowdall, G., Moeykens, B., & Castillo, S. (1994). Health and behavioral consequences of binge drinking in college: A national survey of students at 140 campuses. *JAMA: Journal of the American Medical Association, 272,* 1672–1677.

Weems, C. F., Costa, N. M., Watts, S. E., Taylor, L. K., & Cannon, M. F. (2007). Cognitive errors, anxiety sensitivity, and anxiety control beliefs: Their unique and specific associations with childhood anxiety symptoms. *Behavior Modification, 31,* 174–201.

Weinberger, D. R. (1997). On localizing schizophrenic neuropathology. *Schizophrenia Bulletin, 23,* 537–540.

Weinhold, B. (2006). Epigenetics: The science of change. *Environmental Health Perspectives, 114*(3), A160–A167.

Weiss, M., & Murray, C. (2003). Assessment and management of attention-deficit hyperactivity disorder in adults. *CMAJ: Canadian Medical Association Journal, 168,* 715–722.

Weiss, R. D. & Mirin, S. M. (1987). *Cocaine.* Washington, DC: American Psychiatric Press.

Weiss, R. D., & Mirin, S. M. (1994). *Cocaine* (2nd ed.). Washington, DC: American Psychiatric Press.

Weiss, R. D., Mirin, S. M., & Bartel, R. L. (1994). *Cocaine* (2nd ed.). Washington, DC: American Psychiatric Press.

Weissman, M. M., Bland, R. C., Canino, G. J., Greenwald, S., Hwu, H.-G., Joyce, P. R., . . . Yeh, E.-K. (1999). Prevalence of suicide ideation and suicide attempts in nine countries. *Psychological Medicine, 29,* 9–17.

Weissman, M. M., Markowitz, J. C., & Klerman, G. L. (2000). *Comprehensive guide to interpersonal psychotherapy.* New York: Basic Books.

Weissman, M. M., Wolk, S., Goldstein, R. B., Moreau, D., Adams, P., Greenwald, S., . . . Wichramaratne, P. (1999). Depressed adolescents grown up. *JAMA: Journal of the American Medical Association, 281,* 1707–1713.

Weisz, J. R., McCarty, C. A., & Valeri, S. M. (2006). Effects of psychotherapy for depression in children and adolescents: A meta-analysis. *Psychological Bulletin, 132,* 132–149.

Welch, M. R., & Kartub, P. (1978). Socio-cultural correlates of incidence of impotence: A cross-cultural study. *Journal of Sex Research, 14,* 218–230.

Weltzin, T. E., Cameron, J., Berga, S., & Kaye, W. H. (1994). Prediction of reproductive status in women with bulimia nervosa by past high weight. *American Journal of Psychiatry, 151,* 136–138.

Wender, P. H., Rosenthal, D., Kety, S. S., Schulsinger, F., & Welner, J. (1974). Crossfostering: A research strategy for clarifying the role of genetic and experiential factors in the etiology of schizophrenia. *Archives of General Psychiatry, 30,* 121–128.

Wente, M. (2006, July 6). Post-traumatic stress is felling more troops than the enemy. *The Globe and Mail,* p. A15.

Westen, D., & Shedler, J. (1999). Revising and assessing Axis II, Part I: Developing a clinically and empirically valid assessment method. *American Journal of Psychiatry, 156,* 258–272.

White, J. (2005). A summary of suicide risk and protective factors (youth and young adults). *Visions: B.C.'s Mental Health and Addictions Journal, 2*(7), 8.

White, J., & Jodoin, N. (1998). *Before the fact interventions: A manual of best practices in youth suicide prevention.* Vancouver: University of British Columbia, Mental Health Evaluation and Community Consultation Unit, Suicide Prevention Information and Resource Centre.

Whittington, C. J., Kendall, T., & Pilling, S. (2005). Are the SSRIs and atypical antidepressants safe and effective with children and adolescents? *Current Opinion in Psychiatry, 18,* 21–25.

Wickelgren, I. (1997). Marijuana: Harder than thought? *Science, 276,* 1967–1968.

Widiger, T. A. (1991). DSM-IV reviews of the personality disorders: Introduction to special series. *Journal of Personality Disorders, 5*, 122–134.

Widiger, T. A. (1992). Generalized social phobia versus avoidant personality disorder: A commentary on three studies. *Journal of Abnormal Psychology, 101*, 340–343.

Wieman, C. (2001). An overview of Six Nations mental health services. In L. J. Kirmayer, M. E. MacDonald, & G. M. Brass (Eds.), *The Mental Health of Indigenous Peoples: Proceedings of the Advanced Study Institute* (pp. 177–185). Montreal: McGill Summer Program in Social & Cultural Psychiatry.

Wiersma, D., Jenner, J. A., van de Willige, G., Spakman, M., & Nienhuis, F. J. (2001). Cognitive behaviour therapy with coping training for persistent auditory hallucinations in schizophrenia: A naturalistic follow-up study of the durability of effects. *Acta Psychiatrica Scandinavica, 103*, 393–399.

Wiersma, D., Nienhuis, F. J., Slooff, C. J., & Giel, R. (1998). Natural course of schizophrenic disorders: A 15-year follow-up of a Dutch incidence cohort. *Schizophrenia Bulletin, 24*, 75–85.

Williams, J. B., Gibbon, M., First, M. B., Spitzer, R. L., Davies, M., Bolus, J., . . . Witchen, H.-U. (1992). The Structured Clinical Interview for DSM-III-R (SCID): II. Multisite test-retest reliability. *Archives of General Psychiatry, 49*, 630–636.

Williams, J. M. (1984). *The psychological treatment of depression: A guide to the theory and practice of cognitive-behavior therapy*. New York: Free Press.

Williams, P., Narciso, L., Browne, G., Roberts, J., Weir, R., & Gafni, A. (2005). The prevalence, correlates, and costs of depression in people living with HIV/AIDS in Ontario: Implications for service directions. *AIDS Education and Prevention, 17*, 119–130.

Wilson, G. T. (1994). Behavioral treatment of childhood obesity: Theoretical and practical implications. *Health Psychology, 13*, 371–372.

Wilson, G. T., & Fairburn, C. G. (1998). Treatments for eating disorders. In P. E. Nathan & J. M. Gorman (Eds.), *A guide to treatments that work* (pp. 501–530). New York: Oxford University Press.

Wilson, P. (2000, May 16). Keeping pain at a distance. *The Hamilton Spectator*.

Winnicott, D. W. (1953) Übergangsobjekte und Übergangsphänomene: eine Studie über den ersten, nicht zum Selbst gehörenden Besitz. (First presented 1951). *Psyche, 23*, 1969.

Winston, A., Laikin, M., Pollack, J., Samstag, L. W., McCullough, L., & Muran, J. C. (1994). Short-term psychotherapy of personality disorders. *American Journal of Psychiatry, 151*, 190–194.

Wolfson, C., Wolfson, D. B., Asgharian, M., M'Lan, C. E., Østbye, T., Rockwood, K., & Hogan, D. B. (2001). A reevaluation of the duration of survival after the onset of dementia. *New England Journal of Medicine, 344*, 1111–1116.

Wolpe, J. (1958). *Psychotherapy by reciprocal inhibition*. Stanford, CA: Stanford University Press.

Wong, T. P. T. (2002). INPM: Who we are and what we do. International Network on Personal Meaning. Retrieved April 13, 2003, from http://www.meaning.ca/about_us/june02_letter.htm

Wood, J. M., Bootzin, R. R., Rosenham, D., Nolen-Hoeksma, S., & Jourden, F. (1992). Effects of the 1989 San Francisco earthquake on frequency and content of nightmares. *Journal of Abnormal Psychology, 101*, 219–234.

Wood, J. M., Lilienfeld, S. O., Nezworski, M. T., Garb, H. N., Allen, K. H., & Wildermuth, J. L. (2010). Validity of Rorschach Inkblot scores for discriminating psychopaths from non-psychopaths in forensic populations: A meta-analysis. *Psychological Assessment, 22*, 336–349.

Wood, J. M., Nezworski, M. T., & Stejskal, W. J. (1996). The comprehensive system for the Rorschach: A critical examination. *Psychological Science, 7*, 3–10.

Wood, J. M., Nezworski, M. T., & Stejskal, W. J. (1997). The reliability of the comprehensive system for the Rorschach: A comment on Meyer. *Psychological Assessment, 9*, 490–494.

Woodside, D. B., Bulik, C. M., Halmi, K. A., Fichter, M. M., Kaplan, A. S., Berrettini, W. H., . . . Kaye, W. H. (2002). Personality, perfectionism, and attitudes toward eating in parents of individuals with eating disorders. *International Journal of Eating Disorders, 31*, 290–299.

Woodside, D. B., Garfinkel, P. E., Lin, E., Goering, P., Kaplan, A. S., Goldbloom, D. S., & Kennedy, S. H. (2001). Comparisons of men with full or partial eating disorders, men without eating disorders, and women with eating disorders in the community. *American Journal of Psychiatry, 158*, 570–574.

Woody, S. R. (1996). Effects of focus of attention on anxiety levels and social performance of individuals with social phobia. *Journal of Abnormal Psychology, 105*, 61–69.

Wootton, J. M., Frick, P. J., Shelton, K. K., & Silverthorn, P. (1997). Ineffective parenting and childhood conduct problems: The moderating role of callous-unemotional traits. *Journal of Consulting and Clinical Psychology, 65*, 301–308.

Working Group for the Canadian Psychiatric Association and Canadian Alliance for Research on Schizophrenia. (1998). Canadian clinical practice guidelines for the treatment of schizophrenia. *Canadian Journal of Psychiatry, 43*(Suppl. 2), 25S–39S.

World Health Organization. (2001, June 25). ICD-10 Description. Geneva, Switzerland: Author. Retrieved from https://apps.who.int/whosis/icd10/descript.htm

World Health Organization. (n.d.). WHO definition of health. Retrieved from http://www.who.int/about/definition/en

Wright, J. H., Wright, A. S., Albano, A. M., Basco, M. R., Goldsmith, L. L., Raffield, T., & Otto, M. W. (2005). Computer-assisted cognitive therapy for depression: Maintaining efficacy while reducing therapist time. *American Journal of Psychiatry, 162*, 1158–1162.

Y

Yatham, L. N., Kennedy, S. H., O'Donovan, C., Parikh, S. V., MacQueen, G., McIntyre, R. S., . . . Gorman, C. P. (2006). Canadian Network for Mood and Anxiety Treatments (CANMAT) guidelines for the management of patients with bipolar disorder: Update 2007. *Bipolar Disorders, 8*, 721–739.

Yirmiya, N., & Sigman, M. (1991). High functioning individuals with autism: Diagnosis, empirical findings, and theoretical issues. *Clinical Psychology Review, 11*, 669–683.

Young, M. A., Fogg, L. F., Scheftner, W. A., & Fawcett, J. A. (1994). Interactions of risk factors in predicting suicide. *American Journal of Psychiatry, 51*, 434–435.

Z

Zakzanis, K. K., & Heinrichs, R. W. (1999). Schizophrenia and the frontal brain: A quantitative review. *Journal of the International Neuropsychological Society, 5*, 556–566.

Zakzanis, K. K., Poulin, P., Hansen, K. T., & Jolic, D. (2000). Searching the schizophrenic brain for temporal lobe deficits: A systematic review and meta-analysis. *Psychological Medicine, 30*, 491–504.

Zanardi, R., Franchini, L., Gasperini, M., Perez, J., & Smeraldi, E. (1996). Double-blind controlled trial of sertraline versus paroxetine in the treatment of delusional depression. *American Journal of Psychiatry, 153*, 1631–1633.

Zanarini, M. C., Frankenburg, F. R., Hennen, J., & Silk, K. R. (2003). The longitudinal course of borderline psychopathology: Six-year prospective follow-up of the phenomenology of borderline personality disorder. *American Journal of Psychiatry, 160*, 274–283.

Zhong, C.-B., & Liljenquist, K. (2006). Washing away your sins: Threatened morality and physical cleansing. *Science, 313*, 1451–1452.

Zhou, J.-N., Hofman, M. A., Gooren, L. J., Swaab, D. F. (1995). A sex difference in the human brain and its relation to transsexuality. *Nature, 378*, 68–70.

Zhu, A. J., & Walsh, B. T. (2002). Pharmacologic treatment of eating disorders. *Canadian Journal of Psychiatry, 47*, 227–234.

Zilberman, M., Tavares, H., & el-Guebaly, N. (2003). Gender similarities and differences: The prevalence and course of alcohol- and other substance-related disorders. *Journal of Addictive Diseases, 22*, 61–74.

Zimmerman, B. J., & Schunk, D. H. (2002). Albert Bandura: The man and his contributions to educational psychology. In B. J.

Zimmerman & H. Schunk (Eds.), *Educational psychology: A century of contributions* (pp. 431–459). Mahwah, NJ: Erlbaum.

Zotter, D. L., & Crowther, J. H. (1991). The role of cognitions in bulimia nervosa. *Cognitive Therapy & Research, 15*, 413–426.

Zubin, J., & Spring, B. (1977). Vulnerability— A new view of schizophrenia. *Journal of Abnormal Psychology, 86*, 103–126.

Zucker, K. J. (2005). Gender identity disorder in children and adolescents. *Annual Review of Clinical Psychology, 1*, 467–492.

Zucker, K. J., & Blanchard, R. (1997). Transvestic fetishism: Psychopathology and theory. In D. R. Laws & W. T. O'Donohue (Eds.), *Sexual deviance: Theory, assessment, and treatment*. New York: Guilford.

Zucker, K. J., & Green, R. (1992). Psychosexual disorders in children and adolescents. *Journal of Child Psychology and Psychiatry, 33*, 107–151.

Zuckerman, M. (1980). Sensation seeking. In H. London & J. Exner, Jr. (Eds.), *Dimensions of personality*. New York: Wiley.

Zuckerman, M. (2007). The Sensation Seeking Scale V (SSS-V): Still reliable and still valid. *Personality and Individual Differences, 43*(5), 1303–1305.

Zweig-Frank, H., & Paris, J. (1991). Parents' emotional neglect and overprotection according to the recollections of patients with borderline personality disorder. *American Journal of Psychiatry, 148*, 648–651.

Note: Entries for notes are followed by "*n*."

A

Abas, N., 260
Abdulrehman, R.Y., 332
Abi-Dargham, A., 375
Abikoff, H., 415
Abraham, K., 154
Abrahamson, L.Y., 160
Abramowiz, J.S., 120, 126
Abramson, L.Y., 159, 162
Abramson, P.R., 345
Abugel, J., 196, 198
Acampora, A., 285
Achenbach, T.M., 54
Adams, C., 384
Adams, G., 206
Adams, P.A., 365
Addington, D., 388
Adlaf, E.M., 142, 250, 251*n*, 258, 263
Adler, A., 25
Adler, J., 252
Afifi, T.O., 145, 154
Agras, W.S., 301, 306
Ahern, J., 115
Ahn, H., 83
Ainsworth, M., 418
Akbarian, S., 376
Akhtar, S., 217
Akiskal, H.S., 153
Alden, L.E., 109, 110
Aldous, J., 386
Aldrich, M.S., 310
Aleman, A., 377
Alford, J., 376
Ali, A., 300
Allderidge, P., 11
Allen, A., 129
Allen, M., 327
Allen, P., 366
Alloy, L.B., 160, 162
Alpert, J., 173
Alterman, A.I., 283
Althof, S., 351–352
Altman, L.K., 274
Aluma, M., 364
Amass, L., 282
Ambramson, L.T., 161
Ames, M.A., 331
Amick, A.E., 332
Amminger, G.P., 380
Ancoli-Isreal, S., 310
Andreasen, N.C., 361
Andreski, P., 275
Andrews, B.P., 220
Angermeyer, M.C., 66
Angier, N., 402
Anglin, M.D., 289
Angold, A., 147, 416, 421
Anisman, H., 154
Annis, A.H., 288
Anthony, W.A., 387
Anton, R.F., 282
Antonova, E., 378
Antonuccio, D.O., 167

Antony, M.M., 108, 109, 110, 120–121, 125, 129, 130, 132, 134–135, 245
Appelbaum, P.S., 91
Arango, V., 422
Arboleda-Florez, J., 16
Arendt, T., 427
Arieti, S., 369, 385
Armesto, J.C., 381
Arnett, J.L., 33
Arnett, P.A., 221–222
Arnold, E.H., 413
Arnow, B., 306
Aronson, T.A., 225
Arthur, N., 6, 84
Asaad, G., 365
Asarnow, J.R., 422
Asherson, P., 413
Ashtari, M., 413
Asmundson, G.J., 123, 204, 205, 206, 208
Asnis, G., 129
Astin, M.C., 134
Astley, S.J., 263
Aston, R., 264
Atkeson, B.M., 339
Atkinson, M.J., 22
Aubry, M., 177
Auinger, P., 413
Ayllon, T., 372
Ayoub, C.C., 200
Azrin, N.H., 443, 443*n*

B

Baack, M.J., 129
Bach, A.K., 349
Bachman, P., 364
Badger, T.A., 425*n*
Baer, J.S., 288
Baer, L., 72
Bagby, R.M., 49
Bahammam, A., 311
Baillargeon, R.H., 414
Baker, D., 198
Baker, E., 277
Baker, L., 302
Baker, R.C., 54
Baker, R.W., 424
Bal, P., 94
Baldwin, A.R., 277
Baldwin, D.S., 125
Balvin, R., 396
Bandura, A., 31, 39, 75, 239, 248
Banno, K., 310–311, 314
Banyard, P., 256
Barbaree, H.E., 330, 335, 338
Barbaresi, W.J., 412
Barch, D.M., 377, 378
Bardwell, W.A., 310
Barlow, D.H., 108, 125, 135, 345, 349
Barnes, G.E., 259
Baron, I.S., 413
Baron-Cohen, S., 398
Barongan, C., 338, 339
Barrett, S.P., 250
Barry, D.T., 83

Barry, J.J., 206
Barsky, A.J., 205
Bartecchi, C.E., 267
Bartel, R.L., 256
Barton, S., 366
Bartoshuk, L., 298
Basch, M.F., 75*n*
Basoglu, M., 439
Bassarath, L., 416
Bassett, Anne, 375
Bassetti, C.L., 310
Basson, R., 353
Bastiaansen, J.A., 398
Bates, J.E., 416
Bateson, G., 381
Bateson, G.D., 381
Baucom, D.H., 351
Bauer, C., 205
Bauer, L., 222
Bauer, L.O., 287
Baumal, Z., 147
Baumann, C.R., 310
Baxter, L.R., 134
Baylis, P.J., 7–8, 33
Bear, M.F., 402
Beard, K.W., 256
Beasley, C.M., 384
Beaudet, M.P., 258, 262
Bebbington, P., 5
Beck, A.T., 31, 32*t*, 39, 54, 78, 79–80, 79*n*, 121–122, 157–158, 158*n*, 160, 168, 169*n*, 179, 244, 278, 387
Beck, C.A., 144, 150
Beck, J.G., 351, 352
Beck, R., 160
Becker, D., 234
Beech, A.R., 337–338
Begin, P., 250, 258
Behar, E., 105
Beidel, D.C., 63, 80, 229
Beiser, M., 84
Beitman, B.D., 81
Bellack, A.S., 229, 383, 386, 444, 444*n*
Belland, J.C., 256
Belmaker, R.H., 241
Benitez, J., 71
Benjamin, J., 241
Benjamin, L.S., 225
Bennett, C.M., 340
Bennett, S., 295
Bentall, R.P., 365
Berchick, R.J., 179
Berenbaum, H., 366
Berga, S., 298
Bergeron, S., 351
Bergida, H., 364
Bergin, A.E., 83
Berlim, M.T., 70
Berlin, I.N., 260
Bernstein, D.P., 214, 225
Bernstein, E.M., 196, 196*n*
Bertelsen, M., 388
Best, C.L., 339
Bettelheim, B., 397
Beutler, L.E., 353
Bewernick, B.H., 175
Bexman, R.J., 413

Bezirganian, S., 214
Bibby, R.W., 4
Bick, P.A., 366
Bickel, W.K., 282
Biederman, J., 404, 412, 415
Binder, J.L., 83
Binet, A., 43
Binik, Y.M., 343
Biran, M., 81*n*
Birchwood, M., 388
Bjorlin, G.A., 424
Blair, C.D., 327
Blais, M.A., 47, 244
Blake, C., 84
Blakeslee, S., 272, 273, 409
Blanchard, E.B., 75
Blanchard, R., 327, 329, 332
Blanchette, K., 218*n*
Bland, R.C., 175, 218, 218*n*, 255*n*, 264, 360
Blankstein, K.R., 55
Bleuler, E., 359–360, 396
Blier, P., 129, 172
Bloch, M., 148
Block, D.R., 105
Bloom, B.L., 44
Bloom, H., 88
Blouin, A.G., 300
Bodnar, L.E., 349
Boeck, P.D., 241
Boetsch, E.A., 408
Boggs, C.D., 47
Boksman, K., 378
Bolwig, T.G., 70
Bond, G.R., 386
Bond, L., 92
Bond, M., 166
Bondi, M.W., 427
Bondolfi, G., 172
Boney-McCoy, S., 332
Bonnano, G.A., 116
Boos, H.B., 377
Bootzin, R.R., 312
Boreham, J., 267
Borkovec, T.D., 105
Bornet, A.R., 288
Bornstein, M.R., 444, 444*n*
Bornstein, R.F., 70, 230–231, 238
Bottonari, K.A., 168*n*
Botvin, G.J., 277
Bouchard, S., 44
Bouchard, T.J. Jr., 240
Bourgault, C., 260
Bourgon, L.N., 174
Boutros, N.N., 366
Bowlby, J., 418–419
Boyce, P., 148
Boyle, A.J., 147
Boyle, M., 116
Boyle, M.H., 147, 416
Bracha, H.S., 376
Bradford, A., 344, 345, 353
Bradford, J.M., 93
Bradford, J.M.W., 335
Bradley, E.A., 400, 404
Bradley, J.D.D., 51
Brähler, E., 204
Brandon, T.H., 281

Brass, G.M., 147
Braswell, L., 421
Braun, J.M., 413
Braver, T.S., 240
Braxton, L.E., 47
Breier, A.F., 384
Brekke, J., 388
Brems, C., 289
Brennand, K.J., 20
Brent, D.A., 177–179
Breslau, N., 275
Breslin, C., 289
Breslow, N., 334
Breuer, J., 205
Brickman, J., 337
Briere, J., 337
Brink, D.C., 77*n*
Brodsky, B.S., 225
Brody, J.E., 149*n*, 263, 344, 402, 403, 421–422
Brook, J.S., 214
Brown, G., 179
Brown, G.M., 302
Brown, J., 225
Brown, J.S., 178
Brown, R.A., 289
Brown, R.J., 205, 207
Brown, S., 277
Brown, S.A., 283
Brown, S.L., 338
Brown, S.M., 125
Brown, T.A., 63
Brownell, K.D., 307
Bruce, A.E., 154
Bruce, K., 303
Bryant, R.A., 116
Bryson, S.E., 400
Buchanan, R.W., 384
Buhr, K., 122
Buis, T., 49
Burgess, E.S., 289
Burke, R.S., 277
Burns, D., 158
Burns, D.D., 79*n*
Busatto, G.F., 376
Bush, G., 413
Busheikin, J., 386
Butt, J.C., 333
Butzlaff, R.L., 382
Buysse, D.J., 314

C

Caffier, P.P., 310
Cahn, W., 377
Cairney, J., 150
Calamari, J.E., 65, 120
Cale, E.M., 218
Calhoun, K.S., 332, 339–340
Calhoun, P.S., 47
Caligiuri, M.P., 384
Callaway, H., 72
Callender, J.S., 297
Callinan, P.A., 18
Camara, W.J., 51
Cameron, J., 298
Campbell, L.A., 63
Camper, P., 178
Camplair, P.S., 44

Canli, T., 241
Cannon, M.F., 420
Cannon, T.D., 364
Cantor-Graae, E., 379
Cantwell, D.P., 410
Capps, L., 396
Carey, G., 240
Carey, M.P., 262, 341n, 347
Carey, T.S., 282
Carlin, J.B., 300
Carlson, G.A., 422
Carney, C.E., 172, 316
Carpenter, L., 105
Carr, J.L., 338
Carrera, M.R.A., 272
Carson, A., 202
Cartensen, L.S., 422
Carter, J.C., 301, 305, 307
Carter, J.R., 378
Casanova, M.R., 377
Casey, D.E., 384
Caspi, A., 124, 154, 164,
    241, 274, 379
Cassano, G.B., 173
Cassiday, K.L., 65
Castellanos, F.X., 413
Castelnuovo, G., 44
Castillo, S., 252
Catalan, J., 351
Celis, W., 338
Centeno, S., 334
Cerletti, U., 70
Cernovsky, Z., 260
Chagnon, F., 178
Chaimowitz, G., 90
Challen, P., 332
Chambless, D., 243
Chan, M., 423
Chand, P.K., 193, 197
Chandrashekar, C.R., 207
Chang, L., 273
Chang, S.C., 65
Charcot, J.-M., 15, 205
Charney, D.S., 66, 163
Charter, A., 6, 7
Cheine, M., 384
Chen, L., 404
Chen, W., 413
Cheng, C., 313
Cheng, S.T., 206
Cheung, A., 150
Chevron, E.S., 167n
Chilcoat, H.D., 275
Chiles, J.A., 178
Chipperfield, B., 277
Chodirker, B.N., 403
Chou, C., 256
Chow, E.W.C., 375
Chowdhury, A.N., 206
Christiansen, B.A., 277
Chu, J.A., 199
Chung, S.A., 311
Ciccarelli, S.K., 400n
Cicchetti, D., 7
Clark, D.A., 111–112, 120,
    121–122, 121n, 123n,
    134, 160
Clark, D.M., 208
Clark, W., 285
Clarke, G.N., 421
Clarren, S.K., 263
Clay, K.L., 283
Clayton, P.J., 71
Cleckley, H.M., 190, 218,
    219, 221
Cleghorn, J.M., 365
Cloninger, D.F., 71
Cloos, J.-M., 128
Cockerham, W.C., 280
Coffey, C., 300

Cohen, B.M., 225
Cohen, F.L., 310
Cohen, N.L., 70
Cohen, P., 214, 225
Cohen-Kettenis, P.T., 324
Colapinto, J., 324
Cole, D.A., 420
Cole, T.B., 337
Collerton, D., 366
Collins, A., 387
Colpe, L., 148
Combs, D., 368
Compas, B.E., 305, 420
Condron, L., 256
Cone, J.D., 53
Conley, R.P., 384
Coolidge, F.L., 232
Cools, A.R., 364
Cooney, N.L., 287
Coons, M.J., 208
Coons, P.M., 197
Cooper, P.J., 297
Cooper, S.E., 345
Cooper, Z., 295, 297
Coplan, J.D., 125
Corbitt, E.M., 225, 230
Cornblatt, B.A., 364
Cornelius, J.R., 282
Corr, P.J., 241
Corte, C., 145–146
Cortoni, F.A., 331
Cossette, L., 407
Costa, N.M., 420
Costello, E.J., 147, 416, 421
Cotton, A.J., 116
Cottraux, J., 132
Coursey, R.D., 376, 388
Cox, B.J., 103, 107, 119, 145
Cox, D.N., 88
Cox, W.M., 278
Coyne, J.C., 156–157
Craddock, B., 413
Craighead, L.W., 169
Craighead, W.E., 169
Craske, M.G., 105
Crews, F.T., 282
Crisp, A.H., 297
Crow, S.J., 305
Crow, T.J., 305
Crowther, J.H., 300
Crowther, R., 313
Crozier, W.R., 109, 110
Crum, T.A., 51
Cruysberg, J.R., 365
Cullen, W., 101
Cullumbine, H., 264
Cummings, J.L., 427
Cunningham, C.E., 416
Curran-Celentano, J.,
    296, 304
Currie, S.R., 262, 281
Curry, S., 287
Cuthbert, B.N., 219
Cutter, C.J., 83
Cuvo, A.J., 406

Dadds, M.R., 416
Dahl, R.E., 311–312, 314
Daiuto, A.D., 351
Daley, M., 309
Daling, J.R., 263
Dallaire, R., 115
Damasio, A.R., 163
Dancu, C.V., 63
Daskalakis, Z.J., 71, 174
Davenport, G., 252
David, A.S., 198
Davidson, P.R., 134

Davidson, S., 176
Davies, B.A., 295, 301, 301n
Davies, M.F., 30
Davis, D., 198–199
Davis, D.D., 244
Davis, J.O., 376
Davis, K.L., 218
Davis, R., 301, 304, 305
Davis, S., 93
Davis, T.L., 305
de Bruin, N.M., 364
De Freitas, K., 88
De Luca, R.V., 332
de Queiroz, V., 173
de Zwaan, M., 301
Deckel, A.W., 222
Decker, S.N., 409, 410n
Decouflé, P., 404
Deforce, D., 129
DeFries, J.C., 409, 410n
DeKeseredy, W.S., 337
Dekker, J., 351
Delespaul, P., 376
Dell'Osso, B., 129
Demers, A., 250
Demming, B., 278
Dennerstein, L., 340
Dennis, A.B., 297
Denov, M.S., 331
Denys, D., 129
Desmond, E.W., 285
Desrocher, M., 126
Deter, H.C., 305
Detera-Wadleigh, S.D., 375
Devanand, D.P., 70
Devlin, B., 421
Di Nardo, P.A., 63
Diamond, F.R., 396
Diamond, S., 396
DiChiara, G., 272
Dickens, B.M., 288
Diemel, A., 173
DiLalla, D.L., 240
Dilk, M.N., 386
Dimidjian, S., 156, 167
Dimsdale, J.E., 310
Dinges, N.G., 65
Dingle, G., 258, 262n
Dinh, K.T., 277
Dix, D.L., 12
Dobson, D.J.G., 386
Dobson, K.S., 78, 168
Dodge, K.A., 239, 416
Dohrenwend, B.P., 114
Dolhanty, J., 305
Doll, B., 416
Doll, H.A., 295, 301, 301n
Doob, A.N., 288
Dopke, C.A., 351–352
Dowdall, G., 252
Downey, G., 422
Dozois, D., 46n, 49n, 78
Draijer, N., 114
Drevets, W.C., 163
Drewnowski, A., 300
Drews, C.D., 404
Drislane, F.W., 409
Drummond, D.C., 276–277
Dryden, J., 33
Dryden, W., 30, 78, 80
Duclos, E., 407
Dugas, M.J., 122
Dulberg, C., 7
Dulit, R.A., 225
Dunner, D.L., 149, 169, 171
Dussault, D., 121
Dwork, A.J., 70, 376
Dyce, J., 233

Dykens, E.M., 304,
    304n, 404
Dzokoto, V.A., 206

E

Earnst, K.S., 370, 376
Eberhardy, F., 395n
Ebstein, R.H., 241
Eccles, A., 334–335
Edward, G.H., 413
Edwards, H.P., 67
Edwards, V., 152n
Egeland, B., 445
Ehlers, A., 229
Ehud, K., 148
Eifert, G.H., 167
Eisenberg, L., 396
Eisler, I., 304
Elbert, T., 116
el-Guebaly, N., 22, 258
Elkashef, A., 282
Elkin, A., 163
Elkin, I., 70
Ellason, J.W., 197
Ellenbroek, B., 364
Ellinwood, E.H., 267
Elliot, R., 77
Ellis, A., 30–31, 39, 78, 80
Emerson, S., 296
Emery, G., 31
Emery, R.E., 428n
Emslie, G.J., 421
Engelsmann, F.F., 63
English, S., 220
Enns, M.W., 145
Eranti, S., 174
Erikson, E., 372
Erkanli, A., 147
Erlenmeyer-Kimling, L., 379
Esch, R.A., 282
Eshler, B., 310
Espósito-Smythers, C., 176
Essali, A., 384
Evans, D.M., 289
Everett, B., 16, 65, 66
Exner, C., 72
Exner, J., 223n
Eysenck, H.J., 241
Eysenck, M.W., 241

F

Fairburn, C.G., 295, 297,
    301, 301n, 302,
    304–305, 307
Fairley, C.K., 340
Faraone, S.V., 404,
    412–413, 414
Farber, B.A., 77n
Farberman, R.K., 67
Farberow, N.L., 181
Farley, M., 116
Farmer, A., 163, 374n
Farmer, A.E., 373
Farmer, R.F., 232
Farrell, A.D., 44, 280
Farrell, M., 258
Fawcett, A.J., 407
Fawcett, J.A., 176
Fazzino, T., 83
Federoff, J.P., 313
Feinberg, A.P., 18
Fenichel, O., 344
Ferrans, C.E., 310
Fichner-Rathus, L., 336, 340n
Fiedorowicz, C., 409
Field, A.E., 301
Fiez, J.A., 51
Fine, S., 335
Finkelhor, D., 330, 332

Finney, J.W., 287
Firestone, P., 46n, 49n
First, M.B., 65, 204
Fischer, B., 255, 283
Fisher, L., 92
Fisher, R.S., 206
Fisher, S., 70
Fitzgerald, J.R., 406
Fitzgerald, P.B., 71, 174
Flament, M.F., 129
Fleetham, J., 310
Fleischhaker, W., 373
Fletcher, B.W., 289
Flett, G.L., 158
Foa, E.B., 114
Fogg, L.F., 176
Folstein, M., 425n
Folstein, M.F., 424
Folstein, S., 425n
Folstein, S.E., 424
Fombonne, E., 396
Forde, D.R., 114, 114n
Forth, A.E., 338
Fortier, I., 414
Foster, S.L., 53
Foubert, J.D., 339
Fountain, S., 174
Fowles, D.C., 222
Frackowiak, R.S.J., 366
Frances, A.J., 225
Franchini, L., 171
Francis, D.J., 416
Frank, G.K.W., 302
Frank, H., 225
Frank, J., 407
Frankenburg, F.R., 224
Frankenfield, G., 303
Fraser, F., 6
Freedman, R., 364
Freeman, A., 244
Freeman, C.P., 300
Frenkel, E., 380
Freud, S., 15, 22–25, 23f,
    26, 39, 72–74, 101, 118,
    154, 178, 201, 205, 235,
    279, 372
Freund, K., 327
Frey, L.M., 199
Frezza, M., 259
Fricchione, G.L., 424
Frick, P.J., 415, 416
Friedlander, L., 126
Frith, C.D., 366
Fritzley, V.H., 400n
Froehlich, 413
Fromm-Reichmann, F., 381
Fuchs, C.S., 262
Fukumoto, H., 428
Fung, K.P., 84
Furst, J., 284–285
Fyer, M.R., 225

G

Gaggioli, A., 44
Gagnon, J.H., 321
Galaburda, A.M., 409
Galea, S., 114
Gallagher, S.M., 402
Ganzel, B.L., 199
Garand, L., 250
Garb, H.N., 234
Garbutt, J.C., 282
Gard, M.C., 300
Gardner, C.O. Jr., 63
Gardner, D.M., 128
Garfield, S.L., 81
Garfinkel, P.E., 300, 303
Garland, E.J., 415
Garland, O.M., 415

Garner, D.M., 296
Garnet, B., 83
Gasperini, M., 171
Gatehouse, J., 116*n*
Gauthier, J.G., 68
Gawin, F.H., 267
Gaziano, J.M., 264
Geer, J.H., 351
Geist, R., 301, 304
Genel, M., 413
Gerhardt, G.A., 413
Gerrard, M., 304, 304*n*
Gershuny, B.S., 194
Gersons, B.P., 114
Gettler, L., 220
Gfellner, B.M., 260
Ghizzani, A., 344
Gianoulakis, C., 283
Gibbon, M., 65
Gibbs, N., 414
Giel, R., 362
Gigante, R.A., 190
Gilbertson, M.W., 116
Gilchrist, P.T., 121
Gillberg, C., 413
Girgus, J.S., 420, 421
Glancy, G.D., 90, 93
Glaser, P.E., 413
Glasgow, R.E., 269
Glass, V.L., 83
Glautier, S., 276–277
Gleaves, D.H., 191, 300
Gliksman, L., 250, 258
Glynn, S., 386, 386*n*
Goering, P.N., 16
Gohm, C.L., 337
Gold, J.R., 51
Gold, L.J., 238
Goldapple, K., 163
Goldberg, T.E., 364
Golden, C.J., 51
Golden, R.N., 16, 148
Goldfarb, L.A., 304, 304*n*
Goldfield, G.S., 300
Goldfried, M.R., 81
Goldman, L.S., 413
Goldman, M.S., 277
Goldman, R.N., 77
Goldman-Rakic, P.S., 377
Goldner, E.M., 101
Goldstein, A.J., 243, 265
Goldstein, I., 352
Goleman, D., 227–228,
    227*n*, 230, 297, 420
Goodstadt, M., 33
Gooren, L.J., 326
Gordon, C.M., 262
Gordon, J.R., 287–288
Gorman, C., 414
Gorman, J., 125
Gorman, J.M., 335*n*
Gotlib, I.H., 162
Gottesman, I.I., 240, 373,
    374*n*, 401
Gove, W., 218*n*
Graber, B., 343
Graham, J.R., 47, 279
Grant, B.F., 101, 103
Gratzer, T.G., 91
Gray, J.A., 241, 248
Gray, J.E., 91, 92
Gray, J.J., 300
Gray, J.R., 240
Green, P.A., 408
Green, R., 323–324, 329
Greenbaum, P.E., 277
Greenberg, D.M., 335
Greenberg, J., 155–156
Greenberg, L.S., 28–29, 77
Greenberg, M.D., 70

Greenberg, R.P., 70, 231
Greenhouse, J., 424
Greenspan, E.L., 93
Greenwood, K.M., 316
Greeven, A., 208
Gregg, L., 366
Gregoire, J.P., 309
Greist, J.H., 44
Grekin, E.R., 259
Grenier, D., 418
Griesinger, W., 14, 17, 22
Griez, E., 129
Griffin, J.D., 12
Griffiths, M., 44, 256
Grilo, C.M., 224
Grissett, N.I., 301
Groleau, D., 84
Gross, A.M., 337
Gross, S.R., 250
Grosscup, S.J., 156
Grover, S., 174
Grunberg, N.E., 269
Guertin, T.L., 298
Gunderson, J.G.,
    222–224, 225
Gunewardene, R., 71
Gupta, N., 174
Gur, R.E., 375, 376
Gurley, J.R., 205
Gutheil, T.G., 91
Guthrie, D., 422
Guydish, J., 285
Guzder, J., 84
Guze, S.B., 71

H

Haaga, D.A., 305
Habib, R., 129
Habif, V.L., 332
Haggarty, J., 260
Halbreich, U., 148
Halek, C., 297
Haley, J., 381
Hall, G.C., 338, 339
Hall, S.M., 287
Hall, T.M., 65
Halliday, R., 283
Hamid, S., 84
Hamish, J.D., 416
Hammeke, T.A., 51
Hammen, C., 145, 154,
    420, 445
Hammond, D.C., 344
Hammond, M., 417
Hancock, L., 414
Haning, W., 273
Hankin, B.L., 418
Hanley, W.B., 403
Hanrahan, G.E., 383
Hansen, K.T., 376
Hansen, T.E., 384
Hare, R.D., 88, 219–221
Hariri, A.R., 125
Harkness, K.L., 154
Haroutunian, V., 376
Harpur, T.J., 219–221
Harrigan, T.R., 400*n*
Harris, S., 30
Harrow, M., 364
Hart, S.D., 88, 219–221
Hartikainen, A.-L., 380
Hartung, C.M., 225
Harvey, A.G., 116
Harvey, P.D., 363
Hasselbrock, V., 222
Haugh, J.A., 154
Haughton, E., 372
Havassy, B.E., 287
Hawaleshka, D., 144

Hawkrigg, J.J., 102
Hawton, K., 351–352
Hay, P., 72
Hayashida, M., 283
Hayes, R.D., 340, 341
Hayward, C., 301
Hazen, A.L., 114, 114*n*
Heath, A.C., 252
Heatherton, T.F., 301
Hebb, D.O., 29
Heffelfinger, S.K., 120
Heikkila, K., 313
Heiman, J.R., 351
Heimberg, R.G., 229
Heinmaa, M., 301, 304
Heinrichs, R.W., 375, 377
Hellstrom, W.J.G., 341, 343
Hen, R., 124
Henggeler, S.W., 417
Hennon, J., 224
Herbert, J.D., 229
Hercz, R., 220
Herman, P., 299
Hernandez, E., 191
Herold, E., 336
Herrmann, N., 70
Hersen, M., 444, 444*n*
Herzog, W., 305
Hester, R.K., 285
Hetherington, 421
Hewitt, P.L., 158
Hickey, A., 148
Higgins, G.J., 282
Hill, A.L., 405
Hiller, W., 204, 243
Hinshaw, S.P., 413–414
Hiripi, 294
Hochhausen, N.M., 224
Hodapp, R.M., 404
Hodgins, D., 288
Hodgson, G., 353
Hoefnagels, W.H., 365
Hofmann, S.G., 229
Hoffmann, W.F., 384
Hoffmann, W.L., 397
Hofman, M.A., 326
Hogan, M.E., 160, 162
Hogarty, G.E., 385
Holbrook, A.M., 313, 314
Holland, A.J., 303
Hollander, E., 129
Hollins, S., 263
Hollon, S.D., 55, 55*n*,
    169, 172
Holmes, E.A., 193–194
Holt, C.S., 229
Honig, A., 365
Hooley, J.M., 382
Hope, D.A., 229
Hopkins, I.M., 399
Hopko, D.R., 167
Hops, H., 167
Horne, L.R., 296
Horney, K., 25, 166
Hotaling, G., 330
Hough, M.J., 277
Houston, D.A., 331
Howard, C.E., 307
Howard, S., 33
Hsu, L., 101
Hsu, L.K., 297
Hua, J.M., 394
Huang, W., 406
Hubbard, E.M., 328
Hubbard, R.L., 289
Huber, K.M., 402
Hubley, A., 16
Hublin, C., 313
Hucker, S., 88
Hucker, S.J., 332–333

Hudson, 294
Hudson, J., 225
Hudson, J.I., 190, 307
Hudson, S.M., 337
Hudziak, J.J., 233
Huffman, J.C., 208
Hulshoff Pol, H., 377
Humphrey, L.L., 302
Hundelby, J.D., 260
Hunter, E.C., 198
Huntsman, S., 71
Hur, Y.-M., 311
Hurd, H.M., 11
Hurt, R.D., 282–283
Hussain, M.R., 311
Hutchinson, E.R., 70
Hwang, S.W., 16
Hy, L.X., 427

I

Ianoco, W.G., 413
Iglesias, H., 189
Ilardi, S.S., 169
Ingraham, L.J., 380
Ingram, R.E., 156
Insel, K.C., 425*n*
Iolomiteanu, A.R., 251*n*
Irle, E., 72
Isaac, M., 193, 197
Isohanni, M., 380
Ittig-Deland, V., 289

J

Jablensky, A., 6, 63, 360, 378
Jackson, C., 388
Jackson, D.N., 240, 381
Jackson, H.J., 327
Jackson, J., 332
Jacobi, C., 301
Jacobsen, 395
Jacobsen, B., 373
Jacobson, N.S., 167, 169
Jairam, S., 311
James, W., 242
Janca, A., 208
Janeck, A.S., 120–121
Jang, K.L., 123, 162–163,
    205, 233, 240, 274
Januszkowski, T., 84
Jarvis, E., 84
Jefferson, J.W., 44
Jeffrey, R.W., 75
Jellinek, E.M., 260
Jenner, J.A., 387
Jensen, P.S., 410, 421
Jeppesen, P., 388
Jeste, D.V., 384
Jetté, J., 378
Jilek, W.G., 294
Jodion, N., 180*n*
Joe, G.W., 289
Joffe, R.T., 128, 147, 302
Johns, L.C., 366
Johnson, B.R., 33
Johnson, C.L., 297
Johnson, J.G., 225
Johnson, M.E., 289
Johnson, P.A., 33
Johnson, S.L., 150, 154,
    163, 172, 178
Johnson, V.E., 342, 348,
    350, 351
Johnson, W.G., 304
Joiner, T.E., 157, 178, 179
Jolic, D., 376
Jones, E., 15
Jones, H.E., 263
Jones, J., 404
Jones, J.M., 225, 295, 300

Jones, P.B., 380
Joober, R., 389
Jorm, 144
Joubert, N., 7–8, 33
Jourden, F., 312
Jouriles, E.N., 416
Jung, C., 25
Jurkovic, G.L., 422

K

Kaback, M., 403
Kahan, B., 33
Kahn, M.W., 260
Kahn, R., 377
Kahn, R.S., 379
Kaiser, M.D., 398
Kajander, R., 12
Kane, J.M., 375, 379, 384
Kanne, S.M., 399
Kanner, L., 396
Kaplan, A.S., 297, 298, 301,
    302, 303–304
Kaplan, H.S., 344–345, 349
Kaplan, L., 236
Kaplan, S.J., 417*n*
Kaprio, J., 313
Kapur, S., 375–376, 384
Karkun, S., 148
Kartub, P., 347
Kasari, C., 396
Kaskenvuo, M., 313
Kasper, M.E., 365
Katzelnick, D.J., 44
Katzman, D.K., 304
Kavanagh, D.J., 277
Kay, S.R., 370
Kaye, W.H., 298
Kazdin, A.E., 239, 417,
    421, 444
Keane, T.M., 116
Kearins, J.M., 45
Keefe, F.J., 305
Keel, P., 301
Keel, P.K., 305
Keiller, S.W., 47
Keilp, J.G., 364
Keith, S.J., 361
Keller, D.M., 427
Kellner, C.H., 174
Kellner, C.HR.., 226
Kelly, M.M., 105
Kenardy, J., 306
Kendall, P.C., 55, 55*n*, 421
Kendell, R., 63
Kendler, K.S., 63, 123–124,
    154, 155, 162–163, 218,
    274, 303, 373, 375,
    379, 441
Kennedy, S.H., 70, 174
Kent, A., 301
Kent, J.M., 125
Keon, W.J., 13, 16, 33, 66
Kermeen, P., 260
Kernberg, O., 236
Kerr, S.L., 367
Kershner, R., 339
Kessler, 294
Kessler, D.A., 267
Kessler, R.C., 2*n*, 103,
    252, 422
Kety, S.S., 373, 374, 375
Keys, D.J., 63
Khalifé, S., 343
Khan, R.S., 413
Khan, S., 259
Khan, S.A., 413
Khatami, R., 310
Khatri, N., 168
Kiehl, K.A., 222

...eser, M., 173
Kihlstrom, J.K., 189, 191–193, 197
Killackey, E., 389
Kilpatrick, D.G., 339
Kim, S.C., 353
Kimerling, R., 339–340
King, D., 313
King, J., 414
Kinon, B.J., 383
Kinsbourne, M., 366
Kippin, T.E., 334
Kirby, M.J.L., 13, 16, 33, 65
Kirmayer, L.J., 63, 84, 147, 204, 205
Kirschenbaum, D.S., 54
Kissel, R.C., 406
Klein, D.N., 149
Klein, M.H., 243
Klein, R.G., 415
Kleinman, A., 5
Kleinplatz, P.J., 352
Klerman, G.L., 166, 167n, 385
Klesges, R.C., 270
Klim, P., 403
Klinger, E., 278
Knoll, J.L., 376
Knudson, D.D., 330
Kobak, K.A., 44
Koegel, R.L., 397
Koenigsberg, H.W., 224
Koenraadt, F., 94
Koerner, K., 244
Kohnen, R., 173
Kohut, H., 235, 248
Kolassa, I.-T., 116
Kolbert, E., 312
Koning, K., 129
Koob, G.F., 272
Koppiker, N., 353
Koren, D., 148
Koss, M.P., 339
Kotler, M., 274
Kovacs, M., 421
Kraatz, J., 258
Krabbendam, L., 376
Kraemer, H.C., 301
Kraepelin, E., 14, 17, 22, 359, 360
Krahn, D.D., 300
Krasner, L., 238, 372
Kresin, D., 343–344
Kring, A.M., 367, 370, 376
Krueger, R.F., 124
Kruesi, M.J., 335
Kruth, C.L., 300
Kryger, M.H., 310–311, 314
Kuehn, B.M., 265
Kugelmass, S., 380
Kuiper, A.J., 324
Kulkarmi, J., 71
Kumari, V., 378
Kumra, S., 413
Kunz, G., 280
Kupfer, D.J., 171, 314
Kurtz, J.E., 47
Kwon, S.-M., 160
Kymalainen, J.A., 381

L

Labouvie, E., 284
Ladouceur, R., 256
Lahey, B.B., 415
Laird, R., 239
Laishes, J., 221
Lakhan, S.E., 72
Lalonde, J.K., 190
Lam, R.W., 70, 147–148, 174

Lamacz, M., 334
Lamb, S., 234
Lamberg, L., 303
Lambert, M.J., 83
Landau, S.M., 428
Landy, S., 241
Lang, 54
Lang, P.J., 56, 219
Lang, R., 327
Lange, K.L., 427
Langeland, W., 114
Langenbucher, J., 284
Langevin, R., 327
Langford, S., 414
Lanphear, B.P., 413
Lanyon, R.I., 327
Larimer, M.E., 288
Laroi, F., 366
Lau, E., 297, 297n
Laumann, E.O., 321, 340
Lavallée, C., 260
Lawson, D.M., 288
Lawson, M.L., 295
Lazovik, 54
Leary, W.E., 287
LeBlanc, M., 309
Ledley, D.R., 125
Lee, J.K.P., 327
Lee, S., 63
Lee, T.H., 270
Leff, J., 382n
Lefley, H.P., 6
Lehman, C.L., 63
Lehman, D.R., 198
Lehmann, H., 12
Lehmann, H.E., 383
Leibing, E., 243
Leiblum, S.R., 343, 349, 352
Leibson, C.L., 412
Leichsenring, F., 83, 243
Leit, R.A., 300
Leitenberg, H., 305
Lejuez, C.W., 167
Lenhart, L.A., 417
Lentz, R.J., 385–386
Lenzenweger, M.F., 364
Leon, A.C., 225
Leonardo, E.D., 124
Leszcz, M., 22
Letendre, A.D., 6
Letourneau, E.J., 339, 341, 351
Levitan, R.D., 302
Levitt, A., 150
Levitt, A.J., 147, 302
Levy, S.R., 422
Lewinsohn, P.M., 156, 162, 167, 420, 421, 422
Lewis, I.A., 330
Lezak, M.D., 192
Li, S., 289
Liberman, R.P., 385, 387
Libert, J.M., 156
Lichtenstein, E., 269
Liddle, P.F., 370
Lieberman, J.A., 379, 383
Liebowitz, M.R., 129
Lilienfeld, S.O., 60, 190, 196, 218, 220
Liljenquist, K., 120
Lindahl, V., 148
Lineham, M.M., 244
Linehan, M.M., 178
Links, P.S., 245
Liotti, G., 225
Lipps, G., 407
Liss, A., 109, 125
Litman, L.C., 326
Litman, R.E., 181
Litt, M.D., 287

Little, R.E., 263
Litvin, E.B., 281
Livanou, M., 439
Livesley, W.J., 123–124, 163, 232–233, 240, 245, 248, 274
Livingston, J.D., 92
Livingstone, M.S., 409
Lo, H.T., 84
Lochman, J.E., 239, 416, 417
Lockwood, G., 80
Loftus, E.F., 198–199
Lohr, K.N., 282
Lohr, N.E., 238
London, H., 223n
Long, J.D., 388
Loo, C.K., 174
Looper, K.J., 204, 205
Lopez, A.D., 267
LoPiccolo, J., 343, 351
Loranger, A.W., 242
Lorenz, A.R., 224
Lorrain, D., 309
Lotter, A., 313
Lovass, O.I., 397, 399
Lowe, M.R., 300
Luermans, J., 129
Lueschen, G., 280
Lukassen, J., 258, 262
Lumley, M.N., 154
Lund, C.E., 370
Luntz, B.K., 239
Luria, A.R., 51
Luthar, S.S., 7
Lydiard, R.B., 125
Lykken, D.T., 221
Lynn, S.J., 190, 196
Lynne, J., 116
Lyons, J.S., 302
Lyons, M.J., 123, 124n

M

MacDonald, C., 303
MacDonald, K.R., 288
MacKenzie, R., 22
MacKenzie, T.D., 267
MacLatchy-Gaudet, H.A., 277
MacLeod, C., 123
Macnaughton, E., 84
MacPhillamy, D.J., 156
Maddever, H.M., 332
Magiskan, A., 7, 7n
Magnusson, A., 147
Mahamedi, F., 301
Maher, B.A., 9
Maher, W.B., 9
Mahler, M., 236, 248
Maier, S.F., 161
Makris, N., 413
Malan, J., 103
Maletzky, B.M., 335–336, 335n
Malla, A.K., 389
Maltzman, I.M., 288
Mamdani, M., 70
Manber, R., 316
Mancini, C., 116
Maner, J.K., 122
Mangano, R., 129
Manion, I.G., 176
Mann, J.J., 177–179, 422
Mann, R.E., 251n
Manson, S.E., 65
Mantovani, F., 44
Marchi, M.M., 205
Marcus, D.K., 157, 205, 208
Marcus, S., 173
Marder, S.R., 384, 385

Marengo, J.T., 364
Maric, A., 338
Marin, A., 115
Marino, L., 60
Markon, K.E., 124
Markowitz, J.C., 166
Marks, I., 439
Marlatt, G.A., 278–279, 279n, 287–288
Marques, T., 305
Marquette, C., 178
Marsh, R., 303
Marshall, A.D., 116
Marshall, D., 321
Marshall, W.L., 331, 334–335, 337
Marsteller, F., 134
Martin, D., 410
Martin, R.L., 71
Martinsen, E.W., 172
Masten, A.S., 7
Masters, W.H., 342, 348, 350, 351
Matas, M., 91
Matefy, R., 270
Math, S.B., 207
Mathes, S., 51
Matheson, K., 154
Mathews, A., 123
Mattoo, S.K., 174
Maxwell, J.C., 266
Maxwell, S.E., 420
Mayo-Smith, M.F., 282
Mazurek, M.O., 399
McCabe, M.P., 296, 299
McCabe, R.E., 130
McCarthy, B.W., 349
McCarty, C.A., 175
McCaul, M.E., 284–285
McCleery, A., 387
McCord, J., 239
McCord, W., 239
McCormick, R.M., 6
McCracken, J.T., 399
McCrady, B.S., 275, 284
McCullough, L., 44
McDonald, R., 416
McDougall, G., 386
McEachin, J.J., 399
McEwan, K., 394
McGlashan, T.H., 224
McGue, M.K., 413
McGuffin, P., 163, 373, 374n, 401, 402
McGuire, 421
McGuire, A., 33
McGuire, P.K., 366
McHugh, P.R., 424
McInnes, R., 353
McIntosh, D.E., 398
McKay, D., 120, 126
McKay, J., 283
McKay, J.D., 84
McKeith, I., 366
McKenna, P.J., 370
McLellan, A.T., 281
McMahon, F.J., 375
McMain, S.F., 244
McMurray, L., 69
McNally, R.J., 65
McNaughton, N., 241

Mead, M., 4
Meador-Woodruff, J.H., 376
Meagher, D.J., 423
Meana, M., 343
Medalia, A., 364
Medicine, B., 65
Mednick, S.A., 380, 437
Meehl, P.E., 377

Meichenbaum, D., 32, 39, 78, 80, 175
Meister, A.W., 347
Mellings, T.M.B., 109
Menein, M., 93
Mercier, P., 309
Merette, C., 309
Merriam, A.E., 364
Merskey, H., 189–190, 197, 260
Messenger, J., 321
Meston, C.M., 344, 345, 353
Metsänen, M., 368
Meyers, B.S., 144
Michael, R.T., 321
Michaels, S., 321
Mickley, D., 302
Miklowitz, D.J., 150, 154, 163, 172, 178, 379, 382
Milavsky, J.R., 422
Milberger, S., 404
Miles, J.H., 399
Miller, E., 206
Miller, I.W., 289
Miller, K.B., 305
Miller, K.J., 284
Miller, L.K., 405
Miller, T.I., 83
Miller, W.R., 283, 285, 288
Millon, T., 237
Milner, P., 29–30
Milos, G., 294
Milstone, C., 16
Minas, H., 63
Mineka, S., 103, 119
Minuchin, S., 82, 302
Mirin, S.M., 256, 268n, 276n
Miron, J., 11
Mirsky, A.F., 380
Mischel, W., 237
Mitchell, I.J., 337–338
Mitchell, J.E., 305
Mitchell, P.B., 174
Mitte, K., 135
Moeykens, B., 252
Moffitt, T.E., 124, 154, 164, 274, 379
Mohamed, S., 368
Mohan, R., 206–207
Moher, D., 414
Mohr, D.C., 353
Monahan, J., 88
Monahan, S.C., 287
Mondin, G.W., 83
Money, J., 324, 334
Montgomery, S., 171–172
Monti, P.M., 276–277
Moody, M., 83
Moon, E.C., 163
Mooney, G., 207
Moore, B.A., 83
Moore, R., 310
Moretti, M.M., 418
Morgenstern, J., 284
Morin, C., 314
Morin, C.M., 309
Morris, R., 378
Morrison, M., 416
Morrissette, P.J., 7
Morrow, D.J., 352
Morse, P.A., 287
Mortimer, A.M., 370
Mosconi, L., 427
Moskowitz, A.K., 369
Motiuk, L.L., 218n, 221
Moulden, H., 337
Mower, O.H., 118
Muckle, W., 16
Mueller, T.I., 289

Mueser, K.T., 351, 383, 385–386, 386n
Mukerji, P., 421
Mukherjee, R.A.S., 263
Müller, N., 376
Muñoz, R.F., 288
Murphy, C.C., 404
Murphy-Eberenz, K.P., 300
Murray, C., 413
Murray, H., 50
Murray, R.M., 366
Murray, R.P., 259
Murstein, B.I., 51
Murtagh, D.R.R., 316
Myin-Germeys, I., 376

N

Najavits, L.M., 134
Nandi, A., 114
Nardone, M.E., 157
Nasser, E.H., 154
Nathan, J.S., 51
Nathan, M., 380
Nathan, P.E., 335n
Natowicz, M., 403
Navarro, M., 272
Neale, J.M., 367
Needles, D.J., 159
Neeren, A.M., 162
Nehra, A., 341
Nehta, P., 416
Neill, J., 381
Nelson, C.B., 252
Nemiah, J.C., 189
Nesbitt, N., 388
Nestadt, G., 129
Neufeld, R.W.J., 378
Neugebauer, R., 10–11
Nevid, J.S., 336, 339n, 340n, 350
Newman, J.P., 219, 221, 224
Newman, M.G., 229
Newman, S.C., 218, 218n, 255n, 264
Newton-Taylor, B., 250
Nezu, A.M., 154, 406
Nezu, C.M., 154
Nezworski, M.T., 50
Nicholson, R., 49
Nicklason, F., 423
Nicolson, R., 398
Nicolson, R.I., 407
Nides, M.A., 289
Niemz, K., 256
Nienhuis, F.J., 362, 387
Nigg, J.T., 238
Nolen-Hoeksema, S., 145–146, 165, 312, 420, 421
Norcross, J.C., 81
Norman, R.M.G., 389
Norton, G.R., 103
Norvell, N.K., 301
Nowell, P.D., 314
Noyes, R., 233
Nunes, J., 177n

O

O'Brien, C.P., 282, 283
O'Brien, P.C., 412
Ochs, R., 263
O'Connor, 421
O'Connor, B., 233
O'Connor, M.E., 301, 301n
O'Donohue, W., 341, 351–352
O'Donovan, M.C., 401
Oei, T.P.S., 160, 277
O'Farrell, T.J., 287

Offord, D.R., 218, 218n, 394
Ogloff, J.R.P., 88, 89, 90
Oldham, J.M., 238
O'Leary, S.G., 413
Olff, M., 114
Olfson, M., 173
Olley, M.C., 89
Olmsted, M.P., 295, 301, 305
Oltmanns, T.F., 366, 428n
O'Neill, P., 34
Onstad, L.E., 277
O'Reilly, M.E., 302
O'Reilly, R.L., 91, 92
Orn, H., 218, 218n
Osborne, L., 65
Öst, L., 107n
Overholser, J.C., 154
Overmier, J.B.L., 161
Owen, M.J., 401, 402

P

Paglia, A., 142
Pagnin, D., 173
Paik, A., 340
Palepu. A., 16
Panzarella, C., 162
Parides, M., 302
Paris, J., 225, 238, 245
Parker, K.C.H., 134
Parnas, J., 380
Partinen, M., 313
Partonen, T., 147
Pasquini, P., 225
Patrick, C.J., 219, 222
Patten, S.B., 144, 154
Pattison, P., 327
Patton, G.C., 300
Paul, G.L., 385–386
Paulesu, E., 366, 409
Pavlov, I., 25, 26, 26f, 39
Pearlson, G.D., 375
Pearson, J.L., 148
Pendery, M.L., 288
Penn, D.L., 368, 370, 385, 386
Pennington, B.F., 408
Perez, J., 171
Perkins, A.M., 241, 388
Perkins, T.S., 160
Perlis, R., 173
Perlman, S.D., 345
Perry, B.C., 339
Perry, E., 366
Petersen, L., 388
Petersen, T.J., 172
Peterson, A.L., 443, 443n
Peterson, A.V., 277
Peterson, C., 298
Peterson, E.L., 275
Peto, R., 267
Petronis, A., 19, 36
Pett, M.A., 344
Pettit, G.S., 416
Petty, S.C., 157
Pfaus, J.G., 334
Pham, B., 414
Philips, M.L., 198
Phillips, D., 243
Phillips, D.P., 422
Phillips, K.A., 224
Phillips, R.A. Jr., 335
Phillipson, E.A., 310
Pianta, R.C., 445
Pihl, R.O., 250, 275
Pike, K.M., 302
Pincus, H.A., 173, 204
Pine, D.S., 66
Pinhas, L., 300
Pini, S., 173

Piotrowski, C., 47
Pipe, B., 116
Piper, A., 189–190, 197
Pleva, J., 245
Plomin, 421
Plomin, R., 402–403, 409
Podymow, T., 16
Polaschek, D.L.L., 337, 338
Polivy, J., 299
Pollack, M., 421
Pontieri, F.E., 272
Poonwassie, A., 6, 7
Pop, V.J.M., 148
Pope, 294
Pope, H.G. Jr., 190, 225, 272, 300
Porporino, F.J., 218n, 221
Porter, S., 198
Porzelius, L.K., 307
Potvin, J.H., 384
Poulakis, Z., 301
Poulin, P., 376
Power, M., 25
Prence, E.M., 403
Prescott, C.A., 123–124, 154, 155, 162–163, 274, 373, 375, 379, 441
Prince, R.H., 63, 260, 261
Prior, M.R., 397
Przybeck, T., 219, 221
Ptito, A., 177
Puente, A.E., 51
Pull, C.B., 129, 133
Purdon, C., 120–121, 121n
Purisch, A.D., 51
Putnam, F.W., 196, 196n
Pyszczynski, T., 155–156

Q

Quay, H.C., 222
Quigley, L.A., 288
Quinsey, V.L., 328

R

Rabheru, K., 71
Rabung, S., 83
Radomsky, A.S., 121
Rae, D.S., 361
Ramachandran, V.S., 328
Ranjith, G., 206–207
Ransom, J., 412
Rantakallio, P., 380
Rapin, I., 396, 398–399
Rapoport, J.L., 335
Rapoport, M.J., 70, 71
Raskin, P.M., 77n
Raspe, R.E., 200
Rathod, S., 387
Rathus, S.A., 336, 340n, 342n, 350, 352n
Ratti, L.A., 302
Ravindran, A.V., 70
Rayner, R., 26
Read, J.P., 168n
Rebgetz, M., 416
Rector, N.A., 365, 387
Redner, J.E., 162
Regev, L.G., 351–352
Regier, D.A., 361
Rehm, J., 251n, 255, 283
Reich, J., 233
Reid, D.H., 406
Reid, J.B., 278
Reid, W.J., 222
Reisner, A.D., 174
Reiss, 421
Reiss, S., 406
Reissing, E.D., 343

Remington, G., 384
Renaud, J., 178
Renneberg, B., 243
Resales, G.A., 381
Resnick, H.S., 339
Reuter, M., 240, 241
Rey, J.M., 415–416
Reynolds, C.F. III., 314
Reynolds, J.R., 302
Rhonde, P., 162
Ricciardelli, L.A., 296, 299
Richard, M., 403
Richards, C., 421
Ridenour, T.A., 270
Ridgway, B.A., 383
Rieber, R.W., 189
Rief, W., 204, 205
Riemann, B.C., 120
Rimland, B., 405
Ritter, B., 75
Ritterband, L.M., 316
Riva, G., 44
Rivas-Vazquez, R.A., 244
Roberts, J.E., 168n
Roberts, M., 337
Robins, L.N., 219, 221
Rocha, B.A., 273
Rochlen, A.B., 44
Rock, C.L., 296, 304
Rockert, W., 305
Rodgers, D.D., 260
Rodin, G., 295, 303
Rodin, J., 298, 302
Rodríguez de Fonseca, F., 272
Rogers, C., 39, 76–77
Rogers, R., 365
Rohde, P., 420
Romano, E., 414
Ronald, J., 311
Rorschach, H., 50
Rosa, M.A., 71
Rose, D.T., 162
Rosen, G.D., 409
Rosen, R.C., 340, 343, 351–352
Rosenberg, H., 288
Rosenberg, M., 93
Rosenham, D., 312
Rosenthal, D., 373, 375
Rosman, B.L., 302
Ross, C.A., 196–197
Ross, D., 239
Ross, H.E., 255
Ross, S.A., 239
Rotenberg, N., 148
Roth, W.T., 229
Rothbaum, B.O., 134
Rotter, J.B., 31
Rounsaville, B.J., 167n
Rousseau, F., 402
Rowa, K., 109, 121, 132
Rowland, D.L., 345
Ruggiero, K.J., 167
Rush, A.J., 31
Ruskin, P.E., 44
Russell, J.M., 255n, 264, 265, 267, 271
Russell, L.B., 16
Rüther, E., 72
Rutter, M., 7, 124, 164, 397, 421

S

Sachdev, P., 72
Sachs-Ericsson, N., 157
Sackeim, H.A., 70, 173
Safarjan, B., 376
Salkovskis, P.M., 208
Sampson, P.D., 263

Samtani, P., 258
Sanchez-Craig, M., 288
Sanders, G.L., 333
Sanders, M.R., 416
Sanislow, C.A., 224
Santiago, N.J., 149
Sarason, I.G., 277
Sass, L., 223, 225
Satir, V., 82
Saunders, B.E., 339
Sawka, E., 250, 258
Scamvougers, A., 206
Schachar, R., 414
Schachter, H.M., 414
Schaefer, A., 241
Schafer, J., 277
Schaffer, A., 150
Schank, D., 298
Scheftner, W.A., 176
Scheier, L.M., 277
Schellberg, D., 305
Schepis, M.M., 406
Schiavi, R.C., 344
Schliebs, R., 427
Schmidt, K., 250
Schmidt, M., 337
Schmidt, N.B., 122
Schneider, K., 360
Schneider, R.D., 93
Schnyder, U., 294
Schoeneman, T.J., 10
Schreibman, L., 397
Schreiner-Engel, P., 344
Schruers, K., 129
Schuckit, M.A., 256, 274
Schuller, R.A., 88, 90
Schulsinger, F., 240, 373, 375, 380
Schultz, L.R., 275
Schulze, B., 66
Schulze-Rauschenbach, S.C., 71
Schumacher, A., 19, 36
Schunk, D.H., 31
Schwartz-Mette, R., 65
Scott, K., 260
Sdao-Jarvie, K., 289
Sealy, P., 13
Seeley, J.R., 162, 420
Seeman, M.V., 365
Seeman, P., 375–376
Segal, D.L., 232
Segal, Z.V., 55, 172
Segarra, P., 241
Segraves, R., 344
Segraves, R.T., 351–352
Seibenmorgen, E., 93
Seidman, L.J., 413
Selemon, L.D., 377
Seligman, M.E.P., 160–161, 421
Selkoe, D.J., 427
Selten, J.-P., 379
Seltzer, M.H., 243
Selzer, R., 300
Semans, J., 351
Serene, J.A., 413
Serin, R.C., 219, 331n
Serran, G.A., 331
Seto, M.C., 330, 331, 337–338, 353
Shabsigh, R., 341
Shah, G.M.S., 366
Shapiro, B., 365
Shapiro, C.M., 311, 313, 313n
Shapiro, C., 134
Sharlip, I.D., 341
Sharma, T., 378

arpe, M., 202
Shaw, B.F., 31
Shaw, E., 418
Shaywitz, S.E., 407, 408, 409
Shea, M.T., 243
Shearin, E., 178
Shedler, J., 233
Sheitman, B.B., 383, 384
Shelton, K.K., 415
Shelton, R.C., 172
Shepherd, C., 415, 418
Shepherd, C.A., 394
Sher, K.J., 259, 274–275, 279
Sherman, D.K., 413
Shields, M., 109
Shiffman, S., 287
Shneidman, E.S., 180–181
Shoham, V., 351
Shott, M.E., 302
Sicotte, N., 303
Siegel, J.M., 309
Siegel, S., 276
Sierra, M., 198
Siever, L.J., 218, 224
Sigman, M., 396
Sigmon, S.T., 200
Silk, K.R., 224, 238
Silverthorn, P., 415
Simeon, D., 196, 198
Simmie, S., 86n, 177n, 358n
Simmons, H.G., 71
Simon, G.E., 175
Simon, T., 43
Simpkins, J.W., 349, 353
Simpson, D.D., 289
Singh, A.N., 84
Singh, N.N., 84
Sipila, P., 380
Sitharthan, G., 277
Sitharthan, T., 277
Skinner, B.F., 25, 26, 27, 28, 39
Skodol, A.E., 65, 214, 224
Slanetz, P.J., 413
Slob, A.K., 345
Sloof, C.J., 362
Slovenko, R., 200, 208
Slutske, W.S., 416
Smailes, E.M., 225
Smeraldi, E., 171
Smith, C., 330
Smith, D., 76
Smith, D.A., 367
Smith, D.B., 7
Smith, G.N., 376, 379
Smith, G.T., 277
Smith, K.M., 310
Smith, M.D., 353
Smith, M.L., 83, 403
Smith, R., 311
Smith, S., 275
Smith, S.B., 222, 405
Smith, S.S., 219, 221
Smith, T., 399
Smith, T.L., 274
Smith, Y.L.S., 324
Smith-Warner, S.A., 264
Smits, D.J.M., 241
Smyth, R., 202
Snell, M.E., 404
Sobel, E., 388
Sobell, L.C., 288
Sobell, M.B., 288
Söchting, I., 114
Söderpalm, B., 259
Söderpalm Gordh, A.H.V., 259
Sohn, C.-H., 147

Solhan, M., 65
Solms, M., 25
Solomon, R., 258
Somers, J.M., 101
Sorensen, J.L., 285
Southwick, L., 262
Southwick, S.M., 163
Spakman, M., 387
Spanos, N.P., 10, 190–191, 196
Spector, I.P., 341n
Speed, J., 207
Spencer, T., 413
Speyer, 44
Spindler, A., 294
Spirito, A., 176, 422
Spitzer, R.L., 65, 153n, 306, 330
Spreen, O., 407
Spring, B., 377
Stauffer, V., 384
Steele, C.M., 262
Steer, R.A., 179
Stefanatos, G.A., 413
Steiger, H., 299, 303
Stein, D.J., 25
Stein, M.B., 110, 114, 114n, 123, 124n, 163, 171
Steinhauser, C., 335
Steinmetz Breckenridge, J., 167
Stejskal, W.J., 50
Stephane, M., 366
Stephens, D., 304
Stephens, R.S., 277
Stephens, T., 7–8, 33
Stern, T.A., 208
Stewart, B.L., 179
Stewart, J., 6, 84
Stewart, S.E., 176
Stewart, S.H., 122, 275, 277
Stick, F., 83
Stickle, T., 351
Stiles, T.C., 243
Stipp, H., 422
Stock, W.E., 338, 351
Stoller, R.J., 324
Stone, J., 202
Stone, M.H., 224n
St-Onge, M., 309
Stonnington, C.M., 206
Stowell, K.R., 204
Strachan, A.M., 382
Strassnig, M., 204
Strenger, V.E., 279
Stricker, G., 51
Striepe, M., 301
Strober, M., 302
Strosahl, K., 178
Strupp, H.H., 74, 83
Stuart, F.M., 344
Stuart, H.L., 16, 66
Stuckless, N., 300
Sullivan, G.M., 125
Sullivan, H.S., 25, 166, 372
Sullivan, J.M., 156
Sulloway, F.J., 15
Sussman, S., 11, 12
Sutandar-Pinnock, K., 301
Suzdak, P.D., 262
Svartberg, M., 243
Swaab, D.F., 326
Swagerty, W.R., 6
Swallow, S.R., 109
Swingen, D.N., 351
Swinson, R., 109, 110, 120, 125, 129, 134–135, 245
Swinson, S., 439
Sysko, R., 302
Szanto, K., 176

Szasz, T.S., 17
Szatmari, P., 398, 407
Szechtman, H., 126
Szegedi, A., 173
Szeszko, P.R., 413
Szyf, M., 36
Szymanski, S., 379

Tadic, V., 16
Taft, C.T., 116
Tait, C.L., 147
Takooshian, H., 189
Talbot, J.D., 69
Tam, K.K., 241
Tamura, R.N., 384
Tanda, G., 272
Tashman, N.A., 160
Tavares, H., 258
Taylor, C.T., 109
Taylor, E., 413
Taylor, L.K., 420
Taylor, S., 101, 103, 107, 116, 117, 119, 120, 122–123, 126, 128, 129, 132, 133, 134–135, 163, 171, 204, 205, 206, 208, 339–340
Teasdale, J.D., 161, 172
Teichner, G., 51
Teri, L., 167
Terman, L., 43
Teunisse, R.J., 365
Thapar, A., 401
Thayer, J.F., 194
Thielen, K., 72
Thigpen, C.H., 190
Thomas, A.M., 343
Thomas, S.N., 168n
Thompson, A., 400
Thompson, J., 173
Thompson, J.K., 299
Thordarson, D.S., 205
Thorpy, M., 314
Thun, M.J., 263, 267
Tiefer, L., 342
Tien, G., 92
Tienari, P., 379
Tipp, J., 219, 221
Tjepkema, M., 259, 260, 269n, 308
Tobin, D.L., 297
Toichi, M., 396
Tolin, D.F., 114
Tollefson, G.D., 384
Tolomiczenko, G.S., 16
Toneatto, A., 288
Toner, B.B., 300
Tood, P., 388
Tough, S.C., 333
Townsley, R.M., 229
Tragesser, S.L., 65
Trajanovic, N.N., 313
Tran, P.V., 384
Trask, P.C., 200
Treasure, J., 303, 304
Treffert, D.A., 405
Tremblay, R.E., 415
Trigger, B.G., 6
Triggs-Raine, B., 403
Trimble, J.E., 65
True, W., 124n
Trull, T.J., 65, 279
Tryon, W., 364
Trzepacz, P.T., 423, 424
Tsoh, J.Y., 304
Tupker, E., 289
Turecki, G., 70, 178
Turk, J., 263

Turkington, D., 387
Turnbull, J., 16
Turner, S.M., 63, 80, 229
Tyhusrt, J.S., 13
Tzanis, E., 129

Ullmann, L.P., 238, 372
Underwood, M.D., 422

Valenti-Hein, D., 406
Valera, E.M., 413
Valeri, S., 175
Valladares, L., 335
Van Ameringen, M., 116
van de Willige, G., 387
Van Goozen, S.H.M., 324
Van Heck, G.L., 148
van Honk, J., 25
van Luijtelaar, E.L., 364
Van Meter, R., 349, 353
Van Nieuwerburgh, F., 129
Van Orden, K.A., 157
van Os, J., 376, 378
Van Son, M.J.M., 148
Van Vactor, J.C., 296
VanDeusen, K.M., 338
Varnado, P.J., 304
Vaughn, C., 382n
Vazza, G., 375
Veldhuizen, S., 150
Verbeek, A.I., 365
Verkerk, G.J.M., 148
Vernon, P.A., 123, 233, 240, 274
Vial, J.H., 423
Vidrine, J.I., 281
Viens, M., 309, 314
Vine, C., 332
Vissers, L.E.L.M., 401
Vitello, B., 421
Vlahov, D., 114
Vocci, F.J., 282
Vogel-Sprott, M., 277
Vogler, G.P., 409, 410n
Volkow, N.D., 267
Vollick, D., 378
Volpicelli, J.R., 283
Vythilingam, M., 163

Waddell, C., 394, 415, 418
Wadden, T.A., 307
Wade, T.D., 245
Wagner, B.M., 422
Wahlbeck, K., 384
Wahlberg, K.-E., 379
Wahlund, L.A., 424
Wakefield, J.C., 60
Wald, J., 133, 206, 208
Waldram, J.B., 7, 65
Walker, J.R., 110, 114, 114n
Wallace, J., 284
Walld, R., 310
Waller, G., 301
Walsh, B.T., 302, 305
Walsh, D., 218
Walshaw, P.D., 162
Wampold, B.E., 83
Wang, Q., 364
Waraich, P., 101
Ward, A., 304
Ward, T., 327, 337
Warlow, C., 202
Warme, G., 17
Warner, M.S., 191
Warren, S.T., 402

Warwick, O.H., 288
Wasel, N., 403
Wasserman, D.A., 287
Wasylenki, D., 13, 16
Waters, A.M., 105
Watson, J.B., 25, 26
Watson, J.C., 77
Watson, M., 375
Watson, N.T., 283
Watts, S.E., 420
Weakland, J., 381
Webber, C., 401
Webster, C., 88
Webster-Stratton, C., 417
Wechsler, D., 43
Wechsler, H., 252
Weems, C.F., 420
Weinberger, D.R., 378
Weinhold, B., 18
Weisman, A.G., 381
Weiss, F., 272
Weiss, M., 413
Weiss, R.D., 256, 257, 267, 268n, 273, 275
Weiss, R.M., 276n
Weissberg, M., 243
Weissman, M.M., 166, 167n, 175, 420
Weisz, J.R., 175, 417, 421
Welch, M.R., 347
Welch, S.L., 301, 301n
Welner, J., 375
Weltzin, T.E., 298
Wender, P.H., 373, 375
Weniger, G., 72
Wente, M., 115
Werdegar, D., 285
Werth, E., 310
Wertheim, E.H., 301
West, L.J., 288
West, S.L., 282
Westen, D., 233
Westenberg, H.G.M., 129
Western, D., 238
Weyer, J., 11
White, D., 344
White, J., 180n
White, K.S., 280
Whitehead, P.C., 13
Whitehouse, W.G., 160
Whitley, M.K., 239, 417
Whitman, T.L., 406
Whittington, C.J., 175
Wickelgren, I., 272
Widiger, T.A., 225, 229, 230, 233, 243
Widom, C.S., 239
Wieman, C., 6
Wiersma, D., 362, 387
Wilkins, V.M., 154
Wilkinson, D.A., 288
Williams, D.A., 305
Williams, J.B., 42
Williams, J.B.W., 65
Williams, J.E., 47
Williams, J.M., 156
Williams, J.V.A., 150
Williams, M.G., 172
Williams, N.A., 259
Williams, P., 154
Williams, R.J., 299
Wilson, D., 92
Wilson, G.T., 304–305, 307
Wilson, P., 188n
Wincze, J.P., 347, 349
Winegard, W.C., 288
Wingate, L.R., 178
Winnicott, D.W., 328
Winslett, A., 337
Winston, A., 243

Wise, M.G., 423
Wisenthal, S., 22
Wolfe, R., 300
Wolfson, C., 426
Wolk, S., 420
Wolpe, J., 129–130
Wonderlich, S.A., 225
Wong, T.P.T., 29
Wood, J.M., 50, 312
Woodside, B., 297, 298
Woodside, D.B., 294, 300, 301, 302

Woody, E.Z., 126
Woody, S.R., 109
Wooten, V., 314
Wootton, J.M., 415
Wright, C.L., 75
Wright, J.H., 82
Wynne, L.C., 379

Y

Yatham, L.N., 70, 172–173

Yeargin-Allsopp, M., 404
Yee, D.K., 300
Yirmiya, N., 396
Young, D.A., 375
Young, J., 80
Young, J.E., 158n
Young, M.A., 176
Young, R., 277
Yuille, J.C., 198
Yung, A.R., 389
Yurgelun-Todd, D., 272

Z

Zack, J.S., 44
Zakzanis, K.K., 376–377
Zanardi, R., 171
Zanarini, M.C., 224, 238
Zborowski, M.J., 70
Zelli, A., 239
Zhong, C.-B., 120
Zhou, J.-N., 326
Zhu, A.J., 305
Zilberman, M., 258

Zimmerman, B.J., 31
Zinbarg, R., 103, 119
Zitman, F.G., 365
Zotter, D.L., 300
Zubin, J., 377
Zucker, K.J., 323–324, 329
Zuckerman, M., 223, 223n
Zvolensky, M.J., 122
Zweig-Frank, H., 225, 238

Note: Entries for tables are followed by "*t*," entries for figures are followed by "*f*," and entries for notes are followed by "*n*."

A

A-beta, 426–427
abandonment, fear of, 222–223
abdominal migraine, 306
abnormal behaviour
  biological perspectives, 18–22
  criteria for determining abnormality, 3–6
  cultural differences, 5–6
  current perspectives on, 18–22
  defining, 3–8
  historical perspectives, 9–17
  interactionist perspectives, 35–36
  personal costs of poor mental health, 8
  prevention, 8
  psychological perspectives, 22–32
  resilience, 8
  risk factors, 7
  social costs of poor mental health, 8
  sociocultural perspectives, 34
abnormal psychology, 2, 87–94
Aboriginal Head Start (AHS), 404
Aboriginal peoples
  Aboriginal healing, 7
  alcoholism, 260–261
  Canadian Aboriginal perspective, 6–7
  depression, 146–147
  mainstream treatment of Aboriginal illnesses, 6–7
  posttraumatic stress disorder, 114
  residential schools, 114
  smoking, prevalence of, 269
  smudging ceremony, 7
absolutist thinking, 278
abstinence-violation effect, 287
acculturation hypothesis, 261
acetylcholine, 22, 427
acquaintance sexual assault, 338
acrophobia, 107
acute stress disorder, 102*t*, 113–117
adaptive sleep habits, 315
addiction, 255–256, 257
adjustment disorders, 112–113, 113*t*
Adler, Alfred, 25
adolescence
  and depression, 420–423
  suicide, 421–423
adoptee studies, 441–442
affect, 360
age
  and alcohol dependence, 259
  suicide in childhood and adolescence, 422
aggravated sexual assault, 336
agoraphobia, 5, 80–81, 102*t*, 103–104
  behavioural treatment, 132–133
  diagnostic criteria, 104*t*
Al-Anon, 284

alcohol, 250, 257–264
  see also alcoholism
  absolutist thinking, 278
  intoxication, 252
  moderate drinking, 263–264
  outcome expectancies, 277
  and physical health, 262–263
  psychological effects, 261–262
  and tension reduction, 275–276
  and young people, 258
Alcohol, Drug Abuse, and Mental Health Administration (ADAMHA), 242
alcohol-induced persisting amnestic disorder, 263
alcoholic hepatitis, 263
Alcoholics Anonymous (AA), 284
alcoholism, 258–259
  see also alcohol
  as behaviour pattern, 261
  conceptions of, 260–261
  controlled social drinking, 288
  cue-exposure training, 277
  as disease, 260
  and ethnicity, 260–261
  genetic factors, 274
  as moral defect, 260
  one-drink hypothesis, 278, 279*f*
  oral-dependent personality, 278
  questionnaire, 259
  risk factors, 258–259
all-or-nothing thinking, 158
Alzheimer's disease, 21, 268, 427–428, 428*f*
ambivalence, 360
ambulatory, 56
amenorrhea, 297
American Association on Intellectual and Developmental Disabilities, 401
amnesia
  dissociative amnesia, 191–192
  localized amnesia, 192
  malingering, 192
amphetamine psychosis, 266
amphetamines, 266
amygdala, 377
amyloid plaques, 426–427
analgesia, 265
analogue measures, 54
angel dust, 270–271
anomie, 178
anorexia athletica, 306
anorexia nervosa, 295–297
  amenorrhea, 297
  biological factors, 302–303
  causes, 299–303
  defined, 294
  diagnostic criteria, 296*f*
  family factors, 302
  medical complications, 297
  psychosocial factors, 300–302
  sociocultural factors, 299–300
  subtypes of, 298
  treatment, 303–305
anti-anxiety drugs, 68–69
antidepressants, 69–70, 128, 169–172, 171*f*, 208, 282

antipsychotic drugs, 69, 173, 375, 383, 385
antisocial personality disorder, 218–222
  see also personality disorders
  and alcoholism, 259
  biological factors, 221–222
  craving-for-stimulation model, 222
  criminality, 220–221
  defined, 218
  diagnostic criteria, 220*t*
  emotional responsiveness, lack of, 221–222
  gender differences, 218
  lifetime prevalence, estimates, 218*t*
  limbic abnormalities, 222
  origins of, 237
  profile of the antisocial personality, 219
  profile of the psychopathic personality, 219
  psychophysiological factors, 221–222
  restraint on impulsivity, lack of, 222
  risk factors, 238–239
  sociocultural factors, 221
  and socioeconomic status, 241–242
anxiety, 100*f*, 104, 239
anxiety disorder
  acute stress disorder, 102*t*, 113–117
  adjustment disorders, 112–113, 113*t*
  agoraphobia, 5, 80–81, 102*t*, 103–104, 104*t*, 132–133
  anxiety sensitivity, 122
  behaviour-based approaches, 129–135
  behavioural perspectives, 118–120
  biological perspectives, 123–126
  biological therapies, 128–129
  causal pathways, 126–127
  in childhood, 420
  cognitive-behaviour therapies, 131–132
  cognitive perspectives, 120–123
  defined, 100
  diagnostic criteria, 102*t*
  generalized anxiety disorder, 102*t*, 104–105, 106*t*, 118, 135
  genetic factors, 123–124
  gradual exposure, 130–131
  humanistic approach, 128
  irrational beliefs, 120–121
  misattributions of panic sensations, 122–123
  multiple factors, 127*f*
  neurotransmitters, 124–125
  obsessive-compulsive disorder, 102*t*, 110–112, 120, 125–126, 129, 134–135
  oversensitivity to threat, 121–122
  panic attack, 100, 101–103, 122, 136
  panic disorder, 100, 101–103, 122–123, 123*f*, 135

  phobic disorders, 107–112, 119
  posttraumatic stress disorder, 102*t*, 113–117, 119, 123–124, 124*t*, 133–134
  prepared conditioning, 119
  psychodynamic perspectives, 118
  psychodynamic therapies, 128
  self-defeating thoughts, 120–121
  social phobia, 102*t*, 108–110, 110*f*, 132
  specific phobias, 102*t*, 107–110, 109*t*
  systematic desensitization, 129–130
  theoretical perspectives, 118–126
  treatment, 128–136
  tying it together, 126–127
  types of, 101–117
anxiety sensitivity, 122
anxiolytics, 68–69, 313
anxious behaviour, 228–232
apnea, 310
APP, 426–427
applied behavioural analysis, 167
arousal disorders, 349–350
assessment
  analogue or contrived measures, 54
  Automatic Thoughts Questionnaire, 55, 55*t*
  behavioural assessment, 52–54
  behavioural rating scales, 54
  brain, workings of, 56–58
  clinical interview, 41–43
  cognitive assessment, 54–56
  intelligence tests, 43–45
  methods of assessment, 41–58
  neuropsychological assessment, 51–52
  personality tests, 47–51
  physiological measurement, 56
  projective personality tests, 50–51
  psychological tests, 43–51
  psychometric approach, 52
  reliable, 63
  self-monitoring, 53–54
  thought records, 54–55
associations, 359
asylums, 11
attachment problems, 337–338
attention-deficit and disruptive behaviour disorders
  attention-deficit/hyperactivity disorder, 410–414
  conduct disorder, 414–415
  oppositional defiant disorder (ODD), 415–418
attention-deficit/hyperactivity disorder, 410–414
  defined, 410
  diagnostic criteria, 411*t*
  theoretical perspectives, 413
  treatment, 413–414
attentional deficiencies, 364
attributional style, 161
attributional theory, 160–162
atypical antipsychotic drugs, 384
auditory hallucinations, 365

autism, 395–399
    autistic thinking, 396
    defined, 395
    diagnostic criteria, 397t
    features, 396
    lateralization, 398
    theoretical perspectives, 396–398
    theory of mind, 398
    treatment, 398–399
autism (schizophrenia), 360
autistic disorder. *See* autism
autistic spectrum disorders,
    395–399
autistic thinking, 396
autoerotic asphyxiation, 332
automatic thoughts, 160, 170t
Automatic Thoughts Questionnaire,
    55, 55t
aversive conditioning, 287,
    334–335
avoidant personality disorder,
    228–229
axon, 20

B

bad trips, 270
Bandura, Albert, 31
barbiturates, 264–265
baseline, 53, 442
Beck, Aaron, 31, 31f, 32t, 79,
    157–160
behaviour modification,
    285–287, 307
    see also behaviour therapy
behaviour therapy, 28, 75–76
    agoraphobia, 132–133
    anxiety disorder, 129–135
    aversive conditioning, 287,
        334–335
    cognitive-behaviour therapies. *See*
        cognitive-behaviour therapies
    gradual exposure, 75, 130–131
    modelling, 75, 179, 277, 443, 444
    mood disorders, 167–168
    obsessive-compulsive disorder,
        134–135
    paraphilias, 334–335
    personality disorders, 243–244
    posttraumatic stress disorder,
        133–134
    rehearsal, 443, 444
    self-control strategies, 286, 286t
    social phobia, 132
    social skills training, 287
    somatoform disorders, 208
    substance-related disorders,
        285–287
    systematic desensitization, 75,
        129–130
Behavioural Activation (BA), 167
behavioural approach system
    (BAS), 241
behavioural approach task
    (BAT), 54
behavioural assessment, 52–54
    analogue or contrived
        measures, 54
    behavioural rating scales, 54
    self-monitoring, 53–54
behavioural diaries, 53
behavioural inhibition system
    (BIS), 241
behavioural interview, 52
behavioural perspectives, 25–29
    see also genetics
    anxiety disorder, 118–120
    behaviourism, 25–26
    classical conditioning, 26–27, 27f
    evaluation of, 28

neo-humanistic perspective,
    28–29
    operant conditioning, 27–28
behavioural rating scales, 54
behavioural treatment approaches.
    See behaviour therapy
behaviourism, 25–26
Belak, Wade, 177
la belle indifférence, 201–202
benzodiazepines, 125, 128, 282, 314
bereavement, 143f, 155
Bernardo, Paul, 219f
beta amyloid, 426
Bianchi, Kenneth, 186, 191, 191f
bigorexia, 306
bilateral ECT, 174
Binet, Alfred, 43
binge-eating disorder (BED),
    305–307
biochemical factors, 163
    dopamine theory, 375
    schizophrenia, 375–376
biofeedback training, 316
biological factors
    anorexia nervosa, 302–303
    antisocial personality disorder,
        221–222
    bulimia nervosa, 302–303
    eating disorders, 302–303
biological perspectives, 18–22
    antidepressants, 208
    anxiety disorder, 123–126
    genetics, 18–20
    mood disorders, 162–163
    nervous system, 20–22
    obsessive-compulsive disorder,
        125–126
    panic disorder, 125
    personality disorders, 239–241
    schizophrenia, 373–377
    sexual dysfunctions, 343–344
    somatoform disorders, 208
    substance-related disorders,
        273–275
    suicide, 179
biological therapies, 68–72
    anti-anxiety drugs, 68–69
    antidepressants, 69–70,
        169–172, 171f
    antipsychotic drugs, 69, 173
    anxiety disorder, 128–129
    electroconvulsive therapy,
        70–71
    electroconvulsive therapy (ECT),
        173–175
    lithium, 70
    male sexual dysfunctions,
        352–353
    mood disorders, 169–175
    personality disorders, 244
    prefrontal lobotomy, 71
    psychopharmacology, 68
    psychosurgery, 71–72
    schizophrenia, 383–385
    sleep disorders, 313–314
    substance-related disorders,
        281–284
biopsychosocial (systems) model,
    35–36
bipolar, 141
bipolar disorder, 14, 150–152
    bipolar I disorder, 150
    bipolar II disorder, 150
    lithium, 172
    manic episodes, 150, 151t
"blaming the victim," 230
Bleuler, Eugen, 359
blind, 438
blind interpretation, 48
blocking, 363

Board of Examiners in Sex Therapy
    and Counselling in Ontario
    (BESTCO), 352
body dysmorphic disorder, 204
body image, 300
bondage, 337
Bono, Chastity, 323f
Boogaard, Derek, 177
borderline personality disorder,
    222–225, 238, 244
    see also personality disorders
the brain
    amygdala, 377
    deep brain stimulation, 72
    dementia, 426–427
    and hallucinations, 366
    hippocampus, 377
    imaging techniques, 57–58t
    neurofibrillary tangles, 427
    neuroscience theory of personal-
        ity, 240–241
    schizophrenia, 376–377, 377f
    study of workings of, 56–58
brain electrical activity mapping
    (BEAM), 58
breathing-related sleep disorder,
    310–311
brief psychodynamic therapies, 74
Briquet's syndrome, 204
Broca's area, 366
bulimia nervosa, 297–298
    biological factors, 302–303
    causes, 299–303
    defined, 294
    diagnostic criteria, 298t
    family factors, 302
    medical complications, 298
    psychosocial factors, 300–302
    sociocultural factors, 299–300
    treatment, 303–305
bupropion, 283

C

Canadian mental health
    services, 245
Cannabis sativa, 271
case studies, 442–444
CASPER, 44
castration anxiety, 333
cataplexy, 309
catastrophize, 30
catastrophizing, 159
catatonic type, 368, 369
categorical model (schizophrenia),
    370–371
causal relationship, 437
cause-and-effect relationship, 437
Charcot, Jean-Martin, 15
child abuse
    child sexual abuse, 332, 337
    Münchausen by proxy syndrome
        (MBPS), 200
Child Behaviour Checklist
    (CBCL), 54
child sexual abuse, 332, 337
children
    anxiety disorders, 420
    attention-deficit/hyperactivity
        disorder, 410–414
    autism, 395–399
    conduct disorder, 414–415
    depression, 420–423
    learning disorders, 407–410
    mental retardation, 400–407
    Münchausen by proxy syndrome
        (MBPS), 200
    oppositional defiant disorder
        (ODD), 415–418

pervasive developmental
    disorders, 395–399
separation anxiety disorder,
    418–419
suicide, 421–423
time out, 417
*The Chinese Classification of Mental
    Disorders (CCMD)*, 63
Chinese Society of Psychiatry
    (CSP), 63
choleric, 9
Chrétien, Jean, 92
chromosomal abnormalities,
    401–402
chromosomes, 440
chronicity, 162
chronological age, 43
Church of Scientology, 60f
Cialis, 352
cigarette smoking, 252, 267–270,
    269f, 276
circadian rhythm sleep
    disorder, 311
cirrhosis of the liver, 263
civil commitment, 87–88
clanging, 363
classical conditioning, 26–27, 27f,
    276–277
classification
    developmental delay, 400t
    DSM system, 59–66; *see also
        Diagnostic and Statistical
        Manual of Mental Disorders
        (DSM)*
    importance of, 41
    New View classification
        system, 342
    personality disorders, and clas-
        sification problems, 232–234
    sexual dysfunctions, 342
    substance-related disorders,
        252–257
    systems of classification, 41
claustrophobia, 107, 130–131
client-centred therapy, 96
clinical interview, 41–43
clinical psychologist, 2
clinical psychologists, 67
cocaine, 255, 266–267, 268t
Cocaine Anonymous, 284
cognitive assessment, 54–56
    Automatic Thoughts Question-
        naire, 55, 55t
    evaluation of methods of, 56
    thought records, 54–55
cognitive-behaviour therapies,
    78–81
    anxiety disorder, 131–132
    cognitive-behavioural therapy
        (CBT), 80–81
    cognitive restructuring, 131–132
    cognitive therapy, 79–80
    generalized anxiety
        disorder, 135
    mood disorders, 168–169
    National Sex Offender
        Program, 336
    panic disorder, 135
    rational-emotive behaviour
        therapy (REBT), 78
    sleep disorders, 314–316
cognitive behaviour therapy, 31
cognitive-behavioural perspectives,
    29–32
    Aaron Beck, 31, 31f, 32t
    Albert Bandura, 31
    Albert Ellis, 30–31, 30f
    Donald Meichenbaum, 32
    evaluation of, 32
    personality disorders, 239

...itive-behavioural therapy (CBT), 32, 80–81, 135–136
childhood and adolescent depression, 421
eating disorders, 304–305
schizophrenia, 387
sleep disorders, 316
with social-skills training, 387
cognitive-behavioural modification (CBM), 32
cognitive distortions, 32, 79, 158–160, 170t
cognitive perspectives
anxiety disorder, 120–123
anxiety sensitivity, 122
irrational beliefs, 120–121
learned helplessness theory, 160–162
misattributions of panic sensations, 122–123
mood disorders, 157–162
outcome expectancies, 277–278
oversensitivity to threat, 121–122
panic disorder, 123f
self-defeating thoughts, 120–121
self-efficacy expectancies, 278
sexual dysfunctions, 345–346
somatoform disorders, 208
substance-related disorders, 277–278
cognitive restructuring, 131–132, 316
cognitive schemas, 158
cognitive therapy, 31, 79–80, 131–132
see also cognitive-behaviour therapies
cognitive triad of depression, 157–160, 158t
College of Registered Psychotherapists, 67
Columbine High School massacre, 115
command hallucinations, 365
commitment, 87–88
communication deviance, 381–382
community programs, 387
competency to stand trial, 93–94
compulsion, 111
compulsive behaviour patterns, 111t
compulsive overeaters, 307
computer-assisted therapy, 82–83
computerized clinical interviews, 44
computerized tomography (CT scan), 57t
concordance, 441
Concordia University shootings, 115
concussions, 35, 177
conditioned response, 26
conditioned stimulus, 26
conditioning model of cravings, 276–277
conduct disorder, 414–415
confidentiality, 436
conjoint family therapy, 82
conscious, 23
contrived measures, 54
control, 433–434
control group design, 439
control subjects, 438
controlled social drinking, 288
conversion disorder, 15, 201–202, 201t, 205, 208
coping responses, 135t
Coping With Depression (CWD) Course, 167
coprophilia, 333
correlation, 436–437
cost-containment constraints, 245
countertransference, 74
crack, 266–267
crashing, 267

craving-for-stimulation model, 222
cravings, conditioning model of, 276–277
Criminal Code of Canada, 92, 93
criminal responsibility, 91–94
criminality, 220–221
critical thinking, 444–446
cross-dressing, 328
cross-fostering study, 374
Cruise, Tom, 60f
crystal meth, 266
cue-exposure training, 277
cultural differences in abnormal behaviour, 5–6
cultural factors, and substance abuse, 279–280
cultural-familial retardation, 404
culture, and sexual performance, 347
culture-bound disorders, 65, 190, 206–207
culture-bound dissociative conditions, 207
cyclic vomiting syndrome, 306
cyclothymia, 152
cyclothymic disorder, 152–153
cytomegalovirus, 403

D

Daily Record of Dysfunctional Thoughts, 54
Dallaire, André, 92
Dallaire, Roméo, 115
dangerous behaviour, 5
dangerousness, predictions of, 88–89
date sexual assault, 338
Dawson College shootings, 115
de Sade, Marquis, 333
death instinct, 178
debriefed, 436
decision making, and substance abuse, 277–278
deep brain stimulation, 72
defence mechanisms, 24–25, 24t, 50
deinstitutionalization, 12–13, 16
delirium, 254, 423–425, 424t, 425t
Delirium Rating Scale (DRS), 424
delirium tremens, 254
delta-9-tetrahydrocannabinol, 271
delusions, 5, 111
dementia, 425t, 426–429
dementia praecox, 14, 268, 359
see also schizophrenia
demonological model, 9
dendrites, 20
denial, 24t
dependence. See substance dependence
dependent personality disorder, 229–231
dependent variables, 438, 438t
depersonalization, 193, 194
depersonalization disorder, 193–194, 195t
depressants, 257–266
alcohol, 257–264
barbiturates, 264–265
defined, 257
opiates, 265–266
sedatives, 264
depression
see also mood disorders
in adolescence, 420–423
attributional theory, 160–162
in childhood, 420–423
cognitive distortions, 158–160
cognitive triad of depression, 157–160, 158t
common features of, 142

and concussions, 177
diathesis-stress model, 164f
double depression, 149
ethnicity, 146–147
features of, 425
gender differences, 145–147
interactional theory, 156–157
learned helplessness theory, 160–162
lithium, 172–173
major depressive disorder, 142–149, 143t
postpartum depression, 148
psychodynamic theory, 154–155
reinforcement, 156
screening tests, 149
seasonal affective disorder, 147–148, 147n
self-medication, and drugs, 275–276
stress, 154, 164
and suicide in childhood and adolescence, 422
treatment-resistant depression (TRD), 70–71
derealization, 193
description, 433–434
detoxification, 281–282
developmental delay, 400t
see also mental retardation
developmental theory of persistent sexual offending against children, 331, 331f
deviation IQ, 43–44
Dhat syndrome, 206–207
diabetes, 343
diagnosis
see also specific disorders
example diagnosis, 62t
use of term, 63–65
Diagnostic and Statistical Manual of Mental Disorders (DSM), 41, 59–66
see also specific disorders
advantages and disadvantages, 63–68
axes, 61
evaluation of DSM system, 63
example diagnosis, 62t
features of the DSM, 60–61
fifth edition, 64–65, 215, 326
fourth edition, Text Revision, 59
multiaxial classification system, 61
Dialectical Behaviour Therapy (DBT), 244
diathesis, 35, 164
diathesis-stress model, 35, 35f, 164f, 197, 377–380, 378f
dimensional model, 65
direct observation, 52–53
disorder of written expression, 407
disordered eating attitudes and behaviours, 295
disorganized dimension, 371
disorganized type, 368
disorientation, 254
displacement, 24t, 73
disqualifying the positive, 159
dissociation, 116
dissociative amnesia, 191–192
dissociative disorders, 187–199
depersonalization disorder, 193–194, 195t
dissociative amnesia, 191–192
Dissociative Experience Scale (DES), 196
dissociative fugue, 192–193
dissociative identity disorder, 187–191, 190t
theoretical perspectives, 194–196

treatment, 197–199
tying it together, 196–197
Dissociative Experience Scale (DES), 196
dissociative fugue, 192–193
dissociative identity disorder, 186, 187–191, 190t
distribution of IQ scores, 46f
disturbances in content of thought, 363
disturbances in form of thought, 363–364
disturbances of thought and speech, 362–364
disturbances of volition, 368
disulfiram, 282
diversity
Canadian Aboriginal perspective, 6–7
multicultural issues in psychotherapy, 84
Dix, Dorothea, 12
dizygotic (DZ) twins, 274, 441
DNA, 18
Doctor of Medicine (MD), 67
dopamine, 22, 273, 302
dopamine theory, 375
double-bind communications, 381
double depression, 149
Down syndrome, 401–402
downward drift hypothesis, 34
dramatic behaviour (personality disorders), 218–228
dream anxiety disorder, 311
drug-induced hallucinations, 366
drugs
anti-anxiety drugs, 68–69
antidepressants, 69, 169–172, 171f, 208, 282
antipsychotic drugs, 173, 375, 383, 385
anxiolytics, 313
attention-deficit/hyperactivity disorder, 413–414
atypical antipsychotic drugs, 384
disulfiram, 282
drugs of abuse. See drugs of abuse
historical perspective, 12–13
lithium, 70, 172–173
major tranquillizers, 375
methadone, 283
naloxone, 283
naltrexone, 283
tardive dyskinesia, 384
drugs of abuse
see also substance-related disorders
alcohol, 257–264, see also alcohol
amphetamines, 266
barbiturates, 264–265
cocaine, 255, 266–267, 268t
depressants, 257–266
drug use, selected Canadian age groups, 251t
hallucinogens, 270–272
inhalants, 272
LSD (lysergic acid diethylamide), 270
marijuana, 271–272
nicotine, 267–270
opiates, 265–266
phencyclidine (PCP), 270–271
polydrug use, 250
psychoactive, 252
stimulants, 266–270
Durkheim, Emile, 178
duty to warn, 90
dysgraphia, 407
dyslexia, 407, 408, 410f

dyspareunia, 343, 351
dyssomnias, 308–311
    breathing-related sleep disorder, 310–311
    circadian rhythm sleep disorder, 311
    defined, 308
    hypersomnia, 309
    insomnia, 308–309
    narcolepsy, 309–310, 314
dysthymia, 149
dysthymic disorder, 149–150

E

Early Autism Study, 398
early-intervention programs, 389
early psychosis intervention programs, 387–388
eating disorders, 294–307
    anorexia nervosa, 294, 295–297
    binge-eating disorder (BED), 305–307
    biological factors, 302–303
    bulimia nervosa, 294, 297–298
    causes, 299–303
    defined, 294
    family factors, 302
    genetics, 303
    psychosocial factors, 300–302
    related conditions, 306
    sociocultural factors, 299–300
    treatment, 303–305
eccentric behaviour (personality disorders), 214–218
eclectic orientation, 67
eclectic therapy, 81
École Polytechnique, 115
ego, 23, 24
ego dystonic, 214
ego ideal, 23, 24
ego syntonic, 214
the elderly. *See* older adults
electroconvulsive therapy (ECT), 70–71, 72, 173–175
electrodermal response, 56
electroencephalograph (EEG), 56, 57t
electromyograph, 56
Ellis, Albert, 30–31, 30f, 78
emotion-focused therapy (EFT), 29, 77
emotional behaviour (personality disorders), 218–228
emotional disturbances, 367
emotional intelligence, 29
emotional reasoning, 163
emotional responsiveness, 221–222
endogenous morphine, 265
endorphins, 265, 273–274
epidemiological method, 439–440
epigenetics, 18–19
epigenome, 18, 19f
erectile disorder, 342, 352–353
erectile dysfunction model, 345, 346f
Erikson, Erik, 372
erratic behaviour (personality disorders), 218–228
ethanol, 257
ethics in research, 435–436
ethnicity
    alcoholism, 259, 260–261
    depression, 146–147
    suicide in childhood and adolescence, 422
ethyl alcohol, 257
etiology, 101
exhibitionism, 327–328
Exner system, 50
exorcism, 10, 186

expectancies, 31, 32
experimental method, 437–439
experimental subjects, 438
experimentation, 256
explanations, 433–434
exposure. *See* gradual exposure
expressed emotion, 382
external attribution, 161
eye movement desensitization and reprocessing (EMDR), 134

F

Facebook, 300
FaceSay computer program, 399
factitious disorder, 200
family factors
    see also family perspectives
    alcoholism, and family history, 259
    anorexia nervosa, 302
    bulimia nervosa, 302
    cultural-familial retardation, 404
    eating disorders, 302
    and gender identity disorder, 325–326
    schizophrenia, 382
    suicide in childhood and adolescence, 422
family-intervention programs, 387–388
family perspectives
    see also family factors
    communication deviance, 381–382
    double-bind communications, 381
    expressed emotion, 382
    and personality disorders, 238–239
    schizophrenia, 380–382
    schizophrenogenic mother, 381
family therapy, 82
faulty perception of reality, 4–5
fear, 99–100, 107
fear network, 125
Fear of Fat Scale, 304
fear-stimulus hierarchy, 129–130
fearful behaviour, 228–232
feedback, 443, 444
feeding disorder of infancy or early childhood, 306
female orgasmic disorder, 343
female sexual arousal disorder, 342
"Female Sexual Dysfunction (FSD)," 342
fetal alcohol syndrome (FAS), 263
fetishism, 328–329
fight-flight-freeze system (FFS), 241
first-rank symptoms, 360
flashbacks, 198, 270
flat affect, 367
forced-choice formats, 47
fortune teller error, 159
four As, 359–360
fragile X syndrome, 402–403
François, Lorne, 198
fraternal twins. *See* dizygotic (DZ) twins
free association, 73
free floating, 104
freebasing, 267
Freeman, Walter, 71
Freud, Sigmund, 15, 22–25, 22f, 72–74, 101, 104, 118, 154–155, 178, 235, 372
    see also psychoanalysis; psychodynamic perspectives
frotteurism, 330
Fuller, Thomas, 405
functional magnetic resonance imaging (fMRI), 57t

G

galvanic skin response (GSR), 56, 221–222
gamma-aminobutyric acid (GABA), 124–125, 262
Garland, Judy, 265
gay people, 324, 324n
gender affirmation, 322
gender differences
    adolescent depression, 421
    alcoholism, 258–259
    antisocial personality disorder, 218
    "blaming the victim," 230
    borderline personality disorder, 224
    coping styles, 163
    dependent personality disorder, 230
    depression, 145–147
    dysthymic disorder, 149
    gender identity disorder, 323–324
    histrionic personality disorder, 225
    narcissistic personality disorder, 227
    obsessive-compulsive personality disorder, 231
    paraphilias, 326
    pedophilia, 331
    savant syndrome, 405
    sexist biases, 234
    suicide in childhood and adolescence, 422
    suicide risk, 176
gender dysphoria, 322
gender identity, 322
gender identity disorder, 322–326
    defined, 322
    diagnostic criteria, 323t
    gender dysphoria, 322
    theoretical perspectives, 324–326
    vs. transvestic fetishism, 329
gender reassignment, 322, 324
gene–environment interactions, 379
gene expression, 18
gene silencing, 18
general paresis, 15
generalized anxiety disorder, 102t, 104–105, 106t, 118, 135
genes, 440
genetics, 18–20
    anxiety disorder, 123–124
    cross-fostering study, 374
    defined, 440
    dyslexia, 409
    eating disorders, 303
    epigenetics, 18–19
    human genome, 18
    mood disorders, 162–163
    personality disorders, 240
    schizophrenia, 373–375, 374f
    stem cells, 19–20
    substance-related disorders, 274–275
genome. *See* human genome
genotype, 440–441
Global Assessment of Functioning (GAF) Scale, 62t
global attribution, 161
global factors, 161
gourmand syndrome, 306
gradual exposure, 75, 130–131, 135t
Greenberg, Leslie, 28, 29f
Griesinger, Wilhelm, 14
group therapy, 81–82
gustatory hallucinations, 365

H

hallucinations, 3, 364–367
hallucinogens, 270–272
    defined, 270
    LSD (lysergic acid diethylamide), 270
    marijuana, 271–272
    phencyclidine (PCP), 270–271
Hamid, Sarah, 144
harmful dysfunction, 60
hashish, 271
health. *See* physical health
Health Canada, 33, 175, 262
Hebb, Donald, 29–30
hebephrenic type, 368
heredity. *See* genetics
Hillside strangler, 186, 191, 191f
hippocampus, 377
Hippocrates, 9
historical perspectives, 9–17
    asylums, 11
    demonological model, 9
    drugs and deinstitutionalization, 12–13
    medical model, origins of, 9
    medieval times, 10
    moral therapy, 11–12
    pathways to the present, 13–17
    reform movement, 11–12
    witchcraft, 10–11
histrionic personality disorder, 225–226
Hitler, Adolf, 222f, 223
Hoarding Disorder, 64–65
homelessness, 16
homosexual, as label, 324n
hopelessness, 179–180, 422
Horney, Karen, 25, 166
hospitalization, 284–285, 304
human genome, 18, 19f
Human Sexual Response Cycle model, 342
humanistic approach, 28–29, 128
humanistic-existential therapies, 76–77
humours, 9
Huntington's disease, 427
hyperactivity, 410
Hypericum perforatum, 173
hypersomnia, 309
hyperventilation, 125
hypnagogic hallucinations, 309
hypnosis, 15
hypoactive sexual desire disorder, 341
hypochondriasis, 202–204, 202t
hypocretin, 310
hypomanic episodes, 142
hypothesis, 435
hypoxyphilia, 332
hysteria, 15, 201, 205
    see also conversion disorder
hysterical neurosis, 201

I

ice, 266
id, 23
ideas of persecution, 5
ideas of reference, 217
identical twins. *See* monozygotic (MZ) twins
identification, 23, 24
ill humour, 9
impulsivity, 222
in vivo exposure, 75
incidence, 439
independent variables, 438, 438t
individual education plan, 409

...ence, 434
informed consent, 435–436
inhalants, 272
Inis Beag, 321
insanity defence, 91–93
insomnia, 308–309
intelligence, 43
intelligence quotient (IQ), 43, 45
intelligence tests, 43–45
interactional theory, 156–157
interactionist perspectives, 35–36
internal attribution, 161
internal factors, 161
internalizing, 124
International Classification of Diseases (ICD), 41
International Journal of Existential Psychology and Psychotherapy, 29
International Network on Personal Meaning, 29
International Personality Disorder Examination (IPDE), 242
International Society for Existential Psychology and Psychotherapy (ISEPP), 29
interpersonal psychotherapy (IPT), 166, 172
intervention
  early-intervention programs, 389
  early psychosis intervention programs, 387–388
  family-intervention programs, 387–388
  learning disorders, 409
  mental retardation, 404–406
interview formats, 42–43
intoxication, 252
irrational beliefs, 120–121

J

Jack Project, 14
Jack Windeler Memorial Fund, 14
Jacobson progressive relaxation approach, 316
James, William, 242
Johnson, Virginia, 348
  see also sex therapy
jumping to conclusions, 159
Jung, Carl, 25

K

Kajander, Ruth, 12
Kennedy, Joseph, 71
Kennedy, Rosemary, 71
Kernberg, Otto, 236
Kids Help Phone, 14
Kierkegaard, Søren, 223
Killinger-Johnson, Suzanne, 148
kinship studies, 440–442
Klinefelter's syndrome, 402
klismaphilia, 333
knobs, 21
Kohut, Heinz, 235–236
Koro syndrome, 206
Korsakoff's syndrome, 263
Kraepelin, Emil, 14, 359
Kruze, Martin, 332

L

labelling, 159
lateralization, 398
Lau, Evelyn, 297
the law
  competency to stand trial, 93–94
  criminal responsibility, 91–94
  insanity defence, 91–93
  legal commitment, 87–88

M'Naughten rule, 92
NCRMD, 92
NGRI, 92–93
sexual assault, 336–340
Lawrence, T.E., 223
learned helplessness, 160–162
learned helplessness effect, 161
learning-based approaches
  schizophrenia, 385–387
  social skills training, 386–387
  token-economy systems, 385–386
Learning Disabilities Association of Canada (LDAC), 408
learning disability, 407, 408
  see also learning disorders
learning disorders, 407–410
  defined, 407
  disorder of written expression, 407
  dyslexia, 407, 408, 410*f*
  intervention, 409
  mathematics disorder, 407
  reading disorder, 407, 408, 410*f*
  theoretical perspectives, 409
  types of, 407–409
learning perspectives
  alcohol, and tension reduction, 275–276
  classical conditioning, 276–277
  gender identity disorder, 324–325
  interactional theory, 156–157
  mood disorders, 156–157
  observational learning, 277
  operant conditioning, 275
  paraphilias, 334
  personality disorders, 236–238
  reinforcement, 156
  schizophrenia, 372–373
  sexual dysfunctions, 345
  somatoform disorders, 207
  substance-related disorders, 275–277
  suicide, 178
  withdrawal, and negative reinforcement, 276
legal commitment, 87–88
legal safeguards, 88
Lehmann, Heinz, 12
lesbian people, 324, 324*n*
Levitra, 352
limbic abnormalities, 222
lithium, 70, 172–173
"Little Albert" study, 26–27
"Little Hans" case, 118
localized amnesia, 192
longitudinal study, 437
looseness of association, 359
loss of ego boundaries, 368
LSD (lysergic acid diethylamide), 270, 366
lung cancer, 268
Luria, A.R., 51
Luria-Nebraska Test Battery, 51

M

madhouses, 11
Madoff, Bernie, 89*f*
magical thinking, 217
magnetic resonance imaging (MRI), 57*t*, 163
magnetoencephalography (MEG), 58*t*
magnification, 159
Mahler, Margaret, 236
mainlining, 265
mainstreaming, 404–406
major depressive disorder, 142–149, 143*t*
  see also depression; mood disorders

double depression, 149
environmental factors, 163
genetic factors, 163
risk factors, 145–147
major tranquillizers, 375, 383
maladaptive behaviour, 5
male erectile disorder, 342, 352–353
male orgasmic disorder, 343
malingering, 192, 200
Mangaia, 321
manic, 142
manic-depressive psychosis, 14
manic episodes, 150–152, 151*t*
marijuana, 271–272
marital therapy, 82
mashing, 330
Masters, William, 348
  see also sex therapy
mathematics disorder, 407
medical model, 2, 9, 14–15
  see also biological perspectives
medieval times, 10
Meichenbaum, Donald, 32, 80, 80*f*
melancholia, 9
mental age, 43
mental disorders. *See* psychological disorders
mental filter, 158
Mental Health Commission of Canada, 14
mental health professionals, 67–68
mental health promotion, 33
mental retardation, 400–407
  causes, 401–404
  chromosomal abnormalities, 401–402
  classification of developmental delay, 400*t*
  cultural-familial retardation, 404
  cytomegalovirus, 403
  Down syndrome, 401–402
  fragile X syndrome, 402–403
  intervention, 404–406
  Klinefelter's syndrome, 402
  mainstreaming, 404–406
  mild mental retardation (MMR), 400–401
  and other psychological disorders, 406
  phenylketonuria (PKU), 403
  prenatal factors, 403–404
  prevalence, 400–401
  savant syndrome, 405
  severe mental retardation (SMR), 400
  Tay-Sachs disease, 403
  Turner's syndrome, 402
mental status examination, 43
meta-analysis, 83
methadone, 283
methadone maintenance programs, 283
methods of assessment, 41–58
mild mental retardation (MMR), 400–401
mind, structure of, 22, 23*f*
mindfulness-based cognitive therapy (MBCT), 172
Mini Mental State Examination, 424, 425*t*
minimization, 159
Minnesota Multiphasic Personality Inventory (MMPI), 47, 48–49, 49*t*
misattributions of panic sensations, 122–123
mislabelling, 159
M'Naughten rule, 92
modelling, 75, 179, 277, 443, 444

models, 6
  dimensional model, 65
  medical model, 2, 9, 14–15
  psychodynamic model, 15, 22–25
  psychological models, 15
  sociocultural models, 15–17
moderate drinking, 263–264
monoamine oxidase (MAO) inhibitors, 69, 171
monozygotic (MZ) twins, 274, 441
Monroe, Marilyn, 223, 265
mood disorders
  antidepressants, 169–172, 171*f*
  attributional theory, 160–162
  behaviour therapy, 167–168
  biochemical factors, 163
  biological perspectives, 162–163
  biological therapies, 169–175
  bipolar disorder, 150–152
  cognitive perspectives, 157–162
  cognitive therapy, 168–169
  cyclothymic disorder, 152–153
  defined, 141
  dysthymic disorder, 149–150
  electroconvulsive therapy (ECT), 173–175
  genetics, 162–163
  interactional theory, 156–157
  learned helplessness theory, 160–162
  learning perspectives, 156–157
  lithium, 172–173
  major depressive disorder, 142–149, 143*t*
  postpartum depression, 148
  psychodynamic model, 154–156, 165–167
  reinforcement, 156
  seasonal affective disorder, 147–148, 147*n*
  stress, 154
  suicide. *See* suicide
  theoretical perspectives, 153–163
  treatment, 163–175
  tying it together, 163–164
  types of, 141–153, 141*t*
mood thermometer, 142*f*
moods, 141
moral principle, 23, 24
moral therapy, 11–12
mourning, 155
Mowrer, O. Hobart, 118
multicultural issues in psychotherapy, 84
multiple personality disorder, 186
  see also dissociative identity disorder
Münchausen by proxy syndrome (MBPS), 200
Münchausen syndrome, 200
Murray, Henry, 50
muscle dysmorphia, 306
must statements, 159

N

naloxone, 283
naltrexone, 283
narcissistic personality disorder, 226–228, 235
narcolepsy, 309–310, 314
narcotics, 265
Narcotics Anonymous, 284
Narkissos, 227*f*
National Depression Screening Day, 149
National Sex Offender Program, 336
naturalistic-observation method, 436
NCRMD, 92
necrophilia, 333

negative correlation, 436
negative dimension, 370–371
negative emotionality, 124
negative reinforcement, 276
negative reinforcers, 27
negative symptoms, 370
neo-Freudians, 25
neo-humanistic perspective, 28–29
neologisms, 363
nervous system, 20–22
neurofibrillary tangles, 427
neuroleptics, 69, 375, 383
neurons, 20, 20f
neuropeptide, 310
neuropsychological assessment, 51–52
neuropsychological factors, and personality disorders, 240–241
neuropsychological test performance, 428f
neuroscience theory of personality, 240–241
neurosis, 101, 186
neuroticism, 124
neurotransmitters, 21, 124–125, 171, 273–274
neutral language, use of, 15n
New View classification system, 342
NGRI, 92–93
nicotine, 267–270
 see also smoking
nicotine replacement therapy, 282–283
night-eating syndrome, 306
nightmare disorder, 311–312
nocturnal sleep-related eating disorder, 306
nonprofessional support groups, 284
nonspecific treatment factors, 83
noradrenergic and specific serotonergic antidepressant (NaSSA), 69
norepinephrine, 21
normal obsessions, 120, 121t
normal perfectionism, 232
normal self-interest, 227t

O

objective tests, 47, 155
obscene phone calls, 333
observational learning, 277
obsession, 110, 118
obsessive-compulsive disorder, 102t, 110–112, 120, 129
 behavioural treatment, 134–135
 biological aspects, 125–126
obsessive-compulsive personality disorder, 231–232, 245
obsessive thought patterns, 111t
odd behaviour (personality disorders), 214–218
Oedipus complex, 235
older adults
 Alzheimer's disease, 21, 268, 427–428, 428f
 delirium, 423–425, 424t
 dementia, 426–429
olfactory hallucinations, 365
one-drink hypothesis, 278, 279f
One Flew Over the Cuckoo's Nest, 89, 91f
online information, 446
operant behaviours, 27
operant conditioning, 27–28, 275
opiates, 265–266
oppositional defiant disorder (ODD), 415–418
 theoretical perspectives, 416
 treatment, 416–418
optimum level of arousal, 222

oral behaviour problems, 231
oral-dependent personality, 278
The Organization of Behaviour (Hebb), 29
orgasm disorders, 343, 350–351
orthexia nervosa, 306
osteoporosis, 297
outcome expectancies, 277–278
overgeneralization, 158
oversensitivity to threat, 121–122

P

pain disorder, 204–205
panic attack, 100, 101–103, 122, 135
panic disorder, 100, 102t
 biological aspects, 125
 cognitive-behavioural treatment, 135, 135t
 cognitive models, 122–123, 123f
paranoid, 4
paranoid personality disorder, 215–216
paranoid type, 369
paraphilias, 326–336
 exhibitionism, 327–328
 fetishism, 328–329
 frotteurism, 330
 hypoxyphilia, 332
 other paraphilias, 333
 pedophilia, 330–332
 sexual masochism, 332–333
 sexual sadism, 333
 theoretical perspectives, 333–334
 transvestic fetishism, 328–329
 treatment, 334–336
 types of, 327–333
 voyeurism, 330
paraphilic disorder, 326
parasomnias, 311–313
 defined, 308
 nightmare disorder, 311–312
 sleep terror disorder, 312
 sleepwalking disorder, 312–313
Parkinson's disease, 427
partialism, 333
pathological gambling, 60t
pathways to drug dependence, 256–257
patients' rights, 89–91
Pavlov, Ivan, 25, 26, 240–241
PCP, 270–271
pedophilia, 330–332
peer pressure, 280
penis envy, 344
PEPP: Prevention and Early Intervention Program for Psychoses, 388
perception, 4–5
perceptual disturbances, 364–367
performance anxiety, 347
perseveration, 363
person-centred therapy, 76–77
personal costs of poor mental health, 8
personal distress, 5
personality
 neuroscience theory of, 240–241
 oral-dependent personality, 278
 structure of, 23–24
 traits, 236–237
Personality Assessment Inventory (PAI), 47
personality disorders
 anxious or fearful behaviour, 228–232
 avoidant personality disorder, 228–229
 Axis 1 vs. Axis II disorders, 232–233
 behaviour therapy, 243–244

biological perspectives, 239–241
biological therapies, 244
borderline personality disorder, 222–225, 238, 244
Canadian treatment services, 245
classification problems, 232–234
clusters, 214
cognitive-behavioural perspectives, 239
defined, 214
definition change, and DSM-5, 215
dependent personality disorder, 229–231
dramatic, emotional, or erratic behaviour, 218–228
family perspectives, 238–239
genetics, 240
histrionic personality disorder, 225–226
learning perspectives, 236–238
narcissistic personality disorder, 226–228
neuropsychological factors, 240–241
obsessive-compulsive personality disorder, 231–232, 245
odd or eccentric behaviour, 214–218
overlap among disorders, 233
paranoid personality disorder, 215–216
psychodynamic perspectives, 235–236
psychodynamic therapies, 243
schizoid personality disorder, 216–217
schizotypal personality disorder, 217–218
sexist biases, 234
sociocultural views, 241–242
theoretical perspectives, 235–242
treatment, 242–245
types of, 214–234
variations in normal behaviour vs. abnormal behaviour, 233
personality tests, 47–51
personalization, 159
pervasive developmental disorders, 395–399
phencyclidine (PCP), 270–271
phenothiazines, 12, 375
phenotype, 440
phenylketonuria (PKU), 403
phlegmatic, 9
phobic disorders, 107–112, 107t, 119
phototherapy, 148
physical health
 and alcohol use, 262–263
 and moderate drinking, 263–264
physiological dependence, 255–256
physiological measurement, 56
pica, 306
Pinel, Philippe, 11–12, 12f
placebo, 438–439
pleasure principle, 23
polydrug use, 250
polygenic, 440
polysomnographic (PSG) recording, 308
population, 440
pornography, and sexual aggression, 338
positive correlation, 436
positive reinforcement, 156
positive reinforcers, 27
positive symptoms, 370

positron emission tomography (PET scan), 57t, 134–135, 163
possession, 9
postpartum depression, 148
posttraumatic stress disorder, 102t, 113–117, 119
 behavioural treatment, 133–134
 genetic factors, 123–124, 124t
 sexual assault, 339
Prader-Willi syndrome, 306
preconscious, 23
prediction, 433–434
predictive validity, 63
prefrontal lobotomy, 71
pregnancy
 and alcohol consumption, 263
 cytomegalovirus, 403
 and mental retardation, 403–404
premature ejaculation, 343, 351
premorbid functioning, 370
prenatal factors, and mental retardation, 403–404
prenatal rubella, 376
prepared conditioning, 119
pressured speech, 151
presynaptic, 21
prevalence, 439
prevention
 abnormal behaviour, 8
 relapse-prevention training, 287–289
 sexual assault, 339
 suicide, 181
primary gains, 206
primary insomnia, 308–309
primary narcissism, 372
primary process thinking, 23, 24
primary reinforcers, 28
proband, 441
problem-solving therapy, 239
prodromal phase, 362
projection, 24t, 118
projective personality tests, 50–51
promotion of mental health, 33
proteins, 18
psychedelics, 270
 see also hallucinations
psychiatric commitment, 87–88
psychiatrist, 2
psychiatrists, 67–68
psychic, 23
psychoactive, 252
psychoactive drugs. See drugs of abuse; substance-related disorders
psychoanalysis, 72, 166, 385
 see also psychoanalytic theory
psychoanalysts, 72
psychoanalytic theory, 22–25
 defence mechanisms, 24–25, 24t
 mind, structure of, 22–23
 personality, structure of, 23–24
psychodynamic model, 15, 22–25
psychodynamic perspectives
 anxiety disorder, 118
 depression, 154–155
 evaluation of psychodynamic perspectives, 25
 gender identity disorder, 324
 mood disorders, 154–156, 163–167
 neo-Freudians, 25
 paraphilias, 333–334
 personality disorders, 235–236
 psychoanalytic theory, 22–25
 schizophrenia, 371–372
 sexual dysfunctions, 344–345
 somatoform disorders, 206–207
 substance-related disorders, 278–279

...odynamic theorists, 25
psychodynamic therapies, 72–75
anxiety disorder, 128
brief psychodynamic therapies, 74
displacement, 73
free association, 73
modern psychodynamic approaches, 74–75
paraphilias, 334
personality disorders, 243
psychoanalysis. *See* psychoanalysis
substance-related disorders, 285
transference, 73–74
psychogenic amnesia, 192
psychogenic fugue, 192
psychological approaches. *See* cognitive-behaviour therapies
psychological dependence, 255–256
psychological disorders
see also specific disorders
and criminal responsibility, 91–94
defined, 2
psychological models, 15
psychological perspectives, 22–32
behavioural perspectives, 25–29
cognitive-behavioural perspectives, 29–32
sexual dysfunctions, 347–348
psychological tests, 43–51
psychometric approach, 52
psychopath, 219
psychopathy, 219
see also antisocial personality disorder
Psychopathy Checklist, 88
Psychopathy Checklist-Revised (PCL-R), 219
psychopharmacology, 68
see also drugs
psychophysiological factors, and antisocial personality disorder, 221–222
psychosis, 25
Psychosis Sucks, 388
psychosocial factors
anorexia nervosa, 300–302
bulimia nervosa, 300–302
psychosocial factors, and eating disorders, 300–302
psychosocial rehabilitation, 387
psychosurgery, 71–72
psychotherapy
see also psychodynamic model; treatment; specific therapies
defined, 67
effectiveness of, 83–86
interpersonal psychotherapy (IPT), 166
multicultural issues, 84
psychotic dimension, 370
Public Health Agency of Canada, 33
punishments, 28, 238
Pussin, Jean-Baptiste, 11

R

R. v. François, 198
R. v. Swain, 93
random sampling, 440
rape, 336
see also sexual assault
rapid flight of ideas, 151
Raspe, Rudolf Erich, 200
rational-emotive behaviour therapy (REBT), 31, 78
rationalization, 24t
Rayner, Rosalie, 26
reaction formation, 24t
reading disorder, 407, 408, 410f
reality principle, 23, 24

rebound anxiety, 69
rebound insomnia, 314
receptor site, 21
reciprocal determinism, 31, 32
recovered memories, 198–199
reform movement, 11–12
reformulated helplessness theory, 161
refusal of treatment, 91
Registered Mental Health Therapists, 67
regression, 24t
rehearsal, 443, 444
reinforcement, 27, 156, 238
reinforcement sensitivity theory (RST), 241
relapse, 287
relapse-prevention training, 287–289
relationship problems, 346
relaxation techniques, 316
reliable, 63, 232
religious experiences, and hallucinations, 365–366
religious factors, and substance abuse, 279–280
REM sleep, 309
remission, 15n
repetitive transcranial magnetic stimulation (rTMS), 71, 174
repression, 24, 24t, 25
research ethics boards (REBs), 435
research methods
adoptee studies, 441–442
case studies, 442–444
causal relationship, 437
correlation, 436–437
critical thinking, 444–446
description, 433–434
epidemiological method, 439–440
ethics in research, 435–436
experimental method, 437–439
hypothesis, 435
inference, 434
kinship studies, 440–442
longitudinal study, 437
naturalistic-observation method, 436
population, 440
random sampling, 440
reversal design, 442, 442f
sample, 440
scientific method, 434–435
significant, 435
single-case experimental designs, 442–444
survey method, 439
theories, 434
twin studies, 441
residential treatment approaches, 284–285
residual phase, 362
resilience, 8
reversal design, 442, 442f
reverse anorexia nervosa, 306
right to refuse treatment, 91
right to treatment, 89–90
risk factors
abnormal behaviour, 7
alcoholism, 258–259
antisocial personality disorder, 238–239
major depressive disorder, 145–147
Ritalin, 413, 414
Rogers, Carl, 76
Rorschach, Hermann, 50
Rorschach Comprehensive System (RCS), 50
Rorschach inkblot test, 50, 50f

routine use, 256
rumination, 146
rumination disorder, 306
Rypien, Rick, 177

S

Sacher-Masoch, Leopold von, 332
sadistic rapists, 333, 337
sadomasochism, 333
sample, 440
sanguine, 9
savant syndrome, 405
scatologia, 333
schizoid personality disorder, 216–217
schizophrenia
affect, 360
ambivalence, 360
associations, 359
attentional deficiencies, 364
autism, 360
biochemical factors, 375–376
biological perspectives, 373–377
biological therapies, 383–385
brain abnormalities, 376–377, 377f
catatonic type, 368, 369
categorical model, 370–371
clinical features, 359–371
cognitive-behavioural therapy (CBT), 387
communication deviance, 381–382
costs of, 360–361
defined, 359
diagnostic criteria, 361t
diathesis-stress model, 377–380, 378f
disorganized type, 368, 369
disturbances in content of thought, 363
disturbances in form of thought, 363–364
disturbances of thought and speech, 362–364
double-bind communications, 381
early-intervention programs, 389
early psychosis intervention programs, 387–388
emotional disturbances, 367
expressed emotion, 382
family factors, 382
family-intervention programs, 387–388
family theories, 380–382
first-rank symptoms, 360
flat affect, 367
four As, 359–360
genetics, 373–375, 374f
hebephrenic type, 368
high-risk children, 379–380
historical contributions to concepts of schizophrenia, 359–360
learning-based approaches, 385–387
learning perspectives, 372–373
major features, 362–368
vs. multiple personality, 191
negative symptoms, 370
other types of impairment, 367–368
paranoid type, 369
perceptual disturbances, 364–367
phases, 361–362
positive symptoms, 370
premorbid functioning, 370
prevalence, 360–361
prodromal phase, 362
psychoanalytic approaches, 385

psychodynamic perspectives, 371–372
psychosocial rehabilitation, 387
residual phase, 362
schizophrenogenic mother, 381
second-rank symptoms, 360
social skills training, 386–387
social stigma, 358, 362
stupor, 368
subtypes, 368–370
theoretical perspectives, 371–383
token-economy systems, 385–386
treatment, 383–389
Type I, 370
Type II, 370
undifferentiated type, 369
viral infections, 376
waxy flexibility, 369
schizophrenogenic mother, 381
schizotypal personality disorder, 217–218
Schneider, Kurt, 360
school shootings, 115
science, 13–17, 433–434
scientific method, 434–435
seasonal affective disorder (SAD), 147–148, 147n
second-rank symptoms, 360
secondary gains, 206
secondary process thinking, 23, 24
secondary reinforcers, 28
sedatives, 264
selective abstraction, 158, 169
selective serotonin-reuptake inhibitors (SSRIs), 69, 170–171, 175, 335
self, 23, 24
self-control strategies, 286, 286t
self-defeating behaviour, 5
self-defeating narcissism, 227t
self-defeating thoughts, 120–121
self-efficacy expectancies, 278
self-focusing model, 155–156
self-fulfilling prophecy, 279f
self-help books, 245
self-help therapy, 133, 209
self-monitoring, 53–54, 135t
self-mutilation, 225
self psychology, 235
self-report inventories, 47, 49
self-spectatoring, 350
semi-structured interviews, 42
sensate focus exercises, 349
Sensation-Seeking Scale, 223
separation anxiety disorder, 418–419
separation-individuation, 236
September 11, 2001 attacks, 115–116
serotonin, 22, 270, 273, 302
serotonin-norepinephrine reuptake inhibitors (SNRIs), 69, 128–129, 172, 175
severe mental retardation (SMR), 400
sex offenders, treatment of, 335, 335t
sex reassignment, 322
sex therapists, 352
sex therapy, 348–352
arousal disorders, 349–350
dyspareunia, 351
evaluation of, 351–352
orgasm disorders, 350–351
premature ejaculation, 351
sensate focus exercises, 349
sexual desire disorders, 349
vaginismus, 351
sexist biases, 234
sexsomnia, 313
sexual abuse, recovered memories of, 198

sexual arousal disorders, 342
sexual assault, 336–340
  acquaintance sexual assault, 338
  aggravated sexual assault, 336
  date sexual assault, 338
  defined, 336
  effects of, 338–339
  incidence of, 337
  prevention, 339
  theoretical perspectives, 337–338
  treatment of sexual assault
    survivors, 339–340
sexual aversion disorder, 341–342
sexual desire disorders, 341–342, 349
sexual disorder not otherwise
  specified, 324
sexual dysfunctions, 340–353
  arousal disorders, 349–350
  biological perspectives, 343–344
  biological treatments, 352–353
  cognitive perspectives, 345–346
  common features of, 340t
  defined, 340
  dyspareunia, 343, 351
  estimated prevalence, 341t
  female orgasmic disorder, 343
  female sexual arousal
    disorder, 342
  hypoactive sexual desire
    disorder, 341
  learning perspectives, 345
  male erectile disorder, 342
  male orgasmic disorder, 343
  orgasm disorders, 343, 350–351
  premature ejaculation, 343, 351
  psychodynamic perspectives,
    344–345
  psychological perspectives,
    347–348
  relationship problems, 346
  self-spectatoring, 350
  sex therapy, 348–352
  sexual arousal disorders, 342
  sexual aversion disorder,
    341–342
  sexual desire disorders,
    341–342, 349
  sexual pain disorders, 343
  sociocultural perspectives, 347
  theoretical perspectives,
    343–348
  types of, 341–343
  vaginismus, 343, 351
sexual fulfillment, 345
sexual masochism, 332–333
sexual orientation, 324
sexual pain disorders, 343
sexual relations, 346
sexual sadism, 333
shadowing, 236
shock therapy, 173
  see also electroconvulsive therapy
    (ECT)
should statements, 159
significant, 435
Simon, Theodore, 43
single-case experimental designs,
  442–444
Sirionó, 322
Sizemore, Christine Costner, 189,
  190f
Skinner, B.F., 25
sleep apnea, 310–311
sleep disorders, 308–316
  anxiolytics, 313
  biological therapies, 313–314
  breathing-related sleep disorder,
    310–311
  circadian rhythm sleep
    disorder, 311

cognitive-behaviour therapies,
  314–316
  defined, 308
  dyssomnias, 308–311
  hypersomnia, 309
  insomnia, 308–309
  narcolepsy, 309–310, 314
  nightmare disorder, 311–312
  parasomnias, 308, 311–313
  sleep apnea, 310–311
  sleep terror disorder, 312
  sleepwalking disorder, 312–313
  treatment, 313–316
sleep disorders centres, 308
sleep terror disorder, 312
sleep terrors, 312
sleeping pills, 314
sleeping techniques, 315
sleepwalking disorder, 312–313
smoking, 252, 267–270, 269f, 276
social-cognitive theory, 31, 32,
  178–179
social contagion, 179, 422
social costs of poor mental health, 8
social isolation, 216
social norms, 3–4
social phobia, 102t, 108–110,
  110f, 132
social-reinforcement model, 191
social skills training, 287, 386–387
social workers, 68
socially unacceptable behaviour, 3–4
society, and abnormal psychology,
  87–94
sociocultural factors
  anorexia nervosa, 299–300
  and antisocial personality
    disorder, 221
  bulimia nervosa, 299–300
  eating disorders, 299–300
  sexual assault, 338
  stress, 164
sociocultural models, 15–17
sociocultural perspectives, 34
  personality disorders, 241–242
  sexual dysfunctions, 347
  substance-related disorders,
    279–280
sociodemographic factors, and
  alcoholism, 259
sociopath, 219
soma, 20
somatic hallucinations, 365
somatization disorder, 204
somatoform disorders, 199–209
  body dysmorphic disorder, 204
  conversion disorder, 15, 201–202,
    201t, 205
  culture-bound dissociative
    conditions, 207
  defined, 199
  hypochondriasis, 202–204, 202t
  pain disorder, 204–205
  somatization disorder, 204
  theoretical perspectives, 205–208
  treatment, 208–209
soul loss, 5
specific attribution, 161
specific phobias, 102t, 107–110, 109t
split personality, 188, 191
  see also dissociative identity
    disorder
splitting, 236
St. John's wort, 173
stable attribution, 161
stable factors, 161
standardized interviews, 42
Stanford-Binet Intelligence Scale
  (SBIS), 43, 400
Statistics Canada, 109

stem cells, 19–20
stimulants, 266–270
  amphetamines, 266
  attention-deficit/hyperactivity
    disorder, 413–414
  cocaine, 255, 266–267, 268t
  nicotine, 267–270
stimulus smokers, 276
stop-and-go technique, 351
stop-start technique, 351
stress
  depression, 154, 164
  diathesis-stress model, 35, 35f,
    164f, 197, 377–380, 378f
  family factors, and schizophre-
    nia, 382
  mood disorders, 154
  sociocultural factors, 164
stressful life events, 422
structural family therapy, 82
structural hypothesis, 23
structured interviews, 42–43
stupor, 368
subject expectancies, 438–439
sublimation, 24t
substance abuse, 253–255, 422
  see also substance-related
    disorders
substance dependence, 253–255,
  253t, 255t, 256–257, 257
  see also substance-related
    disorders
substance-induced disorders, 252
substance-related disorders
  addiction, 255–256
  antidepressants, 282
  aversive conditioning, 287
  behaviour therapy, 285–287
  biological perspectives, 273–275
  biological therapies, 281–284
  classical conditioning, 276–277
  classification, 252–257
  cognitive perspectives, 277–278
  cravings, conditioning model of,
    276–277
  cue-exposure training, 277
  decision making, and substance
    abuse, 277–278
  delirium tremens, 254
  detoxification, 281–282
  disorientation, 254
  disulfiram, 282
  drugs of abuse. See drugs of
    abuse
  genetics, 274–275
  learning perspectives, 275–277
  methadone maintenance pro-
    grams, 283
  naloxone, 283
  naltrexone, 283
  neurotransmitters, 273–274
  nicotine replacement therapy,
    282–283
  nonprofessional support
    groups, 284
  observational learning, 277
  operant conditioning, 275
  outcome expectancies, 277–278
  pathways to drug dependence,
    256–257
  physiological dependence,
    255–256
  psychodynamic perspectives,
    278–279
  psychodynamic therapies, 285
  psychological dependence,
    255–256
  relapse-prevention training,
    287–289
  residential approaches, 284–285

self-control strategies, 286, 286t
self-efficacy expectancies, 278
social skills training, 287
sociocultural perspectives,
  279–280
substance abuse, 253–255
substance dependence, 253–255,
  253t, 255t, 256–257
substance-induced disorders, 252
substance-use disorders, 252
theoretical perspectives, 273–280
tolerance, 254
treatment, 281–289
tying it together, 280
withdrawal, and negative reinforcement, 276
withdrawal syndrome, 254
substance-use disorders, 252
sugar pill, 439
suicide, 175–181
  adolescent suicide, 421–423
  anomie, 178
  children, 421–423
  and concussions, 177
  gender differences in suicide
    risk, 176
  hopelessness, 179–180
  prediction of, 179–181
  prevention, 181
  protective factors, 180t
  reasons, 176–178
  social contagion, 179, 422
  suicide risk, 180t
  theoretical perspectives, 178–179
Sullivan, Harry Stack, 25, 166, 372
superego, 23, 24, 235
survey method, 439
Sybil, 189
Sybil, 190
symbiotic, 236
synapse, 21, 21f
syndromes, 61
systematic desensitization, 75,
  129–130
systems model, 35–36
systems of classification, 41
  see also classification
systems perspective, 302

T

tachycardia, 254
tactile hallucinations, 365
taijin-kyofu-sho (TKS), 65
Tarasoff v. the Regents of the University of California, 90
tardive dyskinesia, 384
Tay-Sachs disease, 403
tension reduction, and alcohol,
  275–276
Terman, Louis, 43
terminals, 21
testosterone, 343, 344
Thematic Apperception Test (TAT),
  50–51
theoretical perspectives
  anxiety disorder, 118–126
  attention-deficit/hyperactivity
    disorder, 413
  autism, 396–398
  dissociative disorders, 194–196
  gender identity disorder, 324–326
  learning disorders, 409
  mood disorders, 153–163
  oppositional defiant disorder
    (ODD), 416
  paraphilias, 333–334
  personality disorders, 235–242
  schizophrenia, 371–383
  sexual assault, 337–338

...tical perspectives (*continued*)
sexual dysfunctions, 343–348
somatoform disorders, 205–208
substance-related disorders,
   273–280
suicide, 178–179
theories, 434
theory of mind, 398
therapy. *See* treatment; treatment
   (specific disorders)
Thonga, 322
thought broadcasting, 363
thought disorder, 359, 363
thought insertion, 363
thought records, 54–55
thought withdrawal, 363
The Three Faces of Eve, 189,
   190, 190*f*
thyroid, 343
time out, 417
tobacco use, 252, 267–270,
   269*f*, 276
token economies, 76
token-economy systems, 385–386
tolerance, 68, 254
trait theorists, 236–237
transference, 73–74
transference neurosis, 73
transference relationship, 73
transgender, 322
transsexual, 322
transvestic fetishism, 328–329
traumatic events, 114*t*
treatment
   see also treatment (specific
     disorders)
   behaviour therapy, 75–76
   biological therapies, 68–72
   cognitive-behaviour therapies,
     78–81
   computer-assisted therapy, 82–83

deep brain stimulation, 72
eclectic orientation, 67
eclectic therapy, 81
family therapy, 82
group therapy, 81–82
humanistic-existential therapies,
   76–77
marital therapy, 82
mental health professionals, types
   of, 67–68
phototherapy, 148
psychodynamic therapies,
   72–75
psychotherapy, effectiveness of,
   83–86
residential treatment approaches,
   284–285
right to refuse treatment, 91
right to treatment, 89–90
self-help therapy, 133
sexual assault survivors,
   339–340
virtual therapy, 133
treatment-resistant depression
   (TRD), 70–71
treatment (specific disorders)
   Alzheimer's disease, 428
   anorexia nervosa, 303–305
   anxiety disorder, 128–136
   attention-deficit/hyperactivity
     disorder, 413–414
   autism, 398–399
   bulimia nervosa, 303–305
   childhood and adolescent depres-
     sion, 421
   dissociative disorders, 197–199
   eating disorders, 303–305
   mood disorders, 165–175
   oppositional defiant disorder
     (ODD), 416–418
   paraphilias, 334–336

personality disorders, 242–245
schizophrenia, 383–389
sleep disorders, 313–316
somatoform disorders, 208–209
substance-related disorders,
   281–289
trephining, 9
tricyclic antidepressants (TCAs), 69,
   70
tricyclics, 69
Turner's syndrome, 402
twin studies, 441
two-factor model, 118–119

U

UBC Twin Project, 240
unconditional positive regard, 76
unconditioned response, 26
unconditioned stimulus, 26
unconscious, 23
undifferentiated type, 369
unilateral ECT, 174
unipolar, 141
unobtrusive, 436
unstable attribution, 161
unstructured interviews, 42
urophilia, 333

V

vaginismus, 343, 351
validity, 63, 232
validity scales, 47
variables, 436, 438, 438*t*
vascular surgery, 353
Viagra, 352–353
viral infections, 376
virtual therapy, 133
visual hallucinations, 365
voyeurism, 330

W

Wain, Louis, 365
war veterans, 114–115
Watson, John B., 25, 26
Watts, James, 71
waxy flexibility, 369
Wechsler, David, 43–44
Wechsler Adult Intelligence
   Scale, 45*t*
Wechsler Intelligence Scale for
   Children (WISC), 400
Wechsler scales, 44–45
When Perfect Isn't Good Enough
   (Antony), 245
Windeler, Jack, 14
witchcraft, 10–11
withdrawal, and negative
   reinforcement, 276
withdrawal syndrome, 254
women
   see also gender differences
   "blaming the victim," 230
   New View classification
     system, 342
   sexist biases, 234
   and sexual dysfunctions, 342
World Health Organization (WHO),
   59, 242, 267
World Trade Center attacks,
   115–116
world view, 9

Y

Yu, Edmond, 84–85, 86*f*

Z

Zeta-Jones, Catherine, 70*f*
zoophilia, 333